איך בין ניט קיין יידישיסט, וועלכער גלויבט, אז דאָס

לשון [...]עלם מיט זיך פאר אַן אבסאָלוטן ווערט

אבער [...]בין איך יאָ, און איך ווייס, אז הייליק[...]

קייט און [...]קייט זיינען ניט אַלעמאָל אידענטיש

די הלכה האָט פאָרמולירט צוויי אידעאן פון קדושה: 1

גופי קדושה; 2) תשמישי קדושה. זי האָט אָפּגעפסקנט

אז מען דאַרף ראַטעווען פון אַ שרפה שבת, ניט נאָר ד

ספר תורה נאָר אויך דאָס מענטעלע, אין וועלכן זי אי

איינגעוויקלט; ניט בלויז די תפילין, נאָר אויך דעם זעקל

אין וועלכן זי ליגן. ממילא, יידיש ווי אַ שפּראַך, ני

קוקנדיק וואָס זי איז ניט פאַררעכנט צווישן גופי קדושה

געהערט זיכער צום קלאַס פון תשמישי־קדושה, וועלכ

זיינען אויך הייליק און וועלכע מען מח באַזיצן מיט אַל[...]

כוחות. איז דען דא אַ שענערער „תיק", אין וועלכן ד

הייליקסטע ספרי־תורה זיינען געווען און זיינען נאָך אַלי[...]

איינגעוויקלט, ווי יידיש? אויף דער שפּראַך האָט דער

רמ"א, דער מהרש"ל, דער ווילנער גאון, ר' חיים וואָלאָ[...]

זשינער און אנדערע גדולי ישראל מיט זייערע תלמידים

תורה געלערנט. אויף יידיש האָט דער בעל־שם־טוב, דער

מעזעריטשער מגיד און דער אלטער רבי — סודות פו[...]

מעשה בראשית דערקלערט. אויף פשוטן מאַמע־לשו[...]

האָבן די יידישע מאַסן זייער אמונה, פשוטע ליבע או[...]

טריישאַפט אויסגעדריקט. עד־היום זאָגן גרויסע ראָש[...]

ישיבות זייערע שיעורים אויף יידיש. אזא „תיק" איז זי[...]

כער הייליק, כאָטש זיך קדושה איז ניט קיין אבסאָלוטע[...]

נאָר אַן אָפּגעלייטעטע, אין דעם גדר פון תשמישי־קדושה

אויפהאַלטן דעם „תיק" איז אַ גרויסער זכות!

NEVER SAY DIE!

לא אמות כי אחיה

Contributions to the Sociology of Language 30

לא אמות כי אחיה

טויזנט יאָר ייִדיש אין ייִדישן לעבן און שאַפֿן

שיקל פֿישמאַן, רעדאַקטאָר

Never Say Die!

*A Thousand Years of Yiddish
in Jewish Life and Letters*

Edited by JOSHUA A. FISHMAN

MOUTON PUBLISHERS · THE HAGUE · PARIS · NEW YORK

Library of Congress Cataloging in Publication Data
Main entry under title:

Never Say Die!

(Contributions to the sociology of language, 30)
English and Yiddish.
Bibliography: p.
Includes index.
1. Yiddish language—Social aspects—Addresses,
essays, lectures. 2. Jews—Languages—Addresses,
essays, lectures. I. Fishman, Joshua A. II. Series.
PJ5111.N4   437'.947   81-3957

ISBN 90-279-7978-2   AACR2

Publication of this book was made possible, in part,
by subventions obtained by the League for Yiddish, Inc.

Designed by Arie Bornkamp
Jacket design by Jurriaan Schrofer
Jacket photograph by Hans de Boer with the cooperation of the
Jewish Historical Museum, Amsterdam.

Printed in Great Britain at the University Press, Cambridge

מײַנע קינדער און איה"ש קינדסקינדער:
זאָל זייער אהבֿת-יִשׂראל זיך נישט ענדיקן
פֿון דרויסן פֿאַר דער שוועל פֿון ייִדיש,
און זאָל עס זיך נישט ענדיקן מיט ייִדיש אַליין!

JEWISH EASTERN EUROPE
1830-1914

⊙ Provincial Capital ★ Major City • Settlement

--·--· Border ········· Provincial Border

▨ Congress Poland ▨ Pale of settlement in Czarist Russia

The major Eastern European Yiddish dialect areas: to the left of the north–south line, the 'central dialect' (popularly referred to as 'poylish/galitsyaner'); to the north of the east–west line, the 'northern dialect' (popularly referred to as 'litvish'); south of the east–west line, the 'southern dialect' (popularly referred to as 'volinyer/podolyer/besaraber'). Arrow points to Tshernovits.

וועגן ייִדיש

איך בין ניט קיין ייִדישיסט, וועלכער גלויבט, אז דאָס
לשון אַליין שטעלט מיט זיך פאַר אַן אַבסאָלוטן ווערט.
אָבער אַ גמרא־ייִד בין איך יאָ, און איך וויס, אז היילי־
קייט און אבסאָלוטקייט זיינען ניט אַלעמאָל אידענטיש.
די הלכה האָט פאָרמולירט צוויי אידעאָן פון קדושה: 1)
גופי קדושה; 2) תשמישי קדושה. זי האָט אָפּגעפּסקנט,
אז מען דאַרף ראַטעווען פּון אַ שׂרפה שבת, ניט נאָר די
ספר תורה נאָר אויך דאָס מענטעלע, אין וועלכן זי איז
איינגעוויקלט; ניט בלויז די תפיליָן, נאָר אויך דעם זעקל,
אין וועלכן זיי ליגן. ממילא, ייִדיש ווי אַ שפּראַך, ניט
קוקנדיק וואָס זי איז ניט פאַררעכנט צווישן גופי קדושה,
געהערט זיכער צום קלאַס פון תשמישי־קדושה, וועלכע
זיינען אויך היילִיק און וועלכע מען מח באַשיצן מיט אַלע
כוחות. איז דען דאָ אַ שענערער „תיק", אין וועלכן די
הייליקסטע ספרי־תורה זיינען געווען און זיינען נאָך אַלץ
איינגעוויקלט, ווי ייִדיש? אויף דער שפּראַך האָט דער
רמ״א, דער מהרש״ל, דער ווילנער גאון, ר׳ חיים וואָלאָ־
זשינער און אַנדערע גדולי ישראל מיט זיערע תלמידים
תורה געלערנט. אויף ייִדיש האָט דער בעל־שם־טוב, דער
מעזעריטשער מגיד און דער אַלטער רבי — סודות פון
מעשׂה בראשית דערקלערט. אויף פּשוטן מאַמע־לשון
האָבן די ייִדישע מאַסן זיער אמונה, פּשוטע ליבע און
טריישאַפט אויסגעדריקט. עד־היום זאָגן גרויסע ראשי
ישיבות זיערע שיעורים אויף ייִדיש. אזא „תיק" איז זי־
כער היילִיק, כאַטש זיין קדושה איז ניט קיין אַבסאָלוטע,
נאָר אַן אָפּגעלייטעטע, אין דעם גדר פון תשמישי־קדושה.
אויפהאַלטן דעם „תיק" איז אַ גרויסער זכות!

Abstract of Yiddish text on page VII

About Yiddish. Rabbi Joseph B. Soloveitchik, one of the world's foremost rabbinic authorities, declares that although Yiddish is not holy in-and-of-itself, it nevertheless possesses holiness-by-association, in view of its centuries-old relationship with traditional Jewish piety, scholarship, exemplary leadership, and authentic way of life. Accordingly, it is a great privilege for Jews to exert themselves to protect Yiddish with all the power at their command. (*Der tog*, February 24, 1961)

Preface

JOSHUA A. FISHMAN

During the past two decades, I have devoted considerable effort to the sociology of Yiddish, on the one hand, and to more general sociolinguistic theory and research, on the other hand. In this volume I have tried to bring these two aspects of my work into a closer and more total relationship with each other than has ever been the case in the past. In doing so I have tried to create a volume on Yiddish for my sociolinguistic students and colleagues and, simultaneously, a volume informed by sociolinguistic theory and research for my students and colleagues from the field of Yiddish. However, since both volumes are actually one, I have also hoped that sociolinguistic specialists would find in its sociolinguistic component some materials and concepts that they would consider to be stimulating, whereas Yiddish specialists would, similarly, find in its Yiddish component a number of exciting and valuable suggestions and ideas.

The last few years have witnessed a substantial growth of Yiddish studies at the tertiary (college and university) level throughout the world, but particularly in the United States. However, most of the students benefiting by this development have concentrated on literary and linguistic materials. As a result, the full world of Yiddish, as it was and as it is, is frequently never focused upon or merely vaguely glimpsed. It was (and is) a world that deserves to be inspected directly and exhaustively, if only that its language and literature might be more fully understood and appreciated, but also, most basically, because, like every other human world, it gives testimony to the complexity, the resilience, the creativity, and the conflictedness of society in general and of language in society in particular.

Since it is my hope that a variety of readers may be interested in this volume, differing greatly from each other in area of specialization as well as in level of advancement within their field of special expertise, I have tried to include some basic introductory data, some information of a moderate degree of advancement, and some highly specialized material throughout the interrelated and mutually reinforcing sections of this volume. My own 'prologue' is multi-tiered accordingly, and my 'epilogue' seeks to address itself to further studies in the sociology of Yiddish as a fruitful field for sociolinguistic and Yiddish specialists alike.

The Holocaust of the Nazi years has taken from us the bulk of the world of Yiddish. As that world recedes into history, at best, and into forgetfulness, at worst, it becomes even more subject to either deification, as the epitome of all that was and is holy, noble, wise, and genuine in the Jewish tradition, or to satanization, as the epitome of all the dislocation, pain, poverty, and persecution in Jewish history. It is my hope that this volume will add perspective to most popular reactions to Yiddish – whether pro or con – by providing a dimension of realistic depth and an appreciation for the internal struggles and external pressures that this world continually experienced. Far from being either superhuman or subhuman the world of Yiddish was – and still is, for it is far from over and done with – brimful of very human ambivalences: extremism and compromise, idealism and materialism, shortsightedness and eternal verities, tenderness and cruelty. It was and is a complete world: a full-woven tapestry; a varied world: a multicolored tapestry; a creative world: a still unrolling tapestry. The sociology of language – and, I am convinced, mankind in general – will be richer for becoming more familiar with it.

Of the many who have encouraged and enabled me to undertake and complete this volume, I want to single out for public thanks the Yivo, particularly its library, and most particularly Dina Abramovitsh, head librarian of the Yivo, for locating many dozens of items that I needed to examine, as well as Mordkhe Shekhter, Columbia University, for his friendly criticism and assistance in connection with dozens of queries, Robert Cooper, Hebrew University (Jerusalem), for his very helpful comments on an early draft of the Foreword to this volume, Leyzer Ran for permitting me to make use of so many of the splendid illustrations in his exemplary publications *Fun eliyohu bokher biz hirsh glik* (1963) and *Yerushelayem delite ilustrirt un dokumentirt* (1974), and, most importantly, members of my immediate family who helped me assemble the readings and check the bibliography, and, above all, who convinced me to include readings in Yiddish per se, so that through this volume the language would not merely be 'read about' – but would actually be read and studied directly. In the last analysis, language is not only a socioaffective referent but a cognitive–expressive system first and foremost. Like all languages, but somehow even more than most, Yiddish pleads to be and needs to be read, spoken, laughed, cried, sung, shouted. It is a breath of life itself. This volume, therefore, is, in part, also a contribution to those who will continue to breathe it, to use it, rather than just admire or long for it, and an attempt to add to their ranks.

January 1980

Contents*

* All *reprinted* material has been left as *originally* published in order to accurately reflect the varying conventions of documentation, transliteration, and spelling observed by their authors and publishers, whether in English or in Yiddish.

PART VI MAINTENANCE AND SHIFT

...we dare not abandon one of the foundations of national unity in the very hour that the languages of the peoples around us rob our people of thousands and tens of thousands of its sons, so that they no longer understand the language used by their parents. We must not destroy with our own hands the power of our folk language to compete with the foreign languages which lead to assimilation. Such destruction would amount to suicide. There being no hope of converting our ancient national tongue into the living and daily spoken language in the Diaspora, we would be committing a transgression against our national soul if we did not make use in our war against assimilation of the great counterforce stored up in the language of the people.

...When the language problem is posed in all its ramifications and when it is clarified not from the viewpoint of one party or of one literary clique or another, but from the general national viewpoint, then there will be no place for such errors in this matter. Insofar as we recognize the merit of national existence in the Diaspora, we must also recognize the merit of Yiddish as one of the instruments of autonomy, together with Hebrew and the other factors of our culture.

Shimen Dubnov (Simon Dubnow). Khiyev hagoles; vegn shliles hagoles fun akhed hoom [Affirmation of the Diaspora; Concerning Aḥad Ha-'am's Negation of the Diaspora], in his *Briv vegn altn un nayem yidntum* [Letters Concerning Old and New Jewry]. Mexico City, Mendelson Fund, 1959 [1909].

The Sociology of Yiddish: A Foreword

JOSHUA A. FISHMAN

PART I: SOCIOHISTORICAL PERSPECTIVE ON YIDDISH

Two major viewpoints underlie most reflections about Yiddish across the centuries, be they by adherents or detractors, clergy or laity, language specialists or laymen. One view is that Yiddish is 'just another' Jewish diaspora vernacular – just one more member in a club whose membership has been both rather unselective and fleeting. The other holds that it is much more than that, whether for good or for evil. In relatively recent years, aspects of both views have come to be held simultaneously and dialectically by the same observers, so that the insights of both have been brought together in an intriguingly complementary perspective.

What all three of the above views have in common is their implicit contrastivity. Indeed, the aura of contrastivity accompanies Yiddish throughout the entire millennium of its existence (S. Birnboym 1939, 1968; Opatoshu 1950; Shiper 1923, 1924; M. Vaynraykh 1973) and leads both to a heightened componential consciousness *intra*linguistically (i.e. to a consciousness even among many ordinary members of the speech community as to the fusion nature of the language as a whole as well as of the 'origins' – real or purported – of particular words or structures) and to exaggerated efforts with respect to sociohistorical comparativity *inter*linguistically. Thus, Yiddish speakers in the United States are minimally aware, if not totally oblivious, of the hybrid or fusion nature of English (Acher 1902) e.g., but are fully aware of (even mesmerized by) that fact *vis-à-vis* Yiddish. Similarly, even those who have no more than a nodding acquaintance with Yiddish have a ready-made paradigm with respect to its componentiality (as well as with respect to its longevity), even though they have absolutely no such paradigm for languages with which they are far more familiar from the point of view of personal use and fluency. The foregoing observations are meant not merely to imply that 'a little knowledge is a dangerous thing', which is true enough, but that Yiddish is 'one of those things'

The sections of this Foreword correspond to the sections of this volume.

about which there are readily available *Weltanschauungen*, conceptual maps, which it is exceedingly difficult to penetrate, to alter, to restructure. There is something about Yiddish that stimulates most 'beholders' to act as if they were comparative sociolinguists. Yiddish excites comparative and prognostic tendencies.

The fact that Yiddish has so obviously been the major Jewish diaspora vernacular of modern times – certainly it was such until the early 40s when the Holocaust savagely diminished the number of its users by some 75 per cent – led many polemicists (and even some scholars) who were more basically concerned with *other* Jewish languages to pursue their interests with one eye on Yiddish. Reminders that *loshn koydesh* was the holy tongue basically served to stress that Yiddish was not (Levinzon 1935). Reminders that Hebrew was an eternal language served to underscore that Yiddish was not (Levinson 1935). The emphasis on the continued growth of modern Hebrew constantly pointed to the 'obviously' shrinking base of Yiddish (Bachi 1956; Hofman and Fisherman 1971; Maler 1925). Other Jewish vernaculars have regularly been explored in the light of questions, problems, prejudices, and findings initially derived from the intellectual, political or emotional sphere of Yiddish (e.g. Birnboym 1937; Blanc 1964; Bunis 1975; Faur 1973; Jochnowitz 1975; Shaykovski 1948; Vidal 1972; Ziskind 1965; etc.).

A related pattern is apparent in scholarly work pertaining to Yiddish per se. The view that it should be considered as a language in its own right, a language with systematic characteristics, relationships, functions, and concerns that are particularly and peculiarly its own within its community of users, is constantly 'clinched' by the view that Yiddish is a language *like* all other languages, *equal* to others, as *good* as others, whether the others be Jewish or not. Tsinberg, the major historian of Jewish literature, begins his treatment of Yiddish literature (1975 [1935]) with a chapter on the status of Yiddish in the period of early Yiddish literature. The chapter does *not* give extensive treatment to this topic, although the English translator pretended that it *does* by entitling it 'Languages Among the Jews: The Origin of Yiddish'. Somehow neither Tsinberg nor his translator considered it possible to jump into the beginnings of Yiddish literature without at least a brief, comparative, sociolinguistic excursus. M. Vaynraykh, the master of modern Yiddish studies, does exactly that, and most thoroughly, whether he deals with Yiddish literature (1923b, 1928) or language (1973). The work on the variety of early names for Yiddish (including zhargon – jargon – and ivre-taytsh – translation of Hebrew) quickly points out that both the lack of naming consensus and the lack of self-acceptance (among its users) that are revealed by many of the early designations for Yiddish are quite like those obtained for many languages, including many Jewish languages (S. Birnboym 1942), the world over, and that this condition was even more widespread in centuries gone by and in the very heartland of Europe to boot (e.g. Dubnov

1929b; Prilutski 1938b, 1935; Spivak 1938). Even the YIVO (originally Yiddish Scientific Institute-YIVO and, since 1955, YIVO Institute for Jewish Research), in its widely distributed brochure entitled *Basic Facts about Yiddish*, is quick to point out that Yiddish 'is about the same age as most European languages' (1946), a claim that would concern only specialists, at best, in conjunction with English, French or Polish.[1]

Componentialism, contrastivity, language relativism within and relativism without: these are all the marks of a language that arose among a people already literate (even biliterate) and the conscious and conscientious carriers of a classic tradition, as well as of a classic and seemingly inescapable burden, among the nations of the Euro-Mediterranean world. Both the tradition and the burden have fostered insecurities or, at the very least, sensitivities and awarenesses *vis-à-vis* Yiddish among its lay-devotees (Grosman 1974a; Samuel 1971a), that few other language communities of similar size and creativity have retained for anywhere near as long. However, the sublimation of these cognitive and conative tensions surrounding Yiddish has led to some of the century's major works on linguistics in general (Mizes 1915; U. Vaynraykh 1953), on Jewish interlinguistics more specifically (S. Birnboym 1951; Gold 1974; Paper 1978), and on Yiddish per se within a comparative framework (in particular M. Vaynraykh 1954,

---

1. The appreciable historicity of Yiddish is necessarily based upon historical reasoning and analogy in so far as its earliest beginnings are concerned (M. Vaynraykh 1973). The earliest datable *written* evidence of Yiddish stems from the thirteenth century (M. Vaynraykh 1963; Sadan 1963), although the likelihood that earlier written records existed and were lost due to lack of interest as well as because of expulsions and other adverse circumstances of Jewish life is great indeed. The deeper problem, which Yiddish shares with all *ausbau* languages, is that of arriving at a balance of criteria, psychological, social, and linguistic, according to which 'beginnings' can be validated or verified. Thus, dating the beginning of Yiddish *vis-à-vis* German, presents an issue that is also of interest to Slovak (*vis-à-vis* Czech), Croatian (*vis-à-vis* Serbian), Ukrainian and White Russian (*vis-à-vis* Russian), Urdu (*vis-à-vis* Hindi), and most particularly, Macedonian (*vis-à-vis* Bulgarian) and Indonesian (*vis-à-vis* Malaysian). Both subjective and objective criteria are of concern in this connection, although they will not always agree. Objective criteria alone are not enough for they tend to overstress the significance of structural linguistic features which may have had little or no social or psychological visibility or significance at the time. However, subjective criteria alone are equally fallible, given that language consciousness is commonly so rare (or, if present, so easily influenced by community leaders or even by outside authorities) among ordinary rank-and-file members of speech communities, probably even more so in centuries past than in modern times. The fusion nature of Yiddish (its componentiality) makes both objective and subjective dating easier and more reliable. Nevertheless, this entire topic remains one that deserves and requires additional attention both within Jewish interlinguistics and within the sociolinguistics of *ausbau* languages more generally. Now that the topic of 'language-death' has recently received well-deserved attention (see *International Journal of the Sociology of Language*, 1977, no. 12, entire issue), it may be hoped that language birth will also receive more attention. Most of the recent attention given to the latter topic has been in connection with problems of pidginization and creolization. It would be premature at this time to conclude that this is the only sociopsychological-linguistic context in which language birth takes place. Whereas it has been proposed that Yiddish might best be considered a pidgin in its earliest stages (Jacobs 1975), this would seem to be questionable, or at least highly atypical for pidgins, given (a) the biliterate nature of most of its male speakers, (b) the fact that they did not lack prior, fully fashioned intragroup language varieties while Yiddish was coming into being as such (i.e. while it was leaving behind its initial intergroup functions and characteristics), and (c) the fact that no 'reduced stage' of the language has ever been evinced.

1973). This endless contrastivity – amounting almost to the assumption that comparison is the *only* intellectual stance, that multiplicity of languages (dialects, varieties) is *the* human condition (Goldsmit 1968), and that the moral triumph over inner bias and outer rejection is *the* bittersweet compensation of the disadvantaged – serves to make the sociology of Yiddish a stimulating field for many who have neither a direct nor an indirect affiliation with it. All who are interested either in other insecure language communities today or in the earlier, more temporary periods of insecurity that all languages have faced, including the great languages of this day and age before arriving at their currently uncontested social functions, can recognize in Yiddish parallels to frequently glossed-over parts of their own stories.

However, it would be highly unlikely for any vernacular of a chosen people not to be perceived as incomparable as well, particularly if this vernacular uniquely accompanied and fostered this people's modern national awakening. The deep involvement of Yiddish in modern Jewish authenticity movements (most of them being, naturally enough, modernization-plus-authenticity movements) has indelibly associated it with the chosenness, the specialness, the heightenedness of Jewishness. Professors, poets, and prose masters alike have ascribed to it a unique cultural impact (Mark 1969), an elevating individual role (Leyvik 1957), and an updating, softening, and universalization of the classic Jewish contribution to civilization (Shtif 1922, 1924; Opatoshu 1949b). Thus, it is not only claimed that Yiddish reflects *yidishkayt*, the entire life-pattern and world view of traditional Ashkenazic Jewry (e.g. M. Vaynraykh 1953, 1959, 1967, 1972, 1973; Fishman 1974, 1976a; Tsaytlin 1973) but that it is/was itself a contributor to the creation, development, and preservation of Jewish values, Jewish traditions, and of the survival of the Jewish peoplehood itself (Golomb 1962a, 1962b, 1970; Niger 1928b; Lerer 1940; Bez 1971a). Indeed, every Yiddish word has been viewed in quintessential Herderian perspective, i.e. as not only denoting but as embodying Jewish values (*yidishe verter: yidishe vertn*), wit, humor, and Jewish eternity itself. Significantly, the richness of Yiddish words – their emotional loadings, their innuendos, their diminutives, their endlessly nuanced connotations of collective experience – has been admired, envied and regretted by modern Hebraists faced by the comparative artificiality of Israeli Hebrew (Epshteyn 1910; Kazenelson 1960; Megged 1966; for several additional citations see M. Vaynraykh 1973, vol. 3, p. 262).

Indeed, the presumably unmediated character of Yiddish, making it an instrument of something akin to Jewish phatic communion, its seemingly natural, impulsive involvement in emotional stances, led to early and continued attacks upon it by most of those who championed enlightenment (Nusboym 1882), Zionism (reviewed by Pilovski 1973, 1979), and traditional or reform religion alike (Feder 1815 [in Lifshits 1863], Hakohen 1902; Mendelssohn 1783). Yiddish has long touched and still touches an emotional nerve. It is close to the vital and volatile likes and dislikes of a threatened people, of insecure protoelites, of insufficiently recognized intellectuals. As such, it is rarely reacted to dispassionately.[2] Just as Jews themselves stand accused in the eyes of many outsiders of simultaneous but opposite derilictions (capitalism *and* communism, clannishness *and* assimilation, materialism *and* vapid intellectualism) so Yiddish stands accused – within the Jewish fold itself – of being a tool of the irreligious *and* of the ultraorthodox, of fostering ghettoization *and* rootless cosmopolitanism, of reflecting quintessential and inescapable Jewishness *and* of representing little more than a hedonistic differentiation from the ways of the gentiles, of being dead or dying, *and* of being a ubiquitous threat to higher values. In all cases, however, the claims made and the association played upon are more extreme, more articulated, and more uncompromising in the case of Yiddish than any that are made pertaining to other Jewish post-exilic languages. 'There is probably no other language. . . on which so much opprobrium has been heaped' (Weiner 1899, p. 12). Perhaps this is the fundamental uniqueness of Yiddish. Perhaps it is this enmeshment in never-ending controversy and deep feeling that prompts so many comparisons: the status of most exceptional post-exilic language of an exceptional people; the most itinerant language of an itinerant people; the constantly self-renewing language (its demise being predicted – desired? – generation after generation for centuries) of a constantly self-renewing people.

PART II: ORTHODOXY: THEN AND NOW

The relationship between Yiddish and Ashkenazic Orthodoxy has traditionally been ambivalent and bimodal. Obviously, Yiddish arose at a time when Orthodoxy not only reigned supreme, but also was identical with the Jewish way of life, and when Ashkenaz itself was just coming into being as a relatively self-sufficient Jewish civilization with its own normative authorities *vis-à-vis* the

---

2. The Yiddish literary critic and historian Bal-makhshoves contrasted Yiddish and Esperanto primarily in connection with the emotional dimension that he considered so vital for an understanding of the significance of Yiddish. Writing over 70 years ago (1953b [1908b]) he suggested that Yiddish and Esperanto were really polar opposites in the family of languages. Whereas Esperanto, he contended, was intended to serve superficial and ahistorical human interactions, Yiddish was related to deep emotions and to a millennium of history. Furthermore, whereas Esperanto served primarily for communications between culturally dissimilar interlocutors, Yiddish not only served those who shared intensely a thousand concerns and experiences, but served to bring back to the community those who had unfortunately drifted away from it. Setting aside the fact that not only Yiddish and Esperanto but all mother tongues and Esperanto can be differentiated along very much the same lines that Bal-makhshoves advanced, it is of interest to point out that Zamenhof, the inventor of Esperanto, was himself a Yiddish speaker and writer. Not only did he see to it that a Yiddish translation of his proposal for a world language was published the very year after Esperanto itself was 'born' (Esperanto 1888), but he was sufficiently interested in the state of Yiddish to urge that its grammar and orthography benefit from early codification and standardization (Dr. X 1909). A detailed Yiddish–Esperanto, Esperanto–Yiddish dictionary was completed thanks largely to the efforts of Yiddish-speaking Esperantists in Israel (Rusak 1969, 1973).

classical halakhic tradition. (For the whole sociocultural matrix of this earliest period see M. Vaynraykh 1973; for its earliest extant linguistic clues see M. Vaynraykh 1963; Sadan 1963.) Thus, for nearly a millennium, Ashkenazic Orthodoxy and Yiddish were intimately intertwined and, with the dispersion of Sephardic Jewry in the fifteenth century, this duo ultimately came to be viewed as a phenomenological identity. This apparent identity carries along with it both some of the greatest assets and some of the greatest burdens of Yiddish today. As the vernacular – and, more belatedly and more meagerly, as a language of written and printed communication – of Ashkenazic Orthodoxy, Yiddish was (and to some extent still is) protected by a sociocultural configuration least likely to change and, therefore, least likely to exchange Yiddish for other vehicles of oral communication. The link of Yiddish to *yidishkayt* derives from this origin and from the uncontested centuries in which Yiddish reigned supreme as the intragroup vernacular of Central and Eastern European daily Jewish life.

Supremacy, however, has its functional boundaries. The world of Orthodoxy also clamors and cleaves most assiduously to the two-in-one languages of holy and sanctified writ – ancient and medieval Hebrew and (Judeo-)Aramaic – together: *loshn koydesh*. These alone were long considered completely qualified to be the process languages of worship and the target of textual study, in short, for all traditional, text-anchored activity and, by natural extension, for all serious intracommunal written and printed communication. And yet, Orthodox Jews spoke to each other only (or almost only) in Yiddish; unmediated supplications poured forth from their hearts and mouths in Yiddish (Freehof 1923); they argued the Talmudic law and its interpretations in Yiddish; they testified in intracommunal litigations in Yiddish; they sang in Yiddish, they issued their intracommunal and intercommunal regulations in Yiddish (Dubnov 1929a) and increasingly – certainly as the modern period draws nigh – read both for entertainment and for moral instruction in Yiddish, leaving a printed record half a millennium old in these various functions. Thus, the original 'language problem' of Ashkenazic Jewry has long been that of how far to admit Yiddish into the realms of serious, ritualized, scriptified, and, ultimately, printed functions. However, if this was a 'problem', it long had exceedingly low saliency among the rank and file. Their view was that current in all traditional diglossia settings: attitudinal priority is clearly given to elevated H but most of life proceeds in cozy L. 'The traditional Jew who saw Yiddish always as *mame-loshn* and Hebrew as *loshn ha-koydesh* never felt the need to choose between the two' (Jacobs 1977).

Although the process of Orthodox acceptance of Yiddish as textually co-sanctified is both slow and ultimately incomplete, it progressed for centuries. The acceptability of Yiddish as the *obligatory* language of testimony in intra-communal litigation, as long as both parties admit to knowing Yiddish and at least one party requests its use, is documented in print as of 1519 (Rivkind 1928).

Of approximately similar vintage is a Yiddish concordance to the Bible, *Mirkeves hamishne* (1534), and even a prayer book in Yiddish (1544). Beginning toward the end of the sixteenth century, there are abundant indications of a widespread rabbinic view that it was far preferable to use Yiddish books for prayer and study than to use *loshn koydesh* uncomprehendingly or, what was worse, than not to be able to pray or study at all (see M. Vaynraykh 1973, vol. 3, p. 272). By the end of the sixteenth century the rights of Yiddish begin to be explicitly guaranteed in community records for the above advocated purposes (Balaban 1912, 1916), and various rabbinic educational authorities appear whose championship of Yiddish is open, explicit, and lifelong (Nobl 1951).

For several centuries such efforts continued and slowly multiplied, but usually under the apologetic guise of being intended for women (Niger 1913a) or for uneducated men. (Note, e.g. the *tsene-urene* [Shatski 1928] a 'women's edition' of the Pentateuch first published in 1628 and still in print today.) However, these disguises (protective of the status of *loshn koydesh* and of the latter's gatekeepers) were also increasingly dropped – first with respect to the avowed restriction to women and then with respect to the focus upon the uneducated more generally. By the eighteenth century 'the author of *Emunas yisroel* declared that all that the school boy can acquire from a teacher, he can just as well read...in Yiddish "for nowadays we have the whole Law and the precepts in Yiddish"' (Zinberg 1928 [1946]). Similarly, the *Zohar*, the central source of modern Jewish mysticism, was rendered into Yiddish by 1711, with the explicit indication that scholars might well study it in that language 'for the original itself is not in Hebrew but in the vernacular of the land of its origin [i.e. Aramaic]'.

However, if Orthodox use of Yiddish in a few of the traditional functions of *loshn koydesh* begins early and develops continually, Orthodox opposition thereto long compensates (or overcompensates) therefor. Yiddish books of ritual or scholarly significance are explicitly banned (and even burned) as late as the eighteenth century (see, e.g. Tsinberg 1928, M. Vaynraykh 1973, p. 278), and the protective coloration of proposed focus upon females or upon the unlearned male therefore continues not only into the twentieth century but – to some extent – is encountered to this very day. Certainly, it is unwarranted to claim that the early Orthodox adherents of Yiddish were – with very few exceptions – Yiddishists in the modern sense of that term, since, regardless of the focus of their various works, they did not in any way seek to more generally displace *loshn koydesh* from its central sanctified prerogatives in prayer and ritual (Pyekazh 1964). This is true even with respect to Hasidism, whose use of Yiddish for the purpose of spreading its views (and the wonder stories of its rabbis) among the masses was truly massive (Finklshteyn 1954; Hager 1974). Even in this connection, however, some two centuries elapsed, and other social movements – some of them non-Orthodox and others anti-Orthodox in nature – had already begun to make ample use of Yiddish for mass-propaganda purposes, before the

בקשה

למוצאי שבת

נמצא בכתבי קודש של הרב הקדוש רבי לוי יצחק מברדיטשוב זצ״ל,
בעל המחבר ספר „קדושת לוי״ וזה לשונו:

סגולה גדולה להצלחה

שיאמרו אנשים ונשים וטף בקשה זו בכל מוצאי שבת קודש
קודם הבדלה שלש פעמים. ובטוח אני שיצליחו בודאי אי״ה:

איך בין פֿערזיכערט אַז זײ. װאָלטן אי״ה בֿעגליקֿן.

גאָט פֿון אברהם און פֿון יצחק
און פֿון יעקב.

בֿעהיט דײַן פֿאָלק יִשְׂרָאֵל פֿון אַלֶעם בײנעם אין בײנעם
לויב אז דָער לִיבֶּער שַׁבָּת קוֹדֶש גײט. אז די װאָך און דָער
חוֹדֶש. און דָער יָאר זאָל אונז צוא קומֶען צו אֱמוּנָה שְׁלֵימָה
צו אֱמוּנַת חֲכָמִים צו אַהֲבַת חֲבֵרִים. צו דְבֵיקַת הַבּוֹרֵא ב״ה.
מַאֲמִין צו זײַן בִּשְׁלוֹש עֶשְׂרֵה עִקָּרִים שֶׁלָּךְ. וּבִגְאוּלָה קְרוֹבָה
בִּמְהֵרָה בְּיָמֵינוּ. וּבִתְחִיַּת הַמֵּתִים. וּבִנְבוּאָת מֹשֶׁה רַבֵּינוּ עָלָיו
הַשָּׁלוֹם.

רִבּוֹנוֹ שֶׁל עוֹלָם דו בִּיסְט דאָךְ הַגּוֹסֵן לַיַצֵף כֶּם .
גיב בײַנֶע לִיבֶּע יוֹדִישֶׁע קִינְדֶערְלִיךְ אויך כֶּם דיך צו לויבֶּען.
אִין נאָר דיך צו דִינְגֶען און קײַן אַנְדֶערִין חָלִילָה נישט. און
אז די װאָך און דָער חוֹדֶש און דָער יָאר זאָל אונז קומֶען
צו גֶעזוּנְד און צו מַזָּל און צו בְּרָכָה וְהַצְלָחָה. און צו חֶסֶד
און צו בָּנֵי חַיֵּי אֲרִיכֵי וּמְזוֹנֵי רְוִיחֵי וְסִיַּעְתָּא דִשְׁמַיָּא לָנוּ
וּלְכָל יִשְׂרָאֵל וְנֹאמַר אָמֵן:

"Kodesh Hilluiim" Yeshiva, Jerusalem named on Rabbi Hillel of Kalamey P.O.B. 1247 — Jerusalem	ישיבת „קודש הילולים״ ירושלים ע״ש הרה״צ ר׳ הלל מקאלאמיי זצ״ל ת.ד. 1247 — ירושלים

Figure 1. '*Supplication as the Sabbath Ends*....From the holy writings of the holy Rabbi Levi Yitskhok of Berditshev [1740–1809]...to be said by men, women and children.' The explanatory introduction cited above is in Loshn Koydesh. The supplication itself is in Yiddish, with many traditional learned phrases. This supplication can be bought (on a laminated card) to this very day in Orthodox bookshops in Jerusalem.

nineteenth century avalanche of Yiddish Hasidic publications really got underway. Even this avalanche – precisely because it was intended for the masses – did not establish a serious scholarly or ritual niche for Yiddish among the Orthodox, but rather, primarily a popular emotional one (Liberman 1943).

As we have seen, Eastern European Orthodoxy's ambivalence with respect to Yiddish continued past the late nineteenth century and into the twentieth (see Feder 1815 [in Lifshits 1863]; Shnayd 1956). By then, however, Yiddish had to be, on the one hand, defended among the Orthodox, its adherents pointing to it as a bulwark against coterritorial vernaculars with their penchant for detraditionalizing and secularizing Ashkenazic life (Anon 1931b; N. Birnboym 1913, 1931; Likhtnshteyn 1872 and 1878; Shenirer 1931).[3] On the other hand, Yiddish had by then become an article of faith of Eastern European Jewish secularism in its various political manifestations and, as such, also a new danger for Orthodoxy (Poll 1965; Shatski 1932). As a result, Orthodox defenders of Yiddish tended to relate it increasingly to a glorious and romanti-

---

3. The Yiddish advocacy of Nosn Birnboym deserves special mention and, indeed, further investigation in connection with the topic of reethnification of elites. Such reethnification and accompanying relinguification is a common process in the early stages of modern ethnicity movements and exemplifies both the protoelitist return to (or selection of) roots (often after failure to transethnify 'upwardly' in accord with earlier aspirations) as well as the masses' groping toward mobilization under exemplary leadership. However, modern ethnicity movements are essentially attempts to achieve modernization, utilizing 'primordial' identificational metaphors and emotional attachments for this purpose. Thus, they are not really 'return' movements (not really nativization- or past-oriented). They exploit or mine the past rather than cleave to it. Partially transethnified elites can uniquely serve such movements because of their own double exposure. Birnboym is therefore exceptional in that he ultimately rejected his secularized, Germanized, Europeanized milieu on behalf of a genuine return to ultra-Orthodoxy. By the second decade of this century he had rejected modernization (in the guises of socialism, Zionism, and Diaspora nationalism), all of which he had once charted, as hedonistic and as endangering Jewish (and world) survival. There is about the latter Birnboym a Spenglerian aura foretelling the 'decline of the West' and cautioning Jews that their salvation (and the world's) would come only via complete immersion in traditional beliefs, values and practices (Birnboym 1946). He viewed Yiddish as a *sine-qua-non* in that connection, rejecting its use for modern, hedonistic purposes such as those which he himself had earlier espoused

(Alpern 1977), both immediately before and after the Tshernovits Language Conference of 1908 (Birnboym 1931; see section IV, below). This rare combination of complete Orthodoxy and uncompromising defense of Yiddish within an Orthodox framework have made Nosn Birnboym into something of a curiosity for both religious and secular commentators (Anon. 1977b; Kaplan and Landau 1925; Kisman 1962; Mayzl 1957). Such genuine returners to roots also exist in the context of other modernization movements (for example, in the nineteenth and twentieth century Greek, Arabic, Slavophile, and Sanskrit contexts) and represent a vastly overlooked subclass within the study of ethnicity movements. Even in their case it would be mistaken to consider them as no more than 'spokes in the wheels of progress' merely because they frequently represent an attempt to attain modernization without Westernization. A contrastive study of Birnboym and other such 'genuine returners' would be most valuable for understanding this subclass as well as the more major group of 'metaphorical returners'. Note, however, that Birnboym remained a committed advocate of Yiddish even when he embraced ultra-Orthodoxy, whereas 'true returners' in other cases embraced their respective indigenized classic tongues. To revive Hebrew was long considered antitraditional and was not possible except in speech networks that were completely outside of the traditional framework – ideologically, behaviorally (in terms of daily routine) and even geographically. The dubious Jewish asset of complete dislocation and deracination was denied the unsuccessful advocates of Sanskrit and classical Greek, Arabic or Irish.

cized past, when Orthodoxy reigned uncontested (Elzet 1929; Toybes 1950, 1952) and when its way of life was whole and uncontaminated (A. Levin 1976). Indeed, by mid-twentieth century the bulk of Orthodoxy per se had already wholeheartedly adopted modern participationist life-styles and had already made the difficult transition to the coterritorial vernaculars (including Ivrit in Israel), not only for conversational but for scholarly purposes as well. Since then a transition that had never been completely made before – certainly not in so far as Eastern-European Ashkenaz was concerned – has been made in the course of two generations of exposure to English, French or Spanish. Modern neo-Orthodoxy now views Yiddish wistfully, at best, and derisively at worst, but definitely allocates to it an even lower priority than that assigned to the study

די תקופה פון גלות מצרים און מתן תורה
ביז צום אריינגאנג פון אידן אין ארץ ישראל

ווי עס איז באשריבן אין די ספרים

שֵׁמוֹת־דְּבָרִים

איבערגעזעצט און בעארבעט
לויט די ערשטע מפרשי התורה

הוצאת
"כנות ירושלס"
מרכז לחנוך חרדי מסורתי לבנות בא"י
בעיה"ס ירושלם ת"ו

מהדורא ד', תשכ"ז

Figure 2. Yiddish textbook ('The period from the Egyptian exile and the Giving of the Law until the entrance of Jews into the Land of Israel, as it is related in the books of Exodus–Deuteronomy, translated and edited in accord with the first commentators on the Torah') for ultra-Orthodox schools for girls in Jerusalem. Fourth edition, 1967. The full series of Yiddish texts for these schools covers Yiddish language per se, arithmetic, history, and ethics.

of *loshn koydesh* originals via the coterritorial vernaculars (Fishman 1972; Fishman and Fishman 1977). With respect to safeguarding the future of Yiddish, neo-Orthodoxy does too little and does even that too late. Once coterritorial vernaculars become the process languages (i.e. the L varieties) of *yidishkayt* then it becomes patently unclear to Orthodoxy what Yiddish should be used for, since it 'obviously' cannot be used for H purposes. Even unreconstructed ultra-Orthodoxy the world over has recently begun to utilize a variety of non-Jewish languages in order to reach a wider public with the message of traditional life. Thus, for the first time, Yiddish is now encountering other instructional vernaculars even within the very classrooms, study halls and prayer houses of ultra-Orthodoxy that were its undisputed turf, and where even Sephardic and Western-secularized newcomers would learn Yiddish by dint of constant and intensive exposure. The next generation will reveal whether ultra-Orthodoxy will follow the path of neo-Orthodoxy with respect to Yiddish or whether it will remain a distinctive bastion of Yiddish rather than merely a nostalgic, ambivalent admirer from a distance.[4] Here it is still possible to take steps to alter the drift toward coterritorial monolingualism (Elberg 1962, Susholtz 1976). Ashkenazic Orthodoxy might have become a launching-pad for the spread of Yiddish to

4. I have pointed out elsewhere (see final chapter of this volume) that Israel represents a particularly good context for studying this particular topic. This is so not merely because of the well-entrenched enclaves of Yiddish speaking ultra-Orthodoxy there (Bogoch 1973; Poll 1980) but because the coterritorial population consists largely of fellow Jews (most of them secularized and some of them fervently antireligious) and the coterritorial vernacular is *ivrit* (= modern Israeli Hebrew), a modernized version of *loshn koydesh*. Both of the latter are therefore ambivalent referents for ultra-Orthodoxy and a classical double approach-avoidance dilemma surrounds interactive communication with or via them. This context is not only substantially different from the usual context of interaction with coterritorial non-Jews and use of coterritorial non-Jewish languages, but it is even different from the context of interaction with coterritorial secularized/assimilated Jews via Yiddish or the coterritorial non-Jewish vernacular. Ultra-Orthodoxy in Israel alone views Yiddish in a context where the brunt of secularization/ assimilation is expressed in Hebrew. The traditional ultra-Orthodox reluctance to profane *loshn koydesh* for secular affairs may thus endow Yiddish with an additional edge (although in doing so it reinforces the Israeli stereotype of Yiddish as a marker of antimodern and antistate extremism within the religious fold). One escape-hatch open to ultra-Orthodoxy in this context is to view *ivrit* as sufficiently dissimilar from *loshn koydesh* as to be regarded as a quite separate (and, therefore, unobjectionably permissable) vernacular in the traditional diglossic sense. If *this* interpretation is adopted – and there is evidence that many are doing just that, particularly as they reach out to influence non-Ashkenazic Israelis – Yiddish may ultimately be as expendable for Ashkenazic ultra-Orthodoxy in Israel as it is beginning to be in the United States and elsewhere in the Diaspora. Thus, it is the linguistic status of *ivrit vis-à-vis loshn koydesh* that may be crucial for the future of Yiddish among Ashkenazic ultra-Orthodoxy, this being a twist on the more usual problem of Yiddish *vis-à-vis* non-Jewish coterritorial vernaculars. In Likhtnshteyn's end of the nineteenth century's defense of Yiddish (1882–1887) he advised his ultra-Orthodox readers that far from being a corrupted German, Yiddish was purposely and desirably different from German so that Jews could more easily maintain themselves separate from non-Jews. (A similar view had also been expressed somewhat earlier by the famous Rabbi Khsam Soyfer of Presburg/Bratislava). He also admonished parents 'not to send their children to such yeshives where the rabbi is a secularized Jew [a *goyisher yid*]...who easily abandons and changes the Yiddish language to German'. The phenomenological applicability of such admonitions in Israel, particularly to ultra-Orthodoxy, is deserving of special attention since it expresses in the most succinct terms the ultimate functional role of Yiddish, namely as a guardian of *yidishkayt*. Once that role too is denied to it, then it is truly but another unexceptional vernacular.

others, particularly to *baley-tshuve* (those who return to religion). Failing that, it might at least have become the fortress of uncompromising language-maintenance. Instead, it is in danger of becoming neither the one nor the other.

PART III: MODERNIZATION MOVEMENTS AND MODERN ATTITUDES

In the latter part of the nineteenth century, Jewish Eastern Europe was caught up by the spirit of change. The coterritorial peoples, both those who were in political ascendancy and those who were politically powerless, reflected this spirit. Increasing urbanization, industrialization, massification of educational efforts, politicization of economic differences, movements for cultural autonomy and for national liberation made headway slowly but surely as the century began to draw to a close. The unification of Germany in 1865, the Junker victory in the Franco-Prussian War almost immediately thereafter, the subsequent Dreyfus case in France, the gathering *Drang nach Osten* of a militaristically intoxicated Germany, the increasingly evident internal problems of the multiethnic Austro-Hungarian, Czarist and Ottoman empires, all of these prompted a host of questions and answers among Eastern European Jewry. These questions and answers went far beyond the limited and guarded modernizing capacity of traditional Orthodoxy per se. New would-be elites (proto-elites) arose, as they did in all of the coterritorial modernization movements, to bring answers to the people (as well as the people to the proffered answers) and thus greatly heightened the issue of the language(s) to be used for these purposes. Under these circumstances it became impossible for any modern school of Jewish thought to avoid having a view with respect to Yiddish.

The mildest position – because it was least politicized – was taken by the initially inchoate forces referred to as the *haskole* (Enlightenment). These 'forces' (writers, journalists, educators) viewed general education, surface Westernization (in dress, in facial hair styles, in the privatization of religion), public vernacularization and a smidgeon or more of manual productivization as cure-alls for anti-Semitism, Jewish 'backwardness' and urban/small town poverty. (For a telling portrayal of the diversity of Jewish Eastern Europe that the *haskole* commonly overlooked see S. Birnboym 1946.) The *haskole* in Eastern Europe[5] came to employ Yiddish in its efforts to reach the widest possible public

5. This designation (usually in the form *haska-la(h)/haskolo(h)*) had also been used earlier in the late eighteenth and early nineteenth centuries in conjunction with a similar movement to Europeanize German (and, more generally, Western European) Jewry. The Western European *haskole* also vigorously opposed Yiddish (Kayserling 1862; Altman 1973), although it is an exaggeration to ascribe to it, or, as is more frequently done, to Moses Mendelssohn's translation of the Bible into German (so that the earlier Yiddish translations would no longer be needed), the decisive role in displacing Yiddish there. Although the Eastern European haskole inherited from its Western European predecessor a distinctly negative view of Yiddish (see Liptsin 1944 for the tradition of German dictionaries that define Yiddish in accord with the bias of the Western Enlightenment) the two *haskoles* ultimately took far different developmental paths. In the West the *haskole* led to mass

with its critiques and prescriptions, but commonly did so 'against its better judgement', half-heartedly, viewing Yiddish as a debased instrument at best. Debased, crippled, corrupted or not, it was the only way of reaching those most 'in need' of its message (Miron 1973a, 1973b). 'We will not wait until wags ask and prefer to say immediately that our simple Yiddish can certainly not be considered a language because it is no more than a corrupted German' (*Kol mevaser*, Nov. 15, 1862, p. 79). This is a view that appears early and retains adherents to this very day, as does the equally early view that it is unjust to

say that a language in which many thousands, a whole people, live, trade and work, is corrupted. Only something that was once better and became spoiled can be called corrupted. But where is the evidence that other current languages were initially better? Were they given on Mt. Sinai? They are all derived, as is our language, from various prior languages. Why, therefore, are they not called corrupted?...As soon as one of us begins to learn a foreign language he becomes an expert concerning the corruption of our language and begins to poke fun at it, and, finally, at us as well (Y. M. Lifshits in *Kol mevaser*, June 6, 1863, p. 326).

The facts of life were such that Yiddish *had* to be used, even by those self-proclaimed intellectuals who despised it, used even against itself; if the common man was to be reached, there simply was no alternative. Theoretically, elegant Hebrew would have been much preferable to the *maskilim* (the enlightened purveyors of *haskole*), but there was no real alternative to the use of Yiddish (indeed only via Yiddish could one lead the masses back to Hebrew if that was one's goal). Those like the renowned German-Jewish historian Heinrich Graetz, who were so ashamed of Yiddish as to refuse to use it at all, finally came to be viewed as full of self-hate and, therefore, as themselves a liability to the *haskole* and a source of general shame (Dinezon 1888).[6]

assimilation and apostasy (although not without difficulty; see, e.g. J. M. Cuddihy's *The Ordeal of Civility* [1974]) with an elitist intellectualistic focus upon Hebrew and Judaism as areas of scholarly inquiry. In the East the *haskole* led initially to the (reluctant) use of Yiddish as a vehicle for the spread of enlightenment, and finally to mass modernization movements of diverse but deeply Jewish orientation. Some of these movements, as we will see, became staunchly pro-Yiddish, while others wavered and finally opted otherwise. However, all of them pursued *kiyem ha-ume* (the continuity of the people) as an uncompromising and organized goal, a stage to which the Western *haskole* never attained.

The contextual reasons for the highly contrasted modernization routes of the *haskole* in Western and Eastern Europe need to be sought not only in terms of the Jewish formations in each (even in that connection it should not be overlooked that there *were* strong bastions of Orthodoxy in the German lands far into the nineteenth century, just as there *were* avowed asimilationists in the East at

a very early date). The entire coterritorial socio-economic context was different for Yiddish in the West and in the East, particularly in so far as the speed and depth of social mobility that was possible given detraditionalization. The entire view of the link between language and ethnicity in general, of the *possibility* of reethnification, was different in West and East, and these differences necessarily impacted the developmental path of the *haskole* and its relationship to Yiddish in both locales. For a model treatment of the influence of such pervasive differences upon a modernizing and potentially integrative language movement, see J. Das Gupta 1970.

6. Graetz called forth the wrath of several Eastern European *maskilim* because from his German (and Germanized) perspective it was both manifestly impossible and absolutely undesirable to use Yiddish for serious educational purposes. By the latter part of the nineteenth century, while this may well have been true in Germany proper, it obviously ran counter to the main thrust of *maskilic* efforts in Eastern Europe.

Once the initial reluctance to 'dirty one's pen' with Yiddish gave way, many Eastern European *maskilim* needed but a few decades or so to traverse the path from using (and advocating) Yiddish only for purposes of popular education and satire (see N.Z. 1944), to viewing it as a serious bridge to modernization (e.g. Lifshits 1867; for ample detail, see D. Fishman 1981), to valuing it as a means of moving masses toward Hebrew (or some other 'reasonable' language) as a spoken, written and read vernacular (Levinski 1889), to marveling at it as a surprisingly effective medium for even the most subtle communications from the intelligentsia to the masses (Bernfeld 1900; Sirkin 1900). By the end of the century several had gone further to accord it national, cultural/symbolic significance in its own right.

That the above-sketched *maskilic* progression was not uncontested is clearly indicated by the two contradictory quotations from *Kol mevaser* (within the period of a year). The latter view represented, more fully the basic view of the publication's editor, Aleksander Tsederboym, but it was frequently necessary for him to compromise with it and even to display the opposite stance, in order to avoid antagonizing the Czarist authorities and the small but influential russificatory/polonizing/germanizing circles (Shtif 1932, particularly pp. 29–33) that did not hesitate to report and defame pro-Yiddish tendencies to those authorities. Thus, whereas Mendele (the 'grandfather of modern Yiddish – and Hebrew – literature') proclaimed 'may God remember him for good, because he came to the help of his people with his newspaper *Kol mevaser* (1889 p. 26)' others were equally ready to condemn him for doing so, going so far as to suggest to the authorities that the modern education of Jews in the Czarist Empire could proceed only if all Yiddish publications whatsoever were prohibited (Tsinberg [1937] 1966: 148). That such recommendations did not fall upon deaf ears is clear from the record, although, fortunately, the Czarist authorities themselves were divided between those who believed that the modernization of Jews could proceed only *without* Yiddish and those who believed that only *through* Yiddish could the masses be led to Russian (or German, or even Polish) and to modernity. Tsederboym himself skillfully played upon this division within the Czarist ranks by admitting in 1862, the year that *Kol mevaser* began, that '...enlightened folk of this day and age stress that the masses must be dehabituated from speaking Yiddish and must become used to speaking the language of the country. Perhaps they are not entirely wrong, because one must understand the language of the country in which one resides; but in what language should one speak to simple folk, so that they will learn that which is necessary for everyone to know,

if after all is said and done, they understand nothing but Yiddish?' (Tsinberg [1937] 1966: 148–149). However, even the small group of contemporary Jewish polonizers felt that they could invoke Czarist support for their goals and against Tsederboym. 'Away with dirt, with spider-webs, with *zhargon* and with all kinds of garbage! We call for a broom! And whom the broom of satire will not help, him will we honor with the stick of wrath! Quem medicamenta non sanant, ferrum et ignis sanant!' (*Jutrzenka* 1862, no. 50, 428; also see Tsinberg [1937] 1966, 101). As fate would have it, the polonizers themselves became suspect in the eyes of the Czarist authorities, due to the Polish independence revolt of 1863, and their publication *Jutrzenka* was closed, whereas the *Kol mevaser* prospered for many years and ceased publication in 1872 (primarily due to Tsederboym's neglect after his moving from Odessa to St. Petersberg and leaving the paper in other, far less experienced hands).

Of course, the above sketched early opposition to Yiddish is less than half of the story, since it does not encompass the Hebrew invested opposition to Yiddish which was developed by yet other *maskilim* (e.g. Aḥad Ha-'am 1910) and, subsequently, by both Orthodox and secular Zionism (see below). The closest parallel to this complex picture of opposition to the vernacular of the masses on the part of an internal H language of classical sanctity, on the one hand, and on the part of several different European vernaculars, on the other hand, is the case of modern Somali. Faced by Arabic, on the one hand, and Italian and English, on the other, the recent triumph of Somali (but note: to be written in Latin rather than in Arabic script) is presented in all of its conflicted intricacy in David D. Laitin's *Politics, Language and Thought: The Somali Experience* [1977]). Cases such as these are significantly different from those of European vernaculars that succeeded in coming out from under the sociocultural-political shadow of languages of foreign influence or control (e.g. Slovak vs. Hungarian, Czech vs. German, Ukranian vs. Russian, Catalan vs. Spanish, Frisian vs. Dutch, etc.). The category to which the cases of Yiddish and Somali belong (as well as, e.g. the vernaculars of India vs. Sanskrit and English, modern Greek vs. Katharevusa and French or English, modern 'middle Arabic' vernacular vs. classical Arabic and French or English, modern Irish vs. classical Irish and English, etc.) is characterized by the existence of an *indigenized classical* H. Significantly, only in the case of Yiddish did the classical (Hebrew) also experience genuine vernacularization and modernization in its own right at the very same time as the vernacular (Yiddish) too was undergoing modernization and symbolic elaboration and codeification.

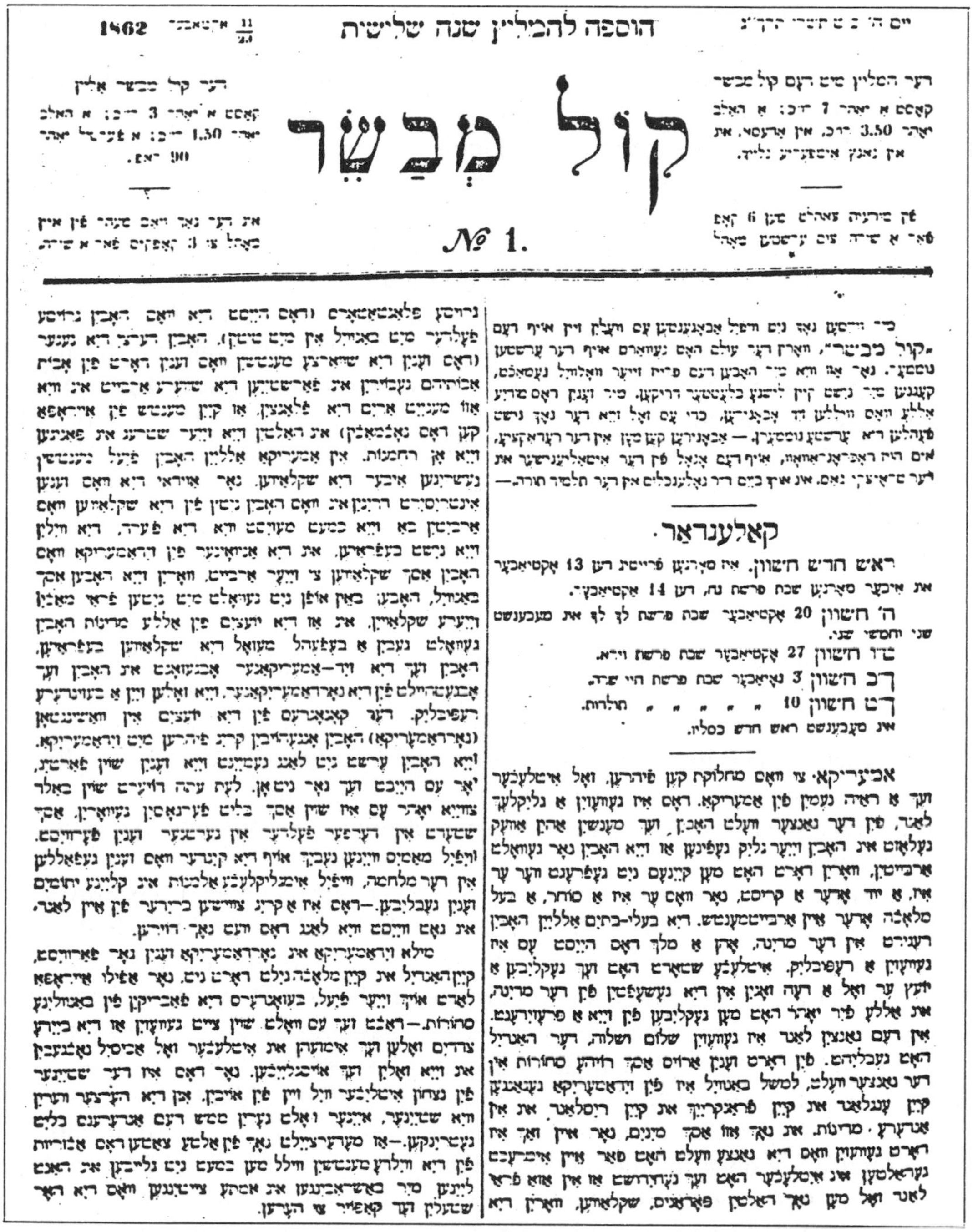

Figure 3. Front page of the first issue of *Kol mevaser* which initially appeared in 1862 as a supplement to *Hameliz*, a Hebrew weekly also owned and published by Alexander Tsederboym. 'We don't know how many subscribers there will be…but because we have made the price very inexpensive we cannot print any gratis copies. We are notifying all who want to subscribe so that later they will not be lacking the first issues…October 11–23, 1862.' The lead story deals with the American Civil War, with the widows and orphans and the grief and suffering that it has occasioned, and expresses hope that the two sides will come to an early understanding and cease further bloodshed ('frightful enough to curl one's hair').

The ranks of willing or begrudging 'educators of the masses' via Yiddish ultimately came to include most (or nearly so) of the illustrious *maskilim* of the late nineteenth and early twentieth century. Never uncontested, indeed always stoutly resisted almost every step of the way (e.g. Aḥad Ha-'am 1912; Drozdov 1959; Zilbertsvayg 1956), the use of Yiddish for *maskilic* communication early began to create true believers in Yiddish (e.g. Lifshits 1863; also note Prilutski 1917a re an 18th century 'Yiddishist' and ftn. 14, p. 380, this volume). By the beginning of the twentieth century, the young Germanized *maskil* (and future academic) Matesyohu Mizes achieved notoriety for his advocacy of Yiddish as a reflection of authentic Jewish creativity in the modern world, and for his temerity in saying so in the very den of renascent Hebraic journalism and in open opposition to some of its most renowned spokesmen (Mizes 1907; Mizes 1910; Kresl 1957; for his exemplary academic works see Mizes 1915 [in refutation of Loewe 1911] and 1924). A similar change of heart occurred early in the Russified historian of Eastern European Jewry, Shimen Dubnov, later to become the major theoretician of a multicentric view of Jewish cultural autonomy (Dubnov 1909, 1929b; Maler 1967a; Mark 1962a; Rotnberg 1961). Countless others followed suit – more or less altruistically/exploitatively – but in conjunction with political passions that finally flowered in a wide variety of directions.

The late nineteenth–early twentieth century politicization, mobilization, and fractionation of the *haskole* into seemingly opposed *diaspora cultural-autonomist* and *Zionist* camps (albeit the majority in both were at an early point socialists) led to a further heightening and sharpening of the conflict pertaining to Yiddish. Both camps foresaw a deterioration of the Jewish position in Eastern Europe – some spokesmen, indeed, had glimmerings of a holocaust to come, particularly as it pertained to the viability of the *shtetl*, on the one hand, and to urban anti-Semitism, on the other – and, therefore, feverishly set about advocating and devising 'a better future for the Jewish people'. Although most of them had come to agree as to the *immediate* utility of Yiddish, such agreement was hardly possible with respect to its long-range future. Finally, in the post-World War I era, the image of the desired, quasi-messianic future also fed back sharply on the implementation of the present. Blatantly pro- as well as anti-Yiddish activity was vigorously pursued 'as a matter of principle'. Thus, Yiddish became the only post-exilic Jewish vernacular to become symbolically (rather than merely functionally) involved in the modern, nationalist 'rebirth' of diaspora Jewry. From this involvement is derived the major advocacy and opposition to it to this very day. However, as we have seen, this involvement was inescapable.

The *diaspora cultural-autonomist* pro-Yiddish position did not develop easily out of the *haskole*'s ambivalence toward Yiddish. Socialism's dream of a united proletariat initially pointed toward Russian, German, or even Polish as the language(s) of the supraethnic brotherhood to come among all exploited nations of Eastern and Central Europe (Goldsmith 1976a; Hertz 1969; Pinson 1945).

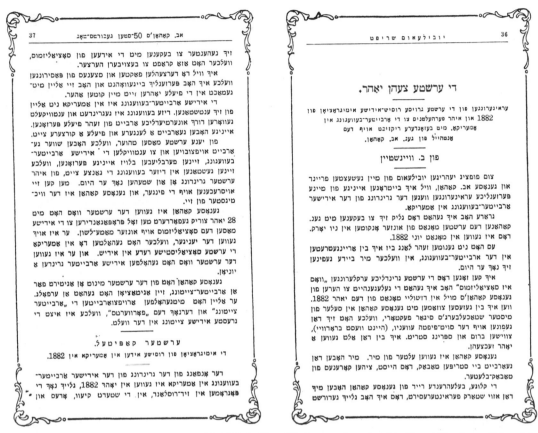

Figure 4. The first socialist lecture in Yiddish in New York was given by Ab Kan (Abraham Cahan) in 1882. 'The intellectuals almost laughed out loud at this odd suggestion: "To propagandize in Yiddish!?...Where will you get propagandists in Yiddish?", Mirovitsh asked. "Would you yourself be willing to lecture in Yiddish?" he asked Comrade Kan. Comrade Kan accepted...That was the beginning of Comrade Ab Kan's popularity, which continues to grow to this very day (Vaynshteyn 1910).'

However, the increasingly exceptional attitude toward Jews within the ranks of the coterritorial exploited bore unexpected fruit *vis-à-vis* Yiddish. The clearer it became that only Jews had been allotted no definite future as an ethnocultural entity in the proletarian heaven to come, and that, more immediately, Jews remained unwelcome even as proletarians in the coterritorial urban centers attracting growing numbers of unemployed Polish, Ukranian, Russian, Lithuanian, etc., ex-peasants, the more necessary it became for the 'Jewish Workers Bund of Russia, Poland, and Lithuania' to take an unambiguous position on behalf of Jewish cultural autonomy and economic activity in Yiddish, both for the here and now and for 'the better future' to come (Mendelsohn 1970; Tobias 1972). Although the non-Zionist radical camp was never fully united on this issue (not even among Bundists) – e.g., note the determined Soviet policy of cultural genocide toward Yiddish since the mid 1930s – the view that socialism and Yiddish culture (usually referred to as 'Yiddish secular culture') should and could flourish symbiotically became increasingly more popular, both prior to the first World War as well as during the interwar period. From weak origins in the last two decades of the nineteenth century (Bloom 1971, Kazhdan 1956a, 1956b) a truly amazing combination of pro-Yiddish literary–educational–political talent was assembled. No matter how typical such an assemblage was for all other Eastern European vernacular-based revolutionary movements of the time, it was essentially novel in the annals of Jewish history. Indeed, socialist Yiddishism gathered influential spokesmen from the ranks of popular educators (Zhitlovski 1900, 1912, 1923, 1940),[7] literary aspirants (Nomberg 1931) and budding linguistic specialists (Shtif 1933), to become one of the major paths of modern Jewish life prior to the Holocaust, and, to remain such for some to this

7. The seminal role of Dr. Khayim Zhitlovski in transforming Jewish socialism from a fixation upon Jewish amalgamation with the supraethnic proletariat into an acceptance of the legitimacy of Jewish peoplehood even in the socialist hereafter (not to mention during the 'long haul' till then) is belatedly becoming more apparent even to those for whom the bulk of his Yiddish writings are still largely inaccessible (thanks to Goldsmith 1975, 1976a, 1976b; Gutman 1976; Howe 1976; Knox 1945). From early beginnings in laborite Zionism, Zhitlovski first moved into Diaspora-oriented socialism-nationalism, and finally moved abruptly leftward into the fellow-traveler camp in the late thirties, to the consternation of most of his earlier admirers who remembered over half a century of pioneering Zhitlovskian formulation and advocacy of Yiddish based, secular, cultural-autonomism (Pinski 1935; Rivkin 1935). Both in Europe and in America Zhitlovski's moving and meticulously systematic lectures and articles (Robak 1935) swayed thousands of Jewish socialists and 'folk intellectuals' to divest themselves of opposition to Yiddish and Jewish ethnicity and, instead, to oppose assimilation (as well as the 'blue-white terror' of Hebraism via the 'blood-red counter-terror' of revolutionary Yiddishism [Zhitlovski 1923]). Although a committed exponent of dialectical materialism, Zhitlovski has been accused of 'Yiddishism without dialectics' (Maler 1967b) in view of his refusal to accept a lesser role for Yiddish in the 30s than that which he had envisaged at the beginning of the century. What most needs to be remembered today, however, rather than one or another of his extreme formulations, are his reconciliation of socialism and Jewish national-cultural creativity, his pioneering and positive formulation of modern Jewish secularism as a 'poetic-national rejuvenation of Jewish peoplehood' (see P. Matenko's English translation of this crucial early essay in Goodman 1976: 149–158, as well as Goodman's translation of Zhitlovski's early essay 'What is Jewish secular

culture?' 47–56; for a bibliography of Zhitlovski's writings up to a decade before his demise, see Roznboym 1929), the vital inspiration that he provided to the organizers and builders of Jewish secular schools in the United States and Canada (Novak 1948) and his early contributions to the terminological modernization and purification of Yiddish via his own voluminous writing on philosophical and sociopolitical topics. For similar careers of pioneering and extremism – such that ideological initiatives ultimately remained more important than actual accomplishments, many of which were vitiated by subsequent ideological initiatives – see Einar Haugen's 'Language planning in modern Norway' (1961) (particularly: the treatment of Ivar Aasen), and Jack Fellman's treatment of Eliezer ben Yehuda in his *The Revival of a Classical Tongue* (1973). Like both Aasen and ben Yehuda, Zhitlovski remains a controversial figure, subject to both adulation and sharp criticism to this very day, some forty years after his demise.

Zhitlovski's intercontinental role (he settled permanently in the United States soon after the Tshernovits Language Conference [1908] with 20 years of leadership already behind him) is an excellent example of the extent to which the ideological positions originally developed in Eastern Europe were quickly replanted and took root anew in the early postimmigration years in the United States and elsewhere. The Jewish socialist ('labor') secular scene in the Eastern European immigrant 'colonies' in the New World long witnessed many of the same debates, allegiances, schisms, and quandaries of its counterpart origin in the old country. Ab Kan (Cahan) claimed to be the first to give socialist speeches in Yiddish in the United States (in 1882) and, what is more, to demand that Yiddish (rather than Russian, German or English) be used for educating Jewish workers with respect to their socialist responsibilities and American opportunities (Vaynshteyn 1910; Higham 1975). Ab Kan's Yiddish speeches

very day. (On the need to keep in mind the assimilated bourgeoisie and attempt to attract it back to Yiddish see Zilberfarb 1928.)[8]

If the final and general socialist–autonomist *acceptance* of Yiddish had to struggle valiantly until its path was clarified even unto itself, the final and general Zionist *rejection* of Yiddish came more naturally, more easily, although, at least on the part of some, not without deep regret. Zionism and Hebraism were a natural pair and sprang full-blown, so to speak, from the brow of Jewish tradition into the modern activist arena. Even the assimilationist ripple in the Zionist sea, that ripple that saw in Zionism no more than an opportunity to be 'like unto (all) the gentiles' (or, as Aḥad Ha-'am put it, who saw in Zionism

were consciously peppered with Anglicisms and Germanisms (as were his many articles in the daily *Forverts* which he edited for so many years [1902–1951]) and its use at all was originally motivated pragmatically, in line with the views toward Yiddish of most early *maskilim*. After Irving Howe's volume on this topic (1975), it is not necessary to go into detail here concerning the long, sometimes conflicted, but remarkably creative and uplifting role of Yiddish in the American Jewish labor movement and its related cultural, philosophical, and ideological offshoots. Unfortunately, Howe tends to slight the role of Yiddish in nonsocialist circles during the same early immigrant period – the Orthodox and Zionist milieus being overlooked in particular, as well as a good bit of the communist oriented activity on behalf of and through Yiddish. Also somewhat paler than desirable is Howe's treatment of Yiddishism per se and, therefore, of the transformation or spillover from laborite *use* of Yiddish (admittedly, often enough, creative use) to laborite (and finally more than laborite) *symbolic elaboration and cultivation* of Yiddish (see, e.g. A. Tsh 1939 re B. Faygnboym's laborite-Yiddishism of the mid-1880s and Trunk 1976). The very process of elevation of Yiddish into a value and a cause in its own right, that had occurred in Eastern Europe between 1880–1920, also occurred, somewhat later on the whole, in the United States, and much of its impetus came from nationalist-secularist laborite circles (Levenberg 1974). This also tends to be the case to this very day, even though the designation 'laborite' must be understood more as an indication of sympathy and weltanschauung than of actual station in life (Doroshkin 1970). Nevertheless, we must take care not to commit the error *vis-à-vis* Yiddish that American laborite Yiddish secularism itself committed, namely, to assume that laborite Yiddish secularism was as central to the total world of Yiddish as the latter obviously was to the former.
8. The dual process of symbolic elaboration and spillover to new networks is evident in all successful language (and language and nationalism) movements and has been documented several times. I have attempted to delineate the theoretical grounds for both, but particularly the process of symbolic elaboration and cultivation, in my *Language and Nationalism* (1972b) and in my 'Ethnicity and language' (1977b). The Yiddish case is worthy of special attention because of the advanced biliteracy of its early ideologizers, thus enabling them to more rapidly formulate and disseminate their views as well as more rapidly to develop the capacities of their linguistic instrument while so doing. On the other hand, two themes that have been well developed in other contexts are, as yet, little developed in conjunction with the Yiddish case: (a) the extent to which the rhetoric/metaphor of symbolic cultivation is shared (e.g. Herderian) or indigenous (e.g. biblical, talmudic) and how the former source comes to be connected to the Yiddish scene; (b) the objective factors *distinguishing* between early pro- and anti-Yiddish protoelites, given that they shared so many sociocultural and politico-economic characteristics.

Due to the multiple tragedies that have befallen Eastern European Jewry and the doubly dislocative mobility that its 'colonies' have experienced, Yiddish secularist-cultural-autonomism failed to accomplish those social, political, and economic goals and safeguards that it generally recognized as necessary or desirable in its pre- and post World War I period of greatest growth and consolidation. As a result it presents a very advantageous case for the study of the course of ideological reformation and reinterpretation. Similar ideological revisions are going on in Norway (*vis-à-vis* Landsmaal or Nynorsk) and in Ireland (*vis-à-vis* Irish) today. An interesting comparative study is thus possible dealing with those elites who *do* and those who do *not* change their views, and what changes as well as what does not, when the objective circumstances surrounding language movements become drastically (and negatively) altered.

merely a solution to 'the Jewish question' – i.e. finding a place where persecuted Jews could live in safety – rather than a solution to 'the Jewishness question' – i.e. creating a society in which Jewish culture could develop without dislocative interference), could confidently prefer Hebrew to Yiddish (Heller 1974, 1977). Few Hebraists expected them to cultivate the former – which was fully alive only in the far away 'Land of Israel' – whereas the latter was ubiquitously present (Kazhdan 1956b) and called for use rather than merely admiration. 'Russian or Hebrew' 'Polish or Hebrew' were slogans that could unite Zionists, neo-Orthodoxy, and assimilationists both prior to and after the first World War, since their common element was hostility to Yiddish. Nevertheless, notwithstanding the obvious linguistic implications of the Zionist dynamics of 'returning to origins', to the wellsprings of eternal Jewish greatness in the Ancient Land, of the 'ingathering of exiles' including non-Ashkenazim as well, and of the striving for 'normalization' in all respects, including monolingualization[9]

9. The Zionist identification of multilingualism with Jewish exceptionality and the Zionist striving toward the monistic model of 'one language, one people' requires further elucidation. The objective need for a homeland and the subjective need for the original homeland do not necessarily imply monolingualism in Hebrew as Klatzkin ([1914] 1960) and so many others implied. The omnipresence of multilingual peoples throughout Jewish and general history (see Glyn Lewis's 'Bilingualism: the Ancient World to the Rennaissance' in Fishman 1976c: 150–200) could not have escaped the attention of Zionist theoreticians and activists. Some analysts and critics would derive the Zionist rejection of traditional Jewish societal multilingualism from its more inclusive rejection of the Diaspora experience as a whole (*shlilut hagalut*) and of Jewish exceptionality more generally, whether in the homeland or in the Diaspora. However, to the extent that that is so, Zionism manifests a tension present in most nineteenth century European nationalist movements, all of which took the putatively monoethnic Western European polities as their models of Europeanism and modernity.

Social theorists in eighteenth–nineteenth century England, France, and Germany (and even in Spain, Holland, and Scandinavia) spuriously viewed their own societies as ethnically homogeneous. They ascribed all sorts of benefits to such homogeneity, which they also advocated for the rest of Europe, thereby recognizing the fewest possible state-building and state-deserving nationalities. As I have indicated elsewhere (see Fishman 1972b, 1980a), it was the process of political consolidation and stabilization that Western social theory postulated as legitimately formative of ethnicity. Whereas Central and Eastern European nationality movements adopted the opposite stance (namely that ethnicity is and should be the creator of the state, rather than its by-product) they nevertheless adopted the Western ideal of ethnic and linguistic homogeneity as hallmarks of modernity. Unlike Third World compromises with multilingualism since the end of World War II, nineteenth-century nationality and state-building movements neither allowed for diglossia 'within' nor for multilingualism 'between' ethnicity collectivities. Rather than accept one or more languages of special communication for controlled intragroup and intergroup functions, as is the modern stance (see Fishman 1977c), they assumed that their own preferred vernaculars could and should suffice for all purposes, particularly at the intragroup level, very much as English, French or German could in *their* respective establishments.

Thus, the predominant Zionist rejection of either integrative or subethnicity symbolic functions for Yiddish and other post-exilic Jewish vernaculars is part and parcel of its late nineteenth-century (Eastern) European social theory heritage. To this more general stance one must add Zionism's particular distaste for Yiddish as the language associated with both ultra-Orthodox and secular rejection of Zionism. Note however the long continuing search for some positive accommodation with Yiddish in certain (particularly laborite) Zionist circles and the recent (post-Holocaust and particularly 70s) general mellowing toward Yiddish in Zionist/Israeli circles described below. For one of the few Zionist thinkers who has consistently viewed Zionism as the means of preserving and furthering all Jewish cultural diversity see Sadan 1977, 1978.

(Fishman 1979), the Zionist abandonment of Yiddish was not uncomplicated. Some trotted out the Orthodox argument of Hebraic eternity (Aleksander 1914; Byalik 1931; Bileẓki 1970; Golomb 1943; Liptsin 1970; Sirkin 1923), even though they were themselves far from Orthodoxy. Others, like Sokolov, stressed the purported superiority of Hebrew for the ingathering of exiles from non-Ashkenazic settings (Malakhi 1961; Ben-tsvi 1956), although Yiddish speaking Ashkenazim were by far the bulk of early Zionist leaders, pioneers, supporters and settlers, and they could, therefore, have converted the non-Ashkenazim to Yiddish – just as they converted them to vernacular Hebrew and to many other secular-socialist Zionist ideals – had they wanted to do so. Still others 'innocently' claimed that Yiddish simply lacked the 'dynamism' to become the language of the new *yishuv* (settlement) (Ben-tsvi 1956), even though punitive methods frequently had to be resorted to in order to 'discourage' settlers from using this purportedly undynamic tongue (e.g. Aleksander 1914a; Kaẓenelson 1919) and in order to provide Hebrew with some of the punch that it apparently lacked in purely verbal interaction.[10]

And still it did not come easy. Not only had some of the leading diaspora *ḥaverim* (comrades) made major contributions to the study and cultivation of Yiddish (e.g. Borokhov 1913a, 1913b; also see Alpern 1977; Maler 1967c; and Zerubovl 1966), and not only did socialist colleagues (from inside and outside

10. For a detailed analysis of the first decade and a half of the *riv haleshonot* (the language dispute) see Pilovski 1973, 1977, 1979. The details concerning the second decade and a half have not yet been integrated. Among the interesting pro-Yiddish reflections of the latter period see Anon. 1935a ('Yiddish in Erets-Yisroel must be tolerated, respected and legalized'), Kendzherski 1937, and Zerubovl 1936. The dispute provides ample data for the student of language attitudes. On the pro-Hebrew side an article by Sirkin (1923) handily summarizes (in Yiddish) the major Zionist stereotypes concerning Yiddish then current (and largely repeated to this very day): Yiddish is no more than an ephemeral 'daughter of the earth' whereas Hebrew is the true and eternal 'daughter of heaven'. Although Yiddish is demonstrably little different from German (except for its Hebraisms; note Sirkin's elaborate 'proof' for laymen) it can nevertheless fill several important functions, e.g. to help make the masses conscious of Hebrew, to lead them to it, and, finally, to abdicate in favor of her heavenly sister.

Writing at the same time and in the same journal, Tshermer articulates the two major Yiddishist counterclaims: Yiddishism seeks its language for the masses; Hebrism seeks the masses for its language. Without Yiddish a new generation must arise in Erets Yisroel that has no connection either with *yidishkayt* or with world Jewry.

The Yiddish vs. Hebrew claims and counter-claims differ interestingly from those advanced in certain other diglossic settings but are strikingly similar to yet others. Commonly, where no deeply classical tradition exists, L-advocates claim greater authenticity, i.e. symbolic relatedness to the original and uncontaminated *volksgeist*. This is true in conjunction with Landsmaal vs. Riksmaal, Turkish vs. Persian/Arabic, Guaraní vs. Spanish, etc. However, where such a classical tradition *does* exist the L cannot claim to be as directly related to it as is the H (note the cases of Sanskrit, Katharevusa, classical Arabic). L, therefore, is defended as useful, natural, unmediated, affect-laden and sanctified-by-association, whereas it is attacked as ephemeral, irregular, irrational, contaminated by foreign influences, unpolished and demeaned/demeaning. All of these respective attitudinal composites can be discussed in terms of the absence or presence of one or another of Stewart's dimensions (vitality, historicity, autonomy, and standardization) but it is the reversal with respect to historicity that I would like to stress here in comparing the view of Ls, even among many of their own adherents, when we view Ls in the absence and in the presence of classical indigenous or indigenized Great Traditions.

'the movement' proper) appeal for cultural democracy *vis-à-vis* Yiddish, but within the movement itself, and within the Holy Land itself, the debate continued well into the 1930s (Zhitlovski 1914; Yehoyesh 1917; Pilovski 1973, 1977, 1980). Meyerzon cautioned against a Zionism that was intolerant and that rejected its Yiddish speaking mothers and fathers as if they were contaminated (1919), offering them neither simple decency nor Jewish recognition. Loker argued against the schizophrenia of exploiting Yiddish in the diaspora (for fund raising, resettlement agitation, and Zionist education more generally) while exterminating it in the Homeland, even though it still possessed thousands upon thousands of speakers in the latter locale (1920). Left-wing Zionist pioneers claimed that 'free expression in Yiddish in all areas of cultural life is required for the satisfaction of our spiritual needs; it is not a reaction against anyone, but rather, an organic necessity of life. We neither can nor will we stop short of the greatest sacrifices in order to satisfy our needs in this respect' (Anon 1928a). Others were convinced that Marxism itself, not to mention the whole course of modern history, demanded the triumph of the proletarian vernacular (Maler 1925, 1947). Even today, after the struggle is considerably muted (Fishman and Fishman 1977), when all that Yiddish asks or can hope for in Israel is a fairly minimal symbolic nod (Herman 1972, 1977), its echoes continue to reverberate in more poetic form in conjunction with memories of cadences lost, of songs and expressions borrowed but not acknowledged, of sensitivities denied, of laughter stifled and spontaneity yet to return (Hameiri [1950] 1973; Megged 1966; Pat 1960; Sadan 1972c).

If the pre-World War II Zionist struggle against Yiddish has led to no major, post-Holocaust Zionist *mea culpas* (and, indeed, to continued anti-Yiddish activity in the diaspora – particularly in Latin America – under the slogan of 'Hebraizing the diaspora') the same cannot be said of the pro-Yiddish cultural–autonomist camp. Here we find regrets aplenty, particularly that traditional life was unnecessarily abandoned or destroyed, without adequate thought as to what, if anything, could take its place, as a daily pattern that would shield Yiddish in modern, interactional urban life on a minority (and often immigrant minority) footing (Golomb 1947; Saymon 1954a, 1954b, 1970). Nevertheless, the life-urge among secular Yiddishists continues, only slightly the worse for wear, and plans or pleas for the revitalization of Yiddish abound. Among some, it reveals an unabashed Yiddishism in all of its pristine secularism and linguocentrism (Pen 1941; Robak 1958a, 1958b). In others, it takes on a more all-inclusive 'united front' guise and an anti-assimilationist focus (Kozlovski 1967; Mark 1970; Tsanin 1966; Shteynberg 1968). In still other

◄ Figure 5. 'The League for the Rights of Yiddish in Palestine' (1935–1939) attracted both Zionist, non-Zionist and anti-Zionist members. One of its major accomplishments: the establishment and maintenance of a Yiddish printing establishment in Ramat Gan, necessary because most printers were too frightened by Hebraist strong-arm tactics to agree to print Yiddish books or periodicals.

cases, it is espoused more metaphorically, in terms of its most subtle (and elusive?) connotations, associations, and implications with respect to the total complex of Ashkenazic Jewry (Landis 1962; Winer 1961; M. Vaynraykh 1951a; Golomb 1967). Whether it is fated to disappear or not, the struggle for Yiddish is far from over as far as the true believers are concerned. For them it has become not merely an article of faith but a faith per se (Hesbacher and Fishman 1965).[11]

PART IV: HISTORIC MOMENTS

The flow of events from the last quarter of the nineteenth century to the last quarter of the twentieth century has witnessed both the heights of attainment and recognition for Yiddish, as well as the depths of annihilation and rejection. So much in one century! A few dramatic events represent the peaks of what was, as well as pay homage, often belatedly, to what might have been.

Perhaps the loftiest peak of all was the Tshernovits (Chernovtsy, Chernowitz)

---

11. The advocacy of Yiddish, the strong bonds of affection that continue for it even among some of those who rarely speak it, as well as the tender fondness for it that often springs up among some who never spoke it (and who may even only have seldom heard it) and who will probably never come to speak it, is an important phenomenon of considerable sociolinguistic generality. This phenomenon deserves further clarification at least on three levels. Most generally put, affect toward language seems to be only weakly related to knowing or using it. This is evidenced both positively and negatively, in connection with classical tongues, vernaculars, and languages of wider communication, and has been documented most extensively in recent days in conjunction with English (see Fishman 1977d) and Irish (see Anon. 1975). Classical languages such as Hebrew, Latin, Arabic, Sanskrit, etc. have benefited from mass attitudinal haloization unrelated to usage for centuries, and vernaculars are also capable of affective functional autonomy along similar lines.

However, in the case of Yiddish and other rather disadvantaged vernaculars there is more involved in such affective 'after-life' than all of the great and beautiful societal ideals, cultural/literary monuments and movements, or acknowledged integral life patterns with which it was (and often still is) associated. Yiddish also seems to represent *gemeinschaft* lost, the intimate and unconscious attachment to place and people, the touching particularism of premodern interdependence, in short, the sight and sound and smell of primordiality that so moved the peripathetic Ulysses when he once again caught a distant glimpse of the smoke slowly rising out of his own homey chimney. Yiddish, therefore, even when unspoken, can represent not only an antedeluvian High Culture which must be appreciated, salvaged, and reconstructed, but it quintessentially represents (as does, for some, Irish, Breton, Occitan, Romansch, Frisian, etc.) not so much emotion or mirth alone (both of which have been much overstressed) as the *weltschmerz* and longing for intimate roots and relationships that modern life both denies and exacerbates, counteracts and reinforces. The paradise of primordiality may be both false and unregainable, but the longing for it is destined to flicker on and to flame up anew as the benefits of modernity fall short of our aspirations and as the problems of modernity (most of them, unanticipated system linkages tied into the benefits thereof) multiply endlessly.

Thus does the past remain an emotional dynamic in our perception of the present and in our program for the future. Yiddish, however, is not only relatable to an idyllic past and Messianic future (dynamics evident also in conection with other similarly disadvantaged vernaculars), but it is the possession of a people that has long incorporated and several times experienced rebirths, returns, and recoveries. The faith in Yiddish seems, therefore, to be triply protected, both general and unique dynamics being at play and reinforcing each other in the conscious behavior of the faithful. In Fishman 1966 (see particularly chapter 12) I have tried to explain why such ethnicity-related language-faith is so difficult to hand on intergenerationally. In Fishman 1977b, I have tried to indicate why such ethnicity-related language-faith is self-renewing in modern contexts, even in the absence of overt language use.

Language Conference of 1908 (Lerner 1957; Goldsmith 1976b), a brainchild of S. Birnboym, Zhitlovski and the Labor-Zionist oriented writer, David Pinski (Pinski 1948). It left behind it a whirlwind of commentary, memoirs, and expectations – and, as with all things that touch upon Yiddish, a huge gamut of opinion. Now, over seventy years later, it is still not clear, as it was unclear even at the Conference and immediately thereafter, just what it accomplished. Its concrete recommendations never materialized, for it had no follow-through apparatus. However it did signal a change in mood, focus, and level of self-regard along the entire spectrum of Yiddish activists and devotees (Mayzl 1928b). At Tshernovits, Yiddish was proclaimed *a* (not *the* but *a*) national language of the Jewish people. As such it deserved respect, cultivation, protection, recognition, and calculated promotion, for both secular and traditional functions, both among Jews as well as between Jews and non-Jews (e.g. with governmental agencies, in legislative bodies in which other minority languages were recognized, and in government-subsidized cultural efforts). Its writers, teachers and advocates were to be viewed as engaged in a great national mission of furthering the identity and fostering the creativity of the Jewish masses (Mizes 1931). A panoply of schools, theaters, modern and traditional genres (including a modern translation of the Bible, see Ash 1931, Elzet 1951), and organizations would arise to serve it and through it to serve the people. Verbiage? Certainly. Mysticism? Perhaps. But the spirit of the times was such as to take note! Even in distant America the daily Yiddish press tried, albeit not very successfully, to explain how the Tshernovits principles could (or could not) relate to American Jewish realities (Rothstein 1977). Closer at hand, in Austro-Hungarian Galicia and Bukovina, both Zionists and Bundists intensified their pre-Tshernovits campaign to declare Yiddish as their 'national mother tongue', even though replies to this effect in the 1910 Census were not only to be discounted but were punishable by fines (Shveber 1911; Sokal 1942). However, the spirit of Tshernovits marched on. The initial published reports (not only in Yiddish, as e.g. A.R. 1908; Prilutski 1908a; Zhitlovski 1908; Perets 1909; and, more generally, Anon 1931a, but also – and, of course, more negatively – in Hebrew, e.g. Aḥad Ha-'am 1908; Epshteyn 1910; as well as at the so-called 'Hebrew Language Conference', Zaydman 1910)[12] have been ritually followed up every decade (except perhaps,

---

12. Aḥad Ha-'am refused to join a planned protest by Hebrew writers outraged at the 'excesses of Tshernovits'. He termed the whole Conference a *purim shpil* (Aḥad Ha-'am 1908; also see Drozdov 1959) and cautioned that it would be far better to ignore it since to attack it would be to dignify it and to publicize it. If only Jews had followed similar advice in connection with Jesus and Hasidism, he concluded, both would have received far less attention and experienced far less success than they did. Aḥad Ha-'am tended to take the Tsher-

novits Conference far less seriously than it deserved to be, given the configuration in which it transpired. The utility of language conferences for the quite separate purposes of (a) language promotion for demographically and functionally strong languages and (b) language maintenance for demographically and functionally weak ones is discussed in my paper on the 1976 World Conference for Yiddish and Yiddish Culture (Fishman 1976b). In general the former have been quite successful (or, better put, related to successful

for the first, when much of Eastern Europe was still reeling from war [but note Shtif 1919]). There have been articles commemorating: twenty years since Tshernovits (Vislevski 1928; Pludermakher 1928; Prilutski 1928; Mayzl 1928a; Zhitlovski 1928; Golomb 1928; Kan 1928a, 1928b; and a list of others in Anon 1931; note the negative evaluations at that time by Kazhdan 1928 and Khmurner 1928), thirty years since Tshernovits (Vays 1937), forty years since Tshernovits (Niger 1948; Pinski 1948) – the Congress for Jewish [= Yiddish] Culture coming into being in connection with this date – fifty years since Tshernovits (Kisman 1958; M. Vaynraykh 1958) – the Committee for the Implementation of the Standardized Yiddish Orthography pegging its initiation to this date – sixty years since Tshernovits (Rozenhak 1969; Mark 1968; Kazhdan 1969) and, most recently, seventy years since Tshernovits (Bez 1976). As with all unforgettable crescendos, future admiring commentary can be predicted with absolute confidence.

In comparison to Tshernovits other moments are paler but yet clearer. At the 1919 Peace Conference in Paris, it was agreed to require that public elementary schools for Jewish children in the new Poland be conducted in Yiddish, the mother tongue of the children (Tenenboym 1958; somewhat similar provisions also pertained in the Baltic region). Unfortunately, the Polish constitutional convention in 1920 adopted a far weaker provision, not only with respect to the language of schooling of minority children but with respect to public or official usage of minority languages more generally (Tikotshinski 1937). Seven years later (1927) Yiddish was once more slighted, and this time in Jerusalem. There the newly established Hebrew University decided *not* to establish a chair in Yiddish (Anon 1928b, 1928c). Retrospectively this was attributed to fear of

movements) whereas the latter have been singularly unsuccessful.

Calls for another international conference to be concerned with furthering 'Yiddish culture' began to be issued quite soon after Tshernovits (see, e.g. Sh. N. 1922; Pludermakher 1928). At that time the demographic-functional role of Yiddish in Eastern Europe was even more favorable than it had been during Tshernovits. Such calls multiplied after the Second World War, particularly as it became clear that neither the Congress for Jewish [= Yiddish] Culture (founded 1948) nor the left-wing YIKUF (Yidisher Kultur Farband, founded 1937) could mobilize the funds or the manpower that was required if Yiddish was to recover from the decimation of its heartland. Such calls inevitably harkened back to Tshernovits (e.g. Zhitnitski 1952; Mark 1968; Zelitsh 1968) but, unfortunately, did not grasp the diminished possible significance of language conferences for languages under adverse demographic-functional circumstances. Conferences necessarily relate best to the affective (liking) and cognitive (knowing) levels of language behavior, since the means of fostering attitudes and familiarity are most easily influenced. However, not only is the link between liking and using an extremely tenuous one (see note 12, above) but the link between knowing and using is even more tenuous (viz the millions of students who spend years learning languages that they never use, not so much because they have not learned them well enough but because their interpersonal networks neither substantially require nor reward such use). The major problem facing demographically/functionally weak languages is not that they are unliked and not that they are unknown, but, rather, that they are unused for crucial life functions, particularly as mother tongues and as vernaculars of crucial status-role interactions. Thus, what is needed, basically, is to bring about the demographic renativization and the functional renaturalization of such weak languages and this is both more difficult to attain and usually not appreciated by the literary, artistic, educational, activist oriented leaders of, and participants in, language conferences.

drawing upon the still fledgling University the fire of the militantly Hebraist *gedud m'giney hasafa*, which had alerted the public that 'an idol was about to be brought into the Sanctuary' (Shwabe, in Anon. 1951; Pilovski 1977). However, nearly a quarter century thereafter (1951), that wrong was righted and a chair in Yiddish *was* finally established in Jerusalem, accompanied by all of the academic and governmental pomp and circumstance normally associated with expiations of guilt (see particularly the remarks by Dinaburg, Greenberg, and Sadan in Anon. 1951). Nearly another two decades slipped by before an Israeli Prime Minister could admit – at a private ceremonial rather than at a governmental substantive initiative – that

the spirit of the murdered millions lives in Yiddish culture. We dare not commit the offense of not having provided our youth with a consciousness of deep attachment to those millions and to the great cultural treasure they created...It is now much easier to do so than it was a few decades ago...This is a wonderful youth and it would be the greatest injustice for them not to recognize the great Jewish-national values that Jews have created in Yiddish (Meir [Meyer] [1970] 1973).

Figure 6. The Hebraists' response to the Tshernovits Language Conference of 1908 was, in part, to studiously ignore it (Aḥad Ha-'am's advice) and, in part, to counter with a conference of their own, held in Berlin, December 19–21, 1909. A Yiddish brochure was published (in a first edition of 10,000 copies) to make sure that the Jewish masses would learn of the conference's efforts to revitalize the Hebrew language.

And finally, six years later, in 1976, yet another Yiddish language conference took place. Almost seventy years after Tshernovits, and 50 years after the original refusal to establish a Yiddish chair at the Hebrew University, a World Conference for Yiddish and Yiddish culture took place in Jerusalem and was officially greeted by the Minister of Education as follows:

Together with the Jewish people that was incinerated in the Nazi crematoria, both languages [Yiddish and Hebrew] went up in flames. And many generations will be unable to fill the vacuum which was created in our national life. We cannot bring back the communities that were destroyed in the Holocaust. However, we *can* preserve their great spirit and their rich and glorious culture. In my opinion that is the duty and the responsibility of the State of Israel. It is our responsibility to exert ourselves to gather all of the cultural treasures that the Jewish people has brought with it from the diaspora. This is a noble but a difficult responsibility, but it is clear to us that what the State of Israel will not manage to do in this area...will simply not be done (Yadlin 1976).

Just prior to this conference, and as an obvious move in setting the mood and preparing the ground for it, the Ministry of Education announced that the study of Yiddish and Judesmo could count toward high school graduation for those students who wished to study yet another foreign language in grade 10 (in addition to English, the study of which is begun in grade 5). If this too, not unlike modern Orthodoxy's 'change of heart', was too little and too late (Sheyntukh 1977), it was at least, a markedly new tune. (For an earlier solitary 'breakthrough' of Yiddish into the Israel high school world see Zamir 1968.) It still remains to be seen, however, whether the Conference in Jerusalem will have significantly more tangible results than did the one in Tshernovits some seventy years earlier, or whether it will remain at the level of plans, promises, and party politics (Anon. 1977a; Botvinik 1976; Fishman 1976b; Pelts 1976) at a time when there is no longer any hinterland such as the one that Tshernovits possessed and when nativization and naturalization are the crying needs, rather than more propaganda and more publications.

PART V: FORMAL INSTITUTIONS OF LANGUAGE

Yiddish journalism

Beleaguered and bedeviled as it always was and is, both from without and from within, a modern world of Yiddish nevertheless came into being, boasting many of the modern urban institutions of cultural expression and development. Almost all of these institutions had their modern beginnings toward the end of the nineteenth century, but, if carefully examined, their origins can be found much earlier. Thus, though the *Kol mevaser* is ostensibly the first Yiddish weekly with any stability in the Czarist empire, beginning publication in 1862 (Arz 1869; Malakhi 1965), the roots of the Yiddish press date back hundreds of years earlier – indeed to 1687 – and to Western Europe per se (see e.g. Hal 1975; Probst 1922;

די ייד. פרעסע פון גאר דער וועלט אין פארש. שפראכן

(* 1557—1920 אין די יארן)

די דריי טאבעלעס, מאָס װערן װײטער געבראכט װײ... די טאבעלעס זיינען צונויפגעשטעלט צוריק מיט עט־
נען א סך־הכל פון מײנער א גרעסערער אַרבעט... העלכע לעצע חדשים און פאר דער צײט זײנען אין מיינע רשי־
...נטהאָלט אויכפירלצכע רשימות פון דער גאָנצער ייב... מות פאָרעקומען אײניקע ענדערונגען. דעריבער סמיכען
שער פרעסע אין פאַרשיידענע לענדער אין דריטיק פאָר... נישט די בך־הכלס אין די די טאבעלעס אין קלײניקײטן.
סיירדנסטע שפראכן אין די יארן פון 1557 בין 1920.

איבערדרוקן פארבאָטן.

ט אַ ב ע ל ע   1

די יידישע פרעסע אין פאַרשיידענע שפראכן פון יאר 1557—1920.

סך־הכל																				שפּראך	נומער
635	145	6	6	17	47	29	42	2	2	30	5	—	137	33	1	113	3	5	12	העברעיש	1
1443	216	160	20	—	179	67	30	—	—	9	1	—	136	63	1	382	19	5	150	ייִדיש	2
103	—	—	—	—	33	1	1	—	—	—	1	—	5	8	1	49	—	3	1	שפּאניאָליש	3
54	1	—	—	—	19	—	6	—	—	1	—	—	9	4	—	14	—	—	—	אונגאַריש	4
29	—	—	—	—	14	—	2	—	—	—	1	—	10	1	—	1	—	—	—	איטאַליעניש	5
30	—	—	—	—	12	—	—	—	—	—	—	—	4	1	—	8	1	1	3	אראַביש	6
1	—	—	—	—	—	—	—	—	—	—	—	—	—	—	—	—	—	—	?1	בוכאַריש	7
13	—	—	—	—	8	—	1	—	—	—	1	—	—	1	—	2	—	—	—	בולגאַריש	8
1	—	—	—	—	—	—	—	—	—	—	—	—	—	—	—	—	—	—	—	גרוזיניע	9
6	—	—	—	—	1	—	—	—	—	—	—	—	5	—	—	—	—	—	—	גריכיש	10
538	31	—	—	—	129	16	61	3	—	8	3	—	103	45	3	131	2	1	2	דײטש	11
4	—	—	—	—	2	—	1	—	—	—	—	—	—	—	—	—	—	—	—	דעניש	12
49	1	—	—	—	9	—	8	—	—	1	—	1	7	1	—	21	—	—	—	האָלענדיש	13
1	—	—	—	—	—	—	—	—	—	—	—	—	1	—	—	—	—	—	—	ווייסרוסיש	14
8	—	—	—	—	5	—	—	—	—	—	1	—	1	1	—	1	—	—	—	סערביש	15
6	—	—	—	—	1	—	—	—	—	—	—	—	3	—	—	2	—	—	—	טשעכיש	16
4	—	—	—	—	3	—	—	—	—	—	—	—	1	—	—	—	—	—	—	מאַהראַטיש	17
1	—	—	—	—	1	—	—	—	—	—	—	—	—	—	—	—	—	—	—	נאָרוועגיש	18
4	—	—	—	—	—	—	—	—	—	—	—	—	1	—	—	3	—	—	—	סעראַביש	19
495	2	—	—	—	152	7	23	—	1	14	6	2	142	18	—	124	2	—	3	ענגליש	20
1	—	—	—	—	1	—	—	—	—	—	—	—	—	—	—	—	—	—	—	פאַרטוגעזיש	21
54	3	—	—	—	6	3	2	—	—	2	—	—	9	4	—	20	—	—	4	פויליש	22
2	—	—	—	—	2	—	—	—	—	—	—	—	—	—	—	1	—	—	—	פערסיש	23
2	—	—	—	—	2	—	—	—	—	—	—	—	—	—	—	—	—	—	—	פיניש	24
105	2	—	—	—	42	4	12	—	—	4	1	—	21	5	—	14	—	—	—	פראַנצויזיש	25
1	—	—	—	—	—	—	—	—	—	—	—	—	1	—	—	—	—	—	—	קאַאָטש	26
32	—	—	—	—	13	—	4	—	—	—	—	—	3	2	—	10	—	—	—	רובעניש	27
200	13	—	—	—	43	20	5	—	—	44	—	—	25	21	—	64	4	—	1	רוסיש	28
2	—	—	—	—	2	—	—	—	—	—	—	—	—	—	—	—	—	—	—	שוועדיש	29
2	—	—	—	—	—	—	—	—	—	—	—	1	1	—	—	—	—	—	—	שפּאַניש	30
3827	414	166	26	17	725	147	198	5	3	73	19	3	626	216	6	950	31	15	177		

Table 1. 'The worldwide Jewish press in various languages for the years 1557–1920' (Probst 1922). Of the 3827 publications listed, 1443 are in Yiddish, 635 in Hebrew, 538 in German, 495 in English, 200 in Russian, 105 in French, 103 in Judesmo, etc. Of the 177 dailies identified, 150 are in Yiddish.

טאַבעלע II

די יידישע פרעסע לויט שטעט און לענדער:

אונגאַרן: (13)		**אַרגענטינע: (19)**		נעוויעד	2	בירלסק	1
בודאַפעסט	8	אָכבו	1	פֿירט	1	בענדין	3
מאַרמאָראָש	2	בוענאָס אײרעס	17	פֿראַנקפֿורט	1	גראָדנע	5
קעסטהעלים	1	קאָלאָניע קלאַרא	1	קעניגסבערג	2	וואַרשע	308
פּרעסבורג	1	**ארץ-ישׂראל: (21)**		**דענעמאַרק: (3)**		חעלצלאַמעק	1
קאַשוי	1	יפֿו	3	קאָפּענהאָגן	3	זאַגלעבביע	2
אוקראַינע: (121)		ירושלים	17	**ווײסרוסלאַנד: (50)**		לאָדז	19
אָדעס	31	ראשון-לציון	1	באַברויסק	5	לובלין	3
ביעלאַ-צערקאָו	1	**בוקאָווינע: (9)**		בערדיטשעוו	5	פּינסק	2
זשיטאָמיר	5	טשערנאָוויץ	9	פּינסק	40	פּיעטריקאָו	2
קאַרקאָו	16	**בעמען: (3)**		**זיבנבירגן: (1)**		טשענסטאָכאָו	5
פּאָלטאַוע	2	פּראג	3	ביסטריץ	1	ראַדאָם	1
פּרילוקי	3	**בעלגיע: (3)**		**ליטע: (118)**		ראָוונע	1
קיעוו	63	אַנטווערפּן	2	ווילנע	107	שעדלעץ	2
אינדיע: (4)		גענט	1	פֿאַניעוויעזש	1	**פֿראַנקרײַך: (8)**	
באָמבײַ	3	**בעסאַראַביע: (1)**		קאָוונע	8	פּאַריז	8
קאַלקוטאַ	1	קישינעוו	1	שאַוועל	1	**קאַנאַדע: (4)**	
אַמעריקע: (303)		**גאַליציע: (119)**		שירווינט	1	סאַראַנטאַ	2
אורעגאָני	2	בראָד	2	**ליפֿלאַנד: (8)**		מאָנטרעאַל	2
אַטלאַנטאַ	1	דראָהאָביטש	3	האַלק	1	**קאַווקאַז: (2)**	
באַלטימאָרע	4	זלאָטשעוו	3	ליבאַווע	1	באַקו	2
באָסטאָן	7	וישלקיעוו	1	ריגע	6	**רומעניע: (26)**	
בראָנזוויל	1	סאָרנאַצאל	4	**מעהרען: (1)**		באָטאָשאַני	3
ברוקלין	6	סימיעניץ	2	בריןן	1	בוקארעסט	13
דעטראָיט	1	טשאָרטקאָוו	2	**מצרים: (1)**		גאַלאַץ	2
וואָרטשעסטער	1	לעמבערג	45	קאַיראָ	1	יאַסי	8
הינדזבג	4	נאַדוואָרנע	2	**עלז.-לאָטרינגען: (2)**		**רוסלאַנד: (89)**	
לואיסוויל	2	סאַנאָק	1	מעץ	2	באַריסאָגלעבסק	1
מילוואָקי	2	סטאַניסלאַווֿאָוו	15	**ענגלאַנד: (56)**		דווינסק	1
ניו-יאָרק	215	סטרי	4	גלאַזגאָו		האָמעל	8
נואַרק	1	פּשעמישל	3	לאָנדאָן	52	האַראָדאָק	1
סאַן-פֿראַנצ.	3	קאַלאָמיי	7	ליווערפּאָל	1	חיטעבסק	5
ס״ט לואיס	6	קראָקע	20	לידס	2	יעקאַטערינאָסלאַו	5
פּראָווידענץ	1	ראסעסאָ	6	**עסטרײך: (21)**		פּאַסקאָוו	16
פּיטסבורג	3	**דײטשלאַנד: (27)**		ווין	21	מוראָם	1
פֿאַסטאָרסאָן	1	בערלין	16	**פּוילן: (357)**		סאַראַטאָו	1
פֿילאַדעלפֿיע	15	דירנפֿורט	1	אָסוואָצ	1	פ״ב	50
קליוולאַנד	4	האַמבורג	1	בינאַליסטאָק	11	**שווײץ: (4)**	
קענטאָקי	1	לאַצבוי	1			גענף	3
ראָטשעסטער	1	קעניג	2			לוצערן	1
סיקאַגאָ	26					**שוועדן: (2)**	
אַפריקע: (6)						שטאָקהאָלם	2
יאָהאַנעסבורג	6						

ט א ב ע ל ע III

– די אנטוויקלונג פון דער יידישער פרעסע לויט די יארן:

סך־הכל																יאר
1	—	—	—	1	—	—	—	—	—	—	—	—	—	—	—	1667
1	—	—	—	—	—	—	—	—	—	—	—	1	—	—	—	1686
2	1	—	—	1	—	—	—	—	—	—	—	—	—	—	—	1751—52
1	—	—	—	—	—	—	—	—	—	—	—	1	—	—	—	1771—72
1	—	—	—	—	—	—	—	—	—	—	—	1	—	—	—	1776
1	—	—	—	—	—	—	—	—	—	—	—	1	—	—	—	1789
1	—	—	—	—	—	—	—	—	—	—	—	1	—	—	—	1797
1	—	—	—	—	—	—	—	—	1	—	—	—	—	—	—	1802
2	—	—	—	—	2	—	—	—	—	—	—	—	—	—	—	1814
2	—	—	—	1	—	—	—	—	—	1	—	—	—	—	—	1816—25
5	—	—	—	1	—	—	—	—	—	3	—	—	1	—	—	1846—55
8	—	—	—	1	—	1	—	—	1	5	—	—	—	—	—	1856—65
8	—	—	—	3	—	—	—	—	3	2	—	—	—	—	—	1856—70
15	—	—	—	4	—	—	—	—	1	—	—	—	—	—	10	1871—75
24	1	—	—	1	—	2	—	—	5	—	—	12	—	1	2	1876—80
20	—	—	—	5	—	—	—	—	1	—	—	12	1	—	1	1881—85
49	5	—	—	4	—	3	—	—	2	3	—	27	2	1	2	1886—90
54	6	3	—	5	—	4	1	—	8	3	—	21	—	—	3	1891—95
66	2	—	—	6	10	2	1	—	11	3	1	20	—	1	9	1896—00
45	2	1	—	2	15	—	—	—	3	2	—	13	1	—	6	1901—03
69	1	12	—	10	6	2	2	—	7	—	—	18	—	—	11	1904—05
245	45	42	—	21	5	3	1	—	23	9	—	65	1	—	30	1906—10
314	81	99	—	10	4	10	1	—	26	5	—	56	2	—	20	1911—14
53	22	3	—	4	1	—	1	—	3	3	—	7	—	—	9	1915—16
59	5	3	—	7	8	—	—	—	5	—	—	22	—	—	9	1917
320	27	6	20	58	16	—	2	1	39	27	—	75	5	2	42	1918—20
59	6	—	—	31	1	—	—	—	6	2	—	10	—	—	3	אומבאקאנט
1426	204	169	20	175	67	29	9	1	135	67	1	371	16	5	157	**סך־הכל**

בערלין, סעפטעמבער 1922.　　　　　　　　　　　מענדל פראבסט

צו די טאבעלעס:

די דריי טאבעלעס, וואָס זיינען אויבן אפגעדרוקט, זיינען אויספירן פון א גרויסער ארבעט, מיט וועלכער מ. פראבסט פארנעמט זיך יארנלאנג.

עס לוינט זיך אפשטעלן אויף איניקע פרטים פון די דאזיקע אנקעטעס.

אין דער ערשטער טאבעלע זיינען נפברפכט די יידישע פרעסע אין 30 פארשיידענע שפראכן. ס'זיינען געווען 3827 אויסגאבן, פון זיי אין י י ד י ש — 1443.

ד. ה. 37,7% פון דער גאנצער צאל. דערביי אָבער בא- דארף מען אונטערשטרייכן, אז די צאל ט א ג ב ל ע ט ע ר – דער סאמע חירקנדיקסטער און פארשפרייטסטער ארט־פרעס— איז אין יידיש געווען 150, ד. ה. העכער 10% פון דער צאל אויסגאבן אין יידיש, אין דער צייט, וואָס א י ן ה ע ב ר ע י ש איז געווען אינגאנצן ט א ג ב ל ע ט ע ר—22 אויף 635, ד. ה. מיניקער פון 2%. די צאל פון ט א ג- ב ל ע ט ע ר אין פארשידענע שפראכן איז 177—פון זיי אין יידיש 150, ד. ה. כמעט 85%.

Shatski 1932; Shaykovski 1970). From the outset, however, the Yiddish press was a supplier of more than news (Fishman 1960). It printed poetry, novels, and short stories (Frostig 1910). It published commentaries on the biblical and prophetic portions of the week. It sought to educate its readers and to prepare them for both Jewish and general responsibilities. Ultimately it drew them into the political process as well and activated them on behalf of innumerable Jewish and general causes. The Yiddish press has been a trusted friend, an advisor, an ally of the reader, no less so in the United States and in other centers of mass immigration than in 'the old country', and, indeed, perhaps even more so (B. Z. Goldberg 1971; Margoshes 1965). The first Yiddish newspapers in the United States began appearing (first in New York) in 1870, i.e. less than a decade after *Kol mevaser* began appearing in Odessa (Rischin 1962; Shaykovski 1970; Lifshits 1974). These newspapers quickly spread to most centers of Jewish population concentration throughout the country (e.g. Selavan 1976; Marmer 1928; Khaykin 1946a) and reached a combined paid circulation of three quarter million in the second decade of this century (Fishman 1965b; Goldberg 1941, 1943, 1945; Shelyubski 1945). They very gradually abandoned their archaic and Germanized linguistic idiosyncrasies (Hurvitsh 1917 [1902]; Shulman 1936; Kobrin 1976), but very quickly pursued various political and cultural goals (Hurvitsh 1917 [1909]), including Americanization (Soltes 1924; Dawidowicz 1963), biculturism (Fishman and Fishman 1959), Zionism, socialism (Rappaport 1957; Dawidowicz 1964), Orthodoxy, etc. Much diminished in recent years, the Yiddish press still reveals occasional noteworthy spriteliness (Fishman 1960) and, in spite of difficulties, an ability to keep going that is truly remarkable (note the *Forward's* 80th anniversary in 1977).[13] Remarkable too is the fact that

13. Similarly noteworthy accomplishments are evident in connection with the Yiddish press in Palestine/Israel (Feyges 1928; Kresl 1951), Roumania (Sh"s-roman 1929) and Poland-Russia. The latter is particularly outstanding in the annals of Yiddish journalism both for its literary quality and its virtually overpowering quantity. After 1917 both Hebrew and Russian journalism for Jewish audiences continued, particularly under Zionist auspices (Yashunski 1922), but quickly became relatively minor in terms of number of publications and readers, due both to governmental prohibition (in the USSR) and the overriding and recurring need of all Jewish political parties to rally their followers. As a result, Yiddish journalism in interwar Poland alone consisted literally of thousands of periodical publications (Shayn 1963, 1974).

The educating and activating role of the Yiddish press has not remained unnoticed by social scientists and specialists in minority affairs more generally (see, e.g. Witke 1957 and Y. L. Chyz 1959).

However, what has been largely overlooked is the extent to which the Yiddish press represents the acme of mass Yiddish literacy. With the double exception of a very few extremely popular authors, on the one hand, and Yiddish commentaries and translations of religious staples, on the other hand, the masses of Yiddish readers associated reading Yiddish with the newspaper and the newspaper alone. Thus, whereas even the most popular of Yiddish books and booklets may have reached only hundreds of thousands of readers, the Yiddish press reached millions and did so regularly. This in itself would not be so noteworthy (since the periodical press of all vernaculars regularly reaches vastly more readers than does the world of books) were it not for the fact that in the minds of many, Hebrew (or a coterritorial language) remained identified with serious books and bookishness while the image of Yiddish was tied to the ephemeral, popular press. I suspect that this was (and even is) so, notwithstanding the fact that most Yiddish authors were/are also the mainstays of the

Table 2. During the year of the Revolution and the year immediately thereafter, 187 Jewish periodical publications appeared in the area of the former Czarist Empire. Eighty-six of these were in Yiddish. Only General Zionists published a considerable number of periodicals in Hebrew (n = 6) and more than twice as many periodicals in Russian (n = 36) as in Yiddish (n = 16).

טאַבעלע I

ייִדישע פּעריאָדישע אויסגאַבעס פֿאַר די יאָרן 1917–1918

ס"ה									ערשיינונגס־אָרט
26	7	4	2	6	—	1	4	2	קיעוו
13	1	—	3	4	3	—	—	2	פּעטערבורג
13	1	—	—	2	3	3	1	3	מאָסקווע
7	1	—	—	2	1	1	—	2	אַדעס
6	2	—	—	—	—	1	1	2	כאַרקאָוו
5	—	1	1	1	—	—	1	1	ווילנע
4	1	—	—	1	1	—	—	1	האָמל
3	—	—	—	—	—	—	3	—	קאַטערינאָסלאַוו
2	—	—	—	—	—	—	1	1	באַקו
1	1	—	—	—	—	—	—	—	באַרדיטשעוו
1	—	—	—	—	—	—	—	1	בעלאָסטראָוו
1	—	—	—	—	—	—	1	—	ביאַלי־באָאַק
1	1	—	—	—	—	—	—	—	האַלק
1	1	—	—	—	—	—	—	—	וויטעבסק
1	—	—	—	1	—	—	—	—	גראָדנע
1	1	—	—	—	—	—	—	—	זשיטאָמיר
1	—	—	—	—	—	—	—	1	ריגע
1	—	—	—	—	—	—	—	1	כאַרקאָוו
1	—	—	—	—	—	—	—	—	סומ
1	1	—	—	—	—	—	—	—	
91(86)	17	5	5	16	9	6	12	17	ס"ה

טאַבעלע II

ייִדישע, העברעישע און רוסישע־ייִדישע פּעריאָדישע אויסגאַבעס פֿאַר די יאָרן 1917–1918

ס"ה	רוסיש	העברעיש	ייִדיש	פּאַרטיקולאַריזם
27	10	—	17	בונד
15	3	—	12	פֿאַראייניקטע
13	7	—	6	פּועלי־ציון
9	1	—	8	קאָמוניסטן
58	35	6	16	ציוניסטן
7	2	—	5	אָרטאָדאָקסן
1	—	1	—	גענעראלע, און פרײ
25	20	—	5	אָרגאַניזאַציעס, אינסטיטוציעס און
32	11	4	17	פֿאַרטיידיקנע
187	90	11	86	ס"ה

Yiddish periodical press. The modern world of Yiddish books is to a large extent a by-product of the Yiddish press, for had not the latter subsidized the former (both in the sense of paying wages/honorariums to the authors and being the first arena in which new books, in serialized fashion, saw the light of day) the books themselves would frequently not have appeared. However, for the lion's share of readers of the press, the books remained unseen and unknown and only the press itself remained to typify the world of Yiddish-in-print.

The foregoing is of more general theoretical significance in that it demonstrates the influence of diglossic pressures. As I (Fishman 1976a) and others before and after me (M. Vaynraykh 1973; Gold 1980) have noted, it is not at all accurate to say that the functional division between Hebrew and Yiddish was that between writing/print and speech or that between sacred and secular. Nevertheless, there was/is a strain in that direction in traditional social networks. The popular associa-tion of Yiddish with journalism and of Hebrew with books represents an attempt to clarify and simplify their functional specificity in accord with the lines or domains of their predominate legiti-mation. As long as some such complimentary dis-tribution is maintained, even if it is not completely accurate, both languages are needed and no 'either/ or' choice is necessary. Under these cir-cumstances bilingual readers (and particularly writers) are not at all unusual. However, when these diglossic tensions are eased and the functional differences ignored, than tendencies toward inter-group monolingualism are fostered and both readers and writers increasingly line up, on one side of the fence or the other. Sadan's plea for a return to the bilingual literary pattern of the beginning of this century and the end of the last (1972b, also see below) thus represents more than a restructuring of literary and literacy habits but, rather, a fargoing functional reallocation of both Hebrew and Yiddish in Jewish life.

דאָס יידישע בּוך אין יאָר 1923

טאַבעלע I

דאָס יידישע בוך אין יאָר 1923

% אלע	סך־הכּל 100%		אַמעריקע 6,5%		עסטרייך 1%		לעטלאַנד 1%		ליטע 2,1%		דייטשל. 13,3%		רוסלאַנד 5,4%		פּוילן 70,6%		
	צוזאמען	אריב. ערג.	אריב. איב.		אריב. איב.		אריב. איב.		אריב. איב.		אריב. איב.		אריב. איב.		אריב. איב.		
8,5	31	4	27	—	3	—	2	—	1	—	2	—	4	—	5	4	10	פּאָעזיע
24,4	89	24	65	1	3	—	1	—	—	—	1	4	9	—	—	19	51	בעלעטריסטיק
8,8	32	11	21	—	1	—	1	—	—	—	2	1	—	—	1	10	16	דראמאטישע ווערק
4,7	17	1	16	—	3	—	—	—	—	—	—	3	—	—	1	10	קריטיק, ליט. געש.
6,6	24	11	13	—	—	—	—	—	—	—	5	3	—	—	6	10	געש. און ביאגראפיע
5,2	19	22	7	3	1	—	—	—	—	—	4	2	—	—	5	4	וויסנשאפט
5,2	19	4	15	—	2	—	—	1	—	1	—	1	1	—	3	10	פאליט. און געזעלש.
1,6	6	—	6	—	—	—	—	—	—	—	—	1	—	—	—	5	סטאטיסטיק
11	40	6	34	—	1	—	—	—	—	1	3	1	2	2	1	29	לערנביכער
13,5	49	17	32	—	1	—	—	—	—	—	1	2	1	6	15	23	קינדער,יוגנט ־ ליט.
5,8	21	—	21	—	1	—	—	—	1	—	—	—	—	—	1	17	זאמלהעפטן
4,7	17	—	17	—	2	—	—	—	—	—	—	5	—	—	1	9	פארשיידענע
100%	364	90	274	4	18	—	4	—	3	—	8	18	31	4	16	64	191	סך־הכל
		364		22		4		3		8		49		20		258		צוזאמען

טאַבעלע II

דאָס יידישע בוך אין די יאָרן 1921, 1922 און 1923 לויט די געביטן פון בוך

	1923				1922(*)				1921			געביט פון בוך
%	סך־הכל	איבערז.	אריג.	%	סך־הכל	איבערז.	אריג.	%	סך־הכל	איבערז.	אריג.	
8,5	31	4	27	9,9	42	2	40	10,3	43	1	42	פּאָעזיע
24,4	89	24	65	26,6	113	30	83	19,1	80	31	49	בעלעטריסטיק
8,8	32	11	21	8,7	37	14	23	6,7	28	9	19	דראבמאטישע ווערק.
4,7	17	1	16	4,4	19	1	18	2,4	10	—	10	קריטיק און ליט. געש.
6,6	24	11	13	6,8	29	10	19	2,7	11	—	11	געטיכטע און ביאגר.
5,2	19	12	7	—	—	—	(**)	1,9	8	6	2	וויסנשאפטסלעבע
5,2	19	4	15	4,2	18	5	13	6,7	28	10	18	פאליטיש און געזעלש.
1,6	6	—	6	1,6	7	—	7	0,7	3	1	2	סטאטיסטיק
11	40	6	34	9,4	40	10	30	8,1	34	4	30	לערנביכער
13,5	49	17	32	20	84	40	44	34,0	142	70	72	קינדער־און יוגנט ליט.
5,8	21	—	21	4,7	20	—	20	5,0	21	—	21	זאמלביכער
4,7	17	—	17	3.7	16	—	16	2,4	10	—	10	פארשיידענע
100%	364	90	274	100%	425	112	313	100%	418	132	286	סך־הכל

Table 3. 'The Yiddish book in 1923' (Mayzl 1923). Of 364 Yiddish books published in 1923, 24.4% were belles-lettres, 13.5% were for young readers, 11% were textbooks, 8.5% were poetry, 8.8% were dramas, etc. Twenty-five of these books were translations from other languages. Over 70% were published in Poland, 13% in Germany, 6% in the USA, and 6% in the USSR.

outside of Israel all Jewish *dailies* are in Yiddish. Their number may be getting smaller, but they represent an intensity of Jewish commitment that no others can match. (For a wealth of additional scholarly detail on the American Yiddish press from its earliest beginnings through the 1970s, see Shtarkman 1979 and his extensive bibliography and notes.)

Of wider repute throughout the world (primarily because of translations and dramatizations) is the Yiddish literary scene – particularly insofar as some of its leading lights are concerned – although the extent of the latter's dependence on the Yiddish daily and periodical press, for both sustenance and audience, remains largely unrecognized. Indeed, the partnership is often a tripartite affair and includes not only the press and the literary world, but the world of ideological–political efforts as well. This dovetailing goes back to the very beginning of organized efforts not only to educate the masses via Yiddish (note, e.g. the editorial on 'Yiddish bibliography' in *Kol mevaser* [Anon. 1869], urging readers to buy the compilation of Goldfaden's plays, the book about the Rothschilds and other 'truly worthwhile Yiddish books' that the periodical had undertaken to publish on a regular basis), but to activate them and, thereby, simultaneously, to build both 'a better world' and to foster 'Jewish cultural work' (see, e.g. Frostig 1910; Lyesin 1954; Litvak 1921; Mendele 1959 [1889]; Niger 1914). The rhetoric quoted above is late nineteenth and early twentieth century, but the goal and, particularly, the intimate tie between the creators of journalism and the creators of literature, originates far earlier.

Yiddish literature

Just as the origins of the Yiddish press may be found in Western Europe, with the modernization, expansion, and social activation thereof coming towards the end of the nineteenth century in Eastern Europe, so also the developmental path of Yiddish literature more generally (see, e.g. Erik 1928; Madison 1968; Robak 1940; Tsinberg 1937, vol. 9; Reyzin 1923; Shatski 1936; Viner 1940; etc.). Even in Eastern Europe, however, far from the blandishments of Reform and massive assimilation, its path was conflicted, particularly at the outset, with leading lights of the *haskole*, of Orthodoxy, of Zionism, of Hebraism, and of socialism all asking, in chorus as it were, 'is a Yiddish literature necessary?' (Ravnitski 1889a). Various merits and justifications were advanced (e.g. Ravnitski 1889b) – originally quite innocuous and artistically unpretentious or self-effacing ones – but the controversy raged on for decades (see e.g. Verses 1938; Kresl 1954) and has been renewed, on occasion, even in post-Holocaust years (see e.g. Niger-Charney 1955). Although the drift and needs of the day led more and more late nineteenth-century writers of stature to write in Yiddish (while, in most cases, also continuing to write in Hebrew), it was many decades, indeed not until after the First World War, before it was generally felt no longer

פאַרלאַג „קולטור-ליגע“, װאַרשע

באַריכט

פון דער פאַרלאַגס-סטאַטיסטיק פאַרן יאָר 1923

נומ.	מאַטעריע װערק	די צאָל בויגן אין בוך	געדרוקט עקז.	סך הכּל דרוק-בויגן
	בעלעטריסטיק			
1	שלום-עליכם—כּתבים פון 8 קאַמיוואָיאַזשער	14	1500	21000
2	„ לכּבוד יום-טוב . .	16½	1350	22000
3	„ יידישע קינדער . .	12	1500	18000
4	„ בלוטיקער שפּאַס 1-טע טייל	27	1500	40500
5	„ „ „ 2-טע טייל	19	1500	28500
6	„ מאָטל דעם חזנס 2. אויפל.	14	650	9100
7	„ „ „ „ 3. „	14	1000	14000
8	„ יאָסעלע סאָלאָוויי . .	14	1500	21000
9	„ קינדער-שפּיל . .	7	1500	10500
10	שלום אַש—קידוש-השם 1 אויפל.	12¼	1500	18375
11	„ קידוש-השם 2-טע אויפל.	12¼	1000	12250
12	„ כּשוף-מאַכערין 1-טע אויפל.	10	1500	15000
13	„ „ 2-טע אויפל.	10	1000	10000
14	„ מאָטקע גנב 1-טע אויפל.	20	2000	40000
15	„ „ 2-טע אויפל.	22	1000	22000
16	„ אַנקעל מאָזעס . .	14	1500	21000
17	„ וועג צו זיך . .	15½	1500	23250
18	„ סאָציאַלע דראַמען . .	21½	1000	21500
19	„ נאַציאָנאַלע דראַמען .	21	1000	21000
20	„ מאָטקע גנב (דראַמע) .	5½	1000	5500
21	„ גאָט פון נקמה . .	6	500	3000
22	„ בונד פון שוואַכע . .	4	500	2000
23	„ יחוס . . .	6	500	3000
24	„ משיחס צייטן . .	5	500	2500
25	„ אונזער גלויבן . .	5¼	500	2625
26	„ אַ שנירל פערל . .	5	500	2500
27	„ אַ שיטער מענטש . .	5½	500	2625
28	י. אָפּאַטאָשו—פּוילישע וועלדער 6-טע אויפל.	22	1000	22000
29	אַ ראָמאַן פון אַ פערד-גנב	15	2000	30000
30	פּ. הירשביין—פאַרן מאָרגנשטערן	6¼	1500	9375
31	מנחם—זאַהל רימער . .	14	1500	21000
32	ה. לייוויק—אין קיינעמס לאַנד	12	1500	18000
33	ב. שימאָן—דראַמען 2 א.	4¼	1000	4250
34	א. פראַנס—טאַיס 3-טע אויפל.	12	1000	12000
	סך-הכּל .	85½		530350
	קריטיק און וויסנשאַפט			
35	ה. שמידט—איינשטיין-טעאָריע .	9	1600	14400
36	ז. רייזען—פון מענדעלסאָן ביז מענדעלע	26¼	2000	52500
37	ה. קיטעל—תּנ״ך-וויסנשאַפט .	19	1500	28500
38	נ. פּרילוצקי—דאָס געוועט .	12	1500	18000
39	ד״ר י. שיפּער—געשיכטע פון טעאַטער	14	1500	21000
40	ב. שפּינאָזאַ—עטיק . .	20	1500	30000
41	א. בערגסאָן—אַריינפיר אין מעטאַפיזיק	4	1500	6000

נ׳	מאַטעריע װערק	די צאָל בויגן אין בוך	געדרוקט עקז.	סך הכּל דרוק-בויגן
	איבערגעטראָגן .	104¼		170400
42	װ. נאַטאַנסאָן—שפּינאָזאַ און בערגסאָן	3	1500	4500
	סך-הכּל .	107¼		174900
	יוגנט-און קינד. ליטעראַטור			
43	שלום עליכם—טביה 2 אויפל.	11½	1000	11250
44	מענדעלע מו״ס—מסעות בנימין השלישי 2-טע אויפל.	6⅛	1000	6125
45	הויפס מעשהלעך . .	10½	2000	21000
46	ה. הויף—ליליפוט-נאָז .	3	1000	3000
47	קליינער מוק . .	2	1000	2000
48	סאַיד . . .	3½	1000	3500
49	קאַליף בישעל . .	1¼	1000	4250
50	פּ. הירשביין—מעשהלעך .	2	1000	4000
51	ב. איגנאַטאָוו — בערל פראַגער	2	2000	3000
52	שלום עליכם — מעסערל .	2	1500	2000
53	ש. אַש — אָרעמער און רייכער	2	1000	3000
54	פּ. מאַרקיש—זאַנג-גאַנג .	2	1000	2000
55	מ. קיפּניס—חברים . .	1	2000	2000
56	קעצל-קאָטער . .	1	2000	2000
57	קאַהענדל . : .	¾—	2000	1500
58	ש. גיטעלעס—אַריע ריז .	¾—	2000	1500
59	ל. קוויטקאָ—לידעלעך . .	1	2000	2000
60	מ. ליסיצקי—חד-גדיא . .	2	1000	2000
	סך-הכּל .	54⅜		76125
	לערנביכער			
61	יעקב פּאַט—מעטאָדישע אָנווייזונגען	1¼	1200	1500
62	ראָב. זיידל—אַרבעטס-שול .	4	1000	4000
63-68	י. פּאַט—לייענען און שרייבן 1-6	6	3000	18000
	סך-הכּל .	11¼		23500
	זשורנאַלן			
69-72	„ביכער-וועלט“ 6, 2-1, 3-4, 5	35	2000	70000
73-74	„נייע שול“ 2-3, 4-5 . .	18	800	14400
75-77	„שול און לעבן“ . .	13	1200	15600
	סך-הכּל .	66		100000
	בעלעטריסטיק . .	85½		530350
	קריטיק און וויסנשאַפט	107¼		174900
	יוגנט און קינדער ליט.	54⅜		76125
	לערנביכער . .	11¼		23500
	זשורנאַלן . .	66		100000
	צוזאַמען דרוק-בויגן	324⅜		904875

necessary to justify or explain why one felt it proper to do so. Such justifications are to be found by Mendele (Miron 1973a, 1973b; Sadan 1965), Sholem Aleykhem (Novershtern 1971; Sholem Aleykhem 1889), and Perets (Byalestotski 1940; Kalmenovitsh 1949; Rabinovitsh 1946; Shveyd 1955a; Turkov-Grudberg 1965), the three great giants of modern Yiddish literature, and obviously also for many writers who ultimately found their way primarily to the Hebrew side of the fence: Byalik (Sadan 1974; Biletski 1970; Byalik 1931), Berditshevski (Mayzl 1965), Agnon (Agnon 1969; Sadan 1969) and others. And, nevertheless, Yiddish literature blossomed and did so on literary–aesthetic rather than only on the utilitarian–educational–political grounds that movement after movement encouraged (Shtif 1924). That this was so was beginning to be recognized even before the turn of the century (Sholem Aleykhem 1892).

The Yiddish muse is not a figment, which lives only in the imagination of hot-headed advocates of Zhargon, not a fable that corresponds to no reality, but she really exists...(and is) one of the heavenly daughters sent down to sweeten the lives of our people. Yes, the Yiddish muse lives and will always live, and the flowers that she strews upon Zhargon grow up on holy soil. This should not be forgotten by all who cast haughty glances at our Ivre-taytsh and who consider it below their dignity to speak of it as one speaks of a literature (Lerner 1889).

Up to the beginning of the Second World War, Yiddish literary productivity continued to grow at a rapid rate (Mayzl 1923; Meyer 1922a, 1922b; Shalit 1913), although the economic rewards for its participants were slim indeed (Prilutski 1908b; Tsitron 1923).

   In America too Yiddish literature goes back quite far (Marmer 1928 and Shtarkman 1939 discuss the first book that appeared in 1877) and begins to attract critical recognition quite early (Wiener [1899] 1972). However among the English reading public it has only recently begun to receive the popular recognition (Howe and Greenberg 1954, 1969, 1975, 1977; Howe 1976; Singer 1979) and the professional scholarly attention (e.g. Miron 1973a, 1973b) that it deserves. Its sole support and acclaim has long come from the small circle of Yiddish writers, critics, and readers who have focused upon it both as a literature with problems and processes of its own (Opatoshu 1954; N. Goldberg 1940) and as a superb record of Jewish life (Gliksman 1966; Nobl 1954; Rabinowicz 1965; Stillman 1977). Although, due to its primary role as literature, it probably should not be taken uncritically as either a faithful or a balanced record of Jewish history, Yiddish literature can nevertheless be a significant reflector of Ashkenazic history for American Jewry, from the history of the printing press and publishing

◄ Table 4. 'Kultur-liga Publishing House, Warsaw. Report of Publishing activity for 1923.' An advertisement of one of the largest and highest quality Yiddish publishing houses in interwar Poland. Approximately one million pages had been set in type, 59% were belles-lettres (including poetry and drama), 19% were science and literary criticism, 8% were for young readers, 3% were textbooks, and 11% were periodicals. A volume by Sholem Aleykhem and another by Sholem Ash each appeared in an addition of 40,000 copies.

itself among Jews (Rabin 1969; Madison 1976), through to the early, middle and most recent days of immigration to the New World (Hapgood 1966 [1902]; Ronch 1975; Landis 1975).

Two views have increasingly come to the fore as post-Holocaust perspectives on Yiddish literature. The first is that Yiddish literature should be viewed jointly with Hebrew literature – 'one literature in two languages' – as an inextricably intertwined flowering of one and the same national genius (Bal-makhshoves 1953 [1908]; Golomb 1967; Niger 1957 [1941]; Ravitsh 1958; Shtarkman 1965). The other is that Yiddish literature has had (and still has) a particular moral, humanistic, and even redemptive message focused upon the sanctity of human life and the nobility of justice (Pomerants 1966; Opatoshu 1949b; Leyvik 1963 [1957]). Although literary analysis per se is not our concern here, but rather the social context and implications of literary efforts, literary goals, and literary response, it is worth stressing that views such as both of the foregoing imply that Yiddish literature, far from being a minor, off-beat concern, is a unifying and eternal repository of the very best that the Jewish people as a whole has created (Leyvik 1963 [1948]; Ravitsh 1947, 1951; Niger 1939, 1950; Friedman 1957–1958).[14]

Yiddish theater

Another pillar of the world of modern Yiddish, and one that has brought it great recognition and considerable acclaim of late, is the theater. Although the theater, as an art medium, may have had a later start among Jews than among coterritorial gentiles (Ernst 1930a; Prilutski 1945), perhaps precisely because theater in Europe originally had christological associations that made it seem even more morally questionable in Jewish eyes than it was for others, it nevertheless grew to massive proportions after its modern beginnings in Roumania a century ago (Berkovitsh 1976). Even more so than Yiddish journalism or Yiddish literature, Yiddish theater became a truly popular vehicle.

---

14. Ravitsh's view that Yiddish creations too belong in a new Book-of-Books (to encompass the very worthiest literary creations of Jews during the past two thousand years) represents a complete reversal relative to the view of Yiddish literature that still predominated a century ago. From the view that the language itself was deficient and that nothing particularly refined, noble, subtle or uplifting could be said or written in it (note even Hapgood's view [1902] that Yiddish was so defective as an instrument of expression that it impeded the thought processes of its users), Yiddish literary work has now come to be viewed as fit to be included among the very best that the Jewish people has created during its entire Diaspora experience. 'And the nature of the matter, of *this* matter, naturally leads to the conclusion that the language of the second Book-of-Books will be primarily – although not entirely – Yiddish, *mame loshn*. And in this fashion the language of the martyrs will remain alive eternally. In a Book-of-Books it is not only the contents that becomes hallowed but the form as well, and the form, the garb of a book, is its language' (Ravitsh 1951: 98). Ravitsh's attitude would be shared by most Yiddish writers today as would the view, probably shared with Jews the world over, that that which is included between the covers of such a book is destined for (is automatically an example of) eternal life.

It called upon spoken expression – much more the language's true metier in the popular mind than even its most widely known written works – and audience empathy (which, not infrequently, became audience participation) and presented not only folk-comedy and melodrama but the greatest works of world and Jewish literature alike. Thus, in the United States, while Broadway was cultivating the American musical comedy, barely literate Jewish immigrants on the Lower East Side were reverberating to versions of Ibsen, Shakespeare, and Tolstoy, in addition to Gordin (*Mirele Efros*), Gutskov (*Uriel Acosta*), Goldfadn (*The Witch*), and, of course, Hirshbeyn (*Green Fields*), Leyvik (*The Golem*), and many, many others of major dramatic worth (Clurman 1968; Gorin 1913). Yiddish theater is most active today in Israel (Fishman and Fishman 1977; see Ernst 1930b for the beginnings of Yiddish theater in Palestine), but its texts (Bez 1977; Landis 1966; Lifson 1965; Warembud 1975), its techniques (Lifson 1965) and its talents (Rosenfeld 1977), have come to be most widely appreciated in the United States, both by memorists and by the nostalgic grandchildren of the theater's original devotees (see e.g. Adler 1959; Kaminska 1973; Kobrin 1925; Rumshinski 1944; Turkov 1951; Tomashefski 1937; Yung 1950; Yablakov 1968, 1969).

As its audience shrank and anglified, Yiddish theater in America attempted to draw an audience opting almost entirely for pulp musical comedy. Currently, no more than a mere shadow – quantitatively and qualitatively – of its former self (Kohansky 1977), the Yiddish theater still attracts the interest of serious students (e.g. Manger, Turkov, and Perenson 1968, 1971; Sandrow 1977; Shmeruk 1971; Shayn 1964; Zilbertsvayg 1931–1969), as it did before (Anon. 1926; Beylin 1934; Gorin 1923; Shatski 1930; Y. Sh. 1930; Shiper 1923, 1925), and the devotion of small ensembles that insist on performing 'the better repertoire' no matter how small the audience for it may be. Although the modern heirs of the *purim shpil* have suffered worse reverses than either the Yiddish press or the Yiddish literary scene, probably due to a variety of objective and subjective factors,[15] they still have hopes and make plans for a better theater,

15. The eclipse of the *quality* Yiddish theater, particularly in America, may have more to do with objective theater-industry factors (e.g. the high cost of unionization of stage hands in New York City) and with objective aging per se (an aged clientele can still read a newspaper or book at home but can no longer travel into center-town for attendance at theater performances) than with such matters of subjective culture as the value of the theater. Nevertheless, in conjunction with demographically-functionally weakened languages, a variety of double-bind situations have been noted such that these languages are further weakened both if they *do* as well as if they *don't* take certain corrective steps. In this connection see the issue on 'Language Death' (Dressler and Wodak-Leodolter, eds. 1977). A possible example of this type of bind in the case of Yiddish would be the literary area. In a weakened state the language is further downgraded because of the meager *cultural tradition* of literacy via Yiddish. On the other hand, attempts to foster literacy in Yiddish provide further negative feedback with respect to attitudes toward the language if the literary material given to the learners is rejected by them as being of poor quality, un- or anti-traditional or otherwise ideologically unacceptable.

The Yiddish theater could conceivably be involved in a double-bind relationship *vis-à-vis* Yiddish in general. On the one hand, it might

particularly in the United States and Israel, and also continue to perform regularly in Poland, Roumania, Canada, and Latin America as well as intermittently in the USSR and Western Europe.

As of now, however, only Yiddish vaudeville and musical comedy are generally to be found, and lo and behold, at times found aplenty. Even so, for a medium that was supposed to have died ever so long ago, this phenomenon has prompted general as well as Jewish amazement, if hardly critical acclaim. Interpreting its implications constitutes a veritable projective test: if a popular Yiddish theatrical pulse still beats, much to everyone's surprise, can a 'better' Yiddish theater be far behind? If Yiddish film classics are now once again being widely shown, and they are, then can the return of Yiddish theater classics be far away? Thus while some wonder how long Yiddish dramatic art can continue at all, others wonder how long its second coming can be delayed.

Education in Yiddish

Finally, schooling in Yiddish must be recognized as a major – in former days, *the* major – formal institution (outside of the family per se) involving the language. Certainly this is so if modern literacy-related pursuits are of concern and, some would claim, doubly so if the continuity of the language is of interest. Here again we find very early origins, specifically as the oral process language of education (with a history as old as that of Ashkenaz itself; see Fishman 1973; Roskies 1977; Shtern 1950), and even in written use as well. In this latter capacity it should be remembered that instruction in *writing* Yiddish is also centuries old (e.g. the communal ordinances of Kracow, 1595, call for teaching boys in elementary school to 'write the sounds [of the language] in which we speak' [Asaf 1925, vol. 1, p. 101]). This responsibility came to be entrusted, as early as the sixteenth century, to the *shrayber* (writing teacher), a functionary who continued to serve Jewish education in Eastern Europe to the very threshold of the present century (Kazhdan 1956c). Through this side door other non-classical subjects also found their way into elementary Jewish education for

generally be considered to be less threatening to traditional diglossic functional allocations because of its oral rather than textual nature. On the other hand, being textually unsanctioned and traditionally unprotected, it may be viewed as more frivolous, unworthy, and dispensible than other forms of Jewish cultural expression. Once the negative demographic-functional cycle has begun, and the theater begins to lose its better actors (when was the last time that either Hollywood or Broadway lured away a Yiddish actor 'as in days of old'?, or do failures on the English stage now gravitate toward Yiddish 'slim-pickins'?), *serious*

Yiddish theater compares more and more poorly with its coterritorial rivals, and this further exacerbates the negative (or, at least, the burlesque) aura surrounding the theater and its language. The double-bind dilemma of weak languages further underscores the care that is required to distinguish between them and officially unrecognized or even underdeveloped languages that have a strong demographic base and intimacy-membership function. Poorly chosen language cultivation efforts may actually intensify rather than overcome or avoid the double-bind 'damned if you do; damned if you don't' dilemma.

ייִדישע ביבליאָטעקן אין פּוילן

נ.נ	שטאָט	נאָמען פון ביבליאָטעק	ייִדיש	פּוילישע	רוסישע	העבר.	אַנדערע שפּראַכן	אַלגעמיינע צאָל ביכער	צאָל לעזער	חובר ביכער אויף א לעזער
1	אָזאָרקאָו	בײַ געז. „אָהונט-קורסן"	350	—	—	—	—	350	160	2
2		„יונגט-ביבליאָטעק"	250	—	—	—	—	250	120	2
3	אָוסיאַראָו	„יודישע ביבליאָטעק"	70	—	—	—	—	70	65	1
4	אלעקסאנדער	בײַ געז. „ארב.-הײם"	546	—	—	—	—	546	52	5
5	עסטראָו	יודישע-ביבליאָטעק	1364	1004	789	790	191	4138	500	8
6		בײַ געז. „אָהונט-קורסן"	200	50	—	—	—	250	75	3
7	אפט		350	—	—	—	—	350	120	3
8	באָדזאַנאָ	„פּראָגרעס"	182	42	—	—	—	224	49	5
9	בגצק-לאפינקא	„יודישע פאָלקס-ביבל."	900	—	—	—	—	900	120	7
10	באָדזענטין	„יו. יאָ. באַראָקאָא-ביבל."	105	—	—	—	—	105	81	1
11	באַראַנאָויטש	בײַ געז. „אונזערע קינדער"	195	25	—	—	—	220	90	2
12	בוטשוטשין	בײַם פראָפ. פ. „נאָדל-ארב."	150	—	—	—	—	150	—	—
13	ביאלע	בײַ „דראַמאַטישער גרופע"	415	—	—	—	—	415	193	2
14		„באָראָכאָוו-ביבליאָטעק"	400	—	—	—	—	400	100	4
15	ביאַליסטאָק	„שלום-עליכם-ביבל."	5000	500	6000	1000	1500	14000	1000	14
16	ביעלסק	„ביבליאָטעק אין לעוו-זאַל"	600	700	3500	200	150	5150	125	41
17	בעלכאטאו	בײַ דער ארב.-געז. „קולטור"	180	—	—	—	—	180	50	4
18	בעזושין	ארב.-ביבליאָטעק	300	—	—	—	—	300	60	5
19	בענדין	בײַם פ. פ. „האַנד-אַנג."	560	—	—	—	—	560	85	7
20	ברײנסק	בײַ געז. „אָהונט-קורסן"	100	—	—	—	—	100	55	2
21	בריסק		450	—	—	—	—	450	150	3
22		„אונזערע קינדער"	1000	—	—	—	—	1000	250	4
23	גאָסטינין	„יודישע ביבליאָטעק"	2000	600	—	500	—	3100	355	9
24	גראָדנע	„ארבעטער ביבליאָטעק"	600	200	462	—	—	1262	236	5
25	גראיעוואָ	בײַ געז. „אָהונט-קורסן"	154	—	—	—	—	154	72	2
26		בײַם פ. פ. „נאַדל בראָנושע"	97	—	—	—	—	97	54	2
27	גאָרזשן	„יודישע-ביבליאָטעק"	222	313	55	—	25	615	60	5
28	דאַבושין	בײַ געז. „אָהונט-קורסן"	225	78	—	—	—	303	65	5
29	דאַמבראָוויץ	יודישע ביבל. בײַ דער ק. פ.	380	—	—	—	—	380	203	1
30	דעמביץ	ביבל. בײַם פאַר. „יונגט"	1800	—	—	—	—	1800	203	9
31		יוד. נאצ. קאָלקס-ביבל.	700	—	—	—	700	1800	250	7
32	דענבלין	„קאָלקס-ביבליאָטעק"	360	—	—	—	—	360	90	4
33	דערגענטין	בײַם יוג. „קולטור-פאַרײן"	410	300	50	—	—	760	70	11
34	וואַרשע	בײַם ארב. קלוב. ב. גראַסער	3000	300	—	—	—	3300	325	10
35		„באָראָכאָוו-ביבליאָטעק"	2080	694	820	90	—	3684	516	7
36		בײַם פר. פ. פון דרוק-ארב.	850	—	—	—	—	850	160	5
37		טעקסטיל	2600	—	—	—	—	2600	284	9
38		ביבל. בײַם יוד. כפיטאַל	320	281	101	742	39	1483	—	—
39		„הזמיר"	1161	198	300	487	120	2276	307	7
40		בײַ דער געז. „אָהונט-קורסן"	1000	—	—	—	—	1000	400	3
41		פראָפ. פ. „ב. באַראָכאָא"	267	—	—	—	—	267	133	2
42		„גיטס-פאָכאָהב"	280	—	—	—	—	280	75	3
43		„פרייער-ארב."	800	—	—	—	—	800	—	—
44	וואַרשע-פּראַגע	בײַם קאָאָפּ. „ארבעל"	1547	400	—	—	—	1947	234	8
45		ארב.-ביבל. א. ג. „גראָאסער"	600	—	—	—	—	600	70	9
46	הילוע	בײַ דער געז. „א.מ.ס. גרסן"	531	—	—	—	—	531	115	5
47	הלאָשטשעוק	בײַם פ. פ. פון האַנד-אַנג.	1220	1003	—	—	—	2223	186	12
48	ווענגראָו	„יודישע ביבל. א. טעק"	1216	—	—	208	—	1424	173	8
49	וויסקאָו	יוד. סטאַט-ביבל. „קולטורא"	470	—	—	50	—	570	184	3
50	זאַמבראָו	„ברק-ביבליאָטעק"	1900	1250	1160	296	—	4606	875	5
51		„דינעזאָן-ביבליאָ-טעק"	277	276	—	301	—	834	154	6
52		„קאָלקס-ביבליאָטעק"	922	479	—	389	—	1790	212	8
53	זדונסקא-וואַליע	בײַם טעקסטיל פאַרין	20	30	—	—	40	340	140	2
54	זשעלעכאָו	„לעדער פאַרין"	280	—	—	—	—	280	60	5

Table 5. 'Jewish libraries in Poland' (Meyer 1902b). Jewish communities in large and small localities supported their own Jewish libraries. The table lists 138 localities with a total collection of 147,177 books. Of these 63% were in Yiddish, 15% were in Polish, 13% were in Russian, 6% were in Hebrew, and 3% were in other languages. In 1922 over 23,000 subscribing members borrowed books from these libraries.

היפּ ביכער אױף לעזער	צאָל לעזער	אלגעמײנע צאָל ביכער	צוזעד שפּראכן	העבר.	רוסיש	פּױליש	יידיש	נאָמען פון ביבליאָטעק	שטאט	א. נ.
3	.50	170	—	—	10	—	160	בײ דער געז. „צוקונפט"	זלאטשעוו	55
5	290	1310	—	110	—	300	900	פאַרײן „ביבל. א. לעזע-זאַל"	זשיכלין	56
3	105	350	—	—	—	—	350	„בר. גראסער"	טאמאשאוו *	57
—	—	200	—	—	—	—	200	בײ דער ארג. „יוגנט"	טשענסטאכאוו	58
6	250	1400	150	—	—	250	1000	ב. ארב.-קלוב „פארײניקטע"		59
2	58	123	—	—	—	27	96	באַאאוו"-ביבליאטעק		60
5	125	625	—	—	—	—	625	„יודישע ארב.-ביבליאטעק"	יאנאוו-דראהיטש	61
5	238	1200	—	—	—	—	1200	„יודישע שטאַט.-ביבל."	כבעלניק	62
3	60	200	—	—	—	50	150	בײ דער ארג. „יוגנט"		63
9	80	750	—	—	—	—	750	ארבעטער-ביבליאטעק	כעלם	64
4	400	1511	120	16	—	570	805	באַאאוו"-ביבליאטעק		65
6	600	3795	281	—	404	1080	2030	ביבל. „ארבעטער-הײם"	לאדז	66
11	400	4500	150	350	800	2300	900	בײם פּראָפ. פאר. האנד.-אנג.		67
5	964	4916	—	—	—	232	4683	„גראסער-ביבליאטעק"		68
8	67	504	—	—	—	—	504	בײ „קולטור-ליגע"	לאנדוואראוו	69
5	61	332	—	—	20	—	312	„לאקאטשאוו-ביבליאטעק"	לאקאטשי	70
4	160	625	110	—	—	95	420	„י. נעקער-ביבליאטעק"	לעמבערג	71
2	156	354	—	—	—	60	294	„יוגנט-ביבליאטעק	לובלין	72
2	312	682	—	—	—	—	682	„ארבעטער-הײם"-ביבל.		73
2	422	1000	—	—	350	50	600	בײם צענט.-ראט פון פּ. פּ.		74
7	242	1767	—	—	—	74	1693	ביבל. בײ „אָוונט-קורסן"	לוצק	75
8	245	2000	—	200	200	400	1200	יוד. לעזע-זאַל און ביבל.	לאוויטש	76
4	28	120	—	—	—	—	120	לאק. קאָמ. אונאפהענ. ב. צ.	לאנצוט	77
5	245	2191	—	225	251	40	1675	בײם צ. ר. פון פּ. פּ.	לאמזשע	78
2	70	150	—	—	—	—	150	ארבעטער-"יוגנט-בונד".	מאקאוו	79
2	400	600	—	—	—	—	600	ביבל. בײ די פּר. קל. פאר.	מעזעריטש	80
16	385	6065	—	1100	2000	65	2900	יוד. שטאָט.-ביבליאטעק	מיר	81
3	40	100	—	—	—	—	100	בײ דער יוג.-ארג. „צוקונפט"	מינסק-מאזאָוו.	82
2	67	135	—	—	—	—	135	„באַ אַאאוו"-ביבליאטעק	מלאוע	83
3	215	705	—	265	—	—	440	יוד. ביבליאָט. „קולטור"	נאָוואגרודעק	84
8	71	582	—	—	—	—	582	בײם צענ. ביוראָ פון פּ. פּ.	נאָוואדוואר	85
4	200	805	—	—	—	120	685	„פּאָלקס-ביבליאטעק"	נאוי-זאמאסטש	86
3	54	180	—	—	—	20	160		נײ-מיש	87
5	150	750	—	—	—	300	450	„מ. ראָזענפעלד"-ביבל.	נײ-כאנג	88
5	200	1000	—	—	—	—	1000	„יוגנט-ביבליאטעק"		89
2	64	136	—	—	60	—	76	יודישע ביבליאָטעק	ניעסמיעזש	90
5	150	650	50	—	—	—	600	„ראָזענפעלד"-ביבליאטעק	סאנאק	91
3	200	600	—	—	—	—	600	בײ דער „ארבײטער-הײם"	סאסנאָוויץ	92
2	150	260	—	—	—	—	260	בײ דער ג. „אָוונט קורסן"	סאקאלאאוו	93
4	130	500	—	100	—	—	400	„ברענער"-ביבל.		94
2	44	86	—	—	—	—	86	„צ. צ.- ביבליאָטעק"	סטארדין	95
3	108	308	—	—	—	—	308	„באַ אַאאוו"-ביבליאטעק	סטרי	96
8	120	1023	106	236	149	13	519	יוד. פאָלקס-ביבליאטעק	סאני	97
6	70	436	47	—	—	39	350	בײ „האָפענונג"	סניאטין	98
4	76	277	57	—	—	52	168	„יוד. ביבליאטעק"	סקאָרושיסקא	99
4	94	421	—	—	—	—	421	יוד. ארב.-ביבליאטעק	סקידל	100
4	123	450	—	—	—	—	450	בײ „ארבעטער-הײם"	פאביאניץ	101
2	140	210	—	—	—	—	210	ביבל. בײם נאָדל-פאַרײן	פארנעשאוו	102
2	142	265	—	—	—	45	220	בײ „אָוונט-שולע	פלאַאוו	103
3	223	582	—	16	—	86	480	„פּרץ" ביבליאָטעק	פולטוסק	104
12	76	875	18	74	—	473	310	יודישע ביבליאטעק	פיעטרקאָוו	105
5	126	647	—	—	—	—	647	„הזמיר" און „אײניקײט"	פלאנסק	106
—	—	100	—	—	—	—	100	„ביבליאטעק"	פלאצק	107
—	—	130	—	—	—	—	130	בײ דער ג. „אָוונט-קורסן"		108

א. נ.	שטאט	נאמען פון ביבליאטעק	יידישע	פוילישע	רומינ.	העבר.	צוזרע שפראכן	אלגעמיינע צאל ביכער	צאל לעזער	חודש ביכער איין אויב לעזער
109	פראשניץ	ארבעטער-ביבליאטעק	20	—	—	—	—	20	—	—
110	פטיסוגא	ביים קולט. פאר. „פראגרעס"	150	—	—	—	—	150	100	2
111	פרוסקאװ	געזעלש. „ביבליאטעק"	342	23	—	—	—	365	50	7
112	צעכאנאװיעץ	„ביבליאטעק"	100	—	—	—	—	100	40	3
113	קאשימיזוס	„בא״אקאװ"-ביבליאטעק	170	—	—	—	—	170	40	4
114	קאזשעניץ	ביים לעדער-פאריין	350	—	—	—	—	350	86	4
115	קאלא	ביי די אהונט-קורסן	983	174	—	—	—	1157	126	9
116	קאלושין	„גראסער"-ביבליאטעק	250	—	—	—	—	250	150	2
117	קאליש	„בצלאװ"-ביבליאטעק	205	—	—	—	—	205	33	6
118	קאליש	בארעאװ	855	—	—	—	—	855	224	4
119	קאנין	געזעלש. „ביבליאטעק	1275	2600	450	300	600	5225	345	15
120	קאטאן	„יוד. געזעל. ביבליאטעק"	1050	—	—	—	—	1050	263	4
121	קארטוז-בעריאזא	„פאלקס-ביבליאטעק"	305	—	280	154	—	739	182	4
122	קיעלץ	„פרק-ביבליאטעק"	1442	1113	226	250	—	3031	180	17
123		„יוגנט"-ביבליאטעק	500	—	—	—	—	500	—	—
124	קלעמסעל	„יוד. געזעל. ביבליאטעק"	380	40	—	—	—	420	87	5
125	קראקאװ	„בארא אוו"-ביבליאטעק	1250	600	—	—	350	2200	828	3
126	קרינקי	„ארבעטער-ביבליאטעק"	1500	—	—	300	—	1800	250	7
127	קאזשעל	„יודישע ביבליאטעק"	220	—	—	—	—	220	65	3
128	קעלק	ביים צענטראל-ביורא	740	—	—	—	—	740	125	6
129	ראדאם	ביי דער ג. „אוונט-קורסן"	500	85	—	—	—	585	112	5
130	ראהא-מאז.	ביים נאדל-פאריין	300	—	—	—	—	300	100	3
131	ראװע	„בעסערכאן"-ביבליאטעק	1580	—	—	50	—	1630	225	7
132	ראשאן	ביי דער געז. „אונט-קורסן"	60	—	—	—	—	60	50	1
133	רעציאנזש	„יוד. פאלקס-ביבליאטעק"	695	827	—	315	—	1837	263	7
134	עידלאװויעק	„יוד. ארב.-ביבליאטעק"	94	—	—	—	—	94	—	—
135	ריפין	„יוגנט"-ביבליאטעק	170	—	—	—	—	170	—	—
136	עעדלעץ	ביבליאטעק ש. לעוו	400	—	—	—	—	400	95	4
137	דערפעץ	ביי דער געז. „אוונט-קורסן"	400	—	—	—	—	400	89	4
138	קעראדזא	ביי די אה.-קורסן פאר ארב.	97	—	—	—	—	97	90	1
	צוזאמען		93115	21342	18742	9164	4814	147177	23312	6

באמערקונג: די סבתם, חעלכע זיינען באצייכנם כיט א שטערנדל, זיינען זוין דערכאנט אין דער איבקטע, האס איז נעדדרוקט אין פאריקן נימער „ביבער-העלט" ,ביבליאטעקסיחסן).

אין פארגלייך מים די 66 ארבעטער-ביבליאטעקן. פון זוגעקוכצן מים די 1500 ביכער. פאר אן אנשטאלט מים צוועלכע העלכע די רעזולטאטן זיינען פארעפיטלעכט געהארן אין קליינע מעגלענקייטן, חי ס׳האט דער ווארשעווער טעקסטיל-פריעדרוקן נעמער „ביכער-וועלט, איז דער פרעצענט-פאר-פאריין, איז דאס זייער פיל. הענטמעניש פון די יודישע ביכער געפאלן פון 68 פרא. די ביבליאטעק פון די יידישע ביים ווארשעווער. יידישן שפיטאל צענו אויף 63. אין די גרעסערע רייכערע אלגעמיינע ביב האט אויף ירע 1483 ביכער קים 320 יידישע. דערפאר ליאטעקן, וועלכע זיינען אין דור פרידערזיקער סאבעל נישט געזיגן, געפינעמ זיך נאכ פט מער ביכער אין פוילנ. דאס איז די איני רוסיש אדער העברעיש חי אין די ארבעטער-ביבליאטעקן. ציקע פון די אלע ביבליאטעקן, חאס האט אנא גרויסן דאס האט נאכמירקם אויף דעם אלגעמיינעם סך-הכל. פרעצענט העברעישע ביכער.

די גרעסטע צאל יידישע ביכער געפינט זיך אין דער די גרעסטע צאל פוילישע ביכער דער האט לאד. זשער אין די האנדלס-אנעטשטעלטע (2300 פוילישע ביבליאטעקער „שלום-עליכם-ביבליאטעק (5000) ווייטער אויף 900 יידישע) און די קאװינער ביבליאטעק 2600 פיי- גייט די לאדזוער און הארשעוער „גראסער" ביבליאטעקן. א גרויסע צאל פוילישע ביכער לישע אויף 1275 יידישע). שער די לעצטע 2½ יאר איז די דער שלום עליכע-ביבלי- האבן אויף די „פרק"-ביבליאטעק אין לאדזוער (1250) טעק אין ביבליסטעק צוגעקיכמען העבער 1000 יידישע ביכער. א. א. ח. די די-„באראקאװ"-ביבליאטעק אין לאדזו (1080). שטארק אנטוויקלט האט זיך איך פאר דער זעלבער ציט ווארשעווער ביבליאטעקן האבן נאר א קליינע צאל פוילישע די ביבליאטעק פון ווארשעווער טעקסטיל-פאריין, ס׳אין ירע ביכער.

boys as well as for girls (Golomb 1957; Shekhter-vidman 1973): e.g. arithmetic, geography, the rudiments of the coterritorial language, etc. From these humble and generally unrecognized functional beginnings of written Yiddish in traditional Jewish education, through various slow and stagewise functional expansions (Shatski 1943), there developed first the thought of Yiddish as the written language of supplementary (secular) Jewish education, under traditional auspices (Reyzin 1933) and then the practice of using Yiddish as a sub-rosa written and spoken comedium of instruction in governmentally supported semitraditional schools (the so-called *kazyone* schools) primarily utilizing Russian or German as language(s) of instruction (Tcherikover 1913; Kazhdan 1956i). Finally, at the very end of the nineteenth century (1898), there came the initiation of schools with Yiddish as their sole medium of written and spoken instruction in conjunction with a totally secular curriculum (Niger

א. סטאַטיסטישע אויספירן

לויט די ציפערן וואָס מיר האָבן אַרויסגעבראַכט אין אונדזער אַרבעט,
באָקומט זיך אַזאַ ציפער־סך־הכל פונעם גאַנצן יידישן שול־בנין אין אומאָפּ־
הענגיקן פּוילן:

אין די דריי סעקטאָרן פון שולן פאַר יידישע קינדער איז געווען (אין
1934־35):

צאָל קינדער	צאָל אָנשט'	ס"ה לויט די סעקטאָרס	ריכטונג
			רעליגיעזער סעקטאָר
			חורב, וואַרשע
71,000	568		און ווילנע
38,000	250		בית יעקב
12,277	184		יבנה
10,300	58		גמינע־שולן
40,000	1,500		חדרים
171,577 קינדער	2,560 אָנשט'		
29.5 פּראָצ'			
			יידי העברי וועלט־
			לעכער סעקטאָר
15,486	169		„צישאָ"
37,000	269		„תרבות"
2,343	16		„שולקולט"
54,829 קינדער	454 אָנשט'		
9.3 פּראָצ'			
			פּוילישער סעקטאָר
			פּויליש־העברי'
6,022	31		גימנאַזיעס
343,671			מלוכהשע פּאָלקשולן
			נישט־יידישע פּרי־
5,398			פּריוואַטע מיטלשולן
355,091 קינדער			
61.2 פּראָצ'			
581,497 קינדער ס ך ־ ה כ ל	100 פּראָצ'		א ל ג ע מ י י נ ע ר ס ך ־ ה כ ל
549			

Table 6. Types of schools attended by Jewish children in Poland 1934–1935. Of the 500,000 unduplicated registrants, approximately 60% received their education completely or partially in Polish. Of the remaining 40% almost all (with the exception of the Hebraist Tarbut and Yavne schools) received their formal education entirely or primarily in Yiddish (Kazhdan 1947).

1913b). Although the first such schools in Eastern Europe were illegal and their teachers were exposed to governmental arrest (Gilinski 1922; Mishkovski 1913) their numbers continued to grow by leaps and bounds, whether under autonomist, socialist, or Zionist auspices (separately or in various combinations). Indeed, even *some* Orthodox schools began to add modern subjects to their official curriculum, and not only to teach these in Yiddish, but to do so consciously and conscientiously (see entire issue of *Beys yankev*, 1931, 8, no. 70–71, 'Yiddish Issue'), in contrast to *others* that demonstratively began to teach both modern and traditional subjects via Hebrew (Beys yankev tsentrale 1933).

The most innovative and forceful cutting edge in the movement for Yiddish as the language of education for Jewish children – both for the bulk of their general education as well as for all of their (secular) Jewish education – doubtlessly occurred under Bundist auspices (Eisenstein 1949a, 1949b; Gilinski 1922; Grosman 1974b; Kazhdan 1956d, e, f; Pat 1954), even though the majority of all children receiving their education via Yiddish continued to do so under Orthodox auspices (Sh'b 1931). 'Yiddish schools' (i.e. secular schools employing Yiddish at least as colanguage of instruction in some grades) also arose under more nonpartisan auspices, i.e. with a more culturist–autonomist and less socialist orientation (Eisenstein 1949b; Kazhdan 1947, 1956g; Kan 1928c). A few arose even under various Zionist auspices (Eck 1947; Tartakover 1926, 1931, 1967), and, briefly, a whole system of such schools came into being during the pre-Soviet period in the Ukraine (Kazhdan 1956h) and, later, during the first two and a half decades of the communist regime itself (Altshuler 1977; Frank 1935; Z. Halevy 1972, 1976; Rotnberg 1973; E. Shulman 1971). Under all of these auspices, education became highly politicized and, at the same time, so was all of life. However, whether the educational goal was that of 'freedom for the Jewish child' (Ester 1910; Perelman 1918), the equality of the Jewish people (Prilutski 1971 [1916]) or the victory of the proletariat – including the Jewish proletariat – against capitalist (including Jewish capitalist) exploitation, or other partisan and non-partisan goals, the assumption that 'normal development and freedom for our children' required Yiddish as the oral and written medium of instruction came to be increasingly self-evident to an ever growing segment of the Jewish population in Eastern Europe (note Bal-dimyen 1908 and Niger 1913b for early Orthodox, Zionist, and 'bourgeois' opposition to Yiddish secular education). Although fascist and communist regimes later restricted and crushed these schools (see Tikotshinski 1937; Valk and Klyonski 1920; and Zr—li 1922 for early Polish opposition; Burd 1938; Mutshnik 1938; Orland 1938; Reminik 1938; and E. Shulman 1971 for Soviet Russification policies and pressures), and, although the internal opposition to them from Orthodoxy and Zionism continued with little abatement, they nevertheless represented the modal approach to *modern* Jewish education in Eastern Europe during the inter-war years. (For brief post-World War II flurries there, see

Kazhdan 1958; Melezin 1948.) Thanks to them the names *Tsisho*, *Kultur-Lige*, and *Shulkult* came to be socioeducational designations that every historian of Jewish education and, indeed, every specialist in modern Jewish affairs must investigate with care.

Many of these school types had their American counterparts too (Fishman 1952; Parker 1973, this volume), but, with the exception of their Canadian (see articles by Vaysman and others in Novak 1935) and Latin American incarnations (Meyern-lazar 1948), they were almost entirely supplementary in nature (Novak 1935; Frank 1935). This fact – as well as the cruel course of Jewish history itself – led to their final concentration on Jewish subject matter alone and, therefore, to a severe narrowing of their impact as originally conceptualized.[16] The

16. The major compendium on Yiddish secular schools is Novak 1935, which not only contains accounts of various types of schools in various countries but also provides educational-philosophical perspective on these schools by major 'theoreticians' and 'statesmen' such as Zhitlovski, Golomb, Lerer and others. Other interesting sources are: (a) on the Labor-Zionist schools, which were the first to attempt Yiddish secular supplementary education in the United States, see Glants 1913, Shapiro 1962; (b) on the Workmen's Circle schools, the largest Yiddish secular school network in the United States, generally with laborite coloring, see Faynerman 1929, Levin 1920, Niger 1940; (c) on the Sholem Aleichem schools, a small, nonpartisan Yiddishist effort limited to New York, Chicago, and Detroit, see Anon. [1927] 1953a, [1953] 1972b, and Gutman [1962] 1967. Sources pertaining to the schools of the pro-communist International Workers Order can be found in Novak 1935 as well as in Parker, this volume.

The Yiddish secular school arena provides a choice vantage point for monitoring the changing interpretations of Yiddish secularism as a whole. The initial stance is one of triumphant modernization. Through this school Eastern European Jewry (and its immigrant offshoots in the Americas and elsewhere) will join the ranks of all modern nations, all of which have switched to their vernaculars as media of education (Goldberg 1914). Not only is this so because 'the revival of Hebrew is impossible in the diaspora and improbable in Palestine', but, more fundamentally, because traditional life and education are 'neither vital nor alive' (Niger 1928a). In the modern world, traditional education, with its emphasis on the dead hand of the past (prayer book, pentateuch, commentaries, Talmud), 'provides a mere foundation, with neither walls nor roof for modern life'. However, the view that grave dangers lurked

in the ahistorical and simplistic 'formula(tion) linguistic-secularistic' began quite early (Lerer 1928a, 1928b, 1940a, 1940b), particularly as the dependence of Yiddish secularism on a strong, surrounding, traditional milieu for the maintenance of Jewish life patterns became clear. This dependence or interdependence led both to a searching reexamination of what Jewish secularism really implied, both for the school and for the adult community that supported it (see e.g. Mark 1948, 1972; Gutman 1972, 1976), as well as to a pervasive (re-)traditionalization under the impact of the Holocaust. Continuing Americanization in language, outlook, and daily rounds (Pen 1958a) finally prompted Yiddish educators to realize the weakness of walls and roofs without foundations.

The postwar recovery of American Orthodoxy merely confirmed the lukewarmness (if not outright hostility) of the daily Yiddish press to the Yiddish secular school (Khaykin 1946b). The religious and Zionist press had generally viewed these schools as radical deviations from their own directions. The laborite and left-wing press, on the other hand, had viewed them as sources of chauvinism and removal from solidarity with the united proletariat. Thus, into the 1930s, with rare exceptions, the Yiddish secular school experienced more criticism than support from the Yiddish press since the daily press was always oriented toward much larger segments of the Jewish population and toward much more massive ideologies than those that Yiddish secularism could control.

The inability of immigrant based Yiddish secular education to build and maintain viable, self-perpetuating speech communities to correspond to its own ideological-philosophical preferences should be contrasted to the school emphases of various language movements. Ben Yehuda, Ivar Aasen, Takdir Alisjahbana, Kemal Ataturk and many other language mobilizers stressed the school as the very basis of their language-in-society

integrative circumstances (both ideological emphases as well as practical opportunities) of American life also required that these schools provide new rationales for themselves, since the rationale that 'Jews are a separate people' became less and less acceptable or even intelligible to American Jewish parents, given the acceptance of the tripartite melting pot and a general view of Jewish ethnicity as merely a narrower intimacy experience within the broader American

goals. However, modern sociolinguistic theory tends to ascribe far lesser potency to the school as an independent factor in language and culture maintenance and spread. More often than not, the school appears to be merely a secondary status system, able to (help) prepare individuals for advanced roles in primary status systems (economy, religion, government), but not, by itself, to replace the latter or substitute for them. (For further details and examples, see Fishman 1980b.) That the Yiddish secular school viewed reality quite differently is probably due to circumstances, only some of which correspond to the circumstances that led other language movements to stress the school as a major sociolinguistic force.

Yiddish secular education arose in the tradition of the 'revolutionary school', i.e. of the school that is part of a movement to rebuild all of society: culturally, politically, economically. When such movements are successful, such schools are, indeed, part of the cutting edge that both destroys and rebuilds. As such, the self-image of the school (including administrators, teachers, pupils, and even parents) is that of a victorious change-agent, i.e. a self-image that does not fully realize the part-whole context that obtains and that ascribes to the self far more causal power than is justified. The larger revolutionary forces often do not reach the young as regularly and as persistently as does the revolutionary school, but if the former forces fail, the roles and statuses for which the school prepares become not only nonfunctional but self-defeating and intrapunative. In this light one might say that in less than a century the Yiddish secular school traversed the distance between riding the crest of a revolutionary transformation of society to serving a society that either no longer existed or no longer existed in terms of adult roles and statuses in which its students could participate.

The original self-image of the Yiddish secular school was probably overblown due to its *narodnik* and its traditional inheritances as well. From the former it inherited an ennobling tradition of serving the masses and activating them via their own language. From the latter it inherited, without knowing it, a stress on schooling as a significant (perhaps even a primary) status system. Unfortunately for the Yiddish school, both of these in-

heritances increasingly lost their viability. The *narodnik* role for Yiddish vanished as coterritorial vernaculars pre-empted not only those functions for which there was coterritorial competition but the intracommunal functions as well. From a practical point of view, the language of coterritorial social status and social mobility for post-Holocaust Jews also determined intracommunal status and roles, thus robbing Yiddish of its functional significance and the Yiddish school of its *narodnik* mission. The Yiddish secular school might still have benefited from the traditional Jewish emphasis on the primacy of education for its own sake. However, the school's own antitraditional emphases led it to pursue modern societal impact directly rather than the continuity of traditional, unmobilized life patterns. Although Yiddish secular schools continued to draw inspiration from the focus on education that *toyre lishmo* provides, they did not create nor relate to a society of their own in which *toyre lishmo* significantly existed and called upon dedication to Yiddish for its implementation.

The 'failure' of the Yiddish secular school, particularly in its post-Holocaust and postimmigration years, needs to be viewed in several mitigating perspectives. The first such perspective is the failure of the schools of all other participationistic immigrant minorities to be effective language maintenance instruments (see my chapter on 'The ethnic group school and mother tongue maintenance' in Fishman 1966: 92–126). The second such perspective is the generally dismal failure of Jewish education to teach even Hebrew successfully enough to make it into a Diaspora vernacular, even with all of the affective positiveness with which it is surrounded. Finally, foreign or second language education as a whole is certainly one of the very least successful branches of all modern education, rarely succeeding in developing spoken facility among pupils *unless clear and powerful functional-demographic reinforcement is present* (see Fishman 1976c, 1977c). Little wonder then that Yiddish secular schools succeeded no better than they did, given that their societal base was so exposed to external and internal onslaught and that Yiddish secularism itself was so weak, so novel and so superficial, either as a movement or as a societal pattern of *yidishkayt*.

dream (Krug 1954; Mark 1948; Yefroykin 1951; Parker 1978). Even in Vilne, Warsaw, Lodz, and elsewhere in the Nazi-organized ghettos, Yiddish teachers continued to be trained specifically so that the remnants of the Jewish school-age child population could receive their education totally or partially in Yiddish (Anon. and Ringlblum 1945; Dvorzhetski 1948, 1970; Gersht 1947). Under the circumstances of American (and Israeli) freedom the need for modern Jewish education in (or even including) Yiddish is neither as clear nor as pressing. (For an affirmation of Yiddish in Jewish education in both of these settings, see Bez 1971b.) As Yiddish secularism and its schools wane (Eisenberg 1968; Rudavsky 1955) – and as Yiddish in education becomes either a marker of unreconstructed Orthodoxy, on the one hand, or a higher educational elective, on the other hand – the Yiddish secular school recedes into history as a memorial to the vicissitudes of Jewish modernization and cultural pluralism. The wealth of love and devotion lavished upon it, by teachers, *shultuers* (school-board members), parents, and children alike, is eloquent testimony to the need that it served.

Yivo: The ministry of Yiddish cultural efforts

The crownpiece and nerve center of the delicately orchestrated Yiddish culture 'movement' – the intellectual and spiritual integrator, elevator, and interpreter of all else that went on in the modern world of Yiddish (except, of course, for its doomed efforts in the Stalinist empire; see Zaretski 1928 for a programmatic

מאָריס ראָזענפעלד אין ניו-יאָרקער „פאָרווערטס“.
(אַ בריוו פון גאַליציען, אַ פּאָר טעג פאַר דער עפענונג פון דער קאָנפערענץ):

„...איך ווייס, אַז מיט דעם אויסנאַם פון איינציקע מענטשן, האָט מען אין אַמעריקע קיין צו-גרויסע אינטערעסע אין דיזן טשערנאָוויצער צוזאַמענפאָר, מחמת פאַרשיידענע טעמים. ערשטנס גלויבט מען, אַז עס וועט דערפון קיין פּראַקטישעס סך-הכּל נישט אַרויסקומען. צווייטנס, איז דער אַמעריקאַנישער יידישער שרייבער, ווי דער יידישער לעזער, נישט צו שטאַרק פאַרקאָכט אין גראַמאַטיקאַלישע כּללים. וואָס מאַכט דאָס אויס, אויב מען שרייבט „גיין“, „געהן“ אָדער „גאַין“, „איד“, „ייד“, „יוד“ אָדער „יאַהודי“, אַזוי לאַנג ווי מען קאָן דאָס איבערלייענען און פאַרשטיין. אַ גראַמאַטיק קאָן דאָך נישט איינגעפלאַנצט ווערן אין אַ פאָלק אָן פאָלקס-שולן. איבערהויפּט אָן העכערע שולן, אָן גימנאַזיעס, וועלכע דערקלערן און גיבן-איבער מיט דורכפרובירטע, פּעדאַגאָגישע עסאָדן און פּראַקטיק דעם גייסט פון דער שפּראַך. טויזנט גראַמאַטיקעס און ביכער איבער רעטאָריק און שפּראַך-לערע וועלן קיין גראַמאַטיקאַלישע שפּראַך נישט שאַפן. ווען עס וועט נישט זיין קיין באָדן, אויף וועלכן די שפּראַך זאָל זיך אַנטוויקלען; קיין שולן, ווו די יוגנט זאָל קומען לערנען. ביי דער מערצאָל אַפילו פון אונזערע גוטע שרייבער ווערט דאָס יידיש באַטראַכט בלויז אַלס אַ פאָרם, וואָס פירט אַריבער צו דער אַנדערער זייט, צו דער לאַנדשפּראַך, וועלכע יעדער איינער פון אונז מוז לערנען אין דעם לאַנד, ווו ער געפינט זיך

אָבער אָט די אַלע טענות, גערעדט מיט אַ „קאַלטן לונג און לעבער“, קאָנען נאָר גילטן אין אַמעריקע. דאָ, אין גאַליציען, זענען זיי מער ווי אַ בלויזע פראַגע וועגן דקדוק, דאָ איז דאָס אַ פּאָליטישע פראַגע, אַ לעבנס-פראַגע...

...ווען עס זאָל אָפיציעל באַשטימט ווערן, אַז לשון-קודש איז די יידישע שפּראַך, דאַן וועלן די יידישע מאַסן פאַרלירן זייער ווערט און זייער שפּראַך וועט איגנאָרירט ווערן. עס וועלן דערפון פּראָפיטירן בלויז די „סנאָבס“, די נאַציאָנאַלע יידישע אַריסטאָקראַטיע צוקער-לעקעך-אידעאַליסטן. דערום זענען די אויגן פון די אמתע פאָלקס-פריינד און אַרבעטער-פריינד אין גאַליציען און אַפילו אין רוסלאַנד געריכטעט צו טשערנאָוויץ; דעריבער האָט יענע קאָנפערענץ אַ וויכטיקע, היסטאָרישע באַדייטונג. איך ווייס נישט פון וועלכן שטאַנד די קאָנפערענץ וועט באַהאַנדלען די שפּראַך-פראַגע, וועלכע אַרגומענטן דאָרט וועלן געפירט ווערן און וועלכן ענדציל מען וועט זוכן צו דערגרייכן. מעגלעך, אַז די קאָנפערענץ זאָל טראָגן אַ מין מלמדיש-בטלנישן כאַראַקטער, אַ זאַך, וואָס לאָזט זיך אַפילו נישט גלויבן, זיכער איז דאָס אָבער, אַז די קאָנפערענץ וועט האָבן אַ שטאַרקן אָפּקלאַנג אויף די יידישע פּאָליטיק אין גאַליציען...“

Figure 7. An excerpt from an advance effort to explain the 1908 Tshernovits Conference to readers of the New York *Forverts* (when it was believed that linguistic–orthographic issues would be of major concern), inserted in the recommendations and demands of the American youth delegation at the '(Jerusalem) World Conference for Yiddish and Yiddish Culture', August 1976.

statement of early hopes there and Choseed 1968 for their abandonment even prior to their official destruction) was to have been the Yiddish Scientific Institute – Yivo. Its special mission was to go beyond explicit ideology, into the higher realms of culture planning, and there to bring to bear the contributions of modern research methods in the humanities and social sciences for the solution of the uniquely difficult sociopsychological, demographic, linguistic, cultural, and even socioeconomic problems of the Yiddish speaking masses (Anon. 1925; Niger 1931; M. Vaynraykh 1936, 1943, 1945). A combination of a think-tank and an action-research center, the Yivo was far more than a university. It was at the hub of the *kultur-bavegung* (Shveytser 1967; Stupnitski 1920). It was part of it; it was involved. While it promised dispassionate, nonpartisan study (although not neutrality *vis-à-vis* the fascist and communist depredations), it was regarded (and self-regarded) as the culmination and fusion of all that Yiddish and its masses hoped for in the arena of modern cultural efforts in interwar Europe and even in its emigration colonies abroad. An extraterritorial people and language prided itself with its extraterritorial *sanctum-sanctorum* in the very capital of Yiddish, Vilne, the Jerusalem of Lithuania.

It would have been miraculous had the Yivo been able to deliver all that was expected of it. In many ways it did accomplish miracles, being associated with the major works of Yiddish scholarship and of research on Eastern European Jewry during the past half century (Fishman 1977). However, the ultimate miracle was denied it. With the Holocaust the Yivo lost not only much of its staff and its archival/library holdings but, more basically and irreplaceably, its sociolinguistic heartland. Although it functions actively to this very day, and is one of the very few Eastern European institutions to successfully relocate in the West, its social mission is largely gone (Gutman 1977). It is a unique interacademic research and teaching agency serving all who have an interest in Eastern European Jewry (Gilson 1976). As such, its routinization follows the typical postethnic lines traveled so often before by formerly ethnic institutions that have 'successfully' outgrown their original missions and clienteles.[17]

PART VI: MAINTENANCE AND SHIFT

Languages the world over are popularly characterized via stereotypes concerning their 'nature'. German is viewed as harsh, and French as precise. Italian is considered musical, and English vigorous. And Yiddish? Yiddish is dead or dying. One must be 'an insider' (of the Yivo, of the Hasidic community, of the

---

17. Of course it is not merely failure that leads to the ideological attrition of routinization but also success. Examples of the latter type of routinization of sociolinguistic institutions are the language academies whose 'charges' have attained full-fledged societal acceptance and functional legiti- mization along the entire range of modern activities. Such academies also have their ideological ground cut out from under them. For case studies of Israel, India, and Indonesia in the latter connection see Rubin et al. 1977.

world of Yiddish *kultur-arbet*), i.e. a member of a very small inner circle indeed, to have a different image or to know enough to question the stereotype. Curiously, this view is infinitely more pervasive than its former companion that *Kol mevaser* alternately so attacked and so espoused, namely that 'Yiddish is a corrupted German'. The latter view has substantially receded as linguistic perspective has seeped down from higher professional spheres. It is also an exceedingly insulting position to take in view of the slaughtered six million who died with Yiddish on their lips (Bez 1971a, 1971b; Faerstein 1965). But that very slaughter, sanctifying and purifying Yiddish in the popular mind, merely adds to the dominant theme of its death (Freidlin 1977). For well over a hundred years that theme has been repeated, as if by a Greek chorus, in conjunction with each and every Yiddish enterprise, until, as with all predictions pertaining to the death of mortals, it might yet come to pass and provide prophets with the additional satisfaction of that final twist of the knife: 'I told you so!' Even repeated exhortations to 'save Yiddish' are an indication of its uncertainty (Tsivyen 1948).

As far as pre-World War II Eastern Europe itself was concerned the prognostication was so completely premature as not only to be unfounded, but to reveal wishful thinking, *schadenfreude* or both. By the time of the *haskole* in Eastern Europe, it was fairly well known that in past generations Yiddish had been displaced in Western Europe (Beem 1954; Landmann 1967; Niger 1959; Shatski 1936; Shaykovski 1939, 1964; Shpirn 1926; Weinberg 1969). This awareness continued to provide an air of expectancy with respect to the future. However, as if in 'perverse disregard of history' the Czarist census of 1897 revealed that almost all Jews in the Empire (97.96 percent to be exact) claimed Yiddish as their mother tongue, the lowest rate of claiming being 95.74 percent in Poland (Goldberg 1905a). Even then, i.e. even prior to the impact of Yiddish secular literature, 49.4 percent of the males and 26 percent of the females claimed that they could *read* Yiddish as well as speak it (Rubinow 1907). However, that was 'before the flood' (World War I). The next Eastern European census for which we have data related to Yiddish is that of 1921 and the area covered is Poland alone (Y. L. [Leshtshinski] 1936). Actually, this census reports religious claiming and nationality claiming. If the latter can be interpreted (as it is by Y.L.) as pertaining primarily to mother tongue then the rate of Yiddish mother tongue claiming among Polish claimants of Jewish religion was slightly under 70 percent. This was lower than the proportion of such claiming in 1897 but it was still substantial. By 1931 the Polish census reported that 79.9 percent of all Jews by religion claimed Yiddish as their mother tongue (with 7.9 percent claiming Hebrew). Lo and behold, the rate of Yiddish claiming had risen, although it was still short of the 1897 rate (Leshtshinski 1940, 1943). However, not only was the total number of claimants a hefty 2.5 million strong, but in certain key urban areas of Jewish cultural and political concentration the rates of Yiddish claiming were actually higher in 1931 than they had been in 1897, e.g. in Warsaw (94.0 percent vs. 84.5 percent) and in Vilne (99.2 percent vs. 97.0 percent; see Goldberg 1905b; Leshtshinski 1940)! Even at the university level in Warsaw, where a previous generation of Jewish students had been almost completely assimilated linguistically, 50.3 percent of all Jewish students in 1931 claimed Yiddish as their current 'home language', with many more doing so in the humanistic, pedagogical, and social science faculties (64 percent, 77 percent, and 83 percent respectively). Interestingly enough, the demographer L. Hersch comments on these figures as follows: 'Ever-broader segments of Jewish diplomaed intellectuals are now derived from those strata where Yiddish is a living language' (Hersh 1931). That this had not always been the case is testified to by Hersh's own student-day memories, as well as by stern warnings of a generation earlier that intellectuals who did not speak Yiddish in their private lives could not be expected to lead the people to national strength and dignity (Olgin 1911). This condition continued into the 30s and it is, therefore, quite clear why there were those who preferred to stress the *empty* half of the glass of water (Mirkin 1939, retrospectively Tartakover 1946).

However, if it could be argued that the demographic-functional position of Yiddish was not deteriorating in Poland prior to the Second World War, this could not be claimed for either the USSR, Palestine/Erets Yisroel or the United States (where the three major concentrations of Yiddish speakers are to be found today). Not only have their absolute numbers and their proportions of Yiddish mother tongue claimants continued to fall (although some 4.1 million out of a worldwide total of 14 million Jews – i.e. 30 percent of the worldwide total – probably would/could claim Yiddish as their mother tongue today [Kloss and McConnell 1978]), but this fall has been even more precipitous than imagined if we seek some more certain indicator of usage than is mother tongue per se. In the Soviet Union the proportion of Jews claiming Yiddish as their 'national language' fell rapidly and continuously, from 72.6 percent in 1926 to 41 percent in 1939 (albeit some 60 percent of Jewish children attended Yiddish schools in the 30s) to 17.9 percent in 1959, to 16.8 percent in 1970 (Lipset 1970; somewhat different figures are reported by Kantor 1962–1963). Even this last figure is little short of miraculously high (as is the fact that some 23 percent of Jews in the RSFSR – *not* a particularly Jewish area of the USSR – claimed in 1970 that Yiddish was their first or second most *used* language; Checinski 1973), given both the 'encouraged' assimilation of Jews and the unabashed repression of Yiddish in the USSR (at least since the mid-thirties; see, e.g. Emyot 1960; Gitelman 1972; Graubert 1974; J. Halevy 1972; Hirzowicz 1974; Korey 1974; Levenberg 1968; Pomerants 1962; Rozental-Shnayderman 1974. For Soviet counterclaims in the mid-30s see Dimanshteyn 1935. For the post-war eradication of the remnants of Yiddish in Poland see Sfard 1974). In Israel, the proportion claiming to speak Yiddish either as their 'principal' or 'additional' language

was only 13.4 percent of the total Jewish population in 1961 and 14.6 percent
of the Jewish population aged 14 or above in 1971 (both being remarkably high
figures, but probably underestimates, given Israeli–Zionist discrimination
against Yiddish in the Holy Land since at least the mid-thirties; Fishman 1973;
Fishman and Fishman 1977; Seikevicz 1976; Tsanin 1974). Finally, in the
United States, Yiddish was claimed as the principal spoken language of only
2.1 percent of the total Jewish population in 1969, even though it was still
claimed as mother tongue by some 1.6 million Jews in 1970 (Ellman 1978), i.e.
by nearly a third of the entire American born Jewish population, comfortably
ensconced though it was by then in thoroughly Anglified suburbia. Differences
in overclaiming fads and underclaiming fads make comparisons across and even
within these three settings quite risky.[18] Even only a relatively small nucleus of
dedicated and creative users could become a serious force (M. Vaynraykh
1951b). Nevertheless, the language is obviously declining with respect to the
number of its overt users and the situation looks even worse if the age
distributions of claimants are examined. These distributions are consistently and
considerably top-heavy, containing few young people and disproportionately
many old people. Similar age trends have appeared in such bastions as Canada

18. Although the precise figures for Yiddish usage
in the USSR, Israel and the United States are not
to be taken at face value, their relative magnitudes
may nevertheless be indicative. All three settings
are characterized by self-fulfilling prophecies concerning the destinies of their respective unifying
languages. Marx is expected to triumph over
Herder in the USSR, notwithstanding the elaborate structure of 'autonomous' republics, regions,
and districts defined on ethnic grounds. As early
as 1927, over half of all those young people being
trained to conduct *politufkler* (political enlightenment) among Jews were non-Yiddish speakers or
seriously deficient in their command of Yiddish (S.
1927). Only a third claimed that their Yiddish was
at least as good as their Russian and early hopes
for party support for Yiddish waned rapidly (Ben
Adir 1919; Shtif 1927), as the party per se turned
out to be the major opponent of Yiddish. In Israel,
Yiddish is spoken much more in private than in
public (Herman 1961) and its speakers have generally as much facility in speaking and reading
Hebrew as does the population at large (Kaz
1972; Fishman and Fishman 1977). Indeed, even
those who champion Yiddish there view Hebrew
as though it were an irresistible superhuman
ocean of the future into which all rivers must
ultimately flow (Sadan 1974). Certainly English
is widely viewed not only as the manifest destiny
of the United States but as the unifying language
of the world at large. Thus, all that can be hoped
for, in the eyes of most, is that Yiddish will provide

a unique flavor to Jewish popular culture (Friedman 1975). In a country in which 'all aspire to
mobility' via English (Fishman 1963), Yiddish
appears to be functionally empty even for most
children of Yiddishists. These still admire it from
afar (Lerer 1961) but have rarely made it their
daily language, not even with the generations
above them, let alone with interlocutors of their
own generation or younger.

Claiming Yiddish usage in the early 70s had an
antiestablishment implication in all three locales
of its major use. Since antiestablishment feelings
were more 'in' than they used to be, Yiddish use
was probably overclaimed, but probably not as
significantly as the overclaiming revealed by
mother tongue statistics of roughly the same years.
(The substantial validity of these claims for estimating Jewish population figures is apparent from
Rosenwaike 1971, 1974.) That the United States
should reveal the least usage claiming for Yiddish
and the USSR the most (16.8 percent vs. 2.1
percent) is testimony to the much greater dislocative impact of immigration, modernization,
social mobility, and interactionism than of most of
the foregoing in the absence of immigration. In the
Yiddish case, voluntary participation in the
world's most sustained social mobility experience
has been far more disruptive of ethnic mother
tongue use than has indoctrination and repression.
This is probably a paradigm for modern days:
more languages are probably enticed into disuse
rather than battered into that condition.

(Yam 1973; Kloss 1977), Latin America (Turkov 1968; Virkel de Sandler 1977), Australia (Medding 1968; Klarberg 1970) and Israel (Hofman and Fisherman 1971; Fishman and Fishman 1977).

The view is similarly grim if we consider such related matters as: the age distribution of Yiddish authors, whether in the United States alone (Fishman 1965) or, comparatively, in the United States, the Soviet Union and Israel (Fishman and Fishman 1977); the market for Yiddish books from the early 30s (M. V. [Vaynraykh] 1934; Z. Reyzin 1931) to this day, as well as the number of such books published (Fishman and Fishman 1977); the number and circulation of Yiddish periodicals (Fishman 1960, 1965a, 1972; also see Soltes 1924; Fishman and Fishman 1976); the number and length of Yiddish radio broadcasting (Fishman 1965a, 1972); the number of Yiddish theater performances (Fishman 1965a, 1972; also see Lifson 1965); and the use of Yiddish as a medium of Jewish education (Fishman 1952, 1965a, 1972; Klarberg 1970). Even the former growth of Orthodox day schools in the United States utilizing Yiddish as *the* (or as *a*) language of instruction of Jewish subjects has slowed considerably (Fishman 1972) and is now considerably outdistanced by the growth in the number of Orthodox day schools teaching Jewish subject matter via English and/or Hebrew. This has probably happened in other countries as well. Nevertheless, both Orthodoxy and ultra-Orthodoxy have clearly become the bedrock of whatever remains of Yiddish-speaking Jewry (Fishman 1972; Saymon 1970), however little interest either the one or the other may have in Yiddish literature or in formal study of Yiddish per se. Yiddish continues to be the language of daily intragroup life and of traditional (Talmudic) study for a very substantial proportion, particularly of ultra-Orthodoxy, although it too may well have turned a corner in this connection, as even part of this sector seeks to reach out and to bring others, particularly wayward adolescents and young folks, back into the fold. For the first time in a thousand years Ashkenazic ultra-Orthodoxy may be conducting more of its work in the diaspora in non-Jewish vernaculars than in Yiddish. The situation in Israel, *vis-à-vis* Hebrew vs. Yiddish as *vernaculars* among the ultra-Orthodox, is probably also approaching the tipping point in so far as actual usage is concerned, if it has not already gone beyond that point. As for 'modern Orthodoxy' whether in Israel or in the United States, its abandonment of Yiddish is well-nigh complete and its return thereto on a nostalgic basis is still retarded by the uneasy and self-conscious emphasis on Orthodoxy's own 'modernity'. The two Orthodox universities (Yeshiva and Bar Ilan) are conspicuous by their peculiar inability to recognize Yiddish either as meeting foreign language requirements ('Does Yiddish have a literature? Is learning Yiddish really a broadening experience, exposing the learner to universal themes, like learning X literature?') or as meeting any part of the Jewish studies requirements ('Yiddish is not a Hebraic study!', even though the specialized study of Judesmo or Yahudic [= Judeo Arabic] *is*).

חודש פאַר יידיש און יידישקייט

ליטעראַדישער פאַמיליען-זשורנאַל

8

אָרגאַן פאַר די אינטערעסן פון די בית-יעקב-שולן
און אָרגאַני/אַציעס בנות-אגודת-ישראל אין פּוילן

יאָרגאַנג

71-72

רעדאַקטאָר: א. ג. פֿרידענזאָן

ב"ה, לאָדזש-קראָקע-וואַרשע, סיון תרצ"א

תוכן פון היאַנטיקן יידיש-בומער:

ידיש אין אַמעריקא

א) תוכן און לבוש

ב) אַ פאָר ווערטער וועגן יידיש: דר. נתן בירנבוים

ג) יידיש (ליד): אליעזר סינדלער

ד) יידיש לשון און יידישער לעבנס-שטייגער: הרב שמשון סטאָקהאַמער

ה) בענטשונג פון צער (ליד): בר נש

ו) דאָס לשון אין מויל פון דער מאַמין: אליעזר גרשון פרידנזאָן

שמואל נאַדלער: דער פילם פון יידיש-פראַנט

ח) שרה שעניגער: יידישקייט און יידיש

ט) הרב שמואל דוד לאַסקי: רעט יידיש

י) די ראָלע פון יידיש אינים חסידות: אַלכסנדר זושא פרידמאַן

יא) יידיש אין דער שול: יהודה לייב אַרלאָזן

יב) יידישקייט פון האַרץ און צונג: אסתר ראוא

יג) גיט מיר לשון (ליד): איש לוי

יד) דאָס מזל פון יידיש: שמואל אסטערזועצער

טו) דאָס אינגעניש מיטן מורה: ריקל בירנבוים

טז) וואָויל איז אונדז (פאָלקס-ליד): בניטין זוסמאַן

יז) פון אַלטע ספרים און פון אַמאָליקן לעבן:
בריוולעך ... 1) אַ יידישע טאַנצסטער אין ביסערע ענוייב; 2) אַ יידיש
שידוך-בריוועל פונים תוספות יום-טוב; 3) אַ בריוועל פונים תוספות יום-טוב
היינ. מחברטיס; 4) אַ ליד פון אַ מירעלע, 5) בת לוי, 6) אַ תּילה לשבת.
תּגלסטעבכייים; 7) דאָ לעזטסע ספר אויף יידיש, 8) אַ תּוש פּאַרן לשון.
תנ"ך צום פּאַרגינינגן; 9) פונים שמואל-בוך, 10) פונים שופטים-בוך; 11)
רדיק פּאָר ג...; 12) צניה ורא...נה אין ארגינאַל; 13) פסוקים אַף ...ריש
דורך פּיניף הונגערער ...יר. 14) אַ ...רושטער רידער.

יח) די ברים און זייער וועג: אליעזר סינדלער

יט) שטהין פון דער מלחמה: שלמה בירנבוים

כ) יידיש וויסן און יידיש רעדן: מאיר האַלף ניעסטצטפאויער

כא) נעפלין (ליד): בר נש

כב) אַמעשה שהי...: משה צבאואל

כג) ווי אלט איז דאָס יידישע לשון? ש"ב

כד) רוסע לבנה (ליד): בר נש

כה) צווי חאווין כל הגוים: דר. שלמה בירנבוים

כו) פאַר יידיש: יצחק מאיר בונים און דר צ. ה: בלוסטעאָן

כז) יידיש - אַ מויער: הרב אליעזר זילבער

כח) יידיש מיט יידישקייט: הרב ישראל ראזנבערג

כט) כנסת ישראל און "יאנג איזראעל": הרב דר ב. רעוועל

ל) פרומע יידן און יידיש: מרדכי דאנציס

לא) דער בונד פון דורות: הרב דר אלי' יונג

לב) שלא שינו את לשונם: הרב דר דוד שפערן

לג) יידיש אין ישיבות און תלמוד תורות

לד) אָוונט (ליד): עזרא גוטמאן

לה) וויפל מענטשן רעדן היינט יידיש ?

לו) וואָס איז יידישקייט: יעקב לאַנדא

לז) אין מערב איז יא דאָ נ...: מאיר שווארצמאַן

לח) דער נצחון פון אונדזער אויסלייב: שב"ן

לט) וועגן ליטווישן דיאַלעקטס אין קאָנגרעס פוילן: נטע ירוחם בערלינער

מ) זייער גירעקס: ב'

מא) פלאַנסטער אין דער נסתה: אשר

סב) לינקע פערל: ס'

מג) ים-מיניאַטורן: וו. לײַבצטער

מד) באַהערשן און באַצווינגען: לייב פיינגאָלד

מה) פנקס פון "יידישקייט און יידיש"

מו) אַלאַרם-רוף צו אונדזערע פרינט

מז) אַלדינענס (ליד): בר נש

מח) וועגן די באַזוכן פון אליעזר סינדלער

מט) הכרזות

נ) מודעות

רעדאַקטירט דורך

דר. שלמה בירנבוים

There *is* one bright spot on the Yiddish maintenance-and-shift horizon at this time, although it is hard to tell whether its significance is real or imaginary. Yiddish as a college-level subject grew tremendously in the decade from the mid-sixties to the mid-seventies (Pen 1958b; Prager 1974; Smolyar 1977). However, all in all, this growth has attracted only two thousand or so students at any one time over the entire world, and did not begin to make up for the loss in attendance at secular Yiddish elementary schools (which have almost become extinct in the United States and which have run into increasing problems of late in Canada and Latin America – fiscally, politically, and in terms of Zionist opposition). At any rate, the likelihood that Yiddish can be functionally mastered via college courses, even among those who *do* enroll, is apparently negligible (i.e. not appreciably more so, nor more permanently so, than it is with respect to achieving mastery of *X* language via college courses). Finally, it does appear that the number of such courses has hit its maximum, given current fiscal and demographic limitations, as well as given the more general rollback of the ethnicity mood which seems to have peaked just a few years ago and is now considerably subdued. Nevertheless the college level texts and dictionaries prepared and planned in conjunction with this erstwhile area of growth will long retain their usefulness and the air of hopefulness with which they were undertaken (Dawidowicz 1977).

Thus the sad prophecies of the last century may yet be realized. Nevertheless, the true and dedicated believers, though fewer and older, remain undaunted, unbowed and unbeaten (see e.g. Ben-adir 1942; Glatshteyn 1972a, 1972b; Robak 1958b, 1958c, 1964a, 1964b; Samuel 1971b, 1972; Toybes 1950. For examples of atypically younger devotion see Yugntruf, particularly 1976, no. 37–37). As with the defenders of all Jewish values, they are blessed with a healthy dose of supernatural and superrational strength which provides unexpected faith, energy, and opportunity.

PART VII: SOCIOLINGUISTIC VARIATION AND PLANNING

More or less dispassionate ('academic') linguistic research on Yiddish began quite early (see e.g. Mansch 1888–1890; Saineanu 1889; Landau 1895; Gerzon 1902) but inevitably, given a language that has always been spoken by a community so many of whose members have been bilingual, and that has been as exposed, as has Yiddish, to social and political pressures from such a variety of coliterary languages, a substantial amount of ink (and, ultimately, even blood) soon came to be spilt over the sociopolitical question of what models Yiddish

◄ Figure 8. Table of Contents of a 1931 issue of *Beys-Yankev*, journal of the ultra-Orthodox Agudas Yisroel schools for girls in Poland. This issue was devoted entirely to advocating maintenance of Yiddish in religious life and education. Among the contributors to this issue are: Nosn Birnboym, Shloyme Birnboym (ed.), Eliezer Shindler and Bernard Revel.

should follow. If successive new English dictionaries are met with storms of criticism and dissonance as to whether certain terms should have been included or excluded (even though the pedigree of English is unquestioned), if French authorities struggle openly and normatively to curb the in-roads of 'franglais' (even though the future of French [in France] is unthreatened), is it any wonder that the counterparts to such normative codification and disagreement should be discernible in the field of Yiddish as well? Although modern language planning theory might imply that Yiddish could not really hope to struggle successfully – given its weak implementational resources – with the vicissitudes of modern social communication, a century's efforts to engage in such planning have, of course, continued, and in so doing have revealed the political and sociocultural biases of the combatants.[19]

One of the earliest and best established modeling tendencies in conscious Yiddish language planning was that of *ausbau* from modern Standard German (e.g. Yofe 1910, 1958; Niger 1912; Sholem Aleykhem 1888b). This effort, carried on during the interwar years under the slogan of 'away from German', sought (and seeks today) to stress that Yiddish follows standardizing conventions and authorities of its own and that these are autonomous from those that pertain to modern Standard German (Kalmanovitsh 1925; M. Vaynraykh 1936, N.P. 1938; Prilutski 1938; Reyzin 1938). The underlying dynamic in this struggle against *daytshmerish* (unnecessary New High German borrowings) is the perennial one of demonstrating that Yiddish is by no means a 'corrupt German', a goal which is still very much alive within Yiddish language planning to this very day

---

19. One of the earliest proponents of Yiddish language planning was Y. M. Lifshits, the compiler of a Yiddish–Russian dictionary (1876) and a consistent, open and vigorous advocate of Yiddish in the otherwise meandering *Kol mevaser*. 'At home' with both French and German, and with the literature of the former and the natural science associated with the latter, he quickly concluded that whatever it was that mid-nineteenth century Yiddish lacked in terms of codification and elaboration was due to the limited scholarly-literary attention devoted to the language rather than to any inherent quality of the language itself. His motto in this connection was: '*Nisht der fidl iz shuldik nor der klezmer*' (The fault lies not with the fiddle but with the fiddler). He rejected the corruption myth with particular vehemence, stressing that all other living languages constantly borrowed from each other and that this was especially true of Russian, a language favored by many of the perpetrators of the corruption myth *vis-à-vis* Yiddish. As with the chief advocate of language planning for Malaysian-Indonesian today, Lifshits did not so much advocate formal codification or elaboration per se as serious literary use of the language in order to advance its cultivation. Other advocates of Yiddish language planning (usually referred to as *shprakhkultur* since the late 20s and early 30s, e.g. Spivak 1931) have often stressed one or another goal, e.g. grammatical codification (Dr. X [= I. Zamenhof, the father of Esperanto] 1909), *ausbau* from all current and past coterritorial languages (Reyzin 1938), standardized spelling and lexical elaboration (Shekhter 1961), etc. All in all, more has been accomplished for the language-in-print in each of these connections, and under the most adverse of circumstances, than might have been expected (Fishman 1979; Shekhter i.p.). However, at the same time, the world of Yiddish-in-print has shrunk to such an extent that the circles of the remaining planners and the circles of those who still publish in Yiddish criss-cross much more fully than they did at the beginning of the century. As in the case of Hindi (*vis-à-vis* Sanskritization) the success of language planning may be advanced at a time of functional-demographic failure due to the fact that the remaining users are both fewer and easier to influence or control.

(Shekhter 1969), even though the stereotype of Yiddish as a 'corrupted German' is somewhat weaker today than it was a generation ago.[20] Similar (although less long-lasting) struggles have been waged against 'excessive' Hebraisms,

20. Although 'away from German' was a generally accepted conscious goal, it was very often also compromised with, as Shekhter (1969) has revealed, even among the 'planners' themselves (for a defense of 'necessary Germanisms' see Mark 1963). The *haskole* per se and the very process of modernization as a whole were themselves powerful forces leading to a massive injection of new German borrowings and calques (see, e.g. M. Vaynraykh 1933 on Tsederboym). In addition some of the early pro-Yiddish activists were willing to accept a German model for spelling even if not for lexical or grammatical development (Herbert 1913; for a similar earlier view by I. M. Dik see Niger 1952). So great was the total onslaught of German influences (we must remember that German represented the major cultural-technological force in Eastern Europe in the latter half of the nineteenth century, for Jews as well as for non-Jews) that some scholars prematurely concluded that Yiddish was actually returning to the womb of German from whence it had emerged (Rubshteyn 1922; note the detailed refutations by Bal-dimyen 1923 and M. Vaynraykh 1923b).

The problem of being engulfed by the very language from which one is seeking to establish distance is not unknown in other settings. French language planning in Quebec faces this very issue today, one of the major problems of the Office de la Langue Française being that technology worldwide is English language dominated whereas it is precisely the technological functions that the Quebecoise movement must seek to control. The problem of Yiddish *vis-à-vis* German was more difficult, however, because, on the one hand, it was an *ausbau* language from shared Germanic origins to begin with and, also, because it so completely lacked either political power or full-fledged internal acceptance. The general problems of seeking purity by *ausbau* from the big brother with whom one shares common origins is analyzed beautifully for Ukrainian and White Russian by Paul Wexler in his *Purism and Language* (1974). The problem of lack of political power to enforce decisions is discussed by Jack Fellman, *vis-à-vis* the early work of the Hebrew Language Committee in his *The Revival of a Classical Tongue* (1973) and by U. Vaynraykh in comparing Yiddish and Romanch (1972). The mutually magnifying interaction of both of these problems remains to be discussed. (Re excesses during the brief period of Soviet political manipulation of Yiddish language planning see Anon. 1935b, Erlich 1973, Redaktsye 1932.)

Two more roadblocks in the rejection of New-High Germanisms remain to be mentioned. During the latter half of the nineteenth century the habitual (even if archaic) Jewish usage of referring to Yiddish as German was externalized. Both Czarist Russian and Imperial Austro-Hungarian permits to publish in Yiddish often referred to the language as German (or as German in Hebrew characters: a designation that was quite appropriate for some much earlier Central European publications) and many *maskilim* hoped to use such publications to slowly lead the masses, step by step, back to 'real German'. This usage fed back upon internal views and readinesses *vis-à-vis* combatting New-High Germanisms.

However, the concept of German itself was also a constantly shifting one, if not for linguists than for more ordinary mortals. Was the more Germanized Yiddish of Kurland, of Western Hungary, of much of Galitsye and Bukovina, Yiddish or German? If it was hard for many to tell *in situ* (since more and less German was a stylistic functional variable present in the linguistic repertoire of many Yiddish speakers) it became even harder *after* immigration when coterritorial German speakers or intellectuals were no longer nearby. Folk interpretations of what were the differences between Yiddish and German abounded. For Zelkovits (1909) it was the difference between *o* (Yiddish) and *a* (German). For Berliner (1931) it was the Litvak dialect in the mouths of Polish Jews vs. either dialect *in situ*. For Toybes (1948) it was the difference between *oy* (Yiddish) and *au* (German). (Toybes points out that those seeking to oppose Yiddish often claim that the *oy* sound is ugly, coarse, uneducated, whereas the *au* sound is beautiful and elegant. However, these same 'phonetic anti-Yiddishists' have no complaints against the *oy* sound in English [as in *boy*, *cloister*]. He concludes that it is not the purported departure of Yiddish from German that troubles the *oy*-haters but, rather, its steadfast association with Jews and *yidishkayt*.) In our own day and age, the continued drive to combat New-High Germanisms is constantly complicated by the fact that most Yiddish speakers are out of touch (or have never been in touch) with German and therefore face additional difficulty in 'recognizing the enemy'. (For the special 'stage standard' in Yiddish see Prilutski 1927; for different approaches to defining a modern literary standard see Shekhter 1977b. For the role of Yiddish-in-print in fashioning this standard see Fishman 1981).

particularly by Soviet planners (Spivak 1935; Shtif 1929, 1931, 1932; Zaretski 1931a; note the counter-struggle in defense of Hebraisms by Hershls 1889; Kalmanovitsh 1925; Nobl 1957/58; Vaynraykh 1931, 1941b, etc.),[21] against 'excessive' Russisms/Sovietisms/Slavicisms (Kalmanovitsh 1931; Niger 1934; Shulman 1937; Tsvayg 1930. For views sympathetic to various degrees of Russification/Slavification see Shapiro 1967; Spivak 1930; Zaretski 1931b; Yofe 1927; for evidence of continued slavophilia in Soviet Yiddish, see S. Birnboym 1979b and Shekhter 1969–1970 and 1971); as well as more restrained struggles with respect to Polonisms (Gelnberg 1930; Prilutski 1938a), Anglicisms (Glatshteyn 1972b; Mark 1938, 1958; Shvarts 1925; M. Vaynraykh 1941a; Yofe 1936), Hispanicisms (Robak 1964c) and internationalisms [= Latinisms in worldwide use] (Prilutski 1938a; Zaretski 1931c).

Of all of the above modeling and antimodeling efforts, the one involving [New-High] Germanisms is not only the most continuous but it is also prototypic for all efforts to reject 'foreignisms' not only in the linguistic but in the ethnoauthentic, sociocultural sense as a whole. Yiddish should be *yidishlekh* (M. Vaynraykh 1942). The burden of the puristic argument here is that there are ample 'good old Yiddish words and Jewish concepts' that predate and are superior to newly introduced, unnecessary and distinctly unwholesome Germanisms (Russisms, Anglicisms, etc.). Obviously, therefore, the struggle for/against Hebraisms is often of a different coloration. Rather than being basically in-group–out-group contrastive it is differential basically on an intra-group basis. However, these two types of stances have often been in complementary distribution. Those who have most opposed Germanisms or other foreignisms have frequently favored Hebraisms since the latter have been viewed as not only representing an old (the oldest) layer of the language-culture

21. It is interesting to note that Hebraisms and Ivritisms have been regarded quite differently by some. Whereas Hebraisms connote authentic ties for Yiddish with 'the way of the *Shas*', i.e. with a millennium of traditional Ashkenaz, Ivritisms are just another kind of unnecessary foreignism, particularly for non-Zionist language planners (Shekhter 1977a; Bogoch 1973b). Pro-Zionist writers, on the other hand, are likely to be quite fond of Ivritisms and to prefer them both because of their modern Israeli connotations as well as because Ivrit appears to them as the natural continuation of *loshn koydesh* (Gros-tsimerman 1962; Ayznman 1976). The human capacity to redefine erstwhile opponents as friends and friends as opponents is evident in the language attitudes field generally and in the sociology of Yiddish particularly. However, similar tendencies are easily found in almost every politicized language planning context. The most obvious example of this capacity to redefine and yet to claim ideological consistency may be found in Ataturk's 'Great Sun Theory'. Believing that his movement to purify Turkish had gone further than was practical (given that modernization-Europeanization was also one of his goals), this theory ennabled Ataturk to consider European languages as being derived from Turkish (the great sun language that had cast its rays over all of Europe) and, therefore, to view the incorporation of French, English, and other Western terms as no more than welcoming back into the Turkish language fold some of its very own long lost children. The general point here is not that language planning rationales are arbitrary, but, rather, that they are intended to advance larger societal purposes and, therefore, are subject to reevaluation and reinterpretation in the light of those purposes, with 'authenticity' frequently remaining officially 'enthroned' but yet quite differently defined.

complex but as representing language use among the most deeply Jewish and scholarly (and, therefore, the most prestigeful) speech and writing networks. Similarly, many of the interwar detractors of Hebraisms were in favor of Sovietisms/Slavisms and of the secularization and Sovietization not only of Yiddish but of Jewish society as a whole (Volobrinski 1930; Gitlits 1934). Just as Ben-yehuda preferred to modernize Hebrew by drawing upon classical Hebrew roots, Aramaic roots, Hebrew roots from other historic periods, and, finally, Semitic roots from other languages (even Arabic), similarly many Yiddish linguists have had their rank ordering from most preferred to least preferred sources for the modernization of Yiddish, e.g. old Yiddish stock (including nonstandard dialects), Hebrew-Aramaic, internationalisms, on the one hand, and Anglicisms, Russisms, Germanisms, on the other.

Although normative efforts in Yiddish have often been ridiculed as either inauthentic in the light of dialectal reality (Tsukerman 1972), or as reflecting no more than one man's (or one group's or one agency's) arbitrary opinion/bias (Itkovitsh 1973; Gutkovitsh and Tsukerman 1977) such efforts have been neither rare nor without effect (Kan 1973; Shekhter 1961, 1975, i.p.), although possible negative effects have never been carefully investigated. Such efforts are certainly far more precedented throughout the world (indeed, they are frequently authoritatively cultivated) than their critics within the Yiddish fold generally recognize or admit. Basically, such efforts and their evaluations reflect sociopolitical–cultural views and assumptions concerning the historic importance of Yiddish in Jewish life, and views toward the Jewish past as such, views concerning the independent validity of Yiddish, and views concerning its future validity. Thus, the advocacy of Yiddish toponymics is not only part of the more general struggle against foreignisms but also an emphasis upon Jewish coterritorial priority and/or permanence (S. Birnboym 1916; Prilutski 1938a; Shekhter 1957; for linguistic analyses see Guggenheim-Grunberg 1965; Stankiewicz 1965).

The lexical and morpho-syntactic concerns that the above efforts have commonly highlighted are paralleled – certainly in so far as broader sociopolitical-cultural inclinations are concerned – in connection with the various Yiddish orthographic conventions and *their* corresponding 'schools of thought'. Although many of the orthographic conventions followed in all Yiddish orthographies predate Yiddish itself (S. Birnboym 1930a, 1931a, 1953) these and more modern conventions are continually reinterpreted in terms of modern rationales of modeling and antimodeling (S. Birnboym 1930b, 1977; Fishman 1976; Sh'b 1928; M. Vaynraykh 1939). Particularly ingrained in Yiddish spelling are certain toward-Hebrew and toward-German tendencies (Sholem Aleykhem 1888) which in modern times, have come under attack from antiforeign, anti-German and anti-Hebrew sociocultural spokesmen and their followers (e.g. Anon. 1930a, 1930b; Litvakov 1928). Although the entire world

Figure 9. *Di yidishe shprakh* [The Yiddish Language], publication of the Institute for Jewish Culture of the Ukrainian Academy of Sciences, Philological Section, subsequently continued under the title *Afn shprakhnfront* [On the Language Front]. The insert announces that, by government edict, the journal is changing its spelling so as to discontinue the use of the five final-letters of the Hebrew alphabet.

of Yiddish orthographic concern is small and specialized, it has produced a relatively huge literature (Shaykovski 1966), replete with broader sociocultural rationales (Gold 1977) as well as with an inevitable degree of interpersonal rivalry (Anon 1959; Robak 1959; M. Vaynraykh 1959b).[22] Today, the Yivo's 'Unified Yiddish Spelling' is widely considered to be the standard. The only other frequently encountered systematic spelling is that of Soviet publications, the formerly popular 'traditional' (= Orthodox) spelling having almost disappeared (although it is still advocated by S. Birnboym 1977, 1979a).

Far less touchy for those within the fold is the topic of Yiddish influences in other languages. Although this has been particularly well-documented with respect to Hebrew (e.g. Ben-amotz and Ben-yehuda 1972; Blanc 1965; Elzet 1956; Koyrey 1967; Kornblueth and Aynor 1974; Oyerbakh 1975; Reisner 1976; Rubin 1945) it has also been noted in connection with English (Dillard 1975; Mencken 1936; Feinsilver 1962, 1970), Dutch (Beem 1954), German (Weinberg 1969), etc.[23] Another 'internal topic' is that of selecting from among Yiddish dialects, particularly insofar as orthoepy and transliteration into non-Hebrew characters are concerned. The literature and altercations on this topic have been reviewed by Shekhter 1977b.

Least examined, but closest to the heart of the entire sociolinguistic enterprise, is the topic of 'oral' functional variation in (or partially in) Yiddish. The 'corruption' stigma has so traumatized and energized several generations of Yiddish linguists, and the language shift threat has so mobilized generations of advocates that the normal fluctuation from one variety to another within

---

22. It seems to be a generally accepted sociolinguistic premise that it is more difficult to alter orthographic systems than almost any other kind of linguistic system (e.g. the lexical or semantic systems). Many hypotheses have been advanced to account for this, e.g., that writing systems, like grammatical patterns, encompass the whole language and, therefore, changing these systems elicits much more opposition since it is impossible to side-step them as one can do with disagreeable lexical change (see Fishman 1977c). The Yiddish experience leads me to question this premise, or, at least, to suggest that it must be qualified by reference to literacy level, depth of literary tradition, magnitude of publishing and typographic investments, etc. My impression of the Yiddish scene is that it has responded more to orthographic change than to purification attempts and more to purification attempts than to lexical modernization (neologism) planning. (For proposals to romanize Yiddish spelling see Acher 1902, Dr. X 1909, and an extensive bibliography in Gold 1977.)

23. There is also a small but important literature concerning Yiddish influences on other literatures (e.g. Cukierman 1977; Eber 1967; Leftvitsh 1977; Mordoch 1972) and theaters (Beck 1972; Zilbertsvayg 1968). My impression is that there is much more to these influences than has as yet been recognized. The influence of Yiddish on the English theater in America must have been both direct and indirect, via personnel that was bilingual/bicultural and via dramatic techniques that were both consciously and unconsciously borrowed. Indeed, American, Soviet, and Israeli literature and theater would probably reveal myriad mutual influences and relationships with the world of Yiddish that have yet to be delineated. The influences and relationships also have their more narrowly linguistic dimensions as well. A host of Yiddishisms have penetrated into English from the Yiddish stage, and, similarly, the English speaking entertainment world has impacted not only Yiddish but most major languages of the world during the past 50 years. Through the impact of Yiddish on 'entertainment English' various Yiddishisms have attained worldwide currency (see Almi 1928 for an early intimation along these lines).

Modern
ENGLISH-YIDDISH

YIDDISH-ENGLISH

DICTIONARY

URIEL WEINREICH

**Professor of Yiddish Language, Literature, and Culture
on the Atran Chair, Columbia University**

YIVO Institute for Jewish Research
McGraw-Hill Book Company, New York, 1968

Yiddish for metaphorical and situational purposes, as well as the inevitable variation from one language to another for these same purposes (as evidenced by at least some speech networks of every multilingual speech community of which there is any record), have been seriously overlooked or, at least, under-examined. The concern for finally arriving at and propagating a standard ('literary', 'cultural', 'scientific') Yiddish has yielded a plethora of advocatory, descriptive, and proscriptive studies focusing upon this acrolectal variety or register alone (e.g. Mark 1941, 1942, 1967; Shtarkman 1958; M.K. 1942) and upon its derivation from the most classical sources in the Yiddish parthenon (e.g. Borokhov 1916; Spivak 1965, 1966; and a fairly endless list of articles by Mark). There is far more meager studied recognition of the differences between spoken and written (i.e. printed) language and of the separate standards that these might pursue (but note: Bikl 1970; Kaganovitsh 1930) and of sociodialectal and sociofunctional variation at least within the former (but note: Kazhdan 1938; Slobin 1963; Shekhter 1977b; Zaretski 1931a, 1931b). Least examined of all is the multilingual repertoire in speech, i.e. the bulk of Yiddish linguistic realization during the entire millennium of its existence. The few studies that we have in this connection reveal highly systematic demographic-functional allocations (Bogoch 1973a; Jochnowitz 1968; Ronch 1969) but do not touch at all on metaphorical alternation and switching. The question here is not that of languages in contact (U. Vaynraykh 1953) or of language purity (Wexler 1974) but of normative pragmatics in face-to-face interaction. While it is clear that the remaining Yiddish speech networks in the United States and in Israel – youth networks and adult networks – tend to use Yiddish and English/Ivrit for quite different but complementary functions, their use of two languages is still undocumented in terms of contrastive emphases: anger, joy, humor, surprise, cynicism, etc. For a language which both Jews and the world at large tend to peg as 'talky' (rather than 'bookish' or 'arty' or 'technical'), what we lack most are studies of Yiddish in conversational action. The sociology of Yiddish is still waiting for a scholar with an ear for dialogue. When he or she arrives, untold additional and generalizeable treasures will doubtlessly be discovered. It has happened before (M. Vaynraykh 1937) and will happen again. Neither Yiddish nor the sociology of Yiddish are about to throw in the towel.

◀ Figure 10. Uriel Weinreich's *Modern English–Yiddish, Yiddish–English Dictionary* seeks to provide terms to cover all aspects of modern daily life. Such updating is crucial 'for those in whose children's mouths Yiddish will continue to live' (from the dedication of Uriel Weinreich's *College Yiddish*, New York, Yivo, now in its fifth edition).

REFERENCES*

Acher, Mathias (1902), 'Hebraeisch und Juedisch', *Ost und West* 2: 458–464.

Adler, Celia (1959), *Celia Adler Recalls*. New York, Committee.

Agnon, Sh'ay (1969), 'Hakdome' [Preface], in his *Shriftn* [Writings], trans. into Yiddish by Eliezer Rubinshteyn, 7–12. Tel Aviv, Hamenora.

Aḥad Ha-'am (1908), 'Letter to A. L. Levinski, November 5, 1908', in *Igerot Aḥad Ha-'am, iv* [Letters of Aḥad Ha-'am, iv], 44–45. Jerusalem–Berlin, Yavne-Moriah. (Excerpted (1931) in *Di ershte yidishe shprakh-konferents* [The first Yiddish Language Conference], 274. Vilna, Yiddish Scientific Institute-Yivo,274.)

— (1910), 'Riv leshonot' [The language struggle], *Ha-shiloaḥ* 22: 159–164.

— (1912), *Selected Essays*, trans. by Leon Simon. Philadelphia, Jewish Publication Society.

Al—r (1914a), 'Lama ragzu?' [Why did they get upset?], *Ha-aḥdut* 5 (37): 3–6.

Aleksander (1914b), 'Teḥiya shel maala u-teḥiya shel mata' [Life on high and life below], *Ha-aḥdut* (40/41): 3–13.

Almi, A. (1928), 'Yidish un english' [Yiddish and English]. *Literarishe bleter* (3): 55–56.

Alpern, Arn, (1977), 'Ershter tsionistisher kongres un yidish' [The First Zionist Congress and Yiddish], *Bay zikh* 9–10: 209–216.

Altbauer, Moshe (1965), 'Zum Rückgang der Slawismen im literarischen Jiddisch', in *Verhandlungen des Zweiten Internationalen Dialekten-Kongress*, vol. 1, 14–18. Wiesbaden, Steiner.

Altman, Alexander (1973), *Moses Mendelssohn: A Biographical Study*. University, Alabama, University of Alabama Press.

Altshuler, Mordechai (1977), 'Jewish studies in the Ukraine in the early Soviet period', *Soviet Jewish Affairs* (1): 19–30.

Anon (1869), 'Yidishe bibliografye' [Yiddish bibliography], *Kol mevaser* (22): 247–248.

— (1886), 'Por verter vegn der shprakh' [Few words about the language], *Nyu-yorker yidishe folkstsaytung* 1 (1): 1, June 25.

— (1914), 'Amar ha-Kuntres': Leshe'eylat ha-safa' [The 'Kuntres' spoke: On the language question], *Kuntres* 5: 28–30.

— (1925), *Di organizatsye fun der yidisher visnshaft* [The Organization of Research on Jewry]. Vilna, Yiddish Scientific Institute.

— (1926), *Goldfadn-bukh* [Goldfadn Book]. New York, Yiddish Theatre Museum. (Note: extensive bibliography.)

— (1928a), 'Undzer onheyb' [Our beginning], *Onheyb* [Jerusalem] August: 1–3.

— (1928b), 'Nokhn shrek' [After the Fright], *Arbeter firer* Jan. 21: 21–26.

— (1928c), 'Arum der yidisher katedre' [Concerning the Yiddish chair (= at the Hebrew University)], *Farn folk* Dec. 28: 3–4.

— (1930a), *Di naye yidishe ortografye; bashtimt fun folkombild, u.s.r.r.* [The New Yiddish Orthography, adopted by The People's Commisariat for Education, Ukrainian Soviet Socialist Republic]. Kiev, Kultur Liga.

— (1930b), *Der eynhaytlekher yidisher oysleyg: materialn un proyektn, ershte zamlung* [The Standard Yiddish Orthography: Materials, and Plans, First Collection]. Vilna, Yiddish Scientific Institute.

— (1931a), *Di ershte yidishe shprakh-konferents; barikhtn, dokumentn, opklangen fun der tshernovitser konferents* [The First Yiddish Language-Conference; Reports, Documents, Commentary Concerning the Tshernovits Conference]. Vilna, Yiddish Scientific Institute-Yivo.

— (1931b), 'Toykhn un levush' [Content and cover], *Beys yankev* 8 (70–71): 2.

* Yiddish transliteration in accord with the Yivo/Library of Congress systems. Authors whose Yiddish works are cited (whether or not their works published in other languages are cited) are listed under the Yiddish transliteration of their names.

— (1935a), 'A geeynikte aktsye far yidish in erets yisroel' [A united effort on behalf of Yiddish in the Land of Israel], *Yiddish* 3: 80–81 (Chicago).

— (1935b), 'Di sovetishe shprakh-politik in onvendung tsu yidish. Tezisn tsu di fortragn fun di khaveyrim m. levitan un e. spivak, ongenumen af der shprakh-baratung dem 11tn may, 1934' [Soviet language policy as applied to Yiddish. Theses in the papers of comrades M. Levitan and E. Spivak, adopted at the language consultation, May 11, 1934], *Afn shprakhnfront* (3–4): 250–269.

— (1946), *Basic Facts About Yiddish*. New York, Yiddish Scientific Institute.

— (1951), 'Tsu der efenung fun der yidish-katedre in yerushelayemer universitet' [On inaugurating the Yiddish chair at the (Hebrew) University in Jerusalem] (Remarks by M. Shneyerson, M. Shvabe, Bentsiyon Dinaburg, Dovid Pinski, Khayem Grinberg, Lui Sigl, and Dov Sadan), *Goldene keyt* 11: 187–202.

— (1959), 'Rezultatn fun an ankete vegn oysleyg' [Results of a questionnaire about spelling], *Yidishe shprakh* 19 (3): 83–96.

— (1972a), 'Principles of the Sholem Aleichem Folk Institute, adopted at the conference of the Institute in 1927', in *Our First Fifty Years: The Sholem Aleichem Folk Institute*, ed. by Saul Goodman, 135–137. New York, SAFI. (Also in Yiddish in same volume, *117–*118.)

— (1972b), 'Basic principles of education in the Sholem Aleichem schools adopted at the 30th school-conference, May, 1953', in *Our First Fifty Years: The Sholem Aleichem Folk Institute*, ed. by Saul Goodman, 138–139. New York, SAFI. (Also in Yiddish in same volume *119.)

— (1975), *Report of the Committee on Irish Language Attitudes Research*. Dublin, Committee on Irish Language Attitudes.

— (1977a), *Barikht fun der velt-konferents far yidish un yidisher kultur* [Proceedings of the World Conference for Yiddish and Yiddish Culture]. Tel Aviv, Ha-vaad le-tarbut yehudit be-yisrael.

— (1977b), 'Nosn Birnboym – der bal tshuve' [Nosn Birnboym – the penitent], *Dos Yidishe Vort* 195: 11–15. (Also see sections on 'Eastern European Jewry', 'Jewish "peoplehood" and Yiddish' and 'From Yiddish to Jewishness' in same issue.)

— and Ringlblum, Emanuel (1944), 'Di yidishe kulturarbet in di getos fun poyln' [Yiddish cultural efforts in the Nazi-imposed ghettos in Poland], *Yivo-bleter* 24: 3–8. (Also translated into English and published separately, 1945.)

Arz [= Aleksander Tsederboym] (1869), 'Tsu undzere geerte lezer un lezerinen!' [To our honorable male and female readers!], *Kol mevaser* 48 (Nov. 9): 333–335.

Asaf, S. (1925–1943), *Mekorot le-toldot ha-ḥinukh be-yisrael* [Sources for the History of Jewish Education], 4 vols. Jerusalem.

Ash, Sholem (1931), 'Vegn ibertrogn di yidishe kultur-giter in der yidisher shprakh' [About translating Jewish cultural treasures into the Yiddish language], in *Di ershte yidishe shprakh-konferents*, 81–82. Vilna, Yiddish Scientific Institute – Yivo. (Note further discussion of this topic, 83–85.)

Ayznman, Tsvi (1976), 'Problemen fun a yidish shrayber baym moln di yisroel-virklekhkeyt' [Problems of a writer of Yiddish on depicting Israeli reality], *Folksblat* (Dec.) 12–13.

Bachi, Roberto (1956), 'A statistical analysis of the revival of Hebrew in Israel', *Scripta Hierosolymitana* 3: 179–247.

Balaban, M. (1912, 1916), 'Die Krakauer Judengemeinde-Ordnung von 1595 und ihre Nachträge, *Jahrbuch der jüdisch literarischen Gesellschaft Frankfort a. Main* (1912) 10: 296–360; (1916) 11: 88–114.

Bal-dimyen (1908), 'Yidish' in der yidisher shul' ['Yiddish' in the Jewish school], *Di shtime* 2: 180–189 (Vilna).

— (1923), 'A bukh vegn yidish' [A book about Yiddish], *Dos naye lebn* 1 (7): 49–57.

Bal-makhshoves (1953a), 'Tsvey shprakhn -eyn eyntsike literatur (1908a)' [Two languages – but only one literature (1908a)], reprinted in his *Geklibene verk* [Selected Works], 112–123. New York, Cyco.

— (1953b), 'Esperanto un yidish' [Esperanto and Yiddish (1908b)], reprinted in his *Geklibene verk* [Selected Works], 124–130. New York, Cyco.

Bass, Hyman: see Bez, Khayim.

Beck, Evelyn T. (1972), *Kafka and the Yiddish Theatre*. Madison, University of Wisconsin Press.

Beem, H. (1954), 'Yiddish in Holland: linguistic and sociolinguistic notes', in *The Field of Yiddish I*, ed. by U. Weinreich, 122–133. The Hague, Mouton.

Ben-adir (1919), *Undzer shprakhn-problem* [Our Language Problem]. Kiev, Kiever Farlag.

— (1942), *An ofener briv tsu undzer yidishistisher inteligents* [An open letter to our Yiddishist intelligentsia], *Afn shvel* nos. 4–5 (13–14), 3–5. (Reprinted (1947). Bucharest, Freeland League [note: epilogue by Eliezer Frenkl].)

Ben-amoz, Don and Ben-yehuda, Netiva (1972), *Milon olami le-ivrit meduberit* [Worldwide Dictionary of Spoken Hebrew]. Jerusalem, Levin-Epstein.

Ben-tsvi, Yitskhok (1956), *Mit der tsveyter aliya* [With the Second Immigration (to the Land of Israel)]. Buenos Aires, Kiyem. (See particularly chapters 4 and 6 on 'The Labor Zionists in the land of Israel in 1904–1907', 50–65; and 'The Third Conference' [1908]; 'The organization of Hashomer and Hakhoresh', 77–99.)

Ben Zvi: see Ben-tsvi.

Berkovitsh, Yisroe (1976), *Hundert yor yidish teater in rumenye, 1876–1976* [A Hundred Years of Yiddish Theater in Rumania, 1876–1976]. Bucharest, Criterion.

Berliner, Note (1931), 'Vegn litvishn dialekt in kongres-poyln' [Concerning the Litvak-dialect in Congress Poland], *Beys yankev* 8 (71–72): 42–43. (Also note the editor's supporting comment, p. 43.)

Bernfeld, Sh. (1900), 'Dos folk un di inteligents' [Ordinary folk and the intelligentsia], *Der yid* (Cracow) 2 (2): 1–3.

Best, Otto F. (1973), *Mameloschen Jiddisch – Eine Sprache und ihre Literatur*. Frankfort am Main, Insel Verlag.

Beylin, A. H. (1934), *Moris Shvarts un der yidisher kunst-teater* [Moris Shvarts and the Yiddish Art Theater]. New York, Biderman.

Beys yankev tsentrale (1933), 'Di yesoydes fun der beys yankev shul: hebreyish oder loshn koydish?' [The foundations of the Beys Yankev school: modern or traditional Hebrew?], *Byuletin* (3): 1–3.

Bez, Khayim (1971a), 'Fir etapn in kamf far der khshives fun der yidisher shprakh' [Four stages in the struggles for the dignity of the Yiddish language] in his *Shrayber un verk* [Writers and Works] 91–104. Tel Aviv, Ha-menora.

— (1971b), 'Far vos yidish?' [Why Yiddish?] in his *Shrayber un verk* [Writers and Works] 548–559. Tel Aviv, Ha-menora.

— (1976), The Czernowitz Yiddish language conference, *World of Yiddish* 8.

— editor (1977), *Di yidishe drama fun 20stn yorhundert* [Yiddish Drama of the 20th century), 2 vols. New York, Congress for Jewish Culture.

Bialik: see Byalik.

Bik, Yankev Shmuel (1833), For his letter of 1815 attacking Tuvye Feder and defending Mendl Levin, *Kerem Khemed* 1: 96–99. (Also see listing under Lifshits, I.M. 1863. Also excerpted in Tsinberg, vol. 9, 1936 [pp. 222–223 of Martin's English translation, 1975]; also excerpted (1957) in Yiddish in *Der yidisher gedank in der nayer tsayt* [Jewish Thought in Modern Times], ed. by A. Menes, 258–260. New York, Congress for Jewish Culture.)

Bikl, Shloyme (1970), 'Geredte un geshribene shprakh' [Spoken and written language] in his *Shrayber fun mayn dor* [Writers of my Generation], 271–282. Tel Aviv, Perets Farlag.

Bilezki, Y. H. (1970), *H. n. byalik ve-yidish* [Kh. n. Byalik and Yiddish]. Tel Aviv, Perets Farlag.

Birnbaum, Nathan: see Birnboym, Nosn.

Birnbaum, Solomon A.: see Birnboym, Shloyme.

Birnboym, Nosn (1931), 'Fayerlikhe efenungs-rede, 1908' [Festive opening speech, 1908], in

Anon. *Di ershte yidishe shprakh konferents*... [The First Yiddish Language Conference...], 71–74. Vilna, Yiddish Scientific Institute. (Also in *Forverts* (1908) September 15 and, reprinted (1968) in *Afn shvel* (1968) 185 (4): 3–4.) (Also see his reminiscences concerning the conference, pp. ix–xi, In Anon., op. cit.)

— (1913), *Der yikhes fun yidish* [The Pedigree of Yiddish]. Berlin, Lifshits.

— (1931), 'A por verter vegn yidish' [A few words about Yiddish], *Beys yankev* 8 (70–71): 2.

— (1946), *Selections from his Writings*. London, Ha-migdal.

Birnboym, Shloyme (1916), *Praktische Grammatik der Jiddischen Sprache*, Wien–Leipzig, A. Hartlebens.

— (1930a), *Yidishkayt un loshn* [Jewishness and language]. Warsaw, Yeshurun.

— (1930b), 'Alef-beyz fun ortodoksishn oysleyg' [Alphabet of Orthodox spelling], *Beys yankev* (59): 17. Reprinted (1930b) in *Der eynhaytlekher yidisher oysleyg* [Standard Yiddish Spelling], 86–87. Vilna, Yivo.

— (1930c), 'Di yesoydes fun yidishn oysleyg' [The foundations of Yiddish spelling], in *Der eynhaytlekher yidisher oysleyg* [Standard Yiddish Spelling], 18–19. Vilna, Yivo.

— (1931a), 'Tsvey vovn kikhol hagoyim' [Two *vovn*, like all the gentiles], *Beys yankev* 8 (71–72): 32–33.

— (1931b), *Geule fun loshn* [Redemption of language]. Lodz, Beys yankev.

— (1937), 'Dzhudezme' [Judesmo] *Yivo-bleter* 11: 192–198.

— (1939), 'The age of the Yiddish language', *Transactions of the Philological Society* 31–43 (London).

— (1942), 'Jewish Languages', in *Essays in Honor of...Dr. J. H. Hertz*...ed. by I. Epstein et al., 51–67. London, Edward Goldston.

— (1946), 'The cultural structure of East Ashkenazic Jewry', *Slavonic and East European Review* 25: 73–92.

— (1951), 'The Jewries of Eastern Europe', *Slavonic and East European Review* 29 (73): 420–443.

— (1953), 'Fun daytshmerizm biz der heyl in der midber yehude' [From Germanism back to the cave in the Judean desert], *Yidishe shprakh* 13 (4): 109–120.

— (1968), 'Vi alt iz yidish?' [How old is Yiddish?] in *Yidishe dialogn: kolokvium fun yidishn velt-kongres* [Yiddish Dialogues: Colloquium of the World Jewish Congress], 245–50. Paris, World Jewish Congress.

— (1977), 'Der traditsionalistisher oysleyg fun yidish in poyln' [The traditionalistic spelling of Yiddish in Poland], *Dos yidishe vort* (Iyar/Sivan): 31–32.

— (1979a), *Yiddish: A Survey and a Grammar*. Toronto, University of Toronto Press.

— (1979b), Soviet Yiddish. *Soviet Jewish Affairs* 9: 29–41.

Blanc, Haim (1964), *Communal Dialects in Baghdad*. Cambridge, Harvard University Press.

— (1965), 'Some Yiddish influences in Israeli Hebrew', in *The Field of Yiddish II*, ed. by U. Weinreich, 185–201. The Hague, Mouton.

Bloom, Bernard H. (1971), 'Yiddish-speaking socialists in America: 1892–1905', in *Critical Studies in American Jewish History*, vol. 3, ed. by R. Marcus, 1–33, Cincinnati and New York, American Jewish Archives and Ktav.

Bogoch, Bryna (1973a), 'A sociolinguistics study of Yiddish and Hebrew in an ultra-orthodox school in Jerusalem'. Manuscript, Hebrew University Communications Program.

— (1973b), 'The influence of *loshn koydesh* and Hebrew on secular and religious Israeli Yiddish texts'. Manuscript, Hebrew University, Communications Program.

Borokhov, Ber (1913a), 'Di ufgabn fun der yidisher filologye' [The tasks of Yiddish philology] in *Pinkes: Yorbukh fun der yidisher literatur un shprakh, far folklor, kritik un bibliografye* [Record Book: Annual of Yiddish Literature and Language, for Folklore, Criticism and Bibliography], ed. by Sh. Niger, 1–22. Vilna, Kletskin. Reprinted (1966) in *Shprakh-forshung un literatur-geshikhte* [Language Research and History of Literature] ed. by N. Mayzl, 53–75. Tel-Aviv, Perets Farlag.

— (1913b), 'Hebreismus militans' [Militant Hebraism] (Reprinted (1966) in *Shprakh-forshung un literatur-geshikhte* [Language Research and History of Literature], ed. by N. Mayzl, 364–367. Tel Aviv, Perets Farlag.

— (1916), 'Undzer "zeyde" – der kolombus fun mame-loshn' [Our 'grandfather' – the Columbus of mother tongue [= Yiddish]], *Varhayt* January 3. Reprinted (1966) in *Shprakh-forshung un literatur-geshikhte* [Language Research and History of Literature], ed. by N. Mayzl, 232–234. Tel Aviv, Perets Farlag.

Botvinik, Leybl (1976), 'Reyd vos hobn ufgerisn' [Words that exploded], *Yugntruf* 36/37: 4.

Bunis, David M. (1975), 'Problems in Judezmo linguistics', *Working Papers in Sephardic and Oriental Jewish Studies* (1).

Burd, Blank (1938), 'Nit lozn tsevalgern di dobroyer yidishe mitlshul' [Do not permit the closing of the Yiddish high school in Dubro], *Der emes* July 4.

Byalestotsky, B. Y. (1940), 'Fun zhargon tsu yidish, fun bildgung tsu shafn' [From Zhargon to Yiddish, from education to literary creativity] in his *Y.l. perets tsum finf un tsvantsikstn yortsayt* [Y. L. Perets on his Twenty-fifth Anniversary], 6–12. New York, Cyco.

Byalik, Khayim Nakhmen (1931), 'Di shprakhnfrage bay yidn' [The language question among Jews], in his *Tsvey redes* [Two Speeches]. Kovne, Merkaz Tarbut. (Excerpted (1957) in *Der yidisher gedank in der nayer tsayt* [Jewish Thought in Modern Times], ed. by A. Menes, 270–275. New York, Congress for Jewish Culture.)

Checinski, Michael (1973), 'Soviet Jews and higher education', *Soviet Jewish Affairs* 3 (2): 3–16.

Choseed, Bernard (1968), 'Reflections of the Soviet nationalities policy in literature: The Jews, 1938–1948'. Unpublished Ph.D. dissertation, Columbia University. (University microfilms no. 69-15, 665.)

Chyz, Y. L. (1959), *225 Years of the U.S. Foreign Language Press*. New York, ACNS.

Clurman, Harold (1968), 'Ida Kaminska and the Yiddish theatre', *Midstream* 14: 53–57.

Cuddihy, J. M. (1974), *The Ordeal of Civility*. New York, Basic Books.

Cukierman, Walenty (1977), 'Isaak Babel's Jewish heroes and their Yiddish background', *Yiddish* 2 (4): 15–22.

Das Gupta, J. (1970), *Language Conflict and National Development*. Berkeley, University of California Press.

Dawidowicz, Lucy S. (1963), Louis Marshall's Yiddish newspaper *The Jewish World*: A study in contrasts. *Jewish Social Studies* 25: 102–132.

— (1964), 'Louis Marshall and the *Jewish Daily Forward*: An episode in wartime censorship', in *In Honor of Max Weinreich on His Seventieth Birthday: Studies in Jewish Languages, Literature, and Society*, ed. by Lucy Dawidowicz et al., 31–43. The Hague, Mouton.

— (1977), 'Heritage: The world of Yiddish (four essays)', in her *The Jewish Presence*, 133–190. New York, Holt, Rinehart and Winston.

Dillard, J. L. (1975). *All-American English*. New York, Random House.

Dimanshteyn, Sh. (1935), *Yidn in FSSR* [Jews in the RSFSR]. Mowcow, Mezhdunarodnaya Kniga and Emes.

Dinezon, Yankev (1888), 'Profeser grets un der yidisher zhargon oder ver mit vos darf zikh shemen?' [Professor Graetz and the Jewish Zhargon (= Yiddish) or who should be ashamed with what?], *Yidishes Folksblat, baylage no. 2* 12 (24): 34–43.

Doroshkin, Milton (1970), *Yiddish in America: Social and Cultural Foundations*. Cranbury, N. J., Fairleigh Dickenson University Press.

Dressler, Wolfgang, Wodak-Leodolter, Ruth, editors (1977), 'Language death', *International Journal of Sociology of Language* 12.

Drozdov, Nakhmen (1959), 'Di yidishistishe bavegung' [The Yiddishist movement] in his *Akhed hoom: shtrikhn fun zayn lebn, kharakter un shafungen* [Aḥad Ha'am: Aspects of his Life, Character and Creativity], 171–172. Tel Aviv, Perets.

Dubnov, Shimen (1959), 'Khiyev hagoles (1909)' [Accepting the diaspora (1909)], *Briv vegn altn un nayem yidntum* [Letters Concerning Ancient and Modern Jewry], ed. and trans. by M. and Sh. Ferdman, 395–409 (trans. from the Russian by Kh. Sh. Kazhdan). Mexico, Mendelson.

— (1929a), 'Tsvey kruzim in yidish funen "vad arbe arotses" in 1671' [Two proclamations in Yiddish of the 'Council of Four Lands' in 1671], *Historishe shriftn* (Yivo) 1: 699–702.

— (1929b), *Fun 'zhargon' tsu yidish* [From 'Jargon' to Yiddish]. Vilna, Kletskin.

Dubnow, Simeon: see Dubnov, Shimen.

Dvorzhetski, Mark (1948), 'Dos kultur-vezn in vilner geto' [Cultural efforts in the Nazi-instituted Vilna ghetto], in his *Yerushelayim delite in kamf un umkum* [The Jerusalem of Lithuania in Struggle and Destruction], 222–259. Paris, Yidisher Folksfarband/Yidish Natisionaler Arbeter Farband.

— (1970), 'Dos kultur-lebn in di getos' [Cultural life in the Nazi-instituted ghettos], in his *Vayse nekht un shvartse teg* [White Nights and Black Days], 301–340. Tel Aviv, Perets Farlag.

Eber, Irene (1967), 'Yiddish literature and the literary revolution in modern China', *Judaism* 16 (1): 42–59.

Eck, Nathan (1947), 'The educational institutions of Polish Jewry', *Jewish Social Studies* 9: 3–32.

Eisenberg, Azriel and Seegar, Jacob (1968), *World Census on Jewish Education 5728–1968*. New York, World Council on Jewish Education.

Eisenstein, Miriam (1949a), 'The Cysho schools', in her *Jewish Schools in Poland 1919–1939*, 18–39. New York, King's Crown.

— (1949b), 'The bilingual schools, in her *Jewish Schools in Poland 1919–1939*, 59–70. New York, King's Crown.

Elberg, Simkhe (1962), 'Geule durkh loshn' [Redemption through language]. *Dos yidishe vort*, 8, no. 78, 8–10.

Ellman, Yisrael (1978), 'The maintenance rate of Yiddish in the United States as compared to German, Polish, Italian and Greek'. *Forum* (30–31): 170–175.

Elzet, Yehude (1929), 'Undzer folks-oytser' [Our ethnic treasure]. *Yidish amerike* [Yiddish America] 1: 233–271.

— (1951), 'Yidish farankert' [Yiddish secured], *Goldene keyt* 9: 177–184.

— (1956), 'Shmusn vegn hebreyish-yidish un yidish-hebreyish' [Chats concerning Hebrew-Yiddish and Yiddish-Hebrew], *Yidishe shprakh* 16 (1): 1–8; (2): 44–55; (4): 114–117.

Emyot, Yisroel (1960), *Der birobidzhaner inyen* [The Case of Birobidzhan]. Rochester, Bogorod.

Epshteyn, Zalmen (1910), 'Ha-sakana ha-zhargonit u-mahuta' [The danger of Zhargon (= Yiddish) and its nature], *Ha-shiloah* 23 (127–132): 512–525.

Erik, Maks (1928), *Di geshikhte fun der yidisher literatur fun de eltste tsaytn biz der haskole-tkufe* [The History of Yiddish Literature from the Earliest Times to the *Haskole* Period]. Warsaw, Kultur-liga.

Erlich, Rachel (1973), 'Politics and linguistics in the standardization of Soviet Yiddish', *Soviet Jewish Affairs* 3 (1): 71–79.

Ernst, Sh. (1930a), 'Tekstn un kveln tsu der geshikhte fun teater, farvaylungen un maskeradn bay yidn' [Texts and sources on the history of theater, amusements and masquerades among Jews] in *Arkhiv far der geshikhte fun yidishn teater un drama* [Archive for the History of Yiddish Theater and Drama], ed. by Yankev Shatski, 5–37. Vilna and New York, Yiddish Scientific Institute – Yivo.

— (1930a), 'Der ershter pruv fun yidishn teater in erets yisroel' [The first attempt at Yiddish theater in Erets Yisroel], in *Arkiv far der geshikhte fun yidishn teater un drama* [Archive for the History of Yiddish Theater and Drama], ed. by Yankev Shatski, 439–440. Vilna and New York, Yiddish Scientific Institute – Yivo.

Esperanto, Dokter (1888), *Di veltshprakh...far dem yidishn volk* [The World Language...for the Jewish People]. Warsaw, Levinski.

Ester [Frumkin] (1910), *Tsu der frage vegn der yidisher folkshul* [Concerning the problem of the Yiddish elementary school]. Vilna, Di velt.

Faerstein, Chana (1965), 'Jacob Glatstein: The literary uses of Yiddish', *Judaism* 414–431.

Falkovitsh, Elye (1973), 'Vegn loshn' [About language], *Sovetish heymland* (Dec.): 157–169.

Faur, Jose (1973), 'A sense of language', *The Sephardic World* 1 (2): 25–32.

Faynerman, Naftoli (1929), 'A bisl geshikhte vegn di arbeter-ring shuln' [A bit of history about the Workmen's Circle schools]. *Fraynd* (Jan.): 9–13.

Feinsilver, Lillian M. (1962), 'Yiddish idioms in American English', *American Speech* 37: 200–206 (Also note (1970), her *The Taste of Yiddish*. New York, Yoseloff.)

Fellman, Jack (1973), *The Revival of a Classical Tongue*. The Hague, Mouton.

Feyges, Motl (1928), 'Di yidishe prese in palestine' [The Yiddish press in Palestine], *Literarishe bleter* (45): 890–891.

Finklshteyn, Leo (1954), 'Di khsidishe bavegung – un yidish' [The Hasidic movement – and Yiddish] in *Loshn yidish un yidisher kiyem* [The Yiddish Language and Jewish Survival], 48–53. Mexico, Fondo Mendelson de la Sociedad pro Cultura y Ayuda.

Fishman, Dovid (1981), 'Di dray penemer fun yehoshua mordkhe lifshits' [The three faces of Yehoshua Modkhe Lifshits], *Yidishe shprakh* 38.

Fishman, Joshua A.: see Fishman, Shikl.

Fishman, Shikl (1951), 'Tsveyshprakhikayt in a yidisher shul: eynike korelatn un nit-korelatn' [Bilingualism in a Yiddish school: some correlates and non-correlates], *Bleter far yidisher dertsiung* (4): 32–42. (Also (1952), abbreviated, 'Degree of bilingualism in a Yiddish school and leisure-time activities', *Journal of Social Psychology* 36: 155–165.)

— (1960), 'New York's non-English dailies and the deliverymen's strike', *Journalism Quarterly* 37: 241–254.

— (1963), 'Yidish un andere natsionale shprakhn in amerike' [Yiddish and other ethnic languages in America], *Tsukunft* 68: 212–216.

— (1964), 'U.S. census data on mother tongues: review, extrapolation and prediction', in *For Max Weinreich on His Seventieth Birthday*, 51–62. The Hague, Mouton.

— (1965a), *Yiddish in America: Sociolinguistic Description and Analysis*. Bloomington, Indiana, Indiana University Center for Anthropology, Folklore and Linguistics.

— (1965b), 'Language maintenance and language shift in certain urban immigrant environments: The case of Yiddish in the United States', *Europa Ethnica* 22: 146–158.

— (1966), *Language Loyalty in the United States*. The Hague, Mouton.

— (1969), 'Language maintenance and language shift: Yiddish and other immigrant languages in the United States', *Yivo Annual of Jewish Social Science* 14: 12–26.

— (1972a), 'Ha-sotsiologye shel yidish be-artsot ha-brit: avar, hove, ve-atid' [The sociology of Yiddish in the United States, past, present and future], *Hug le-yidiot 'am yisrael be-tfutsot* 6 (3). (Also (1972), abbreviated, in *Goldene keyt* 75: 110–127.)

— (1972b), *Language and Nationalism*. Rowley, Newbury House.

— (1973), 'The phenomenological and linguistic pilgrimage of Yiddish' (some examples of functional and structural pidginization and depidginization), *Kansas Journal of Sociology* 9: 127–136. (Also in his *Advances in the Creation and Revision of Writing Systems*. The Hague, Mouton, 1977, 293–306.)

— (1974), 'Vos ken zayn di funktsye fun yidish in yisroel?' [What could be the function of Yiddish in Israel?], *Yidisher kemfer* (2019): 40–46.

— (1976a), 'Yiddish and Loshn koydesh in traditional Ashkenaz: On the problem of societal allocation of macro-functions', in *Language in Sociology*, ed. by Albert Verdoodt and Rolf Kjolseth, 39–48. Louvain, Peeters.

— (1976b), 'Di yerushelayimer "velt-konferents far yidish un yidisher kultur" fun a sotsio-lingvistishn kukvinkl' [The Jerusalem 'World Conference for Yiddish and Yiddish Culture' from a sociolinguistic perspective], *Yidishe shprakh* 35: 16–31.

— (1976c), *Bilingual Education: An International Sociological Perspective*. Rowley, Newbury House.

— (1977a), 'Der yivo in amerike (problemen un dergreykhn in shaykhes mit zayn mehus)' [The Yivo in America (problems and accomplishments in conjunction with its essence], *Goldene keyt* (93): 111–122.

— (1977b), 'Ethnicity and language', in *Language, Ethnicity and Intergroup Relations*, ed. by H. Giles, 15–18. New York, Academic Press.

— (1977c), *The Spread of English*. Rowley, Newbury House.

— (1977d), 'Knowing, using and liking English as an additional language', *TESOL Quarterly* 11: 157–171.

— (1977e), *Advances in the Revision and Creation of Writing Systems*. The Hague, Mouton.

— (1979), 'The sociolinguistic "normalization" of the Jewish people', in *Archibald Hill Festschrift*, ed. by E. Polome, vol. 3. The Hague, Mouton.

— (1980a), 'Neglected perspectives on language and ethnicity in Eastern Europe', in *Language and Ethnicity in Eastern Europe*, ed. by P. Sugar.

— (1980b), 'Ethnicity and language maintenance', *Harvard Encyclopedia of American Ethnic Groups*.

— (1981), 'Why has Yiddish changed?; Reflections on a millennium', in *Toward an Integrated Theory of Language Change*, ed. by James M. Dunn and Andrew W. Conrad. Princeton, Princeton University Press.

Fishman, Joshua A. and Fishman, David E. (1977), 'Yiddish in Israel: a case-study of efforts to revise a monocentric language policy', in Joshua Fishman's *Advances in the Study of Societal Multilingualism*. The Hague, Mouton. (Also abbreviated (1974), in *Yiddish* 1 (2): 4–23, and in (1974) *International Journal of the Sociology of Language* 1: 125–146.)

Fishman, Joshua A. and Fishman, Gella J. (1959), 'Separatism and integrationism: a socio-psychological analysis of editorial content in newspapers of three American minority groups', *Genetic Psychology Monographs* 59: 219–261.

Frank, Herman (1935), 'Di yidishe shul-bavegung iber der velt' [The Yiddish school movement the world over], in *Shul-Almanakh*, 348–364. Philadelphia, Workmen's Circle.

Freehof, Solomon B. (1923), 'Devotional literature in the vernacular', *Yearbook, Central Conference of American Rabbis* 33: 3–43.

Freidlin, Gershon (1977), 'Working on Yiddish', *Ort Reporter* 28 (2): 9.

Friedman, Norman L. (1975), 'Jewish popular culture in contemporary America', *Judaism* 24: 263–277.

Friedman, Philip (1957–1958), 'The fate of the Jewish book during the Nazi era', *Jewish Book Annual* 15: 3–13.

Frostig, M. (1910), *Di folkstseylung un di badaytung far yidn* [The Census and its Significance for Jews]. Lemberg.

Gelnberg, M. (1930), 'Yidish af di varshever gasn' [Yiddish on the streets of Warsaw], *Literarishe bleter* 19 (314): 346–347; 21 (316): 392–394.

Gersht, Y. L. (1947), 'Lererkursn far yidish in Lodzher geto' [Yiddish courses for teachers in the Nazi-instituted ghetto of Lodz], *Yivo-bleter* 30: 152–155.

Gerzon, Jacob (1902), *Die jüdisch-deutsche Sprache*. Frankfort-am-Main, Kauffman.

Gilinski, Sh. (1922), 'Tsu der geshikhte fun yidishn shulvezn in varshe' [Toward the history of the Yiddish school system in Warsaw], *Shul un lebn* 10 (1–2): 68–74.

Gilson, Estelle (1976), 'Yivo – where Yiddish scholarship lives', *Present Tense* (Autumn): 57–65.

Gitelman, Zvi (1977), *Jewish Nationality and Soviet Politics*. Princeton, Princeton University Press.

Gitlits, M. (1934), 'Di shprakh-"boyung" fun di fashizirte yidishistn' [The language-'development' of the fascistic Yiddishists], *Afn visnshaftlekhn front* (5–6): 84–98.

Glants, A. (1913), 'Di natsional-radikale shul' [The national-radical school], *Dos naye lebn* 5: 155–161.

Glatshteyn, Yankev (1972a), 'Lebediker untergant' [Lively death], in *In der velt mit yidish* [In the World with Yiddish], 429–432. New York, Congress for Yiddish Culture. (Also see his 'A loshn af tomid, nisht af dervayl' [A language forever, not temporarily], same volume, 433–436.)

— (1972b), 'Vegn reynikn dos loshn' [About cleansing the language], in *In der velt mit yidish* [In the World with Yiddish], 436–439. New York, Congress for Jewish Culture.

Glicksman, William (1966), *In the Mirror of Literature; Jewish Life in Poland Reflected in Yiddish Literature*. New York, Living Books.

Gold, David (1974), 'Jewish intralinguistics: assumptions, methods, goals, and sample problems'. Paper presented at the Eighth World Congress of Sociology, Research Committee on Sociolinguistics, Toronto, August. Mimeographed.

— (1977), 'Successes and failures in the standardization and implementation of Yiddish spelling and romanization', in *Advances in the Revision and Creation of Writing Systems*, ed. by J. A. Fishman, 317–369. The Hague, Mouton.

— (1980), 'The speech and writing of Jews in the USA', in *Language in the USA*, ed. by Shirley B. Heath and Charles A. Ferguson. New York, Oxford University Press.

Goldberg, B. (1905a), 'Ueber die sprachlichen Verhältnisse der Juden Russlands', *Zeitschrift für Demographie und Statistik der Juden* 1 (6): 1–5. (Also note item entitled 'Juden mit nichtdeutscher Muttersprache in Berlin' in 'Statistisches Archiv' section of same issue.)

— (1905b), 'Ueber die sprachlichen Verhältnisse der Juden Russlands' (Schluss), *Zeitschrift für Demographie und Statistik der Juden*, 1905, 1 (7): 6–8.

Goldberg, B. Z. (1971), 'The American Yiddish press at its centennial', *Judaism* 20: 223–228.

Goldberg, N. (1940), 'Materialn tsum matsev fun yidishn shrayber in nyu york' [Materials concerning the circumstances of the Yiddish writer in New York], *Yivo-bleter* 15: 39–62.

— (1941), 'Di yidishe prese in di fareynikte shtatn, 1900–1940' [The Yiddish press in the United States, 1900–1940], *Yivo-bleter* 18: 129–157.

— (1943), 'Di tsirkulatsye fun yidishe tsaytungen in amerike, 1941–1942' [The circulation of Yiddish newspapers in America, 1941–42], *Yivo-bleter* 21: 252–255.

— (1945), 'Vu zaynen di khilukey-deyes?' [Where are the disagreements?], *Yivo-bleter* 21: 294–297 [A reply to Shelyubski 1945.]

Goldberg, Yitskhok (1914), 'Yidish un hebreyish: di shprakhnfrage in undzer kinder- un folks-dertsiung' [Yiddish and Hebrew: The language question in education for our children and adults], *Dos naye lebn* 6: 33–43, 100–106.

Goldsmit, Shmuel (1968), 'Tsveyshprakhikayt bay yidn' [Bilingualism among Jews], in *Yidishe dialogn: kolokvium fun yidishn velt-kongres* [Yiddish Dialogues: Colloquium of the World Jewish Congress], 428–434. Paris, World Jewish Congress.

Goldsmith, Emanuel S. (1975), 'Zhitlovsky and American Jewry', *Jewish Frontier* November: 14–17.

— (1976a), 'The political impetus' in his *Architects of Yiddishism*, 71–95. Rutherford, Fairleigh Dickenson Press.

— (1976b), 'The Czernowitz Conference' in his *Architects of Yiddishism*, 183–222. Rutherford, Fairleigh Dickenson Press.

Golomb, Avrom (1928), 'Di ufgabn fun yidishizm (20 yor nokh tshernovits)' [The goals of Yiddishism (20 years after Tshernovits)], *Literarisce bleter* (35): 683–684, (37): 726–727.

— (1943), 'Byalik un ben-yehude: tsvey vegn in hebreizm' [Byalik and Ben-Yehude: two paths in Hebraism], *Zamlbukh* 5: 340–352.

— (1947), 'Der yidishizm afn sheydveg (1932)' [Yiddishism at the crossroads (1932)], in his *Geklibene verk* [Selected Works], 77–90. Mexico City, Committee.

— (1957), 'A yidishe meydlshul in tsarishn rusland' [A Jewish school for girls in Czarist Russia] in his *A halber yorhundert yidishe dertsiung* [Half a century of Jewish Education], 67–78. Rio de Janeiro, Monte Scopus.

— (1962a), '*Integrale yidishkayt (teorye un praktik)*' [Integrative Jewishness (Theory and Practice)]. Mexico City, Golomb.

— (1962b), 'Ume veloshn: yidish folk – yidish loshn' [People and language: Jewish nationality and Yiddish language], in *Yorbukh fun der nayer yidisher shul y.l. perets in meksike* [Yearbook of the New Jewish School (named after) Y. L. Perets in Mexico], 13. Mexico City, New Jewish School.

— (1967), 'Der oysgetrakhter shprakhnkamf' [The fictitious language struggle], in his *Tsvishn tkufes* [Between Eras), 312–323. Tel Aviv, Peretz.

— (1970), 'Folk un shprakh' [Nationality and language], part of his essay on yidishkayt, folkishkayt, getlekhkayt [Jewishness, nationhood, godliness], in *Khesed Leavrohom: sefer ha-yovel le-avraham Golomb; tsu zayn akhtsikstn geboyrn-yor* [Grace unto Abraham: Jubilee volume in Honor of Abraham Golomb; for his Eightieth Birthday], ed. by M. Khezkuni-shtarkman, 897–898. Los Angeles, Committee.

Goodman, Saul: see Gutman, Shoyel.

Gorin, B. (1913), 'Der repertuar funem yidishn teater in amerike farn sezon 1912' [The repertoire of the Yiddish theater in America for the 1912 season], in *Pinkes: Yorbukh fun der yidisher literatur un shprakh, far folklor, kritik un bibliografiye* [Record Book: Annual of Yiddish Literature and Language, for Folklore, Criticism and Bibliography], ed. by Sh. Niger, 230–243. Vilna, Kletskin. (In same volume: a similar review by A. M. Mukdoyni concerning Yiddish theater in Russia during 1913, 263–272.)

— (1923), *Di geshikhte fun yidishn teater* [History of the Yiddish Theater], 2 vols. New York, Mayzl.

Graubert, Judah L. (1974). 'The night of the murdered poets', *Reconstructionist* 40 (2 [March]): 17–23.

Grosman, Y. (1974a), 'Fuftsn shprakhn bay yidn-un yidish' [Fifteen Jewish languages – and Yiddish], in his *Eseyen un zikhroynes* [Essays and Memoires], 97–103. Montreal, Grosman.

— (1974b), 'Tsentraler bildungs komitet in vilne' [Central Education Committee in Vilna], in his *Eseyen un zikhroynes* [Essays and Memoires], 148–165. Montreal, Grosman.

Gros-tsimerman, M. (1962), 'Yisroels Yidish' [Israel's Yiddish], in *Almanakh fun di yidishe shrayber in yisroel* [Almanac of the Yiddish writers in Israel], 9–14. Tel Aviv, Organization of Yiddish Writers and Journalists in Israel.

Guggenheim-Grunberg, Florence (1965), 'Place names in Swiss–Yiddish: examples of the assimilatory power of a Western Yiddish dialect', *The Field of Yiddish* 2: 147–157.

Gutman, Shoyel (1967), 'Der morgn fun der yidish-veltlekher shul in amerike (1962)' [The future of the Yiddish secular school in America (1962)], reprinted in his *Traditsye un banayung* [Tradition and Renewal], 330–344. New York, Farlag Matones.

— (1972), 'Half a century of cultural yiddishkayt', in *Our First Fifty Years: The Sholem Aleichem Folk Institute*, ed. by Shoyel Gutman, 102–108. New York, SAFI. (Also in Yiddish in same volume, *97–*102.)

—, editor (1976), *The Faith of Secular Jews*. New York, Ktav. (See particularly two articles by Zhitlovski: 'What is Jewish secular culture?', 47–56, and 'The national poetic rebirth of the Jewish religion', 149–158.)

— (1977), 'Yidishe literatur-forshung un der derekh fun yivo haynt tsu tog' [Research on Yiddish literature and the approach of the Yivo today], *Kheshbn* 33 (89): 9–13.

Gutkovitsh, Yankl and Tsukerman, Rakhmil (1977), 'Derekh-erets farn loshn fun folk' [Respect for the language of ordinary people], *Tsukunft* 83 (2): 72–76.

Hager, Baruch (1974), 'Chassidism and Yiddish', *Jewish Quarterly* 22: 43–44.

Hakohen, Mordechai (1902), 'Sefat ha-galut', *Ahiasaf* 10: 381–391.

Hal, Gershon (1975), 'Dray hundert yor yidish presvezn in der velt, 1675–1975' [Three hundred years of the Yiddish press in the world, 1675–1975], in *300 yor yidishe prese, 1675–1975* [300 years of Yiddish press, 1675–1975], ed. by A. L. Dulchin et al., 18–70. Jerusalem, Zionist World Organization.

Halevy, Jacob (1972), *Genocide of a Culture: The Execution of the 24*. London, World Jewish Congress.

Halevy, Zvi (1972), 'Yiddish schools in the Soviet Union' (Review of Elias Schulman's *A History of Jewish Education in the Soviet Union*, 1971), *Soviet Jewish Affairs* 2 (2): 99–104.

— (1979). *Jewish Schools under Czarism and Communism: A Struggle for Cultural Identity*. New York, Springer.

Hameiri, Avigdor ([1950] 1973), 'Ivre-taytsh – yidish' [Ivri taytsh (= archaic Yiddish of the translated prayer book, etc.) and Yiddish], *Dos yidishe vort* July 7 (Santiago). (Also (1973), in Sh. Rozhansky, *Ivre taytsh, tsene urene* (= Musterverk fun der yidisher literatur, band 53. [Masterworks of Yiddish Literature, vol. 53]), 341–365. Buenos Aires, Ateneo Literario en el Iwo.)

Hapgood, Hutchins (1966), 'Four poets; The stage; The newspapers, A novelist', in his *The Spirit of the Ghetto* (1902), 97–242. New York, Schocken.

Haugen, Einar (1961), 'Language planning in modern Norway', *Scandinavian Studies* 33: 68–81.

Heller, Celia (1974), 'Poles of Jewish background – The case of assimilation without integration in interwar Poland', in *Shtudyes vegn yidn in poyln, 1919–1939* [Studies on Polish Jewry, 1919–1939], ed. by J. A. Fishman, *242–*276. New York, Yivo Institute.

— (1977). 'Assimilationists: Poles in culture and self-identity', in her *On the Edge of Destruction*, 183–210. New York, Columbia. (Also in same volume, see her discussion of Yiddish among 'The Jewish Jews: Orthodox in faith, traditional in culture', 143–182; and among 'The radicalized poor and the Bund', 253–265.)

Herbert, M. A. (1913), 'Der kamf fun a shprakh far anerkenung' [The struggle of a language for recognition], *Dos naye lebn* 5: 155–161, 192–198.

Herman, Simon (1961), 'Explorations in the social psychology of language', *Human Relations* 14: 149–164. (Also in *Readings in the Sociology of Language*, ed. by J. A. Fishman, 492–511.) The Hague, Mouton.

— (1972), *Israelis and Jews: A Study in the Continuity of an Identity*. New York, Random House.

— (1977), *Jewish Identity: A Social Psychological Perspective*. Beverly Hills, Sage. (Re: attitudes toward Yiddish see p. 246.)

Hersh, L. (1931), 'Shprakhlekhe asimilirtkayt bay di yidishe studentn fun di varshever hoykhshuln' [Linguistic assimilation among Jewish students in Warsaw post-secondary schools], *Yivo-bleter* 2: 441–444.

Hershls, Libtse (1889), 'Benemunes a gelekhter' [Upon my word, a laughing stock], *Yidishes Folksblat* (16): 3–7, (17): 3–12 (St. Petersburg).

Hertz, Jacob S. (1969), 'The Bund's nationality program and its critics in the Russian, Polish and Austrian socialist movements', *Yivo Annual of Jewish Social Science* 14: 53–67.

Hesbacher, Peter and Joshua A. Fishman (1965), 'Language loyalty: its functions and concomitants in two bilingual communities', *Lingua* 13: 145–165.

Higham, John (1975), 'Abraham Cohen: novelist between three cultures', in his *Send These to Me; Jews and other Immigrants in Urban America*, 88–101. New York, Atheneum.

Hirzowicz, Lukasz (1974), 'Birobidzhan after 40 years', *Soviet Jewish Affairs* 4 (2): 38–45.

Hofman, John and Haya Fisherman (1971), 'Language shift and maintenance in Israel', *International Migration Review* 5: 204–226. (Also (1971) in *Advances in the Sociology of Language*, ed. by J. A. Fishman, 342–364. The Hague, Mouton.)

Howe, Irving (1976), *World of Our Fathers: The Journey of the East European Jews to America and the Life They Found and Made*. New York, Harcourt, Brace, Jovanovich.

Howe, Irving, Eliezer Greenberg, editors (1954), *A Treasury of Yiddish Stories*. New York, Viking.

— (1969), *A Treasury of Yiddish Poetry*. New York, Holt, Rinehart and Winston.

— (1975), *Voices from the Yiddish: Essays, Memoirs, Diaries*. New York, Schocken.

— (1977), *Ashes Out of Hope: Fiction by Soviet-Yiddish Writers*. New York, Schocken.

Hurvitsh, Y. A. (1917 [1902]), 'Slobodker daytsh un yidishe yidish' [Slobodkian German or Yiddish Yiddish], in his *Oysgeveylte shriftn*, 229–238. New York, Hurvitsh.

— (1917 [1909]), ' Di yidish-amerikanishe gele prese' [Yiddish-American yellow journalism], in his *Oysgeveylte shriftn*, 105–128. New York, Hurvitsh.

Itkovitsh, Moyshe (1973), 'Mi umi hahoylkhim?' [Who and who are those who go (with me in my cause)?], *Sovetish heymland* Sept.: 141–145.

— (1977), 'Far der reynkayt funem loshn' [For purity of the language], *Sovetish heymland* (9): 177–180.

Jacobs, Neil (1975), 'Yiddish origins and creolization'. Unpublished Master's thesis, University of Texas, Austin.

Jacobs, Yaakov (1977), 'Books: The teaching machines of the future/or: some recent books of Jewish interest', *Jewish Life* Summer: 14–19.

Jochnowitz, George (1968), 'Bilingualism and dialect mixture among Lubavitcher Hasidic children', *American Speech* 43: 182–200.

— (1975), 'Judeo-romance languages'. Paper presented at the Association for Jewish Studies Regional Conference, March, Ann Arbor, Michigan. Subsequently published in (1978), *Jewish Languages: Theme and Variation*, ed. by H. Paper, 65–74. Cambridge, Association of Jewish Studies.

Joffe, Judah A.: see Yofe, Yude A.

K., M. (1942), 'A diskusye vegn der shprakh in di oysgabes fun yivo' [A discussion about the language of the Yivo publications], *Yidishe shprakh* 2: 57–49.

Kaganovitsh, Sh. (1930), '"Folks"-shprakh un literarishe shprakh' ['Folk' language and literary language], *Di yidishe shprakh* 4 (2–3): 21–22, 39–48; 4–5 (23–24): 67–74.

Kalmanovitsh, Zalmen (1925), 'Nay yidish?' [New Yiddish?], *Literarishe bleter* (66): 3–4, (67): 21–22, (68): 41–42, (69): 53–55.

— (1931), 'Perspektivn far yidish in ratn-farband' [Prospects for Yiddish in the Soviet Union], *Literarishe bleter* (8): 40–41, 61–62, 78–80, 100–102, 139–141.

Kalmanovitsh, Zelig (1949), 'Y. l. peretses kuk ayf der yidisher literatur' [Y. L. Perets's view of Yiddish literature], *Goldene keyt* 2: 114–126.

Kaminska, Ida (1973), *My Life, My Theater*, ed. and trans. by Curt Leviant. New York, Macmillan.

Kan, Lazar (1928a), 'Af der tshernovitser konferents (eynike perzenlikhe zikhroynes)' [At the Tshernovits conference (Some personal memories)], *Literarishe bleter* (35): 682 (In same issue, also note p. 680: Vos men hot amol geshribn vegn der tshernovitser shprakh-konferents: oystsugn. [What was previously written about the Tshernovits language conference: excerpts].)

— (1928b), 'Di shtile tragediye fun dokter birnboym in tshernovits' [The quiet tragedy of Dr. Brinboym at Tshernovits], *Literarishe bleter* (39): 762–763. (In same issue, also note p. 763: Yoyvl fayerung fun der tshernovitser shprakh-konferents in tshernovits [Anniversary celebration of the Tshernovits language conference in Tshernovits].)

— (1928c), 'Der kamf far yidish un yidishe shuln in letland' [The Struggle for Yiddish and Yiddish schools in Latvia], *Literarishe bleter* (44): 872, (50): 989–990.

Kan, Leybl (1972, 1973), 'Yidishe teminologishe komisyes' [Yiddish terminological commissions], *Yidishe shprakh* 31 (2): 35–42, 32 (1–3): 1–8.

Kantor, Yankev (1962–1963), 'Eynike bamerkungen un oysfirn tsu di farefntlekhte sakh-haklen fun der folkstseylung in ratnfarband dem 15tn yanuar 1959' [Some comments and conclusions concerning the published summaries of the Soviet census of January 15, 1959], *Bleter far geshikhte* 15: 142–154.

Kaplan, A. E., Landau, M., editors (1925), *Vom Sinn des Judentums; Ein Sammelbuch zu ehren Nathan Birnbaums*. Frankfurt, Herman.

Kaẓ, Elihu et al. (1972), *Tarbut yisrael 1970*. [The Culture of Israel, 1970], 2 vols. Jerusalem, Institute of Applied Social Research and Communications Department (mimeographed).

Kaẓenelson, B. (1919). 'Omar ha-kuntres' [The Kuntres said], *Kuntres* 5: 28–30.

Kaẓenelson, K. (1960), *Mashber ha-ivrit ha-modernit*. [The Crisis of Modern Hebrew]. Tel Aviv, Anach.

Kayserling, M. (1862), *Moses Mendelssohn sein Leben und seine Werke*. Berlin, Leipzig, Magdeburg, Institut zur Forderung d. Israelitischen Literatur.

Kazhdan, Kh. Sh. (1928), 'An epizod anshtot a gesheyenish (20 yor nokh der tshernovitser konferents)' [An episode instead of an event (20 years after the Tshernovits Conference)], *Undzer tsayt* (7): 73–77.

— (1938), 'Proletarish yidish amol un haynt' [Proletarian Yiddish past and present], *Yidish far ale* 1: 12–14.

— (1947), *Di geshikhte fun yidishn shulvezn in umophengikn polyn* [The History of Jewish School Systems in Independent Poland]. Mexico City, Kultur un Hilf.

— (1956a), 'Di radikale un di sotsialistishe inteligents-zeyer batsiung tsu yidish' [The radical and the socialist intelligentsia – their attitude toward Yiddish], in his *Fun kheyder un 'shkoles' biz tsisho* [From the Kheyder (traditional orthodox elementary schools) and Shkoles (= Russified schools) to Tsisho (socialist-nationalist Yiddishist schools)], 256–267. Mexico City, Mendelson Fund.

— (1956b), 'Yidish unter tsvey fayern' [Yiddish under attack on two fronts], in his *Fun kheyder un 'shkoles' biz tsisho* [From the Kheyder (= traditional orthodox elementary school) and Shkoles (= Russified schools) to Tsisho (= socialist-nationalist-Yiddishist schools)], 217–255. Mexico City, Mendelson Fund.

— (1956c), 'Di amolike "shraybers" bay yidn' [The 'writing teachers' among Jews in former days], in his *Fun kheyder un 'shkoles' biz tsisho* [From the Kheyder (= traditional orthodox elementary school) and Shkoles (= Russified schools) to Tsisho (= socialist-nationalist-Yiddishist schools)], 76–98. Mexico City, Mendelson Fund.

— (1956d), 'Di ershte vos hobn zikh ayngeshtelt far yidish un take far a folkshul mit yidish' [The first who interceded on behalf of Yiddish and actually for an elementary school in Yiddish], in his *Fun kheyder un 'shkoles' biz tsisho* [From the Kheyder (= traditional orthodox elementary school) and Shkoles (= Russified schools) to Tsisho (= socialist-nationalist-Yiddishist schools)], 109–130. Mexico City, Mendelson Fund.

— (1956e), 'Pruvn fun a shul in der yidisher shprakh' [Attempts to establish a school in the Yiddish language], in his *Fun kheyder un 'shkoles' biz tsisho* [From the Kheyder (= traditional orthodox school) and Shkoles (= Russified schools) to Tsisho (= socialist-nationalist-Yiddishist schools)], 178–193. Mexico City, Mendelson Fund.

— (1956f), 'Der "bund" un der gedank vegn a yidish-veltlekher shul' [The 'Bund' and the concept of a Yiddish secular school], in his *Fun kheyder un 'shkoles' biz tsisho* [From the Kheyder (= traditional orthodox school) and Shkoles (= Russified schools) to Tsisho (= socialist-nationalist-Yiddishist schools)], 268–288. Mexico City, Mendelson Fund.

— (1956g), 'Shimen dubnov un di yidishe shulproblem' [Shimen Dubnov and the Yiddish school problem], in his *Fun kheyder un 'shkoles' biz tsisho* [From Kheyder (= traditional orthodox school) and Shkoles (= Russified schools) to Tsisho (= socialist-nationalist-Yiddishist schools)], 289–305. Mexico City, Mendelson Fund.

— (1956h), 'Di kultur-natsionale oytonomye in Ukrayne un di kulturliga' [Nationality-cultural autonomy in the Ukraine and the 'Culture League'], in his *Fun kheyder un 'shkoles' biz tsisho* [From the Kheyder (= traditional orthodox school) and Shkoles (= Russified schools) to Tsisho (= socialist-nationalist-Yiddishist schools)], 432–440. Mexico City, Mendelson Fund.

— (1956i), 'Di khevre mifitsey haskole, di folkshul un di yidishe shprakh' [The Organization for the Dissemination of Enlightenment, the elementary school and the Yiddish language], in his *Fun kheyder un 'shkoles' biz tsisho* [From the Kheyder (= traditional orthodox school) and Shkoles (= Russified schools) to Tsisho (= socialist-nationalist-Yiddishist schools)], 367–406. Mexico City, Mendelson Fund.

— (1958), 'Yidishe shuln in hayntikn poyln' [Yiddish schools in present-day Poland], *Undzer tsayt* (7–8) (July/August): 22–24.

— (1969), 'Tshernovits-kholem un vor' [Tshernovits: dream and reality], *Undzer tsayt* January: 17–21.

Kendzherski, R. (1937)], 'Der shprakhnkamf-kultur oder politik?' [The language struggle-culture or politics?], *Konferents zhurnal: lige far rekht fun yidish in erets-yisroel* [Conference Journal: League for the Rights of Yiddish in the Land of Israel] 14–16. (See several other articles in same issue on this topic.)

Khaykin, Y. (1946a), *Yidishe bleter in amerike* [Yiddish Newspapers in America]. New York, Shklarski.

— (1946b), 'Di batsiyungen fun yidishe tsaytungen in amerike tsu der bavegung far yidishe folkshuln' [The attitudes of Yiddish newspapers in America toward the movement on behalf of Yiddish elementary schools], in his *Yidishe bleter in amerike* [Yiddish Newspapers in America], 352–363. New York, Shklarski.

Khmurner, Y. (1928), 'Vegn a feler vos khazert zikh iber' [About an error that is being repeated], *Bikhervelt* (7): 1–6.

Kisman, Yoysef (1958), 'Tsum fuftsikstn yoyvl: di tshernovitser shprakh-konferents' [On the fiftieth anniversary: the Tshernovits language Conference], *Undzer tsayt* July/August: 8–13.

— (1962), 'Dokter nosn birnboym – zayne gaystike zukhenishn un vandlungen' [Dr. Nosn Birnboym – his spiritual searches and changes], *Tsukunft* (9): 319–327.

Klarberg, F. (1970), 'Yiddish in Melbourne', *Jewish Journal of Sociololgy* 12: 59–76. (Also in *Jews in Australian Society* (1973), ed. by P. Medding, 103–112. Melbourne, Macmillan. Note: author's first name given as Manfred in the latter source.)

Klatzkin, Jacob (1960 [1914]), 'Boundaries: a nation must have its own land and language' in *The Zionist Idea*, ed. by Arthur Hertzberg, 314–327. New York, Meridian.

Kloss, Heinz (1978), *Die Entwicklung neuer germanischer Kultursprachen* (revised). (Original edition: München, Pohl, 1932.)

— (1977), 'Ein paar Worte über das Jiddische in Kanada', in *Deutsch als Mutter-Sprache in Kanada*, ed. by L. Auburger, H. Kloss and H. Rupp, 129–130. Wiesbaden, Steiner.

Kloss, Heinz and Grant D. McConnell (1978), 'Yiddish', in their *The Written Languages of the World: A Survey of the Degree and Modes of Use*, vol. 1, 571–578a. Quebec City, Laval University Press.

Knox, Israel (1945), 'Zhitlovsky's philosophy of Jewish life', *Jewish Record* 8: 172–182.

Kobrin, Leon (1925), *Erinerungen fun a yidishn dramaturg: a fertl yorhundert yidish teater in amerike* [Reminiscences of a Yiddish Dramatist: A Quarter Century of Yiddish Theater in America], 2 vols. New York, Committee.

— (1976), 'From "daytshmerish" to Yiddish in America', *Yiddish* 2 (2–3): 39–48.

Kohansky, Mendl (1977), 'The curtain comes down: A hundred years of Yiddish theatre', *Forum* 2 (27): 107–121.

Korey, William (1974), 'Assimilation and self-consciousness among Soviet Jews', *American Zionist* 64 (5) (February): 27–29.

Kornblueth, Ilana and Aynor, Sarah (1974), 'A study of the longevity of Hebrew slang', *International Journal of the Sociology of Language* 1: 15–38.

Koyrey, Borekh (1967), 'Yidish – a moker far hebreyish' [Yiddish – a source for Hebrew], in *Almanakh fun di yidishe shrayber in yisroel* [Almanac of the Yiddish writers in Israel], 148–160. Tel Aviv, Organization of the Yiddish Writers and Journalists in Israel.

Kozlovski, Yitskhok (1967), *Bney yidish: undzer ani mamin* [The Sons of Yiddish: Our Fundamental Beliefs]. New York, Bney Yiddish.

Kresl, G. (1951), 'Di ershte yidishe tsaytung in erets yisroel' [The First Yiddish newspaper in the Land of Israel], *Goldene keyt* 11: 216.

— (1954), 'A historishe polemik vegn der yidisher literatur' [A historic polemic concerning Yiddish literature], *Goldene keyt* 20: 228–355.

— (1957), 'Matesyohu mizes un di polemic vegn yidish' [Matesyohu Mizes and the dispute about Yiddish], *Goldene keyt* 28: 143–163.

Krug, Mark M. (1954), 'The Yiddish schools in Chicago', *Yivo Annual of Jewish Social Science* 9: 276–307.

L[eshtshinski]., Y. (1936), 'Di mutershprakh bay yidn in polyn' [Mother tongue among Jews in Poland], *Yivo-bleter* 9: 140–143.

— (1940), 'Di mutershprakh fun di poylishe yidn' [The mother tongue of Polish Jews], *Yivo-bleter* 15: 140–144.

Laitin, David D. (1977), *Politics, Language and Thought: The Somali Experience.* Chicago: University of Chicago Press.

Landau, Alfred (1895), 'Das Deminutivum der galizisch-jüdischen Mundart', *Deutsche Mundarten* 1: 46–58.

Landis, Joseph C. (1962), 'Yiddish: a world in its words', *Judaism* 11: 374–380.

— (1964), 'Who needs Yiddish? A study in language and ethics', *Judaism* 13 (4): 1–16.

— (1966), *The Dybbuk and Other Great Yiddish Plays*, ed. and trans. by J. C. Landis. New York, Bantam. (Note the Introduction, 1–14.)

— (1975/1976), 'America and Yiddish literature', *Jewish Book Annual* 33: 20–32.

Landman, Salcia (1962), *Jiddisch: Das Abenteuer Einer Sprache.* Olten u. Freiburg, Walter. (Also note her 'Ergänzungen', *Zeitschrift Deutscher Sprachforschung* (1967) 23: 115–117.)

Leftvitsh, Yoysef (1977), 'Yisroel zangvil un loshn yidish' [Israel Zangwill and the Yiddish language], *Kheshbn* 32: 88–87.

Lerer, Leybush (1928a), 'Yidishe kultur vi an ideologye' [Yiddish culture as an ideology], *Literarishe bleter* (18): 337–338.

— (1928b), 'Tsayt tsu shafn a kultur-gezelshaft' [Time to organize a culture society], *Literarishe bleter* (26): 500–501, 509.

— (1940a), 'Der blik az yidish iz der tamtsis fun yidishkayt' [The view that Yiddish is the quintessence of Jewishness], in his *Yidishkayt un andere problemen* [Jewishness and Other Problems], 68–79. New York, Matones.

— (1940b), 'Di sakone fun der formule "lingvistish-sekularistish"' [The danger of the formulation 'linguistic-secularistic'], in his *Yidishkayt un andere problemen* [Jewishness and other problems], 94–96. New York, Matones.

— (1961), *Reactions of Second Generation American Jews to Problems of Jewish Living.* New York, Boiberik.

Lerner, Herbert J. (1957), 'The Tshernovits Language Conference: a Milestone in Jewish Nationalist Thought'. Unpublished Master's Thesis, New York, Columbia University.

Lerner, Y. Y. (1889), 'Di yidishe muze' [The Yiddish Muse], *Hoyz-fraynd* 2: 182–198.

Leshtshinski, Yankev (1943), 'Di shprakhn bay yidn in umophengikn poyln; an analiz loyt der folkstseylung fun 1931' [Languages among Jews in independent Poland; an analysis based upon the census of 1931], *Yivo-bleter* 22: 145–162.

Levnberg, S. (1968), 'Yidish in ratnfarband' [Yiddish in the Soviet Union], in *Yidishe dialogn: kolokvium fun yidishn veltkongress* [Yiddish Dialogues: Colloquium of the World Jewish Congress], 179–183. Paris, World Jewish Congress.

— (1974), 'The impact of Yiddish on the Jewish labour movement', *Jewish Quarterly* 22: 47–50.

Levin, Avraham ha-cohen (1976), *Ḥshivota shel sfat yidish* [The importance of the Yiddish language], 14. Hamodia, Tishrey.

Levin, Yankev (1920), *Di yidishe arbeter-ring-shul, ir tsil un program*. [The Yiddish Workmen's Circle school, Its Goal and Program]. New York, Workmen's Circle Education Department.

Levinski, A. L. (1889), 'Sefat ever ve-sefat yehudit ha-meduberet' [Hebrew and the spoken Jewish language], *Ha-meliz* (58) (March 10): 3–4 (conclusion in no. 59).

Levinson, Avrom (1957 [1935]), 'Hebreyish un di goles shprakhn' [Hebrew and the diaspora languages], in his *Ha-tnua ha-ivrit ba-gola* [The Hebrew Movement in the Diaspora], Warsaw. Ed. and trans. into Yiddish by A. Menes in *Der yidisher gedank in der nayer tsayt* [Jewish Thought in Modern Times], 276–279. New York, Congress for Jewish Culture.

Levinzon, Yitskhok-ber (1957 [1935]), 'Hebreyish' [Hebrew], from his *Teuda be-yisrael* Warsaw. Ed. and trans. into Yiddish by A. Menes in *Der yidisher gedank in der nayer tsayt* [Jewish Thought in Modern Times], 267–269. New York, Congress for Jewish Culture.

Lewis, Glyn (1976), 'Bilingualism: The Ancient World to the Rennaisance', in *Bilingual Education: An International Sociological Perspective*. Rowley, Newbury House.

Leyvik, H. (1963a), 'Der yid-der yokhed (1957)' [The individual Jew (1957)], reprinted in his *Eseyen un redes* [Essays and Speeches], 109–124. New York, Congress for Jewish Culture. (Also in English [translated by Emanuel S. Goldsmith] in *The Reconstructionist* (1957) 23 (17): 7–12.)

— (1963b), 'Di yidishe literatur – ophitern fun undzer folks-gantskayt (1948)' [Yiddish literature – guardian of our national unity (1948)], in his *Eseyen un redes* [Essays and Speeches], 158–163. New York, Congress for Jewish Culture. (Also translated into English in *The Faith of Secular Jews* (1976), ed. by Saul L. Goodman, 267–274. New York, Ktav.)

Liberman, Kh. (1943), 'Tsu der frage vegn der batsiung fun khsides tsu yidish' [On the question of the attitude of hasidism toward Yiddish], *Yivo-bleter* 22: 201–209.

Lifshits, Y. M. (1863), 'Di fir klasn' [The four classes], *Kol mevaser* 323–328, 364–366. (Also note the 1815 letter of Yankev Shmuel Bik rejecting Tuvye Feder's attack on Mendl Levin [Satanover]'s translations of the Book of Proverbs and the editor's comments pp. 375–380, as well as the editor's own final comments on Lifshits' article on pp. 392–393.)

— (1867), 'Di daytsh-yidishe brik' [The German-Jewish bridge]. *Kol mevaser* 5 (31): 239–241. (See subsequent issues for editorial comments: 32: 274–249; 33: 259–258; 34: 264–265; 35: 271–273; 41: 305–306 etc.)

— (1876), 'Hakdome' [Introduction] to his *Yidish-rusisher verterbukh* [Yiddish–Russian Dictionary] Zhitomir, Baksht.

Lifshits, Yikhezkl (1974), 'Di yidishe gazetn (1874–1928)' [The *Yudishe gazeten* (1874–1928)], *Di tsukunft* 80 (May/June): 193–196. (Also translated into English by David N. Miller, *Yiddish* (1976) 2 (2–3): 32–38 [1974].)

Lifson, David (1965), *The Yiddish Theater in America*. New York, Yoseloff.

Likhtnshteyn, Hilel (1872, 1878), *Et Laasot*. 2 vols. Lemberg.

Lipset, Harry (1970), 'A note on Yiddish as the language of Soviet Jews in the census of 1939', *Jewish Journal of Sociology* 12: 55–58.

Liptsin, Sol (1944), 'Tsi iz yidish "di shprakhe der ungebildeten yuden"?' [Is Yiddish 'die Sprache der ungebildeten Juden'?], *Yidishe shprakh* 4 (3–6): 120–122.

— (1963), *The Flowering of Yiddish Literature*. New York, Yoseloff.

— (1970), 'Dray shtelungen tsu yidish nokh der ershter velt-milkhome' [Three views about Yiddish after the First World War], in *Khesed le-avrom* [Grace unto Abraham], ed. by M. Kh.-Shtarkman, 93–100. Los Angeles, Committee.

Litvak, A. (1921), 'Di "zhargonishe komitetn"' [The 'jargon (= Yiddish) committees'], *Royter pinkes* 1: 5–30.

Litvakov, M., editor (1928), *Yidishe ortografye: proyektn un materialn* [Yiddish Orthography: Projects and Materials]. Kiev, Kultur Lige. (Note the concluding table comparing 6 proposed and 4 implemented orthographies. Also note the concluding bibliography, characterized as incomplete, listing 54 items.)

Loewe, Heinrich (1911), *Die Sprachen der Juden*. Köln, Jüdischer Verlag.

Loker, B. (1920), 'Tsu undzer shprakhn-frage in erets-yisroel' [Concerning our language question in Erets Yisroel], *Undzer gedank* (Berlin) 91–111.

Lyesin, Avrom (1954), 'Ven yidishe literatur is gevorn sotsialistish' [When Yiddish literature became socialist], in his *Zikhroynes un bilder* [Memoires and Pictures], Cyco. (Also trans. into English and ed. by Lucy Davidowicz in her *The Golden Tradition*, 422–426. New York, Holt, Rinehart and Winston.)

Madison, Charles (1968), *Yiddish Literature: Its Scope and Major Writers from Mendele and Sholem Aleichem to Isaac Bashevis Singer*. New York, Ungar.

— (1976), *Jewish Publishing in America*. New York, Sanhedrin.

Malakhi, A. R. (1961), 'Nokhem sokolov un di yidishe shprakh' [Nokhem Sokolov and the Yiddish language], *Ikuf-almanakh* 466–493.

— (1965), 'Der "kol mevaser" un zayn redakter, in *Pinkes far der forshung fun der yidisher literatur un prese* [Register for Research on Yiddish Literature and Press], ed. by Shloyme Bikl, 49–121. New York, Congress for Yiddish Culture.

Maler, Refuel (1925), 'Vegn der sotsiologye fun hebreyish' [Concerning the Sociology of Hebrew], *Naye arbeter velt* (November 4 and 11): 2.

— (1967a), 'Shimen dubnov' [Shimen Dubnov], in his *Historiker un vegvayzer* [Historians and Guides], 68–99. Tel Aviv, Yisroel Bukh.

— (1967b), 'Di ideyishe yerushe fun khayem zhitlovski' [Our conceptual inheritance from Khayem Zhitlovski], in his *Historiker un vegvayzer* [Historians and Guides], 111–151. Tel Aviv, Yisroel Bukh.

— (1967c), 'Borokhovs teorye un shite in der itstiker tsayt' [Borokhov's theory and approach in the present] in his *Historiker un vegvayzer* [Historians and Guides], 152–183. Tel Aviv, Yisroel Bukh.

— (1947), 'Yidish un hebreyish in likht fun der hayntiker virklekhkeyt' [Yiddish and Hebrew in the light of current reality], *Yidishe kultur* 9 (June): 12–20.

Manger, Itsik, Turkov, Y., Perenson, M. (1968), *Yidishe teater in eyrope tsvishn beyde velt-milkhomes: poyln* [Yiddish theater in Europe between both World Wars: Poland]. New York, Congress for Jewish Culture.

—, editors (1971), *Yidishe teater in eyrope tsvishn beyde velt-milkhomes: sovetn-farband, mayrev-eyrope, baltishe lender* [Yiddish Theater in Europe between both World Wars: Soviet Union, Western Europe, Baltic States]. New York, Congress for Jewish Culture (final editor: Y. Birnboym).

Mansch, Ph. (1888–1890), 'Der jüdisch–polnische Jargon', *Der Israelit* vols. 21–22 (Lemberg).

Margoshes, Sh. (1965), 'Di role fun der yidisher prese' [The role of the Yiddish press], in *Pinkes far der forshung fun der yidisher literatur un prese* [Register for Research on Yiddish Literature and Press], ed. by Shloyme Bikl, 194–205. New York, Congress for Jewish Culture.

Mark, Yudl (1938), 'Yidishe anglitsizmen' [Yiddish anglicisms], *Yorbukh fun Amopteyl* [Yearbook of the American Section (of the Yivo)]. New York, Yiddish Scientific Institute.

— (1941), 'Lomir oyfhitn di ashires fun dem talmed-khokhems shprakh' [Let us preserve the richness of the scholar's language], *Yidishe shprakh* 1: 65–77.

— (1942), 'Undzere fraynd di kritikers' [Our friends, the critics], *Yidishe shprakh* 2: 166–173.

— (1948), 'Yidishkayt un veltlekhkayt in un arum undzere shuln' [Jewishness and secularism in and about our schools], in *Shul-pinkes* [School Record Book], ed. by Y. Kh. Pomerants et al., 9–68. Chicago, SAFI.

— (1958), 'Voz iz a vort in der yidisher shprakh?' [What is a word in the Yiddish language?], in *Yude a. yofe bukh* [Yude A. Yofe Book], ed. by Y. Mark, 287–298. New York, Yivo Institute for Jewish Research.

— (1962a), 'Shimen dubnov un yidish' [Shimen Dubnov and Yiddish], in his *Shimen Dubnov*, 52–60. New York, Workmen's Circle Educational Department.

— (1962b), 'Di natsyonale barekhtikung far der yidisher shul' [The ethnic justification of the Yiddish school], *Bleter far yidisher dertsiung* 1 (6): 1–12.

— (1963), 'Vegn shedlekhe un nitslekhe daytshmerizmen' [On harmful and useful New High Germanisms], *Yidishe shprakh* 23: 65–87.

— (1967), 'Tsu der geshikhte fun der yidisher literatur-shprakh' [Toward the history of the Yiddish literary language], in *Ateres shloyme: shloyme bikl yubiley bukh* [Crown of Solomon: Shloyme Bikl Anniversary Volume], ed. by M. Shtarkman, 121–143. New York, Matones.

— (1968), '60 yor nokh der shprakh konferents in tshernovits' [60 years after the language conference in Tshernovits], *Forverts* (August 25): Section 2, 11 and 15.

— (1969), 'The Yiddish language: its cultural impact', *American Jewish Historical Quarterly* 59: 201–209.

— (1970), 'Vegn motivirungen far yidish' [Concerning justifications for Yiddish], in *Khesed le-avrom* [Grace unto Abraham], ed. by M. Kh. Shtarkman, 615–628. Los Angeles, Committee.

— (1972), 'Secular Jewishness – the basis of the Sholom Aleichem School', in Saul Goodman, (ed.), *Our First Fifty Years: The Sholom Aleichem Folk Institute*, ed. by Saul Goodman, 85–96. New York, SAFI. (Also in Yiddish in same volume *81–*91.)

Marmer, Kalmen (1928), 'Tsvey yubileyen' [Two anniversaries] in *Pinkes*, 38–52. New York, Yivo – American Section.

Mayzl, Nakhmen (1923), 'Dos yidishe bukh in yor 1923' [The Yiddish book in the year 1923], *Bikhervelt* (6): 510–515.

— (1928a), 'Di ershte mobilizatsye' [The first mobilization], *Literarishe bleter* (35): 681.

— (1928b), 'Y. l. perets un di tshernovitser yidishe shprakh konferents' [Y. L. Perets and the Tshernovits Language Conference], *Di yidishe velt* (4): 298–312.

— (1957), 'Dokter nosn birnboym, 1864–1937' [Dr. Nosn Birnboym, 1864–1937], in his *Noente un eygene* [Near Ones and Dear Ones], 53–62. New York, Yikuf.

— (1965), 'Der yidisher mikhe yoysef berditshevsky' [The Yiddish Mikhe Yoysef Berditshevsky], *Yidishe kultur* (9) (November): 18–21.

Medding, Peter Y. (1968), *From Assimilation to Group Survival*. Melbourne, Macmillan.

Megged, Aharon (1967), 'Batrakhtungen iber tsvey shprakhn' [Reflections on two languages], in *Almanakh fun di yidishe shrayber in yisroel* [Almanac of the Yiddish writers in Israel], 65–79. Tel Aviv, Organization of the Yiddish Writers and Journalists in Israel. (Also abbreviated in English: *Midstream* (1966) 12 (8) (October): 31–39.)

Meir, Golda: see Meyer, Golde.

Melezin, Avrom (1948), 'Di itstike yidishe shul in poyln' [The present-day Yiddish school in Poland], *Tsukunft* July–August: 406–410.

Mencken, H. L. (1936), *The American Language*, 4th edition. New York, Knopf. (Re: Yiddish: 633–636.)

Mendele, Moykher Sforim (1959 [1889]), 'Shtrikhn tsu mayn biografye (1889)' [Sketches toward my biography (1889)], in *Dos Mendele Bukh*, ed. by Nakhmen Mayzl, 17–32. New York, Yikuf.

Mendelsohn, Ezra (1970), *Class Struggle in the Pale*. Cambridge, Harvard University Press.

Mendelssohn, M. (1783), *Or la-netiva* [Light on the Path]. Berlin. (Introduction to his *Nitivot hashalom*.)

Meyer, D. (1922a), 'Bibliotek-vezn: di biblyotekn af der provints' [Library system: libraries in the provinces], *Bikhervelt* (3): 331–335.

— (1922b), 'Yidishe biblyotekn in poyln' [Jewish libraries in Poland], *Bikhervelt* 1 (4–5): 467–475.

Meyer, Golde (1973), 'Address at the dedication of the Leivick House in Israel (1970)', *Yiddish* 1: 4–5.

Meyern-lazar, M. (1948), *Dos yidishe shulvezn in argentine* [The Yiddish School Network in Argentina]. Buenos Aires, Meyern-lazar.

Meyerzon, Yaakov (1919), 'Le-reorganizaẓye shel ha-maflaga ha-soẓialistit be-ereẓ yisrael'

[Toward the reorganization of the socialist party in Erets-Yisrael], in *Me-ha-asifa ha-klalit* [From the General Assembly]. Yafo.

Mieses, Matthias, see Mizes, Matesyohu.

Mirkin, M. (1939), 'Yidishe talmidim in di mitlshuln in poyln' [Jewish students in the high schools in Poland], *Yidishe ekonomik* 3 (4–6): 257–265.

Miron, Dan (1973a), 'The commitment to Yiddish', in his *A Traveler Disguised*, 1–33. New York, Schocken.

— (1973b), 'A language as Caliban', in his *A Traveler Disguised*, 34–66. New York, Schocken.

Mishkovski, Niyekh (1913), 'Yidish' [Yiddish], *Dos naye lebn* 5: 89–93.

Mizes, Matesyohu (1907), 'Be-zhut ha-safa ha-yehudit' [On the merit of the Yiddish language], *Ha-olam* 1 (22): 269–270, 1 (23) 281–283. (Note the reply of the editors on p. 83.)

— (1910), 'Le-she'eylat ha-lashon ha-yehudit' [On the Yiddish language question], *Ha-atid* 3: 209–216.

— (1915), *Die Entstehungsursache der jüdischen Dialekte*. Vienna, Löwit. Reprinted 1979. Hamburg, Buske, with an introduction by Peter Freimark.

— (1924), *Die Jiddische Sprache*. Berlin and Vienna, Benjamin Harz.

— (1931), 'Referat vegn der yidisher shprakh (1908)' [Paper on the Yiddish language (1908)], in Anon, *Di ershte yidishe shprakh konferents*, 143–193. Vilna, Yiddish Scientific Institute.

Mlotek, Yoysef (1977), 'Yiddish—loshn fun undzer nehome un yidishe vertn' [Yiddish – language of our soul and Jewish values], *Barikht fun der velt-konferents far yidish un yidisher kultur* [Minutes of the World Conference for Yiddish and Yiddish Culture], 30–34. Tel Aviv, World Bureau for Yiddish and Yiddish Culture.

Murdoch, Brian O. (1972), 'A Yiddish writer and the German cultural hegemony before World War II: Some comments on an essay by Itsik Manger', *Jewish Social Studies* 34 (2): 94–106.

Mutshnik, Y. (1938), 'Rusish in der yidisher shul' [Russian in the Yiddish school], *Der emes* June 5.

N[iger]., Sh. (1922), 'A yidisher kultur kongres' [A congress for Yiddish culture], *Dos naye lebn* 1 (2): 1–4.

Niger-Charney, S. (or Sh.): see Niger, Shmuel.

Niger, Shmuel (1912), 'Daytshmerish' [New High Germanisms], *Lebn un visnshaft* (11/12): 49–55.

— (1913a), 'Di yidishe literatur un di lezerin' [Yiddish literature and the female reader], in *Der Pinkes* [The Record Book]. Vilna. (Reprinted (1959) in his *Bleter geshikhte fun der yidisher literatur* [Pages of History of Yiddish Literature], 37–108. New York, Congress for Jewish Culture; also note postscript by Yitskhok Rivkind in same volume, 431–438.)

— (1913b), 'Tsu der kheyder-frage' [On the question of the kheyder (= the traditional religious elementary school)], *Di yidishe velt* 3: 108–122.

— (1914), 'Krig un kultur-arbet' [War and work on behalf of [Yiddish] culture], *Di yidishe velt* October: 83–93.

— (1928a), 'Poblik skul, talmed toyre, yidishe folkshul' [Public school, talmud toyre (= traditional religious elementary school) and Yiddish (secular-nationalist) elementary school], in *Yorbukh*, 11–17. New York, SAFI.

— (1928b), 'Der yikhes fun der yidisher literatur' [The stature of Yiddish literature], *Der tog* May 25: 17, June 1: 24. (Reprinted (1959) in his *Bleter geshikhte fun der yidisher literatur* [Pages of History of Yiddish Literature], 13–34. New York, Congress for Jewish Culture.)

— (1930), 'Letste oyfblitsn fun yidishn vort in daytshland' [Last sparks of Yiddish literature in Germany], *Der tog* June 13. (Reprinted (1959), in his *Bleter geshikhte fun der yidisher literatur* [Pages of History of Yiddish Literature], 197–203. New York, Congress for Jewish Culture.)

— (1931), 'Yidish-visnshaft un yidishe visnshaft' [The scientific study of Yiddish and the scientific study of Jewry]. *Yivo-bleter* 2: 1–8.

— (1934), 'Sovetishe poteytes' [Soviet potato-yiddish], *Der tog* April.

— (1939), 'New trends in post-war Yiddish literature', *Jewish Social Studies*, 1 (3): 337–358.

— (1940), *In kamf far a nayer dertsiung* [Struggling for a New Education]. New York, Workmen's Circle Education Department.

— (1941), *Di tsveyshprakhikayt fun undzer literatur* [The Bilinguality of our Literature]. Detroit, Lamed Fund. 1941. (Excerpted and Ed. (1957 [1941]) by A. Menes in *Der yidisher gedank in der nayer tsayt* [Jewish Thought in Modern Times], 283–287. New York, Congress for Jewish Culture.

— (1948), 'Fun tshernovits biz nyu-york, 1908–1948' [From Tshernovits to New York, 1908–1948], *Tsukunft* Sept.: 454–460.

— (1950), 'Vegn der natsyonaler role fun yidish un der yidish kultur' [Concerning the ethno-national role of Yiddish and Yiddish Culture], in *Yidish in undzer lebn* [Yiddish in Our Lives], 5–14. New York, Workmen's Circle, Education Department.

— (1952), 'A maskils utopye, araynfir tsu ayzik meyer diks a manuscript on a nomen' [The utopia of an enlightened man; introduction to an untitled manuscript by Ayzik Meyer Dik], *Yivo bleter* 36: 136–190. (See p. 157 for reference to Germanization of Yiddish spelling.)

— (1955), 'Joseph Klausner's "History of Modern Hebrew Literature" and his attitude to Yiddish', *Yivo Annual of Jewish Social Science* 10: 197–211.

Nobl, Shloyme (1951), 'R' yekhil-mikhl epshteyn, a dertsier un kemfer far yidish in 17 yorhundert' [R' Yekhil-Mikhl Epshteyn, an educator and crusader on behalf of Yiddish in the 17th century], *Yivo-bleter* 35: 121–138.

— (1954), 'The image of the American Jew in Hebrew and Yiddish literature in America, 1870–1900', *Yivo Annual of Jewish Social Science* 9: 83–108.

— (1957–1958), 'Yidish in a hebreyishn levush' [Yiddish in Hebrew garb], *Yivo-bleter* 41: 158–175.

Noble, Shlomo: see Nobl, Shloyme.

Nomberg, H. D. (1931), 'Tsu vos a natsyonale shprakh?' [What is an ethnic language needed for?], in Anon. *Di ershte yidishe shprakh konferents*, 255–257. Vilna, Yivo; also excerpted and ed. (1957) by A. Menes in *Der yidisher gedank in der nayer tsayt* [Jewish Thought in Modern Times], 265–266. New York, Congress for Jewish Culture.

Novak, H., editor (1935), *Shul-almanakh* [School Almanac]. Philadelphia, Workmen's Circle Schools.

— (1948), 'Dokter khayem zhitlovski un zayn badayt far der yidisher shul-bavegung' [Dr. Khayem Zhitlovsky and his significance for the Yiddish school movement], in *Shul-Pinkes* [School Record-Book], ed. by Y. Kh. Pomerants et al., 151–169. Chicago, SAFI.

Novershtern, Avrom (1971), 'Sholem aleykhem un zayn shtelung tsu der shprakhn-frage' [Sholem Aleichem and his attitude toward the language question], *Goldene keyt* 74: 164–188.

Nusboym, Hilel (1882), 'Ha-ẓefira v-ha-shaḥar' [The Ha-ẓefira and the dawn], *Ha-ẓefira* 1 (5).

Olgin (1911), 'Di yidishe shprakh in undzer privat-lebn' [The Yiddish language in our private lives], *Fragn fun lebn* 39–49.

Opatoshu, Yoysef (1949a [1936]), 'Yidish' [Yiddish], in his *Yidish un yidishkayt (eseyen)* [Yiddish and Jewishness (Essays)], 17–27. Toronto, Pomerants.

— (1949b [1948]), 'Di ideye fun yidish un fun der yidisher literatur' [The mission of Yiddish and of Yiddish literature], in his *Yidish un yidishkayt (eseyen)* [Yiddish and Jewishness (Essays)], 30–34. Toronto, Pomerants.

— (1950), 'Toyznt yor yidish' [A Thousand Years of Yiddish], in *Yidish in undzer lebn* [Yiddish in Our Lives], 15–27. New York, Workmen's Circle, Education Department.

— (1954), 'Fifty years of Yiddish literature in the United States', *Yivo Annual of Jewish Social Science* 9: 72–82.

Orland, Y. (1938), 'Mer ufmerkzamkayt der arbet tsvishn di natsminderhaytn' [More attention to work among the minority nationalities], *Der emes* February 17.

Oyerbakh, Efrayim (1975), 'Aynflus fun yidish af hebreyish in yisroel' [Influence of Yiddish on Hebrew in Israel], in his *Af der vogshul* [On the Scale], 347–350. Tel Aviv, Perets.

P[rilutski]., N. (1938), 'Zhargonizirung fun yidish' [Jargonization of Yiddish], *Yidish far ale* (1): 3–8.

Paper, Herbert, editor (1978), *Jewish Languages*. Cambridge, Association for Jewish Studies.

Parker, Sandra (1973), 'Inquiry into the Yiddish secular schools in the United States: A Curricular Perspective'. Ed. D. dissertation, Harvard University (Abridged in this volume: 'An educational assessment of the Yiddish secular school movements in the United States'.)

— (1978), 'Yiddish schools in North America', in *Case Studies in Bilingual Education*, ed. by Bernard Spolsky and Robert L. Cooper, 312–331. Rowley, Newbury House.

Pat, Yankev (1954), 'Tsisho' [Tsisho = The Central Yiddish School Organization (in interwar Poland)], in *Lerer-yizker-bukh* [Volume in memory of Teachers], ed. by Kh. Sh. Kazhdan, 465–483. New York, Committee.

— (1960), *Shmusn mit shrayber in yisroel* [Conversations with Writers in Israel]. New York, Der Kval. (Note particularly the interviews with Khayim Hazaz, Avraham Shlonski, Sh. Tsemekh, and Moshe Stavski.)

Pelts, Rakhmil (1976), 'Di mame yidish hot meyn fardint' [Mother Yiddish deserved better], *Yugntruf* (36/37): 12–14.

Pen, Osher (1941), *Yidish in amerike muz geyn barg aruf* [Yiddish in America Must Go Uphill]. Philadelphia–New York, Biderman.

— (1958a), 'Di sholem aleykhem shuln – der veg fun ekstrem yidish-veltlekher kultur tsurik tsu traditsye un...beysmedresh' [The Sholem Aleykhem schools – The road from extreme Jewish secular culture back to tradition and...the house of prayer], in his *Yidishkayt in amerike* [Judaism in America], 376–388. New York, Pen. (Also, note similar articles on the Workmen's Circle [364–375] and Progressive schools [389–400].)

— (1958b), 'Yidish un yidishe literatur als limed in a tsol hekhere ler-anshtaltn fun amerike' [Yiddish and Yiddish literature as a subject in a number of institutions of higher learning in America], in his *Yidishkayt in amerike* [Judaism in America], 539–548. New York, Pen.

Perelman (1918), 'Die frayhayt fun kind', *Dos folk* 32: 1–4.

Perets, I. L. (1909), 'Hebreyish un yidish' [Hebrew and Yiddish], *Yidishe vokhnshrift* 1–2: Jan. 28 (Warsaw). (Also (1957) in *Der yidisher gedank in der nayer tsayt* [Jewish Thought in Modern Times], ed. by A. Menes, 280–282. New York, Congress for Jewish Culture.)

Pilovsky, Aryey Leyb (1973), *Yidish be-erez yisrael 1907–1921* [Yiddish in the Land of Israel, 1907–1921]. Unpublished Master's Thesis, Hebrew University, Jerusalem.

— (1977), 'Di polemik arum dem plan tsu shafn in 1927 a katedre far yidish in yerushelayim' [The dispute concerning the plan to establish a chair for Yiddish in Jerusalem in 1927), *Goldene keyt* (93): 181–220.

— (1979), 'Itonut yidish be-erez yisrael me-thilata ve-ad hofaat "nayvelt"' (1934) [Yiddish journalism in the Land of Israel from its beginning up to the appearance of 'Nayvelt' (1934)]. *Katedra le-toldot erez-yisrael ve-yishuva* 10: 71–101.

— (1980), 'La querella Hebreo-Yiddish en Erez Israel, 1907–1921, y sus proyecciones nacionales, políticas y culturales', *International Journal of the Sociology of Language* 24: 75–108.

Pinski, Dovid (1935), 'Di partey zhitlovski' [The Zhitlovski (political) party], *Yidish* (Chicago) (3): 68–69.

— (1948), 'Geburt fun der tshernovitser konferents, a bletl zikhroynes' [Birth of the Tshernovits Conference, a page of memories], *Tsukunft* Sept.: 499–501.

Pinson, Koppel S. (1945), 'Arkady Kremer, Vladimir Medem and the ideology of the "Bund"', *Jewish Social Studies* 7: 233–264.

Pludermakher, Gershn (1928), 'Di tshernovitser konferents un di ufgabn fun itstikn moment' [The Tshernovits Conference and the Current Tasks], *Literarishe bleter* 40: 777–778.

Poll, Solomon (1965), 'The role of Yiddish in American ultra-orthodox and Hasidic communities', *Yivo Annual of Jewish Social Research* 13: 125–152.

— (1980), 'The sacred-secular conflict in the use of Hebrew and Yiddish among the ultra-orthodox Jews of Jerusalem'. *International Journal of the Sociology of Language* 24, 109–126.

Pomerants, Aleksander (1962), *Di sovetishe harugey-malkes* [The governmentally executed (Yiddish writers) in the Soviet Union]. Buenos Aires, Yivo.

Pomerants, Y. Kh. (1966), *Meshiekh-motivn in der amerikaner yidisher poezye* [Messianic themes in American Yiddish Poetry], Haifa, 'Haifa'.

Prager, Leonard (1974), 'Yiddish in the university', *The Jewish Quarterly* 22 (1–2): 31–40.

Preschel, T., editor (1946), *Nathan Birnbaum. Selections from his Writings.* London, Hamigdal.

Prilutski, Noyekh (1908a), 'Di ershte yidishe shprakh-konferents' [The first Yiddish language conference], *Teater-velt* (1–2), Oct. 8. (Also (1957) in *Der yidisher gedank in der nayer tsayt* [Jewish Thought in Modern Times], ed. by A. Menes, 261–264. New York, Congress for Jewish Culture.)

— (1908b), 'Di materyele lage fun di yidishe shriftshteler in rusland' [The material circumstances of Yiddish writers in Russia], *Togblat* (Cracow) (179–181) Sept.: 16–18. Reprinted (1931) in *Di ershte yidishe shprakh-konferents* [The First Yiddish Language Conference], 135–140. Vilna, Yiddish Scientific Institute – Yivo.

— (1971 [1916]), 'Mir fodern a natsionale shule vayl mir zenen a bazundere natsionalitet' [We demand a nationality school, because we are a separate nationality], in his *Noyekh prilutskys redes, af varshever shtotrat* [1916]. (Reprinted (1916) in *Prakim nivharim be-toldot yehudey polin ben shtey milhamot olam* [Selected chapters on the history of Polish Jewry between the two World Wars]), ed. by Ezra Mendelson, 109–111. Jerusalem, Acadamon.

— (1917a), 'A yidishist fun 18tn yorhundert'. *Noyekh pritutskis zamlbikher far yidishn folklor, filolgye un kultur geshikhte* 2: 1–56.

— (1917b), 'Varshever asimilatorn un yidish mit 50 yor tsurik' [Warsaw assimilationists and Yiddish fifty years ago], *Barg-aruf* 238–258.

— (1927), 'Di yidishe bineshprakh' [Yiddish theater language], *Yidish teater* 2: 129–144 (Warsaw).

— (1928), 'Nokh di tshernovitser fayerungen' [After the Tshernovits celebrations], *Literarishe bleter* (41): 797–799.

— (1938a), 'Internatsionalizmen' [Internationalisms], *Yidish far ale* 5: 129–140.

— (1938b), 'Nemen fun shprakhn un farbn' [Names of languages and colors], *Yidish far ale* (1): 15–20, 142–146.

— (1945), 'Far voz iz dos yidishe teater ufgekumen azoy shpet?' [Why did the Yiddish theater come into being so late?], *Yivo-bleter* 26: 96–104.

Probst, Mendl (1922), 'Di yidishe prese fun gor der velt in farsheydene shprakhn (in di yorn 1557–1920)' [The Jewish worldwide press in various languages (from 1557 to 1920)], *Bikhervelt* 1 (4–5): 438–446.

Pyekazh, Mendl (1964), 'Vegn "yidishizm" in sof fun 17tn yorhundert un der ershter helft fun 18tn yorhundert' [Concerning 'Yiddishism' at the end of the 17th century and in the first half of the 18th century], *Di goldene keyt* 49: 168–180.

R., A. (1908), 'Di ershte yidishe shprakh-konferents' [The first Yiddish language conference], *Di naye tsayt* 4: 89–104.

Rabin, Chaim (1969), 'Liturgy and language in Israel', in *Language in Religious Practice*, ed. by Wm. J. Samarin, 131–155. Rowley, Newbury House.

Rabinowicz, Harry M. (1965), 'Life and literature', in his *The Legacy of Polish Jewry*, 148–169. New York, Yoseloff.

Rabinovitsh, Mikhl (1946), 'Peretses shtelung tsu yidish in 1891' [Perets's attitude toward Yiddish in 1891], *Yivo-bleter* 28: 200.

Rappaport, Joseph (1957), 'The American Yiddish press and the European conflict in 1914', *Jewish Social Studies* 19: 113–128.

Ravich, M.: see Ravitsh, M.

Ravitsh, Meylekh (1947), 'Vegn aynshlisn in a seyfer hasforim di yidishe makhshove un mayse fun di letste tsvey toyznt yor' [About incorporating Jewish thought and experience of the past two thousand years into a book-of-books]. Paper presented at the Yiddish Scientific Institute – Yivo.

— (1951), 'Nokh a vort vegn a tsveytn seyfer-hasforim' [Another word about a second book-of-books], *Goldene keyt* 7: 89–98.

— (1958), 'Eyn literatur – tsvey leshoynes' [One literature – two languages], in his *Mayn leksikon* [My Lexicon], 449–461. Montreal, Committee.

Ravnitski, Y. H. (1889a), 'Ha-yesh tsoreḥ ba-sifrut ha-zhargonit?' [Is Yiddish literature necessary?], *Ha-meyliẓ* (96): 1–2, (97): 1–2, (98): 1.

— (1889b), 'Od be-zeḥut sifrut ha-'am' [More on the merit of folk literature], *Ha-meyliẓ* 130: 1–2, 131: 4–5.

Redaktsye (1932), 'Der revizye-plenum fun der filologisher sektsye funem institut far yidisher proletarisher kultur' [The revision plenum of the philological section of the institute for Jewish proletarian culture], *Afn shprakhn-front* (4) (31): 1–2 (Entire issue on '[self] criticism' re: N. Shtif and A. Spivak.)

Reisner, Yale J. (1876), '*Shivas tsiyon*: Yiddish borrowings from the Hebrew which have returned to the slang of modern-day Israel', *Working Papers in Yiddish and East European Jewish Studies* (21): 1–7.

Reminik, Y. Y. (1938), 'Rusishe shprakh in der yidisher shul' [Russian language in the Yiddish school], *Der shtern* May 15.

Reyzin, Zalmen (1923), *Fun mendlson biz mendele. Hantbukh far der geshikhte fun der yidisher haskole literatur mit reproduktsyes un bilder* [From Mendelsohn to Mendele. Handbook on the History of Yiddish Haskole (= Enlightenment) Literature with Reproductions and Illustrations]. Warsaw, Kultur-lige.

Reyzin, Z. (1931), 'Tsu der statistic fun yidishn bukh' [Concerning statistics about Yiddish books], *Yivo-bleter* 1: 181–185.

— (1933), 'Eynike mekoyrim tsu der geshikhte fun der yidisher dertsiung in der ershter helft 19tn yorhundert' [A few sources for the history of Jewish education in the first half of the 19th century], *Shriftn far psikhologye un pedagogik* 1: 405–406.

— (1938), 'Norme, yoytse min haklal, gramatishe dubletn' [Norm, exception, grammatical doublets], *Yidish far ale* 1 (6–7): 171–182.

Rischin, Moses (1962), *The Promised City: New York's Jews 1870–1914*. Cambridge, Harvard University Press.

Rivkin, B. (1935), 'Der gantser filzaytiker dokter khayim zhitlovski' [The complete, many-sided Dr. Zhitlovsky], *Yidish* (3): 71–76 (Chicago).

Rivkind, Yitskhok (1928), 'Di rekht fun "loshn ashkenaz" bay din-toyres' [The rights of 'the language of Ashkenaz' (= Yiddish) in lawsuits in rabbinic courts], *Pinkes* 1: 156–157. (Also note addenda dealing with (i) the Gaon of Vilna and Yiddish and (ii) the Yiddish of traditional scholarship.)

Roback, A. A.: see Robak, A. A.

Robak, A. A. (1935), 'Dokter zhitlovski der masbir' [Dr. Zhitlovsky the master teacher], *Yidish* (3): 70–71 (Chicago).

— (1940), *The Story of Yiddish Literature*. New York, Yiddish Scientific Institute – Yivo.

— (1958a), 'Ober davenen muz men; vegn metafizishn betokhn', [But one must pray nevertheless; about metaphysical faith], in his *Di imperye yidish* [The Yiddish Empire], 107–146. Mexico, Mendelson Fund.

— (1958b), 'Yidish koydesh [Holy Yiddish] and Libshaft tsu yidish' [Love for Yiddish] in his *Di imperye yidish* [The Yiddish Empire], 147–156. Mexico City, Mendelson Fund.

— (1958c), 'Der goyrl fun yidish; Mit hebreyish hot gehaltn shmoler; a fragele mayne opfregers vegn kiyem fun yidish; der matsev fun yidish; der koyekh fun yidish' [The fate of Yiddish;

Hebrew was formerly in worse condition; A little question for my critics re the survival of Yiddish; The condition of Yiddish; The power of Yiddish], in his *Di imperye yidish* [The Yiddish Empire], 29–34; 97–100; 112–116; 117–122; 320–325. Mexico City, Mendelson Fund.

— (1959), 'Heores tsu der ankete fun verterbukh' [Footnotes to the questionnaire of the Dictionary], *Yidishe shprakh* 19 (1): 16y–21.

— (1964a), 'Untergangizm; Di filozofye fun untergangizm; ven-zhe shtarbt yidish?' [Declinism; The philosophy of declinism; So when will Yiddish die?], in his *Der folksgayst in der yidisher shprakh* [The Ethnic Spirit in the Yiddish Language], 27–49. Paris, Goldene Pave.

— (1964b), 'Folksgayst un shprakh; di neshomedikayt fun yidish' [Ethnic spirit and language; the soulfulness of Yiddish] in his *Der folksgayst in der yidisher shprakh* [The Ethnic Spirit of the Yiddish Language], 298–325. Paris, Goldene Pave.

— (1964c), 'Der latayn-amerikaner yidish; An entfer botoshanskin' [Latin-American Yiddish; An Answer for Y. Botoshanski], in his *Der folksgayst in der yidisher shprakh* (The Ethnic Spirit in the Yiddish Language), 132–141. Paris, Goldene Pave.

Ronch, Judah et al. (1969), 'Word naming and usage for a sample of Yiddish–English bilinguals', *Modern Language Journal* 53: 232–2353.

Ronch, Isaac E. (1975), 'The WPA Yiddish writers project', *Jewish Currents* September: 8–12.

Rosenfeld, Lulla (1977), *Bright Star of Exile: Jacob Adler and the Yiddish Theatre*. New York, Crowell.

Rosenwaike, Ira (1971), 'The utilization of census mother tongue data in American Jewish population analysis', *Jewish Social Studies* 33: 141–159.

— (1974), 'Estimating Jewish population distribution in U.S. metropolitan areas in 1970', *Jewish Social Studies* 36: 106–117.

Roskies, Diane (1977), 'Heder: primary education among East European Jews: A selected and annotated bibliography of published sources', *Working Papers in Yiddish and East European Jewish Studies* 25.

Rotnberg, Yehoshua, editor (1961), 'Di "shprakhn-frage"' [The 'language issue'], in his *Shimen dubnov tsu zayn 100 yorikn geboyrntog: materialn un opshatsungen* [Shimen Dubnov, on His 100th Birthday: Materials and Evaluations], 38–40. New York, Farband.

— (1973), 'A unique phenomenon: Yiddish education in the Soviet Union', *Yiddish* (2): 93 101.

— (1975), 'Yiddish literature and Jewish History', *Yiddish* 2 (1): 1–8.

Rothenberg, Joshua: see Rotnberg, Yehoshua.

Rothstein, Jay (1977), 'Reactions of the American Yiddish press to the Tshernovits Language Conference of 1908 as a reflection of the American Jewish Experience', *International Journal of the Sociology of Language* 13: 103–120.

Rozenhak, Shmuel (1969), 'Hebreyish-yidish (bamerkungen tsu un arum der tshernovitser shprakh-konferents)' [Hebrew-Yiddish (comments on and about the Tshernovits language conference)], *Goldene keyt* 66: 152–169.

Rozental-Shnayderman, Ester (1974), 'Pakhed far yidish loshn' [Fear of the Yiddish language], *Goldene keyt* 84: 144–150.

Roznboym, M. M. (1929), 'Zhitlovski-bibliografye' [Zhitlovski bibliography], in *Zhitlovski zamlbukh* [Zhitlovski Reader], ed. by Y. N. Shteynberg and Y. Rubin, 461–479. Warsaw, Bzhoze. For minor additions see *Yidishe kultur* (1943) June–July, 52–56.

Rubin, Yisroel (1945), 'Vegn der virkung fun yidish afn geredtn hebreyish in erets-yisroel' [Concerning the influence of Yiddish on spoken Hebrew in the Land of Israel], *Yivo-bleter* 25 (2): 303–309.

Rubin et al. (1977), *Language Planning Processes*. The Hague, Mouton.

Rubinow, Isaac M. (1975 [1907]), *Economic Conditions of the Jews in Russia*, 576–583. New York, Arno Press. Originally published (1907) in Washington by Government Printing Office.

Rubshteyn, Ben-tsiyon (1922), *Di antshteyung un antviklung fun der yidisher shprakh: di sotsyologishe un politishe faktorn* [The birth and development of the Yiddish language: sociological and political factors]. Warsaw, Shul un lebn.

Rudavsky, David (1955), 'Trends in Jewish school organization and enrollment in New York City, 1917–1950', *Yivo Annual* 10: 45–81.

Rumshinski, Yoysef (1944), *Klangen fun mayn lebn* [Notes From My Life]. New York, Biderman.

Rusak, H. (1969, 1973), *Encyclopedia vortaro, Esperanto-Jida*, vol. 1 and 2. Jerusalem, Zamenhofa Doma.

S. (1927), 'Vi halt dos mit yidish kenen' [How are things in connection with knowing Yiddish], *Di yidishe shprakh* 1 (3–4): 78.

Sadan, Dov (1963), 'Der eltster gram in yidish' [The oldest rhyme in Yiddish], *Goldene keyt* 47: 158–159.

— (1965), 'Mendele tsvishn beyde shprakhn' [Mendele between both languages], *Goldene keyt* 53: 197–199.

— (1969), 'Sh″ay agnons kapitl yidish' [Sh″ay Agnon's Yiddish chapter], in *Sh″ay Agnon: shriftn* [Sh″ay Agnon: Writings], trans. by Eliezer Rubinshteyn, 589–605. Tel Aviv, Ha-menora.

— (1972a), 'Di taykhn un der yam: a vort baym yidish-simpozyum in tel aviv' [The rivers and the ocean: comments at the Yiddish symposium in Tel Aviv], in *Heymishe ksovim II* [Homey Writings II], 393–400. Tel Aviv, Ha-menora. (Translated into English (1974), in part, in *Jewish Quarterly Review* 22: 29–30.)

— (1972b), 'Vegn tsveyshprakhikayt' [About bilingualism]), in *Heymishe ksovim II* [Homey Writings II], 417–427. Tel Aviv, Ha-menora.

— (1972c), 'Hemshekh, over, yidish' [Continuity, past, Yiddish], *Heymishe ksovim II* [Homey Writings II], 517–524. Tel Aviv, Ha-menora.

— (1974), 'Tsu der sugye yidish in masekhet byalik' [On the topic of Yiddish in the tractate Byalik], in *Tsuzamen* [Together], ed. by Sh. L. Shnayderman, 22–35. Tel Aviv, Perets farlag.

— (1977), 'Kol hakosev lekhayem-beyerushelayim' [All that is written will live – in Jerusalem], *Folk un tsiyon* 26 (18): 20–22.

— (1978), 'Filshprakhikayt bay yidn' [Multilingualism among Jews], *Folksblat* 1–2, 12–15.

Saineanu, Lazar (1889), *Studio dialectologic asupra graiului Evreo-german*. Bucharest.

Samuel, Maurice (1971a), 'The character of Yiddish', in his *In Praise of Yiddish*, 3–15. New York, Cowles.

— (1971b), 'The future of Yiddish', in his *In Praise of Yiddish*, 267–275. Cowles.

— (1956), 'My three mother-tongues', *Midstream* March 18: 52–57. (Also in *The Faith of Secular Jews* (1956), ed. by Saul L. Goodman, 289–293. New York, Ktav.)

Sandrow, Nahma (1977), *Vagabond Stars – A World History of Yiddish Theatre*. New York, Harper and Row.

Saymon, Shloyme (1954a), 'Eygn loshn un redn yidish' [Own language and speaking Yiddish], in his *Tokh yidishkayt* [Substantive Jewishness], 97–118. Buenos Aires, Yidbukh.

— (1954b), 'Yidishizm vuhin?' [Whither Yiddishism?], in his *Tokh yidishkayt* [Substantive Jewishness], 181–204. Buenos Aires, Yidbukh.

— (1970), 'Di marokhe fun yidishn sekularizm' [The condition of Jewish secularism], in his *Emune fun a dor* [Faith of a Generation], 112–132. New York, Matones.

Schaechter, Mordkhe: see Shekhter, Mordkhe.

Schulman, Elias: see Shulman, Eliyohu.

Seikevicz, Channa (1976), 'Yiddish in Israel and present day attitudes toward Yiddish among American Jews'. Unpublished manuscript, Washington, Georgetown University.

Selavan, Ida C. (1976), 'The Yiddish press in Pittsburgh: agency for Americanization or ethnic identification?' *Yiddish* 2 (2–3): 49–53.

Sfard, Dovid (1974), 'Di groyse antoyshung' [The great disillusionment], in *Tsuzamen* [Together], ed. by Sh. L. Shnayderman, 345. Tel Aviv, Perets farlag.

Sh[atski]., Y. (1930), 'Di eltste retsenzye vegn yidishn teater in nyu-york' [The oldest review of Yiddish theater in New York], in *Arkhiv far der geshikhte fun yidishn teater un drama* [Archive for the History of Yiddish theater and Drama], ed. by Yankev Shatski, 431–435. Vilna and New York, Yiddish Scientific Institute – Yivo.

Shalit, Moyshe (1913), 'Statistik fun yidishn bikher-mark in yor 1912' [Statistics concerning the Yiddish book market in the year 1912], in Sh. Niger, ed., *Pinkes: Yorbukh fun der yidisher literatur un shprakh, far folklor, kritik un bibliografye* [Record Book: Annual of Yiddish Literature and Language, for Folklore, Criticism and Bibliography], ed. by Sh. Niger, 299–306. Vilna, Kletskin. (See listing: 278–299.)

Shapiro, M. (1967), 'Eynike bazunderhaytn funem eynhaytlekhn literarishn yidish in sovetn-farband' [Some peculiarities of standard literary Yiddish in the Soviet Union], *Sovetish heymland* 3: 141–147.

Shapiro, Sh. (1962), 'Der onheyb fun di folkshuln' [The beginning of the folkshuln (of the Jewish National Workers' Alliance)], *Bleter far yidisher dertsiung* 6 (1): 27–33.

Shatski, Yankev (1928), 'Dray hundert yor "tsene urene"' [Three hundred years since the appearance of 'Tsene urene'], *Literarishe bleter* (31): 597–599.

—, editor (1930), *Arkhiv far der geshikhte fun yidishn teater un drame* [Archive for the History of Yiddish Theater and Drama]. New York, Yivo.

— (1931), 'A yidish vokhnblat in der tsayt fun der frantsoyzisher revolutsye' [A Yiddish weekly at the time of the French revolution], *Yivo-bleter* 2: 1–2.

— (1932), 'Gedanken fun an odeser balebos vegn yidish' [Thought of a comfortable Odessan about Yiddish], *Yivo-bleter* 3: 466–468.

— (1935), 'Vegn di nemen far yidish' [Concerning names for Yiddish], *Yivo-bleter* 8: 148–154.

— (1936), 'Di letste shprotsungen fun der yidisher shprakh un literatur in holand' [The last sproutings of Yiddish language and literature in Holland], *Yivo-bleter* 10: 232–265.

— (1943), *Yidishe bildungs-politik in poyln fun 1807 biz 1866* [Jewish Educational Policy in Poland from 1806 to 1866]. New York, Yivo.

Shatsky, Jacob: see Shatski, Yankev.

Shaykovski, Zosa (1939), 'Der kamf kegn yidish in frankraykh' [The struggle against Yiddish in France], *Yivo-bleter* 14: 46–77.

— (1948), *Dos loshn fun di yidn in di arbe kehiles fun komta venesen* [The language of the Jews in the four communities of Comtat Venaissin], with a preface by Max Weinreich. New York. Published by the author with the aid of the Yiddish Scientific Institute – Yivo.

— (1964), 'The struggle for Yiddish during World War I: The attitude of German Jewry', *Leo Beck Institute Yearbook* 9: 131–158.

— (1966), *Catalogue of the Exhibition: The History of Yiddish Orthography from the Spelling Rules of the Early Sixteenth Century to the Standard Orthography of 1936*. New York, Yivo Institute.

— (1970), *One Hundred Years of the Yiddish Press in America, 1870–1970: Catalogue of the Exhibition*. New York, Yivo Institute for Jewish Research.

Shayn, Yisroel (1974), 'Materialn tsu a bibliografye fun yidisher periodike in poyln, 1918–1939' [Toward a bibliography of Yiddish periodica in Poland, 1918–1939], in *Shtudyes vegn yidn in poyln, 1919–1939* [Studies on Polish Jewry, 1919–1939], ed. by J. A. Fishman, 422–483. New York, Yivo Institute for Jewish Research. (Also see his 1963 *Bibliografye fun oysgabes aroysgegebn durkh di arbeter parteyen in poyln in di yorn 1918–1939* [Bibliography of publications published by the Workers' parties in Poland in the years 1918–1939], Warsaw, Yidishbukh.)

Shayn, Yosef (1964), *Arum moskver yidishn teater* [Around the Moscow Yiddish Theater]. Paris, Commission du plan d'Action Culturelle.

Sh'b (1931), 'Der nitsokhn fun undzer oysleyg' [The triumph of our spelling], *Beys yankev* 8 (71–72): 40–41.

Shekhter, Mordkhe (1957), 'Vegn nitsn yidishe geografishe nemen' [On using Yiddish geographic designations], *Yidishe shprakh* 17 (1): 1–9.

— (1961), 'Mir shteyen nit af an ort' [We are not at a standstill], *Yidish* (New York, Congress for Jewish Culture) 1: 351–362.

— (1969), 'The "hidden standard"; a study of competing influences in standardization', in *Field of Yiddish III*, ed. by Marvin Herzog et al., 289–304. The Hague, Mouton.

— (1969–1970, 1971), 'Dos loshn fun sovetish heymland' [The language of the Soviet Heymland], *Yidishe shprakh* 29: 10–42 and 30: 32–64.

— (1975), 'Der yivo un yidish: 50 yor institutsyonalizirte shprakhnormirung' [The Yivo and Yiddish: 50 years of Institutionalized language standardization], *Yidishe shprakh* 34: 2–23.

— (1977a), 'Mamterot tsi bashpritser? [Mamterot (= using Ivritisms) or bashpritser (= words derived from established Yiddish roots) for sprinklers (= Israeli realia)?' *Folksblat* February: 15–16.

— (1977b), 'Four schools of thought in Yiddish language planning', *Michigan Germanic Studies* 3: 34–64.

— (i.p.), 'Dem yivos yidish-uftu; roshe-prokimdike obzervatsyes un sakhhaklen tsu a yubiley' [The Yivo's Yiddish accomplishment: outline of comments and conclusions on the occasion of an anniversary].

Shekhter-vidman, Lifshe (1973), *Durkhgelebt a velt: zikhroynes* [Living Through Everything: Memoirs]. New York, Committee.

Shelyubski, M. Y. (1945), 'Vegn der tsirkulatsye fun der amerikaner yidisher prese' [Concerning the circulation of the American Yiddish press], *Yivo-bleter* 21: 290–294.

Shenirer, Sore (1931), 'Yidishkeyt un yidish' [Yidishkayt (= Jewishness) and Yiddish], *Beys yankev* 8 (71–72): 7–8. (Also, reprinted (1933) in *15 yor bukh fun beys yankev*, 34–36. Lodzh, Beys Yankev.)

Sheyntukh, Yekhil (1977), 'Tsu shpet?' [Too late?], *Bay zikh* 9–10: 217–224.

Shiper, I. (1924), 'Der onheyb fun loshn-ashkenaz in der balaykhtung fun onomastishe kveln' [Beginnings of Old Yiddish in the light of onomastic sources], *Yidishe filologye* 1 (2–3): 101–112.

Shiper, Yitskhok (1923/1925), *Geshikhte fun yidisher-teater-kunst un drama fun di eltste tsaytn biz 1750* [History of Yiddish Theater-art and Drama from the Oldest Times to 1750], vol. 1 and 2. Warsaw, Kultur-liga. (Also see extensive review and additions (1928) by Y. Shatski in *Filologishe Shriftn* 2: 215–264.)

Shmeruk, Khone (1971), 'Peretses yeush-vizye: interpretatsye fun y. l. peretses "bay nakht afn altn mark" un kritishe oysgabe fun der drame' [Peret's Vision of Dispair: Interpretation of Y. L. Perets' 'At Night in the Old Marketplace' and Critical Edition of the Drama]. New York, Yivo.

Shnayd, Yekhil (1956), 'A kapitele galitsye' [A brief chapter on Galicia], *Yivo-bleter* 40: 175–184.

Sholem Aleykhem (1888a), 'Vegn zhargon oysleygn' [About spelling Yiddish], *Di yidishe folks-bibliotek* 1: 474–476.

— (1888b), *Shomers mishpet* [Shomer's trial]. Berdichev, Sheftl.

— (1889), 'Le-she'eylat ha-safa' [On the language question], *Ha-meyliz* (80) April 14: 3–4.

— (1892), 'A briv fun der "yidisher folks bibliotek" tsu ir aroysgeber sholem aleykhem' [A letter from the 'Jewish People's Library' to its publisher, Sholem Aleykhem], *Kol mevaser tsu der yidisher folks bibliotek* 1–4. (An enfer [An Answer] 4–4, same issue.)

Shpirn, Tsvi (1926), 'Di yidishe shprakh in ungarn' [The Yiddish language in Hungary], in *Landoy-Bukh* (= *Filologishe Shriftn 1*) [Landoy-Book (= Philological Studies 1)], 195–200. Vilna, Yivo.

Sh"s-roman (1929), 'Di yidishe prese in rumenye fun 1854 biz 1926' [The Yiddish press in Roumania from 1854 to 1926], *Filologishe shriftn* 3: 525–536.

Shtarkman, Moyshe (1939), 'Tsu der geshikhte fun yidish in amerike' [Toward the History of Yiddish in America], *Yorbukh fun amopteyl* 2: 181–190.

— (1958), 'Gemore-yidish' [Talmudic Yiddish], in *Yude a. yofe-bukh* [Yude A. Yofe Book], 265–268. New York, Yivo Institute for Jewish Research.

— (1965), 'Ven yidish un hebreyish zaynen gekumen kayn amerike' [When Yiddish and Hebrew came to America], in *Pinkes far der forshung fun yidisher literatur un prese* [Register for Research on Yiddish Literature and Press], ed. by Shloyme Bikl, 171–193. New York, Congress for Jewish Culture.

— (1979) *Geklibene shriftn* [Selected Writings]. New York, Cyco. See particularly, his chapters on the American Yiddish press 1875–1885 (pp. 56–76) and 1885–1905 (pp. 77–102), on the beginnings of Yiddish proletarian journalism in the United States (pp. 103–127), and on Yiddish bibliography in the United States (pp. 135–153).

Shtern, Y. (1950), *Kheyder un beys medresh* [Kheyder (= traditional elementary school) and Beys Medresh (= traditional synagogue/house of study)]. New York, Yivo.

Shteynberg, Arn (1968), 'Yidish loshn in yidishn velt-kongres' [The Yiddish language in the World Jewish Congress], in *Yidishe dialogn: kolokvium fun yidishn velt-kongress* [Yiddish Dialogues: Colloquium of the World Jewish Congress], 19–27. Paris, World Jewish Congress.

Shtif, Nokhem (1919), 'Yidn un yidish, oder ver zenen "yidishistn" un vos viln zey?; poshete verter far yidn' [Jews and Jewishness, or Who are the 'Yiddishists' and What do they Want?; Simple Words for every Jew]. Kiev, Onheyb. (Also excerpted (1957), in *Der yidisher gedank in der nayer tsayt* [Jewish Thought in Modern Times], ed. by A. Menes, 293–296. New York, Congress for Jewish Culture.

— (1922), *Humanizm in der elterer yidisher literatur* [Humanism in Early Yiddish Literature], 50–60. Berlin, Klal. (Abridged and translated into English by Percy Matenko and Saul L. Goodman in *The Faith of Secular Jews*, ed. by Saul L. Goodman, 275–286. New York, Ktav).

— (1924), 'Ditrikh fun bern. Yidishkeyt un veltlekhkeyt in der alter yidisher literatur' [Dietrich von Bern: Jewishness and Secularism in Old Yiddish literature], *Yidishe filologye* 1–11: 112–122 (Warsaw).

— (1927), 'Di katedre far yidisher kultur' [The chair of Jewish Culture], *Der shtern* January 25–27. (Also, roughly the same text in (1927), *Der hamer* May: 49–54.)

— (1933), 'Oytobiografye' [Autobiography], *Yivo-bleter* 5: 195–225. (Excerpted, edited, and translated into English (1967) by Lucy Davidowicz as 'How I became a Yiddish linguist' in *The Golden Tradition*, 257–263. New York, Holt, Rinehart and Winston.)

— (1929), 'Di sotsiale diferentsiatsye in yidish' [Social differentiation in Yiddish], *Di yidishe shprakh* 3 (4–5) (1918): 1–22.

— (1931–1932), 'Revolutsye un reaktsye in der shprakh' [Revolution and Reaction in language], *Afn shprakhnfront* 1–2 (26–27): 34–54; 6 (1–2): 12–22.

— (1932), 'Af der shvel fun 19tn yorhundert' [On the threshold of the 19th century], *Afn shprakhnfront* 6 (2–3): 29–30.

Shulman, Eliyohu (1936), 'Di konservative yidishe zhurnalistik in nyu-york' [Conservative Yiddish journalism in New York], *Yivo-bleter* 10: 58–63.

— (1971), *A History of Jewish Education in the Soviet Union*. New York, Ktav.

Shulman, M. (1937), 'Vegn sovetizmen in der yidisher shprakh' [Concerning Sovietisms in the Yiddish language], *Emes* iv, ix: 9.

Shvarts, Y. (1925), 'Vegn der farkriplung fun der shprakh af der yidisher gas' [About the crippling of the language on the Jewish street (= in the Jewish neighborhoods, i.e. among Jews)], in his *Literatur un shprakh fun der yidisher gas* [Literature and Language of the Jewish Street], 129–150. New York, Jewish Neighborhood Publishing Co.

Shveber, A. (1911), 'Di folkstseylung in estraykh un di yidn' [The census in Austria and the Jews], *Fragn fun lebn* 61–74 (Vilna).

Shveyd, Mark (1955a), 'Zhargon' [Jargon (= Yiddish)], in his *Dos lebn fun y. l. perets* [The Life of Y. L. Perets], 179–185. New York, Perets.

— (1955b), 'Barg-aruf mit yidish' [Toward the summit with Yiddish], in his *Dos lebn fun y. l. perets* [The Life of Y. L. Perets], 267–276. New York, Perets.

Shveytser, Shloyme (1967), 'Dos yidishe kultur-lebn in poyln tsvishn beyde velt-milkhomes' [Jewish cultural efforts in Poland between both World Wars], *Sefer ha-shana/yorbukh* [Yearbook (of the World Federation of Polish Jews)], 2: 112–209.

Simon, Solomon: see Saymon, Shloyme.

Singer, Isaac Bashevis (1979), *Noble Lecture* (also in Yiddish [Di nobel rede] in same volume). New York, Farrar, Straus and Giroux.

Sirkin, Nakhmen (1900), 'Der zhargon' [Jargon (= Yiddish)], *Der yid* (37): 15; (38): 15; (40–41): 22–23; (42): 14–16; (47): 16.

— (1923), 'Natsyonale kultur un natsyonale shprakh' [Ethnic culture and ethnic language], *Dos naye lebn* 1 (5): 29–37, (6): 22–28. (Note reply by Zhitlovski (10): 1–9, (11): 4–14.)

Slobin, Dan I (1963), 'Some aspects of the use of pronouns of address in Yiddish', *Word* 19: 193–202.

Smolyar, Boris (1977), 'Yidishe yugnt benkt nokh yidish' [Jewish youth yearns for Yiddish], *Forverts*, Oct. 30: 4.

Sokal, Sh. (1942), 'Yidish in der folkstseylung' [Yiddish in the census]. *Yidisher kemfer*, October 30: 20–22, 36.

Soltes, M. (1924), *The Yiddish Press: An Americanizing Agency*. New York, Teachers College.

Spivak, Elye (1931), *Shprakhkultur* [Language Cultivation]. Kiev, Ukranatsminfarlag.

— (1934), 'Vegn dehebreizatsye un vegn dem hebreyishn "element" in Yidish' [About de-hebraization and about the Hebrew 'element' in Yiddish], *Afn shprakhnfront* (second series) 2: 3–22.

— (1938), 'Vegn di gruntnemen fun yidish' [Concerning the fundamental names for Yiddish], *Fragn fun der yidisher shprakh* 1: 71–86.

— (1939), *Naye vortshafung* [Lexical innovation]. Kiev, Ukranatsminfarlag.

— (1965), 'Perets un di literarishe shprakh' [Perets and literary Yiddish], *Sovetish heymland* 7: 138–145. (Reprint, date of original publication not indicated.)

— (1966), 'Sholem Aleykhem un di yidishe shprakh' [Sholem Aleykhem and the Yiddish Language], *Sovetish heymland* 12: 116–122. (Reprint, date of original publication not indicated.)

Stankiewicz, E. (1965), 'Yiddish place names in Poland', *The Field of Yiddish* 2: 158–181.

Stillman, Gerald (1977), 'A defense of 19th century Yiddish literature', *Yiddish* 2: 4–14.

Stupnitski, Sh. Y. (1920), 'Di yidishe kultur-bavegung' [The movement for Yiddish culture], in his *Afn veg tsum folk*, 68–78. Warsaw, Nayer farlag.

Susholtz, Shimon (1976), 'Who needs Yiddish?' *Jewish Observer* June: 18–20. (Note objections and support in September 1976 and June 1977 issues.)

Szaykowski, Zosa: see Shaykovski, Zosa.

Tartakover, Arye (1926), 'Das juedische Mittelschulwesen in Polen', *Der Jude* 79–89 (Berlin), Sonderheft 'Erziehung'.

— (1931), 'Das juedische Schulwesen in Polen', *Monatschrift fuer die Geschichte und Wissenschaft des Judentums* 75: 292–306.

— (1946), 'Yidishe kultur in poyln tsvishn tsvey velt-milkhomes' [Jewish culture in Poland between two World Wars], *Gedank un lebn* 4 (1): 1–35.

— (1967), 'Di yidishe shul in poyln tsvishn tsvey milkhomes' [The Yiddish school in Poland between two wars], *Sefer hashana/yorbukh* [Yearbook (of the World Federation of Polish Jews)] 2: 210–265.

Tartakower, Arieh: see Tartakover, Arye.

Teneboym, Yoysef. (1957/1958), 'Di yidishe shprakh af der tog-ordenung fun der sholem-konferents in pariz, 1919' [The Yiddish language on the agenda of the peace conference in Paris, 1919], *Yivo-bleter* 41: 217–229.

Tikotshinski, Pinkhes (1937), 'Shul- un shprakh-frages in der konstitutsye-debate in poylishn grindungseym' [School and language questions in the constitution debate during the founding assembly of the Polish Sejm], *Yivo-bleter* 12: 433–442.

Tobias, Henry J. (1972), *The Jewish Bund in Russia from its Origins to 1905*. Stanford, Stanford University Press.

Tomashefski, Boris (1937), *Mayn Lebn* [My Life]. New York, Trio.

Toybes, Yankev Shmuel (1948), 'Fonetisher anti-yidishizm' [Phonetic anti-Yiddishism], in his *Af yidishe yesoydes* [On Jewish Foundations], 55–60. London, Narod.

Toybes, Shmuel (1950), 'Vos es kon getun vern far yidish!' [What can be done for Yiddish!], *Kiyem* 3 (11) (35): 1757–1763.

— (1952), *Yidish – nisht hebreyish* [Yiddish – not Hebrew]. New York, 'Yiddish' Publishing Co.

Trunk, Isaiah (1976), 'The cultural dimension of the American Jewish labor movement', *Yivo Annual* 16: 342–393.

Tsanin, M. (1966), 'Dos loshn yidish' [The Yiddish language], in his *Af di vegn fun yidishn goyrl* [On the Paths of Jewish Fate], 77–94. Tel Aviv, Hamenora.

— (1974), 'Der sakhhakl fun a tseshtererisher filozofye' [The sum total of a destructive philosophy], in *Tsuzamen* [Together], ed. by Sh. L. Shnayderman, 333–344. Tel Aviv, Perets Farlag.

Tsaytlin, Arn (1973), 'Undzer yerushe fodert az mir zoln zayn di yorshim' [Our heritage demands that we be its heirs], *Folk un medine* 13: 15–17. (Also translated by Hannah Berliner-Fischthal (1975) in *Yiddish* 1 (4): 1–4.)

Tsh[erikover]., A. (1939), '"Tsum arayngang in a naye periode" (faygnboyms hakdome tsu der broshur "der sotsyalizm fun alef biz tof", 1894)' ['Upon entering into a new period' (Faygnboym's introduction to his brochure 'Socialism from a to z', 1894)], *Historishe shriftn* 3: 757–765.

Tshermer, L. (1923), 'Hebreyish in erets yisroel' [Hebrew in Erets Yisroel], *Dos naye lebn* (8): 51–53.

Tsinberg, Yisroel (1928), 'Der kamf far yidish in der altyidisher literatur' [The struggle for Yiddish in Old-Yiddish literature], *Filologishe shriftn* (Yivo) 2: 69–106. (Also (1946) in *Yivo Annual* 1: 283–293; expanded on in chapter 8, vol. 7 of his *A History of Jewish Literature* [1935]; translated into English (1975) by Bernard Martin, Cincinnati and New York, Hebrew Union College and Ktav.)

— (1975 [1935]), 'Languages among Jews: The origins of Yiddish', in his *A History of Jewish Literature* [1935], ch. 1, vol. 7, trans. into English by Bernard Martin. Cincinnati and New York, Hebrew Union College and Ktav.

— (1929–1937), *Di geshikhte fun der literatur bay yidn* [The History of Literature Among Jews], 8 vols. Vilna, Tamar. (Reprinted (1943) New York, Shklarski, vols. 1–8; vol. 9 [1937] (edited by M. Astur), Waltham and New York, Brandeis University and Cyco, 1966; English translation of vols. 1–8 by Bernard Martin. Cincinnati and New York, Hebrew Union College and Ktav, 1972–78, entitled *A History of Jewish Literature*.)

Tsitron, Sh. L. (1923), 'Honorar-badingungen in der yidisher literatur' [Honorarium conditions in Yiddish literature], *Bikhervelt* 2 (1–2): 15–23, (5): 326–335.

Tsivyen (1948), 'Ven vet yidish untergeyn in amerike?' [When will Yiddish disappear in America?], in his *Far fuftsik yor* [During Fifty Years], 46–53. New York, Laub.

Tsukerman, Rakhmil (1972), 'Me darf shlayfn dos publitsistishe vort' [We must polish the language of journalism], *Yidishe shprakh* 31: 18–19.

Tsvayg, A. R. (1930), 'Lingvotekhnisher "ekizm"' [Linguatechnical extremism], *Di yidishe shprakh* 4 (2–3): 21–22, 49–52.

Turkov, Mark (1968), 'Di marokhe fun yidish in dorem-amerike' [The lot of Yiddish in South America], in *Yidishe dialogn: kolokvium fun yidishn velt-kongres* [Yiddish Dialogues: Colloquium of the World Jewish Congress], 191–196. Paris, World Jewish Congress.

Turkov, Zigmund (1951), *Teater-zikhroynes fun a shturmisher tsayt* [Theater Memories of a Stormy Period]. Buenos Aires, Tsentral Farband fun Poylishe Yidn in Argentine.

Turkov-Grudberg, Yitskhok (1965), 'Di fon fun yidish' [The standard-bearer of Yiddish], in his *Y. l. perets der veker* [Y. L. Perets: The Awakener], 18–25. Tel Aviv, Orti.

V[aynraykh]., M. (1934), 'Af di khurves fun yidish' [On the ruins of Yiddish], *Yivo-bleter* 6: 182–184.

Valk, Y. and Klyonski, A. (1920), 'Di shul af der provints' [The Yiddish school in the hinterlands], *Lebn* (3–4): 21–23.

Valt, Reyzl (1937), 'Der kamf in der khevre mifitsey haskole in vilne 1915–1917' [The struggle in the Organization for the Dissemination of Enlightenment in Vilna 1915–1917], *Yivo-bleter* 12: 420–433.

Vaynraykh, Maks (1923a), 'A nay bukh vegn der geshikhte fun yidish' [A new book on the history of Yiddish], *Bikhervelt* 2 (1–2): 38–47, (3–4): 179–187.

— (1923b), 'Vos mir hobn un vos undz felt [What we have and what we lack], in his *Shtaplen: fir etyudn tsu der geshikhte fun der yidisher shprakh-visnshaft un literatur-geshikhte* [Rungs: Four Studies Toward the History of Yiddish Linguistics and History of Literature]. Berlin, Vostok.

— (1928), *Bilder fun der yidisher literatur-geshikhte, fun di onhoybn biz mendele moykher sforim* [Studies in the History of Yiddish Literature, from the Beginnings to Mendele Moykher Sforim]. Vilna, Tomor.

— (1931), 'Vos volt yidish geven on hebreyish?' [What would Yiddish be without Hebrew?], *Di tsukunft* 36 (3): 194–205.

— (1933), 'A polemik tsvishn tsederboym un perets smolenskin vegn yidishe dialektn' [A polemic between Tsederboym and Perets Smolenskin about Yiddish dialects], *Yivo-bleter* 5: 401–404.

— (1936), 'Form vs. psychic function in Yiddish', in *Gaster Anniversary Volume*, 532–538. London, Taylor's Foreign Press.

— (1937), 'Le Yiddish comme object de la linguistique générale'. Communication au IVe Congrès International de Linguistes, à Copenhague, le 27 août 1936. Vilna, Yiddish Scientific Institute – Yivo.

— (1938), 'Daytshmerish toyg nisht' [Daytshmerish (= New High German influence) is no good], *Yidish far ale* 97–106. (Reprinted (1975) in *Yidishe shprakh* 34: 23–33.)

— (1939), *Di shvartse pintelekh* [The Black Dots (= Writing in Hebrew Characters)]. Vilna, Yiddish Scientific Institute – Yivo. (See chapter 13 'Der yidisher oysleyg haynt un amol' [Yiddish spelling today and in the past].)

— (1941a), 'Vegn englishe elementn in undzer kulturshprakh' [Concerning English elements in our literary standard], *Yidishe shprakh* 1: 33–47.

— (1941b), 'Harbe ivre' [Highbrigh (difficult) language], *Yidishe shprakh* 1: 97–110.

— (1942), 'Vos heyst yidishlekh? analizirt af mendeles an iberzetsung' [What does Jewishly mean? An analysis of one of Mendele's translations (of Pinsker's *Autoemancipation*)], *Yidishe shprakh* 2: 97–113.

— (1943), *Der yivo in a yor fun umkum* [The Yivo in a Year of Annihilation]. New York, Yivo.

— (1945), 'Der yivo un di problemen fun undzer tsayt' [The Yivo and the problems of our time], *Yivo-bleter* 25: 3–18.

— (1951a), 'Ashkenaz: di yidish-tkufe in der yidisher geshikhte' [Ashkenaz: the Yiddish era in Jewish history], *Yivo-bleter* 35: 7–17.

— (1951b), 'Yidisher kiyem in amerike: programen un realitetn' [Jewish survival in America: plans and realities], *Tsukunft* 56 (5): 203–208.

— (1953), 'Yiddishkayt and Yiddish: on the impact of religion on language in Ashkenazic Jewry', in *Mordecai M. Kaplan Jubilee Volume*, 481–514. New York, Jewish Theological Seminary. (Also (1968) in *Readings in the Sociology of Language*, ed. by J. A. Fishman, 382–413. The Hague, Mouton.)

— (1958), 'Fuftsik yor nokh tshernovits: a dermonung un a monung' [Fifty years after Tshernovits: a reminder and an obligation], *Di tsukunft* May/June: 218–223.

— (1959a), 'Inveynikste tsveyshprakhikayt in ashkenaz biz der haskole; faktn un bagrifn' [Internal bilingualism in Ashkenaz up to the *haskole*; findings and concepts], *Goldene keyt* 35: 3–11. (Edited and translated into English (1972) by Irving Howe and Eliezer Greenberg in *Voices from the Yiddish*, 279–288. Ann Arbor, University of Michigan Press.)

— (1959b), 'Der eynhaytlekher oysleyg, zayn geshikhte un verde (der shtumer alef nebekh un di reydevdike problemen hinter im)' [Standard Yiddish spelling, its history and value (The poor silent alef and the very vocal problems behind it)], *Yidishe shprakh* 19 (2): 33–63.

— (1963), 'A yidisher zats fun far zibn hundert yor' [A Yiddish sentence of 700 years ago], *Yidishe shprakh* 23: 87–93.

— (1967), 'The reality of Jewishness vs. the ghetto myth: the sociolinguistic roots of Yiddish, in *To Honor Roman Jakobson*, 211–221. The Hague, Mouton.

— (1973), *Geshikhte fun der yidisher sphrakh* [History of the Yiddish language], 4 vols. New York, Yivo Institute for Jewish Research. (Translated (1980) into English by Shlomo Nobel and Joshua A. Fishman. Chicago, University of Chicago Press. [vols. 1 and 2 of the original 4].)

Vaynraykh, Uriel (1953), *Languages in Contact*. The Hague, Mouton.

— (1972), 'Dos normirn a shprakh: prat-faln un oysfirn' [Standardizing a language: cases and conclusions], *Yidishe shprakh* 31 (1–11): 54–58.

Vaynshteyn, V. (1910), 'Di ershte tsen yor' [The first ten years], in *Yubileyumshrift tsu ab ka[ha]ns 50stn geburtstog* [Jubilee-Publication on Ab. Ka[ha]n's 50th Birthday], 36–72. New York, Committee.

Vays(slonim), Sh. (1937), 'Oys di tsaytn fun der tshernovitser konferents' [From the times of the Tshernovits conference], *Fun noentn over* 1: 57–63.

Vaysman, Sh. (1935), 'Di yidishe folkshuln in montreol' [The Yiddish folkschools in Montreal], in Novak, ed. *Shul Almanakh* [School Almanac], ed. by Novak, 175–182. Philadelphia, Workmen's Circle Schools. (Also see articles by Menakhovski, Katsnelnbogn, Khanin etc. on other Yiddish secular systems in Canada.)

Verses. Sh. (1938), 'Yankev-shmuel bik, der blondzhendiker maskil' [Yankev-shmuel Bik, the groping *maskil* (= bringer of enlightenment)], *Yivo-bleter* 13: 505–536.

Vidal, Sephiha H. (1972), 'Langues Juives, langues calques et langues vivantes', *Linguistique* 8 (2): 59–68.

Viner, M. (1940), *Tsu der geshikhte fun der yidisher literatur in 19tn yorhundert* [On the History of Yiddish Literature in the 19th century]. Kiev, Ukranatsmin. (Second edition (1945) New York, YIKUF.)

Virkel de Sandler, Ana E. (1977), 'El bilinguismo idish-español en dos comunidades bonaerenses', *Vicus* 1: 139–160.

Vislevski, Tsvi (1928), 'Esrim shana le-tshernoviz' [Twenty years since Tshernovits], *Ha-tekufa* 25: 613–620.

Volobrinski, A. (1930), 'Fashizirter yidishizm' [Fascistic Yiddishism], in *Der fashizirter yidishizm un zayn visnshaft* [Fascistic Yiddishism and its Science]. Minsk, Byelorussian Academy of Science.

Warembud, Norman, editor (1975), *Great Songs of the Yiddish Theater*. New York, Quadrangle.

Weinberg, Werner (1969), *Die Reste des Jüdischdeutschen*. Stuttgart, Kohlhammer.

Weinreich, Max: see Vaynraykh, Maks.

Weinreich, Uriel: see Vaynraykh, Uriel.

Wexler, Paul (1974), *Purism and Language*. Bloomington (Indiana), Indiana University Language Science Monographs.

Wiener, Leo (1972 [1899]), *The History of Yiddish Literature in the Nineteenth Century*. New York, Hermon Press. (Introduction by Elias Schulman.)

Winer, Gershon (1971), 'Yiddish: the message in the medium'. *Judaism* 20: 467–475.

Witke, Carl (1957), *The German Language Press in America*. Louisville, University of Kentucky Press.

X., Dr. (1909), 'Vegn a yidisher gramatik un reform in der yidisher shprakh' [About a Yiddish grammar and reforms in the Yiddish language], *Lebn un visnshaft* 1: 50–56.

Yablakov, Herman (1968/1969), 'Arum der velt mit yidish teater' [Around the World with Yiddish Theater], 2 vols. New York, Yablakov.

Yadlin, Aharon (1976), 'An ofitsyele bagrisung' [An official greeting], *Yugntruf* 31/37: 6.

Tam, Joseph (1973), 'Selected data on the Canadian population whose mother tongue is Yiddish', *Canadian Jewish Population Studies* 3 (2).

Yashunski, Y. (1922), 'Di yidishe prese zint 1917 yor' [The Yiddish Press since 1917], *Bikhervelt* 1 (1): 74–79.

Yefroykin, Y. (1951), 'Der ukfum fun yidishe goles shprakhn un dialektn' [The rise of Jewish diaspora languages and dialects], *Kiyem* 1–13, 92–108. (Also see addendum 1952: 329–334.)

— (1952), 'Yidishe leshoynes, fremde shprakhn un yidishe sheferishkayt' [Jewish languages, foreign languages and Jewish creativity], *Kiyem* 231–239.

Yefroykin, Z. (1951), 'Di y. l. perets shuln fun arbeter ring' [The Y. L. Perets schools of the Workmen's Circle], *Bleter far yidisher dertsiung* 4: 1–12.

Yehoyesh (1917), 'Harinte un shifkhe' [Grand lady and maid-servant], in his *Fun nyu-york biz rekhoves un tsurik* [From New York to Rehovot and back], 158–167. New York, Hebrew Publishing Co.

Yofe, Yude A. (1910), 'Shraybn oder shrayben' [Shraybn oder shrayben (= away from or toward a German model in Yiddish orthography], *Literatur* 1: 102–111.

— (1927–1928), 'Der slavisher element in Yidish' [The Slavic component in Yiddish], *Pinkes fun Amopteyl* [Record Book of the American Branch (of the Yivo)] 1: 235–256.

— (1943), 'The development of Yiddish in the United States', *Universal Jewish Encyclopedia* 10: 601–602. (Also note (1936) his earlier 'Yidish in amerike', *Yivo-bleter* 9: 127–145.)

— (1940), 'Hundert un fuftsik yor yidish' [One hundred fifty years of Yiddish]. *Yivo bleter* 15: 87–102. (Somewhat modified (1958) *Yidishe kultur* 20 (5): 21–29.)

Yung, Boaz (1950), *Mayn lebn in dem teater* [My Life in the Theater]. New York, YIKUF.

Z., N. (1944), 'A maskil fun far hundert yorn vegn der yidisher literatur' [A maskil (enlightened man) of a century ago concerning Yiddish literature], *Yivo-bleter* 24: 136–137.

Zamir, Tsvi (1968), 'Yidish in yisroel' [Yiddish in Israel], *Yidishe kultur* 31 (1): 35–38.

Zaretski, A. (1928), 'Vos ken men tun af di erter far yidisher shprakh-arbet?' [What can be done locally on behalf of Yiddish?], *Di yidishe shprakh* 2 (4–5): 11–12, 58–64.

— (1930), 'Problemen fun yidisher lingvotekhnik' [Problems of Yiddish linguatechnics (= language planning)], *Di yidishe shprakh* 4 (1) (20): 1–10.

— (1931a), 'Kegn nepmanishn got' [Against the NEPmanian god] and 'Kegn shovinizm' [Against chauvinism] in his *Far a proletarisher shprakh* [For a Proletarian Language], Kharkov/Kiev, Tsentrfarlag.

— (1931b), 'Shtert nit der dehebreyizatsye fun yidish' [Do not oppose the de-hebraization of Yiddish], in his *Far a proletarisher shprakh* [For a Proletarian Language], Kharkov/Kiev, Tsentrfarlag.

— (1931c), 'Arum a drukfeler' [Concerning a typographical error], in his *Far a proletarisher shprakh* [For a Proletarian Language], Kharkov/Kiev, Tsentrfarlag.

Zaydman, M. F. (1910), *Di hebreyishe kultur konferents* [The Hebrew Culture Conference]. Odessa, Zionist Penny [= Kopike] Library.

Zelitsh, Y. (1968), 'A tsveyte konferents far der yidisher shprakh – 60 yor nokh tshernovits' [A second conference for the Yiddish language – 60 years after Tshernovits], *Afn shvel* 185 (4): 2–3.

Zelkovits, G. (1909), 'Undzer mame-loshn' [Our mother tongue], in his *Literarishe briv* [Literary Letters], 45–46. New York, Hebrew Publishing Co.

Zerubovl, Y. (1936), 'Mir bashuldikn un monen akhrayes!' [We accuse and demand responsibility!], in *Yidish in erets yisroel* [Yiddish in the Land of Israel], 7–18. New York, League for Rights of Yiddish in the Land of Israel.

— (1966), 'Ber borokhov un zayn yidish forshung' [Ber Borokhov and his Yiddish research], in *Shprakh-forshung un literatur-geshikhte* [Language Research and History of Literature], ed. by N. Mayzl, 41–49. Tel Aviv, Perets Farlag.

Zhitlovski, Khayim (1931 [1900]), 'Far vos davke yidish?' [Why necessarily Yiddish?], in his *In kamf far folk un shprakh (gezamlte) shriftn, finfter band* [In the struggle for Nationality and Language (Collected Works, vol. 5)]. Warsaw, Bzhoze.

— (1908–1909), 'Di yidishe shprakh-bavegung un di tshernovitser konferents' [The Yiddish language movement and the Tshernovits conference], *Dos naye lebn* 1: 20–27.

— (1912), 'Di yidishe kultur un di yidishe shprakh' [Jewish culture and the Yiddish language], in his *Gezamlte shriftn* band IV, [Collected Works, vol. 4], 169–171, 179–180, 183. New York, Committee. (Also excerpted (1957) in *Der yidisher gedank in der nayer tsayt* [Jewish Thought in Modern Times], ed. by A. Menes, 288–292. New York, Congress for Jewish Culture.)

— (1914), 'Le-she'eylot ha-yishuv', *Ha-aḥdut* 5 (38/39): 13–21. (Note editorial footnote rejecting author's views.)

— (1923), 'Hebreyizm un yidishizm' [Hebreyism and Yiddishism], *Dos naye lebn* 1 (10): 1–9, (11): 4–14.

— (1928), '"Tshernovits" un der "yidishizm": tsu dem tsvantsik yorikn yoyvl-yontev fun der tshernovitser konferents' ['Tshernovits' and 'Yiddishism': In honor of the 20th anniversary celebration of the Tshernovits Conference], *Tsukunft* December: 735–737.

— (1940), 'Der onheyb fun mayn "yidishizm"' [The beginning of my 'Yiddishism'], in his *Zikhroynes fun mayn lebn, band II* [Memoires of My Life, vol. 2], 80–87. New York, Committee. (In same volume: 'Mayn farlibtkayt in Yidish' [My love for Yiddish], 110–116.)

Zhitnitski, L. (1952), 'Di organizatsye fun der yidisher visnshaft un di organizir-organizatsyes fun der yidisher kultur' [The organization of research on Yiddish and the organizing organizations of Yiddish culture], in his *A halber yorhundert yidishe literatur* [Half a Century of Yiddish Literature], 81–88. Buenos Aires, Eygns.

Zhits, G. (1940), 'Di yidishe bikher-produktsye fun ukrmelukhenatsmindfarlag in 1939 yor un der plan afn 1940 yor' [Yiddish book-production of the ukrmelukhenatsmindfarlag (= Ukrainian Government Publishing House for the Minority Nationalities] in 1939 and plans for 1940], *Sovetishe literatur* (4): 152–157.

Zilberfarb, M. (1928), 'A shedlekhe iluzye' [A harmful illusion], *Bikhervelt* (8): 38–43.

Zilbertsvayg, Zalmen (1956), *Akhed hoom un zayn batsiung tsu yidish* [Aḥad Ha'am and his Attitude Toward Yiddish]. Los Angeles, Elisheva.

— (1968), 'Franz kafke un dos yidishe teater' [Franz Kafka and the Yiddish Theater], *Yidishe kultur* 30, 38–43, 56.

— (1931), *Teater entsiklopedye* [Theater Encyclopedia], first edition. Warsaw, Elisheva. (Second edition (1934) Warsaw Elisheva; third edition (1959), New York, Elisheva; fourth edition (1963), New York, Elisheva; fifth edition (1967), Mexico City; sixth edition (1969), Mexico City.)

Zinberg, Israel: see Tsinberg, Yisroel.

Ziskind, Nosn (1965), 'Printsipn baym forshn yidishe leshoynes' [Principles for researching Jewish languages], *Yidishe shprakh* 25: 1–17.

Zr—li (1922), 'Di ofensive muz opgeshlogn vern' [The offensive must be repulsed], *Shul un lebn* 2 (1–2) (10): 2–6. (See articles in same issue by Y. Lev, H. Erlikh, Kh. Sh. Kazhdan and others on the same theme.)

PART I

Sociohistorical Perspective

Text of the Nobel Lecture by Isaac Bashevis Singer

STOCKHOLM, Dec. 8 (AP) — Following is the text of Isaac Bashevis Singer's Nobel lecture, delivered today before the Swedish Academy.

The storyteller of our time, as in any other time, must be an entertainer of the spirit in the full sense of word, not just a preacher of social and political ideals. There is no paradise for bored readers and no excuse for tedious literature that does not intrigue the reader, uplift his spirit, give him the joy and the escape that true art always grants.

Nevertheless, it is also true that the serious writer of our time must be deeply concerned about the problems of his generation. He cannot but see that the power of religion, especially belief in revelation, is weaker today than it was in any other epoch in human history. More and more children grow up without faith in God, without belief in reward and punishment, in the immortality of the soul and even in the validity of ethics.

The genuine writer cannot ignore the fact that the family is losing its spiritual foundation. All the dismal prophecies of Oswald Spengler have become realities since World War II. No technological achievements can mitigate the disappointment of modern man, his loneliness, his feeling of inferiority, and his fear of war, revolution and terror. Not only has our generation lost faith in Providence but also in man himself, in his institutions and often in those who are nearest to him.

In their despair a number of those who no longer have confidence in the leadership of our society look up to the writer, the master of words. They hope against hope that the man of talent and sensitivity can perhaps rescue civilization. Maybe there is a spark of the prophet in the artist after all.

A New Hope Always Emerges

As the son of a people who received the worst blows that human madness can inflict, I must brood about the forthcoming dangers. I have many times resigned myself to never finding a true way out. But a new hope always emerges telling me that it is not yet too late for all of us to take stock and make a decision.

I was brought up to believe in a free will. Although I came to doubt all revelation, I can never accept the idea that the universe is a physical or chemical accident, a result of blind evolution. Even though I learned to recognize the lies, the clichés and idolatries of the human mind, I still cling to some truths which I think all of us might accept some day.

There must be a way for a man to attain all possible pleasures, all the powers and knowledge that nature can grant him, and still serve God — a God who speaks in deeds, not in words, and whose vocabulary is the cosmos.

I am not ashamed to admit that I belong to those who fantasize that literature is capable of bringing new horizons and new perspectives — philosophical, religious, esthetical and even social. In the history of old Jewish literature there was never any basic difference between the poet and the prophet. Our ancient poetry often became law and a way of life.

Some of my cronies in the cafeteria near The Jewish Daily Forward in New York call me a pessimist and a decadent, but there is always a background of faith behind resignation. I found comfort in such pessimists and decadents as Baudelaire, Verlaine, Edgar Allan Poe, and Strindberg.

Solace in Mystics and a Poet

My interest in psychic research made me find solace in such mystics as your Swedenborg and in our own Rabbi Nachman Bratzlaver, as well as in a great poet of my time, my friend Aaron Zeitlin, who died a few years ago and left a spiritual inheritance of high quality, most of it in Yiddish.

The pessimism of the creative person is not decadence but a mighty passion for redemption of man. While the poet entertains he continues to search for eternal truths, for the essence of being. In his own fashion he tries to solve the riddle of time and change, to find an answer to suffering, to reveal love in the very abyss of cruelty and injustice.

Strange as these words may sound I often play with the idea that when all the social theories collapse and wars and revolutions leave humanity in utter gloom, the poet — whom Plato banned from his Republic — may rise up to save us all.

„דער גרויסער כבוד, וואָס די שוועדישע אַקאַדעמיע האָט מיר אָנגעטאָן, איז אויך אַן אָנערקענונג פֿון אידיש, אַ לשון פֿון גלות, אָן אַ לאַנד, אָן גרענעצן, נישט געשטיצט פֿון קיין שום מלוכה."*

The high honor bestowed upon me by the Swedish Academy is also a recognition of the Yiddish language — a language of exile, without a land, without frontiers, not supported by any government, a language which possesses no words for weapons, ammunition, military exercises, war tactics; a language that was despised by both gentiles and emancipated Jews.

The truth is that what the great religions preached, the Yiddish-speaking people of the ghettos practiced day in and day out. They were the people of the book in the truest sense of the word. They knew of no greater joy than the study of man and human relations, which they called Torah, Talmud, Mussar, cabala.

Ghetto Was an Experiment in Peace

The ghetto was not only a place of refuge for a persecuted minority but a great experiment in peace, in self-discipline and in humanism. As such it still exists and refuses to give up in spite of all the brutality that surrounds it. I was brought up among those people. My father's home on Krochmalna Street in Warsaw was a study house, a court of justice, a house of prayer, of storytelling, as well as a place for weddings and Hasidic banquets.

As a child I had heard from my older brother and master, I.J. Singer, who later wrote "The Brothers Ashkenazi," all the arguments that the rationalists from Spinoza to Max Nordau brought out against religion.

---

*Yiddish typesetting by courtesy of The Jewish Daily Forward.

I have heard from my father and mother all the answers that faith in God could offer to those who doubt and search for the truth. In our home and in many other homes the eternal questions were more actual than the latest news in the Yiddish newspaper. In spite of all the disenchantments and all my skepticism I believe that the nations can learn much from those Jews, their way of thinking, their way of bringing up children, their finding happiness where others see nothing but misery and humiliation. To me the Yiddish language and the conduct of those who spoke it are identical.

One can find in the Yiddish tongue and in the Yiddish spirit expressions of pious joy, lust for life, longing for the Messiah, patience and deep appreciation of human individuality. There is a quiet humor in Yiddish and a gratitude for every day of life, every crumb of success, each encounter of love.

Yiddish Mentality Is Not Haughty

The Yiddish mentality is not haughty. It does not take victory for granted. It does not demand and command but it muddles through, sneaks by, smuggles itself amidst the powers of destruction, knowing somewhere that God's plan for Creation is still at the very beginning.

There are some who call Yiddish a dead language, but so was Hebrew called for 2,000 years. It has been revived in our time in a most remarkable, almost miraculous way. Aramaic was certainly a dead language for centuries but then it brought to light the Zohar, a work of mysticism of sublime value. It is a fact that the classics of Yiddish literature are also the classics of the modern Hebrew literature.

Yiddish has not yet said its last word. It contains treasures that have not been revealed to the eyes of the world. It was the tongue of martyrs and saints, of dreamers and cabalists — rich in humor and in memories that mankind may never forget. In a figurative way, Yiddish is the wise and humble language of us all, the idiom of the frightened and hopeful humanity.

From the text of the Nobel Prize lecture by Isaac Bashevis Singer, December 8, 1978. (*New York Times*, December 9, 1978).

a. What Is Yiddish?

Yiddish is the language of a considerable portion of the Jewish people the world over. It has served as the expression of everyday Jewish life, religious and secular, for a thousand years. It possesses a large literature and folklore and a lively daily and periodic press. It also serves as the primary or subsidiary language of instruction in many Jewish schools of different types. It is the language that most easily connects the Jews of different countries.

b. The Name 'Yiddish'

Yiddish *means ' Jewish' in the language itself. It is the name that Jews themselves have given their language many centuries ago. In English usage, the name was adopted around the middle of the 19th century in England, when Jewish immigrants started coming to that country. With the rising immigration of the Jews to the United States, the name was adopted here also.*

c.
פֿאַר וואָס איז ייִדיש נייטיק פֿאַר דעם בוי און פֿאַר
דער אַנטוויקלונג פֿון אַמעריקאַנער ייִדנטום?
דערפֿאַר, ווײַל ייִדיש איז דער פֿולסטער, דער גאַנצ־
סטער, דער געטרייסטער וועג צו אונדזער פֿאָלק, ווײַל
עס שטעלט מיט זיך פֿאַר די פֿולסטע אַנטוויקלונג פֿון
די שעפֿערישע כּוחות אין דעם ייִדישן לעבן; ווײַל עס
ברענגט צו אונדז האַרציקער ליבשאַפֿט פֿון ייִדישע דורות
וואָס האָבן געבענקט און געשטרעבט; ווײַל ייִדיש פֿאַר־
בינדט אונדז מיט ייִדן פֿון אַנדערע ישובֿים, ווײַל ייִדיש
איז די טרעגערין פֿון דער היסטאָרישער דערפֿאַרונג פֿון
טויזנט יאָר ייִדיש לעבן.

Mottos for Part I

(a) and (b) *Basic Facts About Yiddish*. New York, Yivo Institute for Jewish Research (at that time: Yiddish Scientific Institute – Yivo), 1947. (Reissued over a dozen times in thousands of copies and available today upon request).

(c) 'Why is Yiddish needed for the growth and development of American Jewry?

Because Yiddish is the richest, the most complete, the most faithful path to our people; because it represents the fullest development of the creative forces in Jewish life; because it leads us to heartfelt love of Jewish generations that longed and aspired; because Yiddish unites us with the Jews in other communities; because Yiddish is the bearer of the historic experience of a thousand years of Jewish life.' Khayim Bez. *Shrayber un verk* [Writers and Works]. Tel Aviv, Hamenora, 1971, 558–559.

The Reality of Jewishness versus the Ghetto Myth: The Sociolinguistic Roots of Yiddish

MAX WEINREICH

1. Without a separate community there is no separate language. Yiddish has been the language of the Ashkenazic subculture group of the Jewish people ever since the emergence of that group eleven hundred years ago, when Jews began to settle in the Middle–Rhine–Moselle territory which they called *Loter* (cf. *Lotharii regnum*, *Lotharingia*). The question thus arises of how the Ashkenazic community originated and what forces have kept it alive as a distinct entity ever since. To keep the discussion within limits, no effort will be made to take into account the history of the Sefardic or any other Jewish subculture group; though many analogies and similarities might be adduced, it is preferable to explore one Jewish subculture area more or less thoroughly and only then to proceed to analyze another one on a comparative basis.

2. What was it that made for the peculiar position of the Jews in the Middle Ages and later, until emancipation came along? It was the *ghetto*, we are told and told again, which was at the root of Jewish living during the long centuries of darkness. Time was, so the argument runs, when the Jews in German lands were not distinguished from their compatriots except by their religion. The Jews behaved and spoke as the Germans did and, in the thirteenth century, even produced a German *minnesinger*, Suezkint von Trimberg. But then, under conditions of growing religious intolerance, they were pressed into the ghettos and thus excluded from general society. As a consequence, they deteriorated over the centuries economically, intellectually, and morally. Their German language, which they had previously spoken like every other German person, declined too. The implication was plain. As soon as the sun of tolerance rose, the Jews would again embrace German culture and differ from the bulk of the German population solely by their faith.

The sources and references that might have gone into footnotes to this paper will be found in my two-volume *History of the Yiddish Language: Concepts, Facts, Methods* (1973).
Editor's note: The *History* to which the author referred in 1967 finally appeared as a *four*-volume work (two volumes text and two volumes notes) *in Yiddish* in 1973. An English translation of the first two Yiddish volumes (published in one volume in English) appeared in 1980.

This theory, however, is of rather recent origin. It goes back no further than the second half of the eighteenth century, i.e. the age of Enlightenment, and can be shown to have been developed by the nineteenth-century historians who found themselves fighting for Jewish emancipation.

In preemancipation days, as is well known, the Jews in Central Europe had been largely confined to living quarters of their own. When the repercussions of the French revolution made it possible for the Jews to demand emancipation, restrictions in housing must have appeared to be particularly oppressive. It is then that the ghetto concept became a recurrent topic until it finally was accepted as incontestable evidence. Instead, it must be conceived of as an ad hoc explanation in a political struggle.

3. There would be no point in disparaging historic constructions of bygone days that were intended to serve legitimate political purposes. But it would be equally naïve to accept this kind of fictions at their face value, since they obscure the issue and blur our understanding of the past.

The weakness of the nineteenth-century construction is revealed as soon as one tries to make chronology a bit more exact. When was it that the Jews were excluded from society?

Graetz, the renowned historian of the Jews, believed that this exclusion had begun with the first crusade. But it is only in the ninth century that Jews are again mentioned on German soil after an interval of almost four hundred years. Down to the end of the eleventh century the data are highly fragmentary, to say the least, and with regard to some of the few attestations there is no proof that Jewish communities, and not individual Jews, are referred to. Furthermore, prior to 1096, there is no claim to intellectual excellence in German society from which the Jews allegedly had been excluded. Thus, if we were to follow Graetz, there actually never was any appreciable participation of German Jews in German cultural life until the nineteenth century.

Other representatives of the German-reared 'science of Judaism' would have it that the exclusion of the Jews from German society took place as late as in the thirteenth century or even later. This supposition makes more sense inasmuch as it is common knowledge that in the thirteenth century the legal position of the Jews in German lands began to deteriorate. It was the so-called Lateran church council of 1215 which promulgated a number of restrictive measures, and after some decades of more or less vigorous attempts these measures were enforced. Limitations with regard to the acquisition of land and to trade were imposed; a Jewish hat and, subsequently, the yellow badge were introduced to mark the Jews as members of a group apart. Housing conditions, too, changed for the worse in that separate Jewish living quarters were compulsory in many German cities and towns.

4. The stress in the last sentence, however, is on the word compulsory. A verb like 'introduced' would have been misleading. What happened was that

in the thirteenth century segregated living quarters for the Jews were made compulsory. The fact of the matter is that separate Jewish streets had existed all along ever since the Jews appeared in Loter. Separate dwellings of the Jews are mentioned in all the German cities where the existence of Jews is attested to in the centuries preceding the first crusade, such as Worms, Mayence, Cologne, Ratisbon, Speyer. Kurt Pinthus, in pre-Hitler Germany an ardent student of medieval town layouts and town planning, has been given far too little recognition by sociologists. He has demonstrated both the pertinent facts and their implications on the evidence of more than one hundred cities and towns in Germany and adjacent countries. In the earliest Jewish settlements, while the towns were still in their formative stage, the oldest Jewish streets were located near the principal church and the market place. But the later Jewish settlers in communities already firmly established were given less advantageous dwellings near the gates or even behind the city walls. The inference is plain. The Jews were the typical urban settlers; their part in agriculture must have been insignificant even while ownership of or settlement on the land was not legally denied to them. As town dwellers the Jews were a highly desired element to attract ('*cum ex Spirensi villa urbem facerem, putavi milies amplificare honorem loci nostri, si et Judeos colligerem*', as the bishop of Speyer put it in 1084), and, in view of their urban-type occupations – overland trade and small-scale trading on the spot, money trade – it was very convenient for them to live as close as possible to the town center and the main thoroughfares.

5. If the Jews lived together long before segregated living quarters were imposed upon them, then this segregation must have been voluntary. It was. Living apart, no matter how bizarre this may appear in the light of present-day concepts and attitudes, was part of the 'privileges' accorded to the Jews in conformity with their own wishes. They wanted to be among their own people, to be able to worship collectively, to study, to apply to their own courts of law, not to speak of their urgent need to maintain a ritual slaughterhouse and a ritual bath and to be buried, when time came, in a Jewish cemetery.

Settling in groups, be it by ethnic origin, by religion, or by occupation was an established pattern in the Middle Ages and even much later. There was consequently nothing unusual, let alone degrading, in the very fact that the Jews clung together. There are documented cases to show that every now and then the Jews asked for *permission* to live together in a definite part of the town because they felt safer this way.

To be sure, there was a tremendous difference between conditions at the earlier stage and those which developed after the thirteenth century. Before that, some Jews lived among Christians and, conversely, some Christians lived *apud Iudaeos*, in the predominantly Jewish streets. Later, the Jews were compelled to live only in the assigned areas and were permitted to leave their quarters only during daytime. Even in the forcibly segregated quarters, of course, the houses themselves were constructed of the same material and according to the same design as the buildings in the town, and the Jewish dwellings were distinguishable only by the *mezuzes* attached to the doorposts. But as the Jewish population increased and the area of their settlement remained fixed once and for all, the narrowness in space was felt more severely and it became more difficult to adhere to a modicum of hygienic requirements.

6. But this is not to say that the very fact of living in separate quarters was considered oppressive. Historic periods must be understood in their own frames of reference. Medieval Jewish writings are chiefly concerned with internal problems of Jewish living and thinking, but, naturally, they also reflect massacres, expulsions, tribulations of all kinds. Yet we have still to come across one single complaint about the Jews being 'excluded from society'. There is no statement to that effect and there could not be one. The obvious fact is that at all times the Jews hated oppression and those responsible for it, but, as the societal system gave them no opportunity of outright fight or political struggle, they just tried to offset the consequences of enmity and malice as best they could. Essentially, they wanted to be left alone.

Significantly, before the pre-emancipation period, the term *ghetto*, which originated in Venice in the sixteenth century and spread from there to other Italian cities, was never used, either in a derogatory or in a matter-of-fact manner, to designate the local Jewish living quarters in Central or Eastern Europe. Very infrequent occurrences of *ghetto* in pre-nineteenth-century German sources invariably refer to Italian conditions. In the Jewish environment, the designation was *di yidngas* in Western Yiddish and *di yidishe gas* in Eastern Yiddish, both meaning 'the Jewish street', as opposed to *dos mokem* 'the [non-Jewish] town'. (All Jewish terms in this paper are quoted in their Yiddish versions even if they are of Hebrew-Aramaic origin.) The still popular Yiddish idiom *af der yidisher gas* 'in the Jewish street' is the equivalent of 'among Jews'. It has always been neutral in its connotations, in sharp contrast to the term *ghetto* which is now being associated with the Germans in World War II.

7. German political scientists have worked hard to obscure the issue further. In order to provide the necessary backing for the extermination practices of the years 1939–1945, those scholars gave the German-made Jewish quarters of World War II the name ghetto, which had become habitual, if distasteful, in the last one hundred and fifty years or so, and then proceeded to show that Hitler's policy was only a return to the 'clear-cut separation' (*reinliche Scheidung*), the preestablished social order of the Middle Ages disturbed by eighteenth-century rationalism and its aftermath.

Yet, the purported analogy between the Hitler era and the Middle Ages is a gross injustice to the latter. In the period of voluntary separation, the famous rabbinical scholar Eliezer ben Joel Halevi (born ±1140 in Mayence) wrote: '...We are living among the Gentiles, and [non-Jewish] maid servants and housekeepers and male Gentiles constantly move around in our dwellings'. But even the Jewish living quarters in German towns since the thirteenth century, for all their crowdedness and ensuing squalor, were only half closed; during daytime, the Jews could move freely through the non-Jewish sections of the town and on overland journeys they were allowed to take off their yellow badges so as not to attract the attention of hoodlums looking for easy prey. In contradistinction, the ghettos set up by the Germans during the last war were grandiose concentration camps in which several million Jews were rounded up on short notice so that they be ready for the 'final solution of the Jewish question'. Before the gas chambers took over, the ghettos were hermetically closed to outsiders and whoever tried to escape was shot on sight.

It is a curious contribution to the sociology of knowledge that no German scholar has bothered to expose the fraud of the ghetto protagonists in the twenty-odd years in which, it would seem, a discussion of this matter would no longer have been dangerous.

8. There is just no point in the assumption that such a potent and consistent culture system as that of Ashkenaz was created and sustained by the existence of separate living quarters, compulsory or otherwise. Suffice it to say that roughly comparable 'ghetto' housing conditions in racially troubled northern American cities of today are frequently blamed for working in exactly the opposite direction. It is widely accepted that they lead to the breakdown of family relations, lack of cultural stimulation, reduction of literacy and so on. But if so, how could separate living quarters have led to the rise of a civilization like that of Ashkenaz?

As a substitute for the ghetto theory, the idea is sometimes advanced that Jewish separateness was born from and sustained by Jewish communal autonomy. We may recall the statement of Napoleon supported by one faction of Jewish leaders to the effect that the Jews could expect everything as individuals, but nothing as a 'nation', i.e. as a group. When the Tsarist government, in 1844, in its crude way, decided to put an end to Jewish particularism, it clamped down on the Jewish '*kahals*', and some Jewish progressivists felt this was the right thing to do. It is well known that wherever the Jews lived – and this applies to non-Ashkenazic and pre-Ashkenazic conditions as well – they enjoyed a certain degree of self-government. In the 'privileges' issued by German princes and cities, this point is invariably stressed. The procedure of delegating rights and responsibilities to the inhabitants of the growing urban settlements was customary in medieval Europe; it also applied to merchants, craftsmen etc., and the Jews were no exception.

When in the course of the eleventh and twelfth centuries, the Jews became *servi camerae*, i.e. people placed under the immediate protection of the emperor, the Jews became even more distinguishable among the townspeople. The Jewish community had its own officials (*rosh-hakoel*, *parnes*, *gabe*, *balebos* etc. are

Mendele's last journey. The author of 'Journeys of Benjamin the Third' is accompanied to his heavenly reward by angels carrying gifts of honor, immortality, love of the people, and fame. (*Der groyser kundes*, December 21, 1917)*

* Cartoons provide an avenue through which one can study the affective dimension of social, cultural and political history. Many of the cartoons presented in this volume are taken from *Der groyser kundes*: 'A Journal of Humor, Jest and Satire' (1909–1928), an influential medium of pro-Yiddish social criticism, edited by Jacob Marinoff. It amply reveals the three-front struggle of Yiddishism, rivalled and opposed by adherents of English, Hebrew, and 'vulgar Yiddish'. The brunt of the *Kundes*' critique is aimed at the latter camp (often epitomized by the *Forverts* or its editor Abraham Cahan), with its purported disregard for and antipathy toward standard Yiddish vocabulary, grammar and orthography. Although there are glimmerings of awareness that the fate of Yiddish is being sealed by more major sociopolitical processes in the United States, Europe, and Palestine, and although some Yiddish writers and actors have begun searching for immortality via other languages, nevertheless, *intra*-Yiddish linguistic differences and the struggle with local Hebraists, both crusades epitomized by the figure of Dr. Khayim Zhitlovski, are clearly stressed.

pre-Ashkenazic terms) as well as courts (*bezdn*), whose verdicts in civil matters were unreservedly accepted by the non-Jewish authorities. It goes without saying that the Jews themselves carried the burden of maintaining, on their own terms, their educational and charitable institutions.

It therefore stands to reason that the existence of autonomous communal institutions was linked with Jewish cultural identity. However, cause and effect should be carefully weighed. If there is a community that wishes to perpetuate itself, it establishes institutions for those needs that can be met only on a supraindividual basis. This supreme purpose, the survival of the group, was served in manifold ways. There were institutions like the prayer house or houses, the ritual slaughterhouse, the infirmary, the *tantshous* ('dance house' where weddings were celebrated), the cemetery, and the like. In spheres requiring less centralization, unattached membership organizations (*khevres*) were active, devoted to charity or study, or both. It can be shown, however, that the real nucleus of Jewish life was neither the *kahal* nor the less pretentious *khevre*, but the family. Somewhat precariously, even a lonely Jewish family surrounded by non-Jews could maintain its Jewishness if it wanted to; impressive analogies can be drawn with Jewish villagers (*yishúvnikes*) in nineteenth and twentieth century Eastern Europe.

In short, the basic causes for the rise and the continuing existence of Ashkenaz must be sought not in curbs imposed from outside or in certain institutions but in the vitality of the society which, in spite of seemingly overwhelming odds, managed to keep its head above water.

9. Ashkenazic reality is to be sought between the two poles of absolute identity with and absolute remoteness from the coterritorial non-Jewish communities. To compress it into a formula, what the Jews aimed at was not isolation from the Christians but insulation from Christianity. Although, throughout the ages, many Jews must be supposed to have left the fold, the community as a whole did succeed in surviving and developing. On the other hand, the close and continuous ties of the Jews with their neighbors, which used to be severed only for a while during actual outbreaks of persecutions, manifested themselves in customs and folk beliefs; in legends and songs; in literary production, etc. The culture patterns prevalent among Ashkenazic Jews must be classified as Jewish, but very many of them are specifically Ashkenazic. They are mid-course formations as those found wherever cultures meet along frontiers, in border zones, or in territories with mixed populations.

The most striking result of this encounter of cultures is the Yiddish language. When the Jews entered Loter, their vernaculars were western Laaz and southern Laaz, the Jewish correlates of Old French and Old Italian, while Hebrew–Aramaic was their sacred tongue. But the non-Jewish population of Loter spoke regional variants of German, and it is this German determinant which brought into the new fusion language of Ashkenaz its quantitatively strongest component.

Is this not irrefutable proof of a high degree of contact? On the other hand, the Ashkenazim did not simply become German speakers but fused their acquisitions from German with what they had brought with them in their Hebrew–Aramaic and Laaz determinants. The same applies to the Slavic determinant which made itself felt after the middle of the thirteenth century. Doesn't this, in turn, testify to a remarkable degree of independence?

10. Traditional Ashkenazic Jewishness (*yidishkeyt* is the authentic term) is not coterritorial 'general' culture plus some Jewish additives, but a different sphere of life, a civilization of its own which, to be sure, in many respects resembled that of the non-Jewish neighbors.

In principle, the distance between Jewishness and the culture of the environment was signified by the expression *lehavdl* 'to discern'. An anthropologist approaching the two societies from outside will have to conclude that the Ashkenazic Jews, just as their Gentile neighbors, were preoccupied with helping the needy, with visiting the sick, with praying with a dying person, and with mourning the deceased. But this outward resemblance was of no consequence to the ordinary members or the leaders of the Jewish community. What counted was the fact that Jewish culture patterns could be conceived of in internal Jewish terms, as based on earlier Jewish precepts and practices ultimately grounded in the Talmud and the Bible. Viewed this way, charity is a distinctly Jewish trait; the Jews consider themselves 'the merciful and the children of the merciful', and 'Charity saves from death' is a statement contained in the book of Proverbs. The good deed of visiting the sick (*biker-khoylim*) is mentioned in the Talmud. Confession of sins in one's last hour, though not in its present wording, is known from the Pentateuch. So is mourning the dead, and nobody seems to have worried that some conspicuous Jewish customs in this domain had been taken over from the Christians.

The great Sefardi Don Isaac Abarbanel contended that the Ashkenazic manner of ordaining rabbis (*smikhe*) was patterned after the way the Gentiles granted their doctorates. Serious modern scholars tend to side with Abarbanel. But the accusation was of no concern to the Ashkenazic leaders. They could point to the fact that *smikha* (both the term and the general idea) appear in the Talmud.

To make a long story short: many non-Jewish patterns were incorporated into the Jewish system at an early date and throughout, but the division into Jewishness vs. non-Jewishness was never abolished or questioned. It thus turns out that the very existence of a division is much more important than the actual location of the division line.

To put it even more bluntly, and this applies to any field of culture: more often than not, it appears, the distance between Jewish and non-Jewish patterns is created not by a difference in the ingredients proper but rather by the way they are interpreted as elements of the given system. There was no particular reluctance to use church motifs in the construction and ornamentation of Jewish prayer houses in Loter, and nineteenth-century Western Ashkenaz knows of at least some synagogues (by no means reformed ones!) possessing and using bells.

11. It is the positive factor of striving for meaningful survival, and not the negative one of exclusion or rejection, that is paramount in Jewish cultural history. One would be tempted to speak of Jewish religion if not for the fact that this term presupposes a sphere of life *not* affected by religion. But there is no such division into separate spheres in *yidishkeyt*. Natural sciences, philosophy, law, art, literature – all of them stem directly from the same divine source, just as there is no action so trivial as to escape religiously colored regulation or restriction. Needless to say, there are degrees of sanctity, but, as a matter of course, every nook and cranny of life is sanctified.

In the early days of Ashkenaz the term *derekh-hashás* 'the way of the Talmud' came into being. Though intended as a designation for the way of studying the Talmud, it can conveniently be converted into a term describing the traditional *way of life based upon the Talmud*. The Almighty is our God and the God of our forefathers. He is the God who helped Abraham on Mount Moriah when he was about to sacrifice Isaac. The specificness of Jewish fate became apparent when the two sons of Rebecca, Jacob and Esau, struggled in her womb. Jacob is Israel, identified with the people of Israel, and Esau is Edom, ancestor not only of Haman, but also of Christian Europe. By the same token, the antithesis of Jews and Muslims is expressed in the Isaac vs. Ishmael prefiguration.

In this emotional and intellectual framework, the exclusion-from-society concept simply fades away. Jewish separateness is not even the result of dispersion after the fall of the Second Temple. Jewishness stems from the fact that God made the Jews his chosen people, not for their aggrandizement of course but to sanctify his name. The division into Jews and Gentiles is going to last until the advent of the Messiah. Jewish history thus represents one uninterrupted whole. Past and present converge and merge. Under such circumstances it is easy to fall into what the modern historian calls anachronisms. They are conspicuous by their number. When Jacob arrived in Egypt and met Joseph, he was just in the midst of prayer and could not instantly pause to greet his son. At the courts of King David and King Solomon, the choice dishes were fish and chicken (*Shmuel-bukh, Melokhim-bukh*).

But what to one generation is utter naïveté was plain common sense to another. The *derekh-hashás*, like any pre-modern view of the world, was not overly concerned with historical periods. In most cases, one was satisfied with general indications like *time was* or *in bygone days*. Rabbinical legists are classified as *rishoynim* ('the ancients') and *akhroynim* ('the late ones') but, significantly, the designation is relative. Rabbi Meir of Rothenburg (thirteenth century) belongs to the late ones as compared to Rabbi Gershom the Light of the Exile (who died in the second quarter of the eleventh century), but is an undisputed 'ancient' when related to the great legists of the fifteenth and sixteenth centuries. Time designations are not ignored, but they are not overemphasized either.

Given this relativity, there was the opportunity to explain contemporary events in Talmudic terms and, conversely, to understand the Talmud in the light of contemporary circumstances. By this double-pronged interpretation, the rabbinical writings of all times defy classification as literary works (though Westernized usage refers to 'rabbinical literature'). They were transformed into active elements in the life of all periods and have become a continuum. The Western concept of anachronism holds no longer; panchronism seems to describe the situation much more adequately.

In this system, not every shred of the past is sanctified just because it is time honored. Let us recall that the Samaritans, and later the Karaites, did break away from the Jewish community precisely because they refused to move on. At least this is the picture of the secessions as presented by Jewish tradition; the *altera pars* may have quite a different case to offer. Be this as it may, secessions did occur. The *derekh-hashás* has even set up, as it were, a constitutional procedure for effectuating changes. 'The Tora contains everything', so the Yiddish saying goes, but the Talmud is the oral Tora and thus undisputed in its authority. Actual Jewish life is defined by *dinim* (laws) and *minhogim* (customs). But a breach may occur even in a law if the needs of the hour necessitate it, and certainly no custom is sacrosanct because it is old. The term *silly custom* goes back to the end of the first millennium, and the Yiddish proverb *a minheg brekht a din* ('A custom breaks a law') is modeled after a Talmudic prototype.

To the insider, the *derekh-hashás* is founded upon a set of *norms* derived from tradition, not upon behavior patterns indiscriminately heaped upon each other in an unending sequence of generations.

12. There is no provision for appellate courts, no hierarchy culminating in an infallible head. The tools of remaking the norms are again books, the huge derivative literature beginning in the Talmudic period and reaching into the present. What Mohammed is supposed to have said derisively about Jews (and Christians) has been made by the Jews into unconditional praise: they pride themselves of being 'the people of the book'.

The highest form of literary achievement is the *peyresh* ('commentary'). The authority of the book commented upon is taken for granted, but so is the right of the commenter to elaborate, to point to deficiencies, and to propose emendations. There are quite a number of commentaries on commentaries as well. Every later-day scholar navigates freely in the 'sea of the Talmud'.

With regard to ritual observance, the *decisors* are in the forefront. A learned man is described as being thoroughly versed in *shas un poskim* ('Talmud and decisors'). It is not the modern critical school which found out that the Talmud could not possibly have covered all dubious cases of behavior; the Geonim in Babylonia and Palestine, more than one thousand years ago, used to decide on the basis of precedent and analogy. Later generations of decisors leaned upon the Geonim as well. The *Shulkhn orukh*, compiled in the sixteenth century by the great Sefardi Rabbi Joseph Karo, seemed to subsume the whole halakic wisdom of the Middle Ages, and the annotations of R. Moshe Iserlis of Cracow (the Ramó) to his work seemed to have provided the Ashkenazic version of this impressive codification. But again, new times created new situations, and these in turn called for new clarification in the light of the Tora. In short, the stream of new decisions has never stopped.

It has long been customary that in pondering a difficult problem (*shayle* is the technical term) a rabbi would not rely upon himself but would rather submit the case with the pertinent details to another authority, sometimes to more than one. Many scholars kept records of the inquiries addressed to them and arranged them, together with their replies (*tshuves*) into books. This is the origin of the literary genre of *shayles-utshuves* ('problems and answers') known in Western terminology as *responsa*. Their beginnings reach into the Talmudic period. As time went on, and particularly since the advent of printing, more and more *responsa* were compiled. In many of them, one may surmise, the authors merely used the queries-and-answers form as a literary device to propound halakic problems by way of adducing concrete illustrations.

It is only in retrospect that we can appreciate the role of the halakic books of different types in maintaining the continuity of Jewish thought and action. No less did they contribute to the integration, successful on the whole, of the Jewish community into constantly changing conditions.

Moreover, while there was unremittent insistence on conformity, there was also an implied admission of equally legitimate variants. There is hardly another crisis which shook Ashkenazic society as deeply as the clash between Khasidism and its opponents in the last quarter of the eighteenth century, but one hundred years later the representatives of the two factions felt again as one as they were confronted with the pressing problems of a new day. The smarting awareness of profound dissensions could be soothed by the existence of the Talmudic saying 'Both of these [variants] are the words of the Living God'. To a Westernized mind, it is difficult to grasp the full validity of a pertinent quotation from an authoritative source. But just as in any society, different personality types are to be found in Ashkenaz too. A bold scholar would every now and then contest even the opinion of an outstanding authority.

13. Thus, diversified concepts and practices could be legitimated by leaning upon diversified experiences of the past. This ability to adjust and readjust and to recognize, within prescribed limits, widely differing variants stood the Yiddish speech community in good stead when it was put to its greatest test.

Ultimately as a sequel of the industrial revolution, what may be called the secular sector of Ashkenazic society came into being. Insignificant in numbers at the outset, it has grown gradually and by now elements of secularism have affected even the most traditionally minded member of the community. While the Jew who is consciously antireligious is definitely in the minority, he does exist and may otherwise be closely attached to the community by virtue of tradition, language, nationalism, or political affiliation. Until the secular sector sprang up the antireligious or even nonreligious Jew used to be a *contradictio in adiecto*.

This most divergent version of *yidishkeyt*, 'secular *yidishkeyt*', has come to be accepted as one of the many versions of being a Jew. When looking for the set of historical circumstances that made this extraordinary sociological phenomenon possible, we will see that it was the initial pattern of Ashkenazic Jewry which was laid down in Loter more than one thousand years ago and may be described as legitimate broad diversity within fundamental unity.

14. The distance between the Jewish and the non-Jewish environments was bound to find its reflection in language. Just as the culture out of which it was born, Yiddish, the language of Ashkenaz, cannot be properly understood as 'Gentile plus', i.e. the German language plus some additives like 'Hebrew-Aramaic words' and 'Slavic words'. Yiddish, too, is a mid-course formation or, to remain within the confines of linguistics, it is a fusion language.

As we think of the linguistic determinants from which the components of Yiddish stem, we are immediately struck by a signal qualitative difference between them. Hebrew-Aramaic has been the sacred tongue of the Jews since time immemorial, the carrier of non-Christianity long before Yiddish came into being. To put it differently, Hebrew-Aramaic has been the language of *yidishkeyt* pure and simple, Yiddish has been the specific language of Ashkenazic *yidishkeyt*. Non-Christian, too, were the prelanguages which the settlers from the Romance-speaking countries brought with them to Loter. Old French and Old Italian, to be sure, were 'Christian' languages, but their Jewish correlates, western Laaz and southern Laaz, were not. As opposed to these determinants, Hebrew-Aramaic and Laaz, the other two, German and Slavic, were reflections of Christian cultures.

In the period of Earliest Yiddish (—1250), when Slavic had not yet entered the picture, Christian linguistic influences could come into nascent Yiddish only through German, the language of the coterritorial population. Therefore, figuratively speaking, a border guard had to be established to keep away linguistic items which have specific Christian meanings or connotations, or else to endow these items with Jewish meanings. To quote but one example for each case, Old High German *sëganōn* (cf. Modern German *segnen*) was no good because, at the time, it apparently still evoked the idea of Latin *signare* 'to make the sign (of the cross)'. Thus *bentshn* emerged as a transfer from southern Laaz (cf. Latin *benedicere*) which to this very day is the standard Yiddish verb for 'bless'. On the other hand, *reynikeyt* was taken over from medieval German (cf. Middle High German *reinekeit* 'purity'), but the Yiddish meaning is 'scroll of the Tora'.

Even the unreligious Jew – just as the observant one – is bound by the fact that Yiddish throughout history has been a non-Christian language and that terms like *Trinity, Savior, original sin, purgatory, host, last communion* etc. for a long time did not exist at all, because there was no need for them, while they have been a must in every 'Christian' language. At present, due to the secular sector, words of this sphere do exist, but they are still of a somewhat marginal nature. Their novelty consists in their neutrality, but, as long as there are no Christian Jews within the Yiddish speaking community, the terms can never acquire the emotive overtones which they possess in Christian societies.

15. On the other hand, the secular sector to a large degree must be credited with having contributed to the Yiddish vocabulary thousands upon thousands of new coinages in science and technology, politics, and so on, many of which have made their appearance several hundred years earlier in Western languages but were never required in traditional Ashkenazic society. Be it

די אָרגאַניזאַציע פון
דער יידישער וויסנשאַפט

נ. סטיף. וועגן אַ יידישן אַקאַדעמישן אינ־
סטיטוט./ווילנער טעזיסן וועגן
יידישן וויסנשאַפטלעכן אינסטי־
טוט. / רעזאָלוצע פון צווייטן
שולצוזאַמענפאָר.

אַרויסגעגעבן פון צב׳׳ק אין ווילֹ׳יִב

ווילנע, 1925

פּראָיעקט פון נ. שטיף און „ווילנער טעזיסן" וועגן דער
גרינדונג פון ייוואָ

Project by N. Shtiff and ''Vilna Theses'' about the establishment of YIVO

תוכנית של נ. שטיף ו„תיזות וילנאית" על יסוד „ייוואָ"

Проект Н. Штифа и „виленские тезисы" об осно-
вании „ИВО"   1925

'The organization of Jewish research (by N. Shtif, 1925): about a Yiddish academic institute...Yiddish Scientific Institute (Yivo)...Resolutions of the second school conference.'

remembered that the Yiddish press, the theater, the East European school systems up to the college level with Yiddish as the language of instruction originated almost exclusively in the secular sector. Obviously, once the innovations had appeared on the scene, they also penetrated into the traditional strata and the interstitial areas where the clear-cut ideological distinctions are difficult to apply. At any rate, whatever is in vogue in any part of the speech community is potentially open to any member of the community.

16. The shifting features of Yiddish, but also its panchronic character come to light nowhere more clearly than in the two literary languages it evolved in the course of its history. Primarily, these two formations must be defined by the regional varieties on which they were based. The 'first literary language', which reached its peak in the fifteenth and sixteenth centuries and had not run its full course until the beginning of the nineteenth century, rested upon the regional varieties of Western Yiddish. But as the center of gravity of the speech community shifted to the East, the structure of the literary language became less and less satisfactory, and around 1750 there erupted a new trend which in the nineteenth century brought about the 'second literary language' based almost entirely on Eastern Yiddish. Only slender threads link it directly with the lexical and stylistic devices of the more distant past.

The same developments, however, must also be viewed from a different vantage point. The First Literary Language by no means was used exclusively in strictly religious writings. Old Yiddish literature was all-inclusive to reflect the all-inclusiveness of Ashkenazic society as it existed in the pre-emancipation period. But the Second Literary Language came as the result not only of a regional switch, but also of a social upheaval. Edifying books of the earlier period were now rewritten and republished to suit the East European readers, and new writings of the old types were added. But the new Yiddish poetry and prose which has blossomed since the middle of the nineteenth century and, obviously, uses the new literary vehicle exlusively has been overwhelmingly the product of the secular sector.

This new literary language, as intimated, is the result of fusion with regard to the underlying dialectal substructure. In a social sense, it also reflects an intense process of fusion. On the basis of the *English-Yiddish Yiddish-English Dictionary* by Uriel Weinreich, which YIVO brought out in 1967, these conclusions could even be quantified, but the general qualitative statement is well beyond doubt. Contemporary Yiddish has acquired the preciseness and flexibility of the Western languages, not in the least under their influence. Yet, the imagery has remained to a large degree that of traditional Ashkenazic folk life. For some time it seemed (the 1920s might have given this impression to the outsider) that the secular sector was about to part ways linguistically with the traditional strata since both were driving in opposite directions. No such premonitions are felt now, due to the cohesive forces in the Ashkenazic community which were reinforced by the experiences common to all European Jews in the years of the German war against the Jews. So again, while actual cultivation of Yiddish language and literature is still by and large limited to the secular sector, the traditionalists share in this development in growing measure. So far, Ashkenazic cohesiveness and all-inclusiveness have stood the test in the field of Yiddish as well.

REFERENCES

Weinreich, Max (1973), *Geshikhte fun der yidisher shprakh: bagrifn, factn, metodn.* [History of The Yiddish Language: Concepts, Facts, Methods.] New York, Yivo Institute for Jewish Research.

1

בעל מחשבות
(ד״ר ישראל־איסידאר עליאשעוו)
קאָוונע, ליטע,   1873
קאָוונע, ליטע,   1924

—◆—

אונזער צוויי־שפּראַכיקע ליטע־
ראַטור
דרײַ שטעטלעך
ליטעראַרישע געשפּרעכן
איראָנישע מעשהלעך

———

ליטעראַטור - קריטיקער,
עסייאיסט

2

שמואל ניגער   (טשארני)
דוקאָר, ווייס־רוסלאַנד,   1883
ניו יאָרק. פֿאַר. שטאַטן,   1955

—◆—

וועגן ײִדישע שרײַבער
דערצײַלער און ראָמאַניסטן
י. ל. פּרץ.   (מאָנאָגראַפֿיע)
ה. לייוויק,   (מאָנאָגראַפֿיע)

———

ליטעראַטור־
פֿאָרשער און קריטיקער

3

ד״ר נחום שטיף
(בעל דמיון)
ראָוונע, וואָלין,   1879
מאָסקווע, ראַטנרוסלאַנד,   1934

—◆—

אָרגאַניזאַציע פֿון דער ײִדישער
וויסנשאַפֿט
ײִדישע סטיליסטיק
די אַלטערע ײִדישע ליטעראַטור
ײִדן און ײִדיש, (ווער זײַנען
און וואָס ווילן די ײִדישיסטן?)

———

שפּראַך און ליטעראַטור
פֿאָרשער

4

ד״ר מאַקס ווײַנרײַך
גאָלדינגען, קורלאַנד,   1894
לעבט אין ניו יאָרק, פֿ״שטאַטן

—◆—

שטאַפּלען,   (ליט. געשיכטע)
בילדער פֿון דער ײִדישער
ליטעראַטור געשיכטע
שוואַרצע פּינטעלעך
היטלערס פּראָפֿעסאָרן

———

ליטעראַטור און שפּראַך־
פֿאָרשער

5

זלמן רייזען
קאַדאַנאָוו, ווייסרוסלאַנד,   1887
אומגעבראַכט, ראַטנרוסלאַנד,   1941

—◆—

ײִדישע גראַמאַטיק
לעקסיקאָן פֿון דער ײִדישער ליטע־
ראַטור, פּרעסע און פֿילאָלאָגיע
פֿון מענדעלסאָן ביז מענדעלע
דאָס לעבעדיקע וואָרט, לערן־בוך

———

ליטעראַטור און שפּראַך־
פֿאָרשער

6

אדוו. נח פּרילוצקי
בערדיטשעוו, אוקראַינע,   1882
ווילנע, נאַצי־אָקופּאַציע,   1942

—◆—

מאַמע לשון,   (פֿילאָלאָגיע)
דיאַלעקטאָלאָגישע פֿאָרשונגען
ײִדישע פֿאָלקסלידער   (פֿאָלקלאָר)
ײִדיש טעאַטער,   (קריטיק)

———

שפּראַך און ליטעראַטור
פֿאָרשער
טעאָרעטיקער פֿון פֿאָלקיזם

1. Bal Makhshoves, 1873–1924; Literary critic, essayist; 2. Shmuel Niger, 1883–1955; Literary researcher, critic; 3. Nokhem Shtif, 1879–1934; Language researcher, literary researcher; 4. Maks Vaynraykh, 1894–1969; Literary researcher, language researcher; 5. Zalmen Reyzin, 1887–1941; Literary researcher, language researcher; 6. Noyekh Prilutski, 1882–1942; Language researcher, literary researcher, theoretician of *folkizm*.

The Yiddish Language: Its Cultural Impact

YUDEL MARK

In their long history, the Jewish people have used sixteen or seventeen distinctly Jewish languages, acquired in almost every instance from their non-Jewish environment in the Diaspora. Only three, however – Hebrew, Aramaic, and Yiddish – played a dominant role in the cultural history of the Jews, and only these three can be considered as truly Jewish languages, because they reflect the thinking and the feeling of the greater part of the Jews throughout their history, the formation of their way of life, and the growth and unfolding of their spirit.

The Bible was written in Hebrew, the Talmud in Aramaic, and Yiddish was the language of the most creative part of the Jewish people of the last several centuries. Hebrew is designated as the eternal language, and it has remained through all generations the most important medium for religious and spiritual expression. In the last decades it has become the expression of a multifaceted modern and cultural society. Aramaic was the dominant language in the first millennium of the Common Era. Through the study of the Talmud, and its explanation into Yiddish, a number of its words and concepts came into Yiddish. The Zohar, the compendium of Jewish mysticism, was also written in Aramaic. Aramaic is still used today in the *ketubah* and the *kaddish*. Hebrew, to a great extent, and Aramaic, to a somewhat lesser degree, have found their place in Yiddish.[1]

How old is Yiddish? No exact answer can be given to this question. Languages have no birth certificates. Yiddish was born over nine centuries ago in the communities along the Rhine River, among the immigrants from northern France who spoke a language based on Old French. To adjust to their new environment, they had to adopt the local vernacular, the Germanic dialects,

---

1. Approximately 50 per cent of all three letter roots of classical Hebrew are found in Yiddish. Yiddish-speaking Jews also formed a considerable number of new Hebrew words, first used in Yiddish and later included in Hebrew. Yudel Mark 1958.

retaining, however, a large portion of earlier speech habits in pronouncing the sounds and in vocabulary.[2]

The name Yiddish appeared much later. At first it was called 'the language of Ashkenaz'; somewhat later, simply 'our language'.[3] From the very beginning this new language contained a multitude of Hebrew and Aramaic words, especially in terms concerned with religion, learning, and social life. Thus, Yiddish emerged as a fusion language, with Hebrew, Romance, and Germanic components.

The civilized world does not know of a perfectly pure language. Borrowings from neighboring languages, from those of conquerors, from alien immigrants, from direct and indirect cultural influences are to be found everywhere. Fusion languages are endowed with a special capacity to absorb, to adapt, and to transform new words and give them new meaning. Already in the twelfth century, Yiddish was a distinct fusion language with Germanic as its main component. But Germanic in the mouths of the Jews was very much different from the dialects spoken by the natives along the Rhine. The Jewish communities were always on the run, either because of the evil decrees of expulsion or the more fortunate occasions of matchmaking or commerce, all of which led to changes in their vernacular. There was also a psychological reason. In modern times, Jews everywhere attempt to speak the purest and richest language of the country of their habitation. In the Middle Ages, people gave very little thought to grammar or pronunciation. On the contrary, the pious Jew did everything to be different from his non-Jewish neighbor. Hence, another explanation appears for the formation of Yiddish as a distinct language. Jews lived *among* non-Jews, but they did *not* live *like* them. They consciously kept apart in their religious and social life, and in almost all other areas, except trade and commerce. This desire to be different was the hidden force for Jewish survival in the Diaspora, and here we can also find the answer to the mystery of the many Jewish languages.

In the thirteenth century, a fourth component was added to the three mentioned before – Slavic. At first Czech words and forms appeared, then Polish, later White-Russian and Ukrainian. Russian did not begin to enter until the nineteenth century. These were new words for new situations, and new word-creating elements, suffixes and prefixes were added. The Slavic component in Yiddish created a considerable distinction between Western Yiddish, as spoken in the Germanic lands, and the Eastern Yiddish of the Slavic countries. In the thirteenth century, therefore, Yiddish emerged as a language of four components: Hebrew, Romance (from northern French and northern Italian), Germanic (with words left out and forgotten by the Germans, but preserved in Yiddish), and Slavic.

2. See S. A. Birnbaum 1939; N. Susskind 1953; M. Weinreich 1951, 1954, 1955.

3. N. Shtif 1924; J. Shatzky 1935; E. Spivak 1938.

Besides the aforementioned, nuances from the different locales were also added – from Amsterdam, with its printing center, a number of Dutch words came into Yiddish, from Lithuania, Lithuanian words, and from Roumania, some Moldavian words. Since the eighties of the last century, with the flow of emigration from Eastern Europe, came a new dispersion of Ashkenazic Jewry through every continent. These immigrants once again absorbed words and expressions into their speech – in North America, South Africa, and England – English words and expressions; in South America and Mexico – Spanish words.

The continuous absorption of new words is a natural process, although it does create many problems for Yiddish purists engaged in establishing a standardized language. In the last hundred years, we have also experienced a new influx of words known as internationalisms, which stem from Latin and Greek, and are utilized in all European languages for scientific terminology. Thus in Yiddish, as well, terminology is *terminologie* and linguistics is called *lingvistik*.

The history of Yiddish, like all other cultural languages, is divided into three periods:[4] Old-Yiddish, from approximately the beginning of the second millennium until the middle of the fourteenth century; Middle-Yiddish, from the middle of the fourteenth to the middle of the seventeenth century; and modern Yiddish, from the middle of the seventeenth century on. Yiddish contains a number of dialects, but we shall not concern ourselves here with Western Yiddish.[5] Eastern Yiddish has three principal dialects: Lithuanian, Polish, and Ukrainian.[6]

Yiddish is a very rich language. The number of words and expressions collected to date in our work on the monumental *Great Dictionary of the Yiddish Language* approximates 200,000. This collection represents Yiddish words used in speech and writing by Yiddish-speaking Jews in all countries and at all times.

The wealth of Yiddish can be appreciated by comparison with other cultural languages. Spanish, a language spoken on two continents, has approximately 250,000 words. Russian, a language with an unusually rich literature, contains in its 'Academic Dictionary', that was fifty years in preparation, only 125,000 words.

The question of course arises: How do we explain this wealth of Yiddish vocabulary? One reason has already been noted – the character of the language and its different components. The structure of a fusion language provides great possibilities for enrichment. A second reason is geographical, the dispersion of Yiddish-speaking Jews throughout the world. A third factor is also linguistic in

4. The periodization which is proposed here is not in accordance with M. Weinreich 1939 or N. Susskind 1953. See also Yudel Mark 1967.
5. J. A. Joffe 1954.
6. The dialects are called here by their popular names. In Yiddish linguistic literature, the Lith-uanian dialect is called North-Eastern Yiddish, the Polish dialect Middle-Eastern Yiddish, and the Ukrainian dialect South-Eastern Yiddish. The terminology was introduced by N. Prilutski in his *Dialektologishe forarbetn* (1937).

nature, the large number of prefixes and suffixes enable a multitude of possibilities in the formation of new words and neologisms from old root-words, adding to the language a special flexibility and elasticity which enables us to differentiate the finest nuances.[7] A fourth reason has its roots in the cultural history of the Jewish people.

For hundreds of years, especially in the period when Yiddish was most widely used, the Jews were the most cultured people in Europe. Although such a statement may sound greatly exaggerated, it is nevertheless true that no other people, until the nineteenth century, contained so many scholars, and among no other people during all these centuries did learning and life-long study for the sake of learning play such a prominent role. Until the nineteenth century no other people had an educational system for all male children.

With the widespread availability of printed books in the sixteenth century, almost the entire male population and a considerable number of women could read a printed text. In the Hellenistic period, Jews were called the 'people of the Book', meaning the people of the Bible. In the Middle Ages, the small segment of Christian scholars consisted of priests and monks, but many priests and monks were illiterate. But among the small groups of Jews who lived among them there were thousands of Talmudic students. As late as the seventeenth and eighteenth centuries, there were rulers over powerful nations who had difficulty signing their names to historic documents. At the same time, however, one could hardly find a Jew who could not read the Siddur and a book in Yiddish. For three hundred years Jewish mothers had read the portion of the *teitshḥumesh* every Sabbath afternoon,[8] and through this medium were more acquainted and closer to the history of their people than were the ladies-in-waiting in the palace to their own historical past.

One of the tragedies of human history is the fact that only a small segment of society has ever been actively engaged in its cultural achievements. This often explains the phenomenon of the rise and fall of great cultures, and that periods of unusual growth are followed by extreme barbarism. The rise and fall of the cultures of antiquity and the brief blossoming of the Arabic culture in the Middle Ages are excellent examples. The Jews, especially Ashkenazic Jewry, have escaped this tragedy. In part this was due to the Yiddish language, which absorbed the cultural values of all previous generations. Printed books were accessible to all and in constant use. The Scriptures were taught to all Jewish boys by translating each word into Yiddish. In every community there existed

7. As an example from the root *zog* there are the verbs – *zogn, oyszogn, avekzogn, oyfzogn, unterzogn, iberzogn, onzogn, opzogn, araynzogn, derzogn, farzogn, tsuzogn* and others; substantives – *a zog, zogung, zogekhts, zogenish, zoger, zogerin, zogerke, zogeray,* etc. Compare also the difference between *gutskayt* = goodness, and *gutikayt* = something which is sweet, good; *reynkayt* = cleanliness, and *reynikayt* = scroll of the Torah.

8. צאינה־וראינה by Rabbi Jacob ben Issac, of Yanow; an English translation by Norman C. Gore, has appeared under the title *Tzeenah u-Reenah: a Jewish Commentary of the Book of Exodus* (1965).

ספּאַריק־דרעהער נום. 49.

דר. נ. סירקין, אין אַ לעקטשור איבער די אויסבעסערונג פֿון „זשאַרגאָן":

„איך וויל דאָ סערלירען אַ פֿאַר וואָרטער
וועגען אַ געוויסען קאַרדינאַל־שטריך, וועלכער
איז זעהר באַ־אַקטערריסטיש פֿאַר דעם צושטאַנד
פֿון אונזער ליטעראַטור — איך מיין די
סופּערלאָוינג פֿון וואָרטער, וועלכע האָבען, זאָ
צו זאָגען, מעהר אַן אַרגומענטאַל־
דעקאַראַטיוונען וערטה אַלס סטילי־
סטישע געפֿליגעלטקייטען, איידער אַ ניצליכען
און נוישוענדיגען.

„אַלס אַ שטודענט פֿון דער אידישער
שפּראַך, זשאַרגאָן, האָב איך אַם בעמערקט חן
אין דער פּובליציסטיק, חן אין די בראַנשעס
פֿון בעלל־לעטעריס, אַדער בעלעטריסטיק אַ גע־
ווים שפּאָאַנבאַנע נייגונג, פֿון די אידישע לי־
טעראַטאַרען צו געברויכען אַ —זאָ צו זאָגען—
שפּיראַל־סערמיגע, אונמעגליך־ קאָמפּליצירטע
און עקזאָטיש־אַנקקוירומע, קינסטליך־ערצוי־
גענע שפּראַך־קאָמבינאָאַציאָנען, וואָס זיינען אַב־

דר. נ. סירקין, אין אַ לעקטשור איבער די אויסבעסערונג פֿון „זשאַרגאָן":

סאַלום נים דער ערך צוגעפּאַסט צו די גייסטי־
גע קוואַליפֿיקאַציעס פֿון דעם לעזער, און
וועלכע ווירקט דורך איהר אונקאָנסעקווענטע
שלוסטאַאַלגערונג זעהר סערדעראָבליך אויף די
פּסיכאָלאָגישע אַנלאַגען פֿון די עמפֿענגליכע
סאַנציליטעטען פֿון דעם לעזערס געהירן.

„וואָרום, פֿרעג איך, זאָלען די אידישע
ליטעראַטאָרען נים דעם סאַלק'ם בעגריסם־פֿעהיגקיי־
מען, וועלכע זיינען בשום אופֿן נים צוגע־
פּאַסט צו דער געשליסענקייט פֿון זייער
שפּראַך־מעכניק, אַדער סובסטאַנצועלע געדאַנ־
קען־בעגרינדונג נאָך די עמפֿעירישע פֿילאָזאָ־
פֿיע, אַדער די אונקאָאַקלעאַסטישע סערמסטער־
ריקט פֿון דער מענשליכער אָרעעלעוואַצישא!
אין בעצוג צו די סאָציאַלע אידלען ?

„אידישע ליטעראַטאָרס ! שוין ציים, אַ
איהר זאָלם וערען מענשען !"

Dr. N. Sirkin (in an impossibly involuted and hyperbolic style) appeals to Yiddish writers to write more simply, without embellishments, unnecessary complexities, and linguistic adornments, so that ordinary folk can understand them. (*Der groyser kundes*, March 1, 1912)

societies where the merchant, the artisan, the storekeeper, and even the poorest porter were engaged in pursuit of learning. Questions in the Talmud were debated in Yiddish and it was in Yiddish that rabbis and preachers addressed the people on all occasions. Yiddish was the language spoken not only in the home, in the workshop, and, to a great extent, in the market-place; it was also the expression of a spiritual life in its fullness. Yiddish was born out of a will to make intelligible, explain, and simplify the tremendous complexities of sacred literature. It became a direct expression of feeling, a mode of speech without ceremony or artifice, and a language with intimacy and warmth.

Yiddish, at the same time, was permeated with and continually creating a folklore that had its roots in the legends of previous generations, thus fusing and cementing the wisdom of the pre-Yiddish era with the folk wit of later generations. This treasure of folk wisdom became the strongest weapon in the struggle for an independent cultural existence.[9]

Yiddish is also self-critical. It is full of wise sayings, jokes, proverbs, and derogatory allusions to the fallacies and inadequacies of its own people. For example: 'It is good to partake with one's fellow Jew in a meal, but it is no good to eat with him out of the same plate'.

Two Yiddish expressions, *a yiddish harts* (a Jewish heart) and *a yiddisher kop* (a Jewish head) best exemplify the tendency of Yiddish toward self-characterization. A 'Jewish heart' is one full of compassion for the needy and those in distress; it is always ready to help a fellow man, especially when the other is wronged by either man or nature. A 'Jewish head' describes someone endowed with a quick mind; someone who will always find a way out in a difficult situation.

These characteristics of the Jewish people did not come to them as a gift from heaven, nor did they spring up in one generation, but are the result of the forging of a people of which Yiddish was an integral part.

The plain meaning of words, the straight line of a general rule seemed too shallow, too thin, too narrow to hold the expanding power of their minds.
Ideas were like precious stones. The thought that animated them reflected a wealth of nuances and distinctions...many-faceted ideas shed a glittering brilliance that varied in accordance with the direction in which they were placed, against the light of reason...Concepts acquired a dynamic quality, a color and meaning that, at first thought, seemed to have no connection with one another.
The East European Jews had a predilection...for the flash of the mind, for the thunderclap of an idea. They spoke briefly, sharply, quickly and directly; they understood each other with a hint; they heard two words when only one was said...Jokes without a deeper meaning were considered tasteless; the type of humor that was truly appreciated was a tale from which a meaning suddenly emerged...Puns are almost absent in Yiddish.[10]

The language of a people serves not only as a means of communication, but is also a receptacle of the characteristic traits of the speakers of the language.

9. Y. Mark 1951.   10. A. J. Heschel 1950.

We have already mentioned *a yiddish harts*. There are similar expressions – *es tsegeyt dos harts fun raḥmones* – the heart melts from compassion; *es veynt in mir dos harts* – my heart cries in me. There are scores of expressions of this kind.

Yiddish, as spoken by millions of Jews of many generations, contains also many vulgar words. These are, however, intended to tease rather than hurt. They were never used as a means of entertainment, but rather as an outlet for anger or indignation. Yiddish, it is true, has an abundance of peculiar and comical curse words. But these developed as a reaction to a life of persecution and poverty.

When an exasperated Jewish mother in wrathful indignation over her child's misbehavior gave vent to cursing, she never, even in a fit of rage, forgot to add the negation to the curse, *zolst mir nit geharget vern* – you should not get killed, *zolst nit oysgerisn vern* – you should not become extinct. In general the Yiddish vernacular is very poor in obscenities.

No one ever gave a command to shoot or to kill in Yiddish. The experience of the Yiddish-speaking Jews was not on the battlefield for material or territorial conquest. It was rather a struggle for life and spiritual survival.

It is, in fact, not curses, but countless tender words of endearment that are the predominant characteristic of Yiddish. We can note that the diminutive form constitutes the prevailing form of Yiddish colloquial style. The best example are the names by which Jewish children were called. These names present us with an insight into a sea of emotions. Jewish boys with names of the patriarch Abraham were called: *Avreml, Avremele, Avremenu, Avreminke, Avremche, Avremchik, Avrumche*. Leyb was a common name – but the boy was usually called *Leybele, Leybinke, Leybenu, Leybche, Leybushke*. The same names of endearment were applied to rabbis, especially among the Hasidim.

Yiddish acquired most of the suffixes of endearment from the Slavic languages and added them to those already in use from the Germanic dialects.

The Yiddish-speaking people found and also created new names for their women folk. The most common are: Freyde (joy), Toybe-Taybele (dove), Feygele (little bird), Hindele (little chicken), Ḥayele (little creature), Libe (love), Zisele (sweetness), Shcyne-Sheyndl (beauty), Gute-Gitl-Gutche (goodness), Kreyne (crown) Yentl (gentle), Glikl (happiness), Frume-Frumet (pious) and Paye, Shprintze (hope). They used as names the Hebrew words: Brokhe (blessing), Neḥome (consolation). All these names have a multitude of endearing forms.

Jewish women added part of their piety to the vernacular, and through the Jewish mother Yiddish actually became *mame-loshn*. But this influence was reciprocal. Just as the Jewish woman instilled in Yiddish a certain humanity and kindness, the language in return added much to the spiritual life of the Jewish woman. Judaism was not too generous to women. Men were given six hundred and thirteen commandments to perform, women many less, but Yiddish in part compensated for this. We might say that Yiddish was the first to give Jewish women equal rights. Almost the entire early Yiddish literature was intended to include women readers and many books of this period contain the following inscription on the title page: 'For women and girls – very refined and explicit'.

There even appeared an exclusively women's literature, some of which were *teḥinot*, devotional prayers, composed in some instances by women. Yiddish books intended for women had their own unique style. They were verbose and gentle, and their content was always didactic, attempting to instruct the reader in a life of righteousness and piety. Yet, at the same time, they were also entertaining.[11] As late as the nineteenth century, the popular Yiddish author Isaac Meyer Dik, dedicated his stories to the *libe lezerin* – 'dear woman-reader'. Thus, through Yiddish, Judaism, and Talmudic lore became the property of the entire speaking community.

In his 'Shloime Reb Chayim's', the grandfather of modern Yiddish literature, described the *shtetl* as follows:

a place where Torah has been studied from time immemorial; where practically all the inhabitants are scholars, where the House of Study is full of people of all classes busily engaged in studies, townfolk as well as young men from afar...where at dusk, between twilight and evening prayers, artisans and other simple folk gather around tables to listen to a discourse on the great books of Torah, to interpretation of scriptures, to readings from homiletic or ethical writings like 'Ḥoyves Halvoves' (The duties of the Heart, a work of Jewish morality written by Rabbi Bahya Ibn Pakuda in the eleventh century) and the like...where on the Sabbath and the holidays, near the Holy Ark, at the reading stand, fiery sermons that kindle the hearts of the Jewish people with love for the Divine Presence, for the Shekinah, sermons which are seasoned with words of comfort from the prophets, with wise parables and keen aphorism of the sages, in a voice and a tone that heartens one's soul, and melts all limbs, that penetrates the whole being...[12]

Yiddish-speaking Jews thus possessed a wealth of knowledge and were exposed to the thoughts, ideas, and sayings of many ages. One of the most popular Yiddish proverbs was *toyre iz di beste shoyre* – Torah is the best merchandise. And the most popular Yiddish lullaby included the words: 'My little child, close your eyes: if God will, you'll be a rabbi'. Poorly educated fathers hoped that their children would be scholars, and it was common for women to work, thereby enabling their husbands to devote themselves to the study of the Torah.

In the seventeenth century, the Zohar and other Kabbalistic writings began to influence Polish Jewry. Although the texts were in Aramaic and Hebrew, discussion of this new aspect of Jewish thought and theology were in Yiddish, and a new terminology was added to the everyday vernacular. Similarly, in the eighteenth century, the Hasidic movement found through Yiddish its way to the Jewish masses. Hasidic parables, sayings, stories, and songs flourished, and a new dimension was added to Yiddish folklore and in time new motifs and new sources for Yiddish literature. In the following century, the Enlightenment brought the ideas of secularism and another influx of new expressions.

11. Sh. Niger 1913.   12. See Abramowitz 1911.

Modern Yiddish writers were therefore the heirs to an unusually rich spiritual and cultural legacy. There was enough to suit every talent and every inclination. Shalom Jacob Abramowitz (Mendele Moykher Sforim) was able to standardize the literary language and to create a new style for modern literature. Sholem Aleichem was able to add lively colors and playfulness. Peretz went into the depths of the language of the Talmudic scholar and the Hasidic rabbi. H. Leivick could find a multitude of meanings and allusions in the simplest words. Modern poets coined thousands of neologisms from old roots, and contemporary scientific research added a new element that enabled Yiddish to express both its problems and achievements. Through Yiddish, Jewish literature became an integral part of world literature. It was the medium of all great social movements of the last hundred years. Yiddish was the personal link between our own and prior generations. With the help of Yiddish the East European immigrant, the worker in the sweatshop and the peddler were able to rise to a higher social status.

REFERENCES

Abramowitz, S. J. (1911), *Ale verk* 2: 14 (New York).

ben Issac, Jacob (1965), *Tzeenah u-Reenah: A Jewish Commentary of the Book of Exodus*, trans. by Norman Gore. New York, Vantage Press.

Birnbaum, S. A. (1939), 'The age of the Yiddish language', in *Transcriptions of the Philological Society*, 31–48. London.

Heschel, A. J. (1950), *The Earth is the Lord's*, 59–60. New York, Schuman.

Joffe, J. A. (1954), 'Dating the origin of Yiddish dialects', in *The Field of Yiddish*, vol. 1, 102–121. New York.

Mark, Yudel (1951), 'What is Jewish folklore', *Yidisher Kemfer* April 20: 61–74, May 18: 9–15.

— (1958), 'Yiddish-hebreishe un hebreish-yidishe nayshafungen', in *Shmuel Niger bukh*, 124–157. New York, YIVO.

— (1967), 'Tsu der geshikhte fun der yidisher literaturshprakh', in *Shloyme Bikl Yoyvl Bukh*, 124–135. New York.

Niger, Sh. (1913), 'Di yidishe literatur un di lezerin', in *Der Pinkes*, vol. 1, 85–138. Vilna.

Prilutski, N. (1937), *Dialektologishe forarbetn*. Vilna.

Shatsky, J. (1935), 'On the names of Yiddish', *Yivo-bleter* 8: 148–154.

Shtif, N. (1924), 'Names of Yiddish', *Yidishe filologye* 1: 386–388.

Spivak, E., (1938), 'The principal Names of Yiddish', in *Fragn fun yidisher shprakh*, 71–86. Moscow.

Susskind, N. (1953), 'How Yiddish originated', *Yidishe shprakh* 13: 97–110.

Weinreich, M. (1939), *Algemeyne yidishe entsiklopedye*: Yidn 2, 29–30. Paris.

— (1951), 'Ashkenaz: the Yiddish period in Jewish history', *Yivo-bleter* 35: 7–17.

— (1954), 'Fundamentals in the history of Yiddish', *Yidishe shprakh* 14: 97–110.

— (1955), 'Fundamentals in the history of Yiddish', *Yidishe shprakh* 15: 12–19.

אברהם רייזין: מה קא משמע לן? וואָס־זשע לאָזט איהר מיך צו הע־
רען? אז אידיש איז קיין שפּראך ניט? סטייטש! מיליאָנען שרייבער שטאַרבען
פון הונגער אין אידיש, און איהר שרייט, אז עס איז קיין שפּראַך ניט! אי, וואָס
איהר וועט מיר אויפוואָרפען, אז זי איז אַ שפחה, אַ קאַמענע דיענסט־מויד? וועל
איך אייך זאָגען, אז די נביר'טע איז אַן אויסגעווובטע, אָבנעלעבטע, איינגעקלעפּטע
שלמע כּפּיצע, אָהן ציינהער! האַ? וואָס זאַנט איהר? גראַמאַטיקע? האָט דאָך
זײן בהודער פּערפּאָסט אַ אירישע גראַמאַטיקע.... שאַ, איהר ווילט עס זעהן? אָט
וועל איך אַ זוך טהון אין מײן רעדאַקציע! (טאַפּט זיך ביים בוזעם־קעשענע) אי־
ערשט! איך האָב, דוכט זיך, פֿערביטען מיין פּידזשאָ אין רעסטאָראַן!...

Avrom Reyzin: 'How can you say Yiddish isn't a language? Millions of writers are dying from hunger in Yiddish and you are trying to tell me it isn't a language!...And I tell you the old dowager is a superannuated "has been", a toothless hag...' (*Der groyser kundes*, December 15, 1911)

וועגן דער נאַציאָנאַלער ראָלע פֿון ייִדיש און דער ייִדישער קולטור

שמואל ניגער

SUMMARY: CONCERNING THE ETHNONATIONAL ROLE OF YIDDISH
AND YIDDISH CULTURE BY SHMUEL NIGER

*The major Yiddish literary critic of the first half of the twentieth century (1883–1955)
explains how Yiddish and Yiddish literature formed the national identity and
expressed the national values and aspirations of Eastern European Jewry.*

אין דען איצט נאָך נייטיק צו רעדן וועגן דער ראָלע,
וואָס ייִדיש האָט געשפילט און שפילט אין אונדזער
נאַציאָנאַלן לעבן? איז עס דען אַ פראַגע, וואָס
מען זאָגן, וואָס איז נאָך ניט פאַרענטפערט גע־
וואָרן? און מען וועט אין פלוג זיין גערעכט. שוין
מיט אַ האַלבן יאָרהונדערט צוריק, ווען מען האָט
זיך גענומען אַמפערן וועגן אַ טיטל פאַר דער
שפראַך, וואָס מען האָט זי שוין נישט געקאָנט מער
האַלטן פאַר קיין „זשאַרגאָן", האָבן אייניקע געזען
אין ייִדיש די נאַציאָנאַלע שפראַך פונעם ייִדישן

פאָלק. די טשערנאָוויצער קאָנפערענץ (1908) האָט געפסקנט: „אַ נאַ־
ציאָנאַלע שפראַך". אָבער אפילו יענע, וואָס האָבן געהאַלטן, אַז ייִדיש
איז נאָך אַלץ נישט מער ווי אַ פאָלקסשפראַך, האָבן נישט פאַרלייקנט
און פאַרלייקענען נישט (ווי וואָלטן זיי דען געקאָנט פאַרלייקענען ?) דעם
נאַציאָנאַלן ווערט פון ייִדיש און פון דער גאַנצער ייִדיש־קולטור (די
ייִדישע פאָלקס־שאַפונג, דאָס לערנען אויף ייִדיש אין חדרים און ישיבות,
דאָס זאָגן תורה, און דרשנען אויף ייִדיש, די אַלטע און ניַע, רעליגיעזע
און וועלטלעכע ייִדישע ליטעראַטור, די ייִדישע פרעסע, דער ייִדישער

טעאַטער, דער פֿאַקט, וואָס אַ רוב מנין פֿון יידישן פֿאָלק לעבט זיך אויס
פּריוואַט און געזעלשאַפֿטלעך אויף יידיש). הײַנט צו וואָס זיך טאַקע
אומקערן צוריק צו אַן ענין, וואָס איז לאַנג שוין אויפֿגעקלערט געוואָרן?

דער תירוץ איז, אַז עס זיינען דאָ פֿראַגעס, און דווקא גרויסע פֿראַ־
געס, וואָס אַפֿילו ווען מען געפֿינט אויף זיי אַן ענטפֿער, איז עס זעלטן
ווען אַן ענטפֿער, וואָס ווערט געגעבן איין מאָל פֿאַר אַלע מאָל. עס
שטײַט אָן אַ נײַע עפּאָכע, די אומשטאַנדן ענדערן זיך, — און די אַלטע
פֿראַגע ווערט געשטעלט פֿון ס׳ניי, זי קריגט אַ ניעם, אָפֿט נאָך אַפֿילו
אַ שאַרפֿערן אויסדרוק — און מען מוז זיך אויף איר ווידער אַ מאָל
אומקוקן.

אַזאַ פֿראַגע איז בײַ אונדז די שפּראַכן־פֿראַגע. זי איז לעצטנס
ווידער אַרויסגעשוואומען פֿון אונטער דעם אייבערפֿלאַך — און זי
מאָנט ווידער אַ מאָל אַן ענטפֿער.

דאָס איז דערפֿאַר, ווייל דער בנין פֿון אונדזער פֿאָלקס לעבן איז סיי
פֿון אינעווייניק, סיי פֿון דרויסן אויפֿגעטרייסלט און צעטרייסלט גע־
וואָרן. ווי אַ רעזולטאַט דערפֿון זיינען פֿריערדיקע ספֿקות געוואָרן
זיכערקייטן און, פֿאַרקערט, אמתן, וואָס זיינען געווען פֿעסט און קלאָר,
זיינען פֿאַרנעפֿלט און פֿאַרטונקלט געוואָרן, — און צו אָט די פֿאַרטונקלטע
אמתן געהערט אויך דער אמת וועגן יידיש, דער קולטור פֿון יידיש און
זייער ראָלע אינעם לעבן פֿונם יידישן פֿאָלק.

כדי עס צו פֿאַרשטיין, איז ניט גענוג צו וויסן (און מיר ווייסן
דיער גוט), וואָס עס איז פֿאַרגעקומען אין די לעצטע יאָרן, — וואָס עס
איז אין אונדזער וועלט חרוב געוואָרן און וואָס עס איז אויפֿגעבויט
געוואָרן. עס איז נייטיק צו דערמאָנען זיך אָן דעם אָרט, וואָס יידיש
האָט פֿאַרנומען בײַ אונדז אין פֿריערדיקע צײַטן. אַ קורצע היסטאָרישע
באַטראַכטונג פֿון אָט דער פֿראַגע וועט אונדז העלפֿן באַנעמען, פֿאַר
וואָס זי ווערט איצט ווידער אַ מאָל געשטעלט.

ב

ווי מיר ווייסן, איז דער אָרט פֿון יידיש אין אונדזער קולטור־
באַוואוסטזיין נישט אַלע מאָל געווען אַן אָרט אויבן־אָן... פֿאַר וואָס?
פֿאַר וואָס איז מאַמע־לשון געווען אַזוי אָפֿט דערנידעריקט און פֿאַר־
שעמט? האָט זיך עס גענומען פֿון זיינע רײַן שפּראַכלעכע אייגנשאַפֿטן?
האָט די הויפֿט־ראָלע דאָ געשפּילט דער חילוק צווישן „השפה היפה"
און „שפת עלגם"? ניין, עס האָט זיך גערעדט וועגן אַ סך אַ טיפֿערן

אונטערשייד. אזוי ווי ביי אנדערע פעלקער, איידער די גערעדטע
שפראך איז געווארן זייער לשון שבכתב, די שפראך פון זייערע העכערע
קולטור-ווערטן, איז אויך ביי אונדז דער גורל פון דער פאלקסשפראך
געווען דער גורל פון די פאלקס-מענטשן, פון די פאלקסמאסן, פון די
אלע, וואס זייער טאג-טעגלעכער לשון איז געווען אויך דער לשון פון
זייער שבת און יום-טוב, די שפראך פון זייער שעפערישקייט. אויף אט די
"פראסטע מענטשן", אדער "געמיינע לייט", וואס צו זיי האבן געהערט
ביי אונדז כמעט אלע פרויען און אויך א היפש ביסל מענער, — האט
מען געקוקט ווי אויף נחות דרגאס, — ממילא, האט מען אויך אויף
זייער שפראך געקוקט פון אויבן אראפ. דאס איז געווען א לשון קלילה,
ד״ה א גרינגער, אבער ניט קיין חשובער לשון. אמת טאקע, די רבנים,
די דיינים, די ראשי ישיבהס, די מגידים און אנדערע תלמידי חכמים
האבן גערעדט יידיש, אזוי ווי אלע אנדערע יידן, און עס האט אפילו
געטראפן, אז זיי האבן געשריבן "בלשוננו", אבער ביי זיי אן פאר זיי
איז אונדזער לשון גייסמיק אדער, ווי מיר זאגן איצטער, קולטורעל
געווען נאר א געהילפס-שפראך. דער אמתער לשון פון זייער העכערן
גייסטיקן לעבן, דערהויפט פון די ספרים, וואס זיי האבן געשריבן, פון
די תפילות און ברכות, וואס זיי האבן געזאגט, איז געווען לשון קודש.
אויף יידיש האבן זיי די תורה, די גמרא און אנדערע הייליקע ספרים
בלויז געטייטשט, פארטייטשט און אויסגעטייטשט, און כאטש קיינער
פון זיי האט זיך ניט געשעמט מיט אט דעם לשון, איז עס דאך געווארן
דערהויפט א לשון פאר דברי חול, און אזוי ווי דער עיקר אין לעבן איז
געווען ניט דברי חול, עולם-הזה-זאכן, נאר הייליקע ענינים, תורה, מצוות
און מעשים טובים, — האט מען פאר דער עיקרדיקער שפראך געהאלטן
ניט יידיש, די שפראך פון אין דער וואכן און "אין דערוואכנדיקע" יידן,
נאר לשון קודש, ד״ה העברעאיש-אראמעאיש, דעם לשון פון תורה,
גמרא און אלע אנדערע ספרים קדושים.

יידיש איז געווען א לשון פון דער צווייטער מדרגה דערפאר ווייל
די יידן, וואס יידיש איז געווען די איינציקע שפראך, וואס זיי האבן
פארשטאנען, זיינען געווען יידן פון א צווייטער מדרגה, יידן — עם
הארצים, יידן — יידענעס.

אז עס האט זיך באוויזן חסידות, און מען האט מיט מיט **א פראסטן**
קאפיטל תהלים, מיט דאוונען בכוונה, נישט דווקא מיט לומדות, געקאנט
דערגרייכן א הויכע מדרגה, איז אויך יידיש, די **פראסטע שפראך**,
ניט געווען מער אזוי דערנידעריקט, ווי פריער.

זיינען געקומען די משכילים און האבן אויפן הויכן שטול פון
תורה אוועקגעזעצט חכמה, בילדונג, לשון און די „אומוויסנדיקע" ייד,
די, וואָס קענען נישט קיין דקדוק, האבן אין גאנצן פארלארן זייער
חשיבות, — איז, ממילא, אויך יידיש געווארן „ושארגאן", תחינה-לשון
אד"גל.

חשוב און דערהייבן געווארן איז יידיש ערשט דאן, ווען דער יידי-
שער פאָלקס-מענטש און אויך די פרויען, וואָס האבן נישט געקענט
קיין לשון קודש, זיינען סוף 19טן יארהונדערט ביסלעכווייז אריינגעצויגן
געווארן איינעם מעכטיקן שטראם פון דער סאָציאלער און נאציאנאלער
אויפוואכונג פונעם יידישן פאָלק. ניע גייסטיקע ווערטן האבן זיך גע-
וויזן, ניע אידעאלן, — אידעאלן פון סאָציאלער גערעכטיקייט און
פאליטישער פרייהייט, אידעאלן פון נאציאנאלן זעלבסט-באוואוסטזיין
און זעלבסט-עמאנסיפאציע האבן געצונדן די יידישע פאָלקס-פאנטאזיע,
און כאטש די ניע אידעאלן און אידעאלן האבן געצויגן חיונה אויך פון
אלטן קוואל, דעם קוואל פונעם תורה און נביאים, איז די שפראך, אין
וועלכע זיי האבן געפונען זייער ניעם אויסדרוק, די שפראך, דורך
וועלכער זיי זיינען אריינגעדרונגען אין יידישע מוחות און האבן זיך
אריינגעזונגען אין יידישע הערצער, — געווען יידיש.

יידיש איז געווארן דער מעדיום פון די אידעען און די אידעאלן,
וואָס האבן אויפגעוועקט און אויפגעהויבן דעם יידישן פאָלקס-מענטשן,
— און אין איינעם מיט אים איז יידיש אליין אויך נתעלה געווארן —
און נאך מער ווי אין דער תקופה פון חסידות. זיין ניע חשיבות און
גדולה האט מאמע-לשון נישט געדארפט מער טיילן מיט לשון קודש,
ווי דאָס איז געווען אין די אלטע, גוטע און פרומע צייטן פון חסידות.
עס איז געוואקסן און האט פארנומען אלץ א מער און מער אנגעזעענעם
ארט אין אונדזער קולטור-לעבן די יידישע פרעסע, דער יידישער טעא-
טער, די יידישע ליטעראטור, די יידיש-געזעלשאפטלעכע טריבונע, —
און אין איינעם מיט זיי איז געוואקסן און געווארן אלץ רייכער און
אלץ אנגעזעענער די יידישע שפראך, וואָס זיי אלע האבן באנוצט.

דער יידישער פאָלקס-מענטש און אַרבעטס-מענטש, דער יידישער
פאָלקס-אינטעליגענט און פאָלקס-פירער איז געווארן א טרעגער פון
מאדערנעם סאָציאלן און נאציאנאלן געדאַנק, ער האט אָנגעהויבן זאָגן
דעות און מישן זיך אין יידישע — און נישט נאָר אין יידישע —
קהלשע געשעפטן; אין א סך פרטים איז ער געווארן דער פרוכטבאר-
סטער פראָגרעסיווער כוח פון יידישן לעבן, זיין אוואנגארד, — איז אין

No! It's a Legitimate Love Affair! Hebrew (walking arm in arm with the Hebrew-Yiddish poet Khayim Nakhmen Byalik, who wrote almost entirely in Hebrew toward the latter part of his career): 'Who's that, Khayim Nakhmen, an illegitimate affair?' Yiddish (shouting 'Daddy!'): 'Don't get so upset, madame, Khayim Nakhmen knows me since childhood!' (*Der groyser kundes*, February 5, 1926)

איינעם מיט אים זיין שפּראַך, ייִדיש, אַרויס אויף דער אַוואַנסצענע פֿון דער ייִדישער געשיכטע.

הכּלל, דער וועג פֿון אונדזער פֿאָלקסשפּראַך, סיי באַרג־אַראָפּ, סיי באַרג־אַרויף, איז דער וועג פֿון דעם ייִדישן פֿאָלקס־לעבן, פֿון דעם ייִדישן פֿאָלקס־מענטשן — זײַנע ירידות און זײַנע עליות זײַנען אירע ירידות און אירע עליות.

ג

און אויב עס איז אַ ווידער אַ מאָל געקומען איצט אַ צײַט, ווען מען דאַרף שטיין אויף דער וואַך פֿון דער פֿאָלקסשפּראַך און זען, אַז זי זאָל נישט אַראָפּפֿאַלן אָדער אַראָפּגעוואָרפֿן ווערן פֿון דעם הויכן שטול, אויף וועלכן די געשיכטע האָט זי אַוועקגעזעצט, איז עס צוליב די מפּלות, וואָס די גאַנצע ייִדישע פֿאָלקס־קולטור, דאָס גאַנצע ייִדישע פֿאָלקסלעבן האָט געליטן. איר ווייסט, וואָס איך מיין... איך דאַרף אײַך נישט דערמאָנען, אַז עס איז קאַטאַסטראָפֿאַל קלענער געוואָרן די צאָל ייִדיש־רעדנדיקע, ייִדיש־לייענענדיקע און ייִדיש־שאַפֿנדיקע ייִדן... אויף אַ גאַנצן דריטל קלענער געוואָרן. דער גרעסטער און אייגנ־פֿונדעוווטסטער צענטער פֿון ייִדיש — מזרח־אייראָפּע — איז חרוב געוואָרן, — חרוב געוואָרן פֿיזיש אין די ניט־סאָוועטישע און בײַסטיק אין די סאָוועטישע און סאָוועטיזירטע טיילן פֿון אייראָפּע. אָבער נישט נאָר דער שטח פֿון ייִדיש־לאַנד איז אַזוי טראַגיש אײַנגעשרומפּן געוואָרן, — אויך זײַן צײַט־פּערספּעקטיוו איז, אַזוי צו זאָגן, פֿאַרטונקלט געוואָרן — דורך דעם, וואָס אַפֿילו אין יענע ייִדישע ישובֿים, וואו ייִדיש לעבט און שאַפֿט, לעבט זי, ווי עס דוכט זיך, מיטן הײַנט און שאַפֿט פֿאַרן הײַנט, פֿול מיט זאָרגן פֿאַרן מאָרגן.

און נישט נאָר דאָס אַליין.

נאָך אַ נעגאַטיוווער פֿאַקטאָר איז צוגעקומען — נאָך אַ כּח, וואָס אין אַ סך פּרטים איז ער דווקא האָפֿענונגספֿול, קאָנסטרוקטיוו און שעפֿעריש, אָבער — נישט אין דעם ענין פֿון ייִדיש און דער קולטור פֿון ייִדיש: די חשיבֿות פֿון דער ייִדישער שפּראַך און איר נאַציאָנאַל־שעפֿערישער ראָלע קומט ער צו פֿאַרמינערן... כ'האָב אין זינען די גרויסע געשעעניש פֿון אונדזערע טעג — די עטאַבלירונג פֿון דער ייִדישער מדינה. ווי אַ סך אַנדערע היסטאָרישע פֿאַסירונגען, שפּרייט זי אין איין אָרט ליכט און אין אַן אַנדערן — שאָטנס. בנוגע צו ייִדיש, דער „גלות־שפּראַך", באַשטייט די ראָלע פֿון ישׂראל אין דעם, וואָס זי

צעשטערט דאָס — אַזוי אויך װאַקלדיקע — גלייכגעװױכט צװישן ייִדיש
און העברעאיש. מיט איר גאַנצן געװױכט לייגט זי זיך אויף דער װאָגשאָל
פֿון העברעאיש, — זי זאָל איבערװעגן. הגר, דערמאָנט זי אונדז, איז
אַ שפֿחה, — און כ'טש זי האָט אברהמ׳ען געבאָרן אַ זון, איז זי, אין
איינעם מיט איר קינד, איצט אַן איבעריקע אין הױז. מען טאַלערירט
זי, אָבער די גברת, די בּאַלעבּאַסטע — גיט מען איר אָנצוהערענישן
— איז שרה, װאָס עס איז געשעהן אַ נס און זי איז װידער אַ מאָל
יונג געװאָרן.

העברעאיש איז געװען אַ „גברת", יונג־העברעאיש איז מער װי אַ
„גברת", זי איז אַ „מלכה": כתר מלכות איז אויף איר יונג געװאָרענעם
קאָפּ !

אַחוץ דעם יהוס פֿון מאַכט און אַחוץ יחוס אבות האָט זי יחוס בנים:
די שפּראַך פֿונעם יונגן דור אין ישראל איז און מוז זיין ניי־העברעאיש.

איז עס אַ מיטל אין די הענט און די מיילער פֿון די נעאָ־העברע־
איסטן צו װירקן אויך אויף די דערװאַקסענע — און נישט נאָר
אין ישראל אליין.

הגר, האַלטן זיי אין איין רעדן צו דער פֿילמיליאָנענדיקער „שארית
הפליטה", — הגר, ד״ה ייִדיש און די קולטור פֿון ייִדיש האָט נישט אויף
װאָס צו האָפֿן אַפֿילו אין „מדבר" — אין גלות־מדבר. איר לאָגל אין
איראָפּעאיש מדבר — פֿאַרגיסן זיי אַ טרער — איז אויסגעטריקנט
געװאָרן. און אַזױ — זאָגן זיי פֿינצטערע, אַכזריותדיק־פֿינצטערע
נביאות — װעט ער טרוקן זיין אין דער גאַנצער װעלט... מיר זיינען,
שפּאָטן זיי, געפֿאַלענע, — און זיי כאַפּן אַריין די מיאוסע מצװה פֿון
שלאָגן אַ געפֿאַלענעם... נישט גענוג, װאָס פֿייגטלעבּע כוחות האָבן דעם
בנין פֿונעם ייִדישן לעבן און דער ייִדישער קולטור צעטרייסלט פֿון דרויסן,
— דערװועגן זיי זיך אונטערצוגראָבן זיך אויך פֿון אינעװיניק אונטער די
צעגעשװאַקטע פֿאַזיציעס, סמנדיק אונדז מיטן סם פֿון ספֿקות, גיסנדיק
יאוש אין אונדזערע הערצער...

זיינען מיר עולה קיין ישראל, װערן מיר גלייך יידן־יורדים, אויב
מיר זאָגן זיך נישט אָפּ פֿון אונדזער ייִדיש־בכורה, פֿון אונדזער ייִדיש־
ירושה. בלייבן מיר אין גלות, זיינען מיר ניט סתם אַזױ יורדים, נאָר
יורדי דומה, — און האָבן נישט קיין תיקון און קיין תקומה... אַט
אַזױ זײַט מען אין די נשמות פֿון די מיליאָנען ייִדישע פֿאָלקס־מענטשן אומ־
צוטרוי און — װאָס איז נאָך ערגער — אומאַכטונג צו זיך אליין, —
און (װי אַלע מאָל) אַז זיי װערן דערנידעריקט, װערט אין איינעם מיט

זיי דערנידעריקט אויך זייער שפּראַך, זייער קולטור.

איז, דעריבער, ווידער אַ מאָל, נייטיק געוואָרן צו שטצן זיך קעגן דעם גיפֿט פֿון ביטול און פֿאַראַכטונג צו דעם טויזנטיאָרעדיקן ייִדישן פֿאָלקס־לעבן און פֿאָלקס־שאַפֿן.

ד

ס׳איז ווידער אַ מאָל נייטיק געוואָרן איבערצוחזרן פֿאַרגעסענע אַלף־בית־אמתן.

א. דער נאַציאָנאַלער און מענטשלעכער ווערט פֿון דער ייִדיש־ירושה איז מחמת דער פֿאַרקלענערטער צאָל יורשים נישט קלענער גע־וואָרן. בלויז דער שטח פֿון איר אויסשפּרייטונג, ניט זי אַליין, איז איינ־געשרומפּן געוואָרן ... זיינען דען תנך און תלמוד און קבלה און חסידות און השכלה געשטאַרבן אין איינעם מיט זייערע דורות? יעדע פֿון אָט די גרויסע קולטור־שאַפֿונגען האָט נאָכן טויט פֿון איר תקופֿה אָנגעהויבן צו לעבן, — אמת, אַ שטילערן, אַ טיפֿערן, אַ מער פֿאַרבאָרגענעם לעבן. אָבער זי האָט נישט אויפֿגעהערט צו עקסיסטירן, איר קוואַל איז ניט פֿאַרשטאָפּט געוואָרן. אַזוי איז אויך ניט פֿאַרשאַטן געוואָרן דער ברונען פֿון ייִדיש און דער ייִדיש־קולטור ווען עס זיינען חרוב גע־וואָרן די ייִדישע ישובים, וואָס האָבן אין משך פֿון דורות אים געגראָבן און אַלץ טיפֿער און פֿולער געמאַכט. דער אומ־קום פֿון די, וואָס האָבן דעם קוואַל געגראָבן און פֿון די, וואָס האָבן מיט פֿולע עמערס געשעפּט פֿון אים, האָט נאָר גרעסער געמאַכט די פֿאַראַנטוואָרטלעכקייט און שווערער דעם עול פֿון אות־ה, די לעבן־געבליבענע. די ירושה פֿון ייִדיש און דער ייִדישער קולטור האָט צוליב דעם, וואָס מיר זיינען איצט אירע איינציקע אַפּוטרופּסים, נישט פֿאַר־לאָרן איר ווערט אין אונדזערע אויגן. זי איז אונדז איצט, פֿאַרקערט, טיַיערער, ווי ווען עס איז. זי איז פֿאַר אונדז איצט נישט בלויז דאָס, וואָס זי איז אַליין, נאָר אויך — דער הייליקער אָנדענק נאָך אירע שאַפֿערס. זי איז אַלץ נאָך אַ דינאַמישער כּוח אין דער ייִדישער גע־שיכטע, זי ווירקט און ווערט נישט אויפֿהערן צו ווירקן אויף אונדזער אינעווייניקסטן לעבן, אויף אונדזער שעפּערישקייט.

ב. מיר, אירע איצטיקע טרעגערס, זאָגט מען אונדז, זיינען אַ דור פֿון היַינט, אפֿשר אויך פֿון מאָרגן, אָבער — וואָס איז ,פֿרעגט מען, מכּוח איבערמאָרגן?

מען סטראַשעט אונדז מיט פֿינצטערער נביאות־זאָגעריַי — און

מען פֿאַרגעסט אַז אַ פֿאָלקסשפּראַך און זײַן קולטור איז פֿריִער װי אַלץ,
פֿאַר זײַן לעבעדיקן לעבן, פֿאַר זײַנע נױטבאַדערפֿעניש, פֿאַר זײַן נאַ־
טירלעכער און קאָנקרעטער שעפֿערישקייט, ניט פֿאַר יענער אַבסטראַק־
ציע, װאָס איר נאָמען איז „צוקונפֿט". מען האָט כּלומרשט מורא, טאַמער,
חלילה, װעט דאָס ליכט פֿון לעבעדיקן ייִדן שפּעטער, חלילה, פֿאַרטונקלט
װערן, אײַלט מען זיך צו — און מען לעשט עס שױן איצט, אָנשטאָט
צו טאָן אַלץ װאָס מען קאָן, אַז עס זאָל לײַכטן װאָס העלער — און
װאָס לענגער. מען װיל אונדז פֿאַרזיכערן מיט אַ מאָרגן, דערװײַל שינדט
מען פֿאַסן פֿונעם הײַנט, פֿון אַט דעם ערב־שבת, װאָס איז דער אײַנ־
ציקער כּוח, װאָס קאָן עפּעס צוגרייטן אױך פֿאַרן שבת. מען פֿאַרגעסט
— און דאָס איז נאָך װיכטיקער — אַז מיר האָבן נישט אױפֿגעהערט צו
ציִען חיונה פֿון אונדזער העברעאישער קולטור, װען אונדזער לשון איז
געװאָרן תרגום־לשון — פֿאַרקערט, מיר האָבן דאַן נאָך מער פֿאַרהייליקט
העברעאיש און ס'איז געװאָרן לשון־הקודש. מען פֿאַרגעסט, אַז מיר
האָבן נישט אױפֿגעהערט צו טרינקען פֿון די העברעאישע און אַראַמע־
אישע קװאַלן, װען מיר האָבן אָנגעהױבן צו רעדן (און שפּעטער אױך צו
שרײַבן... אַט אַזױ דאַרפֿן מיר און קאָנען שטרעבן דערצו, אַז
אױב מען זאָל, חלילה, אָפּגעריסן װערן אי פֿון העברעאיש־אַראַמעאיש,
אי פֿון ייִדיש, זאָל מען מיט די לעצטע כּוחות איבערנעמען אי די
העברעאיש־אַראַמעאישע, אי די ייִדישע קולטור־ירושה.

װאָס רײַכער און װאָס לעבנספֿעאיקער די ירושה װעט זײַן, װאָס מער
מיר װעלן אָנזאַמלען און איבערלאָזן, אַלץ מער און אַלץ לעבנס־
פֿעאיקערע יורשים װעלן זיך אָפּזוכן.

ג. אָבער (זאָגט מען אונדז) די ייִדישע מדינה און דער אימפּע־
ראַטיװ פֿון איר שפּראַכלעך־נאַציאָנאַלער גאַנצקייט איז מער שױן נישט
קיין זאַך פֿון מאָרגן, נאָר פֿון הײַנט. איז לאָמיר — ראַט מען אונדז
— ברענגען נאָך אַ קרבן אױף איר מזבח, דעם קרבן ייִדיש. דער הײַנט פֿון
דער ניי־העברעאישער קולטור איז דאָך, זאָגט מען אונדז, אַ מער
זיכערע „אינװעסטירונג", װי דער ייִדיש־הײַנט. דערבײַ טראַכטן נאָר
יחידים און גאָר קלײנע גרופּעס װעגן דעם ייִדיש־קװאַל, װי װעגן אײנעם
פֿון די קװאַלן, װאָס זאָלן פּרוקטבאַר מאַכן דעם באָדן פֿון דער ישׂראל־
קולטור גופֿא. מען װיל ייִדיש מאַכן פֿאַר אַ קרבן עולה, װאָס אױפֿן ניי־
העברעאישן מזבח זאָל ער אין גאַנצן פֿאַרברענט װערן — על ראשו
ועל כרעיו... װייס מען דען ניט, אַז מען װאָלט אין דעם פֿאַל מקריב
געװען אַ רײַכן נעכטן, נישט נאָר דעם הײַנט פֿון גלות? װייס מען

וולאדימיר מעדעם

ליבאווע, לעטלאנד, 1879
ניו־יארק, פ״אר. שטאטן, 1923

◆

סאציאל־דעמאָקראטיע און די
נאציאנאלע פראגע
זכרונות און ארטיקלען
פון מיין נאטיץ־בוך
פון מיין לעבן

◆

עסייאיסט
טעאָרעטיקער פון סאציאליזם

ד״ר יעקב שאַצקי

וואַרשע, פּוילן, 1893
ניו יאָרק, פ״אר. שטאטן, 1956

◆

געשיכטע פון יידן אין וואַרשע
יידישע בילדונגס פּאָליטיק, פּוילן
קולטור - געשיכטע פון השכלה
אין ליטע
ספּינאָזע און זיין סביבה

◆

ליטעראטור, טעאַטער-פאָרשער
היסטאָריקער און ביבליאָגראַף

פּראָפ. שמעון דובנאָוו

מסטיסלאוו, אוקראינע, 1860
אומגעבראכט ריגע, לעטלאנד, 1941

◆

געשיכטע פון יידישען פּאָלק
געשיכטע פון חסידיזם
פון זשארגאָן צו יידיש
בריוו וועגן אלטן און נייעם
יידנטום

◆

היסטאָריקער
טעאָרעטיקער פון אויטאָנאָמיזם

ד״ר יצחק שיפּער

טאַרנע, גאַליציע, 1884
קאצעט מיידאַנעק, פּוילן, 1943

◆

געשיכטע פון יידיש טעאַטער
קונסט און דראַמע
אנהויב פון קאפּיטאליזם ביי יידן
ווירטשאפט-געשיכטע פון יידן
אין פּוילן
קולטור - געשיכטע פון יידן
אין פּוילן

◆

קולטור - היסטאָריקער

ד״ר ישראל צינבערג

דאַרף ביי לאַנאָוויץ, וואָלין, 1873
אומגעבראכט ראטנרוסלאַנד, 1938

◆

געשיכטע פון ליטעראטור ביי יידן
געשיכטע רוסיש־יידישע פּרעסע
געשיכטע פון יידישן טעאַטער
דער „קול מבשר" און זיין צייט

◆

ליטעראטור - היסטאָריקער

ד״ר עמנואל רינגעלבלום

ביטשוטש, גאַליציע, 1900
וואַרשע, געטאָ־אויפשטאַנד, 1943

◆

געשיכטע פון ייד. בוך און דרוק
יידיש לעבן אין פּוילן
יידן אין קאַשטשיוושקא־אויפ־
שטאנד
טאָגבוך פון וואַרשעווער געטאָ

◆

היסטאָריקער

1. Vladimer Medem, 1879–1923; Essayist, theoretician of socialism; 2. Shimen Dubnov, 1860–1941; Historian, theoretician of cultural autonomy; 3. Yisroel Tsinberg, 1873–1938; Literary historian; 4. Yankev Shatski, 1893–1956; Literary researcher, theater researcher, historian, bibliographer; 5. Yitskhok Shiper, 1884–1943; Historian of culture; 6. Emanuel Ringlblum, 1900–1943; Historian.

דען נישט, אַז די יידיש־עפּאָכע, װי יעדע גרױסע תקופה אין אַ פֿאָלקס
געשיכטע, האָט אָבסאַרבירט און אַסימילירט מיט זיך אַלע פֿריערדיקע
עפּאָכעס און אַז אַפּטרײַסלען זיך פֿון איר מײנט אױך פֿון זי זיך
אַפּטרײַסלען — און אָנהײבן אַלץ פֿון ס'נײַ? איז עס געװאָונטשן?
און — דער עיקר — איז עס דען מעגלעך? אַזױ װי אַ פֿאָלק זאָגט
זיך נישט אָפּ פֿון זײַן הײַנט, װײל עס װיל זיך נישט אָנטאָן קײן
מיתה, סײַדן עס איז קראַנק אָדער משוגע, אַזױ לאָזט עס אױך זײַן נעכטן
און אײַערנעכטן נישט אױף הפֿקר, — אַלץ אײַנס צי עס טראָגט דעם
נאָמען „גלות", אָדער אַן אַנדער נאָמען. און װען מען פֿאַרלאַנגט פֿן
אונדזער דור מקריב צו זײַן אױפֿן מזבח פֿון עפּעס אַ װילדן, נישט־
געטלעכן געבאָט זײַן שפּראַך און קולטור, פֿאַרלאַנגט מען אין דער אמתן
פֿון אים, אַז אחוץ זיך אַלײן, זאָל ער מבטל און מבזה זײַן אױך די אָבֿות,
די גאַנצע גאָלדענע קײט פֿון דורות, װאָס זײַנען אין אים מגולגל גע־
װאָרן און װאָס ער גיט זײ אַ תיקון. װײס מען דען ניט, אַז װען ער
זאָל אױפֿהערן צו זײַן טרײַ זיך אַלײן, װאָלט ער אױך זײ פֿאַראָטן?
װײס מען דען ניט, אַז אָן אַ הײַנט איז נישטאָ קײן נעכטן?

װאָס איז שײך צום מאָרגן אָדער איבערמאָרגן, איז שױן פֿריער
געזאָגט געװאָרן, אַז זאָל נאָר דער איצטיקער דור, דער יורש פֿן
נעכטן, היטן שעפֿעריש זײַן פֿאַרמעגן, װעט ער אַלײן אױך האָבן יורשים.
נאָר װען מיר זאָלן עס, חלילה, לאָזן אױף הפֿקר, װעט ניט זײַן, װער עס
זאָל עס איבערנעמען. װעלן מיר אונדזער ירושה טײַער האַלטן, װעלן מיר
נישט לאָזן זי פֿאַרגליװוערט װערן, װעט זי פֿון אונדז און מיר פֿון איר
באַרױכפֿערט װערן, — װעלן געבױירן װערן דורות, װאָס — אין אַזאַ
אָדער אַן אַנדער פֿאָרעם — װעלן זײ שטילן זײער דאָרשט פֿון איר
טיפֿע קװאַלן... ס'איז אַ כלל, אַז װען נאָר ס'איז דאַ אַ הײַנט, װאָס איז
פֿאַרװאָרצלט אין נעכטן, — ליגן אין אים אַלײן באַהאַלטן קערנדלעך פֿון
דער צוקונפֿט...

איז, דעריבער, אונדזער הײליקסטער געבאָט: ניט לאָזן זיך אױס־
װאָרצלען. און דאָס מײנט — ניט לאָזן דערנידעריקן, װי מען האָט ניט
אײן מאָל שױן דערנידעריקט, דעם פֿאָלקס־מענטשן, דעם יידיש־מענטשן,
העלפֿן אים זיך האַלטן אין דער מעלה און האַלטן דעם קאָפּ הױך
אױפֿגעהױבן, — װעט די יידיש־קולטור און איר נאַציאָנאַל־היסטאָרישע
ראָלע זײַן אָנגעזעענער און װערטפֿולער װי װען עס איז אין דער יידישער
געשיכטע...

ווילנער יידישע היסטאריש־עטנאגראפישע געזעלשאפט
אויף דעם נאמען פון ש. אנ־סקי ז״ל

מוזיקאַלישער
פנקס

ניגונים־זאמלונג פון יידישן פאלקס־אוצר

מיט טעקסט און דערקלערונגען

געשאפלט פון א. ב. בערנששיין ז׳לנג

ערסטער בוך

תרפ״ז   ווילנע   1927

„מוזיקאַלישער פנקס״ ניגונים־זאמלונג מיט דערקלע־
רונגען פון א. בערנשטיין

''Musical Journal'' — collection of melodies with
explanations by Z. Bernstein

„פנקס של מוסיקה״ (בייריש), לקט לחנים עם הסברים
מאת א. ברנשטין

„Музыкальная хроника" — сборник песен с об'яснениями
А. Бернштейна

A collection of folk melodies, published by the
Jewish Historical Ethnographic Society, 1927.

אומה ולשון: ייִדיש פֿאָלק, ייִדיש לשון

אַבֿרהם גאָלאָמב

SUMMARY: PEOPLE AND LANGUAGE: JEWISH NATIONALITY AND YIDDISH
LANGUAGE BY AVROM GOLOMB

One of the major Yiddish educators (1888–), formerly professionally active in Poland, Palestine, Canada, Mexico and the USA, argues that without a language of their own (such as Yiddish) Jews have never attained more than fleeting cultural creativity or authentic continuity.

לשון און פֿאָלק

פֿאָלק און שפּראַך זײַנען בײַ אונדז פֿאַרצײַטן געװאָרן
װי סינאָנימען. בחרתנו מכל עם וקדשתנו מכל לשון
פֿאָלק און לשון זײַנען זײַנען דאָ אידענטיש. װען גאָט האָט
געװאָלט צעטיילן די מענטשהייט אויף באַזונדערע פֿעל־
קער, האָט ער צעמישט זײערע לשונות, און װיפֿל שפּראַ־
כן — אַזוי פֿיל פֿעלקער. איך בין אַרײַן אין אַ ספֿרדישע
שול. דערזען „אונדזערע" משגיחות, דאַכט זיך אַלץ װי
אונדזערע, און דאָך זיך געפֿילט פֿרעמד — די שפּראַך
האָט געפֿעלט.

אַזוי איז עס געװוען בײַ ייִדן לאַנגע דורות, איצטער
אָבער זאָגן ייִדן אַנדערש. „רײדעלע יאַק רײדעלע, אַבֿ
דאַברע מײנעלע". מען קען רײדן אויף אַלע שפּראַכן.
אַבֿי נאָר דאָס האַרץ איז אַ ייִדיש; װער רעדט עס הײַ־
טיקע צײַטן ייִדיש ? און נאָך און נאָך שײַנע פֿראַזעם
פֿון דעם מין זײַנען בײַ אונדז גאַנגבאַר. און אַפֿילו פֿרו־
מע ייִדן װאָס האַלטן זיך פֿאַר די „שומרי מסורת" — זײַ
היטן ייִדישקייט, — אויך זיי רײדן מיט קינדער און מיט
אײניקלעך אַלע לשונות אין דער װעלט אַבֿי ניט ייִדיש
און, פֿאַרשטייט זיך, באַלד קומט אַ מאמר חז"ל. אַז שמט
— איז בכל לשון, — מען מעג, הייסט עס, זאָגן קריאת
שמע אויף אַלע לשונות. װײַס איך ניט צי עס איז ריכ־

עטװאָס התנצלות

בײַ אונדז איצט לייענט מען ניט װאָס מען שרײַבט,
נאָר װער עס שרײַבט. איטלעכער מענטש האָט זײַן עטי־
קעט, ער געהערט צו דעם אָדער צו יענעם מין, צו דער
אָדער יענער פּאַרטײ, און מען װייס שוין פֿריער װאָס ער
װעט זאָגן און במילא װי מען דאַרף זיך באַציִען צו זײַנע
רייד. ממה נפשך — איז ער אַן אונדזעריקער, איז אַלץ
װאָס ער זאָגט אָדער אַלץ װאָס ער שרײַבט אומבאַדינגט
אמת וציב, אמת ואמונה. אלא גיט, געהערט ער ניט צו
מײַנע לייט, װײַ איך פֿאַרויס, אַז אַלץ װאָס ער זאָגט
און שרײַבט איז שקר וכזב, און אויב עס אַפֿצולייקענען אָדער פֿאַר־
אמת, איז עס מײַן מצװה עס אַפֿצולייקענען אָדער פֿאַר־
שװײַגן. דאָס איז אונדזער קאָנפֿאַרמיזם. שרײַבט אַט
דעם װיטערדיקן אַרטיקל אַ מענטש װאָס געהערט ניט
צו קיין פּאַרטײ, ער חזרט ניט איבער קיינעמס אמתן, ער
שרײַבט נאָר דאָס װאָס עס זאָגט אים זײַן אייגענער גע־
װיסן און װיסן, און נאָר ער אַליין טראַגט די אחריות
פֿאַר די װיטערדיקע געדאַנקען. איך שרײַב װעגן ייִדי־
שער שפּראַך און איך בין ניט קיין העברעיסט און ניט
קיין ייִדישיסט. איך בין בלויז אַ ייִד װעמען עס איז
טײַער און הייליק די גאַנצע ייִדישע קולטור אין איר
אינטעגראַלער גאַנצקייט און בײַדע ייִדישע לשונות.

טיק, און וואָס דער זאָגער האָט מיט דעם געמיינט; וואָלט
מען ביי חז"ל געקאָנט געפֿינען פּונקט פֿאַרקערטע מאַמ־
רים אויך. אָבער לאָמיר זאָגן — יאָ, מען מעג טאָקע
אָבער פֿון וואַנען איז עס געדרונגען אַז מען דאַרף ? פֿון
מעגן ביז דאַרפֿן איז דאָך אַ וויַיטער מהלך. אָבער זאָלן
זיי מיר מוחל זיין: זיי זאָרגן זיך נאָר פֿאַר זייער פּריוואַטן
חשבון אויף יענער וועלט, זיי זאָרגן אָבער לגמרי נימ
וועגן דעם קיום פֿון כלל אויף ייִדן אויף דער וועלט. און
אַגב, זיי גייען אויפֿן זעלביקן וועג פֿון די קאָנסערוואַ־
טיוו, מער ניט וואָס יענע גייען זיכער און זיי מאַכן
דעם זעלביקן וועג פֿאַמעלעכער. וואָלן מיר זיך צו־
רו און מיר וועלן פּרובירן אָביעקטיוו אַנאַליזירן וואָס
ער מיינונג איז רעכטיקע — די פֿאָרצייטיקע אָדער די
היינטיקע ? איז ריידעלע ווי דו ווילסט אָדער עס איז
אומה ולשון אידענטיש.

❧

שפּראַכן ביי אַ מענטשן אין מויל קענען זיין צווייער־
ליי: עס זיינען פֿאַראַן שפּראַכן וואָס מען רעדט, מען קאָ־
מוניקירט זיך דורך זיי מיט אַנדערע מענטשן און מען
קענען זיין שפּראַכן וואָס מען לעבט אין זיי, מיט זיי.
אַ מענטש לערנט אויס עטלעכע הונדערט ווערטער, זיי־
ערע גראַמאַטיקאַלישע פֿאָרמען, און ער גיסט אַריין אין
זיי זיינע געדאַנקען, וואָס זיינען געבאָרן ביי אים פֿריִער
פֿון די גערעדטע ווערטער. די ווערטער זיינען שפּעטער
פֿון די געדאַנקען. און אפֿילו אפֿשר אויך איינצייטיק,
אָבער די ווערטער זיינען ניט פֿאַרבונדן מיט דעם אינ־
טימען לעבן פֿון דער מענטש. מען קען זיך צונויפֿריידן
אויף אַלע עולעכע שפּראַכן, פֿירן געשעפֿטן. עס איז אַ
ווערטערבוך, אַ מין עספּעראַנטאָ. אָבער דאָס אינטימסטע
אינעווייניקסטע לעבן מיט זיך אַליין איז ניט פֿאַרבונדן
מיט דער שפּראַך, די שפּראַך איז ניט פֿאַרבונדן מיט
דעם איך פֿון דעם מענטשן. זי קען זיין זייער רייך, אָ
די שפּראַכן און דאָך ניט אָרגאַניש, ניט פֿון דער נשמה.
עס איז ווי אַ געקויפֿטער בגד, וואָס מען טוט אָן, אַן אין־
געהאַנדלטן. אַנדערש איז די שפּראַך פֿון לעבן, זי איז
פֿאַרבונדן מיט דעם גייסט פֿון מענטשן. דאָס איז די
שפּראַך וואָס מיט איר קאָמוניקירט זיך דער מענטש ניט
בלויז מיט אַנדערע נאָר אויך מיט זיך אַליין. דאָס
גאַנצע באַוווּסטזיניקע און אומבאַוווּסטזיניקע לעבן פֿון
מענטשן פֿליסט אינעם דער שפּראַך. דאָס איז ניט קיין
געקויפֿטער בגד, נאָר די אייגענע, אָרגאַנישע הויט, ציי־
נער, וואָס וואַקסן און אַנטוויקלען זיך מיט דעם מענטשן
צוזאַמען. אַוודאי קען מען עסן און ריידן אויך מיט
אַריינגעשטעלטע פֿרעמדע ציינער, אָבער ווי קענען
זיי ניט, און דאָך איז זייער פֿרעמדקייט. די אָרגאַנישע

אייגענע שפּראַך הענגט ניט אָפּ ווי דער מענטש לעבט.
ניט פֿון אָרט און ניט פֿון מאָדע. אַן אויסגעלערנטע
שפּראַך איז ווי אַ מאָדע־בגד.

שפּראַך – פֿאַרבינדונג מיט דורות

און נאָך מער: יעדער שפּראַך איז עלטער פֿון אַלע
מענטשן וואָס ריידן זי, וואָס לעבן מיט איר. ווען אַ
שפּראַך איז אָרגאַניש פֿאַרבונדן מיט דעם מענטשן.
ברענגט זי אים זייער אַ רייכע גייסטיקע ירושה. אָט די
ירושה פֿון דורות קען מען ניט אויסלערנען אין קיין שום
שול, זי איז אירראַציאָנעל, ווי די גמרא רופֿט עס „סמוי
מן העין". דאָ קומען אַריין אַ שלל מיט דערפֿאַרונגען
פֿון אַלע פֿריערדיקע דורות, אַלערליי עמאָציאָנעלע רע־
אַקציעס, חכמות, וויצן און נאַרישקייטן. דאָס איז דער
גאַנצער פֿאָלקלאָר. אין דעם איז דער כאַראַקטער פֿון
פֿאָלק, דער גאַנצער געמיט פֿון די דורות. אַזאַ שפּראַך
איז אידענטיש מיט דעם פֿאָלק, דער גייסט און זיין אויסדרוק
די קאָלעקטיווע נשמה און איר שפּיגל. פֿאָלק איז אַ
„קייט פֿון דורות" (מ. קאַפּלאַן). און אָט די פֿאַרגאַנגענע
דורות האָבן אויסגעאַרבעט שטייגער אין שפּראַך, זיטן
און מינהגים, מאָראַל און געדאַנק, אַ געמיינזאַמע פּסיכיק
און געמיינזאַמע האַנדלונגען מאַטעמאַרישע און גייסטיקע.
און דאָס אַלץ קריגט אַ דעם אויסדרוק אין שפּראַך פֿון
פֿאָלק. דאָס אַלץ פֿאַרבינדט באַזונדערע מענטשן אין
איין פֿאָלק, פֿאָלק און שפּראַך — פֿלאַם און קנויט. און
אַיטלעכער מענטש וואָס איז איינגעלעבט מיט דעם לשון
איז שוין במילא אויך איינגעלעבט אין זיין פֿאָלק, צונויפֿ־
געבונדן מיט די פֿאַרגאַנגענע דורות. דער מענטש מיט
דעם אָרגאַניש לשון פֿון זיין פֿאָלק איז אַ קינד פֿון זיין
פֿאָלק מיט אַלע זיינע גייסטיקע אברים, מיט זיין גאַנצן
מהות.

ניסתר און ניגלה אין אַ פֿאָלק

דאָ פֿאַסט זיך זייער אַלטער אונדזער טערמינאָלאָגיע
פֿון קבלה. דאָס צווייטע — דער ניגלה איז אַלץ וואָס
מען קען מעסטן און שאַצן, ציילן און רעכענען. מען קען
עס דעפֿינירן און דערקלערן. דער ניסתר — דאָס איז
דאָס אירראַציאָנעלע וואָס מען קען בשום אופֿן ניט שאַצן
און ניט מעסטן. און דווקא דאָ ליגט די נשמה פֿון אַ
מענטש, ווי אויך פֿון פֿאָלק בכלל. אַ מענטש אַזאַ
אָרגאַנישער שפּראַך איז איינס מיטן פֿאָלק. אַן דעם איז
מען אָפּגעריסן פֿון פֿאָלק, תלישים איז מען, כרת. יאָ,
מען קען זאָגן „שמע" בכל לשון. מען קען דאָך אויך
זיך באַוועגן אָן פֿיס, ניט פֿאַר קיין מענטשן געדאַכט, אַזוי
קען מען, נעבעך, אויך „יעגענען קריאת שמע אויף

אוצרות... אָרעם איז אונדזער נשמה און זי ווערט אַלץ אָרעמער.

די שפּראַך פירט דעם געדאַנק

נאָך מער. מיר האָבן פריער געשריבן, אַז ביי אַן אויסגעלערנטער שפּראַך קומען די ווערטער שפּעטער, נאָך די געדאַנקען און נאָך די געפילן. ביי אַן אָרגאַני-שער שפּראַך זיינען די געדאַנקען, געפילן אַלע מאָל איין-ציטיק מיט די ווערטער, און די ווערטער העלפן דעם געדאַנק געבאָרן ווערן, די ווערטער פירן דעם געדאַנק געפיל, די איבערלעבונגען. עס איז געגליכן צו אַ באַן וואָס גייט אויף רעלסן. דאָס איז דער סטיל, די פאָרעם פון ריידן אָן פון שרייבן. אָבער אָט די רעלסן פון דעם געדאַנק זיינען געלייגט געוואָרן פריער פאַר דעם מאָמענט. זיי זיינען דעם פאָלקס, פון די פריערדיקע דורות. טביה דער מילכיקער האָט זיינע אַלע געדאַנקען און אי-בערלעבונגען אויסגעדריקט אין שפּראַך פון זיין פאָלק, פון זיינע דורות. און דער שפּראַך וואָלט ער געוואָרן אַן אומגליקלעכער פאַרלאָרענער מענטש. אים איז גרינ-גער — ער לעבט זיין גאַנץ לעבן אויף פאַרטיקע רעלסן. איך לערן דאָס אויף פון זיך: איך ריד אין איך שרייב ווי אויף יידיש, אַזוי אויף העברעאיש. איך האָב ניט געלערנט קיין יידיש, עס איז מיין אָרגאַניש לשון. איך האָב אויך ניט געלערנט קיין העברעאיש ווי אַ שפּראַך.. איך האָב זי איינגעזאַפט מיט די ספרים, וואָס געלערנט, וואָס געלייענט אַ גאַנץ לעבן, וואָס געניצט אין בית מדרש און ישיבה. און אַז איך נעם איין טעמע צו שרייבן אויף ביידע שפּראַכן אונדזערע, קומען דאָ אַרויס צוויי פאַרשיידענע שריפטן. די רעלסן פון ביידע שפּראַכן פירן דעם זעלביקן געדאַנק אויף אַנדערע וועגן. ווייל איז דעם מענטשן וואָס האָט זיין סטיל, און נאָך ווילער איז דעם וואָס דענקט און שרייבט אין סטיל פון זיינע דורות. דער סטיל — דאָס איז דער מענטש. דער סטיל, די שפּראַך — דאָס איז דאָס פאָלק. און אַ מענטש מיט אַן אָרגאַנישער שפּראַך, מיט דער שפּראַך פון זיין פאָלק פילט זיך אין איר היימיש. זי — די שפּראַך מיט אירע אויסדרוקן און ניואַנסן — זי איז די אמתע היים פון אַ מענטשן. זי איז די ערשטי-קע היים, דאָס שטיקל ערד איז שוין די סעקונדערע היים. עס ווערט היימיש אויך אין דאַנק דער שפּראַך.

פאַרוואָס פילן זיך אַזוי אָפט היינטיקע יידן ניט היי-מיש אין זייער פאָלק? פאַרוואָס איז אַזוי אָפט שווער די יידישע אידענטיפיקאַציע פון יונגע יידן? פאַרוואָס דאַרף מען אין דער יידישער מדינה אַזאַ גאַנצע פּראָגראַמען צו לערנען מיט די קינדער די יידיש באַוווסטזיין"? אַ זאַך

פרעמדע שפּראַכן. אָבער די גאולה פון פאָלק איז פאַר-בונדן דווקא מיט דעם "שלא שינו את לשונם" — נישט געענדערט די שפּראַך. דאָס איז אויף אַ מאמר חז"ל.

מיר קלאָגן זיך אָפט אויף דעם וואָס עס ווערט איצט פאַרמינערט אונדזער פאָלקישער כאַראַקטער, עפּעס גע-שען זאַך וואָס פּאַסט ניט פאַר אַ יידן, עפּעס ווווּנדערן מיר זיך אַליין אָפט: ווי קומט עס? ווי פּאַסט עס? פון וואַנען נעמט זיך עס?.... מיר זיינען אָפט אַזוי ניט עכט מיט זיך אַליין... עס ווילט זיך ניט צו פיל פאַרשפּרייטן וועגן דעם, אָבער איך גלייב באַאמונה שלמה אַז עס איז פאַר-בונדן מיט דער פאַרמינערונג פון יידיש לשון. די גמרא זאָגט ריכטיק, אַז די גאולה קומט פון אָפהיטן דאָס לשון, די אייגענע טראַדיציאָנעלע נעמען און די שטייגערישע פאָלקישקייט (מסתורין). און דאָס פאַרקערטע געשעט איצט מיט אונדז. דערפאַר טרעפט אַז מיר פאַרלירן זיך אַליין, במילא ווערט די גאולה — די גאולה פון אייגע-נעם גייסטיקן פאָלקישן איך אַלץ ווייטער און ווייטער וואָרעם.

ווי איז די שייכות צווישן דעם ניגלה און דעם ניסתר?

אַ מענטש גיט אַ שמייכל. דאָס איז ניגלה. קען דער שמייכל זיין אַ געמאַכטער, עס פּאַסט אַזוי, "גיט, זייט אַזוי גוט, אַ שמייכל". און עס קען אויך זיין אַן אויסדרוק פון אַ טיפער איבערלעבונג אין הערצן. אָט די איבערלעבונג אינעווייניק דאָס איז דער ניסתר און דער שמייכל איז דער ניגלה. קען אָבער דער שמייכל זיין ליגנעריש, פאַלש, געמאַכט, אומעכט. און מיר זעען דאָס צום באַדוירערן צו אָפט — אין אונדזער קאָלעקטיוון לעבן. גאַנץ מעגלעך אַז עס איז פאַרבונדן מיט אונדזער סיסטעמאַטיש, כסדר-דיקן פאַרלאָזן אונדזער דורותדיקן פאָלקישן לשון.

אַ משל צו וואָס עס איז געגליכן — אַ מענטש גיט אַ טשעק, קען דער טשעק זיין פולווערטיק, און ער קען זיין פאַלש, אָן פּאַנדען אין באַנק און ער האָט נישט קיין שום ווערט. אַזוי קענען אויך זיין אַלע האַנדלונגען פון אַ מענטשן, אַלע ניגלהדיקע טאָאונגען זיינע. זיינע רייד. זיין שמייכל, זיין פריינדשאַפט און שנאה, זיין עקסטאַז און זיין טרויער-אַלץ קען זיין פאַלש, אָן טיפערע איבער-לעבונגען אין דער נשמה, אָן טיפערע נשמה, קענען זיין אויך פול-ווערטיק. עס ווענדעט זיך אין דער רייכקייט פון דעם באַנק. פון דער נשמה, ווען די רייד און די האַנדלונגען אַלע זיינען נאָר די טשעקס, וואָס זיינען צום באַדוירערן צו אָפט פאַלש אָן דעקונגען אין דעם נשמה-באַנק... צום באַדוירערן, זיינען ביי אונדז צו פיל גאַנגבאַר אָט אַזוינע פאַלשע "טשעקס" אָן דעקונגען אין פאָלקישער שפּראַך פאַרלירן מיר אויך אונדזערע נשמהדיקע, אירראַציאָנעלע, ניסתרדיקע,

וואָס קיין עם הארץ, קיין שום יידישער אַנאַלפֿאַבעט האָט
עס ניט געדאַרפֿט. דאָס איז דערפֿאַר ווייל זיי האָבן ניט
אין זייער לעבן, פֿאַר די איבערלעבונגען מיט זיך אַליין
אין דער אייגענער נשמה די נאַטירלעכע „רעלסן" פֿון
זייער פֿאָלק. די נשמה איז ניט היימיש אין דעם פֿאָלק.
מען האָט אַמאָל, פֿאַר דעם דריטן חורבן און פֿאַר דער
מלחמה געטראַכט ערנסט אַז מען דאַרף די יוגנט פֿון
ארץ ישראל שיקן אויף אַ יאָר און מער אויך קיין ווילנע, קיין
וואַרשע, זיי זאָלן זיך דאָרטן אָננעמען מיט פֿאָלקישקייט.
עס איז אויך דעמאָלט געווען אַ טעות. אויך דעמאָלט
זיינען אין ווילנע און אין וואַרשע געווען אָפֿגעפֿרעמדטע
יידן. און די גייסטיקע היימישקייט פֿון אַ מענטשן איז
לגמרי נישט קיין טעריטאָריאַליסטיש: ניט קיין מאַטע־
ריעלע בכלל. די גייסטיקע היים איז די אָרגאַנישע שפֿראַך
פֿון דעם מענטשן, זיין פֿאָלקס לשון, און זי מאַכט היימיש
דאָס אַרט.

די שפֿראַך איז אָפֿט די מוטער פֿון געדאַנקען

וואָס וואָלט געווען טביה דער מילכיקער אָן זיין לשון?
— ער וואָלט געווען אַ באָנטשע שווייג, אַ שטומע נשמה,
אַ פֿאַרלאָרענער אין ליידן און אָן צרות, וואָס עס עסן אים ווי
שטומע ווערעם, און ער ווערט אין זיי פֿאַרלאָרן ווי אַ
שטיק האָלץ וואָס ברענט און ווערט פֿאַרברענט, ווי אַ
שטיק האָלץ וואָס ליגט און פֿוילט און פֿאַסיאָווערהייט. פֿאַר־
וואָס? אָט פֿאַרוואָס:

ניט נאָר אַ „פֿרעמדע נשמה איז אַ פֿינצטערניש" ווי
עס זאָגן די רוסן. נאָר אויך די אייגענע נשמה פֿון דעם
מענטשן איז לגמרי ניט באַלויכטן. דער באַוווּסטזיין בא־
לויכט תמיד ביי אונדז נאָר אַיין קליין ווינקעלע. ווי און־
דזער פֿיזיאָלאַגיע אַזוי איז אויך אונדזער פּסיכאָלאַגיע
אָן אַמתער ניסתר, אַ לאַבירינט, וואָו עס איז זייער שווער
זיך צו אָריענטירן. אַלע אונדזערע איבערלעבונגען קו־
מען ביי אונדז גלאַבאַל, מיט אַיין מאָל גאַנצערהייט, אַ
קנויל. גיי און צי דעם פֿאָדעם אַליין, פֿלאַנטער אים אויס,
ער זאָל זיך ציען גליַיך מיט אַן אָנהייב און אַ סוף. ניט
אומזיסט זאָגט מען אַז דערקענען זיך אַליין איז די שווער־
סטע אויפֿגאַבע. און אָט דאָס דערקענען זיך אַליין איז
קיין מאָל ניט פֿאַר די כוחות פֿון יעדער מענטשן באַזון־
דער, ניט פֿאַר די כוחות פֿון אַיין דור. דאָ קומט די
גיַירשנסטע שפֿראַך פֿון דורות און זי העלפֿט דעם געבוירן
ווערן פֿון די געדאַנקען, פֿון די איבערלעבונגען, און
זיך אָנקליידן אין ווערטער און פֿאַרמען און ווערן אויך
גיגלה. זי העלפֿט צעגלידערן די איבערלעבונגען אויף
זייערע עלעמענטן און זי גיט זיי אַ געהעריקןּ אויסדרוק.

אַבער דאָס קען ניט אויפֿטאָן קיין געלערנטע, קיין
אויסגעלערנטע שפֿראַך; דאָס קען ניט אויפֿטאָן די שפֿראַך
וואָס עלטערן ריידן מיט זייער קינדער אַ שפֿראַך וואָס
זיי האָבן זיך אויסגעלערנט.   די שפֿראַך ביים ערשטן
דור, ביים צווייטן און על פי רוב אויך ביי דעם דריטן
דור ריידער איז נאָר אַ טעכנישע, זיך צונויפֿצוריידן מיט
אַנדערע מענטשן, אָבער ווייט נאָך ניט מיט זיך אַליין,
עס איז נאָך ווייט ניט דאָס לשון פֿון דער אייגענער נשמה.
פֿאַר זיך אַליין האָט דער מענטש נאָך קיין שפֿראַך, קיין
אויסדרוק פֿאַר זיינע איבערלעבונגען. זיין ניסתר בלייבט
פֿאַרבאָרגן פֿאַר אים אַליין אויך. אָט פֿאַרוואָס מיר האָבן
אין אַמאָליקע שטעטלעך געהאַט אַזוי פֿיל שרייבער און
דיכטער, אויך ניט קיין געבילדעטע, און מיר האָבן אפֿילו
ניט קיין צענטשהלק היינט ביי אַ יוגנט מיט בילדונג און
מיט דיפֿלאָמען. משל — עס איז געגליכן צו קינדער וואָס
ווערן ניט געבאָרן, וואָס שטאַרבן אָפֿ פֿריער, אין דער מו־
טערס לייב. דאָס איז דאָס וואָס די גמרא רופֿט אָן „נש־
מות דאָזלין ערטילאין". אַ מענטש קען לערנען און אָן לער־
נען, קען זיין געבילדעט ביז גאָר, קען האָבן אויסגעלערנט
שפֿראַכן אַ צענדליק און מער, — און זיין אייגענע נשמה
בלייבט שטום. אַ מענטש קען ריידן די רייכסטע שפֿראַך
אין דער וועלט, און ביי אים אין מויל איז זי אָרעם, און
זיין אייגענע נשמה איז אומבאַהאָלפֿן דלותדיק. דער מענטש
קען זיך צונויפֿריידן מיט אַנדערע, אָבער ער קען נישט
אַרויסריידן זיך אַליין.

פֿאַראַן ביי ייִדן אַ לעגענדע וועגן גילגול נשמות: זעל־
טן ווען אַ מענטש קריגט ביים געבוירן ווערן אַ נייע (אַ
ניטגעניצטע) נשמה. על פי רוב קריגט אַ מענטש אַ נשמה
וואָס האָט שוין געלעבט אין פֿריערדיקע דורות. רש״יס
נשמה איז געווען אַ גילגול פֿון רבי עקיבאס, און רבי
עקיבא האָט זיין נשמה געהאַט אַ גילגול פֿון משה רבי־
נוס. איז אָט די לעגענדע ווייט ניט פֿאַלש. און די „נייע"
נשמה, ניט פֿון „אָצר הנשמות" איז אומבאַהאָלפֿן צו קע־
נען געבוירן אָן דער הילף פֿון דער דורותדיקער פֿאָל־
קישער שפֿראַך אַלע אירע איבערלעבונגען אויב זי
האָט צו איר   דינסט אַ סך   טעכניש — אויסגעלערנטע
שפֿראַכן.

גייסטיקע קאָמפּלעקסן

און עס איז ניט נאָר אַ פֿראַגע פֿון גייסטיקער אָרעמ־
קייט, פֿון קענען ריידן מיט אַנדערע אָבער ניט מיט זיך
אַליין. עס איז אַ סך מער אַ מקור פֿאַר פֿאַרשיידענע, טי־
פֿערע עמאָציאָנעלע שוועריקייט און קאָמפּלעקסן. די
אָרעמקייט אין אויסדרוק רייסט אַוועק דעם מענטשן פֿון
זיך אַליין. ער זוכט אַלץ זיך אויסצולעבן דרויסנדיק, אין

Evening courses in drawing, for students older than 14...Teachers who complete an eight-month course in drawing and arts and crafts will receive a certificate.

אלערליי געקויפטע אזארטן און שפילן, אבי צו אנטלויפן
פון זיד אליין.

עס ווערט באגלייט מיט א נערוועזקייט, צערודערונג,
אומצופרידנקייט און מיט א פארשיידענע אנדערע גייסטיקע
קראנקייטן. מיט דעם איז אויך אפט פארבונדן דאָס גע־
פיל פון מינדערווערטיקייט. פון נאציאנאלער געפאָלנ־
קייט, וואָס מיר טרעפן ביי יידן אזוי פיל. מיר באשרייבן
דאָס אין אנדערע ארבעטן אונטערן נאמען פון נאציאנא־
לער עגאפאביע, און מיר וועלן דאָ זיד דערמיט ניט פאר־
נעמען. אבער דאָס ברענגט אויך אן א שיעור פריוואטע,
אינדיווידועלע קאָנפליקטן און קאָמפלעקסן, וואָס צערייסן
די פערזאָן, מאכן זי קראנק.

מיר גיבן זיד ניט אָפּ לגמרי קיין חשבון ווי טראגיש

עס איז דאָס פארווארפן די אייגענע שפראד, די שפראד
פון די אייגענע דורות, די אייגענע פאָלקשפראך און וואָס
פאר א וואונדן דאָס איז עלול צו פארשאפן דעם מענטש;
דער מענטש אליין קען זיד ניט אָפּגעבן קיין חשבון
פון זיינע קראנקייטן. מיט אן אנגעריסענעם פינגער לויפט
מען צו א דאָקטער. מיט א צעריסענער, צעפליקטער נשמה
— דאָס ניט. מען ווייס גארניט אז מען איז קראנק. און
וואו איז דער דאָקטאר צו דער קראנקייט, אז די מער־
הייט אליין איז דאָך קראנק.

איז טאקע אומה ולשון — פאלק און שפראך. דאָס
פאלק שאפט די שפראך און די שפראך האלט אויף דאָס
פאלק. און שפראך פארלארן — פאלק פארלארן. דרייען
זיד ארום יידן אן זייער שפראד און אן זייער פאלק, אן

זיין גורל, איז ער אין כעס אויף דעם פאלק וואָס פון אים
שטאַמט ער. "יידישקייט איז אַ טראַגעדיע" — די חכמה
פון אן אומגליקלעך קלוגן משומד (היינע) ווערט צעפּט אזוי
פיל איבּערגעחזרת.   און נאָך מער ווערט זי באַהאַלטן
אונטער פאַרקערטע פראַזעס פון כלומרשטער ליבע און
געטרייעקייט.   און עס טרעפט, אז עס קומט טאַקע יאָ צו
"עקספּלאַזיע-יידישקייט": אַנטוישט אין אַלע אַנדערע
וועלטן קומט אזאַ איינער צוריק צו דער יידישקייט, צום
פאַלק פון זיין אָפּשטאַם, אָן... ער קען ניט אריינלעבּן זיך
אין דעם.   אָן דעם לשון איז אָן דעם פּאַלקישן ניסתר.   איז
מען מיטן באַוואוסטזיין אַ געטרייער ייד, אָבּער אָט דער
יידישער באַוואוסטזיין איז פּרייוויליק אַרויפּגעצוואונגען, אָן
וואַרצלען...   בין איך אַזוינע "הייסע" ייִדן ווייט ניט
מקנא.   ווער קען גאָר אַרומנעמען די טראַגעדיע פון
פרעמדע שפּראַך און איר גאַנצן אַלזייטיקן פאַרנעם?

אַטראָפּיע פון שעפּערישקייט

איך האָבּ פריער דערמאָנט די קנאַפּקייט פון שרייבּער
און דיכטער בּיי יידן וואָס רידן פּרעמדע שפּראַכן.   שאַפּן
קען אַ מענטש נאָר מיט דעם כּוח פון דורות געירשנטער
קולטור.   מיט דער שפּראַך אָן דער גייסטיקער ירושה
אין איר קען מען ניט זיין שעפּעריש.   אָבּער עס איז
שייך ניט נאָר די געבּיטן פון קונסט.   מיר קלאָגן זיך
אָפּט, אז דער צווייטער דור איז בּכלל ניט אויפּטועריש
אויך א. אַ. יף ריין עקאָנאָמישע געבּיטן.   זיינען געקומען אָרע־
מע יונגעלעך פון אָרעמע שטעטלעך אָן שפּראַך און אָן
בּילדונג, אָן דיפּלאָמען און באַקאַנטשאַפט מיט די פעלקער,
— אָן זיי האָבּן אָפט אויפגעבּויט גראַנדיעזע עקאָנאָמישע
פּאָזיציעס.   און די קינדער — מיט שפּראַכן, מיט די־
פּלאָמען, מיט בּילדונג — הלוואַי זאָלן זיי קענען איינהאַלטן
די געשאַפענע פּאָזיציעס פון דעם ערשטן דור אימיגראַנטן.
און נאָך בּולטער איז די שוואַכקייט אויף די געזעלשאַפט־
לעכע געבּיטן.   די ערשטע האָבּן געהאַט אימפעט, מוט,
דערפינדערישקייט, אַן איניציאַטיוו, אַן אָפּהאַלטערס, מיט
דער גאַנצער ענערגיע איז מען געווען שעפּעריש.   דער
צווייטער דור אָבּער מיט זיינע קאָמפּלעקסן, מיט זיינע
אינעווייניקסטע קאָנפליקטן קען שוין ניט זיין שעפּעריש.
יונגע מענטשן גייען אָפט אַרום ווי צעחושעטע.   זיי ווייסן
אַליין ניט וואָס מיט זיי קומט פאַר.   יאָגט עס זיי צו דער־
טרינקען זייערע גייסטיקע נע ואנד אין פאַרווייילונגען.   קענען
זיי זייער אָפּט צעפּרטן וואָס די עלטערן האָבּן געשאַפּן,
אָבּער אַליין קענען זיי שוין גאָרנישט אויפטאָן.   זייערע
צלע גייסטיקע כוחות זיינען אַטראָפּירט.   און אַלץ הייבט
זיך אָן פון דעם אָננעמען דאָס פּרעמדע לשון, וואָס דער מאַטע־
טערן האָבּן זיי איבּערגעגעבּן צוזאַמען מיט דער מאַטע־

דער פאַלקשפּראַך — עלנטע, פאַרוואָגלטע נשמות, נע־
בּעך.   זיי קענען רידן אַ סך רייכע שפּראַכן, אָבּער זיי האָבּן
גאָרניט פון דער רייכקייט — אַן איינגעהאַנדלטער אויפן
שפּראַכן־מאַרק פרעמדער בגד וואָס אַמאָל האָט געטראָגן
אַ רייכער פריץ.   די רייכע שפּראַכן זיינען רייך נאָר פאַר
די קינדער פון דעם פאַלק וואָס האָט די שפּראַך געשאַפּן.
נאָר בּיי זיי איז זי שעפּעריש, פּראָדוקטיק.   בּיי די איבּער־
נעמער איז זי — די רייכסטע שפּראַך — אָרעם, דאַר
און קאַרג און זי שטימט ניט מיט דעם גײערישנטער כאַ־
ראַקטער פון דעם איבּערנעמער.   עלעהיי אַ קאָזאַקישע
היטל אויפן קאָפּ פון אַ חב्रדער חסיד.   וואָלטן ייִדן גע־
פּילט די אייגענע נשמה, די דורותדיקע נשמה אין זיך,
וואָלטן זיי זיך צוגעהערט צו איר, — וואָלטן זיי זיכער
נישט געבּיטן זייערע שפּראַכן ווי די העמדשקעס.   יעדער
שפּראַך איז אייגנטלעך אַ פאַלקשפּראַך, אַ שפּראַך פון אַ
פאַלק.   איר גאַנצע רייכקייט גיט זי אָבּער בּלויז די קין־
דער פון איר פאַלק, די וואָס זייערע דורות זיינען פאַר־
בּונדן מיט דער שפּראַך.   פרעמדע איבּערנעמער געניסן
נאָר די ברעקלעך פון דער איבּערגענומענער שפּראַך.

שפּראַך און אידענטיפיקאַציע

אמאָל האָבּן ייִדן געזונגען "וואָס מיר זיינען זיינען מיר
אַקער ייִדן זיינען מיר".   עס איז טאַקע געווען "שווער צו
זיין אַ ייד", און מען האָט די שוועריקייט געטראָגן גאָר
גרינג, מיט פרייד, מיט גרייטקייט צו ליידן.   איצט איז עס
אַלץ פאַרקערט.   עס איז נישטאָ די אַמאָליקע שוועריקייט
צו זיין אַ ייד, נאָר די יידישקייט גופא איז איצט צו שווער.
וואָס קנאַפּער עס איז איצט דער יידישער אינהאַלט בּיי דעם
ייִדן, אַלץ שווערער ווערט זי.   דער ייד מיטן פרעמדן
לשון אין מויל איז מקנא דעם באַלעבאָס פון דעם לשון,
ער יאָגט זיך נאָך אים און קען נאָך אים דאָך ניט אַײיאָגן.   ער
איז אַ ייד און ער ווייס ניט פאַרוואָס און מיט וואָס.   איז
ער אַ געשפּאַלטענע נשמה.

די גאַנצע טראַגעדיע פון דער יידישער אידענטיפיקאַ־
ציע איז זייער אַ קאָמפּליצירטע, און עס איז אוממעגלעך
זי אויסצושעפּן אין איין פאַראַגראַף.   עס איז אַ שוידער
פאַר אַ מענטשן איבּערצולעבּן אזאַ מין פּראַבּלעם: ווער
בּין איך?   צו וועמען געהער איך?   ווער איז מיין פאַלק?
און ווו איז מיין היים?   ניט די מאַטעריעלע היים, ניט
דאָס לאַנד, נאָר די גייסטיקע היים פון דעם מענטשן.   ווו
און צווישן וועמען ער קען זיך פילן היימיש?   און ער
וואָרפּט זיך ווי אין כף הקלע (קאָף אַקאל).   עס וויל זיך
אים זיין איינער פון דעם לאַנדפאַלק און ער קען ניט, ווייל
ער זיין אַ ייד, און ער קען ווערער ניט: ער האָט ניט
מיט וואָס, אָפּגעריסן פון אַלע וועלטן.   האָט ער פינט

ריעלער רייכער ירושה. אַ שיינער עפל. אָבער מיט אַ
וואָרעם אינעווייניק.

פּאָלקשפּראַך און אינטעליגענץ

אינטעליגענץ איז ניט דעם וויסן וואָס עס האָבן
געזאַמלט אַלע חכמים און געלערנטע פון גאָר דער וועלט.
זי באַשטייט פון צוויי עלעמענטן — קענען געבוירן איי־
גענע געדאַנקען אינטואיטיוו און אין קענען זיי פאַרמו־
לירן און פורעמען אין באַשטימטע, אייגנטימלעכע פו־
רעמס. אַל דאָס געלערנטע און אַל דאָס וויסן, וואָס ווערט
פּאַרדיינט דורך אַ מענטשן און אַלץ וואָס ער ווייסט איז
נאָר אַ מיטל צו קענען אַסאָציאירן ביי יעדער געלעגנ־
הייט אייגענע געדאַנקען, אייגענע פורעמס.

אַן אויסגעלערנטער טעכנישע שפּראַך קען אַרויסברענ־
גען אַלץ וואָס דער מענטש האָט אין זיין וויסן, אין זיין
זכרון, אָבער זי — די שפּראַך — קען ניט העלפן איר
באַנוצער צו געבוירן אייגענע, אַסאָציאַטיווע געדאַנקען
און אידעען. זי קען אים ניט געבן קיין אינטעליגענץ,
סיידן ער האָט געהאַט פריער, אין דער קינדהייט אַ
צווייטע, אַן אָרגאַנישע, ניט קיין אויסגעלערנטע שפּראַך,
אַ שפּראַך וואָס די עלטערן האָבן ניט געדאַרפט לערנען.

דאָס איז די שפּראַך וואָס אַ מענטש רעדט מיט זיך
אַליין, ניט בלויז מיט אַנדערע. נאָר אינטעליגענטער,
אידעעך־רייכער און געדאַנקען־שעפערישער וועט זיין
דער מענטש, ווען זיין אָרגאַנישע שפּראַך איז די אָרגאַ־
נישע שפּראַך פון זיינע פריערדיקע דורות. מיר האָבן
געזאָגט אַז די שפּראַך איז עלטער פון יעדער ריידער,
אַז אין שפּראַך איז אָנגעשפּייכלערט די דערפאַרונג פון
דורות. מיט דער פאָלקישער שפּראַך באַקומט יעדער
קינד די קולטור־דערפאַרונג פון זיינע אָרעלטערן, פון
זיינע דורות, די אינטעליגענץ פון זיין פאָלק.

די פיליאָריקע דערפאַרונג ווי אַ לערער אין פאַרשיי־
דענע יידישע ישובים אין דער וועלט האָט מיר טאַקע
געוויזן אַז דער פּראָצענט פעיקע, אינטעליגענטערע
קינדער איז טאַקע ניט אַזוי אין פאַרגלייך גרעסער צווישן די
וואָס ריידן יידיש פון זייערע היימען. מיט דעם פּאָלקס
שפּראַך האָבן זיי געירשנט אויך דעם פּאָלקס חכמה און
אינטעליגענץ. אין די ערשטע יאָרן פון לערנען איז עס
אפשר ניט אַזוי קענטיק. דאָס ווערט מיט דעם עלטער
אַלץ קענטיקער אַלץ בולטער, קלאָרער.

איך גלייב צוריק אַז די עמאַציאנעלע רייכקייט פון
אַ מענטשן איז פּראָפּאָרציאנעל אָפּט צו זיין אינטעליגענץ
אַט די רייכקייט באַשטייט פון צוויי עלעמענטן: טיפקייט
פון איבערלעבונג און זיי ווערן אַרויסגערופן דורך רייצן,
וואָס זיינען פיזיש שוואַכער, און ניט דווקא דרויסנדיקע.

וואָס דער אינטעליגענטער מענטש, אַלץ מער מעגלעכ־
קייטן פאַר אַ רייכערער און העכערער גאַמע עמאָציא־
נעלע איבערלעבונגען.

מיט דער אפשוואַכונג פון יידיש פאַרלירט דאָס יידי־
שע פאָלק גרויסע טיילן פון זיין אינטעלעקטועלער און
עמאָציאנעלער רייכקייט.

פאָלק אַן שפּראַך

עד כאַן האָבן מיר זיך באַמיט צו באַנעמען אונדזער
שפּראַך־טראַגעדיע ביי די יחידים פון פאָלק. איצט וועלן
מיר פּרובירן באַהאַגדלען די טראַגעדיע ביים גאַנצן קאָ־
לעקטיוו, ביים פאָלק ווי אַזאַ. מיר האָבן אין משך פון
אונדזער געשיכטע צווישן אַזוי פיל פעלקער אויף דער
וועלט גענוצט זייער פיל שפּראַכן. אָבער אַדאַפּטירט
האָבן מיר נאָר דריי פון זיי. אַלע אַנדערע יידישע שבטים
וואָס האָבן איבערגענומען פרעמדע שפּראַכן זיינען פאַר־
לאָרן געגאַנגען. גרויסע, רייכע אוצרות קולטור האָבן
יידן געשאַפן אין די פרעמדע שפּראַכן — אין גריכיש,
אין אַראַביש, אין פראַנצויזיש, אין פּויליש, אין דייטש און
אין רוסיש. זיינען די קולטור־אוצרות יאָ געבליבן — אין
ביבליאָטעקן, אין אַרכיוון. די שבטים אָבער וואָס האָבן
די קולטורן געשאַפן — זיי זיינען ניטאָ. אָדער זיי זיינען
פאַסילן. זיינען די דאָזיקע רייכע ביבליאָטעקן אַ מין
„פּאַלעאָנטאָלאָגישע" רעשטלעך פון ישובים וואָס האָבן
אַמאָל געלעבט, געשאַפן און געשטאַרבן אָן יורשים. עס
זיינען דאָ יידן וואָס ריידן רוסיש, אָבער צו די יידישע
שאַפונגען אין דער שפּראַך האָבן זיי שוין ניט קיין שייכות.
עס זיינען זיכער נאָך אַ סך יידן מיט דייטש אין מויל,
אָבער צו די רייכע אוצרות יידישע שאַפונגען אין דייטש
האָבן זיי שוין ניט קיין שייכות, ניט פאַר זיי איז די ירושה...
אפשר וועט אַ פאַרשער פון אָפּגעשטאַרבענע אַלטערמיט־
לעכקייטן אין זיי זיך נישטערן, זוכן עפּעס. אָבער די
לעבעדיקע יידן מיט דייטש אין מויל — זיי האָבן ניט
צו דעם גאָרניט. דובנאָוו — דער גרויסער היסטאָריקער
פון יידנטום, שרייבט אין דער הקדמה צו זיין „בוך פון
לעבן", אַז די יידישע קולטור אין רוסיש, וואָס ער האָט
אַזוי געטריי געדיינט גאַנצע פערציק יאָר, איז געשטאַרבן.
עס איז זיכער אַ גבורה פון אַן אַלטן מאַן זיך מודה צו
זיין, אָבער עס איז ווייט ניט מוחל צו זיין אַ גרויסן היס־
טאָריקער דאָס ניט פאַרויסצוזען פריער.

און אָט קומט פאַר פאַר אונדז אין די אויגן ווידער
אַזאַ פּראָצעס: יידן ריידן ענגליש און שאַפן אין דער שפּראַך
קולטור. מיט שטאָלץ און מיט גוטן ווילן, מיט צופרידנ־
קייט: איין קלייניקייט: יידישקייט אין אַזוינע רייכע פורעמס
ווי עס איז די ענגלישע אוניווערסאַלע שפּראַך! און איך

נעם זיך די דרייסטקייט צו זאָגן פּאַרויס: אַט די גרויסע שאַפֿונגען פֿון גרויסע יידישע גייסטער וועלן פֿאַרעוציגערט — אַ וויי! — פֿאַר די בית עולמס פֿון אַרכיוון, ניט פֿאַרן לעבעדיקן פֿאָלק. און נאָך מער — דאָס ענגלישע ריידנדי־ קע יידישע פֿאָלק — ניט נאָר דאַרף עס שוין ניט אַט די גאַנצער קולטור (זי ווערט נאָך יאָ געגוצט פֿון די וואָס זיינען געהאַדעוועט געוואָרן אין יידיש), נאָר דאָס פֿאָלק גופֿא, זיי יידן גופֿא, ווערט ביסלעכווייז פֿאַרוואַנדלט אין פֿאַסילן פֿון יידישקייט... ביז עס וועט זיך אויסשטיבן אין ניט ווערן.

און דער זעלביקער גורל דערוואַרט אויך די יידישע ישובים וואָס שאַפֿן נאָך היינט אין שפּאַניש, לאָמיר זאָגן. און עס ניט סתם עפּעס אַ נבֿואה. עס איז אַן אויסשפּיר פֿון אונדזער גאַנצער געשיכטע ביז אונדז. און אַט די דערפֿאַרונג לאָזט זיך פֿאַרמולירן אין היסטאָרישע געזעצן, וואָס איך וועל דאָ פּרובירן פֿאַרמולירן:

1.—אַלע שפּראַכן וואָס יידן ריידן כדי צו זיין ענלעך צו אַנדערע פֿעלקער — אַלע זיי זיינען אַסימילאַציע־מכשירים און זיי מוזן פֿירן צום אונטערגאַנג. נאָר די שפּראַכן וואָס יידן נוצן כדי צו זיין אַנדערש פֿון אַנדערע פֿעלקער, נאָר זיי זיינען שפּראַכן פֿון קיום און לעבן.

2.—בלויז די שפּראַכן וואָס יידן האָבן אין זיי געשאַפֿן אַן אייגענעם פֿאָלקלאָר, אַן אייגענעם פֿראַסט־פֿאָלקישן ניסתּר, קענען ווערן יידישע שעפֿערישע שפּראַכן. אַלע שאַפֿונגען פֿון יידישקייט אויף שפּראַכן וואָס האָבן ניט קיין יידישן ניסתּר זיינען ווי טשעקן פֿון אַ פֿרעמדן חשבון, ריכטיקער — זיי זיינען דעפּאָזיטן פֿון יידן אויף פֿרעמדע חשבונות.

און אויב אפֿילו אַט די ענגליש־ריידנדיקע יידן זיינען זייער פֿרום און היטן אָפּ דעם גאַנצן שולחן ערוך, אפֿילו דעמאָלט זיינען זיי ניט מער ווי פֿאַסילן־יידן, ניט קיין לע־ בעדיקע, שעפֿערישע ישובים. אַזוי זיינען געווען די פֿראַנקפֿורטער פֿרומע יידן, די אונגאַרישע וכדומה. די וועלטלעכע, ניט פֿרומע יידן אין ווילנע האָבן ניט אין פֿאַרגלייך מער געשאַפֿן און מער גע־ לאָזן אַקטיוע לעבעדיקע יידישקייט פֿאַר דורות נאָך זייער חורבן.

לאָמיר דאָ זיך אַ ביסל אָפּשטעלן און באַהאַנדלען דעם טערמין „פֿאַסילן".

יידן-פֿאָסילן

מיט דעם ווערט פֿאַסיל ווערן באַצייכנט פֿאַרשטיי־ נערטע רעשטעלעך פֿון גאָר פֿאַרצייטיקע אָרגאַניזמען, וואָס האָבן געלעבט אין אַמאָליקע געאָלאָגישע תּקופֿות און זיי

זיינען מער ניטאָ צווישן די לעבעדיקע באַשעפֿענישן *) און אַזוי נוצט מען דעם אויסדרוק פֿאַסילן פֿאַר אַלץ וואָס איז פֿאַרשטיינערט, פֿאַרגליווערט, עס איז דאָ, אָבער עס לעבט ניט מער. אין דער נאָנסטער צייט האָט דער היס־ טאָריקער טוינבי געוואָלט באַצייכענען יידן ווי אַזא פֿאַסיל־פֿאָלק. דאָס האָט אַרויסגערופֿן פּראָטעסטן און אָפּ־ לייקענונגען מצד יידן.

מיר דאַכט זיך אָבער אַז ביידע צדדים האָבן געהאַט אַ טעות. מילא טוינבי האָט געמעגט האָבן אַ טעות און מיינען אַז אַלע יידן, אומעטום זיינען אַזוי ווי די וואָס ער זעט אין זיין סבֿיבֿה: טאַקע יידן אָבער אָן כסדרדיקער שעפֿערישקייט. אָבער די קעגנער, די יידישע קעגנער האָבן דאָך יאָ געמעגט אונטערשיידן און וויסן אַז מיר יידן זיינען ניט קיין מאָנאָליט־פֿאָלק, אַז צווישן אונדזערע ישו־ בים זיינען פֿאַראַן לעבעדיקע, אַקטיווע, שעפֿערישע און עס זיינען אויך פֿאַראַן, צום באַדוירען, און גאָר ניט ווי־ ניק גאַנצע ישובים פֿאַרשטיינערטע, אומשעפֿערישע, אַמ־ תּע פֿאַסילן־ישובים. אַ צייט לאַנג פֿאַר טוינבי־ס באַצייכע־ נונגען האָב איך פֿאַרבראַכט עטלעכע טעג אין וועגעציע און געזען די דאַרטיקע יידן, און זיך געמאַטערט צו פֿאַר־ גלייכן — וווּ איז פֿאַראַן מער לעבן — צי אין די שטיינער פֿון פֿאַרום ראָמאַנוס אין רוים אָדער אין דער יידישקייט פֿון יענע וועגעציאַנער יידן ...

אין דעם לעצטן יאָרהונדערט איז דער איינציקער לע־ בעדיק־שעפֿערישער יידישער ישוב דער יידיש־יידישער אַלע אַנדערע ישובים אָן יידיש לשון קען מען מיט מער און מיט ווייניקער רעכט פֿאַרגלייכענען צו די פֿאָסילע ישובים.

קולטור שבעל פה און קולטור שבכתב

צוליב מער קלאָרקייט פֿאַר אונדזער געדאַנק וועגן דעם אונטערשייד צווישן די שעפֿערישע ישובים און די פֿאַר־

*) אין שטעטלעך פֿלעגט מען אַמאָל באַשיטן אַ וווּנד מיט אַ נגעשעבענעמס שטויב פֿון „טייוולס־פֿינגער". אין דער אמתן האָט דאָס רונדע פֿאַרשטיניקרטע שטיינדל קיין שום שייכות ניט צו קיין טייוול (די לעבן גאָר היינט מיט אונדז). עס איז אַ פֿאַרקאַלעקטער סקעלעט פֿון אַ קליין חיהלע פֿון גאָר אַ ווייטער געאָלאַגישער תּקופֿה. דער פֿאַלעאָנטאָלאָגישער נאָמען איז בעלעמניט. אויך די סנאַפֿאַטלער האָבן ניט געקאָנט זיך אַן עצה געבן מיט די רעשטעלעך, און האָבן געגלויבט אין „טייוולשע שאַפֿונגען" ביז קירוווע באַגרינדעט די וויסנשאַפֿט פֿון אויסגע־ שטאָרבענע אָרגאַניזמען — די פּאַלעאָנטאָלאָגיע. סוף אַכצטן און אָנהייב ניינצנטן יה.

שטיינערטע, וואָלט איך געוואָלט אַרײַנברענגען צוויי טער־
מינען וואָס מען באַנוצט געוויינלעך פֿאַר אַנדערע תקו־
פֿות אין דער יידישער געשיכטע. די צוויי טערמינען
זיינען „תורה שבעל פה" און „תורה שבכתב". מיט דעם
צווייטן טערמין באַצייכנט מען די גאַנצע קולטור פֿון דער
הנך תקופה און מיט דעם ערשטן — שבעל פה — די
תלמודישע קולטור. אין תוך אַרײַן פֿאַסן זיך די צוויי
טערמינען אַרײַן אין אַלע תקופות. אין יעדער איז אַ פֿאַ־
ראָן אַ קולטור וואָס איז פֿאַרשריבן, דעפֿינירט, באַשריבן.
דאָס איז די ליטעראַטור און וויסנשאַפֿט. און עס איז
אויך פֿאַראַן די קולטור וואָס איז אין שטייגער, אין די פֿי־
רונגען און אין די ניט־פֿאָרמולירטע טראַדיציעס, אין
ריידן און דענקען. דאָס איז טיילווייז דער ניסתר ווי מיר
האָבן אים פֿריער באַצייכנט, אָבער אויך די גרעסטע טייל
פֿון דעם ניגלה געהערט אַהער. און בדרך כלל פֿירט זיך
ביי אַלע פֿעלקער און אויך ביי אונדז, אַז די קולטור שבעל
פה ברענגט אַרויף די קולטור שבכתב, די לעצטע איז אַ
טאָכטער פֿון דער ערשטער. און אין אַלע תקופות גייען
זיי צוזאַמען — די מאַמע און טאָכטער. פֿאַרן שעפע־
רישן קיום און לעבן פֿון אַ פֿאָלק איז אַלע מאָל וויכטיקער
די קולטור שבעל פה און צוזאַמען מיט איר די שפּראַך
אירע. ניט די קולטור פֿון שבכתב און ניט איר שפּראַך.
די גמרא וואָס האָט די גאַנצע לאַנגע תקופה קולטור שבעל פה
פֿון יענער תקופה האָט אַ שלל מיט אויסדרוק כדי ב̇אַ־
שטעטיקן די העכערע וויכטיקייט פֿון דער בעל פה־קולטור
איבער דער פֿאַרשריבענער. מען דאַרף אָבער כסדר אונ̇־
טערשטרייכן אַז מיר האָבן די צוויי געביטן קולטור אין
אַלע תקופות. אויך איצט און אויך היינט איז פֿאַרן קיום,
פֿאַרן שעפעריש̇ן לעבן פֿון פֿאָלק וויכטיקער די קולטו̇
שבעל פה און אין איר שפּראַך. דאָס איז וואָס מיר האָבן
פֿריער אויסגעדריקט אין די צוויי געזעצן פֿון יידישער
געשיכטע. עס קענען האָבן אַ קיום נאָר די יידישע שב
טים, וואָס פֿאַרמאָגן אַ קולטור שבעל פה. פֿאַרוואָרפֿנדי̇ק
די אייגענע שפּראַך פֿאַרלירט אַ פֿאָלק זיין גאַנצע קול̇
טור שבעל פה און אָן איר איז אומקום און מער ניט.
די קולטור שבכתב — די אַלע ביכער און ווערק וואָ̇
זיינען פֿאַרשריבן געוואָרן זיינען ניט קיין סימן פֿון לעבן.
מען קען נאָך דאָך שאַפֿן ווערק און ביכער אָן אַ שיעור אויך
וועגן דעם לעבן פֿון אַמאָל, וואָס איז געווען אַמאָל און
איז שוין מער ניטאָ. ווערק און ביכער האָבן נאָר דעמאָלט אַ
ווערט פֿארן לעבן פֿון אַ פֿאָלק, ווען זיי ווערן אַ טייל
פֿון לעבעדיקן לעבן. די תורה האָט געהאָלפֿן דעם קיום
פֿון יידישן פֿאָלק נאָר דאַנק דעם תלמוד תורה, ווייל מען

האָט געלערנט כסדר און זי איז געוואָרן כסדר אַ טייל פֿון;
דער תורה שבעל פה. פֿאַרלאַזנדיק די אייגענע קולטור
שבעל פה צוזאַמען מיט איר לשון ווערט די גאַנצע קולטור
שבכתב — אַלע געשאַפֿענע ווערק ניט מער ווי אַ היסטאָ־
רישער עדות פֿון אַ לעבן אַמאָל, ניט היינט.

ווערן די גרויסע ליטעראַטור וואָס יידן שאַפֿן אין
פֿרעמדע שפּראַכן אפשר צושטייערס צו די קולטור פֿ̇ן
יענע שפּראַכן, אויב עמעצער פֿון יענע פֿעלקער וועכ
ווען עס איז האָבן אַ אינטערעס, אָבער קיין יידישע קולטור
איז עס שוין ניט, אין קולטור־קרייז פֿון לעבעדיקע יידן
נעמט עס מער ניט קיין אָנטייל. זיינען די גרויסע און
רייכע ליטעראַטור־אוצרות וואָס יידן האָבן געשאַפֿן אויף
אַלערליי פֿרעמדע שפּראַכן ניט קיין יידישע קולטור און
פֿרעמד זיינען אונדז אַלע שפּראַכן וואָס פֿאַרמאָגן ניט קיין
יידישע קולטור שבעל פה, קיין פֿראַסט־פֿאָלקישע שטיי־
גערישקייט. און פֿרעמד בלייבן אָט די שפּראַכן אויב
אפֿילו די מערהייט יידן וועלן זיי נוצן און ריידן און לער־
נען. און דער גורל — די ביכער, די ווערק — אין אָר־
כיוו־קברים און די יידישע שבטים — צו אַסימילאַצ̇ע
און אונטערגאַנג. אַין כלל; שעפּערישקייט קען זיין אַלע
מאָל נאָר פֿון אייגענעם אָרגאַנישן ניסתר. נאָר ווערק
און ספרים בכלל וואָס זיינען פֿאַרדייט געוואָרן אין ניסתר
אַריין — נאָר זיי קענען באַווירקן די שעפֿערישקייט. און
אָן דער שפּראַך פֿון פֿאָלקס קולטור שבעל פה האָבן זיך
די ווערק ניט קיין קיום מיט וואָס זיך אַסימילירן אין דעם מענ־
טש, ער קען זיי ניט פֿאַרדייען. און אגב, האָט ער ניט קיין
אינטערעסן צו דעם סיי ווי. אַזוינע יידן מחן בלייבן פֿאָ־
סילן. אָבער ווייט ניט אין דער אייביקייט. עס געדויערט
ניט מער ווי ביז זיי ווערן אַסימילירט אין דעם הויפּט־
פֿאָלק פֿון לאַנד. דאָס איז דער גורל פֿון אַלע יידן וואָס
פֿאַרלאָזן זייער פֿאָלקשפּראַך, די שפּראַך פֿון זייער פֿאָלקס
קולטור שבעל פה.

פֿאָלקשפּראַך, קולטורשפּראַך און פֿרעמדע שפּראַך

דאָס זיינען דריי קאַטעגאָריעס שפּראַכן וואָס האָרשן
ביי יידן. און ווי ווי זיינער אַקטיוו אין יידישן לעבן, זייער
צושטייער צום קיום פֿון פֿאָלק? און ווי איז דער גורל
פֿון די שבטים וואָס נוצן זיי?

וועגן פֿרעמדע שפּראַכן איז זייער ווייניק וואָס צו
ריידן. זיי זיינען דער טויער פֿון אַסימילאַציע און אומקום.
זיי הויבן אָן מיט מזל טוב, מיט שטאָלצער צופֿרידנקייט
און מיט אַ געפֿיל פֿון העכערקייט איבער אַנדערע יידן...
אַ, וויפֿל מאָל האָבן יידן דאָס געזונגען מיט גדולה און
גאווה: ווי קענט איר זיך צו אונדז גלייכן? מיר ריידן די

דא איז געווען פֿאָלקישקייט, און פֿאָלקישקייט, קולטור
שבעל פה איז געווען פֿאַרבונדן מיט ייִדיש לשון.

העברעיש ווידער איז שוין אַ קימאַ לן פֿון אַריבער
צוויי טויזנט און פֿינף הונדערט יאָר ניט געווען די רייד
שפּראַך ביי די ייִדן.   עס איז אָבער יאָ געווען די שפּראַך פֿון
אַלע אָנגעזאַמלטע קולטור־אוצרות.   די לעבעדיקע דורות
ייִדן האָבן געפֿורעמט זייערע דירעקטע איבערלעבונגען
ניט אין העברעיש.   עס איז קלאָר פּגֿלש אַז כּלומרשט
איז איצט העברעיש אויפֿגעשטאַנען תּחית המתים.   און
ניט אמת איז עס וואָיל עס האָט טאָקע העברעיש לשון
זייערי אַקטיוו אָנטײל גענומען אין ייִדיש לעבן און איז
אַרײן אַפֿילו אין פֿאָלקלאָר.   און דאָס נאָר ביי דעם ייִדיש־
ייִדישן שבט, פּשוט גערעדט מיינט עס, אַז ייִדיש לשון
האָט אונדז אײַנגעזאָגעהיט העברעיש.   ייִדן זײַנען געווען היי־
מיש אין העברעיש ניט צו לערנענדיק, ניט נעמענדיק קיין
קורסן האָט אַ ייִד אַרײַנגעפֿלאָכטן אַ שלל מיט העברעיש
אין זײַן פֿאָלקלאָר, אין זײַן פּראָסט־פֿאָלקישן לעבן.   דער
ביי דאָרף געזאָגט ווערן אַז דאָס פֿאָלק האָט ניט פֿאַרנאָנ־
דערגעטײַלט צווישן העברעיש און אַראַמיש.   האָבן די
שפּראַכן יאָ געלעבט, אפֿשר מער און מיט לעבעדיקער ווי היינט
מיט די קורסן און אָולפּנים און מיט אַלע אַנדערע מיטלען.
האָבן ייִדן אין אַראַמיש און שפּעטער אין ייִדיש אַרײַנ־
גענומען די קולטור פֿון פֿריערדיקע דורות איז עס געווען
מיט דעם לשון צוזאַמען, האָט ייִדיש אײַנגעזאָעהיט העברעיש
לעבעדיק, ווי פֿריער אַראַמיש, איז אַ דער גאַנצער
תּחית המתים־בום: אַ לעבעדיקער שטײַט ניט אויף קיין
תּחית המתים.   און עס איז קיין מאָל ניט געווען קיין "ריב
לשונות", ייִדיש (אָדער פֿריער אַראַמיש) האָבן זיך קיין
מאָל ניט געקריגט מיט העברעיש: ייִדן האָבן מיט אַלע
כּוחות זיך אָנגעשטרענגט אָפּצוהיטן אַל דאָס וואָס עס
איז געווען הייליק ביי ייִדן, אַלץ וואָס קודש, האָבן זיי גע־
היט דעם לשון פֿון דעם קודש.   איז העברעיש געגאַנגען
דורך יאָרהונדערטער געאָרעמט מיט ייִדיש — ווי דער –-
געזאָגט.   און ביידע צוזאַמען זײַנען געווען למשה מסיני.
און הלוואי זאָל דער קיום פֿון אַט דעם לשון פֿון ייִדישער
קדושה זײַן איצט אַזוי געזיכערט ווי ער איז געווען זיכער
מיט ייִדיש צוזאַמען.   מיט דער אָפּשוואַכונג פֿון ייִדיש
און דער חלילה מיט דעם אונטערגאַנג פֿון דעם לשון, איז דער
קיום פֿון העברעיש אין דער גרעסטער סכּנה.   אָבער וועגן
דעם וועט זײַן נאָך זײַן אַ רייד שפּעטער.   דער עיקר —; אַ ?ֿ
זײַנען ניט גילטיק קיינע סימפּאַטיעס, קיין פֿאַרטייאיש־
קייט, ניט מיט ליבע האָלט מען אויף אַ שפּראַך.   און דאָס
געזעץ איז, אַז דאָרט ווו עס איז ניטאָ קיין ייִדיש, דאָרטן
האָט ניט העברעיש קיין דריסת הרגל.   העברעיש האָלט

שײַנע און רייכע שפּראַך פֿון דעם גרויסן און קולטור־
רײַכן פֿאָלק דעם און דעם !!!   "און זיי ענדיקן מיט אַ שטי־
לער קבֿורה אַפֿילו אָן אַ קדיש, אָן אַ "פּה נקבר".   געווען
געווען אַ ישוב און ניטאָ מער, ניט געבליבן קיין יורש,
קיין קדיש־זאַגער.   יאָ, עס קענען נאָך זײַן גאַנצע דורות
ייִדן וואָס וויסן אַז זיי זײַנען ייִדן, זיי קענען זײַן רעליגיעז
פֿרום, זיי קענען צומאָל אַפֿילו לײַדן פֿון וועגן זייער ייִדער־
קייט, אָבער קיין שעפֿערישקייט איז שוין ביי זיי ניטאָ און
ניט מעגלעך, ווי פֿריער איז דערקלערט געוואָרן.   דאָס
זײַנען ייִדן פֿאַסילן.   ניט מער און ניט אַנדערש.

די שפּראַך פֿון ייִדישן פֿאָלק, פֿון זײַן שעפֿערישן שבט
ישראל איז ייִדיש.   נאָר אין דעם לשון איז פֿאַראַן אַ
ייִדישע קולטור שבעל פה, נאָר אין דעם לשון אַז פֿאַראַן
דער ניסתּר פֿון דעם ייִדישן קאָלעקטיוון "איך", פֿון זײַן
גײַסט.   און נאָר דער דאָזיקער ייִדיש־ייִדישער שבט האָט
געשאַפֿן אַלץ וואָס מיר פֿאַרגﬞאַגן אין ייִדישן לעבן: נײַע
ייִדישע קולטור, נײַע ייִדישע באַוועגונגען.   נײַע אַקטיוונע
ייִדישע ישובים, נײַע ליטעראַטור אין ביידע שפּראַכן, נײַע
סאָציאַלע אָרגאַניזאַציעס און ריכטונגען.   נאָר דער ייִדיש־
ייִדישער שבט האָט געאַרבעט און אויפֿגעבויט די ייִדישע
מדינה מיט אַלע אירע מעלות און חסרונות.   נאָר דער
ייִדיש־ייִדישער שבט האָט אײַנגעהיט העברעיש אַרבעט אין אַ
לעבעדיקן צושטאַנד און אויפֿגעאַרבעט איר ליטעראַטור.
בﬞיט אײַן וואָרט — אַלץ וואָס עס איז לעבעדיק און שעפֿע־
ריש אין ייִדישן פֿאָלק, קומט עס אַﬞץ פֿון דעם ייִדיש־
ייִדישן שבט.   דאָס איז דער העגעמאָן אין ייִדישקייט.   צו
דער משנה אין אבות אַז עס איז געגאַנגען די ייִדישע
קולטור פֿון דור צו דור, פֿון תּקופֿה צו תּקופֿה, און זי
דערפֿירט די קולטור־אַנטװיקלונג ביז די כּנסת הגדולה
(קנאַﬞפּע צוויי הונדערט יאָר פֿאַרן חורבן) קענען מיר איצט
צוגעבן ווי די ייִדישער קולטור איז געוואַקסן אין בבל און
"בבל מסרה לאשכנז".   און פֿון אַשכּנז ביז אונדז.   און
און דער גאַﬞצער מסורה, אין דעם גאַﬞצﬞ גﬞאַנג פֿון ייִדיש־
קייט ליגט דער כּוח טאָﬞקע אין דער פּראָסט־פֿאָלקישער
תּורה שבעל פה.   אודאי האָט די גאָלדﬞענע תּקופֿה אין
ספֿרד געלאָזﬞ אַ פּראַﬞקטיקע ירושה.   און דאָך איז זי באַﬞלד
אויסגעפֿאָלﬞאַשﬞן געוואָרﬞﬞ.   און פֿאַרװאָס ?   — װײַל מיר גע־
פֿינען ניט קײַן שפּורﬞ פֿון קיין פּראַﬞסﬞ־פֿאָלקישﬞﬞ קולטﬞﬞﬞ
שבעל פה.   דאָס ענﬞﬞﬞﬞכﬞ איז געﬞﬞ מיﬞ דﬞﬞﬞﬞ קﬞﬞﬞﬞﬞﬞ
פֿﬞ די צדוקﬞﬞﬞﬞ וﬞﬞﬞﬞ איﬞﬞﬞﬞﬞﬞﬞﬞﬞ מﬞﬞﬞﬞﬞﬞﬞﬞﬞ ניﬞﬞ געﬞﬞﬞ
גﬞﬞﬞ ניﬞﬞﬞﬞﬞﬞﬞﬞﬞﬞ פֿﬞ דﬞﬞﬞ פּﬞﬞﬞﬞﬞﬞ.   אﬞﬞﬞﬞﬞﬞ איﬞ דﬞ הﬞﬞﬞﬞﬞ
כﬞﬞﬞ געﬞﬞﬞﬞ קﬞﬞﬞﬞﬞﬞﬞﬞﬞﬞ הﬞﬞﬞﬞﬞ פֿﬞﬞ דﬞﬞ הﬞﬞﬞﬞﬞﬞ בﬞﬞﬞ
גﬞﬞﬞ.   און — זי האָﬞ אַﬞﬞﬞ קﬞﬞﬞ פּﬞﬞﬞﬞ ייﬞﬞﬞﬞﬞ ניﬞ
געﬞﬞﬞﬞ, בﬞﬞ דﬞ חﬞﬞﬞﬞﬞ הﬞﬞﬞ אַﬞﬞ בﬞﬞﬞﬞﬞﬞﬞﬞ אַﬞﬞ
גﬞﬞﬞﬞ פֿﬞﬞ ייﬞﬞﬞﬞ קﬞﬞﬞﬞﬞ.   און פֿﬞﬞﬞﬞﬞ ?   — ווﬞﬞ

ניסטישע קאַנגרעסן פֿאַרנעמט ייִדיש דאָס ערשטע אָרט,
ניט ווײל מען וויל עס. נאָר מען קען אַנדערש זיך ניט
צונויפֿריידן.

אין אינדיע מיט פֿיל דיאַלעקטן האָט מען גע־
מוזט אָננעמען צו ענגליש ווי די שפּראַך פֿון דער גאַנ־
צער נאַציע ווי אַזאַ. מיר דאַרפֿן ניט קיין ענגליש כּל
זמן מיר האָבן ייִדיש אַן אייגן לשון וואָס ווערט גערעדט
פֿון עטלעכע און ניינציק פּראָצענט פֿון פֿאָלק. אַן ייִדיש
פֿאַרלירן מיר אונדזער אַלוועלטלעכקייט. פֿון איין ייִדיש
פֿאָלק ווערן ברעקלעך פֿון אַ פֿאָלק. מען וויל שלום
מאַכן מיט דעם ווײל מען וויל גלייבן אַז אָט אַזאַ אינ־
טערנאַציאָנאַלע ייִדישע שפּראַך וועט זײַן העברעיש.
וואָלט עס גיווען גוט, ווען מען וואָלט אין דעם געקאָנט
גלייבן. איך גלייב אָבער ניט, אַז די וואָס זאָגן דאָס
זאָלן אַליין גלייבן אין דעם. דערווײַל זעען מיר פּונקט
דאָס פֿאַרקערטע: מיט דער אָפּשוואַכונג פֿון ייִדיש, פֿאַר־
לירן מיר אויף העברעיש ניט געקוקט אויף דעם לערנען
וואָס מען לערנט, אויף דער פּראָפּאַגאַנדע, וואָס מען
פֿירט.

ייִדיש — אַ שאַפֿונג פֿון ייִדישן פֿאָלק

ביאַליק האָט אַמאָל אויסגערעכנט אַז ייִדן האָבן גע־
רעדט אויף עטלעכע צענדליק שפּראַכן. אַלע זיינען פֿרעמ־
דע, נאָר איינע איז אַן אייגענע. ער האָט אָבער פֿאַרפֿעלט
אונטערצושיידן צווישן שפּראַכן איבערגענומענע און
שפּראַכן איבערגעשאַפֿענע. ייִדן האָבן איבערגענומען אַ סך
שפּראַכן מיט אַלע פּרטים, מיט דעם אַקצענט, מיט דער
גראַמאַטיק, מיט אַלע הידורים און פֿליטערלעך, מיט דער
ליטעראַטור — מיט אַלץ. דאָס זיינען שפּראַכן איבערגע־
נומען. זייער גורל בײַ ייִדן: זיי מעקן אָפּ, רײַסן אַרויס בײַ
ייִדן אַלץ וואָס ייִדיש איז מיט זיי הערן די ייִדן אויף צו
זײַן ייִדן, זיי ייִדישן זיך אויס.

אַנדערש איז מיט די שפּראַכן וואָס ייִדן שאַפֿן איבער.
זיי נעמען ווערטער פֿון איין שפּראַך, פֿון עטלעכע שפּראַכן,
מען מאַכט זיי איבער, מען פּאַסט זיי צו צום אייגענעם
געמיט, צו דעם אייגענעם אַקצענט, אינטאָנאַציע. מען
ענדערט זייער גראַמאַטיק, זייער אַלף בית — אַלץ און די
שפּראַך ווערט אַן אייגענע. אַזוי זיינען אַלע הײַנטיקע
שפּראַכן בײַ אַלע פֿעלקער און אַזוי איז אויך ייִדיש בײַ
ייִדן. אַזוי איז אויך געשאַפֿן געוואָרן גאָר פֿאַרצײַטן הע־
ברעיש, ווען ייִדן האָבן גענומען ווערטער פֿון פֿאַרשיי־
דענעם אָפּשטאַם — פֿון מצרים, און פֿון שומעריש, און
פֿון כּלדעאיש און פֿון אַראַמיש, און פֿערסיש און פֿון
גריכיש און זיי אַלע איבערגעשאַפֿן אין אַן אייגן לשון.
פּונקט דאָס זעלביקע איז געשען מיט ייִדיש.

זיך ניט מיט דעם לערנען און ניט מיט די לערנביכער, נאָר
אין שטייגער לעבן. און אַן ייִדיש איז ניטאָ קיין ייִדישער
שטייגער. כּל זמן עס לעבט בײַ אונדז די קולטור שבעל
פּה מיט איר לשון, לעבט אויך די קולטור שבכּתב מיט איר
שפּראַך. אַן דער קולטור שבעל פּה, אַן ייִדיש האָט אויך
העברעיש ניט אויף וואָס זיך צו האַלטן.

נאָר דורך דער קולטור שבעל פּה איז אַ ייִד אַ ייִד.
איך האָב אַמאָל געקענט די רוסישע שפּראַך זייער גוט.
געקאָנט איר גאַנצע ליטעראַטור. געלערנט, געלייענט.
מײַן גאַנצע פֿאַרמעלע בילדונג געקראָגן אין דער שפּראַך.
און אַז עס איז מיר אויסגעקומען דאָס ערשטע מאָל צו זײַן
אין אַן עכט רוסישער שטאַט ערגעץ אויף דער וואָלגע,
האָב איך גלייך אויפֿן וואָקזאַל דערפֿילט, אַז איך בין דאָ
אַ . . . פֿרעמדער: מיט דער גאַנצער רוסישער קולטור
שבכּתב בין איך דאָך ווײַט פֿון צו זײַן אַ רוס. מען
דאַרף האָבן די קולטור שבעל פּה, דאָס וואָס מען קען
גאָרניט אויסלערנען, מען דאַרף עס אײַנלעבן, אין זיך.
איז וואָס איך בין ניט געוואָרן קיין רום, האָב איך איצט
ניט קיין חרטה, איך האָב עס געבראַכט נאָר ווי אַ משל:
זאָלן דאָס געדענקען אַלע די וואָס גלייבן אַז מען קען
ייִדישקייט אויסלערנען דורך לערנען דעם העברעיש.

העברעיש מיט אירע פֿיר טויזנט יאָר לעבן איז אַוודאי
ניט אין פֿאַרגלייך רײַכער ווי ייִדיש מיט אירע טויזנט
יאָר, אָבער קיין קולטור שבעל פּה האָט זי ניט, מוז זי
זיך האַלטן מיט ייִדיש.

וועט מען זאָגן, אַז אין דער אייגענער מדינה שאַפֿט
זיך איצט אַ נייע קולטור שבעל פּה אויף העברעיש און
מען דאַרף ניט קיין ייִדיש. איז עס אויך פֿאַלש. ווי מיר
וועלן עס זען שפּעטער.

ייִדיש די אינטערנאַציאָנאַלע שפּראַך פֿון ייִדישן פֿאָלק

. . . ״אַ ייִד מיט אַ ייִדן פֿאַרשטייט זיך אויך אויפֿן
וווּנק״. אַמאָל איז עס טאַקע אַזוי געווען. מיר זיינען
איצט צעזייט און צעשפּרייט איבער דער גאָרער וועלט,
צווישן אַלע פֿעלקער און אין אַלע לענדער. מיר נעמען
איבער אַלע שפּראַכן און פֿאַרוואַנדערן די אייגענע. ייִדן
פֿון איין לאַנד פֿאַרשטייען זיך ניט מיט ייִדן פֿון אַ צווייטן
לאַנד. קינדער פֿון איין משפּחה וואָס זיינען פֿאַרוואָגלט
געוואָרן אין פֿאַרשיידענע לענדער, פֿאַרשטייען זיך ניט.
קענען זיך ניט צונויפֿריידן . . . ערשט דאָ ווערן מיר אַ
פֿאָלק וואָס איז צעריסן און צעברעקלט. אויף אַלע צווי־

א שפּראך אן איבערגענומענע איז וו ווי א פּאַראזיט אין
אָרגאַניזם, וואָס עס איז אויף דעם אָרגאַניזם און א שפּראך
אן איבערגעשאַפענע איז וי ווי שפּיץ וואָס פון דעם שאַפּט
דער אָרגאַניזם זיין פלייש און בלוט. ייִדיש און העברע־
איש און אראַמיש — דער זעלביקער אויפקום, די זעל־
ביקע אַנטוויקלונג, די ענלעכע אַנזאַמלונג אוצרות קול־
טור — תנך, תלמוד, מאַדערנע ליטעראַטור, די זעלביקע
אוצרות פון נשמה־בת קולות. מער נישט צייט־אונטער־
שיידן: תנ״ך — לאַנג פאַרגאַנגענע צייטן! תלמוד — א סך
גענטער, מער היינטיק; מאַדערנע שריפטן — גאָר היינ־
טיקער.

די טראגעדיע פון העברעיש

איך האַלט אז מיט דער גאַנצער העברעישער קולטור
געשעט ביי אונדז ניט קיין קלענערע טראגעדיע ווי מיט
ייִדיש. איין מזל, איין גורל, א האַר ניט אנדערש. לאָ־
מיר זאָגן — מיר גייען פאַרלירן ייִדיש, מיט דעם צוזאַ־
מען פאַרלירן מיר אונדזער גאַנצע קולטור בעל פּה.
בלייבט דאָך אויף די גאַנצע קולטור שבכתב על בלימה,
אויף גאָרנישט. מיר האָבן שוין געזען אז דער כלומ־
רשטער תחית המתים פון העברעיש לשון איז בלויז א
פיקציע, אָפּנאַרעריי, מען נאַרט זיך אליין. און מען וויל
ניט זען די צווייטע זייט פון דער מטבע. העברעיש האָט
אנגעוואָרן זיין קדושה, געוואָרן וואַכעדיק. מילא, גוט.
אבער מיט יעדער ווערט פון דער שפּראך איז דאָך געוואָרן
פאַרבונדן א שלל מיט קולטור־אַסאָציאַציעס, טאַקע פון די
ספרים האָס זיינען געווען געגעבן צו לעבן אין טאָג
טעגלעכן לעבן. טויזנטער יאָרן קולטור האָבן געשטעקט
אין יעדער אויסדרוק, אין יעדער זאַץ! יעדער וואָרט און
יעדער זאַץ האָט געהאַט א בת קול פון אונדזער
אייביקייט, יעדער זאַץ האָט מיטגעצויגן א קייט פון אום
ענדלעכע דורות לעבן און קולטור: יעדער וואָרט — א
פּלאַש אַלטער וויין מיט אלע טעמים און ריחות פון דורות
און דורות. איז פון דעם אַלעם גאָרנישט געבליבן, וואָ־בע־
דיק געמאַכט, אָפּגעריסן פון אלע זיינע קולטור־אַסאָציאַ־
ציעס, אויסגעליידיקט, ווערטער אַן אַסאָציאַציעס, אַן פאַר־
בינדונג מיט קולטור, אָן באַהעפטונג צום פאַלק. ליידיקע
ווערטער ווי ליידיקע פלאַשן. אָט ווי מען רעדט אַן
אויסגעלערנטע שפּראך, ווי פון א ווערטערבוך אַרויס.
האָט דאָך דעם אויסדרוק "גויים מדברים עברית" גע־
שאַפן ניט עפּעס דאָרטן א ייִדישיסטל, נאָר איינער פון
די גרעסטע קעגנער פון ייִדיש — ד״ר יוסף קלוזנער.
ער האָט אויף דער עלטער דערפילט, דערזען צו וואָס עס
האָט געבראַכט זיין אידעאַל, דערפילט די טראגעדיע אז
מען איז געבליבן אָן א פאָלקשפּראך און אָן א קולטור־
שפּראך. כדי אָפּצורייסן די לשון קודשדיקע ווערטער

פ'ן זייער קדושה פון זייערע קולטור־אַסאָציאַציעס האָט
מען אפילו די אויסשפּראך געביטן. אין לבו חלק ונחלה
בישראל, מיר גייען שאַפן א ניי פאַלק מיט א נייעם לשון
וואָס האָט ניט קיין ריח פון פּאַרצייטיקן שימל ... ווען
מען זאָל זיך אריינלאָזן אין א גענוינערן אנאַליז פון אלע
נייע ווערטער, פון אלע שפּראכנייעסן וואָס עס פאַרמאָגט
צאָט די נייע "עברית חדשה" אָדער "עברית מודרנית",
ווען מען שווער קעגענן דעציזירן וואָס האָט מער גע־
ווירקט: צי די ליבע צו העברעיש אָדער די שינאה צו
ייִדיש און צו אלץ וואָס איז מיט ייִדיש פאַרבונדן ...
איך וועל זיך באנוגענען נאָר מיט איין דוגמא: מען האָט
דאָס אלטע, באליבטע באַגריסונג שלום עליכם פּאַרביטן
מיט "שלום". פאַרוואָס? איז עס דאָך אויך סאַמע העב־
רעיש, טאָ פאַר וואָס איז עס שלעכט? — אלאַי דער תירוץ
אין — זאָגן ביי זיע צינגער — שלום עליכם איז צו פיל
גענוצט געוואָרן אין ייִדישע מיילער, און שלום אַרויסגע־
גערעדט כלומרשט אויף ספרדיש איז דאָך כמעט אזוי
שיין ווי דאָס רוסישע "דאַראוואָ" פאַראן נאָך
אזוינע מוסטערן. און גייט דערקלערט עס מיט
אהבת ישראל און מיט אהבת שפת ישראל ...
איז טאַקע אפשר אמת אז מען האָט ניט אזוי שטאַרק ליב
דאָס אלטע טראדיציאנעלע העברעיש ווי מען האָט פיינט
דאָס ייִדישע לשון מיט אלע זיינע לשון קודשדיקע עלע־
מענטן און טעמים? ... עס איז ביטער אזוינס צו זאָגן,
אַנצושרייבן אויפן פּאַפּיר, אבער די פאַקטן באַשטעטיקן
דאָס, צו אונדזער ווייטיק און חרפה.

איז עפּעס אַ וואונדער, וואָס אָט שוין עטלעכע דורות
רייןן העברעישע דערציאונג אין ארץ ישראל און אפילו
אין דער אייגענער מדינה האָט דערפירט צו כנעניזע
פון דער יוגנט? יונגע העברעער, אויסגעוואַקסן און
דערצויגן אין א לאַנד פון אידעאַליזם, פון הגשמה און
נאָך מער — הקרבה עצמית, און זיי האַלטן אין איין
שרייען מיט קולי קולות, אז זיי זיינען ניט קיין יידן, אז
זיי האָבן ניט קיין שייכות צום ייִדישן פאָלק און זיי ווילן
צו אים קיין שייכות ניט האָבן. איך וויל ניט צו פליי־
קעגענן קיין איין טראפן פון די מעלות פון יענער סאַב־
רישער יוגנט. פאַרקערט, ווייס איך פון זייער פיל מעלות
גייסטיקע און מאַראַלישע. איז דאָך דער פּאַרדרוס נאָך
גרעסער, נאָך טיפער. און עס רעדט זיך ניט וועגן אזא
אָדער א צוויטער גרופּע אָרגאַניזירטער באָוואַ־סטייניקער
גרופּע, וואָס האַבן זיך אזוי א נאָמען געגעבן. עס איז דאָך
א טענדענץ אן אלגעמיינע. זיי ווילן ניט געהערן צום
ייִדישן פאָלק פון כסדרדיקע גלותן, און זיי האָבן פאַר
אים קיינע סימפּאַטיעס. זיי געהערן צו אן אנדער פאָלק,

ווען די פעלקער פון לאנד זיינען נענטער ווי דאס
יידישע פאלק אין די גלות. איז פאר זיי ציוניזם פלוי־
דעריי, פרעמד און דערעסן.

און נאך מער — זיי האבן זיך דאך געהאדעוועט אין
א גאנצער און פולער יידישקייט, אין שולן וואס האבן
א־ין רשות, אין ריכטונג, אין ציל, אין א סביבה פון
יידישקייט אין א לאנד וואו יעדער טריט איז פול מיט
אידעאליזם און איבערגעבנקייט. און דאך! דאך איז
ניטא קיין צובונד צו יידישקייט. פארוואס ? — ווייל עס
פעלט אין דער דערציאונג ווי אין די היימען אזוי אויך
אין שול די קולטור שבעל פה. דאס פשוט פאלקישע, דאס
פרעזענט־יידישע. און אן דעם קען מען זיך ניט צובינדן
צום פאלק דורך קיינע שולן, דורך קיינע פראגראמען און
קורסן מיט עקזאמענס.

אט פארוואס ערנסטע, טיף דענקענדיקע שרייבער
קלאגן זיך אין מדינת ישראל אויף דער פרעמדקייט און
אפגעפרעמדקייט פון דער יוגנט; פארוואס די נייע ליטע־
ראטור איז ניט אויף דער געהעריקער הייך, און נאך און
נאך. א ליטעראטור קען וואקסן נאר אויף דורות קולטור
שבעל פה. אן דעם איז ליטעראטור ווי אן א באדן.

האט די יוגנט ניט קיין צובונד צו א פאלק. דאס
כנעניס־פאלק איז דאך אויסגעטראכט. זיינען זיי פאר־
ליבט אין העברעאיש ? אין דער קולטור פון העברעאיש
— איך ספק זייער. מען האט שוין געזען און באקלאגט
דאס אנטלויפן פון העברעאיש. כל זמן עס זיינען דא
נאך יידישע יידן, פילט מען א געפיל פון העפערקייט
"אתה בחרתנו מכל היהודים", מיר העברעער זיינען פון
א העכערן מין. אבער ווען מען אבסטראהירט זיך פון
אנדערע יידן. טא וואס איז דער יחוס פון העברעאיש ?
איז ענגליש, פראנצויזיש זיכער מער כבוד, מער בא־
קוועם... קענען זיי זיין פארליבט ביז אמונה אין דעם
לאנד, "מולדת". ווי א טראדיציאנעלער ייד, ווי אונדזע־
רער א גלות־ייד פילט די הייליקייט פון דער ערד פון
מדינת ישראל ? —

אויך ניט. אויך דאס ווערט ציט דערגרייכט, און עס
קען ניט דערגרייכט ווערן. דאס "ארץ" איז ליב און
טייער ווען עס איז פארבונדן מיט "ישראל". אן ישראל
— זיינען פאראן א סך בעסערע און באקוועמערע און רייי־
כערע און שענערע ארצות. עס איז דאך טראגיש אט דאס
דארפן אין שולן אריינניפירן א לימוד "יידיש באוווסטזיין"
(תודעה יהודית). און דאס אלץ ווייל עס פעלט אין דער
דערציאונג אין די היימען און אין שול דאס פשוט פאל־
קישע קולטור שבעל פה. און עס וואקס אלץ מער און

מער דער מרחק, דער אפשטאנד צווישן דעם יידישן פאלק
און צווישן דער אין העברעאיש דערצויגענער יוגנט.

און אז איך האלט אן צו טראכטן וועגן דער יידישער
יוגנט אין די גלות וואס מען האדעוועט און מען דערציט
אן יידישער פאלקישער קולטור, ווערט מיר גאר טרוי־
עריק אויפן הארצן. די יוגנט רעדט זיך איין אז
זי געהערט צום פאלק וועמעס שפראך זי רעדט. און עס
איז פאלש. ווייל די גערעדטע שפראך איז דאך בלויז א
טעכנישע אן דער קולטור שבעל פה פון דעם פאלק
וועמעס שפראך מען רעדט. פון יידיש פאלק איז מען
אבער אפגעריסן. והא ראיה — אין גאנץ אמעריקע איז
ניטא קיין אין טאגצייטונג פאר יידן אויף דער שפראך
וואס מיליאנען יידן ריידן. געווען אין בוענאס איירעס א
פרוו און ער האט זיך געענדיקט מיט א גוואלדיקער
פיאסקא. עס אינטערעסירט ניט דאס פאלק, וואס פון
אים שטאמט מען. פאראן יא פארלאנג און אויסגאבעס
פאר יידן אין די "שפראכן פון די קינדער", אבער
ערשטנס לעבן זיי פון גרויסע סובסידיעס, צווייטנס, ווערן
זיי על פי רוב געקויפט פון יידישע עלטערן פאר זייערע
פארגוייישטע קינדער. פריער לאזט מען ארויס די פיי־
געלעך פון יידישן שטייג, נאך דעם וויל מען זיי שיט־
ביסל יידיש זאלק, כדי זיי צוציען צוריק צו זיך ... ווי
זאל א יידיש הארץ ניט וויינען און קלאגן אויף דעם ?
קענען יונגע יידן אן יידיש אין דער וועלט זיך איינריידן
אז זיי געהארן צו די פעלקער, וועמעס שפראכן זיי ריידן,
קענען זיי זיין אפגעריסן פון יידישן פאלק, פון זיין קול־
טור פון זיין ליטעראטור. ביז דער "קבלת פנים" וואס
זיי קריגן פון די אמתע שפראך־בעלי בתים טרייבט זיי
צוריק צום יידישן פאלק און זייער יידישקייט ווערט א
"עקספלאָזיע־יידישקייט", א מין תשובה, וואס איז ניט
ארגאניש.

דאס זעלביקע געפיל און די זעלביקע סיטואציעס
שאפן אין מדינת ישראל אין יענע ספעציפישע באדינ־
גונגען דעם "כנעניזם". די כנענים — זיי האבן ניט די
יידישע פאלק־ווארצלען און צו קיין אנדער "פאלק פון
לאנד" קענען זיי אויך ניט געהערן (דערווייל), האבן די
טיפערע און דענקענדיקע פון זיי אויסגעפונען די כנע־
נים... ארעמע, אויסגעוואָרצלטע יידן אן א פאלק! אפ־
געריסן פון אלע וועלטן.

און דער טראגיזם ציט שוין, רייסט שוין פון אט דער
"כנענישער" העברעאישער שפראך, צו אנדערע פעלקער
מיט אנדערע שפראכן... טיפערע יידישע דענקער אין
דער מדינה, טיפערע יידישע הערצער האבן שוין דער־
פילט די טראגעדיע, ניט אין יידיש הארץ האט שוין

אין אייניקלעך — אַלע לערנען, — און קיינער קען נישט. אײן זאַך טוט מען אויף: פון יידיש דערװײטערט מען. אָבער ניין! ניט פון יידיש, נאָר פון יידישקייט דערװײטערט מען! מען באַמיט זיך צו פאַרמינערן דעם דרך אַרך צו דעם לשון, לשון פון פאָלק, און װער עס האָט ניט ניט קיין דרך אַרך פאַרן פאָלקס לשון, האָט ניט ליב דאָס פאָלק. און אָן ליבע צום פאָלק קען מען קיין גאולה ניט ברענגען.

אויף אַריבער זעקס מיליאָן יידן אין אַמעריקע איז פאַ־ראַן אין גאַנצן אײן העברעאיש װאָכנבלאַט, און ער האַלט זיך נאָר מיט דער הילף פון גרויסע סובװענדיעס. ביכער פאַרקויפן זיך נאָר — אָדער לערנביכער, אָדער פאַרן על־טערן דור, װאָס האָבן זייער העברעאיש געבראַכט פון דער־טן. אַזוי פיל לערנען עברית און אַזוי װײניק קענען! עס איז שוין געזאָגט געװאָרן אַז װאָס מער לערנביכער מען גיט אַרויס, אַלץ װײניקער ליטעראַטור־װערק לײענט מען.

מען איז געקומען מיט אַן אומגליקלעכן לאָזונג: מען דאַרף עברית צו לערנען װי אַ לעבעדיקע שפּראַ. לשון חיה, שפה חיה וכדומה. װאָס מיינט מען אָבער דערמיט?

ערשטנס: אײדער מען גייט צו לערנען קולטור־טעקסטן אין העברעאיש דאַרף מען אויסלערנען די שפּראַך פאַרשטיין.

צװייטנס: דאַרף מען די שפּראַך לערנען ניט צוליב די ספרים, נאָר מען זאָל זיך קענען צונויפריידן אין דעם לשון. דער ציל פון לערנען איז ניט דאָס הספר העברי, נאָר דער הדיבור העברי. יידן זײַנען דאָך קינפטיקע עולים, דאַרפן זיי קענען זיך צונויפריידן אם ירצה השם װען זיי װעלן קומען קיין אַרץ ישראל. און װאָס הייסט "לע־בעדיק"? — װי מען קויפט אַ פעקל שװעבעלעך, װי מען פרעגט אַ גאַס אין תל אביב וכדומה. און דער פועל יוצא?

אײדער די געצײלטע אפשר עולים װעלן יאָ פאָרן קיין מדינת ישראל, פאַרגעסן אַלע לערנערס דאָס ביסל װערטער װאָס מען האָט זיי אויסגעלערנט, און זיי בלײַבן בײַ גאָרניט. קען מען זיך פאָרשטעלן אַ גרעסערע טראַ־געדיע, װען מיט דער הילף אויף פון העברעאיש לשון רייסט מען אָפּ די דורות פון דער העברעאישער קול־טור! ניט קיין בוך, ניט קיין צייטונג, ניט קיין װערטל און ניט קיין װיץ, נאָר "שלום" און דאָס איז אַלץ װאָס עס בלײַבט.

װאַלט מען נאָך אפשר געקאָנט דיסקוטירן װעגן אַזאַ ריין־העברעאישער שול אין אַ װילנע, אין אַ קאָװנער לי־טע. דאָרטן האָט די יוגנט געהאַט אַ פאָלקשפּראַך. גע־לעבט אין איר אין די הימען און אין גאַס; די קינדער האָבן געלעבט אין זייער פאָלק, האָט די העברעאישע שול זיי ניט אָפּגעריסן פון זייער פאָלק, נאָר זיי צוגע־

גענומען קלאַפּן אַלאַרעם אויף דער דערשײַנונג. צוליב געװיסע פסיכישע אייגנשאַפטן אונדזערע איז דער טרא־גיזם נאָך ניט דערגאַנגען צום באַװאוסטזיין פון כלל.

װי גרויס איז די טראַגעדיע אונדזערע, אַז אפילו די געטרײַע זין פון אונדזער פאָלק, פאַרשטייען ניט, װילן ניט אײַנזען, דערשטיקן אין זיך דעם צײַטיק געװאָרענעם האַרץ־געשריי: "װאוהין גייסטו, יידיש װאו פאָלק? אין װאו־סערע תהומים קייקלסטו זיך יידיש פאָלק מיט אַ יוגנט מיט אַלע שפּראַכן אָן יידיש?" (תהומים — אין גייסט פון טראַדיציאָנעלן יידיש, ניט תהומות).

און אָפט, פאַרקערט, דוכט זיך מיר אויס, אַז אין איך פאַרקערטן געשריי: "אַ כפרה דרײַ־פיר־פינף דורות ביז דאָס נײַע העברעאיש װעט דאָך סוף כל סוף יא װערן אַ װאַרצלדיקע פאָלקשפּראַך!"... אַזוי פיל אויך אָפט. הגם אַזוי פרעך האָט מען נאָך דאָס ניט אַרויסגעזאָגט, אָבער אַן װערטער, במסתרים עקסיסטירט דער זאָג זיכער.

און ליידער און ליידער די "האָפענונג" װעט ניט מקוים װערען, היה לא יהיה! עס װעט ניט געשען קיין מאָל: אַן יידיש װערט מען אָפּגעריסן פון יידיש פאָלק אויך אין דער אייגענער, אויסגעחלומטער, אויסגעקעמפטער, מיט בלוט און קדושה אָנגעזאַפטער מדינה. און די אָפּגעריס־נע כלומרשטע כנענים װעלן פריער ־ שפּעטער געפינען, אויסזוכן זיך "גרויסע" לעבעדיקע פעלקער מיט גרויסע, שטאַרק פאַרשפּרייטע שפּראַכן און צו זיי װעט מען זיך רייסן, צו זיי װעט מען זיך ציען אויך אין ציון.

סײַדן, יע סײַדן אויך אין דער מדינה װעט יידיש לשון ראַטעװען די דורות פאַר העברעאיש און פאַר ציון.

...װאו נעמט מען דעם ירמיהו װאָס זאָל באַװײַנען אונ־דזער הײַנטיקן חורבן פון אומה ולשון! װאו?!

און דאָס איז אין דער אייגענער היים, אין דער אייגע־נער מדינה מיט אַן אייגענעם שולװעזן, מיט אַן אייגענעם שטייגער, מיט אייגענע שטעלעס און קאַרי־ערעס אויף העברעאיש מיט אַלץ מיט אַן אַנדער — אַ מדינה איז דאָך אַ מדינה!

און אין דער װעלט? אין אַלע אַנדערע יידישע ישובים? דאָרטן גיסט די העברעאיזם װאַסער אויף אַנדערע, אויף פרעמדע מילן, ער העלפט דעם פּראָצעס פון אויסיידישונג, פון דערװײַטערונג, פון אָפּפרעמדונג, װאָס טראַגט דעם נאָ־מען אסימילאַציע און איז אפילו דאָס אויך ניט.

אַך און װי צו די "גליקן" פון העברעאיש פון אַלע אַנ־שטערענגונגען און באַמיונגען, פון אַלע באַרימערײַען און הורא־הורא־געשרײַען. און אַך און װי: העברעאיש לערנט מען, יונג און אַלט, קינד און קייט, זשוק און זשאַבע, באָבעס

געבן, דערגעבן אויך די קולטורשפּראך צוזאמען מיט
דער קולטור. איז עס אויך דארטן געווען אַ פּעדאגאגי־
שער פעלער — אַ חטא אָדער אַ טעות, ווייל אויך דארטן
האט עס נישט אפֿריסנדיק פון פאלק, דאך יא אַנט־
וויקלט אַ סנאביסטישע באציאונג צום פאלק.

אבער די רייןְ־העברעאישע שולן אויף אויף דעם אַמערי־
קאנער קאנטינענט — דאָ זיינען זיי אַ בפירושער פאר־
ברעכן, ניט בלויז אַ פּעדאגאגישער, נאר אַ נאציאנאַ־
לער פאַרברעכן, אַ פאַראַט. די קינדער האָבן ניט צו דעם
פאָלקס געמיינזאַמס ניט מיטן פאָלק, די
היים און די גאַס — פרעמדע, דאָס גאַנצע לעבן פרעמד
און ווייט, קיין יידישער שטייגער — נישטאָ. די שול —
אפֿילו די יידישע — איז דאָך אין תוך אַריין אַ פרעמ־
דע, אַ מלוכהשע, מיט אַנדערע נאציאנאַלע צילן, צו אַן
אנדער פאַלקישקייט ציט זי. איז זאָ דאָס יידישע אין דער
שול אין בעסטן פאַל נאַר אַ צוגאַב, אַ ביסל כשרע זאַלץ
אין אַ פרעמדן טאָפ. און אָט דער צוגאַב איז נאָך דערצו
אויך ניט קיין גליכבאַרעכטיקטער, אַן אייגעבעטענער,
זען ער אין פּראַקטישן לעבן אַן אומנוציקער... דאָ דאַרף
דער יידישער צוגאַב אָנהייבן פון אָנהייב — דערנענטערן
די קינדער צו זייער פאָלק, אויב נישט צום דירעקטן
היינט, איז צום נאַנטסטן נעכטן. קומט די העברעאישע
שול אָן יידיש ווי אַ באַזיס און זי רייסט אַפ די קינדער
פון דעם היינט און פון דעם נעכטן, פון דעם גאַנצן נאָנטן
יידיש וואָס איז דאָ אין אַרום, פון דעם ביסעלע יידיש
לעבן און יידישקייט וואָס עס איז פאַראַן, מען וויל זיי די
קינדער ברענגען צום ווייטן אַמאָל און צום ווייטן „דער־
טן". איז עס גענליכן צו וועלן אַרויף אויפן דאַך אָן אַ
לייטער וואָס שטייט אויף אויף דער ערד. איז אַזאַ שול — אַפ־
רייסן פון יידן קען זי, ברענגען צום יידישן אַמאָל — דאָס
קאָן זי ניט, דאָס דערגרייכט זי ניט בשום אופן.

און אויב מען לערנט שוין יא אויס עפּעס פון העברע־
איש, איז עס דאָך ניט פון דער קולטורשפּראך, נאָר ווער־
טער וואָס האַבן ניט קיין קולטור־וואַרצלען. עס איז ווי
פלאשן אן דעם וויין אין זיי.

מענדעלע האָט זיך באַמיט אַריינצוגעבן אין דעם הע־
ברעאיש אַ טעם און רירן פון היינטיקן יידיש. אַזוי וואָלט
אויסגעזען דאָס לשון ווען יידן וואָלטן עס גערעדט. ער
האט געוואָלט פון אונדזער קולטורשפּראך מאַכן אויך אַ
פאַלקשפּראך. אין זיין דרך גערעאַגגען נאָך עטלעכע.
אבער עס האָט זיך ניט אַנגענומען, עס איז מער גענעפּעלן
אַ העברעאיש וואָס האָט ניט קיין בת קול פון לעבעדיקער
פאָלקשפּראך און קיין ריח פון לעבעדיקן פאָלק, אפֿילו
ניט דעם פּאָלקס אויסשפּראך. זיינען אַנשטאָט דעם גערו־

מען טרוקענע ווערטער אָן פאַלקישע זאַפטן, און צו אײנ־
האַלטן דערגרייט מען ניט. פאַרגעסט מען די ווערטער,
בלייבט נאָר אַן אָפּגעפרעמדעטיקייט און מער גאָר נישט.
אָפּגעפרעמדט פון יידיש און יידישקייט און די פרעמדע
מלוכה־שפּראך בלייבט דאָך אײנציקער דער האַר און הער־
שער.

אונדזערע ביידע לשונות אויף וויפל זיי טראָגן אין זיך
די אָנגעשפּייכלערטע אוצרות פון אונדזער פאָלקס נשמה
זיינען לשונות חקודש. בײַ יידן באַשטימט דאָך נישט גאָט
די הײליקייט פון עפּעס, נאָר הײליק איז דאָס אַלץ וואָס
טראָגט אין זיך דעם פאָלקס גייסט און זיין נשמה. איז
די קדושה פון יידיש ניט ווייניקער און ניט קלענער ווי
די קדושה פון העברעאיש. אויסגעליידיקט פון פאָלקס
גייסט האָט קיין קיין שפּראך ניט קיין קדושה. ניט קיין רעלי־
גיעזע און ניט קיין וועלטלעך־נאציאנאַלע.

און דער אַלגעמיינער אויספיר:

1.—עס איז ניטאָ בײַ יידן קיין שפּראַכן־קאַמף. אַ האַל־
בן יארהונדערט האָט מען זיך אָפּגעקריגט און דער קריג
איז געווען אויף אַ פאַלשן פראנט: ניט די שפּראַכן —
צוויי לייבלעכע שוועסטער האַבן זיך קיין מאָל נישט גע־
קריגט. עס האָבן זיך געבלאָזן די יוסטע בעלי גאווה פון
אויבן אָן קעגן דעם אונטער דער בימה, וואָס האָט חוצפה־
דיק גענומען פאַרלאַנגען אַן אָרט פאר זיך אין יידישן לעבן.
אבער זיך אָנגעקריגט און גענונג! מיר זיינען אײן פאַלק
מיט אײן קולטור וואָס פאַרמאַגט היפּשע עטלעכע שיכטן
און איטלעכער שיכט מיט זיין לשון.

2.—העברעאיש אַליין איז אָן אַ באַדן אין אונדזער פאָל־
קישער קולטור שבעל פה. יידיש אַליין איז ווי אין די הע־
כערע גאָרנס פון אונדזער קולטור. דער ייד וואָס רעדט
פון קינדווײַז אָן יידיש איז זיכער אַ ייד. דער ייד וואָס
האַט זיך געהאַדעוועט אויף העברעאיש אָן יידיש, דער
זיצט אויפן דאַך פון יידישקייט אָן אַ לייטער צו דעם עצם
פאָלק אונטן. מיט אים דאַרף מען ערשט לערנען „תודה
יהודית" — יידיש באַוווסטזיין.

3.—צוויי ברידער האָבן געלערנט — אײנער יידיש
און דער צווייטער העברעאיש. בײדע האָבן פאַרגעסן. בײם
געהאַדעוועטן אין יידיש, בלייבט די נאַנטקייט צו זיינע
יידן. בײַ דעם צווייטן בלייבט פון יידישקייט גאָרניט.

4.—די יידישע דערציאונג דאַרף באַזירט זיין אויף
דער גאַנצקייט פון אונדזער אײנציקער קולטור מיט איר
אינטעגראַלקייט מיט אירע ביידע שפּראַכן, מיט איר רע־
ליגיעזן און וועלטלעכן אינהאַלט.

5.—די שפראַכן האָבן אַ באַטייט נאָר אַ דאַנק דעם אינהאַלט וואָס אין זיי. אָן די קולטור־אינהאַלטן האָבן די שפראַכן ניט קיין נאַציאָנאַלן ווערט. ליידיקע פלאַשן פון דעם בעסטן ווײַן.

די ייִדישע שול טאָר דערפאַר ניט זײַן קיין שפראַך־שול.

6.—יעדער געדאַנק צו קענען פירן ווײַטער אונדזער קולטור־לעבן אין פרעמדע שפראַכן איז אַ פאַטאַלער טעות, וואָס מוז פירן צו אַסימילאַציע און אומקום.

7.—מען קען אין אַלע שפראַכן פון דער וועלט שרייבן, רײדן און לערנען וועגן ייִדן און ייִדישקייט. אָבער קיין ייִדישע קולטור וועט עס שוין ניט זײַן. מען קען שרייבן אין ענגליש די בעסטע ביכער וועגן יאַפאַן און וועגן אַמאָליקן מצרים, אָבער עס וועט ניט זײַן קיין יאַפאַן און ניט קיין מצרים. מען קען שטודירן אין ענגליש וועגן אַ טויב, אָבער קיין טויב וועט עס נישט זײַן און קיין וואָרקן פון אַ טײבעלע — זיכער ניט. די בעסטע ווערק וועגן ייִדן אין ענגליש זײַנען ניט קיין ייִדישע קולטור.

8.—דער גרעסטער שעדיקער דער ייִדישער קולטור (אין ביידע שפראַכן) איז די סנאָביסטישע באַציאונג צום ייִדישן לשון הן ווען זי קומט פון אָפֿן־אַסימילאַטאָרישע צדדים און הן ווען זי קומט אײַנגעהילט אָן אַ נאַציאָנאַלן מאַנטל פון אַ קיקיון דיונהדיקן העברעאיש. נישט דעם לשון ייִדיש שעדיקט דער סנאָביזם נאָר דער ייִדישקייט אין גאַנצן.

9.—און דער סוף פסוק — דער קיום פון ייִדישן פאָלק איז אונדזער אמונה. דער אמונה דינען מיר. דער קיום האומה איז צפֿהענגיק פון קיום פון דער אינטעגראַלער ייִדישער קולטור. דער קיום פון דער קול־טור איז ווי דער פלאַם מיט דעם קנויט פאַרבונדן מיט דעם קיום פון ייִדיש לשון. און דערפאַר איז די מצוות ייִדיש לשון אונדזער ערשטע מצווה פֿאַרן קיום האומה.

10.—מיטן פאַרלירן ייִדיש לשון פאַרלירן מיר נישט קיין שפראַך, — דאָס ייִדישע פאָלק פאַרלירן מיר!

PART II

Orthodoxy: Then and Now

יהואש טהוט אפ די נביאים אויף—אידיש

The characters of the Old Testament are not entirely pleased with Yehoyesh's modern literary translation into Yiddish. E.g. Job (panel at far right): 'If I didn't have enough troubles during my lifetime Yehoyesh had to come along and translate my book into Yiddish.' (*Der groyser kundes*, June 10, 1910)

a. שעטנז אף דַיַן לייב — נישט
און אַ פרעמד לבוש אף דבַין לשון יאָ‏?!

b. אַ פֿאַר ווערטער וועגן ייִדיש / פֿון ד״ר נתן בירנבוים

אמת, פֿאַראַן ייִדן וואָס האַלטן פֿון ייִדיש און דערבַיַ
זענען זיי בּוגדים בּאלקי ישׂראל. דערפֿון איז אָבּער נישט
גידרונגין, אז ייִדיש איז נישט וויכטיק פֿאַר ייִדישקייט.
וואָרן ס־זענין דאָך אויך פֿאַראַן — און אפֿשר נאָך מער
— „העבּראאיסטישע‟ פּושעים. נו, וועט מין זאָגן, אז
לשון־קודש האָט נישט קיין חשיבות פֿאַר ייִדישקייט?
אָדער, אויב אפֿילו ייִדן לומדים ווערן אפּיקורסים, קען
מען דערפֿון דרינגין, אז מיט לימוד התורה ווערט גאָר
נישט אויפֿגיטון פֿאַר ייִדישקייט? ניין, פֿון דעם אַלימין
איז נאָר גידרונגין, אז ס־זענין דאָ פֿינצטערע פּוחות
אזוינע, וואָס בַיַ גיװויסע תנאים ווערן זיי אזוי שטאַרק,
אז זיי זענין גובר די ליכטיקע השפּעה פֿון ייִדיש, פֿון
לשון־קודש און אפֿילו פֿון לערנין תורה. דאַרף מין
מלחמה האַלטן מיט די פֿינצטערע פּוחות, נישט אָבּער
חלילה זיך מיאש זַיַן פֿון ייִדיש, פֿון לשון־קודש. אָדער
גאָר פֿון לימוד התּורה. און דווקא פֿאַר דער דאָזיקער
מלחמה אַלײַן איז ייִדיש זייער אַ שטאַרק כּלי־זַיַן
— נישט נאָר צוליב דעם, וואָס דער עולם פֿאַרשטייט עס,
נאָר נאָך מער צוליב דעם, וואָס ס־איז אָנגיזאַפּט מיט
ייִדישן נשמה־זאַפֿט.
און אַ חוץ דעם, וואָסער אַ חילוק צווישן דעם ייִדיש פֿון
יענע און צווישן אונדזער ייִדיש, דעם אָנגיזאַפּטן מיט
ייִדישן נשמה־זאַפֿט! מיטן ייִדישקייט גייט דאָך אַרויס
דאָס זאַפֿטיקייט פֿון ייִדיש, ווי די קדושה פֿון לשון־
קודש אויסגיוועפֿט...

Mottos for Part II

(a) 'You will not permit upon your body a garment mingled of linen and woolen; will you permit a foreign garment on your tongue?!'

(b) 'It is true; there are Jews who think highly of Yiddish and at the same time they are betrayors of the God of Israel. However, one cannot deduce therefrom that Yiddish is unimportant for Jewishness, For there are also – and even more numerous – "Hebraist" transgressors. Would one say that loshn koydesh has no importance for Jewishness therefore? Or even if Jewish scholars become non-believers, can one conclude therefrom that nothing is accomplished on behalf of Jewishness by means of Torah study? No, what must be concluded from all of the foregoing is that there are dark forces that are so strong under certain circumstances that they overcome the shining influence of Yiddish, of loshn koydesh and even of Torah study. So one must wage war against these dark forces but never forgo Yiddish, nor loshn koydesh, much less Torah study. And precisely for this war Yiddish itself is a mighty weapon; not only because the masses understand it, but even more, because it is saturated with Jewish soul.

Furthermore, what a difference between their Yiddish and our Yiddish that is saturated with Jewish soul! Without Jewishness the very flavor of Yiddish is lost, just at the holiness of loshn koydesh evaporates...'.

Both quotations from *Beys yankev*, 1931, 8, (a) p. 6 and (b) p. 2 (Nosn Birnboym)

A Defense of Yiddish in Old Yiddish Literature

ISRAEL ZINBERG

In the cultural evolution of no other people has the problem of language played so prominent a role as among the Jews. In the course of its long history, the Jewish people has several times changed its vernacular. And these changes were not solely the result of the Diaspora.

As early as in the period of the Second Commonwealth the Jewish community in Palestine had undergone a transformation that had a mighty effect upon its national cultural life; it had adopted a new language, and virtually relinquished the older one. Whereas in the days of Isaiah I (eighth century B.C.E.), Aramaic, the vernacular of western Asia, was – barring the small ruling and aristocratic class – almost unknown to the Jewish people, some four hundred years later it was the current idiom. The sages of the *Mishna* designated this Aramaic dialect, with its admixture of Greek and Latin elements, as the 'common tongue'. This language was the medium of instruction in the Jewish school; in it, the Torah was expounded to the people in the synagogue and at public gatherings. It became a great cultural factor arousing a national feeling in the people and strengthening the triad: God, Israel, and the Torah. The Aramaic dialect, the vernacular and literary language of the people, merged with the language of the Bible to become for generations almost inseparable.

True, there were even then purists that inveighed against the corrupt language of the people, urging the use of either pure Hebrew, or Greek, or Latin. The Talmud formulates this linguistic quarrel thus: The Scriptures say, 'Thus shalt thou say to the house of Jacob' – in the language in which I, God, speak, that is, in Hebrew. The protagonists of Hebrew cautioned against praying in Aramaic, for the angels are not conversant with that tongue. The defenders of Aramaic countered that God himself highly esteemed the Aramaic language. They maintained that Hebrew was not the only chosen tongue, for at the giving of the decalogue God had spoken to the Israelites in the idiom current among them at that time, in Egyptian.

However, it was a futile battle that the purists fought. Life was against them.

The Aramaic dialect, the language of the *Targum* (Aramaic translations of the Bible), had attained almost the same eminence as the language of the Bible; both became sacred in the consciousness of the Jewish people. Together they continued to spin the golden thread of the national culture even in later days, when Aramaic, too, fell into disuse as a spoken tongue. The weekly lection of the Scriptures was in both languages, twice in Hebrew and once in Aramaic. Prayers were written in both languages; one of the most familiar, the *Kaddish* (the memorial prayer for the dead), was in Aramaic. Two works of prime importance, the Talmud and the *Zohar*, were practically all in Aramaic.

Several hundred years after the redaction of the Talmud (sixth century C.E.), the vast majority of the Jewish people again adopted a new language. Under the influence of the newly arisen Islamic culture, the Jewish settlement in western Asia exchanged its Aramaic dialect for Arabic. But the new vernacular did not attain that place of honor in the national Jewish culture that its predecessor, Aramaic, had attained. It did not become a twin sister of the Hebrew language, but its proud rival. For generations the Arabic language remained for the largest part of the Jewish people the most important factor of general culture, but not of national creativeness. That creativeness continued in the old languages, Hebrew and Aramaic.

In the tenth or eleventh century, the Franco-German Jewish settlement began to rise to prominence. Here, however, the cultural level of the surrounding population was much lower than that of Mohammedan Spain. Learning, such as it was, was limited to the monastery and the church school. The medium of instruction in these institutions was Latin, a language that, in the eyes of the Jewish people, was associated with their enemy and deadly persecutor, the Church, and held in abhorrence. The expression, therefore, of Jewish cultural life continued to be in Hebrew and Aramaic. But these languages were no longer intelligible to large segments of the population: the uneducated, the women; briefly, to practically all save the scholars. The vast majority of the people had adopted the vernacular of their surroundings, and their cultural needs had to be supplied in that language. Parts of the Bible, parts of the Passover service, and some prayers were read in the vernacular. This was also the language of instruction in the school. We know that in the fourteenth century there were current among the German Jews not only translations of prayers, but rhymed prayers in the vernacular in the manner of the Hebrew liturgy. Rabbi Jacob Möllen (Maharil, fourteenth–fifteenth century), who alluded to these, was strongly opposed to them. As earlier the question of Aramaic, so later the issue of the other vernaculars was seriously debated. Nachmanides (thirteenth century) was an uncompromising opponent of the vernacular. 'It is not permitted to publish the Holy Scripture in any dialect or language, but in Hebrew'. His contemporary, the pious Jonah Ghirondi, had a different point of view. If one has no Bible with an Aramaic translation, he says, one may substitute in his weekly lection the vernacular for the Aramaic. Another contemporary, Judah b. Benjamin, went even further, stating that 'our vernacular takes the place of the *Targum* (Aramaic) of former days'. The author of *Shibole Haleket* (Ears of Gleaning, thirteenth century) emphasizes that it is a *mizva*, a religious obligation, while the Scriptures are being read to have interpreters expound their contents for the benefit of those not conversant with Hebrew. The *Sefer Hassidim* (Book of the Pious) teaches:

> If there comes to you a man that does not understand Hebrew, but he is a pious and God-fearing man, or a woman, who surely understands no Hebrew, and wishes to pray with the proper devotion, then tell them to pray in the language they understand. For prayer is the expression of the heart, and if the heart knows not what the lips utter, what is the value of such a prayer? Therefore, it is better that every one pray in the language he understands.

This literature in the vernacular was primarily oral. The rhymed prayers, the translations of portions of the Bible, were improvised and transmitted orally from generation to generation. Occasionally, the interpreter would make notes for himself of translations of certain passages in the Bible; the teachers would do it to a larger extent; and from time to time a wealthy patroness would order a written translation of the prayer book. Very little of this literature, however, has been preserved, particularly of secular content. The numerous folk tales, songs, lullabies, riddles, and children's games in their vernacular form have been completely lost.

The end of the fifteenth and the beginning of the sixteenth centuries marked the development of the city in Western Europe and the rise of the burgher class. The aspirations and interests of this class found expression in a new literary form and, primarily, in a new medium. The folk book became the current literary form, and the medium was the vernacular. The famous humanist Ulrich von Hutten tells: 'In the beginning I wrote in Latin, but few people understood me. Now I turn to my people, the German people, in their own language and summon them to battle to avenge the ills inflicted upon them'. Simultaneously, the invention and the spread of the printing press made the book accessible to the large public.

The great changes in the surrounding world inevitably found repercussions in the Jewish world.

The oldest Yiddish book that has come down to us is the *Mirkeves Hamishne*, a concordance to the Bible, published in Cracow in 1534. There is no doubt, however, that at a considerably earlier date Yiddish books had made their appearance in Germany and northern Italy, which had at that time a considerable Ashkenazic colony. These books, popular folk books, were read to shreds, and not a single one has been preserved. We know that Elijah Levita wrote his *Bovo Bukh* in 1507, but the first edition, or possibly editions, has never reached us. Perhaps, Levita was not the only one who attempted to acquaint the Jewish reading public with the literature of the non-Jewish world. Steinschneider, Güdemann, and other historians of literature maintain that practically all German folk books current at that time were also reprinted in Hebrew characters with but insignificant changes. Nor did Jewish publishers limit their output merely to adaptations of foreign subject matter. One of the oldest Yiddish books that has come down to us is the moralistic *Seyfer Mides* (1542).

Typical of the publishers of the period was one Yosef bar Yokor. By his own admission, he was an uneducated and ignorant person. Earlier, it would not have occurred to a man of that caliber to enter into competition with the scholars and to become an author. But the printing press had popularized the book among the wide masses, making the idiom of these masses a literary language. From their midst arose a man with a new cultural message, who consciously emphasized the vast gulf separating him from the scholars and legal casuists, of whom he was somewhat contemptuous. Yosef bar Yokor was the first to issue the prayer book in Yiddish (Ichenhausen 1544). In this edition he no longer confined himself to the mere role of publisher and printer, but assumed the calling of folk writer and champion of Yiddish. And, although he modestly states, 'I have not invented this translation, but chose one from among several, which seemed best to men', the entire work betrays the hand of an experienced editor, and there is little doubt that he himself translated some of the prayers, as is evidenced by the richness of their language.

In his introduction to the prayer book, Yosef bar Yokor expresses his amazement at the multiplicity and unintelligibility of the prayers, and states categorically: 'I consider them but fools who insist upon praying in Hebrew, yet understand not a word of that language. I should like to know what measure of devotion such prayer carries with it?' He, therefore, determined to publish the prayer book and similar books in the vernacular.

Concurrently with Yosef bar Yokor, Cornelio Adelkind began his publishing activities in Yiddish. Adelkind was a man of a considerable general education, for years in the employ of the famous Venetian Christian printer of Hebrew books, Daniel Bomberg. In his later years, he began to feel an urge to enlighten the 'common people'. In his introduction to the translation of the Psalms (rendered into Yiddish at his request by Elijah Levita) he declares:

In my earlier years I have been instrumental in the publication of many valuable and costly volumes, as can be seen in the books published by Bomberg, in which my name is found on the title-page and the last page. Now it occurs to me that I have done nothing for the pious women and those men that had no opportunity to acquire an education in their youth, but would nevertheless prefer to spend the Sabbath or the holidays in the perusal of edifying and pious works than in the reading of the yarns of Dietrich of Bern and the like. For the benefit of these people, who would gladly read the words of God, but find so little in the vernacular that is faithfully rendered, I have commissioned Elijah Levita to translate several books....

In this declaration two elements are of significance. Adelkind decries the subject matter introduced from foreign sources, such as Dietrich of Bern and the like, an opinion which is frequently voiced in the Jewish literature of the period. The scholars and rabbis were hardly satisfied with the courtly romances and fantastic tales, which became widespread with the invention of the printing press and the rise of the 'itinerant bookseller'. But they well knew that to banish the 'fascinating' book was practically an impossible task, hence they found it necessary to furnish the simple reader with works steeped in Jewish lore and tradition, and entertaining as well. The second point worth noting in the declaration is his appeal not only to the 'pious women' but also to the uneducated men. Some Jewish scholars in Germany, Güdemann, Perles, and Steinschneider, constantly speak of the older Yiddish literature as of writings designed for women exclusively. This however, is not so. I have collected some seventy title pages of older Yiddish books and only nine of them are addressed exclusively to the 'pious women and maidens', the others expressly state that they aim also at the 'men and young men'. Some are addressed to the 'dear brethren', 'every man, scholar or common man'.

Nevertheless, it is undeniable that the Jewish woman was a very prominent factor in the rise and spread of Yiddish folk literature. Prior to the development of this literature, the Jewish woman was entirely barred from the national culture by linguistic barriers. With the fall of these barriers, that is, with the rise of a national culture in the vernacular, the woman was incorporated in the national cultural life. Thereby the horizons of that life were perceptibly widened, and the woman gained a new status. The well-known publisher and translator, Isaac b. Aaron Prostitz, in his preface to the Yiddish translation of the Book of Esther, which he published in Cracow in 1590, inveighs against the 'chattering fools, that think the world was created solely for them', and he particularly emphasizes:

The woman is generally deemed of little worth. This represents a point of view that is contrary to the will of God, blessed be He, who does not suffer any of His creatures to be slighted.... When God came to give the Law to Israel he first addressed himself to the women and the children, as we find it in Scripture.

The same motive is also mentioned by Moses Henekhs Altshul, the author of the popular *Brantshpigl* ('Burning Mirror'), and a contemporary of Prostitz. In the first chapter of his work he states that the book is written in the vernacular, for the women and the men that are like women, possessing little knowledge.... 'So that on the Sabbath they may read and understand it. For our books are in Hebrew, and their subject matter is drawn from the Talmud, both of which, content and form, make comprehension difficult'. He also dwells upon the role of the woman in Jewish life and, referring to the passage cited by Prostitz, concludes that she constitutes the flower of the people.

God had first addressed himself to the woman, and then to the man. The Rabbis asked: 'Why had the woman merited to hear God's word first?' and the answer was given: 'Because from their earliest days they instruct the children in the ways of God, taking them to school and inspiring them to study the Law.'

Whereas the publishers of Yiddish books with secular content aimed merely, as Prostitz stated, 'at entertainment', men like Moses Altshul set for themselves a much higher goal. They wanted to educate, to edify, to spread the fundamentals of the Jewish religion and ethics among the widest strata of the people. Typical in this respect is Jacob b. Isaac of Janow, the author of the *Ts'eno Ur'eno*, the so-called Woman's Bible. The title-page of his translation, or rather paraphrase, of the Prophets and Hagiographa reads: '...Hence we have translated the entire Prophets and Sacred Writings so that no man be in need of an exponent to expound to him these works...and named the book *Seyfer Hamagid* (The Exponent)'. The author repeats the same thought in his *Meylits Yosher*: 'People listen to discourses in the synagogue and fail to understand them; they are delivered too rapidly for the ordinary person to follow. A book, however, everyone can read at his own pace'.

Isaac b. Eliakim of Posen, the author of the very popular didactic work *Lev Tov* (seventeenth century), expresses openly his dissatisfaction with the books in the vernacular that 'do not treat of the Law or the precepts'. These he brands as 'scoffers' tales' in contrast to the pious writings. 'A poor man that cannot afford to pay for the services of a teacher should read the Pentateuch, or the Psalms, or other pious works in the vernacular'. He himself wrote such a book, which he recommended as embodying all of Judaism. He, too, disapproved of prayer in an unintelligible language: '...Therefore, it is necessary that everyone understand the prayer he utters....He who does not understand Hebrew should pray in a language that he understands. Better a few prayers with the proper devotion than many unintelligible prayers'.

Rabbi Yekhiel Mekhl Epstein, mystic and author of the seventeenth century, expatiates on this point. In Chapter XXXI of his *Derekh Hayoshor Leoylam Habo* (The Direct Road to Life Eternal) he reiterates the view that it is preferable to pray in a language that one understands. He continues:

There are many women who, upon being told that it is better that they pray in the vernacular, reply: 'We have been informed that the angels understand only the sacred tongue.' They are in error. For the prayer that comes from the depth of the heart and from a contrite spirit is most acceptable to God who probes all hearts...as we find in many books that a word that one understands is more effective than a hundred words not understood....Therefore, my friends, consider that our ancestors have rendered all our prayers, Psalms, penitential prayers, and other supplications into the vernacular. Were the angels not conversant with the vernacular, would our ancestors have wasted their efforts in a futile enterprise?

Just as in respect of divine worship the vernacular is elevated to a new status, so with regard to study, too, it comes to occupy a new position. Khayim b. Nathan, of Prague, the author of *Esrim Vearba* in the vernacular (1674), states: 'There is no difference whether a man studies it [Holy Writ] in Hebrew or in

„שמחת בית השואבה" אין קצבישע קלויז (יאַטקעווער 5)
לערער אליעזר גאָלדבערג האָט גערעדט א.ד.ט „וויַן,
וואַסער און טרערן" חול המועד סוכות

Water Drawing Festival in the Butchers' Synagogue (Butcher Street no. 5)

The teacher Eliezer Goldberg. spoke on the topic: ''Wine, Water and Tears'', Chol Hamoed Sukkot

שמחת בית השואבה בקלויז של הקצבים (רח' הקצבים 5) ;
המורה אליעזר גולדברג נאם בנושא: „יין, מים, ודמעות"

Торжество в молитвенном доме резников (Ятковая ул. 5) Учитель Элиезер Гольдберг прочел лекцию на тему: ''Вино, вода и слезы'' ''Хол Гамоед Сукот''

1942 1/X

In the Nazi-instituted ghetto (1942): the lull before the storm – the traditional water festival. A speaker, a cantor, and a reminder to come to services.

the vernacular. . .it is only a question of comprehension'. And several generations later, the author of *Emunas Yisroel* (eighteenth century) declares that all the schoolboy can acquire from a teacher, he can just as well read in books in Yiddish, 'for nowadays we have the whole Law and the precepts in Yiddish'.

These attainments of the vernacular could hardly please the teachers, the preachers, the exponents of the Law to the common people, and the rabbis – all of whom were thus to a certain extent made superfluous. Their opposition to rendering in the spoken idiom such books as the *Shulhan Aruk* (Code of Laws) is thus understandable. Moses Frankfurt, associate Rabbi in Amsterdam, published in 1722 an edition of the *Menorat Hamaor* (a moralistic work of the fifteenth century) with a Yiddish translation, in the introduction of which he takes exception to those scholars that are of the opinion 'that it is undesirable to translate books in the vernacular that make accessible the contents of the *Gemara* and the *Midrash* to everyone'. On the contrary, the Amsterdam Rabbi maintains, 'it is a *mizva*, a religious obligation, to publish such books in all languages'. And he continues:

More than that, earlier, all the books most difficult of comprehension had rarely been written in Hebrew, but in the language of the common people. Thus the Jerusalem Talmud was written in the language spoken in Palestine, at that time [Aramaic], not in Hebrew. Also, very large parts of the Babylonian Talmud are not in Hebrew. Similarly, the *Targum*, the Aramaic translation of the Scriptures of Jonathan b. Uziel and the version known as the Jerusalem translation, which contains many of the mysteries of the Law, was written in the language of the common man, and the *Zohar*, a most sacred book, was not in Hebrew, but in the vernacular current in Babylonia.

The above advocates of Yiddish, with the exception of Yosef bar Yokor, came from the ranks of the scholars. They were intellectuals with a keen grasp of the cultural needs of the common man. Of an entirely different caliber was Aaron b. Samuel of Hergershausen, a small town in southern Germany. Orphaned in his early childhood, he grew up in poverty and neglect among strangers. In his distress, he tells us, he sought solace in the sacred books, but his knowledge of Hebrew was inadequate for that purpose. True comfort he found only in the 'pleasant books' in Yiddish, in the folk literature. Having found this source of delight, he wanted others to benefit from his discovery. He desired to point out to men and women the way to the source of living waters, which he had found in the Yiddish books. He, therefore, wrote a unique book, *Liblikhe tfile oder kreftige artsnay far guf un neshome* (Pleasant Prayer or Powerful Physic for Body and Soul, Fürth, 1709).

In his introduction the author declares that he anticipates the ridicule of the proud scholar for his simple words, but is not disheartened. In defense, he cites Ecclesiasticus to the effect that a little scholarship combined with the fear of God is better than great wisdom mingled with hyprocrisy. He ends with the hope that all kind and sincere people will recognize the merit of his work.

The author hardly exaggerated when he declared on the title page that his work never had an equal in Yiddish literature. For the author, the common man, as he styles himself, had the courage, in his introduction, to challenge the entire system of education among the Jews at that time. He emphasized the fact that he wrote his introduction in Yiddish so that even the common man could see and appreciate the currently chaotic state of Jewish education. The crux of the difficulty, in his opinion, lay in the exaggerated emphasis upon language at the expense of content.

It is customary with us that in earlier youth the child begins his training in Hebrew, which he completely fails to grasp. . . . Consequently, no true fear of God can be implanted in his heart, for in his early years he does not comprehend the teachings, and in later life, when he reads the translation, his heart is hardened and he profits from it less than from the Hebrew. Thus the root of all evil is the improper training of our children.

To remedy this state of affairs, the author compiled a collection of prayers and some Psalms in Yiddish, which

. . . would penetrate the hearts of men and lead them to mend their ways and to no longer do wrong. . . and thus bring about peace. . . . Furthermore the children will also learn to speak correctly and to write without mistake.

In reality, his *Siddur* was not a translation of the standard version, but a practically new book. With the exception of a few traditional selections and some Psalms, the author filled his work with prayers composed by him, designed to meet the workaday requirements of the common man: 'Prayers for children', 'a prayer of devotion for a man who is not a scholar', 'a beautiful prayer for a servant or maid', 'a prayer for husband and wife for domestic felicity'. The book was printed not in the special 'women's script' type, in which all Yiddish books used to appear at that time, but in Hebrew characters, like the standard prayer books in Hebrew.

Aaron b. Samuel thought that his book would bring about peace, but he was mistaken. The rabbis saw in his enterprise, and particularly in his introduction, nothing but heresy and anarchy; immediately upon its publication, the work was banned. Apparently the ban was effective, for the book was completely forgotten. Over a century later, in 1830, a few hundred copies of the banned work were found in the attic of the synagogue in his native town.

The rabbis did not find it difficult to vanquish an advocate for Yiddish like the 'heretical' Aaron b. Samuel. However, a fresh defense of Yiddish came from entirely new – and from the point of view of orthodoxy, unimpeachable – quarters. In the second half of the seventeenth century, under the impact of the Thirty Years' War in Germany and Central Europe and the massacres of 1648 in the Ukraine, the mystic-ascetic teachings of R. Isaac Luria gained ascendancy in Jewish life. The adepts of the mystic lore aimed to initiate large numbers of people into the mysteries, to disseminate these teachings among all strata of the population. The *Zohar*, the Bible of the mystics, was rendered into Yiddish

(1711), for, in the words of the introduction: 'Salvation cannot take place, unless everyone studies the Zohar according to his ability and understanding'. The translator deemed it necessary to stress that the scholars, too, need not hesitate to study the *Zohar* in Yiddish, 'for the original itself is not in Hebrew, but in the vernacular of the lands of its origin'.

Other students of mysticism concur in this matter. The author of *Abir Yakov* (published in 1700) states in the introduction to his book: 'Even the scholars will find great delight in this book.... Many mysteries will be revealed to you...'. But the mystics went a step further. In the vernacular they waged war on the scholars that were proud of their attainment in Talmudic lore. The author of *Tikune Hamoadim* (eighteenth century) goes so far as to declare that

...not all depends upon the *Gemara*, or the law, or the *Tosafot* (Supplement to the Talmud).... Some think that the knowledge of a page or two of the Talmud constitutes scholarship, but, my dear friends, know that he who possesses a knowledge of all the *Gemara* and the *Tosafot* without a knowledge of the mystic teachings is but as a child that begins his schooling.

While this aspect of the controversy, dealing more properly with the antinomianism of the mystics, would take us too far afield, it is evident that the use of Yiddish had by then become firmly established and found its champions even in the ranks of the aristocracy of learning.

1  **ד״ר שלמה עטינגער** וואַרשע, פוילן, 1801 זאַמאָשטש, פוילן, 1856 —◆— סערקעלע, (פיעסע) דאָס לעכט, (פּאָעמע) פעטער פון אמעריקע, (פיעסע) משלים און קאַטאָוועסלעך —◆— **פּאָעט, משלים־שרייבער,**	**2**  **אברהם־בער גאָטלאָבער** אַלט־קאָנסטאַנטין, אוקראַינע, 1811 ביאַליסטאָק, פוילן, 1899 —◆— דער דעקטוד, (פיעסע) דער בידנע ישראליק, (ליד) דאָס ליד פונעם קוגל דער גלגול, (דערציילונג) —◆— **פּאָעט, דערציילער, דראַמאַטורג**	**3**  **וועלוול זבאַרזשער** (בנימין ־ וואָלף עהרענקראַנץ) זבאַראַזש. גאַליציע, 1819 קאָנסטאַנטינאָפּאָל, טערקיי, 1883 —◆— דער פאָלקס ־ דיכטער דער רבי רב בער דער פילאָסאָף דער באָנקראָט —◆— **פּאָעט (פאָלקס ־ דיכטער)**
4  **אייזיק־מאיר דיק** (אמ״ד) ווילנע, רוסלאַנד, 1807 ווילנע, רוסלאַנד, 1893 —◆— ר׳ חייציקל אליין שמעיה גוט־יומטוב־ביטער יעקעלע גאַלדשלעגער מעשה גר־צדק —◆— **דערציילער**	**5**  **יצחק־יואל לינעצקי** (עלי קצין הצחקואלי) ווניצע, אוקראַינע, 1839 אַדעס, אוקראַינע, 1915 —◆— דאָס פוילישע יינגל, (דערצ.) ניט טויט ניט לעבעדיק ביזער מאַרשעליק, (לידער) דאָס משולחת, (אַרטיקלען) —◆— **דערציילער, פּאָעט**	**6**  **ש מ ״ ר** (נחום־מאיר שייקעוויטש) נעסוויזש, ווייס־רוסלאַנד, 1849 ניו־יאָרק, פאַר. שטאַטעז, 1905 —◆— דער קאַטאָרזשניק, (ראָמאַן) ניט טויט, ניט לעבעדיג, אַ שפרונג אין הימל, (ראָמאַן) די עמיגראַנטעז, (פיעסע) —◆— **ראָמאַניסט, דערציילער, דראַמאַטורג**

1. Shloyme Etinger, 1801–1856; Poet, writer of fables; 2. Avrom-ber Gotlober, 1811–1899; Poet, writer of short stories and plays; 3. Velvl Zbarzher, 1819–1883; Poet, 4. Ayzik-meyer Dik, 1807–1893; Writer of short stories; 3. Yitskhok-yoyel Linyetski, 1839–1915; Writer of short stories, poet; 6. Shomer, 1849–1905; Novelist, writer of short stories and plays.

פּראָפֿ. מאַקס עריק

(זלמן מערקין)

סאָסנאָװיץ, פּוילן, 1898
אומגעבראַכט, קאַצעט וויעט־
לאַסיאַן, ראַטנפֿאַרבאַנד, 1937

קאָנסטרוקטיווע שטודיעץ,
אַלט־ייִדישער ראָמאַן און נאָוועלע
געשיכטע פֿון דער ייִדישער
ליטעראַטור
עטיודן, (געשיכטע פֿון השכלה)

ליטעראַטור - היסטאָריקער
עסייאיסט

יודל מאַרק

פּאַלאַנגע, ליטע, 1897
לעבט אין ניו יאָרק, פֿאַר. שטאַטן

שול גראַמאַטיק
היסטאָרישע געשטאַלטן
דער העברעישער עלעמענט אין
ייִדיש
גרויסער װערטערבוך פֿון דער
ייִדישער שפּראַך

שפּראַך־פֿאָרשער, לעקסיקאָגראָף

ד״ר נתן בירנבוים

װין, עסטרייך, 1864
װאָסענאַאַר, האָלאַנד, 1937

דער יחוס פֿון ייִדיש
גאָטס פֿאָלק
פֿון אַן אפּיקורס געװאָרן אַ מאמין
דער רוף

עסייאיסט
טעאָרעטיקער פֿון רעל. פֿאָלקיזם

ד״ר חיים זשיטלאָווסקי

אושאַטי, װײַס־רוסלאַנד, 1865
ניו־יאָרק, פֿאַר. שטאַטן, 1943

קאַמף פֿאַר פֿאָלק און שפּראַך
ייִד און מענטש
סאָציאַליזם און נאַציאָנאַלע
פֿראַגע
די פֿילאָסאָפֿיע

עסייאיסט, פֿילאָסאָף
טעאָרעטיקער פֿון ייִדישיזם

הלל צייטלין

קאָרמע, װײַס־רוסלאַנד, 1872
אומגעבראַכט װאַרשע, פּוילן, 1942

דער אלף - בית פֿון ייִדנטום
פּראָבלעם פֿון גוטס און שלעכטס
ר׳ נחמן בראַצלעווער
חסידות

עסייאיסט
טעאָרעטיקער פֿון רעל. פֿאָלקיזם

בער באָראָכאָװ

זלאָטאָנאָשי, אוקראַינע, 1881
קיעװ, אוקראַינע, 1917

קלאַסן־אינטערעסן און נאַציאָ־
נאַלע פֿראַגע
װאָס װילן די פּועלי ציון
אויפֿגאַבן פֿון ייִדישער פֿילאָלאָגיע
ביבליאָטעק פֿון ייִדישן פֿילאָלאָג

ליטעראַטור און שפּראַך־
פֿאָרשער
טעאָרעטיקער פֿון פּועלי ציוניזם

---

1. Maks Erik, 1898–1937; Literary historian, essayist; 2. Yudl Mark, 1897–1975; Language researcher, lexicographer; 3. Nosn Birnboym, 1864–1937; Essayist, theoretician of religious *folkizm*; 4. Khayim Zhitlovski, 1865–1943; Essayist, philosopher, theoretician of Yiddishism; 5. Hilel Tsaytlin, 1872–1942; Essayist, theoretician of religious *folkizm*; 6. Ber Borokhov, 1881–1917; Literary historian, language researcher, theoretician of labor zionism.

יידישקייט און יידיש

שרה שענירער

SUMMARY: JEWISHNESS AND YIDDISH BY SORE SHENIRER

The pre-World War II founder of orthodox schools for girls (1883–1935) argues that Yiddish is the language of traditional (Eastern European) Yiddishkayt (= Jewishness) and that to give it up would be dislocating and impoverishing.

דער נומער 62 פון „בית־יעקב" ליגט פאר מיר. איך לייען די החלטות פון זער פאצביניצער קאנפערענץ פון ט׳ טבת און זע צווישן פארשידינע אנדערע קעפּל׳ך, דאָס קעפּל יידישקייט און יידיש". און לייענינדיק די שורות, שטעלט זיך פאר מײַנע אויגן די גאַנצע פאַבּיניצער קאנפערענץ איך הער די התלהבותדיקע ווערטער פון י״ל ארלעאַן, וועגן יידישקייט און יידיש לשון, און הער די פּלאדיסמענטן פון אלע פארזאַמלטע אויף זײַן פירלייג, אז אלע דעלעגאַטנס זאָלן אויף זייערע ערטער מיט אלע חברות רעדן נאר יידיש דורך דרײַ חדשים.

צי האט מין אבער די דאזיקע החלטה באַאמת אַריינגיפירט אין לעבן ?

צי איז זײַן שיינע כּוונה פארשטאַנין גיוואָרן ? זאָלן זיך טאַקע אלע... אלע חברות אָפגעבּן דין חשבון. די הײַנטיקע ספירה־טעג זענין דאך צום בעסטן מסוגל צו אויצלכע חשבונס הנפש.

וואָרן, כ־מיין, אז יעדע חברה האט פארשטאַנין, אז די כּוונה פון י״ל ארלעאַן איז נישט נאר דרײַ חדשים, צו רעדן בלויז יידיש, און דערנאך ווידער פּויליש, נאר ער האט פאַרשטאַנין, אז אויב מע וועט דורך דרײַ חדשים באַאמת זעען, נאר צו רעדן יידיש, וועט מין שוין אזוי דערמיט צוגיוואָאיינט ווערן, אז מע וועט שוין גאר נישט קענין אנדערש רעדן.

אבּער ס־איז אַ וויטיק! איך זע אַ גאר קלײַנע פעולה פונים פּאַבּיניצער התלהבות בײַ דעם ענין...

יא, מײַן אלט גישרײַ, אז קומין אין התלהבות איז זייער לײַכט, אבער צו האַלטן דאָס התלהבות צו יעדער מצווה, צו יעדן מנהג, לאַנג, יאָרן לאַנג, דאָס גאַנצע לעבּן לאַנג, אזוי לאַנג ווי' הקב״ה גיט אונדז כּוח, נאר לויט זײַן רצון, אויסנוצן אין זײַן דינסט – אט דאָס, דאָס פעלט אונדז נאך שטענדיק.

דערפאַר ווייסן שוין אויף אלע, וואָס קעניין מיך, אז איך בין בין אַזַ שונא פון אלע מין צפּלא־ דיסמענטן... דאָס איז עפּיס אַ מין אויסנווייניק התלהבות, וואָס ברענט אין זעל... אבער בּאַלד, ווי מע קומט נאר אויף דער לופט, ווערט עס אָפּגיקילט.

ג. ה.

מיר האָבֶן דעם כבוד איינצולאַדֶן אײך אױף שבת פ׳ שקלים,
יום כ״ז שבט תרפ״ח (18 פעװראַל 1928). 8 אזײגער אינדערפרי

צום חג היובל (50 יאָר)

פון אונזער ניי־אָפּגערעמאָנטירטער קלױז אױף גלעזער גאַס 9.
ס׳וועט דאַוונען דער טאַלאַנטפולער חזן הבחור שמואל שנײדער.
מיר האָפֿן, אַז איר וועט אָנטײל נעמען אין אונזער שמחה.

מיט אכטונג:
די גבאים פון קלױז דרוקער (גרושקין).
ווילנא, גלעזער גאַס 9.

Invitation to attend the 50th anniversary of the newly renovated Printers Synagogue (Vilna 1928).

און איר, מיינע אַלע לערערנס, בנות, בתי׳ – און בֵּית־יַעֲקב־קינדער! איר וועסט דאך יא,
וואָס וויל, ווי אַזױ איך פֿאַרשטײ מיַין דעווײז „עבדו את ד׳ בשמחה״! פֿאַרװאָס פֿאַרשאַפֿט
איר מיר אַזאַ שרעקלעכן עגמת נֶפש ?
פון אַ זַך, אַ סַך שווערערע זאַכן האָט איר אײַך אָפּגיוויינט צוליב אונדזער הײליקן אידעאַל
– און גראָד דאָס ײדיש־רעדן איז אַזאַ שווערער קרבן פֿאַר אײַך ?
איך וויס, איר וועט מיר ענטפֿערן: מיר וועלן... נאָר...
אבער איך זאָג, ווי דער ווילנער גאָון זצ״ל: „וויל נאָר און דו וועסט וואָרן אַ ווילנער גאָון.״
בײַ אַ פעסטן רָצון מוז מין אַלץ אַדורכפֿירן, און צו דעם ברױך מין נאָר בֶּאֱמת וועלן.
זאָל נישט זײן ווי די סון די, וואָס רעדן אַלע מאָל ײדיש, נאָר טאַקע די, וואָס רעדן אַפֿט
פּױליש, צו מײַן גרױס עגמת נָפש. יענע וואָס האָב איך גימוסרט אַ תַּלמִידה, ווייל זי האָט
גירעט פּױליש צו איר חַברטע. האָט זי גיעֶנטפערט: „די לערערן פון דער פּױלישער שול האָט
גיזאָגט, אַז דאָס ײדישע לָשון איז פֿאַר אונדז דאָס זעלבע, וואָס דאָס פּױלישע, ווייל זי איז
דאָך נישט אונדזער, נאָר עפּיס אַ זשאַרגאָן פון דיַטש״. אָט מיט דעם גרױסן טָעות מײן איך,
טוט זיך אױך נישט מיַין צלטערע ײדישע טאַקטער סֶרצענטספֿערן פֿאַר זיך.
ווֶגֶן דעם חשיבות פון ײדיש וויל איך דאַ נאָר זאָגן אַ פֿאַר גידאַנקין, וואָס מיַין ברודער האָט
אַרױסגירופֿען אין מיר.

דער „חובת הלבבות" זאָגט, אַז דאָס לשון איז די פֿעדער פֿון הַלֵּב. מיר װייסן, אַז דער
שרײַבער שרײַבט מיט דער פֿעדער די גיפֿילן פֿון דער טיף פֿון זײַן הַלֵּב. נו, אַז ער רעט
אַ פֿרעמד לשון, זעגען דאָך די גיפֿילן אויך פֿרעמד, װײַל דער דאָזיקער מענטש קלערט דאָך
אויך אַ פֿרעמד לשון, – מיר מוזן דאָך װיסן, אַז דאָס ייִדישע לשון איז אונדז שוין בלויז
דערפֿאַר אַזוי טײַער, װײַל אונדזערע מאַמעס, זײדיס און עלטער-זײדיס האָבן שוין גירעט מיט
דעם לשון. זעגען מיר שוין בלויז צוליב פֿיעטעט פֿאַר אונדזערע עלטערן מחויב צו רעדן
ייִדיש, אָבער אַ הוץ דעם, איז טאַקע ייִדיש פֿאַר אונדז הײליק, װײַל אַזוי פֿיל צדיקים, אַזױפֿל
חסידים, אַזױפֿל גדולי הַדּוֹר האָבן גירעט זיַמַט הונדערטער יאָרן און רעדן נאָך הײַנט מיט
מיט דעם לשון.

די גמרא סנהדרין דף צ״ב דערצײלט אונדז: יוצק זהב רותח לפיו של אותו רשע – ס־זאָל
װערן אַרײַנגיגאָסן הייס גאָלד אינים מויל פֿון דעם רשע, נבוכדנצר – שאלמלא בא מֵלְאַך
וסטרו על פיו – און ס־זװאָלט נישט גיקומין דער מַלְאַך און אים גיפאַטשט מיט זײַן האַנט –
ביקש לגנות כל שירות ותשבחות שאָמר דוד ע״ה מספר תְּהִלִים – ער האָט גיװאָלט פֿאַרמיאוסן
אַלע שירות ותשבחות פֿון דָוִד הַמֶּלֶך ע״ה. פֿרעגן די מְפָרְשִים: ס־איז דאָך שװער צו
פֿאַרשטײַן, קען מין דען קלערן, אַז נבוכדנצר האָט גיקענט זאָגן שענערע שירים װי דָוד
הַמֶּלֶך. זאָגט אײַן גרויסער לַמדן: װײַל נבוכדנצר האָט גיװאוסט, אַז די שירים פֿון דָוד הַמֶּלֶך
װעלן אַדורכגײַין דורך זײַן מויל װעלן זיי פֿאַרלירן אַ טײַל פֿון זײַער קדושה. דורך דעם האָט
ער זיי גיװאָלט זאָגן, אַזוי װי דער „אור החיים" הַקָּדוֹש זאָגט, אַז װען בִּלְעַם איז גינגַנגין
בענטשן די ייִדן, האָט שֵם־יתָּבָּרֵך גימַאכט אַ קינצֵלעכן צװישן שֵׂיד צװישן זײַן מויל און דיבור,
װאָס שֵם־יתָּבָּרֵך האָט אים גיהײַסן רעדן, כְּדֵי שֵם־יתָּבָּרֵכס הײַליקע װערטער זאָלן נישט
אַדורכגײַין דורך זײַן שָפל מויל. דאָס איז דער פשט: וישם ד׳ דבר בפי בלעם – שֵם־יתָּבָּרֵך
האָט אַרײַנגימַאכט אַ קינצֵלעכע זאַך אין זײַן מויל, ס־זאָל זײַן אַ חציצה, אַ צװישן־שֵׂיד צװישן
זײַן טרֵיפה מויל און די װוצֵ,טַר, װאָס ער װעט רעדן גוטס און נביאות פֿאַר די ייִדן.

די גמרא לערנט אונדז װידער צו דעם „מדה טובה מרובה ממידה רעה" – אַ גוטע מידה טוט
זיך מער פֿאַרװירקלעכן, װי אַ שלעכטע.

מֵמֵילא, אַז אַזױפֿל צדיקים רעדן ייִדיש, איז זי בְּמֵילא הײַליק. דאָס לשון איז אויך דער לבוש,
דאָס קלײַד פֿון דער נשמה. שוין אַזױפֿל מאָל האָבן מיר װעגן דעם גישמועסט, אַז בײַ אונדז
ייִדן מוז דאָס חיצוניות זײַן פֿעסט פֿאַרבונדן מיטן פנימיות. אַזוי גוט, װי דאָס צניעותדיקע
ייִדישע קלײַד און דאָס צניעותדיקע פֿירונג, איז דער בעצסטער צײַכן פֿון אמת ייִדישער
נשמה, אַזוי קער אויך דאָס לשון דערצו. איך װייס, אַז נישט אײַנע פֿון מײַנע קינדער װעט
זאָגן: מע קען זײַן פֿעסט ייִדיש אי רעדן פּויליש, אײַנץ האָט נישט קײַן שײַיכות צום צװײַטן...
אָבער דאָס איז נישט אמת. אַזוי װי זײַ ב־האַב עס אויבן גיזאָגט, װײַל בײַ אונדז מוז גײַין דאָס
חיצוניות מיטן פנימיות.

עַל־כֵּן װוענד איך מיך אַצינד צו אײַך אַלֵּע, װאָס איר האָט איר ביז אַצינד אָפּגיטין אַזַ זַאַך,
צו רעדן פּויליש צװישֵן זיך: נעמט פֿעסט אויף אײַך, צו רעדן נאָר ייִדיש. אומיטום! שטענדיק
אין אײַער שטוב, אויף דער גאַס, און גאָר בַּעַצֵיעל אין בית־יַעקב לאָקאל! װײַזט אַז איר
זֵענט אמת ייִדישע טעכטער, איר שֵׁעמט אײַך נישט ערגיץ אין מיט אײַער אײַגן ייִדיש לשון
און עס װעט שֵׁם־יתָּבָּרֵך זיכער צו יאַגן די גאולה.

און נאָך אײַן װאָרט.

נישט אײַנער פֿרעגט זיך, צו װאָס האָט גיטױגט זיך עפֿיס צו פֿאַרדרײַיען דעם קאָפּ מיט אַ נײַער
ייִדישער אָרטאָגראַפֿיע. קען איך נאָר דערויף ענטפֿערן, אַז צװײַ סיבות האָבן אונדז דערצו

גיצוואונגין. ראשית שטאמט די אלגעמיינע ביז־איצטיקע ארטאגראפיע פון די משכילים, ווי
ד״ר שלמה בירנבוים טוט דאָס וויסנשאַפטלעך באַגרינדן אין זיַן בוך „ייִדישקייט און לשון״.
און שנית, בּפרט אין בית־יעקב און בנות־באַוועגונג האָט זיך גילאָזט פילן דאָס פאַרשידנקייט
אין ייִדישן אויסלייג, כמעט, אין יעדער פּראָווינק צו־אַנדער אויסלייג, אונדזער באַוועגונג
מוז אויך האָבּן איין אויסלייג. ווי כ־האָב שוין גיזאָגט גיט דאָך די פעדער איבער דאָס לשון
פון הארץ, זאָלן מיר אויך אלע שריַבּן איינהייטלעך, זאָל אויך דאָס כתב זיַן צ בּאָלכּער
אויסדרוק פון אונדזער איינהייטלעכן גידאַנק. ויעשו כולם אגודה אחת לעשות רצונך
בּלבב שלם...

צינד – אלע, אלע מיַנע לערערנס, בנות, בּתי' און בּית־יעקב תּלמידות בּפרט איר פון
קראָקע, לאָדזש, ווארשע, יאריסליוו, טאַרנע, לעמבּערג, סטרי און בּכּלל דארטן, וווי איר
פילט דעם פעלער פון ביז צינד, צופיל צו באַנוצן זיך מיט פּויליש – נעמט איַך פעסט
פאר, פון היַנט אָן צו רעדן נאר ייִדיש און זיך צו רופן נאר מיט ייִדישע נעמין! קלערט
מעות ווי אַרום דאָס אויסצופירן. אפשר דורך אויסקלויבּן אין יעדער גרופּ צעטונג־געבּערס,
וואָס וועלן תּחלת אפט דערמאָנין, אפשר אויף יעדן טריט גרויסע אויפשריפטן „רעט נאר
ייִדיש!" אדער וואָס איר ווילט צ־אַליין. נאר לאָזט מיך שוין הערן די גוטע בּשורה, אַז
איר האָט זיך דאָס פעסט גינומין, און איך וויִיס דאָך, אַז אויב מע מיינט אמת, העלפט
שם־יתברך

א כּלל, פּראָפּאגאַנדירט אומיטום דאָס ייִדישע לשון!

אזוי ווי מע צייִלט יעדן טאָג טעג ספירה, זאָל מ'זיך יעדן טאָג געבּן דין וחשבּון, צי מ־האָט זיך
דעם טאָג עפּיס גיבּעסערט אינים ענין „ייִדיש". און בעה"ש וועלן מיר זיך זיכער אלע, אלע
לשנה הבּאה צוזאַמין קומין אין ירושלים.

די רעכט פֿון „לשון אַשכּנז" בײַ דין־תּורות.
דער ווילנער גאון און ייִדיש

יצחק ריבקינד

SUMMARY: THE RIGHTS OF YIDDISH IN SUITS IN RABBINIC COURTS
BY YITSKHOK RIVKIND

A well-known historian (1895–1968) cites rabbinic commentaries from the early sixteenth century declaring Yiddish to be the obligatory language of testimony in intra-communal litigation as long as both parties to a suit admit to knowing Yiddish and at least one party requests its use.

אין דער ערשטער העלפֿט פֿון פֿופֿצטן יאָרהונ־
דערט (צייט אומבאַשטימט) איז פֿאָרגעקומען אַ רבנים
פֿאַרזאַמלונג אין נירנבערג. נאָר אייניקע שפּורן
זיינען פֿאַרבליבן אין שו"ת פֿון דעם סינאָד. זע:
גרעץ: „געשיכטע דער יודן", באַנד 8—2, דריטע
אויפֿלאַגע, לייפּציג, 1890, 4,426.

צווישן אַנדערע באַשלוסן האָט די אסיפֿה אויך
אָנגענומען אַ תּקנה וועגן דער יורידישער אָנערקענונג
פֿון ייִדיש (,לשון אַשכּנז") בײַ דין־תּורהס און
פֿעסטגעשטעלט אַ געוויסן רעגולאַמין איבער איר
אָנוועגדונג אין געריכטס־וועזן, בײַ פּראָצעסן. ווייזט
אויס, אַז עס איז געווען אַ צייט באַדערפֿעניש און
נויטווענדיקייט, ווי אַלע תּקנות פֿון די רבנישע סינ־
אָדן זיינען מערסטנטיילס פֿאָרגעקומען דורך ציייּט
אַרויספֿאָדערונגען.

די תּקנה, ווי אייניקע אַנדערע, איז אויפֿגעהיט
געוואָרן אין די שאלות ותשובות פֿון מהר"י וויל
(ווענעציע, 1549), וואָסער פֿאַקט איז אויך אויסגע־
נוצט געוואָרן אַ סך פֿריער פֿון אַ האַנדשריפֿטלעכן
עקזעמפּליאַר אין די פּסקים (געדרוקט דאָרט 1519),

זײַט 10, איבער די זעלטענע אויסגאַבע פֿון די פּסקים
זע דאָ, אויבן, זײַט 30.

בײַ לונסקי אין זײַן „ייִדיש בײַ ר 'יעקב ווײלן"
(,לאָגדוי בוך", 285—288) איז דער געשיכטלעכער
פֿאַקט פֿאַרבייגעגאַנגען אומבאַמערקט, וואָס איז דאָך
זיך ניט פֿון ווייניקער וויכטיקייט, ווי די שפּראַב־
לעכע מקורים זײַנע און האָט פֿאַרדינט גראַד דערט צו
פֿאַרצייכנט ווערן.

לויט דער תּקנה קומט אַרויס, אַז אויב אַיין בעל־
דין וויל זיך אויסטענהן אויף ייִדיש (,לשון
אַשכּנז"), אַ שפּראַך וואָס איז פֿאַר ב י י ד ע בעלי־
דין גלייך פֿאַרשטענדלעך, איז דער אַנדערער מחויב
נאָכצוקומען דער פֿאָדערונג.

און עס קען אים אפֿילו ניט העלפֿן די איינוועני־
דונג, אַז זײַן „מורשה" (באַפֿאַלמעכטיגטער) פֿאַר־
שטייט ניט די שפּראַך. אין דעם פֿאַל מוז ער
דינגען אַן אַנדערן. אויב ניט, וואָלט אויסגעקומען,
דאָס די תּקנה וואָלט פֿון זיך אַליין בטל געוואָרן,
„דכל אדם ישכור מורשה שאינו יודע לכתוב בלשון
אשכנז ויאמר כך I

אפיש וועגן דאַוונען פון ג. סיראָטא
אין שטאָט־שול

Poster announcing services conducted by Cantor G. Sirota in the
City Synagogue

מודעה על תפילת החזן ג. סירוטה
בבית־הכנסת העירוני

Об'явление о молебне в городской
синагоге с Г. Сиротой

A world-renowned cantor will conduct services Saturday morning in
the Large Synagogue. Tickets can
be bought until Friday afternoon
before candle-lighting time.

ספרים מיט יידיש. נאָכמער, ער האָט געהייסן
אין זיי לערנען זײנע קינדער, די זין ווי די
טעכטער. אין זײן בארימטן בריוו "עלים
לתרופה" שרײבט ער צו זײן פרוי איבער דער עטי־
שער דערציאונג פון זײנע קינדער, דאַבײ באַמערקט
ער: "והנה ישלי כמה ספרי מוסר עם
לשון אשכנז יקראו תמיד וכל שבן בשבת
קודש קדשים לא יתעסקו אלא בספרי מוסר והנה
תדריכם תמיד בספרי מוסר — — ובספרים שלי
משלי עם לשון אשכנז למען ה'
שיקראו בכל יום והוא יותר טוב מכל ספרי מוסר"...

[י. ר.] לומדישער־יידיש.

מיט אַ קורצער צײט־צוריק, איז מיר אויסגע־
קומען זען אַ מאַנוסקריפט, וואָס איז אַנגעבאַטן
געוואָרן פון אַ מו״ס, דער ביבליאָטעק פון יידישן
טעאָלאָגישן סעמינאַר צו קויפן. די קניה איז צוליב
פארשיידענע טעמים ניט צושטאַנד געקומען.

דער כתב־יד האָט געהאַט פאָלגנדעם שער: "ספר
ויברך דוד והם שאלות ותשובות ואגר(ו)ת שנשלחו
להגאון הגדול מאור הגולה מו' הר״ר דוד אופנהיים
וכלם ברכו אותו". (ר' דוד אָפּענהיים האָט געלעבט
1664—1736).

אייגנטלעך איז דאָס ניט געווען קיין ז י י נ־
ה י י ט ל כ ע ר מאַנוסקריפט, נאָר אַ זאַמ־
לונג פון פארשיידענע פראגמענטן, ווי בריוו, שו״ת,
חדושים און נאָך. צווישן זיי אויך אַ קונטרס חדושי־
תורה פון מהר״ם מלובלינס (1554—1616) א
ת ל מ י ד, א י נ ג א נ צ ן ג ע ש ר י ב ן א י ן
י י ד י ש.

דער קונטרס האָט 13 בלאַט פאָרמאַט 12°. די
בלעטער זײנען גומערירט פון ק״ס (פון אָנהײב ביז
דעם דף פעלט) ביז קע״ב (ענדע פונם קונטרס). אָנ־
פאַנג בלאַט ק״ס געפינען זיך צוויי פארשניטענע
שורות פון אַ פריערדיקן ענין, אויך אין יידיש.
ווײזט אויס פון דעם, אז עס איז געבליבן נאָר אַ
פראגמענט פון אַ גרעסערן יידישן כתב־יד.

ווי אָבער, אז דער בעל־דין אַלײן פאַרשטײט ניט
די שפראַך, מוז אָנגעפירט ווערן די דין־תורה אויף
אַן אופן, וואָס זאָל פאַר בײדן זײן צוגענגלעך, וואָס
איז, אגב, אין הסכם מיטן תלמודישן גײסט, אָוועק־
צושטעלן בײדע צדדים פאַר די דיגים, אויף אײן
גלײכע, ווי ווײט נאָר מעגלאַך, שטופע.

די תשובה אַלײן (סימן ק״א, דף מ״ב, ע״ב,
ציטירט לויט דער ערשטער אויסגאַבע) לייענט זיך
אַזוי: "ועל מחלוקת רבי טוביה ורבי ורידל, שרבי
טוביה רצה לטעון בלשון אשכנז ור' ורידל השיב
שמורשה שלו אינו יודע לכתו'[ב] בל"א [= בלשון
אשכנז]. הנה כשהיינו בכנופייא בגורנבער"ק תיקננו
תקנות הרבה וזו אחת מהן: "אם אחד מהבעלי דינין
רוצה לטעון בל"א [= בלשון אשכנז], אז בעל דינו
צריך גם הוא לטעון בל"א [= בלשון אשכנז]. ואם
פשמה תקנותינו במקומכם, אז הדין עם רבי טוביה,
א ת ר ב י ו ר י ד ל מ ב י ן ל ש ו ן א ש כ נ ז
ואם המורשה שלו אינו יודע לכתוב בלשון אשכנז.
ישכור מורשה אחר היודע לכתוב, דאי לא אמרת
הכי, א"כ [= אם כן] תקנותינו במילה, דכל אדם
ישכור מורשה שאינו יודע לכתוב בלשון אשכנז
ויאמר כך?! וכ"ש [= וכל שכן] אם איתא כמו
שכתב רבי טוביה, שמורשה של ר' ורידל יודע לכתוב
בלשון אשכנז, שאז הדין עם רב טוביה. אבל אם רבי
ורידל"ל אינו מבין לשון אשכנז, אז הדין עם ר'
ורידל, וזה אין צריך פנים: נאם הקטן יעקב
ווילא".

[י. ר.] דער ווילנער גאון און יידיש.

ס'איז אָנגענומען, אז חסידים און מקובלים זיי־
נען געווען נאָענט צו מאַמע לשון, געהאַט אַ וואַרימע
באַציאונג צו יידיש, דאַגעגן לומדים האָבן געקוקט
מיט אַ בטול, פון אויבן אַראָפּ, אויף עברי־טײיטש,
געהאַלטן פאַר אַ פחיתת הכבוד צו מעיין זײן אין אַ
רעליגיעזן ספר אין יידיש. — זאָל פאַרצייכנט ווערן,
אז צווישן די ספרים, וואָס האָבן זיך געפינען בײ
דעם ווילנער גאון זײנען אויך געווען

אויף זײט קס״ז געפֿינט זיך אזא איבערקעפֿל
„חלוקים אשר קבלתי ממורי הגאון מהר״ם מלוב־
לין״. פֿון פֿארשיידענע נאטיצן איז צו זען, אז
מיר האבן צו טאן מיט א טרײען תלמיד, וואס איז
נאכגעגאנגען זײן רבין אומעטום. אזוי, צום בײַ־
שפּיל, געפֿינט זיך אויף זײט קס״ב אזא צושריפֿט:
„זה שמעתי ביום ראשון למלאכה מן הגאון מהר״ר
מאיר בק״ק ל ב ו ב ״ (אווּ ער איז געווען
הויפּט־רב אין יאר 1595), און אויף זײט קע״א
ווערט באמערקט: „זה שמעתי מהגאון מורי ורבי
מהר״ר מאיר בלובלין ב ל ו ב ל י ן ״ (געווען
דארט ראש ישיבה פֿון 1582—1586, נאכהער אין
קראקא, און ווידער צוריק אין לובלין רב און ראש־
ישיבה פֿון יאר 1613 ביז דעם יאר פֿון זײן טויט
1616). עטלעכע צושריפֿטן געפֿינען זיך נאך אין
אייניקע ערטער.

אז די שאלות ותשובות פֿון מהר״ם מלובלין
זײנען א קוואל פֿאר דער פֿארשונג פֿון ייִדיש —
איז ניט קיין נײַס. די גבית עדותה פֿון דארט זײנען
שוין לאנג אויסגענוצט געווארן פֿאר דער געשיכטע
פֿון ייִדיש און פֿילאלאגישע שטודיעס — אבער די

חדושי־תורה, וואָס איז פֿון אים געזאגט געווארן אין
י י ד י ש אין זײַנע י ש י ב ו ת , ענדע
16טן און אַנהייב 17טן יארהונדערט, פֿארשטארקן
נאך מער דובנאוס באווײַזן וועגן ייִדיש אַלס אוּמ־
גאַנגס שפּראך פֿון די ייִדן אין ליטא און פּוילן אין
יענער צײַט.

עס איז געלונגען, אין א געוויסן מאַס, ביז איצט,
אויפֿצוהיטן דעם ייִדיש־לשון פֿונם מ ל מ ד , די
ארכאַאישקייט פֿון דער ח ד ר ־ שפּראך, אבער די
העברעע אויסדרוק־פֿארמען פֿון דעם ר א ש ־
י ש י ב ה , דעם ל ו מ ד י ש ן ייִדיש פֿון דער
י ש י ב ה , מיט דער גאַנצער תלמודישער טער־
מינאָלאָגיע, מיט דער אייגנארטיקייט פֿון דיאלעקט,
שקלאָ־סטריא, מעטאָדאָלאָגיע — האָבן מיר דערווײַל
נאך גאַנץ ווייניק.

איז אזא קונטרס מיט הדושי־תורה, סמט א
שפּראבלעבער אוצר פֿונם העכסטן ווערט, איינער פֿון
די געצײַלטע דאָקומענטן פֿונם לעבעדיקן לומדישן
ייִדיש, וואָס מיר פֿארמאָגן. און אז אזא מאַנוסקריפּט
וואלגערט זיך ערגעץ וואו אין דער פֿרעמד, איז
כדאי צו פֿארצייכענען.

גאולה פֿון לשון

שלמה בירנבוים

SUMMARY: REDEMPTION OF LANGUAGE BY SHLOYME BIRNBOYM
(SOLOMON BIRNBAUM)

An outstanding linguist (1891–) argues that not only is traditional Jewishness quintessentially linked to Yiddish but that without it Yiddish is debased to unJewish and even anti-Jewish uses and structures.

ס'איז אויסגעפֿאַלן אף אונדז דער גורל, צו לעבן אין אַ צײַט פֿון אַ גרויסער
ירידה פֿון ייִדישן פֿאָלק, וואָס זי ציט זיך שוין באַלד צוויי-הונדערט
יאָר. נאָר מיר האָבן די זכיּ, אַז אין אונדזער צײַט האָט מען זיך גיכאַפּט
און אָנגעהויבן עפּיס צו טון, צו ראַטעווין, צו זען, מע זאָל ווידער קענין גיין
באַרג אַרויף

ס-זעניִן צוועק פֿון דער ייִדישער היסטאַריִע אָן אַ שיעור מענטשן, גיבוירן פֿון
ייִדישע מאַמיס. אַלע אוצרות אונדזערע זעניִן אײַנגישטעלט. צווישן זיי אויך
איִינס פֿון אונדזערע גאָר גרויסע פֿאַרמעגנס – אונדזערע לשונות: לשון-קודש
צוזאַמין מיט ייִדיש, דעם לשון פֿונים גרעסטן טייל פֿונים ייִדישן פֿאָלק, פֿון
דעם טייל, וואָס איז שוין זינט הונדערטער יאָרן דאָס האַרץ און דער מאַרך-
בײַן פֿון דער גאַנצער אומה.

זייער גרויס איז דאָס חשיבות, וואָס ייִדיש האָט פֿאַרן ייִדישקייט. מע קען עס
אָפּשאַצן אף פֿאַשיידינע אופֿנים, מע קען אָנקוקן ייִדיש בנוגע זײַן ווערט פֿאַרן
פֿאַרייִדישונג פֿון לעבן, פֿונים חול, בפֿרט בנוגע זײַן ווערט פֿאַרן אָפֿזונדערונג
פֿון אַנדערע פֿעלקער, ד״ה אמונות, בנוגע זײַן ווערט פֿאַרן רעליגיעזן גיפֿיל
און בנוגע זײַן פּעדאַגאַגישן און אינטעלעקטועלן ווערט.

בַּיַיִם ייִדות איז אין תוך אַרײַן נישטאַ קיין אייביקע גרעניץ צווישן קודש
און צווישן חול. אויך דער חול דאָרף גיהייליקט ווערן. יעדע ברכה

בײַנ-א טרונק דערמאַנט וואַסער דאָס.   אױך דאָס חומריות דאַרף האָבן דעם
חותם פון דער קדושה.

דער דיבור, דאָס לשון איז אױך א חול-זאַך.   ווערט עס גיהײַליקט אין יידישן
לעבן צו-גלײַך מיט אַלע אַנדערע טײַלן פונים עולם-הזה.   און דורך דעם איז
עס ווידער מַשפּיע אפן יחיד און העלפט אים בײַם הײַליקן דאָס לעבן.

מיט אַט דעם הײַליקן דעם עולם-הזה זענין יידן אָפּגישײַדט פון די אומות-
העולם.   דערבײַ ווערן גיניצט אַ סך מיטלין, אָפּצוזונדערן די יידן, כדי
זײ זאָלן נישט אַרײַנפאַלן אין סכנות פאַרן יידישקײַט, זאָלן זיך נישט אָפּ-
לערינין אזױנס, וואָס מע טאָר נישט. דערבעער איז גוט און גיוואונטשן יעדע
זאַך, וואָס העלפּט צום „עם לבדד ישכון". א ייִד מיט א יידישן נאַמין, מיט יי
יידיש לשון, מיט א יידישער הלבָשה – דעם איז ערשט מעגלעך, ער זאָל זיך
אין גאַנצן און באמת פ‘רן יידיש, אף דער גאנצער ברײַט פונים לעבן, אַזױ
ווי ג‘-ט האט גיבאטן.

לשון וואקסט פונים גיפיל אזױ ווי פונים שכל און אמאל נאך מער.
און דעריבער טאַקי איז, פארקערט, אױך זײַער גרױס די השפעה פון
לשון אפן גיפיל. וואָס קען מין נישט פּועלן מיט א ווערטער ? החיים והמות ביד
הלשון... דאָס לשון, וואָס מע רעדט, דאָס מאַמע-לשון, האָט א גרעסטערן כּוח,
ווי אַנדערע לשונות, זײַן גיפיל איז א גלײַכערע, דאַרף נישט אָן-
קומין צו דעם וועג דורכן שכל, וואָס ער איז אַ סך לענגער.

דערפון איז גידרונגין, וואָס פאַר א חשיבות ס-האט פארן רעליגיעזן
גיפיל. מיר האָבן גינוג עדות דערױף.   דער קדושת לוי און אַנדערע גדולים
האָבן באַשאַפן יידישע גיזאַנגין.   „געטלעכע לידער" האָבן גיצױגן, גיפירט,
גיגלעט די יידישע נשמה זינט הונדערטער און הונדערטער יארן. יידישע
תחינות האָבן גיװועקט, גירירט, גיטרײַסט גישטאַרקט די הערצער פון אונדזע-
רע מאַמיס און באָבּיס, א דור נאָך א דור.

אױך בנוגע צום שכליות איז יידיש ז ער וויכטיק פאַרן יידישקײַט. דאָס
ערשטע לערינין מיטן חדר-יינגל און דער שווערסטער פילפּול פון א
גאון-אַלץ איז דאך אין יידיש. נישט קיין קלײַניקײַט, אַז טױזנט יאר גיסט
זיך אַרײַן אין יידיש דער חומש און די גמרא. און וואָס זענין די אַלע ייִדי-
שע ספרים. אױב נישט לערין-כּלים פאַר די, וואָס קענין נישט לערינין דעם
אריגינאַל ? פּארטײַטשונגין פון תנ‘ך, צאינה וראינה, דינים, מוסר-ספרים
א‘אַזױו: א גרױסע און חשובע ליטעראַטור, פון די עלטסטע צײַטן ביז צום
הײַנטיקן טאָג.

דאָס שײַכות פֿון דער טראַדיציע

צווישן די מחברים פֿון דער דאָזיקער ליטעראַטור גיפינין זיך גינוג רבנים
און פֿירער פּונים פֿאלק, פֿון ר' יעקב בן יצחק און ר' ליפמאַן
העלער, דעם תוספות יום־טוב, ביז צום חפץ חיים. דאָס ווײַזט, ווי גוט מ־האַט
פֿאַרשטאַנין דעם ווערט פֿון ייִדיש.

און מע דאַרף נאָך צוגעפֿן, אז דאָס איז נישט גיווען קיין קאַלטער חשבון פֿון
נוץ און הֵיזק. ניין, ס־איז בײַ זײ אויך גיווען אַ האַרץ־זאַך, ווי מע זעט למשל
פֿון אט די ווערטער, וואָס זענין שוין אפֿט דערמאַנט גיווארן: „אם יתן ה'
תמלא אארץ דעה וידברו כולם שפה אחת לשון אשפנז לא יכתבו כי אם
בריסק". [ב־רעדט זיך דאָ אקעגן ייִדן, וואָס רעדן סלאַוויש.] דער, וואָס האָט
דאָס גיזאָגט, איז נישט גיווען אַצי ווער: ס־איז גיווען דער סאַטער פֿונים
ש״ך, ר' מאיר כ״ץ. — „לשון אשכנז" איז אַן־אַלטער לשון־קודשדשער נאָמין
פֿון ייִדיש.

ס־וואָלט נישט גישאַט, אויב מע וואָלט זיך הײַנט אַ ביסל מײַן פֿאַרקוקט אויף
יענע און זײ נאָכניטון אויך אין דעם פֿרט, שו ן צוליב דעם פרינציפֿ „מנהג
אב תינו תורה היא" [מנחות כ' ע״ב, תוספ'], וואָרן לשון גײַט אַרײַן אינים
פֿלֹי פֿון מנהג. איז מין דאָך מחויב צו גיין אין זײַער וועג אויך אין דעם.
נאָר מע גיפֿינט הײַנט אפֿילו בײַ מענטשן, וואָ ז וואָלטן גידאַרפֿט זײַן פֿירער,
אַז זײ פֿאַרשטײַען נישט די פּראָבלעמין, קומין אָ מיט עט און בע און
טוען גאָר נישט.

אַפֿגידראשינע טעות

אײן דאָס נישט קײן בזיון? איז נישט קײן חרפה און בושה, אז זײ האָבן
דערלאָזט, די אויסגידראשינסטע טעות, אַנטקעגן ייִדיש זאָלן זיך קענין
אַרײַנגנבינין אין די מוחות און נשמות פֿון אונדזער עולם — טעות, וואָס
וואָקסן גלײַך פֿון דער משפֿילישער און אפֿיסורסישער פּסיכאָלאָגיע!! טעות,
וואָס בײַ לײַטן קען הײַנט שוין אַ קינד אַ חלוק מאַכן סון אַזוינע „ראיות".

לידליש איז נישט ייִדיש, איז נישט קײן ייִדיש לשון, דאָס איז אײַנע פֿון די
דאָזיקע חכמות, לײַנט זיך צאַסואַווענדן אַזאַ נאַרישקײַט, לײַנט זיך
אפֿילו אָפֿצושפעטן דערפֿון ז דאַכט זיך, ס־איז זײַער פשוט צו פֿאַרשטײַען, אַ
אַזוי ווי ייִדן רעדן, איז ייִדיש. ר' מאיר כ״ץ האָט אויך אַזוי פֿאַרשטאַנין,
דאָס זעט מין פֿון פֿון זײַנע ווערטער. „ייִדן". — מײַנט מין ייִדן, ווי ס־באַדארף

צו זײַן... וואָס דען איז אין ייִדיש, אויב נישט אַ ייִדיש לשון? איז צפשר דאָ אַ
גנאַיש פֿאָלק וואָס רעט ייִדיש?

טייל האָבן דערמיט גימײַנט, אַז ס-איז אַ גלות-לשון, און דעריבּער נישט
אַ:תדיק ״ייִדיש, וואָס איז דאָס פֿאַר אַ סמיכות - הפרשיות? יא, מיר
זענין אין גלות, נאָר דעריבּער זענין מיר שוין נישט קײן ייִדן?! און אונדזער
לשון נישט קײן ייִדיש לשון? איז נישט לשון-קודש אויך אַ גלות-לשון, און
שטענדיק גיווען אַ גלות-לשון? איז דען נישט דאָס ייִדישע פֿאָלק אַלײן גיבּוירן
גיוואָרן אין גלות?

בּייל אַנדערע האָט דאָס'גיהייסן, אַז ייִדיש איז אין תוך אַרײַן דײַטש, האָט
מין גיפֿרעגט: ״סטײַטש. פֿאַרוואָס? דאָס ווײַסט דאָך הײַנט שוין יעדער,
אַז פֿאַרשידינע לשונות וואַקסן פֿן אײַן וֹרש, אָבּער צלק אײַנס זענין זײַ
נישט, פונקט ווי אפֿן זעלבּן פֿעלד וואַקסט ווײַץ און קאָרן. ‏אויבּ ייִדן זענין
נישט קײַ ד ד טשן, איז ייִדיש נישט קײַן דײַטש״.

און אפֿילו, אַז מע קוקט עס אָן ״רײַן״ לינגוויסטיש: איז נישט טשעכיש טויזנט
מאָל נעענטער צו פוֹליש, האָלענדיש טויזנט מאָל נעענטער צו דײַטש, ווי ייִדיש
צו דײַטש? און פֿון דעסטוועגן קומט קײַנים נישט אפֿן זיניין, ער זאָל
זאָגן, פֿוֹליש איז טשעכיש, אָדער האָלענדיש איז דײַטש.

נישט קײַן סך קליגער אין גיווען, אַ טענה, וואָס האָט גיוואָלט צונעמען אַ
שטיקל כבוד בּײַ ייִדיש דערמיט, וואָס מ-האָט עס אָנגירופֿן נאָר אַ
דיאַלעקט, אַ דיאַלעקט פֿון דײַטש. מאַי קמשמע לן? גאָר נישט מיט גאָר נישט.
לינגוויסטיש איז ניטאָ קײַן חילוק פֿון לשון בּיז דיאַלעקט. דאָס איז אַ סאָ-
ציאָלאָגיש ענין, אַ פראַבּלעם פֿון קולטור. צי אַ לשון איז קולטורעל, אין דער
נשמה, זײַער ווײַט פֿון אַנ-צנדערן, דאָס מוז זיך נישט דווקא אָנזאָגן או:ווי
שטאַרק בּײַם פֿראָסטן ״רײַן״ לינגוויסטישן קוק. אַזאַ קוק נעמט קײַן מאָל נישט
אַרום דעם גאַנצן פֿאַרנעם פֿונים ענין ״לשון״. פֿאַראַן אַ:זי לינגוויסטן, וו ס
רופֿן אָן פֿערסיש און גרעקיש און ליטײַן און דײַטש און ענגליש אַאַ׳׳וו אלץ
דיאַלעקטן פֿונים אינדאַגערמאַנישן לשון [כאָטש אַזאַ לשון איז מן-הסתּם קײַן
מאָל נישט גיווען אפֿ דער וועלט].

ווען מיר זעען, וויפֿיל גוֹיאישע גילערנטע און אוניווערסיטעטן אינטערעסירן
זיך מיט ייִדיש, און ס-איז בּײַ זײַ אַ פשיטא, אַז ייִדיש איז אַ לשון
מיט לשונות גלײַך, קומט אויס אין אונדזערע אויגן אַ גרויס טיפשות, אַז מיר
דערמאַנין זיך אין דער פֿאַרשימלטער טענה: ייִדיש איז נישט קײַן לשון, נאָר
אַ ״זשאַרגאָן״ וואָס הײַסט ״זשאַרגאָן״? בּײַ יענע פֿילאָלאָגן: אַ גימישט לשון.
דאָס וואָרט ״גימישט״ האָט גיהײַסט גאָר אַ מיאוסקײַט, אַ פֿאַסקודנע זאַך.

אונדזערע מאַשכּילימלעך מכּל המינים סײַ אַסימילאַטאָרן, סײַ נאַציאָנאַליסטן,
זענין דען גיווען מחויב, צו וויסן עפּיס, צו לערינין זיך, וואָס ס-טוט זיך אַף
דער וועלט ? זײַ האָבן גיוואַלט זײַן כּכּל הגויים – אַבער אויטלערינין זיך בײַ
זײַ אמת וויסנשאַפטלעכע אויפטוען: חלילה וחס ! אין נישט בעסער צו זײַן
בַּעל-סברות – לאָו זײַן אַפילו מיט בויך-סברות... נאָר ס-האָט זײַ גאָר נישט
גיהאָלפן, שפּעטער איז מין גיוואָר גיוואָרן, אַז אַלע לשונות זענין „גימישטע",
פּשוט „זשאַרגאַנין", נישטאָ גידאַכט ! וועלכעס פאָלק האָט דען נישט קײַן
מגא-משא מיט אַנדערע פעלקער, אַנדערע לשונות, אַנדערע קולטורן ? נעמט
מין טאַקי איבער עלימענטן פון יעמים לשון, אײַנס פונים אַנדערן. בלויז אַ
פאָלק, וואָס וואָלט אײַביק גיוואוינט אין אַ מדבר, גאַנץ אַלײַן און אָפּגעריסן
פון דער וועלט, וואָלט גיהאַט אַ „רײַן" לשון. נאָר אַזאַ פאָלק איז נישט
בנמצא.

אַבער דאָס פּוסטע עם-הארצות האָט גיברעגגט דײַטש, צו ווײַזן, אַז ס-איז רײַן,
און יידיש איז צושׁאַליטשיט. און ווי אַזוי דער פאַקט ? דײַטש איז פול און
פול מיט פראַנצויזישע, ליטײַנישע און אַנדערע השפעות, צווישן זײַ אויך
לשון-קודשׁע און יידישע. כ-זאָג השפעות, ווײַל מ-האָט דאַ צו טון מיט אַלע
טײַלן פונים לשון, נישט דווקא מיט „פרעמדע" ווערטער אַלײַן, ווי דער עולם
מײַנט. און דאָס אײַגינע אין מיט אַלע אַנדערע לשונות. פראַנצויז איז אַ
פּועל-יוצא פון פאָלקס - ליטײַנישע, דײַטשע, ליטײַנישע, קעלטישע פאַקטאָרן.
ענגליש איז גימישט פון קעלטיש, סקאַנדינאַווישע פראַנצויז [פֿאַרנעמט דאָס
גרעסטע אָרט אין וואָרט-אוצר] און דײַטש [נישט מײַן ווי צוויײַ זיבּיטל פון
ווערטער-בוך]. פערס שׁ איז אַ צונויפשטעל פון אַלט-פערסיש, און אַראַביש
טערקיש פון אַלט-טערקיש, אַראַביש און פערסיש; אאַ"וו אאַ"וו, אויסצוגײַן ד
גאַנצע וועלט. און אַפילו בײַ די גאָר אַלטע לשונות איז אויך נישט גיווע
אַנדערש, דאָס קענין יר פּאָלט אַרויסזעען, כאַש מיר ווײַטן וועגן זײַ, פאַו
שטײַט זיך, אַ סך ווינציקער ווי מכּח די שפּעטערדיקע אָדער הײַנטיקע.

אויב יידיש איז נישט קײַן לשון, אָדער עפּיס אַ ווילד צומישעכטס, קען ענ
דאָך נישט האָבן קײַן גראַמאַטיק... אַ פּראָסטער שכּל... נאָר אַ משכּי
לישער שכּל.

גראַמאַטיק הײַסט אין אַזאַ קעפּל אַן-אַטיסטאַט, אַז אַ לשון האָט כּללים, דעמלט
איז ׳ס אַ לײַטיש לשון. אַבער אין יידיש רעט יעדער, ווי ער וויל, ס-האָט
נישט קײַן כּללים, הײַסט עס, נישט קײַן גראַמאַטיק, איז עס נישט קײַן
לײַטיש לשון.

פרעגט מין דאָך דאַן, וואָס אין דען אין תּוך די פעולה פון די כּללים ? און מין

ענפערט: דורך זײ ווערט אַ סדר אין לשון, און אײנער פֿארשטײט דעם
אַנדערן. נו, אויב אַזוי, דאַרף מיך דאָך דרינגען פֿאַרקערט: אוז זאַך, וואָס מע
ברענגט זי אַרויס מיט מויל און צונג, און אײנער פֿאַרשטײט אָקוראַט דעם
אַנדערן, מוזן דערבײַ זײַן כּללים, הײסט עס, אַ גראַמאַטיק, מיט לײַטן גלײַך.
אַ כּלל, האָט ײִדיש אויך כּללים, אויך אַ גראַמאַטיק, וואָרן דאָס וועט סײַדן אַ
שונגענער מסוכּן זײַן, אַז אײנער פֿאַרשטײט דעם אַנדערן גאַנץ גוט, אַז מען
רעט ײִדיש צונ-אים...

נאָך אַ טענה איז געווען, אַ ײִדיש איז נישט שײן: האָסטו געהערט: נישט
שײן! אָווא, ״שט שײן!! נו, איז וואָס? בין איך נישט שײן, דאַרף
איך מיר אַנטון אַ מעשׂה און גײ אין דר-ערד אַרײַן?
דאָס איז אײנס, אָ צווײטנס, פֿון וואַניט האָבן זײ געוואָסט, אַז ײִדיש איז
נישט שײן? וואָס פֿאַר אַ ראַי האָבן זײ געברענגט דערויף?
פּשוט אין פּשוט: ס-איז זײ נישט געפֿעלן פּויליש אדער רוטיש אדער דײַטש
איז בײַ זײ געווען שענער. אײַ, דער האָט ליב עפּ', און יענער האָט בעסער
ליב באַרן! אַזוי ווײַט האָבן זײ זיך נישט פֿאַרטראַכט.
און פֿאַרוואָס איז עס זײ נישט געפֿעלן? אויך אַ פּשוטע זאַך, ס-איז געווען צו
ײִדיש, צו כאַראַקטעריסטיש. פּונקט ווי באַרד און פּאות און אַ קאַפּטן. האָבן
זײ זיך אײַנגירעט אַלע מעגלעכע טענות, אין אמתן האָבן זײ נאַר געוואָלט
אנטלויפן פֿון ײִדישקײט.
צװײטן בײַטן זיך, פֿאַראַן הײַנט גענוג גויים, אין טאַקי קינסטלער זײ,
וואָס האַלטן, אַז ײִדיש איז אַ שײן לשון. נאָך מײַן, אַפֿילו דײַטשן ײִדן, דאָ
נישט לאַנג האָט מיר אַ ליבעראַלער דײַטש-ײִדישער פֿירער וואָס האָט זיך מיט
ײִדיש באַקענט אין פּוילן, בשעת מלחמה — אַלײן געזאָגט, נישט געפֿרעגטער-
הײט, אַז ס-קלינגט זײַער זיס.
צום סוף אַ טענה וואָס מע קען זאָגן, אַז קײן משונה-נאַ ישע איז נישט
אַרויס פֿון אַ משׂכּילישן מוח: ײִדיש איז נישט קײן לשון, והראַי קײן
שׁם אַנדער פֿאַלק רעט עס נישט!
ס-איז באמת שווער אַרײַנצוטראַכטן זיך, אין דעם טיפּקײַט פֿון דער
דאָזיקעַי סבֿרא...
נאָר אַז מען טוט עס קומט מען צו ווײַר אַ חשובער מסקנא: ס-זענין בּכלל
נישטאָ קײן לשונות אַף דער וועלט!
אַ נעכטיקער טאָג אַ נ-אויסגיטראַכטע חקירה... די פֿראַנצויזן רעדן אַלשון, וואָס
קײן שום אַנדער פֿאַלק רעט עס נישט, איז עס דאַך נישט קײן לשון. מיט די
דײַטשן איז אויך אַזוי, דאַ קצן מין נישט לײַקינין. די ענגלענדער האָבן
נישט קײן בעסער מזל. רוסן, פּאָליאַקן, כינעזער, טאַטערן, קירגיזן, האָטנטאָטן

אויך נישט. אַ טעות, נישטאָ קיין לשונות.

חוזק. נאָר אַ ביטערער חוזק. ער וויַיזט, וויַ מיט דער השכלה איז אַריַינגי־
בּרענגט גיוואָרן צו־אינעווייניק קנעכטישקיַיט אין דער נשמה פון ייִדן.

לשון־נאַציאָנאַליזם

אָון אינטעריסאַנט, פון דעם דאַזיק נשמה־מצב איז אויטגיוואָקסן אַ שטרעבּונג
צו באַפריַיען זיך ווידער פון דער פ×מדער שליטה. אבּער ס־איז שוין
גיווען צו שפּעט. איך בּין גיגאַנגין ווייטער דעם וועג פון אַסימילאַציע, נאָר
אין אַן־אַנדערן אופן, מיט־ן גאַנצ פונים איַיראָפּאישן נאַציאַנצליום. צווישן די
פאַרשיַידינע צוויַ כּיחות האָט איַינע גיבּוים דעם העברעאיזם, אַן־אַנדערע דעם
ייִדישיזם.

די לעצטע האָבּן גינומין ייִדיש און עס אַריַינגיקוועטשט אין די קעסטעלעך פון
די מאָדערנע טעאַריעס, כּדי צו ווייזן, אַז דאָ איז אַצינד זיַיער רשות, דאָ
זענין ז×? אַצינדערט די בּעל־בּתּים : זיַי זענין די אַמתע נאַציאַנאַליסטן –
און ייִדיש איז דזוך אַ בּאַשאַפונג פון דער ייִדישער פאָלקס־נשמה. אָדער: זיַי
זענין די רעערצוענטאַנטן פון די בּריַיטע מאַסן – און ייִדיש איז דאָך אַ בּאַ־
שאַפונג פון די בּריַיטע מאַט.

ווער איז אָט די פאָלקס־נשמה, וואָס "האָט בּאַשאַפן" ?
ווער האָט דען גזום גולם גיווען, זי זאָל בּאַשאַפן? קען גאָר זיַין אַספּק, אַז דאָס
איז גיווען, דאָס יהדות? ניט קיין מיסטישע "פסיכאַלאָגיע" פון "פאָלק" פון די
נאַציאַנאַליסטישע אָדער סאָציאַליסטישע טעאַריעס, נאָר דעם דת, דאָס ייִדיש־
קיַיט האָט אויסגיטאַרימט ייִדיש. פונקט אַזוי ווי ס־האָט אויסגיפאַרימט די
אַנדערע ייִדישע לשונות. (די השפּעה פון רעליגיע איז אויך דאָ אין די נישט
ייִדישע לשונות).

לשון איז אַ סאָציאַלער פאַקט, אויב ס־זאָל ניט זיַין קיין שייכות צווישן יחיד
און יחיד, אויב ס־זאָל נישטאָ זיַין פאַראַנין אַ ציבּור, וואָלט נישט גיווען קיַין
לשון און וואָס איז דער יסוד פונים ייִדישן ציבּור? די ייִדישע אמונה, דער
ייִדישער דת, זיַי האָבּן בּאַשאַפן דאָס ייִדישע פאָלק, זיַי בּאַשאַפן איַיבּיק דעם
ייִדישן ציבּור. אַרבּיַט זיך אויס אַ לשון, הייסט דאָס, אַז טע וואַקסט פונים
יהדות.

אי, די לינקע טעֶנין, אַז ס־איז אַ טעות, פונקט פאַרקערט, דאָס ייִדישע פאָלק
האָט זיך אויסגיצַרבּיט ז×? "רעליגיע", ממילא איז דאָס לשון נישט אַ×רס
אַ בּאַשאַפונג, נאָר אַן־אויסטן פונים ייִדישן פאָלק? אַף דעם זענין זיַי דאָך

אפיקורסים, אפט תינוקות שנשבו בין העכו"ם, קען מין דאָס פאַרשטיין.

אויב דאָס זאָל נאָר זיַין אַ טעארעטישער וויכוח, וואָלט נאָך נישט אויסגימאַכט.

אבער זיי ווילן האָבן די ממשלה אפן לשון, זיי ווילן גיוועלטיקן אף צלמין,

זיי ווילן האָבן אַ מאָנאָפּאָל. ווילן – נו – וואָלט נאָך נישט גיווען סכנת-נפשות.

אין אבער די צרה, וואָס זיי פועלן טאַקע, אויך ביַי די פרומע איז מין מודה,

אַז אַזוי דאַרף צו זיַין, אַז להם הממלכה.

פאַרשטייט זיך מע טראַכט נישט אָנצונעמין די טאַריעט פונים ייִדישיזם אָדער

העברעאיזם אבער מע לאָזט זיך פירן פון זיי אין לשון אליין, מע טאַנצט זיי

נאָך אין סיגנון, אין וואָרט-אוצר, אין גראַמאַטיק, אין אויסלייג.

וואָס איז די סיבה פון אזאַ-אויסטערלישן פאַקט?

דאָס קען מין זאָגן מיט צוויי ווערטער: ווַיל מיר זענין אין גלות ביַי "ייִדן".

אָט דאָס גלות האָט זיך אָנגיהויבן נאָך אין די ציַיטן פון דער אַלטער השכּלה

און ס-ציִט זיך אויך אין דער תּקופה פון דער ניַיער השכּלה. פון די היַנטיקע

נאַציאָנאַליסטישע און סאָציאַליסטישע רעיונות.

מיר האָבן טענות צו זיי? זעניין מיר נישט גירעכט. צו זיך אַליין דאַרפן מיר

האָבן טענות, מיר אַליין זעניין שולדיק אין גאַנצן. זיי מעגן אַזוי, ווי זיי בצ-

דאַרפן טון, נאָר מיר טוען נישט ווי מיר בצדאַרפן טון.

אַזוי ווי אין אַ סך זאַכן, אַזוי אויך אין לשון. אין לשון קודש און אין ייִדיש.

אונדזער באָכטאַגניש

דל אַלטע משׂכּילים האָבן פאַרשטאַנין, אַז ייִדיש איז נישט קיין לשון, און

ס-איז אַ צוקצעליטשיט דיַיטש, האָבן זיי עט אויסגיבעסטערט רחמנא-ליצלן

פאַרדיַיטשמערט אף וואָס די וועלט שטייט.

וואָ האָט מין גיטון ביַין-אונדז? נאַכגימאַכט. אַ בלאָט, אַ ביכל, דעט האָט

גימוות זיַין אין אט דעם ניַיעם לשון.

נאָך אַ מערכה, וואָס אין פאָלקס-לשון אַליין אין די המפעה ניט גיווען שטאַרק

דער בריַיטער עולם האָט נישט קיין סך גינומען פונים ניַיעם לשון, צו דעד

גמרא האָט מין עס נישט גיניצט, אין חדר האָט מין גיטיַיטשט אפן צלמן

שטיַיגער. אבער ביַים איבערדרוקן פון דער עלטערער ליטעראַטור האָט זיך יאָ

אַר ניגיכאַפט אַמאָל אַ ביסל ניַיס.

די ניַיע משׂכילים האָבן איַינגיפונין אַז די אַלטע משׂכילים האָבן גיטון שלעכט.

ריש דאַרף און טאָר נישט פאַרדיַיטשט ווערן. האָבן זיי אויפגיהויבן אַ גרויסע

מלחמה אפן דיַיטשמעריזם זיי האָבן איַינגינומין דעם שׂונא. אבער דער נצחון

אין נאר נױוען אַלפֿונימדיקער. זײ האבן צרויטגיטריבן בלריז די גרילצנריקע
און אומגילומפֿערטע דײטשמעריזמין. נאר דער עצם דישטמעריזום איז גיבליבן:
מע קען זאגן פֿאַרקערט: זײ האבן ערשט בּאמת אויראפֿעאיזירט דאָס לשון,
און וואס האבּן מזר גיטון ז װידער אַ מאָל דאָס זײגינע; נאטגימאַכט.

אַז מע לויבט הײנט אַבּיכּל אדער מע מאַכט זערפֿאַר פראפֿאַגאַודע, רעט מין
זעגין זײן „ליטעראַרישער שפראך". וואָס לאוט מיך דאָס הערן? דאָס איז
טײטש: שרײבסטו אזױ װי די לינקע שרײבן, בּיסטו ראוי צום הײליקן נאַני,
„ליטעראַטור". שרײבּסטו חלילה אַנדערש, האַט די ליטעראַרישע שכינה נישט
גירוט אף דיר.

דאָס ווײזט, װי גיפֿאַלן מיר זעניין בּײ זיך אַלײן. ס קומט אונז גאָר ניט אפֿן
ג דאַנק, ס-זאָל מעגלעך זײן אַלײן עפּיס אױפֿצוטון, ניט נאָכצוטאָנצן יענים. —
אדער אין אפֿשר טאַק בּײן-אַינדז שױן נישטאָ קײן בּישעפֿערישער כּוח?

וואָטער מוֹ אַדיק מאַרבּלענדיניש און טויבּקײיט הײנט אין אונדזער מחנה, אַז מע
וֶעט עס ניט און הערט עס ניט. און אױב עמיצער װיזט אָן דערױף. װיל מין
נ שט הערן און ניט זעען – אַזױנס קען מין שױן ניט דן זײן לפֿף זכות.

מיט אַקורצער צײט צוריק האַט אַיינער פֿון די רעליגיעזע מַנהיגים פֿון ייִדן
אין פֿױל, גיהאַט אַ טענה צום לשון פֿון אַרטאָדאקסישע שרײבּער, האַט מין
אים גיענפֿערט: „זאָלן מיר אפֿשר שרײבּן צאַינה-וראַינה-לשון?! מיר קעני
זיך דאָך נישט מאַכן צו לײטיש גילעכטער".

לײטיש גילעכטער: דאָס הײיסט. אױב די לינקע לאַכן. אין לײטיש גילעכטע
זײ זעניין די אמתע פֿוסקים...

ילאַ זײ לאַכן דאָך אױך פֿון בּאָרד און פֿיאות, פֿון כּשר און טריפֿה פֿו
טלית און תפֿילין, און רעזן אף נגתּקה אױך? „עט – הער איך דעֶ
ענפֿער – װו? קומט אײַנס צום אַנדערן? דאָס איז צו ג–ט, און יענס איז צֶ
לײט. מיר קעניין דאָך נישט זײן קײן בּטלנים."

אױ, אױב אַזױנער וואַלט גיוואוסט, אַז מיט אַט דער טענה וויזֶט ער עֶש
אַרױס דאָס אמתע בּטלנות, וועל כּולם איז ער מבַטל דעם תוף פֿון ייִדישקײַ
און ווער זעניין די משפּילים, די אַלטע און די נײַע? נאַכטאַנצערס נאַן
אויראפֿעאישע מאַדיס פֿון גידאַנק, מאַדיס, וואָס זעניין דערצו שױן עובו
בטל אין איירעפֿע גופֿא.

און וואָס זעניין מיר? נאַכטאַנצערס נאָך נאַכטאַנצערס פֿון פֿאַרעלטערטע מאַדיק.

אויסלײזונג פֿונים גלות הלשון

מיר זעניין אין גלוֹ בּײַ „ייִדן" אױך מיט אונדזער לשון, מיט אונדזערע

לשונות. מיר דארפן זײ אויסלײזן פונים דאזיקן גלות.

מיר דארף; זיך גאר נישט ארומרײסן מיט די לינקע. מחלוקת איז צו דעם ענין נישט שייך. לאזן זײ טון זײערס. מיר דארפן גײן מיט אונדזער אײגינים וועג. לאזן זײ טענין, אז בײ אנדערע פעלקער איז אויך נישט אזוי, ס-זאלן זײן צווײ לשונות אדער צווײ מינים אויסלײג, אדער – אז מ-האט בײ יענע שוין גימאכט אזא פרװאװ, און ס-איז נישט גיראטן. מע דארף זיך גאר נישט ארײנלאזן אין פרטים און ברענגין אמאליקע און הײנטיקע פאראלעלן – דער עיקר: זענין דען ווי אנדערע פעלקער?

אײנס איז בײ מ.ר ניט קײן ספק: די אײניקלעך פון איצטיקן פרומין ייִדישן פאלק, וואס רעט יידיש, וועלן נאך אין װײטע דורות רעדן ייִדיש – אבער וויפל אײניקלעך פון די הײנטיקע פרײע ייִדישיסטן. וועלן דעמאלט נאך רעדן ייִדיש, און בכלל נאך האבן א שייכות צום ייִדישן פאלק? סײדן מיר וואלטן אויפגיטון א גרױסע זאך; ווידער צוציען די אלע פארפרעמטע צו דער ייִדישער טראדיציע. נאר מיט אונדזער איצטיקן כוח? מיט וואס קענין מיר הײנט צוציען? אזוי גוט איז בײַן-אונדז, אזוי שײן איז בײַן-אונדז? מיר זענין אלײן אזעלכע גוטע היטער פון אונדזער גרױסער ירושה? מיר ווײזן עפיס הײנט דער וועלט א וועג מעלה מעלה?

א שיעור האבן מיר צו טון און צו ארבײטן, מיר זאלן נישט גײן אלץ מער מטה מטה.

ן שטיקאלע פון דער דאזיקער ארבײט דארפן מיר טון ארום לשון. פאר ייִדישקײט אין לשון, צו ליב לשון פון ייִדישקײט.

קלײנע התחלה איז שוין גימאכט גיווארן. דאס איז אונדזער נײער אויסלײ, ך די אלטע יסודות. מע זעט אפילו נאך אויף אים די סימנים פונים גלות בײ ײדן", נאר אין תוך צומײן איז ער שוין אויסגילײזט, שוין ווידער גיווארן א בן-חורין. ס-איז נאך א גרויסער מהלך, ביז מיר וועלן צוקומין צו דער גאנצער גאולה, דערווײל זענין מיר נאך גאר ניט צוגיטרעטן צום לשון גופא. זיך נאך נישט צוגירירט צום סיגנון, ווערטער-בוך, גראמאטיק. דער אויסלײ, איז ערשט א הקדמה. און אפילו בײ דעם איז נאך א סך צ ארבײטן, זײער א סך. א גרויסער טײל פון אונדזער אײגינים עולם איז נאך ניט משיג, וואס דא טוט זיך.

רא דארף צוהעלפן דאס יונגע דור. בײ זײ איז די קדושה פון אפיקורסישן העברעאיש און ייִדיש און פונים משפילישן אויסלײ, פארט נאך נישט אזוי שטארק און אײנגיבאקן אין די הערצער, זײ זאלן נישט קענין פילן און פארשטײן דאס חשיבות פון אונדזער ענין. די צעירים פועלים, בנות, און בית יעקב, – זײ דארפן זײן די פיאנערן אין אונדזער מלחמה.

און מיט פֿרייד זעען מיר, אַז זייַ פֿאַרשטייען דאָס טאַקע, און אַז זייַ זענען
שוין צוגעטרעטן צו טאָן עפּיס. נאָר מיט יאָרן צוריק האָבן זיך צעירים
אַרויסגעזאָגט פֿאַר אַזאַנ־אַרבעט און זיך אויך גענוּמען דערצו. און אין לעצטן
יאָר האָט „בית־יעקבֿ" און „בנות" אָפֿיציעל גענוּמען די פֿאַן אין זייער האַנט.
„בית־יעקבֿ" בכלל און די לערערנס בפֿרט, „בנות" בכלל און די חבֿרות בפֿרט
האָבן זיך מיט התלהבֿות גענוּמען דערצו. און דאָס איז אַ באַזונדערע פֿרייד,
ווייַל דווקא דאָ, אויף דעם אָרט, בייַ די מיידלעך, האָט זיך שוין גיהאַט
אָנגיהויבן צו וואָקלין אונדזער פּראַנט, דער פּראַנט פֿון ייִדישקייט, און ממילא
אויך פֿון ייִדישן לשון, אַריס איז גיגאַנגין נאָך אַריס. כאָטש אַצינד איז ב"ה
גאָר עפּיס אַנדערש, איז אַבער די סכּנה נאָך ווייַט נישט אַריבער. פֿון דעסט
וועגן — מיר האָבן שוין אַ מחנה, וואָס וועט נישט שטייען מיט פֿאַרלייגטע
הענט.

ו זייַ טראָגט זיך אַצינד דער רוף, צו פֿאָרשטאַרקן זייער אַרבעט, אַרייַנצוצויען
ליטין, מסבֿיר זייַן די, וואָס פֿאַרשטייען נאָך נישט, דאָס חשיבֿות פֿון דעם
דאָזיקן טייל ייִדישקייט־פּראַנט.

זאָלן זייַ זוכה זייַן, צו זעען די פֿאַרבונדינע מחנות פֿון צעירים און פּועלים
בייַ דער זעלבער אַרבעט, און זאָלן זייַ אַלע זוכה זייַן צו זעען אַ
פּעוּלה אאַ"וו.

זאָלן זייַ זוכה זייַן צו זען אַ פּעוּלה פֿון זייער אַרבעט, זען, ווי בייַ־אַנאַנדז
קערט מין אום עטרה לְיוֹשנה צו לשון־קודש, און ווי מע ניצט אויך דעם
גאַנצ־ רעליגיעזן ווערט פֿון ייִדיש: בייַם לערנין ייִדישקייט און בייַם
אייַנפֿלאַנצן אמונה אינים לעבּן פֿונים ציבור, און צלן מיט דרך־ארץ לגבי
דעם פֿארים אַ אָט דער כּלי, דעם אייַבערשטנס אַ מתּנה — און ווי מע
העלפֿט אַזוי אַרו־ דעם פֿאָלק ישראל, צו הייליקן זיך מיט דרייַ
קדושות.

אונדזער לשון איז אין גלות. קומט, העלפֿט, לאָמיר עס אייסלייזן! לאָמיר
דערענטערן די גאוּלה פֿון אונדזער לשון!

אַ ל ף־ ב י ת

פֿון אָרטאָדאָקסישן אוֹיסלייג

אַ בייַ אַ קלינגער אין אָנהייב וואַרט אדער טראָף זיך אַ שוואַכער
קלאַנג. אויב דער קלינגער שרייַבט זיך מיט אַ וואו אדער אַ יוד, ווערט
דער קלאַנג איבערגיגעבּן מיט אַן־אַלף: אומגליק, אומה, אומיסטן, פֿאַר־
אומערט. אופֿן, אורחים, אויבּס, אויס, איז, אינדיק, אום.

א אַ שטומע אַלף שטעלט זיך צוליב אַ מחיצה, ס-זאָלן ניט אויטקומין דרײַ
וואָוון אדער דרײַ יודין אויף אײַן מאָל: כ-וואָוין, וואָונדער, פּרוּואָון. יאָיאָיל.

אָ (1) אַ קורצער קלאַנג: גראָבן, וואָג, טאָג, קאַטאָוויס, אַראָפּ, שלאָפּן, הײַקן,
(2) אַן-אויסגיצויגינער קלאַנג: בלאָ, אָדערן, גלאָו, בראָטן, נאָך (דערנאָך),
טאָל, אָן (בלין), מאָס, גאָר.

אַ (1) אַ קורצער קלאַנג: אבער, אדער, (אָו), קאַוין, לאָזן, אָט, גיבראָכן,
וואַלט, דאַמב, סאַסנע, טאַפּ, גישראַקן, דאַרטן וואַרצל, נאַך (עוד). (2) אַן-
אויסגיצויגינער קלאַנג: גיוואָרן, האַרן.

אָ (1) אַ קורצער קלאַנג: אַז, גלאַט, מאַכן.
(2) אַן-אויסגיצויגינער קלאַנג: גראַם, נאַריש.
(3) מע קען אויך שרײַבן: בײַמאַלע, קעפּאַלעך.

ב ג ד ה

ו (1) אין פּוילן, אוקרײַנע אאַ″וו דאַרף מין עס צרויסרעדן ווי אַ קורצע ″י″
אוגערקע, פּלוגתא, מורן, טוק, קוקן, שטופן, זומער, פּול, (מלא): פּוטער.
(2) אַרויסגירעט אין פּוילן ווי די ″אַ″ אין וואָרט ″דארטן″, אין אוקרײַנע
אאַ″וו ווי די ″ע″ אין וואָרט ″וועט″ דורך, קורץ.

ו אין פּוילן, אוקרײַנע אאַ″וו דאַרף מין עס צרויסרעדן ווי אַ לאַנגע ″י″:
ברודער, דער זון, בשורה, הוסן, גווב.

ו (1) מע דאַרף עס צרויסרעדן ווי די קורצע ″אָ″ אין וואָרט ″דארטן″
אורחים, אות.
(2) אַרויסצורעדן ווי ″ו″: אורח, אותיות.

** וו** וואו, וויכּוח, וויספּע, אָוודאי, קאַווע, ברײַוו.

וי אויך, אַזוי, בוים, הויזן, לויט וואָגן), טויב (מרש) לויז ″(שיטער″), רויט.
שוין.

וי אויך, ברוין, הוין, לויט (וועדליג), טויב (פּויגל), לויז (פּנים), טויער, פּויק.

ז, זש, ח.

ט האַנט, וואָנט, הונט (ווײַל מע זאָגט: העַנטל, וועַנטל, הינטל. אבער:
קינד, ווײַל מע זאָגט: לעַנדער, קינדער).

י קורץ: (1) איבער, ציבור, ווידער, איז, מיט, כ-בּין, יינגל, וויסן, שפּיץ,
טיש, ברית, גיסטו, (געבן, געסטו) (2) יאַטקע, יבשה, ייד, יינגל, יערן.

י העַ, מעַ, לעַב, ייד, לער, שטעַוול, העַטן, שײַך מיל, די בעַן, פּער, (4), פּירן
(נהג), גיסטו (גײסן).

י אַ קורצער קלינגער, אין רוב דיאַלעקטן גיראָטן אין אַמן (″י″): א) גיזאַגט,

גיכאַפּט. ב) ער פּראַוויט, הערגיט. ג) קומין, סאַמין, זענין, ריימנים, זינגין,
בענקין, הימלין, שטאַמלין. ד) איידים, בעזים. ה) וויימטיג זונטיג, עליף,
באַרוויס, עפּיס.

לי זיי, דרעי, צווייג, גריין. טייטל (צו וויזן) רייך, הייליק (צויין), רייַן (סאַ),
נייַן (9), שייַן (ליכט), ווייַס (קאָליר), פּייַקל.

יי זיי (זאַלסט זייען), צווייי, היי, טייטל (פּרי), היילִיק (קדוש), רייַן (טהור),
נייַן (לא), שייַן (יפה), כּ-ווייַס.

פ כ ך ל י מ מ נ ן נ י ס

ע עוולה, עולם.

ע קורץ: בעט (צום שלאָפּן), סערפּ, מענטש, קעץ, ווערטל.

Notice! An eight-grade Jewish high school for boys will open, teaching both traditional Jewish and general subjects...The number of students will be limited.

עֶ אויסגיצויגן: לֶעבּן, רֶעדל, כ-בֶּעט (בַּקשה), הֶערן, וֶוערט (רָאוי).

עַ אַקורצער קלינגער, אין רוב דיאַלעקטן גירַאטן אָן אַמֶן „יּ". אין סוף וואָרט; איך פרַצווע, טֶעֱנע, (ב) גרויסע, שֵׁיֱנע, גוטע.

נאָך אַ קלינגער: ג) נֶאענט, רוֶען, צִיֱען, שטרוֹיֶען, בּויֶען, זֶעֱען, זֵיֱען, זֶעֱען.

פ פ ף צ ץ

ק אויך בֵּיֱם אויסלאָז יק: לֶעבּידיק.

ר ש שׂ ת ת

בֵּיֱ ווערטער פון לשון-קודשׁ אָפּשטאַם, שטעלט מין די נְקודה פון דער גיקווֶעטשׁטער הַבָּרה: בָּטל, מַאמר. אויב מע דאַרף, אויך פון דער הַבְרה מָאר אירֹ: הַנָחה גְדולה.

אַנט, אַפ, בַּא, פַאר, צו: אַנטלויפן, בַּאקומען, פַארקויפן, צוטרַיבן.

קֵיֱן שטומע עַיֱנס זֶעניֱן ישׁטאָ: זאָגן, הימל.

אויך ניט קֵיֱן שטומע הֵיֱן: פאָרן, פורן, פֿירן, אָן, מאָן, צאָל. רו טון.

בְּכָלָל נִיֹ קֵין שטומע אותיות: די שטאָט, ער רעט, דאָס אֵייֱביקֵיֱט.

לֹדז, לֹצ, נֹדז, נצֹ,

אונֹדז, הֶעלֹדזל, פֶענֹצטער, עלֹצטער, אאַ"וו.

מע בינט צונויף ווערטער מיט אַ מָק , מזל-טוב, שטאַט-זֵיֱנגער.

בֵּיֱם שרַיֱבּן בּלַיֱבּט בּ, פ אָן אַדָגוש און בּ, פ קומען מיט אַרָפה: בּ, פ-בּ, פ.

לשבת. וועלטלעכקייט: כ) דאָס עלטסטע ספר צוריף יידיש כ״א) א חוש פאָרן לשון כב) תנ״ך צום
פאַרגיניגן כג) פונים שמואל־בוך כד) פונים שוטים־בוך כה) רר״ק פּאַר נטים כו) צאינה וראינה
אין אָריגינאַל · כז) פּסוקים אויף יידיש דורך 500 יאָר כח) צ יידישער ריצער כט) רעט יידיש —
הרב שמואל דוד "אַסקי ל) פון גיפּאַנגינ־צפט — אליעזר שינדלער לא) יידיש לשון און
יידישער לעבנס־שטייגער — הרב שמשון סטאָקהאַמער לב) יידיש וויסן און יידיש רעדן — מאיר
וואָלף נימטשע־פּאָוער לג) פּלאַנטער אין דער נשמה — אשר לד) יידישקייט פון הארץ און צונג
— אסתּר ראָזע לה) פינקס פון יידישקייט און יידיש — לו) וואָס איז יידישקייט — יעקב לצנדא
לז) לינקע ער־ל לח) דער נצחון פון אונדזער אויסלייין — ש״ב לט) וועגן ליטוויישן דיאַלעקט
אין קאָנגר,ס פּוילן — נטע ירוחם בערלינער מ) זייער גירעבט — ב. מא) בצהערשן און
בצצווינגין — לייב פיינגאָלד מב) בענטשונג פון צער, רויטע לבנה, צלדינגס, נפּלן (לידער)
— בריגש. מג) דע־ קואַל סון יידיש — גרשון נורא מד) דאָס באַאַגינגיש מיטן מורח — ריקל
בירנזוים: יידיש אין אַמעריקע: מה) סאַר יידיש — יצחק מאיר בוום און דר. צ. ה.
לוטטפּצן מו) יריש צ מויער — הרב אלעזר זילבּער מז) יידיש מיט יידישקייט — הרב ישראל
ראָזנצרג מח) כנסת ישראל און "יאַנג איזראָעל" — הרב דר. ב. רעווען מט) פרומע יידן און
יידיש — מאַרדכי דצנצים נ) דער בונד פון דורות — הרב דר. אליהו יונג נא) שלא טגוי את
לשונם — היב דר, דוד שטערן נב) יידיש אין ישיבות און תלמוד תורות נג) אָהנט (ליד) —
צורא גוטמאַן — נד) צווי וואָחין פכל הגוים נה) יידיש דער אויסדרוק פון דער יידישער פאַלקס־
נשמה — ר. ל. סויגל נו) ניט גיט מיר לשון... (ליד) —— איש לוי נז) שעהין אין דער מלחמה,
צ בלעטל זכרונות — שלמה בירנפּוים נח) יסם־מיניאַטורן — ח. לייכטער.

דער חפץ־חיים שליט״א וועגן יידיש־לשון און יידישקייט.

דערדאָזיקער רייכער נומער קאָסט 1 גילדן מיט 20 גר.

צו באַקומין נאָר געגן געלט פריערויט! געלט שיקן P. K. O. 67.795
נאָך צו באַקומין: אַלע נומערן פון קוואַרטל ניסן־סיון, דערונטער: יוביליעאום־
אויסגאַבע, קאָנפּערענץ־נומער, קאָנפּערענץ באַריכט און דער יידיש נומער.
צוזאַמין 3 גילדי.

1

מענדעלע מוכר ספרים

(שלום־יעקב אבראמאָוויטש)

קאָפּולע, וווייס־רוסלאַנד, 1836

אדעס, אוקראַינע, 1917

דאָס ווינטשפינגערל
שלמה רב חיים'ס
פישקע דער קרומער
מסעות בנימין השלישי

דערציילער

2

שלום עליכם

(שלום ראבינאָוויטש)

פּעריאַסלאַוו, אוקראַינע, 1859

ניו יאָרק, פֿאַר. שטאַטן, 1915

מאָטל פּייסי דעם חזן'ס
טביה דער מילכיקער
מנחם מענדל
שווער צו זיין אַ ייד, (פּיעסע)

דערציילער, דראַמאַטורג

3

יצחק־לייבוש פרץ

זאמאָשטש, פּוילן, 1853

וואַרשע, פּוילן, 1915

פֿאָלקסטימלעכע געשיכטן
חסידיש, (דערציילונגען)
אדם און חוה, (לידער)
די גאָלדענע קייט, (דראַמע)

פּאָעט, דערציילער, דראַמאַטורג

4

חיים־נחמן ביאליק

דאַרף ראַדי, אוקראַינע, 1873

תל־אביב, ישראל, 1934

פֿון צער און צאָרן
אַ פּריילעקס
דער מתמיד
יידישע אגדות, (אַנטאָלאָגיע)

פּאָעט

5

שלום אש

קוטנע, פּוילן, 1880

לאָנדאָן, ענגלאַנד, 1957

אַ שטעטל, (דערציילונג)
קדוש השם, (דערציילונג)
גאָט פֿון נקמה, (דראַמע)
דער תהילים־ייד, (דערציילונג)

דערציילער, ראָמאַניסט,
דראַמאַטורג

6

אברהם גאָלדפֿאַדען

(גאָלדענפֿאַדים)

אַלט־קאָנסטאַנטין, אוקראַינע, 1840

ניו יאָרק, פֿאַר. שטאַטן, 1908

שולמית, (היסט. אָפּערעטע)
בר כוכבא, (היסט. אָפּערעטע)
די כּשופֿמאַכערין, (אָפּערעטע)
דאָס יידעלע, (פּאָעמען, לידער)

דראַמאַטורג.
גרינדער פֿון יידישן טעאַטער

1. Mendele Moykher-sforim, 1836–1917; Writer of novels; 2. Sholem Aleykhem, 1859–1916; Writer of novels and plays; 3. Yitskhok-leybush Perets, 1853–1934; Poet, writer of short stories and plays; 4. Khayim Nakhmen Byalik, 1873–1934; Poet; 5. Sholem Ash, 1888–1957; Writer of short stories, novels, plays; 6. Avrom Goldfadn, 1840–1908; Playwright, founder of The Yiddish Theater.

The Role of Yiddish in American Ultra-Orthodox and Hassidic Communities

SOLOMON POLL

This is a paper on the role and position of Yiddish among American ultra-Orthodox and Hassidic Jews. The members of these groups consider their goal in life to be the perpetuation of Jewish laws, practices, and observances, and their conduct is entirely defined by religious dogma and principles. Many migrated to the United States after World War II, and most of them settled in Williamsburg, a section of Brooklyn, in New York City.

In this dynamic metropolis with its many ethnic groups, these Jews have vigorously – and so far successfully – opposed acculturation to American social patterns. Resistance to Americanization is such that, although there is no physical or legal wall to isolate them, there is a strong 'social wall' which separates these groups from activities that might encroach on their cultural stability. All institutions are regulated so as to be conducive to a 'religous way of life'. The family, religious organization, social stratification, religious leadership, and all other phases of social structure are oriented to the preservation of group norms and to the strict observance of the *Shulhan Arukh*, the code of Jewish law.

This paper attempts to deal more explicitly with Hassidic Jews of Hungarian extraction because: (1) they are more recent immigrants and may provide a clearer base for analysis; (2) changes in their Yiddish are more easily observable; (3) their attitudes about languages other than Yiddish are known; (4) Yiddish among Hungarian Jews has distinctive characteristics.

Although the major focus in this paper is upon Yiddish, the following four languages must be taken into account: (1) Yiddish, (2) Hungarian, (3) Hebrew, and (4) English. Attitudes towards any one of these languages are interrelated with attitudes towards the other among the groups under study.

Jews in Hungary were emancipated in the year 1867. A decree passed by both houses of the Hungarian Parliament gave the Jews civil and political rights equal to those held by other Hungarians. In 1868 a Jewish Congress met to establish a federated Jewish national organization which could represent the entire Jewish community of Hungary and Transylvania and be the official voice of all Hungarian Jews in matters involving the government and the Hungarian public at large, as well as regulate internal Jewish affairs. It was in this last instance that it experienced its major difficulties.

Hungarian Jewish reformers (Neologs) began to introduce innovations into synagogue practice in the middle of the nineteenth century. Some of their reforms were as follows: removing the *bimah* (reading desk) from the center of the synagogue and placing it in front of the ark; providing the rabbis and the cantors with ecclesiastical garments to be worn during religious services; removing the separating wall between men and women in the synagogue so that they might sit together during religious services; introducing topical sermons in the synagogue services instead of the traditional homilies; these sermons to be in Hungarian instead of Yiddish (Greenwald 1946: 64–84). The Neologs also departed from traditional daily observances. Gradually they came to control the organization of Congressional Congregations (congregations under the jurisdiction of the Jewish Congress).

The Orthodox Jews protested vehemently against the Congressional Congregations, to whom the Hungarian government initially gave jurisdiction over all Jewish congregations and their membership. Their protests were recognized and in March 18, 1870, the Hungarian House of Representatives adopted the following resolution:

In view of the fact that it is contrary to the concept of the free practice of religion in Hungary that a minority religious group (Orthodox) be forced by a majority (Reform) to participate in an organization whose ideology and practice are opposed to their religious principles and in order that the religious disputes be settled as soon as possible, the minister of culture is hereby directed to suspend all religious ordinances until further establishment of law by the legislature takes effect (Ujvari 1929: 668).

Following this resolution, in 1871 the Hungarian legislature ratified the charter of the religious organization Guardians of Faith, and in 1905 recognized the Hungarian Autonomous Orthodox Israelite Religious Denomination as an independent religious body equal to the Congressional Congregation. The legislature specifically stated that 'the Congressional Congregation may have jurisdiction only over those congregations which accept its dictum or principle' (Ujvari 1929: 500).

Thus, the Jewish community of Hungary was effectively divided into three separate religious groupings or bodies:
1. Congressional Congregations or the so-called Neologs;
2. Orthodox or the traditional; and
3. *Status quo ante*, communities that attached themselves neither to Reform nor to Orthodox organizations.

Members of these groupings differed from one another socially as well as religiously and politically. However, in the main, there were two basic positions.

In one camp there were the traditionally observant Jews who held that the *Shulhan Arukh* was the major guide for their lives. The other camp contained the less observant and nonobservant Jews who modified or rejected the *Shulhan Arukh* and its authority. (For a more extensive treatment of this problem see Poll 1962.) The Hassidim were definitely in the former camp. However, in addition to complete adherence to the *Shulhan Arukh*, they also observed many other religious practices. They did not form a separate organization but were part of the Orthodox congregations. The identifying characteristic of Hassidim, in addition to their ultra-Orthodox religious practices, was their affiliation with Hassidic leaders – the celebrated *rebbes* or *tsadikim*.

The division between Orthodox and Reform Jews was so great that there was a ban against intermarriage among them. The usage of Yiddish was one of the major instruments which strengthened the social separation between Orthodox and nonobservant Jews in Hungary. For example, Rabbi Moses Schreiber, one of the outstanding Orthodox leaders in Hungary in the mid-nineteenth century (known as the Chasam Sofer), prohibited the Jewish communities from electing rabbis who were 'readers of a foreign language because [even] the words of the Torah it is forbidden to receive from such a person. It is like putting an idol into the Ark of the Lord' (Schreiber 1872: 74).

Rabbi Ezekiel Benat, another outstanding Orthodox leader of that time, in ordaining one of his students wrote into the diploma that it was granted on the condition that the recipient speak no other language but Yiddish during his tenure of rabbinical office (Greenwald 1946: 67).

Furthermore, 'at the time the great David Reich was rabbi of Ujpest, some people in his congregation wanted to have their children taught the 'language of the non-Jews', and they hired a teacher of Hungarian. When the great rabbi, may his memory be blessed, heard of this he pretended that he had heard nothing. At the afternoon services on the Sabbath, when the rabbi was called up to the Torah the teacher of Hungarian was standing near the reading desk. When the rabbi finished the benediction after reading the Torah, he said in a loud voice: "Our Rabbi Moses gave us this Torah from the hands of God. Ravina and Rabbi Ashi gave us the oral law. Now this intruder, this arrogant man comes and wants to uproot these two Torahs. May he be uprooted. I assure you that any child given into his tutelage will enter upon the wrong path and walk in the ways of sinners". As he said these words, terror seized the hearers and the next morning the teacher of Hungarian was sent back to his home town' (Greenwald 1946: 67).

This, and similar types of social control, not only divided the Orthodox and Reform communities but kept the separation alive, effective, and basic to Hungarian Jewish concerns. The secular and nationalist movements which began to take root among Eastern European Jews prior to World War I had little, if any, impact on Hungarian Jewry even as late as the beginning of the

Second World War. Recent Hungarian-Jewish immigrants to the United States are still far removed from the world of Jewish nationalist secular interests. However, their concern with Yiddish continues almost unabated.

THE ROLE OF YIDDISH IN HUNGARY

Yiddish in Hungary meant different things to different Jews. There were eight distinct categories in the expression of attitudes toward Yiddish.

1. *Opposition to Yiddish.* The liberal Jews or the so-called Neologs fought for Magyarization and advocated that Hungarian, and not Yiddish, be spoken in the synagogues. They considered Yiddish a 'foreign language'; they associated usage of Hungarian with loyalty to the country. The Neologs threatened Orthodox Jewish congregations with intervention by the Hungarian government if Yiddish continued as the official language of the pulpit. They warned Orthodox congregations to introduce Hungarian instead of Yiddish 'voluntarily' before they would be forced to report 'disloyalty' of the Orthodox to the Hungarian government.

The following excerpt from one of the leading literary Jewish journals in Hungary, which appeared in 1866, clearly demonstrates this viewpoint:

The pain cuts deep into our heart to observe that in most of our synagogues not the Hungarian language but German or Judeo-German is spoken. The reason for this is not a religious one, but a superficial attachment to accustomed ways. What right do the Orthodox congregations have to spread God's commandment in a foreign language? No one can give a real answer to this. We do not know when our brethren will come to the realization that this blind and slavish reverence for Yiddish is absurd.

To be sure, in many parts of our land there are Jewish congregations where some of the members do not understand Hungarian, therefore, religious preaching is done in German. But this condition is temporary and affects only a segment of the congregants and not the upcoming generation. The future of our religion depends upon the new generations which, undoubtedly, would be very happy if the Jewish clergy should spread the holy teachings in their native tongue. But it is painful to notice that, particularly among our Orthodox brethren, no attempt to correct this situation has been made thus far.

Throughout the land the German or the Judeo-German language is heard from the pulpits as if the usage of the Hungarian language in the synagogues would, in any way, alter God's worship... We tolerate, in our temples, a situation where the Hungarian language is not considered worthy of expressing the holiest thoughts and ideas.

Do they want to wait, particularly our Orthodox brethren, until this justifiable weakness of our religious service is placed before the House of Representatives?... It is conceivable that the time is not far distant when this will become an issue there. We are willing to allow some time for the introduction of the Hungarian language in the synagogues because the great majority of the rabbis who currently hold office do not know that language. But the time has arrived when the new rabbis must know Hungarian, when the ability to preach in Hungarian must become one of the major prerequisites [for holding office] (Steinherz 1886: 342).[1]

1. Note the interchangeable references to Yiddish, Judeo-German and German. The Neologs were unwilling to accord Yiddish the status of a bona fide language and referred to it as Judeo-German or German to stress its 'impurity' and 'foreignness'.

2. *Yidish-daytsh.* To some Orthodox Jews Yiddish was *yidish-daytsh* or Judaized German. In their case Yiddish was to all intents and purposes German which became Yiddishized through its usage by Jews. This was particularly true among those Orthodox Jews who lived in the Oberland area, near the Austrian border. These Jews mostly spoke German. They occasionally used some well-known Hebrew terms, which made their German 'Yiddish'.

The speakers of *yidish-daytsh* consisted of people who had received some secular education but had little or no formal Jewish education. These people were usually observant Jews who retained traditional Judaism matter of factly, without background knowledge or familiarity with the Law. They recognized the religious function of Yiddish and associated it with religion and with persons who were religiously learned. They themselves had not been exposed to Yiddish at school or in their own homes. Therefore, Yiddish to them was associated either with the learned, or with those who came from such areas of Hungary or Poland where no other language was spoken among Jews. They tolerated Yiddish and, to some extent, even accorded it 'honorable recognition'. However, they did not feel that Yiddish should play an important role in the continuing development of Jewish life in Hungary.

3. *Translation Yiddish.* There were those Jews who spoke only Hungarian in connection with all their activities. When it came to the study of the Scriptures or the Talmud, only Yiddish was employed. These were usually the younger people who had Hungarian schooling and considered Hungarian their 'native tongue'. Most of them attended religious schools where the translation of the Scriptures and of the Talmud was into Yiddish. Thus it was necessary for them to acquire Yiddish in order to comprehend the subject matter at hand.

4. *Yiddish as a Synagogue Tradition.* Orthodox congregations opposed the viewpoint of the liberals. In the synagogues they maintained Yiddish and considered it a part of religious expression. The Orthodox rabbis opposed the innovation of the liberal Jews to such an extent that they prohibited their followers from entering a synagogue in which the sermons were preached in Hungarian.

The following excerpt from the resolutions of a rabbinical convention held in Hungary in 1886 expresses this viewpoint:

These are the resolutions of the Jewish Court, which consists of the elders of our generation, may their merits shield us, Amen. These resolutions were adopted in Hungary in the year 1866, at the convention of rabbis, scholars, and righteous men, may their merits shield us, Amen. . . . These resolutions have been handed down from generation to generation in order to uphold the Jewish customs and laws in Europe and in the Holy Land. They were published in the Holy City in the year 1873, and these are the holy words of the rabbis:

It is prohibited to preach in the language of the non-Jews. Furthermore, it is prohibited to listen to a sermon which is delivered in the language of the non-Jews. Therefore, it is the duty of every Jewish person who hears a rabbi or anyone else preach in a foreign language to leave the synagogue or the house of prayer. The preacher must speak only in the Yiddish language, which is spoken by the honest, honorable, pious Jews of this land.

Signed in the City of Michalovce on the third day of the weekly section *Vayishlakh* in the year 5626, corresponding to 1866. [The signatures of seventy-seven rabbis and three great Hassidic *rebbes* are affixed to the document.] (*Maaseh Avot* 1901).

This category consisted of Orthodox Jews with considerable formal religious education. They considered Yiddish as part of traditional Judaism and wanted to maintain it as the language of the pulpit. In their own realm of communication, however, Yiddish was used only casually, their major language being Hungarian. They insisted that introducing Hungarian into the synagogue would be a sacrilege and a departure from traditional pathways. For them Yiddish had positive religious significance and represented a basic vehicle of religious expression.

5. *Yiddish on the Sabbath and Holidays.* Still another viewpoint was held by those who considered Yiddish as their 'native tongue' and expressed a moral or religious duty to cultivate Yiddish. They spoke Yiddish on the Sabbath and on holidays. They insisted that at least on *shabes redt men yidish* – on the Sabbath Yiddish must be spoken. To these people there was a clear demarcation between Hungarian and Yiddish. Hungarian was considered a secular language, whereas Yiddish had sacred significance. When any religious literature (i.e. written in Hebrew) was studied, it had to be translated into Yiddish. It was through Yiddish that Hebrew was learned and understood.

Subscribing to this viewpoint was the ultra-Orthodox element, people with an extensive formal religious education and devoutly observant. They not only considered Yiddish a part of religious expression in synagogue usage, but they carried Yiddish one step further. They considered it such an important aspect of religious expression that on holy days, when a religious Jew was supposed to be occupied with 'holy things', Yiddish had to be spoken in their homes. Thus Yiddish was considered as within the category of 'holy things'.

6. *Yiddish as the Language of Import.* There were those who used Yiddish in everyday conversation. Ideas of any import and of any social consequence were conveyed in Yiddish. In addition to studying and translating the Scriptures and the Talmud in that language, Yiddish also constituted the major form of communication. Hungarian was only used as a substitute for Yiddish. It was mainly employed when there was a need to recapitulate the meaning of an idea or a phrase.

This category also consisted of ultra-Orthodox individuals. They not only brought Yiddish into their homes to express 'holy things' on holy days, but utilized Yiddish on every occasion when religion was discussed. To them Yiddish had broader significance in their everyday life. Their religious observance was more intense and more frequent than that of the individuals in the former categories. They also utilized Yiddish more frequently than the members of the former categories, because religion itself had a broader application. Because Yiddish had religious meaning and because religion was more extensively invoked, Yiddish too was more frequently and more intensely utilized.

7. *A yid redt yidish.* There were some who considered Yiddish as the 'language of the Jew' which they expressed in *a yid redt yidish* – a Jew speaks Jewish. By no means did they consider Yiddish the language of the poor, or of the scholar, or of the illiterate. They associated Yiddish with all those who observed the Jewish Law.

This category consisted of the Hassidic elements that spoke exclusively Yiddish in all their activites. Since being Hassidic meant being involved in religious practices all day long, Yiddish was part of their daily life. It was utilized in thinking and interpreting life itself. Many Hassidic males did not engage in any worldly activities and did not earn their livelihood themselves. Some were supported by the community and some by their fathers-in-law who considered it a great honor to have a scholar and a religious man as a son-in-law. Still others were supported by their wives who were the breadwinners for the entire family. To these Jews no other language than Yiddish was necessary. They communicated only with members of their Jewish community and within that community Yiddish was quite sufficient. However, other than its usage in daily life and in Talmudical instruction, Yiddish had no supreme value in itself. The ultrareligious Jews in Hungary did not 'cultivate' Yiddish. There was no Yiddish literature other than religious writings. Yiddish poetry, novels, drama lectures, concerts, choirs, or theatre were practically unknown to these Jews who used Yiddish exclusively.

8. *Extreme Use of Yiddish.* Finally there were those who in addition to speaking Yiddish exclusively carried its usage to the extreme. These were those Hassidic Jews who put special emphasis upon the exclusive use of the Yiddish language. They prohibited their children from attending secular elementary schools, even when such attendance was required by law. To meet the requirements of the law, they hired private tutors to instruct their children in a minimum of reading and writing in Hungarian. They considered Hungarian a vehicle of assimilation and forbade their children to speak it. Hungarian was considered a *goyish* language, the language of non-Jews. They forbade reading of Hungarian papers or any other Hungarian literature, regardless of its contents. They even reprimanded people – who might have been strangers – speaking Hungarian in the synagogue.

Hence it can be seen that usage and attitude toward Yiddish moved in a continuum from one extreme to the other. On one polar end were those who expressed antagonism toward Yiddish and viewed it with disfavor. On the other end were those to whom Yiddish was not only a way of communication but a 'way of life'. To them Yiddish was part and parcel of their religious expression. Those who were antagonistic toward Yiddish wanted to cultivate the Hungarian language and considered use of Hungarian a form of patriotism. These were the left wing liberals in religious expression, the enlightened, the Neologs, and the assimilationists, to whom religion was not a binding force.

The usage of Yiddish became more meaningful as the involvement in religiosity was increased. Chart I shows the relationship between the attitudinal expressions toward Yiddish and the categories of Yiddish users.

Chart I. *Attitudinal expressions toward Yiddish as related to its users*

Attitudinal Expressions Toward Yiddish	Categories of the Yiddish Users
1. Antagonistic toward Yiddish	Enlightened, Neologs, and assimilationists
2. Yiddish considered as *yidish-daytsh*	Modern-Orthodox who lived near the Austrian border
3. Yiddish utilized only for translating the Scriptures or the Talmud 4. Yiddish considered part of traditional Judaism in synagogues	Orthodox with formal religious education
5. Yiddish spoken on Sabbath and holidays 6. Yiddish spoken in connection with religious affairs	Ultra-Orthodox with formal religious education and intensive religious observance
7. Yiddish spoken exclusively 8. Yiddish used to an extreme degree; antagonistic toward Hungarian	Hassidim

THE ROLE OF LANGUAGE AMONG THE ULTRA-ORTHODOX AND HASSIDIC JEWS IN HUNGARY AND IN THE UNITED STATES

Yiddish and Hungarian

In the United States Yiddish has broader acceptance. It is spoken by more Jews and by more types of Jews than anywhere else in the world. The Yiddish language in the United States, in contrast to Hungary, is not confined to religious Jews only. Here Yiddish has gained secular status (Fishman n.d.). Its speakers are not doomed to remain physically isolated or socially segregated among a relatively small group because Yiddish is not a language barrier. One has ample opportunities to communicate with other Jews outside of one's immediate social group. Furthermore, because Yiddish is so widely spoken among Jews in America, many ultrareligious do not find it necessary to learn English. For them Yiddish is not a bridge to English. For them Yiddish is a sufficient language for communication. With Yiddish one can be quite mobile in many and diverse social activities. Thus the role of Yiddish has changed from a language of isolation, as it was in Hungary, to a language of broader horizons.

In the United States Hungarian has a different role for the Hungarian Jew.

Here it is no threat to the ultrareligious Hungarian Jews because there is no social intercourse between them and other Hungarians. Even those ultrareligious Jews who speak Hungarian consider the language too 'unimportant and harmless' to pay any serious attention to it. Many Hassidic women speak Hungarian almost exclusively amongst themselves because they do not know Yiddish or speak it very poorly. Some who know Yiddish still prefer to speak Hungarian because it reminds them of the olden days and it expresses strong primary–group relationships. It brings back memories and has sentimental associations. Hungarian speech denotes a common background, a common interest, and a common understanding of things. Hungarian is used much more frequently among women than among men, and it is a convenient vehicle for gossip. Gossiping in Yiddish would sound too serious and might be considered a transgression of the prohibition against talebearing. Gossip, when spoken in Hungarian, assumes a casualness which lessens the degree of sin of gossiping. Because it is not spoken by 'serious' people at all, and because the Scriptures are not translated into that language, it has no religious significance and is considered only as a casual and incidental language.

Yiddish and Hebrew

Hebrew was not spoken in Hungary. It was used exclusively for religious purposes. Hebrew was considered *loshon kodesh* – the sacred tongue; it was deeply revered and was considered the language 'in which God spoke to the children of Israel and gave them the Torah'. It was used for the most serious aspects of life; for example, in issuing additional religious decrees or warnings about observance of religious laws and customs. Hebrew was not employed in conversation; the ultrareligious Jews associated modern conversational Hebrew with Zionism, which was vehemently opposed by most of the ultra-Orthodox leaders. The establishment of a modern political state was considered contrary to Messianic hopes. The ultra-Orthodox religious Jews believed that the Land of Israel would be redeemed through the coming of the Messiah and the establishment of a state would be realized by God's miraculous performances.

Zionism advocated the propagation of Hebrew. The Hebrew that the ultra-Orthodox used for prayer, study, scholarship, and correspondence consisted of both Aramaic or Talmudical Hebrew and classical Biblical Hebrew.[2] Modern Hebrew, with its expansion of vocabulary, its introduction of modern terms, and its appropriate usage of grammar was completely ignored. As a matter of fact, Hebrew as such was not taught in the Hassidic rabbinical schools. Some Hassidic leaders carried this attitude to the extreme. For example, those

2. Just as the Yiddish of learned men was heavily interspersed with Hebrew phraseology so their Hebrew writings showed the influence of Yiddish. Many Hebrew terms and forms were coined by Yiddish speakers and were subsequently incorporated into Hebrew.

passages in which *Rashi*, the most popular exegete of the Scriptures and the Talmud, elaborated on the grammatical form of a word or a phrase were generally skipped. The Hassidic leaders held that one must not study Hebrew grammar; its knowledge was associated with *apikorses* – skepticism or heresy. Since modern Hebrew, on the one hand, was associated with secularism and, therefore, taboo and classical Hebrew, on the other hand, was associated with religious study and prayer and, therefore, too holy for daily use, Yiddish became the most important vehicle of communication among ultra-Orthodox Jews. Such was the role of Yiddish in Hungary and such it continues to be among the Hungarian ultra-Orthodox who came to the United States after World War II.

A change in attitude toward Hebrew was expected among the ultra-Orthodox in America and elsewhere after the establishment of the State of Israel. Contrary to this expectation, Hassidic Jews not only continued their anti-Zionist agitation, but expanded and intensified it. The Hassidim feel that the establishment of the State of Israel represents a great threat to their ultra-Orthodox beliefs. The State of Israel, as a national state, has policies and laws which are not based upon the *Shulhan Arukh*. The leadership of the new Jewish state and the majority of its inhabitants are not religiously observant – certainly not in an ultra-Orthodox sense. The educational system and the social institutions of Israel are based on secular conceptions and not on religious principles. All this presents a tremendous problem to the ultra-Orthodox, who still consider religious laws the major bonds and guiding principles of all Jews. Inasmuch as modern Hebrew is the official language of Israel and is identified with all of the foregoing undesirable developments, Hassidim have been aroused to greater efforts to prevent modern Hebrew from gaining acceptance among ultrareligious Jews. As a result, modern Hebrew is not taught in the Hassidic schools in the United States. It should be pointed out, however, that on this issue there are differences of opinion between the Hassidic and other ultra-Orthodox Jews. Whereas the Hassidim object to modern Hebrew, many ultra-Orthodox Jews consider it basic and not necessarily associated with heresy and irreligion.

Yiddish as a written language

Despite the fact that Yiddish became the major vehicle of communication for ultra-Orthodox Jews in Hungary, Yiddish did not expand into areas other than those of primary communication. Yiddish writing and the cultivation of Yiddish literature were not encouraged, primarily because *belles-lettres* in any language were frowned upon as a nonreligious triviality. Written Yiddish was considered the 'language of the layman', the 'language of women', or the 'language of those who could not read Hebrew'. It was tolerated because it gave those who could not read Hebrew a taste of religious thoughts and laws. Yiddish literature on *musar* – moral edification – as well as Yiddish literature on the Scriptures were intended for those who had a minimal formal religious training. Furthermore, Yiddish was never taught formally as a language. It was considered a language which one just knew by being Jewish. It was expected that every religious Jew would know how to read and write Yiddish without any formal instruction. Little or no attention was paid to its spelling, proper pronunciation, or sentence structure, for it was never intended as a medium for writing on advanced or involved religious topics. This view persists among ultra-Orthodox Jews to this very day, despite their continued positive attitude toward and reliance upon Yiddish.

Yiddish and English

As has been noted above, liberal Jews in Hungary considered Yiddish a 'foreign language' and Hungarian the proper language for communication. Orthodox and Hassidic Jews, on the other hand, referred to Hungarian as a 'foreign language' and considered Yiddish the proper language, at least for specific Jewish behaviors. In the United States, English and Yiddish are related by Hungarian Jews in an entirely different fashion from Yiddish and Hungarian in Hungary. Whereas Hungarian in Hungary was considered by many of the Orthodox and Hassidic Jews as *goyish* – a non-Jewish language – English in America is considered by them neither as *goyish* nor as foreign. It is conceivable that this is due to the fact that Hungarian was a greater threat to religious Jews in Hungary than English is to them in the United States. Or, it may be due to the fact that Orthodox and Hassidic Jews regarded the Hungarian government as hostile and, as a result, considered Hungarian a detestable language. Whereas the Neologs spoke Hungarian as an expression of loyalty, the Orthodox refused to speak Hungarian in the synagogues, thereby expressing rejection of and dissatisfaction with Hungary. Refusing to use a language as an expression of animosity has been observed repeatedly, e.g. in Czechoslovakia during and after the war. Anyone who spoke German in public was in danger of being mistreated by a mob as a German or a German sympathizer.[3]

On the other hand, the American government is regarded by the ultrareligious Jews as being fair and sympathetic toward Jewish religious practices, customs, and beliefs. English in America is a novelty to the Hassidim and does not fall into the same category as Hungarian in Hungary. Its mastery intrigues them, its vocabulary challenges them, and it is generally believed that one's economic position rises in proportion to one's knowledge of English. Many informants[4] stated that 'I would do much better if I could speak English' or 'I could buy

---

3. Based upon personal observation by the author during his visit to Prague in 1946. He was warned on many occasions not to speak Yiddish in public because it might be mistaken for German by the Czechs.

4. Interviewed in connection with my study *The Hasidic Community of Williamsburg*.

merchandise cheaper if I could speak English' or 'I could go into a different line of business if I only spoke English'. Therefore, there is no apparent rejection of English by the ultrareligious as a safeguard against acculturation. Nor is the expression '*goyish* language' applied to English. However, at present it is difficult to predict what attitudes toward English will ultimately crystallize among the ultra-Orthodox when the group will have mastered the English language and its use among them will have increased.

THREAT OF ASSIMILATION — LANGUAGE AS A VEHICLE

Language is one of the major factors contributing to cultural assimilation. Those who migrate to a foreign land and learn its language find it easier to interact with the native population. Through this interaction, facilitated by a common language, migrants may gradually become integrated into the host society. Conversely, the retention of a distinct language by a group makes integration more difficult. An authority on acculturation, Professor Hansen, has stated: 'as long as any community retained its own language, amalgamation with American social life was impossible. From the first, immigrant leaders complained of the eagerness with which the people discarded their mother tongue. Its retention became the cornerstone of all efforts to maintain solidarity' (Hansen 1948: 203). But once the new language is learned, once the foreign accent is no longer noticeable, and once there are no peculiar external signs that distinguish immigrants from the natives, partial assimilation is inevitable.

Throughout history the retention of a Jewish language has been closely associated with the retention of Jewish religious and cultural practices. A 'Jewish language' is defined here as a language which is spoken almost exclusively by Jews. In the course of history, from about 1400 to the fifth century B.C.E., Jews mainly spoke Hebrew; after the fifth century B.C.E., Judeo-Aramaic and Hebrew; in the seventh and eighth centuries, with the Arabic conquests, 'the Arabic language crossed the frontiers of Arabia and spread rapidly among the Jews of other countries. In Egypt, Syria, Palestine and Persia, which were conquested by the second calif, Omar, the Jews soon learned to use the language of the conquerors and adopted it as their mother tongue (Broyde 1906: 49–50). In the twelfth century they spoke Judeo-Spanish and Judeo-German. From the thirteenth century on, this Judeo-German was carried into Poland and Russia. These languages (whether originally Aramaic, Arabic, Spanish, or German) could not have been transformed into 'Jewish' languages if they had not incorporated in them elements of Hebrew as well as specific lexical and syntactic differences which separated them from their languages of origin. Once a language was spoken by Jews in a 'Jewish way', Jews considered it a Jewish language.

Over the centuries Yiddish has come to convey much of Jewish tradition, attitude, and feeling, and to do so in particularly apt and sensitive ways. It is the most recent 'Jewish language' created by the Jewish people.

It has been held, particularly among religious Jews, that language is one of the most important safeguards against assimilation and unless Jews hold to a Jewish language – a language which is mainly used by Jews and through which their religious–cultural values are expressed – the group will inevitably assimilate. Religious Jews throughout the ages advocated the notion expressed in the Midrashic passage stating that the Jews owed their redemption from Egypt to 'four things'. One of the four was the fact that 'they did not change their language' (*Midrash Rabba* 1939: 413–414).

Although ultra-Orthodox and Hassidic Jews did not (and do not) look upon Yiddish as a vehicle of expression for art and literature, they do see it as a language used by Jews to communicate Jewish thoughts, traditions and philosophies, and 'all things Jewish'. Today, they also view it with a certain historical reverence. Yiddish was the language of millions of martyred Jews in Russia, Poland, Rumania, the Baltic states, and Galicia. It has been used in the religious schools and in the Talmudical academies. It gave the Jews a group identification, a matter of no little significance.

There are still groups in America among whom Yiddish is a living language and to whom Yiddish provides the needed support for cultural continuity. Among these groups are the ultrareligious and the Hassidim. In their circles Yiddish is spoken at home, in the synagogues, and in communication with like-minded fellows. Yiddish is spoken from the pulpits and is a medium of instruction in their schools. The Talmud and the Bible and 'everything holy' is taught and studied in Yiddish only.

LANGUAGE CONCERNS AMONG THE ULTRA-ORTHODOX IN AMERICA TODAY

In the United States there are frequently no major behavioral differences amongst Orthodox, Conservative, and Reform Jews. One's identification with these groups is through congregational membership or organizational affiliation. There are usually no differential requirements for membership in a congregation other than the payment of membership fees or dues. As a matter of fact, in smaller communities there are many who express their 'impartiality' by holding membership in two or even three congregations simultaneously. It has been stated, for example, 'that almost fifteen per cent of the 905 Orthodox members [in Milwaukee] retain dual membership in an Orthodox as well as in a Conservative or Reform temple' (Polsky 1958: 328).

There are many phases of Jewish life in which the various religious groups cooperate closely. For example, Jewish charitable and welfare organizations operate on an interdenominational level, and many Orthodox establishments receive financial support from non-Orthodox individuals and groups. There have been closer social contacts between the various Jewish religious groupings and greater success in coordinating and interrelating their activities in the United States than in most other Jewish communities throughout the world. As a result of all of these factors, it is necessary for the purpose of specifying an Orthodox Jew's religiosity to distinguish between the 'Orthodox' and the 'ultra-Orthodox'. 'Orthodox' Jews are those who either belong to an Orthodox synagogue (and by this fact alone are considered to be 'Orthodox') or who merely consider themselves to be orthodox. 'Ultra-Orthodox' Jews, on the other hand, are those who strictly adhere to the laws of the *Shulhan Arukh*.

Both Hassidic and non-Hassidic ultra-Orthodox tend to value Yiddish in view of its continued importance in Talmudical studies and its continued identification with traditional patterns of Jewish life.

Notwithstanding the fact that Yiddish is the daily spoken language of the ultrareligious groups in America, English has penetrated deeply even into the most religious groups. Many English words have been incorporated into the Yiddish vocabulary of all but the most puristically inclined. An analysis of the front page of an issue of August, 1960, of the most Hassidic Yiddish newspaper in America, *Der Yid*, reveals the following English words blended into the Yiddish text:

adoption	justice
appeals	major
association	meeting
confiscated	office
court	official
epidemic	parties
espionage	percent
flier	scandalized
Foreign Claims Settlement	sorts
Commission	storekeepers
frozen	swimming pool

Since English penetrates even into the most ultra-Orthodox and Hassidic Yiddish speaking groups, and since no hostility has been expressed toward the English language on the part of these groups, the following problems deserve brief consideration. (1) Will the Hassidic Jews allow the free usage of English? (2) Into which social areas will English penetrate? (3) Once English is mastered by the Hassidim, will they consider it as representing a threat of assimilation? (4) Will the knowledge of English influence them to participate in non-Hassidic, secular Jewish activities? (5) To what extent will English become a force for their integration into the larger American society?

In order to answer these questions, the following hypothesis is proposed. As long as Diaspora Jews maintain their Jewish identity there will be a language, besides Hebrew, which will be used almost exclusively by Jews. This language will be known to them and to others as a 'Jewish language'. This language may be spoken by a relatively small segment of the Jewish population, but because of its Jewish terminology and because of the fact that it will be mainly spoken by Jews in a 'Jewish way' about 'things Jewish' to Jews, it will be recognized as a 'language of Jews'.

Currently, the 'Jewish language' most widely used in the Diaspora is Yiddish. However Yiddish has been anglicized in the United States and, regardless of how mingled it may become with other languages in other countries, the mere fact that Yiddish is used by Jews to convey thoughts, ideas, philosophies, and 'things Jewish' makes it particularly meaningful to Jews, and makes it *de facto* a Jewish language. It is conceivable that Yiddish in America, after a long period of time, may have a much higher proportion of English elements than currently; but by virtue of the mere fact that it will be used exclusively and particularly by Jews who seek to convey and cultivate Jewish tradition, it will maintain its identity as a Jewish language. Regardless of the number of Jews using it, it will be recognized as a Jewish language even by those who will not have familiarity with it.

1. Upon closer observation of ultrareligious communities, it seems apparent that thus far there are no particular prohibitions against the usage of English. It seems inevitable that English will penetrate more and more into the ultrareligious groups. However, currently, Hebrew and Yiddish are so greatly overemphasized that English will long remain in the background. At present, the group does not speak or read English well, therefore, it is not necessary for the leadership to give serious consideration to what impact English may have upon the members. As a matter of fact, English is considered by the leadership as a very important tool because through it they obtain 'uncolored and unbiased' news about other Jews and other peoples in the world. Some Hassidic leaders and newspaper editors obtain news of the world from English sources and then, in turn, translate and editorialize it so that the news in the Jewish communities is always religiously oriented. Only those items become newsworthy in the religious community which are in some way related to religious, Hassidic, or Jewish life.

2. As to the areas in which English will play the most important role, at the moment it seems that English penetrates mostly into economic activities. As a matter of fact, the English language is considered a necessary means for communication in the economic pursuits of the community. But it is far beyond the Hassidic imagination to conceive of English as a vehicle of literature, drama, singing or, indeed, of using it as a tool for the expression of philosophy and higher learning.

3. Concerning the problem of assimilation, some additional factors must be

considered. Presumably it makes a difference to what ends a language is utilized. If a language is used mainly in economic pursuits, as it is in the case of English in the Hassidic community, and only that part of its vocabulary is mastered which relates to the economic activities, it does not present as much of a threat of assimilation as would be the case if the language were utilized more extensively. If the English language were comprehended by the group to the extent that it could convey ideologies, this might become a problem. In this case it could become a threat of assimilation because the comprehension of ideologies in the English language may have a significant influence on religious behavior.

4. Contrary to all expectation, in the Hassidic community the threat of assimilation is seen as coming not from English but from Yiddish. The Hassidim are not as much concerned with the English-speaking community as they are with the Yiddish-speaking, non-Hassidic community. The Hassidim fear that Yiddish-speaking, nonobservant Jews may have a bad influence upon their children. The following response of an informant expresses a typical view of the matter:

If a *goy* does not behave as a religious Jew should, we tell our children not to worry about him because he is a *goy*, but if a Jew does not behave as a Jew should, what can we say? We cannot tell our children that he is a *goy*. We have to tell them that he is a Jew, but a different kind of a Jew – a Jew who does not observe *yidishkeyt*. Once we have to make this distinction to our children that there are Jews and Jews, we have a real problem about their upbringing (*Hasidic Community of Williamsburg* 1959).

Yiddish in America is spoken not only by observant Jews as was the case in Hungary. The Yiddish language here is not a vehicle for things pertaining to Jewish Orthodox matters only; it does not deal exclusively with things Jewish. Yiddish is utilized in communicating about all aspects of a complex, modern society. Thus, it also communicates 'things a Hassidic Jew ought not to know'.

This is the major reason why reading and subscribing to non-Hassidic Yiddish papers are prohibited in the American Hassidic community. Non-Hassidic Yiddish newspapers are called 'Sabbath desecrating papers' and are said to do the greatest harm to ultra-Orthodox and Hassidic principles. The fact that they are written in Yiddish only makes them more dangerous.

There are many lustful books, novels and joke books, full of filthy pictures and insolent talk which are sold on every corner. Even worse are the books and newspapers printed in a language invented by the 'innovators,' which they call Hebrew or Yiddish, which take the holy letters with which the world was created and debase them to dust. They write heretical material and forbidden things without end. People who were always careful to avoid reading novels, read these newspapers because they want to know the news but unwittingly they also read other things, which bring them to sin. (Blum 1958: 34).

Modern Hebrew also comes under the same category as secular Yiddish and can be equated with it. Hassidic Jews say that 'the holiness has been removed from the language, and it has been altered by secular words borrowed from other languages which do not contain the ancient and holy tradition'. Because of its secularization, modern Hebrew also presents a threat to the Hassidic Jews. This is illustrated by the following interview:

...we have no objection to the kind of training the girls receive in —— school, our objection is to the teaching of Hebrew there. We very definitely object to teaching the Hebrew language.
   (Do you mean modern Hebrew?)
   Of course, I mean that and that only. I have no objection to the "Holy Tongue". I have seen some statistics recently which show that two-thirds of modern Hebrew contain new words which are made up and created by various Hebrew poets and writers. How can we expose our children to a language that contains no spirit and no holiness?
   (But, sir, do you think language has any influence on behavior? Why do you object so severely to it?)
   The Hebrew language is so closely connected with Zionism that once one is exposed to the language he must somehow, some way, associate with Zionism, which is strictly prohibited in the Hassidic community (*Hasidic Community of Williamsburg* 1958).

TRENDS OF YIDDISH IN THE UNITED STATES AMONG ORTHODOX AND HASSIDIC COMMUNITIES

Yiddish has shown a definite upward trend among the ultra-Orthodox and Hassidic communities during the last decade in the United States. Ultra-Orthodox religious schools where Yiddish is taught have greatly increased in number under the auspices of the ultra-Orthodox and Hassidic groups. The files of Torah Umesorah, National Society for Hebrew Day Schools, substantiates this upward trend. This national organization was founded in 1944 to establish and serve affiliated Jewish all-day schools throughout the United States and Canada, and to conduct teaching seminars and workshops for in-service training of teachers. All member schools are Orthodox, or there is at least a positive commitment by the schools to follow Orthodox principles. Schools that hold membership with this organization are known as 'all-day schools' or yeshivas and have either elementary or junior–senior high school departments or both.

An all-day school is defined as an educational system in which the curriculum is divided into English and Hebrew departments. The English department is responsible for secular studies equivalent to that of the public schools. The Hebrew department is in charge of instruction in Hebrew language, religious sources (Bible, prayer book, Talmud), and traditional Jewish customs and ceremonies. This does not mean that all parents who send their children to an all-day school strictly observe traditional Judaism, but it may be assumed that the parents are at least sympathetic toward Orthodox Jewish education, and that at least during the school term the children are exposed and subjected to a traditional Orthodox conceptual interpretation of Judaism. All schools that are associated with Torah Umesorah have Hebrew instruction. Some of them teach Yiddish in addition to Hebrew.

Table 1.   *Elementary and junior-senior Orthodox all-day schools with (a) Hebrew only and (b) Yiddish and Hebrew instruction, 1952–1953 and 1960–61 school years*

States	Hebrew Only		Yiddish and Hebrew		Total	
	1952–1953	1960–1961	1952–1953	1960–1961	1952–1953	1960–1961
TOTAL UNITED STATES	119	146	25	67	144	213
California	4	9	0	3	4	12
Colorado	0	1	0	0	0	1
Connecticut	4	7	0	0	4	7
District of Columbia	1	3	0	0	1	3
Florida	1	1	0	0	1	1
Georgia	1	2	0	0	1	2
Illinois	7	7	0	0	7	7
Kentucky	0	1	0	0	0	1
Louisiana	0	1	0	0	0	1
Maine	1	1	0	0	1	1
Maryland	1	1	2	3	3	4
Massachusetts	9	9	0	1	9	10
Michigan	0	2	1	1	1	3
Minnesota	1	1	0	0	1	1
Missouri	2	1	0	0	2	1
New Jersey	13	14	0	2	13	16
New York	57	63	21	54	78	117
Ohio	3	4	1	2	4	6
Pennsylvania	7	9	0	1	7	10
Rhode Island	1	1	0	0	1	1
South Carolina	0	1	0	0	0	1
Tennessee	2	2	0	0	2	2
Texas	2	1	0	0	2	1
Virginia	0	2	0	0	0	2
Washington	1	1	0	0	1	1
Wisconsin	1	1	0	0	1	1

Table 1 shows comparative data of the number of all-day schools in the United States during the 1952–1953 (*Directory of Yeshiva All-Day Schools, 5713 – 1952–3* 1952) and 1960–1962 (*Directory of Day Schools in the United States and Canada, 5721–1961* 1961) school years. In the 1952–1953 school year, there were 144 affiliated all-day schools in the United States. In the 1960–1961 school year there were 213 affiliated all-day schools,[5] an increase of 47.9 percent. In the 1952–1953 school year there were 119 affiliated all-day schools with Hebrew only (no Yiddish). In the 1960–1961 school year there were 146 affiliated all-day schools with Hebrew only (no Yiddish). Schools that had Hebrew only increased 22.7

5. *Directory of Day Schools in the United States and Canada, 5721–1961*, lists 270 'affiliated' all-day schools in America. Of this number 19 are in Canada, 40 are duplicated in as much as some schools with elementary and secondary programs are listed twice, under elementary and under secondary schools. Since the publication of the *Directory*, two new schools have been established, thus yielding a total of 213.

Table 2.   *Increase in Orthodox all-day schools offering instruction in (a) Hebrew only and (b) Hebrew and Yiddish instruction between 1952–1953 and 1960–1961 school years*

	Total	Hebrew Only	Yiddish and Hebrew
1952–1953 School Year	144	119	25
1960–1961 School Year	213	146	67
Increase between 1952–1953 and 1960–1961 School Years	69 (47.9 percent)	27 (22.7 percent)	42 (168.0 percent)

percent. However, those schools that used Yiddish in addition to Hebrew tripled in the last seven years. In the 1952–1953 school term there were 25 affiliated all-day schools with Yiddish. In the 1960–1961 term there were 67 affiliated all-day schools with Yiddish, an increase of 168.0 percent (see Table 2).

As for the 1960–1961 school year, out of the total of 213 all-day schools, 117 (54.9 percent) were located in New York State. Of these 117, 63 schools have Hebrew only and 54 have Yiddish and Hebrew. These figures compared to their own respective categories of 'Hebrew only' and 'Hebrew and Yiddish' show that of the 146 schools with Hebrew only 63 schools (or 43.2 percent) are located in New York State. Of the 67 schools with Hebrew and Yiddish, 54 (or 80.6 percent) are located in New York State. Thus, schools offering instruction in Yiddish show a heavy concentration in New York State where ultra-Orthodox and Hassidic communities are mainly located. Brooklyn, which has the heaviest ultra-Orthodox and Hassidic concentration, including the Williamsburg area, contains more than half of the entire total of Hebrew-Yiddish all-day schools (35 out of 67). (See Chart II.)

In addition, of the 35 schools that teach Yiddish in Brooklyn 17 (48.6 percent) are Hassidic. Thus, almost half of the schools offering instruction in Yiddish are Hassidic and the rest are ultra-Orthodox. Most of the affiliated all-day schools that offer instruction at the secondary education level employ Yiddish because their main function is to prepare children for higher Talmudical academies where Yiddish is a prerequisite. 'In the Orthodox Yeshivas, Yiddish is the language of instruction, and the lease on life which Yiddish enjoys in this country is only directly due to these Orthodox institutions of learning'.[6] Hence Yiddish is viewed as a necessary means to the attainment of religiosity, higher learning, and further development of Orthodox Jewish life in America.

Another indication of the upward trend of Yiddish usage among ultra-Orthodox and Hassidic Jews in the last decade is the publication of a Yiddish

6. In a letter from the executive vice-president   of Agudath Israel of America, June 12, 1961, in the possession of the author.

Chart II. *Orthodox all-day schools with (a) Hebrew only and (b) Hebrew and Yiddish instruction as of the 1960–61 school year: the United States, New York State, and New York City*

	Hebrew Only	Yiddish and Hebrew	Total
TOTAL UNITED STATES	146 (100%)	67 (100%)	213 (100%)
NEW YORK STATE	63 (43.2%)	54 (80.6%)	117 (54.9%)
New York City	40 (27.4%)	47 (70.1%)	87 (40.8%)
Bronx	4 (2.7%)	5 (7.5%)	9 (4.2%)
Brooklyn	24 (16.4%)	35 (52.2%)	59 (27.7%)
Manhattan	11 (7.5%)	7 (10.4%)	18 (8.5%)
Staten Island	1 (0.7%)	0 —	1 (0.5%)
Other Cities in New York State	23 (15.7%)	7 (10.5%)	30 (14.1%)
OTHER STATES	83 (56.8%)	13 (19.4%)	96 (45.1%)

weekly journal called *Der Yid*, established in 1952, which calls itself 'the organ for religious Judaism in America'. The paper has approximately 3,500 subscribers, who are mostly Hassidic Jews. The paper is considered to be the official voice of the Satmar Hassidic community.

There is another monthly Yiddish periodical called *Dos yidishe vort* published by the Agudath Israel, which according to its executive vice-president 'is primarily concerned with relating classical Torah Judaism to the problems of current Jewish affairs throughout the world so that the Yiddish reading masses receive through [Agudath Israel] an Orthodox analysis of Jewish affairs in the light of Torah ideology'.[7] The journal was founded in 1954 with 5,000 subscribers, mostly Agudath Israel members. As of 1961, the journal has a circulation of 8,000. This is practically the only Yiddish publication in the United States that increased in circulation in many a year. Under the editorial management of *Dos yidishe vort*, an Orthodox publishing house was founded in 1961. Its first publication was a *Passover Almanac*, containing information about the religious observance of Passover. According to its editor, the purpose of this publication house is to spread Orthodox Judaism, not necessarily to strengthen Yiddish. However, the significant fact still remains that its first publication was in Yiddish, which is an indication of the strength of Yiddish among Orthodox Jews.

It is essential to point out in connection with the above indicators of a growth of Yiddish in the last decade that there has been a sizeable influx of Hungarian Hassidic Jews after World War II. Today this Hassidic element – estimated some 12,000 in Williamsburg alone – is an important contributor to the maintenance and continuity of Yiddish. To these Jews, Yiddish is the language through which the practices and beliefs of religious Judaism are transmitted.

THE EXTENT TO WHICH YIDDISH REMAINS CONSTANT

No language has played such an important role among the ultra-Orthodox as Yiddish. Although it is constantly undergoing change, these changes contribute to its maintenance. Today one can hear American Talmudical students speak a language which is half English and half Yiddish. Sometimes the hearer has difficulties determining whether these students are basically speaking English or Yiddish. One thing is certain, however: many English words are increasingly used as part of the Yiddish of ultra-Orthodox Jewish life.

Although English plays a new and hitherto unparalleled role in the life of the ultra-Orthodox and Hassidic Jews, the tendency is merely to master it, but not to the extent where it might take predominance over Yiddish, particularly in areas of Jewish concern.

7. In a letter from the executive vice-president   of Agudath Israel of America, June 12, 1961, in the possession of the author.

There are prohibitions among the ultra-Orthodox against reading 'novels', 'joke books', just as there is serious objection to 'frivolous talk', etc. These prohibitions are currently not against English per se, but rather against 'frivolous talk' in any language. If the Hassidim come to master English to the extent that with it they can and do reach beyond the intellectual and cultural borders of their religious community, the group will most likely react against its use. However, at present English does not present a threat to religious group cohesion.

Presently only Yiddish is cultivated as the vernacular. It is used in almost every aspect of the lives of the ultrareligious Jews. Thus it is and will remain a tool of communication among this ultrareligious group in America for the foreseeable future. On the other hand, a weakening of Yiddish is proceeding apace among less Orthodox and non-Orthodox segments of American Jewry. Ultimately, Yiddish may become the exclusive badge of American ultra-Orthodoxy, as it was among Hungarian ultra-Orthodoxy.

REFERENCES

Blum, Raphael (1958), *Tal Hashomayim*. New York.
Broyde, I. (1906), 'Use of Arabic language among Jews', in *The Jewish Encylopedia*, vol. 2. New York.
Directory of Yeshiva All-Day Schools, 5713–1952–3 (1952), Mimeographed. New York.
Directory of Day Schools in the United States and Canada, 5721–1961 (1961), Mimeographed. New York.
Fishman, Joshua A. (n.d.), 'Yiddish in America, a socio-psychological portrait', in manuscript, part of a study of the Language Resources Project sponsored by the United States Office of Education. [Revised version published (1965) as *Yiddish in America: Sociolinguistic Description and Analysis*. Bloomington, Indiana, Indiana University Center for Anthropology, Folklore and Linguistics.]
Greenwald, Yekutiel Yehuda (1946), *Letoldot hareformazion hadatit begermania wehungaria*. Columbus, Ohio.
Hansen, Marcus Lee (1948), *The Immigrant in American History*. Cambridge.
Hasidic Community of Williamsburg (1958), Data collected from the files on GOS.
Hasidic Community of Williamsburg (1959), Data Collected from the files on HOS.
Maaseh Avot (1901), Jerusalem.
Midrash Rabba (1939), Leviticus. London.
Poll, Solomon (1962), *The Hasidic Community of Williamsburg*. New York.
Polsky, Howard W. (1958), 'A study of orthodoxy in Milwaukee: social characteristics, beliefs, and observances', in *The Jews*, ed. by Marshall Sklare. Glencoe, Free Press.
Schreiber Moses (1871), *Chasam Sofer, Hoshen Mishpat*. Vienna.
Steinherz, Jakob (1886), 'A Magyar nyelu a zsinagogaban' (The Hungarian language in The Synagogue), *Magyar Zsido Szemle* 5: 34.
Ujvari, Peter, editor (1929), *Magyar Zsido Lexikon*. Budapest.

Who Needs Yiddish?

SHIMON SUSHOLTZ

Two debaters were standing before Hadrian. One was extolling the virtues of speech; the other, those of silence. Said the first, 'My lord, there is nothing better than speech. For without it how could the praises of the bride be sung, how could ships go asea, how could there be commerce in the world?'

Then Hadrian turned to the second: 'What have you got to say in favor of silence?'

As he was about to reply, the first reached over and slapped him on the mouth.

'Why did you slap him?'

'Because, my lord, I use speech in favor of speech. But he wants to put my cause to work for his!'

(*Yalkut Bamidbar* 12)

The writer is in a somewhat similar position, using the English language to extoll the virtues of...Yiddish. But there is no need for anyone to reach over and chastise him. I have been in *chinuch* (Torah education) for over a decade, all this while teaching Torah in English. And I would not trade the *zechus* of those years' labors for anything under the sun. But the inescapable necessity of using English for transmitting Torah has not made it any less unnatural – and my mouth does hurt....

WHY THE QUESTION?

We in today's Torah world are living a pronounced paradox. It is true that our generation has seen a tremendous growth of Torah and Torah living; growth in depth – of strong commitment and tenacious dedication; and growth in breadth – of widening horizons and reaching out. But it is also true that, at the very same time, we have been robbed of a whole set of values, attitudes, and standards of conduct and have replaced them with inferior–quality imitations – and we have not even noticed the difference. Admittedly, this is a broad theme, way beyond the scope of this article; but it does apply here, too.

Time was, not so long ago, when a yeshiva *bachur* just *had* to learn Yiddish in order both to hear *shi'urim* and to really belong to his chosen milieu. Time was when every yeshiva couple started out with the firm resolve that, no matter how difficult it may be, the children will be spoken to only in Yiddish. Nowadays, by contrast, in the home and in the street, in *shul*, in yeshiva, and in the *shtiebel*, English is the reigning language. And by all appearances, it has been a 'smooth and orderly transition'. We feel no pangs of conscience about it. What's more, it has become natural to the point where the stickler for Yiddish is on the defensive and must find justification. So be it!

A CAVEAT

Let it be made clear this discussion does not touch upon the comparative merits of *Lashon Hakodesh* and Yiddish is an everyday language (although there is ample room for such a discussion; see, for example, *Mogen Avrohom* and *Chasam Sofer* to *Orach Chaim* 85). Indeed, some of our arguments may apply equally or *a fortiori* to *Lashon Hakodesh*. But we must focus on the reality of time and place, as things stand here and now; for most of us (excepting only our Sephardic brothers), the choice is clearly one between English and Yiddish. *So, why Yiddish?*

THREE LINKS

First, Yiddish is a link in space, connecting lands and continents. There are Jews living all over the face of the globe and, for the most part, they are of one tongue: Yiddish. The idea of *achdus*, of *kol Yisroel chaverim* – unity and true brotherhood – is a most exalted one; but without the ability of two Jews to *talk* to each other, it remains an idea, whereas it could and should be a living, breathing fact.

It is also a link in time, between generations. Thank G–d, we still have in our midst the remnants of pre-*Churban Yiddishkeit*: both the giant of Torah and piety, and the simple Jew whose very life story is a flaming but never–consumed *Sefer Torah*. Again, for the most part their tongue is Yiddish. By making it impossible for our children to drink in from their fountains of wisdom and *yiras shomayim*, are we not robbing them of their patrimony? (See *Sanhedrin* 91b)

On a deeper level, Yiddish is a powerful chain linking the *neshama* of the individual to the *neshama* of *Klal Yisroel*, i.e. the Torah. The collective soul of a people shows its face in figures of speech. For example, colloquial English is replete with Shakespearean quotations, e.g. 'down in the dumps', 'laughing oneself to death', 'a rose by any other name...'. In modern-day America, references to sports abound, e.g. 'getting to first base', 'going to bat for a cause', 'the line-up'. As for Yiddish, it is the language of Torah; besides the many colloquialisms based on *Tanach* well-known and beloved by us, it sparkles with seemingly senseless expressions which, in truth, derive directly from Talmud and

Midrash, e.g. '*a yohr mit a Mitvoch*',[1] '*bezohlen vie a tatte*'.[2] This is what raises it from a mere means of communications to the level of *sichas chulin shel talmidei chachomim* – the ordinary talk of wise men, which according to the Talmud, is also worthy of study.

Granted, the reader, at this point, may refuse to feel a sense of urgency. After all, not everyone travels abroad, not everyone considers himself a *talmid chacham*; and our second argument, though most powerful, has only temporary validity....But the question *is* urgent, in a very basic sense.

IDENTITY AND REDEMPTION

Man possesses three modes of self-expression: *machshava* (thought), *dibbur* (speech), and *ma'aseh* (deed). The first is wholly internal, the last external. The function of speech is to bring thought into the open, to externalize the internal; it thus belongs between the other two, not sequentially, but qualitatively. Together they comprise the entire field of action in which man's free will manifests itself – which is why every *mitzva*, whether positive or negative, must address itself to one of those categories. But we also know that they are not mere messengers and heralds of the inner being. On the contrary, they in turn exert great power in influencing and molding that inner self. 'Man is shaped by his actions' (*Sefer Hachinuch* 16).

With that, let us now turn to a very well-known, oft-quoted, *and just as often disregarded*, saying of *Chazal*: 'By virtue of three things were our forefathers redeemed from Egypt: they did not change (i.e. de-Judaize) their names, their language, or their mode of dress' (Midrash, quoted in the introduction to *Sefer Hameturgemon*). What is a name? A word used to describe an object or phenomenon in terms of its function, or make-up, or shape....What these factors all have in common is that they are something perceived by the namer; what lies beyond his perception cannot possibly be described, i.e. named. One who would describe a human being in terms of his essence and inner core can only go as far as the innermost of his *perceived* parts, which is *machshava*. Thus, 'name' symbolizes thought. The equations of the other two – language/speech and dress/deed (external) – are too obvious to bear elaboration.

'...To take to Himself a nation from amidst another nation...' (*Devarim* IV: 34). The *sine qua non* of redemption from Egypt was the prior existence of *Bnei Yisroel*, of a *Jewish* nation. Had our forefathers *not expressed* their Jewish identity

---

1. An expression for a very long wait, which literally means 'a year and a Wednesday'. It refers to the Talmud's discussion of the significance of 'The maiden marries on the fourth night' (*Kesubos* 2a) – that the usual interval between betrothal and marriage was one year plus a Wednesday, which to the parties involved may have seemed like an interminable wait.

2. *Baba Kama* 5a: 'Said R. Abahu: All (torts) are like *avos* (principals, lit. fathers) in that payment must be made from the best field'. Hence the expression, 'To pay as a father'.

קול קורא
לאחינו בני ישראל

הישיבה הגדולה דע"ש הגאון דאבדק"ק רשכבה"ג כרן יצחק אלחנן זצ"ל מקובנה, המפורסמה בעולם בשם "ישיבת כנסת בית יצחק דסלאבאדקא' שמתנהלת על ידי זה חי שנה יהבתק'מת בזמן האחרון פה בווילנא, הישיבה, שבצלה מסתופפים הרבה בחורים מצוינים גדולים ומופלגים בתורה ויראה, נמצאת עכשיו במצב של מעבר כללי, מפני יוקר צרכי החיים שהולך ומתגבר במדה מבהילה ומפני רבי התלמידים שמתוספסים ב"ה מיום ליום.

הישיבה הק המחזקת זה יותר משלשים שנה, ואשר בין כתליה חנכו לאלפים תלמידי חכמים, ראשי ישיבות ומורי הוראה בישראל, יעומדת עכשיו בפני סכנה להתבטל ח"ו אם לא יבואו לה לעזרה מיד.

אחינו מוקירי התורה! אתם, אשר תמיד הייתם מוסרים נפשכם לקיום תורתנו הק', נשמת אומתנו ורוחה, כלום תתנו את בית-המקלט לתורה שלנו להחרב? אם אשר תמיד הייתם תומכים בכל מכחכם ב'ישיבות שלנו, כלום תתנו את שארית הפליטה של תלמידי חכמינו להתמוטט ח"ו?

דעו, כי בידכם חלוי עכשיו גורלה של הישיבה הק', שאחרי כל חטלטולים הקשים והמכשולים המרובים שעלה בידנו בע"ה להתגבר עליהם ולהציל את דיק התורה מכליון, ובידכם חלוי עכשיו קיומו של אחד ממשירדי מקדשי ה' אם לא להתקים אם חלילה להתבטל ח"ו. אל תתנו את מוסד תורתנו להתמוטט, הצילו את הישיבה מאבדון, שחדו מכחכם וממונכם לטובת הישיבה, נדבו לטובת "כנסת בית יצחק".

ובזכות זה תתברכו מנחתן ותזרה בכל הברכות הכתובות בתורה.

דברי המברכם ברוך דב ליבאוויץ ר"מ ומנהל דמתיבתא בית יצחק מסלאבאדקא בווילנא.

דברי הגאון הצדיק פוה"ר ברוך דב לייבאוויטש הי"ו ראם דכנסת בית יצחק אינם צריכים חזוק, ורבריו היוצאים מן הלב יכנסו בלב חובבי תורה ויוסדיה לחזק את הישיבה הגדולה והחשובה למען תוכל להחזיק מעמד גם לימים יבואו להפיר תורה בישראל. הכו"ח ר"ח כסלו תרפ"ג וילנא.

חיים עוזר גראדזענסקי

ג' כסלו תרפ"ג, וילנא. אדרעס: רחוב סארסאק' 19 №

די באוואוסטע סלאבאדקער ישיבה "כנסת בית יצחק" וועלכע איז געגרינדעט געווארען שוין העכער 30 יאהר אויפ'ן נאמען פון'ם גרוים'ן גרויסען וועלט - גאון דער קאהו'ער רב ר' יצחק אלחנן זצ"ל און וואם שטייט אונטער מיין הנהלה ב"ה שוין 18 יאהר, געפינט זיך די לעצטע צייט אין ווילנא.

צוליעב דעם אונגעהויער שרעקליכ'ן יקרות וואם שטייגט פון טאג צו טאג, און צוליעב די פיל תלמידים וואם קומען-צו ב"ה אין דער ישיבה, לעבט איבער די ישיבה איצט זעהר שווערען מאטעריעלען קריזיס. עם שטעהט פאר די ישיבה, וועלכע האם באוויזען ב"ה אין משך פון איהר 30 יאהריגע עקזיסטירונג ארויס-צוגעבען טויזענדער תלמידי חכמים, רבנים און ראשי ישיבות, א סכנה פון פאלקאמטען אונטערגאנג ח"ו אויב מ'וועט איהר ניט קו מען גליך צו הילף.

ברידער יידען! איר, וועמ'ענס הארץ עס איז שטענדיג פ"ל געווען מיט אהבה צו דער תורה הק', וועם איר דען דערלאוזען חלילה די וויכטיגע ישיבה אונטערגעהן ח"ח איר, וועלכע האם שטענדיג פערשסאנען און געפיהלט וואם די תורה איז סארן יידישען פאלק, איר, וואם האם זיך תמיד מוסר נפש געווען פאר דער תורה און איהר ע לערנער. רופט זיך אויף איצט אפ מיט אייער ווארעמע גיכע הילף פאר אונזער ישיבה, ראטעוועט די בעריהמטע ישיבה "כנסת בית יצחק" פון אונטערגאנג ח"ו.

העלפט און ארגאניזירט הילף פאר די גרויסע ישיבה "כנסת בית יצחק".

Rabin B. B. Lejbowicz, ul Tartaki № 19

Drukarnia St. Lichtmachera, Wilno.

A famous Yeshiva appeals for support (1923) in Hebrew (right) and in Yiddish. 'Due to the unparalleled and horrible inflation which continues to grow from day to day...the Yeshiva is in danger of total collapse, God forbid...'

in thought, word, and deed, this in turn would have permitted that identity to disappear. Then, there would have been no point in saving some Egyptians from amongst the others.

A LOSS OF IDENTITY

The penetrating effect of external identifying features was brought out by a well-known explanation of the Rebbe of Varka: Rashi on *Chumash* relates that when the Amalakites attacked the Jews after Aharon's death (*Bamidbar* 21, 1), they pretended to be Canaanites by speaking their language, so as to confuse the Jews into praying ineffectively – for victory over 'Canaan'. The Jews, however, took note of their Amalekite costumes, and prayed for victory, without specifying over whom.

An obvious question arises here: Why couldn't the Amalekites render their stratagem foolproof by changing their dress, too? The answer: Had they done so, they would have, in truth, been Canaanites....

'Jewish identity' is very much 'in' these days; so much the better! But proclaiming one's Jewishness is a *goyish* tongue, through *goyish* methods, while looking like a *goy*, is self-contradictory and therefore self-defeating. The medium, yes, is the message.

It is a well-known axiom that *Klal Yisroel* is comparable to a long cord, wherein the slightest tug at one end affects the situation at the opposite end. Who knows but that the story of assimilation and intermarriage would be a different one, had *we* heeded the words of *Chazal*!

WHAT TO DO

Certainly, we must continue to reach out to our brothers and sisters, and in the only language they understand. This is the sacred duty of our generation. But there is nothing to keep us from throwing in *Lashon Kodesh* and Yiddish words whenever feasible – and let pedantic purism go to the winds. Lest this be seen as trivial and unimportant, consider, as just one instance, what happens to our intellectual and emotional perception of the *mitzva* when *nichum aveilim* is turned into a 'shiva call...' (It may also be *halachically* advisable to do so; see *Teshuvos Chasam Sofer Even Hoezer* II: 11.)

True, an entire generation of *bnei u'bnos Torah* has grown up having no working knowledge of Yiddish – and yes, which has attained heights of Torah and *yiras shomayim* to rival anyone's. Moreover, their English is distinctly colored by their Torah *chinuch* so that, in the long run, it may even evolve into a new Jewish language – thus following the pattern of other eras and places. In the meantime, however, those of us who do have a command of Yiddish must impart it to our children for all the above-cited reasons – reasons that cannot wait. So, *lema'an Hashem*, let us use spoken Yiddish in communicating with our children! (And while we are on the subject of language, let us also take care that our English accords with Torah. Obviously, I am not just referring to *nivul peh*, obscenities and slander, but to something more subtle and yet of great concern to us. For example, such expressions as 'this test was murder', 'the pain is killing me', and the like have no place on a Jewish tongue (*Shevuos* 36a). This is but one of several ways in which we must be on guard that our English not be de-Judaized.)

Above all, let us not be embarrassed to *want* to be ourselves and speak in our own tongue.

So, who indeed needs Yiddish?

A Yid.

1
יעקב גאָרדין
מירגאַראָד, אוקראַינע, 1853
ניו יאָרק, פֿאַר. שטאַטן, 1909

◆

מירעלע אפרת, (דראַמע)
דער ייִדישער קעניג ליר, (")
גאָט, מענטש און טייוול, (")
קרייצער סאָנאַטע, (דראַמע)

◆

דראַמאַטורג

2
שמעון־שמואל פֿרוג
באָבראַווי קוט, אוקר. 1860
אדעס, אוקראַינע, 1916

◆

פֿריילינגס לידער
זאַמד און שטערן
דאָס ליד פֿון אַרבעט
די פֿאַפֿירענע בריק

◆

פּאָעט

3
יהואָש
(שלמה בלומגאַרטען)
וואָרזשעבאָלאָוו, ליטע, 1871
ניו יאָרק, פֿאַר. שטאַטן, 1927

◆

ייִדיש - ביאור פֿון תנ"ך
לידער און פּאָעמען
פֿון ניריאָרק ביז רחובות
ייִדיש - ווערטערבוך

◆

פּאָעט,
תנ"ך און שפּראַך - פֿאָרשער

4
ה. לייוויק
(לייוויק האַלפּער)
איהומען, ווייס־רוסלאַנד, 1888
ניו־יאָרק, פֿאַר. שטאַטן, 1962

◆

סיבירער לידער
דער גולם, (דראַמע)
שאַפּ, (פּיעסע)
אין טרעבלינקע בין איך ניט
געווען, (לידער)

◆

פּאָעט, דראַמאַטורג, עסייאיסט

5
מאָריס ווינטשעווסקי
(בן־ציון נאָוואַכאָוויטש)
יאַנעווע, ליטע, 1856
ניו יאָרק, פֿאַר. שטאַטן, 1933

◆

קאַמפֿס - געזאַנגען
פֿאַבלעך, אַפֿאָריזמען, פֿאַראַ־
דיעס
דער משוגענער פֿילאָסאָף,
(אַרטיקלען)
דראַמען

◆

פּאָעט, עסייאיסט, דראַמאַטורג

6
דוד עדעלשטאַט
קאַלוגע, רוסלאַנד, 1866
ניו יאָרק, פֿאַר. שטאַטן, 1892

◆

העלדן און מאַרטירער, (לידער)
בילדער פֿון לעבן,
אָ, גוטער פֿריינד ווען איך וועל
שטאַרבן
מיין צוואה, (ליד).

◆

פּאָעט

1. Yankev Gordon, 1853–1909; Playwright; 2. Shimen-shmuel Frug, 1860–1916; Poet; 3. Yehoyesh, 1871–1927; Poet, Bible translator and language researcher; 4. H(ey) Leyvik, 1888–1962; Poet, playwright, essayist; 5. Moris Vintshevski, 1856–1933; Poet, essayist, playwright; 6. Dovid Edlshtat, 1866–1892; Poet.

1	2	3

1

יוסף באָװשאָװער

לובאַװיטש, אוקראַינע, 1873
ניו-יאָרק, פֿאַר. שטאַטן, 1915

———◆———

פֿאַנזיע און פֿראָזע
בילדער און געדאַנקען
לידער אָן געדיכטעטן
צום שקלאַף! (ליד)

———◆———

פּאָעט, דערצײלער

2

מאָריס ראָזענפֿעלד

דאָרף באָקשאַ, פּוילן, 1862
ניו-יאָרק, פֿאַר. שטאַטן, 1923

———◆———

אַרבעטער אין פֿרײהײט לידער
ליריק און סאַטירע
אַרטיקלען און פֿעליעטאָנען
נאַציאָנאַלע און פֿאָלקס-לידער

———◆———

פּאָעט

3

אברהם רייזען

קאָידאַנאָװ, װײַס־רוסלאַנד 1876
ניו־יאָרק, פֿאַר. שטאַטן, 1953

———◆———

העמערל, העמערל קלאַפּ, (ליד)
דער קראַנקער פֿינגער, (דערצ.)
אַ רויקע דירה, (אײנאַקטער)
עפּיזאָדען פֿון מײן לעבען

———◆———

פּאָעט, דערצײלער, עסײַיסט

4	5	6

4

דוד פּינסקי

מאָהילעװ, אוקראַינע, 1872
חיפֿה, מדינת ישראל, 1959

———◆———

אײזיק שעפֿטל, (פּיעסע)
יאַנקל דער שמיד, (פּיעסע)
דער אוצר, (פּיעסע)
דערצײלונגען

———◆———

דראַמאַטורג, דערצײלער

5

א. ליעסין

(אברהם װאַלט)

מינסק, װײַס־רוסלאַנד, 1872
ניו־יאָרק, פֿאַר. שטאַטן, 1938

———◆———

לידער און פּאָעמען
זכרונות און בילדער
יהודה המכבי, (ליד)
הירש לעקערט, (ליד)

———◆———

פּאָעט

6

לעאָן קאָברין

װיטעבסק, װײַס־רוסלאַנד, 1872
ניו־יאָרק, פֿאַר. שטאַטן, 1946

———◆———

דער דאָרפֿס־יונג, (דראַמע)
אימיגראַנטען, (ראָמאַן)
ערינערונגען פֿון אַ יידישן
דראַמאַטורג
פֿון אַ ליטװיש שטעטל, (דערצ.)

———◆———

דראַמאַטורג,
ראָמאַניסט, דערצײלער

1. Yoysef Bovshover, 1873–1915; Poet, writer of short stories; 2. Moris Roznfeld, 1862–1923; Poet; 3. Avrom Reyzn, 1876–1953; Poet, writer of short stories, essayist; 4. Dovid Pinski, 1872–1959; Playwright, writer of short stories; 5. A. Lyesin, 1872–1938; Poet; 6. Leon Kobrin, 1872–1946; Playwright, novelist, writer of short stories.

Sounds of Modern Orthodoxy:
The Language of Talmud Study

S. C. HEILMAN

The speaking of language is...a form of life.
LUDWIG WITTGENSTEIN

Three principles underlie the logic of what follows in this paper. First, human culture and language are in an inherent dialectical relationship with each other. As Peter Berger writes: 'Men invent a language and then find that its logic imposes itself upon them' (Berger 1970: 374). Second, religious outlook is woven into that relationship. Thus, according to Max Weinreich, 'variations in religion may be said to occasion some separateness in culture which, in turn, leaves its mark in the form of language differences' (1980: 392). The third principle is drawn from the work of Erving Goffman. It maintains that the use of language in human interaction provides 'evidence to suggest a functional relationship between the structure of the self and the structure of spoken interaction' (1967: 36).

Building upon these principles, this paper examines the language of those who share the religious, cultural, and personal outlook of modern American Orthodox Judaism. As I have suggested elsewhere (Heilman 1976), these people shift between the modern, secular, cosmopolitan world and the Orthodox, religious, parochial one. Since they ease their alternation by compartmentalizations and reinterpretations or conceptual compromises, one would accordingly expect their language use to echo and abet this movement. This paper aims to demonstrate that such indeed is the case, to elucidate the process, and, in so doing, to shed further light upon the character of American modern Orthodoxy.

THE RESEARCH SETTING

Although there are various social contexts of modern Orthodox life which might yield the necessary information, one in particular is most revealing: the modern

Orthodox Talmud class. Here, in a relatively intimate atmosphere, the time-honored ideas and discussions of the Talmud are translated – both linguistically and conceptually – into the vernacular. In the process, one may discover the cultural and religious influences upon those who are engaged in the study.

In order to understand the social factors in language selection and use, I spent several years as a participant observer in a Talmud class held one evening a week in a suburban, New York, modern Orthodox synagogue. Over the years the number of participants was between eight and ten men, ranging in age from the early thirties (the largest number) to the seventies. These men neatly fit the model of cosmopolitan-parochial, modern Orthodox Jew; they hold strong attachments to the parochial world of Orthodoxy while pursuing a course of life which weds them to the modern American, cosmopolitan milieu. The very attempt to live an Orthodox life while living in a community with few Orthodox institutions and relatively few Orthodox Jews is some indication of the marginal character of their existence. Moreover, while all have had an extensive Jewish education, most have had a college education or beyond, further indicating an immersion in the world outside the Jewish one. Of the ten regular students, three are physicians, one is a businessman, one a shopkeeper, one an art teacher in the public schools, one is in real estate, one a dentist, one a pensioner, and I am an academic. The rabbi who leads the class was ordained by a traditional Orthodox seminary and comes from a family replete with rabbis. Significantly, he also holds a doctorate in education from a major American university, a fact stressed in his title, Rabbi, Doctor.... Finally, although the rabbi and four of the students are immigrants, they, like the other class members, see themselves as *American* Jews for whom English is the accepted language of everyday speech.

I occasionally recorded the audio portion of the class sessions on a small cassette tape recorder. Ironically, this practice was instituted by another student who wanted the tapes to help him review the class material at home. I later made use of his tapes. By the time I began to record, the presence of a tape recorder was no longer an obtrusive element in the setting.

The tapes enabled me to examine more closely the shifts in the language of Talmud study: the shifts between the language of the text and translation and between the speech associated with study and the inevitable digressions occurring during a typical class (cf. Heilman 1976: 233–237). The discussion below grows in large measure out of what the tapes revealed, and I shall later quote from them at length.

THE TALMUD AND THE JEWS

The Talmud, or as it is alternately called *gemore*[1] or *shas*, is regularly studied as

---

1. The orthography used throughout these pages is one that has been standard since 1936. Estab-   lished in the YIVO Institute for Jewish Research and accepted by the Library of Congress, this

part of the ritual and religious life of all Orthodox Jews. 'Without mastery of Talmud, one must be considered as having received an elementary education at best since it is only via the Talmud that one is introduced to the complexities of Orthodox Jewish law and its regulation of every aspect of individual and group life' (Fishman 1965a: 58). '*Lernen*' Jewish study, is the eternal preoccupation which the Orthodox Jews have had with the Jewish book in general and the Talmud in particular. As Max Weinreich puts it, '*lernen* is a lifelong activity...And the maximum of *lernen* is desirable' (1980: 440, 452). So much so has the study of Talmud become a part of Jewish life that the term *derekh hashas*, literally 'the way of the Talmud', was used by Jews for generations to designate their way of life. In this way of life, no sphere of existence was considered beyond the boundary of religion. There were details but no trifles; and hence nothing was irrelevant to Talmudic concern.

The Talmud, a compilation of divinely revealed and rabbinically debated 'Oral Law' transmitted over generations, demands unending study for reasons logical and theological. In the first case, one needs to repeat the words of Talmud to know details of the law in order to act properly. In the second case, as a divinely inspired document, the Talmud is subject to the sacred repetition and study that all such books are endowed with in Judaism. For both these reasons, the Talmud became a document whose every word and idea, however difficult they might be, must be understood. In the final analysis such understanding demands continual study, but in any case it demands simple translation.

The translation of divine precepts into tractates of law resulted in a document whose language is a combination of tongues and replete with loanwords. The *mishna*, the nucleus of the Talmud, was redacted and arranged around the year 200 C.E. It contains the legal codification of the Oral Law and is essentially in Hebrew. The *gemore*, consisting of discussions and elaborations of the *mishna* by the rabbis who lived in Israel and Babylonia between the third and sixth centuries, is divided into two sections – *halakha* (law) and *aggadetta* (lore). In the Babylonian Talmud, which is longer and more influential in the tradition, the text is in Hebrew and Aramaic, the vernacular among the Babylonian Jews. It also contains loanwords from Greek, although these are all transliterated into Hebrew characters. The nearly mandatory commentaries of Rashi, the eminent French-Jewish exegete, and the Tosafot, his kin and disciples, added between the eleventh and fourteenth centuries, are in Hebrew and Aramaic. They also contain elements of the vernacular of the day, primarily Loez – a sort of proto-Yiddish – and Old French.

Around the sixteenth century, Yiddish became the accepted language of

orthography is elaborated upon in Uriel Weinreich's *Yiddish Dictionary*. All letters are sounded. Special note should be made of 'ey' which is sounded like *ey* in '*grey*', 'ay' which is sounded like *i* in '*fine*', and 'kh' like *ch* in '*Bach*'. Although standard only for Yiddish, I have used it for all words using Hebrew letters.

Talmudic discussion and legal disputation among the Ashkenazim, Jews of central and Western Europe whose descendants centuries later would settle in America in the greatest numbers (M. Weinreich 1980: Mark 1954). For the next four centuries, Yiddish remained the primary language of Talmud study. In the twentieth century, when even the Orthodox Jews learned to speak English in America and Hebrew in Israel, the latter languages have begun to supplant Yiddish as the dominant languages of Talmud study.

One might think that the sixteenth century use of Yiddish represented a precedent-setting effort to translate the language of the Talmud into a vernacular all could comprehend – a necessary feature for a people who saw study as an eternal religious and ritual responsibility. However, a closer examination reveals that from its very beginnings the 'Oral Law', which forms the basis of Talmud, incorporated within it the vernacular. Thus, when the Jewish people were in Israel, as they were in Mishnaic times, the text was predominantly Hebrew. When they were exiled to Babylonia, the language of study and debate, as captured in the *gemore* text, became Aramaic – although Hebrew, the 'holy tongue' remained in secondary use. When Jews moved to Europe, Yiddish, a distinct language evolving out of the interference between Hebrew and the indigenous languages and dialects of the region – Loez and Old French, among the most prominent – became the dominant language of Talmud study. Although the Hebrew and Aramaic of the written text remained part of the *lernen* in the form of a recitation, increasingly the latter was followed with a Yiddish translation and discussion. Those Jews who sought and learned to speak in the non-Jewish languages of the area (e.g. German, French, Polish, and Russian) were also ones who generally ceased Talmud study as they ceased all active association with religious matters, and thus these languages generally did not become integrated into the study process except as loanwords which made their way into Yiddish.

Today, in America and in Israel, English and Hebrew (once again), the new vernaculars of a growing number of Jews involved in the study of Talmud, have begun to take greater roles in *lernen* (Fishman 1965a: 59). Yet, Talmud students still recite the Hebrew and Aramaic, while Yiddish phrases, loanwords, syntax, inflection, and intonation become part of the English[2] in ways that are elucidated below.

Thus both the history of the Talmud's evolution and its study manifest a kind of 'supplementary syncretism', wherein prior linguistic elements are incorporated into the current mode (Burger 1966: 103–115). The effect, however, is such that both the prior as well as the contemporary linguistic elements are modified in the process.

2. Although there is some evidence to suggest that among those who study Talmud in Hebrew the same residual influence of Yiddish obtains, the present discussion is based upon research among predominantly English speakers and will therefore concentrate upon them.

Generally, the syncretism has come about through constant translation which – after an oral recitation (more precisely, cantillation) of the text – is the first step of *lernen*. Translation, however, is more than the simple replacement of one word or phrase in one language for its equivalent in another. It requires a penetration of the original 'verbal envelope' of the message and a repacking of it in terms that make sense in another *communication system* (Vološinov 1971: 165). This may call not only for a *semantic extension of meaning*, wherein new interpretations are added to the original meaning of a lexical unit, but also *conceptual transformation*, wherein an ideal meaningful in one culture and expressed through its language is supplanted by a similar but not identical idea in another culture simply because the latter has no exact lexical parallel to the former. In the case of Talmud study in English translation has often meant extending and transforming a 'meaning directly related to Jewishness to another related to the world in general' (Weinreich 1980: 494).

Where the material evokes an emotional charge, translation may also require an *expressive repetition*, wherein the speaker tries to communicate the original emotion through intonational patterns which make sense to those who need the translation. Such intonation constitutes 'a shade of meaning added to or superimposed upon...intrinsic lexical meaning' (Pike 1947: 21). Intonation contours, are, however, indigenous to each language and the culture of its users. Consequently, because 'no language uses a pure monotone', translation often raises intonational difficulties as well (Pike 1947: 20).

As Dorothy Henderson, in her sociological examination of language, sums it all up: 'It is clearly the case that all cultures or subcultures are realized through communication forms which contain their own, unique, imaginative and aesthetic possibilities' (Henderson 1970). This linguistic distinctiveness creates complex problems for translators, and especially amateur metaphrasts like most Talmud students, who must switch from one language and intonation contour to another or several others.

At the same time, however, these very problems of language choice, use, and intonation embedded in the process of *lernen* serve as a rich source of sociological and psychological information about the speaker and his linguistic community. All communities provide their members with a set of linguistic resources and a lexical and intonational repertoire (which an outsider may discover over time as he is exposed to speakers from the same group). Moreover, 'language is both the foundation and instrumentality of the social construction of reality' (Berger 1970: 376). Hence, the choices a speaker makes in any given speech situation reveal a great deal about the group with which he identifies himself and about the speaker himself. His ultimate choices, from the range of open alternatives, can be used as a behavioral index of the speaker's group preferences, except in the case of the speaker – immigrant or neophyte of one sort or another – who involuntarily utilizes old forms of communication because he is incapable of carrying on in the new ones he would otherwise choose. Normally, however, each language and intonational choice identifies the speaker with a particular group to which he belongs or may wish to belong and from which he seeks acceptance (Fishman 1965b: 68).

Not only does speech reveal group preference and reference, it also discloses the speaker's 'state of mind', which is made up of 'all of the relevant contextual information, linguistic and non-linguistic, that the language user needs when carrying on communicative activity (Yngve 1970: 567). Indeed a person's (or group's) talk over a long period of time 'is a record of the means by which that person [or group] tries to achieve, maintain, relieve, or avoid certain intrapsychic states through the verbal management of his [or its] relations with his [or its] social environment' (Soskin 1963: 229). In terms of the concerns here, the problems of language choice and intonation in Talmud study's translation process study reveal that for the students, in some measure, 'what shapes language…is the preoccupation of their minds' (M. Weinreich 1968: 398, n.25).

In the modern Orthodox Talmud class, the language use illustrates the particular preoccupation of this group: its cosmopolitan parochialism, or cultural dualism. Perhaps more boldly than in any other linguistic situation, the class's language intonation contour, syntax, and translation process reveal the way in which the speakers have come to terms with their Jewishness and their American cosmopolitanism.

LERNEN

As practiced in the class studied, *lernen* consisted of the rabbi's reading of the Talmud text, translating it into English, Yiddish or combinations thereof, reading the commentaries of Rashi and occasionally the Tosafot, and translating them in like fashion. Interspersed with the translation and often indistinguishable from it were explanations and exemplifications of the text's significance. Exemplification often required not only an expressive repetition of text contents but also a sort of dramatic enacting of the text in language that was socially and psychologically meaningful to the students.

Thus, for example, one section of text studied describes a man who, while passing through a marketplace, finds a bill of divorcement. The bill lists as correspondents a man and woman with names identical to his and his wife's. He decides on impulse to make use of that document for himself (in contradiction to the law which requires him to have one expressly written for him and his wife). The teacher translates the text into English and Yiddish and then puts into the mouth of the man in question a metatextual monologue which makes the latter sound like a thoroughly modern man: 'Hey, here's a *get* (bill of divorcement) with my name and Janey's. Why don't I use it'? Throughout, the language and cadence of these metatextual remarks which are being used for illustrative and explanatory purposes are distinctly English, lacking the characteristic rise–fall contour of Yiddish (cf. U. Weinreich 1956: 633–643). Moreover, the setting of the marketplace in which the document is found and the circumstances of its discovery are also described in terms that make sense in the contemporary world and can thus be visualized by the modern student.

As the one who reads the text and offers the preliminary translations, explanations and illustrations, the rabbi is the dominant speaker, but the students often add to the class by offering alternative explanations and translations as well as different illustrations. Moreover, they often ask questions about the text or topic, frequently anticipating questions that the text will raise later and thereby signifying their ability to follow precisely the essential point of the text. As such they too add to the language setting.

LANGUAGE CHOICE AND LANGUAGE SHIFT

Because the text is in Hebrew and Aramaic, languages with which most of the students in the class like other Orthodox Jews have some familiarity, and because the discussion of it is in English and Yiddish and combinations thereof, the participants in this class must generally be considered to be polyglots or multilinguals. As moderns, however, their common and everyday language is English, a tongue in which all of them are fluent. Given the choice of any language, all would in the course of normal conversation use English. In the Talmud class, however, such linguistic exclusivity is out of the question, if for no other reason than that the text must be recited. Accordingly, one might say as the situation or purpose of activity (i.e. reading or explaining) changes, so does language.

One might also say that as content shifts so does language.[3] 'A language shift may be defined as the change from the habitual use of one language to that of another' (U. Weinreich 1953: 68). The languages in contact, those used alternately by the same persons, are essentially Hebrew, Aramaic, Yiddish, and English. In addition to the shifts between these various languages there is also phonemic, syntactic, and intonational interference. In the course of a typical class I observed, the language may become so fraught with shifts and interference as to suggest an argot all its own. The notion of a group developing its own special language or argot is one that Arnold van Gennep pointed to long ago when he asserted the principle that: 'The linguistic situation of each language will depend upon the social situation of the group which speaks it' (1908: 328). Moreover, he went on to point out, the more a group is 'organized around a special sacred activity, the more its special language is so organized as well, to

3. Although this is stated in the reverse by S. Ervin-Tripp (1964), the correlation between content and language is the *primary* issue here – and *that* is *not* in question.

the point of sometimes being a veritable argot outside of general usage...' (1908: 329). The sacred and religious character of Talmud study would thus perfectly fit this description, and the particular language of the class should therefore come as no surprise.

The argot serves in some measure as an exclusionary device which helps guarantee that the group will remain relatively homogeneous and at least linguistically protected against the intrusion of heterogeneous elements. Indeed, the surest way for an outsider to signal his presence is through his inability to shift language along with the others in the class, his inability to speak combinations of Yiddish and English or even to understand them, and his faulty intonational contour. Thus, in a very definite way, the argot of the Talmud class serves to distinguish its members as Orthodox Jews, something which their command of English, dress, occupation, education, and residence does not do as clearly. That all of this social marking is done in the absence of outsiders is characteristic of modern Orthodox Jews who choose to privately express their Orthodoxy without publicly (i.e. in the presence of outsiders) endangering their association with modernity.

In any event, the language shifting becomes so frequent as to be taken for granted and becomes unconscious both to the interlocutors, senders and receivers of communication, and the audience, those others present who are not the primary addressees but who nonetheless follow the talk. So much so is this the case that, for example, during one class, as he frequently does, the rabbi stopped in mid-sentence and asked one of the students, 'How ya' doin? By the way, do you understand Yiddish?' only to receive the reply, 'Fine, I thought you were speaking English'.

The literature on language switching among bilinguals described five frequent circumstances of such switching: (1) when an imperfect bilingual tries to turn the conversation to the language in which he is more proficient; (2) when entering or leaving a conversation and setting; (3) when making a direct quotation in another language, that is in reported speech; (4) under the stimulus of a loanword because there is no satisfactory equivalent in the dominant language of the conversation; and finally, (5) when the conversation turns to a topic associated by the speaker with the other language. Additionally, language switching may be used as a rhetorical device where the speaker chooses to emphasize a statement by repeating it in more than one language (common among Yiddish speakers and possibly derived from biblical Hebrew which uses repetition in this way), where he wants to contrast two statements, where he wishes to make a parenthetical remark, or where he wishes to speak of taboo words or topics (Rayfield 1970: 56–57, 155–156). Speakers may also switch language in the presence of those whom they perceive as outsiders in order to exclude those outsiders from understanding and to assure their own differentiation.

Traditionally Talmud students developed their own argot in the course of their study, thereby trying to distinguish themselves from lower status, less learned Jews. 'But the prestige of the students was so high in the society that everyone wanted to be among them or at least their equal as far as possible', so the argot of Talmud study became integrated into the special linguistic style of the entire Ashkenazic Jewish community. Additionally, the entire linguistic

"The Sale of Joseph," Purim play,
Matz Publication House, Vilna

"מכירת יוסף", הצגת־פורים, הוצאת־ספרים מץ, וילנה

„Продажа Иосифа", Пурим-шпиль, изда-
тельство Маца, Вильна

1908

'Joseph's meeting with his brothers, with sweet words and exquisite songs, to sing on Purim with a wine goblet in your hand, in every town and in every land.'

community seemed to adopt 'the Talmudic chant, the habit of answer *why not?* to a question that began with *why?*' as is so characteristic both of the text and its elaboration (M. Weinreich 1980: 472–473).

For all the circumstances of language switching, in the final analysis one must conclude, as did Uriel Weinreich, that 'there are no strictly linguistic motivations in language shifts' (1967: 1). Rather, the roots of switching may be understood in social and psychological terms. The speaker may wish to appear as a member of the local, parochial community on some occasions while identifying with more cosmopolitan values on another, and he can accomplish this transformation in great measure through the medium of language switching. Even where certain spheres of activity are dominated by one language rather than another, the socially and psychologically motivated switcher may nonetheless use the language of his choice to make a statement indirectly about himself and his identity. Thus, for example, he may choose to phrase a medieval Talmudic tale in English, using syntax and intonation, in order to stress the tale's contemporary relevance and applicability; or vice versa, phrasing a contemporary matter in Yiddish with Hebrew or Aramaic loanwords in the distinctive rise–fall cadence that characterizes Talmudic chant, thereby asserting the matter's Jewish character.

THE GROUNDS FOR SWITCHING

In light of the previous general discussion, one might say that, although the circumstances of language switching in the Talmud class conform to the broad rules outlined for code-switching, there are specific explanations which provide insight into the particular character of modern Orthodox switching. In order to arrive at these explanations, however, one needs a clearer idea of the grounds for switching.

To begin, a 'speaker in any language community who enters diverse social situations normally has a repertoire of speech alternatives which shift with the situation' (Ervin-Tripp 1964: 197). Where the speaker is multilingual, and especially where the situation allows (e.g. when there are other multilinguals present with whom he can speak a variety of languages), this repertoire is accordingly enlarged. Given such an array of choice, each language is, in a sense, in competition with the other, and its being chosen represents an indirect victory for the community in which that language is dominant.

Specifically, in the case of the languages in use during the Talmud class, one might suggest that use of Hebrew, Aramaic, and Yiddish – all languages formed in and generated by the Jewish community – represents a victory by that community in its capture of the speaker. Contradistinctively, use of English (along with its syntax, intonation, etc.) represents a victory for the English speaking community, America.

Further, speech that is a combination of all languages represents a stalemate or cultural compromise. The speaker using a language mix indirectly identifies himself with both communities. To discover the precise mechanics and nuance of this compromise, however, one needs to look more closely at the process of switching.

Certain code variations in the Talmud class can be easily explained. These are what J. J. Gumperz calls, 'superposed varieties of speech', such as occupational argots and language indigenous to a particular activity (Ervin-Tripp 1968: 197). The Talmud class uses many such expressions which come from the text. Here I may quote from my previous work on this matter:

The Talmud in its text makes use of shorthand terms for various of its conceptualizations. Such terms act as representations of complex Judaic legal arguments. When translated literally, they make little or no sense, since they are usually composed of key words of the argument. Although these words could be translated into English abstractions, to do so would destroy their codical and referent qualities. Moreover, such efforts are intellectually gratuitous, since they often obliterate important nuances of meaning in the interests of coining some pithy neologism. Accordingly, such terms remain untranslated. For example, in the sentence '*Hasholayach es ha kayn* is the principle working here', the first words refer to a legal principle which mandates one to chase away a mother bird from a next before taking away her eggs. The words themselves make little sense if literally translated. However, they act as simple referents to the complex argument of which they are the opening words. In much the same way as a pope's encyclical may be referred to by its opening words, so certain legal and talmudic principles become epigrammatized (Heilman 1976: 231).

In addition to such mandatory code variations, there are the switches that come from the interspersing of explanation with textual cantillation. Strictly speaking, such recitation constitutes switching, although the switch is governed by very formal rules governing it. Still, as the examples will later make clear, recitation may become expressive repetition and thereby integrated into the discussion and explanation of the text. In this case, it will have to be accounted for differently. Where a speaker uses the text's language as his own, one must assume that at least to some degree he is willing to identify himself with or through the text and its viewpoint.

Topic switches constitute another ground for code variation:

The implication of topical regulation of language choice is that certain topics are somehow handled better in one language than in another in particular multilingual contexts...Thus, some multilingual speakers may 'acquire the habit' of speaking about topic x in language X partially because that is the language in which they were *trained* to deal with this topic..., partially because *they (and their interlocutors)* may *lack the specialized terms* for a satisfying discussion of x in language Y, partially because language Y itself may currently lack as exact or as many terms for handling topic x as those currently possessed by language X, and partially because it is considered strange or inappropriate to discuss x in language Y (Fishman 1965b: 71).

Normally, speakers indicate that they know they have made a topic shift, that they have changed the manifest content or referent of speech. When only one language is in use such shifts are marked by what Goffman calls 'weak bridges', expressions like 'oh, by the way' (1976: 267, n.11). Uriel Weinreich notes as well the marking accomplished 'by special voice modifications (slight pause, change in tempo, and the like) in speech' (1953: 83). In multilingual situations, all these markings may obtain, but in addition there is the assertive and unmistakable sign of the different language in use.

Perhaps an illustration from the Talmud class can be helpful here. The following interchange occurred during a one minute digression from the text. The stimulus for the digression had been a phrase in the text in which the Emperor Vespasian is quoted as asking the great sage Rabbi Yokhanan ben Zakkai, who had just come to him from out of the besieged city of Jerusalem to ask for mercy, why he had not come earlier. The phrasing of Vespasian's question is: '*Ad ho idno a may lo osis le gaboy*'?[4]

Now the digression begins:

R: Amongst Hasidim it's supposedly Reb Aron Karliner, one of the *gdoley khasidus*, one of the giants of our hasidic world, who used to on Rosh Hashono (pause) go before the *omed*. And the story comes back that one year (pause) as he approached the *omed* (pause) to say '*hamelekh*' (pause) he went into a faint (pause) and he actually fainted (pause), and it took quite a to-do to revive him (pause). And when they revived him, he was speechless (pause). And the whole *besmedresh* [house of study (and prayer)], and the whole spirit of the holiday (long pause) – What's with the rebee? What happened? *Hamelekh*? (pause). He says he approached there *lifney melekh malkhey hamlokhim, ot zokh zikh dermant di gemore:* '*eey malko ano*', *oyb ikh bin take got, ikh bin di melekh malkhey hamlokhim* [before the King of all Kings, he reminded himself of the Talmud, 'if I am a King', if I am indeed God, I am the King of all Kings], *ad...*

H: Why did you not come be...

R: '*Ad ho idno a may lo osis le gaboy*', *vus varts di a gans yor*, why didn't you come before now?

There are various sorts of code variations here, including loanwords and superposed varieties of speech, particularly those which name what Max Weinreich (1980: 404) called 'concepts of concrete Jewishness' (the words *omed* [lectern], *besmedresh* [house of study]). There are also referential terms deriving from liturgy. Included here is *hamelekh* (the King), the opening word of the morning prayers with which the cantor begins the service. Additionally, there are the special and traditional names of God which are not commonly translated and could be considered either as a loanword or one that is superposed: *melekh malkhey hamlokhim* (the King of all Kings).

By far, however, the most significant language switch occurs when the topic switches back from a description of the episode of Reb Aron Karliner to a gloss and explanation of the original Talmud text. Here there is a switch into Yiddish, Hebrew, English, interfered versions of each, and, finally, a reversion into the

---

4. To distinguish quoted text from other words, I will surround all such excerpts with quotation marks. When foreign words or phrases are not followed in the utterance by literal translations or are not translated in the ensuing discussion, I will provide such a translation in brackets following the first appearance of the foreign material.

text. And when one of the members of the class, H, tries to translate the phrase from the text into English, he is cut off as the speech is recited first in the original Aramaic (*ad ho idno a may lo osis le gaboy*), followed by a Yiddish gloss (*vus varts di a gans yor* [why have you been waiting for a whole year]) which refers back to the original tale about Reb Aron Karliner, and then finally closed with an English translation of the text.

While H has tried to skip the shift back to the text and keep the whole matter in English, the rabbi who is not only telling the story but who seeks to use it to teach the meaning of the Talmud cuts off this effort by staying in the Aramaic, glossing in Yiddish and thereby rhetorically emphasizing the Jewish character of this episode, and only in the end reverting to English to complete the tale. The Aramaic and Yiddish emphasize solidarity with the text and the Jewish people, while the English leaves the story in the domain of the English speaker, the modern American. It is as if the narrator here was finally overcome by the Jewishness of his story and could no longer hear himself tell it in words other than those associated with the Jewish community.

In a sense the language shifting here is a means of bracketing the Jewishly oriented activity. It represents an instance of 'embedding', a process in which speech of another is reported in its original form and where the reporting is done by means of 'expressive repetition', repeating the words in the manner in which they presumably were originally spoken. Through the language switch one enters fully into the Jewish *domain*.

Were this, however, simply a case of reported speech, the Yiddish gloss would be absent, since the text in the Talmud was not in Yiddish. Moreover, no actual speech is really being reported here but rather an emotion is being put into the terms of the Talmud and Jewish experience. Accordingly, one may conclude that what has happened here is an effort to merge text, Jewishness (as expressed in the Yiddish), and contemporary sense (as signified by the English), precisely the sort of synthesis that is characteristic of modern Orthodoxy which seeks to blend Judaism (faith), Jewishness (parochial ethnicity), and cosmopolitanism.

One last note is in order. I remarked earlier that this speech contained language interference. In intonation contour there can be no question of this fact, since the English which normally does not have a rise–fall cadence characteristic of Yiddish is here being spoken in rise–fall cadence (cf. Pike 1947; U. Weinreich 1956; and Rayfield 1970). The combination of English language and Yiddish intonation contour is, one might suggest, an example of cultural compromise – again a characteristic of modern Orthodoxy.

There are also Yiddish syntactical structures, the most obvious of these being: 'And the story comes back that one year', which is clearly a construction much more at home in Yiddish than in English. The interference results in an unusual English phrase.

Finally, there is the English morphological structure. The word *rebe* which refers to a Hasidic leader has become 'rebee', thus containing morphology which is far more American than the word *rebe*. Here too one discovers the compromise so much a part of modern Orthodox Jewish existence.

These conclusions raise some important questions. If indeed code variation and interference mark the particular cultural dualism and compromise characteristic of Orthodoxy, why do modern Orthodox Jews not always speak in this polyglottal way? One might answer simply that in great measure they do. The syntax and cadence of their speech is filled with interferences from the various languages of their lives. Indeed, one might suggest that through a process of cultural exosmosis the American Jews, and most particularly the New York variety, many of whom once talked this way, have infused American, and especially New York, English with some of the vocabulary, syntax, and cadence of their multilingualism.[5]

Beyond this sort of a simplistic answer, one must note that language choice and switching is also grounded in situational factors; that is, not only topic change accounts for shift, but situational change also does so. Simply defined a situational shift is one which occurs, 'when within the same setting the participants' definition of the social event changes [and] this change [is] signalled among others by linguistic clues' (Blom and Gumperz 1972: 424).

In the case of the Talmud class situational factors may account for switching. We have already seen how, in spite of H's effort to avoid a switch from English to Aramaic and Yiddish, the situation of the class forced him to acquiesce in the switch. One might go further and suggest that, in general, the situation of *lernen* fosters and demands linguistic flexibility and switching to the extent that even those who speak an otherwise essentially faultless English find themselves speaking in a multilingual manner during the course of the class (cf. Heilman 1976: 230). One simply learns that *lernen* calls for its own multilingual argot. Those who fail to make such switches are either neophytes, outsiders, or rebels.

There is a qualification that must be made here. Alternative definitions of the situation may occur within the same setting. In the Talmud class this may be understood when one realizes that for some members the class is essentially a teaching experience, for some a religious one, for others an opportunity to identify themselves with the sacred community of Jewish scholars, for others a chance to meet with friends, for others an opportunity for field research, and so on. Each of these varying definitions of the situation may manifest itself in linguistic terms. Thus the field researcher, emphasizing his marginality may speak in ways that signal that status, an emphasis on English with English morphology, syntax, cadence, and the like. The sacred scholar may infuse his speech with a variety of Hebraisms and other elements of the holy tongue; and so on for each participant. Indeed, in my observations, I discovered just this sort

5. L. M. Feinsilver (1956) has, for example, reported on the plethora of Yiddish words – 'hutzpa' being perhaps the best known – which have infiltrated American English.

of variation in the language use by the various participants. Nevertheless, what united them was a multilingualism which the *lernen* situation, as supported by the rabbi/teacher, forced upon them. Some were predisposed to fewer cases of code variation and some to more, but all did some switching.

Although among Jews who sought to become acculturated to American life and society, English became the 'prestige-language' and preferred, Orthodox Jews generally held on to Yiddish and Hebrew as an antidote to the threat of what Irving Howe has called 'religio-ethnic abandonment' (Rayfield 1970: 95). That holding action eventually evolved into synthetic forms – interlanguage – under the tremendous acculturative pressures of American life. Through the schools, in the streets, and at work Jews learned to speak English, and through it some of the ways of America. Even the most isolationist Orthodox Jews[6] found that the dominant American culture interfered, at the very least linguistically, with Jewish life (cf. Joffe 1943: 601–602).

Modern Orthodox Jews generally associate the Yiddish and Hebrew dominated interlanguage of their more traditional brethren with a manifest parochialism and concomitant lower social status which they, as moderns, eschew. Accordingly, in their everyday discourse and outside the environment where Jewish life is dominant, many adopt the speech patterns of their particular American milieu.

The controlling factor in speech pattern is 'the socio-psychological sense of *reference group membership*' (Fishman 1965b: 68). However, at the same time that the modern Orthodox Jew may in public, outside the synagogue and away from the Orthodox Jewish domain, seek to identify himself with the outside culture, accomplishing this aim at least in part through his speech, he may in the Jewish environment 'employ dialect...to signal his Jewishness to other Jews', or his Orthodoxy to other Orthodox (Dubb 1977: 56). When these worlds overlap, when, for example, he is with Orthodox Jews with whom he wishes to assert some modicum of solidarity at the same time that he wishes to demonstrate his Americanism, he may *in the linguistic sphere* revert to a highly nuanced form of interlanguage, often using only intonational signals rather than the more obvious lexical ones.

The degree to which modern Orthodox Jews continue to strive to signal their simultaneous reference group membership in American and Jewish society is displayed boldly in the Talmud class. Here repeated efforts are made to translate all matters into English and American cultural sense wherever possible, yet at

---

6. Consider for example the following, spoken by a Hasidic rabbi in which he explained the character of his highly isolationist community. 'When we have free time we're sitting in the synagogue learning Torah' (N.Y. Times, May 26, 1978). The language is English and all that remains of the Jewish world is content and a calque or loan translation. Here the calque 'learning Torah', is in fact an interfered version of the Yiddish '*lernen Toyre*'. The interference becomes immediately apparent when one realizes that the construction 'learning Torah' really makes no sense in English where the phrase would more properly be 'studying the Torah'.

the same time the linguistic nexus with Judaism is assiduously maintained. The latter is accomplished through textual recitation, Yiddish translation, and interlanguage. An example is in order.

Much is going on in the following two minute and eighteen second speech event. I wish primarily to focus upon the effort to maintain linguistic ties with both the Jewish and English-speaking societies. This remains the social and psychological motive – whether conscious or not – which seems to explain much of the language choice.

The selection quoted within this extract comes from a section of text which is *aggadetta* (lore), describing an encounter between Abba Sikra and Yokhanan ben Zakkai. The teacher begins with an identification of the characters involved.

> *R:* Abba Sikra who was head, one of the heads of the *biryoni*, the *biryoni* were a group of fanatics or...
>
> *S:* Zealots
>
> *R:* ...people, zealots who refused to take leadership, a peaceful resolve on the basis of the
> 5 spiritual leaders of Israel. Instead they decided, and they forced the issue, to bring about a war between the besiegers as against the inhabitants of the holy land, of *Yerushalayim* [Jerusalem], by burning down all the storehouses of food and forcing the siege to reach the point that the people can't hold out and they have to go do battle.
> In any case, one of their leaders was Abba Sikra. And Abba Sikra turns out to be no less
> 10 than a nephew of *Reb* Yokhanan ben Zakkai.
> *Hertzoch ayn, haynt az men hert a mol a rebe hot epes a mishpokhe vos er iz nisht azoy* hoo-ha-ha *makht men* shh! *Bald zogt men do* [listen to this, today when one hears of a rabbi who has something of a family which is not so hoo-ha-ha one says shh! Presently it says here]; 'Abba Sikra *reysh biryoni*', the whole *tsore-makher e' geveyn* a nephew, a son of a daughter (sic) [text
> 15 says 'sister'] (pause)
>
> *H:* Yeah, but he wasn't a, he wasn't a (pause) a gangster, he was a...
>
> *R:* On this point he was willing to listen to Yokhanan ben Zakkai, But basically, if somebody becomes a general amongst vagabonds, amongst brigands, eh, he must have earned his title as such.
>
> 20 *H:* He wasn't even a vagabond amongst, amongst brigands. He was a leader of the...
>
> *R:* ...'Biryoni.'
>
> *H:* Of the...
>
> *R:* *Shteyt dokh*, '*Reysh biryoni hava.*' [But it says, 'He was the head of the *biryoni*.']
>
> *H:* Meyer Kahane. Something like Meyer Kahane, *nu* not necessarily the, the *loshn* brigands
> 25 (pause). He was a, he was a nationalist, eh...
>
> *R:* The *khazal gebn zogn* [rabbis say] dis *az zey hobn ongebrengen dem khurbn* [that they brought on the destruction]...
>
> *H:* That's right, no question about it.
>
> *R:* Alright, *shoyn.*
>
> 30 *H:* But it's not necessarily that he was a, he was a robber or stealing money.
>
> *R:* *Ober dos vort* [but this word] '*biryoni*' is (*iz*) a very negative term.
>
> *H:* (softly) Yah.
>
> *R:* 'Biryoni'
>
> *H:* He wasn't...
>
> 35 *S:* ...a *bulgan* [ruffian]...
>
> *H:* ...stealing money.
>
> *R:* What? (to S.)

> *S:* A *bulgan.*
> *R:* I like your word better.
> 40 *H:* He wasn't robbing money; he wasn't stealing money (pause).
> *R:* Na, no. No!
> *H:* He was a...
> *R:* No, they had their ideologists...
> *H:* ...a nationalist, eh (pause)
> 45 *R:* But they would not take spiritual guidance, *nu?*
> *H:* That's right; that's right.
> *M:* That wasn't his real name anyway.
> *R:* What, 'Abba Sikra?'
> *M:* No, his name over here was (pause) 'Ben Batya'.
> 50 *S:* That's his last name.
> *R:* *M'vet nisht onheybn lernen haynt mit, mit eym, mit dem,* [we won't start *lernen* today with, with him, with this], with all this historical and literary criticism. (pause) *Shoyn.*
> *H:* (chuckles)
> *R:* *Lomer shoyn onfangn lernen epes* [let's begin *lernen* something].

Perhaps the most striking feature of this speech event is the code variation wherein R speaks in a mix of English, Yiddish, and their combinations along with a heavy dose of textual quotation while H, S, and M speak predominantly in English but make clear in the content of their responses that they fully understand R's words.

Generally, one might describe the entire discussion as an effort to contemporize as well as translate the Talmud, to make it sensible and relevant to moderns. Those who speak in English, H primarily, are trying to explain Abba Sikra and the *biryoni* in terms intelligible to contemporary Americans – a group with whom they choose to identify themselves linguistically – while the rabbi continually tries to bring the intellectual effort back to the text and its particular concerns.

But why it should be of such concern to H, S, M, and the others who, although not among the interlocutors, made up an interested audience to understand the term '*biryoni*' in contemporary terms? One might suggest the motive lies in the fact that to some extent the modernist associates himself with the contemporary world. Insofar as he does so he feels a compelling need to transform and comprehend the various layers of his experience in its terms. Linguistically this need demonstrates itself in the desire to translate, literally and figuratively, everything into contemporary (American) language. To fail to do so is perhaps to signal the division between the world of the Talmud and that of contemporary life, a division which is an anathema to the modern Orthodox, who wish to assume continuity. On the other hand, to succeed in identifying '*biryoni*' in present-day terms is to once again give evidence of the ceaseless relevance of Talmud and, associatively, Jewish tradition.[7]

7. The notion of the relevance of Jewish texts to contemporary life goes back at least as far as Philo (*c.* 20 B.C.E.–50 C.E.), the Alexandrian Jewish thinker who 'developed to its acme the idea that whatever was noble in Greek thinking was to be discovered in the sacred scripture of Judaism' (Moreau, J. L. 1961).

While it is H who leads this effort here, even the rabbi in his initial translation of '*biryoni*' made the effort at contemporization. His effort was far more tentative. Choosing uncommon, if not archaic, words ('vagabonds', 'brigands'), he does not smoothly make the transition from the parochial language of the Talmud to English, leaving the task to be completed by others. Moreover, he reverts frequently to the languages of Jewishness, Yiddish, and textual quotation. In so doing he acts as one would expect him to, as protector of the tradition (and traditional language) and defender of the parochial (through his emphasis on the text).

Repeatedly the rabbi tries to cut off the moves into contemporaneity and its linguistic reflection, English. To English remarks he responds in Yiddish or with text, as if refusing to ratify the American identity of his interlocutors. In addition, twice – at what he considers opportune moments for closure – he tries to end the discussion with '*shoyn*', a Yiddishism which means 'already' but which has come to be a common lexical marker used by Orthodox speakers for framing and closing conversation. '*Shoyn*' often serves as a bridge to something else: another conversation, a change in action, closure. Finally, following his last '*shoyn*' he remarks in Yiddish '*Lomer shoyn onfangen lernen epes*', 'let us begin (already) to learn something', let us begin our study. Speaking in Yiddish constitutes a linguistic emphasis on the need to return the group from its digression into the modern word and world to the traditional words and world of the Talmud page.

Lest one suppose that the rabbi represents a pristine example of the parochial, one ought to note that his speech is heavily dosed with English, indeed predominantly English. Moreover, his Yiddish also displays English interference. Perhaps the most blatant example is in his phrase '*tsore-makher*' which he uses (line 14) early on as an epithet to describe Abba Sikra. The rabbi has undoubtedly meant to call Abba Sikra a 'troublemaker', an epithet that comes from contemporary American English. Rather than using the actual Yiddish word for troublemaker which is, according to the authoritative Weinreich Dictionary, '*shterer*', he has translated literally from English by combining the word *tsore* (trouble) with *makher* (maker) in a structure rooted in American English.

Beyond this example of a calque, there are other illustrations of English (and by association American cultural) interference in the rabbi's speech. For example, the morphological interference that occurs (line 26) in the word 'dis', which more properly should be the word '*dos*'. '*Dos*' is Yiddish for 'this'. 'Dis' thus seems to be a compromise form. Or again (line 31) one discovers a sentence which is part Yiddish and part English. The bridge between these two parts is the word 'is', which may be either English or the Yiddish '*iz*', which means the same thing. The morphological ambiguity is ideal here for the speaker since it serves almost effortlessly to connect a sentence (and idea) which begins by being parochial – spoken about and to a strictly speaking Jewish audience – and ends by being put in contemporary English terms.

One must also not assume that H, as quoted in the above extract, represents a pure form of the cosmopolitan modern. Not only does he respond to Yiddish, but also his English is dotted with Jewish influences. The most prominent of these is intonation pattern about which there will be more to say later. There is also a series of parochial references, both contextual and lexical. For example, the phrase (line 24), 'the *loshn* brigands', contains the Yiddish '*loshn*' (language or words) which serves as a linguistic marker of H's insider status among those who 'speak the language of the Talmud'. He inserts this signal – whether consciously or not is here irrelevant – as if to indicate thereby as an insider he is to be taken seriously by the others. Although he speaks in English and about matters an English speaker might comprehend, he still is Jewish enough to easily throw in a word associated with the parochial setting and situation.

What one finds in all of this code variation and interference is a sense in which the interlocutors comprehend the duality of their lives as modern Orthodox Jews and how that duality plays itself out in the linguistic shifting of the *lernen* situation. Each foray into one world – be it the parochial or the cosmopolitan – seems to bring about a pulling back to the other. Even among those whose speech is *predominantly* Hebrew, English, or Yiddish, the overall effect is one in which the speech is *primarily* multilingual; and it is this multilingualism which is of greatest sociological significance.

In addition to topical and situational factors, role must be considered an influence in language switching. Those who see themselves as linked to a parochial identity and role, like the rabbi, would, for example, adjust their speech behavior accordingly.

To be more explicit, in certain situations, particular behaviors – including language behaviors – 'are expected (if not required) of particular individuals *vis-à-vis* each other', (Fishman 1965b: 76). Thus, for example, in the Talmud class one expects the rabbi/teacher to be conversant with the terminology of the text, making much use of it. Furthermore, one expects him (and the typical extract quoted above demonstrates this) to be tied both linguistically and contextually to the text and its meaning, and that he will therefore try repeatedly to focus discussion and language around it. On the other hand, the students, most of whom in this class and others like it may be considered avocational pupils, may be expected to display some role distance from the Jewish-student role and associated text. Although it is ritually mandated, their *lernen* is still very much a once-a-week, after-hours activity. Displaying distance becomes especially crucial for those modernists who even in this limited period of *lernen* wish to indicate their marginality in the Orthodox world and their immersion elsewhere.

Normally distance is displayed in speech by means of 'side-involving byplays' and other nonverbal signs of one's dissociation from the ongoing discourse

(Goffman 1974: 542). In the case of the Talmud class, there is additionally the use of English: its syntax, grammar, vocabulary, and cadence.

Perhaps the most obvious example of this effect of role upon language choice occurred when one of the physicians in the class translated into modern medical terminology a portion of the text which referred to sickness. Here the vocabulary offered not only translation and explanation but served latently to indicate his immersion in the medical (i.e. non-Jewish) world where he had become familiar with such terminology. Lexically, he succeeded in distancing himself from the role of Talmud student and reminding the others of his doctor role.

Thus one may suggest the principle that: insofar as modern Orthodox Jews comprehend their various social roles, both in the microcosm of the Talmud class and in the larger worlds of American and Jewish life, they will in part display these roles through language. While none of the factors – topic, situation, role, reference group or textual argot – alone can serve to account for all incidents of language choice and shift, together they enable one to make sense out of the language behavior in a modern Orthodox Talmud class. Behind all of these factors is the fundamental cosmopolitan parochial ambivalence and preoccupation that describes the modern American Orthodox Jewish state of mind. The life in several worlds is reflected in the speech in several languages.

INTONATION

One last element of modern Orthodox Talmud study needs to be considered. Earlier repeated references to the role of cadence and intonational contour were made. These need now to be organized and further elucidated.

To understand the importance of intonation in Talmud study one must first realize that the text is essentially a cryptic compilation of the minutes of rabbinic debates on matters of the orally transmitted law and tradition. It is devoid of any punctuation or vocalization and even the basic exercise of reading it properly requires an expertise beyond that available to the unschooled. In part as a result of this situation, a method of cantillating the text developed. This cantillation, or *gemore-nign* (Talmud tune) as it came to be called in Yiddish, served syntactic and interpretive functions. Cadence helped one distinguish between primary and subordinate clauses and ideas, between rhetorical questions and real ones, between one topic and another, between speech and reported speech, and so on. Indeed still today 'melodic variety is used for the phrasing of the Aramic text, which, as it stands, is compressed to the point of obscurity. Since a brief sequence... may encapsulate a major difference of opinion between two authorities, exaggerated pitch contrasts are used to restore syntactic colorfulness to the emaciated, almost "telegraphic" legalistic formulae' (U. Weinreich 1956: 639).

During the great cultural flowering of Jewish life in central and Eastern Europe, study became accessible to increasingly larger numbers of Jews, and along with it came an increasing familiarity with and prestige of *gemore-nign*. In the process the 'chant figures, or analogs of these figures, deprived of singing voice quality, [were] easily transposed...from the reading of the Talmud to oral discussions about it, and thence to ordinary conversation...' (U. Weinreich 1956: 640).

Gradually, as earlier pointed out, the entire community of Ashkenazic Jewry seemed to adopt the Talmudic chant as a feature of speech. Moreover, an examination of intonations of many European languages and of English reveals that the particular contour of this chant, taken over in great measure by Yiddish, is not to be found in them (U. Weinreich 1956; Pike 1947). Thus the intonation pattern of Yiddish and *gemore-nign* may be considered a cultural characteristic by and through which a Jew may identify and present himself.

Basically the pattern consists in the 'rise of the pitch from a low point to a peak, followed by a distinct fall...' (U. Weinreich 1956: 633–634). More precisely, a level intonation is used for an unmarked transition, a partial rise signifies a marked transition and the rise–fall cadence indicates a dramatized transition. The rise–fall plays an especially large part in Talmud since it serves to set the stage for a remark that seems unexpected but is nevertheless instructive. It is the sound of the rhetorical and rather incredulous question which has become closely linked with Yiddish in particular and Jewish inflection in general.

Ironically, the very cadences which for the traditional Jewish community had been a mark of prestige, a sign of one's high status as scholar, became a stigma in the era of acculturation and emancipation. The Jew who did not wish to stand out amongst the other nations had, among other things, to learn to control his intonation.

In America where the rise–fall contour is rarely a part of normal speech, Jewish inflection and cadence are particularly noticeable. Compared to the Yiddish, in fact, the sound of English seems rather monotonic (reflecting perhaps the stoicism of a Protestant heritage rather than the passion of a Jewish one). And although it is undoubtedly true as Pike points out that 'no language uses a pure monotone', to the immigrant Jew the sound of English seemed to approach that (Pike 1947: 20).

'The retention of intonation patterns of the native language constitutes one of the last features of a foreign accent in the speech of a bilingual who speaks the secondary language almost perfectly' (Rayfield 1970: 72). Jews carried their tone with them into English (especially the New York variety) as they had in the European languages. Under the impact of acculturation, however, the influence of English on Yiddish was to make it relatively 'less sing-song in nature' (U. Weinreich 1956: 642). A distinctively American kind of Yiddish arose, one that not only took into it English expressions and some vocabulary but also some cadences of American speech.

To Orthodox Jews, Jewishness was not a stigma. On the contrary, for them the sing-song sounds of *gemore-nign* retained an association with high social status and prestige even in the face of the acculturative pressures in Europe and America. Accordingly, long after the most marked cadences of Yiddish had disappeared from the speech of most American Jews, the Orthodox generally still talked in the distinctive rise–fall intonation pattern. Their exposure to Jewish learning, and even more importantly, their continued reverence for it served to nourish a speech contour clearly at odds with the sound of contemporary America.

As long as Orthodox Jews protected their Jewish way of life through efforts at isolation from American life, they continued to speak Yiddish and sound English in ways that reverberated the *gemore-nign*. Indeed, even today those who stress separation from American society and culture – various Hasidic sects, for example – may be recognized when they speak English. Their word order, choice, and intonation mark them immediately.

When Orthodox Jews began to value modernity and sought accordingly to decrease their remoteness from the world outside the Jewish one, among the aspects of their existence ultimately subjected to change was their language. Yet unlike so many other Jews who in great measure accepted acculturation as a paramount goal and therefore hoped to diminish their separate identity as Jews, modern Orthodox people wished at once to become part of the contemporary world and remain true to the world of their past. Rather than viewing tradition and parochialism as anachronistic, these Jews adopted an attitude that could best be described as panchronistic and cosmopolitan parochial, seeking to include all time and cultural existence in one frame of reference.

In the sphere of language this meant the modern Orthodox evolution of a speech pattern which brought together traditional tongues with contemporary ones. More to the point of intonation, the cadence of modern Orthodox speech, although lacking the extreme rise–fall of Yiddish and *gemore-nign*, still retained many of its features. While it is not possible here to exhaustively trace the intonational lines of the modern Orthodox speech community, measured against the cosmopolitan American ideal of unmusical speech and other systems of pitch control common in American English, the sound of modern Orthodox Jews speaking *amongst and to one another* is quite distinctive. Perhaps the heavy presence of what to the American ear sounds like incredulity and protestation is the most obvious illustration of lingering influences of *gemore-nign*. In addition one also discovers a frequent use of the untransposed word order typical of Talmudic and Yiddish language questions accompanied by the rise–fall cadence, as for example in the rhetorical question: 'This is coffee'?!

On the other hand, in the outside world, when modern Orthodox Jews try to pass as and interact with moderns or when the topic of their discussion is particularly cosmopolitan in character, the language and cadence betrays none of these Jewish influences.

THE SOUND OF LERNEN

The general procedure for explaining and translating Talmud which, as already outlined, evolved most distinctively in Europe, was such that each phrase of text was followed by a long, often free Yiddish translation. In order to maintain the unity of so complex a structure, melody and cadence were used in such a way that subordinate clauses of the same hypotactic level together with their interspersed Yiddish translations and glosses would always revert to the same tone level. The tonic of the scale would be returned to when the main clause and its translation were completed.

Much of this intonation remains in use in the American modern Orthodox Talmud class. Here however the explanations and translations are not always, nor even necessarily most frequently, in Yiddish. They may rather be in English. Nevertheless, even so, they are often spoken in precisely the same cadence as the original Talmud text. This speech has been described as 'speaking English as if it were Yiddish' (Fishman 1965a: 59). Not only are lexical and syntactic structure reflective of Yiddish and *gemore*, but there is also an intonational and accentual interpenetration. It is as if the English were a sort of expressive repetition of the text, even when the content of the English is strictly speaking liminal.

An example is in order here. The section of text quotes an incident during which the rabbis upbraid the sage Yokhanan ben Zakkai for not having asked the Emperor Vespasian to save Jerusalem but rather to have asked simply for the preservation of the small city of Yavneh and its scholars.[8]

<pre>
         2   2 2 3 2   2   2   2 2 2   2   2 2   2   3
R: Fregt di gemore [the Talmud asks]: And Reb Yokhanan ben Zakkai hot nisht
     3 4   4 4   4   4   2
   gevist vegn di zakhn?! [did not know about these things]
     2   3 4 3   2 2   2   2 2 2   2   2 2   3-2
   'Vehu sovar [and he thought]', ober [but] Reb Yokhanan ben Zakkai thought:
      3 2   2   2 2 3-2 2   4 2   3 2   2   2 4 2 2   2   2   2 4-2 2 3-2 3-2   2   2
   'Dilmo kuley hay lo ovid'; Listen, there are limits to what you can ask. He felt there are things
      2   2   2   2 3   2   2   2   2 4-2
   he can get away with and things he can't.
</pre>

What stands out intonationally in this extract is the preponderance of rise–fall

8. No universally agreed upon notation for intonation has yet been established. Accordingly, I will use a combination of Kenneth Pike's numerical notation (lower numbers signify lower pitch, higher numbers high pitch) and Uriel Weinreich's punctuation (?!). I have also used a dash (−) to note a glide, when an intonational contour occurs in a single syllable.

One last point with regard to transcription: since the extract quoted contains words from the text which are being integrated into the utterance, I have framed these with quotation marks to distinguish them from the rest of the utterance.

contours in the English. While much of the English is spoken in the monotone (2) which is characteristic of that language, there are notable exceptions: thought$^{3\text{-}2}$, listen^{3}, limits^{2}, ask^{4}, felt^{2}, there$^{4\text{-}2}$, away$^{3\text{-}2}$ with$^{3\text{-}2}$, can't$^{4\text{-}2}$. These contours are what gives the English its particularly Jewish sound, a sound one discovers to be predominant in the Yiddish and *gemore* material constituting the rest of the utterance.

The rise–fall and the partial rise that occurs in the English seem to add the drama of the text to what is really a metatextual remark in the English. The precise meaning of the text is: 'And he [Yokhanan ben Zakkai] thought that perhaps he would not have been able to gain so much'. The statement beginning with the word 'listen' assumes one to have comprehended the denotational meaning of the previously quoted text and instead of translating it, dramatically elaborates it, using language that speaks to the contemporary American. But, although the language is quite American, the intonation is distinctively talmudic such that the English *sounds* as if it simply continues the text. Indeed, the intonation of the English is interfered with by the intonation of the text, and one might add – sociologically – by the ethos of the text as well.

When one speaks English in a cadence which is Jewish in its genesis, one thereby partially leaves the domain of the English speaking world. That departure cannot be assumed to be accidental. Rather one must suppose that the speaker is swept up by the world of the Talmud and its language and that this involvement is reflected in language. At times the reflection is lexical, at times syntactic or morphological, and at times intonational. Whatever the sign, the fact remains that through language (or paralanguage, if you will) social involvement is demonstrated.

Surely, one might ask, it is just as conceivable that the sound of English would dominate the sound of Talmud. That is precisely what happens among those who study in a primarily cosmopolitan atmosphere. Thus, for example, in the university where Talmud is studied by Jews and non-Jews alike, the rise–fall sing-song so noticeable in the extract here is absent. Instead one hears a Talmud that sounds like English. Indeed, a person who has learned his Talmud in the cosmopolitan university setting rather than in the parochial *besmedresh* reveals this background both by the intonation and language choice of recitation. The former sound English while those who have done their *lernen* in a *besmedresh* sing the words.[9]

By choosing to sing both English and text, the student implicitly identifies himself with the generations of those who have religiously cantillated *gemore*. The signal, although not formal or explicit, is never misunderstood.

9. Dr. Shlomo Noble, the noted Yiddish linguist, tells the story of his first day of Talmud study under the late Professor Wolfson at Harvard. Noble had just asked a question, using a *gemore-nign*. Wolfson replied, using the same cadences, 'Mr. Noble, this is not a Yeshiva, this is Harvard University'. Noble never again made the same intonational mistake.

For the modern American Orthodox Jew, the choice of how to sound, like the choice of what language to speak, is of course affected by role, topic and situation. Ultimately, however, it is affected by his particular state of mind. Generally this is one in which, as already noted, he finds himself somewhere between the parochial Jewish and cosmopolitan American communities. Although at times, in the rush of living, he may momentarily disattend one world in favor of the other, there are other times, such as during the Talmud class, when the two worlds touch upon each other and disattention is simply not possible. At these moments some compromise must be struck. The use of English in a cadence associated with *gemore*, although not necessarily the only means, may be considered as representing something of a compromise. The generating force behind the intonation is the speaker's sensitivity to cultural factors. He speaks the way he does either because he wishes to put things in ways that the listeners will understand or because he wishes to present himself through his language and cadence in a particular way, or both. Generally, those matters which seem to resonate Jewish concerns display Jewish language or intonation while more neutral matters may be spoken in standard American English.

CONCLUSION

Long after most American Jews abandoned the characteristic patois which was neither quite English nor quite Yiddish at least within the context of the Talmud class (i.e. in the community), modern Orthodox Jews still retain remnants of it. The reasons are only in part explained technically and linguistically. They are as well social and psychological. Talmud study is more than an intellectual or ritual exercise; it provides an opportunity for interaction, arrangements during which individuals come together to sustain some sort of intersubjective mental world. The students become 'inhabitants of a partly shared social world, established and continuously modified by their acts of communication' (Rommetveit 1974: 23).

When the others with whom one is talking share the same ethos and state of mind, when their preoccupations are similar, the interplay of talk cannot help but intensify that preoccupation and at times make it manifest. For modern Orthodox Jews this means that the dualism of their existence displays itself in their conversation among themselves. The patois which develops out of this dualism, seen most boldly in the Talmud class but often present whenever modern Orthodox Jews get together to *shmooz*,[10] the term that denotes sociable conversation among intimates, has in a sense become the argot of modern

10. Properly speaking the Yiddish word for a chat is *shmues*. But modern Orthodox Jews 'shmooz'. The variant morphology draws on English as well. Thus even the term itself betrays the compromise linguistic structure that characterizes the modern Orthodox.

American Orthodoxy. As such it serves not only to mark these people as a distinct group, as all argots do, but also provides a linguistic basis for solidarity.

In the outside American world this argot may be camouflaged. But in the intimate environment of the Talmud class, in the *haymish* (homey) atmosphere of the *besmedresh*, the language and all it symbolizes reappears. Here the well-tuned ear will hear the sound of modern American Orthodoxy.

REFERENCES

Bellack, A. A., Kliebard, H. M., Hyman, R. T., Smith, Jr., F. L. (1966), *The Language of the Classroom*. New York, Columbia Teachers College Press.

Berger, Peter (1970), 'Identity as a problem in the sociology of knowledge', in *The Sociology of Knowledge: A Reader*, edited by J. E. Curtis and J. W. Petras, 373–384. New York.

Blom, J., Gumperz, J. J. (1972), 'Social meaning in linguistic structure: code-switch in Norway', in *Directions in Sociolinguistics*, edited by J. J. Gumperz and D. Hymes, 107–434. New York, Holt, Rinehart & Winston.

Burger, H. G. (1966), 'Syncretism: an acculturative accelerator', *Human Organization* 25: 103–115.

Dubb, A. A. (1977). *Jewish South Africans: A Sociological View of the Johannesburg Community*. Grahamstown, S.A., Institute of Social and Economic Research Occasional Paper No. 21.

Ervin-Tripp, S. (1964), An analysis of the interaction of language, topic and listener. *American Anthropologist* 66 (6, 2): 86–102.

Feinsilver, L. M. (1956), Yiddish and American English. *Chicago Jewish Forum* 14: 71–76.

Fishman, J. (1965a), *Yiddish in America*. Bloomington, Indiana University Press.

— (1965b), 'Who speaks what language to whom and when', *La Linguistique*: 67–88.

Gennep, Arnold Van (1908), 'Essai d'une théorie des langues spéciales', in *Revue des Études Ethnographiques et Sociologiques*, Volume 1, 327–337. (Trans. S. C. Heilman).

Goffman, E. (1967), *Interaction Ritual*. New York, Anchor.

— (1974), *Frame Analysis*. Cambridge, Harvard University Press.

— (1976), 'Replies and Responses', *Language in Society* 5 (3) (December): 257–313.

Heilman, S. C. (1976), *Synagogue Life*. Chicago, University of Chicago Press.

Henderson, D. (1970), 'Contextual specificity, discretion, and cognitive socialization: with special reference to language', *Sociology* 4 (3): 311–338.

Herman, S. D. (1977), 'Criteria for Jewish identity', in *World Jewry and the State of Israel*, edited by M. Davis, 163–182. New York, Arno Press.

Joffe, J. A. (1943), The development of Yiddish in The United States. *Universal Jewish Encyclopedia*, vol. x, 601 ff.

Pike, K. L. (1947), *The Intonation of American English*. Ann Arbor, University of Michigan Press.

Mark, Y. (1954), 'Frequency of Hebraisms in Yiddish' in *The Field of Yiddish*, edited by U. Weinreich. New York, The Linguistic Circle.

Moreau, J. L. (1961), *Language and Religious Language: A Study in the Dynamics of Translation*. Philadelphia, Westminster Press.

Rayfield, J. R. (1970), *The Languages of a Bilingual Community*. The Hague, Mouton.

Rommetveit, Ragnar (1974), *On Message Structure: A Framework for the Study of Language and Communication*. New York, John Wiley & Sons.

Sommerfelt, Alf (1962), 'Language, society and culture', in *Diachronic and Syndronic Aspects of Language*, edited by A. Sommerfelt, 87–136. The Hague, Mouton.

Soskin, W. F., Soskin, J. V. (1963), 'The study of spontaneous talk', in *The Stream of Behavior*, edited by R. G. Baker. New York, Appleton-Century-Crofts.

Vološinov, V. (1971), 'Reported speech', in *Readings in Russian Poetics: Formalist and Structuralist Views*, edited by L. Metejka and K. Pomorska, 149–175. Cambridge, M.I.T. Press.

Weinreich, M. (1968), 'Yiddishkayt and Yiddish: on the impact of religion on language in Ashkenazic Jewry', in *Readings in the Sociology of Language*, edited by J. Fishman. The Hague, Mouton.

— (1980), *The History of the Yiddish Language*, trans. by S. Noble and J. Fishman. Chicago, University of Chicago Press (pagination from prepublication typescript).

Weinreich, Uriel (1953), *Languages in Contact*. New York, Linguistic Circle of N.Y. No. 1.

— (1956), 'Notes on the Yiddish Rise–Fall intonation contour', in *For Roman Jakobson*, edited by M. Halle, 633–643. The Hague: Mouton.

— (1967), 'Influences of Yiddish on American English: possibilities of a new approach'. YIVO Conference, unpublished.

Yngve, V. (1970), 'On getting a word in edgewise', in *Papers from the Sixth Regional Meeting, Chicago Linguistic Society*, edited by M. A. Campbell et al., 567–578. Chicago, Department of Linguistics University of Chicago.

This paper was made possible by a research grant from the National Endowment for the Humanities. I would like to thank Professors Roland Wulbert and Steven Cohen for their helpful criticism of earlier drafts and Professors Shlomo Noble and Marvin Herzog for their help in providing me with the necessary linguistic background for my research. Mrs. Norma Gayne was enormously helpful in the typing. This paper is derived from my forthcoming book on the general subject of American Modern Orthodoxy, entitled *Cosmopolitan Parochials* (in press).

PART III

Modernization Movements and Modern Attitudes

By enforcing the 'Trading with the Enemy Act' and censoring the non-English press, Postmaster-General Burlson is creating more socialists every day than Morris Hilquit can create in an entire year of speech-making. (*Der groyser kundes*, October 26, 1917)

a. *It is not true that, with Yiddish, the Jew of the galut went only to the gas chamber. With Yiddish, the Jew of the galut ascended also many a national height. With Yiddish the Jew of the galut went also to the revolutionary barricades, and with Yiddish, the Jew of the Warsaw Ghetto arose in his unequalled revolt against a powerful world-destroyer. The* Baal Shem, *the great Jew of the galut kindled the Hasidic fire in Yiddish. The Yiddish language has developed a great national literature which is incomparable both in its vitality, in its encouragement of Jewish survival, and in its bemoaning the destruction of our people in the Hitler era, in shattering expressions of lamentation.*

If it were true that with Yiddish the Jew of the galut went only to the gas chamber, I would still say: Bow down before this Jew of the galut; bow down and kiss the dust which the boot of this Jew of the galut touched in his holy march to the gas chamber! Justifiably our Yiddish poetry has praised the Jews, who marched to the gas chamber, as shining, 'radiant' Jews.

b. *...we were educated in the spirit of East European Jews and we have retained its ethos. Yet we can never recover what East European Jewry was and we cannot recreate it, imitate it, or make it serve as a functional model for our lives. But if we are to continue the living Jewish tradition from which those Jews were so swiftly and cruelly cut off, if we are to carry over from one Jewish civilization to the next our memories and our lessons, we must deepen our knowledge and understanding of that East European world. If we are to understand ourselves, we need to understand our origins, our parents and grandparents, their languages, cultures and conflicts, their problems and dilemmas, and their mistakes as well.*

Mottos for Part III

(a) H. Leyvik. Der yid – der yokhid (1957) [The Individual Jew (1957)], published in his *Eseyen un redes* [Essays and Speeches]. New York, Congress for Jewish Culture, 1963, 109–124. Translation by Emanuel S. Goldsmith, *The Reconstructionist*, 1957, 23, no. 17, 7–12.

(b) Lucy S. Dawidowicz. The relevance of an education in the Sholem Aleichem schools, in S. Goodman (ed.), *Our First Fifty Years; The Sholem Aleichem Folk Institute*. New York, SAFI, 1972, *117–*123.

די פֿיר קלאסן

י. מ. ליפֿשיץ

SUMMARY: THE FOUR CATEGORIES BY Y. M. LIFSHITS

The first modern Yiddish linguist (1828–78) argues that the fusion nature of Yiddish is no different than that of English, that Yiddish is no more a debased German than French is a debased Latin, and that the language of an entire people cannot be considered a jargon.

די נאַנצע וועלט. דאָס הייסט אונטער ערד מיט דעם
וואָס איז אין אידער אין אויף אידער אדער ווערט אין 4 קלאַססן אנגעטהיילט
וואָס איינע איז העבער פֿון דער אַנדערער. דיא נידריגסטע הייסט
דיא טורדטע קלאַססע (רומם. מינעראַלרייך). דיא העלערע : דיא
מאָקביגענדינע (צמחה. פפֿלאַנצרייך). דיא נאָך העלערע : דיא
לעבעדינע (חי. טהיעררייך); אוֹן דיא העלסטע : דיא רעדענדע
(מדבר. מענש). אין דער ערשטער קלאַססע איז נבלל אלאַרליא
שטיינער, מעטאַלל דיא ערד אונ אלע יסודיח ! און דער אַנדערער
אלאַרליא נעוויעקם ! אין דער דריטער אלע מינים חיח. אָס איך
רעדפֿערטער אללע מענטשען.

וואָס הייסט מיינטש?

יענע אבטהיילונג האָט מען זיך ניט פֿון דעם קאָפּ אויסגע־
טראכט נאָר מען ועהט ארים בחוש או דער. מיטסער פֿון דער
וועלט האָט אויך אוטליבער קלאַססע אין אנרערן סטעמפּעלבלאַנעט.
עס נעפֿינט זיך אין דער ערטער קלאַסע אפֿילו שטיעגער וואָס
עס ראַבט זיך או זיא זאַקטען, און אנדערע חידער (למשל מאָגנעט)
וואָס בעוועגען זיך, פֿון דעסטוענען אז יעניץ נישט קיין האַקסעם.
וויל עס איז נאָר א פֿרנרסערונג פֿון דרויסען, און דאָס קיין
בעוועגונג נישט. דארין עם איז נישט ביצין (ניכט וילקירליך) !
מיט דער דריטער אין פֿערטער קלאַססע אז אוך דאָס אינדענע :
חאַטשע עם נעפֿינט זיך אין מינים אין דער דריטער קלאַססע (חי) וואָס
מען קען וויא אויסלערנען רערין חיא א מרכר (מענטש). פֿון
רעסטוועגען הייסט דאָס אין אָדיה אריין ניט קיין רערען, וויל
דער אָמחער סימן (נדר, דעפֿיניציאן) פֿון רערען אז או מען
פֿרשטעהט וואָם מען רערט. אָדער שכל האָבען, און דעם סימן האָם
נאָר דער מענטש. וואָס ער למשל : פּאַפיר, אָז שטעללט
ער זיך פֿאַר אין קאָפּ וואָם ער פֿערטשטעהרט אונטער דעם חוָארט.
אָבער דיא נאַנצע קלאַססע חי האָט כאַין איפֿן נישט דעם כח

וואָס הייסט שכל?

דער עיקר ארביים פֿון דעם שכל (דיא דענקפֿרינצישען)
אז -אונטערשירשירען אונ פֿערגליבען, ד. ה. אללעוואַבט וואָס דער.
מענטש דערפֿיהלם מים דיא חושים זאָלל דער שכל רערקענען
מים וואָס איינע איז גלייך צו דער אַנדערער אונ מים וואָס נישט.
חאָם מערר וואָבען אונ וואָם גרינדליבער מען קען אונטערשירשידען
אונ פֿערגליבען, האָם מען, הייסט עם, מעהר שכל מערר אויס־
געבילדעט, ארער מען איז נעבילרעטער, ארער מען האָס מערר
שכל, ארער מען אז מערר מענטש. —

וואָס הייסט לשון?

וויל איטליבער מענטש בעזונדער קאָן נאָר וועניג וואָבל
פֿיהלען, דערקענען אונ פֿערשטעהען, ראַריבער אז דיא טבע
פֿון דעם מענטשען או ער חבט זיך מיטטל וואָם דורך וויא אַלל
ער קענין מקבל דיין נעראַנקען פֿון אנדרעע, אונ וויענ נעראַנקען
חידער אַנדערע איבערגעבען. יענע מיטטל ותנין אפֿילן וערד
פֿערשידען, נאָר פֿון רעסטוועתען וריין וויא אללע מים א איין נאָמען
אנגערופֿען, היט ל: לשן : י). דורך דעם לשן פֿון אידיח (ישראל). קאָן

אין ווך. וירפֿין נעמט זיך וואָם מען טאָר טאָר קין שטיטטמען קין
שום אוטראַבט חלילה ניט טוהן גליך וויא אין רעדענדרינען, וואָרין
ער איז אויך בכלל מענטש, ראַם־הייסט : ער האָם וך אויך שבל.
אפֿילו אַ קינד נאָר פֿן איין טאָ האָט אויך כטעיע רעם איינענעם
חערטה וויא א גרויסער מענטש. וויל עם האָם שין רעם שכל
בכח; ר.ה. ער קאָן האַבען שכל.

———

*) אפֿילו דאָס שטיגלשן (סיטיק) הייסט אין מים רעכט לשן,
חאָרין מענטשין קענין זיך טיס אדער אוֹך פֿעל נעראַנקען מיטטהיילען
אז דער איינינער סימן פֿן לשן אז דער : נעראַקטענצייבעט.

די פוילישע יורען ?

דער הסיסטאאט נאליציאנישע מהויל פן יורען (צו נחמת
ער האט אצער מעהר גלוח נעליטען אלץ אללע אנדערע יתהיל,
אוו האבין אללע מאהל צוישען אנדערע פעלקער נעלעבט), צו אצת
מהית אין אנדערער סיבה), האט זיך נעוועהנט אביסיל מיט דער,
אביסיל מיט טענער שפראכע, ועדלת צוישען חאס פאר א פעלקער
ער אין נעהועין ביז עם אזו ענשטאנטרען א נאנץ בעזונדער לשן,
חאס מען רופט עם יודיש, אוו דיא מענטשען האם הערען אין איהר
אויפנעצוויגען אוו לעבען מיט איהר, הייטען, "פוילישע יורען" וועלכע
מען קען זייא אין דעם פאך וויא א באזונדער פאלק בעטראכטן.

די יודישע שפראכע ?

דאס יודישע לשון איז אוצער מיטער-שפראכע פן דעם
אנדערן בעגריף, ר. ה. אוטער ערציהונגס-שפראכע, וואס דורך
איהר קענט מיר זיך איינם דאס אנדערע אם בעסטען פערשטע-
הען*) - הייט וויא אזו קען מען נאך מסופק זיין אוו אוטער בילהונג
אין נאר נעהועטצ אינדער בילהונג פן אוצער שפראכע ? אונ צום
סוף הער איך וויא נאר מבוה זיין אוו פן איהר נאר חוק מאבען.
מען וואס אלען : וויא איו פעראראבען ! איך מיו מודה זיין אוו איך
פערטעה איבערהויפט נאר ניט צו וואס פאר א רעואן מען קען
אויף א שפראכע. וואס עם לעבען, אנצדרלען אונ וצטרלען אין אנדר
אזו פיל צוועעננדער מענטשען, א נאנץ פאלק, זאנען : וויא איו
פעראראבען. פערדראבע נעטיקט זיך נאר צוא-נצע איך נאך אצא
זאך, וואס עם איו בעסער נעהועטען אונ איו קאלע נעוואדן. נאר פן
האנין איו עם אזו נעדריטצען אצו אנדערע שפראכע וענען פן דעם
נרוד אן בעסער נעהועטען ? תענען וויא דען אזו סטיני נעהועט
נעווארין ? וויא דען קוטען דער נאר אויך ארוים, וויא אוטער לשון פן אנדרע
פערשידענע לשונות. נאר פאר וואס דיא הייסין זייא ניט פעראראבען ?
נאר דער איז אמת איז, אוו ביא א לשון נעשיקט זיך ניט צו וואנען
נלאם (אבסאלאט) פעראראבען, חארין א לשון איו דער;נאר צייכען
פן נעדאנקק. דעריבער מען זיך וויך אין פאלק מאבען וואס פאר
צייכען עם וויל צו אבי (אום, ראטש) עם וואל זיך דורך זייא איינס
דאס אנדערע פערשטעהן !

א פעראראבענער בעגריף דער הייסט א אמת פעראראבע.
שוין דער איוניער פעראראבענער בעגריף מאבט פאך פן דעם
איינם וורט. פער ראדבען האט דיא נעביך דיא יודען צו אזו
שלעכטען מענר נעבראבט! הייבט זיך נאר אן איינער פן אדנו
צו לערנין א פרעמע שפראכע, וואו וערט ער שוין באל-א-סבת
אוו אוטער לשון איו פעראראבען, אוו הייבט שוין נעהעריליך אן
חזק צו מאבע פן אוטער לשון, אבער מיט דער זייט זאפט
פן אונו אלין, אוו נאך שפעטער ברענגט דער חזק שאיה מיט
זיך. הייל ער אלין פיהלם אבער ביא זיך, אוו ער איו נאך א
יוד מיט דעם פילען מויל, טוהט ער כל רחמעלות (האטשע עם איו
איהם נעביך תחילת זעהר פריקרט) אבי ער זאל פערשטעללען נליך
ער איו אום יוד, חארין ער מיינטאו דורך דעם וועט ער האבען מעהר
רעבט צו שפעטצן פן יורען אונ צו האסטען וויא. דריען פער-
לאנסט ער זיך נעביך אין דיא בעראיפע פן יורעשקיט אונ פן
מענטשליבקיט. ער מילל אום יוד וערין, אוו וערד נאר אום

_____

*) ווער קען רען דאס אפילוסקעזין אז דיא ערציע סאבע דעם
שטא-קטסמן אגריק אויף דעם נאגטע לעבק פן דעם סנטשען.

מען אזואלע נעראאקען פן פיעל מענטשען. הן פן דיא וואס
לעבען צאך, אוו הן פן דיא וואס וענין שיין לאנג נעשטארבען.
מהאי טעמא דערף מען אללע מענטשען. הן דיא וואס תענין
נעהועטען, הן ריאוואס ועניןרא, אוו דיא וואס וועלין ערשט זיין, וויא
איין מענטש בעטראבטען ; הארין דורך דעם לשון העלפען
זיך אללע מענטשען. איטליבען בעוינדער, מעהר מענטש צו וערין,
דורך איהם וערין אללע מענטשען אנטאיינעם נליך וויא צוואסמענ-
נעשמאלצען. דערפן קען מען שין פערשיי-ירן פאר וואס עם האם
קורער זיך אזו אן דיא בילרונג פן א פאלק מיט דער בילהונב
פן זיין לשון, חארין דאס לשון איז דער דער צייבע פן נעראנקען,
ראריבער מו נעהוענרט זיין איינם אן דעם אנדערן.

וואס הייסט פאלק ?

אזו וויא דיא שטערין, האטשע וויא וירקען איינם אויף
דאס אנדערע דורך איין אצציהונגסקראפט (אטטראקצ'אן) פן
רעמטהדינגען טהיילען וויא זיך אב אין פערשיידענע סיסטעמען, וואס
איטליבעם האט זיך אין אנדארן וועג (באהן), אזו אויך דיא
מענטשען, האטשע וויא וירקען אללע אויך איטליבען מיט איין בח-
השבל. פן רעסטוהדענען צוטהיילען וויא זיך אין פעלקער, וואס
איטליבעם האט זיך אין אנדערן קאראקטער. א פאלק בעשטעהט פן א
סך פאטיליעם וואס קוטען ארוים פן איין שטאם אוו וואס לעבען,
אדער האבען נעלעבט א סך הונדערטער יאהרין אין איינעם אוו
האבען אין דער נאנצער צייט אלצאיונע פארפעללע נעראטא אוו האבען
איינע מנהנים אוו איין לשון.

וואס הייסט מוטער-שפראכע ?

אזו וויא דיא פעלקער אונטערשיירן זיך פן איינאנדער
מיט דיא קאראקטערס, אזו אויך מיט דיא לשונות. דאס לשון וואס
איטליבעם פאלק בעזוינדער האט, רופט מען מוטער-שפראכע. פן
רעסטוהעגען האט, ראבט מיר, דאס ווערט: מוטער-שפראכע נאך
א צווייטען בענריף: היונו ערצעהונגס-שפראכע, ר.ה. דיא שפראבע
וואס מענטשעג רערען מיט אדער אויפנעצוינען. אוו קען זיין אז
איין מענטש זאלל האבען צווייא מוטער-שפראבען, רהיונו : מען
א הייטשט לעטשל ווערט מיט דער פראגעוייטער שפראבע אויפנע-
צוינען ; אלק רייטש, אזו רייטשלאצר זיין פאטערלאצד אוו דאס
רייטשע לשון זיין מוטער-שפראבע ! אלק אויפנעצוינענער פראנצוויז
אבער, איו נאר פראנצעויש זיין מוטערשפראבע וועטין ראם
איז זיין עיקר-לשון : ר. ה. וויארין דורך דעם, אוו נאר דורך
דעם לשון, קען ער אם בעסטען זיינע נעראנקען, אוטערע
איבערנעבען אוו פן אנדערע וויעדער נעראנקען מקבל זיין אוו
ראריבער קען ער מיט רעבט, א פראנצעוישער רייטש הייסען.

די יורען בכלל ?

דיא יורען בכלל מאבען א בעוינדער פאלק אוים, אוו נאך אזו א
פאלק, וואס האט צוויא מוטערשפראבע-מיט דעם ערשטען לשון קורט איו זיין
מוטערשפראבע פן רעם ערשטען בענריף, וועלבעם אללע יורען
האבען עם בכלל :, רערקרקען איז מיט דער מוטערשפראבע פן דעם
אנדערן בענריף אדטירש. מייל דיא יורען תענין זעבנר פערשפרייט
צוישען פערשידענע פעלקער, האם זיך איטליבער טהויל אנגעוואדנט
מיט דער שפראבע פן דעם פאלק וואס ער לעבט צוישען דעם,
ביו עם איו מיט דער צייט נעוואארין זיין עיקר לשון. ר.ה. זיין
ערציהונגס שפראבע. דערפין איז נעטאחין רייטשע יורען אן
פראנצעוישע, ענגלישע... אוו אזו ווייטער.

די ⋆ קלאסען

(פֿאָרזעצונג)

די ניטע רעגיהנע אין ראם ביסעלע אמת ניבילרעטע יודען
טהען נעביך אפֿילו אללע מענליבקיים אַנזיכער שלעבטען מעמד
צו פֿערבעסערען, אַבער וואַם העלבֿט עם אז וויא לעצרעהען
סאַטע ראם רעבטע פינטעלע, אז וויא רעדען צו אונ אויף אֿעלכֿע
שֿ־ראַבען וואָם אַנזער אויהר (פֿאָלקסאָהר) אז ניט נעװערנטע
סיט וויא ! אויף א פֿאָלק בכלל קען מען נאָר דורך זיין
מוטטערשפֿראַבֿע אָרער ערציהונגס־שפֿראַבֿע װירקען, **חֿאָרן**
ראם וואָרט מיט רעם דער מענטשט אז פֿון קינדהײט אָנגעוואָרגם,
וֿעיד אם טיעפֿסטען אײננערנאַבען אין זין אין הארץ, ניט מחמת
לעבֿטזאַפֿט נאָר מחמת נעװאָהנהײט און װירקט איבֿער רעם אם
שטאַרקסטען. נאָ אין אָבֿער ריא ערציהונגס־שפֿראַבֿע בײא אונו
אזוי ניטדריא נאָר נישטא רא, וויל מיר זיין ריא סבה אונ טהען
אין איהר ניט רא, וואָם מען ראַרף אין א שפֿראַבֿע צו טהֿף.
ראריבער זעגין, ראבֿם מיר, אללע מרחות, יודען בכלל צו בל־
דען נאָר אומיסט ! כל זמן מעװעט אונו ניט טוט רער ראָוין ער
אך צו אללע אומיסט נלֿיך מאבֿן: אז אונױער נאָטודליבע שפֿראַבֿע
ר. ה. ריא שפֿראַבֿע וואָם מיר רעדען אין איהר אין רעם נאַטֿר־
ליבֿען אונ ווירקליבֿען לעבֿען, זיא װאַלל פֿאר א שפֿראַבֿע
נילֿסען. וויא וואָלל אויסנעבֿילדעט װערען, בכדי וויא װאָלל ווירר
בֿילֿען קענין, זיא וואָלל אונו קענין אלין נוטער קאַנאָקטאָרי) צווישען

מענטש!װידער מיטשטעט ער זיך אין פֿרעבֿט ... זיך אין ריא צֿעֿ נאָצע
טֿ־ אָבֿער פֿרֿעמרע שפֿראַבֿען, בכדי ער װאַלל פֿעָרשטען יודיש
אן צֿם אומגליק רערט ער נאָר אֿוס'ן שלאַף יודיש, ארער אֿ
ער רֿערשרֿעקֿם זיך פֿ פֿעֿליצים. ניט ער אנֿשטריֿא אויף יֿודיש
יֿודֿיש ... פֿון קֿין פֿרֿעמֿרער שפֿראַבֿע חֿעט ער יֿשֿט בֿאֿן אֿוֿן
ניט מֿאֿבֿען זיֿנֿע, וֿוֿל ער איֿ שֿון איֿן מֿאֿל פֿאֿר אֿלֿע מֿאֿל אֿין
אֿרֿער ניֿט אֿוֿסֿפֿעֿנֿעֿצֿיֿגֿעֿן נֿעֿוֿאֿרֿין, אֿוֿן פֿון זֿיֿנֿער. מֿאֿבֿֿט ער ליֿצֿֿוֿת
אֿוֿן וֿעֿהֿט וֿיֿא וֿוֿם מֿעֿנֿלֿיֿך אֿיֿ זֿיֿך פֿון אֿיֿהֿר אֿבֿצֿעֿהֿעֿנֿהֿעֿן!—
אֿעֿלֿבֿֿע נֿעֿבֿיֿלֿרֿעֿטֿע יֿֿודֿען קֿעֿנֿען צֿוֿיֿשֿען זֿיֿך אֿפֿיֿלֿו, אֿוֿיֿך
ניֿט וֿיֿן ניֿט פֿֿרֿיֿנֿער, חֿאֿרֿין אֿיֿטֿלֿיֿבֿֿער אֿין וֿיֿא הֿאֿט פֿיֿנֿֿא אֿ
יֿֿ

רעם פאָזיטיוון אונ דעם נעגאַטיוון דיענען, ערשט דעמעלט, אַז
נישט פריהער איז צו האָפֿען אַז מיר אַריִמע יורעץ וואַלעק
אַנהייבין בכלל צו געהען גלייך מיט אַללע פעלקער, וו. אין דער
בילדונג, הן אין דעם גליק; וואַסט איך, ראַכט מיר, רא מע־
מענאָגרע: אַ פֿאַלק בכלל אויף אײן אַנרערער שפראַבע ביל־
דען, אַז שוֹער, גלייך וויא מען וויל אַ פֿערד אויף רעם בודרעם
צום הײא אַרוֹיף שלעפפען.

אַנדערע וואָרטֿען אוֹים דער יורישער שפראַכֿע או וֹא
קלינענט וויא ניט נוֹט ; אונ איך האַב אין עך דאָם עוֹוֹת צו
וואַגען או וֹיא קלינעם נאַין שעַרן. איך וֹועל שוֹין, נ. וואַגען
שעַנער, אַוֹ שעַרן וויא דאָם פֿאַגעוואַשע פראַנצעַוויישֿ אֿייֿר וווֹא
דאָם מאַמעטלימֿע ענגלישֿ און כבֿפֿרט פֿאָר רעם יורישע אֿיֿדר, נאַר
דאָם גליק פֿון אֿיֿטליבֿער וֹאַך אין נעמֿענֿרט (אֿנבֿעֿלאֿנֿנֿען) און
וֹואָם פֿאָר אַ וֹוֹעֿנֿעֿלֿע מען פֿער־וֹיֿטֿם וֹיֿא.

או מען וֹועֿם מֿיך אֿשֿער וֹעֿלֿין פֿרעֿנֿען : עם וֹואֿלֿם וֹיֿך
אַ. סֿך גֿלֿיֿבֿעֿר גֿעֿוֹוֹעֿן או מֿיֿר וֹואֿלֿלֿען נאַֿר פֿעֿרֿגֿעֿסֿסֿען אֿן
אֿטֿעֿר וֹשֿאֿטֿאֿ אֿן וֹואֿלֿלֿען וֹיֿך בֿעֿסֿעֿר נֿעֿוֹוֹעֿנֿעֿט מֿיֿט דֿער
גֿעֿבֿיֿלֿדֿעֿטֿעֿר שֿרֿאֿבֿע פֿון רֿעֿם פֿאַֿלֿק וֹואֿם מֿיֿר לֿעֿבֿען צוֹוֹיֿשֿען
רֿעֿם. קֿאֿן אֿיֿך עֿנֿעֿֿרֿן או מֿען רֿצֿרֿף נֿיֿשֿט קֿיֿקֿֿען אֿוֹיֿף רֿעֿם
וֹואֿם חֿאֿלֿם גֿלֿיֿבֿעֿר או וֹואֿף רֿעֿם רֿעֿם וֹואֿם עֿם אֿֿז ;
מֿעֿנֿלֿיֿך עֿם וֹואֿלֿם אֿיֿך גֿלֿיֿבֿעֿר גֿעֿוֹוֹעֿֿן או רֿיֿא נֿאֿֿצֿע וֹעֿֿלֿם
וֹואֿלֿל נאַֿר רֿעֿדֿן אֿיֿן לֿשֿֿן, עֿם וֹואֿלֿל וֹיֿן אֿיֿן סֿלֿוֹבֿה, אֿיֿן
אֿמֿוֹנֿה, אֿֿרֿעֿר עֿם וֹואֿלֿל וֹיֿן אֿמֿֿעֿֿֿם אֿיֿן מֿבֿע, אֿיֿן נֿעֿמֿֿעֿֿם,
אֿיֿן סֿֿֿם, עֿם וֹואֿֿל..... מֿאֿֿלֿע וֹואֿם עֿם וֹואֿֿֿֿם בֿעֿֿער נֿעֿוֹוֹעֿֿם!
לֿעֿֿ עֿֿֿה רֿעֿֿֿן מֿיֿר יֿוֹרֿֿם, אֿֿ וֹיֿא עֿם וֹוֹיֿֿֿם וֹעֿֿֿֿין
מֿיֿר פֿיֿֿֿֿֿע יֿוֹרֿֿן נאַֿֿ אֿֿֿ גֿעֿֿ נֿיֿֿ רֿעֿֿֿן צֿוֹוֹיֿֿֿֿן וֹיֿֿ נֿיֿֿ
קֿיֿֿ חֿוֹֿֿם, נֿיֿֿ קֿיֿֿ רֿֿֿֿם אֿֿ אֿֿֿֿֿֿ נֿיֿֿ קֿיֿֿ לֿֿֿֿ-קֿוֹרֿֿ !
דֿאֿֿֿֿֿֿֿֿ מֿֿ מֿֿ קֿיֿֿֿֿֿ אֿֿֿֿ רֿֿֿ וֹואֿֿ עֿֿ אֿֿֿ אֿֿ מֿֿ וֹעֿֿ וֹואֿֿֿ
בֿעֿֿֿֿֿ אֿֿֿֿֿֿֿֿֿֿֿֿ רֿֿֿ יֿוֹֿֿֿֿֿ שֿֿֿֿֿֿֿֿ, וֹעֿֿֿ סֿֿ נֿֿֿֿֿֿ הֿֿ
רֿֿֿ מֿֿ אֿֿ נֿֿֿֿֿֿֿֿ, אֿֿ וֹיֿֿֿֿֿֿֿֿ אֿֿ אֿֿ בֿעֿֿֿֿֿ אֿֿֿֿֿֿֿ וֹיֿ.

רֿֿ רֿאֿֿֿֿ פֿאֿֿֿֿֿֿֿֿֿֿֿ פֿֿ רֿֿֿ גֿֿֿֿֿֿ טֿֿֿ וֹואֿֿ
עֿֿ אֿֿֿ קֿֿֿֿ רֿֿ בֿֿ יֿֿֿֿ, הֿאֿֿ מֿֿ נֿֿֿֿֿֿ אֿֿ חֿֿֿ
וֹעֿֿֿֿֿֿֿֿ עֿֿֿ רֿֿֿֿֿֿ צֿ טֿֿֿ, אֿ אֿֿ הֿאֿֿ אֿֿֿ בֿֿ אֿֿ נֿֿ
נֿֿֿֿֿ אֿבֿֿֿֿֿֿֿֿ (צֿבֿֿֿֿֿֿֿֿ) אֿֿ הֿאֿֿ פֿֿֿֿֿֿֿֿ צֿֿ
רֿאֿֿֿֿ אֿ אֿֿ וֹואֿֿ רֿֿֿֿֿ עֿֿֿֿֿ פֿֿֿֿֿ פֿֿ אֿ רֿֿֿֿ-
יֿֿֿֿֿ אֿֿ יֿֿֿֿֿ-רֿֿֿֿֿ אֿֿ רֿֿֿֿֿֿֿֿ פֿעֿֿֿֿֿ מֿאֿֿֿ, חֿאֿֿֿֿֿ
עֿֿ קֿֿ רֿֿ נאַֿֿ אֿֿ וֹעֿֿ גֿֿ וֹיֿ, אֿ מֿֿ וֹעֿֿ לֿאֿֿֿ פֿֿ מֿֿ.
נאַֿ, מֿֿֿֿ לֿֿֿֿ לֿֿֿֿ, אֿֿ וֹשֿֿֿֿֿ קֿֿ קֿֿ חֿֿֿֿ נֿֿ מֿֿֿֿֿ!
לֿֿֿ חֿֿֿ עֿֿ הֿאֿֿ נאַֿֿ נֿֿֿֿֿ אֿֿ הֿאֿֿֿ אֿֿ הֿאֿֿ בֿֿ אֿֿֿ לֿֿֿ
אֿֿֿ מֿֿֿֿֿֿֿ בֿֿֿֿ אֿֿ יֿֿֿ בֿֿֿֿ, רֿֿ וֹואֿֿ צֿֿֿֿֿֿ, צֿ
רֿֿ הֿֿֿֿֿֿ אֿֿֿֿֿֿ ! וֹעֿֿ אֿבֿֿ מֿֿ אֿֿֿֿ נֿֿֿֿ גֿֿֿֿ
אֿֿ בֿֿ אֿֿ וֹשֿֿֿֿ אֿֿ וֹעֿֿ פֿֿ רֿֿ וֹעֿֿ קֿֿֿֿ, קֿֿֿֿֿֿ
וֹיֿ אֿֿֿֿ וֹעֿֿ וֹיֿ רֿֿֿֿ פֿֿֿֿֿֿ, חֿאֿֿֿ אֿֿ מֿֿ
חֿֿֿ נֿֿ רֿֿֿֿ צֿ וֹשֿֿ אֿֿֿֿ פֿֿ מֿאֿֿֿ, וֹיֿ בֿֿ
בֿֿֿֿ-וֹאֿֿ מֿֿ קֿֿ מֿֿ אֿֿ רֿֿֿ קֿֿ וֹֿ רֿאֿֿֿ נֿֿ
וֹֿֿֿ.— מֿֿ רֿצֿֿ וֹיֿ אֿבֿֿ חֿֿֿֿ נֿֿ מֿֿ וֹיֿ, אֿ אֿֿ,
וֹיֿ חֿֿֿֿ, אֿֿ מֿֿ וֹאֿֿ לֿֿֿ קֿֿ מֿֿ אֿֿֿ אֿֿֿֿ שֿֿֿֿֿ
נאַֿ פֿֿֿֿֿ אֿֿ וֹאֿֿ נאַֿ יֿֿֿ לֿֿֿֿ. חֿֿֿֿ.!! אֿֿ קֿֿ

נאָר ניט זיין נאָר, איך זאָל דאָם מיינען! אדרבה, אז יודיש
דעם חורין א נעבילדעטע שפראַבֿע וויא עם ראַרף צו זיין, וועם
מען זיך, ווערעלֿע מיר האַבֿען פריהער נעזואַנם, אֿלֿין־רֿינֿא בֿעֿסֿער
פֿעֿרֿשֿטֿעֿהֿען, אֿ אֿ רֿֿ שֿֿ שֿ שֿפֿרֿאֿבֿֿעֿן סֿמֿֿֿ אֿֿ כֿלֿל .—
בֿבֿֿ אֿֿ וֹאֿֿ נֿֿ נאַֿ אֿֿֿ אֿֿֿֿ וֹיֿ אֿ מֿֿֿֿ-נֿֿ,
קֿאֿֿֿֿ רֿאֿ אֿבֿ בֿֿ חֿאֿֿ וֹשֿֿֿ אֿֿ רֿֿ עֿֿֿֿ חֿֿ
יֿבֿֿ עֿבֿ (סֿבֿ כֿֿ רֿ 97) אֿ חֿֿֿ סֿֿֿ וֹֿ נאַֿ רֿֿ אֿֿ אֿֿ הֿאֿֿ
אֿֿ רֿֿ אֿֿֿֿֿֿֿ אֿבֿ רֿ יֿֿֿ שֿרֿאֿ:

(ענדע פֿאָלֿנֿם)

---

*) עם זא אֿ עֿֿֿ אֿ מֿֿֿֿֿ אֿֿ, עֿ וֹאֿֿֿ אֿ וֹֿ נֿֿֿֿֿ
אֿ רֿ מֿֿֿ וֹאֿ עֿ פֿאֿֿ סֿאֿֿ אֿ אֿבֿֿֿ נאַֿ אֿֿ
אֿֿ עֿ וֹיֿ חֿֿ אֿֿ—נֿֿ נֿֿֿֿ נֿֿֿֿ אֿ מֿאֿֿ אֿ יֿֿ-
חֿֿ אֿ רֿֿֿ—יֿֿ אֿֿֿֿֿֿ חֿֿֿֿֿ אֿ סֿֿֿֿֿֿ
בֿֿֿֿֿ אֿֿ יֿֿ חֿֿֿ אֿ אֿֿֿֿֿ אֿ פֿֿֿֿֿֿ
רֿאֿֿֿֿ.   ארֿ

1863, עמ' 364-366

דיא 4 קלאסֿען
פֿון י. מ. ליֿפֿשֿין
(פֿעֿרֿטֿעֿטֿונֿג)
יֿם סֿֿ תֿקֿוֹה כֿֿאֿֿֿ

לֿר טֿוֹבֿיֿהֿוֹ פֿעֿרֿעֿר.

זֿעֿל הֿשֿֿֿ שֿרֿֿֿ בֿֿ הֿֿֿ מֿֿֿֿ תֿֿ לֿ, רֿֿֿ
לֿֿֿֿ חֿֿֿֿ וֹֿֿ חֿֿֿֿֿֿֿ יֿֿ. וֹֿ נאַֿֿֿֿ;כֿ מֿ רֿֿ
אֿֿֿ אֿֿֿ אֿֿֿ בֿאֿֿ פֿֿֿ וֹֿ בֿֿֿ נאַֿֿ שֿֿ, בֿֿ
רֿבֿ וֹֿֿ וֹֿֿ הֿֿֿ בֿֿ רֿֿֿ הֿֿֿֿ הֿֿ וֹֿ
וֹֿ, בֿֿֿ הֿֿ שֿֿֿ כֿרֿ אֿ וֹֿֿ מֿֿֿֿ וֹֿ. רֿֿ
סֿֿֿ בֿֿֿ יֿֿֿֿ נֿֿֿֿ הֿֿֿ חֿֿ א' רֿ וֹֿ רֿֿ
הֿֿֿ שֿֿ חֿֿֿֿ, מֿֿ הֿֿֿ הֿֿ בֿ בֿֿ שֿֿ אֿֿֿֿ.
אֿ לֿֿ אֿֿֿ הֿֿֿ אֿֿ לֿ לֿֿ לֿֿ שֿֿ אֿ הֿֿֿֿ
הֿֿֿ מֿֿֿֿ, הֿֿֿֿ צֿֿ וֹֿֿ, וֹֿֿ צֿֿ, בֿֿֿֿ הֿֿֿֿ
(הֿֿֿֿ לֿֿֿֿ וֹֿֿֿֿ) הֿֿֿ מֿֿֿ מֿֿ, וֹֿ נֿֿ כֿֿ
אֿ רֿ בֿֿ בֿֿ וֹֿֿ הֿֿֿֿ וֹֿֿ. אֿ וֹֿ הֿֿֿֿֿ
הֿֿֿֿ, וֹֿֿ רֿֿ בֿֿ כֿ בֿ מֿ, כֿֿ נֿֿ כֿ אֿ
בֿֿֿ וֹֿ רֿֿ, וֹֿֿֿֿ תֿֿֿֿ בֿ נֿֿ הֿֿֿ צֿֿ
לֿֿֿֿֿ, אֿֿ בֿֿֿ וֹֿֿ סֿֿ עֿ עֿֿ. מֿֿ וֹֿ הֿֿֿ
עֿ הֿֿ הֿֿ מֿ וֹֿ בֿֿֿ יֿ לֿֿ הֿֿ מֿ רֿֿ חֿֿֿ
בֿֿ וֹֿֿ בֿ הֿ אֿֿֿ וֹֿ הֿֿ בֿֿ אֿֿֿֿ
(עֿֿֿֿֿ) מֿֿ : אֿֿֿ אֿֿֿֿֿֿֿ לֿֿ הֿֿ בֿֿֿ אֿ
לֿֿ הֿֿֿֿ סֿֿֿ עֿ הֿֿֿ, אֿ חֿֿֿ וֹֿֿֿֿ
כֿֿ בֿֿ אֿֿֿ הֿֿֿ, וֹֿ יֿֿ קֿֿֿ וֹֿ, יֿֿֿ
הֿֿֿֿ לֿ רֿ מֿ וֹֿ חֿֿ, בֿֿ שֿֿ לֿֿ רֿֿ
בֿֿֿ, לֿֿ יֿֿֿ הֿֿ מֿ מֿֿֿ ; עֿ אֿ כֿֿ
וֹֿֿ לֿֿֿ הֿֿֿ כֿ אֿֿֿֿ אֿֿ יֿֿֿ לֿֿֿ
בֿֿֿ כֿֿֿ בֿֿֿ אֿֿֿ ; בֿ יֿֿ כֿ חֿֿ עֿ תֿֿ

החפצים לעשות טוב עם מתי חלד הנצרכים לעזרתם) זה הא-
השבת נטול הטוב, כי האברים כותע אם יעמול להכן מזן
צידה לחכמים ונבונים, והחכמים מצד היושר והצדק לא ימנעו
סתא מחיה לנפשם, ולון את שכלם בלשון ובדרך שיוכלו להכן
אכן אם יכלא מלהרחיב כפרי חכמתם את אחרם העמלים
בערם ויכמב כל תכירהום בלשון שלא יכלו רלת העם ולא
יועיל להם, אזי יהדאיבו נם הם לשלוח ידם למסחרשות, לאחום
לקרחסם ולהטיב הררכן, ולא יהטרטסו סנית אחרים תם.

הנה לשונות צרפה ואנגליא, שגם הן בלולות מלשונות אשבנ,
שאלא רסו וזני על ירי תיעות חכמי חור חור, זה כטשלש
מאה שנה נסתלסלו מאד : ותחה, כעור בם התהרחמה האמור,
נעש מכשרות לשרים נשבכם וסליות, מטולות ויקרח : זה כמאא
שנה זה לשן אשבנו כמדרתה השפלה הזאת, כשמונים שנה
היתה שפת רסא לשן אברים, נם לשטוה הקרמנים יוזע
רוחי, בראשית תלחהום שפת שלוח היו עד שבא חכמדם,
צרש ומרזו טלהם, בכ בנינים, עשא נוחת עד תרין לשלימוה
תחלה שאנאו מטחוטמסום עלה. ההכן הא מניח הלשן כבל
עם תם, וכראשית הגחת אין הבריל בין שפה לשפה כבחינת
יקרתה, כי אם שבלשון זה האוהות מרומה מרהנעות, בלשניות
הטשניות, ובלשון זה התנועה מרומה על האשרות, בלשנות
הרחשוה : אבל כלם מטומסים רם כראשית, לא חזר ולא
הדר להם, אך רק הפלסדים יעש מרהוזר העולם כל נחסד
וצה נסהאלה ....קצי למילן ! לא טב עשה אד ! כמד
וחשארת לא תגחל, כרהלות השנינה. שלח הבריך אל החכם
רם"ם לביקש מאהו מחילה על עלבונו....... ואת העצה היעוצה
לך מרע החזן כלשוסך חרש טביתך כל הימים.

יעקב שמואל ביק

אנסערקוננ פֿון דער רעדאקציע. דעם בריף אין
לשון הקורש וועלין אסך פון ריא וואס לעוען דעם קול מבשר
ניט פערשטעונ. ראייבער דאלטען מיר עס פאר רעכט אידם
איבערצוטצען, ובפרט ער איז פון וערי א נרוסען מאן ר'
יעקב שמואל ביק ז"ל אין כראאי, א נרוסער למרן, א נרויסער
נעלעהרטער, אוז א פריממער יוד. ווער בריף שזץ קען רייננען
פֿאר א חשובה אלללע וואס דעם לאבען אים פאראסט יודיס. ר'
יעקב שמואל האט דעם בריף נעשריבעו צו ר' טוביה פערדער
וואס ראס חזק נעמאכט אים דעם נעריהמטען ר' מענדיל
לעֿדין אַעֿר ר' מענריל כאטצענאיער, פאר וואס ער האט
איבערנעזעטצט מטלי אויך פארֿסט יודיש ער פֿערענדערט אידם :
חענען דעם וואס ער האט איבערהעצט ספר מטלי פערדריסט
דיך, ריא נליכסט עם צום קרישטען פון פעגעל אוז צים קל
פון כרסוח אז חזח. רעראמאן ריך נאר פֿרינער ! ווא אוז האבן
נערהט אונזערע טאטטס אוז זיידעס, זיום 400 יאהר, יודיש האבן

---

*) תהער רעכט! אז דעטס וועט נענ שרייבט אהה. אהר
טיליט — יהעשט פ־ארנעסטסטן? דער נעמילדער יוד הארץ איז
נישם! אין דעם איבעכמילדעמ*ס העולם אהר נישם, ריא וואס
שרייכען פֿן נעל אֿער פֿן סטר חענעג— דיא ראהנע פֿרם אין
נישם!!....

נערענרט, נעדענקט און נערשדט ריאנאנים, דער ב"ח, דער רס"א
דער סט"ג, דער שד"ך ז"ל, אין דעם לשן האט נערערט דער ר"לנא"ר
נאך ז"ל. דער נעלערהרטער פאבריא, אין דין כך איבער דער
נעטראאליא (ערשטער טהייל ווייסע 274, האללע 1815) צעהלט
ריא שפראבע צווישען ריא טעכטער פן דער רייטשעו שפראבע.
אט וען ריא א לטערע רייכשע שפראבע איז דיר אזוי ליעב.
פאר וואס שרייעסט ריא נים אויף ריא איבערעצוננען פֿן תיד
פֿן דעם המניד, דעם צאינה וראינה און נחלת צבי; און ריא
ספרים (וואם ראבען אוך נענוטם אין ויער צייט און פֿאר
זייער נעטירען) איז ראם לשן טים טאטע גרייוען, מין נעפֿינם
נים פֿעל ווערטער (וואם מין דארֿף האבען אין א שפראבע.
אט עם איז ביא ווא נים ראם וואם וואם וועקט ראם נעפֿיהל
און מאבט איין איינדרוק אויף יעדען מענש וואם האט נעשמאק
אט ביא ר' מענריל סאטינואערס איבערעצוננ נעפינננן מיר
ראם אללעם, וואם וין נעלערנטסקיע פֿיהרט אים אויף רעם
וועג פֿן ריא רײנסטע לשונה, חאטש ריא שפראבע אַללײ
איז נאך ניט אויסנעבעסערם ביא אַצ.— אן ווען נערט נאך
אצט ארוים אללע וואם א צייטוננ אין דעם לשן וואם עס
רעדין ריא ביעיק אט ראם נעטיינע פֿאלק אין עסטרייך. וחן
ראם נעשטעהט פֿאר א פֿאלק וואם ויטצט נארֿט פֿן דער
רעוידענ, און וואם ווערע נעועטצע ועניג נעשריבען אויף רין
רימש, אין דער שפראבע וואם עם רערען וויער קאיוער און ווערע
נרויסע לייט. וחן פֿן ווירעטשענוננ נעבצן דיך ריא נעלערהרטע
מיה ווא וואללען ווא איבערנעבען אויף ווירער לשן קלטע אט
מארעאליטע ווערסער, כריווייא וואללען וויער קענין נאכ-
רערצעהלען אין דערהיים אט וואללען זיך ווא איינקריטצען
אין ווער ובען; סבל שבן. סבל שן פֿאר יורעו וואם ענין
פֿערטוארטעו אין אֿקריינא און קענין נים לעוען אין ריא ביבער
פֿן אין אנדערער שפראבע. אזוי טוהען אללע חכמים
אין איטלעכער נאציע וואם וויללען א טובה טוהן
ריא מענשען וואם דארֿטען וויער לאסקע. אט ראם
הייסט אבנערינענט, וואֿרן ריא טיעין (אן אוך דער פֿראֿסטע
נאֿר) ארכיטטען שער אן ביטצטר ווא וואללען אֿנריכטע
פֿאר ריא חכמים שפיח און לעבענסטטטעל, אוו דער וישר א
ווא ווירער וואללען הרענעטרען וויער נייסט אוז שטיוונ ווישר
שכל אין אזא לשן און אויך אזוי אין איטן וואם אֿטן וואללען
קעננען פֿערשטעטן. אבער אז ווא חעלין זיך צורירק-האלטען
אט חעלין נים חעלין ספֿרים דין טים ריא סֿרות פֿן ווישר
חכמה, ווירער כרידער וואם ארביטען שער אן ביטטער אֿ
ווירטעשוענען, און חעלין שריבען אללע ווירע תּתּרי אין א
לשן וואם דער נעטיינער עולם הענ נישט פֿערשטעטן אן
וועלין ווא דאריבער נים נוטצליך וין, רעטעלם חעלין ווא
אוך מחויכ וין אללין צו אקירין צו וען צו טנירעו, האללן האקען
וכחמה, און וואללען נים אומסט א האאה טוכן פֿן פֿרעם-
רעם ארבים.

נאֿ, פֿראֿצעטירש און ענגליש, וואם ענין אוך אויסעטישט

פֿון רײטש, נאליש, לאטין און גריכיש. נאר דורך דעם װאס
די חכמים אין יעדען דור האבען זיך מיה געגעבען, שוין געגען
300 יאהר, פֿון װיא לײט צו מאכען, װען זײ נעװאָרן אײס-
נעפֿינען, און איצט חאטש װיא האבען נאך אין זיך ראם
נעמיטשען, פֿון דעסטװעגען נוטצען װיא צו די ערהאבענסטע
נעריכטע און צו די נוטצליכסטע מליצות ערשט פֿאר הונערטע
יאר. איז די רײטשע שפראבע ערהער נידרית געשטאנען. פֿאר
אבצית יאהר איז רוסיש געװוען א בײערן-שפראבע. איך די
נאנין אלטע לשונות גריכיש און רעטיש אז װיא װען געמירטן
נעװאך, װען װיא אוך ערער נעטין געמאװען, ביז עם װען
נעקטטטען װיערע חכמים, האבען װיא נעלישערט, און נערײנטט
די װיא חורדער, האבען װיא אבנעהטהעלט אין רענעלן פֿון נראמא-
טיק, ביז װיא װען נעקטטטען צו דער נרעסטער פֿאָללקאָמסמען-
הײט װאם מיר בעװאָנדערן אױ. ראם פֿראָסטע פֿאָלק מאכט
א שפראבע אין אטלעבער נאצע. און אים אנפֿאנ איז אך קײן
שײם חילוק ניט צווישען אין שפראבע און דער אנדערער אין
איהר אײנענטליבער פֿינקים. נאר אין אין לשון װענן מעהר
רא אותיות פֿון צײבען װיא אװ מען רערט װיא אױם. װיא למשל
די שפראבע אין די צרו לענדער, און אין דעם אנדערן
לשון װענן די צײבען מעהר װיא די אותית, װיא װיא װילביט
שפראבען. אבער אלע װענן שטאָלפֿערט אים אָלאָג, האבען
קײן שײנקים און קין פֿאָרם. נאר װיא פֿלוסטין מאכע פֿן
דעם שטאאף א טהײערע כלי אּ װאונדערליך כליר.... טא
אין װאָרט, װיא האטט ניט רעכט נעשון פֿריער! עם העצװער
קײן נרוסטען כבוד מאכען װען דיא חטט דײן װירלעבץ
פֿערטטעטליבען. שיק בעטסטער אּ כריף צו ר' רם אנ בעט
אידם װיער פֿאר דעם װאם דיא האטט אידם בעליידירט. ראם
איז דיא עצה װאם עם גּוט ריר דײן פֿריער װאם װינשט ריר
חטד נוטם.

יעקב שמואל ביק

נאך דעם ארטיקעל פֿן ה' ל'-העבץ, האלטען מיר עם אין דער צײם
אומער רער אָך זיך אויסטורעט. מײ-ן דים מיר הָגע אָננעהוירען
ארוטענעבע דעם יקל סבֿרא. אך אונן נעצ ניט טטעלן נעהטתועצ זיך
אייטטטורערן איבער אתוער צורק, חײל רים טתצנען װענ נעה-היל, טריל
שריעץ נאןעװאלם אונ האבען אָטלי נעטריבעל אז מיר טהעצ אמטעב
װאם מיר רעהיהאלטעל רים פֿעָראומעע טמר-אבע װאם חאלם שיך
צײט נעתיטען לאנ וי אּ צו פֿערדעטעקא, װ-איך װיא מאכם אין אלא
צריח אקע אידר קקן קי יד נים רעכט-רעדן שם לשן אֹ
ניט לע-רת קין שם חכטה; אקער אידר אז ער מהוח בײא אנדערע
נותצט עם און אבעסטרערט פֿון דער װעלט. אנרערע װידער האבען
נעהר נעלקבט אנדער מדה. װיא מינען אּ דאם אה טער נטעלן צ
פֿולדען ראם פֿאַטע פֿאלק װאם נעלט שון ניט נערן אין שולע
טרין לערן אנרערע לטתות. ניט מען מט עט-ענט דיא װיא נעהאלל אן
דעם לשת.נעם. נוטען װיא פֿערישטערת. מיר האבען אבער ניט נעװאלל
מאןען אז מיר טהען נליך. נאר איטצ טעהן אנז זין אז דא ראם
מ-טתח אינטערעם. נאר איצע װאם מיר ליים נעהען װיא ראם װ דער
נעלם איז רים רים טהון נליך. איך האבען מיר זיך אללין
איבערצײנט את אנרער האבען אנץ רערע.הלס װיא טיסטעלע
סנטרטן אתף-.פ-אסטאקים. אלטע ליים און חיימ-ר זיטצען אױך דעם

מאָרק אָרער פֿרײסאַנעאכטם אין שטיב. אָרער בעלי-מלוח, לאָאָם-
ניקים, בעלי-מלאות אין מטאיינים; מענושען װאָם קעגען קײן אנרער
לשן ניט ליינען, ניט פֿערשטעהען אונ זיא ליינען קל מכער טטאאא
טענער. שטעללען אױף מיל און אדרץ, האבען א הנאה פֿן אללעם
װאָם דיא לעזען, זיא פֿרײען זיך צו הערען װאָם עם נעהם פֿאר אין
רער װעלם, את אלץ װאָם מען דערצעהלט זיא, פֿן אלטע נעשעכט-ן
אונ פֿן װיססענשאפֿטען אין כיא זיא ניעם, זיא רעדן דערנאך
איבער את בעאורטהיילען. נו זינ שון שוין איצם לאבען הער עם װילל,
מיר װיסען בײא זיך אז מיר נעהען אױף א װיכערען חּין צו אנטער
מינע אנרטערע בריער אױף מטום יורדיש בעקאנגנט צו מאכען מים דער
חעלם אנ װאם עם מהם אין אױף אהרע, װיא לערנען אורטהיילען
ריכט-ג איבער די ערע פֿאליטישען נעגען װיתער ירעל-נית-ע, נעטנען דעם
קאיסער את דער רענירונג, נעטנען רער טענטליכען נעטעללשאאם בכלל
אנ נעטנען ױהר נאצע בעתולדער, אית נעטנען מענא װיא נאטטם
בעטעלפֿניש. ראכט זיך את ראם הײטט ריא אַמח בּ-יורונ את עם
איו װ-ר לצבלח קין חילוק נים אױף װעלבער שפראבע ראם אה
נעהאנם נעװאָרן. אבי מען פֿערשטערם אנ-ק, את װער שטעפאם פֿאר דיא
װאם קעננען קין אנרערט את עם את דיא אוטמענליך בײא זײנע
יאהרין אין אנרערע צו לערנע. —

א חך דעם את ראם פֿיטסע הלימות װאם מהײל מיטען, עם
חעם אּ מענליככיים רין ירען װאללען זיך אבנעהירענען פֿן יורדיש. מיר
האבען שון נעטרען אז מלכים אה האבען זיך פֿערלענם שפראבן אוים-
טואַסטען את ראם אּ את אוטמענליך נעטהעטן, חיבא טתן זאל ריא 2
מיליאהן ירען את אנרער לאגר צוסהיילען עם 'װאללען קין צװויא
ירען ניט צהאטסטע כלייכען, את ראם װעט ער רעדין ירדיש קין א
נאלטיושען יד. װאנם אך האם איה אהר הללם, ריא שפראבע תטטה
דעם ירדין צ   צם האַרץ אנ אהר װנם עם א הערטל װאם מתן
קאן עם את אין קין אנרערע ניט איבערטטטען.

נאר איטם את מיר הערען שון פֿ-על אמת נעפֿילדעם את
קלינע מענשען, װאם קין קאה את קין שנאה הלם װיא ניט צורק
מרה צ רין רוא מיאארחיים; את דיא ליבכען שון אנרער חסר װאם
מיר מהעטן מים אנרטערע בריער; אדם את אַ שן צײם ميר זאללען
רערן, װאָם אַללן אין אינטעננטטליך אמטטר טהעג צ זאללען מיר ריא
ירדישע שפראבע ביטטעלכװיטם אױסקטטטען אבעסיל רעם דעם אוים-
ליטען את אביכל טיט רײטטען מערטער היכדטע- װאָם טיר זיך אללע מָאהל
אריינעראלען את פֿערטיסעטטט בין אַ רער עדם נעויאדגם װע-ץ
סים װיא, סים רער צײם װעם זיא װע-א אךן אים נע-נע רײטטע
אנ װעם נילטענ פֿאר   א ביכערשפראבע, װיא ריא דײטטע שפ-אבע
אללין װאם האם ענעל-אדעטא אימהעם-ממ אימטטע-אבען. אדער װאללען מיר אנרעא
ירדיש איסמילדעל פֿאר א בעטורערע טפ-אבע.

(ענע פֿאלנם)

1863 עם' 375-380

דיא 4. קלאסטעון
פֿ-ק-מ- ליפשין

אמערקונג. — (ענע) אין דעם פֿאלל, װען מיר
זאללען װעלק אתער ירדיש אױסקילדען פֿאר אּ בעטונרערע שפראבע,
נאר פֿאר זיך, סען װאלל זיך קעננען מים איהר בערטען; דארף סען

מ.כען א גראמאטיק און א ווערטערבוך, און דאס איז נאך דער
שווער, וזארין אם דאם ארימע לשן איז ערשט נעטהיילם
אין עטליכע ארטען — נרוים פוילים, קליין פוילים, ליטוים, את
נעמישם מים רוסים, נאליציש, סאלדאוויש וכדומה. סלא פן איין
מדינה צו דער אנדערער איז נאר א נרויסער חלוק, איינער לאכם
פן דעם אנדערן את פערשטעהט איהם כמעט נים, ווא לסל א
פוילישער דעם ליטואק את פערקעהרם ; נאר אפילו פן איין שטארם
אין דער אנדערער איופ עטליכע מייל, רערם מען אין איטליכער
אנדערם, את מען בעגיונט זיך מיט אנדערע ווערטער. ווא אזוי ראבי
מען הים סוה איז מען ווילל מאכען א גראמאטיק, וועמם לשן וועם
מען אננעמען פא- דעם עיקר ? — סיר נעפינען צוואר אים אללע
פראוויצען סעניצען וואם האבען זיך נעמריהם צו שרייבען יורדיש, ווא
לסל : דר עמשטענער עזה, ר' אבּ נעמטלאבּער, ר' יצעי סאיר
פעקעלשטיין, ה' רירסמאן יכהומה, זיא האבּען אבּער נאר נעמ-יעבּם
נעריכטען (שירים) אויכער דער דד עמשטענער האם נעמריבּען
סמירקעלעם.. את ר' ישראל אקסמנפעלד האם א סך רא.סאנען את
טהעאמערע פערפאסם, רערפ פן לע'נ נאר נעגרוקם דער ערסמער
הדישער רעקרום. נאר איטליכער בּעזונרער האם נעמריבּען ליים דעם
לאגר ווא ער אזז, את האם זיך זיין איינמנע ארטסגראפיע (אויסלענע)
את אויסשפראכע. סילא איטליכער פן זיא את דיע חיטורים סהן
זיך איינצערמען דין לשן את זיין איכלענן אז ריא בּעסמע ארם, את
את זיין נעמנעט ענוג שין רא ננעג סנעצען וזאם פערשטעהען איהם ;
נאר אתק אתק את אם ערנסטען. נער וועלמען נערק אז אתדער צייטענ
זאלל דין נאר אללע נאם, הע, את פוילק, את סולין, את אין נאליציען,
ראסיס סיר וועללען פרעלין וואם סיר וינטען, אללע יודען צו סער.
איינער, איתער וועל זיך אתמענעסמירען פא- רעם אנרעדן את
אללע וועללען קריגען איין רעה, חאם נם את וואם רעכם את לשם
הכלל. א חרן דעם איז אתק אזער שוער אתטערע צייטענ צו ליימען,
וועללען סיר אללען אלל שרייבען, אח שוער, אללע חיך א כימען
אויסשפילללען וכאדעם סיר האבּען נוך א כלאטם. דעם הסלין, צו
רעהינירען, את צוויסטענע האם אוך א נאוועסטע מערר סעם או
עם אם אם איער רא נעראנקען פן פערשיענעע שרייבּער.. נאר א חרן
וואם סערבהרבעטנעסמהילסהאתען דיך אתטערע נעכלדרעטם יודען ני- נעריכטם
צו שרייבען את האלסן פראזא ערק נ-אמען פאר תחינה לשת, חאם
עם שמאהע נים א קין עין נעכילדרעטען סענע, את נאר ונעינעע מאבען
איבערדעטצונען ארער אימ.פעלטצעע, א חרן רעם חייסט סיר זיך פאסט
נים קין צעה צו נעכען מיט ווייע- לשן את אויסלענע. סיר קעננען
רעם עולם נים דעם קאפ פ ערדרייען, כאלד אוזי את כאלד אמי
איסללענען את רערען ; את וזירער איטלעיכען בעזונרער אויסבּעסטערן
איך אתדער שמיינער, אח איך שוער את נים איטללעיכער סחבר
אח רערם סים ציפ-יודען.—
ראריכער בּענמען סיר אז אללע נעכילדעטע סענשען וואם
סעמען זיך נים פ סם פ-אסם יודש את ווִללען סיטאריבּייטעןן ריא

ספראכע צו מאכען פאר א לשן, דיא וואללען אתצ וייער סיתנ
וואנצ, עפּיט א מיטטעלוועג צו נעפּינען, סיר זאללען קעננען יוצא זין
אללע רעות, כרי סיר וואללען קעננען אללנעמיין ווירקען.
איני ראכם זיך אז אתוער ארטאנראפע איז נים שלעכם.
סיר ניכען זיך מה אז איטלעכיער יאלל זיך קענע לעזען ווא ער איז
נעוואהנם. לכסל' איין אלף סים א קמץ (אָ) אח בּיא אתק נליין
ווא איך O אים רייטשען ; איין אלף סים א קמץ את א קסט את א
שטרעכעלע פן אויכ'ן (אָ) אח חא ז, וזידר- אין טהייל הערטער
וואפ דער פּוילישער יוד רערם ווא אוים או (i) את דר ליטוורשער
יוד דער פּוילישער דער דייטש רערט ווא אוים סים אָ (ר)., שריבען סיר
אם ו, ווא לסל' צוקער וכדומה. חידר- לענען סיר אוים חיא חיא סענליך
איופ דער ארם ווא עס אח אח דר- דייטשען איבּערזעמצונג פן
תציך ; וזארינק, אזוי חיא היינם האבּען שין א סך יורען חומשים סים
איבּערזעטצונג, וועם איינם רעם ארערן העלפּן אז סען וועם זיך
נעהוירעגען סים דר ארטאנראפע וואם ר' משה סענדעלסואהן האם
נעמאבעט אין זין צייט את חאם את ענננענוסטען כסינ אין דר נאנצער
וועלם. דאריכער שריבען סיר ס.נכע ווערטער ווא דייטש, את אח א
סאר יארר ארים, אז דאם ועם זיך איינפיר-ען, וועלק אללע ירדען אתק
פערשטעהן את וועלין האבּען איין בּיכערשפראכע. את דאם ווייסם דיך
אוך יעדער נעכילדעטער סענש או אח דייסט את אח רוכרש את
אח אנרערע לשינות, תענק אללע זאכען איתצען אההיילם אין דרייא ארסען,
טהייל ו ערק איכסיערערערס סענליך (לשן זכר)., טהייל ווייכּליך (לשן
נקבה). טהייל אכּליך (נים סענליך אונ נים ווייכּליך) לסמ.בל, דער סים
(אח סענליך) דיא שישסיעל (ווייכּליך), ראם נלאָו (הכליך),אים יורישע
אה אתק אזוי, נאר אזוי ווא בּיא אתק את קין נראסאטיק נים רא,
זאנם סען אתק אויף טהייל ערטער 'דאם נלאָו, את אויף אנרערע .דא
נלאָו., יורם פערר. וכדומה. אח סענליך אן דר אח דייטשער שפראבּי.ַ וואם שארטם
עם ורק סים וען וענינינסטענע אין דיא כּיכּר איק לשן האכּעו ?
ונעינסטענם וועלק זיך אללע פערשטעהן.
ראם אח אתוער סיתנ, סיר ניכען זיא נים אוים פאר ריא
בּעסטע את בּעסטען נעכיל-רעטער סענשען זאללען אתק וזאנען וייער סיתנ,
סיר וועלק אללע וואלעם אהסמלן את דאם א בּעסערער פן איטל'עכען ארומ
נעסטן.. אפשר איז כּאחם ריא צייט וועגם זיך שין א.לין סאכ.ען את דיא
פאראנראן עגים א לשן ווערען.
אלל.ענפאללם אח נעטהרו אז ריא וואם דעהןן אין ריא נוטא-
ליכקים פן רעם "קול סכ.שר", וזאללען זיך נעכ.ען פרילא אבּאַנענ-
טן צו פ.ערשאפּ.ע.. כרי סיר זאללען קעננען בּעסטעןע איהם צו
רערהאלטען את נים דר צייט וועם וועם זיך שין אלין מאכען את ריא
אוצרינג חברותא וועלין כיסלעכוייז פערבעסערט ווערע.
ארו.

Card-reader to Hebrew writer Ruvn Braynin: 'You are in love with a wealthy woman (Hebrew), of old, aristocratic lineage. But beware of a young, attractive servant girl (Yiddish) who will cause you much trouble!' (*Der groyser kundes*, November 25, 1910)

מתתיהו מיזעס און די פּאָלעמיק וועגן ייִדיש

ג. קרעסעל

SUMMARY: MATESYOHU MIZES (MATTATHIAS MIESES) AND THE POLEMIC
ABOUT YIDDISH BY G. KRESL

*A historian of both Yiddish and Hebrew literature (1911–) details the role of the
linguist Mizes/Mieses (1885–1943) in defending Yiddish from Hebraist/Zionist attackers,
many of whom were 'giants of the age'.*

געהייליקט דעם אָנדענק פֿון שלום אַש ז״ל

אין דער טשערנאָװיצער קאָנפֿערענץ, װאָס איז פֿאָרגעקומען אין 1908 (30סטן
אויגוסט — 3טן סעפּטעמבער), האָבן זיך באַטייליקט באַקאַנטע שרײַבער, ניט נאָר פֿון
דער ייִדישער ליטעראַטור אַליין. קיינער האָט זיך אָבער ניט פֿאָרגעשטעלט, אַז די
סענסאַציע פֿון דער קאָנפֿערענץ און איר צענטראַלפֿונקט װעט זײַן אַן איבעראַשנדיקער
רעפֿעראַט, פֿול מיט לומדות און באַהאַװנטקייט, פֿון אַ מענטש װאָס זײַן נאָמען איז
כּמעט װי ניט ניט געװען באַקאַנט ביז דעמאָלט אין דער ייִדישער ליטעראַטור. גאָר אַ יונגער,
אין גאַנצן 23 יאָר אַלט — האָט מתתיהו מיזעס (אין העברעיִש פֿלעגט ער מקפּיד זײַן
אויפֿן אויסלייג: מיזיש) רעפֿערירט אויף דער טשערנאָװיצער קאָנפֿערענץ װעגן די
װיסנשאַפֿטלעכע יסודות פֿון דער שפּראַך־אַנטװיקלונג, און זײַן רעפֿעראַט האָט געמאַכט
אַזאַ געװאַלדיקן אײַנדרוק, אַז י. ל. פּרץ האָט פֿאַרגעלייגט דעם רעפֿעראַט אַרויסגעבן
אין אַ ספּעציעלער בראָשור, מחמת דאָס איז געװען דער ע ר ש ט ע ר װיסנשאַפֿטלעכער
עסיי אויפֿן געביט פֿון דער ייִדישער שפּראַך־פֿאָרשונג אין דער נײַער צײַט. װי באַקאַנט
אין דער פֿאָרשלאַג ניט דורכגעפֿירט געװאָרן אין לעבן; ס׳זענען אויך, װי באַקאַנט,
קיין שום פּראָטאָקאַלן ניט פֿאַרבליבן פֿון דער טשערנאָװיצער קאָנפֿערענץ. מען דער־

• פֿון דער סעריע „די פּאָלעמיק װעגן דער ייִדישער שפּראַך און איר ליטעראַטור אין דער
העברעיִשער ליטעראַטור". די ערשטע אָפּהאַנדלונג אין דער סעריע — זע : די גאָלדענע קייט נומ׳
20, ז״ז 338—355.

צײלט, אַז אײניקע חובבי־שׂפֿת עבֿר האָבן אױף דער קאָנפֿערענץ אױסגעבראַכן אין אַ
געװײן, הערנדיק מיזעסעס רעפֿעראַט, װײל עס איז װי צוגענומען געװאָרן בײ זײ די
װיסנשאַפֿטלעכע באַזע פֿאַר דעם דורכװיסיקן קשר צװישן נאַציאָנאַליזם און דער העברעי־
שער שפּראַך. מיזעס האָט אָנגעװיזן אױף די פֿיל פֿעדעם װאָס בינדן נאַציאָנאַליזם מיט
דער ײדישער שפּראַך.

די איבעראַשונג איז נאָך גרעסער געװען, װען ס׳איז באַקאַנט געװאָרן נאָך אַ
קורצער צײט, אַז מיזעס איז אַן אױסגעצײכנטער שרײבער אין העברעיש, פּױליש און
דײטש, און אַז ער שרײבט דװקא אין די דערמאַנטע שפּראַכן און ניט אין ײדיש.

ס׳איז צו באַװוּנדערן װאָס גראָד אין די דאָזיקע פֿרעמדע שפּראַכן שרײבט ער
זײנע טיפֿע פֿילאָלאָגישע פֿאָרשונגען איבער ײדיש מיט טיפֿער לומדות און קענטעניט,
און — כאַראַקטעריסטיש — אין ײדיש האָט ער כמעט װי ניט געשריבן במשך זײן
גאַנץ לעבן, אַ חוץ אײניקע אַרטיקלען און נאָטיצן, װאָס האָבן ניט קײן גרױסן װערט
אין פֿאַרגלײך מיט זײנע אַרטיקלען אין די אַנדערע שפּראַכן. דער װאָס װיל זיך באַ־
קענען מיט זײנע פֿילאָלאָגישע פֿאָרשונגען װעגן דער ײדישער שפּראַך, מוז אָנקומען
צו דער דײטשער שפּראַך, און דער װאָס װעט עס טאָן, מעג זײן זיכער, אַז ער װעט ניט
חרטה האָבן. גלײך בײ דער ערשטער זײט פֿון די דיקע בענד װעט ער דערפֿילן, אַז ער
האָט פֿאַר זיך אַ געלערנטן פֿון אַ ניט־געװײנטלעכן פֿאַרנעם, אַ פֿאַרשער װאָס זײנע
ידיעות גרענעצן זיך ממש מיט לעגענדאַרישקײט. און בסך־הכל איז מיזעס געװען זײן
גאַנץ לעבן אַ סוחר אין פֿשעמישל, גאַליציע. אַ זאַך װאָס איז ממש שװער געװען צו
גלײבן.

זײן גאַנץ לעבן איז מיזעס געװען זײער טעפֿעריש, אָבער ערשט ניט־לאַנג אין
אונדז באַקאַנט געװאָרן פֿון אַן אַרטיקל פֿון מאיר באַסאָק, װעלכער איז צוזאַמען מיט
מיזעסן געװען אין געטאָ די לעצטע טעג פֿון זײן לעבן („די לעצטע חדשים פֿון מתתיהו
מיזעס" — דבר 25סטן סעפּטעמבער 1950), אַז ער האָט איבערגעלאָזט מאַנוסקריפֿטן
פֿון גרױסע װערק און, לױט װי מ׳האָט געהערט, האָט זײ אַרױסגענומען פֿון זײער באַ־
העלטעניש אַ געװיסער ד״ר קראָנענבערג, װעלכער האָט פֿאַרלאָזט פּױלן און געפֿינט
זיך ערגעץ־װוּ (אפֿשר װעט ער זיך דאָך אָפֿרופֿן און לאָזן װיסן אין דער עפֿנטלעכקײט
װעגן דעם גורל פֿון מיזעסעס מאַנוסקריפֿטן װאָס געפֿינען זיך אין זײן רשות).

אָבער פֿאַר די העברעיש־לײענער איז דער נאָמען פֿון מתתיהו מיזעס כלל וכלל
ניט געװען פֿרעמד אין דער צײט פֿון דער טשערנאָװיצער קאָנפֿערענץ, װײל מיט אַ יאָר
פֿריער איז ער געװען אַרײנגעטאָן אין אַ שאַרפֿער און טיפֿער פּאָלעמיק, אין ה ע ב ר ע י ש,
איבער דער רעכט פֿון דער ײדישער שפּראַך און איר ליטעראַטור. די פּאָלעמיק האָט
זיך געפֿירט מיט דעם נעסטאָר פֿון דער העברעיִשער זשורנאַליסטן־משפּחה, נחום
סאָקאָלאָװ, און װי װי אַ המשך פֿון דעם מיט אַהד־העם, אַ קורצע צײט נאָך דער טשערנאָ־
װיצער קאָנפֿערענץ. דער רעדאַקטאָר פֿון העולם, נחום סאָקאָלאָװ, האָט אָפֿגעגעבן אין
זײן צײטונג אַן אָנגעזעענעם פּלאַץ דער פּאָליטיק װאָס מיזעס האָט אױפֿגעהױבן. ער
דערקלערט פֿאַר װאָס ער קומט ענטפֿערן מיזעסן אױף זײנע אַרטיקלען: „װײל אַלץ
װאָס מען קען זאָגן לטובת דער ײדישער אומגאַנגשפּראַך איז שױן געזאָגט געװאָרן

דורך אים מיט מער וויסנשאפט, באגרינדונג און פארטיפונג, ווי דאס איז ווען עס איז
געזאגט געווארן דורך אנדערע". דאס באווייזט, אז סאקאלאװ האט זיך גלייך דערקענט
אויף דעם יונגן צוויי און צוואנציק יאריקן מחבר.

א פאר ווערטער וועגן דער אכסניה העולם, וווּ מיזעס האט אנגעהויבן זיין פּאָ־
לעמיק, אדער — ריכטיקער געזאגט — זיין פארטיידיקן די ייִדישע שפּראַך און אויפווייזן,
אז זי איז ראוי צו זיין אונטער איין דאך מיט נאציאנאליזם און ציוניזם. געווען איז עס
אן אפיציעלע העברעיִשע אכסניה פון דער ציוניסטישער אָרגאַניזאַציע, וואָס איז
דעמאלט געווען אונטער דער אנפירונג פון דוד וואלפסאָן. דאס איז געווען אין א צייט
ווען סאקאלאװ איז געווען פריי מחמת דאס פארמאכן זיך פון זיין הצפירה, וואס ער
האָט רעדאגירט און אליין אויסגעפילט די גאנצע צייטונג במשך צענדליקער יארן. אין
יענער צייט איז סאקאלאװ געווארן פארבעטן געווארן דורך וואלפסאָנען צו פארנעמען דעם אמט
פון גענעראל־סעקרעטאַר פון דער ציוניסטישער וועלט־אָרגאַניזאַציע, און גלייכצייטיק
האָט ער געשאפן פאר אים דעם העברעיִשן זשורנאל העולם, פאראלעל צו דער דייטשישער
צייטשריפט די וועלט, וואָס האָט שוין געהאט עקסיסטירט צען יאר. סאקאלאװ, וועלכער
האָט געהאַט פארבינדונגען מיט די וויכטיקסטע העברעיִשע און ייִדישע שרייבער, האָט
כמעט זיי אלעמען פארבעטן צו באטייליקן זיך אין העולם. עס איז א סימבאל פאַן
כאראקטער פון העולם אונטער סאקאלאװס רעדאקציע, וואָס דער ערשטער נומער איז
געעפנט געווארן מיט א פראגמענט פון מענדעלעס "פישקע דער קרומער", באארבעט פון
מענדעלען אליין אין העברעיִש. און דא, אין דעם ערשטן יארגאנג פון העולם, אין 1907
הייבט אן מיזעס זיין פארטיידיקונגס־קאמף פאר ייִדיש מיט א סעריע ארטיקלען, וואָס
זענען דערשינען אין די נומערן 22, 23 אונטערן נאמען "אין זכות פון דער ייִדישער
שפּראַך".

ב

נחום סאקאלאװ האט טאַקע רעזערווירט פאר די דאָזיקע ארטיקלען דעם אויבן־
אָן פון העולם, די ערשטע זייטן פון זשורנאל. און דאָך האָט ער געהאַלטן פאר נייטיק
זיך אפצוגרענעצן מיט א באַמערקונג פון דער הקדמה פונעם מחבר אין די ווייטער
דיקע שורות: "מיר ברענגען דערמיט דעם ארטיקל, וואָס באַלייכט א וויכטיקע פראגע
פון נאציאנאל און וויסנשאפטלעכן שטאַנדפונקט און, באזונדערס, צוליב דער וויכטיקער
וויסנשאפטלעכער באלייכטונג. וואָס שייך די נאציאנאלע מאַטיוון, איז אונדזער מיינונג
א גאַנץ אנדערע ווי די מיינונג פונעם מחבר אין געוויסע' ענינים, און מיר וועלן זיך
נאָך אומקערן צו דער פראגע, און זיי באַהאנדלען פון אונדזער שטאַנדפונקט".

די הויפטטעזע קעגן וועלכער מיזעס איז שאַרף ארויסגעטראָטן איז, אַז אחוץ
א קליינער גרופּע פון סימפּאַטיזירער און ליבהאבער פון ייִדיש, "זשאַרגאָניסטן", הערשט
אן אלגעמיינע מיינונג, אַז ייִדיש איז ניט מער ווי "א שלעכטער דייטש, מיט א פאר־
דאַרבענעם צוגאַב פון העברעיִש און סלאַוויש, אן אומנאַטירלעכער געמיש, א זשאַרגאָן".
די דאָזיקע אנגענומענע מיינונג, וואָס די "זשאַרגאָניסטן" לייקענען אין איר, אָט די
מיינונג האָט דערפירט צו דעם, אַז די צוויי קעגנערישע לאַגערן — אַסימילאַנטן און

ציוניסטן — זענען פאראייניקט אין זייער מיינונג וועגן יידיש, אז צי די ייִדן ווילן זיך
אַסימילירן צווישן די גויים, צי זיי ווילן באַנייען זייער יוגנט און אויסלעבן זיך נאַציאָנאַל,
דאַרפֿן זיי פֿריִער ‏„פּטור ווערן פֿון דעם דאָזיקן געל‏ן שאַנדפֿלעק און אַראָפּוואַרפֿן פֿון
זיך דעם שעדלעכ‏ן און נעבעכדיקן איבערבלייב פֿון מיטל‏־עלטער וואָס רירט אָן די
גאַנצקייט פֿון דער נשמה און האַלט אָפֿ די אינערלעכע באַפֿרייונג”.

די דאָזיקע שותפֿות, אויף אַ געביט וואָס איז אַ גוזר אונטערגאַנג פֿון יידיש, קרענקט
שטאַרקט דעם שרייבער. מיינט עס דאָ, אַנגווערן אַ שפּראַך אויף וועלכער עס ריידן
מיליאָנען מענטשן, אין וועלכער עס פֿילן מיליאָנען, און דריקן אויס זייערע פֿרייִדן און
ליידן — — —”. שווער איז עס אים צו פֿאַרדייען די ‏„האַרמאָניע” צווישן גלויבן אין דער
פֿאָלקס־אויפֿלעבונג און צווישן טאָטאָרטייל אויף דער דאָזיקער מאַסנשפּראַך, און ער
וווייטיקט וואָס גראַד די רענעסאַנס־באַוועגונג פֿון אונדזער פֿאָלק הייבט אָן מיט
נעגאַציע, — ‏„אָפּצושניידן אַ גרויס שטיק פֿון דעם פֿאָלקס־אייגנטום”.

און מיזעס זוכט נאָך די וואָרצלען פֿתעם קאַמף וואָס דער ציוניזם האָט געפֿירט
קעגן דער ייִדישער שפּראַך און קען ניט באַגרייפֿן די סיבה דערפֿון. זאָגן אז דאָ איז
פֿאַראַן אַ קאָנקורענץ צווישן העברעיִשער און ייִדישער ליטעראַטור — עקסיסטירט
דאָך אַזאַ זאַך בכלל ניט, אַחוץ אין די מחות פֿון געציילטע פֿאַנטאַזיאַרן. די ייִדיש־
לייענער פֿאַרקלענערן ניט די צאָל פֿון די העברעיש־לייענער, ווייל זיי קומען פֿון גאַנץ
פֿאַרשיידענע פֿאָלקספֿערעס. עד־כאן בנוגע ליטעראַטור. וואָס שייך צום תחום פֿון לעבן,
דאַרף מען דאָך געוויס ניט מורא האָבן פֿאַר קינאה און קאָנקורענץ צווישן די צוויי שפּראַכן.
קיינעם וועט ניט איינפֿאַלן, אז העברעיש קען אַמאָל יִרשענען דעם פּלאַץ פֿון ייִדיש,
ווערן, הייסט עס, די אומגאַנגסשפּראַך פֿון ברייטע פֿאָלקסשיכטן. און אויב מען וועט
אויפֿהערן צו באַנוצן זיך מיט יִדיש, וועט געוויס ניט העברעיש זיין צווישן די קומענדיקע
יורשים — נ‏יערט די־לאַנדשפּראַך. און דאָס וועט זיין אַ שווערער קלאַפּ ניט בלויז ניט פֿאַר
דער ייִדישער שפּראַך, נאָר בעיקר פֿאַרן ציוניסטישן און נאַציאָנאַלן געדאַנק ; ווייל
דעמאָלט וועט די אַסימילאַציע פֿייערן איר גרויסן יום־טוב און נצחון אויף איר פֿייִנד —
דעם ציוניזם. די אַלע דערשיינונגען, קעגן וועלכע דער ציוניזם קעמפֿט, זענען עלול אויף־
צוהויבן דעם קאָפּ, אויב עס וועט פֿאַרווירקלעכט ווערן דער ווונטש פֿון די ייִדיש־קעגנער :
‏„צוזאַמען מיט דער שפּראַך וועט אונדזער פֿאָלק פֿאַרלירן זיין גאַנצן זעלבסטשענדיקן
אינהאַלט, זיין נשמה, עס וועט פֿאַרלאָרן גיין פֿאַרן פֿאָלק אַ וועלט פֿון גייסט און לעבן,
אַ ליבע וועלט, אַן אייגנאַרטיקע, אַ דאַנק דעם כּח פֿון איר זעלישן צויבער — — —”.
און דער ציוניזם וויל דאָך אָנהאַלטן די דאָזיקע נאַציאָנאַלע באַזונדערקייט, צ‏רלהכעיס
די אַסימילאַנטן, ביי וועמען דאָס איז שטאַרק פֿאַרהאַסט.

מיר זעען, זעצט פֿאַר מיזעס, ווי די הדיפט־סיבה פֿון דער דאָזיקער מלחמה קעגן
ייִדיש איז דער אַנטיסעמיטיזם, סיי ווען ער קומט באַוווסטזיניק פֿון די גויים, און סיי
ווען ער קומט אומבאַוווסטזיניק פֿון אחינו בני ישראל. דער בולטסטער אויסדרוק פֿון
אַנטיסעמיטיזם איז, ווי באַקאַנט, פֿאַראַכטונג צו יעדער זאַך וואָס האָט אַ ייִדישן ריח.
דאָס איז די פֿאַראַכטונג וואָס האָט מען שוין אין לאַגער פֿון די אַסימילאַנטן געבראַכט ביז
אַריבערגריין די גרענעצן פֿון ישראל. מיט אַלע הרעג‏ון פֿאַרמען וווּיל די אַסימילאַציע

עוקר זיין פון אונדזער פאלק „אלץ וואס איז יידיש, אפמעקן יעדן זכר פון בני ישעיה
און הלל, פון בני יואב און די חשמונאים". ס׳איז איבעריק יעדער וויכוח מיט זיי, וואַרעם
אויב מען וועט אפילו אויפווייזן מיט באגליייבטע ראיות דאָס פארקערטע, וועלן זיי זיך
ניט אָפזאגן פון זייער ציל. יעדע זאך וואָס באווייזט אַ צייכן פון לעבן ביי יידן און
יידישקייט איז אין אַ וווי אַ דאָרן אין זייערע אויגן, און ס׳איז אַ מצווה און אַ פליכט אוים־
צורייסן אים מיטן וואָרצל.

וואָס האָט אבער דאָס אלץ אַלץ צו טאָן מיטן לאַגער וואָס פרײדיקט נאַציאָנאַלע אוים־
לעבונג, און טוט אַלץ, כדי אַרויסצוברענגען פון דאָס ניי אויך די באזונדערע אנטפלעקונגען
פון אונדזער פאלק וואָס זענען אין פארלויף פון דורות פארדעקט געוואָרן מיט שימלז
„אויב מענטשן — טענהט מיזעס — וואָס ליבן זייער פאלק, האַלטן טײער זיין פאַר־
גאַנגענהייט און קעמפן פאַר זיין צוקונפט, אויב זיי זענען גאָר אויף כרת אויף דער יידישער
שפּראך און נעמען צו דערמיט פון אונדזער פאלק זיין לעבנסשפּראך — טאָר מען עס
ניט פארשווייגן. — — — צוליב נאַציאָנאַלע מאטיוון טאָר מען ניט דורכפירן אָט די
אבסורדישע השמדה וואָס קאן דערשיטערן די פאָלקס־נשמה — — —".

דאָס איז זיין הויפּט־טענה קעגן די מענטשן פון דעם נאַציאָנאַלן און ציוניסטישן
לאַגער. צו זיי ווענדט זיך מיזעס מיט זיינע רייד; דאָ רעדט ער צו זיינע ברידער און
פריינד מיט וועמען ס׳בינדן אים טויזנטער פעדעם.

ג

ווייזט אויס, אז דאָס איז דאָס ערשטע מאָל וואָס עס דערשיינען אין העברעיש
ראשי־פּרקים פון דער געשיכטע פון יידיש, און די אויפקלערונג ווערט געגעבן אויף
סמך פון אַ טיפער באהאָונטסקייט אין די אלגעמיינע יסודות פון דער שפּראַכן־אנס־
וויקלונג אין דער וועלט וואָס דער מחבר ווייזט ארוים. ער רעדט ווי אַ מומחה אין דעם
געביט, ברענגט ציטאַטן פון די בעסטע פאָרשער און דענקער אַזוי, אז מען קען ניט
אָפפרעגן איינס־צוויי זיין ארגומענטאַציע.

די מיינונג פון די העברעיש־ליבהאַבער וועגן יידיש איז דאך באקאנט: יידיש
איז אַ שפּראַכלעכער תהו־ובוהו, אַן איבערבליבעניש פון גלות, וואָס ברענגט אונדז
חרפה מיט זיין באַרבאַריזם. „פרעמד און מאָדנע איז די שפּראך פאַר אונדז. יעדער ייד
אין וועמענס נשמה עס טליעט אַ פונק פון דעם הייליקן באגער צו באַנייען די ערלעבכע
פאַרגאַנגענהייט פון דער גאָלדענער צייט, אומצוקערן זיך צו דער פּרעקטיקער עפּאָכע
פון זיין עבר — דארף אַראָפּוואַרפן פון זיך די לאַסט פון דער דאָזיקער וואָכעדיקייט,
וואָס לאָזט זיך ניט פאַרדײען און ברענגט בלויז צו פאַרדאַרבעניש". מיזעס קאָן ניט
פארשטיין פאַר וואָס און פאַר וועלן זאָל יידיש פאַרעכנט ווערן פאַר אַ פאַרקריפּלעניש
פון אַ פּרעמדער שפּראַך און ניט פאַר אַן אייגנאַרטיקן דיאַלעקט, פּולקום אין זיינע
אינעווייניקסטע געזעצן, אַט אַזוי ווי די שפּראכן פון פראַנקרייך, ענגלאַנד, שפּאַניע
און איטאַליע „וואָס זענען אויך געמישטע שפּראכן" פון דעם זעלבן מין. „די שפּראכן
פון מאָליער, וויקטאָר הוגאָ, סערוואַנטעס, דאַנטע א.אז.וו. זענען פונקט אַזאַ
זשאַרגאָן ווי די שפּראַך פון מענדעלע און מאָריס ראָזענפעלד. שפּראַך־אַנדערשקייט

אין נאָך ניט קיין פֿאָרדאַרבענישן" — דער אַ לעצטער זאַץ איז אַ וויכטיקער
כּלל פֿאַר מיזעסן און פֿאַר דער ייִדישער שפּראַך אין אַלגעמיין און אַ סך באַמיונגען
מאַכט ער, אַז מען זאָל אין דעם אָן ערשטראַנגיקן כּלל אין אַלגעמיינער שפּראַך־
וויסנשאַפֿט; דעם דאָזיקן כּלל נעמט מען, אָבער, ניט אין באַטראַכט ווען מען קומט צו
ייִדיש און דערפֿון דער מיאוסער צונאָמען "זשאַרגאָן". מיזעס פּראָטעסטירט קעגן דער
אַ באַליידיקער און פֿאַלשער באַצייכענונג. "מיר דאַרפֿן שוין אויפֿהערן איין מאָל
פֿאַר אַלע מאָל אָנצורופֿן אונדזער ייִדישע שפּראַך מיטן שפּאָטנאָמען ,זשאַרגאָן'. בלויז
אַנטיסעמיטיזם, באַוווּסטזיניקער אָדער אומבאַוווּסטזיניקער, קען פֿאַראורטיילן די ייִדישע
שפּראַך אַלס זשאַרגאָן, אַלס אַ מיאוסן שפּראַך־געמיש. פֿון פֿילאָלאָגישן שטאַנדפּונקט
איז אונדזער פֿאָלקסשפּראַך ניט הינטערשטעליק מיט איר שיינקייט לגבי די ראָמאַנישע
שפּראַכן — — ".

מיזעס עקספּאַנירט זיינע טענות אין אַ זאַפֿטיקער העברעיִשער שפּראַך, אָנגע־
פֿיקעוועט מיט נייע אויסדרוקן און שפּראַך־קאָמבינאַציעס, וואָס זענען היינט אָנגענומען
אין דעם העברעיִשן סטיל. אָבער דעמאָלט איז עס נאָך געווען אַ חידוש, וואָס בלויז
געציילטע העברעיִשע שרייבער האָבן זיך דערוועגט צו באַנוצן מיט דעם. זעט אויס
אַז דער פֿאַקט וואָס ער שרייבט העברעיִש דערמעגלעכט מיזעסן אָנצוּווייזן אויף אַן
אַנדער מין קעגנערשאַפֿט צו ייִדיש און דאָס איז — דער עטיקעט פֿון פֿרעמדקייט
וואָס די ליבהאָבער פֿון העברעיִש האָבן צוגעקלעפּט צו ייִדיש, כּדי צו באַווייזן אַז אין ייִדיש
איז דאָ אַ פֿאַרשוועבונג פֿון אונדזער נאַציאָנאַלן מהות, פֿון אונדזער יחיד אַלס נאַציע.
"מאריה דאברהם" — שרייט ער אויס פֿאַרביטערט — דער ייִד האָט זיין הונדערטער יאָרן
אויסגעהויכט זיין נשמה אין זיין שפּראַך, האָט זי אָנגעטרונקען מיט טייכן טרערן און בלוט,
געבראַכט אין איר צום אויסדרוק דעם שטורעם פֿון זיין צער, דעם צער פֿון גלות־השכינה,
פֿון גלות־הציבור און גלות־הנפֿש, פֿאַרוואַנדלט זי אין דעם שפּיגל פֿון זיין נשמה, פֿון
זיין ליידנדיקער און האָפֿנדיקער נשמה — — — דער ייִד האָט דערהויבן דאָס בינטל
דייטשע ווערטער און געמאַכט פֿון זיי די בעסטע אינטערפּרעטאַציע פֿון זיין נשמה,
פֿון זיין גייסטיקער וועלט — און זי איז פֿרעמד? ער האָט פֿון איר געמאַכט אַן אמתע
ייִדישע שפּראַך — און זי איז ניט זיינע? — — — ".

מיזעס רעדט דאָ מיט דער שפּראַך פֿון לאָגיק אָן סענטימענט, אָבער ער באַנוגנט
זיך ניט מיט דעם. ער פֿאַרמאָגט נאָך אַ פֿעקל באַווייזן, אַז מען טאָר ניט האַלטן ייִדיש
פֿאַר אַ פֿרעמדשפּראַך. די באַוווייזן הייבן זיך אָן מיט אַן אַקסיאָם, וואָס זיין יסוד געפֿינט
זיך אין אייניקע אייראָפּעיִשע שפּראַכן, קעגן וועלכע עס איז ניט פֿאַראָן קיין שום
אויסזעצונג, ניט קעגן זיי און ניט קעגן זייער באַזונדערקייט. מיזעס טענהט, אַז גע־
וויינטלעך ווערן אַנדערע שפּראַכן באַאַרבעט, ביז עס ווערט פֿון זיי אַ ספּעציפֿישע און
זעלבשטענדיקדיקע שאַפֿונג, און ביז די היינט איז נאָך קיינער ניט געקומען מיט קיין טענה
קעגן דער אָריגינעלקייט פֿון די דאָזיקע שפּראַכן. די פֿראַנצייִשע שפּראַך, למשל,
שטאַמט פֿון דער אַמאַליקער רוימישער שפּראַך און ווערט באַנוצט דורכן פֿראַנצייִזישן
פֿאָלק, וואָס האָט עס ניט, ווי באַקאַנט, קיין שום ראַסן־אַנגעהעריקייט צו דער אַלטער רוים;
עס קומט גאָר אַרויס פֿון דער קעלטיש דייטשער ראַסע. פּונקט אַזוי איז אַנדז דער

לויבט, און עס איז אפֿילו אונדזער חוב צו זען אין יידיש, די טאַכטער פֿון דער דייטשער
שפּראַך, אַ יידישע שפּראַך. „וואָס קאָן באַווײזן — פֿרעגט ער — אַן אוֹצר ווערטער אין
אַ שפּראַך פֿה וועלכן ס׳איז פֿאַלק, אויב דאָס פֿאַלק געהערט עטימאָלאָגיש צו אַן אַנדער
ראַסע? ניט ווערטער מאַכן אַ שפּראַך, נ י י ע ר ט ד ע ר ג י י ס ט ו ו א ָ ס
ב א ַ ל ע ב ט ז י. די מאַטעריע איז פֿאַסיוו — דער גייסט וואָס באַהערשט איז אַלץ".
מיזעס קומט צו הילף זיין אויסערגעוויילעכצ בקיאות אין די וועלטקולטורן און ער
ברענגט אָן אַ שיעור באַווײזן פֿון דער אַלגעבײנער קולטור-געשיכטע אין פֿאַרשיידענע
מדינות, אַז ניט דער רוי-מאַטעריאַל דעצידירט וועגן דער ספּעציפֿישקייט פֿון אַ שפּראַך,
נ י י ע ר ט ד ע ר ג י י ס ט וואָס ווערט אין איר אַרײַנגעהויכט דורך יעדער פֿאַלק.

מיזעס מאַכט זיך ניט לייכט דעם דעם וויכוח. אַלע טענות פֿונעם צד שכנגד שעפּט
ער אויס, כדי זיי צוניישט מאַכן און ניט איבערלאָז פֿון זיי קיין זכר. ער פֿירט דעריבער
ווײטער צום פּונקט וואָס הייסט — פ ר ע מ ד ס, און גיט צו אַז ווען אַפֿילו מען וויים
אַז די שפּראַך איז יאַ אַ זעלבשטענדיקע שפּראַך קלעפּט מען נאָך אַלק צו צו איר דעם
עטיקעט פֿון פֿרעמדקייט, ווײל די דאָזיקע שפּראַך האָט געטריי באַגלייט דעם ייד אין
ג ע ט אָ און אַ טיפֿישע אַרום אַ סימבאָל פֿון עכטע ירושה פֿון גע טאָ און פֿון יענעם לעבן,
פֿון וועלכן מיר ווילן זיך באַפֿרייען, דאָס מיינט: די שפּראַך „טראַגט אויף זיך דעם
שטעמפּל פֿון קנעכטשאַפֿט און אַ פֿריי פֿאַלק קען זיך ניט באַנוצן מיט איר. די יידישע
שפּראַך איז אַ שווערע משׂא אויף די נשמה-פֿליגלען פֿון אונדזער פֿאַלק, וואָס האַמעוועט
זיין אויפֿשטייג".

מיזעס זעט אין דעם דאָזיקן מאַטיוו ענגהאַרציקייט און קלייגקעפּלדיקייט. ערשטנס,
פֿרעגט ער, פֿילט טאַקע עמעצער אויפֿריכטיק אין יידיש די אַמאָליקע פֿאַרשקלאַפֿונג,
וואָס האַט געצוווּנגען יידן אַנצונעמען די שפּראַך? אין תוך גענומען איז אָט די שפּראַך
אַ פֿרײַע אין איר גײַסט, און אויב עס זענען אַפֿילו געווען טרויעריקע היסטאַרישע אום-
שטענדן, וואָס האַבן זי אַרויפֿגעצוווּנגען אויף אתדה, זאָגט עס אונדז לחלוטין גאָרנישט.
אויך די אָקופֿאַנט, די רוימישע קאָלאָניסטן, געשיקט דורך די צעזאַרן, זענען זיכער
ניט געוווען ווידיקער גרויזאַם לגבי די אָקופֿאַציע-פֿעלקער, וועלכע זיצן פֿון דער אַנדער
זייט פֿון די אַלפּן, און דאָך זענען, ווי אַ רעזולטאַט פֿון דער אָקופֿאַציע, אויפֿגעקומען
אין אײראָפּע אייניקע שפּראַכן — און דאָס האַט כלל ניט געשטערט צו זען אין זיי די
נאַציאָנאַלע שפּראַכן פֿון אַלע יענע מדינות און לענדער. נאָך מער, די דאָזיקע פֿעלקער
זענען געוווען פֿאַרשקלאַפֿט גײַסטיק און פֿיזיש, בעת די יידן זענען דאָך געוווען אונטער-
געדריקט בלויז פֿיזיש, בלייבנדיק פּאָליטיש פֿרײַ און זעלבשטענדיק אין זייער
גײַסטיקן לעבן. „פּנימיותדיק — שטעלט פֿעסט מיזעס — האָט דער ייד קיין מאָל זיך
ניט דערנידעריקט; אויך דער שפּיגל פֿון זיין נשמה, די שפּראַך, האָט זיך קיין מאָל
ניט דערנידעריקט. און אויב דער פֿראַנצויז, שפּאַניער אָדער ענגלענדער שעמען זיך
ניט מיט זייערע שפּראַכן וואָס די אָקופֿאַנטן האַבן גץעבראַכט, דאַרף זיך נאָך ווייניקער
שעמען מיט דעם אונדזער פֿאַלק".

און דאָ קומען מיר צו אַ טעמע וואָס האַט געזאָלט פֿאַרנעמען גאָר אַן אָנגעזעענעם
פּלאַץ אויף דער טשערנאָוויצער קאָנפֿערענץ, וואָס איז פֿאַרגעקומען פּונקט אַ יאָר נאָך

דער פּאָלעמיק וועגן ייִדיש, אַלס איינע פֿון די נאַציאָנאַלע שפּראַכן פֿון אונדזער פֿאָלק.

ד

מיזעס שטעלט זיך אָפּ אויף דער אָפֿט געשטעלטער פֿראַגע: פֿאַר וואָס זאָלן ייִדן
האָבן צוויי נאַציאָנאַלע שפּראַכן, בעת אַנדערע פֿעלקער האָבן נאָר איין נאַציאָנאַלע
שפּראַך? מיזעס העלפֿט זיך אויך אין דעם פֿאַל אַרויס מיט זײַן אויסערגעוויינטלעכן וויסן,
ער ווײַזט אויף, אַז געוויסע פֿעלקער און נאַציעס האָבן טאַקע מער ווי איין שפּראַך,
למשל, די אירלענדער וואָס האָבן אויסער איריש אויך די ענגלישע שפּראַך. ער דערמאָנט
דערבײַ אַז ענגליש איז פֿאַר די אירלענדער די שפּראַך פֿון דעם פֿאָלק, וואָס האָט זי
אָקופּירט און הערשט איבער זיי; דאָך שטויסן זיי ניט אָפּ די שפּראַך און באַנוצן זיך
מיט איר. דאָס זעלביקע איז מיט די עגיפּטער — זיי באַנוצן זיך מיט דער שפּראַך פֿון
זייערע אָקופּאַנטן, די מאַמעלוקן, און פֿאַרמאָגן צוויי אייגענע אַלטע שפּראַכן: קאָפּטיש
און אַלט־עגיפּטיש. פֿון דאַנען איז שוין קלאָר דער אויספֿיר: „אונדזער ייִדישע
שפּראַך (און מען דאַרף לייגן אַכט אויף דעם וואָרט, 'אונדזער', כּדי אָנצוּווײַזן אַז די
שפּראַך איז א עצם מעצמנו) האָט אַ נאַציאָנאַלן און פֿילאָלאָגישן זכות־הקיום".
מיזעס באַגרונטיקט זײַן טעזע מיט שפּראַכגעזעצן פֿון ייִדיש, וועלכע ער האָט
נאָכגעפֿאָרשט און געפֿונען אין זיי אַ שפֿע פֿון קאָמבינאַציעס און וואָרט־צירופֿים, נײַע
באַדײַטונגען און אויסדרוק־אופֿנים וואָס פֿעלן אין דער אָריגינעלער שפּראַך, כאָטש די
ווערטער זענען די זעלביקע. געוויס איז דער זשורנאַל העולם ניט דער פּאַסיקער פּלאַץ
פֿאַר אַ סך בײַשפּילן. אָבער אויך דאָס ביסל וואָס מיזעס ברענגט איז באַלערנט און
באַלײַכט די נײַע ספּעציפֿיש־ייִדישע באַדײַטונג, וואָס ייִדן האָבן אַרײַנגעבראַכט אין
רײַנע דײַטשע ווערטער. פֿון דאַנען איז קלאָר, אַז די דאָזיקע שפּראַך איז אַסימילירט
געוואָרן דורך די ייִדן, און וואָס זיי האָבן זי אַזוי פֿאַרדרייט אַז עס איז אַרויסגעקומען
אַ נײַ ייִדיש לשון.
מיזעס שילדערט מיט אַ סך חן ווי ווי דער ייִד האָט אָפּגעשלאָסן דעם תחום פֿון זײַן
פּנימיותדיק לעבן פֿאַר דער דרויסנדיקער וועלט און ווי אַלע אויסדרוק, וואָס געהערן
צו דעם דאָזיקן תחום, זענען געוואָרן רײַן־ייִדישע, דאָס הייסט — העברעיִשע. הונדערטער
און טויזנטער אַנדערע ווערטער זענען דאָ פֿון דעם מין, ווי, למשל, נשמה, שׂכל, חכמה,
עילוי, חלום, טעות, שקר א"א. די אידענטיפֿיקאַציע פֿון העברעיִש מיט דעם
פּנימיותדיקן לעבן פֿונעם ייִד קומט אויך צום אויסדרוק אין מוזיק, למשל.
געזונג אָנצוּווײַזן אויף אַזעלכע ווערטער ווי: ניגון, זמר, כּלי־זמר, קול, משורר אדג"ל.
אַזוי קלײַבט מיזעס אויף פֿיל בײַשפּילן פֿון פֿאַרשיידענע שפּראַכצווײַגן און ברענגט
אַרויס קודם־כּל די ייִדישקייט פֿון ייִדיש און איר קשר מיטן נשמה־לעבן פֿון פֿאָלק. מיט
די זעלבע בײַשפּילן ווײַזט ער אויף, אַז דאָס גײַסטיקע לעבן פֿון דעם ייִדישן מענטש,
וואָס איז געוואָרן אָפֿן פֿאַר דער העברעיִשער שפּראַך, איז געוואָרן פֿאַרשלאָסן אויף אַלע
שלעסער פֿאַר די דײַטשע ווערטער. מיזעס האָט געמאַכט פֿון דעם אַ גרויסן כּלל: אין
דרויסנדיקע ענינים פֿלעגט דער ייִד דערלויבן זיך דערנעמען פֿון אַן אַנדער שפּראַך, אָבער
אין זײַן אינעוװיניקסטן לעבן האָט ער זיך באַנוצט, בדרך כּלל, מיט העברעיִשע ווערטער.

אויך אין דעם פֿאַל האָבן די העברעישע שפּראַך־קאָמבינאַציעס דורכגעמאַכט גאָר
אינטערעסאַנטע מעטאַמאָרפֿאָזעס, פֿאַר וועלכע מיזעס האָט געבראַכט באַלערנדיקע ביי־
שפּילן, אויף וויפֿל דער פּלאַץ האָט עס דערלויבט.

די קליינע פֿאָרשונג איבער דער העברעיש אין ייִדיש וואָס דער דאָזיקער
אַרטיקל אַנטהאַלט, איז אַ וווּנדערלעכער אַנאַליז פֿון די העברעישע יסודות אין ייִדיש,
אַ טעמע וואָס האָט שפּעטער באַשעפֿטיקט אַ סך פֿאָרשער. מיזעס באַנוצט זיך אָבער
ניט בלויז מיט ביישפּילן, נאָר ער ווייזט אויך אָן די געזעצן וואָס שטעלן פֿעסט און
דערקלערן די דאָזיקע וווּנדערלעכע דערשיינונג. די שפּורן פֿון העברעיש געפֿינט ער
אויך אין די דיקדוק־געזעצן פֿון דער ייִדישער שפּראַך און ער איז איינער פֿון די
ערשטע וואָס האָבן געפֿרווווט אויפֿקלערן זייער אינערלעכע געוועצמעסיקייט. קעטיק
אַז מיזעס האַלט זיך אָפּ פֿון אָנגעבן דעם גאַנצן מאַטעריאַל וואָס ער האָט ער זיין באַזיץ
(ער האָט עס שפּעטער געטאָן אין ביכער און פֿאַרשונגען, פֿאַרעפֿנטלעכטע איבערהויפֿט
אין דייטש). איז דען אַ וווּנדער וואָס ער איז געווען דער פֿאַסיקסטער מענטש צו
עקספּאַנירן אויף דער טשערנאָוויצער קאָנפֿערעבץ די וויסנשאַפֿטלעכע יסודות פֿון דער
ייִדישער שפּראַך און וואָס זיין רעפֿעראַט האָט אַרויסגערופֿן אַזאַ סענסאַציע אויף דער
קאָנפֿערענץ?

נאָך דעם ווי מיזעס האָט פֿאַרענדיקט מיט זייב באַווייזן, אַז ייִדיש איז אַ **ייִדישע
שפּראַך** אין איר גייסט און תּוך, און מען טאָר זי ניט באַטראַכטן ווי אַ פֿרעמדע צווייג,
נעמט ער זיך צו די העברעיסטן, וועלכע האָבן גהר געווען כּרת אויף דער דאָזיקער
שפּראַך. „מיר, די נאַציאָנאַליסטן, וואָס די צוקונפֿט פֿון אונדזער פֿאָלק איז אונדז טייער
און אונדזער ציל איז צו דערהויבן די נשמה פֿון ייִדישן פֿאָלק, מיר דאַרפֿן זיך קעגן־
שטעלן יעדן פּרווו צו ליקווידירן ייִדיש. אונדזער לאָגער דאַרף זיך באַפֿרייען פֿון די
פֿאָראורטיילן, וואָס האָבן זיך אָנגעקליבן אַרום דעם היסטאָרישן אָפּשטאַם פֿון ייִדיש.
די נאַציאָנאַלע און ציוניסטישע באַוועגונג, וואָס קעמפֿט מוטיק קעגן דער אַסימילאַציע,
דאַרף באַגרייפֿן, אַז ייִדיש קאָן האַמעוווען דעם אַסימילאַציע־שטראָם, וואָס שלעפּט אַוועק
מיט זיך באַדייטנדיקע טיילן פֿון אונדזער פֿאָלק. בלויז אונדזער ייִדישער שפּראַך קאָן
זיין דער פֿאַנצער, וואָס וועט אונדז באַשיצן פֿון דער אַסימילאַציע וואָס ווערט אַלץ
שטאַרקער און אָנגרייפֿנדיקער".

מיזעס לאָזט הערן קעגן דער ציוניסטישער באַוועגונג גאָר שאַרפֿע רייד. דער
ציוניזם האָט ניט אַנגעזירט דאָס פֿנימיותדיקע לעבן פֿון אונדזער פֿאָלק און די
פֿאָלקסמאַסן שטייען אומבאַהאָלפֿן קעגן די מעכטיקע אַסימילאַציע־שטראָמען פֿון איין
זייט, און קעגן די גויישע השפּעות פֿון דער צווייטער זייט. די ייִדישע שפּראַך איז אָן
עפֿעקטיוויות דאָמבע קעגן דעם, ווייל זי איז די ריידשפּראַך פֿון גאַנצן פֿאָלק און טראָגט
אין זיך זיין נשמה, — און דאָ איז שוין מיזעס נאָענט צו דער מסקנה, מיט וועלכער ער
פֿאַרענדיקט זיין אַרטיקל: „אונדזער הויפֿט פֿאָדערונג — די פֿאָדערונג פֿון די נאַציאָנאַלע
ייִדן — דאַרף זיין: אָנערקענען דעם זכות־הקיום פֿון ייִדיש אומעטום ווו עס געפֿינען
זיך ייִדן, איינפֿירן זי ווי אַ לערנשפּראַך אין די שולן, ווי אַ משׂא־ומתן־שפּראַך צווישן
ייִדן. בלויז אַ ייִדיש פֿאָלק וואָס רעדט אַן אייגן לעבעדיק לשון קאָן באַ נייען זיין יוגנט.

בלויז אין דער ײדישער שפּראַך איז די ישועה פֿאַר דער ײדישער
נאַציע״ (אונטערגעשטראָכן אין אָריגינאַל).

ה

דער רעדאַקטאָר פֿון העולם, נ. סאָקאָלאָו, האָט זיך ניט באַנוגנט מיט געבן אַ
קורצע באַמערקונג אין אָנהייב פֿונעם אַרטיקל; ביים סוף לייענען מיר זיינע אַ לענגערע
באַמערקונג מיט דער אונטערשריפֿט „רעדאַקציע פֿון העולם״, וואָס פֿרוווט צעשטערן
מיזעסעס בנין. סאָקאָלאָוס הויפּט־טענה איז, אַז מיזעס האָט איבערגעטריבן בנוגע דעם
צוגאַנג פֿונעם נאַציאָנאַלן לאַגער צו ײדיש. די נאַציאָנאַלע ייִדן זענען ניט קעגן
ײדיש; זיי גיבן נאָר אָפּ די בכורה העברעיִש פֿון נאַציאָנאַלן שטאַנדפּונקט. אָבער לעצם
הענין ווייזט אָן סאָקאָלאָו אַז ײדיש איז דאַך בלויז ײדיש־טייטש, און ס׳איז פֿאַראַן
אויך ײדיש־שפּאַניש, ײדיש־אַראַביש, ײדיש־פּערסיש. דאַקעגן איז פֿאַראַן בלויז איין ײדיש,
אַן קיין שום צוגאַב, און דאָס איז העברעיִש. קנאַפּע טויזנט יאָר האָבן ײדן בייִגעטראָגן
פֿון זייִער גייסט פֿאַר ײדיש — און פֿאַר אַלע פֿרעמדשפּראַכן, מיט וועלכע ײדן באַנוצן
זיך אין גאָר דער וועלט. אָבער וואָס איז שייך העברעיִש האָבן ײדן בייגעטראָגן פֿאַר
דער דאָזיקער שפּראַך פֿיר טויזנט יאָר בערך. און אַחוץ דעם אונטערשייד אין
עלטער׳ איז נאַך פֿאַראַן אַ תוכיקער אונטערשייד: צו העברעיִש זענען געווען שותפים
אַלע ײדישע קיבוצים פֿון דער וועלט. נאָך אַ מאָל שטרייכט סאָקאָלאָו אונטער, אַז
מיזעסעס טענות קעגן די קעגנער פֿון ײדיש זענען פּולשטענדיק גערעכטע, אָבער ער
לייקנט אַז די נאַציאָנאַלע ײדן געהאָרן צו די ײדיש־קעגנער. „אין ציוניזם — זאָגט
ער — איז ניטאָ קיין שום שינאה צו ײדיש און צו עס שטיט ניט די פֿראַגע פֿון קוקן
אויבן אראָפּ אויף דער שפּראַך פֿון פֿאָלק. אַזאַ באַציִונג קאָן מען ניט טרעפֿן ביי די
העברעיִשע שרייבער, ווייניקסטנס ביי דער מערהייט פֿון זיי. פֿאַרקערט, די מערסטע
העברעיִשע שרייבער שרייבן אויך אין ײדיש״. סאָקאָלאָו האָט זיך געקאָנט צורעכענען
צו די דאָזיקע שרייבער, ווייל אויך ער האָט געשריבן אין ײדיש, און ס׳איז שווער געווען
אים חושד צו זיין אין אַ פֿיינדלעכער באַציִונג צו ײדיש. מיט דעם איז ער געווען
גענלעך צו די מערסטע העברעיִשע שרייבער פֿונעם נאַציאָנאַלן לאַגער, וואָס האָבן זיך
באַנוצט מיט ײדיש, אָנהויבנדיק פֿון די גרויסע און פּאָפּולערע, ביז די ווינציקער
באַקאַנטע.

זיכער זענען פֿאַראַן אין ײדיש אַ סך העברעיִשע ווערטער, אָבער דאָס זאָגט נאָך
גאָרנישט לגבי דעם מהות פֿון דער שפּראַך און איר צוקונפֿט. איינצלנע ווערטער שאַפֿן
נאָך ניט די שפּראַך. און וואָס שייך דער צוקונפֿט פֿון דער שפּראַך אַסימילירט זי זיך
דאָך אַלץ מער מיט דער סביבה און ביסלעכווייז פֿאַרשווינדן די בולטע סימנים, וואָס
מיזעס האָט אויסגעברילעך אַרויסגעבראַכט. סאָקאָלאָו זעט אין דער העברעיִשער שפּראַך
דעם לעבנסשטאַם פֿון דער גאַנצער נאַציע, און אויב ס׳מערקט זיך אין גלות אַ דער־
ווייטערונג פֿון העברעיִש, האָט דאָך די שפּראַך אַ גלענצנדיקע צוקונפֿט אין ארץ־ישראל.
העברעיִש בליט דאָרט אויף. מען קאָן זיך קוים פֿאָרשטעלן אַז דאָרט זאָל זיך אויסשפּר
רעמען אַן אַנדער אַלגעמיינע שפּראַך״.

סאָקאָלאָו סומירט זיין שטעלונג אין צוויי הויפּטפּונקטן: א. די ציוניסטישע באַ־

ווּעגונג וועט בשום אופן ניט דערלויבן, אַז העברעיש זאָל אָפּטרעטן איר אָרט יידיש;
פֿאַרקערט, אומעטום וועלן געמאַכט ווערן אַלע מעגלעכע באַמיונגען, כּדי אײַנצופֿירן
אין לעבן העברעיש אַנשטאָט יידיש. אין יעדן פֿאַלאַץ, וווּ עס איז פֿאַראַן אַ ברירה צווישן
יידיש און העברעיש, איז דער ענטספֿער אַבסאָלוט קלאָר: העברעיש; ב. ווען אָבער
פֿײַנד פֿון דרויסן וועלן פֿרוּוון אָנגרײַפֿן די רעכט פֿון דער יידישער שפּראַך און באַ-
צייכענען זי אַ ווי אַ מיאוסן זשאַרגאָן, וועט די נאַציאָנאַלע באַוועגונג פֿאַרטיידיקן יידיש
מיט אַלע כּוחות. די שטעלונג פֿון די ציוניסטן צו יידיש איז ניט צו פֿאַרגלײַכן מיט
דעם צוגאַנג פֿון די אַסימילאַנטן, און מען דאַרף ניט אַרײַנלייגן ביידע אין איין זאַק.
יעדער אײַנער וועלכער געהערט צו דער ציוניסטישער באַוועגונג קאָן זיך ניט באַציען
מיט פֿאַראַכטונג צו יידיש.

ס'זעט אויס, אַז מיזעס איז געוווּן גאָר צופֿרידן פֿון סאָקאָלאָווס קורצע באַמער-
קונגען, ווײַל דאָס האָט אים געגעבן אַ געלעגנהייט אַרויסצוברייטערן זײַנע טעזיסן און
פֿאַרטיפֿן זיי. ער האָט דעריבער גלײַך געענטספֿערט סאָקאָלאָוון אין אַ צווייטן אַרטיקל
אונטערן נאָמען: „נאָך אייניקע ווערטער וועגן דער יידישער שפּראַך" (דאָרט, נומער
26, זײַטן 318‏-320).

ו

אווראי האָט מיזעס געוווּסט, און נאָך ווי די געהדסט, וועגן די פֿאַרשיידענע פֿרעמד-
שפּראַכן, מיט וועלכע יידן אין גאָר אין דער וועלט באַנוצן זיך אַחוץ יידיש. אָבער דאָס
לייקנט לגמרי ניט אָפּ, אַז יידיש פֿאַרנעמט דעם וויכטיקסטן פּלאַץ צווישן די אַלע שפּראַכן.
מיזעסן פֿעלט ניט קיין ראיות און באַווייזן; צו באַכט אַ שפּאַציר איבער פֿעלקער און
לענדער אין גאָר דער וועלט, דערינגט אַרײַן אין די בעהיים‏מענישן פֿון זייערע אָפּשטאַם-
שפּראַכן און ווײַזט אויף, אַז עס איז כּמעט ווי ניט פֿאַראַן קיין פֿאָלק וואָס זאָל ניט האָבן
— אַחוץ זײַן הויפּטשפּראַך — אויך פֿאַרשיידענע דיאַלעקטן. אַלע פֿעלקער האָבן אַ סך
„זשאַרגאַנען", אָבער אין דער גרויסער וועלט איז אָבגענומען, אַז די מינדערהייט קאַ-
פּיטולירט פֿאַר דער מערהייט. פֿון דאַנען איז קלאָר דער אויסספּיר, אַז די יידישע פֿרעמד-
שפּראַכן רײַדן ניט קעגן יידיש נאָר פֿאַר איר. אין‏-און‏-אײנציקער סטאַטיסטישער
פּרט קאָן אונדז עפֿענען די אויגן: „פֿון 11 מיליאָן יידן אין דער וועלט (אין 1907) רײַדן
אַכט מיליאָן יידיש. פֿון די איבעריקע דריי מיליאָן האָבן זיך שוין ביי צוויי מיליאָן
אַסימילירט און קענען ניט קיין העברעיש און ניט קיין יידיש, און דער לעצטער מיליאָן
רעדט די פֿרעמדשפּראַכן וואָס סאָקאָלאָוו דערמאָנט און וועלכע אויך מיזעס רעכנט אויס
אויספֿירלעך. — „וואָס באַדײַטן — פֿרעגט ער — אַזעלכע פֿאַלקס‏-שפּליטערן קעגן
אַ פֿעסטן נאַציאָנאַלן בלאַק פֿון אַכט קום מיליאָן? מען קען זיי קום באַמערקן".

אַחוץ דער קוואַנטיטאַטיווער מינדערהייט האָט מיזעס נאָך מאַטיוון מבטל צו
מאַכן די אַ פֿרעמדשפּראַכן לגבי יידיש: „די אַלע האָבן כּמעט ניט קיין ליטעראַטור,
אויסער שפּאַניש (לאַדינאָ). די דאָזיקע שפּראַך, וואָס קעגנער פֿון יידיש האַלטן זי פֿאַר
אַ קאָנקורענץ‏-שפּראַך צו יידיש, איז להלוטין ניט ראוי דערצו. אין לאַדינאָ פֿעלט די
שפֿע העברעישע ווערטער וואָס זענען פֿאַראַן אין יידיש און שוין מיט דעם אַליין פֿאַר-
לירט לאַדינאָ די נאַציאָנאַלע אייגנקייט. פֿון די געצײַלטע שורות וואָס מיזעס גיט אָפּ

לאַדינאַ ווערט קלאָר, אַז ער האָט זיך פּאָרטיפט ווי געהעריק אין דער דאָזיקער פּראַגע
אָן עס זענען אים גוט באַקאַנט די פּאַרשונגען וועגן דער דאָזיקער שפּראַך אָן אֵיר
ליטעראַטור. ער איז מבטל די ליטעראַטור, ווייזט אָן ווי נישטיק זי איז לגבי ייִדיש,
אָן קלערט אויף אויף פּאַר וואָס: דאָס זענען געוואָרן אָפּגעריסענע אברים אין ייִדישן
פֿאָלקס־אָרגאַניזם, וואָס האָט מיט אַ באַזונדער עקשנות געקלאַמערט זיך אָן דער לאַדינאַ־
שפּראַך, אָן דעריבער האָבן זיך ניט אַנטפּלעקט אין איר, אָדער אין די וואָס באַנוצן זיך
מיט איר, קיין שום סימנים פון שעפּערישקייט. „די — טענהט מיזעס — וואָס ריידן אין
אַנדערע זשאַרגאָנען, זענען פּאַר אונדז פּאַראַליזירטע גלידער, האַלב־טויטע גלידער
אָן לעבנסקראַפט — — — אויב זיי ווילן זיך אומקערן צו אַ נאַציאָנאַלן לעבן, זיך
פּאַראייניקן אונטער אונדזער פּאָן, די פּאָן פון אויפלעבונג, זאָלן זיי זיך ביײגן פּאַר
אונדז, פּאַר דער שפּראַך פון דער פּאָלקס־ליטעראַטור". אויך צו דעם האָט מיזעס אַ
שפּאַר ביסל בײַשפּילן, וואָס ווייזן ווי אַ מינדערהייט־שפּראַך איז זיך מבטל פּאַר אַ
מערהייטשפּראַך. אויב דאָס לאָזט זיך ניט, איז דאָך מעגלעך אַ טאָפּל־נאַציאָנאַלע צוויײ־
שפּראַכיקייט, ווי למשל, אין בעלגיע, וואָ עס גייען אום צווייי שפּראַכן, אָבער ביידע
שטערן ניט דער נאַציאָנאַלער איינהייטלעכקייט.

מיזעס רעדט אויספירלעך וועגן לאַדינאַ, ווייל לאַדינאַ איז די אייניציקע פּאַסיקע
פּרעמדשפּראַך אויסער ייִדיש, כאַטש זי איז ניט קיין קאָנקורענץ פּאַר ייִדיש. נאָך אַ מאָל
שטרייכט ער אונטער די באַזונדערקייט פון ייִדיש, די ייִדישע נשמה אירע, איר אייגנדיקע
גראַמאַטיק. אויף די פּינגער פון בלויז איין האַנט האָט מען געקאָנט אויסרעכענען די
מענטשן, וועלכע האָבן אין יענער צייט גערעדט ריידן וועגן אַ גראַמאַטיק פון דער
ייִדישער שפּראַך, אָן צווישן זיי האָט מיזעס זיכער פּאַרגומען דעם אויבן אָן.

מיזעס באַגונגט זיך ניט בלית ברירה מיט קורצע אויספירן, אַז ייִדיש איז ניט ווי
אַלע אַנדערע זשאַרגאָנען, „וואָס זענען באמת ניט מער ווי פּאַרדאָרבענע שפּראַכן".
ייִדיש האָט זיך פּאַרייִדישט אָן איז געוואָרן אָן אמתדיקע פּאָלקסשפּראַך, אָן בלויז זי
איז מסוגל צו פּאַרהיטן אונדזער פּאָלק פון אַסימילאַציע.

וואָס שייך העברעיִש איז מיזעס זיך מודה ומתודה, אַז ווען ס׳וואָלט געוואָרן אַן
אויסוואַל צווישן ייִדיש אָן העברעיִש וואָלט ער אויסגעקליבן העברעיִש, אָבער אַזאַ
ברירה עקסיסטירט ניט, נאָר עס שטײט די פּראַגע: **ייִדיש אָדער די לאַנד־**
שפּראַך, וואָרעם יעדער איינער, וואָס הערט אויף צו באַנוצן זיך מיט ייִדיש גייט
אַריבער צו דער לאַנדשפּראַך. נאָך מער, ער וואָלט מסכים געוואָן מיט סאָקאָלאָוס
וואונטש, צו פּאַרבייטן די ייִדישע שפּראַך אויף העברעיִש, אָבער די ווירקלעכקייט איז
קעגן דעם אָן מאַכט עס פּאַר אַ פּולשטענדיקע אילוזיע. לויט מיזעסעס חשבון זענען
פּאַראַן אין אַלע אַלע גלות־לענדער אַרום הונדערט טויזנט ייִדן וועלכע קענען העברעיִש,
איז וואָס פּאַר אַ ווערט האָט אַזאַ צאָל אין פּאַרגלייך מיטן גאַנצן פּאָלק? מיזעס האַלט,
אַז מען דאַרף זיך רעכענען בלויז מיט דער ווירקלעכקייט אָן ניט ריידן וועגן צוקונפט־
וויזעס, וואָס האָבן ניט קיין שום אויסזיכט צו פּאַרווירקלעכט ווערן. אַ פּאָלק דאַרף
זיך אָנשפּאַרן אויף אַ ברייטער באַזע אָן פּאַר דעם איז ניט פּאַראַן קיין אַנדער שפּראַך
אחוץ ייִדיש.

צום באַדױערן איז שװער איבערצוהעצן גענױ מיזעסעס מאמר װעגן דער מהות
פֿון ייִדיש, װאָס איז געשריבן אין אַ פּרעכטיקן העברעיִשן סטיל, רײך מיט אַלע אױסדרוק־
פֿאָרמען פֿון דער שפּראַך, — און דאָס אַלץ, כּדי אױפֿצוװײזן די אידענטיפֿיקאַציע פֿון
דער ייִדישער שפּראַך מיט דער נאַציאָנאַלער זעלבשטענדיקייט פֿון ייִדישן פֿאָלק. ער
האָט ניט קײן מורא פֿאַר דעסטרוקטיװע השפּעות מצד דער סביבה, קעגן װעלכע מען
קאָן און מ׳דאַרף שטעלן אַ װידערשטאַנד. און דער זעלבער פּראַקטישער מיזעס לאָזט
זיך שװעבן אױף די פֿליגלען פֿון זײן פֿאַנטאַזיע און זעט, אַז דער כּוח פֿון ייִדיש װעט
אין דער צוקונפֿט גובר זײן אַלע השפּעות װאָס זענען פּרעמד דער שפּראַך. װידער
פֿאַרופֿט ער זיך אױף אַ סך שפּראַכלעכע דערשײנונגען אין דער װעלט, כּדי אױפֿצוװײזן
אַז אין די לענדער פֿון מיזרח־אײראָפּע איז פֿאַראַן גענוג װידערשטאַנד־כּוחות קעגן
אַלע פֿאַקטאָרן, װאָס װילן אונטערגראָבן די יסודות פֿון ייִדיש, הגם ער איז מודה, אַז
אין די אַנדערע לענדער (אַמעריקע, למשל) איז אַזאַ כּוח ניט בנמצא.

מיזעס איז סקעפּטיש בנוגע סאַקלאָוס פאַרדיסזאָג, אַז אין אַרץ־ישׂראל װעט
העברעיִש ירשענען דעם פּלאַץ פֿון ייִדיש. „הלװאי װאָלט עס אמת געװען! רופֿט ער
אױס, װי פֿרײען װעט זיך אונדזער האַרץ צו זען װי עס צעװאָקסט זיך אונדזער קולטור־
שפּראַך, װי די אותיות פֿון פֿאַרשימלטע ספֿרים הײבן אָן לעבן אַ פֿרײ, דערפֿרישנדיק
לעבן״. — — — אָבער דאָס אַלץ איז בלױז האַלוצינאַצײעס. אַ ישׁוב פֿון פֿינף טױזנט
פּױערים איז ניט בכּוח צו מאַכן אַזאַ איבערקערעניש אין דער העברעיִשער שפּראַך.
דערװײיל האָט ער ניט פֿאַר זיך מער װי דאָס װאָס זײנע אױגן זעען, און די אַרץ
ישׂראלדיקע װירקלעכקייט אין יענער צײט, בײם אָהײיב פֿון דער צװײיטער עליה, איז
געװיס געװען אַ גוטער אַרגומענט פֿאַר מיזעסן. ער האָט געקאָנט װיסן, אַז די
צװײיטע עליה מיט איר לאָזונג פֿון כּיבוש העבֿודה, האָט אױך אױפֿגעהױבן די פֿאָן פֿון
אױפֿלעבונג פֿון דער העברעיִשער שפּראַך און באַװיזן צו מאַכן העברעיִש פֿאַר דער
שפּראַך פֿונעם ישׁוב, גענױ אַזױ װי ס׳איז געװאָרן סאַקלאָוס װיזיע און ניט מיזעסעס
רעאַלים.

מיזעס מאַכט חוזק פֿון דער העברעיִשער פלאָפלערײ אין אַרץ־ישׂראל, װאָס צינדט
אָן די פֿאַנטאַזיע, און אַגב קריטיקירט ער שאַרף די בחמאת פֿון דער נאַציאָנאַלער און
ציוניסטישער ליטעראַטור װעגן דעם װאָס װערט געטאָן אין אַרץ־ישׂראל. ס׳אין נײיטיק
אױפֿצוהערזן מיט די לױבגעזאַנגען פֿאַר אַ בלימצעלע װאָס שפּראָצט אױף אין אַרץ־ישׂראל,
װי עס װאָלט געװען אַ צעדערבױם. ס׳איז שױן אױך געקומען די צײט ניט אַרײינצופֿאַלן
אין התפּעלות, װען מען הערט װערט קינדער רײידן העברעיִש אין אַ פֿאַר דערפֿער אין אַרץ
ישׂראל. ער זעט ניט אין דעם קײן באװײיז, אַז העברעיִש װערט די רײידשפּראַך פֿון די
פֿאָלקסמאַסן; אַפֿילו װען די אַלע פֿינף טױזנט װעלן רײידן העברעיִש, — װאָס איז
מיט די מיליאָנען פֿון אונדזער פֿאָלק אין גלות? מיזעס װײיס גאַנץ גוט, אַז דער
אױסשפּיל איז שרעקלעך און אױפֿציטערנדיק פֿאַר יעדן ציוניסט און העברעיִש־ליבהאַבער,
אָבער די אילוזיע װעט ברענגען אַ שװערע אַנטוישונג, און ס׳איז גלײכער צו דערזען דעם
אמת אַ שעה פֿריִער, אײידער אַ שעה שפּעטער. הכּלל, ייִדיש איז די שפּראַך פֿון אונדזער
פֿאָלק אין די תּפֿוצות און די צוקונפֿט אין אַרץ־ישׂראל קאָן דאָ גאָרניט איבעראַנדערשן.

ז

און ווידער גייט סאָקאַלאָוו אַרדיס אין קאַמף, ענטפערנדיק מיזעסן מיט אַ צווייטן
אַרטיקל, אונטערגעשריבן „רעדאַקציע פֿון העולם".

קודם־כּל פֿאַרזיכערט סאָקאַלאָוו נאָך אַ מאָל, אַז אין דעם „קרייצצוג" קעגן ייִדיש
באַטייליקן זיך ניט די ציוניסטן. אין אויסגאַנגפּונקט און עיקרים זענען פֿון איין זייט
די אַסימילאַציע־אימפּולסן, און פֿון דער צווייטער זייט — אַ פֿאַרשטעלטער אַנטי־
סעמיטיזם פֿון ליבעראַלע גוייִם. קעגן אַזאַ „קרייצצוג", — זאָגט סאָקאַלאָוו — וועלן
מיר, די ציוניסטן, הייסט עס, זיך קעגנשטעלן מיט אַלע מיטלען, סיי דערפֿאַר און וייל
גענוי ווי אַלע שפּראַכן אין דער וועלט האָבן אַ זכות־הקיום, אַזוי קען מען ניט אָפּנעמען
דעם זעלבן זכות ביי אַ שפּראַך, וואָס ווערט גערעדעט דורך מיליאָנען ייִדן. עד כּאַן
סאָקאַלאָווס איינשטימיקייט מיט מיזעסן. אָבער פֿון דאַנען אָן גייט ער זיך פֿונאַנדער
מיט אים אין איניקע גרונטזאַכן.

ערשטנס, איז ער קעגן דעם צונאָמען „ייִדיש" סתּם. מען דאַרף די שפּראַך ניט
אַנרופֿן „ייִדיש", נאָר באַצייכענען זי פּינקטלעך און קלאָר: „ייִדיש־טייטש", ווייל עס
זענען דאָך פֿאַראַן איניקע אַנדערע „ייִדישן". ס'איז ניט גענוג מיזעסעס קענען די
אַנדערע „ייִדישן", אויך די סטאַטיסטיק זיינע. דאָס אַלץ וועט גאַנץ ווייניק העלפֿן צו
לייזן די פּראָבלעם: אויב אַפֿילו בלויז אַ „קלײנער" מיעוט פֿון טויזנטער רעדט אַ
טאָטערישן „ייִדיש", צי קאָנען מיר פֿאָדערן פֿון זיי אַריבערצוגיין פּלוצלינג צו אַן
אַנדער שפּראַך, צו אַ ייִדיש־טייטש? צי קאָן מען אין דעם פֿאַל דעצידירן לויט ציפֿערן
פֿון מערהייט און מינדערהייט? צי קאָן מען באַשליסן אַז די שפּראַך איז וועניקער
נאַציאָנאַל פֿון דער אַנדערער? אַפֿילו ווען די דאָזיקע שפּראַכן האָבן ניט אַרויסגעגעבן
קיין שרייבער און ליטעראַטורן — און דאָס, ווייזט אויס, לייקנט ניט סאָקאַלאָוו —
האָט מען ניט ניט קיין שום רעכט זיך צו צו האַלטן העכער פֿון זיי און אָפּפּסקענען, אַז זייער
שפּראַך איז וועניקער ייִדיש ווי ייִדיש־טייטש.

סאָקאַלאָוו גלייבט אויך ניט אין מיזעסעס סטאַטיסטיק וועגן די ייִדיש־ריידנדיקע
אין דער וועלט. איז דען פֿאַראַן אַן „איינהייטלעכער בלאָק" פֿון די ייִדיש־ריידנדיקע
אין לאָנדאַנער וויטשעפּל, אין וואָלין, רומעניע, עלזאַס, האָלאַנד אאַז"וו? באַזונדערס
שאַרף טאַדלט סאָקאַלאָוו מיזעסן פֿאַר זיין פֿאַרקלענערן דעם ווערט פֿון די ייִדיש־
ריידנדיקע אין אַמעריקע און אַריבערפֿירן דעם שווערפּונקט קיין אייראָפּע. דער צענטער
גייט אַלץ מער איבער קיין אַמעריקע — טענהט סאָקאַלאָוו — און דאָרט ווערט ייִדיש
אַלץ מער פֿאַרענגלישט. דער וואָס וויל זיך איבערצייגן ווי ס'זעט אויס דאָרט די ייִדישע
שפּראַך, דאַרף ניט מער ווי דורקוקן די צייטונג־מודעות וואָס זענען באַשטימט פֿאַר
די פֿאָלקסמאַסן: אַ מענטש וואָס קען ניט קיין ענגליש, וועט די מודעות ניט פֿאַרשטיין,
דאָס איגענע איז אויך אין ענגלאַנד. די ייִדישע שפּראַך פֿאַרלירט אַלץ מער אירע
כאַראַקטעריסטישע ייִדישע סימנים. באַזונדערס איז עס קענטיק אין דער „בראַשורך־
ליטעראַטור" און אין דער ליטעראַטור פֿון די ייִדישע סאָציאַליסטישע באַוועגונגען. ער
ברענגט אַ כאַראַקטעריסטישן זאַץ פֿון דער דאָזיקער ליטעראַטור: פֿערוואָרפֿענדיג דעם
פּרינציפּ פֿון דער פּסיכאָלאָגיע פֿון דער דערגרייכעריש־בורזשואַזער וועלטאַנשויונג

און שטעהענדיג אויף די שטאַנדפונקטן פון דער טעאָריע פון דער אָביאַזאַטעלנער פער-
לענדונג פון די ברייטע פאָלקסשיכטן..." וואָס איז אין אַזאַ יידיש געבליבן פון דעם
העברעישן גייסט, מיט וועלכן מיזעס שטאָלצירט אַזוי און אויף וועלכן ער בויט לופט-
טורעמס וועגן דעם מהות פון יידיש און איר צוקונפט? דאָס איז דער רעזולטאַט פון
דרויסנדיקע השפעות, און מען טאָר עס ניט אַװועקמאַכן מיט דער האַנט.

פון דאַנען איז שוין אַ טראָט צו סאַקלאַווס אויספיר, אַז יידיש װערט איינגע-
שרומפן און דער ערשטער בולטער סימן פון דעם איז דער פאַקט, וואָס ס'לאָזן זיך אויס
אין איר די העברעישע װערטער. מיר קענען דעם קװאַל פון די װערטער. דאָס לעבן
און די שפּראַך זענען געװוען דורכגעזאַפט דורך און דורך מיט רעליגיע. איצט, װען
רעליגיע איז אַ װײט װייס ניט דאָמינירנדיק אין יידישן לעבן, װערט אַלץ װייניקער דער שפּראַך-
אוצר פון די העברעישע אויסדרוקן, און די יידישע שפּראַך װערט פון טאָג צו טאָג
אַלץ װייניקער יידיש. אמת, עס זענען פאַראַן גרויסע טאַלאַנטן אין דער יידישער
ליטעראַטור, אַזוי װי זיי זענען פאַראַן אין דער העברעישער ליטעראַטור, אָבער די
ליטעראַטור איז בלױז אַ קלײן װינקל אינעם שפּראַקלעבן פון די מאַסן, און די
דאָזיקע ליטעראַטור װערט ניט געלייענט מער װי די העברעישע, מחמת כדי צו פאַר-
שטיין זי, געזאָגט ניט דער שפּראַקלעכער אוצר וואָס דאָס פאָלק פאַרמאָגט. „פאַראַן פיל
טעמעס, זאָגט סאַקלאַוו, אויף װעלכע ס'איז שװערער צו שרייבן אין יידיש װי אין
העברעיש". דערפאַר אפשר — מיינט ער — איז די יידישע ליטעראַטור פאַרשפּרייט
צװישן װייניק מענטשן, ניט געקוקט אויף איר הויכן ניוואָ.

אוודאי דאַרף מען מאַכן אַלע אַנשטרענגונגען, כדי צו פאַרשפּרייטן די ליטעראַטור,
צו פאַרשענערן און באַרײכערן די שפּראַך, רײניאַכן זי פון װילדגעװוקסן אד"גל.
אָבער — פרעגט סאַקלאַוו: װו זאָלן די דאָזיקע אַנשטרענגונגען געמאַכט װערן —
אין העברעיש אָדער אין יידיש? און ס'איז ניט אַזוי גלאַסיק װי מיזעס שילדערט עס: פון
איין זייט — אַ בלאַק פון זיבן מיליאָן יידיש־רײידנדיקע, און פון דער צװייטער זייט —
אַ הײפל העברעיש־קענער; דאַ — אַ יידישע שפּראַך, רייך מיט אידיאָמען און װערטער-
צרופים וואָס מען קען זיי באַנוצן אין אַלע װיסנשאַפטן, און דאַרט — אַן אָרעמע שפּראַך,
אָן אַ קעגנװוואַרט און אָן אַ צוקונפט. פאַקטיש זעט די זאַך אויס גאָר אַנדערש. ס'איז
ניט פאַראַן אַזאַ מין שפּראַך װאָס הייסט ייִדיש, ס'איז דאָ אַ יידיש־טייטש, וואָס בייט
זיך פון טאָג צו טאָג, איז געבונדן מיט טויזנטער פעדעם צו יעטװועדן פּלאַץ װו מען
באַנוצט זיך מיט איר, און איז דריבער אַנדערס אין יעדן פּלאַץ. מיט העברעיש קען
זעלבעקס ניט געשען, העברעיש װערט פאַרטאַנענ אומעטום און איז ניט אונטערגע-
װאָרפן די באַדינגונגען פון דעם אָדער יענעם אָרט. זי איז אַ פּראָדוקט פון דער גרויסער
און רייכער פאַרגאַנגענהייט פון אונדזער פאָלק און זיין קולטור. און אויב מיר װעלן
אוועקשטעלן די פראַגע: װעלכער פון די צװיי שפּראַכן דאַרפן מיר אָפּגעבן אונדזערע
כוחות, כדי צו אַנטוויקלען און פאַרשענערן זי, הײסט דאַך דער ענטספער זיין אַן אַבסאָלוט
קלאַרער — דער העברעישער שפּראַך, וואָס איר געהאָדט די פאַרגאַנגענהייט, קעגן-
וואַרט און צוקונפט.

מיזעס טענהט אַז די שפּראַך־אויפלעבונג אין אונדזער לאַנד (מיט פערציק יאָר

צוריק!) איז קליין און אָרעם און מען טאָר ניט ליַיגן אויף דעם קיין גרויסע האָפענונגען.
סאָקאָלאָוו גיט צו, אַז די שפּראַך־אויפלעבונג איז טאַקע אָרעם, נאָר אָרעמער ווי מיזעס
מיַינט (זיַין גאַנץ לעבן האָט סאָקאָלאָוו ניט מסכּים געווען מיט בן־יהודה און זיַין וועג
וואָס שיַיך דער שפּראַך־אויפלעבונג, ער האָט תּמיד אונטערגעשטראָכן אַז בן־יהודהס
שפּראַך־אינאָוואַציעס שעפּן ניט פון אונדזער שפּראַך־אוצרות), אָבער דאָס באַוויַיזט
בלויז אַז מען דאַרף טאָן מערער און עפעקטיווער. אין דעם וואָס העברעיִש איז אַזוי
ווייניק פאַרשפּרייט צווישן פאָלק איז שולדיק ניט די שפּראַך, די רייכע, קאָלירפולע
העברעיִשע שפּראַך, נאָר מיר אַליין, וויַיל מיר טוען גאָרנישט אין דער ריכטונג.

ח

סאָקאָלאָוו אַנאַליזירט די ייִדיש־ריַידנדיקע אין מיזרח־אייראָפּע: פון איין זיַיט
די פּרומע וואָס ריַידן ייִדיש, אָבער די שפּראַכפראַגע גייט זיי אָן ווי די פאַראַיאָריקער
שנײ, און פון דער צווייטער זיַיט די בונדיסטן וואָס זעען די שפּראַך ווי אַ מיטל צו
פאַרשפּרייטן זייערע אידעען צווישן די מאַסן און וואָס ביַי אַ סך פון זיי דרינגט אַרויס די
ליבע צו ייִדיש בלויז פון דער שׂינאה צו העברעיִש, צו "לשון קודש", "טראַדיציע",
"ארץ־ישׂראל", "בית־מדרש" אד"גל. איינע פון די זאַכן, וועלכער זיי האָבן דערקלערט
אַ "הייליקע מלחמה" אויף דער ייִדישער גאַס איז — העברעיִש. סאָקאָלאָוו איז טאַקע
אַ "צד" אין דער פּאָלעמיק מיט די בונדיסטן און טענהט צו זיי: "אויב ניט העברעיִש,
ניט תּורה, ניט ארץ־ישׂראל, ניט טראַדיציע, ניט בית־מדרש, — וואָס זשע בליַיבט
אונדז איבער?"

מיזעס האַלט אַז "דאָס מאָדערנע לעבן", העלפט ייִדיש. סאָקאָלאָוו וויל אריַין־
דרינגען אין דעם זינען פון די ווערטער "מאָדערנע לעבן" און קומט צום אויספיר, אַז
די אַלע, וואָס לעבן דאָס "מאָדערנע לעבן", קענען פרעמדע שפּראַכן, אויך העברעיִש
און ייִדיש, און ביידע שפּראַכן ברענגען זיי ניט קיין פול נוצן אין זייער לעבן. דער
מאָדערנער ייִד שיקט זיַינע קינדער אין אַלגעמיינע שולן ווו זיי לערנען אַלע שפּראַכן
פון דער וועלט, אַחוץ העברעיִש און ייִדיש. ייִדיש וועט קיין מאָל ניט קאָנקורירן, וואָס
שיַיך אַלגעמיינער בילדונג, מיט די אַנדערע שפּראַכן — און סאָקאָלאָוו קומט צו אַ
"העברעיִסטישן" אויספיר: די האָפענונג אַז די נאַציאָנאַלע שפּראַך פון אונדזער פאָלק
זאָל ווערן ייִדיש איז אַ סך אַ וויַיטערע פאַנטאַזיע ווי אַז זי זאָל ווערן העברעיִש, וואָס
האָט דאָך ברייטע און טיפע וואָרצלען אין דער פאַרגאַנגענהייט פון אונדזער פאָלק און
אַפילו אין זיַין קעגנוואָרט. די דאָזיקע וואָרצלען שפּייזן זיך סיַי פון זכות־אבות, סיַי
פון רעליגיע און, ניט צום לעצטן, פון ארץ־ישׂראל. ס'איז דעריבער נוטיק, אַז מיר
זאָלן דערמאַנען זיך אַליין און אַנדערע די פליכטן וואָס ליגן אויף אונדז לגבי העברעיִש.
"הגם — פאַרגנדיקט סאָקאָלאָוו — מיר האָבן ליב ייִדיש־טיַיטש און זעען איַין, אַז עס
איז נוטיק צו באַנוצן זיך מיט דער שפּראַך און מיר זענען גרייט צו פאַרטיידיקן זי
קעגן ביחווייליקע אָנגריַיפן פון דרויסן, דאַרפן מיר דאָך אָנערקענען אַז בלויז איין
נאַציאָנאַלע שפּראַך פאַרמאָגן מיר און זי איז — ה ע ב ר ע י ִ ש".

דעם זעלבן יאָר האָט דער העולם פאַרעפנטלעכט אייניקע אַרטיקלען וועגן דער

העברעישער שפראַך און איר יתרון לגבי ייִדיש. די דאָזיקע אַרטיקלען מיט פּאָזיטיװע
אָפּשאַצונגען װעגן ייִדיש און איר ליטעראַטור באַלײַכטן די פּראָבלעם פון אַלע זײַטן.
אָבער דער אױסשפּיר איז געװען: "דאָס ייִדישע פֿאָלק האָט און קאָן האָבן בלױז אײן
שפּראַך — די העברעישע שפּראַך". אײנער פֿון די אַרטיקלען האָט גערופֿן "אַרײַנצר
דרינגען מיט אונדזער שפּראַך אין אַלע שיכטן פֿון פֿאָלק און
פֿאַרװאַנדלען די העברעישע שפּראַך אין דער שפּראַך פֿון אַלע
ייִדן" (אונטערגעשטראָקן אין אָריגינאַל).

די טשערנאָװיצער קאָנפֿערענץ האָט אַרױפֿגעבראַכט די פֿראַגע װעגן אַ נאַציאָנאַלער
שפּראַך, אַלס הױפּטפּונקט פֿון די פֿאַרהאַנדלונגען, און אין אַלע דעבאַטעס האָבן די
רעדנער באַרירט מיזעסעס געדאַנקען, ער האָט זײ געבראַכט צום אױסדרוק אין דעם
װיכּוח, װאָס איז פֿאָרגעקומען אַ יאָר פֿאַר דער קאָנפֿערענץ. ערשט נאָך טשערנאָװיץ
האָט זיך צעפֿלאַקערט אַ' לײַדנשאַפֿטלעכע פּאָלעמיק צװישן בײַדע צדדים, אַ פּאָלעמיק
װאָס האָט נאָך מער פֿאַרטיפֿט און פֿאַרשאַרפֿט די חלוקי־דעות. מיזעס אַלײן האָט זיך
ניט באַטײליקט אין דער פּאָלעמיק. אָבער װען אַחד־העם איז אַרױסגעטראָטן קעגן ייִדיש,
האָט מיזעס אױפֿגענומען דעם קאַמף, און אַזױ האָט ער פֿאַרענדיקט די דעבאַטע, װאָס
האָט זיך געצױגן עטלעכע יאָר.

ט

אחד העמס באַצױנג צו ייִדיש איז באַקאַנט געװאָרן דער עפֿנטלעכקײט אַ פּאָר
יאָר פֿאַר דער טשערנאָװיצער קאָנפֿערענץ. דער אײן־און־אײנציקער אַרטיקל זײַנער,
געשריבן אין ייִדיש (אין יוד, 1899, נומער 7), איז געװען קעגן ייִדיש (אַ קיצור פֿונעם
אַרטיקל האָט זלמן רײזען געבראַכט אין זײַן לעקסיקאָן (ערשטער באַנד, זײַט 59).

"נאָר מיר, — שרײַבט אחד העם — זשאַרגאָן־ייִדען זענען אפֿשר די אײנציגע
מענטשען אין דער גאַנצע װעלט, ניט צו װיסטן דעם זיסען טעם פֿון אַ ליעבער, טײַערער
מוטער־שפּראַכע. די שפּראַכע, אין װעלכער מיר זענען אין דער קינדהײט ערצױגען
געװאָרען, דורך װעלכער מיר האָבן אונדזר'ע ערשטע בעגריפֿע בעקומען אין אונזערע
קינדליכע געפֿיהלען אײן אױסדרוק געגעבן — די דאָזיקע שפּראַכע איז אונז אַלײן ניט
טײַער, ניט אײגען. מיר פֿיהלען צו איהר קײן װאָרעם צערטליכקײט ניט, איהר לעבען און
בליהען אינטערעסירט אונז גאָר ניט — — — ". זומערצײַט, 1902 איז פֿאָרגעקומען אין
מינסק דער צוזאַמענפֿאָר פֿון די רוסישע ציוניסטן, און דאָרט האָט אחד העם געהאַלטן
דעם צענטראַלן רעפֿעראַט װעגן דער קולטור־פֿראַגע און גערעדט באַריכות װעגן ייִדיש.
דער אַ רעפֿעראַט איז שפּעטער אױסגעאַרבײטערטער געװאָרען אין זײַן באַקאַנטן אַרטיקל:
"תחית הרוח" (געדרוקט אין השלוח סוף 1902 אָן אין זײַן באַנד שריפֿטן זײַט 173).

אחד העם האָט אױפֿגעװיקלט אין זײַן רעפֿעראַט דעם גאַנצן קנױל פּראָבלעמען,
װאָס זענען פֿאַרבונדן מיט אונדזער פֿאָלקסקולטור אָן ער האָט דעריבער אױך באַרירט
די פֿראַגע פֿון אונדזערע גײַסטיקע אוצרות אין פֿרעמדע שפּראַכן. געפֿסקנט האָט ער,
אַז אױך יענע שאַפֿונגען, װאָס זענען געװידמעצט אונדזער פֿאָלק און זענען געשריבן אין
פֿרעמדע שפּראַכן, האָבן ניט שום פּלאַץ אין אונדזער נאַציאָנאַלער קולטור. ער
האָט געבראַכט אַלס בײַשפּיל לעװאַנדעס רוסישע דערצײלונגען װאָס זענען פֿאַרגעסן

געוואָרן, בעת די ביכער פון פּרץ סמאָלענסקין, וועלכע האָבן אַ קלענערן ווערט פון
קינסטלערישן שטאַנדפּונקט, ווערן נאָך געלייענט. דאָס איז דערפאַר ווייל לעוואַנדע
האָט געשריבן אין רוסיש און סמאָלענסקין — אין העברעיש. און פון דאַנען איז שוין
נאָר איין טראָט צו „זשאַרגאָן" און זיין ליטעראַטור. ער גיט איבער די הויפּט־טענות
פון די ייִדיש־ליבהאָבער, וואָס ווילן דערהויבן ייִדיש צו דער מדרגה פון אַ נאַציאָ־
נאַלער שפּראַך.

ס'איז גרינג צו פאַרשטיין אחד העמס שטעלונג אין דער דאָזיקער פראַגע. ערשטנס,
גלייבט ער ניט אין דער „ווירקלעכקייט", וואָס איז כלומרשט אין גאַנצן אויף דער זייט
פון ייִדיש. ווייל ס'איז נאָך ניט געשען אַז אַ פּרעמדע שפּראַך, וואָס האָט זיך צו־
געקלעפּט צו אַ פאָלק, זאָל ווערן פאַרעכנט אַלס זיין נאַציאָנאַלע שפּראַך. „אַ פּאַלקס־
קיבוץ, — זאָגט ער — האָט ניט קיין אַנדער נאַציאָנאַלע שפּראַך, אַחוץ דער וואָס ער
האָט שוין געהאַט, בעת ער איז געשטאַנען אויפן שוועל פון דער געשיכטע, נאָך איידער
עס האָט זיך אַנטוויקלט זיין נאַציאָנאַלער באַוווּסטזיין אין דער פולער מאָס; די שפּראַך
וואָס האָט אים באַגלייט אין זיין וועג דורך אַלע תקופות און ער געדענקט זיך ניט אין
קיין שום צייט אָן איר". עד כאַן — דער מאַטיוו נומער איינס. נאָך אים קומען די אַנדערע
מאַטיוון, זייער תמצית איז: „די ייִדישע שפּראַך, וואָס איז איצט די שפּראַך מיט
וועלכער עס באַנוצט זיך די מערהייט פון פאָלק, ווערט ביסלעכווייז פאַרגעסן דורכן
פאָלק און דער דאָזיקער פּראָצעס גייט אָן אין אַ שנעלן טעמפּאָ. דער צווייטער דור
אין ענגלאַנד און אַמעריקע באַנוצט זיך שוין ניט מיט אָט דער שפּראַך און איר פּלאַץ
פאַרנעמט די לאַנדשפּראַך. קיין שום עצה אָדער מיטל איז ניט פאַראַן קעגן דעם דאָזיקן
פּראָצעס, און ניט ווייט וועט איז דער טאָג ווען מיר וועלן באַזיצן צווייי ליטעראַטורן אין
טויטע שפּראַכן, וואָס מיר וועלן זיי דאַרפן לערנען פון שריפט און ניט פונעם לעבן גופא.
פאַרשטייט זיך, אַז לויט דער מיינונג פון אחד העם איז די נאַציאָנאַלע שפּראַך פון
אונדזער פאָלק און אונדזער נאַציאָנאַלער ליטעראַטור נאָר העברעיש. איינער פון זיינע
באַווייזן איז דער פאַקט וואָס ייִדישע שרייבער באַמיִען זיך, אַז זייערע שאַפונגען זאָלן
ווערן איבערגעזעצט אויף העברעיש, כדי צו פאַרשאַפן זיך אַ נאַציאָנאַלע אייביקייט
(ווייזט אויס, אחד העם האָט געמיינט מיט דעם מענדעלע מוכר ספרים, כאַטש ס'איז
אַ גרויסער ספק צי דאָס איז טאַקע געווען מענדעלעס מיין ביים איבערזעצן זיינע
שאַפונגען אויף העברעיש).

אין דעם זעלביקן רעפעראַט האָט אחד העם באַרירט ייִדיש בלויז פאַרבייגייענדיק,
אָבער ער קערט זיך אום צו דעם אין אַ ספּעציעלן אַרטיקל, וואָס איז געשריבן געוואָרן
נאָך דער טשערנאָוויצער קאָנפערענץ, ווען אויף דער ייִדישער גאַס איז נאָך אָנגעגאַנגען
די שטורמישע פּאָלעמיק וועגן ייִדיש־העברעיש. דער אַרטיקל הייסט: „ריב לשונות" און
איז פאַרעפנטלעכט געוואָרן אין השלוח (פּרילינג, 1910). מיטעס איז צום צווייטן מאָל
אַרויס אין קאַמף. אחד העם איז, פידוע, געווען דער וואָרטזאָגער אין דער ציוניסטישער
און נאַציאָנאַלער פּובליציסטיק און זיין מיינונג האָט געהאַט אַ דעצידירנדיקע וואָג אין
דער נאַציאָנאַלער באַוועגונג אין מיזרח־אייראָפּע.

אחד העמס טענות קעגן ייִדיש אין דעם מאמר זענען שאַרף און גייסטרייך.

אין זיין גלענצנדיקן העברעישן סטיל. פֿארטיידיקט ער העברעיש אַלס די נאַציאָנאַלע
שפּראַך פֿון אונדזער פֿאָלק, וואָס ודעט ניט אָפּטרעטן קיין שום אַנדער שפּראַך איר
בכבֿודיקן פּלאַץ. ס׳איז, בכן, קיין וווּנדער ניט וואָס דער איינציקער פֿאַסיקער מענטש
זיך צו פֿאַרמעסטן מיט אים אחד העם, איז געוועון מיזעס — אַן אויך דאָס מאָל אין ה ע-
ב ר ע י ש, אויף די שפּאַלטן פֿון זשורנאַל העתיד, רעדאַגירט פֿון ש״י איש הורוויץ (דריטער
באַנד, 1910/11, זייטן 209—216). דער דאָזיקער זשורנאַל האָט אָפּגעגעבן אַ ברייטן
פּלאַץ פֿאַר אויספֿירלעכע און טיפֿע אַנאַליזן וועגן מהות פֿון ייִדישקייט און ס׳איז אָן
שום ספֿק, אַז דאָס אַרויפֿברענגען דעם ענין פֿון ייִדיש אין אַזַא מין זשורנאַל האָט צוגעגעבן
דער פּאָלעמיק אַ „פּראָפֿעסאָרישן" ניואַנס, וואָס האָט גאָרניט צו טאָן מיט דעם קאַמפֿס-
לוסט וואָס האָט דעמאָלט געהערשט אין דער העברעיִשער און ייִדישער פּרעסע.

‫„ביז איצט — הייבט מיזעס אָן — האָבן מיר געוווּסט, אַז איטלעך פֿאָלק באַגערט
אויסצודריקן זיינע געדאַנקען און געפֿילן אין זיין מוטערשפּראַך. דער דאָזיקער באַגער
איז גערעכטיק און איז אין הסכם מיט די געזעצן פֿון דער קולטורעלער אַנטוויקלונג.
און אָט פֿאַרנעמען אונדזערע אויערן אַ נייע טעאָריע. אחד העם פּראָקלאַמירט: די
מוטערשפּראַך פֿון אַ פֿאָלק איז בכלל ניט די נאַציאָנאַלע שפּראַך זיינע. — אַלע האָבן
מיר אַ טעות געהאַט — באַשליסט אחד העם מיט דער פּולסטער זיכערקייט. כדי אַ
שפּראַך זאָל דערהויבן ווערן צו דער מדרגה פֿון אַ נאַציאָנאַלער שפּראַך, איז ניט גענוג
פֿאַר איר צו זיין אַ מוטערשפּראַך, נאָר זי דאַרף צוזאַמען מיט דעם אויך כולל־זיין אין
זיך דעם גייסטיקן פֿאָלקס־אוצר פֿון אַלע דורות". מיר האָבן שוין געהערט אחד העמס
טענות קעגן ייִדיש און געשפּירט ווי ווײַט זיין האַרץ ווייטיקט דערויף וואָס מיר האָבן
ניט קיין מוטערשפּראַך, וועלכע זאָל זיך צוזאַמענפֿאַלן מיט אונדזער נאַציאָנאַלער
שפּראַך. אָבער מיזעס ווײַזט אויף מיט באַגלויבטע ראיות, אַז ס׳זענען יאָ פֿאַראַן
מוטערשפּראַכן, וואָס הגם זיי זענען ניט די שפּראַכן פֿון די גייסטיקע אוצרות פֿון זייער
פֿאָלק זענען זיי דאָך פֿולשטענדיקע נאַציאָנאַלע שפּראַכן.

מיזעס ווײַזט אָן אויף אָן דער נאַרוועגישער און דער פֿינישער שפּראַך, אין וועלכער
ס׳האָבן זיך זינט דורות אויפֿגעקליבן די גייסטיקע און קולטורעלע אוצרות פֿון פֿאָלק,
און, ניט געקוקט אויף דעם, מאַכן איצט די נאַרוועגן גרויסע באַמיונגען, כדי זיך צו
שאַפֿן אַ נאַציאָנאַלע שפּראַך, וואָס זאָל ניט דווקא זיין פֿיניש; און אָט האָבן מיר די
ליטווינער, די גאונים פֿון דער פּוילישער ליטעראַטור — מיצקעוויטש סענקעוויטש,
אָשעסקאָוו (ווער באַטראַכט זיי היינט אַלס ליטווינער?), וואָס אָנערקענען ניט די
פּוילישע שפּראַך אַלס זייער נאַציאָנאַלע שפּראַך, נאָר דווקא זייער אָרעמע מוטערשפּראַך
וואָס האָט ניט, ווי באַקאַנט, קיין שום נאַציאָנאַל־קולטורעלן עבר. מיזעס אילוסטרירט
זיין געדאַנק נאָך מיט בײַשפּילן און קומט צום אויספֿיר, אַז דעצידירן דעצידירט ניט
דאָס וואָס עס האָט זיך אָנגעקליבן אַ מאָל אין דער שפּראַך פֿון פֿאָלקסגייסט, נייערט
דאָס וואָס קאַן איצט און אין דער צוקונפֿט זיך אָנזאַמלען אין דער דאָזיקער שפּראַך.
אַ פֿאָלק וואָס פֿילט: אַז זיין ליטעראַטור־שפּראַך איז אים געוואָרן פֿרעמד און איז צו
ווײַט פֿון דער לעבעדיקער שפּראַך; אַ פֿאָלק וואָס זעט אַז זיין ליטעראַטור־שפּראַך איז
ניט בכח ווײַטער צו באַפֿרידיקן זיינע נשמה־באַדערפֿענישן — אַזַא פֿאָלק מוז זיך אָפּ-

קערן פון דער אַ ליטעראַטור־שפראַך און דערהויבן די לעבעדיקע שפּראַך, די פאַלקס־
טימלעכע, די גערעדטע, אין וועמען עס קלאַפּט אַן אָדער פון לעבן, צו דער מדרגה פון
אַ נײַער ליטעראַרישער שפראַך".

מיזעס ברענגט אַ רײ כּללים וועגן דער שײַכות צווישן אַ ליטעראַטור־שפראַך
און אַ לעבעדיקער אומגאַנגשפּראַך. ווי לאַנג די ליטעראַרישע שפראַך אידענטיפיצירט
זיך מיט דער אומגאַנגשפּראַך, האַלט אָן דאָס לשון זײַן נאַציאָנאַלן חותם. אָבער אין
יעדער שפראַך איז פאַראַן אַן עפּאָכע, ווען די גערעדטע שפּראַך דערווײַטערט זיך און
טרעט אַריבער די גרענעצן פון דער ליטעראַטור־שפראַך — טייל מאָל גאַנץ ווייט, —
דעמאָלט הערט אויף די ליטעראַטור צו זײַגן פון איר די לעבעדיקן וואָרצל, ווערט אַלץ
מער קינסטלעך און די נײַע שפראַך, אָדער דער נײַער דיאַלעקט, ירשנט דעם פּלאַץ פון
דער ליטעראַרישער שפראַך, כאַטש זי איז נאָך בּמשיך איר קיום. מיזעס ברענגט פיל
בײַשפּילן פון דער דיאַלעקט־געשיכטע אין אײַראָפּע וואָס באַווײַזן, אַז פאַלקסטימלעכע
דיאַלעקטן ווערן דערהויבן צו דער מדרגה פון אַ שפראַך.

פון דאַנען קומט מיזעס צו דער מסקנה, אַז ווען אַ דיאַלעקט דערגרייכט זײַן פולע
רײַפקייט, וועט ניט העלפן קיין שום נאַציאָנאַלע שפראַך און קיין שום זכות־אבות, —
אים און נאָר אים געהערט די צוקונפט, ווײַל מיט אים זענען די ברײַטע מאַסן וואָס
באַנוצן זיך מיט אים און האָבן אים ליב. ווער איז נאָך אַזוי גרויס ווי דאַנטע! דאָך
האָט די אינטעליגענץ אין זײַן דור פון אים אָפּגעשפּאַט און אָפּגעלאַכט, ווײַל ער האָט
געשאַפן זײַן גרעסט ווערק אין אַ פאַראַכטיקן דיאַלעקט, איטאַליעניש, און ניט אין דער
ליטעראַטור־שפראַך פון יענער צײַט — רוימיש. און אָט דער דיאַלעקט איז אין פאַר
לויף פון דער צײַט פאַרוואַנדלט געוואָרן אין איינער פון די שענסטע שפּראַכן אין
דער מערבּדיקער וועלט. און אויב אין דער וועלט איז אַזוי, אַז דער מקור פון די
דיאַלעקטן איז אין דער נאָענטער שפראַך, איז עס דאָך אַוודאי און אודאי אין ייִדיש,
וואָס איז אַזוי ווײַט פון העברעיִש, ווײַל אַ "טיפער פּילאָלאָגישער אָפּגרונט טיילט זי
אָפּ פון דער העברעיִשער שפראַך און די שײַכות אירע צו אונדזער ליטעראַרישער
שפראַך לאָזט זיך ניט פאַרגלײַכן מיט דער שײַכות פון וועלכן ס'איז דיאַלעקט צו זײַן
אָפיציעלער שפראַך".

נאָך דעם ווי מיזעס פאַרענדיקט מיט זײַן פּעקל ראיות פון דער געשיכטע פון דער
אַלגעמײַנער לינגוויסטיק, קערט ער זיך אום צו אוֹחד העמס אַרטיקל און באַהאַנדלט אים
אויספירלעך און גענוי.

י

אוֹחד העם האַלט אַז די שײַכות פון ייִדיש צו העברעיִש איז בּבחינת דיאַלעקט
צו העברעיִש און דעריבער מיינט ער, אַז ייִדיש האָט ניט דעם זכות צו זײַן אַ זעלבּ־
שטענדיקע שפראַך. דאָס איז אַ פּאַראַדאָקס. ייִדיש איז קיין מאָל ניט געווען קיין דיאַ־
לעקט פון העברעיִש. די שפראַך איז טאַקע געווען אַמאָל אַ דיאַלעקט, אָבער ניט פון
העברעיִש, נײַערט פון דייטש. נאָר דאָס ייִדישע פאָלק האָט בּמשך פון הונדערטער יאָרן
אַזוי איבערגעאַרבעט די שפּראַך, אַזוי זי צוגעפּאַסט צו זײַן גײַסט, "צוגעפּאַסט זי צו

די באַדערפעגישן פֿון זיין נשמה, אַריינגעגעבן אין איר אַ נייעם פֿאָלקלאָר, געשאַפֿן אין
איר אַ ספּעציעלע וועלט פֿון געפֿילן און פֿאַרבינדונגס־געדאַנקען, ביז דער דיאַלעקט
האָט זיך פֿאַרוואַנדלט אין זיין אייגענער שפּראַך, באַקומען אַ נייעם נאָמען,
אַ יידישן נאָמען: יידיש אָדער יודיש. אַזאַ שפּראַך איז שוין איצט ניט קיין
"דיאַלעקט", זי איז שוין געוואָרן אַ שפּראַך פֿאַר זיך, אַן אויסאַנאַמע שפּראַך. דאָס
יידישע לשון (יידיש) איז אונדזער לשון, דאָס לשון פֿון אונדזער פֿאָלק. דאָס איז דער
ערשטער פֿאַל, זיטט העברעיש האָט אויפֿגעהערט צו זיין די ריידשפּראַך פֿון פֿאָלק, אַז
יידן זאָלן פּראָקלאַמירן אַ נייע שפּראַך וואָס זיי האָבן באַקומען אַלס אַ יידישע.
ניט אַראַמיש, ניט גריכיש פֿון אַלעקסאַנדריע, ניט לאַדינאָ און ניט קיין איינע פֿון די אַלע
אַנדערע שפּראַכן, מיט וועלכע אונדזער פֿאָלק אין גלות זיך באַנוצט, זענען גע־
קרוינט געוואָרן מיט דעם דאָזיקן בכבֿודיקן נאָמען".

אחד העם זאָגט: "אַפֿילו פֿרויען און עם־הארצים וויסן אַז די דאָזיקע שפּראַך
איז ניט די נאַציאָנאַלע שפּראַך", און דאָך האָבן די אַלע — און מער ווי די אַלע —
באַטראַכט די אַ שפּראַך ווי אַן אינטעגראַלן חלק פֿון זייער איך, אַ בשׂר מבשׂרם. מיר
האָבן קיין מאָל ניט געהערט, אַז אַ ייִד זאָל אָנשרייען אויף זיינע בני־בית וואָס ריידן
יידיש, אַז זיי זאָלן ניט ריידן "גויִש", אַזוי ווי מען טוט דאָס לגבֿי אַנדערע שפּראַכן.
דער ייִד האָט זיך קיין מאָל ניט פֿאַרטיפֿט אין דעם קאָמפּלעקס פֿון דער פֿילאָסאָפֿישער
און פֿילאָלאָגישער טעאָריע, אָבער געפֿילט האָט ער מיט זיין יידישן אינסטינקט, אַז אָט
די שפּראַך, וואָס ער רופֿט אָן "יידיש", איז זיין שפּראַך, זיין אייגנטום, און ער דאַרף
עס אויפֿהאַלטן און אָפֿהיטן. מען דאַרף יידיש ניט "אַוועקזעצן אויף איר שטול" — ווי
אחד העם דריקט זיך אויס — סיי ווי זיצט זי אויפֿן שטול און איז עולה לגדולה געוואָרן
מיט איר אייגענעם כוח און מיטן כוח פֿון איר יידישן האָב און גוטס אין פֿאַרלויף פֿון
דורות.

יידיש דאַרף מען ניט אָפּטיילן פֿון דעם טיפּישן פּוילישן ייִד, און מיזעס ווייזט
אויף, אַז אין אָנבליק פֿון געוויסע געשיכטלעכע אומשטענדן האָט דער פּוילישער ייִד
זוכה געוואָרן צו אַ זעלבשטענדיקן לעבן אין אַ גרעסערער מאָס ווי די ייִדן אין די מיזרח־
לענדער (ספֿרדים און ייִדן אין די אַראַבישע לענדער). אַפֿילו די שפּראַך איז געוואָרן
אַ באַזונדערע, אַן אַנדערע. זי איז געוואָקסן און האָט זיך אַנטוויקלט צוזאַמען מיטן ייִד,
און יעדער בּרעקל יידישקייט וואָס טרעט אָפּ פֿאַר אַסימילאַציע בּרענגט מיט זיך אויך
אַ צוריקטריט פֿון יידיש; און אין דעם איז אחד העם גערעכט: יידיש ווערט אַלץ מער
פֿאַרגעסן, אָבער מען דאַרף בּלויז צוגעבן, אַז ווען מען פֿאַרגעסט יידיש, פֿאַרגעסט מען
אויך ייִדישקייט, און דאָס פּרעמדע ירשנט דעם פּלאַץ פֿון בּיידן. מיזעס באַטאָנט נאָך
אַ מאָל, אַז די יידישע שפּראַך האַמעוועט די אַסימילאַציע, ווייל אַפֿילו די רעליגיע איז
נאָך ניט קיין אָפּהאַלט פֿאַר אַסימילאַציע. דאָס באַווייזט די פֿראַנקפּורטער פֿרומקייט,
וואָס גייט האַנט בּיי האַנט מיט דער אַסימילאַציע. די העברעיִשע שפּראַך קאָן ניט אַראָפּ־
גיין אין יידישן געטאָ און פֿאַרהיטן אונדזער אייגנאַרטיקייט. וועגן דעם קאָן קיינער
ניט חלומען (דאָ שטעלט אַוועק די רעדאַקציע פֿון העתיד אַ פֿרעגצייכן, כדי אָנצוווייזן,
אַז מען קאָן אויסזעצן קעגן דעם דאָזיקן פּסק־דין, ד"ה — עס זענען יאָ פֿאַראַן אַזעלכע

וואָס חלומען וועגן דעם).

אין ייִדיש קענען זיך נאָך אויפֿריידן ייִדן פֿון ריגע ביז בוקאַרעשט, פֿון אַדעס
ביז קראָקע. אַנדערש וועט אָבער זײַן די לאַגע אויב ייִדיש וועט ניט פֿאַרנעמען דעם
אויבן אָן. עס וועלן זיך דעמאָלט שאַפֿן ייִדישע פֿאָלקער מיט פֿלערליי שפּראַכן — „און
אַזעלכע קהילות. וואָס וועלן זיך אויספֿרעמען נאָך דעם ווי עס וועט ליקווידירט ווערן
דאָס פֿאַראייניקטע ייִדנטום — צי וועלן זיי קענען ממשיך זײַן די טראַדיציע פֿון זייער
קולטור?" ייִדיש האָט אַ טאָפּעלן זכות, סײַ מיט דעם וואָס זי היט אויף העברעיש און
סײַ מיט דעם וואָס זי איז פֿאַר העברעיש. ייִדיש איז ניט צעקריגט מיט העברעיש. דער
געראַנגל פֿון ייִדיש איז בלויז מיט די פֿײַנד פֿון דרויסן, וואָס ווילן פֿון איר פּטור
ווערן. דעם קיום פֿון ייִדיש שטעלן אין סכנה די פֿאַרבעדע שפּראַכן און יעדער קלײַנער
בצחון איבער ייִדיש מיינט צעשטערונג פֿון אונדזערע גרונטפֿעסטן. די וועלכע גרייפֿן
אָן ייִדיש מחמת פֿאַנאַטיזם צו העברעיש אַז „ווען עס וועלן אײַנ־
פֿאַלן די פֿונדאַמענטן וועלן אַרײַנדרינגען די צעשטערנדיקע ווינטן אין די העברעישע
הייליקטימער. די שוועֶרד וואָס הייבט זיך אויף אויפֿן לעבן פֿון דער ייִדישער שפּראַך,
ניט בלויז קעגן איר איז זי געשליפֿן, זי פֿאַרמעסט זיך אויף אונדזער גאַנצן נאַציאָנאַלן
קיום". באַזונדערס דאַרפֿן עס געדענקען די העברעיסטן.

קאַטעגאָריש און שאַרף טרעט מיזעס קעגן אַרויס קעגן אַחד העם, וועלכער האָט בטחון אין
אַ פֿאַרבאַרגענעם כּוח, וואָס וועט שוין פֿאַרזיכערן די צוקונפֿט פֿון אונדזער נאַציאָנאַלער
עקסיסטענץ. מיט אַחד העם שפּראַך שרייט ער אויס: „ניט דאָס איז דער וועג! מיט
מײַנע ווערטער וועַנד איך זיך אויך צו די העברעיסטן וועלכע קעמפֿן קעגן זייערע ברידער,
די ייִדישיסטן — — — מען ווייזט אײַך אָן אויף אַ שפּראַך וואָס קאָן פֿאַרהיטן דאָס פֿאָלק
פֿון אומקום און וואָס דאַרף דערפֿילן די דאָזיקע שליחות, אַ זעלבסטפֿאַרטיידיקונג שליחות,
און איר, מיט אייער שטערנזעעריי, זײַט פֿאַרקוקט אין עפּעס אַ פֿאַרבאַרגענעם כּוח, וואָס
וועט קומען און באַשיידן די פֿראַגע פֿון אונדזער נאַציאָנאַלן קיום. העברעיסטן! וואָס
וועט איר פֿאַרלייגן דעם פֿאָלק, ווען עס וועט דערפֿילט ווערן אייער ווונטש און עס
וועט אונטערגיין די ייִדישע שפּראַך? אײַערע שווערע ראַנגלענישן מיט די „זשאַרגאָן"
ניסטן' לייגן אַרויף אויף אײַך אַ גרויסע אחריות. זעט, אַז די קומענדיקע דורות זאָלן
אײַך ניט טאָדלען פֿאַר אייער איבערגעאײַלטקייט; די געשיכטע איז אַ ריכטערין און
זי וועט אײַך מישפּטן!"

מיזעס באַנוצט זיך מיט דעם הערצלס באַקאַנטן שפּריכוואָרט: „אם תרצו אין זו
אגדה". אויב מען וועט פֿאַרשטיין, אַז ייִדיש איז אַ נויטווענדיקייט, קאַן די דאָזיקע שפּראַך
פֿאַרנעמען אַ באַדײַטנדיקן פּלאַץ אינעם לעבן פֿון אונדזער פֿאָלק און אפֿילו משפּיע
זײַן אויף זײַן נאַציאָנאַלער קאָנסאָלידאַציע. די דאָזיקע שפּראַך קאָן אפֿילו שאַפֿן אייביקע
שאַפֿונגען, הגם זי איז ניט די שפּראַך פֿון אונדזער אור־אַלטער ירושה. אויך דער תּלמוד
איז ניט געשריבן אין העברעיש, און דאָך איז ער אַ האָפּטיקער יסוד פֿון דעם גאַנצן
ייִדנטום אין דער גאָרער וועלט. וואָס שייך דעם אפּשטאַם פֿון דער דאָזיקער שפּראַך,
דעם קוואַל איר ארן, וואָס איז, ווי איז באַקאַנט, ניט גאָר זויבער פֿון ייִדישן שטאַנדפּונקט, האַלט
מיזעס אַז מיר האָבן דאָס פולע רעכט צו ריידן וועגן ייִדיש ווי וועגן אונדזער שפּראַך,

כאטש זי קומט ארויס פון דײטש, פונקט אזוי ווי אַנדערע פעלקער, פראנצויזן למשל,
ריידן אין זײערע לשונות, כאטש זיי קומען ארויס פון דער לאַטײנישער שפראַך. עס גייט
אונדז דעריבער בכלל ניט אן ווי ווו יידיש איז אויפגעקומען, און דאָס באַטאָנען דעם ענין
אויף טריט און שריט איז אַ מין איבערגעטריבענע סענסיוויטעט.

מיזעס גרייפט אן אהד העם, וועלכער פאָדערט מוותר צו זײן יידיש אויף אַלס
אַ רעקאָמפּענסאָאַציע_ פאַר נאַציאָנאַלע רעכט. אבער אַ יידישער שפריכווואָרט זאָגט: ביז
עס וועט קומען די נחמה וועט ארויס די נשמה. אויב עס וועט פאַרשווינדן די יידישע
שפראַך, איז פאַראן אַ סכנה, אַז אונדזער עצם קיום אלס פאָלק וועט געשטעלט ווערן
אונטער אַ פרעגצייכן און עס וועט שוין בכלל ניט נוֹיטיק זײן קיין נאַציאָנאַלע רעכט.
און ער פאַרענדיקט מיטן רוף: „זאָל זיך אויפוועקן אַ פונק פון שטאָלץ אין הַאַרץ
פונעם אייביקן פאָלק! לאָמיר ניט צעשטערן אונדזערע פאָלקסווערטן, כדי צו טאָן
נחת־רוח אונדזערע שכנים. אן אייביק פאָלק וואָס זײן מהות איז די ,אבסטראַקטע גע־
רעכטיקייט' דאַרף ניט מוותר זײן אויף זײנע נאַציאָנאַלע ווערטן צוליב אומגערעַכטע
פאָדערונגען פון אנדערע".

מיט דעם האט זיך פאַרענדיקט די פּאָלעמיק אבער ניט ענדגילטיק. מיזעס האט זיך
מער ניט באַטײליקט אין דעם וויכוח איבער יידיש. ער האט זיך פאַרנומען מיט גרויסע
פאַרשאַרבעטן, אין קוואַנטיטעט און קוואַליטעט, ווו ער האט באַגרינדעט זײנע מיינונגען
וואָס זענען דא אָנגעגעבן געוואָרן בקיצור. אין זײנע פאַרשונגען האט זיך ער פאַרנומען
מיט דער אלגעמיינער לינגוויסטיק און די פאַרעפנטלעכע ווערק זענען אן אוצר פון
וויסן וואָס איז לײדער וויניק באַקאַנט, אבער זיי קענען דינען ווי אַ פּראַכטפולער
דענקמאָל פאַר דעם וויסנשאַפטלער און גרויסן פאָליהיסטאָריקער מתתיהו מיזעס.

*

די פופציק יאָר, וואָס זענען פאַרבײי זינט יענער פּאָלעמיק, האָבן געוויס געטאָן
זייערס, כדי צו באַלײכטן אייניקע פאַרויסזאָגונגען און פאַקטן, וואָס זענען אָנגעוואָרפן
געוואָרן אין שטורעם פון דער פּאָלעמיק. אבער זיכער איז מיזעס ראוי, אַז זײן קאַמף
פאַר יידיש אויף דער טשערנאָוויצער קאָנפערענץ און נאָך איר זאָל אין פופציק יאָר
ארום דערמאָנט ווערן בײ אונדז אין לאַנד, אין אַ יידישער צײטשריפט וואָס דערשײנט
אין אונדזער מדינה. זאָלן די ווערטער דינען אַלס נר־זכרון פאַר דעם מענטש, וואָס האט
אין די תחומים פון נאַציאָנאַליזם און העברעיִש און העברעיִש געקעמפט פאַר די רעכט פון דער יידישער
שפראַך.

אידישיסטן פון אלע לענדער, לאטיייניזירט זיך! (צו
זשיטלאָוּסקי'ס נייַ־אַלטן אַרויסטריט אין ״טאָג״ פאר אידיש
אין לאַטיינישע בוכשטאַבן).

Zhitlovsky and American Jewry

EMANUEL S. GOLDSMITH

Chaim Zhitlovsky, who was born in a small *shtetl* near Vitebsk, Russia, in 1865, was the outstanding thinker of the Jewish cultural renaissance in the Yiddish language in the twentieth century. He was a leading theoretician of Jewish socialism, nationalism, and radical secularism and the principal exponent of Yiddishism in Eastern Europe and the United States.

In 1904, Zhitlovsky visited the United States together with Catherine Breshko-Breshkovskaya, the 'grandmother of the Russian revolution', in order to gain American support for the Russian Social Revolutionary Party. The assassination of the Russian prime minister. Wenzel von Plehve, by a member of the party had brought it tremendous prestige among socialists outside Russia. The delegation of Breshkovskaya and Zhitlovsky was sent to the United States to capitalize on those sentiments. Since the party leadership considered New York 'Jewish territory', it was deemed advisable to have a Jew who was a good lecturer accompany Breshkovskaya. The party agreed to permit Zhitlovsky to advocate his own Jewish nationalist program among American Jews during his stay. Thus, in addition to his lectures on socialism, he also spoke on Jewish questions.

Zhitlovsky discovered that the East European Jewish immigrants in the United States were under the influence of an intelligentsia dominated by assimilationist and cosmopolitan ideas. They viewed Yiddish culture as a passing phenomenon and were unable to combine radicalism and nationalism in their thinking. Zhitlovsky set about contesting these views with all the force and vigor at his command. From the lecture platform and from the pages of every American Yiddish newspaper and magazine that would publish his writings, he called for a synthesis of international socialism and national culture, of political

◄ *He Who is for the Lord, Stand with Me!*
'Yiddishists of all countries, Latinize yourselves!' Concerning Khayim Zhitlovski's new–old advocacy, in *Der Tog*, of writing Yiddish in Latin characters. (*Der groyser kundes*, September 30, 1926)

radicalism and Yiddish culturism. His influence was tremendous, altering the thinking of a section of the immigrant intelligentsia and working class that was assimilationist, cosmopolitan, far from Jewish thought and culture, and opposed to Zionism.

Zhitlovsky analyzed the *Haskalah* slogan, 'Be a man on the street and a Jew at home', which posits a conflict between humanity and Jewish identity. The Jewish radicals had carried that slogan to its logical conclusion and dissociated themselves from Jewish life. The more human one was, the radicals had felt, the less Jewish. While this may sometimes be true, said Zhitlovsky, frequently Jewishness and humanity were not in conflict. There were even occasions where the more Jewish one was, the more human.

Cosmopolitanism has missed the fact that there are many branches of culture which each people expresses in a different national way but which are nevertheless all equally human, all of equal value and can all possess the same degree of truth, justice, beauty and human dignity. For that reason there is no sense in demanding of any people that it cease to be a people and become human. In all mankind there is no form in which an aspect of culture expresses itself that has more of a right to a people's love than its own national form.

Abandoning one's own nationality was not cosmopolitanism but surrender to the chauvinism of a foreign nationality. The more interested in culture one became, the more natural it was to feel bound to the national forms of one's own people. The more human a Jew became, the more Jewish he became. His love for his own culture was an expression of his humanity.

In a masterful survey of the Jewish cultural heritage, Zhitlovsky demonstrated the historical and contemporary significance of the Bible, the Talmud, Gaonic literature, medieval Jewish philosophy, Hebrew poetry, mysticism, Hasidism, Jewish historical research in the nineteenth century, *Haskalah* literature, and modern Hebrew and Yiddish writing. Lack of familiarity with all of this was not proof of a Jew's humanity, said Zhitlovsky, but of his ignorance.

The concept of humanity also implied the freedom of a people to develop itself in all those areas of culture where universal human reason could not dictate a common rate of progress for mankind. It was therefore necessary for each people to determine its fate and be autonomous in the cultural sphere and, at times, in the political sphere as well. This was not segregation from the rest of mankind but 'the realization of universal human progress which had no executors other than the individual peoples'. Cultural domination of one people by another was an affront to that sense of justice which was essential to humanity. Every people had the duty to fight for its own freedom, independence, and cultural progress. For the Jewish people to become more human, it would have to become more Jewish, assert itself, and fight for its own dignity.

In 1908 Zhitlovsky settled in the United States and continued to elaborate his Yiddishist theories. He wrote that, if membership in the Jewish people was to be as 'natural and voluntary' as that in any other nation, there had to be a common cultural atmosphere in which all kinds of thinking, both secular and religious, could be included. 'Language is that cohesive power which makes of an individual person a uniform organism and clearly delineates his independence and uniqueness for the surrounding world'. Zhitlovsky admitted that the theoretical bickering between Yiddishists and Hebraists was of little avail to either side. Practically speaking, however, the Yiddishists had every reason to be optimistic. They had the upper hand, because even the Hebraists, if they desired to reach the masses, had to use Yiddish. Moreover, they were compelled to fight for Yiddish and treat it as the national language of Jewry wherever and whenever they fought for national rights for their people.

New enemies of Yiddish had arisen in those Jews who championed Jewish cultural creativity in the languages of their respective countries. According to their views, language was the means, not the end, of the national culture of any

The Movers of Our Movement. Dr. Khayim Zhitlovsky (Don Quixote?) – the knight who battles for his beloved Yiddish to the last drop of...ink! (*Der groyser kundes*, October 22, 1922)

people. Zhitlovsky pointed out, however, that as long as talented Jews continued to produce their works in non-Jewish languages their works would be attributed to other peoples. The Jewish people would then continue to be considered impoverished by other nations no matter how many geniuses it produced. The struggle for the development of Yiddish was therefore 'the struggle for a normal, free, comprehensive, rich and fertile culture of the Jewish people; the struggle for its life and development, for its respect and value'.

Zhitlovsky continued to argue that a dispersed people required the voluntary spiritual unity provided by a common culture. American Jewry, he felt, should strive to become the avant-garde of world Jewry. It would also be able to increase its own changes for national survival if it drew closer to other Jewish communities. But if American Jewry was to create an all-embracing, highly developed, and creative culture, it would have to do so in Yiddish. The one-sidedness of a Jewish culture in English, devoted exclusively to Jewish themes, precluded the attainment of excellence because it could hardly expect to attract Jews of genius. Nor could such a culture be fertile. It would fail to attract the masses which were always more concerned with universal human matters than with specific national ones. An Anglo-Jewish culture in America would lead to 'Judaic assimilation', whereas one in Yiddish would lead to the development of a comprehensive, rich, and fertile cultural life.

Zhitlovsky was active in a large number of American Jewish organizations of both a political and cultural character, including the Socialist-Territorialist party, the Labor Zionist party, the Workmen's Circle, and the Jewish National Worker's Alliance (Farband). He also headed a group known as 'Serp' which combined some of the ideas of the Bundists with those of the Territorialists. It sought Jewish cultural autonomy everywhere and political autonomy wherever Jews lived in compact masses. In 1908 and 1909 conferences were held to unite the Labor Zionists, the Territorialists, and the 'Serpists' into one larger party. The merger took place in Chicago in September, 1909. There were a number of heated arguments during these conferences between Zhitlovsky, the Yiddishist, and Nachman Syrkin, the Hebraist who headed the Socialist-Territorialist movement. Zhitlovsky got the new party to engage in work in the Disaspora and to conduct its cultural activities in both Yiddish and Hebrew. He prepared the way for the eventual establishment of the 'national radical' supplementary schools for Jewish children in the United States sponsored by the Labor Zionist movement. When this idea finally took hold, it was duplicated by the Workmen's Circle and other organizations, and a secular Yiddishist school system developed in the United States and Canada. Zhitlovsky also played an important role in the establishment of the American Jewish Congress in 1915.

In 1937 Zhitlovsky participated in the establishment of the politically leftist Yidisher Kultur Farband (YKUF). Although opposed to Bolshevism, he was heartened by the prospects of a Jewish agricultural territory in Birobidzhan and by Stalin's determination to create a multinational country which seemed to augur well for Jewish culture in the Soviet Union. He also saw in Russia a potential ally of the Jewish people against Hitler. Although Zhitlovsky left YKUF during the period of the Nazi-Soviet pact (1939–1941), he returned to it after Hitler attacked Russia, and remained associated with it for the rest of his life. A pro-YKUF address, 'Religion, Culture, Language', delivered in several American cities, was Zhitlovsky's most extreme formulation of his Yiddishist and secularist doctrines.

A Jew who lives in the language sphere of Yiddish can be a Jew by religion, a Christian by religion, of no religion or even against religion. He still remains a Jew and all cultural works by Jews in the Yiddish language will belong to the Jewish people, will be part of the Jewish spiritual national home now being created in Yiddish...

For Zhitlovsky the essence of secularism was the idea that religion is a private matter. Church and state had to be kept separate. Since the Yiddish language was the Jewish people's substitute for a state, it too had to be kept free of religion. 'No religious faith must make the pretense of representing official Judaism which every Jew must accept in order to be considered a Jew'. All religious and antireligious faiths and ways of life were to have equal rights in the spiritual-national home of the Jewish people which was the Yiddish language.

From 1941 on, Zhitlovsky served as chairman of the pro-Soviet 'Committee of Jewish Writers and Artists'. He disavowed communism but called upon his fellow American Jews to support the Soviet Union in its war against Hitler. Unfortunately, Zhitlovsky's blind faith that the Soviet Union was solving the problems of its Jewish population in accordance with his own theories also blinded him to even the grossest miscarriages of justice in the U.S.S.R. and turned him into a pro-Soviet propagandist.

Zhitlovsky died a controversial figure in May, 1943, abandoned by many of his former disciples who now considered him a traitor to his former principles and to the Jewish people. Following his death and for several years thereafter, articles and books appeared evaluating his contributions to Jewish life from various points of view. Despite the controversial nature of many of his views, the contribution he made to American Jewish life and thought at a critical turning point in American Jewish history cannot be gainsaid.

טהעאַטער און קריטיק

א שטורעם אין א גלאָז טינט

אָט־דאָ־אַ װערט באַשטימט, אױב די קינדער פֿון ישראל זאָלען אין זײער אײגנ־
נער מלוכה אין ארץ־ישראל רײדען אידיש אָדער העברעאיש...

A Storm in a Glass of Ink. Dr. Sirkin (Hebraist) and Dr. Zhitlovski (Yiddishist) argue it out. Right here the question is being settled as to whether the children of Israel should speak Yiddish or Hebrew in Erets Yisroel. (*Der groyser kundes*, March 22, 1918)

מיר באַשולדיקן און מאַנען אחריות!

זרובבל

SUMMARY: WE ACCUSE AND DEMAND RESPONSIBILITY!
BY ZERUBOVL

A leader of left-wing Labor Zionists (1886–1967) attacks those pre-World War II Zionist leaders and settlers who destroyed Yiddish printing presses, burned kiosks selling Yiddish papers and used other terrorist and totalitarian methods against Yiddish speakers, writers and advocates in Erets Yisroel.

פון צייט צו צייט קומען־אָן פון ארץ־ישראל ידיעות וועגן בלוטיקע
איבערפאַלן אַף פאַרזאַמלונגען אין יידיש, וועגן שענדלעכע האַנדלונגען לגבי
די, וואָס פירן אָוועלכע עס איז קולטור־אַרבעט עפנטלעך אין יידיש, וועגן
אָפיציעלע רדיפות; ווערן יידישע מאַסן אין חוץ־לארץ אויפגעבראַכט און
מען הויבט אַן פראָטעסטירן: היתכן ? יידן אַליין זאָלן רודפ׳ן די שפראַך
פון מיליאָנען יידישע מאַסן אין דער נאָרער וועלט ?

דערשיינען אָבער באַלד די שלוחים פון די ציוניסטן, ספעציעל, פון
דער אַלגעמיינער אַרבעטער אָרגאַניזאַציע (הסתדרות) און נעמען לייקענען
שטיין און ביין : ס׳איז אַ בילבול, אַן אויסטראַכטעניש פון שונאי ציון,
וועלכע ווילן אונטערשטעלן אַ שטרויכל־פיסל דעם אַרבעטנדיקן ארץ־
ישראל . . . אַזוי איז אין אַמעריקע דערשינען פאַראַיאָרן אַ דערקלערונג
פון דער הסתדרות־דעלעגאַציע, זלמן רובאשאוו און ברוך צוקערמאַן, אזוי
איז איצט געקומען אַן אָפיציעלער בריוו פון אויספיר קאָמיטעט פון
הסתדרות גע׳חתמ׳עט דורך ישראל מערעמינסקי, אדרעסירט צו דער מיטל
מערב קאָנפערענץ פון די קולטור געזעלשאַפטן אין שיקאַגאָ.

האָבן מיר באַשלאָסן דעם גאַנצן ענין ארויסברענגען פאַר דער עפנט־
לעכקייט און די לינע האָט אויפגעפאָדערט דעם שליח פון דער הסתדרות און
אַ פאָרשטייער פון די הינע רעכטע פועלי־ציון, וועלכע פירן אַן מיטן געווערק־

שאפטן־קאמפיין, זיי זאלן קומען אהער, פנים אל פנים מיט אונדז, געבן
זייערע דערקלערונגען.   מיר האבן געשריבן צו ווקערמאַנען אויסדריקלעך,
אז מיר לייגן אים נישט פאר צו "פארטיידיקן די רדיפות", נאר אויפקלערן
און פארטיידיקן דעם אפיציעלן שטאנדפונקט פון דער הסתדרות אין דער
פראגע יידיש.   דאס זעלבע האבן מיר געשריבן חיים גרינבערגן, דעם
רעדאקטאר פון "אידישן קעמפער".   אדרבא, זאלן זיי ענטפערן דירעקט, אן
פארדרייערניש און אויסמיידעניש, אן פאלעמישע שטיקלעך, צי די פאקטן,
וואס מיר גיבן־אן זענען ריכטיקע.   עס קאנען דאך נישט זיין קיין צוויי
אמת'ן.   דריי־צענדליק יאר פיר איך מיין געזעלשאפטלעכע ארבעט עפנטלעך
און טראָג אחריות פאר מיינע ווערטער.   איז אדרבא, זאלן זיי האבן דעם
מוט דא צו דערקלערן וועגן דער "צעשטערערישער כוונה" פון די ראפאל־
סעמס, ערעמס און זרבבלס און זייערע חברים, וואס האבן סיי דאס פער־
זענלעכע לעבן און סיי דאס לעבן פון א גאנצער באוועגונג פון יידישע אר־
בעטער אין דער גארער וועלט פארבונדן מיטן אידעאל און מיט דער טאט
פון טעריטאריעלן יידישן ארבעטער־צענטער אין ארץ־ישראל.   די "הדואר"־
לייט וועלן דא נישט אפקומען מיטן פאליציאיש אויסגעשריי: "נישט
מישן זיך" אין די ענינים פון ארץ־ישראל; ארץ־ישראל איז נישט מער קיין
ענין פון יחידים און גרופקעס.   מיטן לעבן דארט איז פארבונדן דאס לעבן
פון מיליאנען יידן, אפילו פון יענע, וואס וועלן בלייבן תמיד מחוץ
פאלעסטינע.

מיר קומען זיך נישט באקלאגן פאר אייך, הלמאי מען האסט אויס
שויבן, צי מען שפאלט אמאל קעפ, אדער מען צעריייסט יידישע צייטונגען.
מיט כוליגאנישע אנפאלן וועלן מיר זיך אליין אן עצה געבן.   אז דער
כוליגאן הרג'עט, גיט מען אים איין מאל און א צווייטן מאל איבער די העלנט,
פאלט ביי אים אפ דער חשק צו "העלדישקייט" אפן דריטן מאל. געזעל־
שאפטלעך גייט אונדז וועגן דעם סיסטעמאטישן פאגראם אין דער אידע־
אלאגיע און פסיכאלאגיע, אין יענער פארפעסטעטער און פארגיפטעטער
אטמאספער, וואס ווערט געשאפן דורך דערציאונג און דערמוטיקונג צו די
כוליגאנישע אויסברוכן.   דאס מוז אויך אייך אלע דא אנגיין.   דאס האט
נישט צו טאן מיט איינצלנע בויאנעם.   פאר דעם טראגן אחריות די
אויטאריטאטיווע אנשטאלטן און געזעלשאפטלעכע כחות פון ארץ־ישראל.

נעווים מ'קאן ברענגען פאקטן פון איבערפאלן אף א יידישער פארשטע־
לונג אין חיפה, פון א בלוטיקן אנפאל אף דעם קלוב פון פועלי־ציון אין תל־
אביב, פון פאנראמירן א פארזאמלונג פון יידישן ליטעראטן און זשורנא־
ליסטן פאריין אין תל־אביב, פון אן איבערפאל אף א יוביליי־פייערונג פון
דר. חיים זשיטלאווסקי.   פאקטן באקאנטע, וואס געהארן צו פארשידענע
יארן, ביז צו די נאר נאענטע יארן.

איז דאָס געווען אין פלוג אַ שענדלעכע טאַט פון די איבערפאַלער.
אָבער ווי אזוי האָט רעאגירט די געזעלשאַפטלעכקייט ?   דער ארבעטער־
אָרגאַן פון דער הסתדרות „דבר" האָט געהאַלטן פאַר נויטיק אויסצודריקן
זיין אומצופרידנקייט, וואָס מענטשן נעמען זיך צונויף אין תל־אביב און
האַלטן אָפּ פאַרזאַמלונגען אין יידיש וועגן יידיש ; די צייטונג האָט קלאָר
און אומצוויידייטיק גערעדט וועגן דעם, אז דאָס איז אַ „צווייפלהאפטע
אַרבעט", אן אומניטיקע.   אין דעם אָפיציעלן אָרגאַן פון דער ארץ־ישראל'־
דיסקער ארבעטער פארטי (מפא"י) איז דעם 11טן יאנואר, 1935, פארעפנט־
לעכט געוואָרן דער אויפרוף פון דער אָרגאַניזאַציע אייגצופירן די העגעמאָניע

פון העברעאיש אומעטום (אגוד להשלמת העברית), וואו עס ווערט
בפירוש אונטערגעשטראָכן, אז מען דאַרף מיט אלע מיטלען אויסווארצלען
די יידישע שפּראַך.   די רעדאַקציע האָט נישט צוגענעבן קיין שום באַ־
מערקונג פון זיך.   זי האָט נישט געגעבן אלע אונטערשריפטן, ווייל דאָרט
זענען געווען די אונטערשריפטן פון אזאַ פאשיסט ווי דר. קלויזנער, אן
אונטערשריפט פון הרב קוק; דער ארבעטער־אָרגאַן האָט בלויז געזאָגט, אז
עס זענען פאראן אונטערשריפטן פון טויר און לערער.

ס'איז געווען אַ שענדלעכער פאל מיטן דר. ראפאלקעס, וועלכער איז
אויסגעשלאָסן געוואָרן פון דער פארוואלטונג פון דער אדוואָקאטן פאראייני־
קונג נאָר דערפאַר, וואָס ער איז ארויסגעבער פון אַ צייטונג אין יידיש.
דער ארבעטער־אָרגאַן האָט אפילו אין דער כראָניק נישט געבראכט אָט די
ידיעה.   הפנים ער האַלט, אז די ידיעה איז נישט אזוי וויכטיק, ווי דאָס
אָנקומען פון גערער רבי'ן קיין ארץ־ישראל.

וואָלט אן ענלעכער פאקט געשען אין וועלכן אנדער לאנד, וואָלט מען
דאָך געזען אין דעם אן אויסברוך פון בארבאריי, פון אנטיסעמיטיזם פון
ערגסטן מין.   בנוגע ארץ־ישראל שוויינגט מען און דאָ זוכט מען דעם גאַנצן
ענין צו פארדרייען. דאָ שעמט מען זיך מיטן אמת ארויסקומען. מען שעמט
זיך צוגעבן און מודה זיין, אז אין דער הסתדרות גילט ביז היינטיקן טאָג דער
כלל, נישט צו לאָזן עפנטלעך זיך באנוצן מיט יידיש דעם, וואָס איז
איבער צוויי יאָר אין לאנד.   מערעמינסקי ליקענט עס אין אן עפנטלעכן
בריוו.   ער וויים נעבעך נישט וועגן אזאַ זאך.   איז צו באוואונדערן די
קליינמוטיקייט, אדער די חוצפה.   אָט האָט די רעדאַקציע פון „נייוועלט"
פארעפנטלעכט אין ארץ־ישראל איר תשובה צוקערמאַנען און רובאשאָוון און
דאָרט איז געבראכט אַ בריוו פון משה שפּיראַ אין נאָמען פון חיפה'ר
ארבעטער־ראַט צו דעם פראָפעסיאָנעלן פאַריין פון הויז־דינערינס, וואו עס
שטייט געשריבן שווארץ אף ווייס :

„מיר האָבן באַקומען אַ בריוו פון דער פרויען־קאָמיסיע, וואו
זיי באקלאָגן זיך אף דעם, וואָס איר רעדט און פירט פארזאַמלונגען

פון פאריין אין יידיש. מיר מאכן אייך אויפמערקזאם אף דעם,
אנגענומענעס כלל אין דער הסתדרות, אז יידיש מעגן רעדן נאר
חברי־טעס, וועלכע זענען ווייניקער ווי 2 יאר אין לאנד. די פארזיצערס
און פארוואלטונגס־מיטגלידער מוזן אויסשליסלער רעדן העברעאיש,
ווען זיי קומען אף אן עפנטלעכער פארזאמלונג פון דער הסתדרות.
אויב איר וועט נישט אפהיטן אין דער צוקונפט די דאזיקע אנגענו־
מענע כללים פון דער הסתדרות, וועלן מיר זיין געצוואונגען אנצונע־
מען אלע נויטיקע מיטלען קעגן דער פארוואלטונג פון פאריין. מיר
    בעטן אייך זיך רעכענען מיט דער דאזיקער ווארענונג".
ביז היינטיקן טאג האט קיינער אין ארץ־ישראל נישט אפגעלייקנט
די אויטענטישקייט פון דעם ציטירטן דאקומענט. טא ווער־זשע זאגט
אמת : משה שפירא, וועלכער רעדט אויסדריקלעך וועגן "אנגענומענעם כלל
אין הסתדרות" און "ווארנט" אפילו דער פארוואלטונג פון פאריין מיט
"מיטלען" פאר "נישט אפהיטן די אנגענומענע כללים", אדער ישראל
מערעמינסקי, וועלכער לייקנט אין שיקאגע, אז אזא כלל גילט אין הסתדרות?
בעת דעם פאנגראם אף דעם יידישן קלאנג־פילם "די יידישע מאמע",
האט דער יידישער נאציאנאל־ראט געשיקט א בריוו צום גדוד מגיני השפה
אין ירושלים, וואו עס איז געשריבן :

"ג. ה.   מיר באשטעטיקן דערמיט די קבלה פון אייער בריוו פון
דעם חודש נומער 72,226 און קאנען אייך מעלדן, אז מיר נעמען אן
פארשיידענע מיטלען כדי נישט צו שטעלן קיין זשארגאנישע טאן־פילמען.
די רעזולטאטן פון אונדזער אינטערוועניץ וועלן מיר אייך תיכף מיטטיילן".
גע'חתמ'עט זענען אף אט־דעם אפיציעלן דאקומענט פארן "הועד
הלאומי לכנסת ישראל", י. בן צבי און חיים סאלאמאן.
דאס האט פאסירט אין יאר 1930. אבער אין יאר 1934 האבן מיר
ווידער א בריוו, אן אפיציעלן, פון זעלבן כאראקטער:
    "צום הער האפענקא, תל־אביב.
אין דער לעצטער מינוט האבן מיר זיך דערוואוסט, אז איר האט
אפגעגעבן דעם זאל יאשא חפץ איינצואר דנען אן עפנטלעכע פאר־
זאמלונג, וואס וועט געפירט ווערן אין זשארגאן.
מיר דריקן אויס אונדזער שארפסטן פראטעסט קעגן אפגעבן
דעם זאל פון דער מוזיק שול שולמית אף איינצוארדנען די דער־
מאנטע פארזאמלונג כדי צו פארמיידן שטערונגען און אומארדנונגען.
מיר האפן, אז איר וועט וועט עס וויסן אפצושאצן און איר וועט אף
ווייטער פארמיידן אזא זאך זאל זיך איבער'חזר'ן".
גע'חתמ'עט איז דער בריוו "מיט פיל כבוד" ישראל רוקח, וויצע־
בירגערמייסטער.

ווען אן ענדעקישער אנטיסעמיטישער בירגערמייסטער פון א װאר־
שעװער שטאַט־ראַט װאָלט געװאַגט שרײבן אָפיציעל װעגן זשאַרגאָן, װאָלטן
אפילו די „גלות'דיקע אידעלעך" פון פּױלן געפֿונען בײ זיך מוט און װירדע
צו שטעמפּלען אַזאַ אַנטיסעמיטישע אַרױסטרעטונג בנוגע דער שפּראַך פון
מיליאָנען יידישע בירגער אין פּױלן. קומט אָבער אַזאַ פאַרװעניו, אַז סנאַב,
װעלכער האָט זיך אַרױפּגעאַרבעט אַפֿן קאַרק פון די יידישע מאַסן, און
שפּײט אין פּנים גראָביאָנגיש: „זשאַרגאָן", איז נישטאָ קײן מוט אפילו בײ
דער אַרבעטער־פּראַקסיע אין תּל־אבֿיבֿ'ער שטאָט־ראַט רופן אים צו
אָרדנונג. . . .

נײן, נישט װײל איר פעלט מוט, נאָר װײל איר פעלט פאַרשטענדעניש
פאַר אָט־דער באַלײדיקונג און דערנידערונג. דאָס איז דאָך דער הערשן־
דיקער קורס לגבי דער יידישער שפּראַך, װעלכער פאַראײניקט אין אײן
חבֿרותּא די מיטגלידער פון מפאי מיט די ביטערסטע רעאַקציאָנערן און
פאַשיסטן. זײ אַלע צוזאַמען דאַרפֿן עס אָפּהיטן די נאַציאָנאַלע קולטור
אין העברעאיש, אָדער װי עס האָבן איצט אױסגעפֿונען פֿירער פון מפאי
צו באַטאָנען, אַז העברעאיש איז דער קלאַסן־אינטערעס פון דער יידישער
אַרבעטערשאַפֿט. פּונקט װי בן יהודה און יהודה גראַזאָװסקי װאָלטן דורך
זײער פֿאַנאַטישן העברעאיזם געזוכט און אױסן געװען דעם פּראָלעטאַרישן
קלאַסן־אינטערעס פון יידישן אַרבעטער קלאַס. . . .

דאָס איז אַ קורם. אַ ליניע, אַ ריכטונג. דערפֿאַר װעט איר אין די
העברעאישע שולן פון דער הסתדרות נישט געפֿינען דעם לימוד פון יידיש,
אָדער דעם לימוד פון יידישער ליטעראַטור. דערפֿאַר װעט איר כמעט נישט
געפֿינען אין דעם אָרגאַן פון דער הסתדרות אַן אַרטיקל, װאָס זאָל רעדן
װעגן די שאַפֿונגען און דערגרײיכונגען פון דער יידישער שפּראַך און ליטע־
ראַטור אין אַנדערע לענדער, בעת אין זעלבן אָרגאַן זעגען געדרוקט געװאָרן
שענדלעכע און נידערטרעכטיקע אַרטיקלען װעגן יידיש, װי זעלינגמאַנ'ס און
רעגעלסאָנ'ס:

„יידיש איז די שפּראַך פון איטשע מאיר, דעם הפקר־מענטש.
די שפּראַך, װאָס ער באַנוצט, איז אַ הפקר־שפּראַך, אָן כּללים, אָן
געזעצן. די ביכער, װאָס ער שרײבט, זענען הפקר־ביכער, אָן גע־
װיסן, אָן לאָגיק, אָן װיסנשאַפֿטלעכער פֿאַראַנטװאָרטלעכקײט. די
שטענדיקע גרײזן אין די זשאַרגאָנישע צײטונגען באַצײכענען די
צינישע באַציאונג פון איטשע מאיר'ן צו יעדן געדאַנקן־מענטש און
צו אַלץ, װאָס האָט צו טאָן מיט געדאַנקן בכלל".
און אים האַלט אונטער זײן קאָלעגע רעגעלסאָן:

„די שפּראַך פון יידיש איז אין בית־מדרש, אין כּשר'ער מקוה,

מיטן שטאַט־באַק, מיט פּסח׳דיקע ניסלעך און תשעה־באָב׳דיקע
שישקעס."

אַט דער נובול־פּה ווערט געעצט און געדרוקט אַף ליינאָטיפּס און
ראָטאַציע־מאַשינעס, געשענקטע פֿון יידישע אַרבעטער אין אַמעריקע, צו
וועמען מען האָט אַפּעלירט אין יידיש און וועלכע האָבן אין יידיש אויפֿ־
גענומען די שײנקײט און גרױסקײט פֿון אַרבעטנדיקן ארץ־ישראל.   טאָ
זאָלן אַט־די יידישע אַרבעטער אין אַמעריקע כאַטש וויסן, וואָס אַזוינס מען
שרײבט וועגן זיי, די איטשע מאײרס, און זייער שפּראַך אין דער צײטונג,
וואָס זיי האָבן געהאָלפֿן אױפֿשטעלן !

דאָ האָבן מיר נישט צו טאָן מיט כולינאַנעם און אומפֿאראַנטוואָרטלעכע
יינגלעך.   האָט זענען אויטאָריטאַטיווע אָרגאַנען און אַנשטאַלטן, וועלכע
טראָגן אחריות פֿאַר דער אַטמאָספֿער, וואָס האָט זיך אויסגעבילדעט אַרום
יידיש.   אין דער אַטמאָספֿער דערצײטאָ מען ביטול און פֿאַראַכטונג צו יידיש,
און דורך דעם ביטול און פֿאַראַכטונג צו די, וואָס רעדן און באַנוצן יידיש.
דער קלימאַקס פֿון אַט־דער באַציאונג האָבן איצט מיר אין דעם
צירקולאַר 202 פֿון עליה־דעפּאַרטמענט פֿון דער יידישער אַגענץ וועגן
העברעאיש־עקזאַמען ביים באַקומען אַרבעטער־סערטיפֿיקאַטן.   אומעטום
אין דער גאָרער וועלט, אויך אין די שטאַטן איז גענוג צו קאָנען יידיש,
כדי נישט צו גילטן אַלס עם־האָרץ, אַלס אַנאַלפֿאַבעט, און אַרײנגעלאָזן
וואָרן אין לאַנד.   די יידישע אַגענץ האַלט בנוגע ארץ־ישראל אַנדערש.
מען מוז אָפּגעבן אַן עקזאַמען אין העברעאיש כדי אַרײנצוקומען אין לאַנד.
נאַטירלעך האָט מען דעם עקזאַמען אין העברעאיש באַשטימט נאָר פֿאַר
אַרבעטער.   קאַפּיטאַליסטן האָבן זייער אָפֿיציעלע שפּראַך, וועלכע ענטפֿערט
אַף אַלץ.   הכסף יענה את הכל.   די יידישע אַגענץ אָנערקענט די שפּראַך
פֿון געלט אָן העברעאיש.   אָבער די שפּראַך פֿון אַרבעטער־מאזאָליעס און
פֿראַצע גילט נישט אָן דער העברעאישער סמיכה.   מען האָט צוערשט גע־
וואָלט אויך אַט־דעם פֿאַקט לייקענען.   זלמן רובאַשאָוו האָט איבערגעגעבן,
אַז ס׳איז אַ בילבול און ס׳וועט קומען אַ הכחשה.   זעגען אַריבער עטלעכע
וואָכן.   די הכחשה איז נישטאָ.   דערפֿאַר אָבער האָט שוין אַפֿילו אַ העב־
רעאישער שרײבער, זלמן עפֿשטײן, פּראָטעסטירט קעגן דער נבלה פֿון דער
העברעאיש־גזירה לגבי אַרבעטער־סערטיפֿיקאַטן.   די יידישע אַרבעטער־
מאַסן פֿון אַמעריקע שווײגן.   די מיטגלידער פֿון רעכטע פּועלי־ציון, וואָס
האַלטן־אויס יידישע שולן אין אַמעריקע, שווײגן.   זיי טראַכטן נישט וועגן
דעם, וואָס וועלן זיי ענטפֿערן שפּעטער די קינדער, וועלכע ווערן
דורך זיי דערצויגן אין יידיש, ווען יענע וועלן פֿרעגן: ווער האָט אויסגע־
טראַכט אַט־די שענדלעכע גזירה קעגן יידישע אַרבעטס־מענטשן, ווער, אויב

משה-לייב האלפערין
זלאטשעוו, גאליציע, 1886
ניו-יארק, פאר. שטאטן, 1932

◆━━━━◆

אין ניו יארק, (לידער)
די גאלדענע פאווע, (לידער)
גינגעלי, (פאעמע)
יצחק לייבוש פרץ, (פאעמע)

◆━━━━◆

פאעט

משה נאדיר
(יצחק רייז)
נאראיעוו, גאליציע, 1885
ניו-יארק, פאר. שטאטן, 1943

◆━━━━◆

פון מענטש צו מענטש
מעשהלעך מיט א מאראל
א לאמפ אויפן פענצטער,
(לידער)
מיינע הענט האבן פארגאסן
דאס דאזיגע בלוט, (קריטיק)

◆━━━━◆

עסייאיסט, פאעט, דערציילער

איטשע-מאיר ווייסנבערג
זשעליכאוו, פוילן, 1881
ווארשע, פוילן, 1938

◆━━━━◆

א שטעטל, (דערציילונג)
דער טאטע מיט די בנים, (")
דריי שוועסטערלעך, (מעשהלע)
ר' יואל (דראמאטישע בילדער)

◆━━━━◆

דערציילער, ראמאניסט

הערש-דוד נאמבערג
אמשינאוו, פוילן, 1874
אטוואצק, פוילן, 1927

◆━━━━◆

פליגלמאן, (דערציילונג)
פון א פוילישער ישיבה, (")
די משפחה, (דראמע)
ס'לויפן, ס'יאגן שווארצע וואלקן,
(ליד)

◆━━━━◆

דערציילער,
פאעט, דראמאטורג, עסייאיסט

יעקב דינעזאן
ניי-זאגער, ליטע, 1856
ווארשע, פוילן, 1919

◆━━━━◆

יאסעלע, (דערציילונג)
הערשעלע, (דערציילונג)
שווארצער יונגנרמאנטשיק, (")
א שטיין אין וועג, (ראמאן)

◆━━━━◆

דערציילער, ראמאניסט

מרדכי ספעקטאר
אומאן, אוקראינע, 1858
ניו-יארק, פאר. שטאטן, 1925

◆━━━━◆

דער יידישער מוזשיק, (ראמאן)
העניים ואביונים, (ראמאן)
שטרייק פון קבצנים, (דערצ.)
מיין לעבן, (זכרונות)

◆━━━━◆

ראמאניסט, דערציילער

---

1. Moyshe-leyb Halpern, 1886–1932; Poet; 2. Moyshe Nadir, 1885–1943; Essayist, poet, writer of short stories; 3. Itshe-meyer Vaysnberg, 1881–1938; Writer of short stories, novelist; 4. Hersh-dovid Nomberg, 1874–1927; Writer of short stories, poet, playwright, essayist; 5. Yankev Dinezon, 1856–1919; Writer of short stories, novelist; 6. Mordkhe Spektor, 1858–1925; Novelist, short story writer.

נישט די יעניקע, וואָס טראָגן די גאַנצע אחריות פֿאַר דער היינטיקער
ציוניסטישער עקזעקוטיווע און יידישער אגענטור?

מוז קומען די באַשולדיקונג נישט בלויז קעגן די, וואָס טוען די נבלה,
נאָר אויך קעגן די, וואָס נעמען זי אויף שוויינענדיק און גלייכגילטיק.

זענען עס רדיפות אף יידיש? גערעכט איז דוד פינסקי, וועלכער
האָט אין אן אַרטיקל אין „אידישן קעמפּער" דערקלערט, אז „רדיפות איז
נאָך אַ צו שוואַך וואָרט". דער זעלבער פינסקי ווייסט, אלס קינסטלער,
אז „יידיש איז בלויז (אין פאַלעסטינע) פאַרהאַסט און פֿאַרעקלט, מוקצה
מחמת מיאוס". ס'איז נישט סתם מורא פֿאַר יידיש. „האָט דען דער
וויסער אין דרום פון די שטאַטן מורא פֿאַר דעם שוואַרצן? ער האָט
נאָר צו אים אַ געפֿיל פון פֿאַראַכטונג". דאָס זעלבע איז דאָס געפֿיל, וואָס
די העברעאיסטן פֿלאַנצן איין ביי דער געזעלשאַפֿטלעכקייט בנוגע יידיש.
מען דאַרף זיך שעמען צו רעדן יידיש אין דער עפֿנטלעכקייט. די מאַמע
קומט אין שול אריין און וועונדט זיך צום קינד אף שטום-לשון, ווייל דאָס
קינד האָט זיך געבעטן ביי דער מאַמען, זי זאָל אין שול נישט רעדן
„זשאַרגאָן" און נישט פֿאַרשעמען עס פֿאַר די איבעריקע קינדער. מיינען
די העברעאיסטישע קולטור-טוער דערפֿון צו דרינגען, אז די מאַמע דאַרף
זיך וואָס גיכער אויסלערנען העברעאיש, און מיר מיינען, אז די לערער
דאַרפֿן זיך וואָס גיכער אויסלערנען אַכטונג און דרך-ארץ פֿאַר דער שפּראַך
פון יידישע מיליאַנען און פֿאַר אָט יענע מאַמעס, וועלכע זענען זיך אין
פֿאַרשידענע לענדער מוסר נפש ביים אויפֿשטעלן און אויפֿהיטן די יידישע
שול און בילדונגס אינסטיטוציעס פֿאַר די יידישע קינדער כדי אויפֿהיטן
דעם לעבעדיקן אָרגאַנישן קאָנטאַקט צווישן אלע טיילן פון אונדזער נאַ-
ציאנאַלן קאָלעקטיוו.

ערגער ווי רדיפות איז דער סיסטעמאַטישער פּאָגראָם, דער פּסיכישער
און אידעאַלאָגישער, וואָס ווערט געפֿירט פון דער אָפֿיציעלער געזעלשאַפֿט-
לעכקייט אף די עפֿנטלעכע רעכט פון דער יידישער שפּראַך. נישטאָ נאָך
אַ לאַנד אין דער וועלט, וואו מען זאָל נישט טאָרן אויסהענגען קיין שילד
אף יידיש, וואו מען זאָל מורא האָבן צו פֿאַרדינגען אַ זאַל אף אַ פֿאַרזאַמלונג
אין יידיש.

געוויס ווערט יידיש אַ סך געלייענט אין ארץ-ישראל. טויזנטער עקזעמ-
פּליאַרן פון יידישע צייטונגען ווערן פֿאַרשפּרייט אין ארץ-ישראל, עס ווערן
פֿראַנק און פֿריי פֿאַרקויפֿט אין די גאַסן אפֿילו שונדישע און האַלב-פֿאָרנאָ-
גראַפֿישע צייטונגען אין יידיש, אבי זיי דערשינען ערגעץ אין ווסטן גלות.
דער ארץ-ישראל'דיקער באָדן טאָר אָבער נישט דולדן קיין אייגענע צייטונג
אין יידיש. מען דערלאָזט נישט די „ניוועלט" פֿריי אף דער גאַס. מען
דראָעט דעם דרוקער, מען דראָעט די צייטונגס-פֿאַרקויפֿער, מען באַפֿאַלט

די ארבעטער, וואָס פֿאַרקויפֿן אַליין פֿרייוויליק, נישט צוליב פּרנסה, די
„נייוועלט", און יידישע פּאָליציאַנטן האַלטן עס וואָרשיילעך פֿאַר אַ פֿאַקט־
ריאַטישער טאַט צו ערעסטירן אַזעלכע פֿאַרקויפֿערס און נאָכקאָנטראָלירן
בעת מעשׂה זייערע פּאַפֿירן, צי זיי זענען אַרייַנגעקומען אין לאַנד אויף אַ
לעגאַלן וועג. . . .

געוויס ווערט יידיש אַ סך גערעדט אין אַרץ־ישׂראל. אויף אַ באַראַטונג
פֿון דער הסתדרות מוז מען צוגעבן, אַז יידיש ווערט גערעדט אַלץ מער
אין די וואָרשטאָט, אין די פֿאַבריקן, אויף אַרבעטס־פּלעצער. ס׳איז געוואָרן
אַ סימן פֿון „גוטן טאָן" ביי אַרבעטער צו רעדן יידיש. אָבער דאָס
בלייבט אין די ראַמען פֿון פּריוואַטן פֿאַרקער. מען רעדט יידיש דערפֿאַר,
ווייל טויזנטער און צענדליקער ניי־אָנגעקומענע קאַנען זיך נישט אויסלעבן
אַנדערש ווי אין יידיש, און ווייל אָט־די קוואַליע פֿלייצט און ברייטערט זיך
אויס און פֿאַרכאַפֿט אויך יענע, וועלכע זענען הונדערט פּראָצענטיקע העברע־
איסטן. האָט מען געמאַכט דעם אויסשפּיר אויף אַ דער קאָנפֿערענץ, אַז מען
דאַרף זיך נישט אָפּשטעלן פֿאַר ברוטאַליטעט און אַרויפֿצווינגען העברעאיש
מיט געוואַלט. דאָ וועט אָבער קיין געוואַלט נישט העלפֿן צום אויסלערנען
זיך און אויך איינלעבן זיך קולטורעל מיט העברעאיש; דאָ קאָן מען דערגרייכן
בלויז איינס: אָראָפֿדריקן די מאַסן צו אַ נידעריקערן קולטור ניוואָ, אָוועק־
רויבן ביי זיי די מעגלעכקייט צו געניסן פֿון קולטור און פֿאַרטרייבן זיי
ווייט אַוועק פֿון עפֿנטלעכן לעבן און טעטיקייט. אַזוי פּאַסירט מיט נאָר
אַ גרויסער צאָל מענטשן, וועלכע זענען אין דער היים געווען אַקטיוו אויף
פֿאַרשידענע געביטן און וואָס אַ דאַנק אָט־דער אַקטיוויטעט זענען זיי גע־
קומען אין לאַנד. דאָ האָט מען זיי אויסגעשניטן די צונג און פֿאַרשטאָפּט
די אויערן און זיי דעגראַדירט צו דער מדרגה פֿון אַנאַלפֿאַבעטן, פֿון פּרימי־
טיוע בריות, וואָס ווייסן נאָר צו האָרעווען שווער, אָבער נישט צו געניסן
אַליין נייסטיס פֿון דער קולטור, וואָס זיי גופֿא שאַפֿן.

אָבער אויב די מאַסן נויטיקן זיך אין יידיש, פֿאַרוואָס־זשע זעט מען
נישט זייער בונט קעגן די אונטערדריקער, זייער קאַמף קעגן די רדיפֿות?
ס׳איז דאָך נישט מער, ווי אַ קליין הייפֿל לינקע פּועלי־ציון, וואָס טומלט
וועגן יידיש. אָבער זיי זענען איזאָלירט פֿון דער געזעלשאַפֿט, פֿון דער
גרויסער מערהייט טאַקע פֿון די אַרבעטער־מאַסן גופֿא. אַ סברא, אַז די
מאַסן ווילן ברענגען דעם קרבן פֿון יידיש, ווייל זיי ווייסן, אַז דורכדעם
וועט אויפֿגעשטעלט ווערן די איינהייט און גאַנצקייט פֿון דער נאַציאָנאַלער
קולטור. . . .

אַזאַ טענה איז פֿאַלש און אומגערעכט. געווען אַ צייט, ווען אין
צאַרישן רוסלאַנד האָבן די „מאַסן" נישט געוואָלט הערן פֿון סאָציאַליסטי־
שער אַגיטאַציע. . . . מען האָט די ערשטע סאָציאַליסטישע „טומלער" אָנ־

געבראָכן די ביינער, געבונדן אין שטעריק און איבערגעגעבן אין די הענט
פון די צאַרישע סאָטראַפן און די הענקערס. האָט מען דערפון געדאַרפט
דרינגען, אַז די פאָדערונגען פון די סאָציאַליסטן זענען פאַלשע, באַשר די
„מאַסן זענען דאָך בפירוש קעגן"? דערפון האָט מען געדרונגען נאָר דאָס,
אַז די מאַסן ווייסן נישט תמיד אַליין, אין וואָס זיי נויטיקן זיך, און מען
מוז זיי דעריבער עפענען די אויגן, אויפקלערן, אָרגאַניזירן און מאָביליזירן
צום קאַמף פאַר זייערע רעכט.

די „לינג פאַר רעכט פון אידיש אין ארץ-ישראל" נעמט אַרום מענטשן
און גרופן מיט פאַרשידענעם בליק אַף אַלגעמיינע און יידישע פּראָבלעמען,
ממילא זענען אין איר פאַראַן אויך מענטשן מיט פאַרשידענער באַציאונג
צום פּראָבלעם ארץ-ישראל אין יידישן לעבן. איך אַליין געהער צו אַ
פּאָליטישער באַוועגונג אין דער יידישער אַרבעטער גאַס. מיט 30 יאָר
צוריק, ווען מיר, פּועלי-ציון, זענען געקומען מיט אונדזער באַראַכווייסטיש
פּראָגנאָז וועגן דעם אויפקום פון יידישן טעריטאָריאַלן אַרבעטער-צענטער
אין פּאַלעסטינע און זיין ראָל אין לעבן און קאַמף פון די יידישע מאַסן,
זענען מיר אויך געווען איזאָלירט. סיי צווישן די סאָציאַליסטן האָט מען
געלאַכט פון די „כותל-מערבי-סאָציאַליסטן" און סיי צווישן די ציוניסטן
האָט מען גע'חוזק'ט איבער דעם „קלאַסנקאַמף" קעגן דער צדקה-פושקע
פון נאַציאָנאַל פאָנד, איידער דאָס „הויז איז אויפגעבויעט". איז וואָס געווען
דערפון צו דרינגען? אַז די איזאָלירטע גרופע, די נישט אַנערקענטע פון
סאָציאַליסטיש אינטערנאַציאָנאַל און נישט באַטייליקטע אין ציוניסטישן
קאָנגרעס, איז אומגערעכט? היינט צו טאָג וועט עס קיינער נישט זאָגן,
אפילו די גרעסטע קעגנער פון ארץ-ישראל, אָדער פון קלאַסן-שטאַנדפונקט
בנוגע פּאַלעסטינע. דאָס האָט נאָר אַן איבעריק מאָל באַוויזן, אַז אַ פּאָ-
ליטישע באַוועגונג פרעגט זיך נישט ביי די מאַסן, וואָס זיי זאָגן, נאָר זי
זוכט אויסצוגעפינען וואָס עס פאָדערן די לעבנס-אינטערעסן פון די מאַסן,
ווען אפילו די מאַסן פאַרשטייען נאָך אַליין נישט צו ליענען די שפּראַך
פון זייערע איינענע אינטערעסן.

פאַראַן אַ סך פּראָבלעמען אין ארץ-ישראל, וואו די מערהייט גייט אָן
מיט אַן אנדער וועג. אָט איז איינע פון די וויכטיקסטע פּראָבלעמען, לויט
מיין טיפּסטער איבערצייגונג, די גורל-פראַגע פון אונדזער ווייטערדיקן
לעבן אין פּאַלעסטינע, די פראַגע וועגן יידיש-אַראַבישע באַציאונגען.
דערמיט איז אויך פאַרבונדן די פראַגע וועגן דער באַציאונג צו דער ברי-
טישער מאַנדאַט-מאַכט. איז געקומען בן גוריון און דערקלערט עפנטלעך,
אַז „ווער עס איז קעגן קאָאָפּעראַציע מיט דער מאַנדאַט-מאַכט איז אַ
פאַרראַטער פון יידישן פאָלק און פון ארץ-ישראל'דיקן אויפבוי". מיין
איך, אַז ריכטיקער איז די באַהויפטונג, אַז אַ פאַררעטער איז דער, וואָס

בינדט צונויף די באפרייאונג פון דעם יידישן פאלק מיטן קיום פון אים-
פעריאליסטישער מאכט און ענגלישער קאלאניאל־פאליטיק אין ארץ־ישראל.

אט האט בן גוריון געשלאסן אן אפמאך מיט זשאבאטינסקין און דער־
מיט אויפגעהויבן א האנט אף דעם קלאסנקאמף פון די יידישע ארבעטער
אין פאלעסטינע. אב. קאהאן וויל נישט „שטערן דער הסתדרות". ביי
אים איז הייליק אלץ, וואס די „פאלעסטינער ארבעטערשאפט" טוט. און
מיר, אלס מיטגלידער פון דער הסתדרות, האבן גרייליך אויפגענומען א
קאמף קעגן יענעם שענדלעכן אפמאך פון די פירער. ביי די „הדואר־לייט"
מיט אב. קאהאנען מיינט עס „שטערן", „טומלען", „צעברעכן". און איך
באהויפט, אז אט־דאס ערשט מיינט אויפבויען די יידישע ארבעטער־
באוועגונג און ממילא דאס נייע לעבן אין ארץ־ישראל. געוויס דארף מען
„שטערן" יעדן „שלום" צווישן דער ארבעטערשאפט און אירע בלוט־
זוינגערס, געוויס דארף מען צעברעכן יעדן פאקט צווישן ארבעטער און
פאשיזם אפילו אונטער דער מאסקע פון בנין־הארץ. ס'איז אונדזער שטאלץ
און גליק, וואס די יידישע ארבעטער האבן אונדזער רוף פארשטאנען און
בן גוריון'ס אייגענע חברים האבן געשטימט אפצעוווארפן דעם שענדלעכן
אפמאך, וועלכן זייער באליבטער פירער האט גע'חתמ'עט. מיר האבן זיך
נישט אפגעהאלטן פון „צעשטערן" דעם „שלום" אין הסתדרות און אין
ישוב, ווייל אט־דער „שלום" איז קעגן די אינטערעסן פון קומענדיקן
ארבעטנדיקן ארץ־ישראל.

אויך אין דייטשלאנד הערשט איצט אחדות און שלום. אלע שטייען
הינטער דעם „פירער". ס'ווערט אפגעהיט הונדערט פראצענט ריין־אַרישע
ארבעט און ס'הערשט איין נאציאנאלע דייטשע שפראך. וועלן מיר מיטן
גאנצן פייער פון אונדזער נשמה קעמפן און רופן די יידישע מאסן אין
דער גארער וועלט צו קעמפן קעגן אזא „פרייען" יידישן לעבן אין פאלעס־
טינע. די פירער פון דער הסתדרות זענען איינגעשטעלט אף די פרינציפן
פון „כיבוש עבודה" פון עבודה עברית במאה אחוז (הונדערט פראצענט
ריין־יידישע ארבעט), פון תוצרת הארץ, וואס ביי זיי מיינט עס תוצרת
עברית (ארטיקע פראדוקציע — יידישע פראדוקציע), פון שלום און קא־
אליציע מיטן יידישן קלעריקאליזם, מיט דער העברעאיסטישער פיינטשאפט
און פאראכטונג צו יידיש.

ווילן מיר צעשטערן אט־די אלע פרינציפן, ווייל ס'איז אונדזער טיפסטע
איבערצייגונג, אז זיי זענען דער גרעסטער אומגליק פאר ארץ־ישראל און
פארן גאנצן יידישן לעבן. איז דאך אויך ארץ־ישראל די זאך פון יידישן
לעבן אומעטום, און נישט נאר פון די עטלעכע הונדערט טויזנט יידן, וואס
זענען צופעליקע היינט אין לאנד. הונדערטער טויזנטער וועלן נאך קומען.
הונדערטער טויזנטער וועלן באאיינפלוסט ווערן פון דעם, וואס דארט קומט

פאר.   מוזן מיר אלע זיך אריינמישן און אכטונג געבן, אז עס זאל נישט
אויפגעשטעלט ווערן קיין שטער פאר דער נאציאנאלער און סאציאלער
באפרייאונג פון יידישן פאלק אין דער גארער וועלט.

די יידישע מאסן קומט־אויס שווער און ביטער צו קעמפן קעגן א
וועלט מיט שונאים פאר רעכט אף לעבן, פאר רעכט אף נאציאנאלער עק־
זיסטענץ.   א פארברעכן באגנייען יענע, וואס זייען אומגלויבן אין די אויפ־
גייענדיקע כחות פון יידישן לעבן אומעטום א חוץ פאלעסטינע, יענע, וואס,
פארשטעלט אדער אפן, אריענטירן זיך אפן אויטערגאנג פון אומעטומעדיקן
יידישן לעבן.   זיי ווילן אלץ קאנצענטרירן בלויז און אויסשליסלעך אף
ארץ־ישראל.   זיי פראקלאמירן, אז דער קאמף קעגן פאגראמען אין אלע
לענדער איז אויסזיכטלאז, אז דער קאמף קעגן אנטיסעמיטיזם איז נישט
מער ווי א באבסקע רפואות.   אויב אזוי איז אויך קלאר, אז די אלע דערגריי־
כונגען פון די יידישע מאסן וועלן אומקומען אין רעזולטאט פון שטייגנדיקן
פאשיזם אין דער וועלט.   פונדאנען די פאראכטונג צום „גלות", צו די
„גלות"־יידן, צו דעם „גלות"־לעבן, צו דער „גלות"־שפראך.

איז עס נישט נאר קורצזיכטיקייט און פאליטישע נאאיווקייט, נאר א
פארברעך פון פראפאגאנדירן פארברעכערישע רעאקציאנערע אידעען, פון
אריענטירן זיך אף דעם זיג פון היטלעריזם.   וואלט אט־די אנשויאונג
געווען א ריכטיקע, וואלט עס געמיינט נישט נאר אונטערגאנג פון „גלות",
נאר אויך פון ארץ־ישראל גופא.   היטלעריזם ווייזט זיינע נעגל אויך אין
פאלעסטינע, און ס'איז נישט אויסגעשלאסן, אז דער אימפעריאליזם זאל
זיך מיט אים באנוצן־קעגן דעם אויפשטייגנדיקן יידישן ארבעטער־לעבן
אין ארץ־ישראל.

מיר זעען פאראויס דעם אויפשטייג פון ארבעטער־כחות אין דער גארער
וועלט.   היטלעריזם וועט געבראכן ווערן דורכן אויפקום פון ארבעטער־
כחות, סיי אין דייטשלאנד און סיי אין אנדערע לענדער.   אט־דאס שעפן
מיר גלויבן און זיכערקייט אויך אין דעם אויפקום פון ארבעטנדיקן ארץ־
ישראל.   אבער דא זענען די קוואלן פון אונדזער זיכערקייט, אז אויך דאס
יידישע לעבן אין אנדערע לענדער וועט נישט אונטערגיין.   דער בעסטער
באווייז: די דערגרייכונגען אין ראטנפארבאנד און די שטעלונג פון דער
ראטנמאכט לגבי דער אנטוויקלונג פון יידישן נאציאנאלן לעבן.   איז דאס
אויך אונדזער אלגעמיינע ליניע בנוגע די ברידעלעכע און חבר'שע באצי־
אונגען צווישן יידישע און אראבישע ארבעטער און הארעפאשניקעס;
אונדזער איבערצייגונג איז פעסט, אז דער יידישער טעריטאריאלער ארבע־
טער־צענטער וועט אויפקומען נאר אין א פרייער אומאפהענגיקער פאלעסטינע
פון ארבעטער און פויערים, יידן און אראבער, פאראייניקטע אין אינטער־
נאציאנאלער פראלעטארישער סאלידאריטעט.

אָט־די פּאָליטישע אײנשטעלונג און אָריענטאַציע מוז אויפגענומען
װערן פון יעדן ערלעכן ייִדישן אַרבעטס־מענטש, פון יעדן קולטור־מענטש,
װאָס זוכט פאַר'זיך אַ װעג אין דעם װיסטן מדבר פון די איצטיקע אינטער־
נאַציאָנאַלע פאַר־העלטעניש; מען מוז פאַרשטיין און באַנעמען די קאָלאָ־
סאַלע ראָל, װאָס אַרץ־ישׂראל שפּילט שוין און װעט נאָך שפּילן אין ייִדישן
לעבן. אָבער פּונקט אַזוי מוז יעדער פאַרשטיין, אַז אַרץ־ישׂראל טאָר נישט
אָפּגעריסן װערן פון דעם קאַמף פון ייִדישע מאַסן פאַר זײערע נאַציאָנאַלע
און סאָציאַלע רעכט און לעבנס־מעגלעכקײטן אויך אין אַנדערע לענדער.

אין פּאַלעסטינע גײען איצט צענדליקער טויזנטער ייִדישע מאַסן.
זענען מיר פאַרפּליכטעט צו אינטערעסירן זיך מיט זײער לעבן דאָרט. דאָס
װעט זיך אָפּרופן אַף אונדזער לעבן איבעראַל. מען קומט און מען פאָדערט
אײער הילף בנוגע אַרץ־ישׂראל. מיט אײערע געלטער האַלט מען אויף אין
„גלות" הכשרה־פּונקטן, װאו מען דערציט לכתחילה אַ העברעאישטישע
יוגנט, װעלכע קערט זיך אָפּ מיט פאַראַכטונג צו דעם קאַמף פאַר אונדזער
מאַסן־קולטור אין די לענדער, װאו זי געפינט זיך. דערנאָך שטיצט מען זיך
אין אַרץ־ישׂראל אַף דעם העברעאיזם פון דער זעלבער יוגנט כדי צו שטיקן
און דריקן ייִדיש, און אײך הײסט מען זיך „נישט מישן". מיט אײער
געלט בויט מען עליה־אַמטן, אין אײער אַלעמענס נאָמען רעדט מען צו
די פעלקער און צו דער מאַנדאַט־מאַכט, און אַלס אײערע רעפּרעזענטאַנטן
קריגט מען סערטיפיקאַטן, און דערנאָך שטעלט מען אויף אַ װאַנט פון
העברעאיש־גזירות כדי נישט דורכלאָזן אַרבעטס־מענטשן, װעלכע נויטיקן
זיך אין אַרץ־ישׂראל און אין װעמען אַרץ־ישׂראל נויטיקט זיך נישט װײניקער.

מיט היטלערן שליסט מען „טראַנספער"־אָפּמאַכן כדי צו ראַטעװען
פאַרמעגנס פון דײטשע ייִדן, װעלכע װעלן דערנאָך אין אַרץ־ישׂראל גופא
אײנפירן היטלעריסטישע פּרינציפן בנוגע אַרבעטער; אָבער אַף די ייִדישע
אַרבעטער, אַף די לעבעדיקע האַרעפּאַשניקעס װילן די „רעטער פון ייִדישן
פאָלק" אַרויפלײגן אַ געלע לאַטע, אַ נײעם חרם, באַשר זײ קאָנען נישט
קײן העברעאיש.

זאָלט איר שװײגן? האָט איר אַ רעכט צו שװײגן?
מיר מאָנען בײ אײך אחריות. הײבט אויף אײער פּראָטעסט־שטימע.
איר האָט אָפּגעשריען גענונג גזירות, װאָס זענען געקומען אַף ייִדן מצד
„גוים", זענט איר מחויב איצט אָפּשרײען די גזירה, װעלכע קומט מצד
דעם קעמפּנדיקן העברעאיזם. דאָס װעט זײן אַ טובה פאַר די ייִדישע מאַסן,
װעט עס ממילא זײן אַ טובה אויך פאַרן ייִדישן ישׁוב אין אַרץ־ישׂראל.

מ'טאָר זיך נישט באַנוגענען מיט רעזאָלוציעס. ס'איז צײט צו שאַפן
פאַקטן, נײע, אַנדערע פאַקטן. קעגן די פאַקטן פון רדיפות זאָלן עס זײן
פאַקטן פון אונדזער אַלגעמיינער אחריות

האידיש אינה מתה בבריסל

עתיד 25

עתיד 15.11.70 א' יום

מאת אריה יאס, בריסל

בבריסל, בירת נאט"ו והשוק
האירופי המשותף יש קהילה
יהודית חשובה, ענף כרות מגזע
האם של יהדות פולין. ויש בה
שחקנית מהתיאטרון היהודי של
מזרח אירופה, בלה שאפרן.

בריסל איננה עיר נכחדת. אדרבא,
בירת השוק האירופי המשותף ונאט"ו,
עיר המחר, יש בה קהילה יהודית חשו־
בה, ענף כרות מגזע העץ־האם של
יהדות פולין שנמצאה לה הציפור השו־
מרת על הגר הישן בדמותה של בלה
שאפרן. "האידיש אינה שפה מתה, אנח־
נו הורגים אותה, אמרה, איננו מדברים
בה, אין אנו מחנכים ומגדלים בה. רוצ־
חים אנחנו. רוצחים על ידי התבוללות,
על ידי גסות־לב גשמית של חיי יום־
יום".

שחקנית לשעבר בתיאטרונים האידיש־
איים של פולין ורוסיה ומשוגעת לדבר
החלה בלה שאפרן לארגן סביבה קומץ
של חובבי־תיאטרון. ובעקשנות בלתי־
נילאית, במסירות, כאחזת קדחת, קלפה
מעל חסידיה את שכבות הגשמיות של
חיי גלות יומיומים וגילתה בהם את
אותו ניצוץ של נשמה יתירה.

אלה ששמעו על כך משכו בכתפיהם:
ברכה לבטלה, אמרו, היא תתעייף לב־
סוף כרבים אחרים לפניה ותתפזר לענף
אחר. אלא שהמפכפקים שכמה פרט קטן.
המוהיקנים האחרונים אינם אנשים רגי־
לים, הפועלים על פי חוק תורת ההגיון.
ולכן גדולה היתה הפתעתם כשהעלה

תיאטרון "יקולט" ("יידיש קולטור תיא־
טער — תיאטרון תרבות אידיש) במשך
4 שנות קיומו את "קידוש השם", "היור־
שים", "מוטקה גנב" מאת שלום אש,
את "ענך" ו"טוביה החולב" מאת שלום
עליכם בנוסף להספקנים וקטעי האמונה
גדלה עוד יותר משהעלה התיאטרון
קומדיה של לאון קוברין, מחזאי יהודי
אמריקאי, "נשות הרופא". קומדיה ש־
עלילתה סובבת סביב שיוויון הזכויות
לנשים בארה"ב של שנות העשרים, כפי
שהבעיה משתקפת במשפחה יהודית ב־
ניו־יורק. התפקידים הראשיים גול־
מו בידי צעירים, ברובם ילידי בלגיה
שלאחר המלחמה. ועל כך רבתה התמיהה
וההתפעלות: צעירים — ומשחקים באי־
דיש! וכה גם שבין צעירים אלה ותרבות
האידיש מרחק שלם של עולם ומלואו.
אנט היא פקידה בהנהלת חשבונות.
מישל — סטודנט לסוציולוגיה. בטי — מזכירה
במשרד עורך־דין ואסתר לומדת שפות.
ואם הללו, ששפתם, חינוכם ותרבותם
צרפתית, מופיעים באידיש הרי שלא
אלמן ישראל.

היה משהו פתאטי, מרגש, לראות
את ההצגות של התיאטרון שבו נוטלים
חלק צעירים שהאידיש שבפיהם נשמעת
זרה משהו, ושתפקידיהם נכתבו למענם
באותיות לטיניות אם לא בצרפתית
משהו נוגע ללב ומעיד משום שידעת:
כך כבר אין משחקים, וכך לא ישחקו
עוד לעולם. כבר אין מתנועעים כך,
כבר אין מהלכין כך ואין מדברים כך
ובשפה הזו, באידיש, אפילו לא מאחורי
הקלעים. ועלה.

האָבן יידישע אַרבעטער און פֿאָלקס מענטשן געסאָנט אויפֿשטעלן אין
ארץ־ישראל דרוקערייען, וואו מען דרוקט אין העברעאיש שעגדלעכע אר־
טיקלען קעגן יידיש, — דאַרפֿט איר זיך איצט דערהויבן אויפֿשטעלן אַ נייע
דרוקעריי, וואו עס זאָל געדרוקט ווערן די צייטונג „נייוועלט", אייער אייגנס,
וואו עס זאָל קומען צום אויסדרוק אייער אייגן פֿלייש און בלוט, און דורך
דעם זאָלט איר זיך נאָך מער דערנענטערן און פֿאַרהיימישן מיטן נייעם,
נישט רעאַקציאָנערן, נישט קלעריקאַלן, נאָר פֿרייען, אַרבעטנדיקן ארץ־
ישראל.

ראַטעוועט דעם נייעם דור, וואָס קומט אויף אין ארץ־ישראל פֿון סנא־
ביזם, פֿון פֿרעמדקייט צום יידישן לעבן, ראַטעוועט אים פֿאַר די פֿראָבלע־
מען פֿון דעם אַלוועלטלעכן יידישן נאַציאָנאַלן קאָלעקטיוו, ראַטעוועט ארץ־
ישראל פֿון דעם ביטול און פֿאַראַכטונג צום אייגענעם מקור, צום ברייט
פֿאַרצווייגטן יידישן מאַסן לעבן אומעטום.   נעמט־צו ביי די היטלעריסטן
דאָס געווער צו באַרעכטיקן זייערע רדיפֿות אַף אונדזער שפּראַך און קולטור
דורך די רדיפֿות אַף דיזעלבע מצד די אייגענע אין פֿאַלעסטינע.

העלפֿט אונדז אויפֿשטעלן קולטור־פּאָזיציעס, ממשות'דיקע ווערטן,
העלפֿט אונדז צו קעמפֿן פֿאַר די רעכט פֿון יידיש אין ארץ־ישראל !

ס'איז נישט קיין קאַמף קעגן העברעאיש, נאָר קעגן אַגרעסיוון פֿאָלקס
פֿיינטלעכן שאָוויניסטישן העברעאיזם, ס'איז אַ קאַמף פֿאַר די רעכט פֿון
די, וואָס קענען און ווילן זיך אויסלעבן אויך אין ארץ־ישראל אין דער יידי־
שער שפּראַך, ווייל אויך ארץ־ישראל איז ביי זיי ניט אַ ענין פֿאַר זיך, נאָר
ענג און אָרגאַניש איינגעוועבט אין דעם גרויסן קאַמף פֿאַר איבעראַנדערש
דאָס גאַנצע אומעטומיקע לעבן פֿון די יידישע מאַסן אַף נייע געזונטע פּראָ־
דוקטיווע יסודות.

העלפֿט מאַראַליש דורך אייער פּראָטעסט קעגן רדיפֿות, העלפֿט פֿינאַנ־
ציעל דורך אויפֿשטעלן פֿעסטע פּאָזיציעס פֿאַר יידישער קולטור אין
ארץ־ישראל.

◄ *Yiddish Isn't Dead in Brussels.* A major Israeli newpaper and its readers are surprised that Yiddish theater is still alive. After predicting, fostering, and reporting the death of Yiddish for decades Zionist establishment circles are shocked to relate the view that 'Yiddish isn't a dead language. We are killing it.' (*Maariv*, November 15, 1970)

1

זאלקינד שניאור

שקלאװ, אוקראאינע, 1887
ניו יארק, פאר. שטאטן, 1959

◆

שקלאװער ייִדן, (דערצײילונגען)
50 יאר, (לידער און פּאעמען)
פּעטער זשאמע, (ראמאן)
קיסר און רבי, (ראמאן)

◆

פּאעט, דערצײילער, ראמאניסט,
עסײיסט

2

ש. אנסקי

(שלמה-זאנװל ראפּפּאָרט)
װיטעבסק, ױיס-רוסלאנד, 1863
װארשע, פּוילן, 1920

◆

דער דיבוק, (דראמע)
חורבן גאליציע, (מעמואַרן)
פֿון איייביקן קװאל, (פֿאלקלאר)
די שבועה, (הימן פֿון „בונד")

◆

דראמאטורג, פֿאלקלאריסט,
עסײיסט, פּאעט, דערצײילער

3

פּרץ הירשביין

ישוב ביי גראדנע, רוסלאנד, 1880
לאס אנדזשעלעס, פּ. שטאטן, 1948

◆

די גרינע פֿעלדער, (דראמע)
די פּוסטע קרעטשמע, (דראמע)
ב ב ל, (ראמאן)
אַרום דער װעלט, (רײיזעס)

◆

דראמאטורג, פּאעט, דערצײילער

4

דוד איינהארן

קארעליטש, ױיס-רוסלאנד, 1886
לעבט אין ניו יארק, פּאר. שטאטן

◆

שטילע געזאנגען, (לידער)
צו אַ ייִדישער טאכטער, (")
שטילע יוגנט, (לידער)
צביה, (דראמאטישע פּאעמע)

◆

פּאעט

5

אליעזר שטײנבארג

ליפקאן, בעסאראביע, 1880
טשערנאװיץ, רומעניע, 1932

◆

מ ש ל י ם
אלף - בית, (קינדער פּאעמע)
יוסף מוכר שבת, (אפּערע)
אברהם אבינו, (מעשהלע)

◆

פּאעט, דראמאטורג

6

איציק מאנגער

טשערנאװיץ, בוקאװינע, 1901
לעבט אין ניו-יארק, פּאר. שטאטן

◆

שטערן אויפֿן דאך, (באלאדן)
לאמטערן אין װינט, (באלאדן)
חומש-און מגילה-לידער
האצמאך-שפּיל, (פֿארשטעלונג)

◆

פּאעט, עסײיסט, דראמאטורג

1. Zalkind Shneyer, 1887–1959; Poet, writer of short stories, novelist, essayist; 2. S(hin) Anski, 1863–1920; Playwright, folklorist, essayist, poet, writer of short stories; 3. Perets Hirshbeyn, 1880–1948; Playwright, poet, writer of short stories; 4. Dovid Aynhorn, 1886–1973; Poet; 5. Eliyezer Shteynbarg, 1880–1932; Poet; playwright; 6. Itsik Manger, 1901–1969; Poet, essayist, playwright.

דער בליק אַז יִידיש איז דער תּמצית פֿון יִידישקייט. די סכּנה פֿון דער פֿאָרמולע „לינגוויסטיש־סעקולאַריסטיש"

לייבוש לעהרער

SUMMARY: THE VIEW THAT YIDDISH IS THE QUINTESSENCE OF
JEWISHNESS – THE DANGER OF THE FORMULATION
'LINGUISTIC-SECULARISTIC' BY LEYBESH LERER
(LEIBUSH LEHRER)

*A leading psychologist and Yiddish secular-traditional educator (1887–1964)
warns that the conviction that Yiddish alone constitutes Jewishness, endangers
Jewish cultural and national continuity. Not only does this view impoverish
Jewishness, but, by doing so, it endangers Yiddish as well.*

7

עטלעכע צרגאַניזירטע און אומאָרגאַניזירטע גרופּירונגען אין ייִדישן
לעבן האָבן פֿאַרמראָמען די וועלטלעכקייט אידיע. אָבער וואָס עקסטרעמער
די דאָזיקע אידיע איז אויסגעדריקט געוואָרן אַלץ שוואַכער איז אין יענעם
ווינקל געוואָרן דער נאַציאָנאַלער טאָן, אַלץ לויזער די פֿאַרבינדונג מיטן
פֿאָלק, זיינע ווערטן און זיינע האָפֿענונגען.

און ייִדיש? איז דען ניט ייִדיש געקומען אויסצופֿילן דעם ליידיקן
חלל וואָס די פֿאַרטריבענע רעליגיע האָט איבערגעלאָזן? יאָ, אָבער די
אונטערגעמונג האָט זיך ניט געענדיקט מיט גרויס הצלחה. איך האָב
מורא אַז פּונקט ווי בי וועלטלעכקייט, האָבן מיר אויך דאָ צו טאָן מיט
אַ לאַזונג וואָס איז געבראַכט געוואָרן פֿון דער פֿרעמד, אין איר פֿרעמדן
לבוש, זון האָט דעריבער בי אונדז ניט געקענט אַרויסוייזן קיין גרויסע
גבורות.

עס איז כּדאי אונטערצושטרייכן דעם פֿאַקט אַז שפּראַך־ייִדישיזם —
ייִדיש ווי אַן איינציקער גייסטיקער פֿאַרבינדונג־פֿאָדים, לויט ושיטלאַווסקיט
פֿריער־געבראַכטער דעפֿיניציע — האָט ניט געשלאָגן קיין וואָרצלען אין

אונדזער לעבן. עס איז געוואקסן א ייִדישע ליטעראטור, א ייִדישע שול,
ייִדיש איז געווארן א קולטור־שפּראך, אָבער שפּעטער ייִדישיזם איז אַלץ
געמליכן דאָס טעאָרעטישע אייגענום פֿון עטלעכע געצײלטע אידעאָלאָגן
און א קליינער גרופּע באַוואוסטזיניקע אָנהענגער. גרויסע אַרבעטער
פּאַרטיִען האָבן אָן א שיעור מיטגעהאָלפֿן צו קולטיווירן ייִדיש, אָבער זיי
זענען געבליבן קאַלט, אפֿילו קעגנערייש, צו דער אידעאָלאָגישער אויפֿפֿאַ־
סונג פֿונם שפּראך־ייִדישיזם.   די אַרטאָדאָקסן לעבן אינטים מיט ייִדיש,
אָבער די אידעאָלאָגיע האָט זיי אפֿילו ניט אָנגערירט. וועגן אנדערע
גרופּידירונגען אין אונדזער וועלט איז דאָך שוין אָפּגערעדם.

עס איז אינטערעסאַנט אַז פֿרומע ייִדן זענען ווײט פֿון ייִדישן קינסט־
לערישן וואָרט. לחלוטין אַנדערש ווי די שכנות׳דיקע פֿרומע קריסטן.
דאָס דערקלערם זיך מיט באַקאַנטע היסטאָרישע סיבות. אָבער עס האָט
זיך ניט געפֿונען קיין גרופּע, אפֿילו ניט קיין יחיד, וואָס זיין באַגייס־
טערונג פֿאַר דער הײלער ייִדיש־אידעאָלאָגיע זאָל גרייכן אַזוי ווייט אַז
ער זאָל זיך באַמיען צו דערגענצטערן די ייִדישע אָרטאָדאָקסיע — האָט
לעבם דאָך אַזוי בלוט־הײמיש מיט ייִדיש — צו דער מאָדערנער ייִדישער
ליטעראַטור, לכל הפּחות צו ווערק וואָס זענען לכל הדעות כּשר. דאָס
פֿאַרדינסט פֿון אַזא באַוועגונג פֿאַר ייִדיש צווישן פֿרומע ייִדן איז ממש
ניט אָפּצושאַצן. אָבער קעגנטיק אַז שפּראך אַליין האָט ניט גענוג כּוח
בײ אונדז צו שטויסן צו אַזעלכע געפֿילן און מעשים.

העברײיזם, ווי א רייִנע שפּראך־אידעאָלאָגיע האָט אויך געהאָט אַן
ענלעכע, כאָטש אַביסל אַ בעסערע, מערכה. העברײיש האָט געפֿונען
א טיפֿן אָפּקלאַנג, האָט אַרויסגערופֿן באַגייסטערונג און ענערגישע טעטי־
קייט, אָבער שפּראך־העברײיזם האָט גענען קאַלט. ווי געזאָגט איז
בנוגע העברײיש די מערכה אַביסל אַ בעסערע, מיר וועלן באַלד זען
פֿאַרוואָס דאָס איז אַזוי. אָבער אין לעצטן סך הכּל זעט עס אויס אַז
שפּראך־נאַציאָנאַליזם בכּלל איז בײ ייִדן ניט אַזא אָנגעלייגטער גאַסט ווי
בײ אנדערע פֿעלקער. פֿאַרוואָס?   לאָמיר זיך באַנוגענען מיט עטלעכע
באַמערקונגען כדי צו בעסער צו פֿאַרשטיין אונדזערע איצטיקע פּראָבלעמען.

צווישן די קלאַסישע קולטור־פֿעלקער איז דאָס אידישע פֿאָלק דאָס
איינציקע וואָס האָט, בעת עס האָט נאָך געלעבט אין אייגענעם לאַנד, זיך
באַנוצט מיט א פֿרעמדער שפּראך, און אין משך פֿון הונדערטער יאָרן
געשאַפֿן אין איר גראָנדיעזע קולטור אוצרות. דאָס ייִדישע פֿאָלק האָט
בעת זייניִקן טאָג ניט אויפֿגעהערט אַרויסצואווייזן א רירנדיקע צוגע־
בונדנקייט צו העברײיש, אָבער ניט ווי צו אַ שפּראך, נאָר ווי צו אַ לשון
קודש ; זי איז געווארן א מין העכערער סימבאָל פֿון נאַציאָנאַל־גייסטיקער

אייגנאַרטיקייט, וואָס דאָס איז לחלוטין ניט מחויב מען זאָל איר איבער־
געבן געווינטלעכע שפּראַך־פונקציעס, זי זאָל ווערן די שפּראַך פון
לעבן.   דער לעבנס־שטייגער און די תורה־אידייע וואָס יידן האָבן דערמיט
אָנגעפילט זייער גייסטיקע עקזיסטענץ, האָט גענוג באַפרידיקט זייער
אינטענסיוו פאַלק־באַוואוסטזיין.   עס איז געווען אַ לעבן פון מעשים,
געפילן, ניט פון פאַרמעלע שייכותן.   אינטענסיווע צוגעבונדנקייט צו אַ
שפּראַך וואָלט געמוזט אָפּציען די אויפמערקזאַמקייט פון אינהאַלטלעכע
מעשים, וואָלט געווען אַ סתירה צום אָנגענומענעם דרך אַז מען זאָל אַזוי
אייגנגעשפּאַרט לייגן דעם טראָף אויפן אינווייניק, אויף אינהאַלט.   דאָס
ווייזט זיך אויך אַרויס אין דער באַציאונג צו טראַדיציאַנעלע יידישע
נעמען, וואָס דאָס איז דאָך אַן אַספּעקט פון שפּראַך.   צווישן די העכער
צוויי טויזנט תנאים און אמוראים פון תלמוד בבלי און ירושלמי — אַן
עפּאָכע פון אַכט הונדערט יאָר — געפינט מען אין גאַנצן ניט אַזעלכע
נעמען ווי אברהם און משה, בעת עס זענען יאָ פאַראַן אַרום הונדערט
און פופציק גריכישע און רוימישע נעמען.   די זעלביקע יידן וואָס האָבן
זיך אַזוי עקשנות׳דיק קעגנגעשטעלט, ביז קידוש השם, ווען עס האָט
זיך געהאַנדלט וועגן עיקרים פון יידישקייט, האָבן, ווען עס איז געקומען
צו שפּראַך, אַרויסגעוויזן אַ קאַלטע גלייכגילטיקייט וואָס ווערט אַזוי קלאַ־
טיש אויסגעדריקט אינם פאָלקס־ליד : „לאָז איך מיך באַרעגענען און פרעג
קיין קשיות ניט.״

אפילו ווען פון אַזעלכע „רעגנס״ זענען אויסגעוואָקסן אייגענע שפּראַכן,
אפילו ווען די געמען האַט אַרייגעגאַנגאַסן דאָס פיינסטע פון יידישן בלוט אין
אַ פרעמדן דייטעטישן דיאַלעקט, און ס׳האָט זיך פאַנאַנדערעועבליט אונדזער
יידיש, אפילו דעמאָלט האָט דאָס יידישע פאָלק ניט געטיבטן זיין אינערלעכע
באַציאונג צום ענין שפּראַך.   מען קען געפינען אַ מדרש אָ יידן זענען
אויסגעלייזט געוואָרן פון מצרים און ווייל זיי האָבן ניט געביטן זייערע נעמען
און זייער לשון, פונקט ווי מען קען געפינען חסידישע גדולים וואָס האָבן
אייגגעזען דעם אומגעהייערן ווערט פון יידיש פאַר קיום האומה, אָבער
דאָס בייט ניט דאָס גאַנצע בילד.

בלויז מיט אַזאַ פסיכישן הינטערגרונד האָט אַ וואָרעמער ייד ווי
י. ל. גאָרדאָן געקענט שרייבן צו שלום עליכמ׳ען : „איך פרעגט מיין
מיינונג וועגן דעם זשאַרגאָן ?...   דאָס איז דער שאַנד־צייכן פון דעם
געטריבענעם נע ונד׳ניק, און איך האָב עס גערעכנט פאַר אַ חוב פון
יעדן געבילדעטן יידן צו באַמיען זיך אַז ער זאָל ביסלעכווייז אָפּגעווישט
ווערן און פאַרשווינדן פון אונדז...   דעם אמת געזאָגט וואונדערט מיך אויף

אייך, איר שרייבט גוט רוסיש, און באהערשט פּראַכטפֿול אונדזער ליטע־
ראַרישע שפּראַך (העברייאיש), ווי אזוי־זשע קאָנט איר זיך אַפּגעבן צו
דער קולטור פֿון דעם זשאַרגאָן?״   געווען שוין, פֿאַרשטייט זיך, אין יענער
צייט אַזעלכע וואָס זייער באַציאונג צו יידיש איז געווען גאָר אַן אַנדערע,
אָבער אפֿילו ווען אַזעלכע רייד האָבן אַרויטגערופֿן קעגנערשאַפֿט, האָבן
זיי ניט באַליידיקט, ניט געקרענקט, אזוי ווי מען וואָלט באַשעדיגן אַן איינ־
געבאַקענעם נאַציאָנאַלן קנין.

מען קען אַנווייזן פֿאַרשיידענע סיבות פֿאַר אַזאַ פֿסיכישן איינשטעל.
אין יענע צייטן ווען ביי יידן זיך געשאַפֿן און זיך אַנטוויקלט דאָס
פֿאָלקישע באַוואוסטזיין איז די ראַלע פֿון דער נאַציאָנאַלער שפּראַך ניט
געווען, און ניט געקענט זיין, דאָס וואָס זי איז היינט ביי מאָדערנע
פֿעלקער.   אין מיטלאַלמער איז די אַרומיקע באַפֿעלקערונג, צווישן וועלכע
יידן האָבן געלעבט, געווען גלייכגילטיק צו זייערע דיאַלעקטן, די לאַגע
איז געווען אַזאַ אַז עס האָט זיך ניט געקענט שאַפֿן דאָס באַוואוסטזיין
אַז אַן אייגענע שפּראַך איז אַ סימן מובהק פֿון אַ באַזונדער נאַציאַנאַליטעט.
אַחוץ דעם אין נייטיק צו האָבן אין זינען אונדזער לאַגע אין גלות וואו
מיר האָבן זיך תמיד געדאַרפֿט צופּאַסן צו די מורא׳דיקסטע באַדינגונגען
כדי זיך צוויפּצוהאַלטן ווי אַ פֿאָלק.   ווען מיר וואָלטן אפֿילו געהאַט אַן
אייגענע שפּראַך אין אַלע גלות־לענדער וואָלטן עס געווען אַ שרעקלעכע
נאַציאָנאַלע סכּנה ווען אונדזערע פֿירער שאַפֿן אַזאַ לאַגע אַז מיטן אַריבער־
גיין צו דער לאַנד־שפּראַך זאָל זיך ענדיקן די פֿאַרבינדונג מיטן יידישן
פֿאָלק.

אין קיין חידוש ניט וואָס אין די שבעה מדורי גהינום פֿון אונדזער
לאַנגער מאַרטירער געשיכטע האָט זיך איינגעשטעלט די פֿריער־דערמאַנטע
באַציאונג צו אַן אייגענער שפּראַך.   עס וואָלט דעריבער געווען זייער
ניט־שכל׳דיק, ממש געפֿערלעך, ווען אַ נייע אידעאָלאָגיע וואָס וויל אַפּעלירן
צום יידישן פֿאָלק זאָל זיך לחלוטין ניט רעכענען מיט אַט די אַלע היסטאָ־
רישע דערשאַרונגען און מיטן גאַנצן פֿסיכישן הינטערגרונט וואָס זיי האָבן
געשאַפֿן.   ווינט ווי זשע קומט עס וואָס שפּראַך־יידישיזם האָט זיך געלאָזן
אויף אַזאַ דרך?   שפּראַך ווי די דער איינציקער, אָדער אפֿילו ווי דער וויכ־
טיקסטער, פֿאַרבינדונג־פֿאָדים?   און ביי וועמען, ביי יידן?   ווען דאָס
ווערט געזאָגט אין דער היך פֿון פֿאָלעמיק, אין דער עמאָציאָנאַלער אויפֿ־
געברויזטקייט ביים איינשטעלן זיך פֿאַר דער באַליידיקטער, ניט־אָגע־
שאַצטער ״שפֿהה״, איז דאָס נאַטירלעך און פֿאַרשטענדלעך.   אָבער ווי אַ
דורכגעטראַכטע אויפֿפֿאַצונג וועגן דער ראַלע פֿון אַן אייגענער שפּראַך
אין אונדזער קולטורעלן אויפֿהאַלט?   דאָס גייט דאָך להיפּוך צו אַלע

אמת'ן וואָס אונדזער געשיכטע האָט אויסגעשמידט.

ווען מען כאַפּט זיך אָבער וואָס עס איז פאָרגעקומען ביי אַנדערע
אייראָפּעיִשע פעלקער, ספּעציעל אין ניינצנטן יאָרהונדערט, זעט מען
גלייך פון וואָנען די דאָזיקע אידעאָלאָגיע שטאַמט. זי שטאַמט פונם
זעלביקן קוואַל פון וואָנען עס איז געקומען צו אונדז דער קריסטלעכער
סעקולאַריזם, און איז ניט מער צוגעפּאַסט צו אונדזער לעבן ווי יענער
באַגריף.

דאָס ניינצנטע יאָרהונדערט איז דאָס יאָרהונדערט פון אויפשטייגנדיקן
נאַציאָנאַליזם. דעמאָלט זענען אימאַליע און דייטשלאַנד געוואָרן גרויסע
פאַראייניקטע מלוכות; דעמאָלט האָבן אַסך קליינע פעלקער זיך „דער־
וואוסט" וועגן זייער נאַציאָנאַלער באַזונדערקייט; דעמאָלט האָט מען
געזוכט די הויפט אַטריבוטן וואָס דעפינירן אַ פאָלק; דעמאָלט איז שפּראַך
אויעקגעשטעלט געוואָרן אויפן העכסטן פעדעסטאַל ווי אַ הויפּט־סימן פון
פאָלקישער עקזיסטענץ.

געבוירן געוואָרן איז דער דאָזיקער געדאַנק נאָך אַביסל פריִער און
גענומען שפּילן אַ מאַסן־ראָלע אין דער פראַנצויזישער רעוואָלוציע. די
רעוואָלוציע האָט טאַקע געזאָגלט אונטער אַלגעמיין מענטשלעכע לאָזונגען,
אָבער אַיר פּיערדיקער נאַציאָנאַליסטישער אינהאַלט האָט ניט לאַנג גע־
לאָזט וואַרטן אויף זיך. דאָ באַנוץ איך שוין „נאַציאָנאַליזם" אין אַנגריי־
פערישן און אונטערדריקערישן זינען פון וואָרט. דאָס איז אייגנטלעך
געווען דער ניט־ריינער קוואַל פון וואָנען עס האָט לכתחילה אַרויסגעשלאָגן
די פאַרגעטערונג פאַר פראַנצויזיש. אַזוי געפינען מיר אינם באַריכט פון
קאָמיטעט פאַר עפנטלעכער זיכערקייט, וואָס באַרער, דער יאַקאָבינער, גיט
אָפּ דער נאַציאָנאַל־פאַרזאַמלונג אין יאַנואַר 1794: „בירגער, די שפּראַך
פון אַ פריי פאָלק דאַרף זיין די זעלביקע פאַר אַלע... מיר האָבן באַמערקט
אַז די דיאַלעקטן וואָס מען רופט נידער־בּרעטאָניש, דער באַסקישער
דיאַלעקט און די דייטשישע און איטאַליענישע שפּראַכן האָבן פאַראייניקט
די הערשאַפט פון פאַנאַטיזם און אַבערגלויבן, פאַרזיכערט די איבערהאַנט
פון גלחים און אַריסטאָקראַטן"... אאז"וו. אזוי האָט די רעוואָלוציע
רעאַגירט אויפן היסטאָרישן פאַקט וואָס פראַנקרייך איז ניט קיין לינגוויס־
טישע איינס. עס זענען פאַראַן ברעטאָנען, פּראָוװענסאַלן, באַסקן, קאָר־
סיקאַנער, פלעמער, דייטשן, און די אַלע באַנוצן זייערע אייגענע לשונות.
אָט דער אָפּנייג פון אוניפאָרמיטעט האָט שאַקירט די יאַקאָבינער, און זיי
האָבן זיך גענומען אויסשפּרייטן אויף אַלע בירגער דאָס וואָס מען האָט
דעמאָלט גערופן: „די שפּראַך פון פרייהייט", ד"ה, פראַנצויזיש.

די שפּראַכן פון די גרויסע אייראָפּעיִשע קולטור־פעלקער זענען

שײן געװען גענוג צײטיק און רײַך אַז די אידענטיפֿיקאַציע צװישן פֿאָלק
און שפּראַך זאָל ניט בלויז אַרויטרופֿן די באַגײַסטערונג פֿאַרן אמת װאָס
אין דעם שטעקט, נאָר זאָל אויך דערװעקן די װאַרעמע געפֿילן פֿאַר די
אײגנשאַפֿטן פֿון נאַציאָנאַלן אידיאָם, פֿאַרן נײַ-אַנטפּלעקטן אינטימסטן
אויסדרוק פֿון גײַסטיקן לעבן פֿון פֿאָלק.

די ליבע און באַגײַסטערונג פֿאַר דער נאַציאָנאַלער שפּראַך האָט זיך
שנעל פֿאַרשפּרײטיד איבערן איבערן קאָנטינענט. פֿרידריך פֿאַן שלעיגעל דערקלערט
קעמפֿעריש: "אַ פֿאָלק װאָס קוקט שטיל צו װי מען רויבט פֿון אים
אװעק זײַן לשון פֿאַרלירט דעם דרך ארץ װאָס אומאָפּהענגיקײט פֿאַרדינט;
װערט דערנידעריקט אין דער מדרגה פֿון ציװיליזאַציע." בענטעם, דער
שאַפֿער פֿונם װאָרט "אינטערנאַציאָנאַל", דער קילער און באַטראַכטער
קאָפּ װאָס ער איז געװען, האָט פֿונדעסטװעגן געהאַלטן אַז ענגליש שטײט
העכער פֿון אַלע שפּראַכן, און זי װאָלט געדאַרפֿט װערן די װעלט-שפּראַך.

דאָס האָט נאַטירלעך אַרויסגערופֿן אַן ענגלעכע דערשײנונג בײַ קלײנע,
אונטערדריקטע פֿעלקער. בײַ זײ איז די שפּראַך געװאָרן ניט בלויז אַ
סימבאָל פֿון פֿאָלק, נאָר אויך פֿון זײַן באַפֿרײַאונג. אַזוי שטרעבט נאָר-
װעגיע צאַפּצואװאָרפֿן פֿון זיך יאָך פֿון דעניש. די פֿינלענדער
הײבן אויף אַ באַװעגונג קעגן שװעדיש. געלערנטע לינגװיסטן און קינסט-
לער בײַ די קלײנע פֿעלקער פֿאַרשן און באַרײכערן דעם נאַציאָנאַלן אידיאָם
פֿון קעלטיש און אירישע, אין ענגלאַנד. פֿון קאַטאַלאַניש אין שפּאַניע, אאַז״װ.
עס הייבן זיך אויף באַװעגונגען פֿאַר דער אַנטװיקלונג פֿון די קלענערע
סלאַװישע שפּראַכן. עקסטרעמיסטן זוכן זיך צו דערװײַטערן אפֿילו פֿון
אינטערנאַציאָנאַל-אָנגענומענע פֿרעמד-װערטער. בקיצור, שפּראַך דאָס
אַלטע מיטל פֿון מענטשלעכן פֿאַרקער, הייבט אָן צו שפּילן אַ נייע ראָלע
אין דער װעלט-געשיכטע.

פֿון שפּראַך צו דער שריפֿט-פֿאָרם איז אַ קלײנער מהלך. אַזוי האָבן
די װיכוחים װעגן דער לאַטײנישער און גאָטישער שריפֿט אין דײַטשלאַנד,
און װעגן דער לאַטײנישער און קירילישער שריפֿט בײַ סלאַװישע פֿעלקער,
אָנגענומען אַ נאַציאָנאַלן כאַראַקטער. דער טערקישער נאַציאָנאַליזם
האָט געפֿירט צו דעם מען זאָל אין טערקיי אָפּשאַפֿן די אַראַבישע שריפֿט.
די טשעכן, די לעטן און די עסטן האָבן זיך מחמת דעם זעלביקן טעם
אָפּגעזאָגט פֿון דער גאָטישער שריפֿט. דאָס איז געװען אַ פּראָטעסט
קעגן דער דײַטשישער קולטור-הערשאַפֿט. רומעניש האָט אײַנגעפֿירט
די לאַטײנישע שריפֿט, און זיך אָפּגעזאָגט פֿון דער קירילישער, אַ מין
אװעקקרײַטן זיך פֿון רוסישן אײַנפֿלוס.

דער ענגלישער געלערנטער י. מ. ראָבערטסאָן, אין זײַן בוך "די

אַנטװיקלונג פון שטאַטן", פאַרגינט זיך צו דערפירן דעם געדאַנק װעגן
דעם ענין נאַציאָנאַלע שפּראַך ביז זײַן װײַטסטן פּונקט. נאָך דעם װי ער
דערקלערט אַז דער הױפּט־חילוק צװישן ציװיליזירטע פעלקער ליגט דער
עיקר אין שפּראַך, באַשליסט ער: „װען מען אַנאַליזירט דעם ענין קומט
אױס אַז מענטשנס באַגײַסטערונג פאַר זײַן פאָלק אין זײַן גופא איז
אַ באַגײַסטערונג פֿאַר זײַן שפּראַך... אַזױ אַז די אױסגעדױכטע ענטיטעט
װאָס שפּילט אַזאַ גרױסע רעלע אין געװײַנטלעכן לױף פון געדאַנק —
דאָס פאָלק װי אַן אַנהאַלטנדיקער און פערסאַנאַליזירטער אָרגאַניזם —
איז על פּי רוב אַ מעטאַפֿיזישער חלום, און די געפֿילן װאָס לעבן זיך
אױס אין דעם טראָגן אַסך פֿונעם כאַראַקטער פון אַבערגלױבן". לױט דעם
קומט אױס אַז שפּראַך איז סײ דער דרױסנדיקער שײַן, סײ דער אײנער־
לעכער פֿונדאַמענט פון נאַציאָנאַלן זײַן. די נאַציאָנאַלע שפּראַך איז די
אײנציקע רעלע מאַטעריע פון גײַסטיקן לעבן פון אַ פאָלק װי אַ באַזונ־
דערע סאָציאַלע אײנס.

װי מיר זעען איז די דערהײַבונג פון שפּראַך צום העכסטן שפּיץ
פון דער נאַציאָנאַל־קולטורעלער פּיראַמידע, געװען אַ פֿועל יוצא פון
שטרעבונגען און לעבנס־תנאים װאָס קענען מיטן ייִדישן לעבן קײן שײַכות
ניט האָבן. קודם כל איז דאָס געװאָרן אַ אידעאַל פון הערשנדיקע פעל־
קער, װי פֿראַנצױזן און ענגלענדער, װאָס בײַ זײ האָבן די קלײנע נאַציאָ־
נאַלע מינאָריטעטן געשטערט די לינגװיסטישע אײן־פֿאָרמיקײַט פון הער־
שנדיקן פאָלק. די נאַציאָנאַלע שפּראַך איז אױך געװאָרן אַן אױסדרוק
פֿונעם אידעאַל פון פּאָליטישער אײניקײַט בײַ די דײַטשן און איטאַליענער.
אמת, דער זעלביקער אידעאַל האָט זיך אױך דערהױבן צו אַן ענלעכער
מדרגה בײַ זונטערדריקטע פעלקער. זײ האָבן דערפֿילט אין זײער שפּראַך
דעם באַזונדערן גײַסטיקן טעם פון זײער עקזיסטענץ, ממילא איז דאָס
אױך געװאָרן דער סימבעל פון זײער באַפֿרײַאונגס־קאַמף. אָבער דאָ איז
נײטיק אױסצורעכענען כאָטש די װיכטיקסטע אונטערשײדן פון ייִדישן
און ניט־ייִדישן לעבן, אפֿילו בײַ אונטערדריקטע פעלקער, כדי אײַנצוזען
אַז מען קען ניט, אַן ספּעציעלע באַװאָרענישן און געהעריקע ענדערונגען,
אַריבערנעמען געזעלשאַפֿטלעכע אידײַען און אידעאַלן פון אײן פאָלק צום
צװײטן.

בײַ יענע פעלקער איז די העכסטע פאָרם פון אײנטים־גײַסטיקן לעבן,
רעליגיע, ניט נאַציאָנאַל, סײ לױטן קװאַל פון װאַנען זי שטאַמט, סײ לױט
די אידעאַלן און שטרעבונגען װאָס זי שטעלט אַװעק פאַר יעדן יחיד.
ממילא רײַסט זיך די אײיגענע שפּראַך אַרױס מיט אַ מין עקספּלאָדירנדיקן
„אָהאַ!" װי אַ קענטיקער עפֿנטלעכער אױסדרוק פון אַ נאַציאָנאַל־פֿאַר־

ברידנגדיקן כּוֹת. יענע פעלקער פֿאַרמאָגן ניט קיין אַלטע, טיף־דורכ־
דרינגענדיקע באַוואוסטזיניק־פֿאָלקישע טראַדיציע וואָס האָט אין משך
פֿון טויזנטער יאָרן צוזוימפֿגעהאַלטן דאָס פֿאָלק אָן שום טראָף אויף שפּראַך.
יענע פֿעלקער זענען טעריטאָריעל קאָנצענטרירט, און דער אייגענער
אידיאָם שפּרייט זיך אויס אויף אַלע טיילן וואָס פֿילן זיך אײנס מיטן
פֿאָלק. פֿאַרגלייכט די דאָזיקע דריי פּונקטן מיט אונדזער לאַגע, און די
אַנדערשקייט וואַרפֿט זיך ממש אין די אויגן. מיר האָבן ניט קיין דרויסנ־
דיקע רעליגיע ; מיר פֿאַרמאָגן אַלטע ריזיקע אוצרות וואָס האָבן אונדז
געמאַכט ייד־באַוואוסטזיניק מיט שטענדיקן דרוק אויף אינהאַלט ; ביי
אונדז, הייסט עס האָט תמיד געלעבט אַ נאַציאָנאַלע אײנפֿאָרמיקייט, דערצו
נאָך אַזאַ וואָס איר העכסטע שטרעבונג. איז געווען נאַציאָנאַלע אויסלייזונג ;
מיר זענען „מפֿוזר ומפֿורד בין העמים", און דער הוילער געדאַנק אַז
צווישן די „כּל תפֿוצות ישראל" זענען פֿאַראַן קהילות, וואָס מיר קענען
אפֿילו זייער לשון ניט, כאַטש זיי זענען מיט בלוט און פֿלייש אונדזערע,
שוין דאָס אַליין קען דאָך פּשוט ניט דערלאָזן — אין נאָמען פֿון גרויסע
נאַציאָנאַלע אינטערעסן, פֿון פֿילן זיך פֿאַרקניפֿט מיטן כּלל ישראל —
אַז מיר זאָלן צוזעקשטעלן שפּראַך ווי אַן איינציקן ייִדיש־נאַציאָנאַלן סימן.
אָבער דאָס איז וויַיט, וויַיט נאָך ניט אַלץ.

בעת ביי יענע פֿעלקער איז די רעליגיע די דרויסנדיקע אינסטיטוטסיע,
איז ביי אונז געווען אַ פֿסיכישע מעגלעכקייט אַז אַזאַ געפֿיל ווי צו עפּעס
דרויסנדיקס זאָל זיך דערוועקן אין שייכות צו ייִדיש. ראשית דערפֿאַר
ווייל עס האָט שוין סיי־ווי געהערשט אַ הייליקע באַציאונג צו אַ כמו־
שפּראַך, לשון־קודש. שנית, ווייל ייִדיש האָט אויף זיך סימנים פֿון
ענלעכקייט צו אַ שכנישער שפּראַך פֿון אַ הערשנדיק פֿאָלק. אַחוץ דעם
האָט לשון־קודש אויך ניט געקענט דערלאָזן אַז ייִדיש זאָל פֿאַרנעמען
דעם שפּיץ פֿון דער פֿסיכישער געבּיידע צוליב אַן אַנדער טעם. די
הייליקע שפּראַך איז געווען דער סימבאָל פֿון ענדגילטיקער נאַציאָנאַלער
באַפֿרייאונג, פֿונם משיח־געדאַנק, וואָס דאָס איז אייגנטלעך דער מיסטישער
אויסדרוק פֿון אַ ציוניסטיש־טעריטאָריאַליסטישער גאולה. ממילא האָט
שוין דאָ בנוגע ייִדיש געפֿעלט יענער פֿסיכישער תּנאי וואָס האָט ביי
אַנדערע אונטערדריקטע אָדער אויפֿגעוואַכטע פֿעלקער געווירקט אַז די
פֿאָלק־שפּראַך זאָל ווערן דער סימבאָל פֿון נאַציאָנאַלער באַפֿרייאונג, אָדער
פֿון נאַציאָנאַלער רענעסאַנס. אַחוץ דעם איז פֿאַראַן נאָך אַן אומגעהיַיער
וויכטיקער מאָמענט וואָס מען דזאַרף זיך אים מיט זייער שטאַרק רעכענען,
יענע פֿעלקער לעבן אויף זייער אײגן לאַנד. זיי באַנוצן זייער שפּראַך

אינם לאַנד וואו זיי שטרעבן זיך צו באפרייען פון אַ דרויסנדיקער הערשנ־
דיקער מאַכט. די לאַגע פון יענע פעלקער איז אויך אַז עס קענען גאָר
קיין חילוקי דעות ניט זיין וועגן די ענדלעכע נאַציאָנאַלע צילן: ווערן
זעלבסטשטענדיק אין זייער לאַנד. ממילא איז נאַטירלעך אַז די אייגענע
שפּראַך וואָס לעבט אין מויל פון פּאָלק דאָ, אין אייגענעם לאַנד, זאָל
אויך ווערן דער סימבאָל פונם פרייען אייגענעם לעבן צו וועלכן דאָס
זעלביקע פּאָלק שטרעבט דאָ, אין אייגענעם לאַנד. ביי יידן קען אַזאַ
איניקייט בנוגע אונדזער באַפרייאונג ניט זיין. גלות־נאַציאָנאַליזם האָט
תמיד געהאַט אַ קנאַפּערן אָנהאַלט ווי טעריטאָריאַליזם (אַריינגערעכנט
אין דעם אויך דעם משיח־געדאַנק). טייל יידן זענען פון די נאַציאָנאַלע
געפארן געטריבן געוואָרן זיך אָפּצוזאָגן פונם גאַנצן פּאָלקישן כאַראַקטער
פון אונדזער פאַרבונדנקייט. אָט די אומבאַשטימטקייט, און די אומפאַר־
מיידלעכע חילוקי דעות וועגן אונדזער ענדגילטיקער נאַציאָנאַלער פּאָזי־
ציע אין לאַנד וואו מיר לעבן, איז אַ געפערלעכער פסיכישער אבן נגף
אין אונדזערע באַציאונגען צו דער שפּראַך מיט וועלכער דאָס יידישע
לעבן אין אָט אַזאַ לאַנד איז פאַרבונדן. ביי אונדז קען שוין צוליב דעם
אליין די שפּראַך אין זיך גומאַ ניט צוועקגעשטעלט ווערן, מיט אַזאַ
נאַטירלעכקייט און זעלבסטפאַרשטענדלעכקייט, אויף אַן ענלעכער מדרגה ווי
ביי אַנדערע פעלקער.

ווען מיר זענען נאָך מוסיף דעם פאַקט וואָס מיר האָבן דורך
טויזנטער יאָרן געפונען אונדזער היילונג און אונדזער טרייסט אין אַ
שפּראַך, אָדער אין שפּראַכן, וואָס מיר האָבן ניט באַנוצט אין טאָג־טעגלעכן
לעבן, איז שוין ניט שווער צו פאַרשטיין די ספּעציעלע פאַקטאָרן וואָס מוזן
ביי אונדז אויסאַרבעטן גאָר אַן אַנדער באַציאונג צום ענין שפּראַך. אָבער
שפּראַך־יידישיזם האָט דאָס אַלץ ניט געזען. דער יצר הרע אַריבער־
צונעמען אין אונדזער וועלט גייסטיקע ווערטן אָט ווי זיי שטייען און
גייען ביי אַנדערע פעלקער האָט אַלץ אַריבערגעוואויגן. יידיש, ווי אַן
אידייע, וואָס וואָלט געקענט שפּילן ביי אונדז אַזאַ גרויסע פּאָזיטיווע
ראָלע, איז געבראַכט געוואָרן צו אונדז אויף אַ גויאישן אופן, עס איז
געוואָרן אַן עקספּערימענט אין אַ מין: „זאָל איווּאָן בלאָזן שופר".
אָבער איווּאָן — דער יידיש־רעדנדיקער וואָס איז אויסגעטאָן פון יעדן
סאָרט יידישקייט — האָט קלאָר דערוויזן אַז ער קען ניט.

די דאָזיקע פרעמדע באַציאונג צו שפּראַך, וואָס רעכנט זיך להלוטין
ניט מיט די ספּעציפישע תנאים פון יידישן לעבן, ווערט ממש אויף אַ
ספּעקטאַקולאַרן אופן באַשטעטיקט, פון דער באַציאונג צו שריפט. טייל

פירער פון דער סעקולאַריסטישער אידיאַלאָגיע האָבן אָפֿט אײַנגעג׳טענה׳ט
מיט אונדז אַז ס׳איז נײטיק מיר זאָלן זיך אָפֿזאָגן פונם העברייאישן א״ב
און איבערגיין צום לאַטיניש.   דערבײַ האָבן זיי זיך געשטיצט אויף די
פריער־אָנגעוויזענע בײַשפּילן פון פֿעלקער וואָס האָבן געביטן זייער טראַ־
דיציאָנעלע שריפֿט.   אין איין אַרטיקל, געדענק איך, האָט אַ שרײַבער
זיך סומך געוועזן מיט אַ באַזונדערן „אַהאַ!" אויף די טערקן וואָס האָבן
אָבוגענומען דעם לאַטינישן אַלפֿאַבעט.   עס האָט געהייסן אַז בלויז די
אומות העולם קענען זיין מאַדערן בעת מיר בלײַבן אַזוי פֿאַר׳עקשנ׳ט
צוריקגעשטאַנען.

דאָ ווײַזט זיך בולט אַרויס אַז דער אָפֿעטיטלעכער רייץ פונם „נהיה
כלל הגויים" מאַכט בלינד און טויב דעם איינזײַטיקן ייִדישיזם.   ווען מיר
קוקן זיך צו צו די שריפֿט־ענדערונגען בײַ יענע פֿעלקער וועלן מיר
לײַכט איינזען אַז דער עיקר אויפֿטו, וואָס זיי האָבן געוואָלט דערגרייכן,
ליגט ניט אין דער פּאָזיטיווער זייט, נאָר אין דער נעגאַטיווער; ניט אינם
אלבּאַבעט וואָס זיי האָבן אָנגענומען נאָר אין יעגעם פון וועלכן זיי האָבן
זיך אָפֿגעזאָגט.   די אַלטע שריפֿט איז אין אַלע פֿאַלן די שריפֿט פונם
נאַציאָנאַלן שונא, און זיך אָפֿזאָגן פון איר ,איז אַ סימבאַלישער אַקט פון
באַפֿרײַאונג, און פון אַן אָפֿגעהאַלטענעם ניצחון.   פֿאַרשטייט זיך אַז בײַם
אָננעמען אַ נײַע שריפֿט האָבן זיי שוין זיך געקענט פֿאַרגינען צו זוכן
באַקוועמלעכקייט און וועלט־דערנענטערונג.   הײַנט ווי קען מען דאָס
פֿאָר׳גלײַכן מיט אונדזער לאַגע?   ווי קען מען אין נאָמען פון דעם פֿאַר־
לאַנגען אַז מיר זאָלן זיך אָפֿזאָגן פונם העברייאישן א״ב?   אָבער ס׳איז
שווער צו פֿאָדערן מער אײַנזעעניש אין דער פֿראַגע פון שריפֿט בעת
ס׳איז פֿאַראַן אַזאַ פֿרעמדקייט צו אונדזער לעבן אין דער פֿראַגע פון
שפּראַך בכלל.

אַצט זענען מיר שוין גרייט צו פֿאַרשטיין אַז די בעסערע מערכה
פון העברייאיזם נעמט זיך לחלוטין ניט פון דעם וואָס די העברייאיסטן
איז געלונגען צו באַווײַזן אַז שפּראַך איז דער עיקר כל העיקרים.   אפֿילו
די טראַדיציאָנעלע צוגעבונדנקייט צו העברייאיש האָט בײַ ייִדן ניט געקענט
אַרויסרופֿן אַזאַ בליק אויף שפּראַך.   דער אמת איז אַז די אויפֿלעבונג
**פון העברייאיש האָט ניט געשטאַמט פון דער אידיאַלאָגיע אַז די דאָזיקע
שפּראַך קען אָדער דאַרף זיין דער אײנציקער פֿאַרבינדונג־פֿאַדעם פון**
ייִדישן פֿאָלק.   ווי ווײַט איך ווייס האָט קיין העברייאיסט קיינמאָל אַזאַ
געדאַנק אויף די ליפּן ניט געבראַכט.   דער געדאַנק אַז העברייאיש קען
ווערן די שפּראַך פון ייִדישן פֿאָלק אין די גלות־לענדער, אפֿילו דאָס
האָט בלויז געקענט זיין דער חלום פון געצײַלטע העברייאיסטן אין מאַ־

מענטן פון אומקאָנטראָלירטער התלהבות.   ווען יחזקאל קויפמאן טראַכט
אין „גולה ונכר" וועגן פאַרשפרייטן העברייאיש ווי די שפּראַך פון יידישן
פאָלק אין גלות, איז דאָס אויך נאָר מיטן צוועק פון אַ שפעטערדיקער
קאָנצענטראַציע אויף אַן אייגענער טעריטאָריע, וואָס דאַרף, לויט זיין
מיינונג, זיין אַ צוגאָב צו ארץ ישראל.

בכלל, העברייאיזם איז אַ קינד פון ציוניזם און איז אינטים פאַר־
בונדן מיטן הויפּט־ציל פון אַ זעלבשטענדיק לעבן אויף אַן אייגן לאַנד.
ערשט די אַנטוויקלונג פון ציוניזם און פונם ישוב אין ארץ ישראל האָט
געפירט אויך צו דער פאַרשפרייטונג פונם העברייאיסטישן געדאַנק.   הע־
ברייאיזם איז בלויז איין אַספּעקט פון אַ גאַנץ לעבן, ניט קיין אידייע
וואָס איז פאַרענדיקט אין זיך אַליין, ווי דאָס איז שפּראַך־יידישיזם.

אַ גרויסע טייל פון די וויכוחים צווישן יידישיסטן און העברייאיסטן
איז געווען געבויעט אויפן זעלביקן לאָגישן פעלער ווי די מיטלאַלטערלעכע
רעאַנגלאָנישן צווישן יידישקייט און קריסטנטום.   דאָס איז געווען אַ וויכוח
צווישן צוויי ניט־גלייכע צדדים. די העברייאיסטן זענען אָן שום אויסנעם
געווען ציוניסטן, זיי האָבן אין העברייאיש פאַרטייז־יקט בלויז איין אַספּעקט
פון אַן ענטפער אויף דער יידישער פראַגע, אַן ענטפער מיט וועלכן זיג
האָבן אַלע מסכים געווען.   די שפּראַך־יידישיסטן האָבן אַזאַ אַלגעמינעם
איינשטימיקן ענטפער ניט געהאַט, זיי האָבן לאָגיש און פסיכאָלאָגיש
אָפּגעריסן די שפּראַך־פראַגע פון גאַנצן יידישן עלעמענטער, איז געבליבן
אַ נאַקעטע אידייע וואָס הייבט זיך אָן און ענדיקט זיך מיט זיך אַליין.
קומט אויס אַז בעת די יידישיסטן האָבן אָנגעהויבן מיט שפּראַך האָבן די
העברייאיסטן אָנגעהויבן מיט אַ גאַנצן קאָמפּלעקס אידייען וואָס פירן,
לויט זייער מיינונג, דווקא צו העברייאיש אין אונדזער נאַציאָנאַלער אַנט־
וויקלונג.   די העברייאיסטן האָבן דעריבער אַרויסגעשטעלט גאַנץ אַנדערע
פונדאַמענטאַלע טביעות, און האָבן זיך אַזוי ווייט ניט אָפּגעזונדערט, אפילו
אין דער שפּראַך־פראַגע, פון דער יידישער פסיכיק, ווי דאָס האָבן געטאָן
די שפּראַך־יידישיסטן.   העברייאיזם איז, אחוץ זיין פאַרבינדונג מיטן
ציוניזם, געשטאַנען נאָענט צו טראַדיציאָנעלע יידישע ווערטן.   יידישיזם
האָט געשטרעבט צו שאַפן אַ נאַציאָנאַלן חלל און לאָזן יידיש פיגורירן ווי
אַן איינציק ביצל מאַטעריע וואָס שוועבט דאָרט אַרום.

8

טאַציאָלאָגיע, ווי אַ וויסנשאַפט, וועט זיך תמיד מוזן רעכענען מיטן
פאַקט וואָס מען קען ניט אירע הנחות אויספרובירן אונטער לאַבאָראַ־

טאַרישע תנאים.   װען מען װיל, למשל, אין פּסיכאָלאָגיע דערגײן די
װירקונג פֿון פֿיזישער מידקײט אױף אינטעלעקטועלע פּראָצעסן, איז פֿאַראַן
דערױף אַ גאַנץ באַשטימטע עקספּערימענטאַלע טעכניק.   מען נעמט אַ
פּרישן, געזונטן מענטשן, פֿון נאָרמאַלער אינטעליגענץ, און נאָרמאַלע
גײסטיקע אײגנשאַפֿטן בכלל, און מען פֿאַרגיט אים אַן אינטעלעקטועלע
אַרבעט, לאָמיר זאָגן, מאַכן אַריטמעטישע חשבונות.   דערנאָך נעמט מען
דעם זעלביקן מענטשן, װאו אַלע פֿאַקטאָרן זענען נאַטירלעך די זעלביקע
װאָס פֿריער, נאָר מען מאַטערט אים אױס מיט אַ באַשטימטער פֿיזישער
אַרבעט.   נאָך דעם פֿאַרגיט מען אים צו מאַכן ענלעכע אַריטמעטישע
חשבונות.   אױב דער פּועל יוצא אין דער צװײטער פּראָבע איז ערגער
װי אין דער ערשטער, פֿאַרשטײט מען אַז דאָס מוז זײן אַ רעזולטאַט פֿון
פֿיזישער מידקײט.   די אױפֿגאַבע פֿון אַ לאַבאָראַטאָרישן עקספּערימענט
איז דעריבער אױסצומײדן די װירקונג פֿון אַלע מעגלעכע פֿאַקטאָרן אַחוץ
אײנעם.   ממילא איז דער שכל מחייב אַז די באַקומענע רעזולטאַטן זאָלן
צוגעשריבן װערן צו דעם אײנציקן פֿאַקטאָר װאָס בלױז זײן װירקונג
האָט געקענט שפּילן אַ ראָלע.   אין רוב סאָציאַלאָגישע פֿאַרשונגען איז
דאָס כמעט אוממעגלעך.   דאָך זענען פֿאַראַן מאָמענטן װען געזעלשאַפֿטן
און פֿעלקער שאַפֿן אַזעלכע באַדינגונגען װאָס זענען זײער ענלעך צו אַ
לאַבאָראַטאָרישן עקספּערימענט.

װאָס װאָלט געװען װען יידישקײט װערט דערקלערט װי אַ פּריװאַט-
רעליגיע און װערט אין גאַנצן אַרױסגעװאָרפֿן פֿון דער נאַציאָנאַלער
עפֿנטלעכקײט ?   װאָס װאָלט געװען װען אַלע פּעדים פֿונם אַלטן יידישן
געװעב װערן איבערגעריסן, און עס בלײבן בלױז מענטשן פֿון יידישן
אָפּשטאַם ?   װאָס װאָלט געװען װען אַט אַזאַ צוטאַמספּערע װערט
אַרײנגעבראַכט אַן אײגענע שפּראַך, יידיש, װי אַ נאַציאָנאַלער צעמענטיר-
כוח ?   פֿאַלג מיך אַ גאַנג און פֿיר דורך אַזאַ מין עקספּערימענט כדי
אױסצוגעפֿינען װאָס עס װאָלט געװען.   װאָס זשע טוט גאָט ?   קומט דער
סאָװיעמען פֿאַרבאַנד מיט זײנע יידישן פֿאַרשטײער און דערלאַנגען אונדז
ממש אױף אַ טעלער עפּעס װאָס איז זײער ענלעך צו אַט אַזאַ מין
עקספּערימענט.   אמת, אױך דאָרט איז דער עקספּערימענט ניט אין גאַנצן
דײן צו זײטיקע פֿאַקטאָרן.   די אַמאָליקע רוסיש-יידישע סביבה רײסט זיך
נאָך אַלץ פֿון איר לעבעדיקן עבר אין אַלע ריכטונגען.   אָבער אױף
װיפֿיל דאָ איז בכלל מעגלעך אַן עקספּערימענט, זענען דאָס די אידעאַלסטע
לאַבאָראַמאָרישע באַדינגונגען װאָס מען קען צוגרײטן.

ניט געװען קײן פֿאַל אין דער גאַנצער יידישער געשיכטע װען דאָס
גאַנצע יידישע צוזאַמען-לעבן איז געבױט געװאָרן בלױז אױף שפּראַך,

1

יוסף אָפּאַטאָשו

(יוסף אָפּאַטאָװסקי)

מלאװע, פּוילן, 1887
ניו־יאָרק, פֿאַר. שטאַטן, 1954

———◆———

אין פּוילישע װעלדער, (ראָמאַן)
דער לעצטער אויפֿשטאַנד, (")
לינטשעראַי, (דערצײלונג)
אַ טאָג אין רעגענסבורג, (")

———◆———

דערצײלער, ראָמאַניסט

2

דוד איגנאַטאָװ(סקי)

ברוסילאָװ, אוקראַינע, 1885
ניו־יאָרק, פֿאַר. שטאַטן, 1954

———◆———

װוּנדער־מעשׂיות פֿון אַלטן פּראָג
פֿאַרבאָרגענע ליכט, (מעשׂיות)
גדעון, (טראַגעדיע)
אין קעסל־גרוב, (ראָמאַן)

———◆———

דערצײלער, ראָמאַניסט, פּאָעט

3

יוסף ראָלניק

דאָרף זשוכאָװיטש, װײַס־רוס. 1879
ניו יאָרק, פֿאַר. שטאַטן, 1955

———◆———

אַ פֿענצטער צו דרום
אויפֿן זאַמדיקן װעג
צום שטערן נויד
געקליבענע לידער

———◆———

פּאָעט

4

מאַני לײב

(בראַהינסקי)

ניעזשין, אוקראַינע, 1883
ניו־יאָרק, פֿאַר. שטאַטן, 1953

———◆———

ייִנגל צינגל כװאַט, (פּאָעמע)
לידער און באַלאַדן
ייִדישע און סלאַװישע מאָטיװן
געקליבענע לידער און פּאָעמען

———◆———

פּאָעט

5

זישע לאַנדוי

פּלאָצק, פּוילן, 1889
ניו־יאָרק, פֿאַר. שטאַטן, 1937

———◆———

פֿון דער װעלט, (לידער)
לידער
דער בלויער נאַכטיגאַל (פּיעסע)
ס׳איז גאָרניט געשען (פּיעסע)

———◆———

פּאָעט, דראַמאַטורג

6

אײַזיק ראָבאָי

דאָרף זאַװאַליע, פּוילן, 1885
לאָס אַנדזשעלעס, פֿ. שטאַטן, 1944

———◆———

דער גאָלדענבאַרג, (ראָמאַן)
בעסאַראַביער ייִדן, (ראָמאַן)
אין דער װײַטער װעסט, (דערצ.)
איז געקומען אַ ייִד קײן אַמעריקע

———◆———

ראָמאַניסט, דערצײלער

1. Yoysef Opatoshu, 1887–1954; Writer of short stories, novelist; 2. Dovid Ignatov, 1885–1954; Writer of short stories, novelist; 3. Yoysef Rolnik, 1879–1955; Poet; 4. Mani Leyb, 1883–1953; Poet; 5. Zishe Landoy, 1889–1937; Poet, playwright; 6. Ayzik Raboy, 1884–1944; Novelist, writer of short stories.

ווען מען האָט אויך אַרויפגעצוואָונגען מיט שװערסטן סאָציאַלן דרוק
אַז מיר מעגן בלויז לעבן בגשײַנאָל אין „פּאָרם", ניט אין „אינהאַלט",
ווען מען האָט געשאַפֿן אַ לאַגע אַז אַוועק פֿון דער אייגענער שפּראַך
באַטייט זייך צוועק פֿון פֿאָלק בכלל.   ניטאָ קיין איינציקער ביישפּיל אין
דער גאַנצער יידישער געשיכטע ווען מען האָט אויך אונדז אַרויפגעצוואָונ-
גען אַן איינציק דערלויבמע פֿאַרשטייערשאַפֿט פֿון אייגענע ברידער וואָס
זאָל מיט באַגייסטערטער הסכמה, און מיט סאָציאָלן און פֿיזישן צוואַנג,
דורכפֿירן אַזאַ פֿרעמד־וועלטלעכן און שפּראַך־קאָנסעקווענטן עקספּערי־
מענט.   דאָס זעגען דאָך ממש אידעאַל־לאַבאָראַטאָרישע תנאים וואָס אַ
סאָציאָלער טעסט קען זיך נאָר ווינטשן.

די רעזולטאַטן זעגען באַקאַנט ווייט און בדייט.   אַפֿילו די אָפֿיציעלע
סאָוועטישע ציפֿערן לאָזן ניט איבער דעם מינדסטן ספֿק וואו מיר האַלטן
אין דער וועלט.   איך וועל דאָ איבערגעבן בלויז עטלעכע פֿון די רייכע
מאַטעריאַלן וועגן דעם ענין כדי פשוט צו דערמאַנען די פֿאַקטן.   דר.
אוריה צבֿי ענגעלמאַן דערצײַלט („צוקונפֿט", סעפּט. 1936) אַז: „צום סוף
19טן יאָרהונדערט, נאָך דער פֿאָלק־צײַלונג פֿון 1897, האָבן 96.9 פּראָ־
צענט יידן אין רוסלאַנד גערעדט יידיש, און נאָר 3.1 פּראָצענט — אַנדערע
שפּראַכן.   ביז דער באָלשעוויסטישער איבערקערעניש האָט זיך דער
שפּראַכלעכער צושטאַנד ניט געענדערט.   דאָס ווערט באַשטעטיקט פֿון
די ציפֿערן וואָס די „דזשאָינט דיסטריביושאָן קאָמיטע" האָט צונויפֿגעקליבן
אין די מלחמה יאָרן.   אָבער זינט דער רעוואָלוציע גייט אָן די שפּראַכלעכע
אַסימילאַציע צווישן די יידן אין רוסלאַנד מיט אַ שטאַרקן אימפּעט...
אין 1926 געפֿינען מיר אין ראַטן־פֿאַרבאַנד אַז מער ווי 30 פּראָצענט יידן
האָבן זיך אָפּגעזאָגט פֿון יידיש ווי זייער שפּראַך.   אין 9 יאָר נאָך דער
באָלשעוויסטישער רעוואָלוציע איז די צאָל שפּראַבלעך אַסימילירטע יידן
געוואָקסן ניינפֿאַך".   דאָס איז געוועון אין 1926.   ווי עס איז היינט איז
ניט לייכט צו זאָגן, אָבער אַלע סימנים ווייזן אַז די אַסימילאַציע וואַקסט
אין געאָמעטרישער פּראָגרעסיע.   דר. ענגעלמאַן גיט אויך אַן ציפֿערן
פֿון ביאָלאָגישער אַסימילאַציע (געמישטע התונות) פֿון וועלכע עס ווערט
זיכער ניט פֿרייל עכער אויפֿן האַרצן.   וואָרים אין סאָוויעטן־פֿאַרבאַנד,
פּונקט ווי אומעטום, איז דער פּועל יוצא פֿון אַ געמישטער התונה אַז
דער יידישער צד פֿאַרלאָזט זיין פֿאָלק און פֿאַרבינדט זיך מיטן פֿאָלק
פֿונם אַנדערן צד.

געוויינטלעך ווייזט מען אָן אַז דאָס בעמט זיך פֿון דעם וואָס די
סאָוויעטישע רעגירונג האָט געעפֿנט אַלע טויערן פֿאַר יידן, צוגלייך
מיט די אַנדערע פֿעלקער, און דאָס פֿאַרשטאַרקט דעם שטראָם פֿון

אַסימילאַציע. נו, ווי איז אין „אייגענעם" יידישן לאַנד, אין ביראָ־
בידזשאַן? דניאל טשאַרני ברענגט אַ ריי ציפערן פון אָפיציעלע סאָוויע־
טישע קוואַלן וועגן דעם דאָרטיקן יידישן שול־וועזן (,,קולטור און דער־
ציאונג", פעברואר, 1938). דער סך הכל פאַר ביראָ־בידזשאַן איז אַז 2075
יידישע שילער באַזוכן קלאַסן (קלאַסן — ווייל אין ביראָ־בידזשאַן זענען
פאַראַן אַסך געמישטע שולן וואו די פאַרשיידענע קלאַסן האָבן ניט די
זעלביקע אומגאַנג־שפראַך) וואו די לערן־שפראַך איז יידיש, בעת ניין
טויזנט יידישע קינדער לערנען אין רוסישע קלאַסן.

אַזאַ זיכערן, פולשטענדיקן, קאַטאַסטראָפּאַלן דורכפאַל פון אַן עקס־
פערימענט קען מען צו אָפט ניט פאַרצייכענען אין סאָציאַלן לעבן. ווי
זשע האָט דאָס געווירקט אויף די סעקולאַריסטישע שפראַך־יידישיסטן?
אויך דאָס איז אַ טייל פונם עקספּערימענט, וואָרים דאָס דאַרף דאָך באַוויַיזן
דעם פּסיכישן צושטאַנד וואָס די דאָזיקע טעאָריע האָט געשאַפן ביי די
אידיאָלאָגן גופא. וואָס זשע לערנט אונדז דער עקספּערימענט אין אָט
דעם פּרט?

מילא וועגן די פאַרשטייער אין ראַטן־פאַרבאַנד איז אָפּגערעדט. זיי
האָבן זיך לחלוטין ניט מצער געווען. בנוגע ייזן האָבן זיי זיך לייכט
איינגעלעבט מיטן גאַנג פון די באַרימטע ,,סטיכישע" פּראָצעסן, און דער
מיט פאַרענדיקט אַלע חשבונות. פאַרקערט, זיי זענען גרייט געווען צו
באַפאַלן יעדן איינעם וואָס האָט געוואַגט אַרויסצולאָזן אַ זיפץ פון וויַיטאָג
איבער דער לאַגע. אָבער כאַראַקטעריסטיש איז וואָס די סעקולאַריסטיש־
יידישימטישע אינטעליגענץ פון אַנדערע לענדער איז געגאַנגען אויפן
זעלביקן דרך. אפילו די וואָס האָבן זיך דערלויבט צו טײטלען אויף
פאַרשיידענע חסרונות אין סאָוויעטן־פאַרבאַנד האָבן זיך ניט געקענט
אָפּהאַלטן פון אומגעצאַמטער באַגייסטערונג פאַר די קולטורעלע ישועות
ונחמות וואָס זענען געפאַלן אויפן מזל פון די סאָוויעטישע יידן. פאַקטן,
ציפער,ן אפּשאַצונגען, באַריכטן, קיין זאַך האָט ניט געהאָלפן. די רעגי־
רונג האַלט אויס שולן אויף יידיש, יידישע ביכער, יידיש טעאַטער, בקיצור,
יידיש, און דאָס פאַרענטפערט אַלץ. די וואַרעמע צוגעבונדנקייט צום
אַבסטראַקטן לעבן פון אַ דאָגמע האָט אָפּגעקילט די פאַראינטערעסירטקייט
אינם קאָנקרעטן לעבן פון אַ פאָלק.

טייל סעקולאַריסטישע יידישיסטן האָבן אויסגעטיַיטשט רוסיש־יידישע
געשעעניש דערמיט וואָס דער סאָוויעטן־פאַרבאַנד גיט יידן טאַקע די
בעסטע קולטורעלע געלעגנהייטן, נאָר פּשוט די יידן ווילן קיין יידן ניט
זײַן. עס איז באמת געווען אַ רעטעניש ווי אַזוי אינטעליגענטע מענטשן

פארטייטשן דאָס וואָרט „ווילן" ווען עס האַנדלט זיך וועגן סאָציאַלע
געשעענישן.   אויב ייִדן זוילן קיין ייִדן ניט זיין טאָ פֿאַרוואָס האָבן די
סאָוויעטישע לייט ניט געוואָלט זיך פֿאַרלאָזן אויף דעם אַז דאָס אַליין
וועט שוין אונטערברענגען די אַלטע ייִדישקייט?   פֿאַרוואָס האָבן זיי
אַרויסגעוויזן אַזוי פֿיל פֿונם „מענטשנס אוממענטשלעכקייט צום מענטשן",
און ניט בלויז וואָרט־פֿראָפּאַגאַנדע, בעת זיי האָבן צעשטערט, און ניט
באַמיט זיך צו ווירקן כאָטש מיט פּאָזיטיווע רייד ווען מען האָט געוואָלט
נאַציאָנאַל בויען?   פֿאַרוואָס האָבן זיי אַזויפֿיל געאַרבעט צו שאַפֿן דעם
ווילן אויף ניט, און האָבן בשום אופֿן ניט געוואָלט וועקן דעם ייִדישן ווילן
אויף יאָ?   פֿאַרוואָס זענען אין אַלע ישובים פֿאַראַן אַקטיווע ייִדישע גרופּעס
וואָס רייסן זיך מיט אַלע כוחות יאָ צו זיין ייִדן, און אין סאָוויעטן־
פֿאַרבאַנד – ערשט נעכטן דער רעזערוואָאָר פֿון אַלע ייִדישע געדאַנקען
און באַוועגונגען – איז ניטאָ קיין איין באַוואוסטזיניקע גרופּע פֿון דעם
מין?   עס איז בכלל ניטיק טיפֿער אַרײַנצודרינגען אינם פּסיכאָלאָגישן
מעכאַניזם פֿון אַ טאָציאַלן ווילן איידער מען מ־ענגט אַרויס אַזאַ לייכטן
פּסק דין אויפֿן גאַנצן ייִדישן ישוב אין סאָוויעטן פֿאַרבאַנד.   איך בין זיכער
אַז אויך אין יענער מדינה זענען פֿאַראַן גענוג אַזעלכע וואָס קרענקען
און וויטאָגן שטילערהייט אויף אונדזער דערטיקן נאַציאָנאַלן אומגליק,
אָבער זיי קענען דאָס ניט פֿאַרוואָנדלען אין קיין פּאָזיטיווע אַקטן, ניט ווייל
זיי ווילן ניט, נאָר ווייל מען מעַר ניט, און ווייל מען טעראָריזירט מיט דער
גאַנצער אבזריות פֿון דער מאָנאָקראַטישער דיקטאַטור די וואָס ווילן
עס יאָ.

9

וועלטלעכקייט, אָט דער באַגריף וואָס שיידט זיך אָפּ פֿון רעליגיע;
וועלטלעכקייט, וואָס דערקלערט ייִדישקייט פֿאַר אַ רעליגיע, און ממילא
פֿאַר אַ פּריוואַט זאַך (אין דער אמת'ן ווי אַ נאַרישע, אָפֿט אפֿילו ווי אַ
פֿאַרברעכערישע פּריוואַט־זאַך), אָט די וועלטלעכקייט איז געווען אַ מורא־
דיקער טעות ביי אונדז, זי האָט געפֿירט דערצו אַז מען זאָל וועלן אויס־
וואָרצלען ביי אונדז יעדע פֿאַרבונדנקייט מיט אונדזער געשיכטע.   אין איר
נאָמען האָט מען אַנטוויקלט ממש אַן עקל־געפֿיל צו אַלע צערעמאָניאַלן,
פֿײַערלעכקייטן, געדענק־טעג און טרויער־טעג וואָס די אַלטע ייִדישקייט,
ווי אַ געזונטער נאַציאָנאַלער קולטור פּראָדוקט, האָט מיט זיי אַזוי וואונ־
דערלעך באַשיינט אונדזער לעבן.   עס איז דערגאַנגען אפֿילו אַזוי ווייט
אַז ייִדישיסטן וואָס האָבן אַזוי הייס פֿאַרטעסטירט, און מיט רעכט, קעגן

רדיפות אויף יידיש אין ארץ ישראל, האָבן גלייכגילטיק — און טייל אויך
מיט שטילער הסכמה — געקוקט אויף דער אַנטי־יידישער, אַנטי־נאַציאָ־
נאַלער באַציאונג צו העבראיאיש אין סאָוויעטן פאַרבאַנד.

איצט דאַרף שוין זיין קלאָר אַז ווען מען פאַסט אויף יידישקייט ווי
אַ רעליגיע, ווערט מען ממילא געטריבן צו דעם אַז דאָס גאַנצע גייסטיקע
יידישע לעבן זאָל אַוועקגעשטעלט ווערן אונטער דער רובריק "רעליגיע".
און אויב וועלטלעכקייט פאַרלאַנגט מען זאָל זיך פון דעם אָפּזאָגן, וואָס זשע
בלייבט? אויס יידיש לעבן, אויס יידן, צו דעם איז עס טאַקע געקומען.

מיר וואָלטן שוין אויך געדאַרפט זיך צוגעוויינען אַביסל אַנדערש
צו טראַכטן וועגן דעם ענין שפראַך. אַ שפראַך איז ניט קיין חי הנושא
את עצמו, עס איז ניט קיין יש וואָס קען לעבן אין גאַנצן אויפן אייגענעם
חשבון. שפראַך איז פונקט ווי דער ניט־לאַנג אַנטדעקטער טאַבאַק־ווירוס.
אין זיך אַליין איז דאָס אינערט, אַ שטיק אומאָרגאַנישע מאַטעריע. אָבער
אַזוי שנעל ווי עס רירט זיך צו צו אַ לעבעדיקן אָרגאַניזם הייבט עס אָן
אַרויסווייזן סימנים פון לעבן, און ווירקט מיט דער ספּעציפישער קראַפט
וואָס בלויז לעבן פאַרמאָגט. יענע צופרידענע דורכפירער פון סעקולא־
ריסטישער וועלטלעכקייט, וואָס טענהן אַז זיי דאַרפן ניט קיין באַרעכ־
טיקונג פאַר יידיש, אַז יידיש איז ביי זיי ווי אַ נאַטירלעבעד אָבער, יענע
פאַרגעסן אַז אָט די נאַטירלעכקייט האָט צו פאַרדאַנקען זייער יידישקייט
פון אַמאָל, ניט זייער וועלטלעכקייט פון היינט. מען קען פונקט אַזוי
האַלטן אַז הינטער הוילן יידיש זאָל בלייבן אַ יידיש פאָלק, ווי מען קען
גלויבן אַז הינטער עספּעראַנטאָ זאָל ווערן אַן עספּעראַנטיש פאָלק.

זאָל אָבער קיינער ניט דוינגען פון דעם אַלעם אַז וועלטלעכקייט
אין יידיש זענען סתּם פאַלשע אָדער פוסטע לאָזונגען. הינטער יעדן
פון די דאָזיקע געדאַנקען ליגט באַאמת אַ געוווּנטער קערן און אַ וועג־
ווייזעריש ליכט, מען דאַרף בלויז ביטן דעם טראָף, ביטן דעם גאַנצן
אויסגאַנג־פּונקט, און — ווען דורכוויז נייטיק — ביטן טערמינען, כדי
אייַנצוּזען די גרויסע נאַציאָנאַלע ווערטן וואָס אין זיי שטעקט.

יידישקייט איז דורכגעגאַנגען אַ לאַנגע כסדר־דיקע אַנטוויקלונג, האָט
תמיד געדאַרפט אַרפענעמען, צוגעבן און ביטן. ניטאָ אַזאַ יידישקייט
וואָס מען זאָל איינמאָל פאַר אַלעמאָל קענען אָנווייזן מיטן פינגער "אָט
דאָס איז עס!" און ס'זאָל זיין גילטיק אויף אַלע ציטן, און אין אַלע
לענדער. ראַנגלעגנישן צווישן פאַרשיידענע פאַרמען און אויסדרוקן פון
יידישקייט זענען פונקט אַזוי אַלט ווי די יידישע געשיכטע בכלל, דאָס
איז ווייניקער קענטיק ווען מען האַט צו טאָן מיט אַ רעליגיע, אָבער
פאַר אַ פאָלקסטייגער מיט דאָס נאַטירלעך און כאַראַקטעריסטיש.

אַ ייד, וואָס ווערט אין דער הײַנטיקער ניו יאָרק גערופֿן „אָרטאָ־
דאָקס", וואָלט מסתּמא געוועזן אַ קל שבקלים בײַ אַן אָרטאָדאָקס אין אַ
פּוילישן שטעטל, אָדער אין ירושלים.   אַן אַמעריקאַנער „קאָנסערוואַטיוו"
וועט אויסזען ווי אַ „גוי גמור" בײַ אַ גאַליציאַנער חסיד, און אַן אַלט־
פֿראַנקישער ייד בײַ אַ רעפֿאָרמירטן ראַבײַ.   אַ פּראָגראַם פֿאַר ייִדיש־
וועלטלעכע שולן ווי עס וואָלט פֿאָרגעשלאָגן אַ ייד פֿון יואל ענטינעס
שניט, וואָלט מסתּמא באַטראַכט געוואָרן ווי נאַציאָנאַליסטיש־רעליגיעז־
פֿאַנאַטיש־כּלל ישׂראל׳דיק בײַ אַן אַלטן הײַמישן בונדיסט.

הײַנטיקע צײַטן, מער ווי אין פֿריִערדיקע דורות, שטײט פֿאַר אונדז
די גרויסע פּראָבלעם פֿון מאָדערניזירן, צופּאַסן צו צײַט, פּלאַץ, און צו
אונדזער אײגענער געענדערטער פּסיכיק, די גײַסטיקע פֿאָרמען פֿון
ייִדישן אויסדרוק, ייִדישקייט.   דער אויסגאַנג־פּונקט פֿון אַלע ייִדישקייט־
פֿאָרמען איז געוועזן אומבאַוואוסטזיניק, אָדער האַלב־אומבאַוואוסטזיניק,
קיום האומה.   הײַנט דאַרף דער דאָזיקער ציל קלאָר און אָפֿן אויעק־
געשטעלט ווערן, און קיינער פֿון אונדז קען ניט זײַן פּאָזיטיוו ייִדיש,
אַקטיוו ייִדיש אויב ער איז גלײַכגילטיק צו אָט דעם ציל.   עס דאַרף
זײַן אונדזער עובדא קלאָר צו מאַכן אַז יעדע אַלטע לעבנס־פֿאָרם
ברענגט אָפֿט אַרויס אין איר זיגזאַגישער אַנטוויקלונג פּראָדוקטן וואָס
זענען שעדלעך פֿאַר איר אײגענער עקזיסטענץ.   אויך ייִדישקייט איז
ניט, און קען ניט זײַן, קיין יוצא מן הכלל.   מיר דאַרפֿן דעריבער, אַפֿילו
אין שאַרפֿער קריטיק קעגן געוויסע באַגלייטערטע, אָדער סתּם־שעדלעבע
פֿאָרמען, אַרויסרופֿן דעם צוטרוי בײַ ייִדן אַז מיר טוען דאָס אין נאָמען
פֿון קיום האומה.

וועלטלעכקייט האָט געפֿאָדערט אַז מיר זאָלן זיך אָפּזאָגן פֿון אַלץ
וואָס פֿרומע ייִדן האָבן אַמאָל געטאָן.   די מאָדערניזירונג־טענדענץ, וועגן
וועלכער עס רעדט זיך דאָ, וועט האַלטן פּונקט פֿאַרקערט.   יעדער מנהג,
יעדע פֿאָרם, יעדע אַלטע טראַדיציע, איז שוין צוליב דעם אַליין אונדז
טײַער, ווײַל זי איז אַלט, און ווײַל זי איז טראַדיציע, ווײַל זי איז היסטאָריש
פֿאַרוואָרצלט, און ווײַל זי איז נאַענט דער פּסיכיק פֿון פֿאָלק.   שווער אַנצו־
נעמען ווערט זי בלויז דעמאָלט ווען זי פֿאַסט זיך ניט אַרײַן אין די
לעבנס־פֿאָרמען פֿון אַ מאָדערנעם מענטשן.   אַזאַ שטאַנדפּונקט שטעלט
זיך אײַן פֿאַר ייִדישן אינהאַלט, פֿאַר אַלע ייִדישע ווערטן, ער זוכט זיי
בלויז צוצופּאַסן צום לעבן פֿון הײַנטיקן טאָג, ווײַל דאָס ליגט אין די
אינטערעסן פֿון זייער אײגענער עקזיסטענץ.   ייִדיש ווערט דעמאָלט אַ
טייל פֿונעם זעלביקן פֿאַרמעגן, וואָרים אין שפּראַך, אויף וויפֿל זי איז
אַן אויסדרוק פֿון אַן אײגנאַרטיק פֿאָלקיש לעבן, ליגט אַ ריזיקער כּוח

דאָס דאָזיקע לעבן רייכער און שטאַרקער צו מאַכן. קיינער קען ניט, און
טאָר ניט, אָפּלייקענען אַז יידיש לעבט איצט דורך אַ מוראַ׳דיקן קריזיס,
אַז די מניעות וואָס האָבן זיך געשטעלט אין וועג זענען ניט אַזעלכע
וואָס מען קען לייכט בייקומען. אָבער דאָס וואָס איז ריכטיק וועגן יידיש
איז ריכטיק וועגן יידן בכלל. דער זעלביקער גייסט וואָס וועקט אין
אונדז דעם גלויבן אַז מיר, ווי אַ פאָלק, וועלן בייקומען די איצטיקע
לעבנסגעפאַר, דאַרף אין אונדז אויך וועקן דעם גלויבן אינם קיום
פון יידיש. עס מעג זיך פאַרקלענערן די צאָל יידן וואָס וועלן לעבן
מיט יידיש, אָבער דער אונטערגאַנג פון יידיש וואָלט געווען די זיכערסטע
באַשטעטיקונג אַז מיר זענען אונדזערע אַלגעמיינע נאַציאָנאַלע סכנות ניט
בייגעקומען. וואָרים דאָס וואָלט געהייסן אַז דאָס פּולבלוטיקסטע יידישע
לעבן — וואָס אַן אייגענע שפּראַך איז בלויז זיין אויסדרוק — האָט
אומעטום אויפגעהערט צו פונקציאָנירן. בכלל, יידיש איז געבוירן געוואָרן
און זיך אויסגעהאַלטן ווייל יידן האָבן געלעבט יידיש, און וואָס מער
יידן וועלן לעבן יידיש אַלץ לענגער וועט יידיש לעבן.

אַ געדאַנקען־גאַנג וואָס וועל שפּילן אַ פירנדיקע ראָלע אין יידישן לעבן,
און איז מעגליש באַרעכטיקט דערצו, קען דאָך ניט זיין קיין אנדערער
ווי אַז וואָס זיין הויפּט־ציל איז קיום האומה. די וואָס טענה׳ן אַז מען
דאַרף דאָס גאָרניט אונטערשטרייכן, אַז דאָס איז נאַטירלעך, אַז בלויז
קראַנקע מענטשן זענען תמיד באַזאָרגט וועגן זייער געזונט־צושטאַנד,
אאז״וו, אַזעלבע פאַרשטעלן דאָס אמת׳ע בילד פון דער לאַגע. מיר מעגן
זיי אָפן חושד זיין אַז עפעס האַלט זיי אָפּ פון רעדן קלאָרע דיבורים,
אַז אפשר דיקטירט זיי די די געטרייישאַפט צו אַן אַנדער אידיאַלאָגיע צו זיין
באַזונדערס איינגעהאַלטן ווען עס קומט צו יידן און יידישקייט. וואָרים
אונדזער עקזיסטענץ ווי אַ פאָלק, איז אפילו אין די געטאָ־צייטן ניט
געווען אַזוי מילאַדיק און „נאַטירלעך", ווי ביי פעלקער וואָס זענען
ניט אין גלות. אַזעלכע דערשיינונגען ווי שמד און סתם און „אַנטלויפן",
האָבן תמיד געלויערט איבער אונדז. די וואָס ווילן דורכויס פאָרשטעלן
דאָס קראַנקע יידישע לעבן מיט געזונטע גויאישע רייד מוזן מיט דער
צייט ווערן גלייכגילטיק צו אונדזערע נאַציאָנאַלע פּראָבלעמען, ווי מיר
זעען דאָס איצט אַזוי קלאָר. דעריבער ווען מיר רעדן דאָ וועגן מאָדער־
ניזירנדיקע אויפגאַבעס איז דער ציל ניט צו פאַרשטאַרקן די פּאָזיציעס
פון אַן אבסטראַקטן סעקולאַריזם נאָר פון אַ קאָנקרעטער יידישקייט.

עס איז כאַראַקטעריסטיש אַז כאַטש יידישיסטן האָבן זיך איינגע־
שטעלט פאַר וועלטלעכקייט פונקט אַזוי שטאַרק ווי פאַר יידיש פון־
דעסטוועגן האָבן זיי דעם „יום" צוגעטשעפּעט צו דער אייגענער שפּראַך

און ניט צו דער פֿאַדערונג פֿון אַ װעלטלעכן, ד״ה. ניט־רעליגיעזן, אינ־
האַלט. זיי האַבן, װײזט אויס. געפֿילט אַז אַ אידײע װאָס װיל װערן אַ
באַװעגונג און אַפֿעלירן צום פֿאָלק דאַרף קודם כל אונטערשטרײַכן דאָס
װאָס איז פֿאָזיטיװ און נאַציאָנאַל. און דאָס ליגט נאַטירלעך אין יידיש.
עס איז ניט ניט זייער שולד װאָס זענען פֿסיכיש ניט גרייט צו געפֿינען
אין שפּראַך יענע נאַציאָנאַלע װערטן װי מיר באַמערקן דאָס ביי אַנדערע
פֿעלקער.   ממילא איז קיין װאָונדער ניט װאָס די לאָזונג „יידישיזם"
איז בלויז געבליבן דער אידענטיפֿיקאַציע־צייכן ביי עטלעכע געצײלטע
אין אונדזער סביבה, אָדער זײן געצײלטע מאָמענטן. דער פֿאַרשפּרײטסטער
אויסדרוק איז געװאָרן „יידישע קולטור". װאָס איז אַסך כאַראַקטעריסטי־
שער װי מען קען זיך פֿאָרשטעלן.

דער באַגריף יידישע קולטור טוט אויף צװײ זאַכן. ער שליסט אײן
אין זיך יידיש װי אַ טײל פֿון אַ נאַציאָנאַל־קאָנסטרוקטיװער אידעאָלאָגיע.
און ער שטעלט אָף די אַבסטראַקטע. געקינצלטע מחיצה צװישן „רעליגיעז"
און „װעלטלעך" אין דער אַנטװיקלונג פֿון יידישקייט.   יידישע קולטור
איז אַן אײנהײטלעך געװעב װאָס האָט זיך אַנטװיקלט אין משך פֿון
דורות און אין פֿאַרשײדענע תנאים.   אַלע אירע טײלן האַבן אויסגעפֿילט
װיכטיקע פֿונקציעס אין אונדזערע שטרעבונגען צו פֿאַרבלײבן אַ סאָציאַל־
שאַפֿנדיקער אָרגאַניזם.   דעם דאָזיקן באַגריף איז פֿרעמד דער צוגאַנג
פֿון גײנגשעצן און דערהײבן, פֿון חוזק און לויב־געזאַנג, אויפֿן סמך פֿון
אַ סטאַנדאַרט װאָס האָט ניט קיין שייכות צו אַלגעמיין מענטשלעכער מאָראַל
אָדער קיום האומה.

די יידישע קולטור האָט זיך געביטן אין אַלע צייטן לויט די פֿאָדע־
רונגען און באַדינגונגען פֿון לעבן.   איצט האַלטן מיר ביי אַ לאַגע װען
טיפֿע ענדערונגען דאַרפֿן װידער געמאַכט װערן, װערן פֿאַקטיש געמאַכט
פֿון זיך אַליין, און עס איז די אויפֿגאַבע פֿון יעדן צװישן אונדז צו צאַמען
און קאָנטראָלירן דעם דאָזיקן פּראָצעס אין די ראַמען פֿון דער אַלגעמיינער
יידישקייט־סיסטעם.   אַבער דאָס קענען טאָן בלויז די װאָס האַבן אַ
װאַרעם האַרץ פֿאַרן גאַנצן געװעב פֿון דער יידישער קולטור, און זענען
דורכגעדרונגען מיט די צילן װאָס זי האָט תמיד געדינט.

אַט די װאָס פֿאַרשטייען אונדזערע אויפֿגאַבן אויף אַזאַ׳ן אופֿן, און
נעמען אַרײן יידיש אין זייער אַלגעמיינעם פּלאַן, זענען יידישע קולטו־
ריסטן, און „קולטוריזם" איז אַסך אַ פּאַסיקערע באַצייכענונג פֿאַר דעם
װאָס װערט פֿאַקטיש געזאַגט און געטאָן אין אַלע אונדזערע פּראַקטישע
טעטיקייטן און טעאָרעטישע פֿאָרמולירונגען.   דער באַגריף „יידישיזם"
פֿאַרטונקלט אונדזער פּראָבלעם און פֿירט אונדז פֿאַלש אויסצוטײטשן

פֿאַרשיידענע קולטור־דערשיינונגען אין ייִדישן לעבן.

ווי אַזוי דאַרף זיך קאָנקרעט אויסדריקן די מאָדערניזירונג פֿון
ייִדישקייט אין אונדזערע צײַטן? קודם כּל דאַרף זײַן קלאָר אַז אַזאַ
אויפֿגאַבע קען ניט זײַן געבויט אויף אַבסאָלוטע גרענעצן צווישן אַזעלכע
שטײַגערשע אויסדרוקן וואָס זענען נייטװענדיק פֿאַר אונדזער קיום און
אַזעלכע וואָס זענען ניט ניצלעך פֿאַר דעם צוועק, אָדער צווישן דעם
וואָס איז פּאַסיק און דעם וואָס איז ניט פּאַסיק פֿאַר אַ מאָדערנעם מענטשן
אין אַ מאָדערן לעבן. אַזעלכע אַבסאָלוטע גרענעצן זענען ניטאָ און קענען
ניט זײַן. פּרטים פֿון דעם מין זענען פֿאַרבונדן מיט געוואוינהייטן,
מיינונגען, געשמאַקן, אד״ג. בײַם באַשטימען אַזעלכע פּונקטן וועלן
נאַטירלעך זײַן די פֿאַרשיידנסטע חילוקי דעות. דער עיקר איז דאָ דער
אַלגעמיינער פּרינציפּ. אויב מיר שטעלן זיך אײַן פֿאַרן געדאַנק אַז די
צעטיילונג „רעליגיעז־וועלטלעך" איז בײַ אונדז פֿאַלש און פֿאַרפֿירעריש;
אויב מאָמענטן פֿון ייִדישקייט װערן ניט טריף בלויז צוליב דעם וואָס
אין באַוואוסטזײַן פֿון פֿרומע ייִדן װערן זיי אויך סאַנקציאָנירט פֿון איבער־
נאַטירלעכע כּוחות, ווי דאָס איז בכלל כאַראַקטעריסטיש פֿאַר אַלטע טראַ־
דיציעס; אויב די מאָס איז היסטאַרישע פֿאַרווארצלטקייט, אינהאַלטלעכע
רײַקײַט, שיינע פֿאָרם און צוגעפּאַסטקייט צום מאָדערנעם לעבן, דעמאָלט
שאַפֿט זיך אַ קלאָרע ריכטונג סײַ פֿאַר דעם וואָס מען דאַרף אָננעמען,
סײַ פֿאַר פּשרות וואָס מוז געמאַכט װערן.

דער דאָזיקער דרך איז אייגנטלעך דער זעלביקער וואָס איז כאַראַק־
טעריסטיש פֿאַר אַלע ענדערונגען אין דער אַנטװיקלונג פֿון ייִדישקייט,
בלויז צוויי באַװעגונגען האָבן אָפּגעטראָטן פֿון אָ דעם דרך. דאָס איז
די דײַטשישע רעפֿאָרם און דער סעקולאריסטישער שפּראַך־ייִדישיזם.
די ערשטע האָט צעטיילט ייִדישקייט אויף צוויי קאַטעגאָריעס: רעליגיע
און נאַציאָנאַליזם, און זיך אויסגעקליבן די ערשטע. די צווייטע באַװע־
גונג האָט אויך צעטיילט ייִדישקייט אויף צוויי קאַטעגאָריעס: ייִדישקייט
און ייִדיש, נאָר זיך אויסגעקליבן די צווייטע. די ערשטע פֿאַרוואָסערט
דאָס נאַציאָנאַלע בלוט, וואָס דאַרף זײַן אַזוי רויט און אימפּעטיק בײַ אַ
פֿאָלק אין גלות. די צווייטע עפֿנט אויף שטילערהייט די בלוט־געפֿעסן,
רינט אויס דאָס בלוט פֿון זיך אַליין.

ווען דאָס גײַסטיקע לעבן פֿון ייִדישן פֿאָלק וװערט ניט צעהאַקט אין
זײַן ווארצל, ווי דאָס טוען די רעפֿאָרמער און די סעקולאריסטן, דעמאָלט
שיינט פֿאַר אונדז אַרויס דאָס אַלט־אַלטע געוועב, ניט קיין איינצלנער
פֿאַרבינדונג־פֿאָדעם, וואָס באַהעפֿט אונדז ווי אַ פֿאָלק. קודם כּל לײַכט
פֿאַר אונדז טיפֿע באַוואוסטזײַן אַז מיר זענען אַ פֿאָלק און האָבן דעם

ווילן דאָס צו פֿאַרבלײַבן.　מיר האָבן אַ געפֿיל פֿון לאַנגער היסטאָרישער
שותּפֿות, און אַ בשותּפֿות׳דיקע קרובה׳שאַפֿט מיט די גרויסע פֿערזענ־
לעכקייטן און גרויסע געשעעענישן וואָס קוקן צו אונדז אַרויס דורך די
פֿענסטער פֿון אונדזער געשיכטע.　אונדז אַלעמען רעגט אָן דאָס געפֿיל
פֿון צוגעבונדנקייט צו אַלע ייִדישן ישובֿים איבער דער וועלט און זייער
היסטאָריש מזל, צוזאַמען מיט אַ פֿסיכישער גרייטקייט מיטצולעבן זייער
פֿרייד און לײַדן זיי אַרײַן אין קריטישע מאָמענטן.　מיר דריקן אויס
דאָס גײַסטיקע פֿון פֿאָלק דורך מיטלעבן אין קאָנקרעטע סימבאַלישע
און שטייגערשע פֿאָרמען אונדזער גראַנדיעזע היסטאָרישע דראַמע אין
ערנסט, יום טובֿ, און טרויער.　בקיצור, דערמיט דריקט יעדער פֿון אונדז
אויס דאָס געפֿיל אַז „בתוך עמי אַני יושבֿ".

צווישן די קרעפֿטיקסטע אָביעקטיוּוּע סימנים פֿון אונדזער אָרגאַנישער
פֿאַרבונדנקייט, וואָס איז אויך אַ ריזיקער פֿאַקטאָר אין פֿאַרשטאַרקן אונדזער
קיום ווי אַ פֿאָלק, דאַרף מען באַזונדערס רעכענען די אינסטיטוטיעס
וואָס מיר באַשאַפֿן אין יעדן ישובֿ באַזונדער, און ספּעציעל די וואָס זענען
אָרגאַניזירט אויף אַן אַלוועלטלעכן פֿאַרנעם.　פֿון קלענסטן בית המדרש
ביז גרויסע סאָציאַלע און קולטורעלע אונטערנעמונגען, פֿון אַ ליאַדע
צדקה הברה ביז „דזשוינט", פֿון האיאַס ביז ציוניזם, פֿון אַ זשורנאַלכל
אין אַ פֿאַרוואָרינג שטעטל ביז ייווא אָדער ירושלימער אוניווערזיטעט
— דאָס איז אַ קאָלאָסאַלער אַפֿאַראַט וואָס בויט פֿאַר אונדז דאָס ייִדישע
לעבן און בויט אונדז אַלעמען אַרײַן אין אָט דעם לעבן.　יעדע ייִדישע
גרופּע וואָס ווערט ווילנדיק אָדער ניט ווילנדיק אָפּגעריסן פֿון אַלגע־
מיינעם ייִדישן אינסטיטוציאָנעלן לעבן אַ דאָרנדיקע צוווייג אויף
אונדזער בוים.

די ייִדישע וועלטלעכקייט פֿאַרטרעט דעם איינציקן קרייז אין ייִדישן
לעבן וואָס האָט ניט אויסגעבויט פֿאַר זיך קיין געזעלשאַפֿטלעכן צענטער,
קיין אינסטיטוטיע וואָס זאָל פֿאַרבינדן ייִדישע סאָציאַלע און גײַסטיקע
אינטערעסן, וואָס זאָל ווערן אַ שטענדיקער אויסדרוק פֿון אָרגאַניזירט
לעבן.　אומעטום איז פֿאַראַן אַ שול, אַ בית המדרש, אַ סינאַגאָגע, אַ
„צענטער", — די ייִדישע וועלטלעכקייט האָט אין גאַנצן אָפּגעוואָרפֿן
פֿון זיך דעם דאָזיקן עול.　אין די קינדער׳שולן זענען פֿון זיך גופֿא
אויסגעוואַקסן בלאָסע שאָטנס פֿון אָט אַזעלכע צענטערס, און האָבן
געשאַפֿן אַ שטיקל מקום מנוחה פֿאַר די וואָנדערער פֿון דער ייִדיש־
וועלטלעכער סבֿיבֿה.　אָבער סוף כּל סוף זענען זיי בלויז צוטשעפּענישן
צו דערציאונג־אינסטיטוטיעס, און עס איז ניט זייער אייפֿגאַבע זיך צו
פֿאַרנעמען מיט ברייטער פֿאָלק־טעטיקייט.

דער דאָזיקער ווייט־גייענדיקער חיסרון נעמט זיך ניט, ווי מען קען
מיינען, פון צופעליקער נאַציאָנאַלער צעגלאָזונקייט, נאָר דער עיקר פון
דעם וואָס „יידיש־וועלטלעך" איז סוף כל סוף הוילע, אַבסטראַקטע טעאָריע
וואָס קען העכסטנס פירן צו אַ שטאַנדפונקט, אָבער ניט צו אַ קאָנקרעטער
נאַציאָנאַלער פראָגראַם.   דאָס איינציקע קאָנקרעט־פראַקטישע וואָס האָט
געקענט געבוירן ווערן פון אַזאַ טעאָריע זענען די שולן.   זעען מיר
טאַקע אַז די דאָזיקע סביבה צעטיילט זיך אַקוראַט לויט די שול־טיפן
וואָס זי פאַרמאָגט.   ניטאָ קיין אלגעמיינע פונדאַמענטאַלע ליניע וואָס זאָל
זי אויך אַן אָרגאַניזירטן אופן פאַראייניקן.   אַזוי לאַנג ווי עט דער קרייז
וועט פאַר זיך קיין אייגענעם „בית הכנסת" ניט אויפבויען וועט אים
פעלן דער פיזישער יסוד און די סאָציאַלע מעגלעכקייט אַרויסצוברענגען
מכה אל הפועל די נאַציאָנאַלע פאַטענצן וואָס ער פאַרמאָגט.   די טבע
פונם צעזייטן יידישן לעבן איז אַזאַ אַז קיינער פון אונדז קען ניט זינדיקן
קעגן דעם פרינציפ פון סינאַגאָגישער אָרגאַניזירטקייט און בלייבן אומ־
באַשטראָפט.

עס איז אויך אַן אומגליקלעכער סימפטאָם פון אַ ביטער גלות לעבן וואָס
יידן איז נאָך ביז איצט ניט געלונגען צו בויען פעסט־אָרגאַניזירטע
קהילות אין דעמאָקראַטישע לענדער — וואו מיר ווערן באַטראַכט פאַר
יחידים־בירגער — און וואָס אַלע באַמיאונגען צו שאַפן אַן אמת'ן יידישן
וועלט־קאָנגרעס ענדיקן זיך אָן הצלחה.   קאָנגרעס און קהילות זענען
פאַקטיש צוויי זייטן פון זעלביקן אלט־אַלטן געדאַנק וואָס פאַר אים האָבן
זיך אייגגעשטעלט יידן פון פאַרשיידענע ריכטונגען.   יעדער באַוואוסט־
זיניקער ייד קען פאַרשטיין דעם אומגעהייערן ווערט פון אלגעמיינער
אינטערנאַציאָנאַלער אָרגאַניזירטקייט אין אונדזער לעבן.   און כאָטש די
מניעות זענען זייער שווערע און ערנסטע דאָך, האַלט איך אַז אונדזער
וויכטיקסטע אויפגאַבע אין די גלות־לענדער דאַרף זיין צו בויען לאָקאַלע
און לאַנד־אָרגאַניזאַציעס אומעטום צו געשטאַלטן און אַנטוויקלען דאָס
יידישע לעבן.   מען דאַרף דאָס טאָן אפילו ווען אַ קאָנגרעס אויף אַ
וועלט־פאַרנעם באַגעגנט צו גרויסע שטרויכלונגען אויף זיין וועג.   איצט
אין די צייט צו ליגן אַלץ מער דעם טראָף אויף אונדזערע שייכותן צו
„אַ וועלט מיט יידן", ניט אויף די צעשייד־ליניעס פון ריכטונגען.   וואָס
מער מיר וועלן דאָס איינזען, וואָס מער אַלע גרופירונגען פון אונדזער
פאָלק וועלן דאָס איינזען, אַלץ מער וועלן מיר זיין גרייט צו לעבן
ניט בלויז ווי אַ פסיכיש פילנדיק נאָר אויך ווי אַ טעכניש אָרגאַניזירט
יידיש פאָלק.

ווען אָט די אַלע סוביעקטיווע און אָביעקטיווע מאָניפעסטאַציעס פון

נאַציאָנאַלן לעבן ווערן אָנגעטרונקען מיט די זאַפטן פֿון אַן אייגענער
שפּראַך, אין אונדזער פֿאַל ייִדיש, גיט דאָס צי אַ באַזונדער פֿרישקייט,
עפֿנט נײַע קוואַלן פֿון אייגענער שאַפֿנדיקער קולטור, און, דער עיקר,
פֿילט אונדז אָן מיט דער באַרעכטיקטער זיכערקייט אַז דער קאַמף פֿאַר
אונדזער נאַציאָנאַלער עקזיסטענץ וועט זיך ענדיקן מיט אַ נצחון. ייִדיש
ווערט דערמיט אַ פֿונקציע פֿון אַ ברייט פֿאַרצווייגט לעבן, און איז אין
דעם זינען, און בלויז אין דעם זינען, צווישן די אָנגעזעענסטע נאַציאָנאַל־
קאָנסטרוקטיווע כּוחות וואָס מיר פֿאַרמאָגן.

דאָס פּראַקטישע געווינס פֿונעם געגנדערטן צוגאַנג צו וועלטלעכקייט
האָבן מיר שוין געזען, דאָך וועלן ניט זיין איבעריק נאָך עטלעכע באַ־
מערקונגען. קודם כּל וועגן דעם וואָרט גופֿא. דאָס וואָרט "וועלטלעך״
איז שוין זייער אַן אַלטער תּושב אין ייִדיש. אַ ייִד וואָס איז געווען אַביסל
אויפֿגעקלערט, געוואוסט וואָס אויף דער וועלט טוט זיך, געלייענט גויאישע
צייטונגען, אָט אַזאַ ייִד פֿלעג הייסן, אין די צייטן פֿון אונדזערע זיידעס
און עלטער־זיידעס, וועלטלעכער ייִד, אָדער וועלטלעכער מענטש. אין
מיין קינדהייט האָב איך אָפֿט געהערט ווי מען האָט חסידישע רביים
קלאַסיפֿיצירט אויף אַזעלכע וואָס זענען אַרייַנגעטאָן אין די עולמות
עליונים און ווייסן ניט קיין צורת המטבע, און אַזעלכע וואָס זענען וועלט־
לער. אָבער "וועלטלעך״ אינעם זינען פֿון ניט זיין פֿאַרבונדן מיט דער
רעליגיעזער אָרגאַניזאַציע, פֿון זיין אין דרויסן פֿון דער קירך, דאָס איז
אַ ריין דייטשישש וואָרט, און האָט מיט ייִדיש לחלוטין ניט וואָס צו טאָן.
בײַ אונדז איז ניטאָ קיין קירך און קיין "דרויסן״, ממילא האָט אַזאַ באַגריף
גאָרניט געקענט געבוירן ווערן. אַסך בעסער וואָלט געווען ווען דער ניט־
ייִדישער באַגריף וואָלט זיך ניט באַהאַלטן הינטער אַן אַלט ייִדיש וואָרט
מיט אַ נייעם גויאישן טייטש. אַזאַ וואָרט ווי "סעקולער״ וואָלט לכל
הפּחות ניט געווען אַזוי פֿאַרפֿירעריש ווי "וועלטלעך״.

עס איז גענוג אַ טראַכט צו טאָן אויף אַ רגע כּדי אײַנצוזעהן אַז
דאָס וואָס איך האָב אין זינען מיט דער נײַטיקער מאָדערניזאַציע פֿון
ייִדישקייט איז טאַקע צו מאַכן אונדזער לעבן מער וועלטלעך, אָבער אין
אַלטן ייִדישן ניט אין נייעם דייטשישן, זינען פֿון וואָרט. איך וואָלט
דעריבער זיך גאָרניט געשעמט דאָס דאָזיקע זייער פּאַסיקע וואָרט אָנ־
צונעמען, בתנאי מיר זאָלן קלאָר פֿאַרשטיין וואָס מיר מיינען. וועלטלעך
ניט ווי אַ קעגנשטעלונג צו רעליגיע, נאָר ווי אַ קעגנשטעלונג צו אַ מין
טראַדיציאָנעלער פֿאַרגליוווערטקייט, אָדער צו אַן איינגעשפּאַרטער אָרטאָ־
דאָקסיע וואָס וויל אַז איר טעאָריע זאָל זיך באַוואוסטזיניק מאַכן בלינד

צו איר אייגענער פּראַקטיק וואָס די צייט צווינגט אַרויף.

דער געענדערטער צוגאַנג צו יידיש פירט אויך צו גאַנץ באַשטימטע פּראַקטישע קאָנסעקווענצן. דער געדאַנק אַז די איינציקע פאָרם פון נאַציאָנאַל לעבן ביי יידן איז לינגוויסטישע יידישקייט מוז פירן דערצו מען זאָל באַטראַכטן אַלע וואָס לעבן זיך אויס אין דער לאַנד־ שפּראַך ווי אויסגעשלאָסענע פון כלל ישראל. בלויז אַ טעאָריע וואָס האָט זיך אויסגעהאַדעוועט אין דער ספערע פון אַ פרעמער נאָרמאַל פאָלק קען קומען צו אַזאַן אויספיר. ווי אַזוי מען קען אָנוועגן אַזאַ געדאַנקען־ גאַנג אויפן יידישן פאָלק איז פּשוט למעלה מן השכל. עס איז גענוג זיך צו דערמאָנען אַז צווישן די שאַפער און איניציאַטאָרן פון די איצטיקע גרעסמע נאַציאָנאַלע באַוועגונגען ביי יידן זענען פאַראַן אַזוי פיל וואָס יידיש איז זיי געווען פרעמד; אַז טויזנטער, מויזנטער לאַנד־שפּראַכיקע יידן האָבן פאַר אונדז געשאַפן אומגעהייערע פּראַקטישע און טעאָרע־ טישע ווערטן אַט גלייך פאַר אונדזערע אויגן, כדי איינצוזען ווי קאַמיש אַזאַ טעאָריע איז. עס איז גענוג צו טראַכטן וועגן דעם אויף וויפיל אַזאַ טעאָריע שאַפט אַן אייזערנע מחיצה צווישן אונדז און די בעסטע לאַנד־ שפּראַכיקע יידן פון אונדזער דור, כדי איינצוזען ווי שעדלעך זי איז. לינגוויסטישער יידישיזם איז תמיד געווען צו וויניק איבערקליבעריש, צו עקסטראַוואַגאַנט, ביים באַנוצן דאָס ווערט ,,אַסימילאַציע" אין אַזעלכע פאַלן. עס קומט אויס אַז אַ ייד וואָס האָט אַלע האַט אַלע אויסגערעכנטע אטריבוטן פון אַ געטרייען, באַוואוסטזיניקן יידן, נאָר אין ווייט פון דער יידישער שפּראַך, אַזאַ ייד איז אויסגעשלאָסן פון כלל ישראל. אַבער אַ יידיש־ רעדנדיקער ייד וואָס וואַרצלט זיך אויס פון אַלע יידישע אינטערעסן און פאַרבינדונגען, אַזאַ ייד דאַרף אונדז זיין אַ נענטערער נאַציאָנאַלער קרוב.

עס שטעקט אין דעם אַ מערקווירדיקע בלינדקייט צו דער קאָנקרעטער לאַגע אין וועלכער מיר לעבן. די לאַנד־שפּראַכיקע סביבה ווערט סוף כל סוף ניט געשאַפן פון עמיצנס פרייען ווילן. זינער ניט ווי אַ פּועל יוצא פון וועלן אַנטלויפן פון יידישן פאָלק. עס זענען פאַראַן אָביעקטיווע תנאים וואָס אפילו איבערמענטשלעכע אָנשטרענגונגען קענען זיי ניט ביקומען. פּונקט ווי ביי די אידעאַלסטע נאַציאָנאַלע דערגרייכונגען אין ארץ ישראל, אָדער אויף אַן אַנדער טעריטאָריע, וועלן נאָך אַלץ בלייבן מיליאָנען יידן אין די גלות־לענדער, אַזוי וועלן אויך מוזן זיין גרויסע יידישע לאַנד־שפּראַכיקע קאַלאָניעס אפילו ווען יידיש זאָל האָבן די גינ־ ציקסטע און פרייסטע באַדינגונגען זיך צו אַנטוויקלען.

דאָס אַריינרעכענען יידיש צווישן די וויכטיקסטע נאַציאָנאַליזירנדיקע

פאַקטאָרן וואָס מיר פאַרמאָגן איז אַ ביס, און בלי ספק זייער אַ וויכטיקע
נייס, אין יידישן טראַכטן. אָבער מיר וועלן אָנטאָן דעם גרעסטן שאָדן
דער דאָזיקער אידייע גופא, אויב מיר וועלן זי אין דער טעאָריע אָננעמען
ווי אַ מין שטעלפאַרטרעטער אויפן אָרט פונם גאַנצן ברייטן געוועב
פון יידישקייט. אחוץ דעם וואָס דאָס ווערט אָפּגעלייקנט פון אַלע פאַקטן
פון פאַרגאַנגענעם און איצטיקן יידישן לעבן, וועלן מיר דערמיט אָפּשטויסן
די וואָס צו זיי ווילן מיר אַפּעלירן. מיר וועלן אָפּשטויסן מיט אַזאַ
טעאָריע אפילו יידיש-רעדנדיקע יידן, און פאַרלירן זייער צוטרוי.

אויב מיר האָבן אין זינען דאָס יידישע לעבן, די יידישע קולטור אין
ברייטסטן זינען, דעמאָלט דאַרפן מיר מיט מער אָפּגעהיטקייט אונטער-
שיידן צווישן די וואָס זענען און בליבן מיטן פאָלק און די וואָס טיילן
זיך אָפּ. ניט אַלע קענען פאָרן קיין ארץ ישראל אָבער אַלע קענען זיין
ציוניסטן. ניט אַלע קענען לעבן מיט יידיש, אָבער דורכנעמען זיך מיט
דער איבערצייגונג וועגן דעם נאַציאָנאַלן באַטייט פון יידיש, דאָס קען מען.
דאָס איז אַן אומגעהייער וויכטיקע אויפגאַבע, און יעדע הצלחה קען
האָבן אַ קאָלאָסאַלע ווירקונג סיי אויף דער אַנטוויקלונג פון יידישער
קולטור אין יידיש, סיי אויף פאַרשטאַרקן אונדזערע פּאָזיציעס אין פאָלק,
אָבער כדי מען זאָל דאָס דערגרייכן איז קודם כל נייטיק מיר זאָלן
באַטראַכטן יעדע לאַנד-שפּראַכיקע יידישע גרופּע פון שטאַנדפונקט פון
איר באַוואוסטזיניקער מיטשפּיל אין דער נאַציאָנאַלער דראַמע פון יידישן
פאָלק. אַזאַ שטאַנדפונקט וועט אווועקשטעלן גרענעצן און מחיצות אויף די
געהעריקע פּאָזיציעס.

דאָס פּראַקטישע לעבן האָט קלאָר באַוויזן אַז מיר האָבן מער אין
שותפות מיט לאַנד-שפּראַכיקע יידן וואָס האָבן די אַנדערע נאַציאָנאַלע
אַטריבוטן ווי מיט די וואָס די יידישע רייד און זענען לחלוטין ווייט
פון יידישע מעשים. אין אונדזערע באַציאונגען מיט דעם נעענטערן שותף
וועלן מיר, אפילו מיט אונדזער הולער נאַענטקייט צו אים, קלאָר מאַכן
אויף ווי ווייט מיר שאַצן אָפּ יידישע מעשים, און אַז אַז ביי אונדז איז יידיש
אַ לעבעדיקע פונקציע פון אזעלכע מעשים, ניט עפּעס סתם אַ פאַר-
ליבמקייט אין יידיש, ווייל אַזוי דיקטירט אַן אַבסטראַקטע טעאָריע פון
לינגוויסטישן נאַציאָנאַליזם. בלויז דעמאָלט איז פאַראַן אַ האָפענונג
מען זאָל אונדז פאַרשטיין, און זיך צריענטירן אין אַז דעם צוגאַנג ווי אַ
צושטייער צו דער דורות-דיקער אַנטוויקלונג פון יידישקייט.

10

די גאַנצע יידישע פילאָזאָפיע פון דער יידיש-וועלטלעכער סביבה

דריקט זיך אויס אין דער פֿאָרמולע „לינגוויסטיש־סעקולאַריסטיש". בײדע
באַגריפֿן זענען געקומען צו אונדז פֿון דער פֿרעמד, פֿון אַן אַנדער לעבן,
אַנדערע פֿעלקער, אַנדערע האַפֿענונגען און אַנדערע מיטלען אין לעבנס־
קאַמף. אָבער בעת דאָס ערשטע, לינגוויסטיש, איז פֿאַר אונדז לופֿטיקע
פֿאָרם און צעקריכט ווי שפֿינעוועבס ווען מען נעמט עס אין האַנט, האָט
דאָס צווייטע, סעקולאַריסטיש, סתם צו אונדז קיין שײכות ניט. פֿילאָזאָ־
פֿישער סעקולאַריזם, דאָס הייסט פֿרייע וויסנשאַפֿטלעכע פֿאָרשונג, איז
פֿאַרשפּרייט אין פֿאַרשיידענע ווינקלען פֿון יידישן לעבן וואָס ווערן באַ־
טראַכט פֿאַר „רעליגיעז". דערווייל שטאַמען פֿון דאָרט די רייכסטע פֿאַר־
שערישע אוצרות איבער יידישע קולטור פֿאַרבלעמען, און דאָס וואָס זיי
האָבן כּריי־וויסנשאַפֿטלעך אויסגעאַרבעט וועט בלײבן אויף דור דורות. פֿון
דער אַנדערער זייט איז פֿאָליטישער סעקולאַריזם בײ אונדז ניט מער ווי
אַ משונה'דיקע הינטיקע מלחמה מיט נעכטיקע טעג. קאָנסערוואַטיווע
און מאָדערניזירנדיקע ריכטונגען זענען נאַטירלעך, און דער צונויפֿשטויס
צווישן זיי וועט תמיד זיין אַ פֿאַקטער אין אונדזער קולטור־לעבן. אָבער
דאָס האָט גאָר ניט וואָס צו טאָן מיט דער סעקולאַריסטישער פֿילאָזאָפֿיע.

ווען די דאָזיקע פֿילאָזאָפֿיע האָט גענומען ווירן צו פּראַקטישע קאָנ־
סעקווענצן האָט זי טיפֿער טראַכטנדיקע און יידיש־דורכגעדרונגענע אינ־
טעליגענץ זיך דערשראָקן פֿאַר די מוראַ'דיקע סכּנות אין וועלכע עס פֿירט
אונדז אַריין דער לינגוויסטישער סעקולאַריזם. דאָס האָט זיך אַרויסגעוויזן
אין פֿאַרשיידענע אַרטיקלען אין צייטונגען און זשורנאַלן, אין די וויכוחים
וואָס זענען פֿאָרעפֿנטלעכט געוואָרן אין היגן זשורנאַל פֿון אַרבעטער רינג
„קולטור און דערציאונג", און ספּעציעל אין די פּאַריזער זאַמלביכער „אויפֿן
שיידוועג". דאָס זענען טאַקע שטימען פֿון זייער אָנגעוועענע יחידים.
מען דאַרף אָבער דערפֿון ניט דרינגען אַז די אָנהענגער פֿון דער אַלטער
אידעאַלאָגיע וואָס האָט זיך איינגעוואָרצלט אין משך פֿון צענדליקער
יאָרן, מיט אַ טראַדיציע פֿון קעמישער און פֿאַרביטערטער אַפֿיקורסות
הינטער זיך, האָבן שוין טאַקע איינגעזען וואו מיר האַלטן אין דער וועלט,
אָדער האָבן גרויס עגמת נפֿש פֿון אונדזער איצטיקער גייסטיקער לאַגע.

ערשט איצט, בעת איך שרייב די דאָזיקע ווערטער, דערגרייכן צו
מיר קלאַנגען וועגן היציקע וויכוחים וואָס גייען אַן אין געוויסע היגע
יידיש־וועלטלעכע שולן. עס האַנדלט זיך וועגן דעם צי מען מעג זיך
באַנוצן מיט אַ מנורה אין אַ חנוכה יום טוב. ווי איך הער איז דער
לעצטער פּסק דין אַז מען טאָר ניט. אַ מנורה איז ניט גענוג סעקולער.
פֿאַרוואָס יידיש, די שאַפֿונג פֿון די קאַפֿאַטע און שטריימל יידן, די שפּראַך
פֿון די רעליגיעזע תּחינות, פֿון „גאָט פֿון אברהם", פֿאַרוואָס יידיש זאָל זיין

מער סעקולער, וואָלט געווען איבער די כוחות צו פארשטיין. דאָס ווערט
פארשטעגדלעך ערשט ווען מען כאַפט זיך אַז אַזוי האָבן געטאָן געטאָן אויך
די סעקולאריסטן ביי אַנדערע פעלקער, און מסתמא אויך דערפאַר ווייל
דאָס איז דאָך דער איינציקער געבליבענער אָנהאַלט פארן „פינטעלע ייד".

דער פאַקט אַז „עפּעס איז ניט פריילעך דאָ", ווי עס זאָגט זיך אין
מאַני לייבס באַלאַדע, ווערט אויך באַשטעטיקט פונם כאַראַקטער פון די
קולטור־באַוועגונגען וואָס האָבן זיך באַוויזן אין אונדזער קרייז אין די
לעצטע יארן. דער העכסטער ציל פון די דאָזיקע באַוועגונגען זעט אויס
צו זיין צו פארשפּרייטן דאָס יידישע בוך, צו שאַפן אָרגאַניזירטע גרופּעס
וואו מען ליינט דאָס יידישע בוך, צו אַראַנזשירן ראַדיאָ פּראָגראַמען וואו
מען מאַכט באַקאַנט די שאַפונגען פון יידישן בוך, בעקיצור, בוך און
נאָכאַמאָל, בוך. אין אַ צייט ווען פונדאַמענטאַלע טעאָרעטישע הנחות
ווערן אָפּגעפרעגט; אין אַ צייט ווען די גאַנצע עקזיסטענץ פון אַ יידיש־
וועלטלעכער סביבה שטייט אין קאָן; אין אַ צייט ווען די העכסטע
נאַציאָנאַל־גייסטיקע פּראָבלעמען, פּראָבלעמען פון אינהאַלטלעכער יידיש־
קייט, מאַנען אָן ענטפער; אין אַ צייט ווען דאָס טראַגישע לעבן אונדזערס
פאָדערט נייע אינסטיטוציאָנעלע אַפאַראַטן פארן גאַנצן יידישן פאָלק; אין
אַ צייט ווען אונדזער אָפּגעריסנקייט פון אַנדערע טיילן פון פאָלק רעדו־
צירט אונדז צו אַ מין וועגעטירנדיקן ליטעראַרישן קלוב, אין אַזאַ צייט
מאַכן אַזעלכע קולטור־באַוועגונגען באַמת אַ טראַגי־קאָמישן איינדרוק. עס
איז פּונקט ווי מען וואָלט זיך אונטערגענומען אויסצורייניקן אַ שלאַכט־
פעלד מיט אַ צאָן־בערשטל. שוין דאָס אַליין רופט אַרויס טרויעריקע
ספקות אין אונדזער לעבנס־פייאיקייט.

אין זיין ווערק „געשיכטע פון ליטעראַטור ביי יידן", מאַכט צינבערג
אַזאַ מין סך הכל פון דער ראַציאָנאַליסטיש־פילאָזאָפישער באַוועגונג צווישן
די יידן אין שפּאַניע: „אָט דאָס וואָס די פילאָזאָפיש־געבילדעטע אינטע־
ליגענץ, די מתפּלסמים, זענען בשעת דער קאַטאַסטראָפע דעם נסיון ניט
ביי געשטאַנען, און אַסך פון זיי האָבן זייער שטאַם פארלאָזן און איבער־
געגאַנגען צום קריסטנטום — דאָס האָט אין גאַנצן דיסקרעדיטירט אין די
אויגן פון פאָלק ניט נאָר די חכמת יון, די גריכיש־אַראַבישע פילאָזאָפיע,
נאָר אפילו די נאַטורוויסנשאַפטן אויך. אַלץ שטאַרקער זענען געוואָרן
די מיסטישע שטימונגען, און פון דריי פארשיידענע ריכטונגען איז מען
קעגן דעם ראַציאָנאַליסטישן אַריסטאָטעליזם אַרויסגעטראָטן און אים קריג
דערקלערט".

הײנטיקע צײטן האַנדלט זיך ניט וועגן אריבערגײן צום קריסטנטום,
אָבער וועגן אויסוואָרצלען זיך פון דער אינערלעכער ספערע פון ײדישן

פאָלק, ביי דעם האַלט עס יאָ. עס זענען פריִער אָנגעוויזן געוואָרן פאַלן
וועז אַזאַ נסיון איז געווען און די לינגוויסטישע סעקולאַריסטן האָבן אים
ניט אויסגעהאַלטן. מיר זעען פאַר אונדזערע אויגן אַז אַזעלכע נסיונות
הייבן זיך אַרויס אין רוב ייִדישע קיבוצים, און אַלע סימנים ווייזן אַז
די לעצטע נאַציאָנאַלע אידעאַלאָגיע ביי ייִדן וועט זיין די ערשטע צו
פאַלן אויפן וועג.

די צייט ווערט אַלץ קריטישער מיט יעדער מינוט. וואָס וועט דער
מאָרגן ברענגען? דאָס הענגט אָפּ נאַטירלעך פונם וועג וואָס דער היינט
וועט פאַר זיך אויסקלייבן. פאַרשטייט זיך אַז איך האָב דאָ אין זינען
ניט דאָס ייִדישע פאָלק בכלל, נאָר די ייִדיש־וועלטלעבע סביבה וואָס
האָט שוין פאַר זיך געשאַפן זייער בכבוד'ע פּאָזיציעס. סיי פריִער, סיי
נאָכגייער פאָדערן שוין גרינטלעכע רעוויזיעס. אָבער זייער צאָל איז
נאָך אַלץ צו קליין, די ווירקונג ניט גענוג ברייט, און בכלל אין אַ צייט
פון פיזישן חורבן וואָס גייט אַלץ כסדר אָן איז אַ נייער גייסטיקער
אָנהייב אַזוי פיינלעך שווער.

די וואָס זענען געבליבן פאַרוואָרצלט אינם אַמאָליקן ראַדיקאַלן נוסח
האָבן שוין, ווי עס ווייזט אויס, געמאַכט זייערע לעצטע חשבונות מיטן
פאָלק. עס איז אָדער — אָדער, אָדער געטריישאַפט צום נוסח, אָדער —
גאָרניט. און אויב, ווען דער נסיון קומט אָן, האַלט אָפּ דער צווייטער
„אָדער" זיין אומפאַרמיידלעכן נצחון, איז מילא. צו לעצטע חשבונות קען
מען גאָרניט מוסיף זיין, פּונקט ווי מען קען פון זיי גאָרניט אַראָפּנעמען.
אָבער פאַר אַלע אַנדערע איז איצט די צייט צו רעווידירן און איבער־
פאָרמולירן זעם ייִדיש־וועלטלעבן געדאַנקען־גאַנג און ראַטעווען אים פונם
לינגוויסטישן סעקולאַריזם. אויב דאָס וועט ניט געלינגען וועלן מיר
דאַרפן פאַר'ענדיקן אין אַ געפאַלענעם טאָן זייער אַן אינטערעסאַנט קאַפּיטל
אין אונדזער נייסטער געשיכטע: געווען אַ געוואַגטער עקספּערימענט,
אָבער דעם נסיון ניט אויסגעהאַלטן.

The old dowager (Hebrew), on learning that Ruvn Braynin was (also) writing in the Yiddish *Tageblat*:
'I could have understood if he had left me for a young, attractive maid-servant...but for someone like that!?' (*Der groyser kundes*, November 3, 1916)

אַן אָפֿענער בריװ צו אונדזער ייִדישיסטישער אינטעליגענץ

בן־אָדיר

SUMMARY: AN OPEN LETTER TO OUR YIDDISHIST INTELLIGENTSIA BY BEN-ADIR

A major Territorialist leader (1878–1942), in advocating planned and concentrated Jewish settlement in a territory other than conflicted Israel, explains why Yiddishism, without a territorial base of its own, is doomed, particularly given the precarious position of Jewish Eastern Europe.

I.

עס איז שװער זיך אױסמאָלן אַ טיפֿערע טראַגעדיע װי די, װאָס מענטשן, באַהערשטע פֿון שעפֿערישן דראַנג און אידעישן פּאַטאָס, הױבן אָן צו פֿילן, אַז זײיער גײיסטיקער באַדן זינקט אַרגען אין אַ תהום, אַז אַלץ, װאָס האָט אָנגעפֿילט זײיער לעבן מיט גרױסן אינהאַלט און געגעבן אים אַ העכערן זין, גײיט אונטער. װאָרס פֿאַרשװוּנדן און אַרום שאַפֿט זיך אַ פּוסטער חלל פֿון אײַז־קאַלטער פֿרעמדקײט און נשמה־אױסגעלײידיקטקײט.

אַזאַ טראַגעדיע לעבט איצט איבער איבער אונדזער ייִדישיסטישע פֿאָלקס־אינטעליגענץ — אַט־די גאַנצט כּחנה שרײיבער, דיכ־טער, קינסטלער, לערער און קולטור־טוער. נאָך מיט אײן דור פֿריִער — פֿול מוט און גלױבן אין זיך און אין די אױפֿ־געװאַכטע פֿאָלקס כּוחות, פֿול אימפּעט, שװוּנג און געװאוגטן פֿאַרמעסט צו געשטאַלטן בצלמה ובדמותה דאָס גאַנצע מאַ־דערנע ייִדישע קולטור־לעבן — שטײיט זי איצט, אַט־די פֿאָלקס־אינטעליגענץ אונדזערע, געבראָכן, נידערשלאַגן און פֿון פֿאַרצװײיפֿלונג צעפֿרעסן.

און עס איז דאָ פֿון װאָס צו קומען אין פֿאַרצװײיפֿלונג! די לעבנס־ערפֿאַרונגען פֿאַר די לעצטע צװאָנציק־דרײיסיק יאָר האָבן געבראַכט די ביטערסטע ענטוישונג. עס האָט זיך קלאָר און דײטלעך אַרױסגעװיזן, אַז אין די תּנאים פֿון ייִדישער צעזײיטקײט צװישן פֿרעמדע פֿעלקער און פֿרעמדע קולטורן קען ניט געדײיען קײן װעלטלעכע קולטור אױף ייִדיש. זי מוז פֿאַרפֿלײיצט װערן פֿון די מעכטיקע שטראָמען פֿון דעם

אַרומיקן לעבן און פֿאַרשלונגען װערן פֿון די פֿרעמדע הער־שנדיקע קולטורן. אַלײן און פֿאָר זיך פֿאַרמאָגט זי ניט די װידערשטאַנדס־קראַפֿט, װאָס זאָל קענען בײַשטײין דער גװאַל־דיקער אַסימילאַציע־סטיכיע פֿון דער אַרומיקער דרױסנדיקער װעלט. איבערהױפֿט אין אַזאַ ספֿערע װי שפּראַך, װוּ עס פֿאַרקרעפּערן זיך די אומפֿאַרמײידלעכע און כּסדרדיקע פֿיל־פֿאַכע באַציונגען פֿון דעם ייִדישן יחיד מיט דער דרױסנ־דיקער װעלט.

אױב מיט צענדליקער יאָרן צוריק האָבן מיר געהאַט אין די לענדער פֿון די גרױסע ייִדישע מאַסן־ישובים נאָר אַן אױבערשטע דיניקע שיכט פֿון העכערע בורזשואַזיע און אינטעליגענץ, װוּ עס האָט געהערשט די שפּראַך־אַסימילאַציע, אין איצט דרינגט זי דורך און דורך די געדיכטעניש פֿון די פֿאָלקס־מאַסן. דאָ, אין אַמעריקע, האָט אַט־דער אַסימילאַציע־פּראָצעס אָנגענומען אַזאַ ראַשיקן טעמפּ און אַזאַ גרינדלעכע פֿאָרם, אַז עס קען צו לחלוטין קײן שום ספֿק מער ניט זײַן, װוּהין ער פֿירט אונדז. אין אַביסל אַ שװאַכערער פֿאָרם און אַ לאַנגזאַמערן טעמפּ איז דער פֿאָרגעקומען אױך אין די איבע־ריקע לענדער. און אױך דאָרטן איז דער װעג װעג, װוּהין עס פֿירט אונדז אומפֿאַרמײידלעך, קלאָר אָנגעצײיכנט. און עס קען אַפֿילו קײן צװײיפֿל ניט זײַן װעגן דעם פֿאַרסנעלערטן טעמפּ זײַנעם, װען די מחיצות פֿון אומגלײיכהײט און רעכטלאָזיקײט װאָס האָבן דאָרט אָפּגעטײילט די ייִדישע באַפֿעלקערונג פֿו דער אַרומיקער װעלן אָפּגעשאַפֿן װערן.

און עס לעשן זיך אויס די לעצטע פונקען פון דער אי...
לוזיע. אז אנדזער יידישיסטישע פֿאלקס-אינטעליגענץ קע...
אין זי אומשטענדן. אין וועלכע זי געפֿינט זיך. פֿאַרמעכ...
זיך צו פֿאַרהאַלטן אט-דעם פֿאַרפֿלייצנדיקן שטראָם. קיי...
שום אינטעליגענצן קען פֿון זײן אינעווייניק. פֿון זיך אַליין ני...
שעפּן אזעלכע אומגעהײַערע כוחות. סײַדן זי פֿאַרמאָגט אוי...
סער. אין דער דרויסנדיקער ווירקלעכקײט. אין ל...
בעדיקע לעבן. אַ זיכערן אָנהאַלט. אַ בעסטן באָדן. אוי...
וועלכן זי קען שטיין מיט בײדע פֿיס און פֿון אים ציִען ז...
גוטיקע חיות-קוואַלן.

II.

באַטראַכט איר די לאַגע פֿון אַלע זײַטן מיט קלאָרע אױ...
אָפֿענע אויגן און לאָזט זיך ניט פֿאַרפֿירן פֿון פּוסטע אײַנ...
רעדענישן. כדי צו פֿאַרטומלען דאָס אײגענע געוויסן. א...
זײַט איר דורכגעדרונגען מיטן גרויסן און טיפֿן ערנסט פֿ...
דער באמת טראַגישער פּראָבלעם און מיטן לײַנדשאַפֿטלין...
באַגער צו געפֿונען אַ לײַזונג פֿאַר איר. מוזט איר אומב...
דינגט קומען צום אויספֿיר אז ס'איז דאָ נאָר אײן-אײנצי...
קער וועג. וואָס קען אונדז ברענגען די רעטונג. אַז ס'אי...
מעגלעך נאָר אײן-אײנציקע סיטואַציע. וואָ...
קען אַרויספֿירן די יידישיסטישע פֿאלקס-קולטור אויפֿ...
ברייטן טראַקט פֿון געשיכטלעכער אַנטוויקלונג. און דאָ...
איז — שאַפֿן אין אַ וועלכן ניט איז פונקט...
אן אויטאָנאַמען יידישן צענטער מיט יידיש...
אַלס דער אײנציקער שפראַך פֿון גאַנצן...
פּריוואַטן. געזעלשאַפֿטלעכן. קולטורעלן און...
פֿאליטישן לעבן. אַט-דער צענטער וואו קלײן ווי לפֿ"ע ערך...
ער זאָל צוערשט ניט זײַן וועט שוין פֿון אַנהויב אָן געווען...
ניט נאָר פֿאַר זיך אַ זעלבסטשטענדיקער מקור פֿון ברײען ניט...
געשטערטן און אַלזײַטיקן נאַציאָנאַל-קולטורעלן שאַפֿן און...
אַזאַ זיכערס פֿעסטונג. וואָס וואָלט ניט צוגעלאָזט קיינע...
אַסימילאַציע-קוואַליעס—נאָר אויך אַן אויסשליסלעך...
ווירקטיקער שטיק-פונקט פֿאַר דער פֿאלקס-...
קולטור אויף יידיש אומעטום.

האָבן מיר דען פֿאַר זיך אַזאַ לעבעדיקן באַלערעוודיקן...
מוסטער. וואָס רעדט מיט אונדז אַזאַ בילדלעך-קלאָרער און איבער...
צײַגנדיקער שפראַך. אַז ער לאָזט אין דעם פרט ניט איבער...
קיין מינדסטן צווייפֿל. דאָס איז דער ארץ-ישראל-מוסטער...
איז דען דאָרט דער העברעִיש-עקספּעריִמענט אַ דורכאויס...
געקונצעלטע זאַך. אַ דורך און דורך אומנאַטירלעכער אויפֿסט...
וואָס גייט צו היפוך צו די נאַרמאַלע פראָצעסן און טענדענצן...
פֿון סאָציאַל-קולטורעלן לעבן. אויפֿלעבן אַ טויטע שפראַך...
און אַרויסצווינגען זי אויף דער באַטעלקערונג. וועון קײַנע...
נאַטירלעכע לעבנס-באַדינגונגען שטייסן צו דעם ניט. נאָר...
בלױז לױט לױם עפּעס אַן אידעאָלאָגישן באַגער — האָט מען גאָר...

געקענט דענקען. אז אַזאַ עקספּעריִמענס זאָל אין אַ וועלשעכ...
ניט איז מאָס זיך איינגעגבן ? אַז אױף אַזאַ געקינצלטער...
אומאַטירלעכער שפראַך-באַזע זאָל זיך אַנטוויקלען אן אַל...
זײַטיקע לעבעדיקע קולטור ? נאָר אַזאַ גוואַלדיקע קראַפֿט...
פֿאַרמאָגט שוין דאָס אויסגאַנבע נאַציאָנאַלע לעבן. אַז עס קען...
באמת ווונדער שאַפֿן. דער לפֿ"ע ערך קליינער העברעִיזירטער...
ישוב אין ארץ-ישראל (העברעִיזירט איז איינגטלען נאָר אַ...
טייל פֿון דעם ישוב). האָט פֿאַר אַ גאַנץ קורצער צײַט גע...
שאַפֿן אַזאַ ברייטן און פֿעכטן באָדן פֿאַר העברעִישער קול...
טור. וואָס מיט דעם קאָנען גאָר אין קיין שום פֿאַרגלײַך...
ניט גיין די אַלע העברעִישע פֿאָזיציעס. וואָס זענען געשאַפֿן...
געוואָרען איבער דער גאַנצער לענג און ברייט פֿון גרויכן גלות...
אין משך פֿון צעלעכע דורות נאַכאַנאַנד. ס'איז גענוג בלויז...
צו פֿאַרגלײַכן. די פֿאַרשפרייטונג פֿון דער רײַכער און אַזױ...
פֿאַרצווײַגטער העברעִישער פּרעסע און ליטעראַטור אין ארץ...
ישראל. פֿון אײן זײַט. און אין גאַנצן חוץ לארץ. פֿון דער...
אַנדער זײַט. כדי פֿאַר איך זאָל באַשטײנפערטלעך קלאָר ווערן...
דער אומגעהײַערער באַטײַט פֿון דעם נאַציאָנאַל אויטאָנאָמישן...
פֿאַקטאָר פֿאַר דער אַנטוויקלונג פֿון דער נאַציאָנאַלער קולטור.

ס'איז קלאָר פֿון זיך אַליין. אַז גאָר ניט דער עלך גרע...
סער וואָלט געווען די קולטור-שאַפֿנדיקע ראַלע פֿון אַט דעם...
נאַציאָנאַל-אויסגאַנדאַמען פֿאַקטאָר. וועון אַנשסאַט דעם גע...
קינצלטן. אומנאַטירלעכן העברעִיש. וואָס שטעלט אויף אַ...
דיקע וואַנט צווישן אים און דעם קולטור-לעבן און די שאַ...
פֿונגס-קוואַלן פֿון גרויסן איבעריִקן פֿאָלק. — וואָלט די קול...
טור-באַזע געווען די לעבעדיקע. נאַטירלעכע פֿאלקס-שפראַך...
ווו עס פֿולסירט ברײַ דאָס פֿאלבליוטיקע פֿאלקס-לעבן —...
יידיש. דאָס וואָלט ניט נאָר פֿאָנדענט נײַע מעכטיקע קולטור...
קוואַלן אין לאַנד גופֿא. נאָר דאָס וואָלט אומגעהײַער באַ...
פֿרוכפערט דעם באָדן פֿון גער דער מאַדערנער יידישער קולטור...
אין זי יידישע ישובים פֿון גער דער וועלט. דאָס וואָלט...
אויך קאַלאָסאַל געהויבן דעם ווערט און די חשיבות פֿון...
יידיש. געשטאַרקט דעם פֿעסטן גלויבן אין זײַן צוקונפֿט און...
דערמונטערט און באַפֿליגלט די קולטור-טוער.

ווייל איך פֿרעגן אונדזער יידישיסטישע פֿאלקס-אינטעלי...
גענץ — אַט די גאַנצע כהנה שרײַבער. דיכטער. קינסטלער...
לערערדער אין קולטור-טוער. וואָס פֿאַר זײ איז די קולטור אויף...
יידיש דער עיקר-תוך פֿון זייער גײַסטיקן לעבן אין שאַפֿן:...
ווי אַזוי. אויב ניט ווי אַ רעטונג. ווי אַ...
מין גאולה-בשורה וואָלט איר באַדאַרפֿט...
אויפֿנעמען די שטרעבונג צו שאַפֿן אט דעם...
אויטאָנאַמישן יידישן טעריטאָריִאַלן צענ...
טער? ווער. אויב ניט איר. וואָלט באַדאַרפֿט...
זײַן דער איבערגעגעבנסטער. דער באַגײַס...
טערטער אַוואַנגאַרד פֿון אָט דער באַוועגונג ?...
גונג? איז דאָן איז דען קיין צופֿעליקײט געווען. וואָס זי...

העברעישע אינטעליגענץ. די העברעישע לערער און קולטור-
טוער זענען געוואָרן די ערשטע פֿאַנאַטישע אָנהענגער פֿון
חיבת-ציון-ציוניזם און די בלב ונפֿש איבערגעגעבענע פיאָנערן
פֿון דער אויפֿבוי-אַרבעט אין ארץ-ישראל.

III.

און חוץ דעם — און דאָס האָט ניט קיין קלענערן באַ-
טײַט — מיט וואָס אַנדערש קענט איר איצט קומען צום
ייִדישן פֿאָלק, דעם אַזוי אויפֿגעטרייסלטן און אַזוי פֿאַר-
פֿייניקטן? וואָס פֿאַר אַן אנדער טרייסט און האָפֿענונג קענט
איר טראָגן דער אַזוי אויפֿגעשווישדערטער נשמה פֿון אײַער-
פֿעניקן ייִדנטום? קענט איר נאָך אַזעלכע ביטערע און
פֿינצטערע ערפֿאַרונגען און איבערלעבונגען פֿון דער ערש-
טער עמאַנציפאַציע-תקופה ביז איצט קומען צו אים ווידער-
גלײַך ווי גאָרנישט איז געשען, בלויז מיט ס ת ם-לאָזונגען
פֿון פֿרײַהייט, גלײַכהייט און ברידערלעכקייט, פֿון ס ת ם-
דעמאָקראַטיע און אַפֿילו פֿון ס ת ם-סאָציאַליזם?

טראַכט זיך אַרײַן אין אונדזער מאַרטירדער-געשיכטע, וועט
איר שאַרף דערפֿילן די אומפֿאַרמײַדלעכקייט, אז נאָך
יעדער פֿאָלקס-קאַטאַסטראָפֿע, זאָלן ייִדן ליידנשאַפֿטלעך אָנהויבן
זוכן דעם וועג צו זיך, דעם וועג צו נאַציאָנאַלער אויסלײַ-
זונג. דאָס איז דאָך דער זין פֿון די אלע מיסטיש-משיחישע
באַוועגונגען אין אַמאָליקע צײַטן און פֿון "עם-עולם",
"ביל״ו", חיבת-ציון, ציוניזם אין אונדזערע צײַטן. ווען
איר נעמט אין אַכט, אז פֿאַר די לעצטע פֿאַר טויזנט יאר,
זינט דעם צווייטן חורבן, האָט דאָס ייִדישע פֿאָלק נאָך קיין-
מאָל אזא מאָנומדיקע קאַטאַסטראָפֿע ווי איצט ניט דורכגע-
לעבט, דאַרף פֿאַר אײַך קלאָר ווערן, ווי גוואָלדיק וועט איצט
זיין בײַ די ייִדישע מאַסן דער דראַנג צו זיך, צו אן אייגע-
נער היים, צו אַ לעבן פֿאַר זיך נאָך די אלע אינקוויזיציע-
שינוויים אין די געטאָס, קאָנצענטראַציע-לאַגערן, נאָך די
אלע שרעק און פֿורעניות פֿון די בהלה-לויפֿענישן און
וואַגלענישן איבער די אזוי אומהיימלעך געווארענע ימים.
איבער די אלע ווּיסטע און פֿינצטערע וועגן!

ניט בלויז אויפֿגענעמען דעם גרויסן צער און צאָרן פֿון
פֿאָלק, נאָר נאָר אײַנגעזאָפֿן אין זיך אַט דעם טיפֿסטן צאַפֿלדיקן
נשמה-באַגער זיינעם און געבן אים אויסדרוק, געבן אים
פֿאָרם און געשטאַלט, ווערן די פֿירער און וועג-ווײַזער פֿון
פֿאָלק — דאָס איז דאָך פֿון תמיד אָן געווען די גרויסאַרטיקסטע
און הייליקסטע שליחות פֿון אונדזער גײַסטיקער עליטע.
איבערהויפט אין אַזוינע אויסשליסלעכע מאָמענטן פֿון אויס-
שליסלעכן ברוך און איבערבראָך אין פֿאָלקס-לעבן. אין
דעם ליגט דאָך דער סוד פֿון דער אומגעהײַערער ראָלע,
דער איינציקער אין איר ארט, וואָס די אינטעליגענץ, אָט
די נײַסטיקע עליטע אונדזערע האָט אין דער גאַנצער לענג

פֿון אונדזער געשיכטע געשפילט אין לעבן און גורל פֿון
פֿאָלק. •

דער איינציקער אויסנאָס זײַט איר. דאָס איז דער ערשטער
פֿאָל, ווען אונדזער פֿאָלקס-אינטעליגענץ האָט פֿאַרלאָרן דעם
אינסטווינקט, אינסטימען קאַנטאַקט מיטן פֿאָלק, האָט אויס-
געמיטן די גרויסע און געהויבענע שליחות אירע — און איז
דערפֿאַר אַזוי שווער באַשטראָפֿט געוואָרן !... אדרבה,
קוקט זיך צו, צו וואָס איר זײַט געקומען : ווער פֿון פֿאָלק
קערט זיך אָן ביט אײַך ? ווער הערט זיך צו אײַך צו און
ווער קוקט זיך אום אויף אײַך ?... איז מערקווערדיק,
קינער וועט ניט וואָגן צו לייקענען, אז איר האָט אַרײַנ-
געשריבן אַזַ שיין בלאַט אין אונדזער קולטור-געשיכטע, נאָך
מער — ס׳וועט אפֿשר ניט זיין קיין גוזמא צו זאָגן, אז
אײַערע קולטור-שאַפֿונגען פֿאַר די לעצטע פֿאַר דורות קענען
זיך פֿאַרמעסטן מיט די קולטור-שאַפֿונגען פֿון אונדזערע
גלענצנדיקע תקופות. יעדנפֿאַלס, אין גלות-צײַט, אָבער מיט
דעם אַליין קענט איר ניט קומען צו אונדזער פֿאָלק, אונדזער
פֿאָלק באָדערט ניט בלויז קולטור, אויסגעשטיילט און איזאָ-
לירט פֿון דעם קולטור-שאַפֿער, נאָר קודם כל דעם מענטשן
גופֿא, דעם גאַנצן מענטשן, דאָס האַרץ, די נשמה זיינע.
וואָס זאָל זײַן אַרגאַניש באַהאָפֿט מיט אים, מיטן פֿאָלק, און
אויף קיין אין כאַבענט ניט אויפֿהערן צו ווײַטאָגן מיט
זיינע ווײַטאָגן און צו טרוימען זײַנע טרוימען-

דאָס איז די וויכטיקסטע, די צענטראַלסטע לעבנס-נדראַגע
אין דער ערשטער רייַ פֿאַר אײַך גופֿא. ווייל
סוף כל סוף איז אין תמיד גילטיק מרדכיס יאָרענונג צו אכתרן
— ריוח והצלה יעכוד ליהודים ממקום אחר, ות ובית אביך
תאבדו — פֿאָרן ייִדישן פֿאָלק וועט די רעטונג קומען אויך
אָן אײַך, פֿון ערגעץ אנדערש ווו, אַבער איר ?...

IV.

טאנהט איר אבער !

שאַפֿן אַ היים, אַן אויטאנאָמישן ייִדישן ישוב, אויסער
ארץ-ישראל, איז אין אַן אוכמעגלעכקייט, איז אַ אוטאפיע, אַ
חלום. און פֿאַר אוטאפיעס און הלומות קענט איר זיך ניט
באַגײַסטערן און אויף אויבן וועג פֿון אוטאפיעס און הלומות
ווילט איר דאָס פֿאָלק ניט פֿאַרפֿירן, ניט רופֿן אפֿילו — און
דערצו ווייסט איר אויף זיכער, אז דאָס פֿאָלק וויל עס ניט-
וועט עס ניט וועלן...

ווייל איך אײַך פֿרעגן :

האָבן די ערפֿאַרונגען פֿאַר די לעצטע שטלעכע צענדליק
יאר, פֿון אַזעלכע גוואַלדיקע וועלט-איבערקערענישן און
קאַפֿשווענדלדיקע איבעראַשונגען אויף אײַן האַר ניט צע-
טריַיסלט אײַער פֿאַנאַטיש-דאָגמאטיש גלויבן אין דער

אבסאָלוטער גילטיקייט אין אַלמעכטיקייט פֿון אָט דעם אַנט־
שיידענעם „לעצטן אַרגומענט" — דעם אוטאָפּיע־אַרגומענט?
לערנען אייך ניט די ערפֿאַרונגען, ווי פֿאַלש און פֿאַרפֿירע־
ריש אָט־דער פֿאַנאַטיש־דאָגמאַטישער גלויבן איז געווען?
פֿילט איר גאָרניט אַז אפֿשר אין 99 פֿון 100 פֿאַלן זענען דאָס
ניט עפּעס „אָביעקטיוווע געזעצן", נאָר אייער סוביעק־
טיוווער ווילן, אייער נשמה־באַגער געווען דער פוסק
אחרון, די לעצטע אינסטאַנצן, וואָס האָט באַשטימט, וואָס
איז רעאַל און וואָס איז אוטאָפּיש?

און ווי ווילקירלעך, ווי אָפּנאַרעריש איז דער פּאַק פֿון
אָט־דער „לעצטער אינסטאַנץ"! נאָר אין קאָנקרעטן ביי־
שפּיל:

ווען בלויז מיט אַ פֿאַר צענדליק יאָר צוריק וואָלט מען
אייך געזאָגט, אַז אין אַ פֿאַר צענדליק יאָר אַרום וועט די
קאָלאָניזאַציע אין ארץ ישראל דערגרייכן צו דער מדרגה,
צו וועלעכער זי האָט דערגרייכט: קאַנצענטרירן דאָרט אַ
ייִדישן קיבוץ פֿון העכער אַ האַלב מיליאָן און שאַפֿן דאָס־
וואָס דאָרט איז געשאַפֿן געוואָרן — וואָלט איר דעמאָלט
פשוט ניט אויסגעהוזקט אָט־די „ווייסטע אוטאָפּיע" און דעם
„פוסטן חלום"?

וואָלט איר?... באמת איז דאָס ניט קיין היפּאָטעטישער
ביישפּיל, נאָר אַ לעבעדיקער פֿאַקט: איר, מיר אַלע, וואָס
געהערן צו דער מחנה ייִדישיסטישער פֿאָלקס־אינטעליגענץ,
האָבן סיי פֿריִער, סיי דעמאָלט באַוויזן באותות וכופתים
מיט סטאַטיסטיק און „ווינשאַפֿט" אַז אַזאַ קאָלאָניזאַציע
פֿון ארץ־ישראל, אין אַזאַ טעמפּ איז אַ ווייסטע אוטאָפּיע און
אַ פוסטער חלום.

ווען איר זיכער ענטפֿערן דערויף: מיר האָבן דעמאָלט
ניט געקענט פֿאָרויסזען אַזוינע „משונהדיקע" סיטואַציעס,
ווי דאָס שליסן די טויערן פֿון די אימיגראַציע לענדער,
ווי דער אויפֿקום און פֿאַרשפּרייטונג פֿון דער פֿאַשיסטישער
און נאַציאָנאַל־סאָציאַליסטישער מגפֿה און נאָך אַזוינע ווילדע,
אומדערוואַרטע פֿאַקטאָרן, וואָס האָבן גורם געווען די
אויסטערגעוויינלעכע קאָניונקטור, וואָס האָט זיך געשאַפֿן פֿאַר
און אין ארץ ישראל.

געוויס זייט איר גערעכט: איר האָט דעמאָלט ניט גע־
קענט פֿאָרויסזען... נו — און איצט קענט איר פֿאָרויס־
זען? און איצט האָט איר גרונד און רעכט צו באַשטימען
פֿון פֿאָרויס מיט פֿעסטער זיכערקייט, אַז אין דער נייער
וועלט־סיטואַציע, וואָס עס שאַפֿט זיך און וועט זיך שאַפֿן
נאָך דער מלחמה אין אויסגעשלאָסן אַ ייִדישע מאַסן־קאָ־
לאָניזאַציע אין ערגעץ אַ פֿרייִלאַנד, אין אויסגעשלאָסן צו
שאַפֿן אַ ייִדישע היים, אַן אויטאָנאָמען ייִדישן קיבוץ אוי־
סער ארץ ישראל? אמת, איר, יעדנפֿאַלס אַ טייל פֿון אייך,
האָט איבערגענומען ביי די ציוניסטן אַ נייעם און ביז גאָר
טראגיקאָמיש פֿאַר אייך שלאָג־אַרגומענט: אַז דעם נאַציאָנאַלן

ראַמאַנטיזם פֿון ארץ ישראל איז אַ ייִדישע מאַסן־קאָלאָניזאַ־
ציע אויסגעשלאָסן. פֿרעגט זיך אָבער: זענט איר טאַקע
אייַנגעגלויבט אין אמונה שלמה, אַז נאָר הימל און ערד און
ארץ ישראל־ראַמאַנטיזם און אַלץ וואָס חוץ דעם איז פֿון
טייוול? און לעבנס־נויטווענדיקייטן, דרינגענדיקע און פֿול־
וואַגיקע פֿאַלקס אינטערעסן און נאַציאָנאַלע באַדערפֿענישן
האָבן קיין ממשות נישטאָ? ווייסט איר טאַקע אויף געוויס,
אַז ווען אַפֿילו די פּאָליטישע פערספּעקטיוון פֿאַר אַ ווײַ־
טערדיקער ברייטער קאָלאָניזאַציע פֿון ארץ ישראל זאָל נאָך
דער מלחמה זיין האָפֿענונגסלאָז, וועלן דאָך ניט געמאַכט
ווערן קיינע פרוון פֿון אַ ייִדישער מאַסן־קאָלאָניזאַציע
ערגעץ אַנדערש ווו? און טאָמער וועלן זיי געמאַכט ווערן,
וועלן זיי אומפֿאַרמיידלעך זיין אַ דורכפֿאַל?

דאָס אַלץ ווייסט איר ניט און קענט ניט וויסן, דאָס
איינציקע, וואָס איר קענט, איז ווילן, מיטן גאַנצן האַרצן,
מיט דער גאַנצער נשמה ווילן, אַז דאָס זאָל געשען, אַז
אַזאַ קאָלאָניזאַציע זאָל פֿאַרקומען און זאָל האָבן הצלחה,
אַז אַן אויטאָנאַמער ייִדישער ישוב זאָל געשאַפֿן ווערן, און
אַז איר וועט אַזוי וועלן, וועט איר אין דעם גלויבן־
ווייט איר פֿון דעם שאַפֿן מוט און אַקטיוויטעט, וועט איר
זיך אַליין פֿאַר דעם באַגייַסטערן און אויך אנדערע פֿאַר
דעם באַגייַסטערן, אויך ביי אנדערע וועקן גלויבן, מוט און
אַקטיוויטעט — און וועט ווערן אַ גרויסער בוידנדיקער און
שאָפֿנדיקער כוח אין דעם אויפֿבוי פֿון דעם נייַעם ייִדישן
לעבן בכלל און קולטור־לעבן בפֿרט.

איך ווייס, אַז אין אייַערע קריינן, אין די קריינן פֿון דער
ייִדישער אינטעליגענץ, פֿון דער ייִדישער פּרעסע, פֿון דער
ייִדישער געזעלשאַפֿטלעכקייט בכלל דאָ אין אַמעריקע איז
די טעמע טעריטאַריאַליזם ניט נאָר אָפּגעפֿרעגט, נאָר נאָך
ערגער — „ניט אינטערעסאַנט", לאַנגווייַליק, ס'איז פֿאַר
שוואונדן אַפֿילו די פֿריִערדיקע ביטול־באַציִונג צו איר. זי
ווערט גלאַט טויט מיט־פֿאַרשוויגן — וואָרום אין דען כדאי צו
מטפל זיין זיך מיט דעם איר, בשעת די ייִדישע פּרעסע
זיינען דאָ, ביז אריבער די
ברעגן, איבערגעפֿילט מיט אַזעלכע שפּאַנענדיקע, ברענענדיקע
ייִדישע טעמעס און ייִדישע פּראָבלעמעס — אַדרבה, קוקט
איבער בלויז די קעפּלעך פֿון אַ ליאַדער ייִדישער בלאַט־
צייַטונג, וואָס איר דאָס גלייך דערזון באַשיִמפּפּערלעך...

אָבער אַ חוק דער אַמעריקאַנער ייִדישער געזעלשאַפֿט־
לעכקייס און ייִדישער פּרעסע, איז נאָך פֿאַראַן אַ גרויס און
אומגעהײַ־טער סראגישע ייִדיש צו לעבן — און דאָרט קענט איר
איצט מער צו די טעריטאַריאַליטישע פּראָבלעם. די פּראָבלעם
פֿון שאָפֿן אַ היים פֿאַרן היימלאָזן ייִדישן פֿאַלק פֿאַר קיין
פֿאַל ניט אויסגעמיידן, און ניט נאָר פֿאַר דער ייִדישער
וועלט, אויך פֿאַר דער דרויסנדיקער וועלט שטייט זי

בפירוש ווי איינע פֿון אירע אַקטועלע פּראָבלעמעס — אוֹן מיט אײַער ביטול און טײַטס־פֿאַרשווײַגן וועט איר זי שוין פֿון דעם וועלט־סדר־היום ניט אַראָפּנעמען.

אין ווידער אַמאָל — די פֿראַגע שטײט קודם־כל פֿאַר אײַך אַלײן: ווילט איר העלפֿן שאַפֿן דעם פֿעסטן באָדן אונטער אײַערע אײגענע פֿיס, ווילט איר זיך אײַנשליסן אין אַנקומענדיקן לעבנס־שטראָם, ווילט איר סטימולירן אײַער שאַפֿונגס־קראַפֿט, אלֵענען נײַע שפּרודלדיקע קוואַלן פֿאַר

אײַער שאַפֿונגס־גײַסט, ווילט איר אַנפֿילן אײַער לעבן מיט זין, מוט און גלויבן — איז דער וועג אָפֿן פֿאַר אײַך.

* * *

נאָר אפֿשר האָט איר אַנדערע וועגן און אויסוועגן — איז פֿאַרוואָס ווײַזט איר זיי ניט אָן ? פֿאַרוואָס שווײַגט איר ?...

1942

יונה ראָזנפעלד

טשאַרטאָריסק, וואָלין, 1880
ניו־יאָרק, פאַר. שטאַטן, 1944

———◆———

צווישן טאָג און נאַכט, (דערצ.)
אין שאָטנס פון טויט, (דערצ.)
קאָנקורענטן, (דערצ., פיעסע)
אַ ייִד, (מעמואַרן)

———◆———

דערצײלער

ח. רויזענבלאַט

(חיים רויזענבליט)

דאָרף רישאַשע, אוקראַינע, 1878
לאָס אַנדזשעלעס, פ " ש, 1956

———◆———

דאָס לעבען פון אַ ייִדיש יינגל
מיין ליכטיקע נסיעה,
אליהו הנביאס כוס
אין שענסטן טאָג פון האַרבסט

———◆———

פאָעט

מנחם באָרײשאָ

(מנחם גאָלדבערג)

בריסק ד'ליטע, רוסלאַנד, 1888
ניו־יאָרק, פאַר. שטאַטן, 1949

———◆———

דער גייער, (ראָמאַן אין פערז)
זאַול רימער, (פאָעמע)
דער גילגול, (פאָעמע)
תפילות, (פאָעמעד־ציקל)

———◆———

פאָעט, עסייאיסט

ישראל־יעקב שוואַרץ

פעטרושאַני, ליטע, 1885
לעבט אין פלאָרידאַ, פאַר. שטאַטן

———◆———

קענטאָקי
העברעאישע פאָעזיע
אונזער ליד פון שפּאַניע
משה רבינו, (מעשיות)

———◆———

פאָעט

דוד בערגעלסאָן

אַכרימאָווע, אוקראַינע, 1884
אומגעבראַכט, ראַטנרוסלאַנד, 1952

———◆———

נאָך אַלעמען, (ראָמאַן)
דער טויבער, (דראַמע)
ביים דניעפּר, (ראָמאַן)
לא אמות — כי אחיה! (פיעסע)

———◆———

דערצײלער, ראָמאַניסט,
דראַמאַטורג

פרץ מאַרקיש

פאָלאַנאַיע, וואָלין, 1895
אומגעבראַכט, ראַטנרוסלאַנד, 1952

———◆———

די קופּע, (פאָעמע)
דאָר־אויס דאָר־אײַן, (ראָמאַן)
ניט געדאַגהט, (פיעסע)
מלחמה (ראָמאַן אין פערז)

———◆———

פאָעט, ראָמאַניסט, דראַמאַטורג

1. Yoyne Roznfeld, 1880–1944; Writer of short stories; 2. Kh(es) Roznblat, 1878–1956; Poet; 3. Menakhem Boreysho, 1880–1949; Poet, essayist; 4. Yisroel-yankev Shvarts, 1885–1971; Poet; 5. Dovid Berglson, 1884–1952; Writer of short stories, novelist, playwright; 6. Perets Markish, 1895–1952; Poet, novelist, playwright.

Who Needs Yiddish?
A Study in Language and Ethics

JOSEPH C. LANDIS

In the years since the Second World War, Jewish life in America has experienced two major accommodations. First, it has accomodated itself to the American community at large; and as it has done so, it has come to be not only politely tolerated but, to a large extent, accepted by the predominantly Christian society. Second, to the degree that Jews have been accepted as Jews, they have come also to accept themselves as Jews, to accommodate themselves to their Jewishness. But, as they turn inward to inspect what is Jewish in them or in their fellow Jews, they are often dismayed at what they find – or fail to find. And so, with varying degrees of conscious intention in their quest, large numbers of Jews are troubled seekers, and others, with even less real awareness, turn as though by impulse alone to things Jewish.

Thus it is that among the phenomena of this 'return' in the Period of the Third Generation is the increasing evidence of a mounting regard for Yiddish among American Jews, as though they were coming to feel for it the affection for *mame-loshn*: the stream of Yiddish records, the numerous translations from Yiddish, the growth of Yiddish theatrical groups among the native born, the plays translated or adapted from Yiddish – for example, 'The Dybbuk' (on television, in university playhouses, and in the commercial theater), 'The World of Sholem Aleichem', the hit musical 'Fiddler on the Roof' (based on Sholem Aleichem's 'Tevye'), 'The Golem', etc. Even the government of Israel has begun in recent years to relent in its public hostility to Yiddish. Yet the Jewish 'Establishment' here, the *hoykhe fenster* of organized Jewish life, continues to pay scant attention to Yiddish. It is symptomatic that in the calendar of musical months and historical weeks which is proclaimed by the upper echelons of cultural leadership Yiddish has not been found worthy of a single hour, not even of a minute of respectful silence. On occasion a pained protest is heard from a rabbi, crying out, as one did recently: 'The American Jewish community goes about its activities in organization, synagogue and school...as though Yiddish never existed. We consciously refrain from harvesting the rich vines of Yiddish prose and poetry which could do so much to nourish our people's faith and self-respect'. On occasion a Jewish Center schedules a lecture on Yiddish literature. On occasion an organization like the American Jewish Congress publishes a record album for Yiddish instruction. But the solid wall of 'official' intransigeance remains, whether based on ideologically rationalized hostility to Yiddish, or on pathetically misguided contempt, or on sheer indifference. At best, what little official recognition there is remains either sporadic or grudging or condescendingly directed at 'golden-age' groups. In the 'Establishment' the disdainful question, asked or unasked, seems to be, 'Who needs Yiddish?'

Courses in Yiddish or in Yiddish literature have been established in New York City at such schools as Brooklyn College, City College, Queens College, Columbia University, and the New School, in Chicago at Roosevelt College, and, most recently, in Los Angeles at UCLA. Surely, one might have thought, the two large Jewish universities would move with alacrity in the same direction. But again the attitudes prevalent in the Establishment are painfully clear. At Yeshiva University, the Yiddish course is merely an adjunct to the courses in Rabbinic studies. And Brandeis did nothing until tempted by the offer of a $50,000 endowment made by the late Jacob Berg of the Sholem Aleichem Folk Institute of New York to support the chair which bears his name.

If such is the attitude that dominates in the leadership of Jewish community life, one need hardly be surprised that it encourages, even among the multitudes who feel a warmth for the language, a puzzled sense of defeat or of wonder – really, why Yiddish? The answers that are quite readily forthcoming from those who value Yiddish seem not always to convince those at whom they are directed.

Mindful of the Great Catastrophe that destroyed not only six million of our people but the very world that for a thousand years had been a Jewish world, a Jewish civilization, some cry out: Respect for the language of these martyred millions! If Hebrew is our *loshn kodesh*, Yiddish is our *loshn hakdoshim*, as Chaim Weizmann called it, the language of our martyrs. But the skeptic and the utilitarian, as well as the hostile, remain unconvinced. Reverence for the dead comes the reply, does not require knowledge of their language. We can mourn them in another tongue. We do not need Yiddish for our sorrow.

What if one says to them, as many do, that Yiddish is the language of a thousand years of Jewish life, nearly a third of our entire history? Can we blithely ignore the creativity of a thousand years? Are we, as Jews or as human beings, so rich in our cultural heritage, in the bequests of our forebears, that we can afford not to know the language whose literature can be ranked in its achievements no less than among the second literatures of Europe, behind only those of the great nations? Would it not be wasteful and foolish for us not to claim and know those Yiddish writers of the past and present to whom the non-Jewish world is according increasing respect? Yet the obdurately utilitarian will still reply: However imposing the literature, however glad we are to claim it, we can do so in translation; we can enjoy the riches of the past in a more accessible tongue.

The friends of Yiddish, convinced that Jewish life needs Yiddish, add another argument, perhaps even weightier. No one can have an identity without a past, and in Yiddish is contained the record of a thousand years of that past, often the exclusive record. In it are embedded the sufferings and the strivings, the defeats and the victories, the arrivals and departures that are a part, not only of Jewish history but also of the history of the nations. To know ourselves, must we not know the world that shaped us, the experiences that brought us where we are? And is not Yiddish the language in which these experiences are recorded? Still there are those who would reply: let the historian and the scholar serve as the link and interpret the past for us.

Even the argument that Yiddish is still the international language of Jewish life is met with the reply: Ah, but it has no future. If it is the language that is still spoken and understood by Jews the world over, how long will that be so, they inquire. Though it is still the language in which the facts of contemporary Jewish life the world over are recorded by a vigorous and vital press in greater detail than they are available elsewhere, how much longer will that press continue to serve us? 'The dynamic of Yiddish is waning', writes a distinguished editor. It is a dying language, we are informed. As though a language had a life of its own independent of the lives of those who speak it! As though those who speak have no choice of what they speak! As though human determination and obstinacy are helpless! As though there were no exertion of a less admirable obstinacy to ignore the waning 'dynamic' or even to force it to wane.

Nonetheless, in spite of such hostility or indifference, in spite of such deafness to appeals for the defense of a language hallowed by the blood of martyrs, bearer of a rich cultural heritage, channel of a thousand years of the mainstream of Jewish experience, vehicle of communication among the members of a worldwide Jewish community – in spite of such ill-concealed contempt in high or holy places, the sea of Yiddish refuses to dry up. Instead of receding with the decrease in numbers of those for whom it is a first language, Yiddish seems to be reaching out among native American Jews, some of whom persist in sending their children to Yiddish schools, but many more of whom buy the Yiddish books in translation, go to Yiddish plays in English and in Yiddish, and buy the steady deluge of recordings of Yiddish songs, sung by some of our finest singers, both those who know Yiddish well and those whose pronunciation betrays a less intimate knowledge. Is not this the voice of the people expressing a sense that in Yiddish lies something authentically and distinctively Jewish that can help satisfy the hunger for ingredients of Jewish identity in a world whose great pressures are towards uniformity without and loneliness within and the negation of meaningful identity?

Underlying this response is a great but neglected truth: the Yiddish language is not only distinctively Jewish, but it is also uniquely Jewish, and it is, above all, essentially Jewish, so that without it the distinctive identity we recognize as Jewish suffers a grievous loss and a grave alteration. And these qualities of being, uniquely and essentially Jewish, are ultimately incapable of translation into any other language. Without Yiddish our Jewishness is but a puny and a paltry thing. Who needs Yiddish? To anyone examining the language in relation to the qualities that for a millennium and more most Jews have regarded as essential to any conception of Jewish being, one answer seems inescapable. To anyone thinking of communicating these Jewish qualities in a language other than Yiddish, one answer seems unavoidable: Jewish life needs Yiddish as the irreplaceable vehicle of its historic and unique essence. When we are confronted with the cliché expressed by many readers that 'something is lost in translation' or that an artist like Sholem Aleichem is untranslatable, what they are really asserting is not only that the art of a Sholem Aleichem suffers in translation; this is true of most writers, whatever their language. What they are sensing is the loss or serious diminution of the essential *Jewishness* of the work.

The cause of this loss or diminution inheres in the very nature of Yiddish; for Yiddish is not merely a language spoken by millions of Jews. English is too. Nor is it merely a language spoken exclusively by Jews. Ladino is too. It is ultimately a language shaped and developed to embody and express the *Jewish being* of the thousand-year-old civilization built by Ashkenazi Jews and brought to its noblest flowering in Eastern Europe. Two remarkable achievements are to be credited to Ashkenazi Jewry. Animated by a complex of values both implicit and explicit in prior Jewish history and thought, values which in their total constellation are an entity unique in human history, Ashkenazi Jewry proceeded, first, to bring these values to their richest fulfillment. 'I feel justified in saying', writes Abraham Joshua Heschel in relation to this era, 'that it was the golden period in Jewish history, in the history of the Jewish soul'. And it was so golden a period because Ashkenazi Jewry paid not merely lip service to a humane, life-affirming, and man-revering ethic, but to a remarkable degree it embodied that ethic in the pattern of its life, in the structure of its institutions, in the ceremony of its customs and rituals, in the celebration of its holidays, and in the observance of its traditions. Behind all of these is clearly discernible that sense of life and of man, of his duties and obligations, which its values asserted.

But even beyond that achievement lies a second one, fully as remarkable: Ashkenazi Jewry took a Germanic dialect and shaped it into a language in which Jewish ethic and Jewish way of life, Jewish value and Jewish sense of life are embodied in the repatterned sentence style and structure, in the altered pronunciation and word order, in the reshaped inflectional forms and their derivatives, in the enlarged vocabulary, in the created folk expressions and sayings, in the metaphors and allusions. At the heart of the 180,000 words of the language stand the twelve or thirteen thousand Hebrew words and phrases and their derivatives, absorbed orginally from Torah and Talmud, from liturgy and commentary, which pumped the ethical lifeblood of Yiddish. And Yiddish took the Hebrew material and imbedded it in Yiddish contexts. It took the Hebrew words and created new Hebrew from them. And the two elements sustained and nourished each other into a linguistic fulfillment of historic voices and a linguistic embodiment of historic visions, into a bearer of a unique concept and conduct of life. The meanings of Yiddish may more or less be rendered; the experience of the uniquely Jewish values and attitudes and feelings, the ways and the life context which they express and which are vital to Jewish being are left behind.

Yiddish is thus really the language of *teitsh*, as it once was called, of translation of Hebrew writ, not only in a literal sense but in a much larger sense as well; for Yiddish is the translation into language of the ethic of Ashkenazi Jews and of the embodiment of their ethic in a way of life and in quality of being. And they knew it. Is not this the reason why, of all the languages that Jews spoke after they gave up Hebrew, this language alone they called a Jewish language? In this language alone the word for the Jew and his speech are the same: *yidn redn yidish*.

If Yiddish is the linguistic embodiment of Jewish being, then to embrace it is neither a sentimental gesture nor a scholarly attainment nor a cultural luxury; it is an affirmation and acceptance of something vital and essential to the definition of our Jewishness. The very large number of Yiddish words and phrases that persist in English, the expressions that we cling to and that we use, trying to leaven English for ourselves as Hebrew leavened the Germanic dialect that became Yiddish – these are a clue to our sense of the inadequacy of the English approximations of Jewish concepts. To the extent that the 'language habits' that are native to Yiddish sound strange in English, to the extent that these value-laden words, phrases, and constructions that are native to Yiddish sound foreign in English, to that extent is Yiddish an indispensable vehicle of Jewish being and an irreplaceable expression of the uniqueness of the Jewish way. And that extent is indeed considerable. For every principle central to Jewish ethic and Jewish value, to Jewish practice and Jewish character, there are Yiddish words and phrases that defy translation. Explained in English they may be; truly translated, rendered in the same suggestive fullness that the Yiddish context provides, they cannot be.

Is it possible, for example, to translate adequately the phrase *tsar baale khayim*, with its evocation of a quality that was central to the Ashkenazi Jew's sense of himself as a Jew? Will the translation suggest that the consciousness of the Ashkenazi Jew was pervaded by the insistence on compassion for man, on reverence for life; that inflicting needless pain on living things was for him a cause of deep distress; that he was profoundly contented to be regarded as one of the *rakhmonim bney rakhmonim*, the merciful and sons of the merciful? So vital was *tsar baale khayim* that he identified it with his very essence. This is what he referred to when he spoke of *a yidish harts* or *a yidisher oder*. Does a phrase like 'a Jewish heart' or 'a Jewish vein' inevitably suggest such meanings in English? Is the pained disapproval of the delight in killing that is aroused by hunting or fishing as sport native to English as it is to Yiddish? The equivalent of 'God forbid' or 'Heaven forbid!', whatever their sources in primitive consciousness, assume in Yiddish a variety of forms that express, not a faith in their efficacy for warding off evil but a concern for all men, united in a common lot. And, since morality is involved, Yiddish says, in rich variety, not only *rakhmone litslon* or *rakhmone yatsilenu* or *got zol ophitn*, but also *kholile vkhas, khas vsholem, nit do gedakht, nit far aykh gedakht, nit far keyn yidn gedakht, nit far keynem gedakht, nit far keyn mentshn gedakht*. Is there not, then, something disquieting and foreboding in the fate of *nebakh*, that characteristic expression of pity, which has in English become nearly its opposite – nebbish – a term of condescension and derision? Is there not something distressing when *keyn ayn hore*, an expression of rejoicing in another's gladness that has long outlived its source in folk superstition, is rendered into the pidgin Yiddish 'no canary'?

If Yiddish is the language embodying the particularity of the Ashkenazi Jew's valuation of compassion and of human relatedness, it is also the language that expresses his particular valuation of humanity. How can one accurately translate into English a word like *folksmentsh*? It lacks the ambiguity of such phrases as 'the common man' or 'the ordinary man'. Indeed, it suggests something out of the ordinary about the *folksmentsh*; it suggests the rich resources and creativity that are within the man who is of the folk – and therefore the Yiddish admiration for what is *folkstimlekh*. The *folksmentsh*, moreover, is not only *of* the people; he belongs to it and is loyal to it. In the same spirit Yiddish absorbed *amkho* as a synonym for the *folksmentsh*. The respect that is imbedded in *amkho* is understood by the fact that 'Thy people' refers to the people that the Lord chose (or that chose the Lord). It is surely not fortuitous that the greatest figure of Yiddish literature should be Sholem Aleichem's Tevye, the *folksmentsh* and the symbol, in his moral qualities, of the Ashkenazi Jew. It is surely not fortuitous that the major motif of Yiddish literature is its love of the *folksmentsh* and its faith in him.

If Yiddish is the language of the *yidish harts* in its feelings, it is also and of necessity the language of human relatedness in action, of the insistence on man's obligation to be his brother's keeper, of the demand for *maysim tovim*. The Ashkenazi Jew developed and named a large variety of wholly voluntary social services, from the *hakhnoses kale* or the *hakhnoses orkhim* to the *bikur kholim* and the *khevra kedisha*. The far-flung structure of American Jewish philanthropy and our sense of obligation to philanthropy are rooted in these practices. But in the necessary process of modernization of structure and function, our American phraseology loses the clear moral meanings and the specific Jewish quality that the Yiddish expresses or implies. Yiddish uses the word *tsdoko*, knowing that *tsedek* is justice and that *tsdoko* is not charity but the right of the recipient. Yiddish absorbs the word *oyrekh* (stranger, guest) and combines both meanings in action, so that the stranger becomes a guest for the Sabbath or the holiday meal, and *tsdoko* is thus converted from an ethical abstraction into the reality *an oyrekh oyf shabes*. Yiddish creates the phrase *reb meyer baal hanes pushke* to name the little *tsdoko* box that was customary in the Jewish home. Yiddish takes a business-like transaction like an interest-free loan and institutionalizes it into the moral relationship called *gmiles khesed*, which in English sounds not a little quaint and naïve as 'a bestowal of loving-kindness' (or 'grace'). And Yiddish uses the word *yosher* with emphasis not merely on justice in the legal sense but on the individual's feeling for what is right and fair.

Yiddish, the language of human relatedness and man's responsibility for man, is also the language of family relatedness. It is hardly fortuitous that Yiddish had to create the words designating the relationship that exists between the parents of bride and groom – *mekhutonimshaft, mekhutn, mekhuteyneste* – words that are lacking in English. It is hardly fortuitous that Yiddish lacks the word for the impersonal expression 'a parent', and that, though it has the plural form for parents, *eltern*, it prefers the more intimate expression *tate–mame* (and, incidentally, does not use the theoretically possible but more formal equivalent *foter–muter*). In general, Yiddish prefers by far *tate* and *mame* to *foter* or *muter* and uses them in contexts where the English use of 'mama' or 'papa' would sound childish.

Another aspect of the human relatedness which Yiddish embodies is its capacity for tenderness and endearment, within the family as well as outside it. Yiddish is the language in which, for example, a parent can say to an injured child, *mir zol zayn far dir*. The tenderness of such expressions is, in English translation, often mistaken for sentimentality, and, indeed, the words in English do sometimes sound sentimental when in Yiddish they are not. This is especially true of diminutive and affectionate forms in various combinations of the suffixes *ke, she, le, nyu*, which Yiddish eagerly adopted and developed. How can one translate without sounding foolishly sentimental or ludicrous such a progression of diminutives for 'a bit, a drop' as *a kap, a kapele, a kapinke, a kapenyu, a kapichke, a kapinkele, a kapichkele, a kapinyunkele*? How much more sentimental must sound, in English, the variety of forms and phrases that express the warmth of family feeling which is so characteristic of Jewish life and of the Jewish emphasis on the home as a center of Jewish living and Jewish being! In English they must sound sentimental because English does not normally express these feelings in words and must therefore resort to expressions that either sound extravagant or seem drawn from the vocabulary of childhood. In Yiddish, on the other hand, intimacy and affection for parents as well as for children are embodied in numerous and varied diminutive forms. A grandmother is not only a *bobe* but *bobenyu, bobishe, bobichke, bobinke*; and *tate* and *mame* and *zeyde* have a similar variety of forms. A small child is not only a *pitsl* (a tot), but also a *pitsele, a pitsinkele, a pitsinyunkele*, and a *pitsinyunchikl*. A name like Leah became not only *Leye*, but *Leykele, Leyenyu, Leyinke, Leyinkele, Leyke, Leykele, Leykenyu, Leyche, Leychele, Leychenyu*. The English diminutive suffix *y* or *ie*, on the other hand, often cannot even be applied to a name which ends with a vowel sound. Yiddish can even express degrees and kinds of intimacy. A name like *Yosef* is capable of the backslapping affectionate *Yoshke*, the respectful affectionate *Yozifl*, the more intimate *Yosel*, or *Yoshe* (which is also expressive of condescension, as in I. J. Singer's novel *Yoshe Kalb*), the more affectionate *Yosele*, and the tenderly intimate *Yosenyu, Yosinke, Yosinkele, Yoshkele, Yoshenyu*, and *Yoshkenyu*. So great is this internal warmth of Yiddish that even so apparently aloof an inquiry as '*vos makht dos kind?*' is by no means one of indifference, and *dos kind* is not at all rendered by 'the child' and not adequately even by 'our child' or 'your child'. Nor does a phrase like 'my little son' satisfactorily convey the affectionate warmth of such an expression as *mayn yingele* or *yingele mayns*. And what can translate the spirituality of the pleasure, the inner glow, that inheres in the phrase *nakhes fun kinder*? And the affection so easily expressed to members of the family is just as readily communicated at large. Yiddish cannot only add suffixes of affection to nouns and adjectives, it can even make affectionate diminutives of verbs, as Jacob Glatstein brilliantly demonstrated in his poem '*Geto Lid*' ('Ghetto Song'), in which a mother comforts her child with such pleas as '*zingenyu*' (sing), '*shlofele*', '*shlofenyu*' (sleep), and '*lakhele*' (laugh). And in improvisations like '*shazheshe*' (and so hush, little one) the genius of Glatstein and the flexibility in affection are both demonstrated.

If Yiddish is, thus, the language of the *yidish harts* in its involvement with man, whether stranger or kin – a valuation rooted in morality, not sentimentality – Yiddish embodies another of the values vital to Jewishness by being also the language of the *yidisher kop*, of the dedication to learning. And it was a love of learning not for the sake of a diploma nor *smikha* nor income nor even for the sake of heaven, but for the combined and hyphenated spiritual–intellectual–aesthetic experience of the pursuit of Torah as truth. The world in which Yiddish was shaped was one that inaugurated a child's schooling by putting a drop of wine or honey on its tongue, so that its taste of learning might be sweet. It was a world in which it was a father's custom every Sabbath to question his son on the youngster's progress in his studies during the week. How natural then, as Max Weinreich has pointed out, for it to be a world in which the social ladder began with the *grober yung* at the bottom and ranged upward through *a yid fun a gants yor, a sheyner yid, a yid a lamdn* to *a godl btoyre*. What English phrase adequately reflects the profound respect inherent in the words *a godl btoyre*? What English phrase suggests that *a yid fun a gants yor* is not only an ordinary Jew, an everyday Jew, but also a Jew every day of his life and a *folksmentsh*? And while, in English, the man-in-the-street uses 'Doc' as a salutation of familiarity bordering on condescension, in Yiddish, the *folksmentsh* reserved the title *rebbe* for respectful address to any man of learning.

The world which valued this ideal of the *yidisher kop* not only valued the possessor of one but lavished its affection on him and frequently used the affectionate diminutive with his name. How often was the name of a rabbi or a *maggid* or a *khazn* so used? Can English, for example, render properly the name of the most famous of Jewish cantors, Yossele Rosenblatt? Is he to become Little Joey Rosenblatt? Is Sholem Aleichem's famous rabbi of Kasrilevke, Reb Yozifl, to be known as Rabbi Little Joe?

The world which so valued learning and learned men created and named two unique institutions to foster them. It took an institution like boarding a bridegroom in the home of his wife's parents for a stipulated period as part of the dowry and converted it into the uniquely Jewish institution of *kest*, board for the purpose of *study*. And, as Max Weinreich has pointed out, *essn teg* – eating with a different family each day – the unique institution for supporting *yeshiva bokherim* (and a *yeshiva bokher* was not a 'yeshiva student') away from home was really a system of folk scholarships. Indeed, *essn teg* was more than a system of folk scholarships; it was also a system of folk participation in national education which was synonymous with national destiny. And when a housewife could boast that such-and-such a distinguished scholar had once eaten in her home on Wednesdays, it was not merely name dropping on her part, not merely personal pride in having assisted a particular distinguished scholar; it was pride in having participated in a national achievement, in having had a share in adding to a national treasure and to the pursuit of universal truth.

Dedicated as it thus was to the values of the head and the heart, to Torah and *maysim tovim*, the Ashkenazi world was one whose ethic could indeed be called the ethic of *mentshlekhkayt*. In the word *mentsh* it found the summation of its strivings. It could not conceive of the possibility of being a Jew without being a *mentsh*, and it could not conceive of being a *mentsh* without admiring gentleness and being distressed at violence. '*Alle yavonim hobn eyn ponim*', all soldiers (literally 'Greeks') look alike, it said with a clear undertone of contempt for the soldier's function. In fact, the soldier as a symbol stood at furthest remove from the life's ideal and conception of self of the Ashkenazi Jew, as strange and inappropriate as *a yovn in a suke*, as a soldier in a *suke*.

This vision of *mentshlekhkayt*, as well as the loyalty to it, was to the world of Yiddish not merely morally gratifying but aesthetically pleasing, and in the phrase *a sheyner yid* was embodied this fusion of moral and aesthetic fact, for the beauty of the *sheyner yid* lay not in his features but in his *yidishkayt*. If a *mentsh* embodied – or strove to embody – the Jewish virtues, the *sheygetz*, on the other hand, symbolized the opposite: the pugnacity, the cruelty, the unintellectuality, the human indifference and unrelatedness which could only fill with dismay the heart of any *mentsh*. When Yiddish says, '*zay a mentsh*', it is evoking an ideal very far removed indeed from the ideal implied in 'be a man'. Manliness and *mentshlekhkayt* are two wholly different and utterly unrelated visions of desirable human attributes.

If Yiddish is, thus, the language in which *yidishkayt* uniquely expresses its *mentshlekhkayt*, it is also the language in which Jewish *mentshlekhkayt* expresses its religious *yidishkayt*. And if there is, on the one hand, serious doubt that the moral and intellectual values, attitudes, and feelings that constitute the humane sense of life of the Ashkenazi Jew can be transmitted without Yiddish, in whose words and contexts and connotations its central principles are untranslatably embodied, there is, on the other hand, reason for serious doubt whether Judaism as a religious way of life is not gravely limited without Yiddish. That Hebrew is indispensable to Judaism is clear. Yet for how many have the numerous Hebrew words and phrases referring to religous practices and ways descended from their context in Yiddish? How often does their use evoke the overtones of meaning of that Yiddish context? Of the life-style in Yiddish in which they found their home for a thousand years? If we denude them of this rich context, we not only deprive them of meanings rightfully theirs but of history. Even if we were to regard this context as merely incidental, comparable to the cloak and crowns in which are clothed the Scrolls of the Torah, even so, how appropriate these vestments seem! How they, too, become redolent of sanctity, as Rabbi Joseph Soloveitchik has declared.

But far more important than any sanctity that Judaism may impart to Yiddish is the service that Yiddish performs for Judaism: it provides a setting in which the vocabulary of faith and observance is entirely native, just as Judaism is native. More than native – it was the shaping passion. Is Judaism native in English? Is its terminology at home in English, or is it foreign? Has not something inestimable been irretrievably lost when it lives thus as a stranger? And are we not deeply aware of this loss, of the absence of this sense of belonging, of being at home in a full context of ways and values? Is not this loss what we have in mind when we say of anything, '*es hot nit kayn yidishn tam*'? (We must say it, of course, in Yiddish, for that expression itself has, in English, no *tam* either English or *yidish*.) It would indeed be the ultimate irony of a history replete with ironies if one were to contemplate Judaism in America today and be forced to say of so much of it, '*es hot nit kayn yidishn tam*'.

Perhaps not the ultimate irony. The phrase must be reserved for the very real possibility that the God of Judaism might Himself render that judgment. For if Hebrew has been the language of divine prayer, Yiddish has been the language of divine converse. In Yiddish, the God that sometimes speaks fearsomely in Scriptures becomes the gentle Father. And this intimacy with God which the Ashkenazi Jew felt with such immediacy was made possible only by the capacity of Yiddish for intimacy. In Yiddish one can address the Almighty as *gotenyu* or *tatenyu zeeser*, phrases which in English translation ('dear God' and 'sweet Father dear') lose wholly the intimacy that the Yiddish conveys. Even the phrase *riboynoy shel oylem*, so majestic and remote in English translation 'Lord of the universe' is in Yiddish an address that is warm, gentle, and intimate. Yiddish is the language in which the figures of the Bible emerge as near relations and in which *got iz a tate*, a remark which states merely, 'God is a father', and which just as clearly implies that he is *our* Father and that He will do no less than a father should. And though God is our Father – perhaps because He is our Father – He is exempt neither from the righteousness which His Torah commands nor from the rebuke of His children when He fails to fulfill the *mitzvahs* of justice.

From this close relationship that the Yiddish expresses stems what might seem the sacrilegious boldness that runs through the numberless stories about Jews who questioned, accused, indicted, defied, even punished God when He seemed to deviate from the justice enjoined by His Torah. Sholem Aleichem's Tevye questions Him wryly. Levi Yitskhok of Berdichev lays humbly yet firmly before Him the claims of His people for redemption from exile. And Peretz's Reb Shloyme, determined to put an end to the suffering of humanity and the injustice of the world, defiantly refuses to recite the *Havdala* and thus end the Sabbath with its peace and exaltation. The Baal Shem and Reb Nakhman, Leyb of Spola and Shneyer Zalmen of Lyadi all spoke to God in Yiddish, argued with Him in Yiddish, scolded, accused, and blessed Him and gloried in His Torah – in Yiddish. And Itsik Manger, that poet of wonder, marshaling over the gas chambers of Belsen the spirits of Moyshe Leyb of Sossov and Wolf of Zbarazh and Meyerl of Premishlan, proclaimed in their name: '...we, the Galicians, for eternity obliterate Your name from the assembly of True Lovers of Israel'. And he did so in Yiddish. Who can do so in English?

If Yiddish is the language of discourse with God, it is also the language whose designations for His 'functionaries' are far more precisely reflective of Jewish practice and Jewish values than are the English equivalents. Does 'rabbi' in English make clear, as *rov* does in Yiddish, that the bearer of the title is properly neither a priestly mediator nor one who ministers to the soul nor the pastor of a flock, but a teacher, and advisor, and adjudicator? That it is not the *rov* but the *khazn* who is the *sheliakh tsibur* and the one charged with the responsibility of leading the congregation in prayer? Does the English distinguish between the rabbi who is a *rov* and the Hasidic *rebbe*? Can the English distinguish between the *rebbe* who is a *tsaddik* (and if a *tsaddik* is to be translated as 'saint' are all the Christian saints *tsaddikim*?) and the *rebbe* who is a *melamed*? And is *melamed* properly rendered as 'Hebrew teacher' when as a matter of fact he taught Torah and commentary rather than Hebrew as a language? Surely something has been lost when, as Abraham Duker has noted, a *shammes* becomes a 'sexton' and a policeman is a *shammes*. A *rebetsin* is far more than merely a rabbi's wife and a *shaytl* is far more than a wig. A *beys medresh* is far more than a synagogue or a 'sanctuary', and a *minyon* is not a 'quorum'; *bentchn* and *davenen*, as exclusively Jewish activities, are different from 'blessing' or 'praying', which are possible in any faith (and is Judaism merely a 'faith'?); and *shakhris* and *minkhe* and *mayrev*, *mitsve* and *aveyre*, *siddur* and *makhzer* are as distinctively Jewish as the missal used at Mass is distinctively Catholic. And these words are as melodiously at home in Yiddish as 'missal' is in English, and they are nearly as strange in English as 'missal' would be in Yiddish.

And so it is with the thousand-and-one appurtenances and ways of Jewish religious life, for which we either retain the original words in English and lose the native ease and rich meanings of their Yiddish context, or we translate them and in doing so render them hardly Jewish at all. So it is with *tfiln* (a 'phylactery', Webster informs us, is, among other things, 'an indication of Pharisaism or hypocrisy'), and *tfiln zekl* and *yortsayt* and *yortsayt likht*. So it is with *yarmelke*, even when it undergoes a sea-change and emerges as *yamelke*. So it is with *mezuze* ('a door-post amulet'?) and *bris* ('a ritual circumcision'?). With *sandik*. With *pidyon haben*. With *zitsen shive* (*nit do gedakht*, *nit far keynem gedakht*). With *kosher* (which, though it has been naturalized in English has become something of a clown) and *treyf*. With *milkhik* and *fleyshik* and *parev*. With *peysakhdik* and *khometsdik* and *farbrenen dem khomets*. With the whole complex of *dinim* and *minhogim*, for which Yiddish, as a wholly Jewish language, has expressions, idiomatic or abbreviated, while English does not. And whatever shameful connotations may accrue to the word 'Jew' as noun and verb in English (and Webster's *Third* lists them all), in Yiddish the verb *yidishn* has but one meaning – to fulfill the millennial covenant with morality, the *bris* with the Almighty.

Are the very holidays possible without Yiddish? Is the very word 'holiday' a full translation of *yom-tov*, which not merely designates a day of freedom from work or freedom for joy but which embraces all memorable occasions and suggests an inner glow of exaltation? And *gut yom-tov* or *gut shabes* (what shall we do with *a gute vokh*, *a gut yor*?) are as native to the occasion as 'Merry Christmas' is indigenous to English. And just as 'Merry Christmas' is far from *gut yom-tov*, so is *lshono tovo tikhosevu* or *gmar khsimo tovo* far from 'Happy New Year', the difference between an occasion that reemphasizes one's obligation to man and to God and the occasion that emphasizes only the private pursuit of happiness. Need one review the entire calendar of the Jewish year to emphasize the impossibility of translating and the strangeness of transliterating? Indeed, with the likes of *seder* and *praven a seder* or *sukos* and *suke* or *lag b'omer* or *tishe b'ov* or *purim* and *shalakhmones* and *khanuke* and even *khanuke gelt* we have only the choice of using these as natives in their Yiddish setting or as total strangers in English. Yiddish is not only the vehicle through which the life patterns of Judaism find their fullest and richest expression; it is not only the language that knows how to fence off with a *lehavdil* the sacred from the profane; it is, through its idioms, a teacher of Judaism as well. It is not possible to speak Yiddish without acquiring a knowledge of the ways and works of Jewish traditions. *A sheyne, reyne, kapore; a kosher lefl in a koshern top; a nayer ykum pirkon; farbaytn di yotsres; araynfaln vi a yovn in suke; kukn vi a hon in bney odem; makhn emitsn a mi sheberakh; a khokhem fun der ma neshtano; araynzetsn in khad gadyo; shrayen khay vkayem* – these and multitudes of other Yiddish expressions refer to the details of Judaism and provide the materials for metaphor. What in English impels a knowledge of Judaism?

Yiddish is a teacher of Jewish history as well. The span of the centuries unrolls in such phrases as *farkrikhn in goyshn; er hert im vi homen hert dem grager; fun khmelnitskis tseitn; fun melekh sobetskis yorn; a meydl mit an oyringl; hob ikh nit getantst mitn ber; es lebt sikh im vi got in odes.* Yiddish is not only an irreplaceable source of documents and studies pertaining to the whole of Jewish history and a unique source pertaining to the ten Ashkenazi centuries, it is the very embodiment of that history in countless expressions. Does English have expressions rooted in forty centuries of Jewish history? Surely Rabbi Emanuel S. Goldsmith is right in his assertion: 'There can be no renaissance of Judaism in our time without reverence for Yiddish'.

Uniquely and untranslatably, Yiddish is thus the voice of Jewish ethic, the voice of Judaism as a religiously centered pattern of life, the voice of Jewish tradition and celebration, the voice of Jewish loyalty and self-acceptance, the voice of Jewish rejoicing in Jewishness. Which of these are we prepared to dispense with? And all of these become qualities characteristic of the literature of Yiddish and of its folk creativity.

At the moral center of Yiddish literature stands the ethic of Ashkenazi Jewry. Is there a Yiddish writer who does not ultimately affirm it? To a history replete with ironies add one more: Jews, who suffered more at the hands of man than any other people and seemed to suffer more as their history stretched across the centuries, Jews and their writers in Yiddish never lost faith in either man or life, never saw the world as a wasteland, never felt themselves alienated from man. Though there might be but ten righteous men, Jews would not turn their faces from Sodom and Gomorrah. Jewish suffering and Jewish aspiration, Jewish longing and Jewish achievement, Jewish home and Jewish love, Jewish study and Jewish life – these may have been the major subjects of Yiddish literature, but its great theme was and remains the Jewish ethic.

Standing at the moral center of historic experience with the full weight of millennial tradition at his back, the Yiddish writer could observe all the defects of Jewish life, yet never feel himself alienated. Perhaps he perceived himself, in the largest sense, as a continuator of a prophetic tradition which might indeed excoriate man's iniquities, but he never felt that it was either unheeded or defied with impunity. If there was a conflict between the publicly recognized ethic and private greed, it was the greedy who were in defiance of tradition. The Yiddish writer, part of the mighty moral stream, never felt himself irreconcilably at odds with his world, never felt that his was a voice crying in the wilderness. So great was his influence, indeed, that he very often became a folk hero. Is there another literature so entirely steeped in the libertarian tradition, so entirely dedicated to those who suffer, so entirely committed to man's emancipation, so entirely devoted to the values of *mentshlekhayt* as Yiddish literature? And so pervasive was the acceptance of this ethic that it made itself the dominant note in the creativity of the folk. As Y. L. Peretz remarked: 'Did you ever compare our folk songs with those, for example, of the Brothers Grimm? Do you find in ours, as you do in theirs, heroes who are robbers or cunning cheats in seven-league boots?' The efflorescence of Jewish writing which is today brightening English literature on both sides of the Atlantic has its moral and intellectual roots in the world which lived, nourished, and transmitted these values in Yiddish. Bringing to bear on contemporary life, as these writers do, the moral and intellectual values of Ashkenazi Jewry, their work would have assumed an altogether different aspect without the impact of the world of Yiddish, in which these values found the vehicle of their expression and the medium of their nourishment.

The evidence makes it abundantly clear that Jewish life and Jewish identity, whether secular or religious, must be both starved and stunted without Yiddish. These multitudes of really untranslatable expressions are not merely linguistic curiosities. They are the bearers and the shapers of our ethical consciousness into a uniquely Jewish constellation of values. For we are dealing not with ethical abstractions but with operative values, with inner directives that constitute our sense of self. As the phrase 'Christian charity' not only differs in meaning from *tsdoko* and from *tsar baale khayim* but is evocative of an entire tradition of life and values that as an entity is alien to the Jewish consciousness and painful to the Jewish historical memory, so the uniquely Jewish expressions of Yiddish are linguistic embodiments of a uniquely Jewish moral constellation and a uniquely Jewish historical memory. The greater the immersion in Yiddish and its works, the greater the distinctively Jewish qualities; and conversely, the further the remove from Yiddish the greater the distance from those qualities that characterize the most admirable expressions of Jewish being.

Great as the need is for Yiddish here, it is not less great as an element of life in Israel. A century of acrimonious debate and sometimes bitter conflict makes it difficult to keep partisans from falling into the camp of either Yiddishists or Hebraists. Yet such controversy has not only been outmoded by history; it is distinctive to Jewish life, which faces one monumental task: to bring to bear upon itself, upon all who wish to maintain a Jewish identity, the full variety of its resources, the full spectrum of possible choices, the full range of its spaciousness in its three religious dimensions as well as its fourth or secular dimension, so that its future may be creative and meaningful in its continuity with the past; and to bring to bear upon our world the moral vision of *mentshlekhayt*, which for a millennium at least a people strove so hard to incorporate into a pattern of living. If Yiddish is in its own right an indispensable instrument of Jewish continuity, it is not to be regarded lightly even in Israel, where, though the future seems confident, the question of continuity with the past and relatedness with the Jewish communities of the world is not an untroubled one.

Yiddish is not only the language of our six million martyrs, our *loshn hakdoshim*. Yiddish is the language of *kdusha*, of holiness itself. 'In the days of Moses', Professor Heschel reminds us, 'Israel had a revelation of God; in the days of the Baal Shem, God had a revelation of Israel. Suddenly there was revealed a holiness in Jewish life that had accumulated in the course of many generations....' And the language of that holiness, of that moral nobility and humane striving, was Yiddish. If Hebrew was the language in which the Jew blessed God, Yiddish was the language in which he blessed man and strove to be a *mentsh*.

Chaim Zhitlowski long ago insisted, perhaps too harshly: 'He who does not know *loshn kodesh* is an *am horetz*; he who does not know Yiddish is a *goy*'. If we are concerned that Jewish life should continue to aspire to the noblest visions of Ashkenazi Jewry, that it should continue to value those humane and libertarian aspirations that have shaped its Messianic hopes, that it should continue to be imbued with that loyalty that has marked its social conscience, that it should continue to strive for that cultivation of the intellect that has motivated even its daily life, that it should continue to uphold that affirmation of man and that embrace of life that are at its center, that it should continue to bind itself in loyalty to the people that fashioned and dedicated itself to these ideals, then we cannot do without that language in which these values and those visions are indigenous; then we cannot do without that language that was, indeed, shaped to contain them and express them. If the moral and intellectual vision of Yiddish is thus the vision of man's holiness, whether conceived in religious or in secular terms, then Yiddish is indeed our *loshn hakdusha*, the language of our holiness. And if we are to remain true to the historic vision of *yidishkayt*, we must have not only *loshn kodesh* but also *loshn hakdusha*. If to be a Jew is to have meaning rooted in the past, significant and full-bodied in the present, and hopeful of the future, then we cannot do without *loshn hakdusha*. If Jewish life, in the individual and in the group, is to be meaningful in *hemshekh* and promising in *kiyum*, then Jewish life the world over cannot do without *loshn hakdusha*. If language is not only shaped by life but is also in turn a shaper of life, if Yiddish is not merely a passive container of qualities and values but an active shaper of our quintessential Jewish being, of our distinctive Jewishness, then Jews everywhere cannot do without *loshn hakdusha*.

Where Yiddish cannot be the language of daily living, of *vokhedikayt*, it can and must be a language of Jewish living, of that part of their lives which Jews live as Jews. As the vehicle of our essential Jewishness, Yiddish must be at least a language of our formal Jewishness, of our ceremonial and public occasions: wherever we gather as Jews, whenever we celebrate as Jews, whenever we confer with one another at home or with our communities in other lands. And it should be the language of our personal Jewishness, of our family warmth and our human relatedness, of our song and our rejoicing and our *yomtovdikayt*. And it should be a language of our Jewish self-fulfillment, intellectually and aesthetically.

If Yiddish is a road to Jewish being and to the continuum of Jewish history, then it is more than merely a language; then it becomes part of a way of life, an ideology, and a commitment. Whatever the theologians may tell us about the 'faith' of Judaism, it is the living Jew in the qualities of his being, his valuing, his thinking, his feeling, and his doing that must ultimately be the aim of Jewish education and Jewish life. Now, when circumstances conspire to narrow the confines of Jewish consciousness so that tenuous 'membership' adopts, by default, the place of real belonging, when plane service to an 'ould sod' and lip service to an 'ould faith' have become expensive surrogates for meaningful being, when, too often, not only 'Who needs Yiddish?' is asked but the more disastrous 'Who needs Jewish?' – now is the time for the Establishment to speak out for Yiddish on behalf of Jewish life itself.

Who needs Yiddish? The question is not, do we need Yiddish?, but can we, dare we do without Yiddish? Who needs Yiddish? All of Jewish life everywhere, in the individual and in the group, needs Yiddish. There is still time!

PART IV

Historic Moments

1908—1933

25 יאָר נאָך דער 25

טשערנאָװיצער קאָנפערענץ

שבת דעם 4-טן נאָװעמבער 8.³⁰ אָװנט קומם פאָר אין

קליינעם שטאַט-זאַל (קאָנסקע 1)

די פייערונג פון 25-טן יובל פון דער

טשערנאָװיצער קאָנפערענץ

פראָגראַם:

I אָפטיילונג

1) עפענונגס-װאָרט – ד"ר צ. שאַבאַד
2) די הױפטמאָמענטן פון דער טשערנאָװיצער קאָנפערענץ –
רעפעראַט פון ג. פלודערמאַכער
3) 25 יאָר נאָך טשערנאָװיץ – רעפעראַט פון ז. רייזען

II אָפטיילונג

1) אױפמאַרש פון דעלעגאַציעס פון די ייִדישע שולן
2) רחל אײזענשטאַט (שילערין פון 8-טן קלאַס רעאל-גימ.)—דעקלאַמאַציע
3) הירש רייכעל (שילער פון מוזיקאַלישן אינסטיטוט) – פידל
4) באַסיע גאַװורין (שילערין פון מוזיק. אינסטיטוט)–געזאַנג
5) עמא טאַובער (שילערין פון מוזיק. אינסטיטוט) – געזאַנג
9) ביים קלאַװיר – ז. טראַצקאַ.

כאָר פון װיילביג אונטער דער א. סלעפ
אָנפירונג פון

בילעטן צו באַקומען שבת פון 10 פרי
אין קאַסע און קליינעם שטאַט-זאַל.

Druk. „Ekspress" Wilno, Wielka 38

פייערונג לכבוד דעם 25טן יאָרטאָג פון דער טשערנאָװי-
צער ייִדישער שפראַך-קאָנפערענץ

Celebration of the 25th anniversary of the
Chernovitz Yiddish Language Conference

חגיגה למלאת 25 שנים לוועידת השפה היידיש בצ'רנוביץ

Празднование двадцатипятилетия Черновицкой
конференции еврейского языка

A twenty-fifth anniversary celebration of the Tshnernovits Conference, in Vilna, features
talks by famous Jewish spokesmen and writers as well as participation by students
from various Yiddish schools.

a. *Today it seems almost impossible to imagine (unless, of course, one looks at what has since happened to Yiddish in America) that there was a time when in both eastern Europe and America the lovers of Yiddish had to create a* movement *for its defense within the Jewish world. Calling themselves* yidishistn *— some fervent if aging representatives can still be found in every Jewish community of the world — they organized a conference in Czernowitz, Romania, in 1908, at which writers, intellectuals and public figures came together to declare a programmatic adherence to Yiddish, not merely as a language meriting its quotient of respect but as the agent of a national-cultural idea. 'The first conference devoted to the Yiddish language,' they declared, 'recognizes Yiddish as a national language of the Jewish people, and demands for it political, communal and cultural equality . . .'. As if only through the declamations of conference-rhetoric could status be accorded to what in reality was pulsingly alive!*

b. פֿאַרשטייער פֿון דער אידיש-קולטור אין פֿאַרשיידענע
לענדער האָבן שוין געהאַט אַמאָל אַ קאָנפֿערענץ — די
טשערנאָװיצער (1908). זי האָט ניט איבערגעלאָזן קיין
קעגנטייגע שפּורן, אָבער עס איז געװען אַן אויפֿרודע־
רונג אין דער שטילער מחנה, אַן אויפֿמונטערונג, אַן
אָנזאָג, אַ צוזאָג אויף שפּעטער.

פֿון דאַן אָן זײנען צוגעקומען נײע חשבונות, נײע
אויפֿטוען, נײע גרויסע אויפֿגאַבן. און עס איז שוין לאַנג
נויטיג געװאָרן פֿאַר די שאַפֿער און פֿאַרשטייער פֿון אונ־
זער קולטור לעבן זיך װידער אַמאָל צונויפֿצוקומען פֿון
אַלע עקן װעלט און אין איין אָרט, זיך צונויפֿצוקומען
אין אַ גרעסערער צאָל, מער צוגעגרייט, מיט ברייטערע
פֿולמאַכטן און מיט מער קלאָרקייט, זיכערקייט, גבורה,
װי אין טשערנאָװיץ, אויפֿריידן זיך אייניע מיט די אַנ־
דערע און נאָך ענגער צואַמענשליסן די געדיכטער און
מוטיגער געװאָרענע רייען.

עס איז שוין לאַנג נויטיג געװאָרן אַ װעלט-קאָנגרעס
פֿאַר אידישער קולטור צוליב ריין פּראַקטישע, ניט נאָר
דעמאָנסטראַטיװע און דעקלאַריטיװע צילן. מיר זײנען
אַריסגעװאַקסן פֿון דעם פּעריאָד פֿון לויטער דעמאָנ־
סטראַציעס.

And we call out to the world: we are a Jewish nation and Yiddish is our language and we wish to live our lives and create our cultural heritage in this language. This is the language in which we wish to amass our treasure, to fashion our culture, to awaken our soul and to unite with each other across all countries and in all times.

From Y. L. Perets' opening remarks to the First Yiddish Language Conference, Tshernovits, 1908 (*Di ershte yidishe shprakh-konferents.* Vilna, YIVO, 1931, 74–77)

Mottos for Part IV

(a) Irving Howe and Eliezer Greenberg. Introduction, in their (eds.) *Voices from the Yiddish: Essays, Memoirs, Diaries.* New York, Schoken, 1975, 6.

(b) 'Representatives of the world of Yiddish culture have already had a conference – in Tshernovits (1908). It left no noticeable traces, but it provided excitement for the quiet camp, a heightening of the spirit, a portent and a prediction as to the future. Since then new considerations have arisen, new attainments, new major tasks. Therefore, it has long been desirable for the creators and the representatives of our cultural life to get together in one place, coming from all corners of the globe, to get together in large numbers, better prepared, with more inclusive authorization and with greater clarity, confidence, prowess than was the case in Tshernovits, to consult with one another and to unite even more the cadres that have become more numerous and more courageous. A world congress for Yiddish culture has long been needed for purely practical rather than demonstrative and rhetorical goals. We have grown up beyond the period of mere demonstrations'. Sh. Niger. A yidisher kultur kongres [A congress for Yiddish culture]. *Dos naye lebn,* 1922, 1, no. 2, 1.

Attracting a Following to High-Culture Functions for a Language of Everyday Life: The Role of the Tshernovits Language Conference in the 'Rise of Yiddish'

JOSHUA A. FISHMAN

INTRODUCTION

The traditional position of Yiddish in Ashkenaz (= the traditional Hebrew–Aramaic and Yiddish designation for Central and Eastern Europe, Jews living in or derived from this area being known, therefore, as Ashkenazim) was – and in many relatively unmodernized Orthodox circles still *is* – somewhat more complex than the H versus L distinction usually implies. At the extreme of sanctity there was *loshn koydesh*[1] alone, realized via its hallowed biblical and postbiblical *texts*. At the opposite extreme, that of work-a-day intragroup life, there was Yiddish alone: the vernacular of one and all, rich and poor, learned and ignorant, pious and less than pious. Although 'sanctity' and 'work-a-day' existed on a single continuum and were connected by a single overarching set of cultural values and assumptions, they were, nevertheless, clearly distinct overt, cognitive, and emotional composites. In between these two extremes were numerous situations in which (a) *loshn koydesh* and Yiddish co-occurred in-so-far as intragroup life was concerned, and less numerous ones in which (b) co-territorial vernaculars or written languages were employed in-so-far as intergroup activities involving the work sphere, government, and infrequent 'socializing' required.

The traditional *intra*group intermediate zone resulted in a Yiddish oral literature of high moral import and public recognition (sometimes published in Yiddish but, at least initially, as often as not, translated into *loshn koydesh* for the very purpose of 'dignified' publication). It also included the exclusive use of Yiddish as the process language of oral study, from the most elementary to the most advanced and recondite levels. And it included the exclusive use of Yiddish

---

1. Throughout this paper the distinction will be adhered to between the traditional amalgam of classical through medieval Hebrew and Aramaic, referred to by Yiddish speakers as *loshn koydesh* [Language of Holiness] and Modern Hebrew, as developed in Palestine/Israel during the past century as a language of all the functions required by a modern econo-political establishment. Where the distinction between Hebrew and *loshn koydesh* is not clear or is not intended they will be referred to jointly.

as the language of countless sermons by rabbis and preachers and as the language of popular religious tracts (ostensibly for women and uneducated menfolk). Thus, Yiddish *did* enter pervasively into the pale of sanctity and even into the pale of sanctity-in-print (hallowed bilingual texts – *loshn koydesh* originals with accompanying Yiddish translations – had existed ever since the appearance of print and, before that, as incunabula), but it never existed in that domain as a fully free agent, never as the sole medium of that domain in its most hallowed and most textified realizations, never as fully independent target medium but usually as process medium underlying which or superseding which a single *loshn koydesh* text or a whole sea of such texts was either known, assumed, or created (Fishman 1973, 1976).

As a result, when traditional Eastern European Jewry enters significantly into the nineteenth-century drama of modernization, *loshn koydesh* and Yiddish are generally conceptualized, both by most intellectuals and by rank-and-file members of Ashkenaz, in terms of their extreme and discontinuous textified versus vernacular roles, their intermediate co-zones having contributed neither to the substantial vernacularization of *loshn koydesh* nor to the phenomenological sanctification of Yiddish. As the nineteenth century progresses, there are increasing efforts to liberate Yiddish from its apparent subjugation to Hebrew (the latter being metaphorically referred to as the noble daughter of heaven, Yiddish being no more than her handmaiden), particularly for more modern intragroup H pursuits. In addition, there were also increasing efforts to liberate Yiddish from its inferior position *vis-à-vis* co-territorial vernaculars in connection with modern learning and nontraditional life more generally. It is with the former type of language spread that this paper deals most directly (and with its implications for the role of *loshn koydesh*, which was also then being groomed for modern H roles at the intragroup and at the intergroup levels), although the spill-over from the former to the latter type of language spread was often both an objective and an achievement as well. Obviously, when one component of a traditional diglossia (here: triglossia) situation changes in its functions, the societal allocation of functions with respect to the other(s) is under stress to change as well.

The 'spread of language' does not always entail gaining new speakers or users – whether as a first or as a second language. Frequently it entails gaining new functions or uses, particularly 'H' functions (i.e. literacy related functions in education, religion, 'high culture' in general, and, in modern times, in econotechnology and government too) for a language that is already widely known and used in 'L' functions (i.e. everyday family, neighborhood, and other informal/intimate, intragroup interaction). Wherever a speech community already has a literacy-related elite, this type of language spread inevitably involves the displacement of an old elite (the one that is functionally associated with the erstwhile 'H') by a new elite that is seeking a variety of social changes which are to be functionally associated with the prior 'L' and which are to be instituted and maintained under its own (the new elite's) leadership.[2] The last century has witnessed the rise and fall (but not the complete elimination) of such efforts on behalf of Yiddish.

THE TSHERNOVITS LANGUAGE CONFERENCE: SUCCESS OR FAILURE?

Three different positive views concerning Yiddish were clearly evident by the first decade of the twentieth century and a fourth was then increasingly coming into being.[3] The earliest view was a *traditional utilitarian* one and it continues to be evinced primarily by ultra-Orthodox spokesmen to this very day. In accord with this view, Yiddish was (and is) to be utilized in print for various moralistic and halachic[4] educational purposes, because it has long been used in this way, particularly in publications for women, the uneducated, and children. Any departure from such use – whether on behalf of modern Hebrew or a co-territorial vernacular – was/is decried as disruptive of tradition. Another view was a *modern utilitarian* one, namely that Yiddish must be used in political and social education if the masses were ever to be moved toward more modern attitudes and behaviors, because it was the only language that they understand. This view was and, to some extent, still is widely held by *Maskilic*[5] and *Zionist*/socialist spokesmen. A third view was also evident by the turn of the century, namely that Yiddish was a distinctly indigenous and representative vehicle and, therefore, it had a *natural role to play both in expressing and in symbolizing Jewish cultural-national desiderata*. Finally, we begin to find expressed the view that for modern Jewish needs Yiddish is the *only or major natural expressive and symbolic vehicle*.

In the nineteenth century the first two positive views (and the counterclaims

2. The traditional coexistence of a nonvernacular language of high culture (H) and a vernacular of everyday life (L), the former being learned through formal study and the latter in the context of familial intimacy, was dubbed *diglossia* by Charles A. Ferguson (*Word* 1959 15: 325–340). Such contexts and their similarity and dissimilarity *vis-à-vis* other multilingual and multidialectal contexts have been examined by several investigators, among them John J. Gumperz (1964) and in Fishman (1967).
3. For a full treatment of each of these four substantively distinct but also interacting views of Yiddish, see Fishman (this volume; Foreword, parts II and III).
4. Halachic, an adjective derived from *halaḥa* (Yiddish: *halokhe*), refers to the entire body of Jewish law (Biblical, Talmudic, and post-Talmudic) and subsequent legal codes amending,

modifying, or interpreting traditional precepts under rabbinic authority.
5. *Maskilic*, adjective derived from *maskil*, an adherent of *haskala* (Yiddish: *haskole*), an eighteenth–nineteenth-century movement among Central and Eastern European Jews, associated in Germany with the leadership of Moses Mendelssohn (1729–1786), designed to make Jews and Judaism more modern and cosmopolitan in character by promoting knowledge of and contributions to the secular arts and sciences and by encouraging adoption of the dress, customs, economic practices, educational programs, political processes, and languages of the dominant non-Jewish co-territorial populations. For observations as to differences between the *haskole* in central and Eastern Europe, see Fishman (this volume: Foreword, part III).

related to them) were encountered most frequently, but the latter two were beginning to be expressed as well (see, particularly Y. M. Lifshits' writings, e.g. 1863, 1867; note D. Fishman's discussion [1981] of Lifshitz as transitional ideologist). In the twentieth century the latter two views (and their respective refutations) came into prominence and the former two receded and were ultimately almost abandoned.[6] The last public encounter of all four views was at the Tshernovits Language Conference. There the first two views were presented and strongly refuted whereas the last two remained in uneasy balance, neither of them appearing clearly victorious over the other.

PLANNING THE CONFERENCE

The father of the idea to convene an international conference on behalf of Yiddish was Dr. Nosn Birnboym (Nathan Birnbaum) (1864–1936)[7] who came to the United States in 1907 with that very purpose in mind. Birnboym, who had coined the word 'zionism' (in German: *Zionismus*) and had conceptualized much of its mission in the early 1890s, had by then already broken both with Theodore Herzl (1860–1904) and with Herzlian Zionism on the grounds that to save Jews ('to solve the Jewish Question') without aiming at fostering Jewishness ('to solve the Jewishness Question') was tantamount to fostering assimilation under Jewish auspices. In the course of his own Jewish self-discovery, he came to regard Yiddish as a vehicle of genuine, rooted Jewishness and, therefore, as the preferred vehicle of a kind of modernization that would also be particularly attuned to the simultaneous need for continuity of Jewish culture, traditions, and values. He had begun to write in this vein by the beginning of the century in the German periodical *Selbst-Emanzipation* (that he had founded in Vienna in 1885) and continued doing so subsequently in his Yiddish weekly

---

6. Both Zionists and socialists increasingly shifted from the second to the third positive view at or around the turn of the century. In 1889 the Zionist leader Sokolov defended Yiddish merely as a necessary vehicle of mass agitation and propaganda (Roznhak 1969), and even Herzl, who knew no Yiddish, founded a weekly (*Di velt*) in 1900 in order to reach the Eastern European masses. Similarly, socialist spokesmen such as Arkadi Kremer merely advocated the use of Yiddish in order to attain their mass educational purposes in 1893 and organized *zhargonishe komitetn* (Yiddish-speaking committees) in order to foster literacy and to spread socialist publications among Jews in the Czarist empire. Soon, however, a new (the third) tune began to be heard. In 1902 the Zionist editor Lurye (co-editor with Ravnitski of the well-known periodical *Der yid*) wrote that Yiddish must not only be considered as a means of propa-

ganda but as 'a national-cultural possession which must be developed to play the role of our second national language' (Roznhak 1969). In 1905 the Bund adopted its declaration on behalf of Jewish national-cultural autonomy with Yiddish as the language of the Jewish proletariat and of the intellectuals that serve and lead that proletariat. Scholarly literary organizations in the field of Yiddish began to arise soon thereafter: (a) 1908, The Yiddish Literary Organization (St. Petersburg), (b) 1909, The Yiddish Historical-Ethnographic Organization (St. Petersburg), (c) 1908, The Musical-Dramatic Organization (Vilna).

7. For a more detailed examination of Nosn Birnboym's life and thought see my forthcoming *Nosn Birnboym: A Study in Personality, Ideology, and Language* (ms). Also, in connection with his Yiddish advocacy in particular, see note 3 in the Foreword to this volume.

Dokter birnboyms vokhnblat that he had founded in Tshernovits (Czernowitz, Czernowce, Chernovtsy, Cernauti),[8] to which he had moved at the invitation of university students in Vienna who hailed from Tshernovits, were sympathetic toward Yiddish, and who had come under the influence of his writings. However, Tshernovits did not give him the visibility (nor the income) that he required, and he decided to visit the United States in pursuit of both and on behalf of Yiddish, 'the world language of a world people'.

Birnboym's initial host in the United States was the socialist-Zionist Dovid Pinski, already well known as a Yiddish novelist and dramatist, who had read Birnboym's articles in German and was eager to help him reach a wider pro-Yiddish audience. Immediately attracted to Birnboym's cause was the socialist-territorialist[9] theoretician and philosopher Khayem Zhitlovski (for extensive bibliographic details see Roznboym 1929). The three of them formed a curious troika (a neotraditionalist on his way back to full-fledged Orthodoxy, a labor-Zionist, and a philosophical secularist), but together they issued a resolution for a world conference concerning Yiddish, composed in Pinski's apartment on Beck Street in the South Bronx (also signed by the playwright Yankev Gordon and the publisher Alex Yevalenko), and together they brought it to a less than massive public at two 'evenings' (Yiddish: *ovntn* although not necessarily transpiring in the evening) on the Lower East Side. Far more unforgettable than the arguments that they then marshaled for such a conference and more impressive than the proposed order of business suggested in connection with it, was the fact that its chief architect, Birnboym, spoke to the audiences in German (for he could not yet speak standard or formal Yiddish, although he had begun to write Yiddish articles in 1904). His addresses, although purposely peppered with Yiddishisms, struck most commentators as impressive but funny, funny but painful. The intelligentsia was learning its mother tongue so that the latter could fulfill new functions, and thereby provide new statuses to masses and intelligentsia alike.

---

8. Tshernovits is currently located in the Ukrainian SSR. Between the two World Wars it was in Rumania. At the time of the Language Conference, and ever since the Austrian occupation in 1774 (after defeating the Ottoman Turkish occupants), it was in a section of the Austro-Hungarian Empire known as Bukovina (until 1848 administratively a part of Galicia with which Bukovina remained closely connected as far as 'Jewish geography' was concerned).

9. Territorialism acknowledged the need for planned Jewish resettlement in an internationally recognized and protected Jewish territory, but did not consider Palestine to be the only or the most desirable location for such resettlement in view of the conflicting claims and geopolitical perils associated with it. Various territorial concentrations in Eastern Europe itself, in Africa (Angola, Cyrenaica, Uganda), in South America (Surinam), in North America (Kansas-Nebraska), in Australia (Kimberly Region) and elsewhere have been advocated since the latter part of the nineteenth century. At one point Herzl himself was not convinced that a homeland in Palestine and only in Palestine should be adamantly pursued and was willing to consider a 'way station' elsewhere. Most territorialists split with the Zionist movement and set up an organization of their own in 1905, when the Seventh Zionist Congress rejected an offer by the British government to create an autonomous Jewish settlement in Uganda.

But there *was* an intended 'order of business' for Tshernovits, no matter how much it may have been overlooked at the *ovntn* or even at the conference itself. Birnboym, Zhitlovski, and Pinski agreed (primarily at the latter's insistence) to 'avoid politics' and 'resolutions on behalf of Yiddish' (Pinski 1948), particularly since the political and ideological context of Yiddish differed greatly in Czarist Russia, in Hapsburg Austro-Hungary, and in the immigrant United States. Thus they agreed upon a 'practical agenda' and a 'working conference' devoted to the following ten points:

1. Yiddish spelling
2. Yiddish grammar
3. Foreign words and new words
4. A Yiddish dictionary
5. Jewish youth and the Yiddish language
6. The Yiddish press
7. The Yiddish theater and Yiddish actors
8. The economic status of Yiddish writers
9. The economic status of Yiddish actors
10. Recognition for the Yiddish language

The agenda starts off with four items of corpus planning.[10] Yiddish was correctly seen as being in need of authoritative codification and elaboration in order to standardize its usage and systematize its future growth. Major corpus planning efforts for Yiddish – though called for and attempted before – were a sign of its new importance. Point five recognized the dangers that modernization represented for the ethnic identity of the younger generation, particularly if it pursued education and advancement in co-territorial vernaculars to the exclusion of Yiddish. Points six to nine stressed press and theater – their quality and their economic viability – the massive means of bringing modern Yiddish creativity to the public. Finally, the last point recognized something that was certainly on Birnboym's mind. Jews themselves – not to speak of gentiles – were unaccustomed to granting recognition to Yiddish, and, therefore, such recognition was often begrudged it even by democratic or democratizing regimes that gave some consideration to cultural autonomy or to officially recognized cultural

10. Corpus planning is one of the two major branches of language planning: the authoritative allocation of resources (attention, funds, manpower, negative and positive sanctions) to language. Corpus planning entails modifying, enriching, or standardizing the language per se, often via publishing and implementing orthographies, nomenclatures, spellers, grammars, style manuals, etc. Its counterpart is status planning, i.e. attempts to require use of a language for particular functions: education, law, government, mass media, etc. Corpus planning is frequently engaged in by language academies, commissions, or boards. Status planning requires governmental or other power-related decision making and sanctions-disbursing bodies: political, religious, ethnocultural or economic. The two processes must be conducted in concert if they are to succeed and take hold across a broad spectrum of uses and users. Yiddish has constantly suffered due to deficiencies in the status planning realm and, as a result, its corpus planning successes are also limited, although several can be cited (Shekhter 1961). For a detailed empirical and theoretical review of language planning, see Joan Rubin et al. (1978).

pluralism (as did pre-World War I Austro-Hungary). As Pinski in particular feared, the entire agenda of the conference was 'subverted' by the tenth point and, indeed, was dominated by what was in reality only half of that point: *Jewish* recognition for Yiddish.

WHY WAS THE CONFERENCE HELD IN TSHERNOVITS?

Tshernovits was only a modest sized town (21,500 Jews out of a total population of 68,400) and of no particular importance *vis-à-vis* Jewish cultural, political, and economic developments. It was clearly overshadowed by Warsaw, Vilna, Odessa, and several other urban centers in the Pale of Settlement within the Czarist empire. Nevertheless, the recent history of Czarist repressions may have made it undesirable (if no longer clearly impossible) to convene the conference in one of those centers. Even within the Austro-Hungarian Empire, however, such Jewish centers as Kruke (Cracow), Lemberik (Lemberg, Lvov), and Brod (Brody) were clearly of greater importance than Tshernovits. Tshernovits was of course, easily accessible to Yiddish speakers in Austro-Hungary, Czarist Russia and Rumania, but its symbolic significance far surpassed its locational convenience and was two-fold: (a) Not only was it in *frantsyozsefs medine* but many segments of its hitherto significantly Germanized Jewish intelligentsia were already struggling to revise their attitudes toward Yiddish – a struggle that was particularly crucial for that period in Austro-Hungarian cultural politics *vis-à-vis* Germans, Poles, Ukrainians/Ruthenians, and Jews in the Bukovina and in Galicia as well – and (b) Birnboym had already decided to relocate there and had several young followers there (many of whom were students at the university in Vienna during the school year – and had there been influenced by Birnboym). These young followers could provide (on a volunteer basis and during the summer vacation period in particular) the technical/organizational under-pinnings of a world conference for Yiddish. Indeed, these young followers consti-tuted, with Birnboym, the organizational committee that sent out the invitations to individual organizations and committees, secured a hall (not without difficulty), planned a banquet and a literary evening, and disbursed the meager fees that the participants in the conference paid in order to be either delegates (5 Kronen) or guests (1 Krone). Both of these factors (the convening of the Conference in Tshernovits and Birnboym's young but inexperienced followers there in the grips of their own discovery of H-possibilities for Yiddish) influenced the course of the conference. The delicate balance of minority relations in Galicia and Bukovina resulted in more widespread attention being paid to the first Yiddish World Conference than its sponsors had bargained for. The census of 1910 was already being discussed, and it was apparent that the authorities again wanted Jews to claim either German (in Bukovina) or Polish (in Galicia) as mother tongue (as had been done in 1890) in order to defuse or counterbalance the growing pressure from Ukrainians/Ruthenians and Rumanians for additional language privileges and parliamentary representation. Previously, Jews had been counted upon to buttress the establishment out of fear that 'unrest' would lead to anti-Jewish developments of one kind or another. It was equally apparent that young Jews were disinclined to play this role any longer and that they were threatening to claim either Yiddish or Hebrew, even though neither was on the approved list of mother tongues and even though claiming a language not on the list was a punishable offense.[11] Indeed so great was the tension concerning the conference that the president of the Jewish community (*kehile*) in Tshernovits refused to permit the conference to meet in community facilities for fear of incurring official displeasure or worse. Clearly, a new within-fold status for Yiddish would have intragroup repercussions as well: upsetting the former within-group diglossia system was also related to new intergroup aspirations as well and these were, of necessity, political and economic (or likely to be suspected of being such), rather than merely cultural (no matter what the official agenda of the conference might be).

Moreover, meeting in Tshernovits also determined the very nature of the guests and delegates (a distinction that was soon ignored) that could attend, discuss, propose, vote upon, and ultimately implement the conference's deliberations and resolutions. The regional tensions in conjunction with national/cultural rights resulted in attendance by a more substantial number of students and ordinary folk, many in search of something spectacular or even explosive, than might otherwise have been the case. Similarly, because of the characteristics of Bukovinian Jewry per se there were more Zionists and fewer Bundists,[12] more traditionally-religiously oriented and fewer proletarian-politically oriented

11. Vays reminisces as follows (1937, i.e. 30 years after the Conference): 'As is well known, Yiddish was not recognized in Austria as a language, just as the Jewish people was not recognized as such. At the university, e.g., it was necessary to fill out a rubric "nationality" and no Jew was permitted to write in "Jew". The nationalist-oriented Jewish students, not wanting to cripple the statistical distribution in favor of the ruling nationality to the detriment of the minority nationalities, sought various ways of forcing the authorities to recognize the Jewish nationality. Some wrote the name of a nationality that happened to occur to them. There was no lack of entries of "Hottentot" mother tongue and "Malay" nationality.' This context for the Conference led the Yiddish *Sotsyal demokrat* of Cracow to greet the Conference as follows: 'The significance of the Conference is augmented by the fact that it takes place in Austria where Yiddish is closest to official recognition' (Kisman 1958). Tshernovits itself also impressed the delegates and guests from abroad (primarily from the Czarist empire) not only with its ethnic hetero-geneity but with its 'air of relative democracy, where at every step one could feel European culture' (Kisman 1958).

For Eastern European Jewry the late nineteenth–early twentieth century Austro-Hungarian Empire represented Western-style democracy plus nationality-cultural rights, both of which were still sadly lacking in the Czarist empire and both of which were foundational to the conference's goals, although neither was explicitly referred to at the conference itself.

12. The Bund (full name: Jewish Workers Bund [= Alliance] of Russia, Lithuania, and Poland) was organized in Vilna in 1897, the same year as the first Zionist Congress was held in Basel. Always socialist, it adopted a Jewish cultural-autonomist, Yiddish oriented platform in 1905, as a result of which it clashed with Lenin, Trotsky, and other early Bolshevik leaders. The Bund became the mainstay of secular Yiddish educational, literary, and cultural efforts in interwar Poland. For further details and entry to a huge bibliography, see Mendelsohn 1970 and Kligsberg 1974.

delegates and guests than would have been the case elsewhere. Birnboym's youthful admirers and assistants were quite incapable of rectifyng this imbalance via such simple means as sending more invitations to more 'nationally conscious' circles. Indeed, for them, as for most Jewish intellectuals in Tshernovits per se, the idea of a conference *on behalf of* Yiddish and conducted *in* Yiddish was not quite believable even as it materialized. Most local Jewish intellectuals were 'the mainstay of...daytshtum (Germanness), and of a *sui generis* daytshtum to boot, Bukovinian daytshtum. None of the socially and politically active local (Jewish) intellectuals imagined anything like speaking to the people in its language. Indeed, when Berl Loker, who belonged to the exceptions, then a young student, was about to give a lecture in Yiddish, he invited my wife to attend as follows: "Come and you will hear how one speaks pure Yiddish at a meeting!" The best recommendation for a speaker was the accomplishment of being able to speak to a crowd in lovely and ornate German' (Vays 1937). Thus, the lingering disbelief that Yiddish was suitable for H pursuits ('Is Yiddish a language?') *surrounded* the conference and even found its way *into* the conference, and did so in Tshernovits more than it would have in many other, more industrialized and proletarianized centers of Jewish urban concentration and modernization. Bukovinian Jewry and its modernizing elites were then both still relatively untouched by the more sophisticated pro- and anti-Yiddish sentiments that were at a much higher pitch in Warsaw, Vilna, Lodz, or Odessa.

WHO ATTENDED THE CONFERENCE?

The invitations sent by Birnboym's 'secretariat' were addressed to those organizations and communities whose addresses they happened to have. Many *unimportant* societies and clubs were invited, whereas many even more important ones were not. Personal invitations were few and far between. The writer and essayist Y. L. Perets (1852–1915), perhaps the major influence upon the younger generation of Yiddish writers and a conscious ideologist of synthesis between all Jewish values and symbols, modern and traditional, *was* invited and came with his wife (with whom he spoke more Polish than Yiddish). The two other 'classicists of modern Yiddish literature', Sholem Aleykhem (1859–1910) and Mendele Moyker Sforim (1836–1917), were also invited but did not come. Sholem Aleykhem at least claimed to be ill, but Mendele, in his seventies, offered no excuse at all, and, as a result, was sent no greetings by the conference such as were sent to Sholem Aleykhem. Zhitlovski came but Pinski was 'busy writing a book' (Pinski 1948). A young linguist, Matesyohu Mizes (Mathias Mieses), was invited (as were two other linguistics-oriented students, Ayzenshtat and Sotek) to address the conference on the linguistic issues that apparently constituted 40 percent of its agenda. Other than the above individual invitations,

A postcard printed soon after the Tshernovits Conference, showing left to right, A. Reyzin, Y. L. Perets, Sh. Ash, Kh. Zhitlovski, and H. D. Nomberg

a general invitation was issued and broadcast via the Yiddish press and by word of mouth 'to all friends of Yiddish'. All in all some 70 showed up and these were characterized by one participant (and later major critic) as having only one thing in common: 'They could afford the fare...Everyone was his own master, without any sense of responsibility to others' (E[ste]r 1908).

The geographic imbalance among the resulting participants is quite clear:

From the Czarist Empire: 14; among this delegation were found the most prestigeful participants: Perets, Sholem Ash (still young but already a rising star), Avrom Reyzin (a well-known and much beloved poet), D. Nomberg (writer and journalist; later: a deputy in the Polish Sejm and founder of a small political party, *yidishe folkistishe partey*, stressing Yiddish and Diaspora cultural autonomy), N. Prilutski (linguist, folklorist, journalist; later: Sejm deputy), Ester (Bundist; later: Communist [Kombund and Yevsektsiye] leader). Zhitlovski (though coming from the United States) and Ayznshtat (though then studying in Bern) were also usually counted with the 'Russians'.

From Rumania: 1; I. Sotek of Braila (an advocate of writing Yiddish with Latin characters and a student of Slavic elements in Yiddish).

From Galicia and Bukovina: 55; among them eight minor literary figures and 47 students, merchants, bookkeepers, craftsmen, etc., including one 'wedding entertainer' (*badkhn*). This group was the least disciplined and, on its home territory, least impressed and convinced by attempts to keep to any agenda.

At the most crucial votes no more than forty members participated...In the vote on the resolution that Yiddish be considered a national [Jewish] language no more than 36 individuals participated. People always were arriving late to sessions. Some did not know what they were voting about. People voted and contradicted their own previous votes. In addition it was always noisy due to the booing and the applauding of 'guests from Tshernovits'. No one at all listened to Ayznshtat's paper on Yiddish spelling (E[ste]r 1908).

Nor was the banquet or the literary program any more orderly or consensual. When local Jewish workers arrived to attend the banquet

...it was discovered that they lacked black jackets and they were not admitted. They began to complain. Some of the more decently clad ones were selected and admitted without jackets. Some of the 'indecently' clad workers took umbrage and protested so long that the policeman took pity on them and sent them away. As a result, the 'decently' clad ones also decided to leave. After the opening remarks I called everyone's attention to what had occurred. It immediately became noisy and I was told to stop speaking. I left the banquet and a few others accompanied me (E[ste]r 1908).

Attracting an elite to modern H functions for an erstwhile traditional L runs into problems due to the fact that prior and concurrent social issues have brought about allegiances and identities that are not congruent with those that further the interests of the new elite and the new functions. Reformulation of identities and regrouping of allegiances are called for and are difficult for all concerned.

The conference per se

The conference lasted for a little under a week, beginning on Sunday August 30, 1908.

A quarter after ten in the morning there walked onto the stage Nosn Birnboym in the company of Y. L. Perets, S. Ash, Dr. Kh. Zhitlovski and other distinguished guests...Dr. N. Birnboym opens the conference reading his first speech in Yiddish fluently from his notes...He reads his speech in the Galician dialect (*Rasvet*, Sept. 1908: quoted from *Afn shvel* 1968).

Birnboym stressed the fact that this was the first worldwide effort on behalf of Yiddish, sponsored by its greatest writers ('respected even by the opponents of Yiddish') and the beginning of a long chain of efforts yet to come. These opening remarks caused a sensation among local Tshernovitsians:

Everyone knew that he [Birnboym] doesn't speak Yiddish and that the speech would be translated from German. However, all were eager to hear how the 'coarse' words would sound coming from the mouth of Dr. Birnboym who was known as an excellent German speaker...However at the festive banquet in honor of the esteemed guests...he spoke superbly in German, the way only he could (Vays 1937).

Indeed, a speaker's ability to speak Yiddish well and the very fact that Yiddish *could* be spoken as befitted a world conference, i.e. in a cultivated, learned, disciplined fashion in conjunction with modern concerns, never ceased to impress those who had never before heard it so spoken.

Zhitlovski made the greatest impression on all the delegates and guests, both at the conference and at the banquet (which was a great event for Yiddish culture that was still so unknown to most of those in attendance). 'That kind of Yiddish is more beautiful than French!' was a comment heard from all quarters and particularly from circles that had hitherto rejected Yiddish from a 'purely esthetic' point of view (Vays 1937).[13]

Yiddish used adeptly in an H function was itself a triumph for Tshernovits, almost regardless of what was said more substantively.

But of course a great deal *was* said substantively as well. The linguistic issues were 'covered' by Ayznshtat, Sotek, and Mizes. Whereas the first two were roundly ignored, the third caused a storm of protests when, in the midst of a paper on fusion languages and their hybridlike strength, creativity, and vigor, he also attacked *loshn koydesh* for being dead, stultifying, and decaying. Only Perets' intervention saved Mizes' paper for the record as 'the first scientific paper in Yiddish on Yiddish' (Anon. 1931).[14] Obviously, the tenth agenda item stubbornly refused to wait its place in line and constantly came to the fore in the form of an increasingly growing antagonism between those (primarily Bundists) who wanted to declare Yiddish as *the* national Jewish language (Hebrew/*loshn koydesh* – being a classical tongue rather than a mother tongue – could not, in their view, qualify as such) and those (primarily Zionists and traditionalists) who, at best, would go no further than to declare Yiddish as *a* national Jewish language, so that the role of Hebrew/*loshn koydesh* – past, present, and future – would remain unsullied.[15] In the midst of this fundamental

13. The 'esthetic point of view' is dealt with at length by Miron (1973). Although not unknown in connection with other supposedly inelegant vernaculars during the period of struggle to legitimize them for H functions, the vituperation heaped upon Yiddish in terms of its claimed aesthetic shortcomings clearly seems to border on the hysterical. Loathsome, ugly, stunted, crippled, mangled, hunchbacked, gibberish were commonplace. 'Away with dirt, with spiderwebs, with *zhargon* and with all kinds of garbage! We call for a broom! And whom the broom of satire will not help, him will we honor with the stick of wrath! Quem medicamenta non sanant, ferrum et ignis sanant!' (*Jutrzenka* 1862: (50): 428). Note however that the aesthetic metaphor (e.g. the German Jewish historian Graetz refused to 'dirty his pen' with Yiddish or to have his works translated into that 'foul tongue'), interesting though it may be in and of itself, must not obscure from analysis more basic social, cultural, and political goals and loyalties of those that express them. The Yiddish proverb *nisht dos iz lib vos iz sheyn, nor dos iz sheyn vos iz lib* (We do not love that which is lovely, rather we consider lovely that which we

love) applies fully here. By the time of Tshernovits the full force of invective had begun to pass (although it can be encountered in Israel and elsewhere to this very day. See, e.g. Fishman and Fishman 1978) and the countertide of positive hyperbole had begun to rise, assigning to Yiddish not only beauty but virtue, subtlety, honesty, compassion, intimacy, and boundless depth.

14. While it is certainly inaccurate to consider Mizes' comments as 'the first scientific paper in Yiddish on Yiddish', it is not easy to say whose work does deserve to be so characterized, primarily because of changing standards as to what is and is not scientific. One of my favorites is Y. M. Lifshits' Yiddish–Russian dictionary (1876), and his introduction thereto, both of which remain quite admirable pieces of scholarship to this very day. Other candidates for this honorific status abound.

15. Somewhat positive Zionist stances toward exilic Jewish vernaculars had surfaced from time to time well before Tshernovits. Reference is made here not merely to utilizing such vernaculars for immediate educational/indoctrinational purposes, such usage being acceptable to almost the

argument, more primitive views still surfaced as a result of the presence of so many ideologically unmodernized guests. One of the delegates recounts the following tale:

...(T)here suddenly appears on the stage a man with a long, red beard, wearing a traditional black, *kapote* (kaftan) and *yarmelke* (skull-cap). He begins speaking by saying 'I will tell you a story'. The hall is full of quiet expectancy. We all listened carefully in order to hear a good, folksy anecdote. The man recounts in great detail a story about how two Jews once sued each other in court because of a *shoyfer* (ritual ram's horn) that had been stolen from the *beysmedresh* (house of study and prayer). With great difficulty they explained to the gentile judge what a *shoyfer* is. Finally the judge asked: 'In one word – a trumpet?' At this point the litigants shuddered and one shouted to the other: 'Is a *shoyfer* a trumpet?' The assembled participants in the hall were ready to smile at this 'anecdote' which had long been well known, when the man suddenly began to shout at the top of his lungs: 'You keep on talking about language, but is Yiddish (*zhargon*) a language?' (Kisman 1958).

The compromise formulation penned by Nomberg ('*a* national Jewish language') was finally adopted, thanks only to the insistance of Perets, Birnboym, and Zhitlovski, over the vociferous opposition of both left wing and right wing extremists who either favored an exclusive role for Yiddish ('*the* national Jewish language') or who wanted no resolutions at all on political topics.[16]

Very little time was devoted to organizational or implementational issues such as whether the conference itself should sponsor 'cultural work', convene a second conference within a reasonable time, or even establish a permanent office (secretariat) and membership organization. Although the last two recommendations were adopted (the first was rejected due to unified left wing and right wing disenchantment with the conference's stance *re* the *the* or *a* national language issue), and, although Birnboym and two young assistants were elected to be the executive officers and to establish a central office, very little was actually done along these lines. At any rate, the tasks entrusted to the secretariat were minimal and inocuous ones indeed. In addition, Birnboym soon moved ever closer to unreconstructed Orthodoxy and to its stress on matters 'above and

---

entire Zionist spectrum, but to allocating intimacy related and even literacy related functions to them, both in the Diaspora and (even) in Erets Yisroel on a relatively permanent basis. Herzl himself (in his *Diary* 1885), suggests a parallel with Switzerland, such that Hebrew, Yiddish, and Judezmo [= Judeo-Spanish] would be recognized. Except in Labor Zionist circles such views were very much in the minority, remained little developed or concretized, but yet provided the basis for claims at Tshernovits that, since many Zionists/Hebraists had been careful not to reject Yiddish,

so socialists/Yiddishists should do nothing to reject Hebrew/*loshn koydesh*.

16. Interestingly enough, the Balfour Declaration, issued by the British government on November 2, 1917, favoring 'the establishment in Palestine of *a* national home for the Jews, but without prejudice to the civil and religious rights of existing non-Jewish communities' also used the *in*definite (a) rather than the definite article (the) as a compromise between opposite extreme views in the Foreign Ministry.

beyond language'. (He subsequently continued to defend Yiddish as a bulwark of tradition but pointed out that it was the tradition rather than the language that really counted. He therefore metaphorically translated the prayer book phrase *roymemonu mikol loshn* not, as it was usually understood, 'Thou hast raised us above all other languages', but rather, 'Thou hast raised us above all languages', Birnboym [1946]). At any rate, he was not an administrator/executive but an ideologue. He was, as always, pennyless, and the funds that were required for an office and for his salary never materialized. Zhitlovski returned to America and threw himself into efforts there to start Yiddish supplementary schools and to restrain Jewish socialists from sacrificing their own Jewishness and the Jewish people as a whole on the altar of Americanization disguised as proletarian brotherhood. Perets did undertake one fund-raising trip to St. Petersburg where Shimen Dubnov (1860–1941), the distinguished historian and ideologist of cultural autonomy in the Diaspora and himself a recent convert to the value of Yiddish, had convened a small group of wealthy but Russified potential donors. The latter greeted Perets with such cold cynicism that he 'told them off' ('our salvation will come from the poor but warm-hearted Jews of the Pale rather than from the rich but cold-hearted Jews of St. Petersburg') and 'slammed the door'. Thus, for various reasons, no office was ever really established in Tshernovits and even the minutes of the conference remained unpublished (although S. A. Birnboym helped prepare them for publication by editing out as many Germanisms as possible), were soon misplaced or lost and had to be reconstructed more than two decades later from press clippings and memoirs (Anon. 1931).

Intellectuals (and even an intelligentsia) alone can rarely establish a movement. Intellectuals can reify language and react to it as a powerful symbol, as the bearer and actualizer of cultural values, behaviors, traditions, goals. However, for an L to spread into H functions more concrete considerations (jobs, funds, influence, status, control, power) are involved. Only the Yiddishist 'left' had in mind an economic, political, and cultural revolution that would have placed Yiddish on top. But that 'left' did not even control the Tshernovits Conference, to say nothing of the hard, cruel world that surrounded it.

AMERICAN REACTIONS TO THE TSHERNOVITS CONFERENCE

The increasingly democratic, culturally pluralistic, and culturally autonomistic prewar Austro-Hungarian Empire was the model toward which mankind was moving insofar as the leading figures at Tshernovits were concerned. One of the areas of Jewish concentration in which this was most clearly not the case – and where the very concept of a symbolically unified, modernized, worldwide Jewish nationality with a stable, all-purpose vernacular of its own was least understood, accepted, and actualized – was the United States. No wonder then that the Tshernovits Conference was generally accorded a cool reception here and even a derisive one.[17] The idea of teaching people how to spell or write or speak Yiddish 'correctly' was viewed by one journalist as being no less ridiculous than the idea of teaching people to laugh correctly, grammatically (Sambatyen, A falsher gelekhter, gor on gramatik, *Yidishes Tageblat*,[18] Sept. 1, 1908). The *Tageblat* was an Orthodox-oriented paper and in its editorials before and after the conference it stressed that *loshn koydesh* alone was of value for Jewishness, while English (or other co-territorial vernaculars elsewhere) met all of the general and citizenship needs that Jews might have. To elevate Yiddish to H functions was not only ridiculous but blasphemous.

> If the resolutions of the conference declare... that all of the Jewishness will be found in Ash's drama 'God of Vengeance' and in Perets' 'Shtrayml'...will anyone care? Our people decided long ago that we are a nationality and that our national language is none other than that in which the spirit of the Jewish people developed...the language in which the Bible is written, the Book that has made us immortal (Sept. 20, 1908).

If the Orthodox-bourgeois *Tageblat* was unfriendly toward the conference, to say the least, the secular-socialist *Forverts* (still publishing to this very day and now in its 82nd year) was almost every bit as much so. Its correspondent Moris Roznfeld (a famous Yiddish laborite-poet in his own right) wrote from Galicia just a few days before the conference opened:

> I know that with just a few exceptions there is not much interest in America in this Tshernovits Conference and for many reasons. First of all, most believe that nothing practical will come of it. Secondly, the American Yiddish writer, as well as the Yiddish reader, is not terribly interested in rules of grammar. What difference does it make whether one writes גיין, געהן or גאַין [all pronounced geyn/gayn depending on speaker's regional dialect], איד, ייד, יוד or even יאָהודי [the first three pronounced id/yid and the last – utilized only ironically/contrastively in Yiddish – Yahudi, and, therefore not really an orthographic variant in a continuum with the first three], as long as it can be read and understood...? Among the majority of even our good writers, Yiddish is regarded merely as a ferry that leads to the other side, to the language of the land, which each of us must learn in the land in which he finds himself.
>
> But these views, objectively and impartially stated, apply only to America. Here, in Galicia, they are more than merely grammatical issues. Here it is a political issue, an issue of life itself...

17. Several of the references and citations in this section are originally found in Rothstein 1977.

18. Just as Yiddish books commonly carried *loshn koydesh* titles until rather late in the nineteenth century, so Yiddish periodicals commonly bore either *loshn koydesh* or German titles even into the present century. The diglossic implications are manifold even at an unconscious level. The people of 'The Book' was (and in the more unreconstructed-Orthodox circles still is), accustomed to encounter serious H-level writing (and particularly such on intragroup concerns) in *loshn koydesh*.

Thus, a Hebrew title for a Yiddish book is, in part, a visual habit, in part a cultural signal, and in part a disguise (*vis-à-vis* rabbinic criticism and other possibly hostile authorities). Similarly, a relatively ephemeral periodical dealing with the wide world of modern secular events is entitled in German for much the same reasons. Neither *forverts* nor *yidishes* nor *tageblat* were parts of commonly spoken Eastern European Yiddish by well before the nineteenth century. Nevertheless these were perfectly acceptable components of a journalistic title of those times, particularly in the United States.

...If it were to be officially decided that *loshn koydesh* is the Jewish language, then the Jewish masses would lose their power and their vernacular would be ignored. Only the Jewish snobs, the aristocratic, 'let-them-eat-cake' idealists, would gain thereby. Therefore, the eyes of the real friends of the people and of the friends of the workers in Galicia and even in Russia are turned towards Tshernovits. Therefore the conference there has major, historical importance. I don't know from what point of view the conference will treat the language issue...The conference might even be of an academic, theoretical nature...Nevertheless, the conference will have strong reverberations on Jewish politics in Galicia.

Note Roznfeld's total disinterest in either the linguistic portion or any possible American validity of the Tshernovits agenda. In 1908 few American Yiddish writers, few even among the secular laborites among them, aspired to H functions for Yiddish. In their eyes Jews, as workers, were destined to be part of the greater American proletariat and English would, therefore, be its language for higher socialist purposes, and, ultimately, its brotherly interethnic vernacular as well. The Bund's 1905 Declaration, and its positing of Jewish cultural autonomy in Eastern Europe, with Yiddish as the national language of the Jewish proletariat, was considered, at best, to be a politically relevant platform for Eastern European Jewry alone, but one that was irrelevant for those who had immigrated to 'the Golden Land'. Thus, if neither the linguistic nor the political potentialities of the conference applied here then the conference as a whole was merely a distant echo, and either a somewhat funny one or a clearly sacreligious one at that. If it was difficult to assign H functions to Yiddish in its very own massive heartland, where its stability was less threatened (so it seemed) and where all agreed as to its utility, how much more difficult was it to do so in immigrant-America where its transitionality was assumed by secularists and traditionalists alike?

EASTERN EUROPEAN REACTIONS TO THE CONFERENCE

If the brunt of American commentary on the conference was negative, that in Eastern Europe was initially equally or even more so, and on three grounds. As expected, the Hebraist and extreme-Zionist reaction was unrelentingly hostile. In their eyes Yiddish was a language that demoted Jewry from its incomparable classical heights to the superficiality and vacuousness of such illiterate peasant tongues as Ukrainian, Lithuanian, Rumanian, etc. To foster Yiddish struck J. Klausner, Z. Epshteyn, and many other Hebraists as being laughable, if it were not so sad; an exercise in self-impoverishment and self-debasement. A considerable number of those who shared their view urged that a massive counterconference be convened (and, indeed, the First World Conference for the Hebrew Language *was* convened in Berlin in 1910) and that an even more massive propaganda campaign be launched to attack Tshernovits and its infamous resolution. However the veteran Hebraist and philosopher Aḥad Ha-'am (1856–1927) argued vehemently against such efforts on the grounds that they would give Tshernovits more visibility than it could ever attain on its own. According to Aḥad Ha-'am the Jewish people had already experienced two great philosophical disasters in the Diaspora: Christianity and Hasidism.[19] Both of these had mushroomed precisely because Jews themselves had paid too much attention to them by dignifying them with unnecessary commentary. This sad lesson should not be applied to Tshernovits and to Yiddishism as a whole. They were *muktse makhmes miyes* (mukẓe meḥamat mius), *loathsomely ugly*, and the less said about them the better.

If the right wing opposition generally elected to counter Tshernovits with a wall of silence, the left wing opposition apparently decided to drown it to death in a sea of words. From their point of view Tshernovits had been a 'sell out' on the part of those who were willing to water down, render tepid, and weaken the position *vis-à-vis* Yiddish of 'the broad folk-masses' and 'the Jewish proletariat', in order to curry favor among the bourgeoisie, via adopting an uninspired and uninspiring 'all Israel are brothers' approach. The modern, secular, socialist sector of the Jewish people, 'the revolutionary and nationality-building sector', had, by then, already surpassed the meager goals and the luke-warm resolutions of Tshernovits. They, therefore, refused to be compromised and whittled down by a conference that was 'an episode instead of a happening' (Kazhdan 1928) and whose resolution was no more than 'a harmful illusion' (Zilberfarb 1928) and 'a mistake that must not be reiterated' (Khmurner 1928).

The Tshernovits Conference was converted into the opposite of what its initiators had projected. Its isolation from the Jewish labor movement took its revenge upon the Conference...The great masters of Yiddish literature did not possess the magic to convert the Jewish middle class and the bourgeois intellectuals into co-combatants and partners with the Jewish workers in the latter's great national role of limitless loyalty to the Yiddish language. Yiddish cultural life therefore far surpassed the Tshernovits Conference...Neither at the Teachers Conference in Vilna, nor at the organizational convention of the Central Yiddish School Organization (*Tsisho*), nor at the Tsisho-Convention of 1925 where the founding of the Yivo [= Yiddish Scientific Institute; today: Yivo Institute for Jewish Research] was proclaimed, nor at any of the many other [Yiddish] teachers conferences in Poland was there even a word spoken about the Tshernovits Conference...Today, 60 years after Tshernovits we know: Tshernovits was not destined to have any heirs...There was really nothing to inherit (Kazhdan 1968).

19. Ḥasidism: a Jewish movement founded in Poland in the eighteenth century by Rabbi Israel Baal Shem Tov and characterized by its emphasis on mysticism, spontaneous prayer, religious zeal and joy. The various ḥasidic leaders or masters (singular: *rébe*, plural: *rebéyim*, distinguished from *rov*, *rabonim* among non-Hasidim) typically instructed their followers via tales. Yiddish was, therefore, their crucial medium and their tales became an early major component of popular Yiddish publishing (many also being published – first, simultaneously or soon thereafter – in *loshn koydesh*). Although much opposed by most rabbinic authorities for almost two centuries (the latter and their followers being dubbed *misnagdim*, i.e. opponents), ḥasidism finally became generally accepted as a co-valid version of Jewish Orthodoxy and is a vibrant (and the more numerous) branch thereof, as well as a major (but largely unideologized) source of support for Yiddish, to this day.

Even now, over three decades after the Holocaust – when most commentators tend to wax lyrical about Jewish Eastern Europe and to remember it in somewhat rosy terms – there remain Bundist leaders who remember Tshernovits only as a flubbed opportunity.

Even those who were quite satisfied with Tshernovits in symbolic terms soon realized that it was a fiasco in any practical organizational terms. As soon as the First World War was over (and, indeed, in the very midst of the war in anticipation of its conclusion) various Yiddish writers and cultural spokesmen began to call for 'a world conference for Yiddish culture as a result of purely practical rather than demonstrative and declarative goals. We have outgrown the period of mere demonstrations and theoretical debates. There is much work to be done!' (Sh. N[iger] 1922). Zhitlovski himself called for 'an organization to openly unfurl the flag on which it will be clearly written: Yiddish, our national language, our only unity and freedom...a "Yiddishist" organization with the openly unfurled flag of our cultural liberation and national unity' (1928). Others repeatedly reinforced and repeated this view (e.g. Lehrer 1928; Mark 1968; Zelitsh 1968). As a result, most subsequent major nonpartisan or suprapartisan international efforts to organize Yiddish cultural efforts more effectively have viewed themselves as the instrumental heirs of the Tshernovits Conference (e.g. YIKUF-Yidisher kultur farband 1937; Yidisher kultur kongres 1948; Yerushelayemer velt konferents far Yidish un Yidisher kultur 1976). Clearly, however, the realities facing Yiddish after World War I were far different than those that Tshernovits assumed. The multiethnic Austro-Hungarian Empire had been split into several smaller states, each jealously protective of its particular national (= state building) language and quick to set aside the Trianon and Versailles guarantees to Yiddish (Tenenboym 1957/1958). The former Czarist 'pale of settlement' was either in the same situation as the foregoing (insofar as Poland and the Baltic states were concerned) or, ultimately, under even more powerful Russificatory control than before (in White Russia and in the Ukraine). Despite Bundist grievances, a good part of the spirit of Tshernovits lived for two postwar decades in the Yiddish schools, youth clubs, theaters, and cultural organizations of Poland, Lithuania, and Rumania, and, despite Communist attacks, in their regulated counterparts in the USSR. However, by just prior to the Second World War, the former were economically starved and politically battered (Eisenstein 1949; Tartakover 1946), whereas the latter were being discontinued under duress of Russification fears and pressures (Choseed 1968). After the Second World War Jewish Eastern Europe was no more. It became incumbent on Yiddish devotees in the United States and in Israel, i.e. in two locales where Yiddish was originally not expected to benefit from the spirit of Tshernovits, to defend it if possible.

Reevaluating the Tshernovits Conference: shadow or substance?

Notwithstanding Kazhdan's lingering negative evaluation in 1968, distance has made the heart grow fonder insofar as the majority of commentators is concerned. Those few who initially held that the symbolism of Tshernovits had been substantial, i.e. that it had raised Yiddish to the status of an honorific co-symbol, regardless of what its practical shortcomings might have been (for example: Mayzl 1928, Prilutski 1928, Pludermakher 1928), finally carried the day. The views that are encountered today in Yiddishist circles are very much like those that began to be heard when the first commemorative celebrations in honor of Tshernovits were organized in 1928. (In September 1918 the First World War had technically not yet ended and celebrations were presumably not possible.) 'Yes, Yiddishism is a young movement, but it is not all that poor in traditions. One of the loveliest traditions of Yiddishism is the memory of the Tshernovits Conference. No memoirs, pedantry or arguments can darken the glow of that bright cultural dawn's early light that is known by the name: The Tshernovits Conference of 1908' (Pludermakher 1928). Perhaps it was and perhaps it wasn't necessary to compromise in connection with the crucial resolution. In either case, no one was fooled by the compromise: 'The Tshernovits Conference was recorded on the morrow immediately after the last session as the Yiddishist revolt – and that is the only way in which the opponents of the Yiddish language *could regard* it' (Prilutski 1928) for even to claim H *co*-functions *alongside* of Hebrew/*loshn koydesh* was a devastating rejection of what these opponents were aiming at. As a result, Tshernovits deserved to be viewed as 'the first mobilization' (Mayzl 1928) on behalf of Yiddish.

Seventy years after Tshernovits, Yiddishist opinion with respect to it is, if anything, even mellower. Living as they do with the constant if quiet anxiety produced by the continual attrition of Yiddish, Tshernovits has come to be viewed not merely as a milestone in the millennial struggle of Yiddish for symbolic recognition, but as symbolic of the best that Eastern Europe Jewry as a whole achieved and can offer to its far-flung progeny today. Tshernovits is viewed increasingly as a by-product of the confluence of the three organized movements in modern Jewish life: Jewish socialism, Zionism and neo-Orthodoxy. At Tshernovits representatives of all three recognized the significance of Yiddish. Tshernovits was the by-product of a confluence (and, therefore, it disappointed those who wanted it to be all theirs). It was a momentary confluence that quickly passed and, from that day to this, no one has been able to 'put them together again'. Indeed, absence does make the heart grow fonder:

They were three, the convenors of the Tshernovits Conference: the champion of Jewish cultural renaissance and consistent Zionist, Dovid Pinski. He came to the land (of Israel) in advanced age and died here. Khayim Zhitlovski, one of the first Jewish socialists who, after countless reincarnations in search for a solution to the Jewish question, in his old age, sought to attach himself to the 'Jewish' Autonomous Region, Birobidjan. And Nosn Birnboym, the ideologist of Zionism and nationalism, who, after various geographic and ideological wanderings, after various apostasies and conversions, finally reached the shores of Jewish eternity. He waited for the Messiah all his life and suffered terribly the pangs of His delayed coming...He sowed everywhere and others reaped. He gave up this world for the world to come. All three of them served the Jewish people, each in his own way, and as such they [and Tshernovits] will remain in our historical memory (Roznhak 1969).

THEORETICAL RECAPITULATIONS

The late nineteenth/early twentieth century efforts to gain and activate intellectual and mass support for Yiddish, and the Tshernovits Conference of 1908 in particular, illustrate several of the problems encountered in a particular type of language spread: the spread of a former L into H functions in High Culture (education, literature, scholarship), government, technology, and modern literacy-dependent pursuits more generally.

1. Many of those most active on behalf of advocating, rationalizing, and ideologizing this type of language spread will, themselves, have to learn how to use the erstwhile L in H functions, and, indeed, may have to learn the L per se. In this respect the spread of an L into H functions poses similar problems for those who are already literate (and who may, indeed, be the gatekeepers or guardians of literacy) as does the spread of any new vernacular into H functions. Nationalist language-spread movements that are not derived from an intragroup diglossia context (e.g. the promotion of Czech, Slovak etc. in pre-World War I days or of Catalan, Occitan, Irish, Nynorsk, etc., more recently), also often begin with intelligentsias that do not know or master the vernaculars that they are championing. In the Yiddish case many intellectuals of the late nineteenth century were not only *oriented* toward Hebrew/*loshn koydesh* as H for Jewish cultural affairs but *toward* either German, Russian, or Polish as H for modern purposes. Thus Ls existing within a traditional diglossia setting may face double opposition in seeking to attain H functions.

2. One set of factors hampering the spread of Ls into H functions is their own lack of codification (e.g. in orthography, grammar) and elaboration (in lexicon). However, there is a tension between such corpus planning, on the one hand, and status planning needs, on the other hand. It is difficult to turn to serious corpus planning while status planning is still so unsettled (or opposed) and it is difficult to succeed at status planning (particularly insofar as attracting ambivalent or negative intellectuals and literacy gatekeepers is concerned) on behalf of an L that is clearly deficient in terms of corpus characteristics that might render it more suitable for H functions.

3. The vicious cycle that exists between lack of corpus planning and lack of status planning is most decisively broken if a status shift can be forced (by legal reform, revolution, or disciplined social example). The Tshernovits Conference's gravitation toward the 'political (status planning) issue' was a spontaneous

recognition of this fact, so often pedantically overlooked by language technicians and 'experts' who are oriented toward the relatively easier corpus planning task alone.

4. The very same intragroup and intergroup status and power reward systems that previously lead intellectuals to seek/acquire literacy and position via one or more Hs, subsequently hinder the spread of Ls into these H functions. Any such language spread would imply a major dislocation or a change in intellectual and econo-political elites and prerogatives. If Yiddish had achieved H intragroup functions in the cultural-intellectual realm this would have threatened rabbinic/ traditional and modern Zionist/Hebraist hegemony in that sphere. In addition, the spread of Yiddish into H functions would not only have meant the displacement of one power/status elite by another but the popularization/ massification/democratization of intragroup political participation and a deemphasis on elitism as a whole. This too is similar to the dynamics and consequences of many modern nationalist advocacies of vernaculars except that the cultural– political opposition faced in the case of Yiddish may have been more variegated insofar as 'preferred' language is concerned, since not only Hebrew/*loshn koydesh* but Russian, German, and even Polish were its rivals for H functions throughout the Pale.

5. However, just as modern recognition of Ausbau languages (see note 20, below) derives more from their adoption for nonbelletristic than for belletristic functions, so it is the spread into econo-political functions that is particularly crucial in this century if status planning for erstwhile Ls is to succeed. In connection with Yiddish, only the Bundists seem to have glimpsed this truth before, at, or soon after Tshernovits (subsequently the Jewish communists – many of them ex-Bundists – did so as well, but with quite different purposes and results), and even they spoke of Yiddish more commonly in terms of cultural autonomy. Ultimately, however, their design foresaw a socialist revolution: the complete displacement of religio-bourgeois, econopolitical control and the recognition of separate but interrelated/orchestrated culturally autonomous populations *each with control over its own immediate econo-technical apparatus*. Although the political representation of Yiddish speaking Jews *as such* (i.e. as a nationality with its own national [mother]-tongue) in the co-territorial parliaments was advocated also by some Labor Zionists, by minor Jewish parties such as the Folkists and the Sejmists, and even by (some) ultra-Orthodox spokesmen (e.g. those of Agudas Yisroel), only the Bundists had a real economic realignment in mind with educational, political, and cultural institutions deriving from and protected by firm Yiddish speaking proletarian economic control.

6. The weak representation of Bundists at Tshernovits led to the complete neglect of the economic basis of Yiddish as either *a* or *the* Jewish national language and to a complete preoccupation with cultural ideology, cultural

symbolism, and cultural rhetoric. As a result there also arose the view that the conference itself might be an ongoing moving force – either because it would have an executive office for 'cultural work' or because it simply had convened and sent forth its resolutions into the world. However, languages are neither saved nor spread by language conferences. Ideology, symbolism, and rhetoric are of undeniable significance in language spread – they are consciously motivating, focusing, and activating – but without a tangible and considerable status-power counterpart they become – under conditions of social change – competitively inoperative in the face of languages that do provide such. They may continue to be inspirational but – *particularly in modern times* – they cease to be decisive, i.e. they ultimately fail to safeguard even the intimacy of hearth and home from the turmoil of the econo-political arena. The ultimate failure of Tshernovits is that it did not even seek to foster or align itself with an econo-political reality that would seek to protect Yiddish in the new H functions. The ultimate tragedy of Yiddish is that in the political reconsolidation of modern Eastern Europe its speakers were either too powerless or too mobile. They were the classical expendables of twentieth century Europe and, obviously, no language conference or language movement per se could rectify their tragic dilemma. Unfortunately, few. at Tshernovits were sufficiently attuned to broader econopolitical realities to recognize that instead of being en route to a new dawn for Yiddish they stood more basically before the dusk of the Central and Eastern European order of things as it had existed till then.

7. However, it is the delicate *interplay* between econo-political and ethno-cultural factors that must be grasped in order to understand both success and failure in language spread. Any attempt to pin all on one or another alone is more likely to be doctrinaire than accurate. The Yiddish case, because it involves a diglossia situation and multiple possibilities for both L and H functions in the future, is particularly valuable because it makes the co-presence of both sets of factors so crystal clear. Econo-political factors alone are insufficient to appreciate the internal rivalry from *loshn koydesh*/Hebrew and the fact that the latter was undergoing its own vernacularization and modernization at the very same time that Yiddish was being championed for H functions. On the other hand, no amount of internal ethno-cultural insight can explain the allure that German and Russian (and, to a smaller degree, Polish) had for the Jewish bourgeoisie and intelligentsia. Finally, as a capstone to what is already an insuperable burden of opposition, there comes the linguistic relationship between Yiddish and German – the extra burden of all weak Ausbau[20] languages – and the cruel

20. Ausbau languages are those that are so similar in grammar and lexicon to other, stronger, previously recognized languages that their language authorities often attempt to maximize the differ- ences between themselves and their Big Brothers by multiplying or magnifying them through adopting or creating distinctive paradigms for neologisms, word order and grammar, particularly in their

compound of moral, aesthetic, and intellectual caricature and self-hatred to which that lent itself. After being exposed to such an array of internal and external overkill for well over a century, is it any wonder that the 1978 Nobel Prize for literature awarded to the Yiddish writer I. B. Singer often elicits only a wry smile in what remains of the world of Yiddish.[21,22]

written forms. Thus Ausbau languages are 'languages by effort', i.e. they are consciously built away from (= ausbau) other, more powerful and basically similar languages so as not to be considered 'mere dialects' of the latter, but rather, to be viewed as obviously distinctive languages in their own right. The Ausbau process is responsible for much of the difference between (Landsmal) Nynorsk and Bokmal, Hindi and Urdu, Macedonian and Bulgarian, Moldavian and Rumanian, Byelo-Russian and Russian. For the particular difficulties faced in finding, creating and maintaining Ausbau differences, including examples from the Yiddish versus German arena, see Paul Wexler (1974). The original formulator of the term Ausbau (and of its contrast: Abstand) is H. Kloss (1967).

21. Some additional useful secondary sources concerning the Tshernovits Language Conference are Goldsmith (1977), Passow (1971), and Lerner (1957). A literally endless list of other journal articles (pre-1928 and primarily post-1928, this being the date of the Yivo's twentieth anniversary volume (Anon. 1931) remains to be exhaustively catalogued.

22. For their helpful criticism of an earlier draft of this paper, I am indebted to Robert L. Cooper, David E. Fishman, and most especially, S. A. Birnboym. I alone assume responsibility for any errors of fact or interpretation that still remain and hope to correct them in future studies of the Tshernovits Conference, of Nosn Birnboym and of other issues in the late functional and structural modernization of Yiddish.

REFERENCES

Anon. (1931), *Di ershte yidishe shprakh-konferents* [The First Yiddish Language Conference]. Vilna, Yiddish Scientific Institute – Yivo.

Birnboym, Nosn (1908), 'Di konferents far der yidisher shprakh; efenungs rede', *Dokter Birnboyms vokhnblat* (1): 3–7. (Reprinted (1931) in Anon *Di ershte yidishe shprakh konferents* [The First Yiddish Language Conference], 71–94. Vilna, Yiddish Scientific Institute – Yivo.) (Also reprinted (1968) in *Afn shvel* 4 (185): 3–4.)

— (1918), *Gottes Volk*. Vienna, Löwit.

— (1946), *Selections from his writings*. London, Hamagid.

Choseed, B. (1968), 'Reflections of the Soviet nationalities policy in literature: the Jews, 1938–1948'. Ph.D. dissertation, Columbia University, New York. (University Microfilms, (69–75): 665.)

E[ste]r (1908), [Ester Frumkin] 'Di ershte yidishe shprakh konferents' [The first Yiddish language conference], *Di naye tsayt* 4: 89–104.

Eisenstein, Miriam (1949), *Jewish schools in Poland, 1919–1939*. New York, King's Crown.

Fishman, Dovid (1981), 'Di dray penemer fun yehoshua mordkhe lifshits' [The three faces of Yehoshua Mordkhe Lifshits], *Yidishe shprakh* 38.

Fishman, Joshua A. (1967), 'Bilingualism with and without diglossia; diglossia with and without bilingualism', *Journal of Social Issues* 23 (2): 29–38.

— (1972), *Language and Nationalism*. Rowley, Newbury House.

— (1973), 'The phenomenological and linguistic pilgrimage of Yiddish (Some examples of functional and structural pidginization and depidginization)', *Kansas Journal of Sociology* 9: 127–136.

— (1976), 'Yiddish and loshn koydesh in traditional Ashkenaz: the problem of societal allocation of macro-functions', in *Language in Sociology*, edited by A. Verdoodt and R. Kjolseth, 39–74. Louvain, Peeters.

— (forthcoming), *Nosn Birnboym: A Study in Personality, Ideology and Language*.

Fishman, J. A. and Fishman D. E. (1978), 'Yiddish in Israel: a case study of efforts to revise a monocentric language policy', in *Advances in the Study of Societal Multilingualism*, edited by J. A. Fishman, 185–262. The Hague, Mouton.

Goldsmith, E. S. (1976), *Architects of Yiddishism*. Rutherford, Fairleigh Dickenson Press. (See particularly the chapters on Birnboym, Perets, Zhitlovski and the Tshernovits Conference per se.)

Gumperz, John J. (1964), 'Linguistic and social interactions in two communities', *American Anthropologist* 66 (6): 137–153 (part 2).

Kazhdan, Kh. Sh. (1928), 'An epizod anshtot a gesheyenish (20 yor nokh der tshernovitser konferents)' [An episode instead of an event (20 years after the Tshernovits Conference)], (7): 73–77.

— (1969), 'Tshernovits – Kholem un vor' [Tshernovits: dream and reality], *Undzer tsayt* January: 17–21.

Khmurner, Y. (1928), 'Vegn a feler vos khazert zikh iber' [About an error that is being repeated], *Bikhervelt* (7): 1–6.

Kisman, Y. (1958), 'Tsum fuftsikstn yoyvl: di tshernovitser shprakh-konferents' [On the fiftieth anniversary: The Tshernovits language conference], *Undzer tsayt* July/August: 8–13.

Kligsberg, M. (1974), 'Di yidishe yugnt-bavegung in polyn tsvishn beyde velt-milkhomes (a sotsyologishe shtudye)' [The Jewish youth movement in Poland between both World Wars (a sociological study)], in *Shtudyes vegn yidn in poyln, 1919–1939*, edited by J. A. Fishman, 137–228. New York, Yivo Institute for Jewish Research.

Kloss, H. (1967), '"Abstand languages" and "Ausbau languages"', *Anthropological Linguistics* 9 (7): 29–41.

Lerer, L. (1928), 'Tsayt tsu shafn a kultur-gezelshaft' [Time to organize a culture society], *Literarishe bleter* (26): 500–501, 509.

Lerner, H. J. (1957), 'The Hebrew Language Conference: a milestone in Jewish nationalist thought'. Unpublished M.A. thesis, Columbia University.

Lifshits, Y. M. (1867), 'Di daytsh-yidishe brik' [The German–Jewish bridge], *Kol mevaser* 5 (31): 239–241. (See nos. 32, 33, 34, 35, and 41 for subsequent comments.)

— (1863), 'Di fir klasn' [The four classes], *Kol mevaser* (21): 323–328, (23): 364–366. Also see the editor's (Alexander Tsederboym's) comments: pp. 375–380 and 392–393.

— (1876), *Yidish-rusisher verterbukh*. Zhitomir: Bakst.

Mark, Y. (1968), '60 yor nokh der shprakh-konferents in Tshernovits' [60 years after the language conference in Tshernovits], *Forverts*, August 25, Section 2: 11–15.

Mayzl, Nakhmen (1928), 'Di ershte mobilizatsye' [The first mobilization], *Literarishe bleter* (35): 681.

Mendelsohn, Ezra (1970), *Class Struggle in the Pale*. Cambridge, Harvard University Press.

Miron, Dan (1973), 'A language as Caliban', in *A Traveler Disguised*, edited by Dan Miron, 34–66. New York, Schocken.

N[iger], Sh. (1922), 'A yidisher kultur kongres' (A Congress for Yiddish culture], *Dos naye lebn* 1 (2): 1–4.

Nobl, Shloyme (1951), 'R'yekhil-mikhl epshteyn, a dertsier un kemfer in 17tn yorhundert' [R'Yekhil-Mikhl Epshteyn, an educator and crusader on behalf of Yiddish in the 17th century], *Yivo-bleter* 35: 121–138.

Passow, I. D. (1971), 'The first Yiddish language conference' in *Gratz College Anniversary Volume*, edited by I. D. Passow and S. T. Lachs. Philadelphia, Gratz College.

Pinski, D. (1948), 'Geburt fun der tshernovitser konferents; a bletl zikhroynes' [Birth of the Tshernovits Conference; a page of memories], *Tsukunft*, September: 499–501.

Pludermakher, G. (1928), 'Di tshernovitser konferents un di ufgabn fun itstikn moment' [The Tshernovits Conference and the current task], *Literarishe bleter* 40: 777–778.

Prilutski, N. (1917), 'A yidishist fun 18tn yorhundert' [A Yiddishist of the 18th century]. *Noyekh prilutskis zamlbikher far yidishn folklor, filologye un kultur geshikhte* 2: 1–56.

— (1928), 'Nokh di tshernovitser fayerungen' [After the Tshernovits celebrations], *Literarishe bleter* (4): 797–799.

Pyckazh, Mendl (1964), 'Vegn "Yidishizm" in sof fun 17tn yorhundert un der ershter helft fun 18tn yorhundert' [Concerning "Yiddishism" at the end of the 17th century and the first half of the 18th century], *Goldene keyt* 49: 168–180.

Rothstein, J. (1977), 'Reactions of the American Yiddish press to the Tshernovits Language Conference of 1908 as a reflection of the American Jewish Experience', *International Journal of the Sociology of Language* 13: 103–120.

Rozhhak, Sh. (1969), 'Hebreyish-yidish (bamerkungen tsu un arum der tshernovitser shprakh-konferents)' [Hebrew–Yiddish (comments on and about the Tshernovits Language Conference)], *Goldene keyt* 66: 152–169.

Roznboym, M. M. (1929), 'Zhitlovski-bibliografye' [Zhitlovski bibliography], in *Zhitlovski zamlbukh* [Zhitlovski Reader], edited by Y. N. Shteynberg and Y. Rubin, 461–479. Warsaw, Bzozhe.

Rubin, Joan et al. (1978), *Language Planning Processes*. The Hague, Mouton.

Shekhter, M. (1961), 'Mir shteyen nit af an ort' [We are not standing still] in *Yiddish*, 351–363. New York, Congress for Jewish Culture.

Tartakover, A. (1946), 'Di yidishe kultur in poyln tsvishn tsvey velt-milkhomes' [Jewish culture in Poland between two World Wars], *Gedank un lebn* 4 (1): 1–35.

Tenenboym, Yoysef (1957–1958), 'Di yidishe shprakh af der tog-ordenung fun der sholem-konferents in pariz, 1919' [The Yiddish language on the agenda of the peace conference in Paris, 1919], *Yivo-bleter* 41: 217–229.

Vays (Slonim), Sh. (1937), 'Oys di tsaytn fun der tshernovitser konferents' [From the times of the Tshernovits Conference], *Fun noentn over* 1: 57–63.

Wexler, Paul (1974), *Purism and Language*. Bloomington, Indiana, Indiana University Language Science Monographs.

Zelitsh, Y. (1968), 'A tsveyte konferents far der yidisher shprakh – 60 yor nokh tshernovits' [A second conference for the Yiddish language – 60 years after Tshernovits], *Afn shvel* 185 (4): 2–3.

Zhitlovski, Kh. (1928), 'Tshernovits un der yidishizm: tsu dem tsvantsik yorikn yoyvl-yontev fun der tshernovitser konferents' [Tshernovits and Yiddishism: In honor of the twentieth anniversary celebration of the Tshernovits Conference], *Tsukunft* December: 735–737.

Zilberfarb, M. A. (1928), 'A shedlikhe iluzye' [A harmful illusion], *Bikhervelt* (8): 38–43.

די ייִדישע שפּראַך אויף דער טאָג־אָרדענונג
פֿון דער שלום־קאָנפֿערענץ אין פּאַריז, 1919

יוסף טענענבוים

SUMMARY: THE YIDDISH LANGUAGE ON THE AGENDA OF THE
PEACE CONFERENCE IN PARIS, 1919 BY YOYSEF TENENBOYM

*Although originally less than knowledgeable or sympathetic as to the need to write
guarantees for Yiddish into the treaties concluding World War I, the American
delegation is finally convinced and somewhat successful in that connection.*

1

אָנהייב 1919 האָט זיך פֿאַרזאַמלט אין פּאַריז די גרויסע שלום־קאָנפֿערענץ
נאָך דער ערשטער וועלט־מלחמה. דאָס איז געווען אַ גלאָבאַלע קאָנפֿערענץ
נאָך אַ גלאָבאַלן קאָנפֿליקט, דאָכט זיך די ערשטע קאָנפֿערענץ אין דער פּאָלי־
טישער וועלט־געשיכטע פֿון אַזאַ גרויסן פֿאַרנעם. אָבער מער פֿון אַלץ איז
דאָס געווען אַ היסטאָרישע דערשײַנונג אין ייִדישן לעבן, וואָס האָט ניט גע־
האַט איר גלײַכן אין אונדזער לאַנגער גלות־כראָניק.[1]

אַ מאָל וועט אפֿשר דער צוקונפֿטיקער ייִדישער היסטאָריקער ניט נאָר
אָפּגעבן אַ חשובֿן קאַפּיטל דעם אַנטייל פֿון ייִדן אין דער פּאַריזער שלום־קאָנ־
פֿערענץ און דער וויכטיקער ראָלע וואָס זיי האָבן דאָרט געשפּילט (ניט־ייִדישע
היסטאָריקערס טוען דאָס שוין הײַנט), נאָר אפֿילו טאַקע אָנהייבן אַ נײַ בלאַט
ייִדישע געשיכטע פֿון אָט דער תקופֿה.

לאָמיר ניט פֿאַרגעסן אַז אויף דער קאָנפֿערענץ זענען געלייגט געוואָרן
צוויי גרונטבאַזעס פֿאַר אַ נײַ ייִדיש קיבוץ־לעבן. ראשית איז געלייגט געוואָרן
דער יסוד פֿאַרן פּאַלעסטינע־מאַנדאַט, וואָס האָט אין משך פֿון איין דור באַ־
וויזן צו דערפֿירן צו אַ זעלבשטענדיקער מדינת ישׂראל, און שנית איז דאָרט
געבוירן געוואָרן דאָס מינדערהייט־רעכט פֿאַר אַנמלוכישע פֿעלקער. פֿון דער
טריבונע פֿון העכסטן פֿעלקעררראַט איז פּראָקלאַמירט געוואָרן אַ מין נײַע סו־

[1] זען מײַן בוך: צחישן מלחמה און שלום — ייִדן אויף דער שלום־קאָנפֿערענץ נאָך דער
ערשטער וועלט־מלחמה, בוענאָס־אײַרעס, 1956.

ווערעניטעט — די סווערעניטעט פֿון קליינע פֿעלקער אין די ראַמען פֿון דער
מלוכה. מיט איין ווארט, אַנשטאָט די אַלטע טראַדיציע פֿון הערשער־מלוכות,
געשטיצט אויף איין פֿאָלק, איז באַשאַפֿן געוואָרן דער פֿאָליטישער בנין פֿאר
מלוכות מיט פֿאַרשיידענע נאַציאנאַליטעטן, אָדער, לויטן אָפֿיציעלן טעקסט, מיט
קולטורעלע, עטנישע און רעליגיעזע מינאָריטעטן.

אָט דער רעוואָלוציאָנערער שריט האָט געבראַכט אַ גוטע מערכה פֿאר אַלע־
מען, ייִדן און ניט־ייִדן. נחמן סירקין, איינער פֿון די אַמעריקאַנער דעלעגאַטן
צי דער פֿאַריזער שלום־קאָנפֿערענץ, האָט דאָס אַ מאָל זייער געלונגען פֿאָרמו־
לירט. בײַ דער וויכטיקער דעבאַטע צווישן נאַציאָנאַלע ייִדן און אַסימילאַטאָרן
פֿון פֿראַנקרייַך און ענגלאַנד, וואָס איז אָפּגעהאַלטן געוואָרן אויף אַ פֿאַרזאַמלונג
אין פּאַריז דעם 5טן און 6טן אפּריל 1919, האָט סירקין אויסגעשריען: אַ מאָל
איז געווען אַ כלל: cuius regio eius religio, היַנט הערשט נאָך דער
כלל: cuius regio eius natio; בײַדע זײַנען אַלטמאָדיש. מיר פֿאַרלאַנ־
גען אי רעליגיעזע אי נאַציאָנאַלע פֿרײַהייט.[2]

אין דער אמתן דריקט דאָס אויס דעם גאַנצן תהום צווישן דעם עבר און
דעם היַנט און אפֿשר אויך דעם עתיד. אין דעם שלום־אָפּמאַך פֿון וועסטפֿאַלן
נאָך דרײַסיקיאָריקן קריג, האָט דער באַשלוס אַז רעליגיע איז אַ טייל פֿון
דער מלוכה באַטײַט אַ גרויסן פֿאָרשריט לגבי דער אוניווערסאַלער דיקטאַ־
טור פֿון דעם קאַטוילישן קלויסטער. אָבער די רפֿואה איז ניט געווען פֿיל בע־
סער ווי די מכּה, מחמת אַנשטאָט דעם וואַטיקאַן האָט דער פֿרינץ, דער מלך,
איבערגענומען די פֿונקציע פֿון אַ געוויסן־פּאָליציי. עס איז געווען די זעלביקע
בײַטש פֿון צוואַנג און דיסקרימינאַציע קעגן רעליגיעזע מינדערהייטן. עס האָט
גענומען אַ לאַנגע צײַט ביז רעליגיעזע טאָלעראַנץ פֿאר מינדערהייטן האָט זיך
דורכגעזעצט, און ווען דאָס איז שוין געשען, איז אויפֿן פּלאַץ פֿון רעליגיעזן
צוואַנג געקומען דער נאַציאָנאַלער צוואַנג, וואָס האָט זיך ספּעציעל אויסגע־
ברייטערט אין דעם נאַציאָנאַליסטישן 19טן יאָרהונדערט.

2

ביז 1919 זײַנען ייִדן געווען ניט מער ווי אַן אָביעקט בײַ פֿאַרשיידענע שלום־
פֿאַרהאַנדלונגען. ניט אויפֿן וויענער קאָנגרעס פֿון 1815 און ניט אין אַכן אין
1818 און אפֿילו ניט אין בערלין אין 1878, האָבן ייִדן פֿיגורירט ווי דעלעגאַטן
צו אָפֿיציעלע באַראַטונגען אָדער זיצונגען. אין די קולואַרן פֿון דער שלום־
קאָנפֿערענץ האָט געשװויבלט מיט אַלערליי שתדלנים און מעקלערס, וואָס
האָבן געזוכט, אָדער געקריגט, אָדער גאָר אויסגעחנפֿעט פּראָטעקציעס בײַ פֿאַ־
ליטישע יחסנים. אַ קלאַסישער בײַשפּיל איז געווען דער וויענער קאָנגרעס. אַ
קריסטלעכער אַדוואָקאַט, קאַרל אויגוסט בוכהאַלץ, איז געקומען אין שליחות
פֿון די האַנזאַ־שטעט־ייִדן; די ייִדישע שתדלנים יוסף גומפרעכט און יעקבֿ באַ־
רוך (פֿאָטער פֿון לודוויג בערנע) האָבן זיך משתדל געווען אין נאָמען פֿון די

Lithuania Arrives at a 'Compromise'. While both boys (Yiddishists and Hebraists) were fighting to get control of the easy-chair (Lithuanian Ministry for Jewish Affairs), the old, angry uncle (Lithuania) decided to enforce an 'objective compromise' (abolishing the Ministry). (*Der groyser kundes*, March 28, 1924)

פֿראַנקפֿורטער ייִדן; אויך די סאַלאָן־דאַמען, באַראָנעסע פֿאַני (אַ טאָכטער פֿון
דניאל איציג פֿון בערלין) און מאַריאַנאַ (די פֿרוי פֿון לעאָפֿאָלד פֿאַן הערץ)
האָבן מיט זייער גאַסטפֿרײַנדלעכקייט באַצײבערט די פּאָליטישע ווערטזאַגערס
פֿון דעם קאָנגרעס לטובֿת ייִדן.

אַ הונדערט יאָר שפּעטער, אין פּאַריז, האָבן ייִדן מער ניט געשיקט קיין
שתדלנים. געקומען זײַנען אמתע פֿאָלקס־פֿאַרטרעטערס, ייִדישע דעלעגאַטן
וואָס זײַנען אויסגעוויילט געוואָרן פֿון נאַציאָנאַל־ראַטן, קאָנפֿערענצן אין קאָנ־
גרעסן. זיי האָבן געהאַט אַ מאַנדאַט און אַ פּראָגראַם. די מיזרח־אייראָפּעישע
דעלעגאַטן זײַנען געקומען מיט גוט דורכגעטראַכטע ייִדיש־נאַציאָנאַלע תּבֿיעות,
ווי זיי האָבן זיך אויסקריסטאַליזירט אין די לעצטע 40 יאָר ייִדיש־נאַציאָנאַלע
באַוועגונגען. זיי זײַנען ניט געקומען מיט ווייכע בקשות, נאָר מיט האַרטע פֿאָ־
דערונגען. אויך די אַמעריקאַנער דעלעגאַטן האָבן מיטגעבראַכט דעפֿיניטיווע
באַשלוסן פֿון די זיצונגען פֿון אַמעריקאַנער ייִדישן קאָנגרעס וואָס זײַנען אָפּ־
געהאַלטן געוואָרן דעם 15טן—18טן דעצעמבער 1918 אין פֿילאַדעלפֿיע.[3] מען
קען ניט זאָגן אַז עס האָבן געפֿעלט סיכסוכים צווישן די צוויי וועלטן פֿון אַ
מנחם מענדל אוסישקין און אַ לויִ מאַרשאַל, אָדער צווישן אַנדערע דעלעגאַטן
פֿון מיזרח און מערבֿ. אָבער סײַ ווי סײַ האָט דער נאַציאָנאַלער צד זײַנס אויסגעע־
פֿירט. מען האָט שוין געקענט דערפֿילן דעם סוף פֿונעם קוק אויפֿן ייִדישן לעבן
וואָס עס האָט געהאַט דער נאַפּאָלעאָנישער סנהדרין מיט הונדערט און צוועלף
יאָר פֿריִער.[4]

דער קאַמף פֿאַר נאַציאָנאַלע רעכט האָט זיך קאָנצענטרירט אין „קאָמיטעט
פֿון ייִדישע דעלעגאַציעס צו דער שלום־קאָנפֿערענץ אין פּאַריז", וווּ ס'זײַנען
געזעסן פֿאַרטרעטערס פֿון אַלע גרעסערע און אַפֿילו קלענערע ייִדישע ייִשובֿים.
אַפֿילו פֿון אירקוטסק איז געקומען אַ דעלעגאַט. ער איז געקומען מיט אַ יאָר
שפּעטער צוליב גרענעץ־שוועריקייטן.[5]

די ייִדישע נאַציאָנאַלע פֿאָדערונגען צו דער פּאַריזער שלום־קאָנפֿערענץ
האָבן אַנטהאַלטן אַ רײ וויכטיקע פּונקטן, למשל: קולטורעלע און פֿערסאָנאַלע
אויטאָנאָמיע; אַ ייִדישער סעקרעטאַריאַט (מיניסטעריום) בײַ דער מלוכה; אַ
נאַציאָנאַל־ראַט וואָס זאָל דינען ווי אַ ייִדישע רעפּרעזענטאַנץ; אַ פֿאַרשטיער־

---

[3] Bernard G. Richards, "The American Jewish Congress," *Jewish Communal Register, 1917-1918*, New York, 1918, pp. 429-49.

[4] וועגן קאַמף קעגן נאַציאָנאַלע ייִדישע פֿאָדערונגען, זען:
Henry Morgenthau, *All in a Life Time*, New York, 1922, pp. 285-94;
Report of the Delegation of the Jews of the British Empire, London, 1920;
Alliance Israélite Universelle, *La Question Juive devant la Conference de la Paix*, Paris, 1919.

זען אויך די רעדע פֿון סילווען לעוִוי בײַם קבלת־פּנים פֿון דער ציוניסטישער דעלעגאַציע
בײַ דער שלום־קאָנפֿערענץ (יוסף טננבוים, „בוֹעידת השלום 1919", ספר העשור של הדואר,
ניו־יאָרק, 1958, זז' 63—66).

[5] יוסף טעננבוים, צווישן מלחמה און שלום, ז' 93;
The Peace Conference, Paris, 1919.

שאַפֿט פֿון וועלט-ייִדנטום אין פֿעלקערבונד אד״גל.6

אײנע פֿון די קאַרדינאַלסטע פֿאָדערונגען איז געווען זעלבסט-פֿאַרוואַלטונג אויפֿן געביט פֿון ייִדישער דערצײַונג און די רעכט פֿון דער ייִדישער שפּראַך, ניט נאָר אין די שולן, נאָר אויך אין די גערישטן און אין די אַדמיניסטראַטיווע אינסטאַנצן. אין די מעמאָראַנדומס און פֿאָרשלאַגן צו די קאָמיסיעס און קאָמ-צעלאַריעס פֿון דער שלום-קאָנפֿערענץ האָט מען פֿאָרלאַנגט פֿולע רעכט פֿאַר ייִדיש, כאַטש אין די ייִדישע דעלעגאַציעס זײַנען געזעסן אַזעלכע עקסטרעמע העברעיִסטן ווי מנחם מענדל אוסישקין, יצחק נײַדיטש, הלל זלאַטאָפֿאַלסקי און די פֿאַרטרעטערס פֿון פֿאַלעסטינע: דוד יעלין, אליהו בערלין, אהרן אײַזנבערג און יצחק ווילקאַנסקי. די גרויסע מעלה פֿון קאָמיטעט פֿון די ייִדישע דעלע-גאַציעס איז געווען וואָס ער האָט אַרומגענומען פֿאַרטרעטערס פֿון פֿאַרשײדענע פּאַרטײִען און ריכטונגען: דער דיכטער-סאָציאַליסט מאַריס ווינטשעווסקי בײַ אײן טיש מיטן הײסן ציוניסט ד״ר יהושע טהאָן; נחום סאָקאָלאָוו און קאַלאָנעל הערי קאַטלער, ד״ר חיים ווייצמאַן און לוי מאַרשאַל וכדומה. אײן אידעאַל האָט אַלעמען פֿאַראײיניקט.

3

אײדער מיר גייען צו צו דער עצם דיסקוסיע וועגן ייִדיש בײַם העכסטן ראָט (״פֿיררראָט״) איז זיך כדאַי אָפּצושטעלן אויף דער פּראָצעדור פֿון די באַראָטונגען.

בײַ דער שלום-קאָנפֿערענץ האָבן עקסיסטירט פֿאַרשײדענע קאָמיסיעס וואָס האָבן צוגעגרייט די פּראָבלעמען און די פֿאָרשלאַגן וואָס דער העכסטער ראָט האָט געדאַרפֿט באַטראַכטן און דעצידירן. אין העכסטן ראָט זײַנען געזעסן: פּרע-זידענט ווילסאָן, לאַיד דזשאָרדזש, דער איטאַליענישער פּרעמיער-מיניסטער אָר-לאַנדאָ אָדער גראַף סאָנינאָ און דער ״טיגער״, דזשאָרדזש קלעמאַנסאָ, וואָס האָט געפֿירט דעם פֿאָרזיץ. זיי זײַנען געווען די בוררים און די שופֿטים איבער די פֿאָרשלאַגן פֿון די קאָמיסיעס. די מינדערהייט-פֿראַגעס האָבן געהערט צום ״קאָמיטעט פֿאַר נײַע מלוכות און מינאַריטעטן-שוץ״, אונטערן פֿאָרזיץ פֿון די-רעקטאָר פֿון ראָט בײַם פֿראַנצייִשן מיניסטעריום פֿון אויסווייניקסטע ענינים, פֿיליפּ בערטעלאָ. אַנדערע מיטגלידער פֿון דער קאָמיסיע זײַנען געווען העדלאַם מאָרלעי פֿון גרויס-בריטאַניע, די-מאַרטינאָ פֿון איטאַליע און דער בעל-יועץ דייווויד האַנטער מילער פֿן אַמעריקע.7 דער לעצטער האָט געשפּילט אַ וויכ-טיקע ראָלע ווי אַ פֿאַרמיטלער צווישן ייִדישן צד און דער אַמעריקאַנער קאָמי-סיע און האָט אויך געהאַט אַ גרויסע דעה בײַ ווילסאָנען און בײַ קאָלאָנעל הויז,

----

6 זען מײַן בוך:
La Question Juive en Pologne, Paris, 1919.

7 מילֶערס *My Diary at the Conference of Paris,* געדרוקט אין 21 בענ:ה, אין אַן אוצר פֿון אינפֿאָרמאַציע וועגן דער שלום-קאָנפֿערענג. דאָרט געפֿינען זיך אויך אַלֶע בעמעמאַראַנ-דומס און דער גאַנצער מאַטעריאַל וואָס איז פֿאַרגעלייגט געוואָרן פֿאַר די קאָמיביעס אָדער פֿאַרן פּלענום פֿון דער קאָנפֿע-ענץ. פֿאַר דער ייִדישער פֿראַגע אויף דער קאָנפֿערענץ איז דאָס ווערק פֿון גרויס וויכטיקייט.

וואָס איז געווען ווילסאָנס רעכטע האַנט.8 ער אַליין און זײַן מיטאַרבעטער פּראָ־
פעסאָר מאַנלי האָדסאָן9 האָבן אַ סך מיטגעהאָלפן בײַ די פאַרהאַנדלוׁנגען און
פאָרמולירונגען פון די ייׁדישע תבֿיעות צו דער קאָנפערענץ.

ניט אַלע ייׁדישע פאָדׁערונגען זײַנען אָנגענומען געוואָרן. עס איז געווען אַ
שטאַרקע אָפּאָזיציע אי מצד די ייׁדישע אַסימילאַטאָרן אי מצד די רעגירונגען,
וואָס האָבן זיך געוואָרט מיט ציין און נעגל קעגן מינאָריטעטן־רעכט. ס׳איז
געווען אַ שווערער קאַמף פון אַ ייׁדן קעגן אַ מעכטיקן ווידערשטאַנד.

לאָמיר נעמען די פראַגע וועגן י י ׁ ד י ש. אין אַ מעמאָראַנדום, באַקאַנט ווי
„דאָקומענט נומער 822", וואָס די ייׁדישע פאָרטרעטערס האָבן צוגעשטעלט צום
„קאָמיטעט פאַר נײַע מלוכות", האָט זיך געפונען אַ פונקט 4, וואָס האָט פאָר־
לאַנגט אַז יעדער פערזאָן זאָל האָבן דאָס רעכט צו באַנוצן זײַן אייגענע שפּראַך
אויף עפנטלעכע אסיפות, אין דער פּרעסע און אין די שולן; דער ווערט פון
אַ דאָקומענט זאָל ניט געפסלט ווערן צוליב דער שפּראַך אין וועלכער ער איז
געשריבן; אַלע פּריׁערדיקע שפּראַך־באַגרענעצונגען זאָלן אַנולירט ווערן. אין
אַ ווײַטערדיקן אָפּשניט לייענען מיר וועגן עפענען ייׁדישע שולן און אַז זיי
דאַרפן אויסגעהאַלטן ווערן פון דער מלוכה. איינע פון די וויכטיקסטע פראַגעס
איז געווען ווער ס׳דאַרף אָרגאַניזירן און אָנפירן די ייׁדישע שולן. אין דעם
פּרט האָט דער מעמאָראַנדום פאָרגעשלאָגן, אַז די אַדמיניסטראַציע און אויפ־
זיכט איבער די שולן זאָלן געהערן צו אַ נאַציאָנאַלער ייׁדישער קערפּערשאַפט.
דער מעמאָראַנדום איז איבערדיסקוטירט און איבערגעקײַט געוואָרן פון די
אַמעריקאַנער פאָרשטייערס אין דער קאָמיסיע פאַר נײַע מלוכות און דערנאָך
איז די פראַגע געקומען צום העכסטן ראַט וואָס האָט געדאַרפט אָננעמען אַ
באַשלוס.10

דערווײַל איז דער ראַט פאַרפלייצט געוואָרן מיט פּראָטעסט־טעלעגראַמען
פון פאַרשיׁיׁדענע מלוכות און ספּעציעל האָט פּאַדערעווסקי, דער פּוילישער פּרע־
מיער־מיניסטער, געדונגערט און געדראָט אַז ער וועט ניט קומען אונטערשרײַבן
דעם שלום־אָפּמאַך, אויב די מינאָריטעטן־גזירות וועלן ניט בטל ווערן. די

8 *Intimate Papers of Col. House*, ed. by Charles Seymour, New York,
1928 (261 .200—198 ,153־152 'זז ,17 'ב ספעציעל);

זען אויך מילער, דצ״ה, ו, ז׳ 288; ב׳ או, ז׳ 313.

9 וועגן האָדסאָנען זען:

Edward Manley House and Charles Seymour, ed., *What Really Happened
at Paris?* New York, 1921; *Louis Marshall*, ed. by Charles Reznikoff, Philadelphia, 1957, vol. II, pp. 551, 691, 697.

10 וועגן דעם ווי אַזוי די קאָנפערענץ האָט באַטראַכט די ייׁדישע פראַגע און די השפעות
פאַר און קעגן די ייׁדיש־נאַציאָנאַלע פאָדערונגען, זען:

Oscar J. Janovsky, *The Jews and the Minority Rights*, New York, 1933;
Nathan Feinberg, *La Question des Minorités de la Paix de 1919-1920.* Paris-
Genève, 1929; H. W. Temperley, ed., *A History of the Peace Conference*, Lon-
don, 1920.

קאָמיסיע פֿאַר נײַע מלוכות האָט געפרוּווט גיין אויף קאָמפּראָמיסן, אָבער היות
פאדערעוּוּסקי האָט זיך קאַטעגאָריש אָפּגעזאָגט צו פֿאַרהאַנדלען וועגן דעם ענין,
האָבן די מיטגלידער פֿון דער קאָמיסיע באַשלאָסן צו ברענגען זייערע פֿאָרשלאָגן
צום העכסטן ראַט אין איינעם מיט אַ פּראָיעקט פֿון אַן ענטפֿער אויף פּאדע־
רעוּוּסקיס בריוו, און זאָל דער ראַט דעצידירן.

אַגב זאָל דאָ דערמאָנט ווערן, אַז עטלעכע טעג פֿריִער האָט מען זיך גע־
איניקט וועגן דער שבת־רו־פֿראַגע. אין דער דאָזיקער פֿראַגע זײַנען געווען
צוויי שטעלונגען, איינע אַן אַמעריקאַנער, וואָס איז געווען קעגן שבת־רו פֿאַר
ייִדן,[11] און אַ צווייטע אַ בריטישע וואָס איז געווען פֿאַר, און דוקא זי האָט געוווּ־
נען די צושטימונג פֿון פּרעזידענט ווילסאָן. דאָס שבת־רו־געזעץ איז אָנגענומען
געוואָרן און איז אַרײַנגענומען געוואָרן, ווי אַרטיקל 11, אין מינדערהייטס־
טראַקטאַט מיט פּוילן.[12]

4

מאָנטאָג דעם 23סטן יוני 1919 האָט דער העכסטער ראַט, וואָס האָט זיך
פֿאַרזאַמלט אין ווילסאָנס הויז אין פּאַריז, אויפֿגענומען די שפּראַכן־פֿראַגע אין
שײַכות מיט פּאדערעוּוּסקיס בריוו.

מיר גיבן דאָ איבער די דעבאַטע לויט דעם סטענאָגראַפֿישן פּראָטאָקאָל.[13]

ל אָ י ד ד ז ש אָ ר ד ז ש באַרירט דער ערשטער די פֿראַגע וועגן לשון וואָס
דאַרף באַנוצט ווערן אין די ייִדישע שולן אין פּוילן. לויט זײַן מיינונג איז פּאַ־
דערעוּוּסקיס קריטיק אַ גערעכטע. אין אַמעריקע און אין ענגלאַנד, למשל, האָט
מען צוליב ספּעציעלע סענטימענטן פֿון געוויסע סעקטעס געמאַכט הנחות אויף
דעם געביט, אָבער זיי זײַנען געווען אין הסכּם מיט דער דערצײונג־סיסטעם פֿון
לאַנד. ס׳איז אָבער אַ פֿראַגע צי ייִדן דאַרף דערלויבט ווערן צו האָבן ספּעציעלע
שולן אין פּוילן.

ה ע ד ל אַ ם מ אַ ר ל ע י, דער בריטישער דעלעגאַט, זאָגט, אַז לויט דעם
טעקסט פֿונעם מינדערהייטס־טראַקטאַט, וועלן די ייִדישע שולן אין פּוילן דאַרפֿן
אָנגעפֿירט ווערן פֿון ייִדישע קאָמיטעטן.

ל אָ י ד ד ז ש אָ ר ד ז ש פֿרעגט, צי דאָס גיט ניט די ייִדן מער מאַכט ווי
אין ענגלאַנד, וווּ די רוימיש־קאַטוילישע און ייִדישע באַפֿעלקערונג האָבן טאַקע
די אויפֿזיכט איבער זייערע שולן, אָבער דערפֿאַר איז די אַלגעמיינע דער־
צײונג־סיסטעם און די שולפּראָגראַם אַ טייל פֿון דער דערצײונג־סיסטעם פֿון
לאַנד און אונטער דער אויפֿזיכט פֿון דער מלוכה.

[11] מילער האָט געשריבן צו קאַלאָנעל הויז אַז דער שבת־רו־געזעץ וועט אפֿשר שטעלן
אין סכּנה די ראַטיפֿיקאַציע פֿון שלום־טראַקטאַט אין אַמעריקאַנער סענאַט (מילער, דצ״וו,
ב׳ ו, זז׳ 283, 288, 299; ב׳ אX, ז׳ 313.

[12] זען מײַן בוך: *Peace for the Jews*, New York, 1945, p. 174.

[13] *Papers on United States Foreign Policy. The Paris Conference*, U. S.
Printing Office, 1946, vol. VI, pp. 624-28.

העדלאם מארלעי ענטפערט, אז דער טראקטאט איז בכיוון אזוי
פארמולירט געווארן אז דערציונג זאל בלײבן אונטער דער אויפזיכט פֿון דער
פּוילישער מלוכה, אבער די אנפֿירונג פֿון די שולן זאל זײן אין די הענט פֿון
פערזאנענ פֿון יידישן גלויבן. אָט דער פּונקט איז אויפֿגעקלערט געווארן אין
בײגעלייגטן בריוו צו פאדערעווסקין.

פראפֿ' מאנלי האדסאן, דער אמעריקאנער פֿארטרעטער אין קא-
מיטעט, גיט צו, אז די פּרינציפּן וואס קומען צום אויסדרוק אין דעם טראק-
טאַט זײנען זייער עלאַסטיש, אזוי אז זיי לאזן איבער די שולן אונטער דער
קאנטראל פֿון דער מלוכה.

לאיד דזשארדזש פֿרעגט וואר ס'וועט אויסארבעטן די שולפראגראם.

העדלאם מארלעי ענטפּערט, אז די מלוכה וועט האבן די מעגלעכ-
קייט דאס צו טאָן.

לאיד דזשארדזש זאגט, אז דאס איז ניט לויט דעם ווי פאדערעווסקי
האט פֿארשטאַנען דעם טראקטאַט.

האדסאן שלאגט פֿאר, אז אפֿשר וואלט כדאי געווען דאס ברייטער צו
דערקלערן אין דעם בריוו צו פאדערעווסקין.

העדלאם מארלעי גיט איבער, אז ער אליין האט פֿארגעשלאגן (אין
קאמיטעט) אז אנשטאט „קאמיטעטן", וואס דארפֿן האבן די אויפֿזיכט איבער די
שולן, זאל מען בעסער באנוצן „פּערזאנען" (פֿון יידישן גלויבן), מחמת מענטשן
האבן מורא פֿארן ווארט „קאמיטעט". אבער זײנע קאלעגן האבן אים מיט ניט
מסכים געווען. אין דער לעצטער רעדאקציע האָט די קאמיסיע אויסגעמאקט
אומעטום וווּ עס איז געשטאַנען „צענטראלער קאמיטעט", און פֿארביטן דאס
מיטן ווארט „קאמיטעטן".

באלפֿור ווײזט אן אז אין ענגלאַנד איז א רוימיש-קאטוילישע שול ניט
מער ווי א לאקאלע רוימיש-קאטוילישע שול. קיין שום פּראַוויזיע איז דא ניט
געמאכט געווארן. לויטן טראקטאַט קומט אויס אז א צענטראלער יידישער קא-
מיטעט וואלט דווקא יא געקענט געגרינדעט ווערן אין ווארשע.

העדלאם מארלעי גיט איבער, אז ס'זײנען געמאכט געווארן ענדע-
רונגען אין טעקסט, כדי אזא זאך צו פֿאַרמײדן.

באלפֿור שלאגט פֿאר, אז אין ארטיקל 10 זאל דאס ווארט „לאקאלער"
צוגעגעבן ווערן צום ווארט „קאמיטעט". (דאס איז אנגענומען געווארן.)

לאיד דזשארדזש פֿרעגט צי ס'וואַלט ניט כדאי געווען קלאר צו
מאכן אז קיין יידיש זאל מען ניט לערנען. ער האט גאָרניט — האט ער גע-
זאגט — קעגן העברעיש, וואס איז אן אנערקענטע שפּראַך, אבער ער מיינט אז
יידיש דארף ניט געלערנט ווערן.

פּרעזידענט ווילסאן ווײזט דערויף אן, אז יידיש ווערט באנוצט
ווי אן אומגאַנגסשפּראך אין א סך טיילן פֿון דער וועלט, ארײנגערעכנט די פֿאר-
אייניקטע שטאַטן, און אז די פּוילישע מדינה דארף ניט זײן קיין יוצא מן הכלל.

העדלאם מארלעי גיט צו אז די קאמיסיע פֿאר נײע מלוכות איז

אינפֿאָרמירט געװאָרן, אַז װאָס שייך קלײנע קינדער האָט מען ניט געקאָנט באַ־
נוצן קײן אַנדערע שפּראַך װי ייִדיש. זײ האָבן גערעדט ייִדיש אין זײיערע הײי־
מען, און װען זײ זײנען אין אָנהײב געקומען אין שול אַרײן האָבן זײ ניט
געקאָנט קײן שום אַנדערע שפּראַך. מען דאַרף אָבער ניט באַנוצן די ייִדישע
שפּראַך װען ס׳האַנדלט זיך װעגן עלטערע קינדער.

לאַיד דזשאַרדזש פֿרעגט װי אַזױ מען איז זיך נוהג אין ניו־יאָרק?

װילסאָן ענטפֿערט אַז מען האָט אָנגעשטעלט לערערס װאָס האָבן פֿאַר־
שטאַנען ייִדיש, און זײ האָבן געלערנט די קינדער אױף ייִדיש.

לאַיד דזשאַרדזש באַמערקט, אַז ס׳איז פֿאַראַן אַ גרױסער אונטערשייד
צװישן לערנען אױף ייִדיש און לערנען די ייִדישע שפּראַך. מען דאַרף מאַכן
אַלע אָנשטרענגונגען, כּדי צו אינטעגרירן ייִדן אין פּױלן מיט דער פּױלישער
נאַציאָנאַליטעט, פּונקט װי ייִדן אין ענגלאַנד און פֿראַנקרײך זײנען געװאָרן
צונױפֿגעשמאָלצן מיט די ענגלישע און פֿראַנצײזישע נאַציאָנאַליטעטן. ער איז
אינפֿאָרמירט געװאָרן, אַז ס׳איז דאָ אַן אַקטיװ באַװעגונג צו באַהאַנדלען ייִדן
נישט נאַר װי אַ ספּעציעלע רעליגיע, נאָר אױך װי אַ באַזונדערע ראַסע.

פּרעזידענט װילסאָן װײזט אָן, אַז אין דעם פֿאַל האָבן מיר ניט
צו טאָן מיט ענגלאַנד, פֿראַנקרײך אָדער די פֿאַראײניקטע שטאַטן, װוּ די ייִדישע
באַפֿעלקערונג האָט גוט געװוּסט, אַז זי װערט באַהאַנדלט לױט די זעלבע יושר־
דיקע פּרינציפּן װי די אַנדערע בירגערס פֿון דער מלוכה. אױב די פּױלישע
מלוכה װאָלט באַנוצט די זעלבע פּרינציפּן, װאָלט דאָס איצט אַ סך געהאָלפֿן.

העדלאַם מאָרלעי זאָגט, אַז אין פּױלן איז פֿאַראַן אַן עקסטרעם
אַגרעסיװע ייִדיש־נאַציאָנאַלע באַװעגונג.

לאַיד דזשאַרדזש לײגנט פֿאָר די רעזאָלוציע װאָס איז אָנגענומען גע־
װאָרן אין דער קאָמיסיע פֿאַר נײַע מלוכות: ״די קאָמיסיע איז אױך געװוען באַ־
פֿולמעכטיקט צו באַטראַכטן דעם ענין פֿון די נײטיקע ענדערונגען אין דעם
אָפּמאַך־פּראָיעקט מיט פּױלן, כּדי צו פֿאַרזיכערן, אַז אין אַלע שולן, אַחוץ עלע־
מענטאַרע, זאָלן די לימודים פֿאַר ייִדישע קינדער זײַן אױף פּױליש און ניט אױף
ייִדיש, כּדי דורך דעם צו פֿאַרמײַדן די סכּנה אַז דער באַנוץ פֿון ייִדיש זאָל װערן
דערמוטיקט װי אײנע פֿון די נאַציאָנאַלע שפּראַכן פֿאַר אַ טײל פֿון דער באַפֿעל־
קערונג אין פּױלן״. ער אַלײן האָט דאָס געפֿיל אַז מען װאָלט געגאַנגען צו װײט
אױב, װי ס׳איז פֿאָרגעשלאָגן געװאָרן, די קינדער אין די עלעמענטאַרע שולן
זאָלן לערנען ייִדיש.

װילסאָן לײגנט פֿאָר דעם װײַטערדיקן אױסצוג פֿון אַרטיקל 9 פֿון
פּראָיעקטירטן אָפּמאַך מיט פּױלן: ״פּױלן װעט זאָרגן דערפֿאַר, אַז אין די
עפֿנטלעכע ערצײונג־אָנשטאַלטן אין שטעט און אין דיסטריקטן, װוּ ס׳װוינט
פּראָפּאָרציאָנאַל אַ גענוג גרױסע צאָל פּױלישע בירגערס װאָס באַנוצן אָן אַנ־
דער שפּראַך װי פּױליש, זאָלן, לױט די מעגלעכקייטן, געשאַפֿן װערן באַדינ־
גונגען װאָס זאָלן פֿאַרזיכערן, אַז דער לימוד פֿאַר די קינדער פֿון אַזעלכע פּױ־
לישע בירגערס זאָל געגעבן װערן אין זײער אײגענער שפּראַך״. ער לײגט פֿאָר

¦

צו פֿאַרבײַטן דאָס וואָרט „עפֿנטלעכע" מיטן וואָרט „עלעמענטאַרע".

ה ע ד ל אַ ם   מ אַ ר ל ע י   מאַכט אויפֿמערקזאַם, אַז דאָס וואָלט אויך
מעגלעך געמאַכט פֿאַר די דײַטשן (אין פּוילן) צו פֿירן דעם לימוד אין דער דײַ־
טשער שפּראַך. די מערהייט פֿונעם קאָמיטעט פֿאַר נײַע מלוכות, זאָגט ער, האָט
געהאַט דאָס געפֿיל אַז דער באַשלוס פֿון קאָמיטעט האָט זיך באַצויגן נאָר צו
ייִדישע קינדער. די דײַטשן, אין זייערע פֿאַרלוירענע דיסטריקטן, קענען פֿירן
דעם לימוד אין דײַטש, אָבער זיי וועלן ניט האָבן קיין אייגענעם קאָמיטעט,
ווי די ייִדן וואָלטן געהאַט (אַ ייִדישן דערציונגס־קאָמיטעט). וואָס שייך ייִדן,
וואָלט ייִדיש געקאָנט באַנוצט ווערן ווי אַ לערנשפּראַך אין די עלעמענטאַרע
שולן אָבער ניט אין די מיטלשולן. די מערהייט פֿונעם קאָמיטעט האָט געטראַכט
אַז ס׳וואָלט ניט געווען גערעכט צו פֿאַרלאַנגען פֿון פּוילן זי זאָל אויסהאַלטן
מיטלשולן אין דער ייִדישער שפּראַך. אָבער די אַמעריקאַנער פֿאַרטרעטערס
אין קאָמיטעט האָבן ניט מסכים געווען מיט דעם שטאַנדפּונקט.

פּ ר ע ז י ד ע נ ט   ו ו י ל ס אָ ן   לייענט פֿאָר אַן אויסצוג פֿון אַ מעמאָראַנדום,
ווו דער שטאַנדפּונקט פֿון דער אַמעריקאַנער דעלעגאַציע ווערט געמאַכט קלאָר:

אין הסכּם מיט זײַן שבתדיקער דעקלערונג אויפֿן העכסטן ראַט
וויל מ״ר העדלאַם מאַרלעי צוגעבן צום אַרטיקל 10, בנוגע דער ייִדישער
אויפֿזיכט איבער זייערע אייגענע שולן, די ווײַטערדיקע דעקלאַראַציע,
דהײַנו: אַז „קיין זאַך וואָס שטײט אין דעם אַרטיקל קאָן ניט פֿאַרווערן
די פּוילישע רעגירונג צו מאַכן פּויליש די אָבליגאַטאָרישע לערנשפּראַך
אין די העכערע שולן." די אַמעריקאַנער דעלעגאַציע מיינט אַז אָט דער
צוגאַב גייט ווײַט וויַיט איבער זײַן [מאַרלעים] דעקלערונג [אויף דער זיַ־
צונג] פֿון לעצטן שבת. דער פּונקט ווערט שטאַרק באַקעמפֿט פֿון די
אַמעריקאַנער ייִדן און איך בין אויך געגען קעגן — צוליב די וויַי־
טערדיקע טעמים:

(א) ס׳וועט דערמוטיקן די פּאָליאַקן צו פֿאַרווערן דעם לימוד פֿון
ייִדיש אין די העכערע שולן און דאָס וועט שטאַרק פֿאַרמינערן דעם
ווערט פֿון אַרטיקל 10.

(ב) היות די ייִדישע שולן, „דאַרפֿן שטיין אונטער דער אַלגעמיינער
קאָנטראָל פֿון דער מלוכה" שטייט במילא גאָרניט אין וועג פֿון דער
פּוילישער מלוכה, לויט דעם אַרטיקל [10], צו רעגולירן די שפּראַך וואָס
זיי דאַרפֿן באַנוצן.

(ג) די פֿאָרשריפֿטן, לויט ווי זיי זײַנען פֿאָרמולירט געוואָרן, לאָזן
במילא איבער פֿאַר דער פּוילישער רעגירונג די פֿרײַהייט צו פֿאַרלאַנ־
גען אַז אין אַלע העכערע שולן און אוניווערסיטעטן זאָל געלערנט ווערן
אויף פּויליש.

(ד) די איינהייטלעכקייט אין דער פּוילישער מדינה בנוגע שפּראַך
ווערט ממילא גענוגנדיק באַשיצט דורך דער פֿאַראָרדענונג אַז דאָס
לערנען פּוילייש קאָן געמאַכט ווערן אָבליגאַטאָריש.

ס׳איז ניט קיין פֿראַגע, דערקלערט ווײַטער וווילסאָן, צי די קינדער זאָלן
לערנען פּוילייש, עס האַנדלט זיך אין דעם צי פּוילייש זאָל זיַין די איינציקע
לערנשפּראַך אין אַלע עלעמענטאַר־שולן.

ה ע ד ל אַ ם   מ אַ ר ל ע י   ענטפֿערט, אַז ס׳איז געווען די מיינונג פֿון דער

מערהייט פֿון דער קאָמיסיע, אַז היות די קינדער שטאַמען פֿון היימען וווּ ייִדיש
איז די אומגאַנגסשפּראַך, דאַרף ייִדיש אויך זײַן די לערנשפּראַך אין דער ער־
שטער אינסטאַנץ.

סאָנינאָ פֿרעגט, פֿאַר וואָס זאָל דאָס לערנען ייִדיש בכלל זײַן פֿאַרבאָטן?
העדלאַם מאָרלעי דערקלערערט, אַז אַזאַ פֿאַרבאָט עקסיסטירט בכלל
ניט. די איינציקע פֿראַגע איז, ווי ווײַט די פּוילישע רעגירונג זאָל זײַן מחויב צו
שאַפֿן די מעגלעכקייטן פֿאַרן לימוד פֿון ייִדיש אין די שולן.

לאָיד דזשאָרדזש שטערװאַכט אונטער, אַז ער איז קעגן יעדן פֿרוּװ
אַרויפֿצולייגן אויף דער פּוילישער מלוכה אַן אינטערנאַציאָנאַלע התחײַבֿות
פֿאַרן לימוד פֿון ייִדיש. ער וואָלט נאָר געגעבן זײַן הסכּמה פֿאַרן באַנוץ פֿון
ייִדיש אין די עלעמענטאַר־שולן.

סאָנינאָ פֿרעגט ווײַטער, אויב פּוילן זאָל פֿאַרווערן צו לערנען ייִדיש,
צי וואָלט דאָס ניט געברענגט מיט זיך אַ שוועריקייט וואָס מיר ווילן פֿאַר־
מײַדן? ייִדן וואָלטן דעמאָלט ניט געהאַט קיין אַנדערן אויסוועג ווי אָדער לער־
נען ייִדיש אין דער היים, אָדער שאַפֿן ספּעציעלע שולן פֿאַר דעם צוועק.

העדלאַם מאָרלעי האַלט, אַז די ייִדישע באַוועגונג אין פּוילן האָט ניט
דעם צוועק צו אַנטוויקלען אַ רעליגיעזע באַוועגונג, נאָר אַ סעפּאַראַטיסטישן
ייִדישן נאַציאָנאַליזם. אַ ייִדישער פֿרײַנד זײַנער, וואָס איז נאָר וואָס צוריקגעקו־
מען פֿון פּוילן, האָט אים געזאָגט, אַז מען הערט אַלץ מער ייִדיש אין די גאַסן.

נאָך אַ רײַ אויפֿקלערונגען האָט מען זיך געאייניקט אַז (1) בנוגע דעם
שפּראַכן־באַנוץ ווערט דער פּוילישער רעגירונג געגעבן אַ פֿרײַע האַנט אין
אַלע שולן אַחוץ אין די עלעמענטאַר־שולן. דאָרטן וווּ ס׳איז דאָ, לויט די אַר־
טיקלען 9 און 10 פֿון דעם פּראָיעקטירטן אָפּמאַך מיט פּוילן, אַ גרעסערע מינ־
דערהייט פֿון קינדער וואָס רעדן אַן אַנדערע שפּראַך ווי פּוילעש, זאָל זיי זײַ געגעבן
ווערן מעגלעכקייטן, אַז די לערנשפּראַך אין די עלעמענטאַר־שולן זאָל זײַן אין
זייער אייגענעם לשון. די קאָמיסיע פֿאַר נײַע מלוכות ווערט אויטאָריזירט אין
איינעם מיט דעם רעדאַקציע־קאָמיטעט צו מאַכן די נייטיקע שינויים אין די
פּראָיעקטירטע אָפּמאַכן מיט פּוילן... (2) דער פּראָיעקט פֿונעם בריוו צו דער
פּוילישער דעלעגאַציע, וואָס דער קאָמיטעט האָט פֿאַרגעלייגט, איז באַשטעטיקט
געוואָרן מיט שינויים וואָס דאַרפֿן אַרײַנגעפֿירט ווערן אין דעם אָפּשניט וואָס
איז נוגע דעם שולוועזן, אין הסכּם מיט די אָנגענומענע באַשלוסן.

באַלפֿור פֿאָדערט אַז אין דעם אָפּמאַך זאָל מען אַנשטאַט "ייִדן" בעסער
ניצן: "פּערזאָנען פֿון ייִדישן גלויבן". ער איז שטאַרק דערפֿאַר, אַז מען זאָל ייִדן
געבן פּריווילעגיעס צוליב זייער אמונה, אָבער ניט צוליב זייער אומה "(not
fate ער האָט געמיינט ‏‏. "(because they are of Jewish faith [sic!]"

סאָנינאָ איז אַרויסגעטרעטן קעגן דעם, וויַל אויב אַ ייִד וואָלט געוואָרן
אַ קריסט, וואָלט ער מער ניט געקאָנט געניסן פֿון אָט דער שוץ.

5

אָבער מיט דעם איז די ייִדישע שולפֿראַגע נאָך ניט פֿאַרענטפֿערט געוואָרן.
דעם 27סטן יוני 1919 איז פֿאַדערעװוסקי יאָ געקומען צום ראַט אַז דער
פֿאַראַגראַף פֿון טראַקטאַט בנוגע די ייִדישע שולן זאָל געביטן װערן. ער האָט צו־
געזאָגט צו פֿינאַנצירן אַזעלכע ייִדישע שולן װוּ די הצטרכות׳ן פֿון דער ייִדישער
רעליגיע װעלן רעספּעקטירט װערן און אַז די ייִדישע פֿאָלקסשפּראַך זאָל באַטראַכט
װערן ניט מער װי אַ הילפֿשפּראַך. פֿאַדערעװוסקי האָט פֿאָרזיכערט די מיטגלי־
דער פֿון ראַט אַז דאָס איז אַ פֿאָרשלאַג װאָס קומט דוקא פֿון אַן אײנפֿלוסרײכ׳ן
ייִדישן צד. לאָיד דזשאָרדזש האָט געזאָגט אַז דאָס גייט נאָך און װײטער אַפֿילו פֿון
דעם װאָס דער איצטיקער טראַקטאַט פֿאַרלאַנגט, און װילסאָן האָט מוסיף גע־
װען אַז די כּוונה פֿונעם טראַקטאַט איז געװען אַז ייִדיש זאָל באַנוצט װערן װי אַ
לערנשפּראַך נאָר אין די עלעמענטאַר־שולן און אַז קיינער האָט גאָרניט געהאַט
בדעה צו פֿאַרלאַנגען אַז מען זאָל לערנען ייִדיש װי אַ באַזונדערע שפּראַך.[14]

אין די װײַטערדיקע פֿאַרהאַנדלונגען מיט פּוילן בנוגע ייִדישע מינדערהײט־
רעכט זײַנען אַרײַנגעטראָגן געוואָרן װיכטיקע שינויים. דער טעקסט בנוגע ייִדי־
שע שולן װאָס איז אַרײַן אין דעם מינדערהײטס־טראַקטאַט האָט אויסגעזען
אַזוי:[15]

אַרטיקל 8: פּוילישע בירגערס, װאָס באַלאַנגען צו עטנישע,
רעליגיעזע אָדער שפּראַכלעכע מינדערהײטן, זאָלן יורידיש און פֿאַק־
טיש באַהאַנדלט װערן אַזוי װי די אַנדערע פּוילישע בירגערס. ספּע־
ציעל זאָלן זיי האָבן דאָס גלײַכע רעכט צו גרינדן, פֿאַרוואַלטן און קאָנ־
טראָלירן אויף זייער אייגענע קאָסטן צדקה־אַנשטאַלטן, רעליגיעזע און
סאָציאַלע אינסטיטוטיעס, שולן און אַנדערע ערציִונג־אינסטיטוטיעס,
מיטן פֿולן רעכט צו באַנוצן זייער אייגן לשון און אָפּהיטן זײַערע רעלי־
גיעזע מינהגים אָן שום מניעה.

אַרטיקל 9: אין די שטעט און דיסטריקטן, װוּ ס׳װוינען פֿאַר־
פֿאַרציִאַנעל אַ גרויסע צאָל פּוילישע בירגערס מיט אַנדערע לשונות װי
פּוילישׁ, דאַרף פּוילן שאַפֿן אין איר עפֿנטלעכער ערציִונג־סיסטעם
אַזעלכע צופֿרידנשטעליקע באַדינגונגען װאָס זאָלן מעגלעך מאַכן אַז
אין די עלעמענטאַר־שולן זאָל דער לימוד פֿאַר קינדער פֿון אַזעלכע
פּוילישע בירגערס זײַן אין זייער אייגענער שפּראַך. אָט די פֿאָרשריפֿט
זאָל ניט זײַן קיין מניעה פֿאַר דער פּוילישער רעגירונג צו מאַכן אָבלי־
גאַטאָריש דאָס לערנען פּוילישׁ אויך אין די דאָזיקע שולן.

אין די שטעט און דיסטריקטן, װוּ ס׳איז פֿאַראַן אַ גרעסערע פֿאַר־
פֿאַרציע פּוילישע בירגערס, װאָס געהערן צו ראַסישע, רעליגיעזע אָדער

---

[14] טשענעבוים, צװישן סלחמה און שלום, ז׳ 248.

[15] דער מינדערהײטס־טראַקטאַט מיט פּוילן האָט געהאַט 12 אַרטיקלען. 10 פֿון זיי האָבן
געהאַט אַ שײַכות צו אַלע מינדערהײטן אין פּוילן די אַרטיקלען 10 און 11 זײַנען נוגע
געווען נאָר ייִדן, זיי האָבן באַהאַנדלט די פֿראַגעס פֿון ייִדישער ערציִונג און שבת׳דו. מיר
ציטירן דאָ אויך די אַרטיקלען 8 און 9, װײַל זיי באַהאַנדלען ענינים וואָס האָבן אַ
שײַכות צו ייִדן.

שפּראַכלעכע מינדערהייטן, דאַרפֿן אָט די מינדערהייטן קריגן אַ גע־
העריקן טייל פֿון די פֿאָנדן וואָס זײַנען אַסיגנירט געוואָרן פֿון דער
מלוכה אָדער פֿון דער שטאָט־פֿאַרוואַלטונג אָדער פֿון עפּעס אַן אַנדערן
בודזשעט פֿאַר דערצִיונג און פֿאַר רעליגיעזע אָדער צדקה־צוועקן צו
פֿאַרווענדן לויט זייער אײַנזען.

אַרטיקל 10: די לאָקאַלע דערצִיונגס־קאָמיטעטן, וואָס ווערן
באַשטימט פֿון די יִידישע קהילות אין פּוילן, וועלן, אונטער דער אַלגע־
מיינער קאָנטראָל פֿון דער רעגירונג, זאָרגן פֿאַר דער פֿאַרטיילונג פֿון
די עפֿנטלעכע פֿאָנדן פֿון דעם פּראָפּאָרציאָנעלן חלק פֿון דעם געלט
וואָס איז באַשטימט געוואָרן פֿאַר די יִידישע שולן, אין הסכּם מיטן
אַרטיקל 9, און אויך פֿאַר דער אָרגאַניזירונג און אָנפֿירונג פֿון די שולן.
באַשטימונגען פֿון אַרטיקל 9 בנוגע דעם שפּראַכבאַנוץ אין די שולן
זײַנען אויך חל אויף די [יִידישע] שולן.

אַזוי ווײַט די הלכה. ווי אַזוי די פּאָליאַקן האָבן אינטערפּרעטירט דעם
טעקסט און ווי זיי האָבן געהאַלטן דעם אָפּמאַך איז אַ קאַפּיטל פֿאַר זיך.[16]

6

מיר האָבן דאָ אַלץ גערעדט וועגן פּוילישן מינדערהייטס־טראַקטאַט און ניט
דערמאָנט אַנדערע לענדער, ווײַל ערשטנס האָט פּוילן געהאַט די גרעסטע יִידי־
שע מינדערהייט אין גאַנץ אייראָפּע, און צווייטנס, האָבן אַנדערע מלוכות, אַחוץ
פּוילן און ליטע,[17] אָדער אונטערגעשריבן גאָר אַ טייל פֿון די ספּעציפֿיש־יִידי־
שע פּאַראַגראַפֿן, אָדער גאָר אין גאַנצן פּטור געוואָרן פֿון די יִידישע פּאַראַ־
גראַפֿן וואָס זײַנען בדרך כּלל ניט געוואָרן קיין באַליבטער אַרטיקל אויפֿן פּאָ־
ליטישן מאַרק. ס'איז גענוג צו דערמאָנען דעם לאַנגן קאַמף פֿון רומעניע קעגן
די מינדערהייטס־רעכט און צום סוף האָט זי אָנגענומען בלויז דעם פּאַראַגראַף 7,
וואו יִידן ווערן דערמאָנט אין שײַכות מיט בירגערשאַפֿט, אָבער אָן די ספּעציִ־
פֿיש יִידישע שפּראַך־ אָדער שבת־רו־התחַיבֿותן. אויך טשעכאָסלאָוואַקײַ האָט
ניט אָנגענומען די יִידישע פּאַראַגראַפֿן, כאָטש זי האָט יאָ אָנגענומען געוויסע
פּונקטן וועגן טעריטאָריעלער אויטאָנאָמיע פֿאַר די קאַרפֿאַטן־רוטענער. גריכן־
לאַנד האָט אונטערגעשריבן דעם טראַקטאַט אָן דעם דערצִיונג־פּאַראַגראַף. יוגאָ־

---

[16] די פֿראַגע פֿאַר וואָס די מינדערהייטס־טראַקטאַטן האָבן ניט געהאַט קיין גרויסע פּעולה
אין פּראַקטישן יִידישן לעבן, און פֿון וואַנען ס'האָבן זיך גענומען די שטערונגען זיי דורכ־
צופֿירן, זען די אויסגעצייכנטע אַרבעט פֿון:

Dr. Jacob Robinson, et. al., *Were the Minorities Treaties a Failure?* New
York, 1943.

[17] ליטע האָט אונטערגעשריבן דעם טראַקטאַט דעם 12טן מײַ 1922. די אַרטיקלען וואָס
זײַנען נוגע די רעכט פֿאַר מינדערהייטן זײַנען אָנגענומען געוואָרן דורך דער ליטווישער
רעגירונג אין דער פֿאָרעם פֿון אַ דעקלאַראַציע אַנשטאָט אַ ראַטיפֿיקאַציע. עס איז אָבער כּדאַי
צו דערמאָנען אַז ליטע איז געווען די איינציקע מלוכה אַחוץ אוקראַיִנע, וואָס האָט אָנער־
קענט די יִידישע אויטאָנאָמיע לכל־הפּחות אַ שטיקל צײַט און געשאַפֿן אַ מין מיניסטעריום
פֿאַר יִידישע עניִנים.

סלאַוויע האָט דעם טראַקטאַט יאָ ראַטיפֿיצירט, אָבער ניט אָן געוויסע מאָדי־
פֿיקאַציעס.

דער סוף איז געווען אַז די קולטורעלע התחייבֿותן מצד די מלוכות צו
זייערע יידישע מינדערהייטן האָבן ביַי קיינעם ניט נושא־חן געווען און מען האָט
באַלד פֿאַרגעסן אין די יידישע פֿאַראַגראַפֿן און אין יידן בכלל. סיבות זייַנען
געווען אַ סך, אָבער איינע פֿון זיי, אפֿשר די וויכטיקסטע, איז געווען די קליינע
ענדערונג אינעם טעקסט פֿון מינדערהייטס־טראַקטאַט, וואָס מיר האָבן שוין
דערמאַנט אויבן, אַז אַנשטאָט אַ „צענטראַלן יידישן קאָמיטעט״ וואָס זאָל האָבן
די אויפֿזיכט און די אַפֿאָטראָפּסות איבער די יידישע שולן, זאָלן געשאַפֿן ווערן
„לאָקאַלע קאָמיטעטן״. די דאָזיקע המצאה האָט געשטאַמט פֿון לאָרד באַלפֿור.
דאָס באַוויַיזט ווי ווייַט דער פֿאַטער פֿון דער באַוווּסטער באַלפֿור־דעקלאַראַציע
איז געווען פֿון אָנערקענען יידישע נאַציאָנאַלע אינטערעסן. דאָס זעלביקע קאָן
מען אויך זאָגן וועגן לאָיד דזשאָרדזשן. ווען ניט וואָלטאָן וואָלט פֿון דעם גאַנצן
שפּראַכן־פֿאַראַגראַף ניט געבליבן קיין שריד ופליט. אָבער איין זאַך האָט אויך
וואָלסאָן ניט פֿאַרשטאַנען: אויב דער פֿעלקערבונד וועט ווערן דער אַפֿאָטרופּוס
איבער די רעכט פֿון די מינדערהייטן וועט ער אָבער פֿאָרט ניט קענען אַלץ
דערהיטן, ספּעציעל וואָן עס האַנדלט זיך וועגן יידישע אינטערעסן. עס איז
נייטיק געווען אַ פֿאַרטרעטערשאַפֿט פֿון דער מינדערהייט גופֿא, וואָס זאָל אויפֿ־
טרעטן ווי אַ קטיגור אָדער אַ סניגור, און אַז מען זאָל ניט דאַרפֿן זוכן מיט ליכט
אַ מליץ־יושר צווישן מלוכות וואָס האָבן געהערט צום ראַט פֿון פֿעלקערבונד.[18]
און ווער פֿון די מלוכות האָט זיך דען געוואָלט אײַנריַיסן מיט שכנים, סיַידן
ס׳האָט זיך געהאַנדלט וועגן די אייגענע עטנישע גרופּעס וואָס האָבן זיך געפֿונען
אין פֿרעמדע גרענעצן?

און פֿון דעסט וועגן טאָרן די קריטיקערס פֿון מינדערהייטס־טראַקטאַט ניט
פֿאַרגעסן אַז דאָס איז געווען דער ערשטער עקספּערימענט אין דער געשיכטע,
און אַז מיר יידן האָבן געקראָגן אַן אומדירעקטע אָנערקענונג ווי אַ קולטורעל־
עטנישע איינהייט מיט אייגענע אינטערעסן, און צום ערשטן מאָל אין דער
געשיכטע האָט די יידישע שפּראַך געקראָגן די אָפֿיציעלע אינטערנאַציאָנאַלע
„עפֿנטלעך־רעכטלעכע״ אָנערקענונג ווי די שפּראַך פֿון יידן.

<hr />

[18] וועגן פּרעזידענט ווילסאָנס שטעלונג צו אַ יידישער פֿאַרטרעטערשאַפֿט, זען מיַין בוך,
צווישן מלחמה און שלום, זז׳ 141—143.

פּרעזידענט ווילסאָן איז געווען קעגן אַ פֿאַרטרעטערשאַפֿט פֿון דער יידישער מינדערהייט
אין דער פֿעלקער־ליגע. ער האָט דאָס דערקלערט דערמיט, וואָס די זעלבע רעכט וואָלט מען
געמוזט געבן אויך אַנדערע מינדערהייטן, „למשל די דייטשן״. ער האָט אויך געטריַיסט די
יידישע פֿאַרטרייסטערס, און דאָס זעלבע איבערגעחזרט אין דער דיסקוסיע אויפֿן העקסטן ראַט,
אַז סוף־כּל־סוף וועלן יידן אין ענגלאַנד און אין אַמעריקע אַכטונג געבן אויף די יידישע
ענינים אין מיזרח־אייראָפּע און אין פֿאַל דער טראַקטאַט וועט ניט אויסגעפֿירט ווערן וועלן
זיי קענען אינטערוווענירן דורך זייערע רעגירונגען. זען:

Cyrus Adler, *I Have Considered the Days*, Philadelphia, 1941, pp. 313-316.

צו דער עפֿענונג פֿון דער ייִדיש־קאַטעדרע
אין ירושלימער אוניווערסיטעט

מ. שניאורסאָן, משה
שוואבע, בנציון דינאבורג,
דוד פּינסקי, חיים גרינבערג,
לוי סיגאַל, דב סדן

SUMMARY: ON THE INAUGURATION OF THE YIDDISH CHAIR AT THE
UNIVERSITY IN JERUSALEM BY M. SHNEYERSON, M. SHVABE,
B. DINABURG, D. PINSKI, KH. GRINBERG, L. SIGL, D. SADAN

*Seven speakers, at the occasion of the establishment of the endowed chair for Yiddish at
the Hebrew University (Jerusalem 1951) recollect the hostile opposition to such a step
a quarter century before and express their hopes for a growing realization of what Israel
and Jews everywhere owe to Yiddish.*

לכבוד דער ייִדיש־קאַטעדרע אין דער העברעישער אוניווערסיטעט
און דעם דאָצענט דב סדן איז דעם 4טן סעפּטעמבער 1951 פֿאָרגעקומען אין
ירושלים אַ פֿײַערלעכע מסיבה, מיט דער באַטײליקונג פֿון אוניווערסיטעט־
פּראָפֿעסאָרן, פֿאָרשטײער פֿון דער רעגירונג, סוכנות און פֿאַרטרעטער פֿון
דער פּרעסע.
מיר ברענגען דאָ די רעדעס, לויטן סדר ווי די זײַנען געהאַלטן געוואָרן
אויף דער פֿײַערונג.

מ. שניאורסאָן — פֿינאַנץ־דירעקטאָר פֿון אוניווערסיטעט:

קודם־כּל וויל איך באַגריסן דעם חשובן עולם וואָס געפֿינט זיך דאָ, ווי אויך
יענע פֿרײַנד אונדזערע וואָס זענען, צוליב פֿאַרשיידענע סיבות, איצט דאָ ניטאָ מיט
אונדז. באַזונדער האַרציק באַגריס איך דעם סעניאָר אונדזערן, וועלכער באַשײַנט די
שׂימחה — דוד פּינסקי, וואָס איז צו דער פֿײַערלעכער מסיבה געקומען ספּעציעל פֿון חיפֿה.
איך באַגריס אויך די חברים פֿון ייִדיש־נאַציאָנאַלן אַרבעטער־פֿאַרבאַנד און אחרון אחרון —
דב סדן, וואָס האָט באַקומען דעם בכּבודיקן אַמט פֿון אָנפֿירן מיט דער קאַטעדרע פֿאַר ייִדיש.
די טעטיקייט פֿון ייִדיש־נאַציאָנאַלן אַרבעטער־פֿאַרבאַנד איז אַלעמען גוט באַקאַנט.
די קרוין פֿון זײַנע אויפֿטוען איז אָבער דאָס ווערק, וואָס זײַן אַנטשטײונג פֿײַערן מיר הײַנט.
אין מײַן געבוירן־שטאַט איז געוואָרן אַ ייִד אַ גביר, וואָס האָט זיך אויסגעצײכנט מיט

זיין וועלטעטיקייט און מיט זיין פרומקייט — ער האָט אַפֿילו געהאָט אַן אייגענעם בית־
מדרש. אַז ער האָט חתונה געמאַכט זיין טאָכטער פֿאַר אַ גרויסן תלמיד־חכם,
האָט ער זיך אויסגעדריקט: „ערשט איצט ווייס איך, אַז די וועלט איז מיינע". ווילט זיך
מיר זאָגן דעם ייִדיש־נאַציאָנאַלן אַרבעטער־פֿאַרבאַנד: „היינט האָט איר קונה געוואָרן אייער
וועלט".

איך האַלט, אַז מען קאָן פֿאַרבלייבן געטריי געטריי העברעיש און גלייכצייטיק באַטראַכטן
ייִדיש ווי איינעם פֿון די גרעסטע ווערטן, וואָס דאָס ייִדישע פֿאָלק האָט געשאַפֿן אין גלות.
מיין באַציונג צו ייִדיש האָב איך, טיילווייז, צו פֿאַרדאַנקען צוויי ייִדן. איינער פֿון זיי

Because Mendele ('The grandfather of modern Yiddish – and Hebrew – literature) writes in both Yiddish and Hebrew, the Zionist leader M. M. Usishkin refuses to admit him into the Society of Lovers of Hebrew. (*Der groyser kundes*, March 27, 1914)

איז געווען מיין מלמד. דער רבי מיינער האָט געהאַט אַ טבע מקדים צו זיין זיך מיטן אויפֿ־
געמען דעם שבת. פֿרייטיק ביי טאָג פֿלעגט ער שוין אויפֿהערן רייכערן, פֿלעגט אויסשפּרייטן
אַ ווייסן טישטעך איבערן טיש, אַוועקשטעלן די מעשענע לייכטער און אויפֿהערן ריידן
יידיש, די שפּראַך פֿון דער וואָך. געווען אַ גרויסער בן־תורה, אָבער ריידן לשון־קודש
האָט ער ניט געקענט. פֿלעגט ער שווייגן. איין מאָל, געדענק איך, ערב שבת. האָט די קאַץ
גענומען לעקן די חלות, האָט דער רבי, ניט וויסנדיק ווי צו זאָגן עס אויף לשון־קודש, אָנגע־
הויבן שרייען: אי, אוי, קיצי! חלות! אַ גאַנצן שבתדיקן טאָג פֿלעגט ער שווייגן, דער
רבי, ערשט מוצאי שבת האָט ער געעפֿנט דאָס מויל און גענומען זאָגן „גאָט פֿון אברהם,
גאָט פֿון יצחק, גאָט פֿון יעקב" מיט אַזאַ התלהבות, מיט אַזאַ האַרציקן ניגון, אַז דער
וואָכעדיקער יידיש האָט באַקומען אַ מין הייליקייט, אַ קדושה, וואָס לאָזט זיך ניט אַזוי
לייכט פֿאַרגעסן.

דער צווייטער ייִד, וואָס האָט מיך אָנגעשטעקט מיט ליבשאַפֿט צו ייִדיש־לשון, איז
געווען אַ חסיד פֿון מיין זיידן, ביי וועמען איך בין דערצויגן געוואָרן. דער דאָזיקער חסיד
האָט זוכה געווען צו תורה וגדולה במקום אחד — געווען אַ ייד אַ תלמיד־חכם און גלייכ־
ציטיק אַ גרויסער גביר. האָט ער געהאַט אַ טבע דער חסיד — ר' איטשעלע סעמיאַנאָווקער
האָט ער געהייסן — צו פֿאַרטייטשן אויף יידיש דעם „פּאַרטיקין" דאַוונען. און ניט סתם
אויף יידיש, נאָר אויף אַ זאַפֿטיקן יידיש. שבת ווידער פֿלעגט ער נאָכן מעביר זיין די
סדרה, שנים מקרא ואחד תרגום, ליינען דעם טייטש־חומש צאינה וראינה.

„אַל תטוש תורת אמך" — פֿלעגט ער האָבן אַ ווערטל — זאָלסט ניט פֿאַרלאָזן די
תורה פֿון דער מ אַ מ ע ן"...

אָט פֿון די דאָזיקע צווי ייִדן האָב איך געירשנט מיין ליבשאַפֿט צו העברעיִש און די
צוגעבונדקייט צו ייִדיש.

דב סדן, אייך וויל איך זאָגן אָט וואָס: אַ גרויסע זכיה איז אייך צוגעטיילט געוואָרן
צו לערנען דאָס ייִדיש־לשון און די ייִדישע ליטעראַטור אין דער איינציקער העברעיִשער
אוניווערסיטעט אויף גאָר דער וועלט — דאָס איז אַ גרויסע זכיה און גלייכצייטיק אַ גרויסע
פֿאַראַנטוואָרטלעכקייט. איך האָף, אַז דער רעקטאָר און די איבעריקע וויסנשאַפֿטלעכע מיט־
אַרבעטער וועלן אייך פֿיל מיטהעלפֿן, איר, וועט אויך באַקומען די ווייטגייענדיקסטע הילף
פֿון דעם ייִדיש־נאַציאָנאַלן אַרבעטער־פֿאַרבאַנד.

איך ווינטש אייך און אונדז אַלעמען, אַז מיר זאָלן אַלע נחת האָבן פֿון אונדזער ניי
ווערק.

רעקטאָר פּראָפֿ. משה שוואַבע:

איך פֿיל די גאַנצע וויכטיקייט פֿון דאָזיקן היסטאָרישן מאָמענט און כ'בין צופֿרידן
וואָס איך רייד אין נאָמען פֿון אונדזער נאַציאָנאַלער גייסט־אינסטיטוציע דווקא אין דעם
דאָזיקן קרייז פֿון חברים. ווער בין איך — אַ מענטש וואָס איז געקומען צו אונדזער פֿאָלק
פֿון אַן אַסטראַנאַמישער ווייטקייט — אַז איך זאָל דאָ האַלטן פֿאַר אייך רעדעס? ס'פֿאַר־
פֿליכט מיך אָבער מיין אַמט; אויך די אינסטיטוציע וואָס איך פֿאַרטרעט אין ווערט מען זאָל
הערן איר שטים.

איך דאַנק אונדזער חבר מ. שניאָרסאָן פֿאַר זיינע רייד און פֿאַר זיין טעטיקייט. איך

דריק אויך אויס אָנערקענונג אונדזערע חברים פון אַמעריקע, וואָס האָבן מיטגעהאָלפֿן
די קאַטעדרע פון ייִדיש אויפֿצושטעלן.

ווען איך קוק אויף דב סטאָק, דערמאַנט זיך מיר אַ קאַפּיטל געשיכטע. פאַר מײַנע
אויגן שטײַט די גורלדיקע זיצונג פון סוף 1927, ווען ס׳איז באַטראַכט געוואָרן די פּראָגע פון
אַ קאַטעדרע פֿאַר ייִדיש. ס׳האָט זיך דעמאָלט געפֿונען אַ ייִד וואָס האָט זי געוואָלט פינאַנסירן.
אין די גאַסן פון ירושלים האָט זיך אויפֿגעהויבן אַ פּראָטעסט פון „גדוד מגיני השפה
העברית", וואָס האָבן דעמאָלט געפֿירט זייער שטערעריש אַרבעט אין אונדזער שטאָט.
„צלם בהיכל" (אַ צלם אין פּאַלאַץ) — האָט אַלאַמירט זייער אויפֿרוף, און דאָס האָט געפֿונען
אַן אָפּקלאַנג. אוסישקין ז״ל האָט די דאָזיקע מיינונג ענערגיש אונטערגעשטיצט. דער פאַר־
שטאָרבענער ד״ר מאַגנעס איז געווען געצוווּנגען צונויפֿצורופֿן דעם אײַנציקן אַקאַדעמישן
אָרגאַן וואָס האָט דעמאָלט עקסיסטירט. ס׳איז דאָ אַ פּראָטאָקאָל פון יענער זיצונג, און
ד״ר הוגאַ בערגמאַן האָט פֿאַרצייכנט (לויטן דאָזיקן פּראָטאָקאָל האָט ער צייַט אַ שפּעטער
פֿאַרעפֿנטלעכט אין דבר בּיאַלִיקס רעדע אויף דער דאָזיקער זיצונג). מיר האָבן דעמאָלט
אויסגעהערט די זייער אַגרעסיוורע רייד פון אוסישקינען. אין דער זיצונג האָבן אַנטייל גענומען:
ד״ר מאַגנעס, פּראָפֿ. שלום, ח. נ. ביאַליק, מ. מ. אוסישקין, ה. בערגמאַן און איך). ד״ר מאַג־
נעס האָט זיך געפֿונען אין אַ גרויסער פֿאַרלעגנהייַט, ווייַל ס׳איז געווען אַ סכנה, אַז דער
ייִשוב וועט באַריקאַסטירן אונדזער אינסטיטוציע — און דער באַשיידענער קערן פון אונדזער
אוניווערסיטעט האָט זיך דעמאָלט ניט געקאָנט דערלויבן אויף אַ קאַמפֿן. דעריבער זענען
מיר אַוועק פון דער זיצונג מיט אַ פּשרה־באַשלוס, וואָס האָט פאַקטיש דעם גאַנצן ענין
באַגראָבן. מיר האָבן זיך אָפּגעגעבן אַ חשבון, אַז די ייִדישע קאַטעדרע וועט שוין גיך
ניט אַנטשטיין.

פֿאַר גרינדן אַ ייִדיש־קאַטעדרע האָט זיך אויף דער זיצונג ענערגיש אַרויסגעזאָגט
פּראָפֿ. שלום. ד״ר מאַגנעס האָט דעם ענין ניט געקאָנט פֿאַרשטיידיקן צוליב די אַלגעמיינע
אינטערעסן פון אוניווערסיטעט. איך האָב דעמאָלט געזאָגט, אַז קיין שום ייִדישע זאַך איז
מיר ניט פֿרעמד, און דעריבער בין איך פֿאַר דער קאַטעדרע. קיין פֿאַרמעלע אָפּשטימונג
איז אָבער ניט פֿאָרגעקומען. ביאַליק האָט גערעדט האַרב ווערטער וועגן דער געשיכטע
פון ייִדיש און האָט פֿאַרויסגעזאָגט, אַז דאָס דאָזיקע לשון וועט קיין אריכות ימים ניט האָבן.

איך וויל איצט ניט ריידן וועגן געשיכטע. כ׳וויל בלויז זאָגן זאָגן איינס:
בײַם הײַנטיקן טאָג איז איז די לאַגע אַזאַ, אַז מיר קאַנען זיך שוין דערלויבן אויף אַ ייִדישער
קאַטעדרע און ניט בלויז מיר קאַנ ע ן, נאָר מיר מוזן די דאָזיקע שפּראַך שטודירן. אין
יענע צייַטן האָט מען מורא געהאַט, זי זאָל, חלילה, ניט פֿאַרקאָנקורירן העברעיִש. הײַנט
פֿילן מיר זיך אין דאָזיקן פּרט גאַנץ זיכער און מיר אָנערקענען די נייטיקייט צו שטודירן די
ייִדישע שפּראַך און איר ליטעראַטור. איך נעם זיך ניט אונטער נביאות צו זאָגן וועגן דעם
גורל פֿונעם דאָזיקן לשון, מחמת אונדזער גאַנצע געשיכטע — סיי די גייסטיקע, סיי די
מאַטעריעלע — איז דאָך איין גרויסער נס.

די העברעיִשע שפּראַך — און איר ליטעראַטור — איז איצט שטאַרק אַנטוויקלט.
אונדזערע קינדער ריידן אַ לעבעדיק עברית־לשון, וואָס פֿאַרמאָגט שפּראַצונגען פון פֿאַלקס־
טימלעכקייט. ווען איך פֿאַרגלייַך איצט אונדזער לעבעדיקע העברעיִשע שפּראַך מיטן ייִדישן
לשון, ווי איך האָב עס אַמאָל געפֿילט, זע איך די קערנדיקע פֿאָלקסטימלעכקייט פון דער

שפּראַך, וואָס איז געוואָרן געװאָרדעט אין תּחום־המושב. איך וויים ניט, צי די קאַטעדרע אַליין
וועט עס זיין בכּוח צו טאָן — ס׳איז אָבער קלאָר: מען דאַרף אַריבערטראָגן די פּאָלקס־אוצרות
פֿון ייִדיש אין העברעיִש, וואָס לעבט און אַנטװיקלט זיך דאָ. ווי אַזוי וועט איר, סדן, דאָס
מאַכן, וויים איך ניט; איך קען ניט אייער מעטאָד. איך בין אָבער זיכער, אַז איר און אַנדערע
אָריענטירן זיך אין דער פּראָבלעם אַ סך בעסער ווי איך. מיינע ווערטער שטאַמען מער פֿון
בענקשאַפט ווי פֿון וויסן.

נאָך לאַנגע שלעפּעגישן — ווי דער שטייגער איז — האָב איך היינט ענדלעך
אונטערגעשריבן די נאָמינאַציע פֿון דוב סדן, ווייל ערשט היינט זענען פֿאַרענדיקט געוואָרן
אַלע פֿאָרמאַליטעטן — ס׳איז דערהאַלטן געוואָרן די באַשטעטיקונג פֿון דער „ועדת
הביניים" (צווישן־קאָמיסיע). ביים אונטערשרייבן די באַשטימונג האָב איך געהאַט דאָס
געפֿיל, אַז איך עפֿן אַ נייע טיר פֿאַר דער באַרייכערונג פֿון דער העברעיִשער שפּראַך.

איך באַגריס דב סדן, אונדזער אַמעריקאַנער פֿריינד פֿון ייִדיש־נאַציאָנאַלן אַרבעטער־
פֿאַרבאַנד און אויך אַלעמען, וואָס האָבן זוכה געוואָרן צו זיין עדות פֿון אַ גרויסער געשעע־
ניש אין דער געשיכטע פֿון אונדזער אוניװערסיטעט.

בילדונג־מיניסטער פּראָפֿ. בנציון דינאַבורג:

ווי אַזוי איז צוגעגאַנגען די גרינדונג פֿון דער נייער קאַטעדרע פֿאַר ייִדיש ?

מיר האָבן דערלאַנגט דעם פֿאַקולטעט אַ מעמאָריאַל, אונטערגעשריבן דורך רעקטאָר
שוואַבע און דורך מיר, אין וועלכן מיר האָבן געבעטן צו עפֿענען אַ נייע קאַטעדרע פֿאַר
ייִדיש און איר ליטעראַטור. ס׳איז צונויפֿגעשטעלט געוואָרן אַ קאָמיסיע פֿון די פּראָפֿעסאָרן
שלום, בענעט, קאַסוטאָ, טור־סיני און מיר. מיר האָבן דעם גאַנצן ענין זייער ערנסט
באַטראַכט, פֿעסטגעשטעלט עטלעכע פּרינציפֿן און פֿאָרמולירט אונדזער שטעלונג. מיט דער
דאָזיקער שטעלונג, מיין איך, איז כּדאי צו באַקענען די איצטיקע פֿאַרזאַמלונג.

אין דער גאַנצער ייִדישער געשיכטע — האַלטן מיר — לאָזן זיך מערקן צוויי שטראָ־
מען — אַן אייבערשטער און אַן אונטערשטער. ס׳זענען דאָ תּקופֿות, וועז די שאַפֿונג
פֿון פֿאָלק קומט צום אויסדרוק דורך דינאַמישע כּוחות וואָס צי׳ען זייער יניקה פֿון וועלט־
באַנעמען און לעבנס־באַגריפֿן, וואָס געהאָרכן צו זײַנע אײַבערשטע שיכטן. אין אַזעלכע
תּקופֿות זענען די שאַפֿונג־טרעגער נביאים, חכמים, תּנאים, משׂכּילים. דאַקעגן זענען דאָ
תּקופֿות, וועז דער שאַפֿונגסגײַסט קומט צום אויסדרוק דורך די פֿאָלקסטימלעכע עלעמענטן
— אמוראים, מקובלים, חסידים, סאָציאַליסטן. די ייִדישע קולטור־ירושה באַזיצט פֿיל
פֿאָלקס־עלעמענטן און זיי האָבן עס געשאַפֿן דעם יסוד פֿאַר דער לעבעדיקער קולטור אין
ישׂראל. אין גלות אָבער, וועז די ייִדן זענען געווען געצוווּנגען איבערצוּוואַנדערן פֿון לאַנד
צו לאַנד און ראַטעווען וואָס עס לאָזט זיך, — האָבן זיי געמוזט מצמצם זיין די דאָזיקע
פֿאָלקס־עלעמענטן, ווייל די אָנגענומענע לעבנס־פֿאָרמען פֿלעגן צעשטערט ווערן, און אין
די נייע באַדינגונגען האָבן זיי געמוזט אָנהייבן בויען פֿון דאָס ניי. די בוירער זענען אין
אַזעלכע פֿאַלן געווען די חכמים, רבנים און אַנדערע מענטשן פֿון גייסט, דאָס הייסט די
אײבערע שיכטן.

ביים היינטיקן טאָג, וועז מיר האָבן צוריק אונדזער היים, איז אונדזער פֿליכט אויפֿ־
צושטעלן אַ ריזנווערק וואָס זאָל קאָנצענטרירן די גאַנצע דורות־לאַנגע שאַפֿונג פֿון די

ייִדישע מאַסן. דאָס איז אַ תּנאי פֿאַר דער וויטאַליטעט פֿון אונדזער קולטור, פֿאַר איר אײַנ־
װאָרצעלען זיך, פֿאַר איר המשך און פֿאַר איר פֿאָלקסטימלעכקייט.
ווי אַזוי זאָלן מיר עס מאַכן ?

ייִדיש — האָבן מיר פֿעסטגעשטעלט — איז איינער פֿון די יסודות פֿון אונדזער
דורות־לאַנגער פֿאָלקסקולטור ; מיר זעען אין איר אַ גרויסן אויסדרוק פֿון פֿאָלקסאַפֿערישע
כּוחות. מיר שטרעבן צו באַפֿעסטיקן אונדזער העברעיִשע קולטור דורך אַרײַנברענגען אין
איר די פֿאָלקסשאַפֿונג, װאָס איז געקומען צום אויסדרוק אין ייִדיש און אַנדערע שפּראַכן,
מיט װעלכע ייִדן האָבן זיך באַנוצט אין די גלות־לענדער. אַ סך מענטשן האָבן שוין אָנגע־
וויזן אויף דעם שאַפֿערישן פֿאָלקס־כּוח, װאָס קומט צום אויסדרוק אין ייִדיש. אין דעם
פּרט האָט ביאַליק פֿאַרגליכן ייִדיש צו אַראַמיש. מיר האָבן זיך דעריבער געזאָגט : דאָס איז
אונדזער פּלאַן און דאָס װעלן מיר פֿאַרווירקלעכן.

די אויפֿגאַבע פֿון דב סדן װעט זײַן אַרויסצוברענגען די גרונט־עלעמענטן פֿון דער
ייִדישער פֿאָלקסשאַפֿונג אין אַלע דורות און אָרגאַניש זיי אַרײַנפֿלעכטן אין דעם
קולטור־לעבן פֿון דער נאַציע. ווײַל מיר מוזן געדענקען, אַז ניט בלויז ייִדיש אַנטהאַלט
פֿאָלקסטימלעכקייט — אויך אין דער העברעיִשער פֿאָלקס־דערצײַלונג איז דאָ דער דאָזיקער
עלעמענט. ניט מער — דער פֿאָלקסטימלעכער עלעמענט פֿון דער העברעיִשער דערצײַלונג איז
די לעצטע דורות ניט געקומען צום אויסדרוק אין דער אַנטוויקלונג פֿון דער שפּראַך. בא־
זונדער האָט עס אויסגעמיטן די תּקופֿה פֿון דער השׂכּלה. מיר האָפֿן, אַז אין דעם שטח
איז סדן ביכולת פֿיל אויפֿצוטאָן.

איך באַגריס דב סדן, די אוניווערסיטעט און די פֿרײַנד פֿון אַמעריקע. דערבײַ מוז
איך באַמערקן, אַז מיר מוזן זיך באַצײַטנס פֿאַרטראַכטן װעגן די באַדערפֿענישן פֿון דער
נײַער קאַטעדרע. צום שטודירן ייִדיש מוז געשאַפֿן װערן אַ ספּעציעלע ביבליאָטעק און אויך
פֿיל אַנדערע זאַכן. איך האָף, אַז אַרום דער ייִדיש־קאַטעדרע װעט קאָנצענטרירט װערן די
גאַנצע שאַפֿינג אויף ייִדיש אין אַלע אירע פֿאָרמען און אַנטפּלעקונגען.

איך באַגריס אויך דוד פינסקין. גלײַכצײַטיק וויל איך דאָ דערמאָנען אַן אַלטן פֿאַקט.
לעצטנס האָב איך זיך אָנגעשטויסן אויף פינסקיס אַ בריװ, אין אַ נומער װאָסכאַד
װאָס איז דערשינען מיט אַ יאָר 60 צוריק. אין דעם בריװ דערצײַלט פינסקי, אַז אין וויטעבסק
עקסיסטירט אַ גײַסטיקע השׂכּלה־באַװעגונג און אַ „גיין צום פֿאָלק" — און דאָס אַלץ איז צו
פֿאַרדאַנקען דעם חיבת ציון־געדאַנק.

דער דאָזיקער בריװ פינסקיס האָט מיך זייער דערפֿרייט. אַמאָל, װען איך בין
געװעזן אין אַ רוסישער תּפֿיסה, האָב איך זיך פֿאַראינטערעסירט מיט דער פֿאַרגאַנגענהייט
פֿון די ייִדישע רעװאָלוציאָנערן, װאָס זענען מיט מיר צוזאַמען געזעסן. האָב איך אויסגע־
פֿונען, אַז אַלע, אַחוץ די פּ.פּ.ס., זענען פֿריִער געװען ציוניסטן. איין מאָל האָב איך זיך
געפֿרעגט, װאָס האָט אייגנטלעך פינסקין פֿאַרבונדן מיט כּועלי־ציון ? — איצט ווייס איך
שוין : ער איז צוריקגעגאַנגען אַהין פֿון װאַנען ער איז געקומען. ער האָט זיך אומגעקערט
אַהיים.

ווינטש איך דעריבער אים און אונדז אַלעמען, אַז מיר זאָלן דאָ פֿילן ווי אין אַן
אמתער היים. ס'איז קיין שום ספֿק ניט, אַז די קאַטעדרע פֿאַר ייִדיש װעט דאָס היימישקייט
געפֿיל אונדזערס פֿאַרשטאַרקן און באַפֿעסטיקן.

דוד פינסקי:

איך בין אַ ביסל טויבלעך, און ווי איר זעט, העלף איך זיך אַרויס מיט אַ הער־אַפּאַ־
ראַט. אָבער איך האָב אויסגעפונען, אַז ער איז ניט קיין סגולה צו דער הברה ספרדית, איך
כאַפּ אויף איטלעך העברעיש וואָרט, וואָס ווערט אַרויסגערעדט אין אשכנזית און אַ מאָל אויך
אַ וואָרט אין ספרדית, אָבער אַ גאַנצער זאַץ אין ספרדית קלינגט מיר שוין ווי טערקיש. און
אַזוי האָב איך אַלע מיינע פאָררעדנער ניט געהערט. איך קאָן זיך איצטער ניט אַנטשעפּען
אָדער צוטשעפּען און בכלל טשעפּען צו אַ פריערדיקער רעדע, און אויב איך וועל זאָגן עפּעס,
וואָס איז שוין דאָ געזאָגט געוואָרן, וועט עס ניט זיין פון מיין זייט קיין איבערחזרונג. איך
האָב דאָך ניט געהערט   וואָס מען האָט דאָ גערעדט. —

קודם כל וויל איך אויפמערקזאַם מאַכן, אַז איך בין דאָ היינט ניט קיין פאַרטרעטער
פון יידיש און איר ליטעראַטור. איך בין דאָ אַלס געוועזענער פרעזידענט פון דעם יידישן
נאַציאָנאַלן אַרבעטער־פאַרבאַנד אין אַמעריקע, וועלכער האָט גענומען אויף זיך צו געבן זיין
צושטייער אויף די קאַטעדרע־הוצאות. אַלס קרעזידענט פון פאַרבאַנד בין איך געוועזן אַן
אַרויסהעלפער ביי מיין טייערן חבר לוי סיגאַל, דעם גענעראַל־סעקרעטאַר פון דעם פאַר־
באַנד, וועלכער האָט גענומען אויף זיך צו שאַפן אין די קרייזן פון דעם פאַרבאַנד די נויטיקע
פאָנדן פאַר דער קאַטעדרע — און האָט זיי אויך געשאַפן.

אָבער אַלס פאַרטרעטער פון דעם יידישן וואָרט און דער יידישער ליטעראַטור בין
איך געוועזן אויף אַן אַנדער פאַרזאַמלונג לכבוד דער קאַטעדרע פאַר יידיש אין דער
העברעישער אוניווערסיטעט. זי איז פאַרגעקומען אין ניו־יאָרק מיט 24 יאָר צוריק. דער
פאַרשטאָרבענער פאַרלעגער פון דער צייטונג דער טאָג, דוד שאַפּיראָ, האָט מנדב געוועזן
הונדערט טויזנט דאָלער אויף אַ לערשטול פאַר יידיש אין אונדזער אוניווערסיטעט. ד״ר
יהודה מאַגנעס, דער פאַרשטאָרבענער פרעזידענט פון אוניווערסיטעט, האָט די נדבה
אָנגענומען, און לכבוד דעם איז געגעבן געוואָרן אַ באַנקעט אין איינעם פון די פאָרנעמסטע
האָטעלן אין ניו־יאָרק. אויפן באַנקעט האָבן ד״ר מאַגנעס אַלס פרעזידענט פון
אוניווערסיטעט, און איך אַלס פאַרשטייער פון דעם יידישן וואָרט. געוועזן אַ גרויסער
יום־טוב, נאָר וועלכן עס איז געקומען אַ ביטערע אַנטוישונג. דער קוראַטאָריום פון אוני־
ווערסיטעט האָט ניט אָנגענומען די הונדערט טויזנט דאָלער, ווייל ער האָט ניט געוואָלט
אויפעפענען די טירן פון אוניווערסיטעט פאַר יידיש.

דאָס איז געוועזן אַ באַליידיקונג ניט נאָר פאַר דער יידישער שפּראַך און פאַר אַלץ וואָס
זי באַטייט אין דעם לעבן פון אַ סך יידישע דורות, נאָר אויך פאַר דעם שאַפנדיקן יידישן
געניוס. די מאָדערנע יידישע ליטעראַטור איז דאָס ווערק פון דעם יידישן שאַפונגסגייסט,
אַ ווערק, מיט וועלכן יעדער באַוווּסטזיניקער ייד דאַרף שטאָלצירן. זי איז די יינגסטע שאַפונג
פון דעם יידישן פאָלק, און אַ זייער גערעטענער מיזיניק. די שפּראַך יידיש האָט אַרויסגע־
בראַכט פון פאָלק פוחות, וועלכע מען האָט ניט געאַנט. עס איז דער נס פון יידיש. ווען
ער איז געקומען אין באַרירונג מיט דער שפּראַך פון די יידישע מאַסן, האָט דער יידישער
שאַפונגסגייסט באַקומען ריזיקע פוחות, ווי דער מיטאָלאָגישער העלד אַנטעוס, ווען ער
איז געשטאַנען מיט ביידע פיס אויף דער ערד. גאָר אַ גרויסע צאָל פון די יידישע שאַפער,
אויב ניט די גרעסטע צאָל פון זיי, האָבן ניט געשטודירט, ניט דורכגעגאַנגען קיין גימנאַזיעס

און ניט באַזוכט קיין אוניווערסיטעטן, אויך אין אַ ישיבה ניט געלערנט. מענטשן פון
פאָלק, וואָס האָבן אַפילו זייער יידיש קוים געקענט. אַבער זיי האָבן אַריינגעזויגט אין זיך
אַזעלכע שאַפּנדיקע כּוחות פון פאָלק, אַז זיי זענען געוואָרן באַדייטנדיקע וואַרטקינסטלער,
שאַפּער פון גרויסע ליטעראַרישע ווערטן. זיי האָבן באַשאַפן אַ ליטעראַטור, וואָס פאַרנעמט
אַ בכּבודיקן פּלאַץ אין דער וועלט־ליטעראַטור.

איך בין זיכער, אַז חבר דוב סדן, וועמען מען טרויט אָן דעם לערשטול פאַר יידיש,
ווייס דאָס אַלץ, וואָס איך האָב דאָ איצטער געזאָגט. און ער וועט קאָנען אָנפילן זיינע
תּלמידים און צוהערער מיט ליבע צום יידישן וואָרט און מיט באַגייסטערונג פאַר דער
קונסט, וואָס דער יידישער שאַפּונגסגייסט האָט אַרויסגעבראַכט מיטן כּוח פון דעם יידישן
וואָרט.

חיים גרינבערג:

דער רעקטאָר פון אוניווערסיטעט האָט היינט אונטערגעשריבן די באַשטימונג
פון דב סדן פאַר דער יידיש־קאַטעדרע, און איך בין זייער צופרידן וואָס האָבן מיר זיך
דאָ פאַרזאַמלט פאַר אַ באַשיידענער שׂימחה לכבוד דער דאָזיקער געלעגנהייט.

פאַרן אָנפאַנג פונעם אָוונט האָט מיך אַ פריינד אַ פרעג געטאָן: "וואָס פאַר אַ
ברכה, מיינט איר, דאַרף מען היינט מאַכן?" ביי מיר האָט זיך אַרויסגעריסן אַן ענטפער:
"די פּאַסנדיקסטע ברכה, גלייב איך — איז זוקף כּפופים".

איך מיין דאָס גאַנץ ערנסט. כּדי אָנצונעמען אַן ענדגילטיקן באַשלוס און טאַקע
גרינדן די קאַטעדרע, האָבן זיך אייניקע פון אונדז באַדאַרפט באַפרייען פון אַ הויקער,
יעדנפאַלס פון אַ געוויסער "איינגעבויגנקייט".

איך מיין דאָ נאַטירלעך ניט דעם רעקטאָר. כאַטש יידיש איז ניט די שפּראַך פון
דער סביבה, אין וועלכער ער איז געבוירן און אויסגעוואַקסט געוואָרן (ער קומט, כידוע,
פון דייטשלאַנד), האָט ער געפונען פאַר נייטיק זיך אַליין אויסצולערנען אונדזער
פאָלקסשפּראַך. ער האָט אַלע יאָרן געהאַלטן, אַז יידיש דאַרף פאַרנעמען איר פּלאַץ אין
אוניווערסיטעט־פּראָגראַם. איך מיין דאָ אויך ניט אַזעלכע מיטגלידער פונעם סענאַט, ווי
מאַרטין בובער, שׂמחה אַסף, בנציון דינאַבורג, גרשון שלום: יעדער פון זיי האָט געגלויבט,
אַז דאָס פעלן פון יידיש אין אוניווערסיטעט איז פון אַלגעמיין־יידישן קולטור־שטאַנד־
פּונקט אַן אומזין און פון אַקאַדעמישן שטאַנדפּונקט — אַן אומרעכט. איך באַדויער זייער
וואָס פּראָפעסאָר טור־סיני האָט די מעגלעכקייט זיך צו באַטייליקן אין אונדזער
היינטיקער פייערונג. דער פאַקט וואָס אַ געלערנטער פון זיין ראַנג, וועלכער איז
פאַראַנטוואָרטלעך פאַרן לימוד פון העברעישער פילאָלאָגיע אין אוניווערסיטעט, האָט אין
משך פון אַ צאָל יאָרן געפאָדערט דאָס איינפירן פון יידיש, איז פאַר אונדז אַ באַזונדער
שטאַרקע דערמוטיקונג. זאָל דאָ אויך פאַרצייכנט ווערן פּראָפעסאָר קאַסוטאָ, וואָס כאַטש
פאַר אים פערזענלעך איז יידיש אַ פרעמד לשון (די פאַרבינדונג פון אליהו בחור מיט
ווענעדיק איז אַ צופעליקע, און אין איטאַליע האָט מען קיין מאָל קיין יידיש ניט גערעדט),
געפינט ער זיך דאָ היינט מיט אונדז, ווייל ער שאַצט אָפּ דעם באַטייט פון יידיש פאַר
יידישן וויסן, פאַר יידישער פאַרשונג, פאַר יידישער אינטימיטעט.

עס זענען אָבער יאָרן־לאַנג געווען צווישן אונדז און אַרום אונדז אַזעלכע, וואָס זיי

אין „ניט אָנגעשטאַנען", אַז ייִדיש זאָל קריגן אַ פּלאַץ אין אַקאַדעמישן לעבן פֿון דעם
ייִדישן היימלאַנד. זייער קעגנערשאַפֿט צו ייִדיש איז קיין מאָל ניט געוואָען קיין ראַציאָנעלע.
אַלע אַרגומענטן וואָס זיי האָבן אַרויסגעבראַכט קעגן ייִדיש־קאַטעדרע זענען געוועזן ניט
מער ווי ראַציאָנאַליזאַציעס (אויף פּראָסט ייִדיש־לשון) : תירוצים פֿאַר די בעגטשליכט) פֿון
אַ פֿסעוודאָ־העברעיִסטישן סנאָביזם. און וואָס איז סנאָביזם, יעדער סנאָביזם? אַ טאָנדעט־
מאַנטעלע צוצודעקן אַ שיפֿלות־געפֿיל, אַ טריװיאַקער מאַנגל פֿון דרך־ארץ צו זיך אַליין.

אין מיינע ייִנגלשע יאָרן פֿלעגט מען, געדענק איך, אין רוסלאַנד דערציילן פֿון אַ
דאָרפֿס־בחור, וואָס מ'האָט אים גענומען אין דער אַרמיי. מ'האָט אים אויסגעלערנט
לייענען און שרייבן, אויך אַ ביסל רעכענען, און נאָך אַ יאָר צייט האָט מען אים למזל
ולברכה דערהויבן צום ראַנג פֿון אַ פֿעלדפֿעבל. שרייבט ער דענסטמאָל אַ מליצהדיקן
בריװו צו זיין מאַמען אין דאָרף און חתמעט זיך: „וואָס ביוושי סן אַ נינע פֿעלדפֿעבל"
(דיין געוועזענער זון און איצט אַ פֿעלדפֿעבל). זאָל מיך דער אייבערשטער ניט שטראָפֿן
פֿאַרן משל, אָבער אַן אַחד משמים פֿון אַזאַ, כ'בעט איבער אייער כּבֿוד, פֿעלדפֿעבל־
פֿסיכאָלאָגיע האָט געשטעקט אין אַ סך פֿון די אַרגומענטן וואָס מיר האָבן אַ לענגערע
צייט געהערט קעגן דעם איינפֿירן פֿון ייִדיש אין אונדזער אוניװוערסיטעט. די קעגנער
זענען געוועַן „כּפֿוכים", (איינגעבויגענע, איינגעהויקערטע), און די איינגעהויקערטקייט
האָט געזוכט זיך באַפּוצן מיט פֿעדערן פֿון פּוסטער גאװוה. ניט איין מאָל האָב איך
געהאַט דעם מעלאַנכאָלישן איינדרוק, אַז אייניקע אַרגומענטן האָבן שטאַרק געשמעקט
מיט דעם וואָס טעאָדאָר לעסינג האָט אַמאָל אָנגערופֿן: „ייִדישער זעלבסטהאַס". ווען ניט
יענע כּפֿוכים, וואָלטן מיר געהאַט אין דער אוניװוערסיטעט אַ קאַטעדרע פֿאַר ייִדיש
נאָך צוריק מיט עטלעכע און צוואַנציק יאָר, און עס איז בפֿירוש אַ פֿאַרגעניגן היינט צו
זען, אַז זיי האָבן זיך אין משך פֿון דער צייט אָדער באַפֿרייט פֿון זייער הויקער אָדער, לכל
הפֿחות, אויפֿגעהערט מיטן הויקער זיך צו חנדלען.

אַ ייִדישער יום־טובֿ קאָן אָבער ניט באַשטײן פֿון לויטער שׂימחה. איך ווייס
ניט פֿאַר וואָס (און אפֿשר ווייס איך יאָ), אָבער אַ גאַנצן אָװונט פֿאַרפֿאַלגט מיך אַן אַנאַנים
ייִדיש ליד, וואָס איך האָב צוריק מיט אַ סך יאָרן געהערט זינגען אין אוקראַיִנע און וואָס
איך בין זיכער, אַז קיינער דערוועגט זיך ניט דאָרט היינט עס אַרויפֿצוברענגען אויפֿן
מויל. איך רייד דאָ העברעיִש, אָבער די ציטאַטע פֿונעם פֿאָלקסליד וועל איך נאָטירלעך
ברענגען אין ייִדישן אָריגינאַל:

אין מיטן וועג שטייט אַ בוים,
איז ער איינגעבויגן —
פֿאָרט אַ ייִד קיין ארץ־ישׂראל
מיט פֿאַרוויינטע אויגן.

ניט דאָ איז דער פּלאַץ זיך אַריינצולאָזן אין פּסיכאָלאָגישע חקירות און זוכן צו
דערקלערן, פֿאַר וואָס אַ ייִד זאָל גיסן טרערן גראַד אין דעם מאָמענט, וועָן ער האַלט אין
פֿאַרווירקלעכן זיין הייליקסטן טרוים און האָפֿענונג. איך האָב ציטירט דאָס פֿאָלקסליד ווייל
איך האָב דאָס געפֿיל, אַז אויך ייִדיש קומט היינט קיין ארץ־ישׂראל מיט פֿאַרוויינטע אויגן.

ייִדיש מבכה על בניה. ייִדיש באַוויינט די מיליאָנען פֿון אירע פֿאַרטיליקטע
זין און טעכטער, דעם אומקום פֿון אירע יורשים און טרעגער. ערשט ניט לאַנג איז זי

געוועהן אַ צניעותדיקע הערשערין איבער אַ גאַנצער „אימפעריע". אַן מלוכות און אַן כּוח פון מלכות האַט זי „געקיניגט" איבער מיליאָנען מענער, פרויען, קינדער — פון דער וױיסל און דער ווילֹיע ביז צום דניעפער און דניעסטער, פון פרוט און דאַני און צו די ברעגעס פון האָדסאָן און דעלאַווער. איר גייסטיקע ממשלה איז לעצטנס אײַנגעשרומפֿן געװאָרן און איר מערע קינדער זענען פֿאַרמינערט געװאָרן. אױך אַ סך, אַ סך פֿן איר מערע זין און טעכטער, װאָס די האַנט פֿון משחית האָט זיי ניט געקאָנט דערגרײכן, זענען פֿון איר אָפּגעפֿרעמדט געװאָרן. קולטור־און שפּראַך־צוגלופֿטן, געאָגראַפֿיע און סאָציעלע מרחקים האָבן אָפּגעשוואַכט און בלאַס געמאַכט די פֿאַרבינדונג מיט איר. ניט אין אַלע פֿאַלן האָבן מיר דאָ צו טאָן מיט זעלבסטפֿאַרלייקענונג, מיט אַ װילן אָפּגעפֿרעמדט צו װערן; אין די נייע באַדינגונגען פֿון אונדזער עפּאָכע און אין דעם קלימאַט פֿון געװיסע געאָ־גראַפֿישע שטחים, װוּהין דער גורל האָט געבראַכט גרויסע צאָלן ייִדן, האָט דער שָר־השיכחה געקראָגן אַ שטאַרקע שליטה.

װער האָט די דרייסטקייט מיט אַ פֿולן מויל פֿאָרויסצוזאָגן די צוקונפֿט פֿון ייִדיש? װי אָפֿט דוכט זיך, אַז מ'זעט שוין אױף איר דעם טרויער פֿון שקיעה־שטראַלן. אָבער זונען־אונטערגאַנג איז אַ טייל פֿון קאָסמישן לעבן, האַרבסט האָט זײַן אייגענעם חן און פּראַכט, און בלעטערפֿאַל האָט זײַן אייגנאַרטיקן, אומפֿאַרגלײכלעכן צויבער.

ייִדיש קומט היינט קיין אַרץ־ישראל „מיט פֿאַרוויינטע אויגן". ייִדיש וועט דאָ זײַן גלײכצײַטיק אי אין דער פֿרעמד, אי אין דער היים. אַרץ־ישראל פֿאַרמאָגט ניט יענעם לעבנס־עלעקסיר װאָס װאָלט איר געקאָנט געבן אַ נייע יוגנט. ייִדיש ווייס, אַז זי קאָן ניט באַהוילן מיט איר גייסט דעם קינדער־גאָרטן; איר אַנערקענטע רעזידענץ וועט זײַן אין דער אוניװערסיטעט און אין ענלעכע לערן־אַנשטאַלטן. זי קומט אָבער אויך אַהיים. עס איז ניטאָ אַזאַ ייִדישער קולטורווערט, אַזאַ אַנפֿלעקונג פֿון ייִדישן גענוס, אַזאַ טייל פֿון ייִדישער פֿאָלקס־ביאָגראַפֿיע, פֿאַר וועלכן עס זאָל זיך אין דעם ייִדישן לאַנד ניט געפֿינען דער געהעריקער פּלאַץ און די געהעריקע אָפּשאַצונג.

דאָס איז ניט די ערשטע קאַטעדרע פֿאַר ייִדיש אין אַן אוניװערסיטעט. איך ווייס, אַז אַ ייִדישער געלערנטער אונטעררייכט ייִדיש אין אַן ענגלישער אוניװערסיטעט. דאָרט איז ייִדיש אין גאַנצן אין דער פֿרעמד, בלויז אַן אַקאַדעמישער קעגנשטאַנד, פֿרעמד־אַרטיק, עקזאָטיש, װי קינעזיש אָדער יאַפּאַניש. צוריק מיט יאָרן האָט אַ ייִדישער געלערנטער געזוכט אײַנצופֿלאַנצן דעם לימוד פֿון ייִדיש אין דער האַרװאַרד צוזאַמען... מיט רוסיש און „אַנדערע סלאַווישע" שפּראַכן, אין וועלכע ער איז געוועהן אַ ספּעציאַליסט. אַן ערשטקלאַסיקער געלערנטער אונטעררייכט איצט ייִדיש אין ניו־יאָרקער סטאַט־קאָלעדזש, אָבער אויב כ'מאַך ניט קיין טעות, איז דאָרט ייִדיש (בכל אופֿן אַדמיניסטראַטיוו) נאָך אַלץ אַ טייל אַ פֿון ...גערמאַניסטיק. אונדזער אוניװערסיטעט איז די ערשטע, װוּ ייִדיש וועט געלערנט און געפֿאָרשט וערן אַן אַ וױ אַן אייגענער אינטימער עלעמענט פֿון ייִדישער ציװי־ליזאַציע, וי אַ „היימישער" קעגנשטאַנד. און איך גלייב ניט, אַז העברעיש קוקט מיט אַ שלעכט אויג אויף דעם פּלאַץ, װאָס וערט איצט אָפּגעגעבן ייִדיש אין אונדזער אוני־ווערסיטעט. אַ נאָרמאַלע מוטער פֿאַרוװעט ניט קיין אײַפֿערזוכט מיט איר טאָכטער. ייִדיש איז צו פֿיל „אינװעסטירטֹ", אַנגעלאָדן, דורכגענומען מיט העברעיִש, און העברעיִש קאָן ניט פֿאַרגעסן, אַז דער נאָמען װאָס איז פֿאַרצייכנט אין דער מעטריקע פֿון אונדזער

פֿאָלקס־לשון איז עבֿרי־טײַטש: אָן „עבֿרי" וואָלט ייִדיש געבליבן בלויז „טײַטש"
(איינער פֿון אַ סך דײַטשע דיאַלעקטן) און וואָלט שוין לאַנג, לאַנג צוריק אויפֿגעהערט
צו עקסיסטירן.

איך האָב דאָ הײַנט אָוונט געהערט ריידן וועגן פֿאַדערונגען צו דער ייִדיש־
קאַטעדרע, אַז זי זאָל, למען השם, זײַן שטרענג־וויסנשאַפֿטלעך. קום איך אָבער איצט
פֿון אַ לאַנד, וווּ דאָס וואָרט „וויסנשאַפֿט" ווערט גענוצט אין אַ באַשרענקטערן זינען,
ווי איר נוצט עס דאָ און ווי מ'נוצט עס אויך אין דער קאָנטינענטאַלער אייראָפּע. אין
דער אַנגלאָ־סאַקסישער וועלט זענען געשיכטע, ליטעראַטור, פֿילאָלאָגיע ניט קיין וויסן־
שאַפֿט נאָר גיכער „קונסט" (אַרט). דער נאָמען „ייִדישער וויסנשאַפֿטלעכער אינסטיטוט",
וואָס האָט ניט אַרויסגערופֿן קיין שום קשיות אין ווילנע, קלינגט דערפֿאַר אַ ביסל אויס־
טערליש אין ניו־יאָרק. אָבער ניט די טערמינאָלאָגיע אינטערעסירט מיך הײַנט. איך זאָג
דאָ ניט קיין דעות. איך געדענק, אַז מײַן דעה ווי אַ גאָוורנאָר פֿון דער אוניווערסיטעט
איז ווײַט ניט אומבאַשרענקט. איך מעג אָבער אויסדריקן בײַ דער געלעגנהייט מײַנע
אַ פּערזענלעכע מיינונג. איך געהער צו די וואָס זענען ניט שטאַרק פֿאַראינטערעסירט
אין שטרענגער „וויסנשאַפֿטלעכקייט" פֿון דער ייִדיש־קאַטעדרע, אין אַ נעם ספּעציפֿיש־פֿאַך־
מעניש זינען פֿון וואָרט. דער הויפּטצוועק פֿון דער קאַטעדרע, ווי איך פֿאַרשטיי עס,
איז ניט אַזוי פֿיל לינגוויסטישע לומדות (כאָטש אויך דאָס דאַרף מען ערנסט האָבן אין
זינען), ווי די ברייטערע ציוויליזאַטאָרישע זײַט פֿון ייִדיש: ייִדישע ליטעראַטור, ייִדישער
פֿאָלקלאָר, ייִדישער לעבנס־שטייגער וואָס די ייִדישע שפּראַך איז דורות־לאַנג געווען
זײַן אָרגאַן און באַגלייטער. דער בלויז־פֿילאָלאָג איז מסוגל זיך אַזוי צו קאָנצענטרירן אויף
לינגוויסטישע דעטאַלן און פֿאַרשונג־דעליקאַטעסן, אַז דער עיקר זאָל בײַ אים נאָכגע־
לאָזט ווערן. מ'קאָן זיך אַזוי „פֿאַרגאַפֿן" אויף די אײַנצלנע בײַמער, אַז מ'זאָל דעם וואַלד
ניט דערזען און נאַטירלעך אויך אַנדערע אים ניט ווײַזן. זאָלן אויף מיר די בלויז־אַקאַדע־
מיקער ניט פֿאַראיבל האָבן פֿאַר מײַן אויסדרוק: פֿאַר מיר איז די ייִדיש־קאַטעדרע, קודם
כּל, אַ קאַטעדרע פֿאַר… א ה בֿ ת י ש ר א ל — פֿאַר אײַנפֿלאַנצן פֿאַרשטענדעניש, סימפּאַטע־
טישע פֿאַרשטענדעניש, אָפּשאַצונג, כּבֿוד און ליבע פֿאַר דעם היסטאָרישן טרעגער און גע־
שטאַלטיקער פֿון ייִדיש, פֿאַרן „גלות־ייִדן"; פֿאַר די לעבנס־ווערטן און לעבנס־אינהאַלטן פֿון
דורות ייִדן אין מיזרח־אייראָפּע, וואָס ייִדיש איז געווען אַ גרויסער (און אויך אַ שעפֿערי־
שער) טייל פֿון זייער אינטימען לעבן. דער לערער פֿון ייִדיש דאַרף בײַ אונדז דערפֿאַר
זײַן אויך אַן אָפּשאַצער, ניט בלויז אַ בקי און אַ חריף; אויך אַ פֿאַרערער, ניט בלויז אַ
פֿאַכמאַן; אויך אַ וואַרעמער ליבהאָבער, ניט בלויז אַ ספּעציאַליסט אויף שפּראַך־אַנאַטאָמיע.

אונדזער אַקאַדעמישע יוגנט אין ארץ־ישראל דאַרף שטודירן ייִדיש ניט כּדי צו
קענען „נאָך אַ שפּראַך" און ניט בלויז פֿאַר היסטאָרישער פֿאָכפֿאָרשונג, וועלכע איז,
בנוגע געוויסע עפּאָכעס, כּמעט אוממעגלעך, אויב מ'קאָן ניט לייענען טעקסטן אויף
ייִדיש, נאָר אויך כּדי זיך אַליין צו פֿאַרשטיין בעסער, טיפֿער, עכטער און אינטימער.

אָנגענומען, אַז מיר זענען דאָ אַלע „שוללי הגלות"; שולל זײַן דעם גלות הייסט
אָבער ניט אָפּאָנאָרירן אַ גרויסן און פּראָוטיקן טייל פֿון אונדזער פֿאַרגאַנגענהייט, ניט
ווייסן, אָדער (נאָך ערגער) זיך ניט וועלן וויסנדיק מאַכן פֿון גרויסע ווערטן, וואָס ייִדן האָבן
געשאַפֿן אין זייער צעשפּרייטונג טראָץ די קייטן פֿון גלות, אויך צו להכעיס אַלע משחיתים־

קרעפטן וואָס לויערן אויף אונדז אין גלות. י ש ר א ל ס_אַ ב ר א מוז זיך אין זיך אײַנזאַפן די
גײַסטיקע לעבנסוװערטן פון י ש ר א ל – ס ב א, און ייִדיש איז אײַנער פון די דימענטן אין
ישראל סבאס מאַרטירערישער קרוין...

אַ יונגער־מאַן אין מיליטערישער אוניפאָרעם האָט מיר דאָ, די טעג, ביי אַ געלעגנהייט,
אַ זאָג געטאָן וועגן ייִדן: „די ביטול־באַצײַונג צו דער ייִדישער שפראַך נעמט זיך אפשר
ביי אײַניקע דערפון, וואָס ייִדיש איז קיין מאָל ניט געווען די קאָמאַנדע־שפראַך פון אַן
אַרמיי״. נײַן, דאָס איז ייִדיש קיין מאָל ניט געווען. איר ייִחוס איז אַן אַנדערער. זי איז
דורות־לאַנג געווען די שפראַך פון שטילן, אומבאַוואָפנטן אָבער העראָיִשן ווידערשטאַנד
קעגן כוואַליעס, וואָס האָבן געזוכט ייִדן און ייִד־זיין אומצוברענגען; אויך די תחינה־
שפראַך פון אומצייַליקע פרויען, וואָס האָבן מיט ניט־אַפעקטירטער פרומקייט זיך געוואָנדט
יעדן מוצאי־שבת צום גאָט פון אברהם, פון יצחק און פון יעקב. אָבער אויך דער ייִחוס פון
העברעיִש ליגט מער אין „מודה אני״ ווי אין די קאָמאַנדע־ווערטער פון יהושע בן־נון.

„ניט צופעליק״ — האָט דער יונגער־מאַן אין מיליטערישער אוניפאָרעם געענטפערט —
„האָט איר זיך נאָר וואָס באַנוצט מיטן פרויען אימאַזש: אין ייִדיש איז פאַראַן (און געזאָגט
האָט ער עס מיר טאַקע אויף ייִדיש) עפעס ווייבעריש״. איך וואָלט זיך אויף זיין פלאַץ
באַנוצט מיט אַן אַנדער וואָרט: ניט ווייבעריש — נאָר ווייבלעך. דאָס ווייבערישע
איז שמאַלקעפלדיקייט און קליינשטעטלדיקייט, באַגרענעצטקייט און איז אין תוך פאַרגייַיק;
דאָס ווייבלעכע איז דאָס דערהויבענע, דאָס הייליקע, דאָס אייביקע. אָן דעם ווייבלעכן
האָט אַ פאָלק ניט קיין זאַפט, קיין חיות, קיין מאָרגן. אין ליבע צו ייִדיש — אויך אין עצבות־
דיקער, אויסזיכטלאָזער ליבע — ליגט עפעס פון מוטער־נאָסטאַלגיע. שעמען זאָל זיך דער
וואָס שעמט זיך דערמיט...

אַנטשולדיקט מיר, אויב איך האָב זיך געלאָזן היינט „ווילגיין״ מיט מיינע סוביעק־
טיוו־געפאַרבטע, אפשר צו אימפרעסיאָניסטישע באַמערקונגען. אָט דאָס איז מיין געמיט־
צושטאַנד היינט אָוונט, און אין דער דאָזיקער שטימונג ברענג איך דאָ מיין האַרציקע
באַגריסונג ניט נאָר דער נייער קאַטעדרע, נאָר אויך דעם פון דער קאַטעדרע. דב סדן
איז ניט נאָר אַ ייִדיש־קענער; ער איז אויך אַ ייִדיש־ליבהאַבער, אַ ייִדן־ליבהאַבער, אַן
אוהב ישראל. עס איז אַ גוטער־סימן וואָס די קאַטעדרע פאַר ייִדיש ווערט געגעבן אַן
אײַנגעוואָרצלטן תושב פון ארץ־ישראל, אַ בירגער פון מדינת־ישראל, אַ העברעיִשן
פּראָדוקטיקן שריפטשטעלער. איך האָב אמונה, אַז ער וועט זיין קעגנשטאַנד מאַכן באַליבט
ביי אונדזער אַקאַדעמישער יוגנט. זי דאַרף אַזאַ ליבע האָבן — פאַר דער געשטאַלטיקונג
פונעם קולטור־לעבן אין ייִדישן לאַנד, אויך פאַר זיך אַליין.

לוי סיגאַל — גענעראַל־סעקרעטאַר פון ייִדיש־נאַציאָנאַלן אַרבעטער־פאַרבאַנד:

אַ טאָפל געפיל האָב איך דאָ היינט — אַ געפיל פון שׂמחה און אַ געפיל פון טרויער.
שׂמחה — ווייל ס'איז געשאַפן געוואָרן אַ גרויסע זאַך אין לעבן פון ייִדישן פאָלק; און
טרויער, ווייל איך קאָן ניט געפינען קיין ענטפער אויף דער פראַגע: פאַר וואָס איז דאָס
ניט געשען פריִער. און וועגן דעם וויל איך איצט זאָגן אַ פּאָר ווערטער.

איך האַלט, אַז ס'איז אוממעגלעך ניט אײַנצוזען די גרויסע ווערטן פון דער ייִדישער

אונטן — שטאַרקע טענות מיט אַ שוואַכן שטאַנדפּונקט...

A Weak Position for a Strong Complaint. Hebrew writers in Palestine (under the British Mandate) suppress Yiddish while protesting the suppression of Hebrew in the Soviet Union. (*Der groyser kundes*, August 30, 1926)

שפּראַך און ליטעראַטור און ניט אָנערקענען דעם פּלאַץ וואָס יידיש האָט זיך דערוואָרבן אין לעבן פון יידישן פאָלק. ווי אַזוי זשע, פרעגט זיך, איז דאָס געשען, וואָס עס האָבן זיך געפונען יידן, וועלכע האָבן זיך קעגנגעשטעלט דער פאָדערונג איינצופירן דעם דאָזיקן לימוד אין אונדזער אוניווערסיטעט? די לענדער, ווו יידן האָבן געלעבט און גערעדט יידיש, זענען צום טייל אָפּגעמעקט געוואָרן פון דער יידישער גלות־מאַפּע. ס'איז פאַרבליבן בלויז אַ טייל פון דער יידישער וועלט מיטן הויפּטצענטער — אַמעריקע.

גרויסע ספנות לויערן דאָרט ניט בלויז אויף יידיש, נאָר אויפן יידישן לעבן־שטייגער בכלל. און ביי אַזאַ לאַגע איז די פליכט פון יעדן ייד, וואָס ווייל אַז זיין פאָלק זאָל עקסיסטירן ווייטער, צו זוכן מיטלען ווי אַזוי די דאָזיקע ספנה צו באַזייטיקן. איך קאָן ניט זאָגן, אַז אין מיין טאָג־טעגלעכן לעבן בין איך אַ רעליגיעזער ייד. איך בין אָבער גרייט צו טאָן אַלץ וואָס איז מעגלעך, כדי צו שטאַרקן די השפעה פון דער יידישער רעליגיע אין גלות, ווייל איך האַלט, אַז אין די באַדינגונגען פון אַ כסדרדיקער אַסימילאַציע־ספנה איז זי, די רעליגיע, אַ וויכ־ טיקער קעגן־פאַקטאָר. איך שטרייך אונטער, אַז איך אָנערקען דאָס, הגם פערזענלעך בין איך ניט רעליגיעז. איך האָב אויך קיין מאָל ניט געקאָנט פאַרשטיין, ווי אַזוי קאַנען נאַציא־ נאַלע יידן (וועגן אַסימילאַטאָרן רייד איך ניט) ניט זען די גרויסע נאַציאנאַלע השפעה פון דער יידישער שפּראַך און ליטעראַטור און וויפל די דאָזיקע השפעה האָט אויפגעטאָן צו פאַרשטאַרקן דעם ווילן צו זיין אַ ייד.

טײערע פרײנד, איך האָב פריִער געפרעגט, פאַר וואָס איז ניט אַנטשטאַנען די
קאַטעדרע פאַר ײדיש מיט 25 יאָר צוריק. איך האָב דאָס געפרעגט קודם־כל דערפאַר, ווײל
איך קען גוט דאָס ײדישע לעבן אין אַמעריקע פאַר די לעצטע פערציק יאָר און איך ווײס
וואָס פאַר אַ געוואַלדיקע השפעה עס וואָלט געהאַט אויף די אַמעריקאַנער ײדן אַ ײדישע
קאַטעדרע, ווען זי וואָלט דעמאָלט געשאַפֿן. אַזאַ קאַטעדרע אין ירושלים וואָלט דאָרט געהויבן
דעם מעמד פון ײדיש און במילא אויך די צוגעבונדנקײט פון ײדן צו ײדישקײט. לאָמיר
מודה זיין, אַז דורכן אָפּלייגן דאָס איז פאַר אונדז פאַרלאָרן געגאַנגען אַ וויכטיקער אינסטרו־
מענט אויף צו שטאַרקן די צוגעבונדנקײט פון ײדן צום ײדנטום.

אַ לאַנגע צײט האָט געהערשט די פֿאַלשע אײנשטעלונג, אַז ײדיש איז אַ קאָנקורענץ
פאַר העברעיש. אַ טעות האָבן געהאַט די יעניקע, וואָס האָבן געמיינט, אַז אויב זײ וועלן ניט
אונטערשטיצן די ײדישע שפּראַך אין גלות, וועט עס מיטהעלפן צו דער פאַרשטאַרקונג פון
העברעיש. דאָס עצם אויועקשטעלן ײדיש קעגן העברעיש איז געווען אַ טעות. די העברעיִשע
אוניווערסיטעטס האָט געדאַרפט מיטהעלפן אויפצוהײבן דעם אָנזען פון ײדיש, אונטער־
צוהאַלטן דאָס געפיל בײ די ײדן אין גלות, אַז די דאָזיקע שפּראַך איז אַן אָרגאַנישער
טייל פון דער גרויסער ײדישער קולטור.

איך בין צופרידן, וואָס מיר האָבן זוכה געווען דערצו און וואָס דער ײדיש־נאַציאָנאַ־
לער אַרבעטער־פֿאַרבאַנד האָט אַ געוויסן פאַרדינסט אין דער דאָזיקער דערגרייכונג.

פאַר אונדז איז דאָס דאָזיקע ווערק הייליק, און איך בין זיכער, אַז אויך איר זענט
אַזוי איינגעשטעלט. איך דערקלער דאָס פײערלעך אין נאָמען פון אַלע מײנע חברים אין
פֿאַרבאַנד און אויך אין נאָמען פון אַ טייל ײדיש־אַמעריקאַנער געזעלשאַפט וואָס איז ניט
אָרגאַניזירט אין פֿאַרבאַנד.

מיר ווילן האָפֿן, אַז דאָס דאָזיקע ווערק וועט באַלײכטן דעם ניט־באַלויכטענעם (מען
קאָן אַפֿילו זאָגן — דעם פינצטערן) וועג פֿונעם ײד וואָס לעבט אין אַ ניט־ײדישער סביבה,
אין אַ סביבה וואָס איז ניט אַלע מאָל מסוגל צו שאַפֿן אַן אַטמאָספער פון ײדישן זעלבסט־
באַוווסטזײן און ײדישן גלויבן. איר קענט דעם שווערן וועג פון דאָזיקן ײד. געדענקט עס
און שטעלט אויף אַ קאַטעדרע וואָס זאָל צוגעבן כבוד דער אוניווערסיטעטס און די יעניקע,
וואָס האָבן די זכיה און דעם כבוד אין איר זיך צו באַטייליקן.

דב סדן — דאָצענט פאַר דער ײדיש־קאַטעדרע:

מורי ורבותי, דערלויבט מיר אָנצוהויבן מיט אַ וואָרט פון דאַנק פאַר דער עצם
מעגלעכקײט, וואָס ווערט מיר איצט צוגעשאַנצט, די אָנדערע העלפֿט פון מײן לעבן
זיך אָפּצוגעבן לערנען אין זינען פֿון והגית בה. ניט אַז איך האָב אַ שפֿיק חרטה אויף
דער אָפּגעלאָפֿענער העלפֿט. ס׳פֿאַלט מיר ניט אײַן צו באַלאַסטיקן מיט מײן
ביאָגראַפֿיע, אָבער לאָזט מיך אײַך זאָגן, אַז ניט אַזוי ווי איר ערשטער מײן איז געווען איר ווי־
טערדיקער גאַנג. לויט אָפּשטאַם און דערצײ̇ונג, איז מיר באַשטימט געווען צו פאַרוואָרק־
לעכן אַן אַלטן אידעאַל, און וואָס דער ביי צײַטן און זייער געשמאַק האָט אים אַ קאַם
אויפֿגעפֿרישט און צוגעטאַקט אין דער געשטאַלט פון אַן אויפֿגעקלערטן רב וואָס איז, ווי
באַוווסט, געווען דער נאָענטסטער שכן פון חכמת־ישראל. איך האָב ניט קיין חרטה, וואָס

מיין וועג איז אַנדערש געגאַנגען. פּונקט ווי ס׳טוט מיר ניט באַנג, וואָס מיין דעמאָנסט־
רירטער קאַמף פֿאַר ציוניזם און העברעיש אין דער פּוילישער גימנאַזיע האָט מיך פֿון
איר משלח געווען, אַזוי טוט מיר ניט באַנג, וואָס כ׳בין פֿאַרכאַפּט געוואָרן פֿון דער
חלוצישער באַוועגונג, האָב זוכה געווען צו זיין פֿון אירע טוערס און אויפֿטוערס
און האָב מיך אין די יונגע יאָרן געלאָזט טראָגן אין אונדזער לאַנד אַריין אויף דער
שטורמישער כוואַליע פֿון יענער באַוועגונג, וועלכער כ׳האָב געדינט, צו ערשט אין קיבוץ
און דערנאָך, במשך פֿון יאָרן, אין דער טאַגצייטונג פֿון הסתדרות־העובדים, ווו די
אַרבעט האָט זיך מיר אויסגעוויזן ניט ווי ווי אַ באַרוף נאָר ווי אַ באַרופֿונג. אָבער אויך
שפּעטער, ווען מיין ליטעראַרישע און פֿאַרשערישע אַרבעט האָט זיך מער אויסגע־
שפּרייזט, האָט אין מיר תּמיד געטליעט יענע ערשטע ליבע צו לערנען אין זינען פֿון
והגית בה, און כ׳פֿלעג נאָכקלערן, ווען .וועט קומען איר צייט.

די יידיש־קאַטעדרע, וואָס כ׳האָב דעם כּבוד צו איר געראָפֿן צו ווערן, דאַרף
באַטראַכט ווערן פֿון דריי (און אויב איר ווילט: פֿון פֿיר) אַספּעקטן. ערשטנס, דער
אַספּעקט פֿון דער אוניווערסיטעטס גופֿא. זי איז, בדרך הטבֿע, מחייבֿ אין איר ראַם
אַריינצונעמען די פֿולע טאָטאַליטעט פֿון דער פֿאָלקסקולטור אין אַלע אירע אַנטפֿלע־
קונגען, אין אַלע אַלע צייטן און אַלע ערטער. און ווער ס׳כאַפּט אַ טיפֿערן קוק אין דער
אַנטוויקלונג פֿון אונדזער אוניווערסיטעטס, וועט ניט קאַנען פֿאַרלייקענען, אַז דער
דאָזיקער כּלל ווערט בהדרגהדיק דורכגעפֿירט, וסוף הכּבֿוד לבֿא. נאָך מער, אַ היפּש
ביסל גרויסע פֿראָווינצן אין אונדזער קולטור, וואָס מ׳האָט זיי געהאַלטן פֿאַר פֿאַר־
שטויסענע פּראָווינצן, און עטלעכע דורות פֿאַר אונדז האָבן זיך צו זיי באַצויגן מיט
ביטול אָדער גרינגשאַץ, שטייען שוין פֿון לאַנג אונטער דער חופּה פֿון געטרייער
פֿאַרשונג און שטודיע. און אין דעם פֿראַנט, וואָס האַלט אין איין איינשלינגען אין זיך
די דאָזיקע גרויסע היפּאַרכיעס אויף אונדזער קולטור־מאַפּע, געהערט די מסכתּא יידיש,
איר ליטעראַטור און איר שפּראַך .און איר איינגלידערונג איז אַ מחוייבֿדיקע; און אויב
די אוניווערסיטעטס האָט זיך גענעגט קוועטנקלען וואָס פֿריִער און וואָס שפּעטער, האָט
זי ניט געטאָרט איבערהיפּערן, שוין אָפּגערעדט, אַז זי האָט ניט געטאָרט פֿאַרזען.

צו וואָס איז די זאַך געגליכן? צו אַן אַסטראָנאָם, וואָס נעמט באַרעכענען אַ געשטערן פֿון
שטערן און האָט דורכגעלאָזט אַ וואַשנעם שטערן, האָט ער טאַקע אַ טל געמאַכט פֿון זיין
גאַנצער אויסרעכעניש, און זיין חשבון איז קיין חשבון ניט.

דער צווייטער אַספּעקט איז דער אויפֿבוי פֿון דעם כּלל־דיקן יידישן באַוווסטזיין.
די צייט, אין וועלכער ס׳איז אונדז אויסגעקומען צו לעבן, באַצייכענען אין דער געשיכטע
פֿון אונדזער פֿאָלק צווי שטריכן — אונדזער עקסטענסיע אויף דער וועלטמאַפּע ווערט
וואָס מער איינגעשרומפּן: די יידישע קיבוצים אין אייראָפּע זענען דערטרונקען געוואָרן
אין טייכן פֿון זייער בלוט, און דער גרויסער קאָנטינענט, וואָס איז געווען די אַרטעריע
פֿון אונדזער לעבן, איז כּמעט אָפּגעמעקט געוואָרן פֿון אונדזער לעבעדיקער געשיכטע;
די רוסישע יידן האָבן שוין לאַנג אויפֿגעהערט צו זיין אַ פֿאַקטאָר אין כּלל־גורל פֿונעם
פֿאָלק; די איבערבליבענישן אין מיזרח־אייראָפּע, אויב זיי רייסן זיך ניט אַרויס, ווערן
זיי אַרויסגעריסן פֿון אַקטיוון אַנטייל אין אויפֿטו פֿון גאַנצן פֿאָלק. און אונדזער טרייסט
איז, אַז דאָס איינשרומפֿן פֿון דער געאָגראַפֿישער עקסטענסיע אויף דער וועלטמאַפּע

ווערט אויסגעגליכן דורך דער שטאַרקונג פון דער היסטאָרישער אינטענסיע אויף דער
מאַסע פון אונדזער היימלאַנד; נאָך מער, מיר האָבן אין זיך די זיכערקייט, אז די דאָזיקע
אינטענסיע איז דער אַנטשיידנדיקער ווענד אין אונדזער געשיכטע; און זיין סימן איז
דער פּראָצעס פון דער גלות־ליקווידאַציע, וואָס איז אַ נויטווענדיקייט פאַר אַלע גלותן,
און פאַר וועלן איר קיין באַשטאַנד ניט האָבן די כלערליי פּשרות, ווי אַ שטייגער ס׳האָט
געמאַכט דער לעצטער ציוניסטישער קאָנגרעס, אין פאָרעם פון קינסטלעכן אונטערשייד
צווישן גלות און תפוצות; דען ס׳לאָזט זיך ניט אויסדרייען פון דער גזירה: וכל הכתוב
לחיים — בירושלים. און אין דער ציַיט זענען מיר מחוייב צו מאַכן דעם כלל־חשבון
פון אונדזער קולטור, וואָס מיר זענען אירע איבער־און וויַיטער־שפּינערס, און מיר טאָרן
ניט לאָזן אויסגליטשן גרויסע ווערטן פון אונדזער כלל־אינוועונטאַר. לאָזן אויסגליטשן
פון חשבון אַזַא ווערט ווי יידיש, מיט איר האָב און גוטס, הייסט נאָר וועלן פאַראָרעמען זיך
אַליין, פאַראָרעמען מיט גוואַלד און מיט כיוון. מיַינע פריַינד, וואָס האָבן פאַר מיר
גערעדט, האָבן דערמאָנט די מחלוקה מיט אַ פערטל יאָרהונדערט צוריק, די מחלוקה
איבער דעם פּלאַן פון גרינדן אַ יידיש־קאַטעדרע — אָדער, ווי בערל קאַצענעלסאָן האָט עס
קלוג אָנגערופן אין זיַין אויסגעצייכנטן מאמר: קתדרת־המריבה. איך בין דעמאָלט געווען
דער ייַנגסטער צווישן אייך אַלע, און במילא האָב איך מיט מער יוגנטלעכקייט איבער־
געלעבט יענע דיסקוסיע. בפרט געדענק איך דעם דונערדיקן הילך פון ביאַליקס אָפּרוף —
אין דער לופט פון אונדזער יישוב האָט זיך דעמאָלט געטראָגן ניט נאָר די מחלוקה וועגן
דער קאַטעדרע, נייַערט אויך וועגן יידיש, און ביַידע מחלוקות האָבן זיך צוזאַמענגעשטויסן.
מער פון אַלץ געדענק איך אַ לעקציע פון ביאַליקן, וואָס האָט באַהאַנדלט דעם ענין
העברעיש און יידיש און זייערע קעגנזייַטיקע באַצַיונגען. דער דיכטער האָט איבערגעחזרט
זיַין באַקאַנטע הלכה, אַז ווען די העברעישע שפּראַך וואָלט דערהאַלטן אין די גלותן,
ווי אַ שפּראַך פון גאַנג גייענדיקן לעבן, וואָלט זי זיך צעדרויבלט אין כלערליי שפּראַך־
ריטשקעס, יעדער גלות אין זיַין ריטשקע, און ס׳וואָלטן באַשאַפן געוואָרן אַ פּאַר העברעישע
שפּראַכן, ווי אַ שטייגער העברעיש־ראַמאַניש, העברעיש־גערמאַניש, העברעיש־סלאַוויש.
ער האָט אויך געגעבן אַ טייערן משל, פאַרגלייַכנדיק די סכנה צו עוג מלך הבשן, וואָס
זיַינע אומגעלומפּערטע גרויסע אברים זענען אָפּגעפאַלן און זיך צעשיט איבער וויַיטע
וויַיטן. אונדזער חוש־הקיום — האָט ער אויסגעפירט — האָט פאַרהיט, אז דער
ריז זאָל ניט פאַרלירן און ניט פונאַנדערשיטן זיַינע אברים: די שפּראַך, וואָס זענען
דעם פּאַלק אויף וואַנדערוועג צוגעקומען, און בעיקרשט די יידישע שפּראַך, ניט
גענוג וואָס זיי האָבן אונדז געגעבן די מעגלעכקייט פון אַן אייגענעם אויסדרוק פאַר
אַלע באַדערפעניש פון לעבן, האָבן זיי אויך אָפּגעהיט די העברעישע שפּראַך, אז זי זאָל זיך
קאָנען מתייחד זיַין מיט די באַדערפענישן, וואָס זענען בשותפותדיק אַלע שבטים פון
פּאַלק כדי, אז ווען ס׳וועט קומען איר ציַיט, זאָל זי קאָנען ווערן זייער נאַטירלעכע שפּראַך
אין זייער לאַנד.
שיַין האָט דאָ אונדזער פריַינד פינסקי אויסגעמאָלן דעם וועג פון אונדזער פּאַלק,
וואָס האָט אויפגעהויבן אַן אַוועקגעוואָרפענעם דיאַלעקט פון אַנדערע און אים דורכגע־
שפּיקעוועט מיט זיַין גייסט און זיַין אייגנס און האָט אים געמאַכט אַ גאַניץ געביַי.
אָבער זאָל מיר דערלויבט זיַין אָפּצופרעגן זיַין זאָג, אַז דער חילוק פון אַ העברעישן

און אַ ייִדישן שרייבער איז געװען, װאָס דער ערשטער האָט געמוזט קענען אַ סך תּנ"ך און
גמרא און מדרשים וכדומה, און דער לעצטער איז געװען פּטור. דען באמת האָט ער דאָך לפחות
אײן זאַך געמוזט קענען — י י ד י ש. און די קענטשאַפט האָט דאָך בּמילא פֿול געװאָרן אַ גאַנצע
װעלט, װאָס איז אױסגעהאַקט פֿון די גרונטשטײנער פֿון דעם פֿאָלקס תּורה, גלױבן,
טראַדיציע, שטײגער, בּקיצור פֿון זײַן קולטור. װער ס׳קומט אונטערשטרײַכן די װאָגיקײט
פֿון דעם גרױסן און פֿאַרבּיקן העברעיש־עלעמענט אין ייִדיש, איז נאָר אױסן אַ טײל,
װײַל דער פֿולער חשבון מוז אַרײַננעמען אױך די מעטאַמאָרפֿאָזעס, װאָס דער דײַטשישער
און סלאַװישער עלעמענט זענען אַדורכגעגאַנגען אין גײַסט און אין גוסט פֿון סאַמע יסוד
פֿון, אונדזער קולטור, פֿון דער העברעיִשער שפּראַך.

דער דריטער אַספּעקט האָט שױן געפֿונען זײַן שאַרפֿזיניקע דעפֿיניציע אין מױל
פֿון אונדזער פֿרײַנד חיים גרינבּערג: די בּריק צװישן ישׂראל סבא און ישׂראל סברא. פֿון
אַ װײַטער פּערספּעקטיװ װעט מסתּמא אַמאָל די היסטאָריע פֿון אונדזער צײַט געזען
װערן אין איר פֿולער קלאָרקײט, אָבער שױן איצט איז בּולט די גװאַלדיקע חשיבות
פֿון די לעצטע פֿיר אָדער פֿינף דורות, װאָס האָבן אונדז געשמידט צו אַן אַנטשיידנדיקן
איבערבּראָך אין גורל פֿון אונדזער פֿאָלק. פֿאַרשטײן די דאָזיקע ראַנגלעניש איז אַ גרױסע
עובֿדא, און לאָזן זיך ניט פֿאַרשטײן, אױב מ׳װײיס ניט די, סײַ דערענטעדנדיקע
סײַ דערװײַטערנדיקע, באַציונגען צװישן בּײַדע שפּראַכן. די פֿאַרשאַרבּעט פֿון אונדזער
ליטעראַטור אין בּײַדע שפּראַכן איז צומײַסט געמאַכט געװאָרן װי אָפּגעשפּאַלטן אײנס
פֿונעם אַנדערן, אַ שטײגער דער פֿאַרשט זיך אין זײַן װינקל און יענער פֿאָרשט זיך אין
זײַן װינקל, און. צו מאָל געשעט דאָס אין אַ קעגנזײַטיקער פֿאַרפֿרעמדקײַט. דער פֿועל
יוצא דערפֿון איז אַ צעהאַקט און צעהאַקט פֿאָרשן, װאָס בּרענגט זיך מיט אַ צעבּראַכט
און צעהאַקט באַװוּסטזײַן. בּײַ אַ פֿאָרשאַרבּעט, װאָס װערט געמאַכט אין אַזאַ אָפּגע־
שפּאַלטנקײַט, מוזן געניזוקט װערן װיכטיקע דערשײַנונגען, בּעיקר די דערשײַנונג פֿון
שפּראַכלעכער טראַפֿלאַכקײַט, װאָס האָבן געטריבן זײַער פֿיל שרײַבערס — דער שפּאַלט
דערלאָזט פּשוט ניט צו דערגײן אַזעלכע דערשײַנונגען װי די קעגנזײַטיקע השפעה פֿון בּײַדע
לשונות, אײדע לױטן גאַנג פֿון איר אַנטװיקלונג, בּפרט װען בּײַדע האָבן זיך צונױפֿגעקניפּט
אָדער צוזאַמענגעטראָפֿן אין דער זעלבּיקער שאַפּערישער פּערזענלעבּקײַט. בּמילא װערט
אױך געניזוקט דאָס אָפּשאַצן פֿון דעם אָפֿענעם אָדער פֿאַרבּאַהאַלטענעם געראַנגל צװישן
בּײַדע שפּראַכן, װאָס אָן אים קאָן מען ניט פֿאַרשטײן די באַזונדערע דיאַלעקטיק פֿון דער
אַנטװיקלונג פֿון דער העברעיִשער שפּראַך. ניט בּלױז אַזאַ פֿענאָמען װי דער טאָפּלשפּראַ־
כיקער מענדעלע לאָזט זיך ניט אױסשטיטלן בּײַ אַ צעשפּאַלטענער באַהאַנדלונג, נאָר אױך
אַזאַ פֿענאָמען װי בּיאַליק, אפֿילו אין העברעיִשן סעקטאָר, לאָזט זיך ניט דערגרונטעװען,
אױב מען גײט ניט נאָך די אין אים אײַנגעגראַבּענע ייִדיש־עלעמענט. ס׳זענען בּײַ
בּיאַליקן פֿאַראַן בּילדער און בּײַשפּילן, װאָס אױפֿן ערשטן קוק זענען מיר גענױגס זײַ
צו באַטראַכטן װי פֿון דער װײַטנס אױסגעליִענע אָפּשפּיגלונגען, אָבער װען מיר פֿאַרטיפֿן
זיך, אַנטפּלעקט זיך פֿאַר אונדז אַ ייִדיש־בּילד, װאָס אין אים איז פֿאַרקניװלט אַן אונטער־
דערערדיקע ירושה פֿון הונדערטער יאָרן, אַזױ װי ס׳זענען בּײַ אים פֿאַראַן בּילדער, װאָס
נעמען אַ פּשוטן ייִדיש־משל און קערן אים אום זײַן בּראשיתדיקײַט. און בּיאַליק איז אַ
סימבּאָל פֿאַר אַ דערקענטעניש, װאָס איז חל אױף זײַער פֿיל דערשײַנונגען. ,

און צו לעצט, די שטימונגען וואָס פּלאַטערן איצט אין די עקסטע טיילן פון דער יוגנט
ביי אונדז אין לאַנד. די דאָזיקע שטימונגען מאַכן אפילו דעם אַנשטעל פון יונגקייט,
אָבער ס׳איז ניט אַזוי, ווייל די טענדענץ צו פאַרקירצן אונדזער געשיכטע דורך פאַרקירצן
אונדזער קולטור האָט שוין אַ לאַנגע באַרד. פונקט ווי ס׳איז געווען אַ טענדענץ
אונטערצוהאַקן אָדער פאַרגעסן צו מאַכן די ערשטע עפּאָכעס, בפרט מצד די שטרעמונגען,
וואָס האָבן ניט געוואָלט זען אונדזער געשיכטע ווי אַ קרייז, אין וועלכן ס׳באַגעגענען זיך
סוף און אָנהייב — אַזוי איז פאַראַן אַ טענדענץ אונטערצוהאַקן אָדער פאַרגעסן צו מאַכן
לעצטע עפּאָכעס, בעיקר מצד שטרעמונגען, וואָס זעען אפילו אונדזער געשיכטע ווי
אַ קרייז, אין וועלכן ס׳באַצווּנגען זיך סוף און אָנהייב, אָבער זיי ווילן ניט זען וואָס איז דאָ דאַ
צווישן, די מיט. דער פאַרלאַנג איבערצוהיפּערן האָט זיך שוין ניט איין מאָל געלאָזט
הערן — פאַר אייערנעכטן - האָט ער געפּאָדערט איבערצוהיפּערן די גמרא;
אייערנעכטן האָט ער געפּאָדערט אַרויסצושטויסן קבלה; נעכטן האָט ער געפּאָדערט
אָפּצומעקן חסידות. והצד השווה אין די אַלע פּאָדערונגען איז אַ פאַרלייקענען פון אונדזער
געשיכטע ווי אַזוי זי איז געווען. אָבער מיר קאָנען די איבערשפּרינגערס, וואָס ס׳גלוסט
זיך זיי איינאָרדענען אַ באַקוועמערע געשיכטע, גאָרנישט העלפּן, ווייל אונדזער
געשיכטע איז געווען ווי זי איז געווען. און אויך דער פאַרלאַנג איבערצוהיפּערן ייִדיש,
איז אַזאַ מין פּאָדערונג, און דערהויפּט אַ מענטש פון וויסנשאַפט וועט אים האַלטן פאַר
אַן אַטאַק אויף אויף זיין ערשטן און עיקרדיקן חוב, דעם חוב פון אמת.

און וואָס שייך דעם לימוד גופא, מיט וועלכן מ׳האָט מיך איצט מכבד געווען, דוכט
זיך, אַז כ׳בין פּטור צו ריידן דעריבער. דען ס׳איז דאָך ניט אַ זאַך פון ריידן, נאָר פון טאָן,
און בלויז לויטן טאָן וועט זיך אַרויסשטעלן צי אייער צוטרוי צו מיר איז אַ באַרעכטיקטער.
כ׳וועל פאַרענדיקן מיט אַ ווערטל און זאָגן, אַז לעת־עתה פיר איך מיך ווי ר׳ יוסי, וואָס
אַז מ׳האָט אים גערופן צום דוכן, איז ער אַרויפגעגאַנגען. נאָר ער, דער גרויסער, האָט
געמוזט צוגעבן: כאַטש כ׳בין ניט קיין כהן; און איך, דער קליינער, קאָן צוגעבן: און
צופעליק בין איך אויך אַ כהן.

מיר באַגריסן האַרציק די ייִדיש־קאַטעדרע ביי דער ירושלימער אוניווער־
סיטעט און דעם דאָצענט דב סדן. מיר ווינטשן זיי מיט הצלחה און בשלימות
אויסצופירן די גרויסע אויפגאַבע, וואָס עס ליגט אַרויף אויף די ייִדישע
קולטורוועלט.

רעדאַקציע די גאָלדענע קייט

Address at the Dedication of the Leivick House in Israel, May 14, 1970

GOLDA MEIR

There is no doubt that today is a festive occasion. I must confess that when I participate in a celebration to honor the name of a man who is no longer with us and who was near and dear to us all, an illogical feeling penetrates me: What a shame that he can't be here to witness this.

In these great days of hard trials, we deserve his presence; and he certainly earned the right to be with us. He, far more than others, would be equal to the task of giving expression to the state in which the Jews in Israel and throughout the world find themselves. Especially in the land where Jews, who had been silenced for decades, have now begun to speak. It is true that we never believed that the Jews of silence had nothing to say. We knew of the struggle going on in their hearts. Yet there were few who had faith that a time would come when, after the great heroism of silence, these Jews would display the heroism of speech.

We have lived to see a time in which young people were born into an atmosphere where not only was one not supposed to speak, but one was also afraid to think. Now these young people have begun to speak as proud Jews.

I am reminded of what Khaim Greenberg once told me about an old Russian who, at an advanced age, began to study French. When he was asked what use it was to study such a difficult language at so old an age, he answered, 'I'm getting tired of not thinking in Russian'.

Now we hear how these young people, with full national pride, cry out the call of their Yiddishkayt. No one prepared them for this. They speak of a people, not knowing its history, its praiseworthy past. Yet they feel such a strong attachment to the people and to its land. Few artists are capable of expressing the tragedy and the greatness of this young generation.

A heroic chapter of Jewish history is played out before our eyes. Those parents who offer their dearest and best in the struggle for our existence are heroes. With pain in their hearts and with indescribable heroism they bear the sacrifices that they make. Our children have been fated to pay the highest price for the existence of our people.

We often note the phenomenon of being reluctant to give expression to these overwhelming emotions. This is not a matter of weakness. You can admit that your hearts break at the sacrifices that we make daily, not knowing how long we will have to bear this fate.

I knew Leivick, his sensitivity to injustice, his singing out for national and social liberation, and I rejoice that in Israel this magnificent cultural center has been erected in his name. Once it was assumed that Yiddish represented the Diaspora and anti-Zionism, while Hebrew represented Israel and Zionism. Leivick was one of those great poets who, while writing in Yiddish, also expressed, felt, and spoke in Hebrew. He lived and identified with the land of Israel, the great work of construction, and the fight for Jewish survival. This house in his name is an expression of the elimination of the partition between Yiddish and Hebrew. There is no longer a battle between the languages. It is a tragedy that Hebrew no longer faces competition from the millions of Yiddish speakers.

The task of the Leivick House should be to bring the Jewish youth of Israel and the world closer to Yiddish and the cultural treasures of the Jewish past and present.

We have a wonderful youth who do not know the meaning of the word impossible. Every restraint in achieving the tasks and goals set before them is foreign to them. It is our duty to teach them the history and the culture of our millions who are no longer with us, and of the millions who are living and creating Yiddish culture.

We must not forget the injustices done to us by our enemies, and we must guard against doing injustice to our own past. The spirit of the murdered millions lives in Yiddish culture. We dare not commit the offense of not having provided our youth with a consciousness of deep attachment to those millions and to the great cultural treasure they created. The spirit of those Jews must continue to live. It is now much easier than it was a few decades ago. The Six-Day War has strengthened the bond between the world Jewish community and Israel. It has had a tremendous effect that cannot be explained in logical terms alone. Our youth, who confront the Russian tanks and planes with such heroism, have sensed that they are part of all Jews throughout the world. The same sense of belonging was felt by Jewish youth in other countries – those young people whose parents saw to it that they knew nothing of Yiddishkayt, believing that their lives would be easier if they were fully estranged and alienated from Jews and Jewish values. This youth has rebelled. It has drawn closer to Israel and to the Jewish people as a whole. This is a wonderful Jewish youth and it would be the greatest wrong for them not to recognize the great Jewish-national values that Jews have created in Yiddish.

I remember when the founders, the initiators of a Leivick House, came and presented their plan to me. When I asked: 'Where will you get the funds for

'A Jew without Yiddish has no Jewish zest.' Poster announcing free Yiddish courses and drama groups for children and adolescents (Tel-Aviv, 1976).

so large a building?' they answered, 'We haven't thought about that yet'. This reminded me of those early times in the building of the Jewish community in Israel, when Weitzman came to a rich Jew and presented him with the great construction plans. When the rich Jew asked, 'Where will the money come from?' he answered, 'Why, the money is in your pocket.' The rich man responded, 'It's in a secure place'.

I then thought of the pockets that the founders would have to turn to, and was worried whether they, too, would maintain the security of the wealthy Jew. I must confess that I did not then believe that you would succeed with your plan. I knew that writers are not practical people. But now you, the builders of the Leivick House, have shown what can be accomplished through stubborn belief. It is a great honor for us all to have, in Israel, a house bearing the name of the great poet H. Leivick.

(Translated from Yiddish)

Dr. N. Sirkin has called Yiddish 'a jargon...a lie' and Yiddish hands him over to her defenders, the poet Avrom Reyzin and the philosopher-ideologist Dr. Kh. Zhitlovski, so that they can beat some sense into him. (*Der groyser kundes*, July 14, 1911)

דעקלאַראַציע פֿון דער וועלט־קאָנפֿערענץ פֿאַר ייִדיש און ייִדישער קולטור אין ירושלים ... דעם 23סטן־26סטן אויגוסט 1976

SUMMARY: DECLARATION OF THE WORLD CONFERENCE FOR
YIDDISH AND YIDDISH CULTURE IN JERUSALEM...
AUGUST 23–26, 1976

*The totalitarian right and left, as well as the processes of modernization, are
recognized as having seriously weakened Yiddish relative to its pre-World War II
position. Although no mention is made of Zionist sins against Yiddish, an ambitious
program of publication, instruction, theatre support, etc., is drawn up to guarantee
that Yiddish creativity will continue both in Israel and in the diaspora.*

פֿון ירושלים, די אייביקע ייִדישע שטאָט, קומט דער רוף צו די ייִדן אי־
בער גאָר דער וועלט וועגן שטאַרקן און קרעפֿטיקן די ייִדישע שפּראַר און
קולטור. דאָס איז דער רוף פֿון דער וועלט־קאָנפֿערענץ פֿאַר ייִדיש און
ייִדישער קולטור, וואָס איז איז אין די טעג פֿון כ"ז-ל באָב, תשל"ו (דעם 23—
26 אויגוסט, 1976), אין 31סטן יאָר פֿונעם חורבן פֿון דעם אייראָפּעישן
ייִדנטום, אָפּגעהאַלטן געוואָרן אין די מוּיערן פֿון ירושלים, מיטן אָנטייל
פֿון ישׂראלדיקע מלוכה־פֿערזענלעכקייטן, שרייבערס, קינסטלערס און
קולטור־טוער אין דער ייִדישער מדינה און די תפֿוצות — אויסטראַליע,
אַרגענטינע, בעלגיע, בראַזיל, דרום־אַפֿריקע, וועֶנעזוֶעלאַ, מעקסיקע, פֿאַר־
אייניקטע שטאַטן, פֿראַנקרייר, ענגלאַנד, קאַנאַדע, רומעניע און שוועדן.
ביים אָפּשלוס פֿון די פֿאַרהאַנדלונגען איז אָנגענומען געוואָרן פֿאָלגנ־
דיקע דעקלאַראַציע:

1.   די וועלט־קאָנפֿערענץ האָט געבראַכט צום אויסדרוק די ליבשאַפֿט און
צוגעבונדנקייט פֿון ייִדן אין דער גאָרער וועלט צו דער ייִדישער שפּראַך
און ייִדישער קולטור, וואָס זענען געווען און זענען וויַיטער די דאָמבֿ

קעגן אַסימילאַציע און אָפּפרעמדונג, ווי אויך אַן אַקטיוו-שעפּערישער
כוח צו שטאַרקן דאָס נאַציאָנאַלע באַוווסטזיין און טרײַשאַפט צום
פּאָלק.

2. די וועלט-קאָנפערענץ דעקלאַרירט, אַז די קולטור-אוצרות, וואָס יידיש
האָט אָנגעזאַמלט אין איר פיל-הונדערט-יעריקער געשיכטע, האָבן
געקענט אויספירן זייער היסטאָרישע שליחות נאָר דערפאַר ווייל
יידיש איז אַ נאַציאָנאַלע שפּראַך, וואָס האָט אַרײַנגענומען און נעמט
אַרײַן אין זיך אַלע זאַפטן פון דער יידישער קולטור בכלל. די קאָנ-
פערענץ האַלט דעריבער, אַז עס דאַרפן געמאַכט ווערן אַלע אָנ-
שטרענגונגען, כדי דער יידישער שפּראַך און קולטור צו דערמעגלעכן
אַ שעפּערישן המשך.

3. מדינת ישראל, וואָס האָט זיך געשטעלט פאַר אַ ציל צו פאַרזיכערן
נישט נאָר דעם המשך פונעם יידישן פאָלק, נאָר אויך אויפצוהיטן אַלע
גײַסטיקע ווערטן, וואָס יידן האָבן אָנגעזאַמלט במשך פון דורות
אומעטום, ווו זיי האָבן געלעבט, דאַרף העלפן דער שוועֿר-געליטענער
יידישער שפּראַך צו רעסטאַווירירן אירע כוחות. עס ליגט אויך דער
חוב אויף אַלע יידישע קהילות און קולטור-טוער אין דער וועלט צו
ווידמען מי און געפינען מיטלען, אַז יידיש צוזאַמען מיט העברעיש
זאָל ווײַטער זיין דער אויסדרוק פון אונדזערע נאַציאָנאַלע קולטור-
ווערטן.

4. די קאָנפערענץ דעקלאַרירט, אַז יידיש איז נישט בלויז אַ רעזערוואַט
פון גרויסע גײַסטיקע אוצרות, וואָס זענען געשאַפן געוואָרן אין דער
פאַרגאַנגענהייט, נאָר אויך אַ שעפּערישע שפּראַך, אָנגעלאָדן מיט
נאַציאָנאַלע פּאָטענצן און פאַרמאָגט אַ ליטעראַטור מיט גרויסע
קינסטלערישע און עטישע ווערטן, וואָס קענען שטאַרקן דעם יידישן
באַוווסטזיין פון דעם יונגן דור אין אין ישראל און אין די תפוצות. צוזאַ-
מען מיט העברעיש דאַרף יידיש אויפגעהאַלטן ווערן אין מויל פון
דעם יונגן דור.

5. די קאָנפערענץ שטעלט פעסט, אַז די שווערע לאַגע פון יידיש היינט
צו טאָג איז אין דער ערשטער ריי אַ רעזולטאַט פון דעם גענאָסיד מצד
נאַצי-דייטשלאַנד און דעם פיזישן און גײַסטיקן פּאָגראָם אויף יידיש
און דער יידישער קולטור אין סאָוויעטן-פאַרבאַנד.

6. דער שווערער צושטאַנד פון יידיש איז אויך אַ רעזולטאַט פון דעם
אַסימילאַציע-שטראָם, וואָס רייסט לעבעדיקע שטיקער פון אונדזער
פאָלק. מ׳טאָר דערביי אויך נישט פאַרגעסן דעם שרעקלעכן שאַדן

כלפּי ייִדיש און דעם חינוך אין ייִדיש בכלל מצד די, וואָס האָבן נישט
געזען די סכּנה פֿון אַסימילאַציע און אויסוואַרצלונג ביי ייִדן נאָך דעם
חורבן. מיר דריקן אויס אונדזער פֿרייד, וואָס ביים יונגן דור אין צפֿון-
אַמעריקע, מערב-אייראָפּע און אין ישׂראל האָט זיך דערוועקט דער
אינטערעס פֿאַר דעם ייִדישן לשון און די קולטור-אוצרות אין ייִדיש.

7. די וועלט-קאָנפֿערענץ אַפּעלירט צו דער רעגירונג פֿון מדינת ישׂראל,
    צו דער סוכנות, ציוניסטישער אָרגאַניזאַציע, צום ייִדישן וועלט-קאָנ-
    גרעס, צו די ייִדישע סאָציאַלע פֿאָנדן אין פֿאַרשידענע לענדער און
    בכלל צו אַלע אינסטיטוטיעס, וואָס זאָרגן פֿאַר אַ ווייטערדיק נאַציאָ-
    נאַל ייִדיש לעבן, אַז זיי זאָלן העלפֿן שטאַרקן דאָס ייִדישע לשון ביים
    אויספֿירן די שעפֿערישע ראָל פֿאַרן ייִדישן פֿאָלק. כּדי דאָס צו דער-
    גרייכן דאַרף ייִדיש אײַנגעשלאָסן ווערן אין די פּראָגראַמען פֿון ייִדי-
    שער דערציאונג אין די תפֿוצות און אין ישׂראל.

8. די קאָנפֿערענץ דאַרף ווערן אַ היסטאָרישער מײלשטיין אויפֿן וועג צו
    פֿולער האַרמאָניע צווישן העברעיש און ייִדיש. אין דער איצטיקער
    שווערער צייט, ווען אויפֿן יונגן דור לויערט די סכּנה פֿון אַסימילאַציע,
    דערווייטערונג און אָפּגעפֿרעמדקייט, דאַרפֿן מיר שטרעבן צו שלום
    און צוזאַמענאַרבעט פֿאַר דעם קיום און המשך פֿונעם ייִדישן פֿאָלק
    און במילא מדינת ישׂראל.

PART V

Formal Institutions of Language:
The Press, Literature, Theater, Schools

עקידת אידיש

דער „קונדם" (אין דער ראָל פון דעם מלאך) : אברהם, אברהם ! קוילע ניט
דיין איינען קינד. נעם בעסער דעם באָק צו דער שחיטה ! ...

(צו דער קוריאָזער רעזאָלוציע פון א. אָ. ב. אַ. קאָנווענשאָן, אז יעדער מיטגלי־ איז מחויב
צו לייענען א אידיש־ענגלישע צייטונג, אנשטאָט א אידישע.)

The Sacrifice of Yiddish. Angel (to the Independent Order of Brith Abraham, brandishing a resolution against Yiddish): 'Abraham! Abraham! Do not sacrifice your own child (Yiddish). Sacrifice the ram (Anglo-Jewish press) instead.' On the occasion of the curious resolution at the IOBA Convention calling upon members to read the Anglo-Jewish press rather than the Yiddish press. (*Der groyser kundes*, July 6, 1923).

a. נישט בלויז די ישיבות אין פּויזן, אין לובלין, נישט
בלויז די ישיבות אין וואַלאָזשין, אין סלאָבאָדקע, נאָר אויך
די צישאַ-שולן, דער ייוואָ-אינסטיטוט, אונדזערע יידיש-
שולן אין די פאַראייניקטע שטאַטן — דאָס אַלץ איז איין
המשך פון סורא און פומבדיתא.

b. *The basic goal of the schools now, as in the past, is to link our students, children of free Jews in the land of the free, to the four-thousand year old Jewish culture. It goes without saying we must select out of that vast treasure that which we find pertinent and relevant to our times. However, one thing must be made clear; it is not possible to rear an intelligent Jew without Yiddish, Hebrew and the Bible.*

Now, as in the past, we remain committed to Yiddish not because the language is a guarantee for Jewish survival; no, Yiddish, we feel, is essential for a meaningful and creative Jewish continuity. We can and should maintain Yiddish as a language for certain areas of Jewish life ...linked to certain Jewish activities, holidays, Jewish spirituality.

Mottos for Part V

(a) 'Not only the yeshivas in Poyzn (Posen/Poznan), in Lublin, not only the yeshivas in Volozhin, in Slobodke, but also the Tsisho-schools, the Yivo Institute, our Yiddish schools in the United States – all of this together is the continuation of (the academies in) Sura and Pumbadisa (in ancient Babalonia).' Yoysef Opatoshu. Toyznt yor yidish [A thousand years of Yiddish]. *Yidish in undzer lebn* [Yiddish in Our Life]. New York, Workmen's Circle Education Department, 1950, 15–27.

(b) Saul Goodman. Half a century of cultural yidishkayt, in his (ed.) *Our First Fifty Years; The Sholem Aleichem Folk Institute*. New York, SAFI, 1972, *102–*108.

דער „בונד" און דער געדאַנק וועגן אַ ייִדיש־וועלטלעכער שול

ח. ש. קאַזשדאַן

SUMMARY: THE 'BUND' AND THE IDEA OF A YIDDISH-SECULAR
SCHOOL BY KH. SH. KAZHDAN

*A leading Bundist (socialist-secularist-Yiddishist) educator and literary researcher
(1883–1979) documents the early contribution of the Bund to the idea of the
vernacular (= Yiddish) as the medium of education for Eastern European Jewish
children, both for general and Jewish subjects.*

אין 1892 האָט אַ ייִדישער קאָמאַשן־מאַכער אין זיין רעדע אויף אַ
געהיימער 1־מאַי פײַערלונג אין ווילנע צוו. א. געזאָגט: „מיר ייִדן דאַרפן
בײַ זיך נישט אַראָפּפֿאַלן און דאַרפן זיך נישט שעמען, וואָס מיר געהערן
צו דער „שערלעכער" ייִדישער ראַסע ... עס איז ־אויף דער וועלט נישט
געווען נאָך אַזאַ נאַציע, וואָס זאָל אַזוי ווי די ייִדישע קענען מיט אַזאַ
עקשנות גיין שטאַרבן אויף קידוש השם". מיט דריי יאָר שפּעטער האָט
ל. מאַרטאָוו אין דעם זעלבן ווילנע אַזוי גערעדט צו די ייִדישע אַרבעטער:
„מיר דאַרפן אונדזער פֿראָפּאַגאַנדע און אַגיטאַציע צוגעבן אַ מער ייִדישן
כאַראַקטער ... די אויפֿווואַכונג פֿון .דעם נאַציאָנאַלן באַוואוסטזיין און
דעם קלאַסן־באַוואוסטזיין דאַרפן גיין האַנט אין האַנט". אָט אין דעם מאָ־
מענט, ווען עס האָבן זיך דערהערט אין דער יונגער ייִדישער אַרבעטער־
באַוועגונג די נייע נאַציאָנאַלע טענער, איז אָנגעצייכנט געוואָרן איר היס־
טאָרישע ראָל און מיסיע בנוגע דער ייִדישער שפּראַך און וועלטלעכער
קולטור. און ווען עס איז מיט צוויי יאָר שפּעטער נעבוירן געוואָרן דער
„בונד", איז שוין זיין גורל אין דער דערוואַכונג פֿון דער ייִדיש־וועלטלע־
כער קולטור געווען היסטאָריש באַשטימט. דער „בונד" ווערט אַ מעכטיקער
פֿאַקטאָר סיי קענן דער גוטאָ־קנעכטשאַפֿט, סיי קענן דער אַסימילאַציע.

שוין אין 1895 האָבן די פֿיאָנערן פֿון „בונד" באַשאַפֿן „זשאַרגאָנישע
קאָמיטעטן" אין ווילנע, ביאַליסטאָק און מינסק. די דאָזיקע קאָמיטעטן

זענען געוווען א גרויסער שטיץ־פונקט פאר י. ל. פרצן ביים ארויסגעבן און
פארשפרייטן זיינע „יום־טוב־בלעטלעך”.   די דאזיקע זשארגאנישע קאמי־
טעטן מיט זייערע פרואוון פון פארלענגערישער ארבעט און פון לענאלע
ביבליאטעקן — האבן עקסיסטירט עטלעכע יאר.   אין 1897 האט דער
זשארגאנישער קאמיטעט אין ווילנע געפונען פאר נייטיק צו עפענען אן
אייגענע בוך־קראם.   ביי די צארישע באדינגונגען איז דאס געוועך א גאנץ
שווערע אויפגאבע, און ערשט אין 1898 האט זיך אייַנגעגעבן צו לענאלי־
זירן אזא בוכהאנדלונג אויפן נאמען פון אברהם גאסעלניק.   די באדערפע־
ניש אין אזא בוכקראם איז געוועך גרויס: מע האט דא פארקויפט אויס־
נאבעס פון באזונדערע מחברים, גראבע זאמלביכער און דינענע דערציי־
לונגען, לענאל־אריינגעקומענע ביכער פון אמעריקע, די פאפולער־
וויסנשאפטלעכע אויסגאבעס פון קאטיק און ברעסלער א"א.   די גאנצע
ארבעט איז געוווען פארבונדן מיט גרויסע שוועריקייטן און אנשטרעגנונ־
גען.   נאר מענטשן וואס האבן געהאט אן אינטימע באציאונג צו דער
יידישער מאסע און צו איר שפראך, זענען געוווען בכוח דורכצוברעכן אלע
מניעות.   די פיאנערן פון „בונד” זענען אויף אזוי פיל געוווען איבערגע־
נומען מיט דער שפראך־פראבלעם פון דער יידישער ארבעטער־מאסע, אז
ווען זיי האבן צוגעשטעלט זייער באריכט צום אינטערנאציאנאלן סאציא־
ליסטישן קאנגרעס אין לאנדאן אין 1896 (אונטערן נאמען „ווילנער גרופע
סאציאל־דעמאקראטן”), האבן זיי אזוי געשריבן: „די יידישע ארבעטער־
מאסע אין איר גרעסטער מערהייט איז לא די וואס זי קען נישט ליעענ**ן**
קיין רוסיש, נאר זי קען קוים זיך אפילו אויסדריקן אין דער שפראך, און
אונדזער ארבעטער־מאסע קומט אויס זיך צו באפרידיקן מיט דער זשאר־
גאנישער ליטעראטור”.   אין דעם זעלבן באריכט ווערט אויך דערציילט, אז
די ווילנער גרופע האט געשאפן פאר די יידישע ארבעטער א לענאלע בי־
בליאטעק, אויך פון זשארגאנישע ביכער, און די דאזיקע ביבליאטעקס ווערט
אויסגעהאלטן פון די ארבעטער גופא; אין אט דער ביבליאטעקס אין געוווען
נאנצע 250 יידישע ביכער ...

און ווען דער „בונד” האט אין 1907 געפייערט זיין 10־יאריקן יובל,
אין ער געוווען פולשטענדיק בארעכטיקט צו שרייבן אין זיין לענאלן ארגאן
„די האפענונג” (ווילנע, נומ' 14) די ווייטערדיקע שטאלצע ווערטער:
„שוין דער ערשטער טריט פון דער יידישער ארבעטער־באוועגונג, איר
איבערגאנג פון קרייזלער־פראפאגאנדע צו מאסן־אגיטאציע, שוין דער טריט
הייבט זיך אן מיט קולטיווירן די יידישע שפראך.   צו יידן מוז מען יידיש
רעדן. און אלע מוזן מודה זיין, אז דער „בונד” האט א סך אויסגעארבעט
די יידישע שפראך, ער האט זי געמאכט רייכער, בויגזאמער.   ער האט

דעם מארק־זשארגאָן געמאַכט פאַר אַ שפּראַך, אין וועלכער מען קען וועגן
ערנסטע וויסנשאַפטלעכע ענינים רעדן... דער בונד האָט באַשאַפן אַ
גרויסן קרייז לעזער, וועלכער ניטיקט זיך אין אַ גוט בוך, אין אַ צייטונג.
און ער האָט פאַר דעם דאָזיקן קרייז לעזער אַ נייע ליטעראַטור באַשאַפן.
אײַנטלעך, זענען ביידע פּראָצעסן האַנט ביי האַנט געגאַנגען. דער נייער
קרייז לעזער איז געוואָקסן צוזאַמען מיט דער נייער ליטעראַטור״.

ווי זשע האָט געווירקט אָט די גאַנצע נייע אַטמאָספער אויף דער שול־
פּראָבלעם? ווען האָט זיך געשטעלט אין ״בונד״ די פראַגע וועגן דער
ניטיקייט אַריינצופירן די יידישע שפּראַך אין שול, און נאָך מער וועגן אַ
פאָלקסשול אין ייִדיש? ווען האָט זיך אויסנעקריסטאַליזירט אין ״בונד״ אַ
קלאָרע שול־פּלאַטפאָרם?

איר העכסטע ליזונונג האָט די דאָזיקע פראַגע דערגרייכט אויפן זעקסטן
צוזאַמענפאָר פון ״בונד״ (אָקטאָבער 1905), ווען עס איז אין דער באַקאַנ־
טער רעזאָלוציע געוואָנט געוואָרן קלאָר: ״אַ גאראַנטיע קעגן די נאַציאָנאַלע
קאָנפליקטן קען זיין בלויז די באַשאַפונג פון מלוכה־רעכטלעכע אַנשטאַלטן
אין פאָרם פון נישט־טעריטאָריעלער נאַציאָנאַל־קולטורעלער אויטאָנאָמיע;
צו דעם צוועק פאָדערט זיך אַרויסצונעמען פון רשות פון דער מלוכה און
פון די אָרגאַנען פאַר אַרטיסער און ראַיאָניקער זעלבסטפאַרוואלטונג —
יענע פונקציעס, וואָס זענען פאַרבונדן מיט די פראַגן פון קולטור, און
איבערנעבן זיי דער נאַציע אין געשטאלט פון באַזונדערע אַנשטאַלטן —
אַרטיסע און צענטראַלע, וואָס זאָלן זיין אויסגעקליבן דורך אַלע אירע מיט־
גלידער״. פאַרשטייט זיך, אַז צווישן די אָנגערופענע ״פונקציעס וואָס זענען
פאַרבונדן מיט די פראַגן פון קולטור״ פאַרנעמט דעם אויבנאָן די פאָלקס־
שול. און עס איז נאַטירלעך, אַז אין אָט דעם פעריאָד ווען דער געדאַנק
פון קולטור־נאַציאָנאַלער אויטאָנאָמיע האָט זיך אין ״בונד״ אויסגעקריס־
טאַליזירט, האָט זיך אויך געשטעלט אַלץ אין אַ קאָנקרעטערער פאָרעם די
שול־פראַגע אין אַלע אירע פרטים, און דער עיקר בנוגע דער ראָל פון דער
מוטערשפראַך אין פאָלקסשול. וואָס ווייטער ווערט די שול־פראַגע אַלץ מער
אַ פּראַקטישע פּראָבלעם. אין די ריען פון דער אַרבעטערשאַפט און
אינטעלינענץ, און אווודאי צווישן די טעטיקע לערער, דיסקוטירט מען אַלץ
מער וועגן דער דערציאונג פון יידישן קינד, וועגן דער אָרגאַניזאַציע פון
דער פאָלקסשול בכלל און דער עיקר וועגן דעם, ווי אַזוי צו אָרגאַניזירן
דעם לימוד פון יידישער שפּראַך אין די עקסיסטירנדיקע שולן, ווי אַזוי צו
פאַרוואַנדלען די אומאַנגשפּראַך אין דער שול אין ייִדיש, און ווי אַזוי צו
שאַפן נאָרמאַלע עלעמענטאַרע שולן אין דער יידישער שפּראַך.

ווי אַזוי האָט די בונדישע פּובליציסטיק אויועקגעשטעלט און דער־

הויבן די שול־פראגן ? וואָס פאַר אן אָפּקלאַנג האָט דאָס געהאַט אין דער
בונדישער מאַסע און באַוועגונג ?

דער ערשטער, וואָס האָט ערנסט און ברייטער אַוועקגעשטעלט דעם
שול־פּראָבלעם אין דער בונדישער פּרעסע, איז געווען יוסף בעקער; דער
שפּעטערדיקער מיטערדאַקטאָר פון ווילנער „טאָג" און מחבר פון דער
געשיכטע פון דער „גרויסער רוסישער רעוואָלוציע" (2 טיילן). י. בעקער
האָט נאָך אין 1905 פאַרעפנטלעכט א גרויסע אַרבעט א. נ. „די פּאָלקסשפּראַך
און איר באַדייטונג" (חודש־זשורנאַל „דאָס לעבן", ב. 4), אָבער דאָ האָט
ער נערעדט וועגן דער ראָל און באַדייטונג און אויך וועגן דער אַנטוויקלונג
און וואוקס פון די פּאָלקס־שפּראַכן בכלל און בײַ די קלענערע פעלקער
בפרט; ער האָט דאָ אָבער איננאַנצן נישט נערעדט וועגן דער יידישער
שפּראַך. ערשט אין מערץ 1906 גיט ער אין דער ווילנער „פּאָלקסצייטונג"
(נו' 18, 21, 24, 27) א גרויסע אָפּהאַנדלונג, אין וועלכער עס איז שוין
קאָנסרעט באַרירט די יידישע שפּראַך און איר ראָל אין פּאָלקסשול. דער
נאָמען פון דעם אַרטיקל איז „פּאָלקסשפּראַכן און פּאָלקס־שולן". ער פּאָ־
לעמיזירט דאָ מיט אחד העמן און זיין אָנהענגען די נאַציאָנאַלע דערציאונג
נאָר אין דער העברעאישער שפּראַך. „לשון קודש, זאָגט ער, איז נישט נאָר
וואָס זי איז (נישט) קיין מוטערשפּראַך, נאָר זי איז א גאַנץ פרעמדע
שפּראַך" פאַרן קינד. „דער כלל (פון נאַציאָנאַלער דערציאונג) לאָזט זיין
אָנוועגדן אויף יידיש, וואָס איז די אמתע מוטערשפּראַך פון די יידישע
קינדער". דער מחבר טרעט דאָ אַרויס שאַרף קעגן דער מעטאָדע פון
עברית בעברית, ער האַלט זי פאַר א העכסט אומנאַטירלעכער מעטאָדע. ער
ברענגט אויסצוגון פון דער פּרעסע פון די נאַציאָנאַלע מינדערהייטן. אינעם
דעמלטיקן רוסלאַנד, וואו די קאַווקאַזער, אוקראַינער און אנדערע דערציילן,
וואָס פאַר א פּיין און אומרעכט עס איז לגבי דעם קינד די פרעמדע רוסישע
שול, וועלכע די רעגירונג וואַרפט אן מיט געוואַלד אַלע פעלקער. צום
שאַרפסטן איז די דאָזיקע באַציאונג נעקומען צום אויסדרוק אין דעם אויס־
רוף פון די קאַווקאַזער לערער: „מיר זענען נישט קיין לערער, נאָר נלונים
פון די קינדער. די רוסישע שול פאַר די אנדערע פעלקער איז א חדר פאַר
אָפּעראַציעם, וואו מע באַנוצט זיך מיט זייער שלעכט געצייג. די שטומע
און טויבע קינדער זענען פיל גליקלעכער פאַר די געזונטע קינדער". און י.
בעקער פאַרענדיקט זיין אַרטיקל אזוי: „ס'איז קלאָר אז א נאָרמאַלע אַנט־
וויקלונג קען דאָס קינד באַקומען נאָר ווען מען לערנט אים אין זיין מוטער־
שפּראַך. די פּאָלקסשול קען קיין אנדערע נישט זיין, און טאָר אַנדערש נישט
זיין, ווי אין דער מוטערשפּראַך. דער פראַווענסאַלער דיכטער רו מאַניל
האָט געזאָגט: „נעבענשט זאָל זיין דאָס איידעלסטע ווארט, וואָס קלינגט בײַ

אונדזער וויגעלע". די ווערטער פון דעם דיכטער דארפן זיין אויסגעקריצט
ביי אלעמען, וועלכע טראכטן וועגן דער בילדונג פון פאלק און ווילן באמת
ארבעטן פאר דער פאלקסבילדונג. אין דעם ווארט, וואס האט געקלונגען
ביי אונדזער וויגעלע, ליגט די הילף פאר דער בילדונג פון פאלק".

אין דער זעלבער צייט טרעפן מיר אלץ אפטער די יידישע שול־פראגע
אין די לייט־ארטיקלען און רעדאקציאנעלע נאטיצן ביי פארשידענע גע־
לעגנהייטן אויף די שפאלטן פון דעם בונדישן לעגאלן ארגאן. אין יולי
1906 קומט פאר אין ווילנע א קאנפערענץ פון יידישע לערער, מע רעדט
דארט וועגן די שולפראגן, אויך וועגן גרינדן א פראפעסיאנעלן פאריין
פון יידישע לערער אין רוסלאנד*). אין צוזאמענהאנג מיט דעם גיט די
„פאלקסצייטונג" א גרעסערן ארטיקל, אין וועלכן עס ווערן אוועקגעשטעלט
און טיילווייז פארענטפערט די ברענענדיקע פראגן וועגן א יידישער שול.
דער מחבר, אונטערן פסעוודאנים עמנואל, האט אנגערופן זיין ארטיקל
„פון דער זייט", און דאס איז דערפאר ווייל ער איז נישט קיין לערער נאר א
פאליטישער טוער אין „בונד". דאס ארטיקל איז אפגעדרוקט אין צוויי
נומערן (190 און 191, 26 און 27 אקטאבער 1906), און עס איז טאקע
געווידמעט דעם דערמאנטן געפלאנטן לערער־פאריין און זיין גרינדונגס־
צוזאמענפאר. מיט רעכט ווייזט אן דער מחבר אויף דעם, אז דער געפלאנט
טער צוזאמענפאר פון די יידישע לערער טאר בשום אופן נישט טראגן
קיין ריין־פראפעסיאנעלן כאראקטער, ווייל ער האט א גרויסע געזעלשאפט־
לעכע באדייטונג. ער זעט פאר, אז אויפן צוזאמענפאר וועלן זיך באגע־
גענען פנים אל פנים די דריי שטרעמונגען אין דער שול־ארבעט: די רעלי־
גיעז־העברעאישע, די רוסיש־אסימילאטארישע און די יידישיסטישע.
ער באטראכט די שעדלעכע ווירקונג אויפן קינד פונעם חדר, סיי דעם
אלטן טראדיציאנעלן און סיי דעם מאדערניזירטן חדר מתוקן; ער באהאנדלט
אויך די „אומנארמאלע שעדלעכע באדינגונגען, וואס ווערן באשאפן פאר
דער אנטוויקלונג פון מוח און נשמה פון יידישן קינד" אין די רוסיש־צי
פויליש־יידישע שולן; ער רופט די לערערשאפט זיך צו שטעלן מיט דער
גאנצער אנטשיידנקייט אויפן באדן פון א שול אין דער יידישער שפראך.
און דער מחבר פארענדיקט זיין ארטיקל אזוי:

„וואס וועט אונדז געבן דער צוזאמענפאר? עס איז שווער פאראויס־
צוענטפערן אויף דער פראגע. איך נעם דעם ערגסטן פאל, אז דער ערשטער
צוזאמענפאר וועט אויפטאן ווייניק רעאלעס אין דעם פונקט פון באשאפן
א נייע יידישע שול. ווי עס וויזט אויס, וועט דאס טאקע גיכער זיין אזוי.

*) זע דאס קאפיטל אין בוך: „די לעערערשאפט — א ניער געזעל־
שאפטלעכער כוח".

A Lynching in Hester Park. Medem, (leader of Jewish Worker's Bund, Poland):
'Comrade Kan (Cahan), what are you doing? Yiddish is your own child!' Ab Kan
(Abraham Cahan, Editor of the *Jewish Daily Forward*): 'Chauvinism, reaction,
Zionist teachers, potatoes, tickets (prattles on in senile fashion).' *Forward* building
at 175 East Broadway in background. Bulletin-board clippings use highly anglicized
Yiddish to advertise circulation-building features: 'Secrets of the bedroom every day
in the *Forward*,' 'About Turkish operations read the largest socialist paper, the
Forward.' (*Der groyser kundes*, May 20, 1921)

די נייע ריכטונג געפֿינט זייער ווייניק סימפּאַטיע אין דער בורזשואַזער
מפֿיצי־השכלה־געזעלשאַפֿט, וועלכע וואָלט אפֿשר געקענט אויפֿטאָן עפּעס
וואָס. די ייִדישע לערער זאָלן האָבן די מאַטעריעלע מעגלעכקייט די גרינדן
שולן אויפֿן אייגענעם חשבון, איז אַ גרויסער ספֿק. וועגן רעגירונגס־שטיצע
איז דאָך געוויס נישטאָ וואָס צו רעדן. נאָר דאָס אַלעס קען אויף אַ האָר
נישט פֿאַרקלענערן די באַדייטונג פֿונעם צוזאַמענפֿאַר. נישט אין דער זייט
ליגט דער שווערפּונקט זיינער. גרינדן אַ גרויסע צאָל שולן אין דעם מאָ־
מענט, ביי דער איצטיקער פּאָליטישער לאַגע, איז בכלל אוממעגלעך. דער
צוזאַמענפֿאַר וועט פֿאַר זיך האָבן די אויפֿגאַבע צוצוגרייטן די פֿאַרווויר־
קלעכונג פֿון דער ייִדישער שול... ער וועט אָנמערקן די אַרבעט אויף
ווייטער, ער וועט זיך נעמען באַשאַפֿן אַ זשאַרגאָנישע לער־ליטעראַטור,
וועלכע איז אַזוי נייטיק, און דער עיקר איז — דער צוזאַמענפֿאַר וועט
פּאָפּולאַריזירן די אידעע פֿון אַ אמתער פֿאָלקשול אין די ברייטע ייִדישע
מאַסן. די ייִדישע לערער וועט אויסקומען אויסצושטיין פֿיל נסיונות, פֿיל
שוועריקייטן... די גרויסע אַרבעט זייערע וועט אָבער געפֿינען אַ טיפֿן
אָפּקלאַנג אין די אונטערדריקטע שיכטן פֿון ייִדישן פֿאָלק".

נישט געקוסקט אויף דער איבערלאָדנקייט מיט פּאָליטישן און ריין־
פֿאַרטייאישן מאַטעריאַל, נישט געקוסקט אויף די ברענענדיקע פּראָבלעמען
פֿון דער רעוואָלוציע און נאָך־רעוואָלוציע־צייט מיט דער גאַנצער אַטמאָס־
פֿערע אַרום די מלוכה־דומעס; נישט געקוסקט אויף דער אומזיכערקייט פֿון
דער לעגאַלער פּרעסע בכלל, — האָט דאָך דער בונדישער אָרגאַן פֿון צייט
צו צייט אָפּגעגעבן פּלאַץ צו די שול־פּראָבלעמען.

דער אָרגאַן פֿון בונד איז האָט לאָזט נישט דורך קיין געלעגנהייט אָפּצוענטפֿערן
די קעגנער פֿון ייִדיש און פֿונעם געדאַנק וועגן אַ שול אויף ייִדיש. אין
„וועקער" נום. 14 פֿון 11־טן יאַנואַר 1906 לייענען מיר אַ כאַראַקטע־
ריסטישן אין דעם פּרט שאַרפֿן אַרטיקל פֿון הי צביו אונטערן טיטל „די
קראַמאָלע אין דער פּעטערבורגער בילדונגס־חברה" (מפֿיצי השכלה). ער
שרייבט:

„דעם 6־טן דעצעמבער (1905) איז געוועזן אַן אסיפה פֿון דער חברה.
אַ שטורעמדיקע אסיפה איז עס געוועזן. אַ מלחמה צווישן דעם אַלטן
שטאַרקן שימל מיט אַ שטראָם פֿרישע לופֿט, וואָס האָט זיך פֿון נאַס אַריין־
געריסן. די רעוואָזיאַנס־קאָמיסיע האָט באַוויזן אין איר באַריכט, אַז די
חברה האָט בכלל קיינמאָל נישט געלעבט און קיינמאָל קיין נוצן נישט
געבראַכט און בפֿרט איצטער. די חברה האָט יאָ וואָס פֿאַרשפֿרייט, אָבער
אַלץ וואָס איר ווילט נאָר נישט בילדונג צווישן דער ייִדישער מאַסע. די
קאָמיסיע איז באַשיידן, זי וויל קיין רעוואָלוציע נישט מאַכן. זי לײַגט נאָר

פֿאַר געוויסע נייטיקע רעפֿאָרמעס און צווישן זיי אויך אַ רעפֿאָרמע וועגן
דער יידישער שפּראַך. די קאָמיסיע געפֿינט אַז די אַרבעט פֿון דער חברה
האָט דעריבער קיין נוצן נישט געבראַכט, ווייל זי האָט זיך געפֿירט אויף
אַ שפּראַך וועלכע איז נישט פֿאַרשטענדלעך דער מאַסע, און דעריבער
לייגט זי פֿאָר אַז דער יידישער שפּראַך זאָל אָפּגעגעבן ווערן (אין שול) אַזאַ
פּלאַץ, וואָס מע גיט אָפּ דער רוסישער און דער העברעאישער שפּראַך...
האָבן זיך אונדזערע פּעטערבורגער געשוואָרענע „בילדונגס־מענער" שטאַרק
און זייער שטאַרק דערשראָקן.   זיי האָבן דערזען אין דעם פֿאָרלאַנג אַן
אַטענטאַט אויף דער קאָזיאָנער בילדונג, פֿאַר וועלכער די חברה האָט זיך
נעהאַלטן אַזוי פֿיל יאָרן. ד״ר קאַצענעלסאָן אַלס עסטעטיקער קען בכלל
נישט פֿאַרטראָגן דאָס לשון פֿון דער יידישער מאַסע. ער ווערט פּשוט נער־
וועז ווען ער הערט רעדן וועגן יידיש, און אויף דער אסיפה איז ער טאַקע
אַזוי נערוועז געוואָרן, אַז ער האָט שוין אַליין נישט געוואוסט וואָס ער
האָט גערעדט. „זיי פֿאַרלאַנגען פֿון אונדז — טענהט ה׳ קאַצענעלענסאָן —
אַז מע זאָל לערנען אין דער יידישער פֿאָלקסשול אויף יידיש. ס׳קען זיין —
באַלד וועלן זיי פֿאַרלאַנגען, אַז מע זאָל לערנען תּנך און גמרא אויך אויף
יידיש"...

„די יידישע שפּראַך — פֿאַרענדיקט צבֿיון — ווערט נישט אויף
הסכּמות פֿון דער פּעטערבורגער פֿאַרשימלטער בילדונגס־חברה; נישט די
אַלטע פֿאַרשימלטע משׂכּילים וועלן געבן בילדונג דער יידישער מאַסע. די
יידישע מאַסע איז שוין פֿון אירע ווינדעלעך אַרויס, זי דאַרף מער קיין
אָפּעטונעס נישט. ס׳איז אויסגעוואַקסן אַ שטאַרקער יידישער רעוואָלו־
ציאָנערער פּראָלעטאַריאַט, וועלכער האָט גאַנץ אַנדערע השׂגות פֿון פֿאָלקס־
בילדונג"...

אין דער שפּעטערדיקער בונדישער „האָפֿענונג" (נומ׳ 42, 29־טן אָק־
טאָבער 1907) געפֿינען מיר אַן אַרטיקל פֿון א—ר (אסתּר) אונטערן נאָמען
„צו דער פֿראַגע וועגן דער יידישער פֿאָלקסשול", אין וועלכן זי פּאָלעמיזירט
מיטן ד״ר ש. ג. בערנשטיין און זיין אַרטיקל אין „פֿריינד" וועגן דעם נאַ־
ציאָנאַלן ווערט פֿון די ספּעציעלע יידישע לימודים. א—ר באַרירט דערביי
די פֿראַגע וועגן העברעאיש און זאָגט אַרויס איר מיינונג, אַז אין דער
עלעמענטאַרער שול דאַרף דער דאָזיקער לימוד קיין אָרט נישט פֿאַרנעמען.
און דעם דערמאָנטן דאָקטאָר זאָגט זי: „מענטשן וואָס רעדן און וועגן יידישער
פּסיכיק און וועגן נאַציאָנאַלע ווערטן און פֿאַרגעסן אין דער זעלבער צייט,
אַז אַ פֿאָלקסשול קען נאָר זיין אויף דער מוטערשפּראַך פֿון די קינדער, —
האָבן קיין שום שייכות נישט צו דער באַנייאונג פֿון דער יידישער שול...
די נייע שול, וועגן וועלכער עס דאַרפֿן טראַכטן די יידישע לערער־פֿאַריינען,

איבער וועמעס ערשטע שוואכע שפּראָצונגען (אַוונט־שולן, אונטעררריכט פֿון
ייִדיש אין טענגלעכע שול, לערנביכער) ס'הייבן אָן צו אַרבעטן איינצעלנע
קרעפֿטן — דיזע נייע שול וועט זיין אַ ייִדישע פֿאָלקשול, אַ שול וואו
ס'וועט געלערנט ווערן אויף דער מוטערשפּראַך פֿון די קינדער, אַ שול
וואו ס'וועלן נישט זיין קיין ספּעציעלע ייִדישע לימודים, ווייל זי וועט
איננאַנצן זיין אַ ייִדישע... וואו מע וועט נישט רעדן וועגן דער ייִדישער
פֿיסיק, וועגן דעם נאַציאָנאַלן ווערט פֿון ספּעציעלע ייִדישע לימודים, ווייל
זי וועט איננאַנצן צונעפּאַסט זיין צו דער ייִדישער פֿסיכיק, ווייל זי וועט
איננאַנצן זיין אַ נאַציאָנאַלע שול״.

אין 1908 איז שוין קיין טענגלעכע צייטונג פֿון „בונד״ מער נישט
געווען: די צענזור־באַדינגונגען פֿון דער פֿאַרשטאַרקטער רעאַקציע האָבן
דאָס נישט דערלויבט. אין ווילנע גיט אַרוים „דער טאָג אויף שבת״ — אַ
ליטעראַריש־געזעלשאַפֿטלעך וואָכנבלאַט, וואָס איר רעדאַקטאָר איז געווען
א. ליטוואַק און אַרוסיגעבער — ישראל מיכל קאָפּלינסקי. און אויך דאָ
טרעפֿן מיר עטלעכע נאָטיצן און אַרטיקלען, געווידמעט דער ייִדישער שול.
דער וויכטיקסטער פֿון זיי איז דער לייט־אַרטיקל אין נומ' 2 פֿון 18 סעפּ־
טעמבער 1908. ער איז געווידמעט דער מעלדונג פֿונעם וואַרשעווער שול־
קוראַטאָר צו דער ייִדישער גמינע וועגן דעם, אַז אין אירע שולן איז דער־
לויבט צו לערנען אויף רוסיש אָדער אויף ייִדיש, אָבער בשום אופֿן נישט
אויף פּויליש. „די פֿאַראָרדענונג פֿונעם וואַרשעווער קוראַטאָר, לייענען
מיר דאָ, גיט אונדז די מעגלעכקייט אָנצוהויבן בויען אַ ייִדישע שול...
מיר ווייסן, אַז איבעררערדן די איצטיקע גמינע־פֿאַרוואַלטונג איז אַ שווערע
זאַך, אַז די פֿירער פֿון דער גמינע וועלן בעסער אוסקלייבן רוסיש, טערקיש
אפֿילו, נאָר נישט קיין ייִדיש. מיר ווענדן זיך אָבער נישט צו זיי, נאָר צו
דער ייִדיש־געזאָמענער אינטעליגענץ, און צו די באַוואוסטזיניקע מענטשן
פֿון דער מאַסע. מען מוז ווירקן אויף דער גמינע־פֿאַרוואַלטונג, נויטן זי
זיך רעכענען מיט אונדזערע נאַציאָנאַלע פֿאָדערונגען. די פֿאַראָרדענונג פֿונעם
קוראַטאָר איז נוגע נאָר גמינע־שולן. וועגן פּריוואַטע שולן רעדט זי נישט,
און מיר ווייסן נישט צי מען מעג אין פּריוואַטע שולן פֿירן די לערע אויף
ייִדיש אָדער נישט. מען קען אָבער רעכענען, אַז דאָס וואָס מען האָט
דערלויבט די גמינע־שולן, וועט מען אויך פּריוואַטע שולן נישט אָנטזאָגן.
מען מוז זיך פּרואווון״.

אָט אַזוי האָבן די בונדישע פּובליציסטן אויסגענוצט יעדע געלעגנ־
הייט, כּדי אויפֿצושטעלן פֿאַר דער עפֿנטלעכקייט די ייִדישע שול־פּראָבלע־
מען, און טאָקע אויפֿשטעלן זי ווי אַ פּראַקטישן ענין.

* *

*

אין 1908 הייבן אָן אַרויסצוגיין די בונדישע זאַמלביכער — **נישט**
פּעריאָדיש, אונטער פאַרשידענע נעמען, — גרעסערע זאַמלביכער, מיט טעאָ־
רעטישע אַרטיקלען אויף אַלערליי טעמעס. און אין אָט די זאַמלביכער קומען
אויך ערנסטע אַרבעטן איבער דער שול־פראַגע. דער עיקר געהערן די אַלע
אַרטיקלען דער פעדער פון צוויי מחברים: ב. ב.—סקי און אסתר.

ב. ב.—סקי איז דער פּסעוודאָנים פון באָריס לעווינסאָן, אַן אָנגעזעע־
נער בונדישער טוער אין יענער צייט. ער איז טאַקע געווען באַרופן צו דער
דאָזיקער שול־טעמע, ווייל ער האָט פאַרמאָגט פעדאַגאָגישע בילדונג, האָט
געענדיקט דעם ווילנער לערער־אינסטיטוט און אַ געוויסע צייט געאַרבעט
אַלס פּאַרוואַלטער פון אַ תלמוד־תורה אין קרים. אחוץ די אַרטיקלען, וועגן
וועלכע מיר וועלן באַלד רעדן, האָט ב. ב.—סקי אָנגעשריבן אַ בראָשור,
וועלכע איז אַרוים אין 1917 אין בונדישן פאַרלאַג „די וועלט", פּעטער־
בורג. די בראָשור הייסט: „וועגן בילדונג בכלל, יידישער פאָלקסשפּראַך און
יידישער פאָלקסבילדונג בפרט" (16 ז"ז).

אין נומ' 1 פון „די נייע צייט" (ווילנע, 1908) איז אָפּגעדרוקט אַ
גרוים אַרטיקל פון ב. ב.—סקי א"נ „די יידישע פאָלקס־שול". דער מחבר
ניט אַן איבערזיכט איבער אַלע טיפן שולן, וואָס באַדינען דאָס יידישע
קינד. אַ טרעפלעכע כאַראַקטעריסטיק האָבן מיר דאָ פון דעם חדר מתוקן:
„דער חדר מתוקן איז געבוירן געוואָרן אין דעם שום פונעם פּאָליטישן
ציוניזם. די ערשטע קאָנגרעסן מיט דעם גלויבן אין דער באַלדיקער פאַר־
ווירקלעכונג פון דער יידישער מלוכה אין פּאַלעסטינע — האָבן אַרויסגע־
רופן אַ ציוניסטיש־געפאַרבטע קולטורעלע כוואַליע: ציוניסטישע לידער,
העברעאישע און יידישע, זענען געוואָרן אין דער מאָדע, „פריילנס" פלעגן
זיך פאַרייניקן אין קרייזלעך און לערנען העברעאיש. דאַן איז אויך אַרוים
אויף דער סצענע דער חדר מתוקן. האָפענונגען האָט מען אויף אים גע־
לײנט גרויסע, אָבער ער איז געבליבן באַנקראָט. אויב אין אַזאַ גרויסער
יידישער שטאָט ווילנע אָדער מינסק קען עקזיסטירן נאָר איין חדר מתוקן
און ווען ער האָט נאָך נישט דערצו די טענדענץ צו פאַרגרעסערן זיך, —
קען מען זאָגן, אַז דיזע פרי האָט זיך נישט צוגענומען צום יידישן באָדן.
די איניציאַטאָרן פון חדר מתוקן האָבן אַרויסגעטריבן פון אַלטן חדר די
רעליגיעזע נשמה און אַריינגעטראָגן אין אַלטן חדר די אויסווייניקסטע
פאַרמען פון דער וועלטלעכער שול. עס פאַרשטייט זיך, אַז אַזאַ געמי־
שעכטס האָט קיינעם נישט געקענט באַפרידיקן: נישט די אויפגעקלערטע
עלעמענטן, וואָרעם מען לערנט דאָרט נישט קיין וועלטלעכע לימודים, נישט
די פרומע עלטערן, ווייל כאַטש מע לערנט נישט מער ווי   „יידישקייט",
אָבער מע האָט פון איר צוגענומען די גאַנצע הייליקייט. אין חדר מתוקן

ניט מען אָפּ פיל אויף צייט אויף דער העברעאישער שפּראַך, מען לערנט דעם
קינד רעדן אויף העברעאיש, אָבער דער פּרומער שעצט דאָס נישט...".
ב. ב—סקי פאַרגלייכט דעם לערנען עברית בעברית מיט דעם אמאָליקן
דרך פון די „קלאַסיקער": מע האָט נעשטאָפּט די קעפּ פון די תלמידים מיט
דער לאַטיינישער און גריכישער גראַמאַטיקע און מע האָט פאַרזען די בעס=
טע ווערק פון דער לאַטיינישער און גריכישער ליטעראַטור. פּונקט אַזוי
איז ביי דער מעטאָדע פון עברית בעברית: „מע נעמט ביי ׳די קינדער די
בעסטע יאָרן פון זייער לעבן און מען ברענגט זיי אויס אויף פּעדאַגגישע
קונצן".

אין אַ ווייטערדיק קאַפּיטל שטעלט זיך אָפּ ב.—סקי אויף דער
יידישער קאַזיאָנער שול. ער כאַראַקטעריזירט דעם רוסישן און רוסיפיצירנ=
דיקן אינהאַלט פון דער דאָזיקער שול, וואָס ווערט אָנגעפירט דורך לערער=
טשינאָווניקעם און וואָס פאַרבלייבט פרעמד סיי די קינדער, סיי די עלטערן:
וואָס נוגע ווידער די יידישע לימודים אין דער קאַזיאָנער שול, זענען זיי
נישט מער ווי אַ קאָמעדיע. „און דערפאַר איז די קאַזיאָנע שול געבליבן
פרעמד דער יידישער באַפעלקערונג, כאַטש די שול עקזיסטירט שוין פון
צענדליקער יאָרן, דער לערער מעג זיין ווי טריי און איבערגעגעבן דער שול,
דאָך קוקן אויף אים די עלטערן ווי אויף אַ „טשינאָווניק", דאָס ווייסן אַלע
יידישע לערער. און די קינדער אויפן הויף זענען אויך צופרידענער ווען
דער לערער לאָזט זיי אַליין, כדי זיי זאָלן קענען רעדן צווישן זיך אויף
יידיש. און אויך אין קלאַס שלינגט דער שילער אָפּט אַראָפּ אַ פראַגע,
וועלכע ער וואָלט שטעלן ׳דעם לערער, ווען ער וואָלט געקענט ׳רעדן מיט
אים אויף יידיש".

ב. ב—סקי כאַראַקטעריזירט אויך אין זיין אַרטיקל די תלמוד־תורה
— די טראַדיציאָנעלע און די נייע, רעפאָרמירטע. רעדנדיק וועגן דער
לעצטער, דערציילט ער ווי וועגן אַ צייכן פון דער צייט אַזאַ פאַסט: אַ
פאַרוואַלטער פון אַ גרויסער רעפאָרמירטער תלמוד תורה — אַליין אַ
ציוניסט און אַ קענער פון דער העברעאישער שפּראַך — האָט אין איין
קלאַס איינגעפירט עטלעכע שעה אַ וואָך יידיש. „ער האָט דאָס געטאָן...
ווייל דאָס לעבן פאָדערט דאָס; ער האָט מיר געזאָגט, אַז די קינדער וועלן
דאַרפן ליענען יידישע צייטונגען, וועלן דאַרפן שרייבן יידישע בריוו, און
אויב די תלמוד תורה וועט עס זיי נישט אויסלערנען, ווייס ער, אַז די
אָרעמע עלטערן נעמען דאַן פּריוואַטע לערער (שרייבער) וועלכע לערנען
די קינדער יידיש. און מיט די רעזולטאַטן איז ער זייער צופרידן, די קינדער
באַציען זיך מער ערנסט צו דיזע שטונדן. זיי דריקן אויס שריפטלעך זייע=
רע געדאַנקען אויף יידיש פיל בעסער און לייכטער איידער אויף רוסיש".

1. Leyb Kvitko, 1893–1952; Poet; 2. Dovid Hofshteyn, 1889–1952; Poet; 3. Izi Kharik, 1898–1939; Poet; 4. Shmuel Halkin, 1899–1960; Poet, playwright; 5. Itsik Fefer, 1900–1952; Poet; 6. Meyer Viner, 1895–1941; Writer of short stories, novelist, literary researcher.

ב. ב—סקי באהאנדלט ווייטער די ענדערונגען אין יידישן קולטור־
לעבן פאר די לעצטע פאר צענדליק יארן; ער דערציילט בארוכות וועגן דער
גרויסער ראל וואס עס האבן געשפילט אין דעם פרט די אוונטשולן, און
ער קומט צום אויספיר: „א יידישע פאלקשול וועלן מיר האבן דאן, ווען
אין דער וועלטלעכער שול וועט אלץ געלערנט ווערן אויף יידיש". און צום
שלוס שטעלט ב. ב—סקי אוועק פאר די לערער די פראקטישע אויפגאבע,
ווי אזוי פון איין זייט צו באשאפן א נייע יידיש־וועלטלעכע שול, און ווי
אזוי פון דער אנדערער זייט אריינצופירן יידיש אין די פארשידענע טיפן
עקזיסטירנדיקע שולן, וואס דאס איז ביי יענע באדינגונגען געווען דאס
לייכטסטע און דרינגנדסטע.

אין די יארן 1909—1910, ווען עס גייען ארויס די בונדישע זאמל־
ביכער „צייט־פראגן", איז שוין דאס יידישע שול־פראבלעם א סך רייפער
און די צאל אנהענגער פון א שול אין יידיש איז גענוג גרויס נישט נאר
צווישן דער ארבעטערשאפט, נאר אויך ביי דער אינטעליגענץ, געוועזענע
רעוואלוציאנערן און סתם־פאלקיסטן.

צוזאמען מיט דעם האט זיך אויך אנגעהויבן די דיפערענציאציע
אויפן שול־געביט. אין די „צייט־פראגן" ווערט שוין פון איין זייט געפירט
א פאלעמיק מיט די סתם־אנהענגער פון יידישיזם; פון דער אנדערער זייט,
ווערט דא צום ערשטן מאל אויסגעשטעלט די פראגע וועגן פראלעטארי־
שער דערציאונג פון קינד סיי אין דער פאמיליע און סיי אין דער שול.
עס ווערט דא געשטעלט און באהאנדלט די פראגע וועגן דעם, וועלכע פא־
דערונגען דארף דער יידישער ארבעטער ארויסשטעלן צו דער ניי־אויפקו־
מענדיקער יידישער וועלטלעכער שול. אין אן ארטיקל א״נ „צו דער כא־
ראקטעריסטיק פון א נייעס שטרעמונג" פאלעמיזירט אסתר זייער שארף
מיט די מענטשן פון „פריינד" און סתם־יידישיסטן, און זי ציטירט דערביי
מיט פארביטערונג די ווערטער פון ה. ד. נאמבערג, וועלכער האט דעמאלט
געשריבן: „געפינט מען — א יידישע שול, וואס ס׳איז איצט נישטא די
מינדסטע האפנונג אויף איר. געפינט מען, אז זי איז דאס די „רעאלע אין־
טערעסן"... צוליב א יידישע שול — עס איז וויער, זייער טרויער
צו זאגן — איך וויים נישט אויב א גראשן, איך וויים נאך נישט אויב
בחינם ווילן זיי דאס, אונדזער ביסל יידעלער" („צייט־פראגן", ב. 2, 1910).

אינעם ערשטן באנד „צייט־פראגן" (1909) איז אפגעדרוקט א
גרויס ארטיקל פון אסתרן „וועגן נאציאנאלער ערציאונג". אסתר האלט,
אז פאר דער יידישער ארבעטער־פאמיליע שטייט נישט די פראגע וועגן
נאציאנאלער דערציאונג, נאר וועגן דערציאונג בכלל, ווייל אין דער יידי־
שער ארבעטער־פאמיליע איז די דערציאונג ממילא נאציאנאל. „זאל דער

יידישער ארבעטער נאר בכלל ערציען זיין קינד, און אזוי ווי אין זיין
גאנצער באוועגונג, פונעם ערשטן טריט ביזן לעצטן, איז ער געווען טיף
נאציאנאל, האט ער געשאפן נאציאנאלע אוצרות, נאציאנאלע קולטור,
נישט שטעלנדיק זיך דאס פאר א ציל, — אזוי וועט אויך זיין ערציאונג
זיין נאציאנאל, כאטש ער וועט זיך דאס פאר א ציל נישט שטעלן. און
דאס איז דערפאר, ווייל ער אליין איז טיף נאציאנאל".

אסתר שטעלט אין דעם ארטיקל די פראקטישע פראגע: וואס זאל די
יידישע ארבעטערשאפט שוין איצט טאן אויפן שולגעביט, נישט ווארטנ־
דיק ביז וואנען עס וועט פארווירקלעכט ווערן די קולטור־נאציאנאלע
אויטאנאמיע ? וואס זאל די יידישע ארבעטערשאפט און סאציאליסטישע
אינטעליגענץ טאן פאר דער שולזאך, אחוץ דער לעבאהאפטער אניטאציע ?
ברענגנדיק א צאל ביישפילן פון דער דאמאלסטיקער יידישער ווירקלעכ־
קייט, באווייזט אסתר, אז עס לאזט זיך אויף דעם געביט גראד זייער א סך
אויפטאן. זי דערציילט וועגן דעם פאקט, וואס מיר האבן שוין אויבן דער־
מאנט, וועגן דער גינסטיקער באציונג פון דער אדמיניסטראציע אין פולן
צו דער יידישער שפראך, און זי לייגט פאר דאס אויסצונוצן: ״מ׳דארף
אויסנוצן די ווירקונג פון פראלעטאריאט, פון די ברייטע פאלקסמאסן און
פאדערן אין דער קהילה, ביי די געזעלשאפטלעכע איינריכטונגען, עס זאל
וואס מער אונטעריכטעט ווערן יידיש אין די תלמוד־תורהס, געזעלשאפט־
לעכע און יידישע פריוואטע שולן. דא דארף מען זיך פאר זאך קיין נישט
אפשטעלן, מ׳דארף יעדע קלייניקייט אויסנוצן, מ׳דארף פאר יעדע איבע־
ריקע שעה אין און וואך פירן א מלחמה, און אין דער מלחמה וועט דער פראָ־
לעטאריאט האבן די שטיצע אויך פון א טייל — אמת נישט קיין גרויסן —
אויפגעקלערטע און באוואוסטזיניקע יידישע לערער, וועלכע פילן שוין, אז
זייער טעטיקייט אין דער פרעמד־שפראכיקער שול איז פארלארענע מי...
די דערפארונג האט אונ באוויזן, אז אפילו אין דער ליטע איז אויך מעגלעך
וואס צו טאן אין דער זאך. אין איניקע שולן ווערט יידיש אונטעררריכ־
טעט אנשטאט דעם אפיציעלן ״שיינשרייבן", אין אנדערע — אנשטאט
זאקאן באזשיי; און ס׳עקזיסטירן אפילו אוונטשולן, וואו דער גאנצער אונ־
טערריכט כמעט אין יידיש. מ׳געפינט זיך שוין אן עצה".

אסתר מערקט אן א גאנצע פראגראם פון שול־און קולטור־טעטיקייט
פאר . דער ארגאניזירטער יידישער ארבעטערשאפט, צוגעפאסט פאר די
דאמאלסטיקע באדינגונגען פון צארישן רעזשים נאך דער רעוואלוציע פון
1905. אסתר לייגט פאר צו גרינדן נייע און אויסצונוצן די עקזיסטירנדיקע
געזעלשאפטן פאר קינדער־שוץ און ענלעכע קולטור־און דערציאונגס־ארגא־
ניזאציעס. זי רופט צו ארגאניזירן פארלעזונגען פאר עלטערן, אויך אוונט־

סורסן פֿאַר ייִדישער שפּראַך און ליטעראַטור, קינדער־ביבליאָטעקן, שפּיל־
לעצער פֿאַר קינדער, קלובן, עקסקורסיעס הינטער דער שטאָט, און דער
עיקר שטעלט זי אַוועק דאָס פּראָבלעם פֿון שאַפֿן קינדער־גערטנער אין
דער ייִדישער שפּראַך — אַ זאַך, וואָס איז דעמאָלט געווען איינגאַנצן אַ
נײַעס אויף דער ייִדישער גאַס.   זי רופֿט אויך די ייִדישע אַרבעטער צו
ווירקן אויף די עקזיסטירנדיקע געזעלשאַפֿטלעכע אינסטיטוטיציעס, זיי זאָלן
אײַנפֿירן ייִדיש און ייִדיש־לימודים אין די שולן, וואָס שטייען אין זייער
רשות. אין דער גרינדונג פֿון די פֿאַרשידענע מינים דערציונגס־אַנשטאַלטן
אויף ייִדיש זעט אויך אַנב אסתּר אַ מיטל צו דערנענטערן די קינדער פֿון דער
ייִד' אינטעליגענץ מיט די קינדער פֿון דער אַרבעטערשאַפֿט און אָרעמשאַפֿט:
„דאָרט וועלן זיך די קינדער פֿון דער אינטעליגענץ זיך שעמען, ווען זיי וועלן
נישט קענען רעדן קיין ייִדיש, און וועלן זיך לערנען ליבן זייער נאַצ' שפּראַך
און קולטור. דאָ ווידער וועלן די אַרבעטער־עלטערן קענען וויפֿל נישט איז
באַקאַנט ווערן מיט די פֿאָדערונגען פֿון פּעדאַגאָגיק."

אינעם צווייטן באַנד פֿון די „צײַטפֿראַגן" האָט ב.—סקי געענטפֿערט
מיט „אײניקע באַמערקונגען צום אַרטיקל פֿון א—ר ווענן נאַציאָנאַלער
ערציונג".

ב. ב—סקי פֿאָלעמיזירט מיט אסתּרם שטעלונג, אַז דער ייִדישער אַרבע־
טער דאַרף רעדן נישט ווענן נאַציאָנאַלער דערציונג, נאָר ווענן דערציונג
בכלל. ער ווײַזט אָן אויף דער נייטיקייט זיך אויסצולעבן נאַציאָנאַל, ער
וויקלט אויף די שוועריקייטן און די פּראָבלעמען פֿון שאַפֿן אַן אייגנטימ־
לעך ייִדיש לעבן. זיין אַרטיקל אַנטהאַלט אין זיך אַ סך אַפֿיקורסות און
ער איז באַצייכנט ווי אַ „דיסקוסיאַנס־אַרטיקל". מיר וועלן דאָ ברענגען נאָר
צוויי ציטאַטעם פֿון ב. ב—סקים אַרטיקל:

„די אינטעליגענץ אונדזערע און די אויפֿגעקלערטע אַרבעטער מעקן
אָפּ אַלע פֿאַרבן פֿון זייערע לעבנספֿאָרמען, אַלץ איז גראָ און וואָכעדיק.
איך ווײַס נישט קענען וועלכן פּונקט פֿון אונדזער פּראָגראַם וועלן זיך
פֿאַרזינדיקן, ווען שבת וועט לינג אויפֿן טיש אַ גאַנצן טאָג אַ ווײַסע טיש־
טוך, ביינאַכט וועט מען אָנצינדן ליכט (מען קען אָנצינדן ליכט אָן אַ ברכה
און אָן טרערן), ווען אום פּסח, דעם יום טוב פֿון פֿרילינג און פֿרייהייט,
וועט אין אונדזער וווינונג אַלץ שײַנען און לײַכטן, ווי אין יעדער ייִדישער
שטוב, ווען שבועות וועט זיין אין שטוב גרינס, ווען תּשעה באָב וועט זיך
אויך בײַ אונדז פֿילן אַ נאַציאָנאַלער טרויער אא"וו.

„...באַשאַפֿן אַ ייִדישע ליטעראַטור אין אַלע וויסנשאַפֿטן, פּאָפּולאַרי־
זירן די נאַנצע ייִדישע געשיכטע, אַרויסגעבן אָריגינעלע ייִדישע און אי־
בערנעזעצטע שריפֿטן, וועלכע שפּיגלען אָפּ דאָס ייִדישע לעבן איצט און

אין דער געשיכטע, איבערזעצן די קלאסישע ווערק פון דער אלוועלטלעכער
ליטעראטור, זאמלען יידישע פאלקסלידער און ניגונים, פאלקס-מעשיות
אא"וו — דאָס איז אַ פראָגראם נישט אויף אַ יאָר; אָבער דאָס דארף ווערן
אַ לאָזונג פאַר אַ ברייטער און שטארקער געזעלשאַפטלעכער אָרגאַניזאַציע,
און מען דארף צו דער פאָרווירקלעכונג פון פראָגראם וואָס פריער צו
טרעטן" ("צייטפראגן", 2, מערץ, 1910).

* *
*

די אכטע קאָנפערענץ פון "בונד" (לעמבערג 1910) האָט קאָנקרע-
טיזירט די שפראַך-און שול-פאָדערונגען פון יידישן ארבעטער-קלאַס. צווי-
שן אנדערע פאָדערונגען פאָרלאַנגט די רעזאָלוציע: "...ביז עס וועט
ווערן פאַרווירקלעכט די קולטור-נאַציאָנאַלע אויטאָנאָמיע, וועלכע גיט
איבער דן פירונג פון די שול-און קולטור-ענינים צו די נאַציעס גופא,
— מוז מען זען זען קעמפן, אז די מלוכה-שולן פאַר יעדער נאַציאָנאַלער גרופע
פון דער באַפעלקערונג זאָלן געשאַפן ווערן אויף דער מוטערשפראַך. עס
מוז אָפּגעשאַפט ווערן די נגישות בנוגע דעם באַנוצן זיך מיט דער מוטער-
שפראַך אין דעם געזעלשאַפטלעכן לעבן, אויף פאַרזאַמלונגען, אין דער
פרעסע, אין די געזעלשאַפטע, פריוואַטע שׁולן וכדומה". און, כדי צו פאָ-
פולאריזירן און אריינגעבן אַ קלאָרן אינהאַלט דאָזיקן פּראָבלעם
פון גלייכבארעכטיקונג פאַר יעדן פאָלק אויפן שפראַך-געביט, — האָט
אסתר ווייטער פאַרעפנטלעכט אַ גרויסע אָפּהאַנדלונג א"נ "גלייכבארעכטי-
קונג פון שפּראַכן"*).

זי שטרייכט דאָ אונטער, אז די פאָדערונג פון אַ יידישער נאַציאָנאַל-
קולטורעלער אויטאָנאָמיע איז נישט קיין ענין פון "מיסטישן נאַציאָנאַלן
גייסט", פון דעם "אייביקן תוך פון דער נאַציע". אסתר שטעלט אַוועק
די פראַגע רעאַל-פּאָליטיש, זי מאַכט קלאָר דעם פעסטן צוזאַמענבונד
צווישן דעם לאָזונג "יידיש" און דעם לאָזונג "אויטאָנאָמיע": "אין דעם
מאָמענט — זאָגט זי — וואָס (ווען) די יידישע ארבעטער האָבן די פאָ-
דערונג פון דער יידישער נאַציאָנאַל-קולטורעלער אויטאָנאָמיע ארויס-
געשטעלט, האָבן זיי זיך ארויסגעזאָגט פאַר יידישער קולטור, איז פאַר
זיי דאָס שפראַך-פּראָבלעם געלייזט געוואָרן. אין די יידישע שולן מעגן
זייער אַ ברייט אָרט פאַרנעמען פרעמדע שפראַכן, אין די יידישע ביבליאָ-
טעקן מעגן זיך געפינען זייער פיל ביכער נישט-יידישע. די שפּראַך, די
קולטור, וועלכע וועט בילדן דעם אינהאַלט פון דער יידישער נאַציאָנאַל-

קולטורעלער אויטאָנאָמיע וועט זײַן די ייִדישע שפּראַך, די ייִדישע קול־
טור. — אָדער. די ייִדישע נאַציאָנאַל־קולטורעלע אויטאָנאָמיע וועט קיין־
מאָל נישט מקוים ווערן".

עס איז געווען יעמאָלט די צײַט, ווען אין דעם רוסישן פּאַרלאַמענט
(נאָסור. דומאַ) איז געשטאַנען אויפן סדר היום די פראַגע וועגן פאָלקשולן.
עס האָט זיך געפאָדערט אַ פעסטע און קלאָרע שטעלונג בנוגע דער פראַגע,
וואָס פאַר אַ פאָלקשול איז נייטיק פאַר די ייִדישע מאַסן: אַ העברעאישע
אָדער אַ ייִדישע. דער ייִדישער דעפּוטאַט פרידמאַן האָט אין דער דומאַ־
קאַמיסיע אויף דער פראַגע געענטפערט: "זאָלן דאָס ייִדן אַליין באַשטי־
מען". אסתר רעאַגירט אויף דעם זייער שאַרף און זאָגט, אַז מיט דעם
דאָזיקן ענטפער פרידמאַנס "לייקנט ער שטיי:ער אויפן וועג צו דער בא־
שאַפונג פון אַ ייִדישער שול און צו דער גלײַכבאַרעכטיקונג פון דער ייִדי־
שער שפּראַך. אַ פאָלק וואָס האָט נאָך נישט באַשלאָסן, וועלכע איז זײַן
נאַציאָנאַלע שפּראַך, איז נאָך נישט דערוואַקסן צו נאַציאָנאַלער גלײַך־
באַרעכטיקונג... דער ייִדישער באַוואוסטזיניקער פּראָלעטאַריאַט האָט
אָבער אויף דער פראַגע געענטפערט און דאַרף זען, דאָס זאָל ווערן אַן
ענטפער פון פאָלק".

אסתר מערקט אָן די פּראַקטישע פּאָליטיש־געזעלשאַפטלעכע פאַרשלאָגן,
וועלכע דאַרפן געמאַכט ווערן אין דער שול־קאָמיסיע בנוגע דער שפּראַך־
פראַגע אין דער פאָלקשול. "עס מוז פעסטגעשטעלט ווערן — זאָגט זי —
אַז די אונטעררריכט־שפּראַך פון יעדער שול דאַרף זײַן די מוטער־שפּראַך
פון די קינדער, אַז פאַר יעדער נאַציע דאַרפן זײַן באַזונדערע שולן איינ־
געאָרדנט, און די נאַציאָנאַלע שולן דאַרפן זיך געפינען אינעם רשות פון
די נאַציאָנען; אַז ביז וואַנען ס'וועלן באַשאַפן ווערן נאַציאָנאַל־קולטורעלע
אָרגאַנען דאַרף יעדע נאַציאָנאַלע גרופע אין שטאַט אָדער וואָלאָסט בילדן
אַ באַזונדער שולראַט געקליבן אויפן גרונט פון געהיימען, גלײַכן, דירעק־
טן און אַלגעמיינעם .וואַלרעכט... מ'מוז באַזונדערס שטאַרק באַטאָנען,
אַז צווישן אַלע שפּראַכן אין רוסלאַנד, וואָס ווערן דערלאָזן אַלס אונטער־
ריכט־שפּראַכן אין די פאָלקשולן, דאַרף אָנערקענט ווערן די ייִדישע
שפּראַך". און אסתר רופט אַלע ייִדישע אַרבעטער, זיי זאָלן שיקן צו דעם
סאָציאַל־דעמאָקראַטישער פראַקציע אין דומאַ "וואָס מער רעזאָלוציעס מיט
חתימות, וווּ עס ווערט געפאָדערט די אָנערקענונג פון דער ייִדישער אונ־
טעריכט־שפּראַך און די באַשאַפונג פון ייִדישע שולן, וווּ אוי ייִדיש זאָל
פאַרנעמען אַ פּאַסנדן אָרט. זיי דאַרפן צושיקן דער פראַקציע וואָס מעהר
מאַטעריאַלן וועגן דער ייִדישער קולטורעלער באַוועגונג, וועגן דער אַנט־
וויקלונג פון דער ייִדישער שפּראַך און ליטעראַטור, כדי די פראַקציע זאָל
מיט פאַקטן אין די הענט אימשטאַנד זײַן צו ענטפערן אויף די באַהויפ־

Dzis w teatrze Ludowym Zydowski Seminarjum Nauczycielski
urządza przedstawienie p. t. „Nowa gra Purymowa" w 4 aktach
na zakończenie balet.

לכבוד פורים!

הינט מיטוואך 8 אונט

אין פאָלקס ־ טעאטער

ווערט אויפגעפירט פון יידישן לערער ־סעמינאר

אַ נייע פורים ־שפּיל

אין 4 אקטן

אַ באַלעט "יציאת מצרים"

אין 4 בילדער

בילעטן פון 50 גראָשן אָן

Drukarnia L. Efrona w Wilnie

In honor of Purim the Yiddish Teachers Seminary presents a ballet,
'The Exodus from Egypt' in four acts (1928).

טוננגען אז יידיש איז קיין שפּראַך נישט און האָט קיין ליטעראַטור נישט...
ס'דאַרף אויך פיל אויפמערקזאַמקייט אָנגעווענדט ווערן אויף דער פּאַ־
דערונג, אז אַלע שפּראַכן און אויך די יידישע זאָלן דערלאָזן ווערן אלס
אונטעריכט־שפּראַך אין די פּריוואַטע שולן,—די פאָדערונג האָט דעם נרעס־
טן פּראַקטישן ווערט"*).

מיר וויסן נישט, וויפיל אַזעלכע רעזאָלוציעס זענען דורך יידישע
אַרבעטער צוגעשיקט געוואָרן צו דער סאָץ. דעם. פּראַקציע פון דער נאָם.
רומא. מיר וועלן אָבער ברענגען אַ מוסטער פון אַזאַ ועלדונג. דאָס איז,
דער בריוו צו דער סאָץ. דעם. דומאַ־פּראַקציע, וועלכער איז ארויסגעשיקט
געוואָרן אין נאָמען פון דער אַלגעמיינער פאַרזאַמלונג פון דער בונדישער
אָרגאַניזאַציע אין ווילנע („אָטקליקסי בונדא", פעברואַר 1911, נום' 5, צי־
טירט אין דער כרעסטאָמאַטיע פון א. קירזשניץ „דער אידישער אַרבע־
טער", דריטער באַנד). די נעהעריקע שטעלן וואָס האָבן אַ שייכות צו
אונדזער טעמע לייענען זיך אזוי: „נעערטע חברים! לויטן באַשלוס פון

*) „צייט־פראַגן", 5־טער באַנד 1911.

דער, אַכטער קאָנפערענץ פון „בונד", האַלטן מיר פאַר נייטיק אַרויסצו-
זאָגן זיך אייער טעטיקייט פאַר די ערשטע צוויי חדשים פון דער,
פערטער דומע־סעסיע... מיר באַגריסן דאָס אַקטיווע אָנטיילנעמען פון
דער ס' ר' פראַקציע אינעם באַהאַנדלען דעם שול־געזעץ־פּראָיעקט... אי־
נעם קאַמף, וועלכן אונדז קומט אויס צו פירן אויף דער יידישער גאַס קעגן
דעם נאַציאָנאַליזם און קעגן דער הערשונג פון דער רעליגיע אין דער
פאָלקסשול, באַקומען מיר אין אייערע אַרויסטרעטונגען אַ באַדייטנדיקע
שטיצע. אייערע אַרויסטרעטונגען אין דומע קעגן דעם רעאַקציאָנערן אין־
האַלט, וועלכן די רעגירונג און די דומע־מערהייט לייגן אַריין אין דער
פאָרמולירונג פון די שול־אויפגאַבן; אייערע שאַרפע רעדעס קעגן דער
הערשונג פון דעם אדעל אין דער שול־פאַרוואַלטונג — דאָס אַלץ וועט
אומבאַדינגט העלפן אויפצוקלערן די מאַסן... איר האָט ריכטיק געטאָן,
ווען איר האָט קעגן די נישט־קלאָרע און נישט־פולשטענדיקע אויסבעסע־
רונגען פון פאַרשידענע אַפּאָזיציאָנעלע פאַרטייען — קלאָר און געניוי גע־
זאָגט אין אייער אויסבעסערונג, אַז די שפּראַך פון דער שול דאַרף זיין
די מוטערשפּראַך, אַז די שול דאַרף זיין צוגעפּאַסט צו די לעבנסבאַדינגונ־
גען פון דער אָרטיקער באַפעלקערונג. אין אייערע אויסבעסערונגען וועלן
מיר, בונדישע אָרגאַניזאַציעס, געפינען אַ שטיצפּונקט אין אונדזער קאַמף
פאַר דער קולטור־נאַציאָנאַלער אויטאָנאָמיע, וועלכע איז דער איינציקער
קאָנסעקווענטער וועג אויף אויף צו דערגרייכן די צילן, וועלכע איר שטעלט זיך
מיט אייערע אויסבעסערונגען"...

אַזוי אַרום, איז דער פּאַרדינסט פון „בונד", וואָס ער האָט נישט נאָר
קלאָר געמאַכט דאָס פּראָבלעם פון שולוועזן פאַר די יידישע מאַסן און
אַריינגעלייגט אַ קאָנקרעטן קולטור־דערציעריש אינהאַלט אין דעם לאָזונג
פון אַ יידיש־וועלטלעכער שול, נאָר ער האָט צום ערשטן מאָל אַרויפגע־
בראַכט דאָס דאָזיקע פּראָבלעם אויפן פּאַרום פון דער געזעצגעבערשאַפט,
ער האָט עס דערהויבן צו אַן אַלגעמיין־מלוכהשער פראַגע.

* * *

*

די קרוין פון דער בונדישער שול־ליטעראַטור אין יענער צייט איז
געווען אסתרס בוך, וואָס איז אַרויסגעגעבן געוואָרן אין 1910 דורכן פאַר־
לאַג „די וועלט" אין ווילנע (ז"ז 97) און איז שפּעטער אַרויס נאָך אין צוויי
אויפלאַגעס (די דריטע אויפלאַגע אין פעטערבורג אין 1917). אסתרס
אַרבעט האָט געטראָגן דעם נאָמען „צו דער פראַגע וועגן דער יידישער
פאָלקסשול" און האָט געהאַט פיר אָפּטיילונגען, 1) די מוטערשפּראַך און
די פאָלקסשול, 2) די פּרעמדע שפּראַך אין דער יידישער שול, 3) יידיש —
אַן ענטפער אויף די טענות קעגן יידיש, 4) די יידישע פאָלקסשול און דאָס

יידישע פּאָלק. אסתרם ארבעט האָט דערצויגן אַ גאַנצן דור פון נייע פּראָ־
לעטאַרישע שולטוער*). זי האָט נישט איינעם פון די לערער אין די רו־
סיש־יידישע שולן געצווונגען איבערצוריסן מיט דער נעגאַטיוּער באַציונג
צו יידיש און צו ווערן אַ באַוווסטזיניקער אָנהענגער פון יידיש אין שול
— צי ווי אַ לימוד, צי ווי די אומגאַנג־און אונטעריכט־שפּראַך פון די
אַלגעמיינע לימודים. פֿאַר אונדזער הײַנטיקן לייענער וועט עס נעוויס
זײַן אינטערעסאַנט און באַלערנדיק צו הערן די פֿאָרמולירונגען און דעם
אופן פון ארגומענטירן, אַזוי ווי מיר זעען דאָס איינעם שלום־קאַפּיטל פון
אסתרם ארבעט:

„די פֿאָדערונג, דער אונטעריכט אין דער פֿאָלקשול זאָל פֿאָרקומען אין
דער מוטערשפּראַך פון די קינדער, איז נאָר אַ גאַנצער רייע פֿאָ־
דערונגען, וועלכע בילדן דאָס שולפּראָגראַם פונעם באַוווסטזיניקן פּראָלע־
טאַריאַט.   די פֿאָדערונג, די פֿאָלקשול זאָל נישט זײַן קיין אָרעמאַן־שול
לויט איר פּראָגראַם; עס זאָל זײַן איינע און די זעלבע עלעמענטאַרע ביל־
דונג סיי פֿאַרן צוקונפֿטיקן טאַגלוינער און שוסטער, סיי פֿאַרן צוקונפֿטיקן
סוחר, דאָקטאָר, מיניסטער; די מיטלשול זאָל זיך אָנהייבן פון יענעם על־
טער, ווען אַ קינד ענדיקט די פֿאָלקשול און זאָל זײַן אַ דירעקטער איבער־
גאַנג פון איר ...; די פֿאָדערונג, די פֿאָלק־שול זאָל זײַן וועלטלעך ...;
די פֿאָדערונג, אַז ווייניקסטנס די עלעמענטאַר־בילדונג זאָל זײַן פֿאַר אַלע־
מען אומזיסט און אָבליגאַטאָריש, די לערנדויער זאָל זײַן ווייניקסטנס אַכט
יאָר; ... די פֿאָדערונג, די תלמידים זאָלן אומזיסט באַקומען אין שול וואָ־
רעם עסן און אַלע אַלע לערמיטלען; די פֿאָדערונג, דער אונטעריכט זאָל זײַן
פֿריי פון דער אדמיניסטראַטיוּער השגחה; די פֿאָדערונג, די עלטערן זאָלן
האָבן אַ ברייטע ווירקונג אויף די שול־ענינים ...; ענדלעך, די פֿאָדערונג,
דער גאַנצער ענין פון פֿאָלקסבילדונג זאָל איבערגעגעבן ווערן אין די הענט
פון אויטאָנאָמע נאַציאָנאַלע פֿאַרבאַנדן, וועלכע באַזיצן אין דעם פּרט אַ
געזעצגעבערישע מאַכט (נאַציאָנאַל־קולטורעלע אויטאָנאָמיע), — די דאָזי־
קע הויפֿט־פֿאָדערונגען און אַ ריי אַנדערע, וועלכע באַרירן דירעקט אָדער
אומדירעקט די פֿאָלקסבילדונג און פֿאָלקסדערציונג, מוז דער יידישער פּראָ־

*) ווי עס דערצײַלט בן ציון כ״ץ אין זײַנע לעצטנס פֿאַרעפֿנטלעכטע
„זכרונות" („סטָג־מָארגנזשורנאַל", 24־טן יולי 1955), איז אסתר געווען
אין דער יוגנט אַ סטודענטין אויף די פּעדאַגאָגישע קורסן אין פּעטערבורג.
אין דער צײַט פון דער ערשטער וועלט־מלחמה, דערצײַלט ער, איז אסתח
געווען אַ לערערין אין אַ יידישער שול אין אַסטראַכאַן, פֿאַר די פּליטים־
קינדער.

לעטאריאט אַרויסשטעלן בנוגע צו דער יידישער פּאָלקסשול"(*).

און ווייטער:

"דער יידישער פּראָלעטאריאט איז דער ערשטער מיטן לאָזונג פון דער
גלייכבאַרעכטיקונג פון ייִדיש אַרויסגעטראָטן; דער ערשטער פֿאָרמולירט
די פֿאָדערונג פון דער יידישער פֿאָלקסשול; די דאָזיקע פֿאָדערונג האָט אים
דיקטירט די אייזערנע נויטווענדיקייט, די אינטערעסן פון זיין קלאַסן־
קאַמף, זיין ברענענדער דורשט נאָך בילדונג און ליכט. — דורך שפּאַט
און גענעכטער פון איינע, דורך קאַלטע גלײַכגילטיקײַט פון אַנדערע —
האָט דער פּראָלעטאריאט זיין אַלטן לאָזונג דורכגעטראָגן ביז איצט, ווען
ער הערט אויף צו זיין איינזאַם, ווען אַ שיכט פון דער יידישער אינטעלי־
גענץ הייבט אָן איבערצוחזרן אים. די יידישע פֿאָלקסשול ווּעט זיין אָן
אַרבעט פון דער נאַציע; דער פּראָלעטאריאט אָבער קען פון אָנהייב אָן זיין
שטעמפּל אויף איר אַרויפּלײַגן; דער פּראָלעטאריאט מוז זען, זיין לאָזונג
זאָל נישט ווערן אין די הענט פון אַנדערע געפעלשט און פֿאַראומרייניקט;
ער זאָל נישט ווערן קיין מיטל אין די הענט פונעם נייעם מין רעאַקציאָנערן
שאָוויניזם. — דער פּראָלעטאריאט קען נישט דעם אַליין פון בנין פון דער
יידישער פֿאָלקסשול שאַפֿן; ער איז אָבער גענונג שטאַרק צו ווירקן, דאָס
זאָל זיין אַ בנין פון דער נייער לעבעדיקער אַלמענטשלעכער קולטור, —
דער בנין זאָל דינען נישט דעם אַלטן חלום פון אַ טויטער פֿאַרגאַנגענהייט,
אָבער (נאָר) דעם ליכטיקן געדאַנק פון דער לעבעדיקער צוקונפט"(**).

אַזוי אַרום האָט אסתר אין איר אַרבעט אויך אויסגעלייגט דעם יסוד
פֿאַר אַ זעלבשטענדיקער פּראָלעטאַרישער פּאָליטיק אויפ׳ן שולגעביט און
פֿאַר דער אידעאָלאָגיע פון אַ סאָציאַליסטישער דערציונג פונעם יידישן
קינדער.

*   *

*

פֿאַר די בונדישע טוערס פון יענע יאָרן, ערב דעם ערשטן וועלט־
קריג, איז די שול־פֿראַגע נישט געווען קיין ענין פון סתם טעאָרעטישע
באַהאַנדלונגען, זיי האָבן אויסגענוצט יעדע געלעגנהייט כדי אויסצושטעט־
לן די שול־פֿראַגע ווי מעגלעך פּראַקטיש. "די צייַט", דער בונדישער לעגאַ־
לער אָרגאַן אין פּעטערבורג, האָט אין אַן אַרטיקל פון 26־טן פעברואר 1913
געשטעלט די אַנהענגער פון אַ יידיש־וועלטלעכער פֿאָלקסשול — די פֿראַגע:
"ווי לאַנג נאָך?". די דאָזיקע פֿראַגע האָט באַטײַט: ווי לאַנג נאָך וועלן
זיי פֿאַרטײדיקן ייִדיש מיט ווערטער און נישט דורך שאַפֿן אַנשטאָלטן

ממש. „אײן ײדישע מוסטער־שול װאָלט מער געערדט צום ברייטן עולם,
אײדער צענדליקער פֿיערדיקע רעדעס. זאָל דער פֿאָטער נאָר דערזען װאָס
אַזאַ שול ניט זײנע קינדער, װעט ער זיך שוין האַלטן פֿאַר איר שטאָל און
אײזן. דאַרף מען זי אים אָבער װײזן. װאָרעם דער אױפֿטו איז נײַ אומ־
געװײנלעך, אָן אַ בײשפּיל אין דעם בזאַהעריקן לעבן... אַזאַ שול װאָלט
איצט אױך נישט געװען אוממעגלעך צו גרינדן. אױסערע שטערעניש
לאָזן זיך װי עס איז, אױב ניט באַזײטיקן, טאָ צײַטװײליק פֿאַרטושן. שי־
לער און לערער װאָלט זיך געפֿונען. ביכער? טײלװײז איז דאָ, טײלװײז
װאָלט זיי די נאָכפֿראַגע געשאַפֿן". און דער מחבר פֿון דעם אַרטיקל אַפּע־
לירט צו דער אַרבעטער־אינטעליגענץ און צו די ברייטע שיכטן פֿון דער
ײדישער דעמאָקראַטיע, „װעלכע זענען אי קעגן דער אַסימילירטער שול
אי קעגן דעם רעליגיעזן חדר", אַז זיי זאָלן נעמען אױף זיך און מאַכן דעם
ערשטן פֿרואװװ צו גרינדן די ערשטע ײדישע שול.

דאָס װאָס דאָ זוערט דערמאָנט דער „רעליגיעזער חדר" — איז נישט
קײן צופֿאַל. עס איז דאַמאָלסט אין דער ײדישער בירגערלעכער פּרעסע
אָנגעגאַנגען אַ באַװעגונג צום קאַמף פֿאַרן חדר. „מען דאַרף פֿאַרװאַנדלען
דעם חדר אין אַ שול — האָט געשריבן מ. קריינין אין „פֿרײנד", — אָנ־
הײבן דאַרף מען פֿון אױסבעסערן דעם חדר פֿון אױסװײניק, און מען דאַרף
אַזױ גײן וװיטער ביז מען װעט אין חדר אַריינטראָגן אַלע עלעמענטן פֿון
אַ גוטער שול". אױך אין „ראַזסװיעט" און אין דער „ײדישער װעלט"
האָבן זיך געהערט שטימען, אַז די נייע ײדישע שול דאַרף זיין „אַ סינטעז
פֿון צװײ עלעמענטן — דעם חדר און די שול". „די צייטי האָט שאַרף
פּאָלעמיזירט מיט די דאָזיקע שטימונגען. אין נומ. 24—25 שרײבט מ. ר.:
„די זעלבע ײדישע ליבעראַלן װעלכע זענען אַזױ ליבעראַל בעת עס רעדט
זיך װעגן גאַנץ רוסלאַנד, װערן רעאַקציאָנער בעת זיי קומען צו זייער
פֿאָלק... און פֿון זייערע גרױסע רייד װעגן בילדונג לאָזט זיך אױס אַז מען
דאַרף זיך אומקערן צוריק, צוריק צו די אַלטע צייטן, צום חדר, צום בית
המדרש... װי אַנדערע דעמאָקראַטישע אױפֿגאַבן, פֿאַלט אױך דער קאַמף
פֿאַר אַן אמתער פֿאָלקס־בילדונג — אױפֿן ײדישן אַרבעטער־קלאַס און זיין
פּאַרטי. אױפֿהײבן דעם אינטערעס צו דער פֿאָלקסבילדונג אין ײדישן לעבן,
אַפֿרייניקן די פֿראַגע פֿון אַלע אירע נאַציאָנאַליסטישע פֿראַזן, אַרױסרוקן
קעגן דער נאַציאָנאַליסטישער שול־פֿראָגראַם פֿון דער גרױסער און קלײנער
בורזשואַזיע זײן אייגענע שול־פֿראָגראַם — דאָס איז די אױפֿגאַבע פֿון דער
ײדישער אַרבעטער־דעמאָקראַטיע"... „די ײדישע שולפֿראַגע דאָס איז אַ
פֿראַגע װעגן דעם, װאָס פֿאַר אַ שול דאַרף באַשאַפֿן װערן נישט פֿאַר דעם
אָדער יענעם הײפֿל קינדער, נאָר פֿאַר דער גאַנצער ײדישער פֿאָלקסמאַסע...
די ײדישע שולפֿראַגע איז פֿריער פֿון אַלץ אַ פּאָליטישע פֿראַגע, אַ פֿראַ־

גראם־פראנע.‏ און דערום איז שוין דאָס אויך א פאַרטיי־פראנע.‏ נישט
צופעליס איז דאָס, וואָס די אָדער יענע פאַרטייאישע יידישע ריכטונג קוקט
אזוי אָדער אנדערש אויפן חדר, און ניט אזא אָדער אן אנדער ענטפער
אויף דער פראנע וועגן יידיש אָדער העברעאיש אין דער פאָלקסשול.‏ דער
ענטפער פון יעדער גרופע איז ענג פאַרבונדן מיט איר אלגעמיינער וועלט־
אָנשויאונג.‏ די שולפראנע איז א פאָליטישע פראנע.‏ אויסארבעטן דעם איי־
נעמם שול־פראָגראם הייסט פאַר דער יידישער ארבעטער־דעמאָקראטיע
פאָרמולירן די פאָליטישע פאָדערונגען אירע, מיט וועלכע זי האָט זיך צו,
וועגדן צו דער מלוכה, פאַרבינדן די פאָדערונגען מיט איר אלגעמיינעם
פּראָגראם".‏

אזוי האָט דער „בונד" דערצוויגן זיינע אָנהענגער אין דער שול־פראנע.‏
אינעם קאַפּיטל, וועגן דער חברה מפיצי השכלה און איר באַציונג צו יידיש
דערציילן מיר, געגוי וועגן די ברייט־פאַרמאַסטענע קאַמפן וואָס די בונדיסטן
האָבן יענע יאָרן געפירט אין די אָרטיקע אָפּטיילונגען פון דער חמפ״ה און
אויף אירע יערלעכע קאָנפערענצן אין פּעטערבורג.‏

נישט נאָר איז געווען גרוים די ראָל פון „בונד" אינעם אויסקריסטאַלי־
זירן דעם געדאַנק פון א יידיש־וועלטלעכער פאָלקסשול.‏ ער איז געווען דער
ערשטער ארויסצוברענגען דעם דאָזיקן געדאַנק אויף דער וועלט.‏ ער האָט
די שולפראנע פאַרוואַנדלט אין א גרוים געזעלשאפטלעך פּראָבלעם פון
יידיש־נאַציאָנאלער גלייכבאַרעכטונג.‏ ער האָט די יידישע לערערשאפט
אויפגעוועקט צום באַוווסטזיין פון זייער דערציערישער פליבט צום יידיש
פאָלק.‏ ער האָט די שול דערהויבן צו א ברייטער פּאָליטיש־סאָציאלער אויפ־
גאַבע.‏ ער האָט אָנגעצייכנט די פאָרמען פון פּאָליטישן קאַמף פאַר דער
אידעע פון א יידיש־וועלטלעכער שול־סיסטעם, ווי אויך די פאָרמען פון
דער זעלבסטעטטיקייט און זעלבסט־אָרגאַניזאַציע פון די נידישע מאַסן
פאַר אן איינענער שול.‏ ער האָט פאַרבונדן דעם שול־קאַמף מיט דעם גאַנצן
סאָציאלן און באַפריאונגס־קאַמף פונעם יידישן ארבעטער־קלאַס.‏

די געשילדערטע טעטיקייט פון „בונד" האָט צוגעגרייט דעם באָדן און
די מעטאָדן פון דער שפּעטערדיקער „צענטראַלער יידישער שול־אָרגאַני־
זאַציע" אין פּוילן, אין וועלכער דער „בונד" האָט געשפּילט אזא גרוימע
היסטאָרישע ראָל.‏

The writers and artists of *yung vilne* (Young Vilna) march onto the stage of Yiddish literature (cover pages of their first two annual publications).

צוויי שפראַכן – איינאיינציקע ליטעראַטור

בעל־מחשבות

SUMMARY: TWO LANGUAGES – ONE LITERATURE (1908)
BY BAL-MAKHSHOVES

*A major literary critic of the early part of the twentieth century (1873–1924)
explains traditional Jewish diglossia (= societal bilingualism) and the widespread
concomitant pattern among writers of writing both in Hebrew and in Yiddish. As a
result, he considers both languages, together, to constitute one Jewish literature, just
as Jews, with two languages, constitute one people.*

I

די בין גיט האָניק, און די ליטעראַטן – ליטעראַטור.
זוכט נישט ביי דער בין אַ באַזונדער כּוונה. זי איז מהנה דעם
מענטשן נישט ווילנדיקערהייט מיט איר זיסן האָניק. און ס׳איז
איר אפילו נישט באַקאַנט, אַז זי ברענגט מיט איר האָניק אַ שטיקל
דערלייכטערונג פאַר קראַנקע לונגען. און ווער ווייס? ווען אַ בין
וואָלט געקאָנט רעדן, וואָלטן מיר אפשר געהערט אירע טיפע
זיפצן און די קללות, מיט וועלכע זי פאַרשילט איר ביטערן מזל,
וואָס צווינגט איר צו געבן דעם זיסן האָניק.

אַנטקעגן וואָס זאָג איך דאָס? אַנטקעגן אונדזער ליטעראַטור
אין די לעצטע יאָרן.

ביי אונדז איז באַשאַפן געוואָרן אַ נייַער סאָרט מענטש, וואָס
איז אַ שרייַבער אי מאָנטיק, אי דינסטיק, סיי אַ גאַנץ יאָר. אָט
דער סאָרט מענטש האָט זיך גענומען אַ פעסטן הסכּם אַרויס־
צוגעבן פון זיך ליטעראַטור. זיינע אויגן זעען נאָר דאָס, וואָס
טראָגט אויף זיך די סימנים פון אַ ליטעראַרישער טעמע. זיין

הארץ קלאָפט גאָר דעמאָלט, וועגן עס באַקומט אַ ליטעראַרישן איינ־
דרוק, און איטלעך וואַכעדיקע זאַך נעמט אָן ביי אים אַ ליטע־
ראַרישע פאָרעם. און דער סאָרט מענטשן, ווילנדיק צי נישט,
באַשאַפן מיט מי און מאַטערניש דאָס, וואָס מען רופט אָן ליטע־
ראַטור. זיי האָבן מיר צו פאַרדאַנקען, וואָס פון צייט צו צייט
באַוויזן זיך ביי אונדז גראָבע און דינע ביכלעך, וואָס היינט
טראָגן זיי אויף זיך דעם נאָמען „ספרות", מאָרגן „ליטעראַרישע
מאָנאַטשריפטן" און איבערמאָרגן „קונסט און לעבן"; אַ „מעורר"
אין לאָנדאָן, אַ „רביבים" אין לעמבערג, אַ „רשפים" אין וואַרשע
און אַ „העתיד" אין בערלין־קראַקאָו.

און זוכט נישט, ליבע לייט, עפעס אַ צוזאַמענבונד ,אַן איינציקע
טענדענץ אין אַלע די זאַמלביכער. ד"ר י. קלויזנער, ש"י איש הורוויץ
און זיין אייביקער קעגנער האַראָדעצקי זיצן אַלע ביי איין טיש פון
„העתיד"; הלל צייטלין און ראובן בריינין פאַרייניקן זיך צוזאַמען מיט
ד. פרישמאַן אין די געצעלטן פון „ספרות". הער ח. ברענער אין זיין
„המעורר" און אין זיין „רביבים" פאָרט צוזאַמען מ. קליינמאַן מיט מ. י.
בערדיטשעווסקי. אין די „ליטעראַרישע מאָנאַטשריפטן" האָבן זיך פאַר־
אייניקט דריי זינגערלעך פון דריי יידישע פאַרטייען, ה' וויטער, גאָרעליק
און ניגער, צו איין איינציקן כאָר. און אין „בירנבוימס וואָכנבלאַט"
האָבן זיך צוזאַמענגעטראָפן י. ל. פרץ, עפעס אַיינער אַ א. קליינמאַן און
בירנבוים אַליין. דער „השלוח" איז געווען דער איינציקער זשורנאַל, וואָס
איז אַ צייט געווען ריין ווי גאָלד און האָט זיך מיט קיינעם חלילה נישט
אויסגעמישט. נאָר זייט ה' נ. סאָקאָלאָוו האָט זיך באַוויזן אין אַמאָליקן
אחד־העם'ס אָרגאַן, האָט ער פאַרלאָרן זיינע תמימות און אונטערשיידט
זיך שוין נישט פון אַנדערע זאַמלביכער. אויך ער איז געוואָרן אַ דעפאָ
פון אַלערליי ליטעראַטור, וואָס ווייס נישט פון קיין שום טענדענצן און
פניות.

II

מען באַקלאָגט זיך וואָס אונדזערע ליטעראַרישע אונטערנעמונגען
האָבן אָפּגעשניטענע יאָרן. מען איז זיך מצער אויף ,דעם יונגן „המעורר",
וואָס האָט זיך גיך אַזוי אָפּגעטראָגן פון דער וועלט, אויף ,די ליטע־
ראַרישע מאָנאַטשריפטן" וואָס האָבן נישט דערלעבט אַרויסצוגיין פון די
וויקעלעך א. אז. וו.   אָבער איך אַלס געטרייער לייענער טראַכט נישט

אזוי. איך האב זיך איבערצייגט, אז מיר האבן גארנישט פארלארן. עס
האבן זיך נאר געביטן ביי אונדז די נעמען און די שפראכן פון אונדזערע
אויסגאבן, אבער די שרייבער האבן זיך ביי אונדז נישט געביטן. אויב
דער שלעכטער מזל פון די שרייבער האט געבראכט דערצו, אז איינער
פון די אלמאנאכן איז אוועק שלאפן, — האבן זיי זיך באלד צונויפגעקליבן
אין אן אנדערן, וואס אונטערשיידט זיך פון ערשטן נאר דורך זיין נאמען
און זיין שפראך. אויב מען מאכט היינט צו פאר זיי די ליכטיקע זאלן
פון די „ליטעראַרישע מאַנאַטשריפטן" — קלייבן זיי זיך צונויף אין אן
אנדער זאַמלבוך, — מיינעטוועגן אַ העברעאישן — און שרייבן העב־
רעאיש. אויב איינער אַ פאַרלעגער מאכט־צו היינט זיין זשאַרגאַניש
קרעמל, עפנט זיך אויף באלד אַ העברעאיש קרעמל מיט דער אייגענער
סחורה אויף העברעאיש. האט אייך צייטלין געעגבן אויף יידיש אין
„היינט" זיינע פיערדיקע מוסר־ארטיקלען, גיט ער אייך מארגן דאָס
אייגענע אין דער נביאים־שפראך אין די „רשפים". ח. י. ברענערס
מאמרים אין „רביבים" געפינט איר אין „היינט" אונטער דעם נייעם
טיטל „שטילע ווערטער". נאָמבערג געפינט אפילו נישט פאר נויטיק צו
בייטן דעם נאָמען, ווען ער שרייבט איבער אויף העברעאיש דאָס, וואָס
ער האט פריער געשריבן אין זשאַרגאָן. דאָס וואָס האָט אין „יוד" ע״ה
געהייסן „אויף אַיין קוואַרטיר" באַווייזט זיך היינט אין „ספרות" אונטער
דעם טיטל „במעון אחד".

די יידישע ליטעראַטור גייט, חלילה, נישט צו גרונד. זי איז איינע
און איר נאָמען איז איינער. נאָר זי קומט צום לייענער אין צוויי גע־
שטאַלטן און ווי די שאָלן אויפן וואָגשאָל שאָקלען זי זיך צוויי איינער
אנטקעגען דער אנדערער. און אזוי ווי אין דער נאטור איז קיין זאַך
נישט אבסאָלוט — באַוועגן זיך די שאָלן ארויף און אראָפ. אמאָל זיגט
די ערשטע, אמאָל די צווייטע שאַל. היינט קומט ברענער אין אַ זשאַר־
גאַנישן בגד. מאָרגן שלום עליכם אין אַ העברעאישן. פאַראיאָרן איז
נאָמבערג געוואָרן אַ העברעער אין „הזמן", היינט איז ער אַ זשאַרגאַן־יִיד
אין „אונדזער לעבן" און אין „ראָמאַנצייטונג". צי שפילט טאַקע אַ ראָלע
אין אַ זאַמלבוך דער נאָמען, דער טיפּאָגראַפישער פּנים און דער פּאָר־
לעגער? אין די לעצטע יאָרן איז אַנגענומען געוואָרן, אז אזוי ווי אַ
קאָרעספּאָנדענט אין אַ קאָנטאָר מוז קענען פרעמדע שפּראַכן, אזוי מוז
דער יידישער שרייבער קענען לכל הפחות צוויי שפּראַכן, דערמיט ער
זאָל קענען פריי שאַפּן. צום יוביליי פון י. ל. פּרץ זיינען ארויס צוויי

אויסאַבן פון זײַנע "געזאַמלטע שריפטן", אײַנע אין העברעאיש, אײַנע
אין ייִדיש. און אַז מען האָט געפּרעגט דעם יוביליאַר, וואו פון די ביידע
אויסגאַבן קען מען געפינען דעם אמתן פּרץ, האָט ער געעַנטפערט מיט
גרויס עניוות, אַז אין ביידע "געזאַמלטע שריפטן" זײַנען צעשפּרייט די
פונקען פון זײַן גײַסט. און ווער עס וויל באַנעמען זײַן גרויסקייט
און די אײַנציקייט פון זײַן נשמה — מוז זיך פאַרטיפן אין ביידע
"געזאַמלטע שריפטן". איצט קלייבט מען זיך אַרויסגעבן אַ ייִדיש זאַמל־
ווערק פון ד. פרישמאַנס שריפטן. און איך בין זיכער, אַז ווען ר'
מענדעלע וועט ווערן אַ 75־ער, וועלן זיך געפינען מענטשן, וואָס וועלן
אים פּראָקלאַמירן פאַר אַ העברעער און אַרויסגעבן זײַנע "געזאַמלטע"
אין העברעאיש.. און שלום עליכם האָט נישט לאַנג אַליין געזאַגט, אַז
כל זמן ער וועט נישט איבערזעצן אַלע זײַנע שריפטן אין העברעאיש,
וועט דער מלאך־המות קיין שליטה אויף אים נישט האָבן! אויך נ.
סאָקאָלאָוו איז נישט זיכער, אַז ער וועט נישט באַקומען זײַן זשאַרגאַנישן
פּנים. זײַנע אַרטיקלען אין "טעלעגראַף" וועלן אויספילן אַ באַנד נישט
דינער פון אַ סלאַוויטער גמרא. אונדזער ליטעראַטור האָט זיך אין איר
שאַצקאַמער אַ זשאַרגאַנישן ביאַליק, אַ זשאַרגאַנישן בערדיטשעווסקי ;
אפילו אויך אַ זשאַרגאַנישן ... קלויזנער. נאָר אַין אַחד העם מאַכט אַן
אויסנאַם. נאָר אַחד העם זאָגט דאָך אַליין וועגן זיך, אַז ער איז נישט
קיין שרײַבער (זע זײַן על פּרשת דרכים), און דעריבער טאַקע האָט זײַן
"אמת מארץ ישראל" נישט קיין זשאַרגאַנישן נאָמען, כאַטש אין זשאַרגאַן
לאָזט זיך דאַס אויך כמעט נישט איבערזעצן מיט אַנדערע ווערטער,
ווי "אַן אמת וועגן ארץ ישראל".

III

עס געפינען זיך ביי אונדז צעפלאַמטע לייענער, וואָס ווילן נישט
מודה זײַן, אַז אונדזער אײַן־אײַנציקע ליטעראַטאָר האָט אַ טאָפּלטע
שפּראַך. נאָר דער טשערנאַוויצער קאָנפערענץ האָט אײַנער אַ העברעאי־
שער שרײַבער (ער געפינט זיך איצט אין אַמעריקע) זיך אַ נדר געטאָן
פון היינט אָן נישט צו באַפלעקן זײַן פעדער מיט אַ זשאַרגאַניש וואָרט.
און אַזאַ נדר איז ביי אים נישט געווען קיין קלייניקייט! דען ער האָט
דערמיט צעריסן זײַן בונד צווישן זיך און זײַן מאַמען, וואָס וואוינט אין
רוסלאַנד, און צו וועלכער ער איז אַ געטרייַער זון. און ווידער איז מיר
באַקאַנט אַ פאַקט, ווען אַ פאַרברענטער זשאַרגאַניסט האָט נאָך ש. אשש

דרשה אין טשערנאָוויץ אָנגעהויבן לערנען זיין ייִנגל דעם „מודה אני"
אויף אַ ריינעם זשאַרגאָן. נאָר אויך דאָס איז אים אָנגעקומען נישט
מינדער שווער, ווי יענעמס נדר, ווייל דער „מודה אני" קומט אַרויס
אויף ייִדיש אָן געשמאַק, אָן פעפער און זאַלץ. איבעריקנס, זייער
פאַנאַטיזם האָט לאַנג נישט געהאַלטן. דער העברעאישער שרייבער איז
אין גיכן געװאָרן אַ רעדאַקטאָר פון אַ ציוניסטיש בלאַט. און דער
פאַנאַטישער זשאַרגאָניסט איז אָנפאַנג זמן אַריין אין אַ „אַגודת מלמדים"
אַלס חבר; און װי באַקאַנט לערנט מען דאָך ביי די ניי־מאָדנע מלמדים
„עברית בעברית".

די טשערנאָוויצער רעזאָלוציע איז װי אַ רויך צעקראָכן. דער טשער-

His Yiddish muse to Yehoyesh, prior to his departure for Palestine: 'Bon voyage, my dear. But do not run away with Madam Hebrew, with whom you carried on a love affair in your youth.' (*Der groyser kundes*, December 19, 1913)

נאָוויצער צוזאַמענפאָר, וואָס איז 90 פּראָצענט באַשטאַנען פון שרייבער,
האָט אַ ווײלע פאַרגעסן, אַז ס׳איז דאָ שרײבער בײ ייִדן. זײ, די שרײַ־
בער, האָבן מיט אַ מאָל פאַרגעסן, אַז ס׳איז שוין אַזוי זייער מזל צו
קלײַבן שטרוי פאַר צווייערליי ציגל, צו באַאַקערן צווייערליי שפּראַכן.

עס איז שוין אַן אַלטע מעשה, אַז מיטגלידער פון קאָנגרעסן זײַנען
געוואָלטיקע אידעאַליסטן און זײ האָבן אַ נייגונג צו ווערן אַ ביסעלע
סענטימענטאַל. עפּעס אַ קלייניקייט! עס שיקט זיי דאָך אַ כּלל ייִדן,
און זיי קעמפן דאָך פאַר די נאַציאָנאַלע פאָדערונגען! די דאָקטוירים
האָבן שוין לאַנג באַמערקט, אַז דער פּולס בײ אַ מיטגליד פון אַ צוזאַמענ־
פאָר קלאַפט מיט 10 שלעג שטאַרקער ווי געוויינלעך, און אַז זײַן
פאַנטאַזיע אַרבעט מיט 5 פּראָצענט קרעפטיקער ווי אַ גאַנץ יאָר. אַ סך
אַמעריקאַנישע דאָקטוירים זײַנען מיט דער מיינונג, אַז קאַלטע אָפּ־
רײבונגען, אַ רייזע אין אַ לופט־באַלאָן און אַן אָנטיילנעמען אין אַ
צוזאַמענפאָר זײַנען די בעסטע מיטלען קעגן מידע נערוון און בלוט־
אָרעמקייט.

אַ פּשוטער מענטש קאָן זיך גאָר נישט פאָרשטעלן, וואָס פאַר
אַ מחיה דאָס איז אויף אַ פּאָר טעג אין יאָר אַוועקצואוואַרפן די אייגענע
דאגות און נאָר טאָן און דאגהנען וועגן אַנדערע. למשל, וועו שלום אַש
וואָלט זיך נישט געאײַלט שרײַבן זײַן „שבתי צבי" פאַרן טשערנאָוויצער
צוזאַמענפאָר, בשעת ער איז געווען צופיל פאַרטאָן מיט זיך און מיט
זײַנע איבערזעצער, וואָס האָבן געדאַרפט איבערזעצן זײַן נייע שאַפונג
אין זיבעציק שפּראַכן; וועו ער וואָלט געשריבן זײַן ווערק אין די טעג
פון צוזאַמענפאָר, בשעת די נשמה איז אַזוי פול מיט אידעאַלן, —
אפשר וואָלט דאָס ווערק אַרויס אַ סך בעסער, אָדער, וואָס איז וואַר־
שײַנלעכער, עס וואָלט אפשר גאָר נישט דערזען די שײַן פון דער
וועלט. איך חזר איבער מײַנע פריערדיקע רייד. אַ פּראָסטער מענטש
האָט גאָר נישט קיין באַגריף, ווי וואויל און גוט עס איז צו פאַרגעסן
אויף אַ ווײַלע די אייגענע זאָרגן, און זיך ברעכן דעם קאָפּ וועגן
פרעמדע צרות! וועו די טשערנאָוויצער שרייבער וואָלטן מער געטראַכט
וועגן זיך, ווי וועגן פרעמדע עסקים, וואָלטן זיי דעמאָלט, ערשטנס,
זיך געטאָן אַ האַרבן נדר צו שרײַבן נאָר אין איין שפּראַך; צווייטנס,
וואָלטן זיי באַקאָטירט איטלעכן, וואָס שרײַבט אין העברעאישע בלע־
טער; דריטנס, וואָלטן זיי געצוואונגען די העברעאישע בלעטער די
זשאַרגאָנישע אַרטיקלען נישט אויסצוגעבן אַלס אָריגינעל.   מיט איין

Wealthy dowager Hebrew (to I. L. Perets, walking arm in arm with Yiddish): 'Woe unto me that I have lived to see such things in my old age! My Perets, at the age of 60, is romancing the servant girl.' Perets: 'Come, we will ride in the chariot of time...we will spin gold and silver...we will build palaces of marble...' (*Der groyser kundes*, June 16, 1911)

וואָרט, זיי האָבן זיך געדאַרפט מוסר נפש זיין פאַרן זשאַרגאָן און פאַר־
קלענערן די מעגלעכקייט צו קריגן אַן איבעריקן אָרעמען האָנאָראַר
דורך דעם, וואָס זיי דרוקן זיך צוויי צוויי מאָל: יידיש און העברעאיש. זאָל
זיך זיי נישט גלוסטן היינט צו זיין אין "ספרות" און מאָרגן אין "די
ליטעראַרישע מאָנאַטשריפטן" און אַ . וו. א. אַז. וו. אָבער אָנצונעמען
ביי זיך אַזאַ הסכם איז פיל שוועערער, ווי אָנצונעמען אַ רעזאָלוציע, אַז
דער זשאַרגאָן איז אונדזער נאַציאָנאַל־שפראַך. ס׳איז לייכטער צו זיין
דער גורם פון צעבלוטיקטע קעפ ביי די טשערנאָוויצער סטודענטן, וואָס
זיינען זיך מפקיר פאַר אַ טשערנאָוויצער רעזאָלוציע, ווי צו באַשליסן
זיך נישט צו זיין אין דער זעלבער צייט אַ מיטאַרבעטער אין "טעאַטער־
וועלט", "יוגנט־וועלט" און אין אַ "ספרות". אַוודאי, איז פיל גרינגער
אַ שרייבער דעם צווייטן צוצודריקן צו דער וואַנט מיט אַ רעזאָלוציע,
ווי אָפצוזאָגן זיך פון אַ האָנאָראַר פון אַן אָרעם יידיש בלעטל.

איך מיין נישט חלילה עמיצן פוגע בכבוד צו זיין. איך וויל נאָר
אָנווייזן, אַז די טשערנאָוויצער פון גרויס אידעאַליזם און פון גרויס
ליבשאַפט צום פאָלק האָבן אויף אַ רגע פאַרגעסן, אַז פריער פאַר אַלץ
זיינען זיי יידישע שרייבער, און זיי לעבן און עטעמען צווישן צוויי
שפראַכן, ווי אַ חתן צווישן צווויי מחותנים־אונטערפירער.

IV

און צי עטעמט און לעבט דער שרייבער נאָר צווישן צוויי שפראַכן?
צי טראָגט זיך נישט פון אונדזערע בעסערע קריטיקער דער גייסט פון
דער דייטשער שפראַך? און ביי אונדזערע יינגערע שרייבער, וואָס האָבן
זיך דערצויגן אויף דער רוסישער ליטעראַטור, צי הערט מען נישט
דעם גייסט פון דער רוסישער שפראַך? און צי הערט מען נישט ביי
אונדזערע קאָלעגן די פאַלעסטינער שרייבער (בן־אבי, חרמוני) דעם
אָפקלאַנג פון דער פראַנצויזישער שפראַך?

אמת, עס געפינען זיך ביי אונדז שפראַך־קינסטלער, ווי ביאַליק, נ.
סאָקאָלאָוו, אַבראַמאָוויטש, שלום־עליכם, וואָס שרייבן צייטנווייז אין אַזאַ
שפראַך, אַז מען קאָן מיינען, דאָס אין יידישן תחום איז נאָך נישט
אַריינגעדרונגען קיין וואָרט, וואָס זאָל נישט דורך און דורך זיין יידיש־
נאַציאָנאַל. געווויס געפינען זיך ביי אונדז אַ סך טאַלענטירטע שרייבער,
וועלכע מיען זיך צו באַשאַפן אַ העברעאישן שפראַך־גייסט, וואָס זאָל
זיין די נאַטירלעכע צוזאַמענפליסונג פון תנ״ך־לשון, פון דער נביאים־

שפּראַך, פֿון דער שפּראַך פֿון משנה, מדרש און דער יוריסטישער,
פֿילאָסאָפֿישער, מיסטישער שפּראַך פֿון גמרא, מיטלאַלטער־פֿילאָסאָפֿיע,
קבלה און חסידות. אחד־העם, בערדיטשעוּוסקי, צייטלין און אַנד. זיינען
די דאָזיקע טאַלענטן, וואָס מען זיך צו באַשאַפֿן אַזאַ צוזאַמענפֿליסונג
פֿון די פֿאַרשידענע ריינע עלעמענטן אין דער העברעאישער שפּראַך.
דערווייל אָבער איז אויך העברעאיש אַן אויסמישעניש פֿון צענדליקער
שפּראַך־גייסטער. און ס׳איז נאָך אַ גרויסער ספֿק בײַ מיר, צי וועט
דער קינפֿטיקער ארץ־ישׂראלדיקער דור, וואָס איז שוין ווייט פֿון רוסיש
ווי פֿון אַ רוסישן פּאָגראָם, פֿאַרשטיין גאָר די שפּראַך פֿון ברענער,
שאַפּמאַן און אַנד.

דער גייסט פֿון דער דייטשער שפּראַך איז אוּמעטום גלייך.   עס איז
קיין חילוק נישט ווער עס שרייבט אויף איר: צי אַ דייטש, אַן אַמערי־

Three in one: Osip Dimov. His friends (right) claim that two literatures (Russian and Yiddish) are eager to have him. His enemies (center) claim that he has actually been torn in half by the struggle. The truth (left) is that he is the hero of one of his own dramas (The Eternal Wanderer) with his constant alternation between one literature and the other. (*Der groyser kundes*, May 5, 1916)

קאָגישער דייטש, צי אַ שוװייצער. דאָס אייגענע איז מיט דער פראַנ־
צױזישער, קאַטש די בעלגיער, ־די פראַנצױזישע שװייצער און די
פראַנצױזן אַליין שטאַמען אײטלעכער אָפּ פון אַן אַנדער שבט. אַנדערש
איז דאָס מיט דער העברעאישער שפּראַך, װאָס איר גייסט איז אַנדערש
אין יעדער מדינה. פון אונטער דער מאַסקע פון די װערטער שפּאַרט
אַרױס דער גייסט פון אַ פרעמדער שפּראַך. און װאָס אָנבאַלאַנגט דעם
זשאַרגאָן איז דאָס נאָך ערגער. איר ריינקייט איז נאָך טױזנט מאָל
פאַרדעכטיקער, װי ביי דער העברעאישער שפּראַך. דען העברעאיש
האָט נאָך אױסער דער געגנװאַרט אַ געשיכטע און אַ ליטעראַטור פון
טױזנטער יאָרן, און אַדאַנק דעם קאָן זי נאָך האָפן צו באַשאַפן אַמאָל
אַ שפּראַך מיט אַ ריינעם נאַציאָנאַלן גייסט. דער זשאַרגאָן האָט אָבער
נאָר אַ געגנװאַרט. מאַכן אַ סינטעז צװישן ״צאינה וראינה״, אייזיק
מאיר דיק, אַקסענפעלד, עטינגער, שמ״ר, יידישע פאָלקס־לידער, אליקום
צונזער, די ציוניסטישע, בונדיסטישע בראָשורן און די אַמעריקאַנישע
ליטעראַטור — װעט מען הסתּם קיינעם נישט איינפאַלן. אױב זאָלן
פאַרגלייכן די העברעאישע שפּראַך מיט אַן אינדזל אין אַ ים פון
פרעמדע לשונות, װאָס װילן זי איינשלינגען, טאָ מיט װאָס זאָלן מיר
שױן פאַרגלייכן דעם זשאַרגאָן? אפשר צו אַן איינפאָר־הױז אױף אַ מיטן
שליאַך, װאו איטלעכער שטעלט זיך אָפּ װי ביי זיך אין דער היים,
אָבער קיינער בלײבט דאָרט ניט לענגער, װי אַ קורצע װיילע? נאָר די
געגנװאַרט קאָן מאַכן פון זשאַרגאָן אַ ליטעראַרישע שפּראַך, נאָר פון
דער געגנװאַרט ציט זיך איר חיות. אָבער אונדזער געגנװאַרט איז פון
דעם מין, װאָס װיל נישט און קען נישט באַשאַפן אַ ממשותדיקע זאַך.
באַשאַפן אַ שפּראַך, װי יעדע נייע שאַפונג, קאָן מען נאָר דאָרטן, װאו
עס איז רואיק און שטיל, װאו עס ־דרינגען נישט אַריין די קולות פון
מאַרק און די זיפצן פון נױט. אַ פּאָלק אַ װאַנדערער איז אָבער נישט
בכוח צו בילדן אַ שטילע סביבה אַרום זיך. נישט גענוג װאָס ער קאָן
גאָר נישט טאָן פאַר דער שפּראַך, פאַראומרייניקט און פאַרשװעכט ער
זי נאָך אױף איטלעכן שליאַך פון זײן אייביקער װאַנדערונג.

⁂

״אונד װאָס איזט דער רעדע קורצער זין?״ — אַז שפּראַכן האָבן
מיר צװיי און אַ טוץ גײסטער פון פרעמדע שפּראַכן, אָבער אַ ליטעראַטור
האָבן מיר נאָר איינע. און דעריבער טאָר דער לײענער, װאָס װיל זיך
באַקענען מיט שטרעמונגען פון יידישן לעבן, באַגרייפן דעם גײסט פון

ייִדישן המון און דעם יחיד, ווי דאָס דריקט זיך אויס אין אונדזער
ליטעראַטור, — דעריבער טאָר ער נישט מאַכן קיין חילוק צווישן אַ
העברעאישן און אַ זשאַרגאָנישן שרײַבער. ר' מענדעלע, ביאַליק, שלום־
עליכם, בערדיטשעווסקי, פּיערבערג און אַז. וו. — אַלע זיינען זיי די
פאַרשטייער פון אונדזער ליטעראַטור, אַלע פאַרקערפערן אַ שטיק ייִדיש
לעבן אין דער ליטעראַטור, אַלע זיינען זיי ייִדישע קינסטלער, כאָטש
נישט אַלע באַנוצן זיך מיט די צוויי שפּראַכן, אויסצודריקן זייערע
קונסט־מאָטיוון.   1918

(*V

איבער די ברייטע גאַסן פון אַ דרום־רוסישער
שטאָט האָט דער המון יום־טובדיק געטראָגן דאָס בילד פון שעוטשענקאָ,
באַקראַנצט מיט לאָרבער־בלעטער, אַרומגערינגלט מיט נאַציאָנאַל־
אוקראַינישע פאָנען. פון דערווייַטנס האָט מען געקאָנט מיינען, אַז דאָס
באַוועגט זיך אַ רעליגיעזע פּראָצעסיע, אַז דאָס טראָגט מען די הייליקייטן
פון אַ קאַסטיאָל, אָדער די „באָזשע מאַטקאַ".

אָט אַזוי גיבן איצט כבוד אָפּ די פריי־געוואָרענע נאַציעס אין
רוסלאַנד זייערע גייסטיקע פאַרטרעטער, זייערע שאַפער פון אַ נאַציאָ־
נאַלער ליטעראַטור.

וואָרום די באַדײַטונג פון דער ליטעראַטור אין דעם איצטיקן
מאָמענט איז נישט גענוג אָפּצושאַצן. זי איז דער סימן פון אַ נאַטיר־
לעכער אָפּגעשיידטקייט פון אויסן און אַ צוזאַמענגעבונדנקייט פון
אינעווייניק. אַלץ, וואָס שיידט אָפּ — פאַרבינדט, און דאָס, וואָס פאַר־
בינדט נאַטירלעכע, ריין־אָרגאַניש, באַקומט דאָס רעכט צו פאַרלאַנגען,
אַז מען זאָל דאָס באַטראַכטן אַלס עפּעס אַזוינס, וואָס דאַרף און מוז זיך
פריי אַנטוויקלען.

כל זמן אַ פאָלק האָט נישט קיין ליטעראַטור, קאָן מען זאָגן, אַז
דאָס איז שטום. דער איינצלנער רעדט, דאָס פאָלק איז אָבער שטום —
שטיל. אַן אמתע ליטעראַטור איז דאָס צויבער־קעסטעלע, וואו עס איז
זיך מצמצם דער גייסט פון פאָלק אין אַלע זיינע צרות, האָפענונגען,
צוקונפט־אידעאַלן, און געגנוואַרט־אידעאַלן. ליטעראַטור איז די תורה

---

*) דער טייל פון אַרטיקל: „צוויי שפּראַכן—איינאיינציקע ליטעראַטור", וואָס
הייבט זיך אָן מיט קאַפּיטל V, איז געשריבן געוואָרן מיט יאָרן שפּעטער.

שבעל פּה, וואָס ווערט אַ תּורה שבּכתב און וואָס וואָקסט די ערשטע
תּורה נאָך שטאַרק, שטאַרק אַריבער. די וואָס בלייבן אייביק בּיי זייער
תּורה שבעל פּה ווערן אין גיכן פֿאַרגליווערט און ווערן אויסגעמעקט
פֿון ספֿר האומות. דער בּעסטער בּיישפּיל זיינען די קאַראַאימען. דוכט
זיך, דער אייגענער אָפּשטאַם, וואָס מיר, אפֿשר קאָן אַ היינטיקער
שאַפּשאַל ציִעﬞ זיין יחוס פֿון דוד המלך אָן. און פֿון דעסטוועגן רעכנט
זיך קיינער נישט מיט די קאַראַאימען, ווי מיט אַ נאַציע. אין דעם כאַר
פֿון די פֿעלקער, וואָס וועט קלינגען אין דער גרינדונגס־פֿאַרזאַמלונג,
וועט זייער שטים נישט מיטזינגען.

פֿאַר אונטערגעדריקטע פעלקער איז שטענדיק געווען זייער ליטע־
ראַטור אַ מין אייגענע טעריטאָריע, וואו זיי האָבן זיך געפֿילט, ווי אין
דערהיים. ווייניקסטנס איז דאָס געווען אַ מין עקס־טעריטאָריאַליטעט,
אַזוי ווי דער פּאַלאַץ פֿון פֿראַנצויזישן אָדער אַן ענגלישן געזאַנדטן
ערגעץ אין אַ פֿרעמד לאַנד. ביים שוועל פֿון פּאַלאַץ האָט שוין דאָס
פֿרעמד לאַנד נישט געהאַט קיין שליטה אויף אים. הינטער די טירן
פֿון זיין פּאַלאַץ האָט ער געלעבט אין טערקיי, אָדער פּערסיע, ווי ביי
זיך אין דערהיים, נישט האַבנדיק איבער זיך קיין שום מאַכט, חוץ זיין
אייגענער נאַציאָנאַלער מלוכה.

אויך מיר יידן האָבן נאָר געקאָנט אַריבערלעבן די **היסטאָרישע**
צייטן צוליב אונדזער עקס־טעריטאָריאַליטעט. היינע האָט אַמאָל פֿאַר־
גליכן די ביבל ביי יידן מיט אַ פֿאַטערלאַנד. וואָס גייט מיט אין באַגאַזש
(די ביבל איז „דאָס פּאָרטאַטיווע פֿאַטערלאַנד"). און אין דעם טיטול
„עם הספר", מיט וואָס די געשיכטע האָט אונדז געקרוינט, ליופֿט קלאָר
דורך דער געדאַנק, אַז אונדזער ערד, אונדזער היים איז שטענדיק
געווען אונדזער ליטעראַטור. זעלבסטפֿאַרשטענדלעך, דאַרף מען באַ־
נעמען דאָס וואָרט „ליטעראַטור" אין ברייטערן זין פֿונעם וואָרט. אַלץ
וואָס דריקט אויס די גייסטיקע באַוועגונגען פֿון אַ פֿאָלק, סיי וויסנשאַפֿט,
פֿילאָסאָפֿיע, פּובליציסטיק, פּאַעזיע א. אַז. וו.. און ווערט אָנגענומען
פֿונעם פֿאָלק, איז דאָס, וואָס מיר רופֿן אָן מיט שטאָלץ נאַציאָנאַלע
ליטעראַטור.

VI

אונדזער ליטעראַטור איז אָבער פֿון אייביק אָן כמעט געווען אַ צוויי־
שפּראַכנדיקע, און די דאָזיקע לייט ביי אונדז, וואָס קאָנען קיינמאָל נישט
אָפּטיילן די ליטעראַטור פֿון דער שפּראַך, ד. ה. דאָס גייסטיקע, וואָס
איז אָנגענומען געוואָרן פֿון די פֿאָלקס־מאַסן, פֿון די שפּראַכן, אויף
וועלכע עס רעדט די אינטעליגענץ און דאָס פֿאָלק, ווילן בשום אופֿן
זיך נישט רעכענען מיט דער דאָזיקער טאָט־זאַך. זיי ווילן נישט מודה
זיין, אַז די צוויי־שפּראַכיקייט ביי אונדז איז שוין אַזאַ אַלטע קראַנק,
אַז די קראַנק איז געוואָרן אַזוינע, וואָס זי האָט שוין אויפֿגעהערט צו
זיין אַ סכנה פֿאַרן יידישן אָרגאַניזם. זיי פֿאַרמאַכן די אויגן פֿאַר דעם,
וואָס איז באַקאַנט אַיטלעכן יידן, וואָס האָט זיך באַקענט מיט דער
געשיכטע פֿון אונדזער 2000־יעריקער ליטעראַטור.

Association des Ecrivains et Journal. Juifs
à VILNO

CERTIFICAT Nr.

Le porteur de ce certificat

M.

à

est membre de l'Association des
Ecrivains et Journalistes Juifs à Vilno

Valable jusqu'au

Vilno, le 193

Le Président:

Le Sécrétaire:

Membership card
Бленский билет

פֿאַראיין
פון יידישע ליטעראַטן און זשורנאַליסטן
אין ווילנע

לעגיטימאַציע №

דער באַזיצער פון דער דאָזיקער לעגיטימאַציע

ה׳

אין

איז אַ מיטגליד פון פֿאַראיין פון יידישע ליטעראַטן

און זשורנאַליסטן אין ווילנע.

גילטיג ביז

ווילנע, דעם 193

פֿאָרזיצער:

סעקרעטאַר:

לעגיטימאַציע
כּרטיס-חבר

Membership card: Association of Yiddish Writers and Journalists in Vilna (1930s).

ווארום די דאָזיקע צווייי־שפּראַכיקייט געפֿינען מיר שוין אין תנ״ך,
ווען דאָס חדר־יינגל דערגרייכט אין זיינע לימודים ביז דניאל און נחמיה,
און ער פֿאַלט פּלוצים אריין אינעם כאַלדעאיש פון אַ יידיש־פּערסישן
היסטאָריקער, וואָס פֿרואָוט דערציילן זיין היסטאָריע. און לערנט דאָס
יינגל די פּרקים פון די אַנשי כנסת הגדולה, איינעם פון די שענסטע
קאַפּיטלעך אין דער יידישער ליטעראַטור, מוז ער זיך וויייטער אַפּ־
שטעלן ביי אזוינע ווערטער, ווי: „על דאַטפת אטפוך וסוף מטיפיך
יטופון". און וואַקסט דאָס יינגל אויס אין אַ גמרא־בחורל, דעמאָלט
דערפֿילט עס ערשט ווי עס דארף צו זיין, וואָס פֿאַר אַ טבע עס האָט
געהאַט דער ייד צו ריידן כּסדר אויף צוויי שפּראַכן. אונטער דער
קליינער משנהלע וואַקסט אויס אַ בריייטלייביקער ייד, וואָס רעדט נאָר
אַראַמעאיש, אָן אַ שום ברעקל עברי.

און די אייגענע צווייי־שפּראַכיקייט דרינגט אריין אין אַלע פֿעלבעלעך
פון יידישן גייסטיקן פֿרומען לעבן. דער תרגום אונקולוס האָט אַ דריט־
חלק היייליקייט פון חומש. איטלעכער ייד איז מחויב מעביר קריאה

צו זיין ‏די סדרה פרייטיק צוויי מאָל אין דער שפּראַך פון משה רבינו
און איין מאָל אין תרגום אונקולוס. אין די סידורים געפֿינען מיר אויך
תפילות און זמרלעך, וואָס זיינען געשריבן אין דער שפּראַך פון „אתקינו
סעודתא".

שפּעטער, אַז דאָס יידנטום ווערט אַריינגעשטויסן צווישן די אַראַבער,
באַווייזט זיך ביי יידן א גאַנצע פילאָסאָפֿישע ליטעראַטור אין אַראַביש.
אויך דאָס באַרימטע פילאָסאָפֿישע ווערק פון מיימאָנידעס (רמב״ם).
„מורה נבוכים", וואָס האָט געשפּילט אַזאַ גרויסע ראָלע אין יידישן
גייסטיקן לעבן נאָך גאָר, גאָר נישט לאַנג, כאַטש דאָס ווערק האָט שוין
כמעט מתושלחס יאָרן, איז געווען געשריבן אַראַביש.

פון 15טן יאָרהונדערט אָן הויבט אָן זיך צו אַנטוויקלען אַ גייסטיקע
ליטעראַטור אין דער צווייטער שפּראַך — יידיש. אַקוראַט ווי אַמאָל
האָבן די יידן צוגעפּאַסט די אַראַבישע שפּראַך צו זייערע טאָג־געשעפּטן
און שפּעטער צו זייערע גייסטיקע אינטערעסן, אָט אַזוי פאַסט זיך דער
ייד צו ‏די אַלט־דייטשע שפּראַך, זינט זיין וואַנדער־לעבן האָט אים ענג
פאַרקניפּט מיט די גערמאַנען.

די בעסטע יידישע גייסטיקע קרעפּטן האָבן פון 15טן יאָרהונדערט
אָן געזוכט צו געבן דעם פאָלק ביכער אין דער יידישער שפּראַך. פון
אָן אליהו בחור ביז אַן אַבראַמאָוויטשן האָט מען זיך געמיט, אַז די
יידישע מאַסן זאָלן האָבן כאַטש א טייל פון דעם, מיט וואָס עס קוויקט
זיך דער גייסט פון ‏דער יידישער אינטעליגענץ. און דער „צאינה
וראינה" איז געוואָרן פאַרן פאָלק מיט דער צייט דאָס, וואָס דער תרגום
אונקולוס פאַר דעם ייד אין ‏דער צייט פֿאַרן צווייטן חורבן, ווען די
פֿאָלקס־מאַסן האָבן שוין נישט געקאָנט פֿאַרשטיין די ביבל־שפּראַך און
האָבן געמוזט האָבן אין די שולן אַ ספּעציעלן מתורגמן.

פון די קורץ־אָנגעמערקטע פֿאַקטן דערגייען מיר, אַז די צוויי־
שפּראַכיקייט האָט דעם ייד באַגלייט נאָך פון זייער אַלטע צייטן, נאָך
דעמאָלט, ווען ער האָט נאָך געהאַט אַ לאַנד, און איז נאָך נישט געווען
דער נע־ונדניק וואָס איצט. און דערפון איז אויך צו זען, אַז די שפּראַך,
אַלס באַזונדער היַליגטום (ווי למשל איצט ביי די פּוילן), האָט ביי
אונדז קיינמאָל נישט געשפּילט אַזאַ גרויסע ראָלע. קורץ פֿאַרן חורבן
און שפּעטער האָט ‏די פֿאַרם שוין נישט געשפּילט ביי אונדז די ערשטע
פֿידל. דער וואָנטש טיפֿער איינצופֿלאַנצן געוויסע גייסטיקע אוצרות
איז שטאַרקער געווען, ווי איינצוהאַלטן דאָס פֿאָלק אין ראַם פון אַן

איינציקער שפּראַך. און ווײל דער דאָזיקער וואָונטש האָט שטענדיק
געטראָגן אויף זיך דעם שטעמפּל פֿון — מען קאָן דרײַסט זאָגן — אַ
מאָדערנעם דעמאָקראַטיזם, דערום האָבן אונדזערע גייסטיקע פֿירער
נישט געמאַכט קיין גרויסן פּירוש פֿון דער שפּראַך. בעסער אַ צוויי־
שפּראַכיקע אומה, איידער אַזוינע, וואָס האָט נאָר איין־איינציקע שפּראַך,
אָבער נאָר פֿאַר דער אינטעליגענץ, אָן דעם פֿאָלק.

דאָס יידנטום אַלס מאָראַל־רעליגיעז־פֿילאָסאָפֿישע תורה איז נישט
עפּעס אַזוינס, וואָס ליגט אין די הענט פֿון אײנצלנע. זײן קראַפֿט איז
די קראַפֿט, וואָס עס ווערט פֿאַרשפּרײַט צווישן אַלע קלאַסן פֿון פֿאָלק.
שוין אין חומש געפֿינען מיר די שטעלע, וואו משה רבינו, דערגייענדיק,
אַז אלדד און מידד זאָגן נביאות פֿאַר די יידישע געצעלטן, זאָגט : הלוואי
זאָלן אַלע יידן זײן נביאים

און דערום האָבן די גייסטיקע פֿאַרטרעטער פֿון פֿאָלק קיינמאָל נישט
אויפֿגעהויבן די שפּראַכן־פֿראַגע, און האָבן זיך שטענדיק צוגעפּאַסט צי
דער שפּראַך, אויף וועלכער עס רײדן די גרויסע פֿאָלקס־מאַסן.

(„פּעטראָגראַדער טאַגעבלאַט", 1918.)

לערערקורסן פֿאַר ייִדיש אין לאָדזשער געטאָ

י. ל. גערשט

SUMMARY: YIDDISH SOURCES FOR TEACHERS IN THE (NAZI) GHETTO
OF LODZH BY Y. L. GERSHT

*In the Nazi-instituted ghetto of Lodzh refresher and training courses for teachers covered
Yiddish grammar, spelling, literature and folklore. Attention to Yiddish, even among those
educators not accustomed to attending to it before, was considered a contribution to
strengthening the child's identity and resistance in the face of Nazi annihilation.*

די לאָדזשער געטאָ, ווי אַלע געטאָס, האָט צו פֿאַרצייכענען פֿאַרשיידענע צײַטן און מדרגות.
מען קען נישט פֿאַרגלײַכן, למשל, דאָס ערשטע יאָר צו די לעצטע יאָרן פֿון איר פֿינפֿסטהאַלבן־
יאָריקער עקסיסטענץ. במילא איז אויך דאָס גײַסטיקע לעבן צוגעפּאַסט צו די באַדינ־
גונגען און מיגלעכקייטן וואָס האָבן זיך געהאַלטן אין בײַטן.

נאָך במשך די ערשטע ווינטער-חדשים פֿון דער מלחמה, איידער די געטאָ איז פֿאַרשלאָסן
געוואָרן, איז די פֿראַגע פֿון שולחינוך געווען אין צענטער פֿון ייִדישע פּראָבלעמצו. אָפֿיציעל
האָט די דײַטשע מאַכט די ייִדישע שולן נישט פֿאַרמאַכט, פֿאַרקערט, מען האָט נאָך אַפֿילו
געצוווּנגען די קינדער צו גיין אין די שולן אום שבת. אָבער ס׳האָט וועגן נאָרמאַלער שול־
טעטיקייט ניט געקענט זײַן קיין רייד. די לערערס האָבן נישט געקענט גיין אין די שולן
ווײַל זיי זענען נישט געווען זיכער אַדורכצוגײַן אַ פֿאַר טריט איבער דער גאַס נישט וועראַנדיק
געכאַפּט און פֿאַרשלעפּט צו שווערער אַרבעט און פּײַניקו03נגען. די עלטערן האָבן אויך בעסער
באַהאַלטן די קינדער אין שטוב, ווײַל יעדער טאָג האָט געמט האָט אָנגעיאָגט נײַע גזרות און
גירושים אַזוי אַז מען איז נישט געווען זיכער מיט דער חיל־שעה.

אַנדערש איז געוואָרן מיט דער שאַפֿונג פֿון דער געטאָ דעם 1טן מײַ 1940. די פֿאַר־
צוימונגען אַרום דער געטאָ וועגן זענען געוואָרן שטרענגע צוגעהיטן פֿון דײַטשער פּאָליציי פֿון אויסן־
ווייניק און פֿון ייִדישער פֿון אינעווייניק. אַ ייִד האָט ניט געקענט בּאין אופֿן אַרויס פֿון אַט
דער פֿאַרשלאָסענער שטײַג און אַ פּאָליאק אָדער אַ דײַטש האָט ניט געטאָרט אַרײַנקומען
אָן דער אָפֿיציעלער דערלויבעניש פֿון דער געשטאַפּאָ און געטאָ־פֿאַרוואַלטונג. דאָס האָט גע־
מאַכט פֿון דער געטאָ אַן אמתע תפֿיסה. אָבער אין די ערשטע צײַטן איז דאָס געווען, אין

פּלאַקאַט פֿון 6טן פֿאַרגעלייענטן „פֿאָלקסגעזונט" „זשורנאַל"

Poster concerning the sixth oral journal "Public Health"

כרזה על כתב ־ העת הששי המוקרא „בריאות העם"

Плакат о 6—ом читанном номере „Фолксгезунт"

1942 7/XII

In the Nazi-instituted ghetto (1942): the lull before the storm – popular medical lecture concerning nutrition, infections, high temperatures, and medical superstitions or folk cures.

אַ געוױסן זינגען, אַ מין פֿאַרלײַכטערונג, װיבל מען האָט לכל הפּחות אײנהײיניק אין געטא
געקענט פֿרײַער אַרױסשטעקן דעם קאָפּ און נישט מורא האָבן געשלאָגן אָדער געכאַפּט צו
װערן.

די אַמביציע פֿון מ. ח. רומקאָװסקי, װעמען די דײַטשן האָבן געמאַכט פֿאַרן Älteste
der Juden, איז געװען צו שאַפֿן אַן אָפֿיציעלע שולונק, װוּ ס׳זאָלן אַרײַנגעצױגן װערן אַלע
קינדער — װי ס׳פּאַסט פֿאַר אַ מלוכה אין מיניאַטור. באַלד װי די געטא איז געשלאָסן גע־
װאָרן און ס׳האָט זיך אָנגעהױבן דעם „פּרעזעס” רומקאָװסקיס ממשלה איז דער ערשטער
אױפֿסו זײַנער געװען צו שאַפֿן דעם אַ״ג שולזשטעל.[1] אין דער שפּיץ האָט ער אַװעקגעשטעלט
דרײַ מענטשן: שמואל לעה, אליהו טאַבאַקסבלאַט און משה קאַרא.

לעה איז געװען אַ ייִד אַ זקן שױן און האָט אין שול־ענינים כּמעט קײן מאָל ניט גע־
האַט צו טאָן. זײַן זכות איז געװען, װאָס ער איז געװען זײַער נאָענטע גוטע־פֿרײַנד מיטן
„פּרעזעס”. על כּל פּנים איז ער געװען אַן אָרנטלעכער מענטש, מיט גוטע כּוונות, כאָטש
מיט קלײנע השגות. טאַבאַקסבלאַט איז געװען אַן ענערגענטער שולטוער פֿון פֿריִער, אַ פֿאַר־
װאַלטער פֿון אַ „פּאַדשעכנער” רעגירונגס־שול פֿאַר ייִדישע קינדער ביז דער מלחמה. די
לערנשפּראַך אין דער דאָזיקער שול איז געװען פּױליש, אָבער ער איז געװען אַ ליבהאָבער
פֿון דער ייִדישער שפּראַך און געשטאַנען נאָענט צו די ייִדישיסטישע קרײַזן. פּאָליטיש האָט
ער געהערט צו די פּױלי־ציון, אָבער ער איז געװען גענוג טאָלעראַנט צו אַנדערע ריכטונגען
אױך און האָט זיך געפֿלײַסט צו זײַן ערלעך אין דער דאָזיקער אַטמאָספֿער פֿון געטא. דער
דריטער, משה קאַרא, איז ביז דער מלחמה געװען סעקרעטאָר פֿון דער ציוניסטישער גימנאַזיע
אין לאָדזש. הגם ער איז געװען, פֿאַרשטײַס זיך, מער אָריענטירט אױף העברעִיש האָט ער
זיך פֿאָרט צוגעפּאַסט צו די באַדינגונגען און סאָלידאַריש צוזאַמענגעאַרבעט מיט טאַבאַקסבלאַטן.

אָט דער שולאַפּטײל האָט קאָנצענטרירט אַרום זיך אַלע טיפּן שולן: רעליגיעזע, פּױליש־
ייִדישע, ציוניסטישע און ייִדישיסטישע. װעגן פּריװאַטשולן האָט יעמאָלט נישט געקענט זײַן
קײן רײד, װיבל ס׳איז נישט געװען װער ס׳זאָל האָבן די מעגלעכקײטן זײ אױסצוהאַלטן. האָט
זיך געשטעלט די האַרבע שאלה: װי אַזױ רעגירט מען מיט אַזעלכע פֿאַרשײדנדמיניקע שולן
און דער עיקר, אױף װאָס פֿאַר אַ שפּראַך דאַרפֿן פֿאָרקומען די לימודים. דײַטש ניט, װיבל
די דײַטשן האָבן דאָס בָארניט געװאָלט. פּױליש װידער האָט געשמעקט מיט פּרעמדן פּאַטריאַטיזם,
און „ליצמאַנשטאַט” איז דאָך גאָר געװען אינקאָרפּאָרירט אין רײַך. האָט דעריבער געקענט זײַן
זײַן אַ רײד װעגן ייִדיש אָדער העברעִיש. חוץ דעם האָט מען געדאַרפֿט באַשליסן, װוּ נעמט
מען לערערס װאָס װאָלן זײַן פֿעיִק פֿאַר די אַלגעמײנע לימודים. דער רוב פֿון די פֿאַראַנענע
לערערס האָבן ניט געקענט קײן גוט ייִדיש, און קײן העברעִיש אַװדאי ניס. דאָס זײַנען דאָך
דער עיקר געװען אַזױנע װאָס האָבן ביז דער מלחמה געאַרבעט אין די פּאָװשעכנע שולן פֿון
דער רעגירונג, װוּ ס׳איז אַלץ געפֿירט געװאָרן אױף פּױליש. פֿאַר יודאַיסטישע לימודים האָט
מען נאָך געקענט אָפֿזוכן װי עס איז אַ געװיסע צאָל לערערס װאָס אַ ייִדיש לשון, אָבער בשום
אופֿן נישט װאָס שײך אַלגעמײנע לימודים.

די דאָזיקע שװעריקײיטן האָבן אפֿילו בײַם בעסטן װילן נישט געקענט באַזײַטיקט װערן.
האָט זיך דעריבער לכתּחילה, אין די ערשטע חדשים פֿון זומער 1940, אײַנגעשטעלט אַ מין
סטאַטוס־קװאָ, ד״ה די לערערס האָבן געלערנט אין דעם לשון װי זײ זענען געװױנט געװען.
צו דעם גענמיש איז נאָך צוגעקומען די פֿאַרשײדנקײט פֿון ריכטונג. די לערערס מיט אַסימי־
לאַטאָרישע נטיות זײַנען זײער געגאַנגען זײַער װעג, און דאָס איז געקומען אין סתּירה

---

[1] װעגן דער טעטיקײט פֿון דעם דאָזיקן אָפּטײל זען ישׂראל טאַבאַקסבלאַט, חורבן לאָדזש
(בוענאָס־אײַרעס, צענטראַל־פֿאַרבאַנד פֿון פּױלישע ייִדן אין אַרגענטינע, 1946, 203 זז׳), זז׳
68—72.

רעם 15 זולי 1942 קומט פאר אין געטא-טעאטער

דער ספארט - יום - טוב

אין פראגראם: צום 2טן מאל

1. ג׳מנאסטיק.
2. ר׳טמיק (פלאסטישע טענץ)
3. באקס
4. באסקעטבאל.
5. נעץ-באל

נעמען אנט״ל 14 גרופן(200 מאן)

אנהויב 20 אז״גער.

דער פארקויף פון ב״לעטן קומט שוין פאר אין
סעקרעטאר״אט פון דער ספארט-אבט״לונג, ספארט-פלאץ
סטראשונא 6 טעגליך פון 18 ביז 20 אז.

In the Nazi-instituted ghetto (1942): the lull before the storm – gymnastics, rhythmic dancing, boxing, basketball, volley ball.

פלאקאט: ספארט-פעסטיוואל אין געטא-טעאטער

Poster: Sports Festival in the ghetto theater

כרזה: חגיגת-ספורט בתיאטרון-הגיטו

Плакат: спортивный фестиваль в театре в гетто

1942 15/VII

מיט די טענדענצן פון אלע יודאיסטישע לימודים, אלץ איינס צי מיט א רעליגיעזער, העברעיש־
טישער אדער יידישיסטישער באפארבונג.

דער דאזיקער מצב איז געווארן וואס א מאל געשפאנטער, און מען האט געדארפט גע־
פינען אן אויסוועג. איך בין בין ארײנגעטרעטן אין דער שולארבעט באלד אין מײ 1940 ווי א
לערער און פראגראם-צונויפשטעלער. בין איך דארטן געווען אן עדות פון דער סתירותדיקייט סײַ
אין פראגראם און סײ אין לערן-לשון. די געטא-באדינגונגען זענען אבער געווען אַזעלכע, אז
א סך האבן זיך דאס ניט גענומען צו שטארק צום הארצן. מען האט געטראכט: סײַ ווי איז
דאס אלץ אויף דערווײל און ווען מען וועט אויסגעלייזט ווערן וועט מען שוין אלץ
אויסבעסערן.

עס זענען אבער געלאפן חדשים, און דער זומער איז אַוועק. מען האט געמוזט אין

שולאַפּטייל צוגרייטן אַ פּלאַן פֿאַר אַ ניַ שוליאָר און עס פֿאָרשטעלן דעם פּרעזעס צוב
באַשטעטיקן, וויַל אָן אים האָט גאָרנישט געטאָרט פּאַסירן אין דער געטאָ־מלוכה. פֿונעם קלענסטן
ביזן גרעסטן ענין און אַפֿילו אין זאַכן, האָט ער האָט ער אין זיי נישט געהאַט קיין שום
ידיעה. מיט זיַן שאַרפֿן פּרימיטיוון חוש־הריח האָט רומקאָווסקי דערשפּירט די קאָנקלעיניטן
וועגן די שוועריקייטן פֿון לשון און ריכמונג און ער האָט גענומען דיקטירן. ער האָט אַפֿ־
געמאַכט, אַז די לערנשפּראַך פֿון אַלע לימודים דאַרף זיַן נאָר ייִדיש. ערשטנס איז עס געוועזן
דערפֿאַר וואָס ער אַליין האָט עס ניט געקענט קיין אַנדער לשון און צווייטנס האָט ער געהאַלטן
פֿאַר פּראַקטיש צו האָבן אַן אייגענע "מלוכה־שפּראַך". פֿאַר העברעיש האָט ער באַשטימט אַ
געוויסע צאָל שעהען ווי אויך פֿאַר רעליגיעז לימודים אין אַ געהעריקער מאַס.

איצט האָט דער שולאָפּטייל "אָפֿיציעל" איַנגעפֿירט די ניַע פּראָגראַם מיט ייִדיש ווי דאָס
לערן־לשון פֿאַר אַלע לימודים. פֿאַר וואָס נאָר "אָפֿיציעל"? וויַל פֿאַקטיש זיַנען פֿאַרן וויַטער
געבליבן ממשותדיקע שוועריקייטן, נישט צים באַזיַטיקן. די לערערס פֿון די אַמאָליקע פּוילישׁ־
ייִדישע שולן האָבן, ווי געזאַגט, ניט געקענט גענוג ייִדיש. אויך האָבן געפֿעלט לערנביכער
פֿאַר די פֿאַרשיידענע לימודים. זעענדיק די שוועריקייטן האָט די טאַבאַקסבלאַט גענומען פֿאַרהאַנדלען
מיט מיר וועגן לערערקורסן פֿאַר ייִדיש ווי אויך וועגן אַ לערנביכל פֿון ייִדיש פֿאַר די ערשטע
קלאַסן. ווי אַ רעזולטאַט דערפֿון האָב איך בּאַשלאָסן צו מאַכן אַ פּרווו פֿון אַ לערנביכל פֿאַרן
לימוד פֿון ייִדיש, ביַ דער מיטהילף פֿון שמואל ראָזנשטיין, שפּעטער דער רעדאַקטאָר פֿין
דעם בלעטעלע וואָס האָט זיך גערופֿן געטאָ־צייטונג.

מיר האָבן צוגעגרייטס דעם ערשטן אין צווייטן טייל פֿון אַזאַ שולביכל, און מען האָט
אָנגעהויבן קלערן וועגן צוזאַמענקלאַבֿן אַ ביסל שריפֿט אויף צו דרוקן עס אין דער געטאָ־
דרוקעריַ. ביני לביני האָט אָבער דער פּרעזעס זיך אַ ביסל צוריקגעצויגן פֿון אַרויסגעבן אַזאַ
ביכל, משמעות צוליב מורא פֿאַר דער דיַטשער מאַכט, און די זאַך איז בטל געוואָרן.
עס איז אָבער יאָ געבליבן וויַטער דאָס שאַפֿן די לערערקורסן פֿאָרן ייִדישן לשון, פֿאַר
די לערערס פֿון די אַלגעמיינע לימודים, אַריַנגערעכנט אויך שפּראַך־קענטעניש. דאָס קליינע
ביסל לערערס וואָס האָבן יאָ געפֿאַסט דעם ייִדישן לימוד, ווי למשל די "בית־יעקב"־לערער:ס
און די צישא־לערערס, האָבן בשום אופֿן נישט געקענט באַפֿרידיקן דעם סום באַדאַרף.

פֿון דעם פּלאַן ביזן פּראַקטישן אַדורכפֿירן די זאַך איז אָבער דעמאָלט געוועזן אַ שפּאַרער
מהלך. אַלע מאָל האָט מען פֿריש מורא בּעהאַט אַדער "נישט געהאַט דעם קאָפ" צוליב אַ
ניַער צרה וואָס האָט צוגענומען די חושים. דאָס האָט זיך אַזוי געצויגן דורכן גאַנצן שוליאָר
41/1940, ביז פֿרילינג. דעמאָלט ערשט זענען די לערערקורסן געוואָרן אַ פֿאַקט.

געררופֿן האָבן זיך די קורסן סעמינאַר פֿאַר ייִדיש־קענטעניש. צוהערערס זענען געוואָרן
דורכויס אַמטירנדיקע לערערס פֿון אַלגעמיינע לימודים. זיי האָבן זיך געטיילט אין 4 גרופּעס.
דריַ גרופּעס, בערך צו 25 פּערזאָן אין יעדערער, זענען אָנגעפֿירט געוואָרן, איטלעכע באַזונדער,
פֿון יוסף זעלקאָוויטש (באַוווסטער ייִוואָ־זאַמלער און זשורנאַליסט), אײבעשיץ און נעלקען.
די פֿערטע גרופּע, מיט אַן ערך 65 צוהערערס, האָב איך אַנגעפֿירט.

דאָס ערשטע מאָל האָב איך געהאַט די געלעגנהייט צו קומען אין אַ דירעקטן קאָנטאַקט
מיט אַן עולם גאַנץ אַדער אַלב אַסימילירטע לערערס, וואָס זייער באַציַונג צו ייִדיש איז
געוועזן אַ פֿיַנדלעכע אַדער אין בעסטן פֿאַל אַ גרינגשעצנדיקע. אויף דער ערשטער לעקציע
מיַנער איז געקומען די אָנפֿירונג פֿון שולאָפּטייל מיטן אינספּעקטאָר ד"ר א. ש. קאַמעניעצקי,
אַ באַוווסטער סעמיטאָלאָג, בכדי צו זען דעם רושם. ווי מיר דאַכט זיך איז אין דער רושם געהאַט
אַ גוטער, און די וויַטערדיקע לעקציעס האָב איך געקענט פֿירן אין דער בעסטער אַטמאָספֿאַר
פֿון אויפֿריכטיקער פֿאַראינטערעסירטקייט מצד די צוהערערס, צווישן וועלכע ס'איז געוועזן אַ
רוב פֿרויען.

כ׳געדענק דעם ערשטן שטארקן איַינדרוק וואָס עס האָט אויף זיי געמאַכט דאָס פֿאַר־
ליַיענען אַ מעשׂה פֿון ר׳ נחמן בראַצלאַווערס סיפורי מעשׂיות. זיי האָבן געהאַט גאָר אַן אַנדערע
פֿאָרשטעלונג וועגן די חסידישע רביים, און דאָ האָט זיך פּלוצעם פֿאַר זיי אַנטפּלעקט אַזאַ
עשירות פֿון געדאַנקען און חנעוודיקייט פֿון פֿאַנטאַזיע. אַנדערע האָבן נאָר באַדויערט, וואָס
ערשט אין די געטאָ־באַדינגונגען זענען זיי געווויר געוואָרן פֿון דעם אָריגינעלן יידישן קהל.
בעת די לעקציעס האָט מען באַהאַנדלט פֿראַגעס פֿון גראַמאַטיק, פֿון לעקסיק און פֿון יידישער
ליטעראַטור. פֿאַרגליַיכונגען מיט אַנדערע שפּראַכן וואָס שייך אָריגינעלע יידישע שפּראַך־
רעסורסן האָבן אַ שפּאַר ביסל פֿאַרחידושט דעם עולם.

דער סעמינאַר האָט געגעבן די לערערס־צוהערערס די מעגלעכקייט תיכף אויסצובעסערן
זייער לערנען אין קלאַס, ווַיַל זיי האָבן באַקומען אַ גענוגע צאָל טערמינען פֿאַר די פֿאַר־
שיידענע לימודים. זיי האָבן זיך באַריַיכערט מיט פֿאָלקסלידער און זיי דערנאָך איבערגעגעבן
זייערע אייגענע תלמידים מיט חשק, כאַטש דער מאָגן איז געווען ליידיק און די אויגן האָבן
געשווינדלט פֿאַר הונגער.

די דאָזיקע לערערקורסן האָבן זיך געצויגן אַן איבעררײַס פֿון 15טן מײַ ביזן 21סטן
סעפּטעמבער 1941. בטל געוואָרן זענען זיי נישט חסִ־ושלום צוליב אינעווייניקסטע סיבות
נייַערט צוליב דעם מבול פֿון נײַע גזרות און דער עיקר צוליב דעם גרויסן צושטראָם דעמאָלט
פֿון טראַנספֿאַרטן פֿאַרשלעפּטע יידן: מען האָט זיי געבראַכט אין לאָדזשער געטאָ אַרײַן פֿון
דײַטשלאַנד, עסטריַיך און טשעכיע. דאָס איז געווען דער סוף פֿון דער כלומרשטער „אויטאָ־
נאָמער געטאָ". נישט נאָר דער סעמינאַר איז דעמאָלט געשלאָסן געוואָרן, נאָר די גאַנצע
שולסיסטעם אין געטאָ איז בכלל אָפֿיציעל בטל געוואָרן.

ס׳איז נאָך שפּעטער אויך ווימטערגעפֿירט געוואָרן אַ געהיַיסע שול־טעטיקייט, אַבער דאָס
איז שוין געהאָן פֿאַרבאַהאַלטן, אין די אַרבעט־רעסאָרטן גופֿאַ.

י. ל. געורשט

The Night of the Murdered Poets

JUDAH L. GRAUBART

'Earth, O earth, do not cover my blood', were the last words of Dovid Bergelson, one of twenty-four Jewish intellectual and cultural leaders executed in Moscow's Lubyanka prison on the night of August 12, 1952. The execution of these men, which occurred at the height of Stalin's post-war anti-Semitic campaign, has thus come to mark the nadir of Jewish life in the Soviet Union during the tragic period known as 'The black years of Soviet Jewry' (1948–1952).

But despite the perverse significance of that event, the 'night of the murdered poets' remains little more than a footnote in the tragic history of Soviet Jews. Indeed, the fact that the executions themselves occurred was not even known until 1956 when, during Khruschev's 'de-Stalinization' program, the Warsaw Yiddish daily, *Folkshtimme*, made mention of the executions in a series of memoirs by the wife of a late Jewish poet who had been imprisoned by Stalin.

Today the amount of information surrounding the events of August 12th remains so scant that the probable names of only nine of the victims and perhaps a tenth are known. These nine were: Itzik Feffer, Dovid Bergelson, Solomon Lozovskii, Dovid Hofshteyn, Peretz Markish, Shmuel Persov, Leib Kvitko, Eliahu Spivak, and Yitzhak Nusinov. The possible tenth was Binyamin Zushkin.

To understand the circumstances surrounding the murder of the twenty-four Jewish intellectuals, one must begin by very briefly touching upon certain aspects of Soviet Jewish history, beginning with the Revolution and continuing through the 'black years'.

PRACTICE DEFIES RHETORIC

While the Revolution of 1917 was to have inaugurated a permanent era of minority tolerance in the new Union of Soviet Socialist Republics, there is often times a tragic gap, as history has so tragically demonstrated, between the rhetoric of principles and the practice of policy. And so, under Lenin, and especially under his successor, Josef Stalin, a campaign of brutally forced Jewish assimilation was begun, which has remained unabated to the present.

There was, however, one notable period of cultural freedom for Soviet Jews, that which was instituted by Stalin with the German attack on the Soviet Union in 1942. At that point, confronted with the necessity of a united home front against the Nazis, Stalin took steps to insure maximum nationalities support of the Soviet war effort, particularly as regarded the Jews. In the latter case he did so by ordering the formation of the Jewish Anti-Fascist Committee (JAC) of the Soviet Information Bureau, an event which would have a direct bearing on the events of the night of August 12. Colonel Solomon Lozovskii was appointed the director, while the chairman was dramatist Shlomo Mikhoels; Itzik Feffer, the writer, was the secretary. Writers Ilya Ehrenburg and Dovid Bergelson were among its other prominent sponsors. Within ten years all, with the exception of Ehrenburg, would perish in the Lubyanka prison.

The purpose of the JAC, according to Shakhno Epshtain, writing in *Pravda* in February, 1943, was to '...enlighten...the Jewish masses in all countries about the great historical accomplishments with which Soviet reality is replete'. In other words, the agency was to generate pro-Soviet propaganda, in both the East and West. To achieve these ends in the West, primarily Britain, Canada, the United States, and Mexico, there were daily cablegrams, radio broadcasts, and other forms of communication, including plays and songs. Within the Soviet Union, the triweekly paper *Einigkeit* was published, which became a vehicle for some of the leading Jewish literati.

STALIN'S 'CUP OF HAPPINESS'

As an additional part of the JAC's program, Feffer and Mikhoels visited the United States, Canada, and Mexico in 1943 and, according to Feffer, succeeded in raising two to three million dollars, while also receiving substantial amounts from Jewish organizations for field hospitals and childrens' homes.

In fulfilling their wartime roles, the men who are the subject of this paper did so both because of their profound loyalties to their people and to their country, and because of their belief that Stalin as a leader, and socialism as a system of government, offered the greatest hopes to the Jewish people for living in an environment free of persecution. These attitudes were reflected in their writings as well as in the fact that all of them returned to the USSR after 1917 from their pre-Revolutionary 'exile'. Thus, Itzik Feffer wrote that for him, 'Yiddish is a language like other languages, not homeless on the road...and that is why it is dear to us'. He wrote in equal praise of Josef Stalin; 'Stalin's name, like the sun, will ever shine in the world....' During the war, Feffer's religious, cultural, and political loyalties were manifested in his poems, 'I am a Jew', he wrote, 'The angry sword of pain and sadness has not destroyed my possession, my fold, my faith...From under the sword I shouted, "I am a Jew...who has drunk from Stalin's magic cup of happiness...".'

Dovid Bergelson shared Feffer's loyalties to the Soviet Union, as well as his belief that it offered the greatest hope of becoming a state totally void of anti-Semitism, and thus returned to the USSR in 1933 from New York where he had written for the left-wing Yiddish daily, the *Freiheit*. In so returning, he urged his colleagues to do likewise, stating that Jewry's only hope lay in '...the emerging Jewish center in the Soviet Union'. Indeed, at one point Bergelson wrote a friend, 'Here I feel happy and free and young, and needed, and appreciated, and full of energy to work, happy about myself...about the surge of Soviet Yiddish literature'. Later, in a pamphlet titled *The Jews and the War With Hitler*, Bergelson wrote that the Jews, 'Together with Russians, Ukrainians, Georgians, Americans, in their fights...with the fascists, created new legends about Jewish heroes'.

FAITH IN REVOLUTION

Dovid Hofshteyn was also inspired by the Revolution of 1917 and dedicated his first published poem to it. In 1925, he returned to the Soviet Union from Palestine. Like the other poets, Hofshteyn had a deep Jewish commitment, which, due to his literary impetuosity, sometimes led him afoul of the censors, as manifested by one of his lines, 'A quiet hour of rest...far from the city of Kiev, so what if once a small boy studied a bit of Job?' Like his fellows, Hofshteyn saw the destinies of the Jewish people and the USSR as being intertwined. In 1944, of the Soviet war effort he wrote, 'Soviet Russia saved our Jews and some of those near to us...'

Peretz Markish, born in 1895 in Vohlynia, had also left imperial Russia, but returned in 1926. Like Hofshteyn, Markish also occasionally ran afoul of the censors, but this was not a major detriment to his writing or to its recognition by the state. Markish's loyalties to his people and state were manifested not only in his now famous exhortation to his coreligionists to 'carry your gun as you carry your Sefer Torah', but even more strongly in his poem, *The Jewish Army Man*. There he wrote, 'You have made a solemn declaration with fire and blood...pain – you the Jew! the soldier! You! The Jew! The Red Army man...!

Shmuel Persov, whom the Yiddish literary historian Charles Madison calls 'a relatively minor (fiction) writer', left Russia in 1906 at the age of seven and returned with the outbreak of the Revolution. During World War II he wrote extensively about the partisan units, and based one of his stories, 'Your Name is People' on actual events.

Of all these literary figures, however, the man with the broadest appeal was

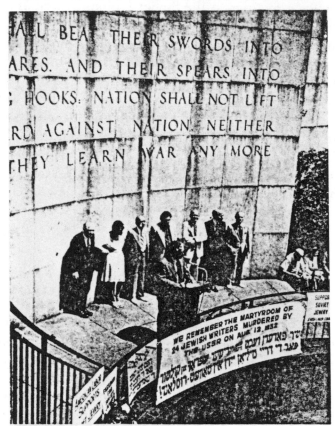

On the 22nd anniversary (in 1974) of the murder of a score of Yiddish writers in the Soviet Union (in 1952). The Arbeter Ring (Workmen's Circle, major Yiddish secular–socialist fraternal organization) conducts an annual demonstration in front of the UN 'demanding the right for Soviet Jews to be able to give their children a Jewish education, to have Yiddish schools, newspapers, and theaters, to immigrate to any country of their choosing.'

the children's poet, Leib Kvitko, who returned to his native Kiev from Berlin in 1925. His works were widely published in the USSR, and in 1938 he was awarded the 'Red Worker Flag' for his contributions. With the German attack in 1941, Kvitko proclaimed. 'This is the first time in the dispersion of the Jewish people when it became possible for them to organize openly and en masse...against the destroyer'.

One of the nine Jewish leaders was not an intellectual per se, but nonetheless fulfilled a leading role in the Soviet society. Colonel Solomon Lozovskii, the aforementioned director of the JAC, was a prerevolutionary contemporary of Lenin and Stalin and filled, among other positions, that of the Red Trade Union International.

ELIMINATION OF JEWISH CULTURE

With the end of World War II, Stalin renewed his anti-Semitic campaign, but in such a way as to belie its existence to the West. Thus, ostensibly maintaining viable Soviet Jewish cultural institutions, while in reality paving the way for their total obliteration, Stalin had the remaining manifestations of such intellectual creativity concentrated in Moscow, which became the Jewish 'showplace'. So, for example, the Yiddish publishing house Emes produced 110,000 books and pamphlets between 1946 and 1948, the year of its demise. Similarly, Binyamin Zushkin and Shlomo Mikhoels of the Moscow State Theater were awarded Stalin Prizes.

Yet, while some concessions were made to Jewish culture, they were few in number and scope beside the deprivations which existed. Indeed, as early as 1944, when Feffer and Mikhoels transmitted a request to Stalin through Lazar Kaganovich (the highest ranking Jew in the USSR) that a Yiddish daily be reestablished, the request was denied. After the war, the government similarly refused to reestablish Yiddish journals and publishing houses in such centers as Lithuania, the Ukraine, and White Russia, which had been destroyed by the Nazis.

Even the Moscow State Theater itself was subject to *sub-rosa* discrimination. As Zushkin thus confided to a visiting Hungarian diplomat, first the theater was 'relocated' on an unpaved street, then assessed higher taxes, and then fined for alleged fire and sanitation ordinance violations. He predicted that 'soon...the group will collapse and we, too, shall have been purged'. In 1949 he was arrested and the theater was permanently closed.[1]

In early 1948, Stalin's *Kulturkampf* was launched in full force with the murder of Shlomo Mikhoels, who was dispatched to Minsk, ostensibly to present the

---

1. There are two versions of Zushkin's death. One is that upon learning of his arrest he committed suicide; the other is that he was executed on August 12, 1952.

Stalin Prize to the White Russian State Theater. While out for a stroll on the night of January 13, he was thrown in front of an oncoming truck by agents of Lavrenti Beria and was killed. Writing in his memoirs about this incident, Ilya Ehrenburg commented that Beria chose this brutal method of execution, because 'it was his idea of fun'.

STALIN'S FEAR OF ISRAEL

Subsequent to Mikhoels' murder, in May, 1948, the State of Israel came into being, and thus created what Stalin saw as a distinct domestic difficulty in terms of the dangers of a possible resurgence of Jewish nationalism and Zionism. His anxieties were heightened in September of that year when thousands of Moscow Jews defied Soviet police and, in a spontaneous demonstration, escorted Israeli Ambassador Golda Meir to the Choral Synagogue for the high holiday services.

In response to the situation, Stalin issued a stern policy statement through Ilya Ehrenburg, who at the 'invitation of the editor of *Pravda*', wrote a scathing attack against Israel and Zionism. On September 21, 1948, Ehrenburg denounced the Zionists as '...the ideologists of race hatred, those adepts of inhumanity, those anti-Semitics (sic) who uprooted Jews from their long established homes...' With respect to Israel, Ehrenburg warned that Soviet Jews '...are bound every inch to Soviet soil...and must look to the Soviet Union...alone...'

The article caused much consternation in the Jewish community. So strong was the revulsion, that on October 19, *Einigkeit*, in one of its last issues, published a sharp rebuttal of Ehrenburg, especially attacking his denigration of the new Jewish state. In November, Stalin responded by dissolving the JAC which the authorities alleged had become a 'nest of folk traitors', and along with it, *Einigkeit*.

Concomitant with the aforementioned postwar developments came the initial arrests of the 'black years'. And among the first to be imprisoned were the former leaders of the JAC, Itzik Feffer, Leib Kvitko, and Dovid Hofshteyn.

'ROOTLESS COSMOPOLITANS'

Peretz Markish, the former secretary of the JAC, was not arrested until the night of January 27, 1949, and was one of the few, if not the only one, of the writers to succeed in preserving some of his unpublished works for posterity. Forewarned of his imminent arrest, he was able to have some of his manuscripts smuggled from his apartment at the virtual moment of his midnight arrest by the secret police.

At the time of Markish's arrest, Stalin began to escalate his campaign with his new attacks on the 'rootless cosmopolitans', a euphemism for the Jewish people. Beginning with the discovery of a group of allegedly subversive Jewish drama critics, Yiddish theaters were soon accused of having produced unpatriotic plays. The list of 'culprits' was then expanded to include prominent Jews in related fields such as cinematic direction, film review, etc. A short time later, in a move unprecedented in Soviet Jewish history, leading citizens were exposed as 'enemies of the state' and of having Russified their real names which, when 'revealed', were all Jewish.

While Stalin's anti-Semitic campaign was exacting its toll within the USSR, virtually nothing was known of it in the West. Indeed, the first hints of the Jewish purge did not come until 1949 at the World Congress of Jewish Peace Partisans in Paris, when certain Jewish writers were conspicuous by their absence and were surmised by some to have been arrested.

By 1950, the Soviet Union was, culturally speaking, '*Judenrein*'. The *American Jewish Yearbook* describing the situation wrote that, 'there are no Jewish communal institutions of any kind in the Soviet Union except for a few remaining synagogues'.

A 'ZIONIST REPUBLIC'

Stalin continued his anti-Jewish purges, and on July 11, 1952 brought to trial twenty-five of the Soviet Union's leading Jewish cultural and communal leaders, who were charged with being 'national bourgeois Zionists', and attempting to establish a 'National Bourgeois Zionist Republic'.

In addition to these charges, Itzik Feffer was accused of having conspired with American Zionists 'and other fascists' during his 1943 visit.

Although twenty-four were executed, the probable ten mentioned at the outset of this paper and fourteen others, a twenty-fifth person was also tried, Dr. Lena S. Shtern. Like her codefendants, she was actively involved in the JAC, but for unknown reasons, received a sentence of life imprisonment. She was 'rehabilitated' in 1954 and appointed to the highly prestigious Soviet Academy of Sciences. Dr. Shtern also served as the Director of the Soviet Institute of Physiology. Born in 1878, she died on March 8, 1968, after spending her remaining years in seclusion.

While the aforementioned charges were fabrications, the one concerning the establishment of a 'Zionist republic' is one that deserves elaboration. During the war, Stalin removed thousands of Tartars from the Crimea because of their alleged collaboration with the Nazis. As a result of this situation, the JAC suggested, in a paper submitted by Lozovskii to Stalin, that the Jews be permitted to re-populate the Crimea since it was far more desirable than the 'Jewish Autonomous Region of Birobidjhan', and, indeed, some Jews had lived there prior to World War II anyway.

Stalin responded negatively and, according to Nikita Khrushchev, 'let his imagination run wild in this direction', viewing it as part of a Zionist plot to establish an 'outpost of American imperialism on Soviet shores'. So, it was on the basis of that particular incident and Stalin's paranoia that the twenty-five were found guilty of attempting to found a 'National Bourgeois Zionist Republic'.

THE TRIAL

Little is known of the actual proceedings of the trial. It has been reported that Dr. Shtern conducted a very spirited defence on her own behalf, returning each accusation with counterstatements of her own. In contrast, Solomon Lozovskii is said to have remained absolutely silent. Itzik Feffer is reported to have broken down under the pressure of the pre-trial torture, and confessed. Undoubtedly the most tragic figure was Dovid Hofshteyn; already insane from four years of imprisonment and deprivation, he had let his hair and beard grow while spending his evenings chanting the Psalms generally recited in mourning for the destruction of the Temple. Hofshteyn went to his execution alternately laughing and singing.

Although Stalin's excesses, including the subsequent notorious 'Jewish Doctors' Plot' were roundly denounced in the de-Stalinization program inaugurated with Khruschev's 'secret speech' of 1956, the events of the night of August 12 were never acknowledged by the Soviet authorities. Indeed, since 1952 Soviet spokesmen have gone to great lengths to deny that any such incident as the execution even occurred. For example, in October, 1955, the Foreign Ministry Press Chief, while attending a session of the UN General Assembly, openly denied 'rumors' about the disappearance of the writers. In a subsequent conversation with the *Jewish Daily Forward*'s correspondent S. L. Shneiderman, the spokesman claimed he had only recently seen Peretz Markish in the *Pravda* office.

However, on November 27 of that same year, the government did make a small concession to the memory of the writers and 'rehabilitated' them in a private Kremlin ceremony. On the aforementioned date, their widows were summoned to the Soviet high court where they were informed that their husbands had been 'shot by enemies of the people'.

THE CHARADE OF DEATH-LIFE

But with that one exception, official Soviet policy has been publicly to deny the reality of the night of the murdered poets. *Sovetish Heimland* recently carried this policy of non-acknowledgement to bizarre extremes with their issue celebrating the seventieth anniversary of Itzik Feffer's birth. In that issue, editor Aaron

Vergelis and contributor Abraham Gontar, the latter who knew Feffer well, completely ignored his death and carried the charade to such an extent that according to a contemporary scholar, Elias Shulman, '...one gets the impression that Feffer is alive and well in Moscow...and that he continues writing'. And, as if to make the non-demise of the Soviet writers complete, the immediate relatives of Itzik Feffer and Leib Kvitko were even denied permission to erect gravestones for these men.

In late 1972, the final chapter of the night of the murdered poets was written when, after years of efforts, the remaining families of Peretz Markish and Itzik Feffer left the Soviet Union for Israel, where some of Markish's unpublished works will be printed by Tel Aviv University. And with the close of that tragic event perhaps the most fitting epitaph for those men, their works, and all they signified can be taken from the title, based on the Psalms, of one of the last books by Dovid Bergelson: *Killed, I Will Live*.

1	2	3

1 — משה קולבאק
סמאָרגאָן, ווייס־רוסלאַנד, 1896
אומגעבראַכט, ראַטנרוסלאַנד, 1937

מאָנטאָג (ראָמאַן)
דיסנער טשיילד האַראָלד
(אויטאָביאָגראַפישע פּאָעמע)
זעלמעניאַנער (דערציילונג)
ב ו י ט ר ע (פּיעסע)

פּאָעט, דערציילער, ראָמאַניסט

2 — דער נסתר
(פּנחס קאַהאַנאָוויטש)
בערדיטשעוו, אוקראַינע, 1884
אומגעבראַכט, ר״פ, 1951

מעשהלעד אין פערזן
געזאַנג און געבעט, (לידער)
געדאַכט (מעשיות און וויזיעס)
די משפּחה מאַשבער, (ראָמאַן)

פּאָעט, דערציילער, ראָמאַניסט

3 — יעקב גלאַטשטיין
לובלין, פּוילן, 1896
לעבט אין ניו־יאָרק, פאַר. שטאַטן

שטראַלנדיקע ייִדן,
אין תּוך גענומען, (עסייען)
ווען יאַש איז געקומען, (דערצ.)
די פרייד פון ייִדישן וואָרט,
(לידער)

פּאָעט, דערציילער, עסייאיסט

4	5	6

4 — א. לעיעלעם
(אהרן גלאַנץ)
וואָלצלאַוועק, פּוילן, 1889
לעבט אין נ־י־יאָרק, פאַר. שטאַטן

פאַביוס לינד (פּאָעמען)
יונג האַרבסט, (לידער)
שלמה מולכו, (דראַמע)
אשר לעמלען, (דראַמע)

פּאָעט, עסייאיסט, דראַמאַטורג

5 — נחום־ברוך מינקאָוו
וואַרשע, פּוילן, 1893
ניו יאָרק, פאַר. שטאַטן, 1958

א שטערן בליט, (לידער)
אליהו בחור, (עסיי)
ייִדישע קלאַסישער פּאָעטן, (״)
פּיאָנערן פון דער ייִדישער
פּאָעזיע אין אַמעריקע

פּאָעט, עסייאיסט
ליטעראַטור־פאָרשער

6 — אפרים אויערבאַך
בעלץ, בעסאַראַביע, 1892
לעבט אין ניר־יאָרק, פּ״ש

קאַראַוואַנען, (ישׂראל לידער)
לויטער איז דער אַלטער קוואַל
(לידער)
פאַר גרויס און קליין, (דערצ.)
געטראַכט מיט עברי־טייטש,
(עסייען)

פּאָעט, עסייאיסט

1. Moyshe Kulbak, 1896–1937; Poet, writer of short stories, novelist; 2. Der Nister, 1884–1951; Poet, writer of short stories, essayist; 3. Yankev Glatshteyn, 1896–1971; Poet, writer of short stories, essayist; 4. A. Leyeles, 1889–1966; Poet, essayist, playwright; 5. Nokhem-borekh Minkov, 1893–1958; Poet, essayist, literary researcher; 6. Efrayim Oyerbakh, 1892–1973; Poet, essayist.

An Educational Assessment
of the Yiddish Secular School Movements
in the United States

SANDRA PARKER

The Yiddish secular movement, as a phenomenon on the American scene, is unknown to most American Jews today and probably would elicit no sign of recognition at all among non-Jews, with the possible exception of those familiar with the history of the American labor movement. Such information as is readily available would most certainly be related to the role of Yiddish-speaking groups in the development of American unions and to the general struggle for economic and social equality by working men and women from the turn of the century up to the Second World War.

In view of a common tendency (less marked in the last decade), on the part of Americans to identify their fellow countrymen by religion, it is not surprising that those Jews who chose to stress the nonreligious aspects of their group attributes should receive such minimal attention, and consequently acquire almost no visibility. Within the national 'table of organization' there were no legitimate ethnic or cultural slots until quite recently. Now that these categories are respectable, even highly regarded, the number of Yiddishists who might qualify has dwindled considerably, although changes in governmental and educational policies could alter the present situation dramatically.

It, therefore, seems important to examine what the Yiddish secularists were attempting to accomplish in spheres other than the political and economic arenas in which their achievements are fairly well documented and recorded. One might describe a wide gamut of cultural activities in the performing arts, journalism, literature and education. However, the prime concern of this writer is an exploration of the educational endeavors of the Yiddish secularists. Due to the constraints of space and scope, this examination will highlight major objectives, procedures, and problems, in an effort to provide a context for consideration of the question of the viability of ethnic education in the modern era, within the matrix of mainstream American culture.[1]

1. For additional details see Parker 1973.

The goal that was common to the four Yiddish secular school movements in the United States was the creation, through Yiddish secular education, of community identification and commitment based upon common cultural and ideological values. Yiddishists conceived of this sense of community as a telescopic one that began with the close family unit and extended to encompass ethnic (peoplehood) and universal (general-humanistic) dimensions. In their view the quality of the ideal relationship to each of these overlapping communities was identical, and this is to be understood as the meaning of the assertion that a Yiddish secularist education treats the Jew and the human being as an integral whole. Related to this major goal were others, like (1) the maintenance of a distinctive, linguistically based, dynamic culture in exile, whose healthy functioning would serve as a source of ethnic pride and self-delineation by individual Jews, (2) the transmission of a social and ethical value system whose principles were identical whether applied to the family unit, the ethnic group (folk) or humanity as a whole, and (3) the acceptance on the part of individual members of the group of a level of commitment that would assure active involvement in the perpetuation of (1) and (2).

The educational program which was designed to implement these goals was consequently ideologically based, value-oriented, with a strong emphasis upon behavioral activity and inspirational, emotional, attitude-inducing materials and experiences. It is important at this point to describe the major ideological factors that separated the various Yiddish secular school movements and to mark their evolution in direction and emphasis. As external environmental factors grew increasingly influential, they affected the autonomy and integrity of the Yiddish schools as well as the ideology of different Yiddish secular school movements.

Ideology

The major initial issues which distinguished the Yiddish secular school movements and caused the establishment of four rather than one Yiddish secularist educational movement were (1) cultural versus territorial nationalism, (2) the place of Hebrew in the curriculum, (3) the place of religious tradition in the curriculum, (4) political versus educational emphasis, and (5) the nature of universalist affiliations. The first and second issues separated the Sholem Aleichem, Workmen's Circle, and International Workers' Order schools from most of the Farband which believed in the establishment of a Jewish homeland and in the traditional heritage – both of which focused heavily upon Hebrew. The third separated the more tradition-oriented Farband and the Sholem Aleichem from the Workmen's Circle and the International Workers' Order. The fourth divided the Sholem Aleichem from the others because they desired their organization to be apolitical and focused primarily upon educational matters, regardless of the affiliations of individual members. The fifth isolated the International Workers' Order from the others because of International Workers' Order identification with the Soviet Union up to World War II, and the total rejection by the other Yiddish secular school movements of the USSR variety of socialism.

The ideological differences that existed among the Yiddish secular school movements in the early years of their activity on the American scene narrowed considerably by mid-century, and the curricular modifications which followed this shift made the schools of each of the Yiddish secular school movements less distinct – one from the other – than they had ever been before.

Even before these changes began to occur, however, it was clear that the curricula of the Yiddish secular school movements could not be expected to transmit to young children the specifics of the ideological positions which separated the movements. In spite of this (and perhaps because of an under-estimation of the socioeconomic forces arrayed against them, and the persistence of the old ideological fanaticisms characteristic of the late nineteenth and early twentieth centuries), the Yiddish secular school movements did not carefully analyze or fully appreciate the position, the needs, and the vulnerability of an ethnic school system. They, therefore, placed ideological considerations before educational priorities and maintained their schools in a manner which proved to be pedagogically rickety once the supportive external Yiddish linguistic environment no longer existed.

It would seem that, in order to survive, the educational system of a minority group must be as broadly based as possible, concentrate upon educational essentials and the transmission of common rather than distinct ideological elements. Had there been the necessary ideological assessment of common essentials, and a unified educational effort, the decline of the Yiddish language and environment in the aftermath of the Holocaust and the establishment of the State of Israel would not necessarily have resulted in the simultaneous decline of secular Yiddish education in the United States.

The assessment of the quality of the internal elements of the Yiddish secular school movements schools (namely, materials, methodology, teachers, and structure) which follows may help explain their vulnerability to the external social forces which competed with them for the interest of the secularly oriented American Jew.

Materials

In the area of ethnic language the following trends were observable among all the Yiddish secular school movements:

1. a change in curricula emphasis from literature to language;
2. a change in emphasis from authentic materials to educationally contrived materials;

3. a change from a substantive to a structural emphasis which resulted in less use of affective and more use of cognitive and skill-oriented materials;

4. a shift from immersion in literature which reflected distinctive life styles and a language which was used for communication to an appreciational approach to both literature and language (sometimes in translation or transliteration).

In spite of the evidence of shrinkage and decline which the trends referred to above seem to suggest, there is today less denial of the importance of ethnic language among Jews than there was in the pre-World War II era when Yiddish speaking branded the immigrant as a foreigner. The status of ethnic language is, therefore, not the issue it once was. The crucial issues have become which ethnic language, the synchronization of expectations, intensity of exposure, and linguistic approach. Except in day schools, the Yiddish secular school movements have not been able to offer real immersion in both Hebrew and Yiddish. It is clear that the latter is losing ground to the former, probably due to the destruction by Hitler of the largest Yiddish language center in the world in Eastern Europe, and the development of a Hebrew cultural center in Israel. In one-day-a-week schools, achievement in both languages is negligible and most textual materials are unusable.

An examination of history materials suggests the following trends:

1. Except in one or two instances, the ideological views of the Yiddish secularists increasingly received less and less emphasis in the materials used for teaching history.

2. With the decline in Yiddish comprehension, the most effective materials available to the Yiddishists – their Yiddish nontextual, affective sources, e.g. dramatizations and recitations – became useless, and English materials of the same quality were not developed and/or used to the same extent.

3. Material on Jewish history in the twentieth century is largely non-existent. In its absence too much of the responsibility for interpreting the history of the modern era to pupils has fallen upon the classroom teacher, with the result that the period gets much less attention than it warrants (if children are to acquire an understanding of the problems of the modern Jew).

4. History increasingly had to be taught in English, as Yiddish comprehension declined. Teachers became more and more dependent upon materials available in English that were published almost exclusively by Jewish religious denominations. It is likely that a pooling by the four Yiddish secular movements of resources and personnel might have resulted in more distinctive, appropriate, and up-to-date materials than are now available. A more ecumenical spirit would have, at the very least, permitted the dissemination of the International Workers' Order history series in English, which, while far from perfect, is ideologically more appropriate to Yiddish secularism than those used by Jewish religious groups.

The desire to develop a Yiddish secularist tradition and ritual was somewhat obstructed by the duplication and fragmentation resulting from the variety of materials produced by the Yiddish secular school movements for this purpose. It would seem that a basic ingredient of a successful tradition or ritual is acceptance of its standardized form, whatever that may be, by a group large enough to give it stability. In the case of the Yiddish secularist school movements no effort was made to achieve a unified ritual. This fact, in combination with the categorization of Americans by religious affiliation (which was common in the forties and fifties), and the absence of a standardized secular ritual, caused a return among most of the Yiddish secular school movements to some of the elements of the standardized Orthodox ritual.

The exit of many Jews from the working classes caused the modification of their proletarian universalist position to one of liberal humanism. This change resulted, in a curricular sense, in the reduction of behavioral possibilities for participation in militant universalist causes and reduced the usefulness of previously effective models and heroes for which no new substitutes were offered.

If the materials of the Yiddish secular school movements are assessed as a whole, it can be said that, except for the use of excellent primary sources in literature, and of affective, nontextual, and community resources, there was not enough development of appropriate education materials at times when they would have been most useful. This lack of materials and the constant lag between changing needs and the availability of new materials were due to limited human and physical resources as well as to the ideological loyalties which kept the Yiddish secular school movements from pooling their facilities and talent. Most Yiddishists also resisted (even when Yiddish usage was already in severe decline) analysis and examination of their curricula in a manner which would focus on, and invigorate, aspects of Yiddish secularism other than Yiddish language learning.

Methodology

The primary methodological strength of the Yiddish secular school movements lay in their ability to relate nontextual and community resources to the formal aspects of the curriculum and thereby to increase affective learning. It was this factor more than any other that gave a dynamic quality to their schools, and this element was the most difficult to retain when environmental conditions altered.

The austere conditions under which the Yiddish secular school movements began their activity were probably partially responsible for their emphasis upon content rather than upon the process of transmission of that content. While pupil comprehension of Yiddish remained high, and the Yiddish and proletarian environments were supportive, methodological weaknesses were not so apparent.

Cover page of the Workmen's Circle *Kinder tsaytung*, one of four Yiddish children's magazines currently appearing in the USA. The alphabet chart shows several orthographic conventions (e.g. those for v, oy, ay, ey, zh and tsh) that differentiate between Yiddish and Hebrew. At lower right: stanza from Yiddish folksong: 'Children, when you become older you will understand by yourselves how many tears these letters contain and how much weeping.'

As these supports disintegrated, the need for methodologically sound approaches to subject matter became manifest.

Limited resources and personnel, as well as a constant preoccupation with coverage of material in the face of growing anxiety about reduced study time, appear to be more responsible for the absence of methodological sensitivity than for the outright rejection of the significance of this factor in the educational process. International Workers' Order language and history materials reflect more attention to this matter than do those of the other Yiddish secular school movements, but not enough. Furthermore, this groups' willingness to offer Yiddish literature in translation gave their pupils a knowledge of Yiddish culture (that was denied to some of the children in the other Yiddish secular school movements) as well as an opportunity to engage in substantive discussion about both subjects.

In spite of a considerable body of literature about child-centered learning and some early experimentation in this area by the four movements, it is clear that the Yiddish supplementary school was a traditional rather than a developmental learning environment. The Yiddish teacher emphasized group rather than individual instruction, and utilized primarily standardized methods and materials. However, flexibility of approach and integration of general and Jewish subject matter were apparent in many day-school classes, and a few talented afternoon school teachers were able to include some of these elements in their teaching.

It seems clear that, as in the area of materials, the Yiddish secular school movements depended too heavily upon ideology, a supportive community, and the teacher and did not provide adequate methodological direction and guidance.

Teachers

Many of the teachers of the Yiddish secular school movements entered their profession without academic credentials, but, supported by a conducive ideological and ethnic environment, they were willing to assume an instructional leadership role in a community-oriented school. While Yiddish teachers' seminars helped prepare candidates for the intellectual tasks they were to face, the meagerness of financial resources and the heavy reliance on voluntary rather than paid maintenance and office staff added a multitude of responsibilities to the academic burdens of the Yiddish teacher. During the decades when the Yiddish school was a neighborhood cultural center for adults and children, low wages, long hours, and a variety of distasteful tasks were compensated for by some sense of achievement as reflected in successful programs, numbers of children graduating and continuing into Yiddish High Schools, adult interest in cultural activities, and a sense of communal intimacy.

As the nature of the Jewish community changed, however, the relationship between it and the schools was affected. Yiddish became a foreign language, and the activities which were related to it were no longer of interest. Old adult workers moved away or died and were not replaced by younger newcomers. Pupil numbers and school hours declined. Few graduates of the Yiddish secular school movements chose to make Yiddish teaching their professional career. As the Yiddish teacher grew older, he was forced to put aside most of the Yiddish literary heritage that he had earlier shared with his pupils and interested adults and turn to the teaching of introductory Yiddish. As the Yiddish school became more and more removed from the mainstream, the Yiddish teacher grew increasingly isolated. In the absence of adequate supervision and methodological assistance, the few new teachers who were recruited and hired (often without satisfactory backgrounds) were sometimes less equal to the instructional responsibilities than some of their older colleagues. Rapport between some youthful teachers and their pupils, while initially beneficial, did not prove durable without content expertise and pedagogical competencies.

The most crucial problem facing the Yiddish secular school movements today is a lack of able teachers who have good substantive backgrounds, sensitivity to the child and his context, and the commitment and the ability to relate the former to the latter.

Structure

The schools of all the Yiddish secular school movements were community schools in the pre-World War II period. The involvement of school workers and the common struggle to keep the school in existence gave the enterprise a personal quality, and an internal resourcefulness which more efficiently operated institutions with secure financial support from governmental agencies do not always have. (Glazer (1970) makes the point in *Beyond the Melting Pot* that the welfare system and television may well have contributed to the disintegration of the social fabric of Puerto Rican life in New York City.) The schools of the Yiddish secular school movements were vehicles for the creation and strengthening of social and communal bonds.

When the communal–cultural center quality began to break down under the impact of changes in neighborhood and life-style, the Yiddish schools became more limited, both educationally and structurally. Many schools in the old neighborhoods closed for lack of pupils; others became less intensive until the typical pattern was no longer five days a week of study but one to three days a week. Only the day schools and a few exceptional supplementary schools maintained the type of curricular immersion which had existed in earlier years. As supportive structures in the larger community disappeared, the ability of the Yiddish school to be somewhat self-contained, i.e. to constitute a minicommunity and offer cultural and social as well as educational opportunities, became even more important than it had been during earlier times. The trend to limited structures, however, reduced the flexibility and variety of contact and activities which were possible at the very time when they were most needed.

The relatively small student body that was characteristic of each local neighborhood school in the pre-World War II period made it extremely sensitive to slight variations in the immediate vicinity. The advantage of a small student body, however, was that pupils probably gained a sense of personal contact and intimacy with the teacher in small classes, which often did not exceed ten children.

It is evident from what has been said about materials, methodology, teachers, and structure that, although the Yiddish secular school movements utilized community and affective resources very sensitively when these were available, their schools were never really internally sound institutions, from an organizational point of view. The weaknesses resulting originally from limitations in conditions and facilities, and more recently from limitations in structure and intensity of program, became increasingly obvious as the facilitative climate of the first half of the twentieth century disappeared.

Accomplishments and failures

Great faith existed among educators of the Yiddish secular school movements in the power of substantive content (offered in affectively suitable forms) to develop strong convictions and commitments. Perhaps because of the long tradition among Jews of strong communal ties and mutual responsibility, Yiddishists took them for granted, paying little attention to structure, processes, means, and vehicles of operation. They concentrated instead upon goals, principles, and the transmission of a unified value system and life-style. This was an ambitious set of objectives in a country without strong communal traditions. It reflected a naïve misinterpretation of a period in which industrialization increasingly encouraged conditions which stressed process, structure, vehicles of change, and mobility and created fragmentation and atomization. Furthermore, if Fishman (see documentation in Parker 1973) is correct in suggesting that Americanization was supraethnic, neutral, nonideological and nonvalue-oriented, and it is for this reason that Jews did not view its acceptance as a form of ethnic betrayal, then the nonvalue-oriented value system of American society was indeed the greatest saboteur of Yiddish secularism. However, the vast Yiddish-speaking Jewish community of the Lower East Side of New York in the first quarter of the twentieth century did not clearly assess its vulnerability, nor could it predict the abrupt extermination of its well springs in Eastern Europe and adequately prepare for the circumstances it would have to face after World War II.

Once the distinctive linguistic, ideological, and communal aspects of the Yiddish secular school movements' education were undermined by the processes of assimilation and social change, the most significant achievements of the Yiddish secular school movements, the behavioral and affective quality of the relationships fostered among pupils, adults, the community school, and the larger community was grossly impaired. Except in the few day schools and intensive supplementary programs that are still in existence, and have usually gifted and sensitive teachers and administrators, the dynamic aspects of the schools have disappeared, and the programs are, at best, oriented to academic knowledge and appreciation, and, at worst, are strongly fragmented by a skill-based program which has lost its coherence and distinctive direction.

The discrete ideological differences which separated the Yiddish secular school movements in the early years of their activity were not reflected in conspicuous differences in the quality of educational approach, either in terms of materials or methodology. In general, all the Yiddish secular school movements have become more ethnocentric in the last two decades.

Relevance for the child

At its best Yiddish secular education was probably a relevant experience for pupils because it provided a sense of continuity, group identity, and pride, all of which are necessary to emotional stability and a positive self-image. In addition, the strong emphasis upon behavioral and affective elements offered abundant opportunities for meeting developmental needs of children, which fell within the realms of the perceptual, emotional, aesthetic, and psychomotor, as well as within the cognitive, domain. Close relationships with adults within the context of the Yiddish school, and in the larger community, provided children with real as well as vicarious models, and also afforded visibility and recognition among concerned, familiar adults who were somewhat more objective and less emotionally involved than their own parents.

The loss of the extended environment of the Yiddish school probably resulted in a loss of relevance of Yiddish education to the child, and this became more true as the activities of the school grew more limited. The decline in Yiddish language comprehension was not as severe an instructional problem, because flexible teachers can cope with this deficiency up to a point. It was, however, a loss of one of the basic elements that gave the Yiddish school environment its distinctiveness.

The remoteness of textual references also did not appear to pose problems of relevance as long as the teacher was aware of them and utilized powerful elements, taken from the child's experience, to help give them meaning and context. The increasing lack of excellent teachers seems, therefore, to be a greater cause of pupil dissatisfaction than the quality of instructional material. However, more appropriate resources would be of considerable help to inexperienced teachers whose guidance has come primarily from the materials which they use.

Relevance for the ethnic group

Societal factors seem to have arrayed themselves in such a manner on the American scene as to have made the ideas and the activities of the Yiddish secular school movements largely invisible to the Jewish mainstream. That there are large numbers of nonreligiously oriented, noninstitutionally affiliated, philosophically liberal, secular Jews on the American scene, who continue to identify themselves as Jews, seems beyond dispute. Whether they would have found, had they known about its existence, or would now find, some form of Yiddish secular education relevant to their needs is difficult to judge.

The decline in emphasis upon universal and current aspects of life has not only resulted in a loss of ideological distinctiveness for which no new substitute has been found, either in terms of content or in terms of useful models and heroes, but it has also strongly affected the relevance of the ethnic material which *is* offered. It would appear that the underlying factors which were responsible for the relevance and effectiveness of these schools are related to the sensitive employment of universal elements within ethnic subject matter and within extracurricular activities. Regional, suburban Yiddish schools that have emerged in new Jewish population areas, operating a one- or two-day program, find themselves physically unable to organize many on-going curricular, social action, and humanistic programs, either for older classes of pupils or for adults.

Is ethnicity a divisive element?

In some quarters there is the feeling that to encourage the strengthening of ethnicity and cultural pluralism is to court civil strife and extremism. And indeed, a perusal of history and the daily newspaper will provide ample evidence to support this contention. It is easily proven then that in many places in this country, and abroad, ethnic allegiances have been responsible for unrest and even turmoil. Careful examination of these situations, however, indicates that in a substantial number of such cases the minority, rather than the majority, have been in some way victimized and the upheaval is an effort to right a long-standing injustice.

The fundamental question is whether ethnicity in its essence is necessarily ethnocentric, and whether ethnic groups will under all circumstances place their own perceived needs before and above those of others; in other words, whether ethnicity and universalism must be antagonistic forces. Scrutiny of the behavior of the Yiddish secular school movements may shed some light on this subject. Although Yiddish secularism was an ideological movement (with various points of view) and was engaged in political and economic activity within the larger society, it sought to perpetuate its ethnicity primarily through educational and cultural means. It viewed the task of persuading Jews to commit themselves to a Yiddish secularist, ethnic identification as a major goal rather than as a vehicle for the attainment of economic and political equality. Examination of the history of this movement, since the turn of the century, suggests that the period of greatest emphasis on universalism was congruent with the period of greatest ethnicity and that both declined together. Increasing curricular focus upon Jewish material, at the expense of universalist material, is a reflection not of increased ethnicity but of an effort to stem the tide of loss of ethnicity. Clearly, the example of the Yiddish secularist experience strongly suggests that ethnicity need not necessarily be a danger to the larger society.

The Jewish Torah in Yiddish. Finally, Jewish children will be able to utter 'a Yiddish word'. (Honoring the modern Yiddish translation of the Bible by Yehoyesh, shown giving the Ten Commandments on 'Mt. Bronx'.) (*Der groyser kundes*, September 30, 1926)

IMPLICATIONS OF THE YIDDISH SECULAR SCHOOL MOVEMENT'S
EXPERIENCE FOR ETHNIC EDUCATION

During the last few years, there has been a growing awareness of the fact that minority groups face common educational problems. It is not always acknowledged, however, that groups which are no longer the victims of socio-economic or political discrimination are ethnic minorities, and may have experience to contribute that can be of value to others.

The following conclusions, which are based upon the experience of the education activity of the Yiddish secular school movements, may have some bearing on educational efforts to create and maintain cultural identity. The Yiddish secular school movements seemed to achieve their own goals best when:

1. They had a supportive ethnic environment with a variety of cultural structures upon which they could depend.

2. They maintained an active relationship with the larger world, while simultaneously preserving their inner distinctiveness which, though unique, was not parochial in the pre-World War II period.

3. Their schools were neighborhood–community cultural centers rather than when, in later years, they became more limited types of institutions.

4. They were functionally dependent upon voluntary, nonprofessional, often inefficient, adult help in the maintenance of the schools.

5. Ethnic language competency was at a level which made it possible to use Yiddish for delineating a unique linguistic environment in the schools. As Yiddish comprehension declined, the conflict between those who were willing to compromise some substance for retention of a Yiddish environment and those who stressed the importance of content over environmental factors sharpened. The importance of language to the quality of the school environment cannot be minimized, however, and the desire or need to maintain such an environment and to teach the cultural heritage in the original rather than in translation has implications for the depth of ethnic education which is possible.

6. The curricular and extracurricular experiences which they offered were more value-oriented and ideologically delineated, and affective materials were used in great abundance, in contrast with the later period (post-World War II) when content was treated more scholastically.

7. They were able, because of appropriate structure and personnel, to correlate ethnic and general content.

The Yiddish secular school movements seemed to grow educationally less effective when:

1. They failed to search for ways to reinterpret their ethnicity and universalism in a manner which would offer pupils relevant involvements with issues and models within their *present* ethnic and general community *at home* as well as in areas remote from their own physical residence. This issue seems crucial because,

for example, traditional heros like Jewish sweatshop workers, although they continue to be important elements of the Yiddish secular heritage, are not powerful enough to induce a sense of current identification or affect communal participation, during a period in which Jewish life-styles and problems are very different from those of the early twentieth century. All cultures in transition (among them many minority groups in this century) face the dilemma of the nature, direction, and degree of adaptation and reinterpretation which a cultural heritage can sustain without losing its essential character. However, unless this issue is realistically faced at an appropriate time, ethnic education runs the risk of becoming parochial, out-moded, and ethnocentric.

2. The status of the Yiddish teacher sank so low that only the rare individual considered Yiddish secular teaching as a possible professional goal. Talented, elderly Yiddish teachers who retire or die are irreplaceable, and this situation is not unique to Yiddish or even to Jewish education, nor is it totally solvable from within the ethnic group. The crucial shortage of competent teachers is probably the most serious problem facing the Yiddish secular school movements, and finding the means to increase the commitment to ethnic teaching, as well as the status and rewards that are connected with it, is not simple in a nation whose government does not even adequately support mainstream cultural endeavors in the arts and in education.

3. They failed to improve the quality and appropriateness of the method and materials they used.

4. They failed to guarantee the type of structural organization, except in a limited number of cases, which would provide the kinds of activities and involvements within the school community which in earlier years had been possible as a result of dependence upon frameworks external to it.

The Yiddish secular school movements developed schools that contained many of the human, social, ideological, and value-oriented elements which are essential to a good educational process. However, they lacked some of the qualities which provide an educational institution with internal stability, namely, the coherent provision of appropriate materials, methods, personnel, and structure to sustain an educational program without excessive reliance on the existence of conducive external, environmental factors. The proper combination of a values-based curriulum, on the one hand, and an orderly structure on the other, is difficult to achieve. Most public educational systems suffer more from a lack in the former dimension (of Yiddishist strength) than in the latter dimension which proved to be the Achilles heel of the Yiddishists. Due to their fragility, ethnic schools must, in order to guarantee their own survival, offer an education which is of superior quality in both of these areas, and the two dimensions must be properly articulated. Otherwise, ethnic schools will neither be able to withstand the impact of the forces of change nor be able to provide the quality of education which they have the potential to provide.

Implications for American society

There is certainly evidence of disenchantment with aspects of the American dream which three or four decades ago so enticed the immigrant. The feelings of alienation, lack of identity, sense of powerlessness, and lack of sense of community which are expressed by American youth today were not so apparent a half century ago. On the contrary, the writings of pupils from the early days of the Yiddish secular school movements, and undoubtedly of other young people of the pre-World War II era as well, are full of optimism, a sense of human solidarity and community, and powerfulness. The differences in attitudes between then and now can probably be attributed to the complexity of current issues and to a loss of naïveté about them. To some extent, however, the impact on individuals and groups of a skill- and process-oriented society which deemphasizes strong communal relationships and commitments, and reinforces competition and the formation of many short-term, associational ties, must be compared to that of the Yiddish secular school movements' form of education which stressed historical continuity, community responsibility, consideration and acceptance of a value system, and behavioral commitment to the improvement of man's physical and cultural life.

It is probable that the decline experienced by the Yiddish secular school movements in recent years is largely a result of the clash between the former and the latter constellations of social elements, and that the Yiddish secularists, like members of other ethnic groups, were not able to withstand the force and momentum of the American mainstream. It may be argued, however, that the disappearance of the qualities inherent in a Yiddish secular education, rather than the specifics of its program, have resulted in a loss not only to the Yiddish secular school movements but also to the quality of American society. If the words and actions of the youth are to be believed, the need for these elements within a constructive educational system and a healthy society are manifest.

Given the unequal strength of the adversaries, it is clear that the survival of ethnic education as a valuable essence, rather than as a temporary expedient for economic and political mobility, cannot be left either to the efforts of the cultural minorities or to instinctive responses alone. Facilitating external conditions which once existed, but have largely disappeared, may have to be restored in some form, and this could become an awesome task of revising social and economic priorities. Provision of support for the improvement of internal ethnic educational facilities may also be necessary in greater measure than has been available. There is no doubt that all this will require governmental planning and involvement at a level, and with a degree of sensitivity, which shows that there is as much national concern for human and cultural resources as now exists for economic and environmental resources. Properly understood, this effort, to encourage ethnic identity and community commitment, will be viewed as a program to rehumanize and repersonalize American society rather than as a philanthropic gesture toward a few minority groups.

REFERENCES

Alter, R. (1969), 'The Jewish Community and the Jewish Condition', *Commentary* (February).

— (1940), *Amol Un Haynt* [Long Ago and Today] Collection of Essays of Mitlshul Students. Chicago, Workmen's Circle.

Bez, Kh. (Kh. Bezprozvani) (1949), 'Yidishe geshikhte un natsyonale dertsiyung' [Jewish History and National Education], *Bleter far yidisher dertsiyung* June–September. New York, Congress for Jewish Culture.

Bez, Kh. (1951), 'Di program fun a yidisher shul' [The Program of a Yiddish School], *Bleter far yidisher dertsiyung*. June–September. New York, Congress for Jewish Culture.

Chanin, N. (1944), 'Kultur tetikayt in un arum di shuln', [Cultural Activity in and Around our Schools], *Kultur un dertsiyung* (April): 6–7. New York, Workmen's Circle.

Curriculum of the Jewish Secular Schools (1962), prepared by teachers of the Los Angeles Kindershuln. Los Angeles, California.

Derekh [The Way] (1969–1971), New York: Sholem Aleichem Folk Institute, February, 1969; May–June, 1970; November–December, 1970; January–February, 1971; November–December, 1969.

Di arbeter kinder (1935), [The Child Workers] (play in one act). New York: Workmen's Circle.

Dushkin, A. (1918), *Jewish Education in New York City*. New York, Bureau of Jewish Education.

Dushkin, A., Engelman, Z. (1959), *Jewish Education in the United States*. New York, American Association for Jewish Education.

Eisenberg, A. (1968), *World Census on Jewish Education 5728–1968*, ed. by World Council on Jewish Education. New York.

Fishman, J. (1953), 'Summary of findings reported in a study of attitudes held by teachers in Jewish schools toward children and toward various other aspects of Jewish teaching work', in *Jewish Education Survey*. New York, Jewish Education Committee.

— (1965a), 'Yiddish in America', *International Journal of American Linguistics* 3(2) (April). Indiana University Research Center.

— (1965b), 'Language maintenance and language shift', *Sociologus* 16(1). Berlin, Dunker and Humblet.

Fishman, J. et al. (1966), *Language Loyalty in the United States*. The Hague, Mouton.

Friedman, G. (1968), *The End of the Jewish People?* New York, Doubleday.

'Fun di kinder in america – far di kinder in poyln' [From the Children in America – For the Children in Poland) (1940), *Kinder-tzaytung*, January. New York: Workmen's Circle.

Glazer, N., Moynihan, D.P. (1970), *Beyond the Melting Pot*. Cambridge, Massachusetts, M.I.T. Press.

Goldberg, I. (n.d.), *Di naye hagode* [The New Hagaddah]. New York, Service Bureau for Jewish Education.

Goldberg, I. (1961), *Jewish Secular Education: Its Values and Meanings*. New York, Kinderbuch Publications.

Goodman, H. (1961), *Our People through the Middle Ages*, vols. 1 and 2. New York, Kinderbuch Publications.

Hagaddah (n.d.), New York, Service Bureau for Jewish Education.

Hagode shel peysekh [Hagaddah of Passover], *A New Hagaddah for Passover, Festival of Freedom* (n.d.), Brookline, Massachusetts, Y. L. Peretz Children's School of the Workmen's Circle.

In dinst fun folk [In the Service of the People] *Almanac of the Jewish People's Fraternal Order* (1947), New York, Jewish People's Fraternal Order Press.

Jewish Schools in America: A Description of Types of Jewish Schooling in Jewish Communities in the United States and Canada (1947), New York, American Association of Jewish Education.

Kallen, H. (1950), *Jewish Education for American Jews*. Boston, American Association for Jewish Education.

'Kinderklangen' [Children's Sounds] (1942), Montreal, Committee of School Pupils of Jewish People's Shul.

'Labor Zionist Organization of America Statement on Jewish Day Schools' (1964), *Jewish Education* 34 (4).

Lehrer, L. (1928), 'Boiberik', in *Yearbook*. New York, Sholem Aleichem Folk Institute.

Mark, Y. (1956), *Veltlekhe yidishkayt un di sholem aleykhem shuln*, [Secular Jewishness and the Sholem Aleichem Schools]. New York, Sholem Aleichem Folk Institute.

Mlotek, J. (1967), 'Zorg farn yidishn lerer' [Concern for the Yiddish Teacher], *Kultur un dertsiyung*. New York, Workmen's Circle.

Parker, Sandra (1973), 'Inquiry into the Yiddish secular schools in the United States: a curricular perspective'. Unpublished Ph.D. dissertation, Harvard University, Cambridge, Mass.

Scheffler, I. (1969), 'Reflections on Educational Relevance', *The Journal of Philosophy* 26 (21): 764–773.

Schiff, A. (1966). *The Jewish Day School in America*. New York, Jewish Education Committee Press.

S.A.F.I. Views (1969–1971). New York: Sholem Aleichem Folk Institute (April, May, September–October, December, 1969; February, September–October, November–December, 1970; January–February, March–April, June, 1971).

Shapiro, J. (1970), *The Friendly Society, A History of the Workmen's Circle*. New York, Media Judaica.

Shloyme vaysman bukh [Shlomo Wiseman Book] (1961). Montreal, Yidishe Folk Shuln.

The Suburban Jewish School (1958), New Jersey, Cooperative Enterprise of Parent Body.

Yidishe dertsiyung (Jewish Education) (1938), New York, Jewish National Workers' Alliance (see also March, 1939; May, 1940; No. 1; 1950, No. 8; December, 1962.)

Yidisher lerer seminar [Yiddish Teacher's Seminar] *Naye klasn un naye kursn* (New Classes and New Courses) Catalog–Brochure (1929), New York.

Yugntruf [International Jewish Youth Journal] (1964–1972), New York, Yugntruf.

Zaltz, P. (1950), 'Traditsye in undzere shuln' [Tradition in our schools], *Yidishe dertsiyung* 101–107. New York: Jewish National Workers' Alliance.

Why Yiddish for our Children? (1956), New York, Sholem Aleichem Folk Institute.

פּרֺאגרֺאם פֿון דער פֿײַערונג אין טעאַטער „פּאַלאַס" רעדנער: —
מ. שאַליט, מ. װײַנרײַך, ז. רײַזען; 1טער אַקט — ד"ר עטינגערס
„סערקעלע"; 2טער אַקט — מענדעלע מוכר ספֿרים — „דער
פּריזיװ", גאָלדפֿאַדענס מוזיק.

Program of the celebration in the "Palace" Theater.
Speakers: M. Schalit, M. Weinreich, Z. Reisen: 1st
act — Dr. Ettinger's "Serkele"; 2nd act — Mendele
Mocher Sforim's "The Draft", Goldfaden's music

One-hundredth anniver-
sary of the Yiddish press:
a celebration organized
by the Association of Yiddish Writers and Journal-
ists of Vilna (1924).

The American Yiddish Press at Its Centennial

B. Z. GOLDBERG

The first Yiddish newspaper in America, *Di Yiddishe Tseitung*, which appeared in 1870, was by no means the first Yiddish newspaper in the world, nor, of course, the first Jewish publication in this country.

The very firstborn of the Yiddish press saw the light of day close to two centuries earlier, back in 1686, only some decades after the first appearance of newspapers in Western Europe. That newspaper, *Courant*, was published in Amsterdam to serve the commercial interest of the Ashkenazi, Yiddish-speaking Jewish community, just as the *Gaceta De Amsterdam*, in Ladino Spanish, established ten years earlier, had been serving the same interests of the Sephardic Jewish community of that city.

In America, the first Jewish publication was *The Jew*. It came out in 1822 and its purpose was not commercial, but antidefamation, to counteract the scurrilous attacks by some Christian missionaries upon the Jewish religion and the practicing Jews. Then, with the wave of Jewish migration from Germany and Central Europe during the turbulent period of the Revolution of 1848, came the impetus for the rise of a Jewish press in this country. Primarily in English, but also in German, with some of the English publications carrying sections in German to bridge the gap between the generations, these publications, surprising for their time, had both a wide scope and an enlightened aproach to the problems of their community. *The Asmonian*, which began publication in 1849 and which could well compare with the best Anglo-Jewish weeklies of our time, represented itself as 'a family journal of commerce, politics, religion and literature, devoted to the interests of American Israelites'.

To see the Yiddish press in its full perspective one must place it in the framework of the Jewish press as a whole. Ever since the turn of the eighteenth century the Jewish press consisted, linguistically, of three categories, Hebrew, Yiddish, and the non-Jewish languages of the countries in which Jews lived. And each category had its own characteristic and purpose.

The Hebrew press, which may be said to have begun with *Pri Etz Hayim*, published by the Amsterdam Rabbinate in 1728, and *Koheleth Musar*, founded by Moses Mendelssohn in Berlin in 1750, was concerned more with Judaism than with Jews, a sort of modern extension of Rabbinic literature. While these early publications came to include mundane matters dealing with the Jewish condition, their *raison d'être* was ideological, the major issue being the developing struggle between Enlightenment and Reform Judaism and historical Orthodoxy. The pacemakers in this duel were the *Bikurei Haitim* of Vienna, for Reform, 1820, and *Hamaggid* of Berlin, 1850, for the Orthodox.

In its upsurge in the 1860s the Hebrew press took a more modern turn. Still dealing with the ancient verities, its methods were analytical rather than dialectic, and its major concern was with the Jewish situation. Limited, because of the language, to the Talmudic elite, this new Hebrew press sought to guide them into the nineteenth century. Of the various efforts to establish a daily newspaper in Hebrew – one of them in this country – to provide current news and comment for the Hebrew readers, only one, *Hazman*, of Vilno, managed to struggle along for a number of years, despite its proper ideology of Zionism, nationalism, and the furtherance of renascent Hebrew. It was only in Palestine, after Hebrew became the living tongue of the people, that daily newspapers appeared – still on an ideological basis, reflecting the political parties or social movements.

The Jewish press in the non-Jewish languages of the Diaspora, which has included most languages of Europe and some Asian tongues, generally followed the pattern of the Hebrew press. Circumstances, however, imposed certain characteristic changes. Judaism was still the *raison d'être*, but since it catered to a potential mass of ignorant, assimilated Jews it concentrated on religious practices rather than on learning and deep meaning. As the readership was not presumed to have a wide interest in Jewish affairs, the coverage of Jewish news was meager, abbreviated, without background or comment, and, of course, it brought no general news. Strictly a community press, its preoccupation was with local activities and personal trivia. Speaking in a voice that was intelligible to non-Jews as well, it was ever conscious of the non-Jewish presence, and sensitive to interfaith relations, anti-Semitism, and defamation. Hence, the impression, not always justified, of its being parochial and on the defensive. The rise of Israel gave a new dimension to the Diaspora Jewish press, widening its scope and adding, perforce, interest in certain areas of world affairs. But it has always and everywhere assumed that its readers follow the general press of the land.

Unlike the Hebrew and Diaspora Jewish publications, the Yiddish press was, from its very inception, a general press for Jews. *Courant* of 1686 contained no articles on Judaism, no material dealing with internal Jewish problems. Its objective was to bring to its readers those world events that might concern them because of their direct or indirect connection with particular parts of the world. In the issue of August 27, 1687, for example, *Courant* featured on its front page

The Jewish Daily Forward
Introduces Four Pages of
English and is oblivious to
its own impending doom
by so doing. (Note: the
English pages were sub-
sequently discontinued as
having no impact on cir-
culation but were reintro-
duced, in the Sunday
edition, as of 1980). (*Der
groyser kundes*, April 30,
1926)

the invasion of Turkey by a Venetian fleet, the arrival of Dutch ships in Moscow, a terrific storm in France (Bayonne), and a mishap in a race in England. A little over a century later, in 1798, we have an echo of the French Revolution in the Yiddish *Discours* of Amsterdam, in its complaint that 'no king is as sovereign as Kahal', meaning the authorities of the Jewish community. Similarly, the *Beobachter an der Weichsel* (Observer on the Vistula) of Warsaw, 1823, reflected the mood of its time, while a Roumanian Yiddish newspaper with a Hebrew name, *Eys Ledaber* (Time to Speak Up) Bucharest, 1850, issued a call for democracy within the Jewish community, with the heading, *Liberty, Equality, Fraternity!*

The Yiddish press was oriented, not towards the intellectual elite, but towards the plain people, the toilers, artisans, and petty traders, who had neither the advantage of years of study in a yeshiva, where they might have acquired a command of Hebrew, nor any schooling in the language of the country where they might have picked up a reading knowledge of that language. The Yiddish newspaper was the only one which these people could read. But it was more than a newspaper to them. It was their only window to the world, their guide, their teacher, and their entertainer.

The Yiddish press always devoted twice as much space to general reading matter as it did to spot news, which was of current events in the world, in the country, and, of course, of happenings to Jews everywhere. The general reading matter, however, was varied in content and depth. Sensational news items, human interest stories, bits of interesting information such as one might find in popular magazines, originated there. Central in these columns was what one might call Jewish educational material, such as discussions of Jewish problems, reviews of trends in Judaism, surveys of Jewish movements, the retelling, as the occasion might warrant, of dramatic events in Jewish history, and biographies of great men of the Jewish past.

The great pride of the Yiddish press has always been that it was the first publisher of many, if not most, of the major works of Yiddish literature, thus giving them at once a mass readership of many tens of thousands, and, no less important, providing a livelihood for the authors. Beginning with the grandfather of modern Yiddish literature (and of modern Hebrew literature as well), S. J. Abramowitz, over a century ago, down through the years to our own day, all of the great Yiddish writers have been professionally connected with the Yiddish press, not writing especially for it, but publishing whatever they wrote first and exclusively in particular newspapers, with novels appearing serially. Almost all of the works of Sholom Aleichem and of Scholem Asch, to name only those best known to non-Yiddish readers in this country, first appeared in print in newspapers.

Surprising as it may seem today, both Russia and the United States were latecomers to the Yiddish press. For Russia the date is 1862, with the lateness due to Czarist restriction. Jewish books, in Hebrew or Yiddish, could be published freely, requiring only the stamp of the censor, but a periodical, which was also subject to the censor's approval, had to have a permit from the highest authority, the minister of education, who often referred the matter to the Czar himself. So it was with the application by Alexander Tsederbaum for permission to issue *Hamelitz*, the first Hebrew publication in Russia. Czar Alexander II returned the application to the minister with a notation in his own hand, reading as follows: 'In my opinion, a new journal in Hebrew is entirely unnecessary, for the Jews, with the exception of their Rabbis, have forgotten that language almost completely. But to publish a newspaper in Judaeo-German would be, in my opinion, very very useful in educating the Jews and would cure them of

Yiddish (reflecting on R. Braynin's Hebrew sales-pitch for his new weekly *Hadoar*): 'What is he saying? He wants ten cents for something or other. It appears to be in my alphabet but I can't make head nor tail out of it.' (*Der groyser kundes*, September 8, 1911)

their sickness of fanaticism. But the matter does not interest me. Do as you may find necessary'. After struggling for two years, the *Hamelitz* was about to close, having only 500 subscribers, but Tsederbaum saved it by adding a Yiddish supplement, actually a new publication, the first Yiddish periodical in Russia, *Kol Mevaser*. He said he wanted a newspaper 'in plain Yiddish so that the plain people, and even women, might know what was going on in the world'. He had also realized, of course, that 'while one man in a town might read Hebrew, the whole town could read Yiddish'. *Kol Mevaser* soon covered the deficit of the *Hamelitz*.

The tardiness of the Yiddish press in America was due primarily to the paucity of Yiddish speaking immigrants in this country prior to the exodus from Russia that began in the 1880s. The exact number of Jews in this country in 1870 cannot be determined with certainty, for the census bureau has had no ethnic or religious entries, and the immigration records, which would be a major gauge for an intelligent estimate, first included Jews as a separate entity only in 1899. The usual estimate for the Jewish population for the period is 50,000 in 1840 and 260,000 in 1880. The Jewish immigration estimate for the 1840–1880 years is 200,000, with the 1870 figure, itself, being close to 100,000. While the first East European Jewish congregation in America dates from 1819, only seventeen years after the first German Jewish one in 1802, the bulk of Jewish immigration to this country up to 1870 came from the Germanic countries.

Another obstacle to the emergence of a Yiddish press in this country was the absence of an intellectual element to produce it. In the early years it was regarded improper for a respectable person to emigrate to America. A father, boasting of his parental achievement, was said to have claimed that none of his sons was a worker, a soldier, or an emigrant to America, all three being considered social denigration. If a learned Jew did go to America in those years, he would first qualify as a *shohet*, so that he could provide his own kosher meat, and bring along his own scroll of the Torah, as though going into a spiritual wilderness.

The first publishers and editors of the Yiddish press in this country were stray, restless souls from Rabbinic families, or uprooted intellectuals. The editor-publisher of the very first Yiddish newspaper in this country, J. K. Buchner, was an itinerant journalist who had, in 1865, edited a Jewish annual in Stuttgart called *Volkskalendar für Israeliten* and, in 1867, had edited the first Yiddish paper in London, *Londoner Yiddishe Tseitung*. In 1870 he came to New York, where he started *Di Yiddishe Tseitung*. Since the only Jewish printing shop in the city would not undertake such a formidable job, and no Jewish type was to be had, Buchner produced his newspaper on a lithograph. The publisher-editor of the second Yiddish newspaper, Z. H. Bernstein, imported type from Vilno and Vienna to issue *Di Post*. These early Yiddish publisher-editors were not content with merely providing the news; they also championed social causes. Through his London

Yiddish paper, Buchner organized an Association for the Resettlement of the Holy Land – thirty years before the first Zionist congress. In New York, his *Yiddishe Tseitung* called for tenants to unite against rent increases, and for workers to organize against misuse by their employers. Bernstein carried the fight for his cause even across the ocean. The issue was the direction which Jewish emigration from Eastern Europe was to take. The German Jews in America preferred that East European Jews go anywhere except the United States. One of their publicists planted a story in *Hamaggid* warning potential emigrants from Eastern Europe not to come to these shores, for the people in the country would be unfriendly, there would be nothing for the newcomers to do and many who had come were already homeless and starving. The editor of *Di Post* refuted these statements in a communication to the *Hamaggid*, quoting from the American

He Speaks 'Plain Yiddish'. Ab Kan attacks obscene language, but at the same time he feeds his readers a steady diet of vulgarity drawn from the barrel of 'underworld material'. The reader: 'What does he want? I speak the way he writes!' (*Der groyser kundes*, February 17, 1922)

press on the desirability of immigration and of the availability of jobs, so that 'even a girl, if she only knows how to sew, could find work here'.

In the course of the century the Yiddish press had its ups and downs, with, for a time, as many as half a dozen dailies in New York and as many more in the other major cities of the land. Since every Yiddish newspaper had to have an ideological justification there was actually room for five: two Orthodox of different shades, two socialist, also of different shades, one being straight socialist and the other communist, and one bourgeois-liberal-Zionist-cultural. An anarchist weekly, which began publication seventy years ago, is still appearing regularly. The heyday of the Yiddish press was, of course, during the years of mass migration and the period thereafter. Every ship landing immigrants at Ellis Island brought additional readers. For a while, as many as 100,000 East European Jews came annually. The total circulation of the Yiddish press at that point may have gone beyond the 400,000 mark, with a readership perhaps three times that large. But after the immigration quotas were introduced, and some of the earlier arrivals had died, or turned to the English press, the circulation reached a plateau of close to a quarter of a million. Today, the circulation figure

The poet Avrom Reyzin's new journal *Dos naye land* (The New Land) does not live up to its prospectus. Yiddish (on viewing the chick): 'Is that all? Such a large egg has produced such a tiny chick?' (*Der groyser kundes*, September 22, 1911)

Masthead of *Der groyser kundes* reveals a feather-like pen that tickles, both impishly and in jest, at many sensitive points. Although the title is translated as 'The Big Stick' a more accurate translation would be 'The Great Prankster'.

is just under 100,000, with a readership of more than twice that figure, for three daily newspapers: one socialist by commitment, one bourgeois-liberal-Zionist-cultural, with a commitment to historical tradition and a predilection for modern Orthodoxy, and one pro-communist with a minuscule circulation.

Strange as it may seem, the Yiddish press here has never enjoyed more prestige, not to say yielded greater influence, nor had a more intelligent readership, and, *mirabile dictu*, as many young, American born readers, than it does today. No longer does the Yiddish reader *have* to read his Yiddish newspaper. He can, and does, read his local English newspaper, and listens to newscasts and commentators on the television and radio. And Jewish news has become world news. Still, he reads his old Yiddish newspaper because he finds therein what he cannot find in the English newspaper: more detail and greater in-depth coverage of news about Israel, of the status and struggles of the Jews in the Soviet Union, and of Jewish life everywhere. Even the general news which he finds in the Yiddish newspaper is presented more to his liking, in wider scope and with more perceptive analysis. Other factors may play a role here, such as force of habit, the Yiddish newspaper having become part of the reader's life, perhaps also a barely conscious sense of gratitude.

For it was the Yiddish newspaper that met him on his landing on the shore of the Promised Land, and led him by the hand into this new world. Like other immigrants, the East European Jew came here with practically no worldly goods and very limited education. Within his own lifetime he advanced from ignorance to knowledge and rose several rungs on the economic ladder. For this socio-economic cultural advance he has America to thank, of course, but, also, to a considerable degree he has to thank the Yiddish press.

אויסערגעוועגליכע נייעס!

לכבוד דעם 30 יעהריגן יובילעאום

פֿון די גרינדונג פֿונם

אידישען קונסט פֿעראיין פֿון קאירא

גרויסע

טעאטער פֿארשטעלונג

אין דעם קעגטליכען אפערא טעאבער

דינסטאג דעם 12 מאי 1942, 5, 30 און אבענדט

אונטער דעם הויכען פאטראנאזש

פֿון זיין עהסעלענץ אחמד נאגיב הילאלי בעי

בילדונגס מיניסטער

און פֿון זיין עהסיעלענץ גענעראל סער כ. אוהנדעק

הויפט גענעראל פֿון די בריטישע טרופען אין מיטטעל-מערען

עס ווערט געשפילט

די כישוף-מאכערין

בארימטע מוזיקאלישע קאמעדיע

מיט געזאנג, קאר און גרויסער אָרקעסטער

אין 5 אקטן און 8 בילדער, פֿון א. גאלדפֿאדען

דער ערלעבס פֿון דעם אוועגד זיי פֿאר דעם

קאמפֿארטס פֿאנד פֿאר אידישע סאלדאטען

An announcement of a dramatic presentation
of A. Goldfaden's musical comedy, "The En-
chantress," in Cairo, Egypt, on May 12, 1942.
The play was given at the Royal Opera House
and was under the patronage of the Egyptian
Minister of Education and Sir C. Auchinleck,
then commander of the British troops in the
Mediterranean theatre of war.

Extraordinary news: in honor of the thirtieth anniversary of the Jewish Art
Association of Egypt: colossal theater performance, proceeds to be awarded to The
Comfort Fund for Jewish Soldiers.

Ida Kaminska and the Yiddish Theater

HAROLD CLURMAN

The Jewish State Theater of Poland, under its artistic director and leading actress, Ida Kaminska, was scheduled to play a four-week season at New York Lyceum Theater beginning on the 19th of October [ed: 1967]. Due to its success the engagement was extended to nine weeks. By the end of the run, which played to ninety per cent of capacity, more than sixty thousand spectators had attended the performances.

Theatrically speaking the two productions left much to be desired. Yet this hardly counts as the salient factor in estimating the season's significance. A great part of the audience came to see Ida Kaminska and her company as a tribute to the valiant troupe and even more as a manifestation of its nostalgia.

The first play the sixty-eight-year-old actress-director presented herself in was Jacob Gordin's *Mirele Efros*, originally produced in 1898. It has often been referred to as 'The Jewish Queen Lear'. It is the story of a matriarch whose sons and daughter-in-law, having been taken into their mother's prosperous household, seek to undermine her authority, force the resignation of her administrator and lifelong friend, dismiss her loyal servant, and connive for her fortune.

The old woman yields her home to the cantankerous clan, takes up lodgings with her administrator, refuses any further contact with her children. In time their incompetence and wastefulness lead them into difficulties and they return to the great lady for help. She remains adamant. But she is brought around to forgiveness by the appeal of her little grandson.

Mirele Efros is a portrait of a woman of power and probity. Kaminska emphasizes her kindness. We see little of her strength and everything of her gentility. This is as much a result of the actress' personal character as of her interpretation. As far as may be judged by the two roles she chose to play in New York and by her appearance in the Czech film *The Shop on Main Street*, Kaminska's most striking trait as an actress is a sweet delicacy. At first I supposed that her fragility in 'Mirele' was a sign of her age, but on seeing her more vigorous performance in Brecht's *Mother Courage*, her second production, I realized that making Mirele an essentially mild person was deliberate.

A soft Mirele weakens the play. The forbearance and kindness of a strong person is more impressive than the moderation of a refined old lady. Mirele Efros is written as a dominant person of formidable will: when she found that her husband had died bankrupt she took charge of his business and reconstituted his wealth. Such a person may be scrupulously just but she is above all a battery of determination.

I imagine that for all her goodness Mirele has a fierce eye! What Kaminska replaces this with is a bit of shrewd humor, a trait in which Gordin's own caustic pen sustains her. Indeed, everything said about Mirele applies to Gordin himself. He possessed a kingly bearing, a proud spirit, a sharp tongue and an indomitable will. For such a person to be temperate and indulgent of weaker beings is noble and dramatic. A smile on a severe face is manna. The enchanting smile on Kaminska's lips was no surprise.

Other members of the Kaminska company gave creditable performances – especially Juliusz Berger as Mirele's older son and Ruth Kaminska (Ida's elder daughter), who managed to avoid italicizing the daughter-in-law's nastiness. Marian Melman as Mirele's administrator also pleased by an unostentatious dignity. On the whole the company, though not particularly striking, made a good impression.

In Brecht's *Mother Courage* – a difficult play for any company but the Berliner Ensemble – the Jewish State Theater of Poland is out of its element. The style and quality of this play – except for its being an antiwar piece – are wholly foreign to the Kaminska players. In their treatment *Mother Courage* is sentimental rather than astringent. It becomes only the tale of a long suffering and forever enduring mother but, touching though this may be, it diminishes the play's originality. Brecht's approach to the stage was classic in a modernist sense; the Jewish State Theater of Poland is the product of and heir to the nineteenth-century Yiddish theater tradition.

At certain dramatically neutral points of *Mirele Efros* I found myself moved. This occurred when Gordin reflected aspects of Jewish folk wisdom: those everlasting standards of *menschlichkeit* which people today hesitate to state with any forthrightness. And I was very near tears at the scene in which the family and friends of bride and groom with lighted candles in their hands went forth to the wedding. My emotion stemmed from two sources: the depth of warm feeling which Jews bring to such occasions and, perhaps even more specifically, the memories that were stirred in me of the old Jewish theater of New York. That is the nostalgia to which I alluded at the beginning of this article.

I was seven when my father, then a physician on the East Side, took me to the theater for the first time to see Gutzkow's *Uriel Acosta*, starring Jacob Adler.

I was ignorant of the language and was too young to understand the matter, but I was so fascinated that for years I never ceased clamoring to be taken to the Yiddish theater.

Much later, when I had become professionally involved with the stage, I grew to understand the causes for my consuming interest in the many performances I had seen. Not only had Jacob Adler been an actor of inescapable magnetism, but at that time the Yiddish theater was in the judgment of such men as Lincoln Steffens and Norman Hapgood 'about the best in New York, in stuff and in acting'. Broadway then was not receptive to Hauptmann, Tolstoy, Gorky, Andreyev, Sudermann, and other contemporary Europeans; the Yiddish theater was.

I have never forgotten the actors who played those dramatists, as well of course as specifically Yiddish playwrights like Goldfaden, Gordin, Kobrin, Asch, Shomer, Libin. I have just mentioned Adler with his gift of characterization, his wily humor, his affecting voice, his imposing stature, his regality. There was also David Kessler, Adler's 'rival' and in the opinion of some his equal if not his superior: Kessler who in the late thirties Jed Harris named as the best actor he had ever seen. Kessler possessed something like an animal force, a peasantlike strength which could be as reassuring as the caress of a benevolent giant. He was less picturesque than Adler but more realistic, though never vulgarly so. Even the 'matinee idol' Boris Thomashevsky, apart from his slightly oily good looks, had a winning good nature – like a cunning flirt – with a surprising empathy for old men's parts.

I remember one of the first important actors of the Yiddish stage and the greatest of its comedians, Zelig Mogulesco, with his endearingly piping voice (he had been a choir boy), his disarming smile, his intimacy, and his ability to say the most hilarious things as if they were a matter of course. He could play grannies as effectively as clowns. He spread a twinkling cheerfulness as heartening as the Sabbath light on a table laden with the finest vintages and victuals.

The arrival of Rudolf Schildkraut from the Reinhardt theaters of Germany brought to the Yiddish stage an actor of magnificent scope and craftsmanship. In a Yiddish so 'pure' that it was controversial (by the time he appeared I had learned Yiddish chiefly through playgoing), he startled his audiences with a humorously 'wicked' Shylock, in contrast to Adler's, which was heroic. Schildkraut could transform a bit part, that of a gourmand wedding guest in an all but forgotten play by Theodor Herzl, for example, so that it took shape as a universal type.

Then there was Jacob Ben-Ami, whose delineation in the Danish play *Samson and Delilah* of the suffering of an artist betrayed by the Philistinism of his environment became a memorable event on Broadway, as it had previously been in Yiddish performance. In the expression of an off-beat lyricism as in Peretz Hirschbein's plays and in certain eccentric character parts as well as in the embodiment of spiritual humiliation – for instance in Ossip Dymov's *The Eternal Wanderer* (with one of the great casts of the era: Thomashevsky, Celia Adler, Lazar Fried, Rubin, Bina Abramovitz, Sigmund Weintraub) – Ben-Ami was a superlative artist.

I must not fail to mention the actresses I can recall from that blessed epoch. I saw Rachel Esther Kaminska (Ida Kaminska's mother) in Sudermann's *Home* with David Kessler. The elder Kaminska as an actress was much more authentically European (that is, cosmopolitan) than her daughter, and her emotionalism had a haughty sweep.

I met but never saw the majestic, deep-voiced *prima donna* Bertha Kalish on the stage. On the other hand, Keni Lipzin's fiery intensity, on and off stage, held one as in a vise. Of small stature with a kind of Toulouse-Lautrec head crowned (off stage) by burning red hair, she became in a Gordin play a compact mass of passion without a trace of stagey flashiness. Sarah Adler was simplicity itself, the very emblem of complete womanliness, reserved yet unequivocally authoritative, sensuous and discreet, with deep stores of elemental feeling which could emerge in a torrent of pathos or in the most acute shafts of perceptiveness.

Despite the individual brilliance of these actors (and I am obliged for lack of space to neglect a host of others – for example, Leon Blank, Maurice Moskovitch, Ludwig Satz), despite too their fiercely competitive spirit, all of them formed companies notable for their interplay, their spontaneous sense of one another – their *ensemble*.

*

The secret of this rare theatrical virtue – seldom achieved in our theater today – points to the heart of greatness and value in the theater as a cultural event. The excellence of the old Yiddish theater was not simply a happy accident. It was the consequence of an historical circumstance. Due to the difficulty and peril of life for the Jews of Russia, Poland, and Rumania in the late nineteenth century, a great many emigrated to America. They were concentrated in those parts of the big cities – particularly New York – where they could set up a tight community life.

Some were orthodox in religion, more were children of the Enlightenment; some were politically conservative, others inclined toward socialism; a great many were almost illiterate, others had already become familiar not only with the Yiddish classics (Mendele Mocher Sforim, Peretz, Sholem Aleichem etc.) but with Gogol, Tolstoy, Dostoievsky, Chekhov, and Gorky. Where else but in the theater, that melting pot of national consciousness, could all these disparate and still basically interrelated forces fuse and find integrated cultural expression? The theater, even more than the lodge or the synagogue, became the meeting place and forum of the Jewish community in America between 1888 and the early 1920s, at which time immigration was curtailed by an act of the United States government.

This is a universal theater pattern. 'Not until actors and spectators are united in a common belief', Gordon Craig once said, 'can plays become a revelation of the inner life and values'. One cannot affirm that the Yiddish theatergoers shared a 'common belief', but more than any other alien conglomeration in America at the time they had a common background and destiny in the new land, a common identity and need.

The immigrants of the time were an eager, energetic, ambitious, gifted, economically and socially growing group, and the focal point of their community existence, I repeat, was, almost had to be, the theater. That is why the Yiddish theater of the period flourished and produced such rich fruit. But despite the coming of the Vilna Troupe, the brave efforts of Maurice Schwartz and the spunkiness of the left-wing Artef, the Yiddish theater in the thirties fell into a precipitous decline. The Jewish audience today is largely a Broadway theater audience.

As a sidelight on this thesis it is worth noting that when the Russian Jews were released (for a while) from their bondage after the Revolution, at least two new theatrical movements sprouted from the seed. One was that of the Hebrew-language Zionist sector, which became the Habimah, whose natural destination was Israel. The other was developed by those who took the road of the new Russian theater of highly stylized (Meyerhold-influenced) modernism; the Jewish Chamber Theater of Moscow, first under the ultrasophisticated Alexander Granowsky and later under Solomon Michoels, whose *King Lear*, in conjunction with Radlow's direction in 1935, Gordon Craig proclaimed the best production of a Shakespeare play he had ever seen.

Stalin destroyed Michoels and his theater. What then is the Yiddish theater situation today? It crops up increasingly in Israel where Joseph Bulov was permitted to introduce it after the use of Hebrew was well established. The Yiddish language, which produced a vivid and humanly robust literature, is part of the Jewish heritage and could not be permitted to wither. On a popular level, Bulov's performances contribute something of the same service which the recently initiated courses in the Yiddish language and literature do at the Hebrew University in Jerusalem.

In New York today there is very little left of the best Yiddish theater. Still there are some young folk – organized as The New Jewish Theater Workshop produced by the Herzl Institute and the Information Department of The Jewish Agency – bent on saving or reviving it. Nor should we forget the perennial efforts of The Workmen's Circle *Folksbiene* to maintain it at the Educational Alliance on East Broadway. There are also traveling companies which play brief seasons in Buenos Aires and other South American cities. Bulov and Ben-Ami found responsive audiences there for a while. But it is more than likely that these audiences will dwindle and the appetite for Yiddish theater will abate.

The Jewish State Theater of Poland represents the remnant of a once healthy vein of the theater world. There are only 30,000 Jews left in that country. An even greater number in the audiences which attend the Kaminska performances in Warsaw and elsewhere in Europe require earphone translations than in New York. In the production of *Mirele Efros* an American-born young fellow was enlisted to play the part of Mirele's grandson. He spoke Yiddish far less well than the erstwhile *shabas goy* Jimmy Cagney! Have the roots for a Yiddish theater been entirely cut? Can they be revitalized?

Whatever the answer, the many people who attended the Kaminska season came in fond recollection of something which still dwells within them as a yearning, or if they were too young to harbor such feelings, then to spin a cultural tie between themselves and those who did.

Yiddish in the University

LEONARD PRAGER

AMBIVALENCE TOWARDS YIDDISH

Anyone who has taught Yiddish language or literature at a university and has had occasion to announce the fact to friends or acquaintances is familiar with their bemused or bewildered reactions. Whether delighted or puzzled, or both, one's listeners seem to discover an element of incongruousness in the coupling of 'Yiddish' with 'university'. One has long steeled himself against this response, which though irksome is nonetheless quite understandable. There *is* something incongruous in removing Yiddish to a university, and something disturbing as well. For a thousand years Yiddish carried its own vitality within itself and was a natural, never a hothouse, growth. Much of its charm lies in its ease of utterance ('*Yiddish ret zikh*' – 'Yiddish speaks itself') and in its unselfconsciousness. For the vast majority of Yiddish speakers throughout the centuries, Yiddish had been simply one of life's givens, a fact of life deserving neither contempt nor awesome regard.

The notion that one's native speech could serve as a vehicle for serious writing was incongruous to many of Dante's contemporaries. A similar feeling as regards the vernacular lingered on into Renaissance England. Indeed, such feelings continue to haunt many a modern non-Western nation whose 'classical' language is unsuitable for the expression of actual experience. Isolated from its native Germanic environment, Yiddish had created a rich 'secular' literature in late fifteenth- and early sixteenth-century Italy, but history and geography conspired to extinguish this tradition. Elye Bokher (Elias Levita), like Chaucer in English literature, had to be rediscovered by scholars. When a 'modern' Yiddish literature began to appear in the second half of the nineteenth century, basing itself on Eastern as opposed to Western Yiddish, the Yiddish language still possessed no viable standard such as Luther had provided for literary German three centuries earlier. Yiddish was perhaps the last European vernacular spoken by many millions which waited well into the nineteenth century to become a 'literary' language.

The reasons for this state of affairs are pretty well understood, although the phenomenal growth of modern Yiddish literature has by no means been adequately investigated. The depressed socioeconomic, political, and educational conditions of the mass of Yiddish speakers; the religion-permeated culture in which 'literature' was an alien concept; the status of Hebrew as the language of serious, written expression; the competitive appeal, for the better situated, of various national tongues such as German and Russian; the erroneous yet widespread view of Yiddish as a corrupt form of Modern High German – these provide the major reasons as to why Yiddish could not have become a secular literary medium earlier than it did. These reasons may be conceived as barriers holding back great sources of creative energy seeking release from pre-Enlightenment confinement, yet they by no means 'explain' the absorption of much of this energy in the rapid creation of a modern Yiddish literature.

Three in one: Mendele Moykher Sforim. His friends (right) claim that he is the grandfather of modern Yiddish literature. His enemies (center) claim that he has transformed the Jewish people into an old gray mare ('The Mare' is the title of one of Mendele's novels). The truth (left) is that Yiddish literature has outgrown him. (*Der groyser kundes*, December 29, 1916)

When people, even those quite knowledgeable in Jewish matters, respond with amazement to the statement, say, that modern Yiddish poetry is highly sophisticated and reflects the major currents in Western literature during the past century, they are unconsciously echoing their parents or grandparents or great-grandparents for whom 'literature' was not a value and for whom Yiddish was merely the language of ordinary speech. The case of Yiddish is somewhat special. No major Yiddish writer came to Yiddish 'naturally' despite the fact that Yiddish was his natural vernacular. The roots of the Yiddish writer's own ambivalence toward his medium are so deep that they have not been altogether eradicated even after a century of literary creation in Yiddish. There is probably no literature in the world where the *motif* of impassioned love of one's language is as prominent as it is in Yiddish literature. This is the obverse of an equally widespread aversion to Yiddish. A huge anthology could be constructed of Yiddish poems to and about Yiddish, which is praised, bewailed, commiserated, cajoled, mocked, extolled, even apotheosized. Whether invoked as person or as mysterious Presence, Yiddish itself is the chief muse of the Yiddish writer, a muse chosen consciously from among contending muses. Modern Yiddish poetry may be said to begin with Y. L. Peretz's *Monish*, where the author self-mockingly denies that romantic love can be voiced in Yiddish. Though Yiddish literature has long since demonstrated its enormous expressive range and is generally admitted to be far superior to Modern Hebrew for delineating the subtlest shades of feeling, Yiddish writers continue to be champions and not merely users of their linguistic medium. These writers know that, in multilingual world Jewry, the status of Yiddish as a literary language has never been secure and stigma-free.

The optimal conditions for the creation of a great literature probably require the existence of formal traditions which can work on living speech and thus draw sustenance from below as well as above. For both Yiddish and Hebrew writers in the late nineteenth century, Yiddish provided the necessary nutrient soil. Their endeavors, however, never concerned more than a tiny minority of Eastern-European Jewry. Yiddish literature was made possible by the living speech of the masses, but was not actually created by or for them – despite its declared educational intentions. Yiddish literature enriched popular speech with idioms and locutions which empathic writers had discovered in popular speech itself, yet these writers were always in some respect estranged from the people. Assimilationist pressures, on the one hand, and Hebraist hostility, on the other, placed Yiddish on the defensive. Quite illogically, the overwhelmingly plebeian character of the Yiddish-speaking populace caused Yiddish itself to be indelibly stamped as plebeian. With the rise of Jewish populism and socialism, this very stigma was consciously transvalued, thereby merely confirming the stigma in the eyes of many. Surprise at the achievement of Yiddish letters or at the place of Yiddish in universities reflects deeply embedded associations of Yiddish with a lower order of cultural life, with poverty, with parochialism, and, often, with radical ideologies. Most typically, Yiddish is associated with what by Western standards would be regarded as the generally limited cultural development of one's own parents or grandparents. Familial feelings, an area where ambivalence is often rife, may be the most powerful psychological determinant of attitudes towards Yiddish. In any event, one can still generalize that the swift and impressive rise of Yiddish literature has not effaced older negative views.

The status of Yiddish

The co-ordinates of time and place must be reckoned with in assessing the status of Yiddish. In such Jewish centers as Vilna, where most intellectuals spoke and wrote Yiddish and breathed in a virtually total Yiddish-speaking milieu, the status of Yiddish and Yiddish literature were high. The current prestige of Yiddish is more in evidence in America than anywhere else in the Jewish world, including Israel. The attachment to Yiddish on the part of many Russian Jews is largely a result of a complex political situation and may be more symbolic than real.

The older the person the more surprised he is that Yiddish is being studied at universities. The young, especially in America, spurred on by identity problems and temperamentally predisposed to value what their parents may have scorned, are more likely to be without preconceived notions as to the nature and status of Yiddish. In an educational environment where virtually everything may be studied and where Black America has been vigorously transvaluing a largely sordid past, it is no wonder that Yiddish, too, should enter the curriculum. For many older Jews this development is in certain respects a sad one, since it suggests that a living organism has become fossilized. Yet I have never met an older Jew who was not also pleased that Yiddish was being studied in universities. For was this not a kind of belated recognition for that which the older Jew himself had in most instances undervalued? He, too, had doubtless never achieved the linguistic consciousness of the Yiddish writer who chose Yiddish rather than Hebrew, Russian, Polish, or German. Rarely does the ordinary person choose his language; his language chooses him.

Among many older and younger Jews, there is today a certain awareness of Yiddish as one of the great monuments of the past millennium of Jewish life. This awareness often includes the sense of a tragic rupture with the past and reveals an effort to somehow relate to that past. Post-Enlightenment ideological issues have lost their relevance, thus facilitating the objective study of Yiddish and Yiddish literature. At the same time the relevance of such study, focused as it is on the past, continues to be questioned.

'PHILOLOGISTS' AND 'LINGUISTS'

Sixty years ago Ber Borochov, who in addition to his fame as a socialist-Zionist theoretician must be credited as a serious Yiddish scholar, reviewed the achievements of four hundred years of Yiddish studies in his compendious and still valuable bibliographical survey 'Di bibliotek fun yidishn filolog' (Niger 1913: cols. 1–65). Since Borochov uses the term *philology* in an earlier and broader sense which includes literature as well as language, his survey is of literary as well as linguistic importance. In the same volume of *Der Pinkes*, Borochov also contributed the opening article – 'Di uyfgabn fun der yidisher filologye' (The Tasks of Yiddish Philology) (Niger 1913: cols. 1–22). More recently, the Yiddish literary historian and textual scholar, Khone Shmeruk, has provided an abbreviated report 'State of Research and Bibliography' in his article 'Yiddish Literature' (*Encylopaedia Judaica* 1971: cols. 826–833). To the companion article 'Yiddish Language', the late Uriel Weinreich appends a bibliography (*Encyclopaedia Judaica* 1971: col. 798), permitting himself to be brief, since in his first two items he includes sources which cover a large part of his subject.[1]

Shmeruk's listings were of necessity more extensive, since nothing comparable to Weinreich's linguistic guide exists for Yiddish literature – a fact whose import will be considered later in this article. First I should like to scan the Borochov and the Weinreich-Shmeruk surveys as a convenient way of gauging certain crucial changes which have occurred during the past six decades.

Borochov dedicated his essay to an earlier and forgotten student of Yiddish, Dr. Philip Mansch (1838–1890), which may serve to remind us of a salient feature in the history of Yiddish scholarship – its discontinuities, its disruptions, and its relative lateness on the academic world scene. The academization of Yiddish studies, a necessary condition for systematic research and sound knowledge, developed slowly and suffered from all the convulsions which have shaken Jewish life in this century.

When S. Niger launched his *Der Pinkes* in 1913, with the subtitle 'An Annual for the History of Yiddish Literature and Language, Folklore, Criticism and Bibliography', he as well as other contributors to the venture (especially Borochov) were well aware of the need for some central body or organ to coordinate the efforts of scattered individuals and to provide authority in such vexing matters as orthography. Though Nahum Shtif is credited with having formulated the original proposal for a Yiddish academic body (in his brochure *Di organizatsye fun der yidisher visnshaft*, 1925), a proposal which is linked with the founding in the same year of the Yidisher Visnshaftlekher Institut (YIVO), Borochov in *Der Pinkes* clearly states: '...individuals can cultivate particular

---

1. Weinreich writes: 'The main works up to 1958 are inventoried in Uriel and Beatrice Weinreich, *Yiddish Language and Folklore: A Selective Bibliography for Research* (1959). The most important current literature is covered in the annual bibliographical issues of the *PMLA*'.

ביבליאטעק
און לייען־זאל אויפ׳ן נאמען פון
בראניסלאװ גראסער
ביים איד. ארבעטער־קונסט־פאראיין.

№ ....

ח׳ ....

ערב׳ת־געלד .... רוב. .... ק.

אײנגעשריבן 191.... .

1. די ביכער דארף מען האלטן
פארזיכטיג, ניט באשעדיגען און
ניט איינריכטן.

2. א בוך קאן מען האלטן ניט
מער פון 2 װאכן.

ביבליאטעק און לייען־זאל א״נ פון בראניס־
לאװ גראסער ביים ארבעטער־קונסט־פאראײן

Library and reading room in the name
of Bronislaw Grosser at the Workers'
Art Association

הספרייה ואולם־הקריאה ע״ש ברוניסלב
גרוסר ליד איגוד־הפועלים לאמנות

Библиотека и читальный зал имени Брони—
слава Гроссера при Союзе работников
искусства

1918 – 1916

Library membership card stipulates that 'books must be handled carefully, not damaged nor dirtied.'

branches, and be initiators, but only a social institution can organize the philological work in its entire scope...Until we possess a national organization devoted to philological efforts, Yiddish philology will remain incapable of properly fulfilling its tasks' (Niger 1913: col. 18). War and revolution may help to explain why only a single volume of *Der Pinkes* appeared and why it was not until the mid-1920s that Borochov's vision could begin to materialize.

The decade and a half from the founding of the Yiddish Scientific Institute (YIVO) in Vilna until that organization's removal to New York in 1940 following the outbreak of World War Two were years of enormous productivity. These years saw the appearance of Yivo's impressive three-volume series, *Filologishe Shriftn*, of its *Historishe Shriftn*, of *Yidishe Filologye* (Kultur Lige, Warsaw, 1926), of Z. Reyzen's *Leksikon fun der Yidisher Literatur, Prese un Filologye* (4 vols., Vilna, 1928–1929) of Max Weinreich's *Bilder fun der Yidisher Literatur Geshikhte* (Tomor, Vilna, 1928). During the same period (especially its first half) in the Soviet Union, a talented group of scholars worked within the framework of research institutes in Minsk and Kiev and – admittedly with a Marxist bias – produced works of solid value. One thinks here of such men as Nahum Shtif, Max Erik, Meir Wiener, to mention but a few. World War II, the Holocaust, and the Soviet suppression of Jewish culture destroyed the research institutes in Eastern Europe which in an amazingly short period had produced basic works in virtually all departments of Yiddish studies. The establishment by the YIVO (in 1938) of a standardized orthography was not the least of this period's fruits, one not negated by the short-lived Sovietized system of spelling. The training of a small body of scholars, the publication of *Yivo Bleter* (1931–), the collection of archival materials – these were among the achievements of YIVO in its Vilna period, working with a relatively small group of professional scholars and enjoying only modest financial support from communal sources.

Yiddish studies

During the war years and afterwards, YIVO in New York assumed direction of research activities, which were not limited to Yiddish language and literature, but placed considerable emphasis on the social sciences. *Yivo Bleter* continued to appear, though with decreasing regularity in the past decade. Starting in 1941, Yudel Mark began to issue his language journal *Yidishe Shprakh*, which in the past few years has also undergone the difficulties involved in a shift of editors. But a major turn in Yiddish studies took place after World War II – the introduction of Yiddish courses in several American universities, principally in New York City, and especially at Columbia University's Department of Linguistics. The place which Yiddish earned at Columbia and the rich crop of Yiddish scholarship executed under the aegis of that university are largely the personal achievement of Uriel Weinreich.

In 1952 the Hebrew and Yiddish scholar and critic Dov Sadan was appointed to the Chair of Yiddish Literature at the Hebrew University, Jerusalem, where in the course of two decades there developed a small but distinguished Department of Yiddish Literature. That department's present chairman, Khone Shmeruk, and two additional Sadan students, Benjamin Hrushovski and Dan Miron, have also made significant contributions to Yiddish studies. Gradually, the center of Yiddish studies has been shifting from New York to Jerusalem. The immigration to Israel of Yudel Mark and others, and the transfer of the *Great Dictionary of the Yiddish Language* project to the Hebrew University illustrate this shift. YIVO itself has altered visibly, attempting now to function in cooperation with various universities and to become a graduate center with emphasis on training of doctoral candidates. Isolated scholars in Germany, Holland, England, Hungary, and elsewhere are also occupied in Yiddish research, almost invariably within the framework of academic institutions and particularly within the discipline of Germanic studies.

From Borochov's call for institutionalized direction of Yiddish research to the creation of university departments of Yiddish, this is the story of the academization of Yiddish – but with the passions, the travail, the hopes, the living issues left out. Borochov, and most Yiddishists with him, were interested in something more than the transformation of Yiddish studies into an academic discipline.

The distance between *Der Pinkes* and the *Encyclopaedia Judaica* surveys cannot be measured by mere chronology. Borochov in *Der Pinkes* writes in Yiddish for an audience part of which had only just begun to master the disciplines of Western scholarship, yet all of which lived in intimate relationship with Yiddish-speaking Ashkenazic Jewry. Borochov regards philology as a tool of national liberation and as a means of teaching Jews to value their folk tongue and to refine it so that it might express every area of human experience. He is scornful of detached scholarship and bemoans the fact that existing works on Yiddish are almost all written in languages other than Yiddish. He cites work after work and his scholarly acumen is great, but it is always overlaid by a sense of practical purpose. A philological literature which neither the general public nor the intelligentsia can use lacks 'national value'. Borochov actually complains of some of the works he reviews that are 'academic', removed from real life and lacking in educational goals. He regards certain Greek and Czech philologists as folk heroes and 'philology' becomes a banner word. 'He who does not believe in the survival of the Yiddish language', he writes, 'can perhaps be a Yiddish linguist, but not a Yiddish philologist' (Niger 1913: col. 2).

One is here reminded of the definition of *philology* offered by the University of Chicago's John Matthew Manly – 'It's life'. Borochov would have agreed. Borochov's distinction between 'linguist' and 'philologist' continues to be a meaningful one for the rapidly diminishing Yiddishist circles in North and South America whose members truly live in Yiddish as a primary, or at least a home and community-centered, second language. The pages of the territorialist *Oyfn Shvel*, for instance, pour scorn on those for whom Yiddish is merely an object of academic interest. Yet secularist Yiddishism of the Bund and communist varieties has long ceased to be a viable mode of Jewishness and has been rendered doubly absurd by the destruction of Polish Jewish life and the forcible suppression of Yiddish culture in the Soviet Union. Jewish education in the

YIDDISH AIN'T JUST FOR BUBBES!

If **you too** would like to:
* hear some Yiddish music
* buy a "ש״דיי" T-shirt
* get a free mini-lesson in Yiddish
* buy a "Speak Yiddish to me" button
* or just find out what's happening in the world of Yiddish

—then <u>come</u> <u>right</u> <u>over</u> to the <u>YIDDISH</u> <u>BOOTH</u> at Section D2

The 'Flyer' of the Yiddish booth at an Israel Independence Day/Jewish Heritage Day celebration in Central Park, Manhattan, Spring 1978.

Diaspora has consistently moved in the direction of Hebrew and some sort of religious traditionalism and away from Yiddish and conceptions of secularist Jewishness. Hasidic and ultra-Orthodox Jews who actually live in Yiddish have remained as unconcerned with Yiddish philology as their forebears have always been with Hebrew grammar. Yiddish is, ironically, most alive, most un-threatened, among those Jews who have rejected modern Jewish ideologies, have never felt the need for a 'national philology', and who do not regard Yiddish as a primary value. For the ultra-Orthodox, Yiddish is essentially an additional defence with which to ward off the gentile world, including that of assimilated Jewry. One of the original purposes of YIVO at its founding in 1925 was to bring modern European scholarship to Jews in their own language, in Yiddish, and, in general, to make Yiddish a means through which Jews could explore all realms of thought and learning.

The chief languages of general Jewish scholarship today are English and Hebrew, and this statement is becoming increasingly applicable to Yiddish scholarship as well. The situation lamented by Borochov – that Yiddish philology is pursued in languages other than Yiddish – is gradually being restored, albeit with the difference that today's Yiddish scholars tend not to share the assimilationist outlook of their German predecessors. It is hardly surprising that the most authoritative recent resumés of Yiddish scholarship have appeared in English, the language spoken by the world's largest Jewish community and, by virtue of its international status, the one language most understood by Jews all over the world. Only a few decades ago Yiddish could rightly claim to be the Jewish Esperanto. Today, the pressure of the powerful and prestigious English language on Hebrew has many Israelis worried. As Israel's unofficial second language, English is the medium in which Hebrew-speaking and non-Hebrew-speaking Jews normally communicate – even on subjects of Jewish scholarship.

The context of Borochov's appeal has altered so drastically that it must at first glance seem quixotic to suggest that Borochov's distinction between 'linguist' and 'philologist' is still meaningful. Yet no one can fail to recognize the difference, say, between Ugaritic or Akkadian studies and Yiddish studies. Hundreds of thousands of Jews continue to speak Yiddish, the Yiddish press, radio, and theater somehow stubbornly survive, and not to be able to read what is currently being written in Yiddish is to disqualify oneself from serious involvement in Yiddish studies. For the past decade many of the most important contributions to Yiddish scholarship have appeared in *Di Goldene Keyt* (Tel Aviv), and even *Sovetish Heymland* (Moscow) has scholarly value for those who know how to use this politically motivated journal. *Yidishe Shprakh* and *Yivo Bleter* are not yet extinct and even *Di Tsukunft* and *Yidisher Kemfer* occasionally publish material of research value. Several other Yiddish periodicals may be added to this list, and a small number of books in Yiddish appear year after year which the Yiddish scholar cannot afford to ignore.

A matter of survival

The crucial term, of course, in Borochov's distinction between 'linguist' and 'philologist' is *survival*. All Yiddish scholars, regardless of ideology, value the fruits of Yiddish creativity and the great marvel of the Yiddish language itself. Their very enterprise argues some mode of 'survival' for Yiddish. The objective Yiddish scholars whose academy-supported research is published in reputable journals no longer need to polemicize or be defensive. The *Encyclopaedia Judaica* articles from this point of view are a fulfillment of Borochov's vision. The fact that their bibliographies list so many works in Yiddish is further proof of this fulfillment.[2] Here we have a reverse paradox: no one can aspire to Yiddish

2. Yet one must for objectivity's sake note that for many years a major portion of the material published in *Yivo Bleter* was translated into Yid- dish – without explicit acknowledgement of this fact – from other languages.

scholarship without acquaintance with the studies *in Yiddish* of the past half century.

When Yiddish was most alive as a total culture, organized Yiddish scholarship in Yiddish was either nonexistent or in its infancy; today when Yiddish culture is in decline the major works of Yiddish scholarship are found to be in Yiddish, a fact which renders the Yiddish language a *necessary tool for the scholarly investigation of the source materials*, which are, of course, in Yiddish. The Ugaritic scholar does not read contemporary works in Ugaritic in order to interpret original Ugaritic texts. All this is obvious enough, yet the point is often lost by those who do recognize the importance of Yiddish primary sources. The secondary sources may not always meet the most stringent standards of modern scholarship, yet they cannot be safely ignored – not even in those areas where Yiddish has least distinguished itself, literary theory and literary criticism.

For all their shortcomings as critics, S. Niger and Jacob Glatstein, to cite two of the best, are necessary reference points for any current reassessment of Yiddish letters. The scholar of Yiddish literature is thus continually thrust into the company of a generation of writers for whom the critical act as applied to a Yiddish work was inevitably tinged with Borochov's sense of 'philological tasks'. As more and more of the significant works of Yiddish scholarship and criticism are rendered into Hebrew and English, itself an effect of the decline of Yiddish culture, much of the force of the original is lost by virtue of the altered medium itself. Writing about Yiddish in any other language but Yiddish somehow changes the very assumptions underlying the act of writing itself. Thus again Borochov is not wholly wrong in insisting that Yiddish scholarship in the languages of Western Europe is necessarily alien to its subject, which becomes mere object, and, no matter how scientific, lacks 'national value'.

The early YIVO scholars were sometimes guilty of a certain tendentiousness, which had unfortunate effects on their critical formulations. Their search, for instance, for an older secular literature and their mode of interpreting it were obviously influenced by ideology. Yet the scholarly function which these men assumed was informed by a sense of relevance whose loss can hardly be compensated by the values of objectivity or exactitude. In short, in moving out of non-university institutes and organizations and into the modern university, Yiddish scholarship left behind its sense of purpose and gained merely in sophistication of method.

One cannot, however, argue with history. A somewhat denatured Yiddish scholarship is the logical accompaniment of a declining Yiddish culture, and if it lacks Borochov's 'philological' goals it must at least define for itself the most meaningful 'linguistic' ones. Just as the twentieth-century poet has ceased to view himself as seer and oracle in the manner of his romantic predecessors without abandoning his calling, so the Yiddish scholar, though he can no longer imagine himself a hero in a struggle for national liberation, can still function meaningfully. Uriel Weinreich, who, like several great English romantic poets, died young, was perhaps the last of the heroes as well as the ideal type for the 'linguist' of the present and future. In his *Modern English-Yiddish Yiddish-English Dictionary*, he created a work which embodies the philological ideals of almost a century of predecessors, a dictionary which insists on calling itself 'modern', which includes scores of inspired coinages, which prescribes a Standard Yiddish destined perhaps to be spoken by few, yet which redeems for generations to come the plasticity and strength of a language whose monuments are all too inaccessible and whose continued growth and refinement have been tragically impaired. One may argue with the prescriptive character of Uriel Weinreich's *Dictionary* and find it less a reflection of the rich variety of actual speech than a guide to some imagined language of power and precision. Yet without roots in Borochov's world of 'national value' the lexicographical and linguistic acumen of Uriel Weinreich would doubtless never have been released to pattern and probe with scholarly rigor that language which he loved as no Sumerologist could love his baked clay hieroglyphic tablets. Passion lay behind Uriel Weinreich's work, passion for the living Yiddish language, and his reason and training contributed merely the method, the skills. Academic Yiddish studies, even at their unimaginable best, will nurture no such love.

YIDDISH STUDIES TODAY

At every stage of its development Yiddish scholarship has faced enormous problems, both external and internal. The academic status of Yiddish studies today, whether assessed in statistical or critical terms, is by no means secure. This judgement is at variance with the widely held impression of a great surge of interest and activity.

Fully constituted, degree-awarding departments of Yiddish are exceedingly difficult to establish at present. Only the Hebrew University can claim such a department, though moves in this direction are being made at the University of Haifa and at Tel Aviv University. Yiddish language is also being taught at the University of the Negev. In North America, Columbia's offerings have been most significant at the graduate level in the field of Yiddish linguistics. McGill University, CCNY, Brooklyn College, Queens College, and at least a score of other institutions maintain departments or programs of Jewish studies in which Yiddish language and literature are studied. The recently established journal *Yiddish* emanates from Queens College and may contribute to making that school an active center of Yiddish studies. YIVO, of course, with its Max Weinreich Graduate Center and its other activities remains the chief center for Yiddish studies in North America. At numerous American universities, both on and off campus, Yiddish courses are given sporadically, often by instructors who are themselves self-taught. However, despite its admirable energy and proliferation,

American academic activity in the field of Yiddish studies has yet to demonstrate its scholarly mettle.

The problems of establishing Yiddish as a major study in a university can hardly be exaggerated. Without the supporting periphery of Judaic disciplines (Hebrew language and literature, Jewish history, Talmud, etc.) and non-Judaic ones (Germanic and Slavic studies), the effort is likely to be perfunctory. Without an array of courses covering all periods of Yiddish literature and examining the Yiddish language in all its permutations, the program is doomed to be superficial. Trained specialists who can teach advanced courses are in short supply and the necessary supporting texts and study materials are either nonexistent or expensive to acquire. Had we not been fortunate enough to possess Uriel Weinreich's *College Yiddish* (now finally translated into Hebrew), Yiddish might not have penetrated the university at all.

Satisfactory texts in Standard Yiddish orthography exist for only a minority of authors (e.g. Itsik Manger); increasingly, such texts will have to be subsidized. The Xeroxing of scarce materials for advanced courses can also prove very expensive. Outside of a few centers (e.g. Jerusalem, New York) libraries are inadequately equipped for advanced work in Yiddish. To compound the problem, few collections have printed catalogs. Furthermore, as was indicated above, there is no bibliographical guide to Yiddish literature to assist the student. Neither in Hebrew, English, Yiddish or any other language can the student find a satisfactory one-volume history of Yiddish literature. There are no complete bibliographies of any of the major authors (though the Mendele Project in Jerusalem is slowly remedying this lack with regard to the 'grandfather' of Yiddish literature). There are few academic editions of Yiddish works (Shmeruk's recent study of Peretz's *Bay nakht afn altn mark* (New York, Yivo 1971) is an admirable exception). There are few indexes to periodicals (the Hebrew University's Yiddish department is currently indexing all literary materials from Yiddish periodicals which appeared between 1823–1903). Many works by the major figure, Sholem Aleichem, have never been published in book form (a lack which the Bet Sholem Aleichem archives in Tel Aviv may partially attend to in the next few years), and that master's correspondence is still in the process of being cataloged. This list of what is lacking can be multiplied tenfold, but the point should be clear: Yiddish scholarship must create basic teaching and research tools. Advanced grammars and readers in standardized spelling, texts with critical apparatus, concordances, bibliographies, indexes – all the paraphernalia of literary study which exist in abundance in most Western languages – remain to be produced.

Yiddish in translation

The research picture is by no means altogether bleak. The forthcoming publication of the Columbia-based *Linguistic and Cultural Atlas of Ashkenazic Jewry* should have an immense impact on Yiddish scholarship. Max Weinreich's monumental *History of the Yiddish Language*, in four volumes, has appeared and a fifth index volume and an English translation of at least part of the work are promised. Tsinberg's *History of Jewish Literature* is currently being translated at Wayne State University and several volumes have already appeared. The Mendele Project mentioned earlier will ultimately make available an academic edition of all of Mendele's works in Hebrew and Yiddish, together with concordances in both languages and, possibly, a new set of translations. The *Great Dictionary of the Yiddish Language* has, regrettably, only published three of its projected twelve volumes, but the encyclopedic scope of these volumes renders them enormously valuable to the trained user. We may hope to see the *Leksikon fun der nayer yidisher literatur* (seven volumes to date) completed if and when funds become available – despite its shortcomings as a work of reference. The joint publication by C. Shmeruk and S. Werses of the bilingual *Hasidic Tales and Letters* of Joseph Perl (Jerusalem, 1969) created both a precedent and a standard for the editing of parallel Hebrew and Yiddish texts. Jerusalem will also shortly provide a scholarly edition of all extant Biblical dramas in Yiddish. Fortunately the list of significant work-in-progress can be much extended. Especially in Israel, important research is going forward.

Most Yiddish courses offered in America are actually courses in Yiddish literature in translation. Only the supercilious will deny the value of such studies for those who know no Yiddish. In the hands of a skillful instructor capable of mediating between translation and reader, the sense and flavor of the original can at least be approached. In such courses, fortunately, Yiddish literature is studied as literature and lack of Judaic knowledge is often compensated by critical sophistication.

The problem of translation tends to be an intractable one. Sholem Aleichem is an important writer in the Soviet Union because his works in Russian translation are of a high order. Sholem Aleichem in English is a reputation, perhaps even a legend, but certainly not a significant figure in English writing. Isaac Bashevis Singer *is* a figure in American writing by virtue of the highly literate renderings of his works into English. Yet the liberties which that author takes in supervising his own translations has created a body of writing which is often at variance with the Yiddish original. The Yiddish Bashevis is at times barely recognizable as the English Singer. Not one of the great Yiddish 'classical' triumvirate – Mendele, Sholem Aleichem and Peretz – is experienced in English with any force. The anthologies of Howe and Greenberg have raised the level of translation immensely, without however substantially altering the fact that Yiddish literature in English has still a long way to go to achieve the highest standards.

Under the stars and stripes: four pieces of good news. Wilson proclaims Jewish relief day (to help Jews in war-torn Europe), Brandeis nominated to the Supreme Court, Meyer London becomes Speaker of the House, and Yiddish recognized at Columbia University. (*Der groyser kundes*, February 4, 1916)

Lack of scholarship

The training of translators must find a place in Yiddish studies, but should not at present command a high priority. There are simply too many more basic tasks demanding attention. Here we see sharply the division between public as opposed to internal needs. Regardless of how small the community of Yiddish scholars may be, it must emphasize the Yiddish language text. Nor can Yiddish researchers neglect the scholarly monograph because of the absence of popular surveys. The meretricious popular works on Yiddish language and literature which have appeared in the past three decades might not have been so bad had they been able to draw on specialist works. Had someone attended to the basic chore of compiling adequate bibliographies of existing scholarship, the popularizations might have proved more knowledgeable. This is not the place to review these books in detail but a few examples might illustrate the point I wish to make. In the only full-scale history of the American Yiddish theater available in English, a work based on a doctoral dissertation and thus presumably reflecting Yiddish in the academy, we read such astounding statements as the following:

An organization called Haskalah was started by a German philosopher, Moses Mendelsohn (Lifson 1963: 24).
Yiddish literature in substance is purely Jewish (Lifson 1963: 29).
Yiddish literature started and was nurtured on the dreams, ideals and aspirations of Jewish nationalism (Lifson 1963: 30).

Lifson's book is also full of factual errors and ignores the best scholarly sources. The last stricture could be applied wholesale to all the book-length surveys of Yiddish literature published in English in the past three decades.[3] Though far more reliable than Lifson on the factual level, none of these works grapples with its material in a critical spirit. The recent popular books on the Yiddish language are not on a much higher level than those dealing with general Yiddish literature.[4]

The kind of loose and unsubstantiated generalizations about the *shtetl*, Ashkenazic culture, the Yiddish language, and the traditions of Yiddish literature that one runs across in American essays and book reviews indicate that scholarship isn't filtering down to those who should be using it. An adequate critical evaluation of Yiddish literature as of any literature must rest upon a certain body of scholarship, and it is for Yiddish scholars in universities to create that scholarship and to assist in making it available. Unfortunately, academic association per se cannot assure the requisite quality and Yiddish scholarship

3. Including works by A. A. Roback, Sol Liptzin, and Charles S. Madison.
4. These capsule condemnations will have to be defended elsewhere. Reference to the language books is principally to Leo Rosten's vulgar *Joys of Yiddish*, Lillian Feinsilver's strident and typographically monstrous *The Taste of Yiddish*, and the literate yet ultimately impressionistic and ill-informed *In Praise of Yiddish* by the late Maurice Samuel.

must thus undergo a conscious process of professionalization to safeguard its standards. At the most obvious level this means that those who teach Yiddish should be specifically trained to do so. It also means that no university should approve a dissertation in Yiddish studies without consulting expert opinion. The notion that one must encourage anyone who is so disinterested and noble as to lend a hand in so unrewarding a field as Yiddish studies – such a craven notion – must finally be rejected. Yiddish studies make rigorous demands and their intellectual rewards are not less than those of any other humanistic discipline. The Shmeruk–Weinreich surveys should make abundantly clear that modern Yiddish studies have nothing in common with apologetics.

REFERENCES

Encyclopaedia Judaica (1971), vol. 16. Jerusalem.
Lifson, David S. (1963), *The Yiddish Theatre in America*. New York.
Niger, S., editor (1913), *Der Pinkes*. Vilna. (Note separate pagination at end.)

PART VI

Maintenance and Shift

Why Girls Run Away from Home. While leftists, rightists (Orthodoxy), Yiddishists and Hebraists are 'busy' with petty rivalries, Assimilation comes to court and to corrupt Jewish youth. (*Der groyser kundes*, March 20, 1926)

a. אונדז דארף זיין קלאר: דער קאמף פאר יידיש דארף
אנגעפירט ווערן אינגאַנצן מיט אַנדערע מיטלען ווי מיר
טוען עס איצט, און אונדזער אידעאַלאַגישער צוגאַנג דארף
זיין אינגאַנצן אַן אנדערער. מיט אַגיטירן יידיש לשם
יידיש, יידיש לשם עקזיסטענץ פון פאָלק וועלן מיר ווייט
נישט אַוועקגיין.......... די וואָס זענען מודה אין
דער הנחה, אַז עס וועט אַלעמאָל זיין אַ תפוצות-ישראל
מוזן באַנעמען, אַז די הנחה איז מחייב אַ גייסטיקן וועלט-
באַנעם, וואָס שאַפט אַן אייגנאַרטיקן לעבנס-שטייגער.
שפראַך און ליטעראַטור איז דער נאַטירלעכער פועל-
יוצא פון אַן אייגענעם לעבן. די עקזיסטענץ פון יידיש,
ווי אַ גערעדטער לשון, איז פאַרבונדן מיטן רענעסאַנס
פון יידיש לעבן און יידישקייט אין תפוצות-ישראל.

b. און דאָס איז אונדזער פאַראַדאָקסאַלער מצב. אין
דער זעלביקער צייט, ווען יידיש און יידישע ליטעראַטור
אין ענגלישער איבערזעצונג האָבן דערגרייכט צו דער
העכסטער רום און אַנערקענונג, ווערן אונדזערע קינדער-
שולן, די באַזע פון יעדער פאָלקס-קולטור, קלענער און
אייגנעשרומפענער און די, וואָס עקזיסטירן קענען אין די
פאַר זונטיק- אָדער נאָכמיטאָג-שעהען, נישט איבערגעבן
צו די תלמידים אונדזער גרויסע פאָלקס-ירושה. אַ יידיש
בוך, דאָס סאַמע בעסטע און פונעם גרעסטן מחבר, דער-
שיינט אין פינף הונדערט, העכסטנס אין טויזנט עקזעם-
פלאַרן ·

Mottos for Part VI

(a) 'This should be clear to us: The struggle for Yiddish must be conducted by entirely different measures than those we now employ, and our ideological approach must be an entirely different one. We will never get very far by agitating on behalf of Yiddish for its own sake or for the sake of the existence of our people... Those who accept the premise that there always will be a Jewish diaspora must realize that this premise implies a cultural outlook which results in a unique way of life. The maintenance of Yiddish as a vernacular is related to the renaissance of Jewish life and yidishkayt in the Jewish diaspora.' Shloyme Saymon, Eygn loshn un redn yidish [Our own language and speaking Yiddish], in his *Tokh yidishkayt* [Substantive Jewishness]. Buenos Aires, Yidbukh, 1954, 97–118.

(b) Our paradoxical situation is as follows: at the very time when Yiddish and Yiddish literature in English translation have attained the very height of recognition, our elementary schools, the very basis of every national culture, are becoming smaller and fewer and those that remain cannot hand on our rich national heritage to their pupils in the few available Sunday or weekday afternoon hours. The very best Yiddish book by the most outstanding author is published in five hundred, or, at the very outside, in a thousand copies...' Yosl Mlotek. Yidish – loshn fun undzer neshome un yidishe vertn [Yiddish – language of our soul and of Jewish values] *Barikht fun der velt-konferents far yidish un yidisher kultur* [Report of the World Conference on Yiddish and Yiddish Culture]. Tel Aviv, World Bureau for Yiddish Culture, 1977, 30–34.

די ייִדישע שפּראַך אין אונדזער פּריוואַט־לעבן

מ. אָלגין

SUMMARY: THE YIDDISH LANGUAGE IN OUR PRIVATE LIFE
BY M. OLGIN

A literary critic who later became a leading figure in Yiddish communist circles in the USA (1878–1939) is among the first to point out that Yiddishist intellectuals commonly speak co-territorial non-Jewish languages to their families and intimate friends and that this does not augur well for the future of Yiddishism.

I.

טעערעטיש האָט ביי אונד די אַסימילאַצע קיינמאָל ניט געהאַט קיין קרעדיט. פּראַקטיש זענען מיר נאָך עד היום פון אַסימילאַצע ניט ריין.

„מיר" — מיינען איך יודישע אינטעליגענטען, דעמאָקראַטישע, ראַדיקאַלע, „איניסטע לינקע" טהוער און העלפער און מיטהעלפער פון'ם אינטעליגענטישן לאַגער — די אַלע, וואָס באַהערשען די רוסישע אָדער פּוילישע שפּראַך און זענען נאָהענט צו דער רוסישער אָדער פּוילישער קולטור*).

אין עפענטליכען לעבען זענען מיר דוקא קאָנסעקװענט: אויף אַרביי־ טער־פאַרזאַמלונגען, אין געזעלשאַפטען און פאַרויינען רידען מיר יודיש, אין אונזער פּרעסע שרייבען מיר דאָם רוֹב יודיש (דעם גרעסטען טייל פון דער סאָ־ ציאַל־פּאָליטישער און עקאָנאָמישער ליטעראַטור אויף יודיש האָבען מיר גע־ שאַפען, פאַר אונזער נאַציאָנאַל־שפּראַך ערקלערען מיר יודיש. מיר רידען פעסט און זיכער פון אַ נייער יודישער וועלטליכער קולטור, וועלכע שטאַמט פון די

---

*) איך מוז באַמערקען, אַז מיטצ אייניגנע באַאַבסטונגען זענען נור אווייב אינטעליגענטען, האָם קעגען רוסיט און האָבען אײנגעזאַפט אין זיך עלעמענטען פון דער רוסישער קולטור. בלי-ל-שי-יודישע לינקע אינטעליגענטען אין מיר יעדער דעניע אייכ־ געקומען צו יעדן.

טיעפּעניטשען פֿון דעם פֿאָלק און העלפֿט דעם ארבעטס־פֿאָלק צו אויסהויבּען זיך
אויף אַ העכערע שטופֿע פֿון געזעלשאַפֿטליכען און פּאָליטישען בּאַוואוסטזײן.
און ניט נאָר מיר רײדען – מיר טהוען אַזאַ אַרבּעט, וואָס אָהן איהר וואָלען
די יודישע קולטור קיין קיום ניט האָבּען. מיר וועקען אין די מאַסען אַ אינטערעס
און אַ שטרעבּוג צו דעם לעבּען לעבּענס־פֿאָרמען – ד. ה. מיר בּעאַרבּײטען דעם
בּאָדען, אויף וועלכען עס וואַקסט יעדע נאַציאָנאַלע קולטור.

דאָס איז אָבּער נאָר אין עפֿענטליכען לעבּען, דאָרט וואו מיר בּעריה־
רען זיך מיט דעם פֿלל. אין וועו מינוט, ווען עס הערט־אויף אונזער גע־
זעלשאַפֿטליכע אַרבּעט און עס הויבּט זיך אָן דער פּריוואַט־מעניט, בּיטטען מיר
די נאַציאָנאַלע צרה' און ווערען... יעדענפֿאַלס ניט דאָס, וואָס פֿאַלגט פֿון
אונזער איינגענער פּראָפֿאַגאַנדע.

אַ פֿאַקט איז, אַז בּײ אונזערע אינטעליגענטען איז יודיש נאָך ניט זײער
איינענע שפּראַך. יעדען פֿון אונז איז ניט איינמאָל אויסגעקומען צו בּאָאָבּאַכ־
טען, ווי אין דער פֿײנע אינמיטען אַ יודישען רעפֿעראַט רעדט דער רעפֿערענט
מיט זײנע פֿריינד אויף רוסיע, ווי אַ טהיער, וואָס האַלט פֿלאַס־פֿיערדיגע
רעדעם וועגען דעם וואַכען און בּלײהען פֿון דער יודישער ליטעראַטור, רעדט ניט
וואָגענלאַנג קיין איין יודיש וואָרט. איך האָבּ ניט געזעהען קיין איינצינען אינ־
טעליגענט, וואָס זאָל אין דער היים, מיט ווײבּ און קינד, רײדען אויף יודיש.
ערווואַקסענע אינטעליגענטען, וואָס לערנען זיך אויף דער עלטער יודיש,
איז יעדען פֿון אונז, מסתמא, אויסגעקומען צו בּעגעגענען. אָבּער אַז אינטעליגענטען,
וואָס קענען יאַ יודיש, זאָלען לערנען די שפּראַך זײיערע קינדער – אַזאַ
ערשיינונג איז אַ זעדער זעלטענע אויסנאַהמע, אויבּ מען קאָן זי יאַ עריין געפֿינען.

און אַזאַ בּעציהונג צו יודיש וועט אידה בּעמערקען ניט נאָר צווישען „נײיט־
ראַליסטען", נאָר אויך צווישען זײיערע געגנער. דאָס איז איבּערדויפֿט ניט קיין
פּועל־יוצא פֿון לאָגישע אויספֿיהרונגען און טעאָרעטישען ישובֿ־הדעת. לאָגיש
האָבּען מיר שוין לאַנג אַ שטײן אויף אַ שטײן ניט איבּערגעלאַזט אין אַלע ראיות
פֿון די אנטיי־שׁוואַרצאַניסטען". מיר פֿיהרען דעם קאַמפֿף אי געגען די העבּרע־
איסטען, אי געגען די אַסימילאַטאָרען און זעגען פֿעסט איבּערצײגט אין דער
ריכטיגקײט פֿון אונזערע ארגומענטען. מיר האָבּען אויספֿיהרליך און מיט דעם
גרעסטען ערנסט געענטפֿערט אויף די טענות וועגען דער „אָרימקײט" פֿון דער
יודישער שפּראַך און קולטור, וועגען דעם, וואָס זי האָט ניט קיין „ט־אַדיציעס".
וועגען דעם, וואָס זי איז ניט „נאַצאָנאַל" און אַז אז. וו. קײנעם וועט ניט קומען אויף'ן
געדאַנק, אַז אונזער קאַמפֿף פֿאַר יודיש איז ניט אויפֿריכטיג, אַז מיר „בּע־
גליקען" מיט דער יודישער קולטור די „אָרימע בּרידער", בּשעת אַליין ווילען מיר
טאַקי שטענדיג בּלייבּען אין אַן'אַנדער קולטור־וועלט.

און פֿונדעסטוועגען... די יודישע קולטור איז פֿאָרט ניט אונזער אייגענע
קולטור, די יודישע שפּראַך איז בּײ אונו נאָך אַלץ אַלק אַ יום־טובֿ־דיגער פּנג, וואָס
מען טהוט איהם אָן, ווען מען דאַרף זיך ווייזען פֿאַר ליטען. און ווי שטאַרק
איינינע פֿון אונו זאָלען זיך ניט בּעגײסטערען מיט דעם זאוקם פֿון דער יודישער

קולטור און ליטעראטור — א בעדערפעעניש איז דאָס בײַ אונז נאָך ניט
געוואָרען, צונויפגעװאָקסען דערמיט זענען מיר ניט, און אַלצדינג, וואָס
מיר טראָגן אויף דעם געביעט, האָט אַנאינװעניעמסטען רים.

צוויי זעעלען וואוינען אין אונזער ברוסט: די זעעל פון א פ ר א ג ר א ם ־ מ ע נ ש,
פאָן אַ קעמפפער פאַר אַ געוויסער וועלט־אַנשויאונג — און די זעעלע פון אַ
ג ע מ י ה ט ס ־ מ ע נ ש, וועלכע איז ארויסגעשפינען און ארומגעוועבט מיט די
פאָדים פון אַ געוויסער קולטור־סביבה אין לעבט זיך, טאָג איין, טאָג אויס.

כ'וואָלט אפשר ניט פדאי געוועזן וועגען דעם צו רײַדען, ווען דאָ גופא וואָלט
ניט געוועזן איין וויכטיגע געזעלשאפטליכע זײַט: די ערצידונג פונ'ם יינגען
דור.

מיר אַסימילירען אונזערע קינדער! אין דעם פרט זענען מיר,
„לינקע" יודישע אינטעליגענטען, ניט בעסער פון אַלע אַנדערע אַסימילאנטען. מיר
מאַכען הזק פון די ציוניסטען, וואָס רעדען רײַדען זיי פון העברעאיש אין אין
פראַקטישען לעבען קולטיווירען זיי רוסיש אָדער פויליש. און מיר — ווי
טוען מיר מיט יודיש ? אמת, צווישען איגעו און זיי איז דאָ דער גרוסער פרינצעפיעלער
אונטערשיעד, וואָס אונזער געזעלשאפטליכע אַרבײַט איז אין הסבב מיט
אונזער פראָגראַם. אָבער צו זענען מיר אײַנגאַנצען רײַן פון דעם חטא, וואָס
מיר וואַרפען אויף אונזערע געננער ? צי איז דען די ערצידונג ניט קיין גרויסע
געזעלישאפטליכע אַרבײַט ?

II.

די סבּה פון אונזער קולטורעלער „צוויי־פּנימ'דיגקײט" ליעגען אין די אַל־
געמיינע בעדינגונגען פון אונזער לעבען. מיר זענען אויסגעוואָקסען און האָבען
זיך ערצויגען אויף פרעמדע קולטורען. מיר האָבען אָפט געמוזט לאַנגע יאָהרען
אונטערדריקען אין זיך די ווירקונג פון דער היימישער יורישער סביבה. כן די
היימישע געוואָהנהײטען, מיר האָבען אָפט געפיהרט א פערביסענעם קאמפף גע־
גען אָט דער סביבה, כדי צו קענען אומגעשטערט אַרײַנזאפען אין זיך די רוסישע
אָדער פוילישע קולטור, וועלכע איז פאַר אונז דעמאלט געוועזן דער אײַנצעגער
קװאל פון קולטור איבערהויפּט. פיעלע פון אונז האָבען אויסגעבילדעט זייער
געסטעטינע פערזענליכקײט נאָך אין יענער צײַט, ווען די קולטור־בערײַטונג פון יו־
דיש איז געוועזן זעהר קלײַן, אויב ניט גאָר אינגאַנצען נישטיג. דער גרעסטער טײַל
פון אונזערע אינטעליגענטען איז פון קינדהויז אויף געוואָהנט צו טראַכטען אויף
רוסיש אָדער פויליש, די בעגריף־שפּראך, די שפּראך פון ערנסטען דענקען
אין בײַ אונז ניט יודיש אפילו דעמאלט, ווען מיר בעהערישען יאָ די יודי'שע שפּראך.
דאָס איז א פסיכאָלאָגישער פאַקט, וואָס קײַנער איז אין איהם ניט שולדיג.

אָבער אויך אין דער הײַנטיגער צײַט ווירקען פערשיעדענע פאַקטאָרען, וואָס
דערהײַטערן יודיש פון אונזער אַלטעגליבען לעבען. מיר, אינטעליגענטען, דרעהען
זיך ס'רוב צווישען אינטעליגענטען, דאָס הײַסט צווישען מענישען, וואָס דער
גרעסטער טײַל ווײַערער אינטערעסירט זיך וועניג מיט דער יורישער קולטור און

מיט דעם גייסטיגען יודישען לעבּן. געגען וועלכן ווילען מיר אַרוּמאַרין-
געלט מיט אַזאַ אַטמאָספֿערע, וואָס די בּאַצילען פֿון אַטמילאַציע פֿערזפֿערען זיך
און מעהרען זיך. מיר זײ איינמאַל אויסגעקומען הערען, ווי איינער פֿון אוּנזערע
חבֿרים האָט גערעדט געגען העבּרעאיש און פֿאַר יודיש אויך אַ פֿערזאַמלוּנג פֿון
ציוניסטען. די געגנער האָבּען גערעדט ווער אויף רוּסיש, זיער אויף לשון-קוֹדש,
דער חבֿר, נאַטירליך, אויף מאַמע-לשון. נאָך דער פֿערזאַמלוּנג האָבּען זיך אָנגע-
הויבּען פֿרײוואַטע געשפּרעכלען, וואוּ ער האָט אויך געוואָלט רײזען יודיש – איז
דאָס אָבּער געגאַנגען אונמעגליך, הײל פֿיעלע פֿון די דערבּײגעוועזענע האָבּען טאַקן
זעהר שלעכט פֿערשטאַנען, וואָס מען רעדט צו זײ אויף יודיש. און אַזוי אין
טויזענדער פֿאַלען. וויפֿיעל מאָל טרעפֿט גאָר, אַז מיר פֿערטייָדיגען די יודישע שפּראַך
און די יודישע קולטור – אויף ר ו ס י ש!

אינגער בּעשעפֿטיגוּנג איז געוואָדגליך אַזאַ – אויב מיר זענען נאָר
ניט קיין יודישע שרײבּער און קיין דאַקטוירים און פֿעלדשערס אין די אָרמאַן
יודישע גאַסען – אַז די יודישע שפּראַך האָט צו איהר ניט קיין הירעקטע שיִלוּת,
מיר זענען לערער, יוריסטען, אינושענערען, האַנדעלס-אָנגעשטעלטע, סטוּדענטען,
חסידישע אָדער פֿיליוּשע זשוּרנאַליסטען. אַלס אַזעלכע – דאַרפֿען מיר די
יודישע שפּראַך כמעט ניט האָבּען. איך האָבּ ניט גערעדט פֿון גרויסע יודישע
פֿירמעס, יודישע קאַנטאַרען, וואוּ די קאָרעספּאָנדענין און די בּוּכער זאַלען זיך
פֿיהרען אויף יודיש. אויב עס זענען יאָ דאַ איינינע אַזוינע געשעפֿטען, זענען זײ
געווים אַ יוצא מן הכּלל. דער גרויס-קאַפּיטאַל, די רײַכע קאַנטאָרען, די בּע-
רייטענדע בּענק, וועלכע בּעשעפֿטיגען אינטעלינענטען פֿערסאַנאַל, האָ-
בּען יעדענפֿאַלס אַ קנאַפּע פֿערבּינדוּנג מיט יודיש.

אין אַזאַ סבֿיבֿה דאַרף מען האַבּען אַ סך מוּט און אַ סך עקשנוּת, כּדי
צו האַלטען זיך, ווי ווײַט דאָס איז מעגליך, פֿאַר יודיש.

נעהמט מען די ערציהוּנג פֿון די קינדער – טרעט דאָ אַרוֹים אַנאַנדערער
פֿאַקטאָר, וועלכער איז ניט ווענינער וויכטיג. יעדער פֿאַטער וויל קוֹדם כּל אַזוֹי
ערציהען זײַן קינד, אַז זײַן קולטוּר-מצבֿ זאָל זײַן העכער און דער קאַמפֿף
פֿאַרן לעבּן זאָל איהם אָנקוּמען וואָס וואָס גרינגער. די יודישע מאַסען האָבּען נאָך ניט
דערגרײוֹבּט צו אַזאַ מדרגה פֿון ענטוויקלוּנג, אַז ס'זאָל שוֹין איצט לוֹינען צו
לערנען יודיש אויס מאַטעריעלע אינטערעסען. מיט דער צײַט וועט דאָס געווים
אַזוֹי זײַן; כמניס דערפֿוּן בּעמערקען מיר שוֹין איצט אויך*). אָבּער דערווײַל איז
דער תּכלית – לערנען מיט דעם קינד די לאַנדעס-שפּראַך, ערציהען עם אויף
דער לאַנדעס-קוּלטוּר. טרוּען דאָס אַפֿילו אַזוֹינע עלטערן, וואָס זענען גענג פֿער-
בּוּנדען מיט דער יודישער קולטוּר. וואָס טרוּט מען ניט צוֹליעב קינדער?

אַז אויף דעם בּאָדען וואַקסען אוֹים אוּננאָרמאַלע, אַפֿטמאָל העסליכע ער-
שײנוּנגען – איז אַלעמען בּעקאַנט. אַ יודישער „האַלבּ"-אינטעלינענט בּרענט זיך

*) זעה די נעטיע אויספֿיהרוּנגען פֿון אסתּר: „צו דער פֿראַגע וועגען דער יי-
דישער פֿאָלקסשוּל". קאַפּיטעל IV, בּעזוּנדערס זײַטע 86–93.

דער ווערטער ווערטער מאגנאט

אלעקסאנדער האַרקאַווי, וואָס האַלט, אַז אויב אידיש
דאַרף גיין פון דער וועלט, זאָל זי כאטש האָבן וואָס מיט־
צונעמען אויפ'ן וועג צום לייענען.

(צו דער דערשײַנונג פון האַרקאַווי'ס
אידיש־העברעאיש־ענגלישן ווערטערבוך)

The Worthy Word Magnate. Alexander Harkavy, who believes that if Yiddish is destined to depart from this world it should at least have something to take along to read on the way. (On the publication of Harkavy's *Yiddish–Hebrew–English Dictionary*, subsequent to the appearance of his *Yiddish–English, English–Yiddish Dictionary*, and several other volumes). (*Der groyser kundes*, October 15, 1926)

דעם צונג כדי צו רעדען מיט'ן קינד דוקא אויף רוסיש, לאטש אוז אַך און
ווען וואָס פאַר אַ ח׳סיש דאַס איז. אַ ייִדיש קינד געוואוינט זיך פֿון דער פֿריִערע־
סטער יוגענד אָן צו קוקען אויף ייִדיש ווי אויף אַ ניִדעריִגע שפּראַך און אויף
די, וואָס רײדען ייִדיש — ווי אויף ניִדעריגע ברואים. פרעגסט דעם פֿאָטער, צוליעב
וואָס טהוט ער דאָס, וועט ער אײַך ענטפֿערן: כדי דאָס קינד זאָל האָבען אַ גו־
טע ח׳סישע אויסשפּראַכע...

„איך האָב גענוג געליטען, אײַדער איך בין געוואָרען אַ קולטור־מענש, זאָל
טײַן קינד פֿערשפּאָרען דורכגעהן דעם זעלביגען גיהנם", — אַזוי האָט ערקלעֶרהט
זײַן „סיסטעם" אײַנער פֿון מײַנע בעקאַנטע, וואָס מיט מיר האָט ער גערעדט ייִדעֶריש
און מיט זײַן צוויי־יאָהריגען מײדעֶלע האָט ער כסדר „געבראָקט" רוסיש אויף אַ־
עלט ייִדישען וויטעבסקער שטײַגער.

דעֶרצו איז נאָך די ייִדישע ליטעֶראַטור ניט צוגעפֿאַסט צום געברויך אין
דער פֿאַמיליע. ניטאָ קײַן לעזע־ביכער פֿאַר קינדער, ניטאָ קײַן געזאַמעֶלטע פֿאָלקס־
מעשיות און ליעדער, וואָס מ׳זאָל זײַ קעֶנען געבען אַ קינד אין די הענד. ניטאָ קײַן
געזאַמעֶלטע ביכער, וואָס זאָלען פֿערשאַפֿען אַ עסטעֶטישען פֿאַרגעניגען: ביכער
מיט שעֶנע בילדעֶר, אויף גוט פאַפיר, וואָס מ׳זאָל זיך וועֶלעֶן זײַ נעֶדעֶמעֶן אין
האַנד אַרײַן.

און דער תּוך כּל התּוכין, — די אָרימקײַט פֿון דער ייִדישער קולטור. וואָס מיר
פֿעֶרמאַגעֶן באַאמת און אין־ספּעֶצ און וואָס ס׳קעֶן מעֶהר אָדעֶר וועֶניִגעֶר בע־
פֿריעדיגעֶן די בעֶדערפֿעֶנִישעֶן פֿון אַ מאָדעֶרנעֶם קולטור־מענשען איז — די שעֶנע
ליטעֶראַטור און די זשורנאַליסטיק. פֿון ייִדישען טעאַטעֶר לאָמיר בעֶסעֶר ניט רײַדעֶן:
אַ מעֶנש מיט אַ שטיקעֶלע עֶסטעֶטישעֶן געֶשמאַק מוז דאָך לײַדעֶן אין אונזעֶרע
טעאַטעֶרס פֿאַר מגושמדיגקײַט אין קולטורלאָזיגקײַט, ווי אײַנעֶר לײַדט פֿאַר צאָהן־
וועֶהטאַג. קײַן ייִדישעֶ קונסט, קײַן ייִדישעֶ מוזעֶען איז ניטאָ. די ייִדישעֶ מוזיק מוז
עֶרשט בעֶאַרבײַט וועֶרעֶן און איז דערווײַלע נאָך ניט קײַן זעֶלבסטיגעֶר קולטור־
פֿאַקטאָר. פֿעֶרלאָזט מעֶן דאָס געֶביעֶט פֿון קונסט און מעֶן נעֶהמט זיך צו וויסעֶנ־
שאַפֿט — איז דאָ שוין גאָר אײַנגאַנצעֶן לײַדיג. וויסעֶנשאַפֿטליכעֶ וועֶרק
אַפֿיִלו וועֶניִג וועֶרעֶן יודעֶן אויף ייִדיש ניט געֶשריעֶבעֶן, אַפֿיִלו דעֶלעֶט איבעֶרזעֶצוינגעֶן
זעֶנעֶן בײַ אונז זעֶהר זעֶלטעֶן.

דער ייִדישעֶר אינטעֶליגעֶנט מוז לעֶבעֶן אין אַנ׳אַנדעֶר קולטורדעֶר־וועֶלט, אַ ח ו ץ
דעֶר ייִדישעֶר, אויב ער וויל בלײַבעֶן אַ קולטור־מעֶנש. דעֶרין איז, אויב איהר ווילט,
די טראָגעֶדיע פֿון אונזעֶרעֶ אינטעֶליגעֶנטעֶן.

III.

צי קעֶן מעֶן אָבעֶר די דאָזיִגעֶ טראָגעֶדיעֶ ניט מאַכעֶן קלעֶנעֶר? צי וועֶנדט זיך
ניט אָן אונזעֶר אײַגעֶנעֶם ווילעֶן פֿטרן אַ גרויסעֶן טײַל פֿון די וויעֶדעֶר־שפּרוכעֶן,
וואָס מאַכעֶן אַזוי אומגעֶלימפּעֶרט אונזעֶר גאַנצעֶ אַרבײַט?

צוויי! זאָבעֶן מוז מעֶן זיך קלאָר מאַכעֶן קודם כּל, וועֶן מעֶן וויל ענט־
פֿעֶרעֶן אויף אַט דעֶר פֿראַגעֶ — און בײַדעֶ געֶהעֶרעֶן, לײַדעֶר, צו די כלי־זין, וואָס
מיר בעֶנוצעֶן אין אונזעֶר קאַמפֿף געֶגעֶן די קריטיקעֶר פֿון ייִדיש. אויב דאָס

זעלבּע געװער קעגן אױסגעניצט װערען אױך געגען אונז אַלײן — אין נאַר אַ
בעװײז, װי אונגאַרטמאָל עס איז אונזער לאַגע.

דער װעג פֿון דעם יודישען פֿאָלק — לכל הפחות דער װעג זײַנער אין
דער געהענטער צוקונפֿט — פֿירהרט ניט אין דער ריכטונג פֿון אַטמיללאַציע. די
גרױסע מאַסען, דער קערן פֿונ'ם יודישען פֿאָלק, דער הױפֿט-פֿונדאַמענט פֿון זײַן
לעבּען, בּלײבּט יודיש.

פֿון די דאָזיגע מאַסען, פֿון דער טיעפֿעניש פֿונ'ם פֿאָלקס-לעבּען, אַדאַנק דער
קלאַסען-דיפֿערענצירונג, אין דעם — עקאָנאַמישען, פּאָליטישען, קולטורעלען און
גײַסטיגען — קאַמפֿף, װאָס איז מיט איהר פֿערבּונדען, װאַקסט אַ נײַ-יודישע װעלט-
ליכע קולטור, — װאַקסט און װערט אַלעמאָל ריכער און עראַבּערט זיך אַלעמאָל
מעהר פּלאַץ און אָנזעהן אין דעם יודישען לעבּען. דאָס איז אַ פֿאַקט, װאָס װערט
ניט געלײַקענט אין אונזער לאַגער. אַניט װאַלטמען מיר דאָך באַמת געדאַרפֿט
צוזיקלעגען „שער און אײזען" און געהן זיך לערנען אינ'ם חדר פֿון די אַסי-
מילאַנטען.

דאָס איז אָבּער ניט נאַר אַ נאַיװעאַקטיװ ער „פֿאַקט", דאָס איז אױך אַ סאָ־
ציעל-פּסיבּאָלאָגישער פֿאַקטאָר. דאָס בּעשאַפֿט אַזאַ פּסיבּאָלאָגישע אַטמאָספֿערע,
אַזאַ סבֿיבֿה, װאַס כ'טערען מעגליך און נאַטירליך פֿועלע ערשײַנונגען, װעלכע
װענען פֿריהער געװען אונמעגליך — ספּעציעל אין די אינטעליגענטישע קרײזען.
יעדער אינטעליגענט, װאָס איז אַזױ אָדער אַנדערש פֿערבּונדען מיט'ן לעבּען פֿונ'ם
פֿאָלק, פֿיהלט דעם דופֿק פֿון אָט דעם לעבּען, פֿיהלט די אונרוהיגע בּעװעגונגען,
די װירקונג פֿון די מאָלעקולאַרע קרעפֿטען דאָרטען טיעף אין די מאַסען. דאָס
שפּיעגעלט זיך אָפּ — אָפֿט אונבּעװאַוסט — אױף זײַן פּסיבּיק.

און דאָס איז אין דער גרונד, פֿאַר װאַס דער יודישער אינטעליגענט קעגן הײַנט
זיך אומקעהרען צי דער יודישער קולטור און צו דער יודישער שפּראַך. דאָס
איז די געגען-שטרעמונג, װעלבּע שװאַלט-אָפּ די אַטמיללאַציאַנס-װירקונג פֿון
דער בּעשעפֿטיגונג און פֿון דעם פֿערקעהר מיט אַסימילירטע אינטעליגענטען. דאָס
איז דער װאַרימער װינד, װאָס ציהט פֿון דעם „סאַמע געדיכטען" פֿאָלקס-לעבּען און
בּלאַזט אַראָבּ אַ סך שטױבּ פֿון די אינטעליגענטישע נשמות און צעשמעלצט
ניט אײן דיקע קאַרע (איך רעד, נאַטירליך, װעגען אַזױנע אינטעליגענטען, װאָס
האַבּען ניט אַבּגערריסען יערעל צובינד צו די מאַסען).

און דאָס איז אין דער גרונד, פֿאַר װאַס אַ הײַנטיגער אינטעליגענט, אַפֿילו אַזױנער,
װאָס האַט קײן יודיש ניט געשמעקט, װעט שױן ניט מאַלען קײן אירראַנישע מינע,
װען ער װעט הערען רײַדען פֿון דער יודישער ליטעראַטור. און דאָס איז אין דער
גרונד, פֿאַר װאָס מיר אַלײן האַבּען לכל הפחות אין אונזער עפֿענטליכ ער
אַרבּײַט אַנגעהױבּען בּענוצען נאָר די יודישע שפּראַך (אחוץ אױסנאַהמען, װאַ
ס'זענען שולדיג אױסװעניגסטע מניעות). און דאָם איז דער גרונד, פֿאַר װאַס
אײניגע יודישע אינטעליגענטען, װען זײ בּענעגענען זיך אין פּריװאַטען לעבּען
אַפֿילו, האַלטען שױן פֿאַר נױטיג צו רײַדען צװישען זיך יודיש; די צאָהל
פֿון אַזױנע אינטעליגענטען איז נאַך װעדר קלײן, אָבּער ס'איז אַ פֿאַקט, אַז ס'איז

דאָ אַזוינע אויך) און דאָס איז די דער גרונד, פֿאַר וואָס אַזוינע עָרשטײַנוּנגעָן װאַנדעָרן
ניט קײַנעָם און פֿאַר וואָס מען קוקט ניט אויף אַזוינע אינטעָלי-געָנטעָן זיך אויף
לעים – וי וי מען וואָלט געָוויס געָטהאָן פֿריהעָר מיט צוואַנציַג יאָהר. און דאָס איז
אויך דעָר גרונד, פֿאַר וואָס פֿיעָלעָ אינטעָעָלי-געָנטעָן נעָהמעָן זיך איצט אויף דעָר
עלטעָר לעָרנעָן יודיש אָדעָר סטאַרעָן זיך אָפּ-פֿרישעָן אין זייעָר אין זיכן זבהון דאָס, וואָס
זיי האָבעָן אַמאָל געָקעָנט און מיט דעָר צייט פֿעָרגעָסעָן.

דאָס איז איינס. און דאָס צװייטעָ איז נוגע דעָר מעָגליכקײַט צו בע-
פֿרעָדיגעָן אַלעָ קולטור-בעָדעָרפֿעָנישעָן אויף יודיש. דאָ מוז מען ווידעָר איבעָרי-
חזר'ן דאָס, וואָס מיר רעָדעָן אַזוי אָפֿט אין אונזעָר פּאָלעָמיק מיט אַנדעָרעָ.
מיר אַנטעָרשטרייַסעָן דאָך שטעָנדיג, אַו קייַנעָר הייסט ניט, פֿעָנוגצעָנדיג יודיש,
זיך אָבזאָגעָן פֿון אנדערע שפּראַכעָן. מיר אַליין דערטאָנעָן דאָך אַלע-
מאָל, אַו איבעָרהויפּט קעָן דעָר מאָדעָרנעָר מעָנש זיך ניט בעָגיהעָן מיט איין מוטעָר-
שפּראַך, נאָר עָר מוז קעָנעָן מינדעָענסטעָנס נאָך איין קולטור-שפּראַך. מיר אַליין
האָבעָן ניט איינמאָל דערוויזעָן, אַו אַפֿילו ווען מען שיקט אַ קינד אין אַ פֿרעָמד-
שפּראַכיגעָ שול, איז דאָס נאָך ניט קייַן מוז, אַו די שול-שפּראַך זאָל בײַ
איהם ווערעָן די מוטעָר-שפּראַך. מיר האָבעָן דאָך ווי-פֿיעָל מאָל געָמאַכט חוז פֿון די
אַלבעָ מעָנשעָן, וואָס האָבעָן ניט ניט קייַן אייַגעָנעָ שפּראַך, ניט קייַן אייַגעָנעָ
קולטור – און העָלפֿעָן עָנטװיקלעָן פֿרעָמדעָ קולטורעָן, װי-או מען קעָן זיך בע-
געָהן אָהן זייעָר טובה, בשעת די קולטור פֿון די יודישעָ מאַסעָן איז פֿעָרװאָהר-
לאָזט און אָרים.

לאָמיר זיך נאָר געָוועהנעָן אָנװעָנדעָן די זעָלבינעָ קריטיק אויף אונז גופֿא–
װעָלעָן מיר װעהעָן, אַו זעָהר פֿיעָל פֿון דעָם, וואָס מיר האָבעָן געָקעָנט טהאָן,
האָבעָן מיר ניט געָטהאָן.

די כּבה: פּסיכאָלאָגישע אינעָרציע, די מאַכט פֿון געָוואָהנהײַט. דאָס ניט
װעָלעָן רעָוװידירעָן די אייַגעָנעָ סימפּאַטיעָס און אַנטיפּאַטיעָס אויפֿ'ן   געָפֿיעָט
פֿון קולטור, דאָס ניט װעָלעָן זיך אָנטהאָן אַ כּח.

און מיט דעָם אַלעָמעָן מוזעָן מיר מאַבעָן אַנעָק, אויב מיר װילעָן ניט.
אַו אונזעָר אַרבײַט זאָל זיַן דאַלבעָ אַרבײַט.

מיר, אינטעָעָלי-געָנטעָן, געָפֿינעָן זיך איבעָרהויפֿט אין אַו אַזאַ פּאָזיציעָ, אַו מיר מוזעָן
דורך אונזעָר אייַגעָנעָם וייַלעָן עָרוואַרבעָן פֿיעָלעָ פֿון די אייַגעָנשאַפֿטעָן,
וואָס אַנדעָרעָ געָועָלשאַפֿטליכעָ שיכטעָן האָבעָן זיי אַדאַנק זייעָר קאַציאַעָלעָר לאַגעָ.
שטאַמעָן – שטאַמעָן מיר דעָרהויפֿט פֿון דעָר מיטעָל-און קלייַן-בורזשואַזיעָ –
און געָשטעָלט האָבעָן מיר זיך „אויף דעָם פּראָלעָטאַרישעָן שטאַנדפֿונקט". פֿעָר-
אינטעָרעָסירט זעָנעָן מיר דעָרהויפֿט אין פּאָליטישעָר פֿרײַהײַט – און קעָמפֿעָן
קעָמפֿעָן מיר פֿאַר אַ אידעָאַל פֿון עָקאָנאַמישעָר געָרעָכטינקײַט. לעָבעָן – לעָבעָן
מיר איצט געָוועָהנליך אין אַ בירושוטאַוער סביבה – און די דאָזיגעָ כבֿיבה װילעָן
מיר דורך אונזעָר טעָטינקײַט פֿעָרניכטעָן. דאָס איז אַזאַ לאַגעָ, וואַ אַ מעָנש
דאַרף זעָהר פֿיעָל זיך מיט זיך קעָמפֿעָן, זעָהר פֿיעָל אין זיך איבעָרמאַכעָן, זעָהר
פֿיעָלעָ פֿעָרטיליגעָן, בּיז עָר בעָשאַפֿט פֿון זיך דעָם נייַעָם מעָנשעָן, דעָם קעָמפֿעָר

פֿאַר אַ ניַי לעבּעֶן

און אַזוי דאַרפֿעֶן מיר וועהעֶן פֿעֶרטיליגעֶן אין אונז, אויף וויפֿיעל דאָס איז
איצט מעֶגליך, דעם אַלטעֶן אַסימילאַטאָר.

און מעֶגליך איז איצט זעהר פֿיעל. עֶס איז דאָ אַ גרויסע צאָהל אינטעֶליגעֶנטעֶן,
וואָס קעֶנעֶן כּמעֶט אָהן שום שוויריגקייטעֶן איבּעֶרגעֶהן פֿון אַ פֿרעֶמדעֶר שפּראַך
אויף יודיש אין זייעֶר אַלטעֶגליכעֶן לעבּעֶן. עֶס איז פֿאַראַהן נאָך אַ גרעֶסעֶרע צאָהל
אַזוינע, וואָס וואָלטעֶן געקעֶנט מאַכעֶן די יודישע שפּראַך פֿאַר אייזנעֶר פֿון זייעֶרע
הייטישע שפּראַבּעֶן אין אַ יודיש בּוך פֿאַר אַ שטעֶנדיגעֶן גאַסט אויף זייעֶר שרייבּ-
טיש. און עֶס איז כּמעֶט ניטאָ קיין איינציגעֶר, וואָס זאָל ניט קעֶנעֶן לעֶרנעֶן זייַן
קינד יודיש, אַזוי אַז דאָס קינד זאָל רעֶכעֶנעֶן יודיש פֿאַר זיין מוטטעֶר-שפּראַך און
זאָל האָבּעֶן אַ בּעֶדעֶרפֿטעֶניש צו לייעֶנעֶן יודיש.

ווילטיג איז בּעֶזונדעֶרס דער לעֶצטעֶר פֿאַקט. מיר מוזעֶן לעֶרנעֶן אונזעֶרע
קינדעֶר די שפּראַך פֿון דעם יודישעֶן פֿאָלק. מיר האָבּעֶן דאָס רעֶכט ניט אָבּצורייסעֶן
אונזעֶרע קינדעֶר פֿון דעם יורש, פֿון וועֶלכעֶן מיר ציהעֶן אונזעֶר אידעֶאַליום און
אונזעֶר בּעֶגייסטעֶרונג און אונזעֶרע האָפֿענונגעֶן אויף אַ בּעֶסעֶרע צוקונפֿט. מיר
טאָרעֶן ניט קאַליעֶטשעֶן אונזעֶרע קינדעֶר, מאַכעֶן פֿון זיי צושפּאַלטעֶנע בּעֶשעֶפֿעֶני-
שעֶן, גייט-אַרין-ניט-אַהער-מעֶנשעֶן. מיר דאַרפֿעֶן זיך היטעֶן, אַז אונזעֶרע קינדעֶר זאָלעֶן
אונז שפּעֶטעֶר ניט וואַרפֿעֶן אין פּנים אַרין די פֿעֶרבּיטעֶרטע פֿראַגע: וואָס האָט
איהר געהאַט צו אונו?

און מיר קעֶנעֶן איצט לעֶרנעֶן אונזעֶרע קינדעֶר יודיש, מיר דאַרפֿעֶן נאָר
וועֶלעֶן.

מ'האָט פֿיעל געשריעבּעֶן וועֶגעֶן נאַציאָנאַלעֶר עֶרציהונג, וועֶגעֶן אַ יודישעֶר
סבֿיבֿה. איך וויל די פֿראַגע דאָ ניט בּעֶריהרעֶן. מיר דאַכט: אַ סבֿיבֿה קעֶן
מעֶן אויף אַ קינסטליכעֶן אופֿן ניט בּעֶשאַפֿעֶן. בּיי אינטעֶליגעֶנטעֶן — צו וועֶלכעֶר
נאַציאָן זיי זאָלעֶן ניט געהעֶרעֶן — האָט די סבֿיבֿה אויפֿגעהעֶרט שפּיעלעֶן אַזאַ ראָלע,
ווי בּיי אַנדעֶרע פֿאָלקס-שיכטעֶן. יעדעֶנפֿאַלם קעֶנעֶן מיר דאָ אויפֿטהאָן ניט פֿיעל.
וואָס כּ'איו יאָ מעֶגליך — דאָס איז געבּעֶן אונזעֶרע קינדעֶר די נויטיגע קעֶנטניששעֶן,
אַרינפֿיהרעֶן זיי לכל הפּחות דורך דעם בּוך, אויבּ ניט דורך דעם לעבּעֶדיגעֶן
לעבּעֶן, אין דעם קריים פֿון יודישעֶ איבּעֶרלעבּונגעֶן, שטימונגעֶן, געדאַנקעֶן, מאַכעֶן
אַזוי, אַז קיין שום יודישעֶס זאַך זאָל זיי ניט פֿרעֶמד זין.

און דאָס איז אָבּיעֶקטיוו מעֶגליך. דאָ דאַרף, נאַטיורליך, יעדעֶרעֶר אויסקלייבּעֶן
די יעֶניגע לעֶרן-מעֶטאָדע, וועֶלכעֶ עֶר געפֿינט פֿאַר פּאַסעֶנד. אָבּעֶר צוויי גרונד-
עֶלעֶמעֶנטעֶן קעֶנעֶן מיר אָנווייזעֶן שוין איצט: די יודישעֶ געשיכטע און די יודישעֶ
ליטעֶראַטור. דאָ איז פֿאַראַהן גענוג שטאָף: מעֶן דאַרף נאָר קומעֶן און שעֶפּעֶן.

און דאָס איז מעֶגליך אַפֿילו דאָרט, וואו די קינדעֶר בּעֶזוכעֶן אַנ'אַלגעֶמיינע —
ניט-יודישעֶ שול. נאָר איין זאַך דאַרף מעֶן זיך נאָר היטעֶן: אַז דאָס לעֶרנעֶן מיט
די קינדעֶר יודיש זאָל ניט בּעֶקומעֶן אַזאַ פּנים, ווי דאָס לעֶרנעֶן העֶברעֶאיש בּיי
איינינע „נאַציאָנאַל-געשטימטע" יודישעֶ אַסימילאַנטעֶן, וואו אי די עֶלטעֶרעֶן, אי די

קינדער קוקען אויף דעם „זוברעװען" (פקדה, פקדתי) װי אויף אנ׳אבקומעניש און
פון דעם לערנען קומט געװעהנליך גאר ניט ארױס.

נאר דערפֿאר איז אפֿשר ניטא װאס מורא צו האבּען: יודיש איז א לעבּעדיגע
שפראך, בשעת העברעאיש שטארבּט־אב און קען װערען קאנסערװירט נאר דורך
געלעהרטע יחידים. דער עיקר – אױף יודיש רעדט דאך דער גרעסטער טײל
פֿון אונזערע אינטעליגענטען, ד. ה. מען קען רעדען. איך בּין זיכּער, אז אין
די הײזער, װאו די קינדער װעלען אנהױבּען לערנען (בּיַי אינטעליגענטע לעהרער)
די יודישע שפראך, װעלען אױך די עלטערען בּיסלעכװײז זיך אימקעהרען צו
יודיש. נױטיג איז נאר דער ערשטער שטוס...

אבּער קודם כל איז נױטיג, אז מיר זאלען זיך אבזאגען פֿון א טײל אלטע
שטימונגען, װעלכע לעבּען נאך האלב אונבּעװאוסט אין אונזער נשמה. למאי זאלען
מיר נארען: מיר אלײן האבּען זיך נאך ניט געװעהנט קוקען אױף יודיש
געװען ערנסט, אין פֿיעלע פֿון אונו װעט אידז נאך געפֿינען שפּורען פֿון דער
אלטער פֿעראכטונג צום „אונקולטורעלען" זשארגאן.

און דאס מוזען מיר אײנמאל פֿאר אלעמאל אױסראמען פֿון אונזער נשמה.

שװער? געװיס. ס׳קאסט קרבּנות? אודאי. אבּער װען האבּען מיר זיך אבּגע־
שטעלט פֿאר שװעריקײטען, װען האבּען מיר מורא געהאט פֿאר קרבּנות, בשעת
ס׳האט זיך געהאנדעלט װעגען דורכפֿיהרען אין לעבּען די פּרינצ(יפּ)ען פֿון אונזער
װעלט־אנשױאונג?

מען װעט מיר אנװײזען אױף טעכּנישע שװעריגקײטען. איך קען זײ. איך האב
זײ אױסגערעכענט אין דעם פֿריהערדיגען קאפּיטעל. דאס איז אבּער נאר ט ע כ ־
נ י ש ע שװעריגקײטען. בּײצוקומען זײ איז גאר ניט אזוי שװער.

IV.

נאר דא װעט קומען דער „נײטראליסט" און װעט זאגען: צו װאס טױג
די גאנצע ארבּײט? דאס, װאס ס׳טהוט זיך אין די אינטעליגענטישע קרײזען, איז
דאך נארמאל, װאס זשע מאכט מען דא פֿאר א געפּילדער? און ס. װעלצער
װעט אונז דערמאנען דעם אלטען אמת, אז „ס׳איז פֿאראהאן אינטערנאציאנאלע
קולטור", נאר אין פֿערשיעדענע פֿארמען, אז „די אדער יענע פֿארם פֿון קולטור האט
פֿאר אונז ניט קײן אבּסאלוטען װערט", אז „מיר װעלען נישט מאכען פֿון איהר
קײן אבּגאט, מיר װעלען די נישט קולטיװירען קונסטליך". ער װעט אונז נאך
דערמאנען, אז אנדערש דענקען נאר די, װאס װענען זיך טמך אױף א „מעטאפֿיזיש־
נאציאנאליסטישע קאנצעפּציע"(*). און ער װעט מײנען, אז דאס פֿערענטפֿערט
אלע פֿראגען, בשעת אין אמת׳ן האט ער אפֿילו ניט געפּרוט צוגעהן צו דעם
פּונקט, װאו די פֿראגען װערען בּרענענד.

װארום בּרענענד װערט א פֿראגע ערשט דארט, װאו מען בּעדארף ט ה א ן
דארט װאו מען בּעדארף תיכּף, אהן טענות ומענות, ענטשערען: עט אהין געהען

מיר און אהין געהען מיר ניט. וויסנשאַפֿטליך, טעאָרעטיש, ד. ה. שע־
צענדיג דעם ווערט פֿון דער ערקענטניש, ניט דעם ווערט פֿון דער האַנדלונג,
ד. ה. בלײַבענדיג אײַנאַנצען אָן אַ זײַט פֿון פּראַקטישען לעבען, וואָלטען מיר
אפֿשר געקענט מסכּים זײַן, אַז סּאיז אונז אַלץ אײַנס. וועלכע קולטור, אַבֿי
קולטור, אָז קײן פֿעסטען קריטעריום צו אורטײלען וועגען דער צוקונפֿט פֿון דער
ייִדישער קולטור פֿאַרמאָגען מיר ניט. ווער עס קען זיך בעפֿרידיגען מיט אַזאַ
ערקענטניש – זאָל זיך.

מיר מוזען אַבֿער האַנדלען! מיר זענען ניט קײן קאַבינעט־זיצער, קײן באַנק־
קנעטשער, וואָס קענען זיך בענוגענען מיט דעם ענטפֿער: „מיר פֿאַרמאָגען ניט
קײן גענוים, וויסענשאַפֿטליכען, מאַרקסיסטישען מעטאָר, האָם זאָל אונז ערלױבען
שטעלען אַ פּראָגנאָזן אין דעם געבּיעט", וווי דאָס טהוט ס. זעלצער – און בלײַבּען
בײַ דעם תּירוץ. דאָס לעבּען פֿאַרלאַנגט פֿון אונז מעשׂים – און מעשׂים זענען
קײנמאָל ניט גלײַבּגילטיג, טהאָטען קענען ניט זײַן אַבסטראַקט. האַנדלען מוז
מען אין אַ געװיסער ריכטונג, אהין אָדער אהער, צו דער נאַציאָנאַלער קולטור
אָדער צו דער אַסימילאַציע. פֿון „איך ווײַס ניט" קען דאָ ניט זײַן קײן רעדע.

אײַנס לעבּען פֿון יעדער פּאַרטיי פֿאַרהאַן אזוינע זיטען, וואו די
מעהרצאָל האָט נאָך ניט געזאָנט איהר לעצט וואָרט, וואו סּאיז פֿאַרהאַן חלוקי־
דעות וועגען דעם גאַנג פֿון דער וויטערדיגער ענטוויקלונג. אַ פּאַרטיי אַ לעבּעדיגע
בלײַבּט אַבּער ניט זיצען ניט פֿאַרלעגטער הענד און זאָגט ניט: „איך פֿאַרמאַג ניט
קײן גענוים מעטאָר". מען געדט געװעהנליך אין אַזאַ ריכטונג, וועלכע איז
װאהרשײַנליך צוגעפּאַסט צו דער ליניע פֿון דער ענטװיקלונג. מען האַנדעלט
אַזוי, אַקוראַט װי מען ווײַסט שוין. און קומט דערנאָך די וויסענשאַפֿט,
וועלכע האָט ניט אױפֿגעהערט פֿרעגען און פֿאָרשען, און בעװיזט, אַז מיאיז געגאַנגען
אין אַ פֿאַלשען וועג, ענדערט מען די ריכטונג. דערפֿון נעהמט זיך דאָך די ניט־
װענדיגקײַט צו איבּערקוקען אַלעמאָל און אױספּעסערען דאָס פּראָגראַם און, נאָך
אָפֿטער, די טאַקטיק פֿון פּאַרטײַען.

און אַזױ איז אױך מיט דער פֿראַגע װעגען ייִדיש.

מיר זאָגען: עס איז װאהרשײַנליך, אַז די ייִדישע קולטור װעט עקזיס־
טירען אַ לאַנגע צײַט (פֿאַר „אײביג" קען אײַך אפֿילו די שטאַרקסטע קולטור ניט
גאַראַנטירען). עס איז װאהרשײַנליך, אַז צוליעב דעם ערװאַלען פֿון די מאַסען
צו פּאָליטישען, געזעלשאַפֿטליבּען און קולטורעלען לעבּען װעט די ייִדישע שפּראַך,
די ייִדישע ליטעראַטור, די ייִדישע שול. דאָס ייִדישע טעאַטער זיך ענטװיקלען
און פֿאַרשטאַרקען. עס איז װאהרשײַנליך, אַז די ייִדישע נאַציאָן געהט ניט אונטער.
געניו װויסען מיר דאָס ניט – און עס ווײַסט דאָס ניט קײנער. געפֿינט דאָ דאָך
אפֿילו ס. זעלצער פֿאַר נױטװענדיג נישטװעסטעס מעדדיג צו „בּעטאַנענ אױפֿין קאַטעגאָריאָרישען אופֿן", אַז
„מיר (נעיטראַליסטען) האַלטען ניט, דאָס די אַסימילאַציע איז װאהרשײַנליבּער.
אײַנדער די װעלבּסטשטענדיגע ענטוויקלונג פֿון דער ייִדישער קולטור". און אַזױ ווי
אין דער װעלבּיגער צײַט שטעהען פֿראַגען, וועלבּע פֿאַרלאַנגען שױן, תּיכּף, אױפֿן

שטעל אנ׳ענטפֿער: ײדישע שולען אָדער דאָס רעכט פֿון ײדישע קינדער צו לערנען
אין רוסישע שולען, שבת־רוה, אָדער זונטאָג־רוה, נאציאָנאל־קולטורעלע אויטאָנאָמיע
אָדער בירגערליכע גלײכבערעכטיגונג. און אז. וו., — דערױבער קענען מיר ניט
וויצען אין פֿילאָזאָפֿירען: „מיר האָבען ניט קײן פֿראָגנאָז". מיר ענטפֿערן אזוי, ווי
עס איז אונז וואהרשײנליך. ניט ענטפֿערן איז ניט מעגליך. מיר נעהמען דערפֿאַר
ניט אָן „אונזערע סוביעקטיװע וואוינטשען פֿאַר אָביעקטיװע אנגאַבען פֿון דער גע-
שיכטע", ווי דאָס מײנט ס. ד. בעצער. מיר קענען זיך בעגעהן אָהן סוביעקטיװע
וואונשען (נעהם יעדער לעבעדינער מענש, אַ נײטראַליסט ווי אַ אנטי־נײטראַליסט,
ה, ד אזוינע וואונשען). אָבער מיר קענען ניט אויסמײדען די אָביעקטיװע פֿאָרערונגען
פֿון אונזער אַרבײט.

און אָט די אָביעקטיװע פֿאָרערונגען פֿערלאַנגען אויך פֿון אונזער אינטעלי-
גענט, אז ער זאָל אויפֿהערען זײן צװײ־פּנימ׳דיג אין קולטור־פֿראַגען.

די ײדישע פֿראָקציע האָט דאָס גערעכט פֿאַר אַ וועג פֿון ײדיש. ווען ניט ד׳
לאָונטש און פֿירדרטאָן האָבען זיך, ענדליך, ארויסגעזאָגט אין רומע פֿאַר אַ ײדי-
שער שול אויף ײדיש. מ׳האָט אָגעוויזען, אז קעמפֿ׳ען פֿאַר עפּ׳ם קען מען נאָר
דעמאָלט. ווען מ׳איז איבערצײגט, אז דאָס „עפּ׳ם" איז ווירקליך נויטיג.

איך וואָלט דאָס געוואָלט דערמאָנען אונזערע אינטעליגענטען.

ווילען זײ, אז זײער קאַמפֿ זאָל זײן קאָנזעקוועענט, ניט צעבראָכען, ניט גע-
פֿעלשט. מוזען זײ אויך פּראַקטיש טהאָן דאָס אײגענע, וואָס זײ האָבען געטהאָן
טעאָרעטיש: ד. ה. אומקעהרען זיך צו ײדיש.

ווארום עס האָט אַ פּנים פֿון חוק און, דער עיקר, עס קען ניט ה א-
בען קײן ערפֿאָלג, ווען איך, למשל, קעמפֿ מיט די העברעאיסטען פֿאַר אַ
ײדישע שול, בשעת אין פּריװואַט־לעבען רײדע איך, גלײך מיט די העברעאיסטען,
אויך רוסיט אָדער פֿויליש. און דאָס ווײסען אי די פֿרינד, אי די געגנער. עס
קען ניט אימפּאָנירען קײנעם, ווען איך זינג שירות ותשבחות לכבוד דער אויפֿ-
בליהענדיגער ײדישער ליטעראַטור. בשעת פֿאַר מיר גופֿא איז אַ נײע ערצעהלונג
פֿון סאָלאָגוב אַ וויכטיגערע געשעהעניש. אײדער צעהנדליגע נײע ײדישע ביכער.
עס קען ניט צעײלט ווערען דער מענש אויף אַ געזעלשטאַפֿט-
ליכען און פּריװואַטען ווי אַלע אנדערע. אז אײנער זאָל סותר זײן דעם צווייטען —
אונזער אײנער נאָך ווענׅיגער ווי אַלע אנדערע. צעשפּאַלטען מיר זיך, — הײסט דאָס.
אז מיר שוואַכען אָב אונזערע קרעפֿטען, אז מיר גיבען אונזערע שונאים אַ גע-
ווער אין האנד, אז מיר טרעטען אָב פֿון אונזער פּאָזיציעס.

ס׳איז שוין צײט. די ײדישע קולטור זאָל אָנהויבען אימפּאָנירען אונזערע
געגנער. און דאָס וועט ניט זײן, כל זמן מיר האַלטען זי ניט פֿאַר אײגענעם. און
וועט זי ניט אימפּאָנירען — וועט זיך קײנער אויך אידער ניט אומקוקען. וועלען די
בעדערפֿענישען פֿון די מאַסען טאָקי אַלץ בלײבען אונבעפֿרידיגט.

דאָ איז ווידער דאָס פּריװואַטע לעבען אונזערס גענג צוזאַמענגעבונדען מיט דער
געזעלשאַפֿטליכער אַרבײט.

שוין צייט זיך אומקוקען, וואוהין מיר געהען.

אין דער שטורעם־און דראַנג־צייט, ווען אַלצדינג האָט געקאָכט און געברויזט און אַ מענשעַנס אַרבעַט האָט געדויערַט ניט מעהר ווי אַ יאָהר, צוויי, דרייַ, אי דאָם מיט גרויסע הסכּמות, איז געוועַן נאַטירליך, וואָס מ'האָט געלעבט אין פיעלע פּרטים ״ווי גאָט גיעט״. מ'האָט אַלץ קיין צייט ניט געהאַט, אַלץ אָבּגעלעגט אויף שפּעטער.

אונזער היינטיגע צייט איז אין פיעלע פּרטים אַ סינטעטישע. מען קוקט זיך אַרום. מען שעַצט־איבּער אַלטע ווערטען. מען זאַמעלט כּהח. מען גרייַט זיך צו אַרבייַטען לאַנגע יאָהרען. מען מוז זיך אויך אַרומקוקען, וואו האַלטען מיר אין אונזער בעַציהונג צו יודיש....

דייטש
העברעאיש
אונד זשארגאן
קענען זיך אייערע טעכטער גרינדליך
דערלערנען נאר אין דיא העברעאישע
קלאססען פיר אידישע
מעדכען
פין דער
נארטהאיסטערן
עדיוקיישאנעל
אינסטיטוט
702 נ. פרענקלין סט.,   פילאדעלפיא.

'German, Hebrew, and Jargon [= Yiddish]: Your daughters can learn these well only in the Hebrew classes for young ladies'. The title page of the highly Germanized prospectus of a Jewish school in Philadelphia around 1900. An item in the Yivo archives.

The Struggle for Yiddish During World War I:
The Attitude of German Jewry

ZOSA SZAJKOWSKI

Before World War I, Yiddish was regarded by most Western Jews as a disgrace. This was a legacy of the Enlightenment which had, also among the more sophisticated and Westernized strata of Eastern Jewry, evoked an overt aversion to this language of the masses. To cite but one example, Professor Heinrich Graetz, who disliked the culture of the *Ostjuden*, refused to permit the publication of a Yiddish translation of his History of the Jews.[1] Only a small group of German Jews, most of them Zionists, refused to look upon Yiddish as a shameful jargon.[2] To them it was a product of the life of the people, and love of the people, the common folk, required also affection for the idiom in which they expressed their

The research for this study was made possible by a grant of the Leo Baeck Institute in New York. The following abbreviations of sources are used in the notes: AA – Archives of the German Ministry of Foreign Affairs (Auswärtiges Amt, Bonn); AZJ – Allgemeine Zeitung des Judentums; DZ – Deutsches Zentralarchiv (Potsdam); IF – Israelitisches Familienblatt (Hamburg); JDC – Archives of the American Joint Distribution Committee; JP – Die Jüdische Presse (Berlin); JR – Jüdische Rundschau (Berlin); LBIB – Bulletin des Leo Baeck Instituts (Tel Aviv); LBIYB – Leo Baeck Institute Year Book (London); NJM – Neue Jüdische Monatshefte (Berlin); VZ – Vossische Zeitung; YIVO – Archives of the Yivo-Institute for Jewish Research (New York); ZA – General Zionist Archives (Jerusalem).

1. Prof. Graetz wrote to Rabbi Dr. Salomon Zwi Skomorowsky: 'Wegen einer Übersetzung meiner volkstümlichen Geschichte der Juden im jüdischen Jargon muss ich entschieden Einspruch erheben. Ein Jargon ist eine grosse Schmach für eine Volksklasse... Ich bitte Sie, geehrter Herr, eine solche Schändung meiner Geschichte zu verhindern' Dr. Josef Meisl, 'Graetz und das Ostjudentum', JP, XLVII (1917), p. 505 (first pub-

lished in *Almanach Zydowski*, 1917). In 1897/98, a Yiddish translation of Graetz's History by I. I. Lerner was published in Warsaw. Other editions and translations were published in later years.
2. '...Die Mehrheit der deutschen Juden empörte sich wohl aus Gerechtigkeitsgefühl und allgemein menschlichem Empfinden bei der Kunde von Pogromen und wirtschaftlichen Verfolgungen, gab Geld her zur Linderung des Elends und zur Förderung der ziemlich planlos betriebenen Auswanderung nach Übersee, verharrte aber in seelischer Unberührtheit und Gleichgültigkeit. So kam es, dass für viele Tausende, die mit unseren Heeren nach den so gut wie unbekannten Ostländern zogen, das Vorfinden einer kompakten jüdischen Volksmasse mit ausgesprochener Eigenart in Tracht, Sprache und Lebensführung eine Entdeckung bedeutete. Eine Entdeckung, die um so widerstreitendere Gefühle auslöste, als sie mit einem Zustande gesteigerter Empfindungen für das schwer ringende Vaterland, seine Kultur und Volksgemeinschaft zusammenfiel'. Dr. Adolf Friedemann, 'Wir und die Ostjuden'. NJM, I (1916), pp. 58–59; see also Max Mayer, 'A German Jew goes East'. LBIYB, III (1958), pp. 344–60.

feelings and worries. Yiddish was considered by this small group to be an integral part of the *All-Judentum*, as formulated by Nathan Birnbaum and Fritz Mordecai Kaufmann. While the Orthodox Jews saw in the East European Jews a considerable source of help in strengthening the religious life of German Jewry,[3] the Zionists welcomed them as allies in the fight for nationalist Jewish ideals. In the culture of the *Ostjuden*, in the Yiddish language, folklore, and literature, they discovered an immense source of inspiration.[4] As early as 1901, Fabius Schach of Karlsruhe had written that Yiddish was not a jargon but a living language spoken by a large population. He advised the Jewish scholars of Germany to study the Yiddish literature, and thus to come to know and love the Jews of Eastern Europe.[5] In 1913, Julius Kaufmann, together with his brother Fritz Mordecai, published the monthly *Die Freistatt*, an *alljüdische Revue* whose object it was to present Yiddish culture to German Jewry.[6] Earlier, and in a less dogmatic way, *Ost und West*, published by the German branches of the Alliance Israélite Universelle under the editorship of Leo Winz, had done the same thing.

For political purposes, Yiddish had been described as a link with the German language, thereby supporting German culture and German influence abroad. In 1911, Davis Trietsch wrote that outside the German Reich there were about eleven million Jews with whom it was possible to communicate in German.[7] When the war broke out in 1914, both Jews and non-Jews in Germany suddenly discovered how useful Yiddish was to German interests in Eastern Europe as

---

3. 'Wer weiss, ob der unergründliche Plan der Vorsehung den osteuropäischen Juden nicht darum zum westeuropäischen Juden schickt, damit eine harmonische Ergänzung sich vollziehe, damit die im Westen entschwundene Thora von neuem erweckt...' *Der Israelit* (Organ of Orthodoxy), LIV, No. 13, 1913, pp. 1–2.

4. Dolf Michaelis wrote in his memoirs: 'Mitleid ohne Tat findet seinen krassen Ausdruck in dem alten jüdischen Witz: "Schafft ihn mir weg, er zerbricht mir das Herz!" Wegschaffen, oder besser: gar nicht erst hereinlassen, das war, wie wir ja wissen, die Reaktion gewisser jüdischer Kreise in Deutschland, die in den Ostjuden eine Gefährdung der deutsch-jüdischen Position sahen. Für meisten von uns aber wurde das ostjüdische Erlebnis, das Zusammentreffen mit diesen Menschen, zur Bestätigung unserer zionistischen Erkenntnis und auch zur Bestärkung unseres eigenen zionistischen Zieles.' Dolf Michaelis, 'Mein Blau-Weiss-Erlebnis'. LBIB, V-17 (1962), p. 44.

5. 'Nein, der Jargon der russischen Juden ist kein Mauscheln. Er ist keine durch willkürliche Verdrehung und Entstellung entstandene Mundart, sondern eine in sich geschlossene Volkssprache, die ihre Geschichte und ihre Entwicklung

hat. Der Jargon ist eine lebendige Sprache einer grossen Bevölkerung...Den jüdischen Gelehrten in Deutschland aber, denen das innere und äussere Leben der russischen Juden noch immer ein Buch mit sieben Siegeln ist, kann ich nur raten, die Jargonliteratur zu studieren. Sie werden erst dann die Juden des Ostens kennen und lieben können.' Fabius Schach, 'Der deutsch-jüdische Jargon und seine Literatur.' *Ost und West*, I (1901), p. 190.

6. For a Yiddishist opinion on *Die Freistatt* see S. Niger, in *Di Judische Welt*, No. 8, 1913; Z. Reizen, *Leksykon*...Wilna, 1929, III, p. 593–99.

7. Davis Trietsch, 'Das deutschsprachige Judentum im Auslande.' JR, XVI 6–7 (1911), pp. 66, 75–76. Franz Oppenheimer wrote on this period: 'Würde es nicht hebräisch geschrieben und gedruckt, so würden die Deutschen es anders beurteilen und vielleicht seine Träger anders behandeln. Professor Hoeniger sagte mir einmal im Berliner Dozentenzimmer: "Es ist ein Skandal, da haben wir das unverschämte Glück, dass das begabteste Handelsvolk der Welt unsere Sprache spricht, und machen es uns zu Feinden. Was würden die Engländer aus dieser ungeheuren Chance gemacht haben?!"' 'Jugendfreundschaften, Erinnerungen'. VZ, July 19, 1930.

well as in neutral countries.[8] A number of Yiddish-German dictionaries[9] appeared in Germany and Austria, and studies of the language,[10] translations of Yiddish writers,[11] essays on Yiddish folklore,[12] etc. were published. Yiddish was often represented as a Middle High German dialect (*mittelhochdeutscher Dialekt*).

At the beginning of the War, an unofficial Jewish nonparty committee, the *Komitee für den Osten* (KfdO), was formed in order to defend the interests of the Jews of Eastern Europe and at the same time to gain their sympathy for the Central Powers. Yiddish was represented by the KfdO as a natural instrument for the propagation of German influence in countries where it was spoken. After the outbreak of war, Dr. I. M. Bodenheimer, a Zionist leader and one of the founders of the KfdO, submitted a memorandum on the Jews of Eastern Europe to the German military and diplomatic authorities. In this he said that Yiddish

8. 'Der Jargon...ist ja vielfach gerade von deutscher Seite bekämpft worden. Man sah in ihm eine Verstümmelung des Deutschen, ein Hindernis, die breiten jüdischen Volksmassen der allgemeinen Kultur zuzuführen, etc. etc. Jetzt aber hat es sich gezeigt, welchen grossen Nutzen gerade diese Sprache der Sache der europäischen Zentralmächte geleistet hat...Die Haltung gewisser jüdischer und nichtjüdischer Kreise gegenüber dem Jargon dürfte infolge des Weltkrieges ganz radikal revidiert werden.' Joseph Kreppel, *Der Weltkrieg und die Judenfrage.* Wien, 1915, p. 20; also in IF, XVII-7, 1915, p. 9; 'Der Krieg hat auch das verachtete Judendeutsch umgewertet...in Russisch-Polen hat sich die Sprache...als eine schätzenswerte Bundesgenossin erwiesen.' Professor S. Kraus (Wien), 'Das Judendeutsch'. IF, XVIII-25 (1916), p. 10; 'Die Sprache der Ostjuden, das Jiddische, ist ihnen unbekannter als ein exotischer Dialekt.' Fritz Mordechai Kaufmann, 'Grenzsperre. Ein Kapitel vom Versagen der deutschen Judaeologie.' *Der Jude*, I (1916–17), p. 14. – Many years later the *Vorwärts* of Berlin wrote: 'Unsere Alldeutschen und Nationalisten sprechen gern von "deutscher Weltgeltung", die sie sich nicht anders denken können, als auf Waffengewalt und Kriegsmacht beruhend. Das Jiddische wird von ihnen natürlich mit Hohn abgetan. Nur wenn die Not gross und zwingend ist, dann erinnert man sich auch dieser verachteten Sprache, wie Ludendorffs berühmter Aufruf An die Jidden in Polen beweist.' H.D., 'Bedeutung und Verbreitung des Jiddischen.' *Vorwärts*, 21.2.1931.
9. For example: E. Bischoff: *Jüdisch-deutscher und deutsch-jüdischer Dolmetscher*, Leipzig, 1916; *Idem*,

*Wörterbuch der wichtigsten Geheimund Berufssprachen. Jüdisch-Deutsch...*Leipzig, 1916; Hermann L. Strack, *Jüdisches Wörterbuch mit besonderer Berücksichtigung der gegenwärtig in Polen üblichen Ausdrücke.* Leipzig, 1916, 204 pp.; *Seiben-Sprachen-Wörterbuch.* Deutsch / Polnisch / Russisch / Weissruthenisch / Litauisch/ Lettisch/Yiddish. Herausgegeben im Auftrage des Oberbefehlshabers Ost. Leipzig, (1918).
10. For example: Moses Cavalry, 'Jiddish,' *Der Jude*, I (1916–17), pp. 25–32; Germano-Judaeus, *Deutsch, Polnisch oder Jiddisch. Betrachtungen und Urkunden zur Ostjudenfrage.* Berlin, 1916; Wlad. Kaplun-Kogan, *Die jüdische Sprach- und Kulturgemeinschaft in Polen. Eine statistische Studie* – Verfasst im Auftrage des 'Komitee für den Osten'. Berlin-Wien, 1917; Dr. Heinrich Loewe, 'Die jüdisch-deutsche Sprache.' *Süddeutsche Monatshefte*, Feb. 1916; *Idem*, 'Vom Leben einer toten Sprache.' *Jüd. Nationalkalender 5677.* Wien, 1916; Max Mayer, 'Rivalen oder Verbündete.' *Der Jude*, I (1916–17), pp. 65–68; Math. Mieses, *Die Entstehungsursache der jüdischen Dialekte.* Wien, 1916; S. J. Stubnitzki, 'Die jüdische Sprache.' JR, XX–42, p. 339; Davis Trietsch, *Juden und Deutsche. Eine Sprach-und Interessengemeinschaft.* Wien, 1915.
11. For example: Herm. L. Strack, *Jüdisch-deutsche Texte.* Lesebuch zur Einführung in Denken, Leben und Sprache der osteuropäischen Juden. Leipzig, 1917.
12. For example: Arno Nadel, 'Jüdische Volkslieder.' *Der Jude*, I (1916–17); 'Aus dem Sprichwörterschatz der Ostjuden.' NJM, I (1916), pp. 18, 41, 82. – F. M. Kaufmann wrote the introduction to the Yiddish edition of *Jüdische Folkslieder.* Flugblätter des Jüdischen Volksheim in Berlin.

was a German dialect, a language of purely German character.[13] In its report
of December 1914, the KfdO referred to Yiddish as a Middle High German
Volksdialekt.[14] The same statement was repeated by the KfdO in a memorandum
of January 1915,[15] as well as in a letter of June 2, 1915 written by Dr.
Bodenheimer from Lodz,[16] in his official report on the visit to Lodz,[17] and also
in the *Kölnische Zeitung*.[18]

In 1914, Dr. Isaac Straus, who was sent by the KfdO to the United States to
gain American Jewish sympathy for the German cause, wrote to the German
Ambassador in Washington to the effect that in case of a German conquest of
Poland the medieval German used by European Jews would be replaced by
modern German within a few decades. The Jews would then form a bulwark
of German speakers against the separatist tendencies of the Poles.[19]
W. Kaplan-Kogan, one of the secretaries of the KfdO, also expressed the
opinion that Yiddish was a German dialect and stressed its usefulness to
Germany's interests.[20]

This was reiterated by many other Jews, for example by the Zionist Dr.
Nachum Goldmann, who in 1915 wrote: 'Originally Yiddish was Middle High
German as it was spoken in Germany in the fifteenth century'.[21] The leaders
of the KfdO, in all their talks with German officials and in their written
memoranda, continually insisted that Yiddish was a German dialect. This was
stated, for instance, in the memoranda of January 17, 1915, addressed to the
Civil Governor of Poland, von Brandenstein,[22] and of July 5, 1915, to von

13. 'Für die Gleichheit der deutschen und der
jüdischen Interessen ist nun von entscheidender
Bedeutung, dass die 6–7 Millionen Juden Russlands einen deutschen Volksdialekt sprechen, der
nur mit wenigen slavischen und hebräischen Be-
standteilen vermischt ist...die Sprache einen
durchaus deutschen Charakter trägt.' According
to the 'Generalbericht für die Mitglieder des
Komitees für den Osten', Dec. 1914 (z A, A 15/VIII/
6; also in AA, 162/1, Russland 73, Bd. 10–11).
14. *Ibid.*
15. '...einen deutschen Volksdialekt sprechen,
der mit wenigen slavischen und hebräischen Be-
standteilen vermischt ist' (z A, A 15/VIII/7).
16. '...sprechen unter sich das sogenannte Jiddish, das einen mit den hebräischen und slavischen
Beiworten vermengten mittelhochdeutschen Dialekt darstellt' (z A, A 15/VIII/8).
17. 'Es kann insbesondere nicht oft genug
wiederholt werden, dass der missachtete jüdische
Dialekt deutsches Sprachgut its.' Bericht über die
im Auftrage des Komitees für den Osten im
Mai-Juni 1915 unternommene Reise nach
Russisch-Polen, von Justizrat Dr. M. I.
Bodenheimer (Köln). Zweite Ausgabe, n.p., n.d.,
pp. 14–15.
18. Dr.   M. I. Bodenheimer, 'Die jüdische

Sprache ein deutscher Volksdialekt.' *Kölnische
Zeitung*, No. 958, Sept. 20, 1915.
19. 'Die Sprache der Juden ist heute noch das
mittelalterliche Deutsch, das in wenigen Jahr-
zehnten unter deutschem Machtbereich der modernen deutschen Sprache Platz machen wird. Die
Juden werden ein deutsch sprechendes, deutsche
Kultur pflegendes Element abgeben, das einen
lebendigen Wall bilden kann gegen die separa-
tistischen Bestrebungen der Polen.' (z A, A/15/
VIII/4, 6).
20. W. Kaplan-Kogan, 'Deutsche und Juden in
Polen.' v z, Aug. 14, 1915 ('Gerade für die Juden
bedeutet der siegreiche Vormarsch der Deutschen
nicht nur einen politischen Wechsel, sondern vor
allem einen engeren Anschluss an die den Juden
längst wohl vertraute deutsche Kultur. Sprechen
doch die Juden des Ostens einen deutschen Dialekt, den Jargon'); see also *Die Juden in Polen. Ein
geschichtlicher Überblick*. Im Auftrage des 'Komitees
für den Osten' von Waldimir W. Kaplan-Kogan,
Berlin, 1915, p. 7.
21. N. Goldmann, in *Frankfurter Zeitung*, Sept.
23, 1915.
22. 'Die Juden Polens stehen nach Sprache und
Kultur dem deutschen Wesen weit näher als dem
slavischen...So erscheinen sie dazu bestimmt, bei

Westarp of the Ministry of the Interior.[23] On August 25, 1915, Professors Franz Oppenheimer and Moritz Sobernheim of the KfdO, in a discussion with a group of Reichstag Deputies, spoke on 'The Jargon as a German language' and 'The German trade interests and the Jargon'. On August 27, 1915, during an audience with the Grand Duke of Baden in Karlsruhe, Dr. Adolf Friedemann and Professor Sobernheim of the KfdO spoke on 'The German character of Jargon'.[24] In a memorandum of January 14, 1918, addressed to the Ministry of Foreign Affairs, Dr. Paul Nathan and Max M. Warburg, two representatives of another Jewish body, the 'Hilfsverein der deutschen Juden' (Hilfsverein) also stated that Yiddish was the German spoken in the Middle Ages by the Jews of the Rhineland.[25]

In most of these instances Yiddish was also represented as a powerful weapon in the defence of the German cultural, economic, political, and military interests in Eastern Europe. On November 29, 1914, Dr. Bodenheimer wrote to von Hindenburg that in the future status of the German Reich the Jews of the Western Russian provinces, because of their culture and language, would be an important pro-German influence.[26] On June 28, 1915, during an audience with von Westarp, Professor Oppenheimer and Dr. Friedemann stated that there were in the Slavonic East many millions familiar with the German language – the Jews.[27] Heinrich Loewe, who frequently wrote on Yiddish, remarked that the enemies of Germany who had recognized far better than the Germans themselves the value of Yiddish to German interests, objected to the use of this language by Jews.[28] In the opinion of Dr. S. Oppenstein the Jews of Eastern Europe formed an important preserve of the German spirit and culture.[29] This position was also frequently adopted in non-Jewish semiofficial documents, as

---

verständnisvoller Behandlung Träger deutscher Gesittung und Kultur im Osten zu werden und zuverlässige Stützen der deutschen Verwaltung zu sein' (ZA, A 15/VIII/7).

23. 'Die Juden Russlands, Galiziens, Rumäniens sprechen als ihre Muttersprache einen altertümlichen oberdeutschen Dialekt, den verbreitetsten deutschen Dialekt überhaupt...Sie waren mit uns dahin einig, dass das Vorhandensein einer so ungeheuren Zahl von Trägern der deutschen Sprache, ganz gleichgültig, welcher Abstammung diese Träger sind, für die Sprache und die Kultur, und da es sich um ein hauptsächlich handeltreibendes Volk handelt, namentlich auch für den deutschen Handel, von sehr grosser Bedeutung ist...das Deutsche Reich und Volk daher ein sehr starkes Interesse daran haben, diese Masse nach Möglichkeit bei ihrer Sprache zu erhalten und vor der Slavisierung zu bewahren' (*Ibid.*).

24. *Ibid.*

25. '...jenes Deutsch, das sie bei ihrer Vertreibung aus den rheinischen Gebieten im Mittelalter nach dem Osten mitgenommen haben' (AA, Der Weltkrieg, No. 14a, K204184).

26. ZA, A 15/VIII/6.

27. ZA, A 15/VIII/7.

28. '...die Feinde des deutschen Volkes haben viel besser als die Deutschen den Wert dieses grossen Vorwerkes deutscher Sprache erkannt. Seit hundert Jahren versuchen die slavischen Barbaren im Osten mit Gewalt und List, mit Versprechungen und Drohungen die polnischen Juden von der jüdisch-deutschen Sprache abzudrängen.' Heinrich Loewe, 'Die jüdisch-deutsche Sprache des Ostjuden.' JP, XLVII-9 (1916), pp. 100–104.

29. Dr S. Oppenstein, 'Die Ostjuden und ihre Beziehungen zur deutschen Kultur.' JP, XLVI-II (1915), pp. 120–22.

for instance in the collection of studies on Eastern Europe published by Dr. Paul Rohrbach.[30]

Even after World War I, some people continued to believe in the role of Yiddish as an influence furthering the cultural and political interest of Germany. One of them was Dr. Ludwig Haas, well known for the part he played as an adviser on Jewish affairs to the German administration in Poland during World War I. His conception of the role of Yiddish fell within the scope of his general political views. Haas believed that there were economic and political possibilities for Germany in Eastern Europe; he fought actively against the Treaty of Versailles and for German–Russian collaboration.[31] In 1930, a similar opinion was also defended by Dr. Hans Schaeffer at a meeting of the Hilfsverein.[32]

However, in most cases the insistence of some Jewish leaders, in their dealings with German authorities, on the importance of Yiddish as a politically valuable factor, was only a tactical manoeuvre in order to enlist Germany's support for East European Jewry. Some, of course, sincerely believed that Yiddish was a language in its own right (*eine Sprache*), as affirmed by Professor Hermann L. Strack, a non-Jew[33] – a true language (*eine wirkliche Sprache*), according to a pamphlet by Dr. Nathan Birnbaum, who, long before August 1914, was enamored of Yiddish.[34] In 1914 the KfdO published a pamphlet on Yiddish by Hermann Struck.[35] A draft of a second edition, dated October 1915 and prepared by Heinrich Loewe, was to have been published under the title *Die*

30. 'Die jüdisch-deutsche Sprache, der Jargon', ist der räumlich am weitesten verbreitete deutsche Dialekt...Bis tief in die Levante und nach Mittelasien hinein streckt durch ihn das deutsche Sprachtum seine Fühler in das sprachfremde Gebiet namentlich der slavischen Welt hinein. Und nicht nur das deutsche Sprachtum; fast alles, was die Juden des Ostens ausser ihren religiösen Schriften an Kulturgütern besitzen, hat ihnen das Deutschtum übermittelt; fast alle Klassiker unseres Volkes, viele Historiker u.a., sind in den Jargon übersetzt worden und haben die Verbindung mit der deutschen Kultur erhalten. Hieraus können sich mit der Zeit Folgen von Bedeutung für das deutsche Interesse ergeben.' *Die Juden in Polen und Westrussland*. (Aus der Denkschrift 'Russisches', herausgegeben von Dr. Paul Rohrbach.) (Berlin, 1915), pp. 4–5.

31. Dr Ludwig Haas stated in 1924: 'Ich kenne die Ostjuden aus meiner Verwaltungstätigkeit in Warschau und muss sagen, dass sie die deutsche Sprache, die sie im Mittelalter aus Deutschland mitbrachten, besser bewahrt haben, als viele aus Deutschland eingewanderte Nichtjuden...Wo die jiddische Sprache gesprochen wird, die zu 60% deutsches Sprachgut enthält, findet sich immer selbst im kleinsten Dorf ein Haus, in dem ein Schiller oder ein Goethe zu finden ist. Dieses

deutsche Kulturgut, das sich bis nach Asien binzieht, könnten wir sehr gut im deutschen Sinne verwerten. Was würden die Engländer daraus machen, wenn es bis nach Asien englisch sprechende Juden geben würde?' – Judith Schrag-Haas, 'Ludwig Haas. Erinnerungen an meinen Vater.' LBIB, pp. 83, 85, 90–91.

32. 'Der Redner würdigte die Verdienste der Juden in Osteuropa um die Verbreitung von deutscher Sprache und Kultur und sagte, das Deutschtum in allen diesen Ländern stehe in Fühlung mit den Juden mittels des Bindegliedes der Sprache.' *Dreissig Jahre Hilfsverein*...Berlin, 1931, p. 23.

33. 'Was von 6 Millionen Menschen an Ausdruckmittel der Gedanken gebraucht und geliebt wird, ist eine Sprache, sogar wenn keine Literatur vorhanden ist. Die jüdische Sprache aber hat eine Literatur.' Prof. Hermann L. Strack, 'Zur Psychologie der jüdischen Sprache.' NJM, I (1916), p. 76. See also Dr. Hermann L. Strack, *Jüdisches Wörterbuch. Mit besonderer Berücksichtigung der gegenwärtig in Polen üblichen Ausdrücke.* Leipzig, 1916, p. iii.

34. Dr. Nathan Birnbaum, *Was sind Ostjuden?* Wien, 1916, p. 11.

35. Hermann Struck, *Über die jüdisch-deutsche Sprache. Eine kurze Einführung.* (Berlin, 1914), 9 pp.

deutsche Sprache der polnischen Juden.[36] However, the work of editing the pamphlet was given to Struck who stated that Yiddish was a German dialect and not a *Mischsprache.*[37] For the actual publication, even the title of the pamphlet was changed to *Die jüdisch-deutsche Sprache des Ostjuden.*[38]

In one respect this expedient representation of Yiddish as a German dialect did actually have some good results. The German policy on Jewish schools in the occupied territories, by which the children's mother tongue was used as the language of instruction, which will be referred to later, was most probably a result of the belief that Yiddish was indeed a German dialect which might later evolve into pure German.[39]

The Yiddishists of Eastern Europe, of course, ridiculed those who said that Yiddish was not an independent language but a German dialect. The founders of the Jewish *Schul- und Volksbildungsverein* in Warsaw, in their memorandum of November 14, 1916 to the German General Government in Poland, asserted that such a view was against all accepted principles of philology. 'Since the Middle High German period, the German and Yiddish languages have developed in two different directions'.[40]

Basically, the attitude of the leaders of the KfdO to Yiddish was determined by their demand for Jewish cultural and national autonomy in Eastern Europe and by their general views on the political future of Eastern Europe. In face of the German military victory, some of them foresaw, and went so far as to advocate, some kind of German influence or even control over part or the whole of the territory between Germany and Russia.[41] Their Jewish policy in respect of Eastern Europe was consequently constructed on these lines. The representation of Yiddish as a German dialect became an important instrument for gaining the sympathy of the German authorities towards Jewish autonomy and for

36. ZA, A 15/VIII/13.

37. 'Wir haben also im Jüdischdeutschen in keiner Weise eine Mischsprache vor uns, sondern einen deutschen Dialekt, der seit drei Jahrhunderten sich selbständig entwickeln musste, der sich aber immer im Zusammenhange mit der deutschen Entwicklung bewegt hat und die nicht so viele fremde Elemente aufgenommen hat, um den deutschen Character der Sprache zu beeinflussen' (*Ibid.*).

38. *Ibid.; Die jüdisch-deutsche Sprache des Ostjuden.* Ein Abriss von Heinrich Loewe. Im Auftrage des 'Komitees für den Osten.' Berlin, Oktober 1915. 25 pp.

39. '...nach vielem Hin und Her einigte man sich stillschweigend dahin, dass sie zwar bestehen blieb, dass aber in der Praxis das Jiddische als deutscher Dialekt betrachtet und der Dialekt der eigentlichen Sprache (wenigstens für eine geraume Übergangszeit) gleichgestellt wurde, so dass nun

in der Muttersprache der Kinder weiter unterrichtet werden konnte.' W. Stein, p. 155 (see note 43); '...Dr. Haas auf dem Standpunkt steht, dass unter deutsch auch das Jiddische zu verstehen sei, und dass deshalb der Unterricht in den jüdischen Schulen trotz der allgemeinen Verfügung der Zivilverwaltung in jiddischer Sprache geführt werden soll. Herr Lazarus Barth bemerkte hierzu, dass etwas anderes auch nicht möglich sei, weil man nur Lehrer, die nur in jiddischer Sprache unterrichten können, zur Verfügung habe.' W. Kaplan-Kogan of the KfdO to Dr. Bodenheimer, Sept. 25, 1915 (ZA, A 15/VIII/2c).

40. ZA, A 15/VIII/9B. The German and Yiddish texts of the memorandum were published in *Di naje schul*, Nos. 6 and 7 (1922), pp. 86–102, 101–116.

41. M. J. Bodmer (Bodenheimer), *Ein neuer Staatenbund und das Ostjudenproblem.* Stuttgart-Berlin 1916. (*Der Deutsche Krieg*, No. 73). 36 pp.

preventing the compulsory Germanization of Jewish schools. The demand for Jewish schools – Yiddish schools – was the first major practical step towards autonomy. Indeed, one of the main arguments put forward by the leaders of the KfdO in their demand for schools in Eastern Europe – and Jewish cultural autonomy in general – was the necessity of saving the Jews from absorption into the Slav culture, which would have run counter to the German interest.[42]

On April 24, 1915, the German authorities in Poland issued an ordinance introducing Polish as the language of instruction in Polish schools and German as the language of instruction in German and Jewish schools. This *ungeschickter Beginn* (clumsy start), as Wilhelm Stein wrote, satisfied no one.[43] The Poles saw in it an expression of separatist tendencies in which the Jews were to play a pro-German role. The Jews, who had previously fought against the Russification and Polonization of their schools, now feared a Germanization. The German-Jewish periodical *Jeschurun* considered that Germanization of the Polish Jews would run counter to German interests since it would be a constant cause of unrest between Jews and Poles.[44]

In Lithuania, an ordinance of Division VIII of the German Administration (Churches and Schools) introduced the mother tongue as the language of instruction, while the teaching of German was to be given a prominent place. An ordinance of March 7, 1916 gave a precise directive that Yiddish should be the language of instruction for Jews.[45] However, German policy was not

---

42. '...eine Poloniseurung der jüdischen Bevölkerung durch die Schulen zu verhindern.' Report of an interview with von Kries, chief of the Civil Administration in Posen, May 6, 1915 (ZA, A 15/VIII/9 A); '...dass man die Juden des Ostens in ihrer kulturellen Eigenart, die ja von jeher durch Deutschland beeinflusst sei, erhalten müsse, um sie vor der Slavisierung zu schützen. Darum solle man in den Volksschulen den Jargon zunächst als Unterrichtssprache beibehalten. Report of an interview with the Grossherzog of Baden, Aug. 27, 1915 (ZA, A 15/VIII/7); 'Wir haben den dringenden Wunsch, dass diese natürlichen Träger des deutschen Gedankens im Osten nicht der Slavisierung verfallen. Das muss aber der Fall sein, wenn beim Friedensschluss lediglich die staatsbürgerliche Gleichberechtigung für die Juden gefordert wird, ohne dass ihre Schule und ihre sonstigen kulturellen Institutionen den notwendigen gesetzlichen Schutz finden.' Memorandum of the KfdO to the Auswärtiges Amt, Oct. 11, 1915 (AA, 254/3, *Der Weltkrieg*, No. 11, adh. 2, Bd. 5–6).
43. Dr. Paul Roth, *Die politische Entwicklung in Kongress-Polen während der deutschen Okkupation.* Unter Mitarbeit von Wilhelm Stein. Leipzig, 1919, p. 155.

44. 'Es kann Deutschlands Interesse unmöglich sein, die Juden in Nationalpolen zu verwandeln. Darüber ein Wort zu verlieren, erübrigt sich. Millionen neue Polen zu schaffen, die durch ihre Intelligenz, ihre Regsamkeit und ihre Zähigkeit doppelt und dreifach zählen würden, das scheint uns der Gipfel der Torheit. Es kann aber ebensowenig in Deutschlands Interesse liegen, diese Juden restlos zu germanisieren und sie dadurch in einen verschärften Gegensatz zu den Polen zu bringen. Wir reden gar nicht von dem Interesse der Juden, die doch mit den Polen zusammen leben müssen. Es wird das Lebensinteresse der deutschen Vormacht immer bleiben, jede Verschärfung des Nationalitätenstreites zu verhindern.' 'Deutschland und die Ostjudenfrage'. *Jeschurun*, III–1 (Jan. 1916), p. 19.
45. 'Als Muttersprache hat diejenige Sprache zu gelten, welche die Eltern im häuslichen Umgang mit den angemeldeten Kindern zu sprechen pflegen. Bei den Juden wird das Jiddish-Deutsch in der Regel also Muttersprache anzusehen sein.' Hans Zemke, *Der Oberbefehlshaber Ost und das Schulwesen im Verwaltungsbereich Litauen während des Weltkrieges.* Berlin, 1936, pp. 107, 111.

uniform; it was sometimes determined by local officials. As early as March 1, 1916, an ordinance had introduced German as the official language of instruction in the schools of Grodno. Another ordinance of March 12, 1916 did the same for the schools of Bialystok which was part of the occupied *Ober-Ost* territory.[46]

Thus, the German authorities of occupation forcibly introduced German into the curriculum of Jewish schools, very often as the language of instruction. 'Jewish children started to sing German patriotic and military songs'.[47] On many occasions, e.g. in Lodz, the German authorities arrested Jewish leaders for their work on behalf of Yiddish schools or other Yiddish cultural activities.[48] In Lithuania the Jews, like other nationalities, opposed the forced Germanization of schools. The Germans used not only German civilians and soldiers but also Jews as teachers, and this contributed to tension between Lithuanians and Jews.[49] In 1917, because of united protests by the Jewish and Polish teachers of Vilna, the Germans closed all the schools in the town for a period of six months, giving as an official reason the danger of epidemics. The Jews then opened clandestine schools. In November 1917, the Germans permitted the reopening of the schools, but on condition that six hours each week should be devoted to the teaching of German.[50] In Poland the idea of using German as the language of instruction in Jewish schools was soon abandoned and even in the *Ober-Ost* territories Yiddish became the language of instruction.

Some German Jews agreed to the Germanization of Jewish schools in the occupied territories because, in their opinion, the use of Yiddish would isolate the Jews culturally and economically.[51] German Orthodox Jews often collaborated in the Germanization of Jewish schools. According to a report to the KfdO from Kovno, the German *Feldrabbiner* (Jewish chaplain) there demanded a school where German should be the language of instruction, on the grounds that

46. *Ibid.*, p. 61.
47. Dr. Z. Szabad, in *Pinkes*...Vilna, 1922, pp. 3–4. See also Victor Shulamn, in *Di Jidn in Pojln*. New York, 1946, p. 827; Hirsch Abramowitsch, *Farszwundene gesztaltn*. Buenos-Aires, 1958, pp. 300–301.
48. I. S. Hertz, *Di geschichte fun Bund in Lodz*. New York, 1958, pp. 256–58.
49. C. Rivas, *La Lithuanie sous le joug Allemand*. Lausanne, 1918, p. 302; Azriel Shohat, 'The Beginning of Anti-Semitism in Independent Lithuania.' *Yad Washem Studies*, II (1958), p. 10.
50. Dr. C. Szabad, *op. cit.*, p. 6; Dr. A. Wirszubski, *ibid.*, p. 85.
51. 'Man mag den Kulturwert der jiddischen Sprache noch so hoch anschlagen, eine westeuropäische Verkehrssprache ist sie nicht, und für den

wirtschaftlichen Aufschwung der ökonomisch sehr ungünstig situierten ostjüdischen Volksmassen ist sie von keiner ausschlaggebenden Bedeutung. Die deutsche Unterrichtsverordnung beabsichtigt ja in keiner Weise, in die Sprache des Hauses und der Familie einzugreifen. Dort kann die Jargonsprache ruhig erhalten bleiben und von denen gefördert, werden, welche ihrer zur Erhaltung eines besonderen jüdischen Nationalcharakters zu bedürfen glauben. Die soziale und materielle Lage der russisch-polnischen Juden kann aber nur auf ein höheres Niveau gehoben werden, wenn die Erziehung ihrer Jugend diese zur Beherrschung einer westeuropäischen Kultursprache, wie der deutschen, und damit zur späteren erfolgreichen Betätigung im Lebenskampfe befähigt.' IF, XVII–41, Oct. 14, 1915, pp. 1–2.

Yiddish was no language at all, and that Jews should be exponents of German culture.[52]

On some occasions, even leaders of the KfdO expressed the opinion that the introduction of Yiddish as the language of instruction should be regarded as a temporary policy only. In time, depending upon future military and political events, the Jews of Poland would have to choose between German and Polish.[53] On January 3, 1916, Professor Oppenheimer, on behalf of the KfdO, told Dr. Paul Nathan of the Hilfsverein that the KfdO was opposed to a 'forced Germanization' of Polish Jews but not to a free development of the jargon into German (*Entwicklung des Jargons zum Hochdeutschen*).[54]

However, this too was most probably part of a policy of expediency, in order to obtain first of all a German declaration favorable to Yiddish schools in Eastern Europe. On May 21, 1915, Dr. Bodenheimer, in a memorandum addressed to the German *Polizeipräsident* (Head of Police) von Oppen in Lodz, stated that Germanization of Jewish schools could be dangerous for Germany itself, because only Yiddish could be a strong arm against Polonization of the Jewish masses.[55] An unsigned report of 1916 stated that the introduction of a language other than Yiddish in the Jewish schools was out of the question.[56] In Bialystok, where the

52. '...der Unterricht in Deutsch geführt wird, weil (1) Jüdisch keine Sprache ist und (2) müssen die Juden als Vermittler und Träger der deutschen Kultur dienen' (ZA, A 15/VIII/9 C).

53. 'Die nächste Stufe de oberen Schule ist dann von selbst deutsch, während bei Volksschulen mit polnischem Unterricht das polnische Gymnasium unvermeidlich sei.' Report of an interview with the Grossherzog of Baden, Aug. 27, 1915 (ZA, A 15/VIII/7); 'Wird Kongress-Polen von Russland losgetrennt und ein selbständiges Staatswesen – etwa in Anlehnung an die Habsburgische Monarchie – geschaffen, so stehen die Juden des Ostens vor der Notwendigkeit, deutsch oder polnisch zu werden. Denn der Jargon ist keine entwicklungsfähige Sprache, er reicht wohl für die Volksschule in ihrer gegenwärtigen unentwickelten Form aus, muss aber bei allmählicher weltlicher Ausbildung der Lehrer in einigen Jahren – wahrscheinlich schon in der Volksschule, sicher aber in der auf ihr aufgebauten Mittelschule – ins Deutsche einmünden. Als ein mögliches Mittel zur Verhinderung der Polonisierung der Juden haben wir das System der Matriken-Führung nach den Plänen des Reichsratsabgeordneten Renner vorgeschlagen. Dieser suchte eine Ausschaltung der Nationalitätenkämpfe aus den gemeinschaftlichen Landtagen der Kronländer dadurch herbeizuführen, dass jedem Volksbestandteil vollkommene Autonomie in allen Sprach-und Kulturangelegenheiten gegeben wird ...Die Kulturgemeinschaft wird, wie heute schon

die Religionsgemeinschaft mit eigenem Steuerumlagerecht versehen und regelt autonom ihre eigenen Angelegenheiten.' Memorandum of the KfdO to the Auswärtiges Amt, Oct. 11, 1915 (AA, 254/3, *Der Weltkrieg*, No. 11, adh. 2, Bd. 5–6. – Karl Renner, Leader of the Austrian socialists and one of the principal theorists of national autonomy, became Prime Minister of the first Austrian Republic in 1918 and President of the second in 1945. See note 111.

54. See note 111.

55. 'Eine deutsche Assimilation wäre verfrüht und könnte unliebsame Folgen für das Deutsche Reich und das Deutschtum nach sich ziehen... Das Festhalten an der jüdischen Unterrichtssprache dient ferner dazu, den inneren Zusammenhang der jüdischen Masse zu stärken, die dann ein wertvolles Gegengewicht gegen die polnischen Bestrebungen bilden wird. Die deutsche Sprache wird aber einen breiten Raum als Unterrichtsgegenstand einnehmen müssen, sodass die Kinder die hochdeutsche Umgangssprache beherrschen lernen' (AA, 254/3, *Der Weltkrieg*, No. 11, adh. 2, Bd. 5–6; ZA, A 15/VIII/7). The same idea was repeated by Bodenheimer in: *Bericht über die im Auftrage des 'Komitees für den Osten' im Mai-Juni 1915 unternommene Reise nach Russisch-Polen*, von Justizrat Dr. M. I. Bodenheimer.

56. '...aussichtslos für die nationale Schule eine andere Sprache zu arrogieren als die Muttersprache der Juden, das Jiddisch' (ZA, A 15/VIII/9c).

German authorities forced the introduction of German as the language of instruction, the KfdO reported that the children felt much freer when expressing themselves in Yiddish.[57] The author of an article published in 1917 in the *Neue Jüdische Monatshefte*, which was edited by members of the KfdO, strongly attacked the Germanization of Jewish schools in Eastern Europe. He ridiculed the idea that Yiddish was to be considered only as an introduction to German and that the next generation of East European Jews would speak pure German. The problem of a 'Greater Germany' could not be resolved by means of cheap attempts at Germanization. Germany could gain the Jews' gratitude only by helping them to obtain wholly Jewish schools.[58]

At a very late stage of the war, on September 28, 1918, a statement was made by the German Administration in Lithuania to the effect that it had no interest whatsoever in forcing German culture on the Jews.[59] However, the acts of the German authorities contradicted such a liberal statement, which was made under the influence of the deteriorating German position in the war.

In spite of all the efforts and all the propaganda the Jews of Eastern Europe did not acquire the German language and culture. They were not willing to submit to German assimilation. Three important factors induced them to take such a position: attachment to their own language and culture; the existence of an able and strong Yiddish intelligentsia; general distrust of the drastic economic and political policies of the German occupation forces. The only effect was the introduction of a large number of German words and expressions into spoken Yiddish.[60] Of 73,248 children registered in December 1917 in the Grodno-Bialystok territory, 21,429 were registered as Jewish by religion; 21,387 Jewish children were noted as using Yiddish as their mother tongue. Out of 2,698 children registered as German-speaking only 42 were Jewish.[61] In some regions, for example in Lithuania, the German occupation helped to defeat the tendencies towards Russification among Jews. In many families Yiddish culture replaced Russian. Only later, when Jewish refugees began coming back from

---

57. 'In bialystok konnten wir weider die Erfahrung machen, dass in der Jargonvolksschule die Kinder lebhafter am Unterricht teilnahmen und sich gewandter ausdrückten.' 'Jüdische Schulen in Oberost' (YIVO, NIF 98 B).

58. 'Man könnte verstehen, wenn die deutsche Verwaltung...auch das Deutsche in den Schulen berücksichtigt wünschte...Aber faktisch wenig zweckmässig und sachlich nicht gerechtfertigt erscheint der Standpunkt, der das sogen. Jiddische als nichts anderes als eine Vorbereitung auf das Deutsche betrachten und nun den Schritt vom Mischdeutsch zum sprachreinen Deutsch mir nichts dir nichts, ohne Rücksicht auf den bisherigen Schulcharakter, auf dem Verordnungswege tun zu können vermeint...Eine Politik der Wür-

digung und Berücksichtigung der deutsch-jüdischen Sprache würde den Lebensbedürfnissen des jüdischen Volkes, die in der Schulfrage durch die Sprachpflege des Jüdischen und Hebräischen zum Ausdruck kommt, vollauf Rechnung tragen ...dafür aber würde durch solche eindeutige Schulpolitik in unseren östlichen Grenzbezirken mit Sicherheit ein Wertgut gewonnen und gepflegt...die Erkenntlichkeit und Dankbarkeit.' Schulrat Eberhard, 'Zur Schulfrage der Ostjuden.' NJM, I (1917), pp. 677–80.

59. H. Zemke, *op. cit.*, p. 62.

60. Z. Rejzen, 'Di Yiddische sprach un di okupacje.' *Di Woch* (Vilna), No. 2 (Jan. 17, 1919), pp. 61–62.

61. H. Zemke, *op. cit.*, p. 102.

Russia, was Russification renewed. In Grodno at that time the Jews were the first to publish Russian newspapers.[62]

The attitude of the Russian Jewish leaders to Yiddish does not belong to the subject under discussion. Yet, it should be noted that, while a large proportion of Russian Jewry was militantly Yiddishist, some upper-class Jews looked upon Yiddish as a disgraceful jargon. Thus on May 20, 1916, Baron David Günzburg wrote from Petrograd to Felix Warburg in New York, expressing his strong feelings against Zionism and Yiddishism:

> We find the Yiddishists much worse, firstly because they base their national ideal on a language which is no language but only a jargon, and secondly because in so doing they deepen the ditch which somehow, to our sincere regret, separates Russians and Jews...Yiddishism is patronized by our most radical party which has nothing to do with Judaism and uses Yiddishism as an instrument to gain the sympathy of simple, hopeless and embittered people.[63]

It was during the German occupation that the Yiddish newspaper, *Letzte Najes*, published in Vilna, began a reform of Yiddish spelling.[64]

In fact, there can be no doubt that during the German occupation Yiddish as a language and Yiddish culture in general attained a status they had never held during the Tsarist régime. Jewish libraries and clubs were organized in hundreds of communities where no such activities had previously been permitted.[65] This was not the result of a planned German policy, but of a remarkably self-disciplined Jewish effort to survive that difficult period with dignity and in their own cultural environment. But, of course, this became possible thanks only to the comparative freedom of activity which had not existed under Russian rule.

These years were a period of evacuations, famine, compulsory labor, and other tribulations. The Eastern European Jews manifested a heroic courage and a desire to survive not only as individuals but also as a national entity. Not only did there come into existence in those days a ramified network of free kitchens, free loan societies, and many other relief agencies, but political parties were also formed and many cultural Jewish institutions established.

The KfdO demanded that Yiddish, too, should be used in the official German pronouncements and in the administration of the cities.[66] Similar requests were

62. Z. Rejzen, *op. cit.*, pp. 61–62; *idem*, 'Awek mit der rusifikacje.' *Di Woch* (Vilna), No. 1, Jan. 8, 1919, p. 20; A. Zak, *In onejb fun a friling*. Buenos-Aires, 1962, pp. 200, 225.

63. American Jewish Archives (Cincinnati, Ohio). L. Marshall papers, a copy of Baron Günzburg's letter to Warburg.

64. A. I. Goldschmidt, 'Di Yiddische presse in Vilna in der cajt fun der Milchome.' *Pinkes*... Vilna, 1922, pp. 583–90.

65. See the large number of memorial (*Yiskor*) books published after World War II, where much

information on such activities can be found, e.g., *Pinkes Zyradow, Amszynow un Wiskit*. Buenos-Aires, 1961, pp. 131–32, 435.

66. 'Unterredung der Herren Dr. Oppenheimer und Dr. Friedemann mit Herrn Ministerialdirektor Dr. Lewald und Geheimrat Dr. Schulz im Reichsamt des Inneren am 5. Juli 1915' (ZA, A 15/VIII/7). Dr. Bodenheimer reported on his visit to Lodz in May 1915: 'Die offiziellen Kundgebungen werden von nun an in drei Sprachen veröffentlicht (mit Geh.-Rat Cleinow verabredet)' (ZA, A 15/VIII/9a).

made by the local Jewish population, and in many places the official German ordinances were also published in Yiddish. This was one of the many victories in the advance towards cultural autonomy.[67] The KfdO also advocated the development of the Yiddish theater.[68] Of the greatest value, however, was the help given to the Yiddish press.

The KfdO demanded support for the Yiddish press and other publications. One of the reasons given by the KfdO to the Germans for this was the desirability of making Jewish readers independent of Polish newspapers.[69] Indeed, in Warsaw, the German authorities allowed the publication of Yiddish newspapers which had been closed down by the Russian authorities. New newspapers appeared, either inspired by the Orthodox section of German Jewry, or as Jewish supplements to newspapers published by the Germans.[70] In some instances the Germans tried to dictate a pro-German policy to the Yiddish press or even to Germanize its language. Thus on October 12, 1915, the Jewish press was ordered to print the official German Army *communiqués* in 'Judaeo-German', i.e. German written in Hebrew characters. This order was, however, cancelled on August 13, 1916. (The *communiqués* of the Austrian Army were published in such a 'Judaeo-German' until August 25, 1916.)[71] In Lodz, the German authorities allowed the publication of a newspaper – the *Arbaiter Sztime* – by the Socialist Bund, but they stipulated that in the first issue the editors should state that the publication had been made possible by the victory of the German army. This the editors refused to do and the first issue was published illegally.[72] By order of the German authorities, the issue of January 27, 1917 of the *Letste Najes* in Vilna was printed in gold letters in honor of the Kaiser's birthday.[73] But these were minor difficulties. Actually, the Jewish press became a major factor in Jewish life; it lost its regional character and gained a more respected status.[74]

67. *Wilner Zemelbuch*, II (1918), pp. 8–12, 26, 37–39.
68. Dr. Bodenheimer's report of May–June 1915 (see note 55), p. 15.
69. *Ibid.*, p. 15 ('damit die Masse nicht mehr auf die Zeitungen in der polnischen Sprache angewiesen ist'). – Already in 1907 the German 'Baltic Constitutional Party' financed the publication of a Yiddish newspaper in Riga in order to gain Jewish votes during the elections. D. Druk, *Cu der geschichte fun der yiddischer prese (in russland un pojln)*. Warsaw, 1920, pp. 69–78.
70. N. Prilutzki, 'Der 18ter Juli 1915 in der geschichte fun der yiddischer prese.' *Moment*, Aug. 2, 4, 8, 1935; G. Druk, *op. cit.*, pp. 124–38; M. Grossmann, in *Fun nonten ovar*, II (1956), p. 52; M. Mozes, *ibid.*, pp. 266–67; A. J. Goldschmidt, 'Di Yiddische presse in Wilna in der cajt fun der Milchome.' *Pinkes*, pp. 583–590; Josef Winiecki, 'Fun Zhetler noentzter fargangenajt.' *Ojf di churwes fun milchomes un meumes*. Vilna, 1931, p. 428;

L. Chein-Shimoni, *Nechtn*. Buenos-Aires, 1959, p. 114. – In 1917, the German authorities noted the following 10 Yiddish and 5 Hebrew newspapers: *Czenstochauer Tageblatt, Das Jüdische Volk, Das Jüdische Wort, Das Volk, Hajnt, Lebensfragen, Lodzer Tageblatt, Moment, Schule und Erziehung, Volksblatt, Bino l'ittim, Eiz Chaim, Hazefira, Ohel Josef, Schaarei Tora*. See: *Warschauer Tafeln zur Gegenwartsgeschichte des Königreichs Polen. Herausgegeben von der Presseabteilung des Verwaltungschefs beim Generalgouvernement Warschau*, 1917, p. 4.
71. Druk, *op. cit.*, p. 127.
72. I. S. Hertz, *op. cit.*, p. 242.
73. [Z. Szajkowski,] *Catalogue. Exhibition, Vilna. A Jewish Community in Times of Glory and in Time of Destruction*. YIVO Institute for Jewish Research. New York, 1960, p. 46, No. 501.
74. The attitude of the Yiddish Press in Poland toward Yiddish and schools was often noted in the official bulletin of the 'Presseabteilung des Verwaltungschefs beim Generalgouvernement War-

This was achieved thanks to a highly intellectual group of Jewish journalists; but without the freedom – though a strictly controlled freedom – given by the Germans to the Jewish press this could not have been accomplished. In many respects the Jewish press was well in advance of official Jewish bodies in expressing the wishes of the Jewish population. Thus, for example, representatives of the KfdO reported that more unity and desire not to give in to Polish pressure were observed at a meeting with representatives of the press than at similar meetings with other Jewish leaders.[75]

Among German Jewish spokesmen were many opponents to the use of Yiddish as a weapon in the fight for the rights of East European Jews. Marc Eber, in the *Allgemeine Zeitung des Judentums*, attacked the KfdO's 'phantom of national minority status and the introduction of Yiddish as a main and administrative language in Western Russia'.[76] Dr. Alfred Klee of Berlin severed his relationship with the KfdO, partly because Professor Oppenheimer, in an article published in the *Vossische Zeitung*, had based his conclusions concerning the problem of nationalities in Eastern Europe upon considerations of language.[77] When Dr. N. Goldmann wrote about the relationship between Yiddish and German, the assimilationist Bernard Lauer replied: 'To consider this jargon as a cultural German product is an insult to German culture'.[78] Basically, the discussion on Yiddish was just one aspect of the much wider discussion which took place among German Jewish leaders on the future of East European Jewry between the partisans of assimilation and those who advocated a nationalist point of view. N. Goldmann, in his reply to B. Lauer, stated that the solution of the Jewish problem in Poland was not a question to be left to the Poles, as Lauer had advocated. This matter was of great importance to the Central Powers. The only solution for the Polish Jews would be to maintain themselves as a national organism.[79]

schau': *Tagesbericht aus der polnischen und jüdischen Presse.* No. 1, Jan. 22, 1917, No. 137, July 7, 1917.

75. 'Konferenz der Herren des Komitees für den Osten mit den Vertretern aller jüdischen Blätter Warschaus am 9.2.1916.' (ZA, A 15/VIII/9c).

76. 'Alms im Herbst 1914 unsere Heere nach Russland eindrangen, da bildete sich auf einmal in Berlin ein Komitee zur Befreiung der östlichen Juden. In ihm tauchten plötzlich wieder, mit den Führern der zionistischen Bewegung an der Spitze, die Phantome von nationaler Autonomie und Einführung des Jüdisch-Deutschen als Haupt- und Amtssprache in Westrussland auf...Welche Berechtigung haben gerade die Zionisten, sich sofort auf Polen als neues Feld ihrer Betätigung zu werfen?' Marc Eber, in AZJ, LXXX (1916), p. 451.

77. Dr. Klee to Dr. Bodenheimer, Apr. 1, 1915 (ZA, A 15/VIII/3).

78. Bernard Lauer, *Preussische Jahrbücher*, Band 162, Heft 2 (1915).

79. [N. Goldmann,] Zum Polnisch-Jüdischen Problem. Eine Erwiderung. Sonderabdruck aus den *Preussischen Jahrbüchern.* Band 162 Heft 3. Berlin, 1915, 11 pp.; *Zum polnischjüdischen Problem* (Eine Auseinandersetzung aus den 'Preussischen Jahrbüchern', Berlin, 1915, published by the KfdO). See also Dr. Nachum Goldmann, 'Das polnischjüdische Problem.' *Frankfurter Zeitung*, Sept. 3, 1915. – However, Dr. J. Hirsch wrote in the assimilationist AZJ, 'Die Assimilation der Ostjuden im westeuropäischen Sinne erscheint uns unmöglich,' and he asked 'dass die Eigenart ihnen erhalten bleibt, die ihnen lieb und teuer ist, vor allem auch die Sprache, die sie mit dem Westen, dem Deutschtum verbindet.' *Die Schicksalsfragen der Ostjuden.* AZJ, LXXX-2 (1916), pp. 13, 16.

Initially many non-Jews and Jews in Germany, including some officials of the KfdO, regarded Yiddish as *keine entwicklungsfähige Sprache* (a language with no possibility of development) – as the KfdO wrote in a memorandum of October 11, 1915 addressed to Dr. Arthur Zimmermann, the Minister for Foreign Affairs.[80] Berthold Timendorfer was against the demand to maintain Yiddish. He expressed the hope that Jews could learn High German and forget their jargon.[81] To this Dr. Friedemann replied that the insistence on the use of Yiddish was certainly only a temporary policy. The same opinion was expressed by Professor Oppenheimer.[82] On December 8, 1915, Dr. Friedemann wrote to Dr. Bodenheimer that there was no unity in the KfdO on the question of Yiddish. The majority of the members of the KfdO were in favor of replacing the jargon by High German.[83] On January 7, 1916, Professor Oppenheimer wrote to Dr. Paul Nathan of the Hilfsverein – an adversary of the nationalist Jewish policies advocated by the KfdO – recommending a gradual change from Yiddish to High German with the use of force.[84]

While German officials often expressed their hope for such an assimilation,[85] German-Jewish leaders maintained that this could be done only on condition that East European Jews were granted full economic and political rights.[86] One German official, dealing with the problem of schools in Poland, wrote that every German could easily understand Yiddish. He expressed the opinion that when the Jews had been granted all rights, they would have to choose only between German and Polish. In the German interest, he continued, the language of instruction in the Jewish schools should be changed from jargon to German.[87] Others discussed the problem in the light of the political situation likely to arise after the war. Georg Gotheim, writing on Yiddish as a High German dialect, stated that only if Poland became part of Germany could the Jews, within decades, reach the same status as their brethren of Western Prussia. In an

80. AA, 254/3, *Der Weltkrieg*, No. 11, adh. 2, Bd. 5–6.
81. ZA, A 15/VIII/9B.
82. *Ibid.*
83. 'Im Komitee herrscht keineswegs Einigkeit darüber, ob es nützlich wäre, den Jargon zu einer literarischen Sprache auszubauen. Die grosse Mehrzahl der Mitglieder steht unserer Meinung nach sogar auf dem Standpunkt, dass der Jargon sobald wie möglich verschwinden und dem Hochdeutschen Platz machen solle.' (ZA, A 15/VIII/2d).
84. '...ohne Zwang erfolgende Entwicklung des Jargons zum Hochdeutschen und eine Stärkung des deutschen Gedankens im Osten willkommen heissen würden' (ZA, A 15/VIII/5).
85. 'Wenn hierbei für die Juden die deutsche Sprache als Muttersprache erachtet wurde, so liegt das wohl in der grossen sprachlichen Verwandtschaft des Jiddischen mit dem Deutsch...

Wie die deutschen Dialekte neben dem Hochdeutsch auch in der Literatur die schönen Blüten treiben ... so wird auch das Jiddische neben dem Hochdeutsch seine berechtigte Entwicklung finden.' *Deutsche Warschauer Zeitung*, Dec. 3, 1915.
86. 'Wenn die wirtschaftliche und politische Gleichberechtigung diesen Juden die Möglichkeit gibt, neue Kultur und Bildungsstoffe in sich aufzunehmen, ihrer Religion und ihrem hebräischen Schrifttume treu zu bleiben ... so wird die jüdisch-deutsche Sprache sich nicht bloss ohne Zwang sehr schnell dem Schriftdeutschen nähern, sondern auch zugleich das beste Mittel sein, der deutschen Sprache den Weg in den weiten Osten zu bahnen.' Heinrich Löwe, *Die Jüdisch-deutsche Sprache*... Berlin, Oktober 1915, p. 16.
87. Sonderabdruck aus der Nummer 300 des 'Tags' vom 23. Dezember 1915. Eine Kulturfrage im Osten, vom Gouverneur v. Puttkamer (ZA, A 15/VIII/16).

independent Poland the linguistic assimilation of Jews would be impossible because there they formed a separate nationality. The KfdO reprinted and distributed this article.[88] This was in line also with a pamphlet by Alfons Paquet, who advocated emigration of East European Jews to Palestine. Paquet said that in the future the German language should play the same role as Greek in ancient times and that German should in the Orient replace French and English.[89] Franz Rosenzweig wrote in 1916 in a letter from Poland that the German anxiety about Eastern Jews did not concern the *Ostjuden* as such but only the *Ostjuden* as potential *Westjuden*, i.e. if they became assimilated to German culture. There was not, he concluded, an Eastern Jewish question (*Ostjudenfrage*) but only a Jewish question (*Judenfrage*).[90]

Those German Jews who disliked Yiddish and the idea of a Jewish cultural autonomy had powerful allies among the East European Jews themselves.

The major political bodies of German Jewry met in Poland groups with almost identical ideologies and political aims. Dr. Bodenheimer of the KfdO saw a similarity between his own views and the *Folkspartei* of the Polish Jews, whose main aim was cultural and national autonomy, with Yiddish schools.[91] The KfdO found in the Zionist movement a strong ally in its fight for Jewish autonomy, but most Zionists preferred Hebrew schools to Yiddish ones. Dr. Arthur Hantke of the Zionist Executive in Berlin assisted at the meetings of the Jewish National Club (*Yiddisher Nacionaler Klub*) in Warsaw, which tried to organize a representative nationalist Jewish body to direct all Jewish affairs of a political character.[92]

The Orthodox group of German Jewry was most active in helping to shape the Orthodox Jews of Eastern Europe into a political power. Their attitude towards Yiddish schools often followed the assimilationist line.

Most German Zionists expressed their respect for Yiddish, but did not accept it as a national language (*Nationalsprache*), this role being reserved for Hebrew.[93] This opinion was not unanimous, as can be seen from Dr. Bodenheimer's attitude. The Zionists in Poland, on some occasions (mostly at a later stage) were in favor of either Hebrew or Yiddish as the language of instruction in Jewish

88. *Die Juden in Polen*, von Georg Gothein. Sonderabdruck aus der Wochenschrift 'März', Heft 12, 25.3.1916. 7 pp. (ZA, A 15/VIII/9c).
89. Alfons Paquet, *Die jüdischen Kolonien in Palästina*. Weimar, 1915, p. 34.
90. Franz Rozenzweig, *Briefe*. Berlin, 1935, p. 95.
91. The *Folkspartei* was first organized in 1916 by the Union of Jewish writers and journalists in Warsaw as a 'Folks komitet'. As a party it was officially organized on May 11, 1917. On the attitude of the *Folkspartei* to Jewish schools see N. Prilutzki, *Redes*. Warsaw, 1922, pp. 48, 61–78.

92. The first recorded meeting of the Club was held on November 23, 1916, with representatives of 22 Jewish organizations (according to the minutes, in a private collection).
93. 'Dem Ghettojuden ist sein Jiddisch so lieb und teuer, wie dem mecklenburger, dem badischen und elsässischen Alemannen seine Mundart ...zur Nationalsprache ist das Jiddische auf die Dauer ohnedies nicht geeignet, diese Rolle kann nur das Hebräische übernehmen.' D. Emil Simonsohn-Halensee, in JP, XLVII–1 (1916). See also: J. Kaufmann (from Bern), 'Die hebräische Sprache und unsere nationale Zukunft.' *Der Jude*, 1 (1916–17), pp. 407–08.

schools, according to the parents' wishes.[94] However, their basic demand during World War I was that Hebrew should be recognized as the national Jewish language and the language of instruction in schools.[95] On the other hand, the Yiddishists, and many neutral Jews, demanded Yiddish as the language of instruction. The demand for Yiddish and for Yiddish schools became the flag around which rallied the partisans of Jewish cultural and national autonomy. A sharp conflict broke out between Hebraïsts and Yiddishists. The situation became even more complicated because the assimilationists demanded that Polish should be the language of the Jews. Representatives of the KfdO tried to make peace between the various groups of Polish Jewry, but in vain. One of the leaders of the KfdO, Dr. Bodenheimer, openly favored Yiddish. On October 9, 1915, in a memorandum (*Neubelebung der hebräischen Sprache in den besetzten Gebieten*) addressed to the Ministry of Foreign Affairs, he stated that, during the Palestinian language conflict between Dr. Paul Nathan and the Zionists before World War I, he supported Hebrew as the language of instruction in the schools in Palestine. In Eastern Europe, however, where the Jews spoke Yiddish, they would certainly derive support from the German language and culture.[96] Dr. Bodenheimer sharply criticized the pro-Hebrew

94. *Dos Yiddische Folk*, No. 41 (1918), p. 6.

95. 'In Anerkennung, dass Hebräisch die einzige nationale Sprache des ganzen jüdischen Volkes ist, beschliesst die Konferenz, dass die Unterrichtssprache in den Schulen, die unter der Aufsicht des zionistischen Schulkuratoriums stehen, die Hebräische ist. Dabei wird Jiddisch als einzige Hilfssprache benutzt und ein stufenweiser Übergang zum Unterricht in hebräischer Sprache angestrebt.' *Die Resolution der dritten Zionistischen Konferenz in Polen*. A leaflet (ZA, A 15/VIII/16).

96. 'Dem Bericht über diese Unterredung (mit zwei Vertretern des Comités für den Osten) entnehme ich, dass Euer Exzellenz der Auffassung gewesen ist, als ob ich oder das "Comité für den Osten" die Neubelebung der hebräischen Sprache in dem besetzten Gebiete anstrebe. Es kann hier nur eine Verwechslung mit meiner Stellung in dem palästinensischen Sprachenrecht vorliegen. Damals bin ich entgegen der Politik des Herrn Dr. Nathan, die ich den deutschen Interessen für schädlich hielt, dafür eingetreten, den Wünschen der palästinensischen jüdischen Bevölkerung um Einführung der hebräischen Unterrichtssprache für einige Hauptfächer in Technikum zu Haifa entgegenzukommen. Die Erfahrung hat gelehrt, dass der von mir eingenommene Standpunkt der richtige war. Ganz anders liegen aber die Verhältnisse im russischen Osten. Während in Palästina die hebräische Sprache infolge des Zusammenströmens von Juden aus aller Welt ein notwendiges Verständigungsmittel und lebendige Volkssprache geworden ist, herrscht im russischen Osten ausschliesslich die jüdisch-deutsche Sprache. Diese Tatsache zwingt die Judenheit des russischen Ostens zur Anlehnung an die deutsche Kultur, die deutsche Sprache und die deutsche Politik. Dass ich diesen Standpunkt schon vor 15 Jahren vertreten habe, dafür finden Euer Exzellenz einen Beleg in der Denkschrift, die ich die Ehre hatte, dem damaligen Staatssekretär des Auswärtigen Amtes, Herrn von Bülow, zu überreichen. Ich habe in der Anlage den betreffenden Passus ausgezogen. Die Gründung des Comités für den Osten, dem sich massgebende Vertreter der grossen jüdischen Organisationen Deutschlands angeschlossen haben, ist in erster Linie erfolgt, um den Interessen des Deutschen Reiches durch Erhaltung des jüdischen Volkselementes in Russisch-Polen in seiner Eigenart gegenüber dem Slaventum zu dienen, ihm die Möglichkeit einer wirtschaftlichen und sozialen Hebung zu schaffen und hierdurch einen starken Stützpunkt für das Deutschtum im Osten zu gewinnen. Zu diesem Zweck haben sich deutsche Zionisten und Nichtzionisten vereinigt. Wenn einzelne unversöhnliche Gegner des Zionismus unter Bruch des Burgfriedens das Comité für den Osten bekämpfen, weil demselben einige Zionisten angehören, kann dies weder mich noch meine Freunde abhalten, unsere Kraft in diesem Sinne weiterhin dem deutschen Vaterlande zur Verfügung zu stellen, solange uns das bisher bewährte Vertrauen seitens der höchsten Reichsbehörden auch ferner zuteil wird' (AA, 254/3, *Der Weltkrieg*, No. 11, ad. 2, Bd. 5–6; ZA, A 15/VIII/6).

resolution of the Warsaw Zionists on the language question, in which he saw 'great political danger' for the united front of Polish Jewry in the fight for its national rights. Yiddish is the *Volkssprache* of the Polish Jews, he wrote, and they should fight for it. He asked the Zionists to give up their 'fight for a theory' and to join the pro-Yiddish fight in order to strengthen the future of Polish Jewry.[97] Respect for this language by non-Jews meant also respect for Jews in general and for the Jewish national entity. He ridiculed the position of the assimilationists and Zionists who defined Yiddish – a language spoken by millions – as a German dialect. The fight for the Jewish language in the schools was the most striking expression of the fight for Jewish nationalism in Poland and the Zionists should participate in this fight. He denounced the 'crime' of the Zionist leaders in Poland and Lithuania who had refused to participate in the struggle for the recognition of Yiddish and Yiddish schools. The views of the KfdO were similar to the policy of the Yiddishist *Folkspartei*.[98] Most probably, Dr. Bodenheimer's opinion was not shared by many leaders of the KfdO.

What was the attitude of the German administration towards Hebrew? In Lithuania, according to the ordinance of December 22, 1915, the language of instruction of religion in non-Jewish schools was to be the mother tongue, but in the Jewish schools it was to be Hebrew.[99] The ordinance of January 16, 1916 permitted the use of Hebrew only as the language of instruction of religion.[100] In Vilna, Hebrew was used illegally as a language of instruction for secular studies in the Hebrew *Gymnasium*.[101] This anti-Hebrew policy was, most probably, a result of interventions by the representatives of German Orthodoxy, who had great influence on the German administration in Poland and Lithuania. The Orthodox leader, Rabbi Joseph Carlebach, was appointed by the *Ober-Ost* forces to organize a secondary school system in Lithuania. He organized a

97. 'Und wenn es den jüdischen Massen gelingen würde, diese Forderungen durchzusetzen, dann werden die Zionisten für das jüdische Volk, für seine Erstarkung und für seine Zukunft viel mehr geleistet haben, als den Kampf um eine Theorie, die in weniger stürmischen, friedlichen Zeiten mit Vorteil erörtert werden kann.' Dr. Bodenheimer, in *Warschauer Zeitung*, No. 76, 1916; ZA, A 15/VIII/8 and Z 3/204.

98. '...Halten es die Führer der Assimilatoren und der Zionisten für einen normalen Zustand, das die Sprache von 3 Millionen Bewohnern des besetzten Gebietes als nicht vorhanden betrachtet wird, oder halten sie es für einen gangbaren und der Ehre der jüdischen Bevölkerung gerechten Ausweg, die jüdische Sprache zwangsweise als deutsche Sprache zu behandeln? Erkennen sie nicht die Gefahr, die darin liegt, dass man das Jüdische als ein verdorbenes und verwelschtes Deutsch bezeichnet, dass man die Juden damit sprachlich als minderwertig charakterisiert? Entspringt nicht die Bekämpfung des Jüdischen durchaus der antisemitischen Anschauung von der Minderwertigkeit der Juden...Der Zionismus ist nicht Selbstzweck, er dient lediglich der Erhaltung des jüdischen Volkes. Verbrechen der Zionistenführer in Polen und Litauen wäre, wenn sie nicht die Führung und Organisierung der jüdischen Massen übernehmen und sich mit der Partei vereinigen würden, welche das Recht auf die eigene jüdische Schule und Sprache und den Schutz ihrer nationalen Minderheit durch verfassungsmässige Garantieen bei den gegenwärtigen Erörterungen für die politische Neugestaltung der besetzten Gebiete erkämpfen will...' (ZA, A 15/VIII/8).

99. H. Zemke, *op. cit.*, p. 107.

100. '...zur etwaigen Erlernung der hebräischen (Religions-) Sprache nur die Religionsstunden zu benutzen sind. Andere Unterrichtsstunden dürfen zu diesem Zwecke nicht benutzt werden' (*Ibid.*, p. 117).

101. M. I. Nadel, in *Pinkes*. Vilna, 1922, pp. 757–60.

Gymnasium in Kovno where Hebrew, regarded as the holy language, was not 'taught solely for its own sake or as a vehicle for Jewish studies'. This was in line with the Orthodox view that Hebrew was being used as a Zionist and anti-Orthodox tool. Before the War Rabbi Carlebach had fought in Palestine against teaching in Hebrew. His brother-in-law, Dr. Leopold Rosenak, Rabbi of Bremen, was also active in the same field in Lithuania. (Even after the war the *Agudath Harabbanim* of Lithuania turned to Rabbi Carlebach for help in their fight with the secularist Yiddishists.) A report of the KfdO on the schools of Kovno stated that the assimilationist attitude of the Orthodox group clearly expressed itself in the view of Hebrew as a sacred but not a living language.[102] It is also possible that the Germans considered that Hebrew could be an unyielding obstacle to Germanization, while Yiddish was sometimes regarded as a German dialect, though in need of purification. The Orthodox leaders often preferred Polish to Yiddish: Polish was chosen as the language of instruction for secular teaching in the *hedarim* – the traditional Jewish religious schools. This was in line with the demands of the German Orthodoxy and their friends in Poland.[103]

As for the Jewish assimilationists in Poland, they were filled with hatred for Yiddish, either as a recognized language of instruction in schools or for any other purpose.[104] This may be illustrated by one incident. In connection with a conflict over the distribution of American Jewish funds in Eastern Europe, Dr. Judah Leon Magnes was sent in 1916 by the American Joint Distribution Committee to investigate the situation in Germany and Poland. He told Dr. S. Nathanson, a leader of the Polish assimilationists, that the American Jews desired a more democratic representation of various groups of Polish Jews – including the Socialist Bund – on the Warsaw Relief Committee, which was then controlled by an assimilationist majority. To this, Dr. Nathanson replied that new members 'would start to speak in Yiddish, whereas the assimilationists would not understand Yiddish'.[105] Dr. Paul Nathan and his friends of the Hilfsverein tolerated the assimilationist control of the distribution of the funds.[106] Of course,

102. 'Besonders plastisch wirkt der orthodox-assimilatorische Geist der Schule in Bezug auf hebräisch, das hier in eine "heilige Sprache" verwandelt worden ist' (z a, A 15/vɪɪɪ/9c); Joseph Carlebach, in j p. No. 38–45 (1907); Haim A. Cohn, 'Joseph Carlebach'. l b i y b, v (1960), p. 64. In July 1917, the Prussian Minister of Justice visited the *heder Tora un derech-erec* in Warsaw, where a lesson of Talmud was conducted in Polish. *Israelit*, 1917, p. 29.

103. *Dos Yiddische Folk*, Dec. 27, 1917; Dr. Emanuel Carlebach, *A plan cu reorganizirn dos hederwezn*...Warsaw, 1918. 40 pp. – Dr. H. Nusbaum, an assimilationist leader, spoke out in favor of teaching Hebrew, but not Yiddish. *Kurjer Warszawski*, Sept. 26, 1915. For the attitude of 'Mizrahi' see Jehuda Lejb Zlotnicki, *Tachnit limudim*...Warsaw, 1918, 20 pp.

104. According to an official German estimate there were in Poland 10,000 assimilationists. The Nationalists (Folkists) and Socialists spoke only Yiddish; the Zionists Yiddish and Polish; the Orthodox Jews Yiddish, and seldom also Polish; the Chasidim Yiddish; the Assimilationists Polish. *Warschauer Tafeln* (see note 70), p. 4.

105. JDC minutes, Dec. 14, 1916.

106. This will be the subject of a separate study.

no one – the Zionists and Yiddishists included – was against the introduction of Polish into the curriculum of the Jewish schools. Even the Jewish labor unions who fought for Yiddish recognized this necessity.[107] But the assimilationists demanded Polish instead of Yiddish. The Council of the Warsaw Jewish Community officially requested the German authorities to permit them to use Polish as the language of instruction in the schools and children's homes of the community and also in the private schools, when parents requested this. This the German authorities refused. They did not believe that it was the genuine desire of the Jewish population.[108] In Lodz too, Polish was not permitted as the language of instruction in Jewish schools.[109]

Of special importance was the attitude of Dr. Ludwig Haas, the consultant on Jewish affairs to the Department of Schools and Churches in the German Administration in Poland. It was the KfdO which first proposed the appointment of Dr. Haas to this office, but his ideology was much more similar to that of the assimilationist Hilfsverein than to that of the KfdO. On December 8, 1915, Dr. Haas stated that the introduction of Polish as the language of instruction in Polish schools and German in German and Jewish schools was a disaster. There were no teachers available to teach in German and the children did not understand the language. The Jews would be considered by the Poles as propagators of Germanization and sooner or later the Poles would take their revenge on the Jews. Dr. Haas, who regarded Yiddish only as a political expedient, preferred Polonization to Germanization. As for Yiddish, he considered that 'a perpetuation of the jargon could lead to difficulties in the struggle to include the Jews in Western European culture'.[110]

All these problems were often discussed between leaders of the KfdO and the Hilfsverein in an attempt to find a formula leading to a united action of both bodies for the benefit of the East European Jews. On one occasion Professor Oppenheimer told Dr. Nathan that Polish Jews must be spared a forced Polonization, or even a forced Germanization, and that, unlike the Western Jews, the Jews of the East were 'by language and culture a separate community'.[111] But Dr. Nathan advocated a policy of waiting and of abstaining from the making of definite plans for the future of East European Jewry, because

---

107. *Hajnt* (Warsaw), No. 179, 1915.
108. *Jewrejskaja Zizn*, 1916, 9, 11; Paul Roth, *Die politische Entwicklung in Kongress-Polen während der deutschen Okkupation*. Leipzig, 1919, p. 156.
109. 'Der Polizeipräsident hat verboten, in jüdischen Schulen die polnische Sprache als Unterrichtssprache zu benutzen.' Dr. Bodenheimer's report from Lodz, May 1915 (ZA, A 15/VIII/9 A).
110. ZA, A 15/VIII/2c.
111. '...um so der jüdischen Masse eine erzwungene Polonisierung zu ersparen. Das Komitee wünscht auch keine zwangsweise Germanisierung, sondern Gewährleistung völlig freier Entwicklung.

Eine ohne Zwang erfolgende Entwicklung des Jargons zum Hochdeutschen würde das Komitee willkommen heissen. Das Komitee geht von dem Gedanken aus, dass die Juden des Ostens nach Sprache und Kultur eine besondere Gemeinschaft darstellen, die ein Recht auf den Schutz ihrer Eigenart besitzt, im Gegensatz zu den Westjuden, die geistig in der Kultur ihrer Umgebung wurzeln und wirtschaftlich wie politisch die Interessen ihrer Mitbürger teilen' ('Unterredung des Herrn Dr. Paul Nathan mit Herrn Dr. Franz Oppenheimer, am 3. Januar 1916.' ZA, A 15/VIII/5 and Z 3/204).

of the obscurity of the general political future. This shrewd politician and great German patriot foresaw very early the impossibility of deciding the political future of Poland solely from Berlin, without taking into consideration the will of the Polish people. He did not want to bind the Jewish destiny in Poland to an unrealistic political future. At meetings with the KfdO on April 23, September 11 and 12 and October 6, 1915, as well as at other times, Dr. Nathan stressed that the future of Poland was not yet decided. He stated that Jewish school policy could be determined only when this future would be known.[112] As early as October 1915, the *Deutsche Vereinigung für die Interessen der osteuropäischen Juden* (German Association for the protection of the interests of East European Jews) – an organization supporting the Hilfsverein and opposing the KfdO – stated in a printed memorandum that the major Jewish problems in Eastern European countries, including the problem of schools, could be discussed only when the basis of the political future of these territories had become clear.[113] On September 12, 1915, Dr. Nathan said that Jewish and Polish children should go to the same schools.[114] This opinion was shared by other leaders of the Hilfsverein. In March 1916, Max M. Warburg told Professor Oppenheimer that they could not as yet foresee a German victory as certain and, because of this, no conclusive decisions should be taken.[115]

Dr. Nathan's farsightedness not only had its origin in his discerning mind but was also based on his assimilationist attitude. At a meeting of the KfdO (June 29, 1916), it was noted that the Jewish assimilationists from Poland refused to discuss Polish Jewish problems with the KfdO so long as the future of Poland itself had not yet been decided.[116] Dr. Nathan and others of the same ideology believed in the possibility of a Germanization of the Lithuanian but not of the Polish Jews. This was a result of their attitude towards the political future of

112. ZA, A 15/VIII/2D, 9B, 14. See also: Dr. Paul Nathan, 'Polen und Juden'. *Berliner Tageblatt*, 17. Januar 1916. ('Deutsche und Polen werden sich vorurteilslos auf einer breiten Basis verständigen müssen. Einige Millionen Juden können von dieser Verständigung nicht ausgeschlossen bleiben, wenn eine ruhige Entwicklung den in Betracht kommenden Gebieten beschieden sein soll').
113. '...erst dann vorzubringen, wenn die Grundlagen für die politische Zukunft jener Gebiete sich klar erkennen lassen.' On schools: 'Eine Entscheidung hierüber kann nur im Zusammenhang mit den Beschlüssen über das endgültige politische Schicksal der in Betracht kommenden Gebiete gefällt werden. Und solange diese letzteren nicht vorliegen, wird jede provisorische Massregel grosse Beunruhigung erzeugen, den Gegensatz zwischen Polen und Juden zuspitzen ...Bei den jetzigen ungeregelten Zuständen in Polen wird es als kleineres Übel erscheinen

müssen, wenn die Schulfrage solange in der Schwebe bleibt, bis sie von festem politischen Fundament aus zu abschliessender Regelung gebracht werden kann.' Pp. 2–3 of the memorandum (DZ, Reichsamt des Innern. I.A.O. Bd. 1. Spez., Die jüdische Frage im Osten).
114. 'Dr. Nathan hält es für das einzigmögliche, dass die jüdischen und polnischen Kinder in dieselbe Schule gehen' ('Unterredung der Herren Dr. Nathan, Prof. Sobernheim, Prof. Mittwoch.' ZA, A 15/VIII/9B).
115. 'Protokoll der Unterredung des Herrn Franz Oppenheimer mit Herrn Max Warburg.' 3rd February, 1916 (ZA, A 15/VIII/9c).
116. '...zunächst auf keine einzige Unterredung mit den Berliner Herren eingehen wollten, mit der Ausrede, das Ostkomitee sei mit der Lösung der Judenfrage beschäftigt, während die Polenfrage selbst noch nicht gelöst sei' (ZA, A 15/VIII/9c).

these two countries. They foresaw an independent Poland; at the same time they considered German control of the neighboring Lithuania likely. Indeed, this was the view generally accepted at that time. On January 14, 1918, Dr. Nathan and Max M. Warburg, in a memorandum addressed to the Ministry of Foreign Affairs, stated that the Jewish problem was different in the two countries. In Kurland, with its large number of Baltic Germans, the problem of the social and political status of the Jews would soon find an acceptable solution. Jewish children there would easily take their place in the general schools. It would only be necessary to make it possible for Jews to have additional instruction in their religion and in Hebrew. No mention of Yiddish in Kurland was made in the memorandum. For the Jews of Lithuania the authors of the memorandum asked for schools for Jews where Hebrew or Yiddish, according to the wishes of the parents, should be taught. Dr. Nathan and Warburg did not speak of Jewish schools with Yiddish or Hebrew as the language of instruction, but of 'Lithuanian schools for Jews', where Jews would be able to teach their own religion, Hebrew, and Yiddish. The situation in Poland, they stated, was of a very different character. They favored a policy which would grant the Polish Jews the right to learn Yiddish or Hebrew in their schools, but 'always within the framework of the general Polish school system'. No mention was made of Yiddish or Hebrew as a language of instruction. As for the political aspect, they expressed their belief that Yiddish could play a role in strengthening economic relations between Germany and Poland. But they also strongly objected to the use of Polish Jews as exponents of Germanization. Such a policy would only provoke trouble and sharp conflict between Poles and Jews. German policy should be not to use Polish Jews as an 'element of Germanization' but to make of them 'Poles of Jewish faith' (*Polen jüdischen Glaubens*) – an expression much in favor among the Jewish assimilationists in Poland and other countries.[117] The *Deutsche Vereinigung für die Interessen der osteuropäischen Juden*, in the memorandum of October 1915 mentioned earlier, favored the assimilation of Polish Jews, which it referred to as the *Prozess der Umbildung*.[118]

Dr. Nathan was an outspoken opponent of Jewish autonomy in Eastern Europe. He was against 'building a state within a state', as he wrote in November 1918.[119] On occasion, at a meeting held on February 4, 1918, where Rabbi Rubinstein, a Jewish leader from Vilna, was present, Dr. Nathan expressed his opinion that the Jews could demand only 'some cultural autonomy'.[120] Other Jewish spokesmen were of a different opinion. In April 1918 Theodor Behr (Julius Berger) advocated Jewish schools in Lithuania, with freedom to choose their own language of instruction, as a first step towards

117. AA, *Der Weltkrieg*, No. 14a, K204177–204195. The memorandum was also noted in AA, 729/1, *Türkei* 195, Bd. 18–19.
118. DZ, Reichsamt des Innern, I.A.O. Bd. 1.

Spez. Die jüdische Frage im Osten. p. 4–5 of the memorandum.
119. VZ, Nov. 19, 1918.
120. ZA, Z 3/207 (Minutes of the VIOD).

national autonomy.[121] On April 2, 1918, the VIOD (*Vereinigung Jüdischer Organisationen Deutschlands* – Association of Jewish Organizations in Germany), a body which included representatives of the major Jewish organizations (among them the Hilfsverein and the KfdO), addressed a memorandum on the Jews in Eastern Europe to the Reich Chancellor. The VIOD demanded for them not only civil equality but also a 'linguistic–cultural autonomy', including schools, and even a full national autonomy in the case of such autonomy being granted to another minority.[122] It should be noted that Dr. Nathan advised the authorities not to oppose the introduction of Hebrew where it was wanted by parents.[123]

The struggle of the Jewish masses in Eastern Europe was an important factor in obtaining Yiddish schools. On November 14, 1916, the Jewish *Schul- und Volksbildungsverein* in Warsaw submitted a petition, signed by 32,645 persons of 18 years and over, to the German authorities, demanding that Yiddish should be the language of instruction in Jewish schools. A similar petition from Lodz was signed by 30,000 persons.[124] But the German decisions were naturally determined first of all by consideration of their own interest. They did not favor Polonization of the Jews, whom they considered a possible pro-German influence.

The German administration used Yiddish as a political and military expedient, without particular liking for the language. Sammy Gronemann, in his memoirs, mentions cases of German persecution of those who took the Yiddish language and culture seriously. He was one of a group of Yiddish interpreters to the civil and military administration. Since Yiddish became a *hochpolitische Angelegenheit* (matter of high policy), the role of interpreter was particularly important. Most of these interpreters became enamored of Yiddish. In Kovno, they founded a club in order to learn about the culture of Eastern Europe, particularly Yiddish and Yiddish culture. The club, called *Der Klub ehemaliger Intellektueller* (The club of former intellectuals), held its meeting at the Hotel Levisohn and among its members were S. Gronemann, Hermann Struck, Hans Goslar, Arnold Zweig, and also non-Jews, such as Richard Dehmel, Herbert Eulenberg, Emigelski, and Werth, the theater director. The military authorities did not like the club. Emigelski once wrote an enthusiastic article for the *Kovnoer Zeitung* on the Yiddish theater 'Wilner Trupe'. When, however, the editor made changes in

121. Theodor Behr, 'Die Judenfrage in Litauen'. *Der Jude*, III, No. 1 (Apr. 1918), p. 6.
122. DZ, Stell. des Reichskanzler. II. Kulturpflege 1d, Bd. 1. Juden.
123. Dr. Nathan and Max Warburg wrote in the memorandum of Jan. 14, 1918: 'Es gibt im eigentlichen Polen eine nicht unerhebliche Anzahl von Juden, die nicht eine ausgiebigere Pflege des Jargons, wohl aber des Hebräischen, in der Schule fordern. Es ist nicht abzusehen, warum aus politischen Gründen dieser Wunsch abschlägig beschieden werden müsste' (p. 8 of the memorandum, see note 117).
124. For the Warsaw petition see note 40; for the Lodz petition see Hertz, *op. cit.*, p. 256.

the text and even inserted an anti-Semitic tone, Emigelski refused to sign it. For this, he was relieved of his post and sent to the front. In Bialystok, the German authorities did not permit the publication of a favorable review of the theater in the German press.[125] Some of these interpreters, like Hermann Struck, were among the leading figures of the KfdO and, even while in uniform, were very active in this body. In the postwar years they did much to maintain a friendly attitude in Germany towards Yiddish culture and East European Jewry in general. The leader of German Zionism, Kurt Blumenfeld, mentions in his memoirs the influence on German Zionism of the pro-Yiddish people who had spent the war years in Eastern Europe.[126]

The German administration used German Jews to a large extent as intermediaries between the local populace and the occupation forces (as interpreters, office workers, etc.). In the course of time many people regarded these Jews as 'German agents', while in Lithuania, for instance, German officials, feeling the antagonism of the Lithuanians, accused the Jews of being responsible for this anti-German attitude.[127]

On January 5, 1918, two months after the publication of the Balfour Declaration in Britain, the German Deputy Foreign Secretary, von der Busche-Haddenhausen, in the name of his government, made a statement in favor of the development of the culture of the Jewish minority in Eastern Europe.[128] Professor Franz Oppenheimer commented warmly on this German declaration 'in favour of the linguistic-cultural autonomy of the minorities'.[129] It seems that the Poles protested against Professor Oppenheimer's interpretation and that this caused the Deputy Foreign Secretary to publish a denial.[130] Later, Professor

125. Sammy Gronemann, *Hawdoloh und Zapfenstreich*. Erinnerungen an die ostjüdische Etappe 1916–18. Mit Zeichnungen von Magnus Zeller. Berlin, 1924, pp. 33, 45–55, 120, 171, 199–200, 219. See also M. Szalit's review of the book in *Literarysze Bleter* (Warsaw), Jan. 30, 1925.

126. 'Mit einer Krampfhaftigkeit, die nachträglich schwer zu verstehen ist, separierten sich ausgezeichnete Zionisten, wie Fritz Mordechai Kaufmann, Ludwig Strauss und für eine kurze Zeit sogar auch Werner Senator von der zionistischen Organisation. Sie verlangten mit der gleichen Intensität, mit der sie vorher den Palästinagedanken verfochten hatten, im Namen der arbeitenden Massen, die wie sie sagten, die aus der bürgerlichen Sphäre erwachsene hebräische Sprachrenaissance ablehnten, jiddisches Theater und jiddische Literatur. Die Schrittmacher dieser Bewegung hatten die Kriegsjahre in Litauen und Polen verbracht und waren geradezu betrunken von den dort empfangenen Eindrücken. Sie veranlassten viele Zionisten, sich ihnen anzuschliessen, und wer nicht mitmachte, war in ihren Augen ein Mensch, dem das jüdische Herz und der jüdische

Sinn fehlten.' Kurt Blumenfeld, *Erlebte Judenfrage*. Ein Vierteljahrhundert deutscher Zionismus. Stuttgart, [1962,] pp. 122–23.

127. C. Rivas, *La Lithuanie sous le joug allemand*. Lausanne, 1918, p. 188; Azriel Shohat, 'The Beginnings of Anti-Semitism in Independent Lithuania', *Yad Washem Studies*, II (1958), 9–10. Years later Professor Oppenheimer wrote: 'Die Juden waren denn auch überall die Dolmetscher unserer Truppen; sie hatten dafür später vielfach schwer zu leiden, ohne dass sie von den Deutschen durchschnittlich anständig behandelt worden wären.' 'Jugendfreundschaften'. VZ, July 19, 1930.

128. 'Entwicklung ihrer Kultur und Eigenart gerichteten Wünsche der jüdischen Minderheit in den Ländern, in denen sie ein stark entwickeltes Eigenleben haben.' NJM, II, No. 7 (Jan. 10, 1918), p. 147.

129. *Zur Erklärung der Reichsregierung über die Judenfrage*, von Prof. Dr. Franz Oppenheimer. [Berlin, 1918.] 1 p. Reprinted from NJM, II, No. 7 (Jan. 10, 1918), pp. 148–152.

130. 'Der Artikel kann den Eindruck erwecken, als ob die deutsche Regierung eine jüdische

Oppenheimer explained that the German statement had been made only to record the official view and as a statement of principle.[131] In Lithuania, where the Germans contemplated remaining, the German authorities made at that time a clear statement in favor of Jewish autonomy.[132]

In the confused situation the representations of the KfdO and other Jewish leaders from Germany, in spite of many contradictions, did much to influence the German authorities towards establishing Yiddish schools and other strongholds of Jewish culture. While the local population in Lithuania, troubled by their own national problems, did not oppose Yiddish schools, the situation in Poland was different. On September 21, 1917, the Polish authorities refused permission to open a Yiddish teachers' seminary because Polish law did not provide for Yiddish as a language of instruction.[133] In July 1918 the influential Polish newspaper *Gazeta Warszawska* demanded the prohibition of Yiddish because it was a German dialect and Poland was at war with Germany.[134] However, when Poland became an independent state, the existence of Jewish schools and other organizations was a *fait accompli* facing the Polish authorities.[135] To this achievement, German Jews who had worked in the occupied territory under very delicate and changeable conditions during a cruel war had contributed a not inconsiderable share.

Many other aspects of various problems noted in this paper call for further research by objective historians and also for memoirs written by people who still remember that period. Thus, for instance, the constantly changing attitude of the German administration at various stages of the war should be taken more into consideration. Although this paper deals mainly with the German-Jewish aspect of the problem, the East-European aspect needs more detailed study. But this is beyond the scope of the present essay.

sprachlich-kulturelle Autonomie in Polen schaffen wolle. Das ist nicht der Fall und ergibt sich auch aus der Erklärung des Unterstaatssekretärs keineswegs. Vielmehr wird der polnische Staat darüber zu entscheiden haben…Es ist insbesondere nicht die Absicht Deutschlands, dem polnischen Staat eine bestimmte Lösung der Frage aufzuzwingen.' *Deutsche Warschauer Zeitung*, No. 22, Jan. 23, 1918.
131. NJM, II, No. 11 (March 1918), pp. 260–62.
132. *Eine Erklärung über die Judenfrage in Litauen.* (Berlin, 1918). 1 p. (ZA, A 8/3/1/3). Reprinted from NJM, II, No. 19 (July 10, 1918).
133. *Glos Zydowski*, 1918, 7.

134. *Gazeta Warszawska*, July 12, 1918, No. 189; N. Prilutzki, *op. cit.* (see note 70).
135. See also the following sources: *Von den jüdischen Volksschulen in Polen.* (Berlin) n.d. 1 p. published by the KfdO (ZA, A 8/3/1/3); Max Brod, 'Erfahrungen im ostjüdischen Schulwerk'. *Der Jude*, I (1916–17), pp. 32–36; Germano-Judaeus, *op. cit.* (see note 10); Jacob Robinson, 'Das jüdische Schulwesen in Litauen'. *Der Jude*, No. 2 (1920), pp. 89–92; Prof. M. Sobernheim, 'Die jiddische Schule in Warschau'. NJM, I (1916), pp. 152–54; Joseph Wohlgemuth, *Das Bildungsproblem in der Ostjudenfrage.* Berlin, 1916. 80 pp.

ה ו ד ע ה

אַזױא װיא איצט קומט פֿאַר אַניע פֿאָלקסצײלונג

אין דיא בַרױטקַאַרטעןבֿױרָאַס נאָך די ברױטקאַרטען

און בּיא בּעשטימען דיא נאָציאָנאַלָישטעט רעכינט מען

זיך אױר מיט דעם, אױף װעלכען לשון מען שרייבט

זיך אונטער, בעט מען אז יעדער זאָל זיך

אונטערשרייבען אױף אידיש און ניט אױף קײן

אַנדערע שפּראַך.

Announcement in the synagogue yard asking to register   ה. אױפֿן שול־הױף אָנצוגעבן יידיש װי די מוטער־שפּראַך בעת דער פֿאָלקסצײלונג
Yiddish as the mother tongue in the census

Возвание на „Шул—Гойф" (школьный двор) чтобы при переписи   ה. בחצר בית־הכנסת. הקורא לרשום יידיש כשפת־האם בשעת ספירת האוכלוסיה
населения декларировать идиш как родной язык   1931

Since nationality is determined in accordance with the language in which one signs one's signature, it is requested that everyone sign in Yiddish and not in any other language.

די שפּראַכן ביַי ייִדן אין אומאָפּהענגיקן פּוילן

יעקב לעשטשינסקי

SUMMARY: THE LANGUAGES OF JEWS IN INDEPENDENT POLAND
BY YANKEV LESHTSHINSKI

The major Jewish demographer of the inter-war period (1876–1966) demonstrates regional and chronological differences in Yiddish mother-tongue claiming in Poland. Although there was some loss by 1931 (relative to the very end of the nineteenth century) there were also several noteworthy gains relative to the early twenties.

1

אין מלוכות מיט אַ סך נאַציאָנאַליטעטן, מיט פֿאַרשיידענע נאַציאָנאַלע קולטור־טראַדיציעס און מיט אַ ירושהדיקן קולטורקאַמף שפּילט די שפּראַכן־פֿראַגע אַ גרויסע פּאָליטישע ראָלע. איז דאָך די שפּראַך די עלעמענטאַרע פֿאָרעם פֿון יעדער נאַציאָנאַלער קולטור, איר בולטסטער און אָנזעעוודיקסטער אויסדרוק, איר בפֿירושסטע מאַניפֿעסטאַציע.

אין דעם אומאָפּהענגיקן פּוילן, ווו די פּאָליטיק האָט זיך געפֿירט אין די אינטערעסן פֿון דער פּוילישער נאַציאָנאַליטעט און קעגן די אינטערעסן פֿון די נאַציאָנאַלע מיעוטים, האָט די אָפֿיציעלע סטאַטיסטיק געדאַרפֿט אויסמיַידן געוויסע סכּנות פֿאַר דער הערשנדיקער גרופּע און מען האָט דעריבער בכלל ניט פֿאַרעפֿנטלעכט די רעזולטאַטן פֿון שפּראַכן־סטאַטיסטיק אין דער פֿאָלקס־ציילונג פֿון 1921. נאָך דער פֿאָלקסציילונג פֿון 1931 האָבן מיר געניגע ידיעות וועגן דער שפּראַכן־סטאַטיסטיק. דערפֿאַר אָבער איז יעמאָלט בכלל ניט געווען אין דעם פֿרעגבויגן די פֿראַגע וועגן צוגעהעריקייט צו דער נאַציאָנאַ־ליטעט, וואָס קעגן דעם האָבן בשעתו זייער שאַרף פּראָטעסטירט די פֿאַרשטיי־ערס פֿון אַלע מיעוטים. ביַי ייִדן האָט עס אַרויסגערופֿן אַ הייסע פּראָפּאַגאַנדע, אַז מען זאָל אָנגעבן דעמאָנסטראַטיוו איינע פֿון די צוויי נאַציאָנאַלע שפּראַכן: ייִדיש אָדער העברעיש.

ווי אין אונדזערע פריערדיקע אַנאַליזן [1] פֿון די רעזולטאַטן פֿון די ביידע פֿאָלקס־
ציילונגען (אין 1921 און 1931), קענען מיר אויך דאָ — און דאָ טאָקע נאָך ווינציקער ווי
ביי די אַנדערע פּונקטן! — זיך ניט האַלטן ביי דער אײַנטײלונג אין פֿיר ראַיאָנען, וואָס די
אַפֿיציעלע פּוילישע סטאַטיסטיק האָט זי אָנגענומען, ווײַל אָט די ראַיאָנירונג האָט אַ בפֿירוש
פּאָליטישע כּוונה.[2] ווי אין די באַטראַכטונגען וועגן דער שטאַטישער באַפֿעלקערונג אין פּוילן,
גיבן מיר דאָ אַזאַ אײַנטײלונג פֿון לאַנד :

א) לויטן עטנאָגראַפֿישן פּרינציפּ ווערט דאָס אומאָפּהענגיקע פּוילן געטיילט אין
דרײַ גרויסע ראַיאָנען : אין אַ פּוילישן, ווײַסרוסישן און אוקראַיִנישן ראַיאָן ;

ב) צום פּוילישן ראַיאָן געהערן די וואָיעוואָדשאַפֿטן : די שטאָט וואַרשע (וואָס איז
געווען אַ וואָיעוואָדשאַפֿט פֿאַר זיך), די וואַרשעווער, לאָדזשער, קעלצער, לובלינער און קראַ־
קעווער — זעקס וואָיעוואָדשאַפֿטן וואָס שטעלן צונויף דעם פּוילישן סובראַיאָן א, און די
וואָיעוואָדשאַפֿטן : פּויזענער, פּאָמעריזער און שלעזיע — דרײַ וואָיעוואָדשאַפֿטן וואָס שטעלן
צונויף דעם פּוילישן ראַיאָן ב. אין איינעם זיינען דאָס ניין וואָיעוואָדשאַפֿטן, וואָס דאָרטן
איז דאָס רובֿ באַפֿעלקערונג בלי שום ספֿק פּוילישע ;

ג) צום ווײַסרוסישן ראַיאָן געהערן פֿיר וואָיעוואָדשאַפֿטן : ביאַליסטאָקער און
ווילנער — וואָס זיי שטעלן צונויף דעם ווײַסרוסישן סובראַיאָן א ; נאָוואַרעדקער און פּאָ־
לעסיער — וואָס זיי שטעלן צונויף דעם ווײַסרוסישן סובראַיאָן ב. דאָ איז די באַפֿעלקערונג
זייער אַ געמישטע נאָך די נאַציאָנאַליטעטן נאָך, און די ווײַסרוסן, אויב זיי זיינען ניט
אומעטום דאָס רובֿ פֿון דער באַפֿעלקערונג, זיינען זיי אָבער (אַחוץ אין די שטעט) דער
קוואַנטיטעטסטער עלעמענט ;

ד) צום אוקראַיִנישן ראַיאָן געהערן די פֿיר וואָיעוואָדשאַפֿטן : לעמבערגער, סטאַניס־
לאַווער, טאַרנאָפּאָלער, וואָליניער. דאָס רובֿ באַפֿעלקערונג, אמת ניט קיין גרויסע מערהייט,
איז דאָ אוקראַיִניש.

אין דער טאַבעלע 1 [3] האָבן מיר צונויפֿגענומען די רעזולטאַטן פֿון דער
פֿאָלקסציילונג אין 1931 נאָך אונדזער ראַיאָנירונג נאָך. ס׳באַקומט זיך אַזאַ בילד :

פּאָליאַקן האָבן אַן אַבסאָלוטע מערהייט נאָך דער שפּראַך נאָך אין
צוויי ראַיאָנען : אין פּוילישן און אין ווײַסרוסישן. אין אוקראַיִנישן ראַיאָן
האָבן די אוקראַיִנער אַן אַבסאָלוטע מערהייט, אמת ניט קיין גרויסע,

---

[1] דאָס איז אַ קאַפּיטל פֿון אַ גרעסערער אַרבעט וועגן יידן אין אומאָפּהענגיקן פּוילן
(1919 — 1939), וואָס דער מחבר גרייט פֿאַרן אינסטיטוט פֿאַר יידישע ענינים. אַנדערע טיילן
פֿון דער זעלביקער אַרבעט האָבן זיך געדרוקט אין די ייִוואָ־בלעטער, באַנד XX, נומ׳ 1, זז׳ 1—28
און אין באַנד XXI, נומ׳ 1, זז׳ 20—46. די ביידע דערמאָנטע אַרטיקלען זיינען אַרויס ווי אַ באַזונ־
דערע בראָשור א״נ יידן אין דער שטאַטישער באַפֿעלקערונג פֿון אומאָפּהענגיקן פּוילן, ביבליאָ־
טעק פֿון ייִוואָ, ניו־יאָרק, 1943, 56 זז׳.

[2] זע ייִוואָ־בלעטער, ב׳ XX, נומ׳ 1, זז׳ 6—7 אַדער אין דער דערמאָנטער בראָשור
זז׳ 8 און 13.

[3] פֿאַר דער און פֿאַר די אַנדערע טאַבעלעס (זע זז׳ 153—157) האָבן מיר זיך באַנוצט
מיט מאַטעריאַלן פֿון :

a) *Statystyka Polski*, seria C, zeszyt 62, Warszawa, 1937;

b) Krysiński, Dr. Alfons, "Struktura narodowościowa miast polskich", *Sprawy Narodowościowe*, 1937, No. 3;

c) *Sprawy Narodowościowe*, 1937, 1—2.

אָבער פֿאָרט איז עס דאָס רובֿ — 51.1 פּראָצענט. אָט אין דעם אוקראַיִנישן
ראַיאָן האָבן פּאָליאַקן ניט מער ווי 39.4 פּראָצענט. ווען מען נעמט דעם וואָס-
רוסישן ראַיאָן ווי אַ גאַנצקייט, האָבן דאָרטן די פּאָליאַקן אַ שפּראַכיקע מער-
הייט פֿון העכער 52 פּראָצענט, אָבער אין וווייסרוסישן סובעראַיאָן ב, מיט נאָוואָ-
רעדקער און פּאָלעסיער וואָיעוואָדשאַפֿטן, האָבן שוין פּאָליאַקן ניט מער ווי
32.9 פּראָצענט און זיי זײַנען דאָרטן אַ מיעוט. אמת, אויך דאָ באַקומט זיך
אָפֿיציעל, אַז די וווייטרוסן זײַנען אַ מיעוט, בלויז 22.3 פּראָצענט. אָבער
ווען מען לייגט צו צו דער וווייסרוסישער שפּראַך די „היגע" (tutejsi) — אַ שפּיצל,
עס זאָל ניט זײַן קאַנטיק דער אמתער כאַראַקטער פֿון דעם וואָיאָן — זעמאָלט
באַקומען די וווייסרוסן 54.9 פּראָצענט און זײַנען דאָס רובֿ אין דעם סובעראַיאָן.

אין זייער אייגענעם ראַיאָן זײַנען די פּאָליאַקן העכער 86 פּראָצענט פֿון
דער באַפֿעלקערונג (נאָך דעם סימן פֿון שפּראַך) און אין דעם סובעראַיאָן ב, אין
דעם טייל פּוילן וואָס האָט געהערט ביז נאָך דער ערשטער וועלט-מלחמה
צו דײַטשלאַנד, האָבן פּאָליאַקן אַפֿילו העכער 90 פּראָצענט. בכן איז דאָס דער
פּוילישסטער טייל פֿון פּוילן.

לויט דער אָפֿיציעלער סטאַטיסטיק באַקומט זיך, אַז ייִדיש און העב-
רעיִש אין איינעם זײַנען די שפּראַכן פֿון 8.7 פּראָצענט פֿון דער באַפֿעלקערונג
פֿון גאַנץ פּוילן. אַזוי ווי מען מוז אָננעמען, קענענדיק די סיטואַציע אין פּוילן,
אַז די וואָס האָבן אָנגעגעבן העברעיִש פֿאַרשטייען ייִדיש און רעדן ייִדיש,
וועלן מיר צוליב קלאָרקייט און איינפֿאַכקייט דאָ רעדן וועגן ייִדיש אַליין
(די גענויע ציפֿער וועגן ייִדיש און העברעיִש — זע אַ ביסל וווײַטער).

לויט דער אָפֿיציעלער סטאַטיסטיק אַפֿילו האָט זיך אויך באַקומען, אַז
צווישן די שפּראַכן פֿון דעם אומאָפּהענגיקן פּוילן פֿאַרנעמט ייִדיש דאָס דריטע
אָרט, גלײַך נאָך פּוילש און אוקראַיִניש. אין פּוילישן ראַיאָן מאַכט דער פּראָצענט
ייִדיש-ריידערס אויס 8.7, אין וווייסרוסישן — 9.6, אין אוקראַיִנישן — 7.6; נאָר
אין צוויי סובעראַיאָנען דערגרייכט דער פּראָצענט איבער צען — אין פּוילישן
סובעראַיאָן אַ — 11.4, אין וווייסרוסישן סובעראַיאָן אַ (אין ווילנער און ביאַ-
ליסטאָקער וואָיעוואָדשאַפֿטן) — 10.4 פּראָצענט. דעם קלענסטן פּראָצענט,
אַ נישטיקע צאָל ייִדיש-ריידערס, האָבן מיר אין פּוילישן סובעראַיאָן ב, וואָס ער
האָט אַ קלײנע ייִדישע באַפֿעלקערונג.

2

פֿאַרשטייט זיך, אַז ייִדן האָבן ניט געקענט האָבן קיין אײן ווינקל אין
פּוילן מיט אַן אַבסאָלוטער אָדער אַפֿילו רעלאַטיווער מערהייט. דאָס בילד
ווערט אין גאַנצן אַנדערש, ווען מיר וועגדן זיך צו די שטעט און האָבן צו
טאָן נאָר מיט דער שטאָטישער באַפֿעלקערונג. דאָ בײַטן זיך די שפּראַך-פֿאַר-
העלטענישן בכלל און גאַנץ באַזונדער דער מצבֿ פֿון דער ייִדישער שפּראַך.

די טאַבעלע 2 און 3 גיבן איבער די סיטואַציע אין די שטעט. די טאַבעלע

ב א ר י כ ט

פֿון דער ווילנער יידישער

לערער=געזעלשאַפֿט

פֿאר דער צייט פֿון 1915 ביז 1918.

Zur Verbreitung im Gebiete des Oberbefehlshabers Ost und zur Ausfuhr zugelassen.
Buchprüfungsamt Ob. Ost.

באַריכט פֿון דער ווילנער יידישער
לערער-געזעלשאַפֿט

Report by the Yiddish Teachers Association in Vilna

דו״ח של הברת המורים האידיים
בוילנה

Отчет виленского Общества
еврейских учителей

1918—1915

Report (1915–1918) of the
Vilna Jewish Teachers Association distributed with the permission of the German military
authorities.

2 גיט די צאָל רײדערס און די טאַבעלע 3 זייער פּראָצענט־פֿאַרהעלטעניש.
אויב דאָס בילד בײַט זיך בנוגע אַלע נאַציאָנאַליטעטן, איז עס לחלוטין ניט
צו דערקענען, װען מען קומט צו ייִדן. אין דער צײַט װאָס אין גאַנץ פּוילן
האָבן ייִדיש־רײדערס (אָדער פֿינקטלעכער: ייִדיש־ און העברעיִש־רײדערס)
אויסגעמאַכט נאָר 8.7 פּראָצענט, האָבן זיי צװישן דער שטאַטישער באַפֿעל־
קערונג באַטראָפֿן כּמעט אַ פֿערטל — 24.3 פּראָצענט. אין איין סובראַיאָן
(אין נאָװאָרעדקער און פּאָלעסיער װאָיעװואָדשאַפֿטן, ד״ה אין אונדזער װײַס־
רוסישן סובראַיאָן ב) זײַנען ייִדיש־רײדערס אַפֿילו די רעלאַטיװע מערהייט פֿון
אַלע שטאָטישע אײַנװױנערס: 45.4 פּראָצענט, בעת װען קאַטוליִאַקן זײַנען בלויז
— 36.1 פּראָצענט. אין דעם זעלביקן סובראַיאָן, װו װײַסרוסן זײַנען אַ פֿאַקטישע
מערהייט (װי עס װײַזט, װען מען נעמט צונויף אין איינעם די װײַסרוסישע
שפּראַך מיט דער „היגער"), זײַנען זיי אין די שטעט ניט מער װי 14 פּראָצענט
(אָפֿיציעל װײַסרוסיש 6.6 פּראָצענט און דאָס איבעריקע פֿון דער „היגער"
שפּראַך). אין די שטעט פֿון דעם סובראַיאָן זײַנען פֿאַראַן סך הכּל 17,652
װײַסרוסישע אײַנװױנערס.

די טאַבעלע 3 װײַזט אונדז, אַז דער פּראָצענט ייִדן לויטן שפּראַך־סימן
האָט אין די שטעט פֿון פּוילן באַטראָפֿן:

אין פּוילישן ראַיאָן:

סובראַיאָן א	28.7
סובראַיאָן ב	0.7
אין גאַנצן ראַיאָן	21.5

אין װײַסרוסישן ראַיאָן:

סובראַיאָן א	34.4
סובראַיאָן ב	45.4
אין גאַנצן ראַיאָן	37.4

אין אוקראַיִנישן ראַיאָן:

| אין גאַנצן ראַיאָן | 28.0 |
| אין גאַנצן לאַנד | 24.3 |

דעם קלענסטן פּראָצענט מאַכן ייִדן אויס אין פּוילישן ראַיאָן, דעם העכסטן
אין װײַסרוסישן, אין דעם עקאָנאָמיש אָפּגעשטאַנענסטן. אויב זאָל מען ניט
נעמען אין באַטראַכט דעם פּוילישן סובראַיאָן ב, װו עס זײַנען פֿאַראַן װייניק
ייִדן, האָט דער פּוילישער ראַיאָן אין די שטעט אַ ביסל מער ייִדן װי דער
אוקראַיִנישער — 28.7 לגבי 28.0 פּראָצענט. אין אוקראַיִנישן ראַיאָן איז פֿאַראַן
איין װאָיעװואָדשאַפֿט, װו ייִדן מאַכן אויס אַ רעלאַטיװע מערהייט — דאָס איז
די װאָלינער װאָיעװואָדשאַפֿט — 48.6 פּראָצענט ייִדיש־רײדערס אין די שטעט.

די פּויליש־רײדערס זײַנען דאָס רוב פֿון דער באַפֿעלקערונג אין די שטעט
פֿון אַלע ראַיאָנען:

אין פּוילישן ראַיאָן ————————— 74.6

אין ווײַסרוסישן ראַיאָן ————————— 52.9

אין אוקראַיִנישן ראַיאָן ————————— 52.7

אין גאַנצן לאַנד ————————— 68.3

אַײַנגעטיילט נאָך אונדזערע ראַיאָנען, דערגרייכן די פּויליש־ריידערס דעם מאַקסימום אין פּוילישן סובראַיאָן ב און זעוען דער מינימום לגבי די אַנדערע ראַיאָנען אין דעם ווײַסרוסישן סובראַיאָן ב. פֿון באַזונדערע ווײַעוואָדשאַפֿטן איז דער מאַקסימום פּויליש־ריידערס אין פּויזענער — 94.0 פּראָצענט, דער מינימום אין וואָלינער — 27.5 פּראָצענט.

די טעריטאָריעלע נאַציאָנאַלע מיעוטים, די ווײַסרוסן און די אוקראַיִנער, האָבן אין זייערע אייגענע ראַיאָנען נאָר אַ מיעוט אין די שטעט. אין קיין איין ראַיאָן איז ניטאָ אַ שטעטישע באַפֿעלקערונג וואָס זאָל על־פּי רובֿ רעדן ווײַסרוסיש אָדער אוקראַיִניש. די אוקראַיִנער זעוען אין אַ בעסערן מצבֿ ווי די ווײַסרוסן, זיי האָבן אין זייער אייגענעם ראַיאָן 17.3 פּראָצענט אוקראַיִניש־ריידערס אין די שטעט. דעם העכסטן פּראָצענט גרייכן זיי אין סטאַניסלאַווער ווײַעוואָדשאַפֿט, אָבער אַפֿילו דאָרטן זעוען זיי אַפֿילו ניט קיין דריטל פֿון דער שטאַטישער באַפֿעלקערונג. אין אַט דער אוקראַיִנישסטער ווײַעוואָדשאַפֿט האָבן זיי נאָר 29.7 פֿון דער שטאַטישער אײַנוווינערשאַפֿט נאָך דער שפּראַך נאָך. די ווײַסרוסן זעוען נאָך אין אַן ערגערן מצבֿ און זעוען נאָך שוואַכער פֿאָר־געשטעלט אין די שטעט פֿון זייער ראַיאָן. די אָפֿיציעלע סטאַטיסטיק גיט זיי סך־הכּל 3.4 פּראָצענט אין גאַנצן ראַיאָן און אַפֿילו אין דער ווײַסרוסישסטער, דער נאָוואַרעדקער, ווײַעוואָדשאַפֿט ניט מער ווי 11.4 פּראָצענט.

מיר האָבן פֿון דער זעלביקער פֿאָלקסצײַלונג די דאַטעס לויט דער רעליגיע. דאָס גיט אונדז אַ מיגלעכקייט צו פֿאַרגלײַכן ביידע צאָלן, ווי מיר וועלן דאָס באַלד טאָן בנוגע ייִדן און ניט־ייִדן. אַזוי ווי מיר האַלטן דאָ בײַ די אוקראַיִנער, לאָמיר דערוויַל זען, אַז אין זייער ראַיאָן זעוען געווען אין די שטעט 39.1 קאַטויליקן און 52.7 פּויליש־ריידערס. אַזוי ווי אַלע פּאָליאַקן כּמעט זעוען קאַטוילינקן און חוץ זיי, קען מען אָננעמען, זעוען קיין אַנדערע קאַטוילינקן ניטאָ אין די שטעט פֿון אוקראַיִנישן ראַיאָן, הייסט עס, אַז 13.6 פּראָצענט פֿון די שטאַטישע אײַנוווינערס רעדן דאָרטן פּויליש, הגם זיי זעוען ניט קיין פּאָליאַקן. דאָס זעוען ייִדן, אָבער אויך ניט ווייניק אוקראַיִנער. אין דעם אוקראַיִנישן ראַיאָן זעוען געווען ייִדן אין די שטעט:

לויט רעליגיע ————————— 23.5

לויט שפּראַך ————————— 17.3

דער אונטערשייד איז דאָ 6.2 — דאָס איז דער פּראָצענט ייִדן (לגבי דער גאַנצער באַפֿעלקערונג) וואָס זעוען דאָרטן שפּראַכלעך אַסימילירט. אָבער דאָס איז נאָך אַלין דער קלענערער טייל פֿון די 13.6 פּראָצענט שפּראַכלעך־אַסימילירטע. הייסט עס, אַז ניט אַלין ייִדן אַלין אַסימילירן זיך שפּראַכלעך אין די

שטעט. אגב האבן אין דעם אוקראַיִנישן ראַיאָן אָנגעגעבן דעם קלענסטן
פּראָצענט ייִדיש־ און העברעיִש־רײדערס אין פֿאַרגלײַך מיט די אַנדערע ראַיאָנען
(מיר נעמען ניט אין באַטראַכט דעם פּוילישן סובראַיאָן ב מיט דער קלײנער
צאָל אַמאָליקע דײַטשישע ייִדן).

גאָר אַן אַנדער בילד זעען מיר אין די אַנדערע ראַיאָנען, דער פּראָצענט
ייִדן האָט באַטראָפֿן:

אונטערשייד	לויט שפּראַך	לויט רעליגיע	ראַיאָן
2.2	28.7	30.9	פּוילישער סובראַיאָן א
0.6	37.4	38.0	װײַסרוסישער ראַיאָן

אין װײַסרוסישן ראַיאָן איז פֿאַראַן די קלענסטע שפּראַך־אַסימילאַציע
בײַ ייִדן און אַפֿילו אין פּוילישן סובראַיאָן א איז זי אָפֿיציעל ניט גרויס. מיר
װעלן װײַטער זיך אָפּשטעלן אויף דעם זינען פֿון אָט די צאָלן.

אַזוי װי מען האָט ניט פֿאַרעפֿנטלעכט די רעזולטאַטן פֿון דער שפּראַך־
סטאַטיסטיק אין 1921, איז ניטאָ קיין גרינגער און זיכערער יסוד צו פֿאַרגלײַכן
די דאַטעס מיט אַ צאָל פֿון אַ פֿריִערדיקן צײַטפּונקט כּדי אויסצוגעפֿינען די ריכ־
טונג, אין װעלכער עס גייט די אַנטװיקלונג אין פֿרט שפּראַך־אַסימילאַציע. מיר
פֿאַרמאָגן דאַטעס װעגן דער שפּראַך בײַ ייִדן נאָר פֿון די אַמאָליקע טיילן פֿון
רוסלאַנד, אָבער פֿון אַ פֿאָלקסצײַלונג װאָס איז װײַט אָפּגערוקט אין צײַט
(פֿון 1897), און פֿאַרשיידענע אינעװייניקסטע װאַנדערונגען האָבן אַ היפּש ביסל
איבערגעמישט די באַפֿעלקערונג. בפֿרט נאָך אַז דאָ רעדט זיך װעגן שטעט
װאָס זײַנען במשך פֿון אַ דריטל יאָרהונדערט שטאַרק אויסגעװואַקסן. אָבער
דאָך האָבן מיר אין די דאַטעס פֿון 1897 אָן אַנשפּאַר צו קענען דערזען אַ טענדענץ
און אַ באַזיס פֿאַר אַ פֿאַרגלײַך. װאָס איז שייך די טיילן װאָס האָבן געהערט
צו עסטרײַך איז די מיגלעכקייט פֿון פֿאַרגלײַכן אַ קלענערע. אין עסטרײַך האָט
מען בײַ דער פֿאָלקסצײַלונג פֿון 1910 ניט אָנערקענט די ייִדישע שפּראַך און
מען האָט קיין מאָל ניט פֿאַרעפֿנטלעכט װיפֿל ייִדן אין גאַליציע אָנגעגעבן
דעמאָנסטראַטיװ, אַז זיי רעדן ייִדיש. בכן קענען מיר װײַטער מאַכן דעם פֿאַר־
גלײַך נאָר פֿאַר די געװעזענע טיילן פֿון צאַרישן רוסלאַנד, אַקעגנשטעלנדיק
דאַטעס פֿון 1897 און 1931.

3

ביז גאָר אינטערעסאַנט איז זיך צו אָריענטירן, װי איז געגאַנגען די
אַנטװיקלונג פֿון נאַציאַנאַלן באַװוּסטזײַן בײַ ייִדן אין אומאָפּהענגיקן פּוילן. דאָס
אָנװײַזן די נאַציאַנאַלע שפּראַך איז געװיס אַ מאַניפֿעסטאַציע פֿון נאַציאַנאַלן
באַװוּסטזײַן. מיר מיינען דעריבער, אַז עס איז אַבסאָלוט קאָרעקט צו פֿאַר־
גלײַכן די צאָל ייִדן װאָס האָבן אין דער פֿאָלקסצײַלונג פֿון 1921 אָנגעװיזן, אַז
זיי געהערן צום ייִדישן פֿאָלק, מיט דער צאָל ייִדן װאָס האָבן צען יאָר שפּעטער
אָנגעװיזן אויף אַיינער פֿון אונדזערע שפּראַכן, אויף ייִדיש אָדער אויף העב־
רעיִש, װי אויך זייער מוטערשפּראַך. אַזאַ פֿאַרגלײַך קען אפֿשר ניט אויפֿװײַזן

די טענדענץ אין דער שפּראַך־אַסימילאַציע, אָבער ער קען בולט דעמאָנסטרירן
דאָס אַנטוויקלען זיך אָדער דאָס אַינשרומפּן פֿון דעם נאַציאָנאַלן באַוווסטזײַן.
לאָמיר געדענקען, אַז אין 1931 האָבן אַלע יידישע פּאַרטייען געפֿירט אַ גרויסע
אַגיטאַציע, אַז מען זאָל בײַ דער פֿאָלקסצײַלונג אָנווײַזן אַ יידישע מוטערשפּראַך
און מאַניפֿעסטירן אויף אַזאַ אופֿן די צוגעהעריקייט צום יידישן פֿאָלק. לאָמיר
זשע אַ קוק טאָן, ווי אַזוי דאָס יידישע נאַציאָנאַלע באַוווסטזײַן איז מאַני־
פֿעסטירט געוואָרן:

פּראָצענט לגבי רעליגיע	יידן לויט נאַצ׳ צוגעהע׳ ריקייט אָדער לויט שפּראַך	יידן לויט רעליגיע	יאָר
74.2	2,110,448	2,845,364	1921
87.8	2,732,573	3,113,933	1931

טאַבעלע 1

די באַפֿעלקערונג אין פּוילן אין 1931 לויט מוטערשפּראַך (אין טויזנטער)

%	ווײַס־ רוסיש	%	אוקראַי׳ניש	%	פּויליש	%	סך־הכּל	ראַיאָן
0.0	2.6	1.0	138.8	85.4	11,967.1	100	14,031.5	פּוילישער ראַיאָן א
0.0	0.5	0.0	1.4	90.8	4,071.4	100	4,481.6	פּוילישער ראַיאָן ב
0.0	3.1	0.7	140.2	86.6	16,058.5	100	18,513.1	פּוילישער סך־הכּל
17.0	495.3	0.2	5.0	66.5	1,944.0	100	2,919.9	ווײַסרוסישער ראַיאָן א
22.3	488.9	2.5	55.2	32.9	718.0	100	2,189.1	ווײַסרוסישער ראַיאָן ב
19.2	984.2	1.2	60.2	52.1	2,662.0	100	5,109.0	ווײַסרוסישער סך־הכּל
0.03	2.6	51.1	4,241.2	39.4	3,272.9	100	8,293.7	אוקראַי׳נישער סך־הכּל
3.0	989.9	14.0	4,441.6	68.8	21,993.4	100	31,915.8	אַלגעמ׳נער סך־הכּל

%	אַנדערע	%	יִדיש־ העברעַיִש	%	דײַטש	%	רוסיש	ראַיאָן
0.2	27.7	11.4	1,600.2	1.9	263.5	0.1	11.6	פּוילישער ראַיאָן א
0.1	6.2	0.3	11.8	8.8	389.1	0.0	1.2	פּוילישער ראַיאָן ב
0.3	33.9	8.7	1,612.0	3.6	652.6	0.1	12.8	פּוילישער סך־הכּל
2.9	84.7	10.4	303.9	0.3	8.6	2.7	78.4	ווײַסרוסישער ראַיאָן א
32.5	*712.6	6.7	190.0	0.1	1.4	1.0	23.0	ווײַסרוסישער ראַיאָן ב
15.7	797.3	9.6	493.9	0.3	10.0	1.9	101.4	ווײַסרוסישער סך־הכּל
0.7	47.4	7.6	626.7	0.9	78.4	0.3	24.5	אוקראַי׳נישער סך־הכּל
2.7	878.6	8.7	2,732.6	2.4	741.0	0.4	138.7	אַלגעמ׳נער סך־הכּל

* 707.1 = „היגע" שפּראַך.

טאַבעלע 2

די שטאַטישע באַפעלקערונג אין פוילן אין 1931 לויט מוטערשפּראַך (אין טויזנטער)

אַנדערע*	ייִדיש העברעיִש	וו״צם רוסיש	אוקראַיניש	פּויליש	סך־הכל	וואָיעוואָדשאַפט
				פּוילישער ראַיאָן א		
10.5	333.3	0.6	1.3	825.2	1,171.9	וואַרשע־שטאָט
6.1	170.7	0.1	0.2	405.4	582.5	וואַרשעווער
83.1	329.0	0.1	0.5	691.5	1,104.2	לאָדזער
2.6	219.6	0.0	0.3	527.5	750.0	קעלצער
1.9	162.6	0.1	1.1	268.0	433.7	לובלינער
6.6	111.4	0.0	2.1	459.5	579.8	קראָקעמער
110.8	1,326.6	0.9	5.5	3,178.1	4,621.9	סך־הכל
				פּוילישער ראַיאָן ב		
46.1	3.2	0.2	0.7	788.2	838.4	פּויזנער
24.4	1.7	0.2	0.2	321.8	348.3	פּאָמערנער
54.7	5.9	0.0	0.2	357.6	418.4	שלעזיע
125.2	10.8	0.4	1.1	1,467.6	1,605.1	סך־הכל
236.0	1,337.4	1.3	6.6	4,645.7	6,227.0	פּוילישער סך־הכל
				ווײַסרוסישער ראַיאָן א		
14.0	150.4	5.9	0.5	225.3	396.1	ביאַליסטאָקער
13.1	75.6	7.8	0.3	164.5	261.3	ווילנער
27.1	226.0	13.7	0.8	389.8	657.4	סך־הכל
				ווײַסרוסישער ראַיאָן ב		
2.8	41.3	11.8	0.2	46.6	102.7	נאָוואָרעדקער
25.6	72.7	5.6	0.8	44.1	148.8	פּאָלעסיער
28.4	114.0	17.4	1.0	90.7	251.5	סך־הכל
55.5	340.0	31.1	1.8	480.5	908.9	ווײַסרוסישער סך־הכל
				אוקראַינישער ראַיאָן		
5.7	183.9	0.1	93.9	492.1	775.7	לעמבערגער
6.1	80.9	0.0	87.6	120.6	295.2	סטאַניסלאָווער
0.6	59.6	0.0	53.1	158.5	271.8	טאַרנאָפּאָלער
18.9	122.8	0.3	41.0	69.5	252.5	וואָלינער
31.3	447.2	0.4	275.6	840.7	1,595.2	אוקראַינישער סך־הכל
322.8	2,124.6	32.8	284.0	5,966.9	8,731.1	אַלגעמײנער סך־הכל

*אײַנגערעכנט רוסיש, דײַטש, ליטוויש, טשעכיש, „היגע״ שפּראַך (פּאָלעסיע).

טאבעלע 3

די שטאטיסטישע באפעלקערונג אין פוילן אין 1931 לויט מוטערשפראך

(אין פּראצענטער)

אנדערע*	ייִדיש־העברעאיש	ווײַס־רוסיש	אוקראיניש	פּויליש	סך־הכל	וואוינשאפט
			פּוילישער ראיאן א			
0.9	28.5	0.0	0.1	70.5	100.0	וואַרשע־שטאט
1.1	29.3	0.0	0.0	69.6	100.0	וואַרשעווער
7.6	29.8	0.0	0.0	62.6	100.0	לאדזשער
0.4	29.3	0.0	0.0	70.3	100.0	קעלצער
0.5	37.5	0.0	0.2	61.8	100.0	לובלינער
1.1	19.2	0.0	0.4	79.3	100.0	קראקעווער
2.4	28.7	0.0	0.1	68.8	100.0	סך־הכל
			פּוילישער ראיאן ב			
5.5	0.4	0.0	0.1	94.0	100.0	פּויזנער
7.0	0.5	0.0	0.1	92.4	100.0	פּאמערנער
13.1	1.4	0.0	0.0	85.5	100.0	שלעזיע
7.8	0.7	0.0	0.1	91.4	100.0	סך־הכל
3.8	21.5	0.0	0.1	74.6	100.0	פּוילישער סך־הכל
			ווײַסרוסישער ראיאן א			
3.5	38.0	1.5	0.1	56.9	100.0	ביאליסטאקער
5.0	28.9	3.0	0.1	63.0	100.0	ווילנער
4.1	34.4	2.1	0.1	59.3	100.0	סך־הכל
			ווײַסרוסישער ראיאן ב			
2.7	40.3	11.4	0.2	45.4	100.0	נאוואַרעדקער
17.3	48.8	3.7	0.5	29.7	100.0	פּאלעסיער
11.3	45.4	6.8	0.4	36.1	100.0	סך־הכל
6.1	37.4	3.4	0.2	52.9	100.0	ווײַסרוסישער סך־הכל
			אוקראינישער ראיאן			
0.7	23.7	0.0	12.1	63.5	100.0	לעמבערגער
2.1	27.4	0.0	29.7	40.8	100.0	סטאניסלאווער
0.2	21.9	0.0	19.6	58.3	100.0	טארנאפּאלער
7.5	48.6	0.1	16.3	27.5	100.0	וואלינער
2.0	28.0	0.0	17.3	52.7	100.0	אוקראינישער סך־הכל
3.7	24.3	0.4	3.3	68.3	100.0	אלגעמיינער סך־הכל

*אריינגערעכנט רוסיש, דײַטש, ליטוויש, טשעכיש, "היגע" שפּראך
(פּאלעסיע).

טאבעלע 4

די יידישע באפעלקערונג אין פוילן אין 1931 לויט מוטערשפראך

%	אנדערע	%	העברעיִש	%	יידיש	סך־הכל	וואָיעוואָדשאַפֿט
					פוילישער ראיאָן א		
5.5	19,305	5.6	19,743	88.9	313,611	352,659	וואַרשע־שטאָט
1.9	4,076	6.8	14,891	91.3	200,157	219,124	וואַרשעווער
5.0	19,060	6.1	23,241	88.9	336,194	378,495	לאָדזשער
3.8	12,136	3.7	11,715	92.5	293,169	317,020	קעלצער
17.4	54,803	4.3	13,527	78.3	246,010	314,340	לובלינער
26.2	45,573	17.4	30,232	56.4	97,813	173,618	קראָקעווער
8.9	154,953	6.5	113,349	84.6	1,486,954	1,755,256	סך־הכל
					פוילישער ראיאָן ב		
54.4	3,920	5.0	362	40.6	2,929	7,211	פוידזענער
43.0	1,482	4.1	143	52.9	1,822	3,447	פאָמערנער
65.9	12,471	5.7	1,082	26.4	5,365	18,938	שלעזיע
60.4	17,873	5.3	1,587	34.3	10,136	29,596	סך־הכל
9.7	172,826	6.4	114,936	83.9	1,497,090	1,784,852	פוילישער סך־הכל
					מיזרח־מיטעלער ראיאָן א		
1.2	2,430	11.5	22,771	87.3	172,164	197,365	ביאליסטאָקער
1.8	1,968	12.3	13,649	85.9	95,179	110,796	ווילנער
1.4	4,398	11.8	36,420	86.8	267,343	308,161	סך־הכל
					מיזרח־מיטעלער ראיאָן ב		
7.1	5,847	8.7	7,243	84.2	69,782	82,872	נאָוואָרעדקער
0.9	1,022	14.4	16,452	84.7	96,514	113,988	פאָלעסיער
3.5	6,869	12.0	23,695	84.5	166,296	196,860	סך־הכל
2.2	11,267	11.9	60,115	85.9	433,639	505,021	מיזרח־מיטעלער סך־הכל
					אוקראַיִנישער ראיאָן		
32.0	109,467	6.4	21,936	61.6	211,002	342,405	לעמבערגער
21.7	30,368	5.8	8,122	72.5	101,256	139,746	סטאַניסלאָווער
41.1	55,185	5.2	7,042	53.7	71,890	134,117	טאַרנאָפאָלער
1.1	2,247	15.1	31,388	83.8	174,157	207,792	וואָלינער
23.9	197,267	8.3	68,488	67.8	558,305	824,060	אוקראַיִנישער סך־הכל
12.2	381,360	7.9	243,539	79.9	2,489,034	3,113,933	אלגעמיינער סך־הכל

טאבעלע 5

די יידישע באפעלקערונג אין 12 פוילישע שטעט אין 1931 לויט מוטערשפראך

%	אנדערע	%	העברעיִש	%	יידיש	סך־הכל	שטאָט
5.5	19,305	5.6	19,743	88.9	313,611	352,659	וואַרשע
5.3	10,777	7.1	14,291	87.6	177,429	202,497	לאָדזש
24.4	24,279	7.8	7,796	67.8	67,520	99,595	לעמבערג
18.9	10,687	39.8	22,488	41.3	23,340	56,515	קראָקע
0.7	410	12.9	7,073	86.4	47,525	55,006	ווילנע
2.4	936	3.7	1,452	93.9	36,549	38,937	לובלין
5.4	1,370	1.4	366	93.2	23,852	25,588	טשענסטאָכאָוו
7.8	1,613	4.2	878	88.0	18,314	20,805	סאָסנאָוויצע
72.4	4,139	3.3	189	24.3	1,388	5,716	קאַטאָוויץ
59.2	1,663	6.4	182	34.4	966	2,811	כאָזשוח
45.4	887	4.2	83	50.4	984	1,954	פוזנ

טאַבעלע 6
די שטאַטישע און דאָרפֿישע ייִדישע באַפֿעלקערונג אין פּוילן אין 1931
לויט מוטערשפּראַך

%	אַנדערע	%	העברעיִש	%	ייִד	סך־הכל	שטאם און דערפֿער
12.2	361,360	7.9	243,539	79.9	2,489,034	3,113,933	פּוילן בכלל
10.7	255,464	8.5	202,481	80.8	1,922,130	2,380,075	סך־הכל שטעט וויניקער וי
13.1	121,940	8.5	79,215	78.4	723,697	929,852	20,000 ביז 20,000
9.6	56,014	8.4	49,266	82.0	481,168	586,448	100,000 איבער
8.9	76,846	8.6	74,664	82.5	712,265	863,775	100,000
17.2	125,896	5.6	41,058	77.2	566,904	733,858	דערפֿער

דער אונטערשייד צווישן דעם פּראָצענט לגבי רעליגיע — 13.6 — ווײַזט
אונדז דעם וווּקס פֿון ייִדישן נאַציאָנאַלן באַוווּסטזײַן. אַגבֿ ווערט דאָ אויך דער־
מאָנסטרירט דער פּראָטעסט קעגן דער פּוילישער רעגירונג וואָס האָט ניט
אַרײַנגענומען אין דעם פֿרעגבויגן פֿון 1931 קיין פֿראַגע וועגן דער נאַציאָנאַ־
לער צוגעהעריקייט.

עס איז אוממיגלעך זיך פֿאָרצושטעלן אַ ייִדן וואָס האַלט זיך סוביעקטיוו
פֿאַר אַ צוגעהעריקן צום פּוילישן פֿאָלק און זאָל דערבײַ אָנגעבן ייִדיש אָדער
העברעיִש פֿאַר זײַן מוטערשפּראַך. עס איז אָבער בלתי ספֿק מיגלעך, אַז אַ ייִד
זאָל אָנגעבן זײַן מוטערשפּראַך פּויליש (אָדער אַן אַנדער שפּראַך), וויל דאָס
שטימט טאַקע מיט דער אמתער לאַגע, און דאָך זאָל ער זיך רעכענען פֿאַר אַ
צוגעהעריקן צום ייִדישן פֿאָלק. דער העכערער פּראָצענט ייִדן (לויט דער
מוטערשפּראַך) אין פֿאַרגלײַך צו רעליגיע אין 1931 קען דעריבער אויסגעטײַטשט
ווערן בלויז ווי אַ מאַניפֿעסטאַציע פֿון וווּקס פֿון נאַציאָנאַלן באַוווּסטזײַן, וואָרעם
עס איז דאָך במשך פֿון די צען יאָר צווישן די ביידע פֿאָלקסציילונגען ניט
פֿאָרגעקומען קיין צוריקגאַנג אין דער שפּראַך־אַסימילאַציע, ווען מען זאָל
האָבן אין זינען דאָס גאַנצע לאַנד. די מאַניפֿעסטאַציע פֿון נאַציאָנאַלן בא־
וווּסטזײַן חזרט זיך איבער אין אַלע וואָיעוואָדשאַפֿטן און זי איז אין אַזאַ
פֿאַרנעם, אַז דער כאַראַקטער פֿון אַ בכיוונדיקן אַרויסווײַז כּלפֿי חוץ קען ניט
פֿאַרלייקנט ווערן. די פּרטים גיבן די טאַבעלעס 4 און 5.

איצט לאָמיר נעמען פֿון אײן זײַט צווײ צוויי בײַשפּילן, פֿאַר וועלכע מיר האָבן
נאָך די דאַטעס פֿון 1897 און פֿון דער אַנדער זײַט באַזונדער אויסטיילן די
וואָיעוואָדשאַפֿטן פֿון גאַליציע, כּדי אָנזעעוודיק צו מאַכן דעם דעמאָנסטרא־
טיוון כאַראַקטער פֿון די צאָלן וועגן דער שפּראַך אין 1931:

1) אין דער שטאָט וואַרשע האָבן אין 1897 אָנגעגעבן ייִדיש ווי זייער
מוטערשפּראַך 86.8 פֿון אַלע ייִדן; אין 1921 האָבן דאָרטן אָנגעוויזן זייער צו־
געהעריקייט צום ייִדישן פֿאָלק 81.4 פּראָצענט פֿון אַלע ייִדן. עס איז פֿאַר־
שטענדלעך, ווען מען איז באַקאַנט מיט דער ייִדישער געזעלשאַפֿט, אַז דער

פּראָצענט ייִדן װאָס גיבן אָן ייִדיש װי זייער שפּראַך זאָל זײַן קלענער פֿאַרן
פּראָצענט ייִדן װאָס װײַזן אָן זייער צוגעהעריקײט צום ייִדישן פֿאָלק. עס זײַנען
דאָך פֿאַראַן שפּראַכלעך־אַסימילירטע ייִדן װאָס װעלן בשום אופֿן ניט צוגעבן,
אַז דאָס מינערט װיפֿל ניט איז אין זייער נאַציאָנאַלער צוגעהעריקײט צום
ייִדישן פֿאָלק. װאָס זשע װײַזן אָבער די דאַטעס פֿון 1931 ? אין װאַרשע האָבן
אָנגעגעבן ייִדיש װי זייער שפּראַך 88.9 פּראָצענט ייִדן, דאָס הייסט נאָך מער
װי מיט אַ דריטל יאָרהונדערט צוריק; העברעיִש האָבן אָנגעגעבן 5.8 פּראָ־
צענט, אין איינעם בײדע שפּראַכן — 94.7 פּראָצענט פֿון אַלע װאַרשעװער ייִדן.

(2   אין דער אַמאָליקער װילנער גובערניע זײַנען אין 1897 געװען
צװישן ייִדן 98.73 פּראָצענט װאָס האָבן אָנגעגעבן ייִדיש װי זייער מוטערשפּראַך.
אין דער װילנער װאָיעװאָדשאַפֿט האָבן אין 1921 נאָר 86.9 פּראָצענט פֿון אַלע
ייִדן אָנגעגעבן, אַז זיי געהערן צום ייִדישן פֿאָלק, און אין 1931 האָבן דאָרטן 98.2
אָנגעגעבן ייִדיש און העברעיִש װי זייער מוטערשפּראַך. אַדער די צען יאָר
פֿון פּױלישער הערשאַפֿט האָבן דאָרטן אָפּגעװישט אַלע סימנים פֿון אַסימילאַציע
צװישן 1897 און 1921, אַדער די ציפֿער װעגן שפּראַך בײַ ייִדן האָבן אױך
אַ דעמאָנסטראַטיװו־נאַציאָנאַלן װערט.

(3   די פֿיר װאָיעװאָדשאַפֿטן פֿון ג אַ ל י צ י ע מיט אַ לאָנגיאַריקער שפּראַך־
אַסימילאַציע גיבן אַזאַ בילד :

װאָיעװאָדשאַפֿט	1921 צוגעהעריקײט צום פֿאָלק	1931 ייִדיש און העברעיִש
לעמבערגער	60.8	68.0
סטאַניסלאַװער	63.3	78.3
טאַרנאָפּאָלער	43.5	58.9
קראָקעװער	50.4	73.8

אין די דאָזיקע ציפֿער װערט בלױז ספֿק דעמאָנסטרירט די רעװאָלוציע
װאָס איז פֿאָרגעקומען נ י ט אין ל ע ב ן, נאָר אין באַװוּסטזײַן פֿון די
גאַליציאַנער ייִדן. עס איז גענוג צו זען, אַז אין קראָקעװער װאָיעװאָדשאַפֿט
האָבן 30,232 ייִדן אָנגעגעבן העברעיִש פֿאַר זייער שפּראַך, װאָס דאָס מאַכט
אױס 17.4 פּראָצענט — אַ זעקסטל! דאָס איז אַזױ װײַט פֿון דער װירקלעכ־
קײט, אַז מען דאַרף ניט גיין זיך נאָכפֿרעגן בײַ די קראָקעװער ייִדן, װאָס עס
זאָגן אונדז די דאַטעס פֿון 1931.

4

87.8 פּראָצענט פֿון אַלע פּױלישע ייִדן האָבן אין 1931 אָנגעגעבן אַז זייער מו־
טערשפּראַך איז ייִדיש אָדער העברעיִש; אַז זייער שפּראַך איז ייִדיש האָבן
אָנגעװיזן 79.9 פּראָצענט און 7.9 פּראָצענט — העברעיִש. מעג מען האָבן
ספֿקות אין דעם, צי האָבן טאַקע אין פּױלן קרוב צו אַ פֿערטל מיליאָן גערעדט
העברעיִש. דער גרעסטער רוב ייִדן װאָס האָבן אָנגעװיזן, אַז זיי רעדן העברעיִש,
האָבן ניט ערגער גערעדט ייִדיש. קען מען אָננעמען די צאָל ייִדיש־ריידערס

ווי 87.8 און דעם פּראָצענט לאָמיר האָבן אין זינען שפּעטער, בײַ די פֿאַרגלײַכן
מיט 1897.

עס איז דאָך אינטערעסאַנט צו זען, ווי עס וואַקלט זיך דער פּראָצענט
העברעיִש־רײדערס. פּרטים קען מען זען פֿון די טאַבעלעס 4, 5 און 6. דאָ
שטרײַבן מיר בלויז אונטער, אַז מער פֿון 10 פּראָצענט ייִדן האָבן אַנגעוויזן
אויף העברעיִש אין פֿינף וואָיעוואָדשאַפֿטן, וואָס דרײַ זײַנען אין וווײַסרוסישן
ראַיאָן, איינע אין פּוילישן און איינע אין אוקראַיִנישן: קראַקעווער — 17.4,
וואָלינער — 15.1, פּאָלעסיער — 14.4, ווילנער — 12.3, ביאַליסטאָקער — 11.5.

ווייניקער ווי 5 פּראָצענט העברעיִש־רײדערס זײַנען געווען אין דרײַ וואָיע־
וואָדשאַפֿטן: קעלצער — 3.7, פּאָמערנער — 4.1, לובלינער — 4.3.

און איצט, אָנגעמענדיק וווײַטער דעם פּראָצענט ייִדיש־רײדערס ווי דעם
סכּום פֿון די ציפֿער פֿאַר ייִדיש און העברעיִש, לאָמיר, ווו עס לאָזט זיך, פֿאַר־
גלײַכן מיט די דאַטעס פֿון 1897. ווען מען האָט פֿאַר זיך בלויז די רעלאַטיווע
צאָלן, איז אַזאַ פֿאַרגלײַך דערלויבלעך, האָבנדיק אין זינען די באַוואָרענישן וואָס
מיר האָבן שוין אויסגערעכנט פֿריִער.

ייִדיש ווי זייער מוטערשפּראַך האָבן אָנגעוויזן אַזעלכע פּראָצענטן ייִדן:

1931 (וואָיעוואָדשאַפֿט)	1897 (גובערניע)	גובערניע אָדער וואָיעוואָדשאַפֿט
95.9	90.0	וואַרשעווער
95.0	95.9	פּיעטריקאָווער (לאָדזשער)
96.2	99.5	קעלצער
82.6	99.3	לובלינער
98.8	99.3	גראָדנער (ביאַליסטאָקער)
98.2	98.7	ווילנער
99.1	99.5	מינסקער (פּאָלעסיער)
98.9	99.7	וואָלינער

לאָמיר געדענקען, אַז די וואָיעוואָדשאַפֿטן און די גרענעצן פֿון די שײַכות־
דיקע רוסישע גובערניעס פֿאַלן ניט צונויף אין גאַנצן. אָבער די גרעסטע
שינויים זײַנען פֿאַרגעקומען בנוגע דער לובלינער וואָיעוואָדשאַפֿט, ווּהין עס
קומען אַרײַן טיילן פֿון מיזרח־גאַליציע. און אָט מיט דעם לעצטן מאָמענט
קען מען דערקלערן דעם אויסנעם אין די ביידע פּאַראַלעלע צװ̈עלכעלעך — דאָס
איינציקע אָרט, ווּ עס איז פֿאַראַן אַ גרויסער אונטערשייד צווישן די ביידע
דאַטעס און גראַד אויף א רױף, בעת אומעטום איז פֿאַראַן א מיטשװעכות צווישן
די ציפֿער און אין וואַרשעווער וואָיעוואָדשאַפֿט איז דער פּראָצענט ייִדיש־רײדערס
אין 1931 אַפֿילו גרעסער איידער אין 1897.

די דאַטעס פֿון 1897 שפּיגלען בלתּי ספֿק אָפּ די רעאַלע ווירקלעכקייט,
די צאָלן פֿון 1931 מאַניפֿעסטירן אין א גרויסער מאָס דאָס נאַציאָנאַלע באַ־
וווּסטזײַן פֿון די ייִדישע מאַסן אין אומאָפּהענגיקן פּוילן.

Student identification card for an evening school in Vilna in the mid-1920s.

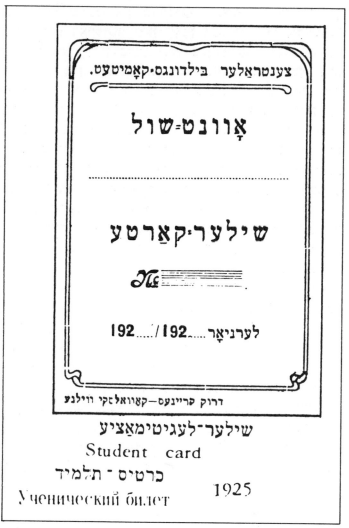

שילער-לעגיטימאַציע
Student card
כרטיס - תלמיד
Ученический билет   1925

5

וואָסערע פֿרעמדע, ניט-ייִדישע שפּראָכן האָבן געערעדט ייִדן אין פּוילן?

מיר ווענדן זיך צו דער טאַבעלע 4. מיר זעען, אַז 381,360 ייִדן, ד"ה 12.2 פּראָ־
צענט האָבן אָנגעגעבן אַ פֿרעמדע שפּראַך.

פּראָצענט פֿון אַלע פֿרעמדשפּראַכיקע ייִדן	פּראָצענט פֿון אַלע פּוילישע ייִדן	צאָל ייִדן וואָס האָבן זי אָנגעוויזן	שפּראַך
97.4	11.9	371,821	פּויליש
1.8	0.2	6,827	דײַטש
0.2	0.0	547	אוקראַיִניש
0.2	0.0	444	רוסיש
0.1	0.0	200	ווײַסרוסיש

ווען מען נעמט באַזונדער שטעט און באַזונדער דערפֿער באַקומט זיך
אַ גאַנץ אינטערעסאַנטער חילוק: דאָרפֿישע ייִדן האָבן געגעבן 17.2 פּראָצענט
שפּראַכלעך אַסימילירטע, שטאָטישע ייִדן בלויז 10.7 פּראָצענט. הייסט עס אין
דאָרף, וווּ ייִדן זײַנען ווינציקער אין צאָל און האָבן ווינציק וואָס צו טאָן מיט
אַנדערע ייִדן, ווירקט קענטיקער די אַרומיקע שפּראַך־סבֿיבֿה. די ציפֿער וועגן
די פֿאַרשיידענע טיפֿן שטעט (זען טאַבעלע 5) באַשטעטיקן, אַז וואָס געדיכטער
ייִדן לעבן, אַלץ מער בלײַבן זיי בײַ זייער שפּראַך. די טאַבעלע 6 ווײַזט אונדז,
אַז דעם גרעסטן פּראָצענט שפּראַכלעך אַסימילירטע אין די שטעט גיבן די
ייִדן וואָס ווינען אין די קלענערע פּונקטן, מיט ווינציקער פֿון צוואַנציק טויזנט
אײַנוווינערס, און די קלענסטע צאָל פֿרעמדשפּראַכיקע איז פֿאַראַן אין די גרעסטע
שטעט מיט מער פֿון הונדערט טויזנט אײַנוווינערס — 13.1 און 8.9 פּראָצענט.

בײַ דעם פּונקט איז ווידער כּדאי צו פֿאַרגלײַכן מיט דער צײלונג אין
רוסלאַנד פֿון 1897. יעמאָלט איז אויסגעקומען אַז אין די גרויסע שטעט איז
דער פּראָצענט פֿרעמדשפּראַכיקע צווישן ייִדן גרעסער ווי אין די קליינע שטעט־
לעך. אין די שטעט פֿון תּחום־המושבֿ זײַנען צווישן ייִדן געווען 3.72 פּראָ־
צענט פֿרעמדשפּראַכיקע, בעת אין די קלענערע קרײַזשטעטעט נאָר 0.44 פּראָצענט.'
מיגלעך, אַז אין 1931 האָט די אַגיטאַציע געווירקט מער אין די גרויסע שטעט,
ווי אין די קלענערע אָדער ווי אין די דערפֿער, און אין דער אמתן איז דער
פּראָצענט שפּראַכלעך אַסימילירטע אויך אין פֿיילן געווען גרעסער אין די
גרויסע שטעט. אָבער מען דאַרף אויך נעמען אין באַטראַכט, אַז אין די גרויסע
שטעט, וווּ דאָס ייִדישע געזעלשאַפֿטלעכע לעבן איז אינטענסיווער און רײַכער,
קערט זיך אום אַ געוויסער פּראָצענט קינדער, וואָס מען האָט זיי דערצויגן
אויף אַ פֿרעמדער שפּראַך, צוריק צו דער ייִדישער שפּראַך, בעת אין דאַרף
אָדער אין דער קליינער שטאָט פֿאַרבלײַבט שוין די אַסימיליר־ווירקונג פֿון
דער שול אויף תּמיד.

די פֿרעמדשפּראַכיקייט בײַ ייִדן לויט ראַיאָנען אילוסטרירט די טאַבעלע
4. לויט די ראַיאָנען איז דאָס בילד אַזאָ:

אין פּוילישן ראַיאָן   —   7.9 פּראָצענט

אין ווײַסרוסישן ראַיאָן —   2.2   „

אין אוקראַינישן ראַיאָן —   23.9   „

אָבער דאָ קומט אונדז זייער צו ניק אונדזער אױטיילן אויף סובראַיאָנען,
וווּ עס קומט צום אויסדרוק דער עובֿר פֿון די באַזונדערע ראַיאָנען. דאָ דאַרף
מען אויך ערטערווײַז נעמען יעדער וואָיעוואָדשאַפֿט באַזונדער. אין פּוילישן
סובראַיאָן א, מיט אַ דורכשניט פֿון נאָר 8.9 פֿרעמדשפּראַכיקע בײַ ייִדן, טיילט
זיך גלײַך אויס די קראַקעווער וואָיעוואָדשאַפֿט וואָס האָט אַ מאָל געהערט צו
עסטרײַך און וווּ די פֿרעמדשפּראַכיקייט דערגרייכט 26.2 פּראָצענט. אין אוק־

'Б. Д. Бруцкус, С т а т и с т и к а   Е в р е й с к а г о   н а с е -
л е н і я , С.-Петербург, 1909, таблица 5.

ראַיאָנישן ראַיאָן, מיטן הויכן פּראָצענט פֿון 23.9 פֿרעמדשפּראַכיקע, טיילט זיך
אויס די וואָלינער וואָיעוואָדשאַפֿט מיט קוים 1.1 פּראָצענט פֿרעמדשפּראַכיקע
ייִדן, וואָרעם וואָלין האָט געהערט צו רוסלאַנד. אין די ראַיאָנען פֿון אַמאָליקן
רוסלאַנד איז די פֿרעמדשפּראַכיקייט רעלאַטיוו די קלענסטע. דערפֿון בעט זיך דער אויס־
פֿיר, אַז די גרעסטע ווירקונג אויף שפּראַך־אַסימילאַציע האָט די פֿרעמדשפּראַ־
כיקע שול, ווי דאָס ווייזן די דאַטעס פֿון די ראַיאָנען וואָס האָבן געהערט אַ מאָל
צו עסטרייַך און צו דייטשלאַנד. אין די אַמאָליקע דייטשע ראַיאָנען, אין אונדזער
פּוילישן סובראַיאָן ב, האָבן ייִדן גערעדט דייטש, און אויב עס וואָלט ניט געווען
אַהין קיין צושטראָם פֿון פּוילישע ייִדן פֿון אַנדערע ראַיאָנען, וואָלט דאָרטן
דער פּראָצענט פֿרעמדשפּראַכיקע געווען נאָך העכער. דער העכסטער פּראָצענט
פֿרעמדשפּראַכיקע אין אוקראַיִנישן ראַיאָן איז אין טאַרנאָפּאָלער וואָיעוואָדשאַפֿט
— 41.1. אין ווײַסרוסישן ראַיאָן ווייזט אַ מאָדנע הויכע פּראָצענט פֿרעמד־
שפּראַכיקע די אָפּגעשטאַנענע נאָוואַרעדקער וואָיעוואָדשאַפֿט. זאָל מען דאָס
דערקלערן מיט דעם, אַז דאָרטן איז די אַגיטאַציע בײַ דער פֿאָלקסציילונג
געווען זייער אָרגאַניזירט? אָדער צייַלערס האָבן דאָרטן געקענט פֿאַרשרייַבן
וואָס זיי ווילן?

ווען מיר ווענדן זיך צו דער טאַבעלע 5, האָבן מיר דאָס בילד פֿון די
עלף גרעסטע שטעט אין פּוילן. דאָ שפּיגלט זיך אויך בולט אָפּ דער עבֿר פֿון
דער שטאָט. די דאַטעס וועגן לובלין באַשטעטיקן דאָס וואָס מיר האָבן שוין
אָנגעוויזן וועגן דער לובלינער וואָיעוואָדשאַפֿט, ווו מען האָט אַרײַנגענומען
פּאָוויאַטן פֿון מיזרח־גאַליציע. אין לובלין גופֿא דערגרייכט די צאָל ייִדיש־ און
העברעיִש־רעדערס ביז 96.3 פּראָצענט.

פֿון די עלף שטעט זײַנען זעקס פֿון אַמאָליקן רוסלאַנד און זיי גיבן
אַלע העכער 90 פּראָצענט ייִדיש־ און העברעיִש־רעדערס. דעם העכסטן פּראָ־
צענט גיט ווילנע — 99.3, דעם נידעריקסטן סאָסנאָוועץ — 92.2 פּראָצענט.
צוויי שטעט זײַנען פֿון אַמאָליקן עסטרייַך — קראָקע און לעמבערג. גיט קראָקע
39.8 פּראָצענט העברעיִש־רעדערס און אין איינעם מיט די ייִדיש־רעדערס 81.1
פּראָצענט (דאָ האָבן מיר אַגבֿ ווידער אַ באַווײַז, סאַראַ גרויסע ראָלע עס האָט
געשפּילט די נאַציאָנאַלע אַגיטאַציע בײַ אַט דער פֿאָלקסציילונג) און אין לעם־
בערג זײַנען געווען מער ייִדיש־רעדערס — 67.8 פּראָצענט, אָבער אַ סך ווינ־
ציקער העברעיִש־רעדערס און דער אַלגעמיינער סכום נאָר 75.6 פּראָצענט.
דרײַ שטעט פֿון די עלף האָבן געהערט צו דייטשלאַנד, און דאָרטן זײַנען פֿאַראַן
די קלענסטע פּראָצענטן פֿאַר די אייגענע שפּראַכן און די גרעסטע פֿאַר די
פֿרעמדע. פּויזן האָט 54.6 ייִדיש־ און העברעיִש־רעדערס, קאַטשווואָ — 40.8 און
אויפֿן נידעריקסטן שטאַפּל איז קאַטאָוויץ מיט בלויז 27.6 פּראָצענט. אַגבֿ זײַנען
דאָס שטעט מיט אַ קלינער צאָל ייִדישע אײַנוווינערס. ייִדיש אָדער העברעיִש
האָבן דאָרט אָנגעגעבן ייִדן, צוגעקומענע פֿון אַנדערע טיילן פּוילן. די רעשטלעך
דייטשע ייִדן האָבן אָנגעגעבן זייער דייטשע מוטערשפּראַך.

„20 יאָר קופּערשטיין־שול", יובל־זאַמלבוך

"Twenty   Years   of   the   Cooperstein
School'' – Jubilee Publication

„20 שנה לבית־ספר קופרשטיין" — פּנקס יובל

„20 лет школы им. Куперштейн"
— юбилейный сборник   1934

Twentieth anniversary of the Cooperstein School, originally founded (1912) as a Russian language
elementary school, and then, after the establishment of an independent Lithuania, reorganized (1920) into
a Yiddish elementary school.

לעבעדיקער אונטערגאַנג. אַ לשון אויף תּמיד, נישט אויף דערווײַל

יעקבֿ גלאַטשטיין

SUMMARY: LIVELY DEATH/A LANGUAGE FOR ALWAYS, NOT JUST
FOR A WHILE BY YANKEV GLATSHTEYN

*A major modernistic poet (1896–1971) comments on the grace, beauty, subtlety
and wisdom of Yiddish even as it seems destined to disappear. Jews seem to have
conceived of it as temporary rather than as eternal and to have begun doing so, as
if that were a natural process, when it was still hale and hearty.*

באַקלאָגט זיך פֿאַר מיר אַן אינטעליגענטער ייד, וואָס איז נאָך אין
די מיטעלע יאָרן, אַז ער מוז אויפֿהערן קומען צו ייִדישע פֿאַרזאַמ־
לונגען. די זאַך איז אַזוי, אין ער מיר מסביר:

בײַ די מײַסטע ייִדישע אַסיפֿות הערט מען שוין נישט קיין ייִדיש
וואָרט. סײַ ציוניסטן, וואָס זענען יאָ מסכים מיט בן־גוריונען, סײַ די,
וואָס קריגן קעגן אים, גיבן צו, אַז דער מקיים־געוואָרענער ציוניזם לעבט
דורך אַ שטאַרקן קריזיס. פֿונדעסטוועגן פֿאַלט זיי נישט אײַן צו רעדן
שטע פֿון שטויסל, אָבער ער, דער טאַטע אָדער זיידע, האָט זיין אייגענעם
המשך, אָפּגעזוגן פֿון דער קײַטלדיקער אייביקייט.

דערלאַנגט מען אים דעם גאַנצן פֿינצטערן אונטערגאַנג אויף אַ
טעלער און מען אַמוזירט אים נאָך דערמיט.

האָט אַזאַ ייד ממש נישט וואו צו גיין — רעדט ווייטער מיט האַרץ
דער אינטעליגענטער טענות־האַבער. זאָל ער גיין צו די פֿאַרזאַמלונגען,
וואו ער ווייסט זיכער, אַז מען וועט נישט הערן קיין ייִדיש וואָרט, אָדער
זאָל ער גיין צו די אַנדערע, וואו מען וועט רעדן לעצט־ייִדיש, וואו מען
וועט הערן קלאָג־און־אונטערגאַנג ייִדיש און וואו מ׳וועט וואַרפֿן אַ מרה־
שחורה אויף אַלע פֿאַרזאַמלטע, בײַ וועמען ייִדיש איז נאָך אַלץ אַ לעבע־
דיקער ענין, בעסער געזאָגט, אַן ענין צום לעבן און נישט צום אונטערגיין?
אַז איך וויל נישט ראָק פֿאַרזאָרגן מײַנע קינדער און קינדסקינדער.

איך בין אויך אַ שטיקל מענטש און איך וויל נישט כסדר אונטערגײן.
בקיצור, וואָס רײסט מען מיר דאָס לעבעדיקע וואָרט פֿון מויל? —
שרייט אויס מיט מיט היץ דער ייד, וואָס איז זיך מתרעם אויף ייִדישע אַסי־
פֿות. „ווען וועט מען מיך אויפֿהערן רודפֿן מיט אונטערגאַנג?"

און איר דאַרפֿט זען מיט וואָס פֿאַר אַ גלאַטע ייִדישע צונגען מען
רעדט וועגן ייִדיש־אונטערגאַנג! ניט נאָר ווייל מען אונטערהאַלטן דעם
עולם, נאָר מען זעט, אַז די אונטערגאַנג־נביאים האָבן דעם אמתן „גוד־
טאַים". זיי אַליין זיינען העכסט אַמוזירט. מען דערקענט עס אין דעם עקס־
טאַז, אין דעם פּאַטאָס זייערן, אין די שיינע ייִדישע ווערטער, ווי זיי
שילדערן דעם אונטערגאַנג פֿון זייער לשון. ס'איז אַ דעמאָנסטראַציע פֿון
וואונדן־קראַצעניש. דער רעדנער קראַצט זיך די וואונדן און ער האָט
הנאה, וואָס אים געלינגט צו שאַפֿן אין גאַנצן זאַל אַן אַרגיע פֿון גסיסה
און אונטערגאַנג. אַלע ווערן איבערצייגט, אַלע ווערן דורכגעדרונגען מיט
דעם געפֿיל, אַז מען האָט געהערט אַ לעצט ייִדיש וואָרט.

ס'איז באמת כדאי צו הערן, ווי דאָס ייִדישע לשון וו לעבט מיט אַלע
רמ"ח איברים אין מויל פֿון קלאָג־אָראַטאָר. יעדער וואָרט, וואָס פֿליט
אים אַרויס פֿון מויל, איז אַ לעבעדיק זינגפֿייגעלע, וואָס פֿייפֿט אויף
אונטערגאַנג־נביאות. דער רעדנער באַמיט זיך צו רעדן שיין און האַרץ־
רייסנדיק און ער שטייגט אַלץ העכער און העכער צו די העכסטע עולמות
פֿון עקסטאַז.

וואָס־זשע בלייבט אַזאַ ייִדן צו טאָן, וואָס האָט נאָר וואָס אויסגע־
הערט אַן איבערצייגנדיקן פּראָגנאָז וועגן דעם אונטערגאַנג פֿון זיין לשון?
דער לאָגישער פֿועל יוצא איז צו העלפֿן דעם רעדנער באַשטעטיקן די
שוואַרצע פּאַרויסזאַגונג. צו וואָס ציען די גסיסה? אַז אַלץ כ'י, ווי
פֿאַרלוירן. דאַרף ער אפֿשר אויפֿהערן לייענען אַ ייִדישע צייטונג אָדער אַ
ייִדיש בוך? אַז אומעטום וואו ער קומט איז זיין לשון אָדער שוין לאַנג
אונטערגעגאַנגען, אָדער ס'האַלט אָט בײ אונטערגײן. און אַלץ דערפֿאַר,
ווייל זיינע קינדער אָדער קינדסקינדער זיינען שפּראַכלער פֿון אים אַוועק־
אַ ייִדיש וואַרט בײ זייערע פֿאַרזאַמלונגען. איר דאַרפֿט זען דעם עולם —
ממש ווי אין אַ מדבר. מען לעכצט, מען חלשט, מען איז דורשטיק, מען
וויל הערן אַ דערפֿרישנדיק ייִדיש וואָרט, אָבער די פֿאַרעקשנטע ציוניס־
טישע מטיפֿים ווילן נישט נאָכגעבן דעם עולם. זיי ווילן אפֿילו ניט אײַנ־
שטעלן, אפֿשר וועט אַ ביסל ייִדיש־טעטיקייט, פּשוטע טאָלעראַנץ צו
ייִדיש, געבן אַ ביסעלע ניי לעבן צו אַ באַוועגונג, וואָס זוכט איצטער
איר אייגענעם טעם און תמצית.

פֿון די ניט־ציוניסטישע פֿאַרזאַמלונגען איז דאָך שוין אָפּגערעדט.
בײ יענע פֿאַרזאַמלונגען, ווען מען קומט רעדן אַבסטראַקט וועגן אַמע־
ריקאַנער ייִדנטום — וועגן דעם דאָזיקן מיטאַלאָגישן פֿיפֿערנאַטער, וואָס

קיינער האָט נאָך קלאָר נישט געזען זיין פנים — רעדט מען אװדאי נישט
קיין ייִדיש. אויף אַזעלכע פאַרזאַמלונגען הערט מען באַמבאַסטישע און
פאַבריטשענע ענגלישע רעדעס, אָבער מ'הערט נישט קיין איין מחיהדיק
ייִדיש וואָרט. פאַר ייִדיש איז אַפילו נישט איינגעפירט קיין פּראָצענט־
נאָרמע, זאָגן מיר — צוין ייִדישע רעדע צו ניין ענגלישע „ספּיטשעס".
קומט מען ווידער צו אונדזערע אייגענע מענטשן, צו די פאַרשידענע
קולטור־אַװונטן, וואו מען איז שוין אויף מער־ווייניקער זיכערער טעררי־
טאָריע, הערט מען שוין דװקא יאָ אַ ייִדיש וואָרט, אָבער — עס פאַלט
אויס באָקאָם.
ביי אַזעלכע פאַרזאַמלונגען געפינט זיך געװיינלעך אַ רעדנער, און אַז
ס'גליקט אָפּ — גאַנצע צוויי, וואָס זאָגן פאַרויס, מיט דער גרעסטער
פּינקטלעכקייט, דעם אונטערגאַנג פון ייִדיש. אַלץ הייסט פאַרויסזאָגז. ווי
אַמאָליקע מגידים משלען זיי אויס דעם אונטערגאַנג מיט אַזעלכע שוועבל־
דיקע רייד, אַז ס'גייט ממש דורך אַ סקרוד. מען זעט בפירוש, ווי עס
שליסט זיך דאָס לעצטע ייִדישע מויל, וואָס רעדט אַרויס אַ לעצט ייִדיש
וואָרט, נאָך דעם ווי ער האָט געקויפט די לעצטע ייִדישע צייטונג און
פאַרמאַכט דאָס לעצטע ייִדישע ביכל.
לאָמיר נישט פאַרגעסן, אַז אַ סך אַוונטן זעגענען נאָך, אַזוי צו זאָגן,
אונטערהאָלטונגס־אַוונטן. זעגנען די דאָזיקע אונטערגאַנגס־פאַרויסזאָגונגען
אַ טייל פון פאַרווײַלונגס־פּראָגראַם. מען אַמוזירט דעם עולם דורך דעם,
וואָס מען דערלאַנגט אים די דאַטע פון אונטערגאַנג.
און מען רעדט אַלץ פון יונגן דור. לאָמיר נישט פאַרגעסן, אַז דאָס
זעגענען נישט קיין ספּעציעלע אסיפות געװידמעט חינוך אָדער דערציִאונג־
פּראָבלעמען. דער טאַטע, אָדער אַפילו דער זיידע קומט צו אַזעלכע פאַר־
זאַמלונגען אפשר נאָר דערפאַר, ווייל ער וויל זיך אָפּרוען פון זיינע קינ־
דער און אייניקלעך. אים פאַרדריסט אַליין, וואָס אים איז נישט געלונגען
איינצופלאַנצן אַ ייִדיש וואָרט ביי זיך אין דער היים. די גאַס האָט אים
באָזיגם. קומט ער אַליין צו אַזאַ אַלײַדישער פאַרזאַמלונג, וואו ער וויל
כאָטש אָטעמען אין ייִדישער אַטמאָספער. ער אַליין איז אויך אַ שטיקל
מענטש. ער וויל נאָך אויך לעבן. אַװדאי זעגנען קינדער דאָס אײַבער־
שטע פון שטײַסל, אָבער ער, דער טאַטע אָדער זיידע, האָט זיין אייגענעם
המשך, אָפּגעזען פון דער קיטלדיקער אײַביקייט.
דערלאַנגט מען אים דעם גאַנצן פינצטערן אונטערגאַנג אויף אַ
טעלער און מען אַמוזירט אים נאָך דערמיט.
האָט אַזאַ ייִד ממש נישט וואו צו גיין — רעדט ווייטער מיט האַרץ
דער אינטעליגענטער טענות־האַבער. זאָל ער גיין צו די פאַרזאַמלונגען,
וואו ער וויסט זיכער, אַז מען וועט נישט הערן קיין ייִדיש וואָרט, אָדער
זאָל ער גיין צו די אַנדערע, וואו מען וועט רעדן לעצט־ייִדיש, וואו מען

A monument for Nokhem Sokolov, 'journalist polygamist', who may play around with French girls, German girls, Polish girls, etc., but, in the end, he is really in love only with Jewish girls (Hebrew and Yiddish). (*Der groyser kundes*, March 14, 1913)

וועט הערן קלאָג־און־אונטערגאַנג יידיש און וואו מ׳וועט וואַרפן אַ מרה־
שחורה אויף אַלע פאַרזאַמלטע, ביי וועמען יידיש איז נאָך אַלץ אַ לעבע־
דיקער ענין, בעסער געזאָגט, אַן ענין צום לעבן און נישט צום אונטערגיין?

אַז איך וויל נישט ראַק פאַרזאָרגן מיינע קינדער און קינדסקינדער.
איך בין אויך אַ שטיקל מענטש און איך וויל נישט כסדר אונטערגיין.
בקיצור, וואָס רייסט מען מיר דאָס לעבעדיקע וואָרט פון מויל? —
שרייט אויס מיט הים היץ דער ייד, וואָס איז זיך מתרעם אויף יידישע אסי־
פות. ״ווען וועט מען מיך אויפהערן רודפן מיט אונטערגאַנג?״

און איר דאַרפט זען מיט וואָס פאַר אַ גלאַטע יידישע צונגען מען
רעדט וועגן יידיש־אונטערגאַנג! ניט נאָר וויל מען אונטערהאַלטן דעם
עולם, נאָר מען זעט, אַז די אונטערגאַנג־נביאים האָבן דעם אמתן ״גוד־
טאַים״. זיי אַליין זיינען העכסט אַמוזירט. מען דערקענט עס אין דעם עקס־
טאַז, אין דעם פּאַטאָס זייערן, אין די שיינע יידישע ווערטער, ווי זיי
שילדערן דעם אונטערגאַנג פון זייער לשון. ס׳איז אַ דעמאָנסטראַציע פון
וואונדן־קראַצעניש. דער רעדנער קראַצט זיך די וואונדן און ער האָט
הנאה, וואָס אים געליינגט צו שאַפן אין גאַנצן זאַל אַן אַרגיע פון גסיסה
און אונטערגאַנג. אַלע ווערן איבערצייגט, אַלע ווערן דורכגעדרונגען מיט
דעם געפיל, אַז מען האָט געהערט אַ לעצט יידיש וואָרט.

ס׳איז באמת כדאַי צו הערן, ווי דאָס יידישע לשון לעבט מיט אַלע
רמ״ח איברים אין מויל פון קלאָג־אַראַטאַר. יעדער וואָרט, וואָס פליט
אים אַרויס פון מויל, איז אַ לעבעדיק זינגפייגעלע, וואָס פייפט אויף
אונטערגאַנג־נבואות. דער רעדנער באַמיט זיך צו רעדן שיין און האַרץ־
רייסנדיק און ער שטייגט אַלץ העכער און העכער צו די העכסטע עולמות
פון עקסטאַז.

וואָס־זשע בלייבט אַזאַ ייִדן צו טאָן, וואָס האָט נאָר וואָס אויסגע־
הערט אַן איבערצייגנדיקן פּראָגנאָז וועגן דעם אונטערגאַנג פון זיין לשון?
דער לאָגישער פּועל יוצא איז צו העלפן דעם רעדנער באַשטעטיקן די
שוואַרצע פּאַרויסזאָגונג. צו וואָס ציען די גסיסה? אַז אַלץ איז כ׳׳י ווי
פאַרלוירן. דאַרף ער אפשר אויפהערן לייענען אַ יידישע צייטונג אָדער אַ
יידיש בוך? אַז אומעטום וואו ער קומט איז לשון אָדער שוין לאַנג
אונטערגעגאַנגען, אָדער ס׳האַלט אָט ביי אונטערגיין. און אַלץ דערפאַר,
ווייל זיינע קינדער אָדער קינדסקינדער זיינען שפּראַכלעך פון אים אַוועק־
געפאַרן. דערפאַר מוז ער אַליין ווערן אַ שפּראַקשטומער אָדער גאָר אַ
קלאָגמוטער. ער טאָר נישט האָבן קיין רואיקע מינוט און הנאה האָבן,
ריין און שיין און יום טובדיק הנאה האָבן פון אַ יידיש וואָרט.

און מעשה שטן גייט גאָר אויף דער שטערן פון יידיש. ס׳איז אַ
ביטערער עסק, די שוואַרצזעערס וועלן עס נישט איבערטראָגן. מען

לערנט ייִדיש אין עטלעכע אוניווערסיטעטן. מען גיט דער ייִדישער
ליטעראַטור אַ גאַנץ חשובן פּלאַץ אין ליטעראַטור־ענציקלאָפּעדיעס. די
ענציקלאָפּעדיע בריטאַניקאַ גיט אַרויס אַן ענגליש ווערטערבוך, איבער־
געזעצט אויף זעקס לשונות, איז ייִדיש איינע פון די זעקס וועלטשפּראַכן
צוזאַמען מיט פראַנצייזיש, דײַטש, שפּאַניש, איטאַליעניש, שוועדיש.

ס׳איז נאָך נישט צו אַלע גויים דערגאַנגען די וויסטע בשורה, אַז
מיר זײַנען שוין לאַנג אונטערגעגאַנגען, אָדער ס׳וועט אָט־אָט זײַן אויס
מיט אונדז. די ייִדישע ליטעראַטור האָט פולע גלײַכבאַרעכטיקונג אויף
די אינטערנאַציאָנאַלע קאָנגרעסן פון וועלט־ליטעראַטורן.

הכלל, אויב ס׳האַלט, חלילה, בײַ לעצט־ייִדיש, געזעגנט מען זיך מיט
אונדז אויף אַ גאַנץ פײַנעם אופן. אפשר וואָלט געווען אַ יושר, אַז מיר
אַליין זאָלן טאַקע שעפּן אַ ביסל נחת פון די אַלע טרייסטמאָמענטן?
אפשר גאָר אַראַנזשירן ימים טובים פאַר אונדזער לשון און פייערן די
נײַע פּאָזיציעס, וואָס אונדזער שפּראַך דעראָבערט להכעיס אַלע שוואַרצע
פאַרויסזאָגונגען?

אפשר וועלן מיר מיט דער מיט דער דאָזיקער פרייד אויך אַנשטעקן אונדזערע
קינדער? אָבער קודם־כל דאַרפן מיר נאָך אַליין זיך לערנען הנאה האָבן
פון יעדער פרייִדיקער בשורה און אויסנוצן די שמחה און עס פאַר־
וואַנדלען אין גוטן פּראָפּאַגאַנדע־מאַטעריאַל.

דערצו זײַנען אָבער נייטיק נייע אויפגאַנג־רעדנערס. ענטוזיאַסטישע
גלייבערס און נישט ענטוזיאַסטישע אונטערגייערס. זאָלן די שוואַרצזעערס
זיך צעּרוען, זאָלן זיי צוריקקומען אין 25 יאָר אַרום און זען, צי זיי
האָבן געטראָפן.

דערווייל לאָמיר כאַטש צווישן זיך, אויף ייִדישע פאַרזאַמלונגען, וואו
מען רעדט נאָך יאָ אַ ייִדיש וואָרט, אויפהערן צו באַקלאָגן, צו באַוויינען
און צו פאַרפינצטערן אונדזער לשון. לאָמיר זיך אויפהערן צו אַמוזירן
מיט אונטערגאַנג.

אַ לשון אויף תמיד, נישט אויף דערווייל

נישט געקוקט אויף די אומזיכערע מאַרגנס פון דער וועלט, מעג מען
פונדעסטוועגן פאַרויסזאָגן, אַז אין דעצעמבער פון יאָר צוויי טויזנט וועלן
ייִדישע שרײַבערס זיך צוזאַמענקומען און אונטערפירן אַ סך הכל פון דער
ייִדישער ליטעראַטור דורכן גאַנצן צוואַנציקסטן יאָרהונדערט. מ׳קאָן נישט
פאַרויסזאָגן, וואו די פייערונג וועט פאַרקומען, אין בוענאָס איירעס, אָדער

Yiddish literature (holding anarchist editor Yanovski by the ear): 'What do you think about that? This little nobody says I am doomed to die!' (At a literary evening in honor of H. D. Nomberg, Yanovski assured everyone that Yiddish literature was bound to die.) (*Der groyser kundes*, April 19, 1912)

איך ניו יארק, אין תל-אביב, צי אין פאריז. מ׳קאָן אויך נישט וויסן,
ווי אַזוי די יידישע ליטעראַטור וועט דעמאָלט אויסזען. אָבער, אַז אַזאַ
קאַנפערענץ וועט אָפּגעהאַלטן ווערן, איז אויך קיין האָר נישט אומזיכערער
ווי די גאַנצע וועלטלאַגע.

אונדזערע יידישע ווערטן, אין אַלע זייערע מאַניפעסטאַציעס און אין
אַלע לשונות פֿון אונדזער צעשטראַלטן „שמע", זענען אַ טייל פֿון דער שענע-
רער וועלטס האָב-און-גוטס, וואָס ווערט איצטער אי אָנגעגריפֿן, אי פֿאַר-
טיידיקט. אָבער דער גלויבן, אַז אויך אין דרייסיק יאָר אַרום וועלן זיין
לעבעדיקע יידישע שרייבערס, וואָס וועלן רעדן וועגן יידיש אויף יידיש,
איז נישט קיין פֿוסטער גלויבן. מיר לעבן אין גענוג פֿינצטערע צייטן,
אָבער נישט אין אַזאַ פֿינצטערער צייט, אַז מענטשן זאָלן בידים הרגענען
לעבעדיקע לשונות. אונדזער לשון האָט די זעלביקע שאַנסן צו בלייבן
לעבן, לויט איר מצב און באַזונדערן פֿאַרנעם, ווי די רייכסטע פֿון זיי —

ענגליש, פראנצייזיש, רוסיש; און אונדזער קאמף מיט דער וועלט, און
פאר דער וועלט, שליסט אויך איין א קאמף פאר דעם לעבן פון אונדזער
יידיש לשון.

מ׳קאן מיט זיכערקייט זאגן, אז איבער דער גאנצער וועלט זוכן
הונדערטער, אויב נישט טויזנטער, יחידים דעם היינט דעם וועג צו יידיש.
עס זענען אויפגעשטאנען באשיצערס און פארטיידיקערס פון אונדזער לשון
אין אזעלכע קריזן, וואו מ׳האט זיי נישט געקאנט דערוואארטן מיט פופציק
יאר צוריק, ווען פינצטער־זעערס האבן אנגעהויבן פינצטערן וועגן און־
טערגאנג. אנטלויפערס באגעגענען זיך איצטער מיט צוריקליפערס. ס׳איז
נאך פאראן א סך לעבנסקראפט און באהאלטענע גבורה אין אונדזער מאמע־
לשון, וואס שלאגט צוריק אלע טענות און מענות, מיט אנטשלאסענער
דויערעוודיקייט, אויף די פארשטייניקטע באדנס.

יידיש איז ביים היינטיקן טאג אונטערגעוואארפן אלע אימות און אלע
האפענונגען פון אלע גרויסע וועלטשפראכן. אוודאי זענען מיר קליין אין
צאל, אבער פון קליינקייט און וויניציקייט איז נאך קיין שפראך נישט
אונטערגעגאנגען. פון אונדזער גרויסן אומגליק, און פון סאמע קאלאויוון,
איז יידיש ארויסגעקומען אנגעגורט און באקרוינט מיט פרישן זכן אום־
דערוואארטן לעבנס־ווילן.

מיר וואארפן אפ קאטעגאריש יעדער געדאנק פון לעבן אויף דערווייל,
אויף געבארגטער צייט, די כלומרשטע טרייסט פון א ציטווייליקער
איבערגאנג־עקסיסטענץ. איבערגאנג איז א סעמאנטישער ליגן; ס׳מיינט
פשוט אונטערגאנג. און די דאזיקע צווישן אונדז, וואס יאגן אונטער דעם
פראצעס, מיט גוטן אדער מיט בייזן, זענען פשוט אומדאנקבאר אונדזער
לשון, וואס האט זיי אזוי ברייטהאארציק און נשמהדיק געגעבן אלץ, וואס
זיי פארמאגן.

דער געדאנק פון א געשלעפטן המשך, וואס דער יידישער שרייבער
איז אין דעם בעל כרחו איינגעשפאנט, ווי ער וואלט דערמיט געמוזט
מקיים זיין תרי״ג מצוות פון יידיש, איז אונדז פונקט אזוי דערווידער
ווי א לעבן אויף דערווייל. יידיש איז נישט קיין מצוה, נאר לופט פארן
יידישן שרייבער און יידישן לייענער. אונדזער המשך איז נישט אונדזער
אנרעג צו עקסיסטענץ, נאר אונדזער עקסיסטענץ איז שוין ממילא המשך,
אן באזונדערער אויגן־גלאצעניש און איבערגעטריבענער קדושה, וואס וויל
מאכן פון ליטעראטור א הייליקע ברודערשאפט.

די יידישע ווירקלעכקייט און די ממש לעגענדארישע אומגליקן און־
דזערע, האבן, פארשטייט זיך, געמוזט געבן אונדזער ליטעראטור דעם
אינהאלט פון אונדזער לעבן. אבער רוי אומגליק איז נאך נישט קיין
מאטעריאל פאר אמתער ליטעראטור. קונסט קאן וואארפן א גרוילשיין אויף
אומגליק און עס אזוי באלייכטן, אז ס׳זאל פון אומגליק אליין ארויס־

שטראַלן טרייסט. קונסט לייזט נישט קיין פּראָבלעמען, נאָר זי דערהייבט
זיי צו אַזעלכע הייכן, אַז אין דעם עצם זוכן אַן ענטפער הערט מען
די מאַרשמוזיק פון די ערנסטע און טרויעריקע מענטשלעכע טריט, וואָס
גייען פאַרט פאַרויס, דורך אַזוי פיל זיגזאַגן און מוראדיקע שטרויכלונגען.

יידישע ליטעראַטור און יידישע שרייבעריי איז, רעדנדיק אַמעריקאַ־
ניש, אַ "פּולער דזשאָב" און נישט "פּאַרט־טאַים". מען קאָן זיך נישט
דורכווינקען און שפּאַרצאָלעך ראַמאַנסירן מיט דעם אייגענעם אונטערגאַנג.
מען קאָן זיך נישט פּאַטאָגראַפירן אין אַן אַלט־פרענקישער שרייבערישער
פּאָזע, אין דעם אָפּשפּיגל פון אייגענעם אַרון און גילטן פאַר אַ לעבעדיקן
יידישן שרייבער. יעדער יידישער שרייבער, וואָס איז ווערט דעם נאָמען
שרייבער, שרייבט מיט דעם מינימאַלן גלויבן, אַז ס'וועט אונדז כאַטש
נישט אונטערגיין דאָס לשון פון אונדזער יידיש־טראַכטן; אָפּגערעדט,
אַז ער טאָר אַליין נישט ווערן זיין אייגענער פינפטער קאָלום, וואָס זוכט
זיך אַרויסצורייסן די צונג, נאָך איידער ס'באַווייזן זיך די אייזערנע,
אַכזריותדיקע צוואַנגען.

די גאַנצע וועלט־ליטעראַטור לעבט איצט דורך אַ מוראדיקן קריזיס,
דער שעפּערישער קינסטלערישער מענטש מענטש איז פּשוט אָנמאַכטיק אַנטקעגן
דעם אימפּעט פון אַזוי פיל אַקטיוון כאַאָס, וואָס האָט געשאַפן אַ פּסיכאָז
פון פאַרמבולדיקייט — אַ געפיל, אַז אַלע אַנגעזאַמלטע גייסטיקע פּאַר־
מעגנס וועלן אַרונטערגעשוועענקט ווערן, ווי די ערד אַליין וואָלט געווען
אין אַ פאַרשווערונג אונדז אַרונטערצורייסלען פון זיך.

אַ שרייבער דאַרף זיין אַ גאָר גרויסער גיבור, אַז ער זאָל נישט,
פריער פון אַלץ און פון אַלעמען, אַוועקגעטראַגן ווערן אין דער פאַר־
פליצונג פון אַזוי פיל רייד, וואָס אויבן אויף זעען זיי אויס צו זיין פון
באַלדיקער לעבנס־נויטווענדיקייט. זיי שטעלן אָבער אַוועק דעם קינסט־
לערס גלייביקן שטאַמל אין אַ האָפענונגלאָזער פאַרשטעטענונג. דער יידי־
שער שרייבער דאַרף זיין גרייט צו באַגעגנען די דאָזיקע וועלט־געשעע־
נישן מיט דער גאַנצער אַחריות און פאַרטיפונג פון אַ וועלטקינסטלער,
וואָס ראַנגלט זיך אַנטקעגן אונטערגאַנג און וואָס זוכט צו ראַטעווען זיין
קול אין דער גרויסער צעטומלעניש און צעמישעניש, אָבער זיין לשון
טאָר קיין מאָל נישט אַרומגעפרעגט ווערן מיט ספקות אָדער אין גאַנצן
אָפּגעפרעגט ווערן. ער מוז זיך זעצן שרייבן מיט גלויבן אין זיין אייגע־
נעם לשון.

מיר גייען אַנטקעגן דעם סוף פון בלוטיק־באַשערטן יאָרהונדערט
אונדזערן, מיט דעם פּולן ווילן בייצושטייערן יידישע מונטערונג און
טרייסט און נישט אויפגעבן צו זוכן קינסטלערישע אויפקלאָרונג פאַר
דעם כאַאָטישן און ווייטאָגדיקן געראַנגל פון דער גאַנצער מענטשהייט.

מיר דאַרפֿן, ווי קינסטלערס, אויפֿזוכן און אַרויסברענגען דעם פֿאַרטונקלטן
דראַנג נאָך גוטס און די ליכטיקע מאָמענטן פֿון דעם יצר לב האָדם,
וואָס רײַסט זיך צו טריאומפֿירן איבער זײַן אייגענער פֿאַרנעפֿלטער פֿאַר־
שאַלטנקייט.

די יידישע שרײַבערס איבער דער גאַרער וועלט ; די אַלע, וואָס
גלייבן באַמונה שלימה אין דער נויטווענדיקייט פֿון יידישן וואָרט ; די
אַלע נישט־שרעקעוודיקע און נישט איבערגעשראָקענע ; די, וואָס זענען
נישט קיין ציטוויייליקע יידישע שרײַבערס, וואָס הינקען נישט אויף
איבערגאַנג און שטאַמלען נישט אויף אונטערגאַנג, נאָר וואָס האָבן טאַקע
די האָפֿענונג איבערצולעבן אונדזער אַטאָמשרעק־עפּאָכע, ווי פֿולע יידישע
שרײַבערס — מוזן נאָך לעבעדיקער, שטאַרקער, הילכיקער, דערהײַבע־
נער און פֿאַרטיפֿטער פּראָקלאַמירן זייער גלויבן אין יידישן וואָרט.

און צו יענע יידישע שרײַבערס, וואָס גלייבן נישט אין קיום פֿון
אונדזער לשון, זאָגן מיר : אַוודאי איז עס מנוחהדיק צו זיצן ווי מאָנאַכן,
אונטער אַ פֿאַלשן פֿײגנבוים פֿון אייביקייט, אין לאַטײיניזירן יידיש,
שרייבן פּאַסיוו און רואיק אונדזער לשון, ווי ס׳וואָלט שוין געווען אַ יאָר
נאָך אונטערגאַנג און צו שאַפֿן ווערק, אין האַלבדרימל פֿון זיסלעכער
בענקשאַפֿט, נאָך עפּעס, וואָס איז פֿאַרגאַנגען און וואָס קאָן שוין מער
נישט צוריקגעבראַכט ווערן. אַזאַ יידיש־שרייבן איז אָפּגעריסנקייט פֿון
קוואַל, רעזיגנאַציע, איז נישט מער ווי אָפֿהענטיקייט און אומבאַוואוסט־
זיניקע ליקווידאַציע.

יעדער יידישער שרײַבער מוז זיך פֿאַרבינדן מיטן יידישן שעפֿערישן
וואָרט אויף דער גאַנצער וועלט און נישט קוקן אויף זיך ווי אויף אַ
פֿאָרזעען, איבערגעבליבן, פֿאַרשעמט, אָפּשטאַרבנדיק און אויסצאַנקענדיק

Yiddish in Melbourne

F. KLARBERG

Until recent times it was common for Jewish communities to develop their own dialect of the local language whether it was Persian, Arabic, Spanish, or German. There have even been suggestions of the development of a Jewish form of English among some groups in New York, though it awaits full documentation. In order to communicate ideas related to Jewish culture, words and phrases not readily available in the local languages were often borrowed from Hebrew. The growth of distinct forms of speech also helped to distinguish the Jews from their neighbors. Thus, two major social functions of language – solidarity and separation – were present.[1]

Since the emancipation of the Jews of Europe in the last century, a search developed for the major factor of Jewish identity. Religion, language, culture, and nationalism were all suggested in various forms, both singly and in combination. One approach postulated that Jews could become an integral part of the new secular society while still maintaining Jewish identity through the Yiddish language and its secular culture. While these assumptions were widely debated in Eastern Europe, adherents of all views established themselves among the immigrant communities in Australia. Between totally secular Yiddishism and ultra-Orthodox Judaism, which also shows a strong preference for Yiddish, the largest group of Australian Jews form an undemarcated middle sector who value Yiddish as part of the total cultural baggage which they brought with them from Europe.[2]

Since the Second World War, the Australian government policy of boosting immigration has led to considerable interest in the adjustment and integration of immigrant groups. An assessment of the level of language maintenance is of prime importance in an appreciation of the Jewish community, since half its members are postwar immigrants or their children. Both individual and group

1. Cf. G. Hammarström 1967.
2. I wish to acknowledge my gratitude to Mr. B. Jernudd, who supervised my research at Monash University. I have also to thank Professor J. A. Fishman who read this paper in manuscript and made valuable suggestions.

studies of the community have been made.[3] These show that over 80 percent of Melbourne's Jews have some acquaintance with Yiddish. However, no study of Yiddish language maintenance within the Jewish community has yet been undertaken.

SCOPE OF INVESTIGATION

For a full survey of the level which Yiddish maintains in Melbourne today, one would have to investigate the whole of the Jewish community's language habits – in homes, businesses, social clubs, synagogues, and religious and secular day schools. In addition, one would wish to find the extent to which Yiddish is known by non-Jews, and its effect on English – whether by vocabulary or other linguistic influence. However, only the institutional environment is considered here, because it is the predominant setting of social activity.

Yiddish was the language of the Jewish masses of Eastern Europe before 1939. A recent survey[4] disclosed that over 25 percent of Melbourne Jews spoke Yiddish at home, about 55 percent claimed various degrees of knowledge of Yiddish, while the remainder were children of non-Yiddish-speaking parents. The last group represents those who are not of immediate Eastern European descent. The 1966 census showed 33,000 Jews to be living in Melbourne.

There are two groups in the community which maintain organizations in which Yiddish is used extensively: the ultra-Orthodox and the secular.[5] Among the ultra-Orthodox, the frequent personal contact resultant from daily synagogue attendance and other religious observances tends to strengthen language maintenance, thus creating factors not present in most immigrant groups.[6] On the other hand, the members of the secular sector identify themselves as belonging to a Jewish culture which expresses itself principally through the medium of the Yiddish language. There seems, therefore, to be more justification for comparing these last with other European immigrants who do not regard religion as being in any way associated with a national language or culture.[7] These secular Jewish groups maintain a number of distinctive Yiddish cultural institutions, which are also patronized in varying degrees by members of the middle sector. It is this patronage which makes the functioning of a regular Yiddish theater possible.

3. Price 1964; Medding 1968; and Jewish Social Service Council of Victoria 1967, work for publication in progress under the chairmanship of Mr. W. Lippmann.
4. 1967 Melbourne Jewish Community Survey, op. cit.
5. 'Ultra-orthodox' is used for those Jews who take their Orthodoxy seriously, as described by J. A. Fishman (1965: 57–63).

6. On this point, Medding suggests that the ethnic church most like Jewry is the Greek Orthodox Church (Medding 1968: 15n).
7. Moreover, I felt I could be more objective in such a study. I am a teacher in an Orthodox school and closely involved in the religious sector. Admittedly this fact could also prejudice my examination of the secular group – but at least I am less involved emotionally in its study.

In addition to the secular institutions, I considered it important to include the Victorian Jewish Board of Deputies and Jewish Press. They serve all sections of the Jewish community and follow a policy of using both Yiddish and English. Through them, the Yiddishists maintain contact with Melbourne Jewry and try to influence its policy and development. As a result, the following were investigated:

1. the Yiddish schools
2. the Jewish press and literature
3. the Jewish National Library 'Kadimah'[8]
4. the Yiddish theater
5. Yiddish clubs
6. the Victorian Jewish Board of Deputies

Interviews conducted with the leading personalities in these institutions yielded important information and insights into the types of people involved. Publications were also obtained; however, it became apparent that the importance of Yiddish lay more in its use as a spoken language than as a literary medium.[9]

THE YIDDISH SCHOOLS

The oldest Yiddish school, Peretz School, was founded in 1935 in Carlton, an inner-industrial suburb, where most of the Jewish immigrants concentrated between the wars. In 1938 the present headmaster[10] took over; the school then had 35 pupils. It expanded steadily, moved to its present spacious premises in 1956, and in 1961 reached its peak enrollment of 262 pupils.[11] This rise in enrollment is in inverse proportion to the trend of the Jewish population in the area during the period 1947–1961. There was an overall growth in the Jewish population in Victoria (mainly in Melbourne) from almost 15,000 in 1947 to almost 30,000 in 1961. Nonetheless, the Jewish population of the inner, eastern, and northern suburbs from which the Peretz School drew its pupils, fell not only

8. 'Kadimah' means 'forward' in Hebrew.
9. I met the principals of both Yiddish schools and some of the teachers, the proprietor of *The Australian Jewish News*, the editor of the Yiddish section, a sub-editor who is also an actor and secretary of the Yiddish theater, a business man who was writing a column for *The Jewish Herald*, and the secretary of the Kadimah. I had a most stimulating two-hour informal discussion with a group of university students, members of 'Zukunft' (Yiddish for 'future'), who all agreed that, as they do not actively use Yiddish among themselves, their ideology needs rethinking. An evening at a meeting of the Victorian Jewish Board of Deputies provided good entertainment, but was also en-

lightening on the structure of the elite of Melbourne Jewry. The individuals mentioned were all generous with their time – some preferring to conduct the conversation in English, others in Yiddish. Many of the publications came to my notice in the course of these interviews. I also attended a lunch-time lecture on the Jewish Press by Monash University's Publications Officer, who was the proprietor and editor of *The Jewish Herald* from 1940 to 1960.
10. At one time Director of the Jewish section of the Latvian Government Education Department.
11. Despite the foundation of Mount Scopus College which taught Yiddish for some years after its inception in 1948.

Parents: register your child in the non-political *shulkult* school, which gives instruction via Yiddish in all general subjects, as well as a truly Jewish education, in renovated classrooms, at a negotiable tuition rate. (late 1930s).

proportionally (from 31.7 percent to 14.2 percent), but even absolutely (from 4,650 to 4,200).[12]

Relationship to Jewish population

The growth of the Peretz School was, then, unrelated to overall population figures. It must be explained by the trend not uncommon in poor immigrant areas in all countries.[13] While the older and better integrated settlers who were not greatly interested in Yiddish moved elsewhere, they were replaced by newcomers who found that the area provided them with readily available Jewish communal facilities, cheap rent traditional in immigrant neighborhoods, and

12. Medding 1968: 18, 20, Tables 1.1 and 1.2.   13. Cf. Price 1964: 25.

proximity to the city center which made it easy to travel to work. These people, mostly D.P.'s from Eastern Europe, had spent the postwar years in the ghetto-like environment of the refugee camps. There they used Yiddish as the lingua franca, irrespectively of whether Yiddish or some local national tongue had been their first language at home. The Peretz School found more supporters among them than among the old-established Jewish inhabitants, so that, despite the reduced Jewish population, school enrollment actually increased.[14] After its peak of 262 pupils in 1961, enrollment dropped to 110 in 1968. This is the result of the continual exodus by immigrants as soon as they are financially able to move.

With the growth of the Jewish population south-of-the-Yarra,[15] a need was felt for the teaching of Yiddish. At first, it was expected that the Peretz School would establish a branch; when this proved administratively inadvisable, a committee of interested parents in St. Kilda founded the Sholem Aleichem School in 1946. Teachers were drawn from graduates of the Peretz School who had attended a teachers' seminar led by the headmaster of the Peretz School, and also from among Polish immigrants. A committee to coordinate instruction was established, so that children being transferred from one school to the other might be able to find an appropriate level. Both schools now teach a uniform syllabus, which is designed to provide supplementary Yiddish education at primary and secondary level for pupils receiving their general education elsewhere. By 1960 the Sholem Aleichem School had reached its optimum level of 200 pupils, allowing the full span of eleven classes to function. It has maintained that level since. The total number of children receiving instruction in the Yiddish language has dropped during the last eight years, from 450 to 300. This constitutes about 7 percent of all Jewish children who attend Melbourne Jewish educational institutions cither part-time or full-time,[16] as compared with 3 percent in the United States.[17] This is not surprising, since the Melbourne Jewish community has a higher proportion of post-Second World War immigrants than American Jewry.[18]

Teaching of Yiddish

The children attend every Sunday morning from 10 a.m. to 1 p.m., with a twenty-minute break. The best proof of the appeal of the school is the fact that teenagers preparing for School Leaving and Matriculation examinations attend regularly, although they can obtain no formal credit for their work. Nevertheless,

14. Mr. Medding has suggested to me in a private communication that this increase may be partly explained by the post-war 'baby boom'.
15. Medding 1968: 18, Table 1.1.
16. Figure derived from statistical information submitted to delegates at the Federal Conference on Jewish Education called by the Executive Council of Australian Jewry, 24–26 August, 1968.
17. Fishman 1965: 25.

18. Medding (1968) Sklare's Introduction p. xxi. However, pupils at the Yiddish schools in Australia are today drawn almost exclusively from post-war immigrant families. If this is also true of the American scene, it could well be that a higher percentage of post-war immigrants in the United States are sending their children to Yiddish schools than is the case in Australia.

conversation between the youngsters during breaks is carried on exclusively in English. In the first four grades (6–10 years age-group), the children are taught Yiddish through conversation and by the use of a textbook and workbook imported from the United States. They are also told Bible stories in Yiddish, so that an introduction to Jewish culture is presented. In grades 5–7, textbook language-learning is continued, but extracts from Yiddish literature are also read and discussed. Some of the prophetic books of the Bible are read in Yiddish translation. Jewish history from Biblical times up to the present day is also taught in the upper grades.

The standards of fluency and cultural awareness are well demonstrated in a wall-newspaper at each school, regular contributions by pupils to the Yiddish press, and occasional school publications. Thus, among twenty pages of essays and poems contributed by pupils of the Sholem Aleichem School to its twenty-year Jubilee celebration magazine published in 1967,[19] we find discussion on such subjects as prophecy, child labor, and the State of Israel, besides many essays based on Yiddish literature. Though these are showpieces by the most outstanding pupils, they indicate the standard towards which the school is striving. In fact, the standard of written expression is high. An inspection of essays which had been corrected ready for return to the pupils at the Peretz School revealed very few spelling errors. This is so because of the simplicity of the spelling system. The few errors were of two types: those due to lack of knowledge of Hebrew, and those due to dialectal deviation from the standard Lithuanian Yiddish. The errors due to dialect influence seem to indicate that these children, like those of the Sholem Aleichem School, are largely from homes where Polish–Yiddish is a living language. Syntactical faults seemed more common, and appeared to be chiefly due to interference from English.

For special occasions such as Passover and end-of-year, the schools stage functions where recitations are made, songs sung, and playlets are performed by the pupils in Yiddish. The Jewish community as a whole also often requests their participation in public functions, as, for instance, at the annual Warsaw Ghetto Revolt commemoration held under the auspices of the Victorian Jewish Board of Deputies. (The commemoration is organized by members of the Kadimah and associated groups of Polish Jews.) Even more, the State Zionist Council of Victoria, although it regards the spreading of Hebrew in the community as one of its prime objectives, considers it appropriate to incorporate an item by the Yiddish schools in the annual Israel Independence Day celebration.

All this does not ensure that the next generation will speak Yiddish, but it does preserve some form of attachment. There is a parallel here with the situation in the United States.[20] It is interesting to note that the Peretz School, faced with a drop in enrollment which might close the school in the foreseeable future, has

19. There was a delay in publishing.   20. Fishman 1965: 25.

acquired a property in Balwyn – a northeastern outer suburb – and is establishing a branch there. If the school manages to become established in Balwyn, its pupils will be drawn from English-speaking homes. This is bound to affect the teachers' approach, and to lower the standards of achievement, but it would ensure some continuity of Yiddish teaching and preserve the possibility of a stronger future interest.

Generational patterns among the pupils

A questionnaire was administered to the 11 students in the highest class of the Sholem Aleichem School. Aged 14–17 years, five of them were born in Australia, four in Poland, and two in Israel. Their parents were all born in Eastern Europe (19 in Poland, one each in Latvia, Russia, and Czechoslovakia). They arrived in Australia between 1948 and 1962. The responses indicate that the parents almost invariably speak to each other and to their children in Yiddish, and often the children also reply in Yiddish. However, 8 of them speak to the brothers and sisters in English – 5 always did, and 3 mainly did. One claimed to speak Yiddish 'always', yet 'mostly' English; one speaks an 'other language', while one has no siblings. The replies seem to indicate that English will probably be the language they will use in their own homes, and that they will not pass Yiddish on as a living tongue to their children. Since this group is what a member of the Zukunft Youth organization described as the 'hard core' of Yiddishists, the outlook for the future of the language is not very promising.

JEWISH PRESS AND LITERATURE

Press

Gilson and Zubrzycki[21] state that the only study of the Jewish press in Australia was published in 1913. Up to the year of that study,[22] all Jewish publications had been in English. *The Australian Jewish News* was founded as *Australier Leben* in 1931; it was a Yiddish publication, and became bilingual under its present name two years later. *The Australian Jewish Herald*, founded in 1870, first added a supplement in Yiddish in 1946. It was called *The Australian Jewish Post* and took some years to reach the scale of *The Australian Jewish News* Yiddish section. Thus during the war years and immediately thereafter, *The Australian Jewish News* monopolized the Yiddish market, and so gained an advantage over its rival, becoming the leading Australian Jewish newspaper: it reached practically every Jewish home. The goodwill of the immigrant readers had been established and was maintained when they started to read English. *The Australian Jewish Herald*, after changing hands a number of times, finally ceased publication in August 1968, amidst widespread political controversy.

21. Gilson and Zubrzycki 1967: vii. 22. Mark 1913.

Being weekly publications, the Yiddish and English sections of *The Australian Jewish News* supplement the daily press in their coverage of events of specifically Jewish interest overseas, and particularly of matters concerning Israel. Topical news is absent from both sections, indicating the fact that the editors expect their readers to keep themselves informed by way of the general daily press; the Yiddish reader, then, is assumed to be bilingual. The more interesting aspect of comparison between the Yiddish and the English sections lies in the difference that while the English section consists mainly of reports of communal happenings and the activities of the clubs, synagogues, and organizations, the Yiddish section may be compared with the weekend supplements published by the dailies. The English-speaking section of the community apparently gets its culture elsewhere, while the Yiddish speakers prefer to read political comment, ideological debate, and literary criticism in a weekly devoted to their own culture. Although ideological and cultural matter is part of Yiddish journalistic tradition, it would appear to me that consumer demand is the most important factor. While both the readers of the English and Yiddish sections can, and do, read the English dailies, those of them whose first language is English can also read the cultural section of the dailies, and require *The Australian Jewish News* purely as a social notice-board. The others, however, whose first language is Yiddish, find that they must make an effort to read the news in the daily papers, and prefer to read cultural matters in their mother tongue.

The Australian Jewish News, it should be noted, is not secular Yiddishist, but addresses itself to all sections of the Jewish community. There are Melbourne and Sydney editions of both the English and Yiddish sections. The Melbourne edition serves all states other than New South Wales. The following are the circulation figures supplied by the paper in June 1968:

	English	Yiddish
Melbourne edition	9,500	4,000
Sydney edition	6,100	1,000

As a result of the closing of *The Australian Jewish Herald* in August 1968, these figures are likely to rise.

In addition to the weekly *Australian Jewish News*, there are two quarterlies – *Der Landsman*, which has been published by the Federation of Australian *landsmanshaften* since 1965, and a Bundist publication called *Unzer Gedank*. *Der Landsman* contains articles on Israel, the Holocaust in Europe, short stories, essays, and reviews.

Literature

Many books have been published in Yiddish in Australia. Some of the authors, such as Herz Bergner, have been translated into English. An interesting piece of Australiana is a Yiddish translation of a Hebrew travelogue[23] which describes a visit to Australia and New Zealand in 1861–1862 after the Gold Rush.

The first Australian Jewish Almanac appeared in 1937, and a second one in 1942. The *Third Australian–Jewish Almanac*[24] appeared in 1967. With the exception of one article in Hebrew, it is a compendium of Yiddish cultural activities in Australia. The first of its five sections deals with Kadimah's activities. The second deals with Jewish life in Australia, and is written by Australian writers; this section includes a fifteen-page article covering the history of Yiddish literature since the first Yiddish writer arrived in 1928 up to the present time. Further sections include 'As Others See Us' (by overseas writers who have recently visited Australia) and 'Stories, Poems, and Drama'. One section consists of essays on contemporary life; these are mostly on topics involving Jewish life. However, as in the United States,[25] the local scene has had a strong influence on writers. There is even an essay in the Almanac which discusses the aboriginal problem.

These books must find their market overseas, and even locally, by private sale: the three Jewish bookstores in Melbourne report selling only 'two or three' Yiddish books annually. Yiddish gramophone records, however, are extremely popular.

Spelling

Yiddish spelling was not standardized until 1936–1937. Previously it had been the subject of heated controversy which had religious and political significance. The major question to be settled was the spelling of words of Hebrew (and Aramaic) origin. These traditionally retain their original spelling, which is at variance with the widespread, but unstandardized, Yiddish spelling based on a phonemic system. The retention of etymological spelling was felt to be a form of identification with Hebrew, reflecting a bond with Jewish religious literature whose authoritative texts are Hebrew or Aramaic, and with nationalist (Zionist) aspirations. In 1936, YIVO (Yiddish Scientific Institute) in Vilna adopted a reformed spelling.[26] Silent graphemes were dropped, the spelling of all non-Hebrew words was rationalized, but the etymological spelling for morphemes of Hebrew origin was retained, even when incorporated in Yiddish words having affixes of Germanic origin. In communist countries, phonemic spelling was adopted even for the words of Hebrew/Aramaic origin. The Australian publications follow YIVO spelling.

The Kadimah is the central organization for the furthering of Jewish culture. It was founded in 1911 to provide a forum for Jewish debates, cultural activities, and to set up a 'national' library. Its fifty-sixth annual report (in Yiddish and

23. Safir 1950.
24. Frydman 1967.

25. Fishman 1965: 35.
26. Weinreich 1968*b*: xx.

English) shows its important contribution to cultural life. Concerts and lecture evenings are arranged on numerous occasions; memorial evenings are held for important departed leaders of Yiddish cultural life. In 1967, the library added 98 books, reaching a total of 8,743 – 5,770 in Yiddish, 2,379 in English, and 594 in Hebrew. There are still over 100 active readers but the number of books read fell from 920 in 1966 to 767 in 1967. Not a single new member joined in 1967, and membership is falling owing to death, emigration, and other causes; there are 1,379 subscribing members listed. The library is open twice a week. It has bought a cinema close to the Sholem Aleichem School in Elsternwick, a southern suburb, and in October 1968 moved from its premises in Carlton. In the past, institutions have been established in new neighborhoods where there was sufficient demand, but only two institutions had actually abandoned their earlier site. The Carlton Synagogue also closed down in 1968. If we assume that there is a parallel between the situation in the United States and in Australia, the Kadimah librarian's hope that the move to the south will revitalize his library might be realized. Fishman, who deals mainly with a community of second-generation immigrants, hardly mentions Yiddish libraries.[27] A swing to Anglo-Jewish culture would appear to be the only prospect of Kadimah's continued activity. A change in this direction appears to be envisaged by some.

Yiddish theater

The Kadimah provides a major Yiddish cultural service to a widespread public through the David Herman Theater Group, which it houses. There are usually two seasons annually, each of 10–12 performances. Plays performed include original Yiddish scripts, as well as translations from English and Hebrew dramatists. The group consists of local Yiddish actors and other theater enthusiasts, who spend many evenings throughout the year preparing and rehearsing for their two seasons. They also stage occasional performances at the Jewish Home for the Aged, and for other charitable purposes. The needs of this group governed Kadimah's choice of a cinema for its new premises. The theater is supported by over 3,000 regular patrons.

YIDDISH CLUBS

The Bund, Zukunft, Skif

The Bund was founded in 1897 as one of the many socialist groups in Russia. It soon broke with the extreme left, and has since been the sworn enemy of the Communists. Its ideology consists of two basic doctrines. These are, first, that

---

27. Fishman 1965. There is no section devoted to libraries. The YIVO library is mentioned in passing on p. 44, and the Los Angeles Yiddish Culture Club library on p. 47.

Jewish culture can be maintained, based on the belief that 'Yiddish can flower in any place where Jews live', and second, the political doctrine that 'socialism is the best form of government'. The Bund conducts various cultural evenings, talks, discussions, and readings, and encourages Zukunft – a group of university students and young adults – to do likewise. In addition to the normal range of cultural and political topics which are debated by intelligent young people, Zukunft meetings often discuss topics related to Jewish affairs. However, with the exception of discussions on Yiddish literature, all meetings are held in English. The reason, I was informed, is that 'it would take us twice as long to say what we think in Yiddish'.[28] This is an example of a sociolinguistic phenomenon of interest. When Yiddish came to Australia, it had not developed the style necessary to deal with the discussions of the milieu in which these young people gained their experience. As they are not sufficiently at home in the language to develop it, they feel the need to use English. On subjects of Yiddish literature, however, they feel Yiddish to be the better vehicle of expression.

The members of Zukunft lead a youth group called Skif, where Yiddish is officially encouraged (but, in fact, not used at their weekly meetings). I was told that at summer camps which the organization runs, the daily line-up and announcements are made in Yiddish. Internal publications are mostly in English, and the Yiddish program for a cultural evening to be presented by the group for their elders was transliterated into roman type.[29]

Landsmanshaften

There are numerous associations known as *landsmanshaften*, which are joined by immigrants hailing from a common town in Poland.[30] These hold occasional cultural functions and fund-raising activities, and many of them conduct an annual memorial evening on the anniversary of the Nazi slaughter of their townsfolk and relatives. All their functions are conducted in Yiddish.

THE VICTORIAN JEWISH BOARD OF DEPUTIES

The Victorian Jewish Board of Deputies is a 'roof organization' which attempts to represent the Jewish community. Though it has no official status, and there are a number of Jewish organizations not represented on it, it is joined by most bodies which qualify (minimum requirements being existence for two years and a membership of 250). In fact, the Bund is not officially represented, but the Yiddish schools and Kadimah are, and further, as a result of the election of direct

28. Professor J. V. Neustupny drew my attention to the importance of this statement: the subjective assessment of one's command of a language is an important factor governing usage.

29. Interestingly, 'helfer' – youth leader – was transliterated as 'helper'. On being questioned, the students laughed with embarrassment, not being certain whether this was a slip or not.

30. The only non-Polish group known as a *landsmanshaft* is one combining all Latvian and Lithuanian Jews. There is also an 'Association of British Jews' and one of Sephardim.

representatives by members of the Jewish public who care to register as voters by paying a levy, a number of Bundists are on the board. The 'Yiddishist' group forms a quite strong vocal bloc. When, in 1948, the board embarked on its greatest enterprise, the establishment of Mount Scopus College[31] – a day school which was intended to cater for the children of all sections of the community – this group was strong enough to enforce the provision of Yiddish as an elective subject. In fact, the school soon abandoned Yiddish classes because of insufficient demand.

At a meeting in March 1960 the chairman ruled that in the future 'no translation of Yiddish speakers will take place where the speaker in the opinion of the chair, could express himself properly in English'. Debate ensued on a motion dissenting from this ruling. The members of the Yiddish bloc felt that they all had the right to address the board in Yiddish, even those who had a fluent command of English. Their opponents (with the support of the chair) felt that it was wasteful of the board's time to have such speeches translated into English. Though the minutes are rather sketchy, the atmosphere of the meeting is indicated by the note following the defeat of the motion. We are informed that 'a number of Yiddish-speaking delegates then withdrew from the meeting'. This apparently was followed by lobbying, for the following minutes report the rescission of this ruling and the reversion to the practice of a member of the board giving an English summary of Yiddish speeches.

A meeting at which I was an observer was attended by over 100 delegates. The reason for this unusually full attendance was the subject of the debate: the demise of *The Australian Jewish Herald*, in which some members of the Executive were involved. Seventeen speeches of varying length were made. Three members of the Yiddish bloc spoke, and the youngest of these, a gentleman of about forty years of age, spoke in English. In contrast, an elderly Zionist delegate spoke in Yiddish. A number of other speakers used occasional Yiddish words or phrases. A university lecturer, who made a number of interjections, chose Yiddish and English, according to circumstance. At least at board meetings, where Jews of many backgrounds come together, Yiddish seems to have a quite definite social function. While the older generation of immigrants may use Yiddish simply in order to express their thoughts and feelings with greater freedom, the young people, who express themselves more easily in English, deliberately throw in phrases of Yiddish in order to identify themselves with their parents of the Eastern European tradition, which they regard somehow as superior to the Judaism of Western European tradition. Even when they reject the ideology of the secular Yiddishists, they use Yiddish as a form of identification with the Eastern European tradition.

31. By 1968, this college consisted of a central primary and secondary school and three branch primary schools. Total enrollment was approaching 2,000.

DISCUSSION

It is noteworthy that there is a considerable overlap among the Yiddish organizations. Most of the members of Zukunft are graduates of the Yiddish schools. The secretary of the theater group is subeditor of the Yiddish section of *The Australian Jewish News*; the headmaster of the Peretz School is a member of the Bund, while some of the contributors to *The Australian Jewish News*, and many of the above, will be found among the delegates to the Victorian Jewish Board of Deputies. These people form the core of the Yiddishist groups:

Yiddish weekly paper circulation	4,000
Yiddish theater patrons	3,000
Yiddish library members	1,374
Yiddish school pupils	300
active Yiddish book borrowers	100

It is very difficult to determine to what extent the Yiddish section of *The Australian Jewish News* is read. In some families, it is likely that two or more of the older members will read it. In others, it may hardly be glanced at – one pays only two cents extra for it to be delivered with the English section. According to the 1967 survey,[32] 30 percent claim to read it. The figures for theater patrons, on the other hand, are more accurate, as the tickets sold represent actual visitors to the theater. However, one requires much less linguistic ability to understand a Yiddish play than to read a Yiddish newspaper. Library membership entitles one to vote at annual meetings, so that it may indicate political affiliation rather than cultural activity. The active Yiddish book borrowers and the Yiddish school pupils, though two generations apart, clearly belong to what an informant described as the 'hard core'. These same people are to be found among the leaders of the Bund and its youth organizations.

It is interesting to note that in the United States Yiddish has fared worse than other comparable immigrant languages.[33] Perhaps the competition with Hebrew, as the language which Jewish schools have traditionally found necessary to teach, is a factor. A more basic factor is the 'low' status of Yiddish as a language. Rarely has a secular institution of higher learning used Yiddish as the language of instruction. A few secondary schools did, but this situation existed only for a short period in some countries by virtue of the provisions for ethnic minorities in the Treaty of Versailles, which were ignored more often than not. Furthermore, it is nowhere a language of government. A number of informants were apologetic about the use of Yiddish. One, a columnist on the defunct *Australian Jewish Herald*, pointed out without my prompting that 'after all, English is also a language which has developed from a number of languages'.

32. Jewish Social Service Council of Victoria 1967.
33. Fishman 1965: 69, 72n.

Finally, it seems that in Melbourne, Yiddish is, relative to the size of the Jewish community, better known and more widely used than is the case in the United States. This is because a greater 'proportion of the Jewish community consists of first generation Australians',[34] while the problem of adjustment is still with us. However, in view of its non-use by the younger generation, even of the hard core, it could well be that it is losing ground faster than it did in the United States among all but the ultra-Orthodox group.

In his introduction to the Yiddish translation of *Iban Safir*, H. Munz suggested that the closed doors of the Ballarat[35] synagogue, and of other country-town synagogues of the last century, proved that those early Australian Jews, by approaching Judaism as a religion and ignoring Yiddish culture, had missed the essence of Judaism, thereby making their assimilation inevitable.[36] Less than twenty years later, every publication of Yiddishist organizations bears marks of the ideological dilemma in which they find themselves. They want their children to retain their Jewish identity, yet are painfully aware of the fact that their children prefer to speak English, even within their own closed circle. On the other hand, one can still meet many of the country-town Jews and their city-born descendants regularly attending synagogue – not in Broken Hill or Shepparton[37] of course, but in the Melbourne suburbs of Caulfield and St. Kilda. The drift to the city is a widespread phenomenon of the twentieth century. Remarkable evidence of this was offered at the centenary celebration of Ballarat's synagogue in 1961. It was preceded by articles on the history of the community in both the Yiddish and English sections of the Jewish press. The Yiddish article in *The Australian Jewish News* dwells purely on the nineteenth-century history. However, the English article by N. Rosenthal, a Melbourne University lecturer who himself grew up in the Ballarat Jewish community, brings the story up to date and points out that 'many of the families who became associated with it in one way or another are names well known in the Melbourne Jewish Community'. He concludes with a list of family names.[38] The following week the paper reported the function as being attended by members and exmembers of the Ballarat congregation. 'The old synagogue was thronged to capacity with many people having to stand. . .',[39] despite the 60-mile distance from Melbourne. *The Jewish Post*[40] estimated attendance at 230, though only 12 Jewish families resided in Ballarat. Urbanization then, not lack of Yiddish, closed the doors of the country synagogues.

No doubt, many Jews did abandon their faith in the small country towns, but this did not destroy the community, nor does it establish the case for Yiddish.

34. Medding 1968, Sklare's Introduction, p. xxi.
35. Ballarat, established as a result of the Gold Rush in 1850, had a Jewish population of 700 in 1890.
36. Safir 1950: 6.
37. Once flourishing rural Jewish communities.

38. *The Australian Jewish News*, March 24, 1961, p. 11.
39. *The Australian Jewish News*, March 30, 1961, p. 3.
40. *The Jewish Post*, March 30, 1961, p. 10.

On the contrary, only when a distinct way of life exists is there need for a language which can give expression to the unique experiences of the group. Ethnic group survival depends on the presence of a multitude of factors. A minority whose other behavior patterns conform with the majority will soon abandon its linguistic distinctiveness. Among the ultra-Orthodox, then, investigation is likely to show greater fluency in Yiddish, and a more active use of the language among members of the younger generation.

REFERENCES

Australian Jewish Herald (Melbourne weekly).

Australian Jewish News (Melbourne weekly, English and Yiddish).

The Bridge (Sydney quarterly, published by The Australian Jewish Quarterly Foundation).

Executive Council of Australian Jewry (1968), Materials and papers presented at Education Conference in Melbourne. August (unpublished).

Fishman, J. A. (1965), *Yiddish in America*. The Hague, Mouton.

Frydman, L., editor (1967), *Third Australian–Jewish Almanac* (Yiddish). Melbourne, Kadimah.

Gilson, M., Zubrzycki, J. (1967), *Foreign Language Press in Australia*. Canberra.

Goldman, L. M. (1954), *The Jews in Victoria in the Nineteenth Century*. Melbourne.

Hammarström, G. (1966), *Linguistische Einheiten im Rahmen der modernen Sprachwissenschaft*. Berlin.

— (1967), 'Zur sozialektalen und dialektalen Funktion der Sprache', *Zeitschrift für Mundartforschung* 24 (3–4): 205.

Jewish Cultural Centre and National Library 'Kadimah' 56th Annual Report (1968), (in Yiddish and English). Melbourne.

Jewish Post (Melbourne weekly, Yiddish).

Jewish Social Service Council of Victoria (1967), *1967 Melbourne Jewish Community Survey* (work for publication in progress).

Jubilee Committee of Peretz School, *25 Yor. I. L. Peretz Shule in Melbourne* (Yiddish).

Jubilee Committee of Sholem Aleichem School and Kindergarten (1967), *20 Yor Sholem Aleichem Shule* (Yiddish), Melbourne.

Mark, P. J. (1913), *The Jewish Press in Australia Past and Present*, Sydney.

Medding, P. Y. (1968), *From Assimilation to Group Survival*. Melbourne.

Peretz School Committee (1946), *Kinder Shreiben in Melbourne* (Yiddish). Melbourne.

Peretz School Committee (1951), *Kinder Shreiben* (Yiddish), Melbourne.

Price, C. A. (1964), *Jewish Settlers in Australia*, Canberra.

Safir, J. (1950), *Iben Safir* (Yiddish edition trans. H. Munz). Melbourne.

Victorian Jewish Board of Deputies Minutes.

Weinreich, U. (1968a), *Languages in Contact*, The Hague, Mouton.

— (1968b), *Modern English–Yiddish Dictionary*, New York.

Yiddish Schools (n.d.), *Hagodah fun Unzer Driten Seder*. Melbourne.

1

ישראל-יהושע זינגער

בילגאריי, פוילן, 1893
ניו-יארק פאר. שטאטן, 1944

יאשע קאלב, (ראמאן, פיעסע)
משפחה קארנאוסקי, (ראמאן)
פון א וועלט וואס איז ניטא מער
די ברידער אשכנזי, (ראמאן)

ראמאניסט, דערציילער,
דראמאטורג

2

יעקב-יצחק סיגאל

סאלאבקאוויץ, פאדאליע, 1896
מאנטרעאל, קאנאדע, 1954

ספר יידיש
מיין ניגון
לידער וועגן לעבען
דאס הויז פון די פשוטע

פאעט, עסייאיסט

3

הערש סעקלער

בראדשין, גאליציע, 1883
לעבט אין ניו יארק, פאר. שטאטן

יזכור, (דראמע)
דעם צדיקס נסיעה, (דראמע)
דער זעער, (דראמע)
סקיצן און דערציילונגען

דראמאטורג,
דערציילער, עסייאיסט

4

פישל בימקא

קעלץ, פוילן, 1890
לעבט אין ניו יארק, פאר. שטאטן

אויפן ברעג וויסל, (דראמע)
גנבים, (דראמע)
דעמבעס, (דראמע)
קעלץ, (דערציילונגען)

דראמאטורג, דערציילער

5

א. לוצקי

(אהרן צוקער)

דימידאווקע, וואלין, 1893
ניו יארק, פאר. שטאטן, 1957

נעמט עס, ס'איז גוט פאר אייך!
בראשית — אינמיטן
אומעטיק און פריילעך
פארטרעטן

פאעט

6

י. באשעוויס-ווארשאווסקי

(יצחק זינגער)

ראדזימין, פוילן, 1904
לעבט אין ניו יארק, פ"שטאטן

דער שטן פון גאריי (דערצ.)
דער קנעכט (ראמאן)
די פאמיליע מושקאט, (ראמאן)
מיין טאטנ'ס בית-דין שטוב

דערציילער, ראמאניסט

1. Yisroel-yehoyshua Zinger, 1893–1944; Novelist, writer of short stories, playwright; 2. Yankev-yitskhok Sigal, 1896–1954; Poet, essayist; 3. Hersh Sekler, 1883–1974; Playwright, writer of short stories, essayist; 4. Fishl Bimko, 1890–1965; Playwright, writer of short stories; 5. A. Lutski, 1893–1957; Poet; 6. Y(ud) Bashevis-Varshavski (Zinger), 1904–   ; Writer of short stories, novelist.

Knowledge, Use, and Evaluation of Yiddish and Hebrew among American Jewish College Students

ALAN HUDSON-EDWARDS

Although Fishman (1965) has traced the expansion in the social roles of Yiddish in the United States during the years of mass European immigration, and its retrenchment since then, there has been little microsociolinguistic analysis of the functional allocation of Yiddish in the United States and none whatever of the societal roles of Hebrew. One exception is a study by Ronch (1968) which found that Yiddish use claiming among older speakers in the New York City area was greatest in the context of Jewish cultural activities, next greatest in the home setting, and weakest in the work domain.

The purpose of the present study is to present data on Yiddish and Hebrew proficiency, use, and attitudes among a group of 191 American Jewish college students, the majority of whom are in the third generation of residence in the United States. More specifically, the paper reports on the students' self-assessments of their abilities in Yiddish and Hebrew, their actual use of either language in each of five social contexts, their desire to use either language in each of these situations given the necessary proficiency to do so, their perceptions of the ability of situationally appropriate interlocutors to speak Yiddish or Hebrew to them if necessary, and, finally, their expectations regarding the likely reactions of these same interlocutors to the use of Yiddish or Hebrew.

METHODOLOGY

A questionnaire containing 131 scorable items dealing with language and Jewish identity was administered to 191 Jewish college students at five institutions in the New York City area. Subjects for the study were selected by means of contacts with teachers in Jewish-oriented courses at the five academic institutions. Questionnaires were distributed during regular class periods either by the investigator himself or by the class instructor. Pretests of the instrument had indicated that it would take a minimum of one hour to complete and this was considered to be an unacceptable imposition upon regular class time. Accordingly, subjects were permitted to take the questionnaire home with them and to complete it at their own convenience. Questionnaires were returned to the instructor approximately one week after distribution.

The questionnaire contained two major components. The first consisted of 78 items dealing with the language background of the subjects, their abilities in Hebrew and Yiddish, their language-use patterns, and their language attitudes. The second component contained 53 scorable items which solicited information regarding religious observance, attitudes toward the State of Israel, participation in Jewish organizations, general attitudes toward Jewish identity, and a variety of other topics. As only the first section of the questionnaire is germane to the topic of this report, further information is provided under the appropriate headings below. The full instrument is reproduced in the appendix to Hudson (1977).

FINDINGS
Language proficiency

As approximate measures of language proficiency, participants in the study were asked to provide self-assessments of their ability to speak, understand, read, and write Yiddish and Hebrew. As measures of their speaking abilities in these languages, participants were asked to indicate on ten-point scales how well they could conduct a conversation at home, first in Yiddish and then in Hebrew, talking to members of their families about family affairs. Separate contexts were provided for the items dealing with ability to understand Yiddish and Hebrew. In the case of Yiddish, participants were asked how well they might understand a conversation about the events of the day between two Eastern European Jews sitting beside them on a bus. In the case of Hebrew, they were asked to report their ability to understand a conversation taking place in a school cafeteria or coffee shop between a group of Israeli students discussing current events. Finally, the participants were asked, separately for Yiddish and Hebrew and again on ten-point scales, how well they could read a newspaper and write a letter to a friend in either language.

The data on all items pertaining to reported proficiency in Yiddish and Hebrew are summarized in Table 1. Although there is some variation between languages and between modalities, it is clear that, on the whole, proficiency in both Yiddish and Hebrew is at an extremely low level.

Yiddish proficiency

On the average, the respondents to the questionnaire report themselves to be familiar with some Yiddish vocabulary beyond a few stock words and phrases, but not quite able to conduct a 'short, halting, conversation' in the language.[1] Approximately one respondent in seven claimed not to be able to speak any Yiddish whatsoever, while a further 37 percent claimed knowledge of no more than a few words and phrases. At the higher end of the scale, on the other hand, some 12 percent of the respondents claimed sufficient facility with Yiddish to at least be able to conduct a 'rapid, extended, conversation' in the language.

The data of Table 1 suggest, not surprisingly, that passive competence in Yiddish runs slightly ahead of competence in the corresponding active modality. Thus, as a group, the respondents appear able, though with difficulty, to understand 'short, slow, conversation'. More specifically in this instance, only 11 percent of the respondents are unable to understand any Yiddish at all while only 30 percent understand 'a few words [or] phrases'. Fully 19 percent of the respondents fall at the average, however, while an additional 22 percent would be able to follow a rapid, extended conversation, apparently without serious impairment of comprehension.

Literacy skills in Yiddish, due no doubt to the problems of mastering an unfamiliar alphabet, are at lower levels than the corresponding oral skills. Fully one-quarter of the respondents can read no Yiddish at all, while almost one-third can write none. A further 26 percent claim to be able to read, and 19 percent to be able to write, only a few words or phrases. Only seven percent and eight percent of the respondents, respectively, claim moderately good or better proficiency in reading and writing Yiddish – this compared with 12 percent and 22 percent, respectively, who could speak and understand the language with some facility.

Hebrew proficiency

Hebrew proficiency, among the students of this sample, compares favorably with Yiddish ability, especially in the area of writing skills, where the average response is indicative of ability to write a 'short, simple, note on some subjects' though 'probably with grammatical errors'. The proportion of respondents claiming moderate, or better, fluency in writing Hebrew (32 percent) is dramatically higher than the corresponding proportion for Yiddish (8 percent) although, at the other extreme, the proportions claiming no knowledge of Yiddish and Hebrew are almost identical (30 percent and 29 percent, respectively).

Reading knowledge of Hebrew is also, on average, one full scale point ahead of reading knowledge of Yiddish, though simultaneous comprehension of text is still reportedly quite limited. As in the case of Yiddish, one-quarter of the respondents report they are unable to read any Hebrew whatever; however, fully

---

1. Unless otherwise indicated, unacknowledged quotation marks indicate direct quotations from the anchor points provided with the self-report scales. See Hudson (1977), Appendix B, for details.

21 percent, as opposed to seven percent in the case of Yiddish, claim sufficient knowledge of Hebrew for 'rapid, extended, reading [with] good understanding' of the text.

Ability to speak Hebrew is also somewhat more widespread than the ability to speak Yiddish, despite the fact that twice as many respondents (32 percent) claim to be unable to speak Hebrew as claim to be unable to speak Yiddish (15 percent). However, in the upper reaches of the proficiency scale, there are more fluent speakers of Hebrew than there are fluent speakers of Yiddish: while 21 percent of the respondents claim to be able to conduct a rapid, extended, conversation in Hebrew, only 12 percent could do so in Yiddish.

Lastly, ability to understand Hebrew exceeds, though not significantly, the ability to understand Yiddish, the average respondent claiming to be able to 'understand short, slow, conversation without difficulty'. Once again, whereas only 11 percent of the sample claim no comprehension of Yiddish, some 27 percent claim no comprehension of Hebrew. On the other hand, however, while only 22 percent of the sample can understand 'rapid, extended, conversation' in Yiddish, 36 percent can do so in Hebrew.

Charity Rescues from Death. Hebrew (old grandmother carrying the struggling, newly founded American Hebrew Weekly *Hadoar*) to Yiddish (modern young lady): 'Don't be stingy, miss. Give us a little publicity.' (*Der groyser kundes*, November 11, 1921)

Relationships between self-reports of proficiency

As might be expected, all of the Yiddish proficiency items are highly inter-correlated as are all of the Hebrew proficiency items. The average Kendall's Tau correlation coefficient for the six nonredundant pairs of Yiddish items was 0.62 and that for the corresponding pairs of Hebrew items 0.76. This differential is almost certainly due to the contrast between the social acquisition contexts for Hebrew and for Yiddish. While Hebrew most typically is acquired in the context of some variety of formal Jewish education, where literacy skills are emphasized along with oral–aural skills, knowledge of Yiddish is much more likely to be acquired in the home setting where reading and writing of the language may play no significant role whatever. Accordingly, those who claim fluency in spoken Hebrew are also likely to claim proficiency in reading the language while, in the case of Yiddish, although the same trend obtains to a lesser extent, there are some native or near native speakers of the language whose literacy skills are quite limited.

Relationships between Yiddish proficiency items, on the one hand, and Hebrew proficiency items, on the other, appear to be random, however. Of the 16 possible correlations between these items, 12 are negative in direction and four positive. Only six correlations even border on statistical significance and none, in any case, exceeds 0.12 in magnitude. Disregarding sign, the average Kendall's Tau correlation coefficient across all possible pairs of items was 0.06.

Generational trends in language proficiency

Table 1 provides a cross-tabulation of Yiddish and Hebrew proficiency by generational status of the respondents. The pattern for Yiddish is clear: under each proficiency category, facility in Yiddish diminishes with increasing distance from the generation of immigration. Indeed, the generational stratification of Yiddish proficiency is so fine as to distinguish consistently, and in the anticipated direction, between native born respondents of foreign parentage, natives of mixed parentage, and natives of native parentage. The Kendall's Tau correlation coefficients between Yiddish proficiency and generational status, as can also be seen in Table 1, are all highly significant and negative in direction.

There is evidence in Table 1 for a curvilinear relationship between Hebrew proficiency and generational status. In all modalities, it is the foreign born who claim the greatest proficiency in Hebrew and the immediately succeeding generations, the native of foreign or mixed parentage, who claim the least. With the advent of the third and later generations, however, there appears an increase in knowledge of Hebrew. One is tempted to speculate, cautiously, that this increase is related to a third-generation resurgence of interest in Jewish identity, in Israeli nationalism, and perhaps also in religious orthodoxy, and that Hebrew

Table 1.   *Self-reports of language proficiency, by generational status*

| | | Self-reports of proficiency | | | | | | | |
| | | Yiddish | | | | Hebrew | | | |
Generation	*n*	Speaking	Under-standing	Reading	Writing	Speaking	Under-standing	Reading	Writing
All respondents	191	2.4[a]	3.2	2.4	2.1	3.1[b]	3.7	3.4	3.5[a]
Foreign born	15	4.7	6.5	4.3	3.2	4.9	4.9	5.0	4.8
Native, of foreign parentage	44	3.8	5.2	3.5	3.4	2.6[c]	3.2	2.9	2.8
Native, of mixed parentage	25	2.2	3.2	2.1	2.0	2.5[d]	3.1	2.7	3.0[d]
Native, of native parentage	62	1.6[e]	2.2	1.8	1.7	3.2[f]	3.6	3.1	3.5
One or more grand-parents native	43	1.5[g]	1.8	1.6	1.3	3.3[h]	4.2	3.8	4.0[g]
Tau		−0.34	−0.43	−0.29	−0.28	−0.00	0.04	−0.03	0.05
P		<0.0001	<0.0001	<0.0001	<0.0001	0.48	0.23	0.30	0.19

[a] $n = 189$ [b] $n = 183$ [c] $n = 43$ [d] $n = 24$ [e] $n = 61$ [f] $n = 59$ [g] $n = 42$ [h] $n = 40$.

is displacing Yiddish as the linguistic expression of these interests. Indeed, Goldstein and Goldscheider (1968) argue that the role of Hebrew in Jewish education as well as pride in the State of Israel have contributed to increased knowledge of Hebrew as a written and spoken language.

In pointing to the apparent revival of interest in Hebrew among later generations of Jews in the United States, however, it is essential also to emphasize that the sample of respondents for this study is susceptible to a very special type of bias. All of these students have already made a deliberate commitment to Judaism by their participation in Jewish religious, cultural, and intellectual life. Many are students of Jewish thought, Jewish literature, and Jewish social history; others are rabbinical students, while still others are active members of Jewish student organizations. As Fishman (1965) has pointed out, it is precisely among such groups – the Orthodox religious, the secular Zionists, and, to a lesser extent, the Conservative and Reform religious, educational, and organizational leadership – that the most complete mastery of Hebrew is to be encountered in the United States. This being the case, it may safely be assumed that the signs of a Hebrew revival among the students in the present study do not necessarily presage a return to Hebrew among the general, less consciously identified, Jewish community.

Table 2. *Situational measures of actual language use, ideal language use, perceived proficiency of interlocutors, and expected reaction to language use*

Item	Context				
	Grand-parents	Parents	Seder	Organi-zations	Rabbi
Actual language use					
Yiddish	1.3	0.9	0.8	0.3	0.3
Hebrew	0.6	0.6	1.2	1.1	0.6
Ideal language use					
Yiddish	6.2	5.0	4.6	4.2	4.8
Hebrew	6.2	5.9	6.1	5.8	6.3
Perceived ability of interlocutors					
Yiddish	5.3	5.7	4.3	3.6	6.7
Hebrew	2.5	2.6	2.9	4.4	7.0
Expected reaction to use					
Yiddish	6.8	6.4	5.6	4.6	6.6
Hebrew	5.3	5.4	5.1	5.5	6.8

Language use: actual and ideal

Twenty items on the study questionnaire enquired as to the participants' use of Yiddish and Hebrew in five different societal domains characterized by situationally congruent combinations of interlocutors, topics, and locales (Greenfield and Fishman 1972; Fishman 1972). The five representative situations selected for inclusion in the study, on the grounds that they would be most likely to reveal differential allocation of Yiddish and Hebrew, were: the home in conversation with grandparents, the home in conversation with parents, at a Passover seder with family and friends, in conversation with a rabbi about religious matters, and in conversation with fellow members of Jewish organizations to which the respondent belonged. These situations resembled closely those employed by Ronch (1968) in his earlier study of word naming and Yiddish claiming among older, first generation, Jews in New York City.

One-half of the items asked the participants to report their actual use of Yiddish and Hebrew in each environment; the second half asked how much Yiddish or Hebrew the participants would like to use in each of the same five situations assuming fluency in both languages on their own part and on the part of all of their interlocutors. The results are summarized in Table 2 above.

Actual language use

Given the extremely severe limitations on language proficiency in the study sample, it comes as no surprise that actual use of Yiddish and Hebrew is minimal or, in most cases, nonexistent. Yiddish language use is greatest in the domestic sphere of activity, and in particular in conversation with grandparents; it is virtually nonexistent, however, outside the home and family setting. Although fully two-thirds of the sample use essentially no Yiddish at all in conversation with their grandparents, some 12 percent use it at least half the time. In conversation with parents and with family and friends at a seder, the proportion of those using no Yiddish rises almost to three-quarters, while the percentage of respondents using Yiddish at least half of the time drops to seven percent. Both in the organizational context, and in conversation with a rabbi, only a handful of respondents report any use of Yiddish at all.

Generational shift in language use is, naturally, everywhere in evidence in the case of Yiddish. Thus, among the 13 foreign born respondents, 46 percent speak Yiddish to their grandparents more than half the time; among the native born of foreign or mixed parentage, the corresponding figure is 22 percent, while, among the later generations, it drops to a mere three percent, In fact, none of the 42 respondents claiming at least one native born grandparent speaks Yiddish to their grandparents more than half the time. Furthermore, for each generational category the proportion of respondents claiming to use no Yiddish with their parents is always greater than the proportion claiming to have used no Yiddish with their grandparents, while the proportion claiming frequent use with parents is always less than the corresponding proportion for grandparents.

Hebrew language use is scarcely more widespread than is Yiddish, though its functional allocation is slightly different. It is used hardly at all in conversations with grandparents, parents, and rabbi, but is apparent, to a very limited degree, in the contexts of the Passover seder and Jewish organizational activities. Some 10 percent of the respondents claim to use Hebrew at least half the time when participating in a seder and an additional 30 percent claim they would use it to some appreciable degree in such circumstances. The situation is not much different in the organizational context, nine percent claiming to use Hebrew half the time and 23 percent claiming to use it at least some measurable portion of the time.

Compared with Yiddish, there is little sign of generational effect upon the extent of Hebrew use claiming. The foreign born, it is true, claim frequent use of Hebrew, in all situational contexts, far more often than do the native born, but this effect is almost entirely due to the presence in the sample of six Israeli students, all native speakers of Hebrew. One other peripheral generational trend is also in evidence in that 10 percent of the third generation respondents, as opposed to only two percent of the second generation, claim to use Hebrew at least half the time in conversation with a rabbi.

Ideal language use

If self-reports of preferred language use can be taken as a guide, then it is clear that affective attitudes toward Yiddish and Hebrew remain quite strong among the study population, despite the severely limited levels of proficiency and the even more limited levels of actual use.

In the case of Yiddish, the contextual variation found with regard to actual use of the language is apparent also with respect to ideal use, the main contrast being that between conversation with grandparents and conversation in other contexts. By a considerable margin, respondents would most be inclined to use Yiddish in conversation with their grandparents about life in the latters' native town. In this particular environment 71 percent of the respondents indicated they would wish to use Yiddish at least half of the time, given fluency in the language on the part of all of the participants in the conversation, while fully one-third declared they would wish to use Yiddish all the time. Among the remaining four environments, the differences are not so substantial, though conversation with parents is clearly more congruent with Yiddish use than is conversation with fellow members of Jewish organizations.

Unlike Yiddish, there is very little contextualization in evidence in the case of the data on ideal use of Hebrew, the difference between the most favored environment, conversation with a rabbi, and the least favored, Jewish organizational activities, being a mere five percentage points. This, in itself, is not particularly surprising given that for most of the respondents in the sample — apart, of course, from the native Israelis — Hebrew, in contrast with Yiddish, has never presented any natural contexts for use other than prayer and recitation of the Jewish liturgy. However, what is surprising in the light of this consideration is the fact that, in every context but one, Hebrew substantially outranks Yiddish in terms of ideal use. Although the respondents indicate they would wish to use Hebrew with their grandparents to the same degree they would wish to use Yiddish, they are more inclined toward the use of Hebrew in conversation with a rabbi, with family and friends at a seder, with parents, and with fellow members of Jewish organizations. Perhaps, as one author noted previously, this is indeed evidence that 'Hebrew is increasingly becoming the cultural emblem *par excellence* of Jewish identity in the Diaspora' (Herman 1970: 82).

Relationships between actual and ideal use

Given the fact, reported earlier, that 52 percent of the respondents in the study knew, at best, only a few words and phrases of Yiddish, it is certainly not surprising to find major discrepancies between self-reports of actual language use and ideal language use. Whereas actual language use is logically constrained by the real limits of language proficiency, reports of ideal language use are predicated upon the assumption of fluency in Yiddish or Hebrew on the part of the respondent and all of his interlocutors in any given situation. Moreover, relationships between actual and ideal use vary considerably from context to context and from language to language.

Table 3 displays the Pearson product–moment correlation coefficients between the ideal and actual language reports in each social context for each language. All of these correlations are significant at or beyond the 0.05 level of probability and five are significant at or beyond the 0.001 level. In the case of Yiddish, the congruence between actual and ideal is greatest in the three domestic settings as reflected in the relatively higher correlations found in the contexts of conversation with grandparents, conversation with parents, and conversation with family and friends at a seder. The relationship between actual and ideal use is rather more attenuated in the context of Jewish organizational activities and is virtually nonexistent, though nonetheless systematic, in the context of conversation with a rabbi.

Contextual effects upon the relationship between actual and ideal use are also evident for Hebrew, though the pattern of relationships appears to be in complementary distribution with that for Yiddish. Thus, within the domestic sphere of interaction all three correlations between actual and ideal use fall markedly below the levels of the corresponding correlations for Yiddish. Outside of the home environment, however, the relationships between actual and ideal are stronger for Hebrew than they are for Yiddish, especially in the organizational context.

Other situational determinants of language use and language attitude

The context-dependent and language-dependent nature of the relationships between actual and ideal use suggests strongly the need to explore other intervening variables which might help to explain this variability. The variable most likely to account for variation in language use, of course, is language proficiency. However, there is no reason to expect a perfectly linear relationship between ability and use. While it is obvious that those who do not know the language cannot, therefore, use it, it is not necessarily the case that all those who do not use it do not know it. Similarly, while those who use the language with some frequency must be reasonably fluent in order to do so, it is by no means necessarily so that all those who are fluent in the language will always use it when the occasion arises. The question that may then be asked, therefore, is: Having controlled for the variability due to language proficiency, what remaining variables, and in what order of importance, contribute to explaining the variance in actual language use? For the purposes of the present report, four such additional variables have been examined: (1) attitude, as measured by ideal language use; (2) opportunity, as indicated by the respondents' perceptions of the ability of various interlocutors, in various congruent situations, to understand Yiddish and Hebrew; (3) situational reinforcement as defined by the respondents' perceptions of the social consequences of using either Yiddish or Hebrew in various situational contexts; and (4) generational status of the respondents.

The first three variables mentioned were examined by asking participants in the study questions of the following sort:

1. Imagine, once again, that you are visiting with your grandparents and are talking about life in their native town. If you were to speak Yiddish to your grandparents in this situation, how well do you think they would understand?
2. How do you think they would respond to your speaking Yiddish to them?
3. Assuming you were *all* fluent speakers of Yiddish, how much Yiddish would you *like* to speak in this situation?

The question was then repeated substituting the word 'Hebrew' for each occurrence of 'Yiddish' in the above example. Subjects responded to the first portion of the question on the same ten-point scale used in reporting their own language proficiency; they responded to the third portion on the same scale as had been used in reporting their own actual use of Yiddish and Hebrew. The scale for the second portion of the question consisted of a set of ten anchor points ranging from extreme hostility, anger, or sarcasm through indifference to extreme pride, enthusiasm, or praise.

The data on ideal language use have already been discussed at considerable length; however, a brief summary of the data on opportunity to speak Yiddish and Hebrew and on the perceived social consequences of doing so is in order at this point (see Table 2).

The data of Table 2 show, in sum, that the use of Yiddish in conversation with parents, grandparents, and rabbi is *feasible* in the sense that all of these potential interlocutors, and especially the rabbi, are perceived, on the whole, to have a more than adequate command of the language for simple conversational purposes. Not surprisingly, therefore, these same interlocutors are the ones from whom the respondents would expect a distinctly positive response to the use of Yiddish. Jewish organizational activities, on the other hand, seemingly provide the least opportunity to use Yiddish as well as the least positive social reinforcement for doing so.

With regard to Hebrew, it is the rabbi, once again, who is expected to have the greatest mastery of the language, followed at quite some distance by fellow organization members. Opportunity to use Hebrew is most circumscribed in the home contexts of conversation with grandparents, with parents, and with family and friends at a seder. Accordingly, by a considerable margin, the rabbi is also identified as the individual most likely to respond positively to the use of Hebrew. While the organizational environment is also seen as the next most conducive to the use of Hebrew, it is only minimally more positive than the three domestic contexts.

Table 3.   *Zero-order correlations with actual language use, by social context*

Context	Ability	Ideal use	Ability of interlocutor	Reaction of interlocutor	Generation
Yiddish					
Grandparents	0.72	0.27	0.32	0.18	−0.46
Parents	0.65	0.37	0.34	0.22	−0.47
Seder	0.60	0.32	0.36	0.21	−0.43
Organizations	0.35	0.21	0.25	0.08	−0.25
Rabbi	0.27	0.13	0.09	0.05	−0.17
Hebrew					
Grandparents	0.37	0.15	0.35	0.14	−0.34
Parents	0.47	0.25	0.54	0.21	−0.34
Seder	0.45	0.18	0.44	0.22	−0.24
Organizations	0.43	0.32	0.46	0.31	−0.16
Rabbi	0.40	0.19	0.15	0.08	−0.21

Table 4.   *Multiple prediction of actual language use in various social contexts*

Actual language use	Predictor variables										Multiple R
	Ability		Ideal use		Ability of interlocutor		Reaction of interlocutor		Generation		
	Order	Δr^2	Order	Δr^2	Order	Δr^2	Order	Δr^2	Order	Δr^2	
Yiddish											
Grandparents	1	0.51	4	0.01	3	0.02	5	0.00	2	0.02	0.75
Parents	1	0.42	2	0.05	5	0.00	4	0.01	3	0.03	0.70
Seder	1	0.35	2	0.03	—	—	4	0.00	3	0.02	0.64
Organizations	1	0.12	4	0.01	2	0.02	3	0.01	5	0.00	0.40
Rabbi	1	0.08	2	0.01	4	0.00	—	—	3	0.00	0.29
Hebrew											
Grandparents	1	0.14	4	0.00	3	0.03	5	0.00	2	0.11	0.53
Parents	2	0.06	4	0.00	1	0.29	5	0.00	3	0.05	0.63
Seder	1	0.20	5	0.00	2	0.06	4	0.00	3	0.04	0.55
Organizations	2	0.08	3	0.03	1	0.22	5	0.00	4	0.02	0.59
Rabbi	1	0.16	3	0.02	5	0.00	4	0.00	2	0.04	0.47

The multiple prediction of actual language use

Table 3 displays the zero-order correlations between actual language use, on the one hand, and ability, attitude, opportunity, social consequences of language use, and generational status on the other. Table 4 displays for each social context the order in which each of the same five independent variables emerges in a stepwise multiple regression of actual language use, as well as the percentage increase in explained variance at the point at which each independent variable was introduced into the regression equation. Comparison of the data in these two tables results in a number of interesting contrasts between Yiddish and Hebrew.

Yiddish ability is always the highest zero-order correlate of Yiddish use and therefore invariably emerges as the most significant independent variable in the multiple prediction of Yiddish use (see Table 4). This is especially so in the case of the three home contexts of Yiddish use with grandparents, with parents, and with family and friends at a seder celebration. Yiddish ability is a far more successful predictor of language use in these environments than any of the other situational or demographic variables. Furthermore, it is a better predictor of language use in these environments than it is in the remaining two contexts of language use with a rabbi or in organizational settings. Lastly, it may be noted that Yiddish ability is a better predictor of Yiddish use in the home contexts than is Hebrew ability of Hebrew use in the same three situational contexts.

Hebrew ability also is the most important single predictor of Hebrew use in three of the five situations studied; in the remaining two situations it is the second most important. In contrast with Yiddish, the relationship between ability and use is relatively stable across contexts for Hebrew, the zero-order correlations ranging from 0.37 to 0.47 across all situational contexts. Although the correlations between Hebrew ability and Hebrew use in the home contexts are slight when compared to those for Yiddish, the correlations in the contexts of organizational activities and conversation with a rabbi are somewhat larger than the Yiddish correlations in these same contexts.

Although generational status is the second highest zero-order correlate of Yiddish language use, the overlap in variance between generation and Yiddish ability is sufficiently great as to minimize its incremental contribution to the prediction of actual Yiddish use. Attitude toward Yiddish, as expressed by ideal Yiddish use, is, in fact, marginally more important in this regard, especially in the context of conversation with parents where it adds some five percentage points to the proportion of variance in actual Yiddish use already explained by language ability alone. Both the ability of the respondents' interlocutors to speak Yiddish, and the perceived social consequences of using Yiddish in various contexts are of scarcely any significance whatever in the multiple prediction of actual Yiddish use. In sum, it may be claimed that the fundamental consideration

Table 5.   *Zero-order correlations with ideal language use, by social context*

Context	Ability	Ideal use	Ability of interlocutor	Reaction of interlocutor	Generation
Yiddish					
Grandparents	0.27	0.21	0.11	0.18	−0.16
Parents	0.37	0.26	0.12	0.12	−0.27
Seder	0.32	0.24	0.30	0.29	−0.25
Organizations	0.21	0.29	0.45	0.45	−0.20
Rabbi	0.13	0.17	0.07	0.32	−0.17
Hebrew					
Grandparents	0.15	0.27	0.08	0.14	−0.10
Parents	0.25	0.29	0.16	0.12	−0.22
Seder	0.18	0.24	0.19	0.21	−0.10
Organizations	0.32	0.17	0.29	0.39	−0.06
Rabbi	0.19	0.08	0.15	0.28	−0.14

Table 6.   *Multiple prediction of ideal language use in various social contexts*

Actual language use	Predictor variables										Multiple R
	Ability		Ideal use		Ability of interlocutor		Reaction of interlocutor		Generation		
	Order	Δr^2	Order	Δr^2	Order	Δr^2	Order	Δr^2	Order	Δr^2	
Yiddish											
Grandparents	1	0.07	5	0.00	4	0.00	2	0.02	3	0.00	0.30
Parents	1	0.14	4	0.00	—	—	3	0.00	2	0.01	0.39
Seder	1	0.10	5	0.00	4	0.00	2	0.05	3	0.02	0.42
Organizations	4	0.01	3	0.03	1	0.20	2	0.03	5	0.00	0.52
Rabbi	4	0.01	2	0.03	3	0.02	1	0.10	5	0.01	0.40
Hebrew											
Grandparents	5	0.00	1	0.08	4	0.01	3	0.01	2	0.01	0.31
Parents	4	0.01	1	0.09	3	0.00	5	0.00	2	0.05	0.38
Seder	4	0.00	1	0.06	5	0.00	2	0.01	3	0.01	0.29
Organizations	2	0.04	4	0.00	5	0.00	1	0.15	3	0.00	0.45
Rabbi	3	0.02	5	0.00	4	0.00	1	0.08	2	0.03	0.36

in understanding Yiddish use is Yiddish ability. In the context of conversation with parents, the addition of the four nonproficiency items yields a multiple correlation of 0.70, a gain of 0.05 over the correlation obtained with Yiddish ability alone. In the context of organizational activities, all five predictors yield a multiple correlation of 0.40, again an increase of 0.05 over the correlation obtained with Yiddish ability alone. In the remaining three environments, the increases in the multiple correlations due to the addition of the nonproficiency items is 0.04 or less.

By contrast, the increase in the multiple correlations with Hebrew use obtained by introducing all five predictors into the regression ranges from 0.07 to 0.16. In the case of conversation with grandparents, for example, proficiency is clearly the most important consideration in predicting actual Hebrew use; however, it is followed in close succession by generational status, which adds an additional 11 percentage points to the proportion of variance explained by ability alone. In the context of conversation with parents, it is the ability of the parents to speak Hebrew that is the most important predictor of Hebrew use, though generational status and the speaker's own proficiency in Hebrew together account for an additional 11 percent of the variance in language use.

The prediction of ideal language use

Table 5 presents the zero-order correlations obtaining between ideal language use, on the one hand, and actual language use, own language ability, interlocutor's language ability, interlocutor's expected reaction to language use, and generational status, on the other. Table 6 shows the multiple correlation obtained by regressing the criterion variable, ideal language use, against the remaining five predictor variables. In addition, Table 6 also shows the order in which each of the predictor variables was introduced into the stepwise multiple regression as well as the increment in explained variance obtained by its introduction at that point. In eight out of ten instances, the multiple correlations with ideal language use are considerably less than those obtained with actual language use as the criterion variable (see Table 4).

In the contexts of conversation with grandparents and parents, it is the extent of *actual* Yiddish use that accounts for most of the variance that can be explained in *ideal* Yiddish use. The more frequently Yiddish is actually used in these two home settings the more likely are respondents to claim to wish to use Yiddish given proficiency in the language on the part of all the interlocutors present. Although this tendency is present, it should be pointed out that it is slight indeed ($r = 0.27$), especially when compared with the relationship between Yiddish ability and actual Yiddish use ($r = 0.72$). Nonetheless, of all the predictors in the equation, actual language use remains the most significant correlate of ideal language use – so much so, in fact, that the remaining four predictors can add virtually nothing to the explained variance in the criterion once actual language use is controlled for.

Actual language use is also the dominant predictor of ideal language use in the context of conversation with family and friends at a seder celebration. However, the remaining predictors are sufficiently independent of actual language use that an additional five percent of the variance in the criterion is explained by the expected reaction of one's interlocutors to the use of Yiddish and a further two percent by the generational status of the respondent. While the zero-order correlation between actual and ideal use of Yiddish in this situation is 0.32, the cumulative correlation obtained by including interlocutor's reaction and generational status is an appreciable 0.42.

Outside the home and family setting, factors other than the extent of actual use take precedence in determining attitudes toward Yiddish use. In the case of Jewish organizational activity, it is the *interlocutor's* ability to speak Yiddish that accounts for the greatest proportion, 20 percent, of variance in Yiddish attitudes. Moreover, the interlocutor's expected reaction to use of Yiddish and the speaker's own proficiency in the language account for an additional three percent of the variance each. In the case of conversation with a rabbi, it is the latter's expected reaction to Yiddish use that is the most important consideration, accounting for 10 percent of the variance; a further three percent of the variance is accounted for by the respondent's own fluency in Yiddish and an additional two percent by the rabbi's perceived fluency. The result is that when the three most important predictors are included in the regression, a multiple correlation of 0.39 is obtained with ideal language use.

The preceding data indicate that where there has been some history of actual use of Yiddish, the abilities and attitudes of the interlocutors are known and largely taken for granted. Accordingly, it is the extent of actual Yiddish use which, more than any of the other variables considered, tends to shape preferences in idealized situations. In contrast, in those situations lacking such a history of Yiddish use it is the more immediate situational considerations of interlocutor's abilities and attitudes that assume primary importance.

As for ideal use of Hebrew, it is the respondent's proficiency in the language that accounts for most of the explained variance in the contexts of conversations with parents, grandparents, and family and friends at a seder celebration. Apart from the fact that generational status accounts for an additional five percent of the variance in the context of conversation with parents, none of the other predictors ever explains more than one percent of the variance in ideal language use. In organizational settings, and in conversation with one's rabbi, it is the reaction of the interlocutors in each of these situations which becomes the most important predictor of ideal language use.

In sum, both for Yiddish and Hebrew, in all situations, such variance in ideal language use as can be explained is attributable largely to one predictor only. For Yiddish, extent of actual use explains between seven percent and 10 percent of the variance in ideal language use in the home settings; other variables have little incremental predictive value once this first variable is partialled out. In conversation with fellow members of Jewish organizations, it is the Yiddish ability of one's conversation partners that is the most important consideration while, in conversation with one's rabbi, since the latter is the person most expected to be able to speak Yiddish (Table 2), it is the interlocutor's perceived attitude toward the use of Yiddish that is most significant. As far as Hebrew is concerned, however, it is the Hebrew ability of the respondent that most accounts for ideal use of Hebrew in the home settings; outside of the home it is the perceived attitude of the interlocutor which is most important.

SUMMARY

This report has shown that, among a group of 191 Jewish college students in the New York area, knowledge of Yiddish and Hebrew is at a relatively low level. Generational distance from immigrant status is associated with a decline in Yiddish skills and, among more recent generations, at least, with a slight upturn in the level of Hebrew skills (Table 1). Actual use of Yiddish and Hebrew is virtually nonexistent, although some slight situational contextualization still remains in evidence: Yiddish is most frequently used with grandparents and with parents while Hebrew is most frequently used with family and friends at a seder and in Jewish organizational activities (Table 2). Given proficiency in Hebrew and Yiddish on the part of all interlocutors in a given situation, respondents would most wish to use Yiddish in conversation with their grandparents. Yet even in this most Yiddish of all situations, the language of Israel ranks on a par with the immigrant language as a language for ideal use. In all other situations Hebrew is viewed more favorably than Yiddish for the purposes of ideal use (Table 2).

Interestingly, rabbis are perceived by the respondents as the individuals most likely to be proficient in Yiddish *and* Hebrew. Parents and grandparents are considered the next most proficient speakers of Yiddish, while colleagues in Jewish organizations are considered the second most proficient speakers of Hebrew. Grandparents, parents, and rabbis are seen as most likely to provide social reinforcement for the use of Yiddish, while rabbis are considered most likely to provide reinforcement for the use of Hebrew (Table 2).

Generally speaking, almost all of the explained variance in Yiddish and Hebrew attitudes and use is attributable to a single predictor variable. The most significant determinant of actual Yiddish use is always proficiency; proficiency is also the best predictor of actual Hebrew use in three out of five social contexts. Ideal Yiddish use is predicted mostly by extent of actual Yiddish use in the home settings and by the abilities and attitudes of the interlocutors outside of the home. Ideal Hebrew use is predicted by the speaker's own proficiency in the language in the three home settings, and by the anticipated social consequences of using Hebrew in other settings.

REFERENCES

Fishman, J. (1965), *Yiddish in America: Socio-Linguistic Description and Analysis*. Bloomington, Indiana, Indiana University Press.

— (1972), 'Domains and the relationship between micro- and macrosociolinguistics', in *Directions in Sociolinguistics: The Ethnography of Communication*, edited by J. Gumperz and D. Hymes, 435–453. New York, Holt, Rinehart and Winston.

Goldstein, S., Goldscheider, C. (1968), *Jewish Americans: Three Generations in a Jewish Community*. Englewood Cliffs, N.J., Prentice-Hall.

Greenfield, L., Fishman, J. (1977), 'Situational measures of normative language views in relation to person, place and topic among Puerto Rican bilinguals', in *Man, Language, and Society*, edited by S. Ghosh, 64–86. The Hague, Mouton.

Herman, S. (1970), *American Students in Israel*. Ithaca, N.Y., Cornell University Press.

Hudson, A. (1977), 'Language attitudes in relation to varieties of Jewish identification'. Unpublished doctoral dissertation, Yeshiva University.

Ronch, J. (1968), 'Word naming and usage scores in a sample of Yiddish–English bilinguals', in *Bilingualism in the Barrio: The Measurement and Description of Language Dominance in Bilinguals*, edited by J. Fishman, R. Cooper, and R. Ma, 564–576. Washington, D.C., U.S. Department of Health, Education, and Welfare.

PART VII

Sociolinguistic Variation and Planning

דער איסט בראָדוויער האמלעט

אידישער שרייבער: װי שרייבט מען: די קאָפּ — דער קאָפּ — דאָס
קאָפּ? — — — דאָס איז די פראַגע!

זעצער: ברעכט זיך נישט ס'קאָפּ, מיסטער! ס'װעט בלייבען, װי איך װעל
עס אויסזעצען. (געװידמעט דער ניי־געגרינדעטער אידיש־אַרבאַגראַפישער געזעלשאַפט.)

a. מען דארף זיך קלאָר מאַכן דעם חילוק צווישן **לינג-
וויסטיק** און **פֿילאָלאָגיע**. לינגוויסטיק איז אַן אַלגעמיינע
וויסנשאַפֿט, פֿילאָלאָגיע — אַ נאַציאָנאַלע. לינגוויסטיק
קאַן זיך באַשעפֿטיקן אויך מיט לחלוטין טויטע אָדער
לחלוטין ווילדע שפּראַכן; די פֿילאָלאָגיע זעצט אָבער פֿאָ־
רויס, אַז אַ שפּראַך, מיט וועלכער זי גיט זיך אָפּ **פֿאַר־
מאָגט אַ** קולטור־היסטאָרישן ווערט לפחות פֿאַר דעם
עבר. געוויינטלעך אָבער גייט די פֿילאָלאָגיע נאָך ווײַ־
טער און שטיצט זיך אויף דער איבערצײַגונג, אַז איר
שפּראַך האָט אַ נאַציאָנאַלן ווערט אין דער צוקונפֿט. ווער
ס'גלייבט ניט אין אינעם קיום פֿון דער יידישער שפּראַך, קאַן
אפשר נאָך זײַן אַ יידישער לינגוויסט, אָבער ניט קיין
פֿילאָלאָג.

b. נאָך אַלע מלחמות און קאַטאַסטראָפֿעס פֿאַרמאָגט נאָך
הײַנט יידיש אַ וויטאַלן כוח וואָס יעדעם פֿאָלק וואָלט
אַזאַ כוח אַנגענומען זוי אַ ברכה. קיין שום לשון וואָלט
נישט אַרויס אַזוי, ווי יידיש איז אַרויס פֿון אַלע פֿאַר־
לענדונג־מלחמות קעגן דעם דאָזיקן אוצר. עס איז נאָך
קיין מאָל אַזאַ בענקשאַפֿט נישט געווען צו יידיש —
נישט בלויז בײַ די וואָס יידיש איז זייער לשון, נאָר
אויך בײַ דער אַמעריקאַנער יוגנט, אויך בײַ די אין
ישראל, וואָס האָבן פֿריִער געפֿירט אַ קאַמף קעגן יידיש
און ערשט איצט הייבן זיי אָן צו פֿאַרשטיין, וואָס יידיש
האָט געמיינט פֿאַרן יידישן פֿאָלק.

c. *The growth of standardized Yiddish has been stimulated
since the middle of the nineteenth century by the precipitous
development of belles lettres and the employment of the
language as a medium of the press, of political movements,
of educational systems up to the college level, of scholarly
research, and occasionally of political administration. This
rapid growth has taken place simultaneously in many
countries, sometimes with only limited planning and coord-
ination. The Dictionary may therefore also have significance
for accomplished speakers and writers of Yiddish as a
checklist of modern terminology in which innovation has
been relatively decentralized. Where the author was faced
with a multiplicity of competing innovations, he generally
elected to recommend those that struck him as most felicitous
from the point of view of precision, idiomaticity of
patterning, and adequacy within a broader terminological
framework capable of further expansion.*

Mottos for Part VII

(a) 'The difference between linguistics and philology must be made clear. Linguistics is a general science, philology – a national science. Linguistics can keep busy with totally dead or entirely primitive languages; philology, however, requires that any language with which it is concerned have a cultural-historical value, at least insofar as the past is concerned. Normally, philology goes even further and bases itself on the conviction that its language is of national value in the future as well. Whoever does not believe in the future of the Yiddish language might perhaps be a Yiddish linguist, but he could never be a Yiddish philologist.' Ber Borokhov. Di ufgabn fun der yidisher filologye [The tasks of Yiddish philology, in Sh. Niger (ed.)]. *Pinkes: Yorbukh fun der yidisher literatur, far folklor, kritik un bibliografye* [Record Book: Annual of Yiddish Literature and Language, for Folklore, Criticism and Bibliography]. Vilna, Kletskin, 1913, 1–22.

(b) 'Even after all the wars and catastrophies Yiddish still has a vital power that any people would consider a blessing. No other language could emerge the way Yiddish emerged from the war of annihilation against its national heritage. Never before was there such a longing for Yiddish – not only among those that speak Yiddish, but also among American youth, and also among those in Israel who formerly engaged in a struggle against Yiddish and only now have they begun to understand what Yiddish has meant for the Jewish people.' Mordkhe Tsanin. Dos loshn yidish [The Yiddish Language], in his *Af di vegn fun yidishn goyrl* [On the Paths of Jewish Fate]. Tel Aviv. Hamenora, 1966, 77–94.

(c) Uriel Weinreich. Preface, in his *English–Yiddish, Yiddish–English Dictionary*. New York, McGraw-Hill, 1968, vii–viii.

Caption to illustration page 654
Hamlet on East Broadway. Yiddish writer (Hamlet): 'How should one write: di kop, der kop, dos kop? That's the question.' Typesetter: 'Don't bother your head (s'kop), mister. It will be spelled whichever way I set it in type.' (Dedicated to the newly-organized Yiddish Orthographic Society). (*Der groyser kundes*, April 5, 1918)

וועגן זשאַרגאָן אויסלייגן

שלום עליכם

SUMMARY: ABOUT SPELLING ZHARGON (= YIDDISH)
BY SHOLEM ALEYKHEM (ALEICHEM)

The most famous, most beloved and most translated Yiddish author (1859–1916), himself an early publisher and editor of modern Yiddish literary efforts, expounds on the need for a standard, unified spelling for Yiddish.

אונדזערע לעזער וועלן דאָ געפֿינען אַ נאָנץ צעטעל דרוקפֿעהלער, וועלכע מיר האָבּען בּעמערקט, פֿאַרבּיילויפֿענדיג איבּער דער „בּיבּליאָטהעק". דאָס זענען די הויפּטפֿעהלער, די גרֹאבּע גרייזען, אין וועלכע עס איז שׁוּלדיג, ווי דער שׁטײגער איז, דאָס בּפֿרה־הוהגדל, דער בּ חור ה ז ע צ ע ר; די איבּעריגע װאָרטער, לְמָשָׁל, װאָס מיר שרײבּען: „אֶרַע"—ניט „אַלֶרע", „פֿאַלֶען"—ניט „פֿאַללֶען", „װיסֶען"—ניט „װיססֶען", „זאַל"—ניט „זאַלל", „צוריק", „צוריקֿק"—ניט„צוריקֿק", „װיל"—ניט „װילל", „קאָן"—ניט „קאָנן", „קומֶען"—ניט „קוממֶען", „אַראפֿ"—ניט „הֶעראבּ", „פֿאַר"—ניט „פֿיר", „וּכְדוֹמָה ... רעכֶנֶען מיר כְּלַל נישׁט פֿאַר קיין גרייזען, דֶענן צו װאָס טויגֶען אוּנז די איבּעריגֶע אוֹתִיוֹת,װאָס שֶׁלֶעפֿען זיך נאָך סְתָּם אין יֶעדֶען װאָרט כְּמֶעט? מְמָה נַפְשָׁךְ, שׁרייבֶּען מיר דַײַטשׁ, דאַרפֶֿען מיר האַלֶטֶען אַלֶע כְּלָלים פֿון דֶער דײַטשׁער שׂפֿראַבֶּע; נו, װעֶר זשׁע װעֶט אוּנז דֶעמאַלֶט פֿאַרשׁטעֶהן? צוֹריק אבֶּער, נאָר אִינגאַנֶצֶען פֶֿערגרֵײַזֶען אוּנזֶער זשׁאַרגאָן, טאָר מֶען אוֹיךֶ ניט אוּן מֶע מוּז דאָךֶ אוֹיסֹאַרבֵּיטֶען עֶטֶליכֶע גֶעװיסֶע כְּלָלים, דאָס הֵייסֶט, גֶעװיסֶע צייכֶענֶם, בִּכְדֵי אַלֶע זאָלֶען שׁרֵײַבֶּען אוֹיף אֵיין שׁטֵײגֶער אוּג אֵינֶער דֶעם אַנֶדֶערֶען זאָל קאָנֶען פֶֿערשׁטעֶהן.

דְרום האָבֶּן מיר אוֹיסֹגֶעקֶליבֶּן אין דֶעם עֶנֶין פֿון אוֹיסֹלֶעגֶען (אָרפֿאַגראפֿיֶע, אָדֶער אָרֶטהאָגראפֿיֶע) פֿוּנֶקט די מיטֶעלֶװֶעג, אוּן די „בּיבּליאָטהעק" האָט זיך גֶעהאַלֶטֶן,

The Simplest Way of Instituting a Correct Orthography in the Yiddish Press: send the editors and writers back to kheyder (elementary school). (*Der groyser kundes*, April 12, 1918)

ווי װײַט מעגליך, דאָס לשון גיט ניט פֿערבריטטשען אָבּער אויך נישט שטאַרק
פֿערגרייזען, נאָר גראַדע אַזוי ווי מע רעדט בײַ אונגז, יודען, דאָ אין רוסלאַנד (ניט
אין דײַטשלאַנד) אין אַלע ערטער. דעם סאָרט אָרטאָגראַפֿיע האָט שׁוין
לאַנג אָנגעהויבֿען אויסצואַרבּײַטען דער „קול מבשׂר" און נאָכדעמדאָס „יוד"-פֿאָלקה-
בּלאַטט, אזוי אז די בּעסטע אונזערע זשאַרגאָניסטען שרײַבּען אַלע אין דעם אופֿן.
מעהר פֿון אַלע האָט און בּאַווינען אונזער גרויסער פֿאָלקסשרײַבּער, אַבּרַמאָװיטש,
כּמעט אין אַ גאַנצען צעהנדלינג גרויסע זשאַרגאָנישע בּיכער, אַז מע קאָן זיך נאָמנ
לײַכט באַגעהן אָהן טיעף דײַטש אָן לשון קודש, נאָר מיט פֿשוט יודיש, אַזוי ווי
מע רעדט. פּונקט אַזוי זעענ זיך נוהג אונזערע בּעסטע מיטאַרבּײַטער פֿון דער
„פֿאָלקסביבליאָטהעק", האַלטענדיג זיך נאָר אין די „עטליכע געצעהלטע כּללים,
דהיינו:

‏1. מע דאַרף שרײַבּן י ו ד י ש , אַזוי ווי מע רעדט .

‏2. מע דאַרף שרײַבּן אַזוי , אַז סאַ דאָר פּוילישער רעזער , סאַ דער ליטוואָק , זאָלען קאָנען פאַרשטעהן .

‏3. יעדער זשאַרגאָניסט דאַרף געדענקען אַז ער שרײַבּט ז ש אַ ר ג אָ ן , ד . ה . מעהר פאָר'ן פֿאָלק , פֿאָר'ן הָמון _עם .

‏4. דאָס אויסלענגען פֿון די דײַטשע וואָרטער דאַרפֿען זיין מעהר נאָהענט צו דײַטש .

‏5. עס דאַרף זיין אַ היליוק · צווישען וואָרטער , וואָס ווערען גלײַך אויסגערעדט און האָבּן צווייערלי בעדײַטונג , למשל : שטײַין · שטעהן—стоять , ואון . шטעהן—стоять Каmень—שטײַין · ; זוбы—צאָהן , און . צעהן—десять , וихъ—זייער , און · זעהר—очень ; וויинингַ · וועניג , און · ווенно—малo ; ציילען—ряды , און · צעהלען—считать ; сынъ—זוהן , солнце—זונן , און · זינן—смыслъ ; ей , ея—איהר · , און · איר—вы ; я везу, я веду—פיהר · , און · איך פיהר—четыре ; это—то—דעם , за , און · אָן—אָהן .

His friends, his enemies, and the truth are all in perfect agreement about Sholem Aleykhem: he took Yiddish from the scrap-heap ('jargon junk') and fashioned it into a thing of beauty ('golden Yiddish language'). (*Der groyser kundes*, May 9, 1916)

דָעם'—ЭТОГО בעזъ ; .װעגְנֶן' ; אוּן „װאַנֶן—вѣсить ; .פֿיעל"
מְנОГО—, אוּן „אִיךְ פֿיהל'—я чувствую—א. ז. וו. . .

מִיר מוּזְען זִיךְ מוֹדֶה זַיְין, אַז דָאס לָשוֹן פֿוּן דֶער „בִּיבְּלִיאָטְהֶעק" בִּכְלַל אִיז
מֶעהְר פּוֹילִיש, אַלְם לִיטְװיש', דָאס הֵייסְט! מֶעהְר װי מֶע רֶעדְט בַּיי אוּנְז אִין
פּוֹילִין, אִין װאָהְלִין, אוּקְרַיְינָא, אַלְם װִי מֶע רֶעדְט אִין דֶער לִיטַא,
װאוּ דִי יוּדֶען הָאבֶּן בֶּעזוּנְדֶערֶע אוֹיסְשְפְּרַאכְבֶּע (произношеніе выговоръ), אוּן
דָאס אִיז דֶערְפֿאַר, װײַל אִין דֶער „בִּיבְּלִיאָטְהֶעק" זֶענֶען דִי שְרַיְיבֶּער מֶעהְרְסְטֶענ-
טְהֵייל פּוֹילִישֶע יוּדֶען .קֵיינֶער זַעט אוּנְז אָבֶּער נִישְט אַיְינְרֶעדֶען, אַז דֶער לִיטְװאַק
פֿעֶרְשְטֶעהְט נִיט אוּנְזֶער פּוֹילִישֶען זְשַאַרְנָאן, אוּן נִישְט נָאר דֶער לִיטְװאַק, אַפֿילוּ
דֶער אֶמֶת'עֶר דַיְיטְשֶער יוּד (נִיט פֿוּן דִי לִיטְװֶענֶשֶע דַיְיטְשֶען) פֿעֶרְשְטֶעהְט אוֹיךְ
אוּנְזֶער לָשוֹן, אוֹיבְּ עֶר װיל נָאר . . .

עֶס טְרֶעפֿט אָפֿטְמָאל צוּ לֶעזֶען, װי אֵייניגֶע מַאכֶּן חוֹזֶק אִיבֶּער דִי אוֹיס-
דְרוּקְע אִינ'ם זְשַאַרְנָאן, לְמָשָל: „בֶּעשִינְפֿעֶרְלִיךְ", „קְלַאמְפֶּעֶרְשְט", „מִשְטֵיינְם גֶעזַאגְט" *)
„סַאי װֶסַאי", „קַאטְאָועֶס", „מֶחַיֵיבֶא תֵּתִי" (מַכְּתִיתִי) „אִי אַהֶער אִי אַהִין", „נִישְקָשָה",
„חָלֶעבֶּען", וּכְדוֹמֶה, אַזֶעלְכֶע װאָרְטֶער, װאָם װעֶרֶען בֶּענוּצְט, גֶעװאָהְנְלִיךְ, נִישְט
אִין הוֹיכֶע פֿיִלָאזָאפֿישֶע, אָדֶער פָּאלִיטִישֶע שְמוּעסֶען, נָאר אִין אַזֶעלְכֶע אֶרְטֶער,
װאוּ עֶס קוּמְט פֿאַר צוּ בֶּעשְרַיְיבֶּען דָאם װירְקְלִיכֶע לֶעבֶּען פֿוּנ'ם פָֿאלְק . מִיר פֿעֶר-
שְטֶעהֶען נִישְט,װאָם קָאנֶען אַזֶעלְכֶע װאָרְטֶער שַאַדֶען ? אַדְרַבָּה,װאָם מֶעהְר װאָרְטֶער,
אִיז גְלַייכֶּער ; אַי, זֵיי הָאבֶּען נִישְט אַזַא שֵאַנֶעם קְלַאנְג , װי אִין דַייטְשֶען,
„שְװאַאמְדְרִיבֶּער !" אָדֶער װי אִין רוּסְסִישֶען !" דָאם אִיז вотъ тѣ фунтъ„
אַ קְלֵיינִיגְקֵייט : עֶס װעֶנְדְט זִיךְ אָן דֶעם, מִיט װאָ סֶ עֶ ר ע אוֹיהְרֶען מֶע הָאְרְט
זִיךְ צוּ . . .

אוֹיךְ הַאלְטֶען מִיר פֿאַר נִישְט אִיבֶּעריג אַרַיְינְצוּפֿיהְרֶען אִין אוּנְזֶער יוּדִיש
פֿעֶרְבֶּ עֶ דֶ ע װאָרְטֶער, נָאר אַזֶעלְכֶע, װאָם זֶענֶען שוֹין אַזוֹי בַּאהְטִיג, אַז מֶע קָאן
זִיךְ אָהְן זֵיי אִין דֶער לִיטֶעראַטוּר נִישְט בַּאנֶעהְן בְּשוּם אוֹפֿן, לְמָשָר : „פָּאעֶזִיע",
„קְרִיטִיק", „יוּבִּילֶעאוּם", „בֶּעלֶעטְרִיסְטִיק", „אָרְטְהָאגְרַאפֿיֶע", „פֿאַנאַטִיזֶם",

_____

*) נָאךְ אוּנְזֶער מֵיינוּנְג נֶעמְט זִיךְ דָאם װאָרְט „מִשְטֵיינְסְגֶעזַאגְט" .נִיט װי _אַנְדֶערֶע_ מֵיינֶען,אַז פֿוּן דַיְיטְש
„צוּ מֵיינְסְטֶענְם גֶעזַאגְט" ד. ה. דָאם הֶעכְסְטֶ ע, װאָם מֶע קָאן דֶערְאַף זָאגֶן . גֵיין , עֶס אִיז נָאר
אַ פֿעֶרקוּרְצְט װאָרְט פֿוּן עֶטְלִיכֶע װאָרְטֶער צוּזַאמֶען ; „אִין דֶעם שְטֵיין גֶעזַאגְט" . דָאם הֵייסְט : גֶעהְ רֶער
צוּם שְטֵיין !" „סַאי אַוודאַי דָא טִים װעֶמֶען צוּ רֶעדֶען מְשֶׁ ... עִ ז אִינְסְג יִינְסְ ם ע. נ א א. מ וּ יְ מָה יְכְדוּמֶה . אַוָו אִיז אִיךְ
פֿעֶרקוּרְצְט דָאם װאָרְט „חָלֶעבֶּען" פֿוּן עֶטְלִיכֶע װאָרְטֶער „אִיךְ זָאל אַזוֹי אַזוֹי לֶעבֶּען" אִיךְ לֶעבֶּען, חָלֶעבֶּען ...
הֵי פֿ ר ו ג שְרַיְיבְּם „כָּלֶעבֶּען" .אוּן אַזוֹי דַאְרף זִיךְ מַאקִי שְרַיְיבֶּען דָאם װאָרְט „כָּלֶעבֶּען, דוּרךְ א כ'.

„קאָבּיזם", אונ נאָך אַזעלכע ; נישקשה, עס מעג אונז אָנשטעהן : שאַנערע
לשונות טאָבּען מעהר,אַלס צו הונדערט טויזענד פרעמדע ווערטער אין זיך .

נאָר נאָך אַלעמען מוזען מיר דעם אמת זאָגען, אז .וויפיעל מיר האָבּען זיך
ניט געפלייטט, אז די „בּיבּליאָטהעק" זאָל דורכאויס האָבּען אין אויסלעגגעכץ, איין
סגנון , אין דאָך אונז פאָרט נישט אינאַנצען געראָטען, דענן עם איז נישט אַזוי
גרינע אויסצופיהרען , אז א בוך פון העכער פערציג פערשיעדענע אַרטיקלען זאָלען
אַלע האָבּען איין אָרטאָגראַפיע , ובפרט אז מיר האָבּען נאָך ניט קיין גראַמאַטיק.
בּיז וואַנען מיר וועלען נישט האָבּען קיין שאַרגאַנישע גראַמאַטיק, וועלען מיר
נאָך לאַנג בּלאָנזען אין דער פינסטער אונ.עם וועט בּיי אונז זיין אַבּהלה אין דער
שפּראַבּע, יעדער וועט זיך האָבּען דאָס רעכט צו שרייבּען, ווי ער וויל .

The Orphan. The ordinary Jew is orphaned by Sholem Aleykhem's death. Sholem Aleykhem, the great humorist, novelist, and playwright, is buried at the Workmen's Circle cemetery in New York, among ordinary folk who were his readers. (*Der groyser kundes*, May 19, 1916)

מיר מאַבֶּען אוֹיפֶמֶערְקְנאם דֶערְאַף אַלֶע אוּנְזֶערֶע לֶעזֶער אוּנ אִיבֶּערְהוֹיפֶּט
די גֶעלֶעהרְטֶע לײט, װאס פֶערְשטֶעהֶען מֶעהר שפֿראַך , אַז זֵיי זאָלֶען זיך נֶעמֶען
גֶרֶעֹנְֹסט אוֹיסְצוּאַרְבֵּייטֶען אַ זשאַרְנאַנִישֶע גראַמאַטיק ; זֵיי װעֶלֶען בֶּעקוּמֶען דֶער־
פֿאַר אַ יַישֶר בֹּח פֿון אוּנְזֶער פֿאָלְק אוּנ פֿון זֵיינֶע שׂרַייבֶּער .

דֶער הערוֹיסגֶעבֶּער.

יאלטע 1 דעקאבֶער.
1888

אונדזער מאַמע־לשון

ג. זעליקאָוויטש

SUMMARY: OUR MOTHER TONGUE BY G. ZELIKOVITSH

A relatively unknown writer (1863–1926) for relatively uneducated readers explains why Yiddish phonological and orthographic conventions are not a whit inferior to those of German or English and why the inability to accept this view is related to minority self-hate and insecurity.

װערהרטהער פריינער דר. ר...... איהר פֿרעגט מיר װאָרום איך זוך ניט צו פֿאַרטײדיגען דיא אידישע שפּראַך מיט מעהר דײַטשע װ.,רטער, אן איהר בעט מיך ענטפֿער אין ענגליש אָדער העברעאיש. איך װעל אײַך אָבער ענטפֿערן אין דער שפּראַך אין װעלכע שרײַב דיא לעצטע 12 יאהר זײַט איך רעדאַקטיר אי־ רישע צײַטונגען אין אמעריקאַ—איך שרײַב צו אײַך אין מאמע־לשון, און איך װעל אײַך זאָגען פֿאַרװאָס:

דיא אײביגע מלחמה צװישען קמץ און פּתח, האָט גענומען אין ענדע. דער פּתח האָט אַרױס געשטעלט אַ װײַסע פֿאָהן אן דער קמץ האָט געזיגענט!

זײַט עס האָט זיך אָנגעפֿאַנגען דיא אידישע אײנװואַנדערונג אין אמעריקאַ האָבען אונזערע דײַטשע ברידער ערקלעהרט קריגען דעם קמץ : זײ האָבען עפֿענט־ ליך פּראָקלאַמירט אַז עס איז אַ שאַנדע צו רײַדען זשאַרגאָן, עס איז אַ שאַנדע צו פֿרײַרינגען זשאַר אָן, עס איז אַ שאַנדע צו שרײַבען זשאַרגאָן אן עס איז דיא נרעסטע שאַנדע צו בילדען דאָס פֿאָלק דורך אַ שפּראַך װעלכע זאַנט ,,וואָ ס'' אַנשטאָם ,,וואָ ס,'' עס איז אײן אוננליק פֿאַר יודענטהום אַז מיר זאָלען אועק־ זעטצען אָרפֿץ מהראָן פֿן בילדונג דעם אונפֿערשעהעסטען קמ ץ!

דיעזע ,,דײַטשע'' אידען װעלכע האָבען פֿערלאַנגט אַז יעדער יוד וועלכער קומט אַהער אריבער פֿן רוסלאַנד זאָל שוין ר ידען אן לעזען ענגליש אָדער דײַטש

—דיעזע יהודים האבן אבער פערגעסטן אז מען סען זאנען אין שרייבען דיא נרעס־
טע חכמות מיט „דאָס" אן „וואָס', פונקט וויא מען קען זאנען אן שרייבען
דיא נרעסט נאַרישקייט מיט „דאָס" אן „וואָס" דיא דייטשע חכטים האבן
פערגעסטן אז מען קען בילדען א מענשען נור אן דיא מוטערשפראך וועלכע ער
פערשטעהט, וועגענסטענטס ביז איהר לערנט איהם אויס דורך זיין מאַמע ־ לשן
אנדערע שפראכען. זיי האבן איבערהויפט אין נאַנצען פערגעסטן דיא פילאָאַפישע
וו תרהיים אז א שפראך איז ניט מעהר וויא א מאַנטעל אין וועלכע מען וויקעלט
אין א נעדאַנק, און דיא שפראך אליין שפיעלט קיין ראַללע פאַרין גרויסֶן
דיִנקטֶר. ועֶ: דער נרויסער איוב וואָלם געשריעבען זיין אונשטערבכיע פּאַעמע אין
זוהרשפּראך, און דער פּרינץ פן אַללע רעדנער דער וועלט, ישעיה, וואָלט נעפרעֶ־
דינט אין האָטענטאָטען־שפּראך, און ותן דער פּאַעט פן אַללע פּאָעטע, ווילליאַם
שעקספּיר וואַלם אויסנענאַסטן זיינע לעבעדינע פּערל אין לימוטש, וואַלטען דיעזע
מייסטערווערס נעוון אזוי שעהן וויא זיי זיינען אין העברעאיש אן ענגליש. וואַס
אַללע האָט צו טהאָן דיא שפראך צו דיא נעפּלינעלמע נעדאַנקען פן דעם
יעניגען וועלכער סודעט זיך מיט מלאכים אדער מיטְן תהום ?

אבער דער דייטשער פתח האָט ניט נעוואָלט וויסען פן דיעזע אַלע ארנומענ־
טען, און ער האָט נעהאַלטען אין איין באַסבאַרדירערן דעם קמץ ! און וואָס האָט
נעטאָהן דער קמץ דיא נאנצע צייט? ער האָט פּאַרטנעזוועצט זיין ערהאַבענע
שליחות נאַנץ רוהיג: האָט נעבילדעט דעם רוסישען אירען דורך זשארנאַנישע

Pictorial Book Reviews.
Writing his 'Worlds De-
stroyed', A.-Sh. Zaks
has, in passing, destroyed
another world: the Yid-
dish language. (*Der groyser
kundes*, August 2, 1918)

צייטוננען, דורך דיא זשארנאַנישע ביהנע, דורך זשארנאַנישץ ביכער אן
דורך רעדנער אין ריין זשארגאָן ביז דער קמץ האם נעזיענם איבעראל מים
גלאַנץ.

יא, ווען מיר ווילען ריידען צו אונזערע ברידער, מחמן מיר עם מאָהן אין
דער שפּראכע אין וועלכע ער האם צום ערשטען מאָל נעזאָנט „מאַמע,” אין דער
שפּראכע אין וועלכע מען האם איהם צום עעשטען מאָל נענעבען א לעקציאָן
וויא צו שטעהען אַקיין אויף זיינע קינדישע פיסעלאַך, אין דער שפּראכע אין וועל־
כע ער האם צום ערשטען מאָל נעלאַכם אן נעוויינם, אין דער שפּראכע אין
וועלכע ער האם נעלערנם האנדלען, וואנדלען, קעמפּפען, לעבטו און ליעבען !

דער פתח האם ארויסנעשטעלם זין וויסע פּאָהן, דער קמץ בענריסט איהם
מים רעספּעקם !

קול מהיכל!

קול קורא מהרבנים דקהלתנו.

אונזער שטאדט ווילנא איז שטענדיג געווען א אכסניה של תורה
און זיא האט שטענדיג הויך געשעצט אונזער היילינע תורה מיט אידרע
לומדים: זיא האט אים געהאלטען 2 ישיבות „ראמיילעס" און „ז״ץ"
(קצבישע) און גרויסע קבוצים ווי „חברה תורה" און „בית שאול".
דעם לעצטען יאהר האט זיך געגרינדעט די גרויסע ישיבה
„קבוץ לומדי תורה" וועלכע האט א נאגצען יאהר אויסגעהאלטען
העבער הונדערט בחורים גדולי תורה וואס זיינען חרוב געווארען אין
די לעצטע מלחמה געשעהעניסען.

ליידער אבער זיינען יעצט די אלע מוסדות זעהר גיפאלען זיי
האבען קיין עקסיסטענץ. אלע פרייהערדיגע הכנסות איז צופאלען
און זיי שטייען היינט אין זעהר א קריטישע לאגע. הונדערטער לומדי
תורה וואס אויף זייא לייגען מיר אונזער נאגצע האפנונג לעתיד,
שטייען אין א הונגער געפאהר ח״ו.

אום צוא ראטעווען אונזער אייגנציגען טרייסט אין גלות־די היילינע
תורה מיט אידרע לומדים פון א גרויסער סכנה, האבען מיר איינגע-
ארדענט דאס היינטינען שבת פ׳ ואר״א זאל מען מאבען מי שברך
אלע עזלי תורה אין אלע בתי מדרשים און מנינים פון ווילנא און
פארשטעדט און יעדער זאל געבען זיין נדבה לטובת מוסדי תורה הנ״ל.

מיר ווענדען זיך צוא אייך אידען אין נאמען פון די מוסדות התורה
הנ״ל, דורך וועלכע עס ווערען געשטיצט פיעלע לומדי תורה, אז
יעדער זאל זעהען צוא שטיצען די מוסדות כפי כחו. פארגעסט ניט אז
ס׳רוב פון די לערנער זיינען פארוואעלט פון דערהיים אהן עלטערן און
פאמיליע און זייער איינצינער לעבענס־קוואל זיינען נור דיעזע מוסדות.

די היסטאריע דערצייילט אונז, דאס ווען אידען זיינען געשטאנגען אין
א גרויסע סכנה, ווען זיי האט געדראהט מלחמה שרעק מיט הונער.
נויט. האבען זיי גראדע יעמאלט געגרינדעט ישיבות און זיי געשטיצט,
דען די אמת׳ע ליעבהאבער פון פאלק האבען גוט פארשטאנען, דאס
ווי און וואס עס זאל ניט זיין, אבער דעם כרם ד׳צבאות מוז מען היטען!
דען דערמיט פארהיט מען דעם גאנצען כלל אומה פון א כליה ח״ו.
דאריבער האפען מיר, אז אפילו ביא א יעצטינע זעהר שווערע לאנע
וועט זיך אויך יעדערער זעהר וואריס אפרופען און יעדער וועט
געבען זיין נדבה בעין יפה.

און בזכות די תורה וואס זי איז געבויט אויף שלום וועלען מיר אין
גיכען ערוואַרטען שלום און ישועות ונחמות אויף כלל ישראל אמן.

ווילנא, טבת, עזרת לפ״ק.

בוכדרוקערייי ד. קריינעס וש. קאוואלסקי, ווילנא.

A Yeshiva appeals for support during World War I: 'In honor of the Torah that is based upon peace, may we speedily welcome peace and deliverance and consolation for all of Israel, Amen.'

וועגן ליטווישן דיאלעקט אין קאנגרעס-פוילן/
זייער גערעכט

נטע ירוחם בערלינער/ב.

SUMMARY: CONCERNING THE LITVAK (= NORTHEASTERN) DIALECT IN CONGRESS
POLAND BY NOTE BERLINER/ABSOLUTELY RIGHT BY B. (= SHLOYME BIRNBOYM)

*An orthodox writer (1897–1945) complains that speakers of the 'central' dialect employ the 'northern'
dialect out of snobbishness and out of an erroneous impression that the latter is somehow 'better', 'nicer',
'purer', 'richer', etc. The editor [B.] declares him to be 'absolutely right'.*

כלל די פרייע איז עס א שיטה: דאָס אייגינע, דאָס היימישע,
סייג נישט און דאָס פרעמדע, דאָס גוֹאישע, איז שיין
און גוט.

און ביי אונדז אין קאנגרעס-פוילן, זענין א סיל פון זיי גינגינין
נאך מיטטער. די האבן גינומען אנדענגן דעם זעלבן כלל: ליב צל
האבן דאָס פרעמדע, אויך אף זאכן, וואָס זענין נישט דוקא
גוֹאיש...

פוילישע יונגע-לייט — ציוניסטלעך, חלוצים און חלוצות, אדער
סתם משכילים-זירלס יונגע-לייט — וואָס זענין גיבוירן אין דער
צוליגן גיהארן אף קאנגרעס-פוילישער ערד, זענען אויפגישטא-
נין אין א גיוויסן פרי-מארגן און גינומען רעדן... מיטן ליטווישן
דיאלעקט.

סאטסט-מאמע האבן אויפגישטעלט אויגן און אויערן, גימיינט, אז
זייערע בנימלעך זענין מיט אמאל אראָפ פון דעת און זענין,
רחמנא לצלן, משוגע גיווארן...

דער סאטס האס, א מיואסדיקער, ארויסגינרומט עסלעכע ווער-
סער, וואָס זענען אריינגיפאלן אין זיין, פריצייטיק גראָ-גיווארינער
באָרד און מיט אים אויפגיריסינע אויגן און אף איר פנים האָס זיך
צוליינגט א משונהדיקע גרימאסע:

— סטייטש, וואָס איז דאָס פאר א נייע צרה? וואָס, זיך שוין
אריינגיהאקט אין קאפ אריין עפיס א פריש משוגעת? ליטוואקיס
גאר גיווארן!

און הברה בנים און בנות האָט גרויס-הא'סטעריש און מיט ביטול
גיקוקט אף די „נישט-אינטעלעגענטע" סאטע-מאמע, וואָס פארשטיי-
ען נעבעך נישט, ווי נישט שיין עס אין דער פוילישער דיאלעקט,
ווי ער „גרילצט" אין אֹיער פונים היינסיקן מענטש...

אזוי אין עס גישעץן ביי די פרייע. ביי זיי איז עס א שיטה,
אדער בעסער גיזאגט: א מהלה, אף וואָס זיי קרענקין שוין לאנגע
יארן און קלאמצארן זיך אן איר מיט אלץ מיאוסקיטן אירע...
„פרעמדס און פרעמדס און נאר פרעמדס!"

אבער ווי קומין מיר צו דער דאזיקער מחלה? פארוואָס גיפעלט
עפיס פוילישע רעליגיעזע יונגע-לייט דוקא דער ליטווישער
דיאלעקט?

אָט שטייט א קאנגרעס-פוילישער יונגערמאן, א פעאיקער, א בא-
וואוסטזיניקער, אן-אין-
לייג אלוֹיס ייִדיש טעליגענטער יונגער-מאן,
אף דער סריבונע און
אף איִידישן אופן! רעט. ער האלט א שיין-
גיבויטן רעפעראַט. זיין
קול קלינגט זיכער און איבערצייגנדיק. אבער ווי-אזוי רעט ער
עפיס, דער דאזיקער יונגער-מאן, וואָס איז גיבוירן און דערצויגן
גיווארן אין קאנגרעס-פוילן און אפן קאנגרעס-פוילישן דיאלעקט,
און וואָס ערשט פאר עטלעכע מינוט האָס ער מיט אונדז גירעט
פשוט מאמע-לשון אינים היימישן דיאלעקט — ווי-אזוי רעט ער
עפיס ווי מיאוס קלינגט דער ליטווישער דיאלעקט אין זיין
מויל!

און אָס פרואוט נאר א קוק-טון אין די ארסאדאקסישע צייטונגין
אין פוילן און איר וועס זיך באלד אנשטויסן דא און דארטן אף
ידיש-ליטוישע לשון פארמין, וואָס זענען ארויסגינאנגין פון און-
סער דער פעדער פון א קאנגרעס-פוילישן ארטאדאקסישן שרייבער,
וואָס האָס נאך זינט ער לעבט דעם דאזיקן לשון-פאריס אין
רעדן נישט באנוצט... א וואָסער גישמאק-ארימקייט פילט זיך
פונים דאזיקן „שטענג"!

אבער נאָך ערגער איז, וואָס די דאָזיקע מחלה האָט זיך שוין
אויך אריינגיכאַפּט אין אונדזערע מיידל-שולן. די לערערינס גי־
פעלט אויך דוקא זיך צו באַנוצן, ביים לערנען, מיטן ליטווישן
דיאַלעקט. עפּיס דאַכט זיך זיי, הייסט אויס, אַז מ-אין נישט גע־
גוג אינטעליגענט, אויב מ-לייענט איבער אַ ייִדיש וואָרט אין
אונדזער פּוילישן דיאַלעקט...

אזוי קומט-אויס, אַז די קינדער רעדן מיט אַן-אַנדער דיאַלעקט
און לייענען מיט אַן-אַנדער דיאַלעקט און דער דיאַלעקט איז נישט
קיין פּוילישער און נישט קיין ליטווישער...

דאָס פירט-אריין, פאַרשטייט זיך, אַ צוטומלונג אין דער אריע־
נטאַציע פונעם קינד. דאָס קינד אַריענטירט זיך שלעכט אינם לשון.
עס לייענט נישט ריכטיק, שרייבט נישט ריכטיק און רעט נישט
ריכטיק.

אַט בין איך לעצטנס גיווען ביי אַן-אַזוינס, וואָס עס האָט איינגע־
אָרדנט איינע פונע די חשובסטע בית-יעקב-שולן. אינס פּראָגראַם
זענען איך גיהערן עטלעכע רעפעראַטן. איך בין גישטאַנין און זיך
צוגיהערט. דער תוכן איז גיווען אַ גאַנץ נישט קשהדיקער, די
האַלטונג — אַן-אויסגעצייכנטע מ-האָט דערקאַנט, אַז די קינדער
פאַרמאָגן פעאיקייטן און אינטעליגענץ, און זענען אויך אַדורכגי־
נומען און אין התלהבות פון זייערע וואָרטער. אבער, רבונו-של-
עולם, אַ וואַסער אַרויסרעדן איז דאָס גיווען! דער ייִדיש האָט דאָ
גיקלונגין פונקט ווי די מיילער פון אונדזערע
היימישע סוחרטים, אין די ציטן פון דער דייטשער אָקופּאַציע...
און דאָס זעלבע איז אויך גישעצן מיטן ייִדיש ביי די ייִדישע
דעקלאַמאַציעס און פאַרשטעלונגין. אַלע האָבן גירעט פּלוצלמרשט,
מיט אַ ליטווישן דיאַלעקט אבער דאָס איז שוין מאָל גיווען
אַ דיאַלעקט, אַז דער אייבערשטער זאָל שומר ומציל זיין!

איז דאָס טאַקע, די תעורה פון אונדזערע לערערנס, צו מאַכן
דאָס ייִדיש לשון פרעמד אינים מויל פון אונדזערע קינדער, אַז
עס זאָל קלינגין אַזוי שיין ווי אַ גוי רעט ייִדיש?.. צי דאַרפן זיי
זוכן, ווי-אַזוי צו באַשיינערן דעם לימוד פון ייִדיש, אָדער אפשר
גאָר פאַרקערט?

ניין! עס טאָר אַזוינס נישט גישעען!

דאָס רעדן מיט אַ נישט-פּוילישן דיאַלעקט פון אַ גיבוירינס אין
אַ דערצוגינגינס אין אַ קאָנגרעס-פּוילן, איז נישט ייִדישלעך, נישט
שכלדיק און נישט עסטעטיש. עס האָט אַן-אַסימילאַטאָרישן טעם..
און מכל-שכן, אַז דאָס אַריינפירן אַזאַ דיאַלעקט אין אונדזערע
שולן אין קאָנגרעס-פּוילן איז נישט עסטעטיש, נישט פּראַקטיש און
ווייס, ווייט נישט פעדאַגאָגיש...

זייער גירעכט   / פון ב.

קלינבער וועט ניט חושד זיין בערלינערן, אַז ער האָט
חלילה צו די ליטואַקעס אָדער צו זייער דיאַלעקט.
זיין מאמר פאַרנעמט זיך בכלל נישט מיט זיי. פאַרקערט, ער
האָט נאָר צו די פּוילישע יורדן.

ער האָט מיט אַ שאַרפן קוק גיפונין דעם אמתן פּסיכאָלאָגישן
יסוד פון דער ליטוויש-מאָדע, וואָס ער זעט זיי אָנהייבן זיך און
ער האָט בולט און קלאָר אויפגעוויזן, אַז דאָס איז פּשוט דער
חשק צו אסימילאַציע. אָבי נישט פּראַסט ייִדיש, ווי אַלע מענטשן
פון דער סביבה. ס-איז צו פּראָסט, נישט גיהויבן, נישט גינוג
פרעמד, מ-האָט זיך נישט גינוג דערווייטערט פון אַלטן שורש,
מ-אין נישט גינוג מאָדערנער מענטש.

אזוי זעט אויס דער יסוד אין דער נשמה. און פאַרוואָס נעמט זיך

דער חשק צו אסימילאַציע ביין-אונדו פונקט אַף אזאַ וועג? דאָס
איז שוין די השפּצה פון לינקס.

דער צענטער פון היינטיקן ייִדישיזם איז חילנע, קען מין זאָגן.
פונקט אזוי ווי אַמאָל אין דאָרסן גיהאָן אַ צענטער פון דער
אַלטער השכלה און בכלל פאַרנעמין ליטוואַקיס אַ גרויס אָרט אין
דער ניער השכלה. אין רוסלאַנד איז די זעלביקע זאַך מיט
מינסק. דעריבער פאַרשטייט זיך במילא, אַז ביי די ייִדישיסטן
הייבט זיך אָן צו פאַרשפרייטן זיך גיפיל, אַז דער ליטוישער דיא־
לעקט איז חשובער, ליטוישער, סאָקי אַן-אינטעליגענץ-לשון. אזוי
ווי ביי אַנדערע פעלקער אויך, און דער אייגינער פּוילישער
דער מזרחהדיקער דיאַלעקט איז נאָר עפּיס אַ מין פּאָלקס-דיא־
לעקט און אָט דער קרומער קוק האָט זיך צו ביסלעך אויך גי־
נומין אַריינגננבינין ביין-אונדז, וואו ער איז נאָך קרומער. מער־
אין דען אזא נאַכמאַכן, אזא צופּאַסונג צום ייִדישיזם נישט ממש
די גרעסטע סתירה צום רעיון פון טראַדיציאָנאַליזם און ייִדיש־
קייט?

צום סוף וויל איך נאָך זאָגן אַ פּאָר ווערטער וועגן גיוויסע מיי־
נונגין, וואָס מע קען אַמאָל הערן בנוגע צום פּוילישן
צום ליטוישן דיאַלעקט.

,דער ליטוישער דיאַלעקט איז עלטער". נו, און דעריבער? איז
וואָס? דעריבער איז ער אַ בעסער, בילעכער, שענער, דאַרף מין
אויפהערן צו רעדן מיט זיין אייגינים דיאַלעקט? אפילו ווען די
הנחה וואָלט גיווען אמת.

איז דאָך נישט גידרונגין דערפון, וועלכער ענגלענדער
וועט אויפהערן צו רעדן ענגליש און ,רעדן דייטש, ווייל
דייטש איז עלטער פון ענגליש?

אבער די גאַנצע הנחה וואָלט זיך גאָר נישט אָן. ס-איז בכלל
אין תוך אריין שווער צו רעדן וועגן ,עלטער' און ,ייִנגער".
אויב מע וויל זאָגן, וועלכער דיאַלעקט ס-האָט אויפגיהיטן מער
סמנים פון אַלטע ציטן, איז עס בלי שום ספק דער ,פּוילישער.

צווי גאַנץ וויכטיקע זאַכן: ס-אין דאָ דער חילוק פון קורצע און
פון אויסגיצוינגע קלינגער: ,מיט — ער מיט זיך', פאַראַן דאַט
דריטע מין: ,דאָס טישל" — בשעת אין ליטוויש זענען אַלע קלין־
גער קורץ: ,מיט — ער מיט זיך', און דאָס דריטע מין איז אין
פאַרלוירין גיוואָרן: ,דער טישל', דערצו נאָך אַ סך פּרטים.

,דער ליטוישער דיאַלעקט איז ריכטיקער. וואָס הייסט דאָס?
כ-קען מיר נישט מאַלן קיין אַנדערן פּשט ווי ,עלטער', דאָס
הייסט נענטער צו די עלטערע פלים, און וועגן דעם האָבן מיר
נאָר וואָס גירעט.

,דער ליטוישער דיאַלעקט איז וויסנשאַפטלעכער". אָסור אויב איך
פאַרשטיי, וואָס מע מיינט דאָ. וואָס איז אַ ,וויסנשאַפטלעך לשון'ז
מע קען זאָגן וועגן אַ בוך, אַז זיין לשון איז וויסנשאַפטלעך, מע
קען נאָך זאָגן, פראַנצייזיש איז ,וויסנשאַפטלעכער' פון קירגי־
זיש: הייסט עס, ס-אין מיין אויסגיאַרבית אַף וויסנשאַפטלעכע
ענינים. אבער דאָס מיינט מין דאָ נישט, פאַרשטייט זיך, בפרט,
אַז מע רעט פּמעט נאָר וועגן אַרויסרעדן. — כ-האָב מורא, אַז
דאָס גאַנצע איז פּשוט עם-אָרצות. מע וויל רעדן ,אינטעליגענט'
און מיינט דאָ זעלבע ווי ,ריכטיקער' און ,עלטער"...

איך חזר איבער: דאָ גייט נישט אין די ליטוואַקיס און אין זייער
דיאַלעקט. כ-הייב נישט אָן צו זאָגן, אַז ער איז ערגער פונם אַן־
,פּוילישן', אָדער די ליטוואַקיס זאָלן אים אַוועקוואַרפן און אַן־
נעמין דעם ,פּוילישן". דאָ גייט נאָר אין דער אַסימילאַטאָרישער

פסיכאָלאָגיע פון פּױלישע ייִדן, אַז אַ ליטוואַק וועט אַגב אורחא
ביװאויער װערן, אַז זײַן דיאַלעקט איז נישט דער „אמתער״, דער
„ריכטיקער״ דער בחור צווישן אַלע אַנדערע, איז דאָס אָװדאי

יװאָונטשן.

.נטע בצרלינערן קומט אַ יישר-כּוח, וואָס ער האָט אַנגיװיזן אַף דער
דאָױקער מכּה דעם סימן פון אונדזער מחלה.

The epitaph of Ber Borokov (1881–
1917), Yiddish linguist and father of
Labor Zionism, is in Yiddish and reads:
'The first priority for any awakening
people is to become the master of its
own language'. Reinterred in Israel in
1963, his second gravestone is inscribed
entirely in Hebrew.

Vulgarity (brandishing 'vulgar spelling' rolling pin and speaking highly anglicized Yiddish): 'If he (Ab Kan) tells me to fix you, I'll fix you, all right! You'll really look swell, damn you!' (The *Forward* appointed a committee of its 'own boys' to 'fix Yiddish spelling.' (*Der groyser kundes*, June 19, 1925)

The 'Hidden Standard':
A Study of Competing Influences in Standardization

MORDKHE SCHAECHTER

0. *Introduction*

0.1. *Definitions*

0.1.1. By *Standard Yiddish* (StY) is generally meant the literary language that conforms to the orthographic, grammatical, and stylistic norms prescribed by modern reference manuals: *Takones* (1937), U. Weinreich (1949, 1968), Stutshkov (1950), and Schaechter-Weinreich (1961).

0.1.2. For the purposes of the discussion that follows, I define *Non-Standard Yiddish* (NonStY) as those varieties of the written language – primarily the journalistic prose of the daily Yiddish press – which have lagged behind in adopting the more modern standards.

0.1.3. *Written Yiddish* (WritY) encompasses both *Standard* and *Non-Standard Yiddish*.

0.1.4. The term *daytshmerish*[1] refers to the tendency to appeal to standard German (*daytsh* 'German') as a model of 'correctness' for the Yiddish language.

0.2. In this paper, I shall examine the competing claims to selection of native-dialectal as against foreign *daytshmerish* forms, and I shall attempt to show, adducing historical[2] as well as geographical evidence[3] in support of this view, that many of the features of contemporary WritY – in contrast to the spoken language in its regional variety – can be attributed to a 'hidden standard', the unconscious preference for those linguistic forms that coincide with standard German (NHG).

---

1. An extensive bibliography on the problem of *daytshmerish*, compiled by the author of this paper, is being prepared for publication.

2. Wherever the instances of usage cited are culled from texts written in the First Literary Language (see below **1.1.**) and in the early Second Literary Language (see **1.2.**), a bibliographic reference to the source is given. However, in order not to burden the bibliography with a large number of nonlinguistic entries, we have refrained from including references for examples of usage common in the writings of journalists, essayists, etc.

3. The maps that accompany this study are based on data drawn from the files of the Language and Culture Atlas of Ashkenazic Jewry (LCAAJ). So are most of the findings cited in the discussion. In order to keep the text uncluttered, no explicit credit is given in addition to this acknowledgment.

0.3. With respect to their susceptibility to NHG influence, three levels can be distinguished in WritY:
1. StY belles lettres – relatively immune.
2. StY nonbelletristic prose – selectively resistant.
3. NonStY[4] – highly susceptible.

1. *The NHG influence*

1.0. Throughout its development, the 'delicate fusion that is Yiddish' (U. Weinreich 1959b: 426, 427) has had to contend with the pressures of various languages, in turn, leaving its imprint on them. One of the strongest influences, that exerted by standard German, has been subject to fluctuations in the course of history.

1.1. The First Literary Language (M. Weinreich 1959: 567) was based on Western Yiddish (WY) dialects of the pre-nineteenth-century period. Patterned on the Middle High German (MHG) model, it adopted not only the imagery of the non-Jewish literature of the period (M. Weinreich 1960b: 109), but many of its standards of linguistic correctness as well.

1.2. On the other hand, the Second Literary Language (M. Weinreich 1959: 567) – Modern Yiddish – which emerged around the turn of the nineteenth century was marked by a more or less conscious turning away from WY towards the spoken Yiddish of Eastern Europe.[5]

1.3. During the second half of the nineteenth century, however, a new trend became apparent: the more or less explicit application of criteria derived from NHG linguistic material to determine the acceptability of Yiddish forms for literary usage. In accordance with the rather unsophisticated view of the nature of complex linguistic relationships prevalent at the time, the advocates[6] of *daytshmerish*, who regarded Yiddish as 'corrupt German', showed preference for those Yiddish forms for which a German cognate could be ascertained. In grammar, the adherence to the 'authentic German language' was explicitly recommended with important normative consequences.[7] However, even at its peak, the *daytshmerish* tendency did not go unchallenged. Yiddish linguists,

4. As in the case of American English, it is important not to equate nonstandard with dialectal. Indeed, of the three levels of WritY described here, it is NonStY that is furthest from the dialects, while StY (1) best reflects the uniqueness of various dialects.
5. M. Markuze (1970; cf. Herzog 1965b: 51), Mendl Lefin (1819), A. B. Gotlober, and other

late eighteenth- early nineteenth-century writers are representative of this tendency.
6. Among them the folk writers Dik, Tsunzer, Shomer; the proletarian poets of the 1890s: Bovshover, Vintshevski, Edlshtat, Roznfeld; the American Yiddish theater, and the American Yiddish daily press.
7. Said Aleksander Tsederboym (1863: 393ff.),

ספּאָריק־דרעהער נום. 41

אברהם שאמער (וויים־פרעזידענט פון אידישען „ליטערשטען קלוב") : —
דחי טינע איז דהים, נעּלאָבטשיק ! דהי אידרייש ליטערטשור סאפפּעערד פון דערפון
וואם מיר יוזען ענטיערלי צופיעל אינגליש ווערדז... וואהאט וי ניער איז : ע קלין
אידרייש וואקעביולערי — סאמטהינג לייק מענדעלי דהי בוק־סעללער... אַדער ווי
אַיהר רופם איהם : מענדעלי מאקער סעמפּאהרים... דהאט איז דחי ריעל סטאָף... אין
דראּמס אין אויך דהי סיים סהינג... ביי דהי ווי : נעהמט זיך אריין אין קאָפּ ענ:
ּאַברדושעפם אַן אירך וועל עם געססען אין צעה קונעסטשענס—סי איף אי דאָנט !

Avrom Shomer (vice-president of the Yiddish Writers Club), in highly anglicized Yiddish: 'Yiddish literature suffers from our use of entirely too many English words. What we need is a pure Yiddish vocabulary, like that of Mendele the Bookseller. That's the real stuff...' (*Der groyser kundes*, June 5, 1912)

normative grammarians, and the great masters of Yiddish prose, Mendele and Sholem Aleichem, made an attempt to stem the tide of NHG loanwords and grammatical forms. Gradually, the tide subsided reaching its lowest ebb in contemporary Yiddish. Indeed, the present linguistic climate may be described as anti-*daytshmerish*.

editor of the pioneering Yiddish weekly *Kol mevaser*, which played a prominent role in shaping Modern StY: 'All educated persons know that in German, Russian, and other languages, all things are divided into three genders...this is also the case in Yiddish, but since we have no grammar, in some places they say *dos gloz* and in other places *di gloz*; *dos ferd, der ferd*, and so on. In such cases we shall adhere to the authentic German language. What harm can come of having a single language at least in our books? At least then we will all understand one another.' It is interesting to note in this connection that a later grammarian (Reyzen 1924: 14) opposes the reliance on the NHG standard in problems of gender.

1.4. Theoretically, in the formative decades of Modern StY, many characteristic features of East European Yiddish were legitimate candidates for adoption as standard patterns. In practice, native forms were most commonly selected where there was full interdialectal agreement. In cases where the major dialects did not agree, forms closer to the NHG model were adopted, leaving an indelible imprint on the language. And though, in the continuing development of Modern Yiddish, the role of *daytshmerish* as a major force has declined, I am inclined to believe that its undeclared and perhaps unrealized influence, referred to above as the 'hidden standard', has been underestimated.

1.5. Linguistic geography provides striking evidence of the preferential treatment accorded to StY to the NHG model. In numerous instances, cited below, where the major dialects disagree, the new literary language has standardized neither the forms used by the majority of Yiddish speakers nor the forms current in any one particular dialect, but rather the forms that coincided with standard German.

1.5.1. *šotn*[8] vs. *sotn* 'shadow'. As can be seen in Figure 1, except in marginal areas, the word is *sotn* [sotn ~ sutn ~ cutn] nearly everywhere. StY gives preference to *shotn* [šotn ~ šutn], the minority form that is closer to NHG *Schatten*.[9]

1.5.2. *im* vs. *em* [em ~ ejm] (Figure 2). The *em* territory embraces by far the larger part of the Yiddish-speaking community – NEY, CY, and WY. Moreover, it was common in older literary usage until well into the nineteenth century.[10] As first noted by M. Weinreich (1939: 80), later writers and editors considered *em* incorrect because no corresponding NHG form was found; *im*, which had the advantage of similarity to NHG *ihm*, became the accepted form despite the attempts of some normativists (e.g. Zaretski 1927: 143) to standardize *em* as an acceptable alternative to *im*.

1.5.3. *mer* vs. *mejn* 'more' (Figure 3) shows that *mejn* occupies most of CY and SEY as well as a small segment of NEY; those areas include such important centers as Warsaw, Radom, Kołomyja, Iași, Cherkas, and Pinsk.

In literary documents, *meyn* goes back to the oldest sources including the MS of 1382 where it appears in the form *mey* (Fuks 1957: 6).[11] Even writers from *meyn*-free areas used the word.[12]

8. Spoken dialectal forms are rendered in a modified IPA transcription: *š* = IPA (ʃ), *ž* = IPA [ʒ], *c* = IPA [ts]. Written forms are given in the transliteration system followed by the Library of Congress.

9. 'Homonymophobia' (cf. Schaechter 1963) may have played some part: cf. *sotn* 'Satan'. But its importance can be exaggerated.

10. *Em* was favored by Etinger, Tsunzer, Ruf, and Basman.

11. See also: the fifteenth century *Shmuel-bukh*; Elye Bokher's 'Hamavdil' (Shtif 1926: 154, stanzas xxvi, xxvii, xxxii); *Pariz un Vyene* (M. Weinreich 1928: 176, 178, 180, 184, 186 et al.; the fifteenth-century MS quoted by Kosover (1964: 362, 365, 367); the Yiddish Psalms translations of 1510, 1532, 1562; the Cracow community regulations of 1604; the Prague letters of 1619 (Landau-Wachstein 1911: 127); the elegy on the Chmielnicki massacres of 1648 (M. Weinreich

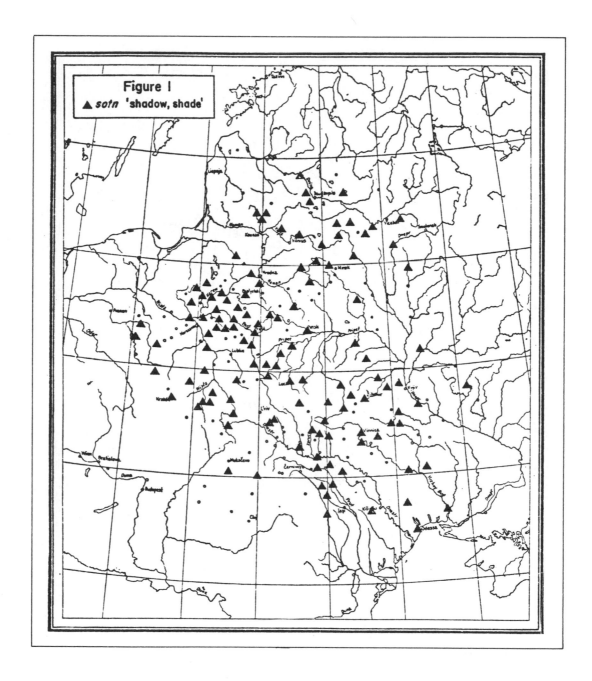

1928: 209, 211, 213); the song on a false Messiah of 1666 (M. Weinreich 1926: 169); the Witzenhausen Bible translation of 1687 (excerpts in Falkovitsh 1940); various seventeenth century songs (M. Weinreich 1927: 185, 192). Also Yente bas Yitskhok (Prilutski 1938: 36, 47); Volfzon (Reyzen 1923: 43, 45, 46); Etinger (M. Weinreich 1925: 11, 15, 45, 55, 65, 68, 71, 90-twice, 113, 195-twice, 228, 284), Makman, Ruf, Shatskes, Basman, Munk, and Goldfadn.

12. E.g. Manashe Ilyer.

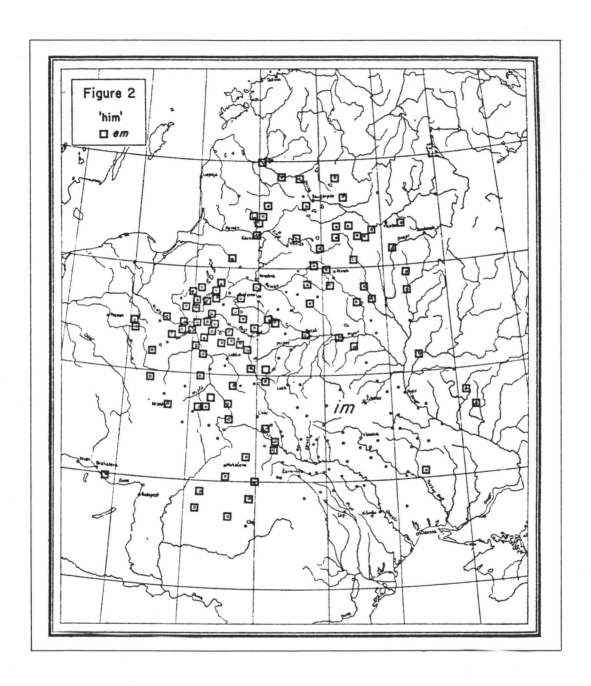

In the nineteenth century, however, *meyn*[13] has become extremely rare in StY[14] and has completely disappeared from NonStY.[15]

13. Also *tsum meynstn, dos meynst, meyner, nish(t) meyn, meynish(t)* (cf. Prilutski 1937: 147–149).
14. Among contemporary writers, I have so far encountered *meyn* only in the works of Broderzon, Driz, Opatoshu, N. Prilutski, and Yehoyosh. The word is listed in U. Weinreich (1968).
15. At the same time, the *daytshmerish* form *mayst* (NHG *meist*) did, for a while, virtually supplant Yiddish *merst*, at least in NonStY.

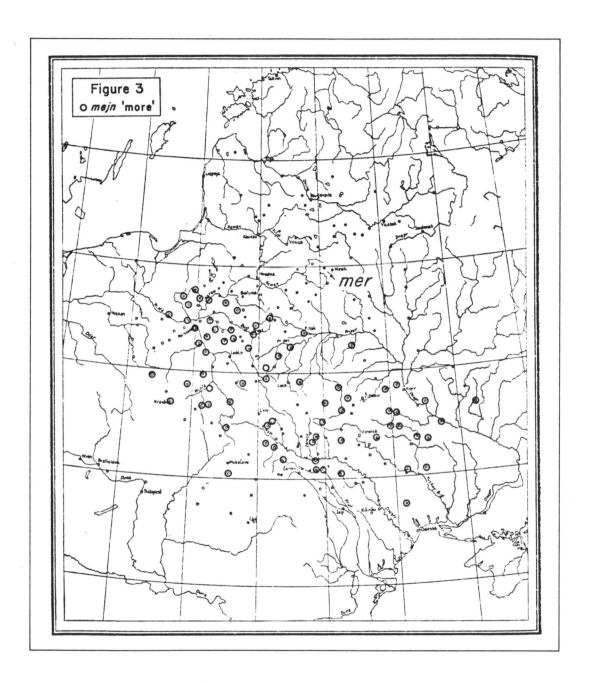

Figure 3
o *mejn* 'more'

1.5.4. *krik* vs. *tsurik* 'back' (Figure 4). The adverb *krik*[16] and its variants, widely used in all the Yiddish dialects, was kept out of WritY in favor of *tsurík* [crik, carik] (cf. NHG *zurück*) also common in most of the dialects. It should be noted, however, that, perhaps as a result of its frequent use by the famous Yiddish novelist Yosef Opatoshu, *krik* has recently gained a foothold in StY.[17]

16. On the regional distribution of *krik* see Prilutski (1933: 349).

17. Other recent users are: Bikl, Demblin, and Diamant.

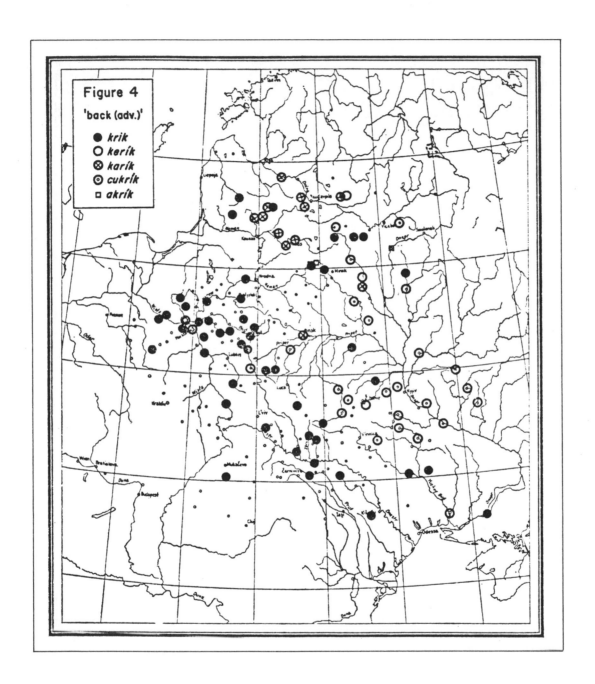

2. Orthography

2.0. After years of preparatory work, the standards of Yiddish orthography were codified in *Takones* (1937), and have since been adopted by responsible publishers in many countries. At this point, it must be emphasized that no revision of the rules laid down in this authoritative manual is suggested here. *Takones* was a major normative achievement, notably free from *daytshmerish* bias. Rather, it is suggested that in a few instances, where other claims to standardization seemed equally valid, *daytshmerish* forms were adopted in recognition of the wide currency they had gained.

2.1. NHG influence may reasonably be assumed (Birnbaum 1930: 55) in the Modern Yiddish rendition of the past participle prefix [gə-], which for almost nine centuries had been spelled *gi-*. Despite efforts by Prilutski, Birnbaum, and Joffe to retain the traditional spelling, it was superseded by *ge-*.

2.2. Traditional spelling was, however, preserved in the StY *oyf*, both for the preposition 'on, upon' and for the separable adverbial complement (as in *oyfkumen* 'get up, rise'), disregarding dialectal differentiation: East Y (comprising NEY and SEY) consistently distinguishes the preposition [af] from the prefixed complement [uf, if]. So does South CY, where they appear as [ouf] and [of] respectively. North CY alone has [of] for both. Thus, in view of the fact that, at various times, the distinction has been noticed and recommended for standardization (Zamenhof 1910:91; Prilutski 1921; M. Weinreich 1930: 38, 39; SYO 328), the choice of *oyf* seems to have been conditioned by its correspondence with NHG *auf*.

2.3. The StY feminine derivational suffix universally rendered [n̩] in Yiddish is written *-in*. Thus, *lererin* (fem.) teacher, *rebetsin* 'rabbi's wife'. Various orthographic projects had unsuccessfully recommended the spelling *-n* (Birnbaum 1932; SYO). The reason given for the standardization of the *-in* spelling, namely the possibility of homonymic confusion with the nominal and verbal plural endings *-n*, is rather unconvincing, since the number of possible homonyms is very small and hardly of any consequence. More likely the *-in* was a concession to the usage of the Yiddish press, which was imitating standard German (*Lehrerin, Schneiderin*).

2.4. Similarly, iotation was accepted in StY only when there was a corresponding form with *j* in NHG. Thus: East Y [id], CY [jid], NHG *Jude*, StY *yid*. East Y [ingl], CY [jingl]; NHG *Jüngling*, StY *yingl*. But: NEY [jir], SEY [ir], CY [ir], NHG *ihr*, StY *ir*.

2.5. The dialectal alternations *shtivl* vs. *shtibl* 'boots'; *borves* vs. *borbes* (NCY) 'barefoot'; *oyvn* (Mieses 1924: 68) vs. *oybn* 'above'; *heyvn* (Prilutski 1917: 86) vs. *heybn* 'midwife' were resolved in favor of the forms nearer to the NHG model (*Stiefel, barfuss, oben, Hebamme*): StY *shtivl, borves, oybn, heybam*.

2.6. Selectivity of a different kind operated in the differential treatment of forms with a posttonic interconsonantal epenthetic vowel, absent in standard German:

Yiddish forms, having a general distribution in all dialects, did become StY: *vorem* 'worm' (NHG *Wurm*), *turem* 'tower' (NHG *Turm*), *zeneft* 'mustard' (NHG *Senf*). On the other hand, both the CY type [barik], [dorif], [hemit], also common in WY, and the even more common SY and WY type [miləx], [hojəx] were not adopted. Their inclusion was recommended by Borokhov (1913: 23), Birnbaum, Prilutski, Gininger, Schaechter.

2.7. With regard to the spelling of affixes, there is a marked difference between StY and NonStY. NonStY continues to use the *daytshmerish* nineteenth-century orthography in: *-likh, -ig, -igkeyt, -nish, -nung, er-* (cf. NHG *-lich, -ig, -igkeit, -niss, -nung, er-*), instead of StY *-lekh, -ik, -ikeyt, -enung, der-*. Similarly, while all Yiddish dialects (Prilutski 1924: 65f. 91f., 107, 109, 115, 117–120, 138, 150) as well as StY use *undz, undzer*, NonStY still uses *unz, unzer* (NHG *uns, unser*).

2.8. In closing this section on orthography, it is interesting to note that attempts of some linguists[18] to standardize the spelling of adverbial phrases, composed of a preposition and an adverb, as a single graphic unit, e.g. *intsvishn, tsuersht*, instead of the traditional *in tsvishn, tsu ersht*, were resisted by others[19] as instances of *daytshmerish* (cf. NHG *inzwischen, zuerst*), and proved unsuccessful.

GRAMMAR

3. *Nouns*

3.1. *Plural Formation*

The Yiddish plural system, or rather plural systems – since we must speak of coexisting systems – are comparatively free of NHG influences. One reason for this relative immunity might be the lack of corresponding plural forms in standard German. Another reason might be that some of the competing alternatives in Yiddish were 'at an equal distance' from standard German. Thus, for instance, in the competition between *nez* and *nezer* 'noses' the German plural *Nasen* was irrelevant (U. Weinreich 1960b). The absence of a strong regulative pull, exerted elsewhere by NHG models to force a degree of uniformity, probably accounts, at least in part, for the relative multiplicity of plural alternatives in StY and NonStY alike.

The following examples illustrate the process of selective adoption and rejection.

3.1.1. While the imported NHG *-e* plurals like *kinste* 'arts', *redaktere* 'editors', having no parallel among Yiddish dialectal forms, did not survive, another clearcut case of NHG influence (Veynger 1926: 59, Zaretski 1927: 27), survives

---

18. SYO: Mark-Joffe (1961).

19. Birnbaum (1915, 1930, 1932), *Takones* (1937), Schaechter-Weinreich (1961).

to this date in the *-n* plural with nouns ending in *-e*, still common in NonStY: *fragn* 'questions', *grupn* 'groups', where StY requires an *-s* plural: *frages, grupes* (cf. NHG *Fragen, Gruppen*).

3.1.2. NHG influence may not unreasonably be assumed in the gradual disappearance of the plural distinction between *manen* 'husbands' and *mener* 'men', attested in WritY in the oldest documents (Shlosberg 1938: 322), leaving *mener* for both 'men' and 'husbands'. This Yiddish development might have been encouraged by the fact that NHG *Männer* is used for both 'men' and 'husbands', while *Mannen* is rarely used and only in the specialized meaning of '(medieval) warrior, knight'.

3.1.3. Of the alternative plurals of *-ung* derivatives: EastY *-ungen*, CY *-unger*, the former, having the benefit of correspondence with NHG *-ungen*, has been selected for standardization.

3.1.4. Similarly, in the alternation between the *-n/-s* ending, on the one hand, and a vowel change, on the other, the plural form closer to NHG has become standardized in WritY: *bruders* 'brothers' vs. *brider*; *floyen* 'fleas' vs. *fley*; *foyglen* 'birds' vs. *feygl*; *hutn* '(ladies) hats' vs. *hit*; *kniyen* 'knees' vs. *kniyes* vs. *kni*; *kuen* 'cows' vs. *ki*; *nusn* 'nuts' vs. *nis*; *zunen* 'sons' vs. *zin*.

3.2. *Gender*

In the clash between the dialectal gender systems preceding and concurrent with the development of StY, the SY three-gender system defeated the NEY two-gender system with the help of its 'shadow ally', the NHG three-gender system. Uniquely Yiddish gender features have been excluded from WritY – the largely EastY mass gender and the NEY intermediate gender.[20] Zaretski (1927: 31) had proposed the latter for standardization.

In other words, in the majority of cases, the gender of a noun in StY is the same as in SY and agrees with that of its NHG cognate. Thus, for example, under the influence of the NHG rule that mass nouns are neuter (Reyzen 1924: 181) WritY has ignored the NEY category of a mass gender of the feminine in favor of the SY neuter. Even many exceptions to the rule are parallel in NHG and WritY e.g., each of the following mass nouns is masculine in StY as well as in NHG:

kez 'cheese'	*shtof* 'material (textile)'	
zamd 'sand'	*vayn* 'wine'	*bronfn* 'brandy'
honik 'honey'	*med* 'mead'	*drot* 'wire'
tsuker 'sugar'	*fefer* 'pepper'	*korn* 'rye'
veyts 'wheat'	*hober* 'oats'	

20. The question whether these two categories ought to be called genders (U. Weinreich 1961), subgenders (Wolf 1969), or noun classes (Herzog 1965a: 156) need not concern us here.

However, within the three-gender system, the treatment of morphological groups and individual items is subject to other considerations. Examples follow:

3.2.1. Where there is full interdialectal agreement StY follows the internal Yiddish pattern regardless of NHG influences: *der aksl* 'shoulder', *der gopl* 'fork', *der gorgl* 'Adam's apple', *der kugl* 'pudding', *der tovl* 'blackboard', *der vortsl* 'root'.

3.2.2. In two noteworthy instances StY adopted a gender form contrary to NHG usage: *hor* 'hair', *kni* 'knee' – in Yiddish dialects *der/di*, in NHG *das*, in StY *der*.

3.2.3. A group of feminines firmly established in literary tradition[21] did not preserve their gender in StY (cf. Reyzen 1924: 316): *krig* 'strife', *pruv* 'test', *royb* 'robbery', *shpiz* 'spear', *shtul* 'chair', *tsoym* 'bridle', *tsvayg* 'branch', *zoym* 'hem'.

3.2.4. A group of old *-ung* derivatives – though neuter in SY (especially CY), and masculine in NEY – is feminine in StY: *farfleytsung* 'flood', *bashraybung* 'description', *bafrayung* 'liberation' (cf. Reyzen 1924: 190). This development is probably due to gender analogy with a large number of NHG feminine loanwords introduced in the last eighty years, e.g. *zitsung* 'meeting', *bavegung* 'movement', *oysshtelung* 'exhibition'.

3.2.5. For other suffixed derivatives of Germanic origin, without an obvious equivalent in NHG, the gender usage of the majority of speakers was accepted as the norm (Reyzen 1924: 192, 303f.): *dos zegekhts* 'sawdust', *dos shpayekhts* 'saliva', *dos kleynvarg* 'small fry', *dos zisvarg* 'candy', *dos guts* 'good', *dos gebrotns* 'roast'.

In his *Modern English–Yiddish Yiddish–English Dictionary*, U. Weinreich (1968) makes an attempt to regulate StY gender usage with more regard for dialectal usage.

4. *Case system*[22]

4.1. German case distinctions have been drastically reduced in Yiddish (Veynger 1926: 198; Zaretski 1927: 10; Mark 1938; Herzog 1965a: 124), more in the dialects, however, than in StY, which like any written language is more conservative.

4.2. The collapse of dative–accusative distinctions in the singular, almost general in NEY but also prevalent in part of SEY and NCY, did not penetrate WritY, with its heavy reliance on NHG standards. But the plural syncretism, being a universal feature in EY, did become the rule in WritY.

---

21. In the devotional literature of past centuries, Nakhmen Broslever, Y. M. Lifshits, Y. Y. Linetski, Y. L. Perets, Sholem Asch, etc.

22. On case and gender variation see now also Wolf (1969: in this volume pp. 102–215).

4.3. The CY and NEY syncretism of nominative, dative, and accusative feminine singular after a preposition – *nokh di milkhome* – was kept out of WritY. The hidden NHG standard has already been mentioned in this connection (Mark 1938: 271).

4.4. The dative and accusative in *-n* with proper names has a NEY dialectal base and was recommended by grammarians (e.g. Zaretski 1927: 28f., U. Weinreich 1949: 305), but is rarely used with feminine proper names, or with last names if either the first name or a title is present.

5. *Adjective derivation*

5.1. With a few exceptions the *daytshmerish* suffixes *-bar*, *-haft*, *zam*, with no basis in Yiddish dialects, have disappeared from StY. They were too obviously foreign and were rejected as such. But covert NHG influence may be helping in the process by which SY *-ekhik*, CY *-edik* is being dislocated by *-ik* in words like *drayekekhik* / *drayeke(kh)dik* 'triangular', *firekekhik* / *fireke(kh)dik* 'quadrangular', *shpitsekhik* 'pointed', *rizedik* / *rizndik* 'gigantic', vs. *drayekik*, *firekik*, *shpitsik*, *rizik*.

5.2. In the competition between NEY *-sh* and SY *-ish* (Reyzen 1929: 596), the latter became predominant in StY and has completely supplanted its counterpart in NonStY. (NHG has only one cognate suffix: *-isch*.)

5.3. The partially CY and partially NEY augmentative plural suffix *-ne* (*gantsene* 'whole', *groysene* 'large'; *hoykhene* 'tall'), has not gained a foothold in WritY, where *gantse*, *groyse*, *hoykhe*, is the rule (cf. NHG *ganze*, *grosse*, *hohe*).

6. *Pronouns*

Among Yiddish pronouns the hidden standard has played a part in more than one detail.

6.1. The fact that the dialect forms *ex*, *jex*, *jix*, *jax*, *ijox*, used by the majority of Yiddish speakers are all represented by *ix* in WritY, can be better understood by taking into consideration German *ich*. According to Prilutski, the stylistic changeover from Yiddish to *daytshmerish* in Purimplay dialogs is signalled by the switch from *jax* to *ix*. The well-known Yiddish poet Yankev Glatshteyn considers *ikh* 'the worst *daytshmerism*' in present-day Yiddish; an objectively undemonstrable but subjectively relevant statement.

6.2. The indefinite pronoun *se* 'it' in preverbal position, e.g. *se klingt* 'it rings' vs. *klingt es*, has its dialectal basis in SEY and the southern part of CY. It was

מלך ראוויטש

(זכריה־חנא בערגער)

רעדים, גאַליציע, 1893
לעבט אין מאָנטרעאַל, קאַנאַדע

◆

קאַנטינענטען און אָקעאַנען
בלוט אויף דער פאַן, (פיעסע)
די לידער פון מיינע לידער
מיין לעקסיקאָן, (פאַרטרעטען)

◆

פּאָעט, עסייאיסט, דראַמאַטורג

חיים גראַדע

ווילנע, פּוילן, 1908
לעבט אין ניו־יאָרק, פאַר. שטאַטן

◆

מוסרניקעס, (פּאָעמע)
דער מאַמעס שבתים, (דערצ.)
ר' צמח אַטלאַס, (ראָמאַן)
דער מענטש פון פייער, (לידער)

◆

פּאָעט, דערצ̈יילער, ראָמאַניסט

אברהם סוצקעווער

סמאַרגאָן, ווייס־רוסלאַנד, 1913
לעבט אין תל־אביב, ישראל

◆

סיביר, (פּאָעמע)
געהיימשטאָט, (פּאָעמע)
מדבר סיני, (פּאָעמע)
ווילנער געטאָ, (חורבן כראָניק)

◆

פּאָעט, עסייאיסט

הירש גליק

ווילנע, פּוילן, 1920
גאָלדפיליע, עסטלאַנד, 1944

◆

אמאל
דאָס זאָנגל
באַלאַדע פון ברוינעם טעאַטער
פּאַרטיזאַנער הימן

◆

פּאָעט

יהושע־מרדכי ליפשיץ

בערדיטשעוו, אוקראַינע, 1828
בערדיטשעוו, אוקראַינע, 1878

◆

יודל און יהודית, (דיאַלאָג)
די פיר קלאַסן, (אַפּהאַנדלונג)
רוסיש ־ יידישער ווערטערבוך
יידיש ־ רוסישער ווערטערבוך

◆

לעקסיקאָלאָג, יידיש־פאָרשער

אלכסנדר האַרקאַווי

נאָוואַרעדאָק, ווייס־רוסלאַנד, 1863
ניו־יאָרק, פאַר. שטאַטן, 1939

◆

די יידיש־דייטשע שפּראַך
כללים פון יידישער אָרטאָגראַפיע
ענגליש — אָן אַ לערער
יידיש ־ העברעאיש ־ ענגלישע
ווערטערביכער

◆

שפּראַך־פאָרשער, לעקסיקאָלאָג

1. Meylekh Ravitsh, 1893–1976; Poet, essayist, playwright; 2. Khayim Grade, 1908–   ; Poet, writer of short stores, novelist; 3. Avrom Sutskever, 1913–   ; Poet essayist, 4. Hirsh Glik, 1920–1944; Poet; 5. Yehoyshue-mordkhe Lifshits, 1828–1878; Lexicographer, language researcher; 6. Aleksander Harkavi, 1863–1939; Language researcher, lexicographer.

used by many distinguished writers including Sholem Aleichem (see Schaechter 1961). The form occurs in the works of natives of areas where *se* was unknown, e.g. M. Kulbak and A. Sutskever. *Se* is widely used in StY, but it is practically unknown in NonStY.

6.3. The indefinite pronoun of the third person sg. *me* 'one' has an even wider distribution than *se*. It seems to be the common form in all Yiddish dialects. In WY it is also used in postverbal position. Common in StY usage, it has not penetrated the NonStY of the press. The form *me* was used by Mendele, Sholem Aleichem, Peretz, Yehoyosh, Sutskever, and other first-rate Yiddish writers and was recommended by various linguists (Zamenhof 1910: 100; Birnbaum 1932: 36; Joffe 1948: 35; Mark 1965: 63), but has not yet completely replaced *men* even in StY.

6.4. Under the heading NHG influence I am also inclined to group:

The rejection by WritY of CY and WY (Stalek 1928: 277) *re* 'he'. WritY *er* (cf. NHG *er*).

The rejection of the CY metanalytic forms *nim* 'him', *nir* 'her', *nes* 'it'.[23] StY *im, ir, es*, NonStY *ihm, ihr, es* (cf. NHG *ihm, ihr, es*).

The rejection of CY and WY *ets* 'you (nom. pl.)', *enk* 'you (dat. pl)', *enker* 'your'. StY *ir* (NonStY *ihr*), *aykh, ayer* (cf. NHG *ihr, euch, euer*).

The rejection of CY and partly SEY *undz* 'we (nom)'. WritY *mir* (cf. NHG *wir*).

6.5. NEY *yetvider* 'each' and uninflected *yeder*,[24] as well as the largely CY *yederer* and the universal Yiddish *itlekher* are all losing ground to the inflected CY *yeder*,[25] which corresponds to NHG inflected *jeder*.

It is worthwhile pointing out that the *itlekher* has a long literary tradition behind it. Thus, in the form *itlekh-*, it was commonly used in the 1382 MS. (Fuks 1957: 4, 6; et al.), although *yeder* is also encountered (Fuks 1957: 6). In the one paragraph of *Mirkeves hamishne* cited by Birnbaum (1965: 12f.) as a sample of sixteenth-century Eastern Yiddish we encounter two instances of *itlekhs*, one of *iklekhen*, and one of *iklekhem*, but none of *yeder*. In the works of Gotlober, one of the forerunners of modern Yiddish literature, we have counted 76 occurrences of *itlekher*,[26] only one of *yeder*.[27] In the first volume of Etinger's works we have

---

23. For the distribution of these forms see Prilutski (1937: 91–94, 101ff., 114ff., 141f., 144, 179).
24. Joffe (1939) attributes this development to NHG influence.
25. But see also U. Weinreich (1949: 313) about StY *yeder* being as a rule uninflected.
26. Reyzen 1927: 5, 20, 28, 29 (twice), 31, 32 37, 41, 51, 55 (three times), 57, 59, 62, 63 (twice),

65, 67, 70, 71, (twice), 75 (four times), 77, 94, 97, 124, 143, 145, 146, 147, 150 (four times), 152 (twice), 153, 154, 158, 164, 170, 172, 182, 187, 188, 194, 195, 201 (twice), 202 (twice), 203 (twice), 208, 210 (three times), 215, 216, 217, 218, 222 (three times), 228, 229, 237.
27. Reyzen 1927: 231.

encountered *itlekh* 81 times, *yeder* – not even once. The prevalence of *itlekher* over *yeder* ('rarely used') was noted by Tshemerinski.

6.6. CY *eynemen, keynemen, yenemen* (Prilutski 1937: 28) have not been standardized: WritY has *eynem, keynem, yenem* (cf. NHG *einen, keinen, jenen*). But *vemen* has become StY in disregard of NHG *wem*.

6.7. With regard to reflexive pronouns the hidden standard was ignored. The EastY uninflected *zikh* is steadily gaining ground, replacing *mikh, dikh, undz* despite their affinity with NHG *mich, dich, uns*. In fact, Brakazh (1951) used similarity to NHG as an argument against the inflected forms. This must be viewed as an expression of the present anti-*daytshmerish* sentiment, which was not strong in the formative decades of Modern StY.

7. *Numerals*

7.1. The distribution of *finef* 'five' (Prilutski 1924: 51, 73, 146f.), *elef* 'eleven' (Prilutski 1920: 88, 153), *tsvelef* 'twelve', includes all of SY, WY (Guggenheim-Grünberg 1969: n. 2), as well as parts of NEY. These forms have a centuries-long tradition of written Yiddish behind them[28] and were recommended by some normativists (Borokhov 1913: 23; Birnbaum 1915: 44; Gininger; Schaechter) and considered admissible by others (Tsvayg 1929: 28; Zaretski 1921: 16, 1929: 32). Modern Yiddish writers have used them.[29] Nevertheless, it is not the 'majority forms' *finef, elef, tsvelef* but the 'minority forms' *finf, elf, tsvelf* that are the more common in present-day WritY (cf. NHG *fünf, elf, zwölf*).

7.2. Similarly, NEY *nayen*, although considered admissible in one orthographic project (Zaretski 1921: 15), lost to WritY *nayn* (cf. NHG *neun*).

7.3. In the case of 'ten' CY *tseyn*, NEY *tsehen* – admitted by Zaretski (1921: 16) and favored by Borokhov (1913: 23) – and SEY *tsan* were all rejected. StY *tsen* has both a solid EastY dialectal basis, and the advantage of conformity with NHG *zehn*.

7.4. Somewhat similar is the case of the compound numerals: dialectal *draysik eyns*, etc., is inadmissible in StY. The WritY *eyn un draysik* is based on the usage of the majority of Yiddish speakers, but it also agrees with the way NHG forms compound numerals.

---

28. Yekusiyel Blits, Glikl Haml (Landau 1901: 33), etc.

29. E.g. Perets Markish, S. Bikl and L. Faynberg.

7.5. In the competition between NEY *fert* 'fourth', *finft* 'fifth', and SY *ferd*,[30] *fift*,[31] the NEY form is clearly the winner, although some SY pockets of resistance still exist (cf. NHG *viert, fünft*).

7.6. Of the geographically equally distributed suffixes *-st* (CY) and *-t* (EastY), as in *zibetsikst* 'seventicth' vs. *zibetsikt*, the former was standardized (cf. NHG *siebzigst*).

7.7. In the case of the ordinal numerals between 13 and 20 the predominant form in WritY is the one ending in *-nt*, e.g. *draytsnt* 'thirteenth' (NHG *dreizehnt*), while the form in *-et*: *draytset* covers practically the whole Yiddish speech territory.[32]

7.8. The CY *eynse* 'one o'clock', *tsveye* 'two o'clock', etc. (Prilutski 1917: 128f.; 1924: 52), and the parallel series *eynsn, tsveyen*, etc. (Mieses 1924: 161), were kept out of WritY.[33] The lack of NHG correspondence was probably a contributing factor.

8. *Verbs*

8.1. Where there is consonantal variation in the verbal stem, StY invariably adopts the form that conforms with NHG, e.g. *hustn* 'to cough', *pasn* 'to fit', *lozn* 'to let', rather than *husn, pastn, lon*. Where an interdialectal alternation does not exist, the NHG form is of no consequence: NHG *messen*, Yiddish *mestn*.

8.2. Some verbs have dropped the historic *-d-* after a nasal: *gefinen* 'to find', *geshtanen* 'stood'. This is a universal feature of Yiddish verbs and has been accepted in WritY, ignoring the NHG cognates *finden, gestanden*. But where the deletion is not universal in Yiddish dialects, the hidden standard comes to the fore. Thus *binen* 'to bind', *tsinen* 'to light', with a fairly wide distribution in SY, did not find their way into WritY, although recommended by one normativist (Birnbaum 1932: 15). StY has *bindn, tsindn* (cf. NHG *binden, zinden*).

---

30. *Ferd* and its older variant *fird* is the traditional form. It is to be found in WY texts, e.g. in the 1382 MS. (Fuks 1957: 6), the sixteenth-century *Seyfer mides* (Mieses 1924: 62), the 1622 edition of the *Tsene-rene* (Shmeruk 1964: 324), the Bible translations by Blits and Vitsnhoyzn (cf. Prilutski 1920: 88; where many other sources are referred to), as well as in the oldest EY texts, e.g. in the excerpt quoted by Birnbaum (1965: 13) from *Mirkeves hamishne* (ca. 1534).

31. The Blits and Vitsnhoyzen translations use *fift, finft, fineft* (cf. Prilutski 1924: 52f., 77). The last one seems to be a spelling convention rather than a reflection of an actual pronunciation. *ferd* and *fift* were used by Y. Aksnfeld, Khaykl Hurvits, Sh. Etinger, Moyshe Nadir, N. Prilutski, etc.

32. Prilutski's (1937: 17–20) preliminary findings about sporadic *-nt* in NEY have not been confirmed by the LCAAJ investigation.

33. U. Weinreich's (1968) is the first dictionary to list these forms without qualifications, in line with current dialect-conscious Yiddish language engineering.

8.3. The impression is strong that some prefixed verbs tend to disappear from NonStY and even from StY in favor of the nonprefixed forms: *farbahaltn*, *fargedenken*, *farhofn* vs. *bahaltn* 'to hide', *gedenken* 'to remember', *hofn* 'to hope'. In some cases NHG influence may be assumed (NHG *behalten* 'to keep', *gedenken*, *hoffen*), which may also be involved in the gradual disappearance of a series of unprefixed forms: *drikn* 'oppress', *glaykhn zikh* 'compare oneself to', *shpetikn zikh* 'be late' vs. *unterdrikn*, *farglaykhn zikh*, *farshpetikn zikh* (Schaechter 1964: 38f.). In this development, however, the Slavic aspect system through prefixation was the primary factor.

8.4. Some verbs formally reflexive in NEY are used without the reflexive pronoun in SY, especially in CY: *fargesn* (*zikh*) 'forget' (transitive), *kniyen* (*zikh*) 'kneel', etc. (Schaechter 1964: 43). Although two of the classicists – Mendele and Sholem Aleichem – as well as a number of other nineteenth-century writers, used the medial-reflexive forms extensively, they have subsequently not been able to withstand the pressure of NHG *vergessen*, *knien*. StY does have reflexive verbs (*plontern zikh*, *shpiln zikh*) in all cases of full agreement among the three main dialects.

8.5. WritY has also rejected the following probably due to the lack of NHG correspondence:

The NEY 2nd person sg. ending [-ste] and [-sti], even in stressed position. WritY *-stu* (cf. NHG *-st du*).

The partly NEY and partly CY *binst* '(you) are'. WritY *bist* (cf. NHG *bist*).

The CY elision of the -(e)*n* ending in the first person plural: *geymir* 'we are going', *homir*[34] 'we are having'. WritY *geyen mir*, *hobn mir* (cf. NHG *gehen wir*, *haben wir*). *-mir* [mər] functioning as a verbal ending (Prilutski 1924: 15–25, 45ff., 143f.) was common in the folk literature of the nineteenth and early twentieth centuries.

Various SY contractions of future tense, auxiliaries *eb*, *ebn*; *lobn*; *em*(*en*); *en*(*en*). (Prilutski 1917: 76; 1924: 34–38, 41, 43, 145f.).

The SY ending *-et* after a diphthong: *boyet* 'builds'; *kayet* 'chews'; *kreyet* 'crows'. StY *boyt*, *kayt*, *kreyt* (cf. NHG *baut*, *kaut*, *kräht*).

8.6. The present participle in *-end*, a *daytshmerish* form without any dialectal basis (Prilutski 1909: 65–68), was very common in the Yiddish press in the late nineteenth and early twentieth centuries. In contemporary StY it has completely disappeared with the exception of *glentsnd* 'outstanding'. It did, however, leave its mark in forms like *dringendik* or *dringlekh* (Schaechter 1959: 106) and in the widespread collapse of the distinction between *-ndik* and *-edik* (Prilutski 1909: 67f.).

34. Used by Y. L. Perets and others.

8.7. The past participle did not escape the powerful pull of the NHG standard. Thus, the dropping of *ge-*, quite common in Yiddish dialects especially in East Y and WY, was well established in the First Literary Language:[35] *gangen* 'gone', *gesn* 'eaten', *kumen* 'come', *gebn* 'given'. The Second Literary Language discarded these forms in favor of the full *ge*-prefixed participle forms: *gegangen*, *gegesn*, *gekumen*, *gegebn* (*cf.* NHG *gegangen*, *gegessen*, *gekommen*, *gegeben*).

8.8. Excluded in varying degrees from StY are: SY *genemen* 'taken', *gebunen* 'bound' (Mieses 1924: 71), *getsun(en)* 'lit' (Prilutski 1917: 139f.); SEY *gegibn* 'given'; CY *gedorfn* 'needed', *farrokhtn* 'repaired'; NEY *gebakt* 'baked', *geborshtn* 'combed', *gebuln* 'barked', *geforbn* 'painted', *gevelt*[36] 'wanted' (Haylperin-Weinreich 1929: vol. 2, p. 35). StY *genumen*, *gebundn*, *getsundn*, *gegebn*, *gedarft*, *farrikht*, *gebakn*, *gebarsht*, *gebilt*, *gefarbt*, *gevolt* (cf. NHG *genommen*, *gebunden*, *gezündet*, *gegeben*, *gedürft*, *verrichtet*, *gebacken*, *gebürstet*, *gebellt*, *gefärbt*, *gewollt*).

8.9. StY did not accept SEY *dertrenken*, *dertronken* (Mieses 1924: 175) 'drowned', but *dertrunken* of the other dialects (cf. NHG *ertrunken*). Nor did it accept CY *geganen*, NEY *gajngjen*, *gegangn* – the choice was *gegangen*. SEY *gegan* is used to a certain extent, especially in poetry, probably due to its value as a rhythmic doublet.

The point should be made here that, where other factors are at work, variant forms of participles coexist, proving the NHG standard ineffective in tipping the balance in favor of one of the two competing forms: *gebrakht* / *gebrengt* 'brought'; *geborn* / *geboyrn* 'born'; *farlorn* / *farloyrn* 'lost'; *gehangen* / *gehongen* 'hung'; *geheft* / *gehoftn* 'fastened'; *gelozn* / *gelozt* 'left'; *geliyen* / *gelign* 'borrowed, lent'; *geshenkt* / *geshonken* 'gave away as a present'; *geshorn* / *geshoyrn* 'cut one's hair'; *geshit* / *geshotn* 'poured'; *geshrign* / *geshriyen* 'shouted'; *geshvorn* / *geshvoyrn* 'took an oath'; *getretn* / *getrotn* 'stepped on'; *gevaksn* / *gevoksn* 'grew'; *gevendt* / *gevondn* 'turned to'.

9. *Adverbs*

9.1. In the morphology of the adverb I am inclined to ascribe to NHG influence:

9.1.1. The rejection in WritY of adverbial forms like *s'beste* 'at best', *s'merste* 'the most', in favor of *tsum bestn*, *tsum merstn* in StY and *am best(e)n*, *am merst(e)n* / *am mayst(e)n* in NonStY (cf. NHG *am besten*, *am meisten*).

9.1.2. The rejection of various equivalents of 'firstly': *s'ershte*, *eyn mol*,[37] *eyns*,

---

35. See texts discussed or reproduced in the following sources: Birnbaum (1938: 173; 1965: 13); Kahan (1931: 204); Fuks (1955: 2, 10); Landau (1901: 43); Reyzen (1923: 43, 57, etc.); Shtif (1926: 152); M. Weinreich (1923: 172, 173, 175, 181, 183).

36. Also WY, cf. texts quoted by Birnbaum (1965: 11); Mieses (1924: 175); Shatzky (1929: 51); M. Weinreich (1923: 189).

37. Used by Y. Aksnfeld, Sh. Etinger, B. Demblin et al.

and 'secondly' *s'endere / s'tsveyte*,[38] in favor of *ershtns, tsveytns* (cf. *erstens, zweitens*).

9.1.3. The rejection of *tsum letst* 'last'; *tsum ersht / tsum ershnt*[39] 'first', etc., in favor of *tsu letst, tsu ersht*, etc. (cf. NHG *zuletzt, zuerst*).

9.1.4. The rejection of *a*-affixed forms which are not common in all dialects: NEY *avu* 'where', *avin* 'where to'; *abald* 'soon'; SEY *ado*[40] 'here'; *adort* 'there', etc. WritY *vu, bald, dort* (cf. NHG *wo, bald, dort*).

9.1.5. The rejection of *-t* suffixed forms: *aleynt*[41] 'alone'; *andersht*[42] 'differently' (Mieses 1924: 64); *azoy arumer(t)* 'thus'; *al(e)molt* 'always'; *eyn molt* 'once'; *keyn mo(l)t* 'never'; *tsu mo(l)t* 'sometimes'; *e(y)ntslt* (Prilutski 1920: 90), etc. Most of these forms were common in the First Literary Language, some still have a SY or a CY distribution. Glückel von Hammeln (Landau 1901: 40) used: *schont, liberst, itsundert, da herumt, aleynt, anderst, eyn malt, ale malt, fon den malt an.* Of these only the universally Yiddish *libersht* and *demolt* have become a part of WritY. The more regional forms could not overcome the analogy of the hidden standard (cf. NHG *alein, anders, herum, mal, einzel, schon*).

9.1.6. The rejection of NEY *-et: aropet, aroyset, araynet, onet, opet.* WritY *arop, aroys*, etc.

9.1.7. The rejection of SY *vu ahin* (Mieses 1924: 186) in favor of the contraction *vuhin*, while other contractions *azoyrumer(t), vuremer(t)*, were rejected in favor of full forms.

9.1.8. The rejection of CY *banezamen* 'together', *fun azamen* 'apart', *mit azam, nokh azam, tsishn azamen, unter azam* (Prilutski 1912; 1937: 104f., 142f.) in favor of *baynand, fun anand, mit anand*, which do not seem to have a Yiddish dialectal source.

9.1.9. The rejection of most of the synonyms and variants for 'now'. The usual form in StY is *itst*, less common are *itster* and *atsind*; the usual forms in NonStY are *itst* and *yetst* (cf. NHG *jetzt*).

9.2. The hidden standard may account for the scarcity in WritY of adverbs of the type *af gevis, af letst*.

10. *Prepositions and conjunctions*

10.1. Redundant prepositions of the type *fun derfun, tsu dertsu* which are common in EastY, were recommended by one linguist (Zamenhof 1910: 100f.) and accepted as correct by others (Schaechter-Weinreich 1961: 25, 59, 76). The

---

38. Used by Y. Y. Linetski, M. Weinreich et al.
39. These forms were used by M. Markuze, Mendele Moykher Sforim, A. M. Sharkanski.
40. *ado* and *avu* do occur in WritY but only in writers from the NEY speech territory.
41. Used by B. Ruf and other nineteenth-century

writers, as well as by the contemporary poet A. Sutskever to evoke an archaic atmosphere.
42. Occurs in the Vitsnhoyzn translation, in the Sabbatai-Zevi poem (M. Weinreich 1926: 167), as well as in works by Nakhmen Broslever, Etinger, Birnbaum et al.

preference of Yiddish writers for the nonredundant forms, which have the advantage of being shorter and more logical, may also be based on the NHG standard.

10.2. The SY *tsun* vs. *tsu* 'to' in prevocalic position has a wide distribution (Prilutski 1937: 99ff., 103, 141). In the nineteenth century it was frequently found in WritY, and was recommended for standardization by one lexicographer (Harkavy 1888). In the twentieth century, though still used by important writers, it is declining. The probable reason – NHG *zu*.

The only exception is *tsun* in *tsunoyf* 'together', with no NHG counterpart to function as an obstacle to the standardization.

Even less successful was the CY *tsun* (Prilutski 1917: 85f.) as the equivalent of StY *tsum* 'to the', i.e. in preconsonantal position. (NHG *zum*.)

Modern StY did accept the traditional *tsuzamen* 'together' (cf. NHG *zusammen*) but not the CY *tsun ezamen*, *tsun ezamet*, *tsun azamen*, *tsu azam*, etc. (Prilutski 1937: 28, 104f., 142f., 145), which had no NHG equivalent.

10.3. *bay* (cf. NHG *bei*), with a small geographic distribution, won out over *ba*, *ban* (Prilutski 1937: 97f., 97–100, 141), and *bar*, the latter two in prevocalic position. WritY *bay*, *baym* (cf. NHG *beim*) won out over CY *barn*, CY, Courland Yiddish (M. Weinreich 1923: 206) and TCpY *ban*, NEY *bayn*, SEY *bam*. Only in Soviet Yiddish Orthography (SYO 21f.) was *bam* standardized.

10.4. SY *vayl* 'because' and *oyb* 'if' have become standardized, while NEY *vayle* and *oybe(r)* have become dialectal (cf. NHG *weil*, *ob*).

11. *Summary*

It has been generally recognized that the overt NHG influence played a decisive part in the standardization of WritY despite many years of anti-*daytshmerish* efforts. In this paper I have attempted to demonstrate the existence of a hidden standard, a covert *daytshmerish* influence, which became a primary regulating factor in the uniformity attained by WritY, but also a major inhibiting force in the development of the unique characteristics of the Yiddish language.

REFERENCES

Avanesov, R. I., editor (1964), *Narysy pa belaruskaj dyjalektalohii*. Minsk.

Ben-Nahum, D. (1964), '[Jewish migration]', *Encyclopedia of Social Science* 2: 20–28. Israel.

Beranek, F. J. (1955–1965), MAJ = *Mitteilungen des Arbeitskreises für Jiddistik*. Butzbach–Giessen.

— (1955–1965), *Westjiddischer Sprachatlas*. Marburg.

Beyer, E. (1964), *La palatalisation vocalique spontanée de l'Alsacien et du Badois*. Strasbourg.

Birnbaum, S. A. (1915), *Praktische Grammatik der jiddischen Sprache*. Vienna–Leipzig. (Second revised edition (1966) Hamburg.)

— (1930), *Yidishkeyt un loshn*. Warsaw.

— (1932), *Yidish verter-bikhl fun oysleyg, gramatishn min, beygung un vort-klas*. Lodz.

— (1938), '[Two Old Yiddish poems]', *Yivo-bleter* 13: 172–177.

— (1954), 'Two problems of Yiddish linguistics', *The Field of Yiddish* 1: 63–72.

— (1965), 'Specimens of Yiddish from eight centuries', *The Field of Yiddish* 2: 1–23.

Borokhov, B. (1913), '[The tasks of Yiddish philology]', in *Der pinkes*, ed. by S. Niger, 1–22. Vilna.

Brakazh, Kh. (1951), '[A note on Yiddish]', *Davke* 2: 239–246.

Braun, M. (1907), 'Die hebräischen Grabschriften schlesischer Juden aus dem dreizehnten und vierzehnten Jahrhundert', *Geschichte der Juden in Schlesien*. Anhang II: vi–xiii.

Brown, Lloyd (1949), *The Story of Maps*. Boston.

Buzuk, P. (1928), *Sproba linhvistyčnae heahrafii Belarusi*. Part I. Minsk.

Curme, G. O. (1922), *A Grammar of the German Language*. 7th edition. 1952. New York.

DABM (1963), *Dyjalektalahičny atlas belaruskaj movy*. Minsk.

Dal, V. I. (1934), *Tolkovyj slovar živogo velikorusskogo jazyka*. Tokyo.

deBray, R. G. A. (1952), *Guide to the Slavonic Languages*. London.

Diver, W. (1958), 'On the diachronic role of the morphological system', *Estructuralismo e historia, miscelánea homenaje a André Martinet* 2: 41–54. La Laguna.

Doroszewski, W. (1958–1965), *Słownik języka polskiego*. Warsaw.

Duschenes, F., editor (1893), 'Die Cultusgemeinden Böhmens', *Jahrbuch für die israelitischen Cultusgemeinden Böhmens* 5654: 153–268. Prague.

Entwistle, W. J., Morison, W. A., (n.d.), *Russian and the Slavonic Languages*. London.

Ettinger, S. (1956), '[Jewish participation in the colonization of the Ukraine]', *Zion* 20: 107–142.

Even-Shoshan, A. (1961), *Milon ḥadash*. Jerusalem.

Falkovitsh, E. (1940), *Yidish: fonetik, grafik, leksik, gramatik*. Moscow.

Ferguson, Charles A., Gumperz, John J., editors (1960), *Linguistic Diversity in South Asia: Studies in Regional, Social and Functional Variation*. Bloomington, Indiana.

Fischer, J. (1936), *Das Jiddische und sein Verhältnis zu den deutschen Mundarten*. Leipzig.

Friedmann, F. (1933), 'Einige Zahlen über die tschechoslovakischen Juden', *Schriften zur Diskussion des Zionismus* 9: 7. Prague.

Fuks, L. (1955), [*All's well that ends well: an 18th-century Yiddish comedy*]. Paris.

— (1957), *The Oldest Known Literary Documents of Yiddish Literature (c. 1382)*. Leiden.

Garde, Paul (1961), 'Réflexions sur les différences phonétiques entre les langues slaves', *Word* 17: 34–62.

Gerzon, J. (1902), *Die jüdisch-deutsche Sprache; eine grammatisch-lexikalische Untersuchung ihres deutschen Grundbestandes*. Frankfurt a. M.

Goldin, Hyman (1939), *The Rabbi's Guide: A Manual of Jewish Religious Rituals, Ceremonials and Customs*. New York.

Grünwald, M. (1923), 'Fünfundzwanzig Jahre jüdische Volkskunde', *Jahrbuch für jüdische Volkskunde* 1: 1–22.

Guggenheim-Grünberg, F. (1954a), 'Alte Grussformeln der Surbtaler Juden', *Schweizer Volkskunde* 44. Basel.

— (1954b), 'The horse dealers' language of the Swiss Jews in Endingen and Lengnau', *The Field of Yiddish* 1: 48–62.

— (1958), 'Zur Phonologie des Surbtaler Jiddischen', *Phonetica* 2: 86–108.

— (1964), 'Überreste westjiddischer Dialekte in der Schweiz, im Elsass und in Süddeutschland', *For Max Weinreich*, 72–81.

— (1966), 'Surbtaler Jiddisch', *Schweizer Dialekte in Text und Ton*. Heft 4. Frauenfeld.

— (1969), 'Endinger Jiddisch', *The Field of Yiddish* 3: 8–15.

Gutmans, T. (1930), 'Consonant assimilation in the sentence', *Filologishe shriftn fun Yivo* 2: 107–110.

Hapanovič, P. M., Mackevič, Ju. F. (1959), '[On the classification of Belorussian dialects]', *Voprosy jazykoznanija* 6.

Harkavy, A. (1928), *Yidish–english–hebreisher verterbukh*. 2nd ed. New York.

Haylperin, F., Weinreich, M. (1929), *Praktishe gramatik fun der yidisher shprakh*. Vilna.

Herzog, M. I. (1964), 'Channels of systematic extinction in Yiddish dialects', *For Max Weinreich*, 93–107.

— (1965a), *The Yiddish Language in Northern Poland: Its Geography and History*. Bloomington, Indiana.

— (1965b), 'Grammatical features of Markuze's *Sejfer refues* (1790)', *The Field of Yiddish* 2: 49–62.

— (1968), '[Language geography as an aid to historical research]', *Proceedings of the Fourth World Congress of Jewish Studies* 2: 189–193. Jerusalem.

— (1969), 'Yiddish in the Ukraine: isoglosses and inferences', *The Field of Yiddish* 3: 58–81.

Ivanov, V. V. (1961), *Kratkij očerk istoričeskoj fonetiki russkogo jazyka*. Moscow.

Jakobson, R. (1953), '[The Yiddish sound structure in its Slavic environment]', *Yidishe shprakh* 13: 70–83. (Reprinted (1958) in *Yuda A. Yofe-bukh*, 207–220. New York.)

For Roman Jakobson (1956), *For Roman Jakobson*. The Hague, Mouton.

JE (1925), *Jewish Encyclopedia*. New York and London.

Joffe, J. A. (1927–1928), '[The Slavic element in Yiddish]', *Pinkes fun Amopteyl fun Yivo* 1–2: 235–256, 296–312.

— (1939), '[*Yeder* or *Yed*]', *Yidish far ale* 2: 23–25.

— (1948), '[Analysis of some YIVO orthographic rules]', *Yidishe shprakh* 8: 33–61.

— (1954), 'Dating the origin of Yiddish dialects', *The Field of Yiddish* 1: 102–121.

Kahan, Y. L. (1931), '[Samples of Yiddish folklore in Burgenland; stories and songs]', *Yivo-bleter* 2: 200–221.

Kaiser, K. (1930), *Mundart und Schriftsprache*. Leipzig.

Karaś, M. (1966), Personal communication to Moshé Altbauer (in the files of LCAAJ). Polish Academy of Sciences. Institute of Linguistics. Cracow.

Karłowicz, J. (1900–1935), *Słownik języka polskiego*. Warsaw.

Kestenberg-Gladstein, R. (1944), '[The census of nonmetropolitan Jews in Bohemia in 1724]', *Zion* 9: 1–26.

— (1968), '[The internal migrations of the Jews of Bohemia in the 19th century]', *Proceedings of the Fourth World Congress of Jewish Studies* 2: 215–217. Jerusalem.

Kluge, Friedrich (1963), *Etymologisches Wörterbuch der deutschen Sprache*. 19th ed. Berlin.

Kobrin, L. (1944), *Fun daytshmerish tsu yidish in amerike*. New York.

Kohn, A. (1852), *Die Notabelnversammlungen der Israeliten Böhmens in Prag*. Mit statistischen Tabellen über die israelitischen Gemeinden...in Böhmen. Vienna.

Kolas, Ja., Krapiva, K. (1953), *Russko-belorusskij slovar*. Moscow.

Kosover, M. (1964), '[Gleanings from the vocabulary of a 15th-century Yiddish manuscript collection of customs]', *For Max Weinreich*, 355–368.

Landau, A. (1895), 'Das Deminutivum der galizisch-jüdischen Mundart', *Deutsche Mundarten* 1: 46–58. (Revised Yiddish version in *Yivo-bleter* 11: 154–172.)

— (1899), 'Holekreisch', *Zeitschrift für Volkskunde* 9: 72–77.

— (1901), 'Die Sprache der Memoiren Glückels von Hameln', *Mitteilungen zur jüdischen Volkskunde* 7: 20–68.

Landau, A., Wachstein, B. (1911), *Jüdische Privatbriefe aus dem Jahre 1619.* Vienna.

— (1927–1929), '[The Slavic elements and influences in Yiddish]', *Filologishe shriftn fun Yivo* 2: 199–214, 3: 615–616.

Leibel, D. (1965), 'On Ashkenazic stress', *The Field of Yiddish* 2: 158–181.

Lefin, M. (1819), Translation of *Sefer Koheleth Shlomo.* (Facsimile edition of 1819 MS. YIVO 1930.)

Lestschinsky, J. (1931), *Jüdische Wanderungen im 19. Jahrhundert.* Rome.

Lexer, M. (1962), *Mittelhochdeutsches Taschenwörterbuch.* 30th ed. Leipzig.

Lowenstein, S. (1969), 'Results of Atlas investigations among Jews of Germany', *The Field of Yiddish* 3: 16–35.

MAGP (1957), *Mały atlas gwar polskich.* Wrocław-Cracow.

Mark, Y. (1938–1939), '[Several particularly important problems of our present-day standard language]', *Yidish far ale* 1: 233–244, 265–272; 2: 80–86, 97–100.

— (1943), '[The gender of nouns]', *Yidishe shprakh* 4–6: 97–136.

— (1944), '[Lithuanian Jews and the neuter gender]', *Yidishe shprakh* 4: 83–94.

— (1945), '[Editorial remarks on A. A. Roback's article]', *Yidishe shprakh* 5: 75–78.

— (1951), '[Our Lithuanian Yiddish]', in *Lite*, ed. by M. Sudarski, 429–472. New York.

— (1965), [Questions and answers], *Yidishe shprakh* 25: 63–64.

Mark, Y., Joffe, J. A., editors (1961), *Groyser verterbukh fun der yidisher shprakh.* New York.

Markuze, M. (1790), *Seyfer refues.* Poryck.

Mieses, M. (1924), *Die jiddische Sprache; eine historische Grammatik.* Berlin–Vienna.

Moulton, W. (1961), 'The dialect geography of *hast, hat* in Swiss German', *Language* 37: 497–508.

Muneles, O. (1966), 'Zur Namengebung der Juden in Böhmen', *Judaica Bohemiae* 2: 3–13.

Nazarova, T. V. (1964), '[The Ukrainian–Belorusian language boundary in the lower Prypjat region]', *Voprosy dialektologii vostočno–slavjanskix jazykov.* Moscow.

Oshry, Ephraim (Rabbi) (1966), Personal interview with the author. Beth Hamedrash Hagodol. New York.

OUD (1955), *Oxford Universal Dictionary.* London and New York.

Paul, Hermann (1916), *Deutsche Grammatik.* Halle.

Pepłowski, Fr. (1966), Personal communication to Moshé Altbauer (in the files of LCAAJ). Institute of Literary Research. Lexicographic Association. Toruń.

Pfeifer, S. (*c.* 1897), *Kulturgeschichtliche Bilder aus dem jüdischen Gemeindeleben zu Reckendorf.*

Posnanski, Ad. (1895), 'Die Cultusgemeinden Böhmens', *Jüdische Chronik* 1: 15–17, 48–53. Saaz.

Prilutski, N. (1909), '[Materials for Yiddish grammar and orthography]', *Lebn un visnshaft* 1: 61–68.

— (1912), '[Dialectological phenomenon]', *Noyakh Prilutskis zamlbikher far yidishn folklor, filologye un kultur-geshikhte* 1: 134–137. Warsaw.

— (1917), *Der yidisher konsonantizm.* Warsaw.

— (1920), *Tsum yidishn vokalizm; etyudn* (= his *Yidishe dialektologishe forshungen* 4). Warsaw.

— (1921), *Dialektologishe paraleln un bamerkungen* (= his *Yidishe dialektologishe forshungen* 3 = *Noyakh Prilutskis zamlbikher far yidishn folklor, filologye un kultur-geshikhte*, vol. II, part 2). Warsaw.

— (1924), *Mame-loshn: yidishe shprakh-visnshaftlekhe forarbetn.* Warsaw.

— (1933), '[On the contrary]', *Arkhiv far yidisher shprakh-visnshaft, literatur-forshung un etnologye*, 347–349. Warsaw.

— (1937), *Dialektologishe forarbetn.* Vilna.

— (1938), '[Yente bas Yitskhok, the unknown Old Yiddish poetess]', *Yivo-bleter* 13: 36–54.

PUS (1958–1960), *Polsko–ukrainskyj slovnyk.* Kiev.

Reyzen, Z. (1923), *Fun Mendelson biz Mendele.* Warsaw.

— (1924), '[Grammatical gender in Yiddish]', *Yidishe filologye* 1: 11–22, 180–192, 303–322.

— (1927), *A. B. Gotlobers yidishe verk.* Vilna.

— (1929), '[Concerning adjective information]', *Filologishe shriftn* 3: 589–598.

Roback, A. A. (1944), '[Why Lithuanian Jews have no neuter gender]', *Yidishe shprakh* 4: 80–82.

— (1945), '[Once again concerning grammatical gender and other matters]', *Yidishe shprakh* 5: 70–74.

Rosetti, A. (1965), *Linguistica*. The Hague.

Ruppin, A. (1930), *Soziologie der Juden*. Berlin.

Şăineanu, L. (1899), *Studiu dialectologic asupra graiului evreo-german*. Bucharest. (Revised French version (L. Sainéan) in *Mémoires de la société linguistique de Paris* 12: 90–138, 176–196.)

Sapir, E. (1916), *Time Perspective in Aboriginal American Culture: A Study in Method*. Ottawa. (Reprinted (1949) in *Selected Writings*, 389–462. Berkeley–Los Angeles.)

Schaechter, M., Weinreich, M. (1961), *Yidisher ortografisher vegvayzer*. New York.

Schaechter, M. (1959), '[Review of the Yiddish section of the *Seven World Languages Dictionary*]', *Goldene keyt* 33: 102–108.

— (1963), '[Homonymophobia]', *Yidishe shprakh* 23: 21–26.

— (1964), *Elyokem Tsunzers verk: kritishe oysgabe*. New York.

Shapiro, M. (1939), '[Grammatical gender in Yiddish]', *Afn shprakhfront* (third series) 3: 111–163.

Shatzky, J. (1929), '[Dirge on the destruction of Worms]', *Filologishe shriftn* 3: 43–56.

— (1938), '[A historical and critical introduction to *Yeveyn metsolu*]', *Gzeyres takh* 5–159. Vilna.

Shiper, I. (1926), *Kulturgeshikhte fun yidn in poyln beysn mitlalter*. Warsaw.

— (1914), '[The settlement of Jews in Poland and Lithuania]', *Istorija evrejskogo naroda* 11: 105–131. Moscow.

Shklyar, H. (1933), '[Yiddish–Belorussian linguistic parallels]', *Lingvistishe zamlung* 1: 65–80.

Shlosberg, B. (1938), '[*Mirkeves-hamishne* – the oldest printed Yiddish document]', *Yivo-bleter* 13: 313–324.

Shmeruk, Kh. (1964), '[The East European versions of *Tsene-rene*, 1786–1850]', *For Max Weinreich*, 320–336.

Shrier, M. (1965), 'Case systems in German dialects', *Language* 41: 420–438.

Shtif, N. (1926), '[A mid-16th century Yiddish manuscript collection in Venice]', *Tsaytshrift* 1: 141–158.

— (1929), '[The dialectological expedition of the chair in Jewish culture]', *Di yidishe shprakh* 19.

Shulman, M. (1939), '[Sholem Aleichem's contribution to Yiddish phonological-dialectological research]', *Afn shprakhfront* (third series) 4: 149–160.

Stalek, R. (1928), '[Materials concerning the Yiddish of Burgenland]' *Filologishe shriftn fun Yivo* 2: 265–280.

Stankiewicz, E. (1965), 'Yiddish place names in Poland', *The Field of Yiddish* 2: 158–181.

Stutshkov, N. (1950), *Der oytser fun der yidisher sphrakh*, ed. by M. Weinreich. New York.

SYO (1932), *Sovetishe yidishe ortografye*. Kharkov–Kiev.

Takones (1937), *Takones fun yidishn oysleyg*. Vilna.

Traub, M. (1919), *Jüdische Wanderungen*. Berlin.

Tsaytshrift (1936–1931), *Tsaytshrift far yidisher geshikhte, demografye un ekonomik, literatur-forshung, shprakhvisnshaft un etnolog? afye*. Minsk.

Tsederboym, A. (1863), *Kol mevaser*. Odessa.

Tshemerinski, Kh. (1912), '[Mendele's grammar]', *Mendele zamlbukh*. Reprinted (1928) in *Der Mendele turem*, 225–238. Warsaw.

Tshernyak, Y. (1930), '[Case government in colloquial speech]', *Di yidishe shprakh* 1: 31–38.

Tsvayg, A. R. (1929), '[Materials for a systematic Yiddish orthoëpy]', *Di yidishe shprakh* 14: 21–28.

Urbańczyk, St. (1966), Personal communication to Moshé Altbauer (in the files of LCAAJ) Polish Academy of Sciences. Institute of Linguistics. Cracow.

Veynger, M. (1926–1928), '[Concerning Yiddish dialects]', *Tsaytshrift* 1: 181–207; 2–3: 613–651.

Vilenkin, L. (1931), *Yidisher shprakhatlas fun Sovetnfarband*. Minsk.

Viler, J. (1926), '[The gender of nouns in Eastern Galician Yiddish]', *Filologishe shriftn fun Yivo* 1: 249–264.

Weinreich, M. (1923), *Shtaplen*. Berlin.

— (1926), '[A Yiddish poem about Sabbatai-Zevi of 1666]', *Tsaytshrift* 1: 159–172.

— (1927), *Shturemvint. Bilder fun der yidisher geshikhte in 17tn yorhundert*. Vilna.

— (1928), *Bilder fun der yidisher literatur-geshikhte*. Vilna.

— (1930), '[Project for standardizing Yiddish spelling]', *Der eynheytlekher yidisher oysleyg*, 20–65. Vilna.

— (1939), *Algemeyne yidishe entsiklopedye*. Supplementary volume *Yidn* 2: 23–90. Paris.

— (1953), '[Outlines of Western Yiddish]', *Yidishe shprakh* 13: 35–69. (Reprinted (1958) with an addendum in *Yuda A. Yofe-bukh*, ed. by Y. Mark. New York.)

— (1954), 'Prehistory and early history of Yiddish: facts and conceptual framework, *The Field of Yiddish* 1: 73–101.

— (1956), 'Yiddish, Knaanic, Slavic: the basic relationships', *For Roman Jakobson*, 622–632.

— (1957–1958), '[Yiddish phonology as a clue to Medieval Hebrew: the aspirate and the velar and palatal spirants]', *Yivo-bleter* 41: 101–123. (Reprinted (1958) in *Shmuel Niger bukh*, ed. by S. Bikl and L. Lehrer, 101–125. New York.

— (1959), 'History of the Yiddish language: the problems and their implications', *Proceedings of the American Philosophical Society* 103: 563–570.

— (1960a), '[The system of Yiddish protovowels]', *Yidishe shprakh* 20: 65–71.

— (1960b), 'Old Yiddish poetry in linguistic-literary research', *Word* 16: 100–118.

— (1965), 'On the dynamics of Yiddish dialect formation', *The Field of Yiddish* 2: 73–86.

For Max Weinreich (1964), *For Max Weinreich on His Seventieth Birthday – Studies in Jewish Languages, Literature, and Society*. The Hague, Mouton.

Weinreich, U. (1949), *College Yiddish*. New York.

— (1952), '*Sábesdiker losn* in Yiddish: a problem of linguistic affinity', *Word* 8: 260–277.

— (1954), 'Stress and word structure in Yiddish', *The Field of Yiddish* 1: 1–27.

— (1958a), 'Yiddish and colonial German: the differential impact of Slavic', *American Contributions to the Fourth International Congress of Slavicists*, 369–421. The Hague.

— (1958b), 'A retrograde sound shift in the guise of a survival: an aspect of Yiddish vowel development', *Estructuralismo e historia, miscelánea homenaje a André Martinet* 2: 221–267. La Laguna.

— (1959), 'On the cultural history of Yiddish rime', *Essays on Jewish Life and Thought*, 423–442. New York.

— (1960a), '[Concerning a new Jewish language and culture atlas]', *Di goldene keyt* 37: 47–57.

— (1960b), '[The plural of *noz*: a chapter in Yiddish grammatical geography]', *Yidishe shprakh* 20: 81–90.

— (1961), 'The seven genders of Yiddish'. Unpublished paper read before the annual meeting of the Linguistic Society of America. Chicago.

— (1962a), 'Multilingual dialectology and the new Yiddish atlas', *Anthropological Linguistics* 4: 6–22.

— (1962b), 'Culture geography at a distance: some problems in the study of East European Jewry, in *Proceedings of the 1962 Annual Spring Meeting of the American Ethnological Society*, 27–39. Seattle.

— (1963), 'Machine aids in the compilation of linguistic atlases', in *Yearbook of the American Philosophical Society*, 622–625.

— (1964a), 'Four riddles in bilingual dialectology', in *American Contributions to the Fifth International Congress of Slavicists*, 335–359. The Hague.

— (1964b), 'Western traits in Transcarpathian Yiddish', in *For Max Weinreich*, 245–264.

— (1965a), 'On the syntax of the Yiddish adjective'. Unpublished paper read before the YIVO Linguistic Circle.

— (1965b), *Ha'ivrit haashkenazit weha'ivrit shebbeyidish: behinatan hageografit.* Jerusalem.

— (1968), *Modern English–Yiddish Yiddish–English Dictionary.* New York.

— (1969), 'The geographic makeup of Belorussian Yiddish', *The Field of Yiddish* 3: 82–101.

Weinreich, M., editor (1925), *Ale ksovin fun Sh. Etinger.* Vilna.

Weinreich, M., Weinreich, B. (1959), *Yiddish Language and Folklore: A Selective Bibliography for Research.* The Hague.

Weinreich, U., editor (1954), *The Field of Yiddish: Studies in Yiddish Language, Folklore, and Literature.* New York.

— (1965), *The Field of Yiddish: Studies in Yiddish Language, Folklore, and Literature,* second collection. The Hague.

Weinreich, U., Herzog, M. I., Ravid, W., editors (1969), *The Field of Yiddish: Studies in Yiddish Language, Folklore, and Literature,* third collection. The Hague.

Wexler, P. (1964), 'Slavic influence in the grammatical functions of three Yiddish verbal prefixes', *Linguistics* 7: 83–93.

Wiener, L. (1893), 'On the Judeo–German spoken by the Russian Jews', *American Journal of Philology* 14: 41–67, 456–483.

Wolf, M. L. (1969), 'The geography of Yiddish case and gender variation', *The Field of Yiddish* 3: 102–215.

Wright, J. (1907), *Historical German Grammar.* Oxford.

Zamenhof, L. (1910), '[Essays in Yiddish grammar]', *Lebn un visnshaft* 7: 89–96, 9: 97–104.

Zaretski, A. (1921), *Klolim fun yidishn oysleyg.* Odessa.

— (1926), *Praktishe yidishe gramatik.* Moscow.

— (1927), *Grayzn un sfeykes; kapitlen stilistishe gramatik.* Kiev.

— (1928), *Yidishe gramatik.* Vilna.

— (1929), '[Concerning Yiddish orthoëpy]', *Di yidishe shprakh* 16: 1–8; 17–18: 21–32.

Zhitlowski, H. (1955), *Geklibene verk.* New York.

Žilko, F. T. (1953), '[Speech varieties transitional between Ukrainian and Belorussian in the northwestern areas of the Černihiv region]', *Dialektolohičnyj bjuletin* 4.

— (1958), '[Some questions of the classification of Ukrainian dialects in the light of data from linguistic geography]', *Filolohičnyj zbirnyk.*

— (1964), '[Peculiarities of dialect boundaries in Ukrainian]', in *Voprosy dialektologii vostočno-slavjanskix jazykov.* Moscow.

Žirmunskij, V. M. (1939), '[On some questions of Yiddish dialect geography]', *Jazyk i myšlenie* 9: 135–145.

— (1962), *Deutsche Mundartkunde.* Berlin.

Zivy, A. (1966), *Elsässer Jiddisch, jüdisch–deutsche Sprichwörter und Redensarten.* Basel.

Zunz, Leopold (1836), *Namen der Juden.* Second enlarged edition in *Gesammelte Schriften.* 1876. Berlin.

משה בראָדערזאָן

מאָסקווע, רוסלאַנד, 1890
וואַרשע, פּוילן, 1956

———◆———

באַגייסטערונג, (לידער)
צונגענלונגען (מאַריאָנטן־שפּיל)
דוד און בת־שבע, (אָפּערע)
י ו ד , (לידער)

———◆———

פּאָעט און קלײנקונסט־שרײַבער

יצחק קאַצענעלסאָן

קאַרעליץ, וויַיס־רוסלאַנד, 1886
פיטיוויע־לאַגער, פראַנקרייַד, 1944

———◆———

די זון פאַרגייט אין פלאַמען (ליד)
תרשיש, (דראַמע)
דאָס ווייסע לעבן (נאָוועלן)
דאָס ליד פון אויסגעהרגטן
ייִדישן פאָלק

———◆———

פּאָעט, דערצײלער, דראַמאַטורג

זוסמאַן סעגאַלאָוויטש

ביאַליסטאָק, פּוילן, 1884
ניו־יאָרק, פאַר. שטאַטן, 1949

———◆———

אין קאַזימיעזש, (פּאָעמע)
זעליגס יאָרן, (ראָמאַן)
די וואַנט, (דראַמ. פּאָעמע)
איצטער, (חורבן לידער)

———◆———

פּאָעט, דערצײלער, ראָמאַניסט

יחיאל־ישעיה טרונק

דאָרף אָסמולסק, פּוילן, 1887
ניו יאָרק, פאַר. שטאַטן, 1961

———◆———

אידעאַליזם און נאַטוראַליזם
אין דער ייִד. ליט. (עסײען)
פּוילן, (היסטאַרישע עפּאָפּעע)
קוואַלן און בוימער, (נאָוועלן)
דער פּריילעקסטער ייִד אין
אין דער וועלט, (פּאָלקס. ראָמאַן)

———◆———

עסײאיסט
דערצײלער, ראָמאַניסט

אהרן צײטלין

אווואָראָוויטש, וויַיס־רוסלאַנד 1889
לעבט אין ניו־יאָרק, פאַר. שטאַטן

———◆———

מטטרון, (פּאָעמע)
יעקב פראַנק, (פּיעסע)
ייִדנשטאַט, (פּיעסע)
געזאַמעלטע לידער

———◆———

פּאָעט, עסײאיסט, דראַמאַטורג

קאַדיע מאָלאָדאָווסקי

קאַרטוז בערעזע, פּוילן, 1894
לעבט אין ניו־יאָרק, פאַר. שטאַטן

———◆———

חשוונדיקע נעכט
דזשיקע גאַס
ייִדישע קינדער
דער מלד דוד אַליין איז
געבליבן, (פּיעסע)

———◆———

פּאָעט, דראַמאַטורג

1. Moyshe Broderzon, 1890–1956; Poet; 2. Yitskhok Katsnelson, 1886–1944; Poet, writer of short stories, playwright; 3. Zusman Segalovitsh, 1884–1949; Poet, writer of short stories, novelist; 4. Yekhil-yeshaye Trunk, 1887–1961; Essayist, writer of short stories, novelist; 5. Arn Tseytlin, 1898–1973; Poet, essayist, playwright; 6. Kadye Molodovski, 1984–1974; Poet, playwright.

Politics and Linguistics
in the Standardization of Soviet Yiddish

RACHEL ERLICH

A few general remarks about the character of Yiddish are necessary in order to present with clarity the controversy over the standardization of Yiddish which took place in Eastern Europe after the First World War, between the Yiddish linguists in the Soviet Union and those living outside Russia.

Yiddish in itself contains the history of Jewish migrations from Asia to Europe and, like English, it is a fusion language, based on a variety of linguistic components. The oldest component is Hebrew, after which come – in order of historical sequence – the Romance, and then the Germanic components. The fourth and newest is the Slavic component; its influence on the Yiddish language as a whole is immense. Its composition contains the history of the Ashkenazi Jews' migration eastward, their contacts with the Slavic peoples, and with the Czech, Polish, Ukrainian, and Byelorussian languages. Tsarist restrictions, barring Jews from settling outside the Pale of Settlement, limited the contact of Yiddish-speaking Jews with the Russian language, and its influence upon Yiddish is minor.

The rapid modernization of Jewish life in the nineteenth and twentieth centuries was reflected in the growing diversification and sophistication of the Yiddish language. On the spoken level, a modern idiom emerged; while the written language developed so as to serve the purposes of literary prose, poetry, political and philosophical essays, and scholarly works. And this in turn led to a lively interest in Yiddish as a whole. Jewish linguists began working on different aspects of the language; and, although they did not always agree with one another's assumptions and conclusions, they all shared a common goal: the need to standardize Yiddish. They all believed that standardization would add to the prestige of Yiddish, raising the social status of both the language and their people. To adapt a recent English coinage, standardization would show that 'Yiddish is beautiful'.

The geopolitical changes in East-Central and Eastern Europe after World

War I affected the members of Yiddish-speaking communities there; and also affected and modified the type of communication between the various spokesmen for standardization. Political developments within the Soviet Union, its changing policy towards national minorities, which was based on the hidden assumption of Great Russian chauvinism in 'revolutionary' disguise, gave rise to a linguistic feud between former friends and coworkers. The Yiddish linguists who found themselves living inside the Soviet Union were forced to declare the Yiddish linguists outside the Soviet Union to be class enemies. But as the controversy became one between a Soviet Yiddish point of view and a non-Soviet one, a common goal still continued to absorb the Yiddish linguists. All of them in Poland, Lithuania, Latvia, Romania, and Soviet Russia, each in his own way, continued working toward the standardization of Yiddish.

There was no conflict between the aspirations of the revolution and those of the Yiddish linguists in Soviet Russia; for the revolution had held out the hope to all formerly oppressed peoples residing within Russian boundaries that they would become free to develop their respective languages and cultures. Moreover, after the revolution, government resources were promised to all the peoples of Soviet Russia to help with the establishment of their respective school systems, newspapers, publications, and scientific research institutes. The Yiddish linguists, intent on standardization, were elated by this, and set out to simplify Yiddish spelling. They had before them as an example the changes in Russian spelling brought about with the help of government power. A plan of simplified Russian spelling, filed away in the Tsarist Academy of Sciences, had been quickly adopted by the Soviet government, and brought into being by its decree.

The first change that came about in Soviet Yiddish spelling concerned words from the Hebrew component which are treated differently in Yiddish than those from other sources. Although, by now, the Yiddish pronunciation, and sometimes also the meaning, of these words is different from that of the Hebrew, they have kept through the years their traditional Hebrew spelling. Often they are only part of a compound word, have affixes or are affixed to other components.

As part of a pedagogical debate on how to teach Yiddish to children ignorant of Hebrew, and how to make it easier for adults unfamiliar with Hebrew to write Yiddish correctly, discussions about changing the Hebrew spelling of Yiddish words had begun long before the Russian Revolution.

The discussion centered on the question of replacing the traditional Hebrew spelling of words belonging to the Hebrew component of Yiddish by a phonetic spelling, and on the question of discarding the five special characters ץ ף ן ם ך reserved for word endings of all components in Yiddish.

Only in the Soviet Union did the adherents of change win out. In 1919, the name of the official Yiddish daily newspaper of the Communist Party in the Soviet Union *Der Emes* (meaning 'truth', the equivalent of the Russian *Pravda*) – a word belonging to the Hebrew component – was still spelt in the traditional way אמת דער but in 1921, in response to the demands of the authorities, the spelling was changed. The word came to be 'naturalized', i.e. spelled עמעס דער phonetically. The second step in the changed spelling of Soviet Yiddish was the elimination of the five special letters used for word endings. This occurred later, and both steps became symbols of the new Soviet Yiddish.

The response outside the Soviet Union was mixed; the naturalized spelling of words of Hebrew origin receiving a more sympathetic response than the dropping of the final letters. Both steps were imitated at one time or another in Yiddish writing in Europe and the United States, but these changes were never formally adopted in the West.

In the Moscow *Emes* of September 15, 1921, there is an article about a newspaper of the same name in New York City, which states:

The name [of the paper] is spelt the new way, but in the text the same word is spelt the old way...Our aim is to implement the new spelling that we have in Russia...It is simpler and more accessible to the masses...it is also a kind of revolutionary symbol,...it shows immediately that there is a difference between the old Yiddish press and the new one. It is especially necessary to show this difference in America where external [things] play such a great role. Let people see that we are breaking down barriers...revolutionary means revolutionary in everything.

Falk Halpern, a Yiddish teacher in Vilna, Poland, wrote:

We have to be a bit more courageous and start to write and print our books with the thoroughly consistent Yiddish spelling, and to teach our children in the schools to read and write the same way (*Literarishe bleter* 1926).

In 1932, the organ of the youth organization of the Bund in Poland, the *Yugnt-Veker*, naturalized the spelling of the words of Hebrew origin, and continued to do so until the outbreak of the Second World War.[1] While the official organ of the Bund, *Di Naye Folkstsaygung*, kept the original spelling, not wanting to change it.

There were also many negative responses; and even within the Soviet Union there was some opposition. In *Der Oysleyg fun Yidish* (Yiddish Spelling), A. Vevyorka writes that although 'carefulness' (by which he means adherence to the old spelling) is considered by some comrades to be a kind of 'orthographic menshevism', a reactionary manifestation, it would be possible to sell Soviet Yiddish literature abroad in much greater quantities, were it not for the difficulties imposed upon the reader by the new orthography.[2] And now that

---

1. The details about the *Yugnt-veker* were kindly supplied to me by its former editor, J. S. Herts, presently residing in New York City.
2. Vevyorka 1926. The statement about the 'difficulties' in reading Yiddish books in the new Soviet Yiddish spelling seems to contradict the claim to simplicity which served as a reason for changing the old spelling system. But a spelling system can be made easier for those who are in the process of learning to read and to spell; it may please those sophisticated users of the language who desire the standardization of the spelling; yet it presents in the beginning some difficulty to older people who are set in their ways and do not like innovations.

we have become familiar with the way non-Soviet sources are used in Soviet publications to express opposition to official policies, we can understand why Max Weinreich, the leading Yiddish linguist outside the Soviet Union – in a booklet entitled *The Soviet Yiddish Orthography* (*Rules of the New Yiddish Spelling*) – was first attacked as 'the pillar of Fascistic Yiddishism', and then quoted:

> For a considerable segment of the Jewish intelligentsia the naturalized spelling means that somebody is exterminating the Jewish tradition, is tearing the language from its Jewish source. Such a sentiment must not be ignored, by any orthographic reform.[3]

Someone within the circle of Yiddish linguists in the Soviet Union wanted readers to know what Max Weinreich of the YIVO in Vilna had to say about the naturalized spelling. And what Max Weinreich had to say was said gently enough to make possible some kind of dialogue between Yiddish linguists on both sides of the Russian-Polish border. For no one wanted to exclude Soviet Yiddish culture from the cultural treasury of the Jewish people.

Nokhum Shtif, the editor of *The Orthographic Dictionary of Soviet Yiddish*, in his preface to the dictionary, takes part in the indirect dialogue:

> This is not an ordinary reform. It is a Soviet reform. It is imbued with the spirit of October, the spirit which conducts a cultural revolution...[without] being afraid of tradition...In the Yiddishist scholarly camp...[they are] afraid to touch the 'delicate' spelling of the 'exalted' [Hebrew] words, they are afraid to touch even such an everyday traditional nuisance as the final letters...with our first steps in the reform – to spell the Hebrew words the Yiddish way – we hit the reaction and the opportunism...like a thunderbolt. This, the whole pious and Hebraistic-Yiddishistic reaction cannot forgive us to this day.[4]

The booklet: *Soviet Yiddish Orthography*, that accompanied the above-mentioned dictionary, states succinctly: '[Soviet Yiddish] Orthography is socialist in content and national in form' (Weinreich 1932: 3).

More complex, however, than that of revised spelling, was the lexical problem. Here the standardization of Yiddish in Soviet Russia was constantly pushed in the direction of creating a new 'revolutionary Yiddish', which could be called a class language, in accordance with demands that affected all languages within the Soviet Union, including Russian.

The first step in 'revolutionizing' the Yiddish vocabulary was – as in the case of spelling – to attack the Hebrew component. This was called 'dehebraization' of Yiddish.

3. *Di sovetishe yidishe ortografye* (*klolim funem nayem yidishn oysleyg*) (Weinreich 1932) was published by the Institute for Jewish Proletarian Culture at the Ukrainian Academy of Sciences, Philological Section, Publishing House for National Minorities of the Ukrainian Soviet Republic.

The term *yidishizm* in the Soviet Yiddish sources has a decidedly pejorative connotation. It was used in the polemics against the Yiddish linguists outside of the Soviet Union who were considered nationalists and counter-revolutionaries.

YIVO: abbreviation for *Yidisher visnshaftlekher institut* which was founded in Vilna in 1925; presently located in New York City under the name of YIVO Institute for Jewish Research.

4. *Ortografisher verterbukh* (Shtif 1932) was published under the auspices of the Ukrainian Academy of Sciences.

In the periodical *Di Yidishe Shprakh*, N. Shtif published an article entitled 'Social differentiation in Yiddish, the Hebrew elements in the language', in which he attempts to show that the emergence of a Jewish working class had reduced the inventory of Yiddish words of Hebrew origin 'both in quantity and in quality', and that Soviet Yiddish reflects this. Shtif then tries to create the impression that the 'rabbinic-merchant aristocracy' is responsible for the presence of the Hebrew component in Yiddish, and that now that their power had been broken it was time to put an end to their rule over the language. It was time to dehebraize Yiddish (Shtif 1929).

In his preface to the dictionary, N. Shtif writes:

In choosing the word material...one principle prevailed: generally we did not include the archaic, the decrepit...many Hebrew words...foreign words and the words of the class enemy...but we have carefully collected the new ones which the revolution, industrialization, collectivization...created...in short, this is a dictionary of the present Soviet Yiddish (Shtif 1932: VII)'.

These new 'carefully collected' words were necessary in order to create a proletarian literary language, as part of the general process in the struggle of the working class for hegemony.

A Homeland in Berditshev. 'Oh, what a pleasure to be at home!' Berditshev City Council recognizes Yiddish as an official language. (*Der groyser kundes*, December 4, 1925)

אויבן — אַ היימלאַנד אין בערדיטשעוו —
אך, ס'אַ מחיה! ביי זיך אין דער היים. (בערדיטשע־
ווער שטאָט־פּאַרוואַלטונג אַנערקענט אידיש, אלס
אָפיציעלע שפּראַד).

The 'dehebraization' of the Soviet Yiddish vocabulary was not very successful. Many Yiddish words of the Hebrew component have no connection with their 'archaic' origin or with religion; some are everyday words, some obscenities, some are used as socially acceptable descriptions of bodily functions. It was impossible to eliminate the Hebrew component from Yiddish. Kh. Holmstok tries to find a way out of this dilemma by justifying the retention of these words: 'if we are dealing with an enemy that we have to fight, we have to know it...its class roots and its social class function (Holmstok 1933: 36–37). And E. Spivak even criticizes N. Shtif for ascribing to the 'Hebrew element' a specific religious function, describing this approach as 'mechanistic' (Spivak 1935).

The only solution was to diminish the importance of the Hebrew component by substituting words of other components for those of Hebrew origin and to bestow some measure of prestige on another component; the natural choice for this was the Slavic one. The 'dehebraization' of Yiddish went hand in hand with the promotion of the Slavic component. If the words of Hebrew origin were considered to be the property of the class enemy, the words of the Slavic component were declared to be the property of the masses.

The discussions on Slavisms in Yiddish were complicated by the fact that although the political directives came from Moscow, Jews lived largely in two Soviet Republics, the Ukrainian and the Byelorussian, and their work on language took place mainly in the Yiddish divisions of the Ukrainian Academy of Sciences and the Byelorussian Academy of Sciences. This situation gave rise to three competing strains in the Slavic component.

Thus in 1929, A. Kushnirov writes in *Der Emes*:

They began to cultivate a 'theory' that there is no unified Soviet Yiddish literature, but there are apparently three separate Yiddish literatures – a Ukrainian, a Byelorussian, and a Moscow one.

He then discusses Ukrainian writing circles where a theory had emerged that Ukrainian literature and culture should not base themselves on '"Muscovite" Asiatic Moscow', but on the cultural West (Kushnirov 1929). Apparently Yiddish writers and cultural activists were trying to take advantage of Ukrainian and Byelorussian opposition to Moscow, to improve their own position. In an article on book production in Yiddish in the Soviet Union during 1932, N. Rubinshteyn of Minsk, writes:

Book production in the national languages generally, and in Yiddish in particular...confirms once more the genius of Stalin's thought that in our country...the national languages not only do not die or merge into one common language, but just the opposite, the national languages develop and begin to bloom! This is what the dialectic of Lenin's point of view in regard to the question of national culture means. 'One should give national culture the possibility to develop and reveal its potentials, in order to create the circumstances for a merger into one common culture with one common language' (Stalin 1933).

But at the same time, there was another official trend: to 'enrich' all the national languages in the Soviet Union with Russian word-material defined as words from Soviet revolutionary reality. To paraphrase Orwell: 'All languages were equal, but the Russian language was more equal than the others'. The Ukrainians, the Byelorussians, and the Jews found themselves in similar positions; on the one hand, they were urged to develop their respective languages, on the other hand, they had to demonstrate that they were not nationalistic and were not driving the Russian words from Soviet reality out of their respective languages.

Because of these contradictions the pitfalls were tremendous. *Der Emes* was criticized for invoking Maxim Gorky's name and his comments on the vulgarization of the Russian language, in an attempt to stop the flooding of Yiddish with Russian words; and instead of using the newly coined Yiddish word *kolvirt* for the Russian *kolkhoz*, and the new Yiddish word *shlogler* as a translation of the Russian *udarnik* (shock worker), *Emes* was told to popularize the Russian terminology, as all the other languages should, and that this in turn would create a common ground for all languages in the Soviet Union, and foster the unity of the Soviet peoples (*Lingvistishe zamlung* 1934: 25). This criticism also reflects an underlying desire to make Soviet Yiddish different from the Yiddish used in the rest of the world, in parallel with the idea of 'Socialism in one country'.

At the Yiddish language conference in the Ukraine in 1934, the Ukrainian Assistant Commissar of Education, A. A. Khvila, speaking in Ukrainian, said:

> The Ukrainian nationalists...did counter-revolutionary work...[they tore] the Ukrainian language away from the brotherly Russian language...In the Ukrainian language there is a bitter struggle going on against so-called Russianisms...*pozhar* and *pozhezha* are both Ukrainian words [both meaning something is on fire]...[but because] *pozhar* is the same in both Ukrainian and Russian only *pozhezha* was used (Khvila 1934).

Khvila's words were meant to underline the analogy between Ukrainian and Yiddish in regard to the resistance against the influx of Russian words entering the national languages. And at that time it sounded like a warning. A new Soviet term had been created to describe the 'reactionaries' who were attempting to secure the integrity of their languages. They were called *natsdemy* (national democrats)[5] in all the national languages in the Soviet Union; and the Byelorussian *natsdems* did the same as the Yiddish *natsdems*: they translated the Russian word *kolkhoz* into the Byelorussian word *supolka*, and they used their own word *dziadzka* instead of the Russian *tovarishch*.

The 'Yiddishists' were accused of shunning Russian Sovietisms because they feared these words might destroy the 'unity' of all the Jewish people and their culture but 'we Bolsheviks do not care about the unity of the Jewish nationality and culture...we Bolsheviks know [that in each nation there are] two nations,

---

5. The word *demokrat* is now considered a compliment in the countries of the Soviet bloc. But it was considered an insult in the Soviet Union of the thirties.

and [in each culture] two cultures...[and we are the one that] serves the construction of socialism in the Soviet Union' (*Lingvistishe zamlung* 1934: 30).

But other opinions still appeared in print, and in the same source quoted above, the so-called 'nationalists' were cleverly defended:

The majority of the Jewish people do not live among Russians, but among Ukrainians and Byelorussians who do not always use the Russian Sovietisms...to demand that only the Russian forms be used, is to reach such a degree of 'leftism' that it smells of Big Power chauvinism (*Lingvistishe zamlung* 1934: 70).

The reply to the defenders of the 'nationalists' was: 'The block of the Jewish and local Byelorussian and Ukrainian nationalists, act together in their support of the language politics of the *natsdems*' (*Lingvistishe zamlung* 1934: 117).

And still Yiddish laid claim to great achievements in the Soviet Union:

...it became a powerful Soviet weapon with the help of which the party [and] the Soviet authorities carry communist proletarian ideas...[Yiddish] conducts a ruthless fight against the clerical-Hebraistic elements on the one hand and against the Russianizing elements on the other (*Afn shprakhfront* 1935).

It was clear that the instructions to promote Russianisms in Yiddish came from above, from Moscow. In order to protect their language and strengthen their position, Yiddish linguists looked for support from the national minorities among whom they lived. But they did not speak of accepting Ukrainianisms or Byelorussianisms instead of Russianisms; they spoke in terms of Russianisms and Slavisms. The Slavisms were considered to be the product of a more desirable social origin, and by accepting them in Yiddish one promoted the unity of the Jewish workers with workers of other nationalities. On the other hand, the Russian language was presented as the language of the Jewish beourgeoisie: 'If [a Jew] speaks Yiddish he is a proletarian *intelligent*, if he speaks Russian he is a bourgeois *intelligent*' (*Lingvistishe zamlung* 1934: 108).

The tendency was to promote the Slavic component as a whole, but to beware of the Russian influx. In the Soviet Union, where proletarian origin was considered an asset, the old Slavisms of the masses were given added prestige by introducing historical evidence of their traditional use. And to this in turn was added the claim of their existence not only on the spoken level, but on the written level as well (*Lingvistishe zamlung* 1936: 73). The acceptance in Yiddish of Slavic words other than the Russian was a linguistic argument with political overtones; it was a dangerous struggle for cultural independence.

Byelorussians, for example, were accused of secessionist desires, of using their language in preparation for cutting their country off from the Soviet Union so as to establish a dictatorship of the bourgeoisie; for this reason they had rid their language of all words which might remind them of Russia, and had even cultivated artificial Polonisms (*Lingvistishe zamlung* 1934: 111).

Despite all the controversy the Russian influx into the languages of all the national minorities continued. And in the case of Yiddish there was even some discussion about using the linguistic material of the Russian-flooded substandard Yiddish (incorrect Yiddish) to create a separate standard Russian-Yiddish language that would be the expression of 'Soviet Internationalism' within the Soviet Union. But this political language theory was declared a 'vulgar deviation', and was dropped.[6] On the standard level, in literary Yiddish there was a deliberate effort to create some sort of barrier to the flood of Russian words.

But the Soviet Yiddish Standard accepted other forms of Russian influence. The Russianization of words of foreign origin in Soviet Yiddish began in the vernacular right after the revolution. 'Internationalisms', as they are called in Yiddish, such as *mitologye* (mythology) and *aritmetik*, are spelled and pronounced the Russian way in Soviet Yiddish: *mifologye* and *arifmetik*. Yiddish has an *h*-sound, while Russian does not; either a *g*-sound or a *kh*-sound is substituted whenever a foreign word containing an *h*-sound is written in Russian. For instance, the Russian pronounciation of Hiroshima is khiroshima, and Soviet Yiddish, despite the fact that it possesses an *h*, spells it in the Russian way. In distinction from the Standard Yiddish outside the Soviet Union, Soviet Yiddish uses the Russian-sounding names of the months of the year (e.g., *Oktyaber*, *Noyaber*, *Dekaber* instead of *Oktober*, *November*, *Detsember*). In non-Soviet Yiddish 'class enemies' would be *klasn-sonim*, but in Soviet Yiddish they are called *klaseve sonim*. This, of course, does not exhaust the subject of the differences between Soviet and non-Soviet Yiddish, but it is an attempt to show some of the elements contained in the specific character of Soviet Yiddish. The Stalinist Russianization policy which had started in the early 1930s toward all non-Russian languages in the Soviet Union had its impact also on the Yiddish sector. But here the situation was more complex due to the tension between the Hebrew and the Slavic components within Yiddish. This would require a separate study.

But Soviet Yiddish could not cut itself off from the rest of the Yiddish language. Soviet Yiddish literature, Soviet Yiddish writings were eagerly read all around the world. And in spite of the name-calling and rude criticisms on both sides, the dialogue between the Soviet and non-Soviet camps continued, as both sides desired that it should.

In 1928, The Ukrainian Academy of Sciences in Kiev established a Yiddish chair, and invitations to the ceremony marking this occasion were sent out to the 'class enemy' in Poland, to YIVO in Vilna, and to the important literary magazine in Warsaw, *Literarishe bleter*. Because of Poland's hostile relations with Communist Russia neither of these invitations could be accepted. But they both sent written congratulations to the Academy and these were published in the *Literarishe bleter*. There we read of YIVO's hope for 'still closer contact' between

6. I came across this information in a handwritten
note by the late Max Weinreich.

the two academic institutions; and of the *Literarishe bleter*'s belief that 'in the future the bonds between us will be strengthened and tightened' (*Literarishe bleter* 1928: 158).

When the first graduation of the Yiddish division of the Second State Institute in Moscow was celebrated in 1928, Perets Hirshbeyn, the Yiddish writer from New York City, attended the ceremony and pleaded with the people of Moscow, in the name of his 27 years in Yiddish literature, not to cut themselves off from the YIVO in Poland:

I have seen how the springs of folk-creativity run from all Polish cities and towns to the YIVO in Vilna, and from there to you, to Minsk, to Odessa, to Moscow, and to all your scientific institutions (*Literarishe bleter* 1928: 459).

In 1928, the Soviet Yiddish writers who were still sending their works to be published in the *Literarishe bleter*, met with disfavor from Moscow. Among these writers was Sh. Gordon who wrote, in response to numerous letters to the editor of *Emes*:

While living in a provincial town, I didn't realize what the *Literarishe Bleter* are...But now [I know] that the *Literarishe Bleter* are a bourgeois (*balebesldike*) nationalistic publication which is certainly not a place for our sort of people, and I admit my error (*Literarishe bleter* 1919: 207–208).

As long as Soviet political developments could be used to justify communication between the spokesmen of Soviet Yiddish and those abroad, they were used to advantage and the dialogue continued. But then came *di tshistkes*, the purges, and the dialogue ended. What happened afterward is beyond the scope of this paper.

REFERENCES

Afn shprakhfront (1935), vol. 2, 6. Kiev.
Holmstok, Kh. (1933), *Lingvistishe zamlung*, vol. 1, 36–37. Minsk.
Khvila (1934), *Ukrainishe yidishe shprakhbaratung*, May 7–11: 14, Kiev.
Kushnirov, A. (1929), *Literarishe bleter* (7): 142. Warsaw.
Lingvistishe zamlung (1934), vol. 2, 25, 30, 70, 108, 111, 117. Minsk.
Lingvistishe zamlung (1936), vol. 3, 73. Minsk.
Literarishe bleter (1926), 333. Warsaw.
Literarishe bleter (1929),(7): 142. Warsaw.
Rubinshteyn, N., editor (1932), *Dos Yidishe Bukh in Sovetn-Farband in 1932*, xxv. Minsk.
Shtif, N. (1929), 'Social differentiation in Yiddish, The Hebrew elements in the language', *Di yidishe shprakh* (4–5): 17–18, col. 1–22. Kiev.
— (1932), 'Preface', in *Ortografisher verterbukh*, V, The Ukrainian Academy of Sciences.
Spivak, E. (1935), *Afn shprakhfront*, vol. 2. Kiev.
Veryorka, A. (1926), *Der oysleyg fun yidish* 6, 26. Moscow.
Weinreich (1932), *Di sovetishe yidishe ortografye*, 3 (note). Institute for Jewish Proletarian Culture.

Some Aspects of the Use of Pronouns of Address in Yiddish

DAN I. SLOBIN

In recent publications, Brown and Gilman (1960), and Brown and Ford (1961), have examined the role of linguistic forms of address in the patterning of social relations, as reflected in more than 20 languages of Europe and Asia. So far, regardless of the linguistic device used to denote the second person (choice of two pronouns, as German *du* or *Sie*; choice of several pronouns, as in Japanese; choice of first name or title and last name, as in English), Brown et al. report that they have found a consistent pattern.

Brown distinguishes two dimensions of social relations relevant to usage of forms of address: status and solidarity (intimacy). Status relations are asymmetrical. In any dyad where status is involved, one individual is higher, or more powerful than the other. This asymmetry is often reflected in a nonreciprocal use of forms of address. A 'polite' form (*Sie, vous, Mr. Smith*, etc.) will be offered upward, a 'familiar' form (*du, tu, John*, etc.) downward. (For convenience, these forms will be referred to below as the V- and T-pronouns, respectively.) Considerations of solidarity, or intimacy, however, introduce another dimension into the system – a symmetrical dimension based on the sharing between individuals of various socially relevant characteristics or past experiences. This symmetry is reflected in a mutual, reciprocal use of forms of address among intimates or individuals solidary on some basis of social importance (e.g. family, common profession, etc.).

Brown et al. have found what may be a 'linguistic universal' in all of the languages they investigated: the form used vertically to address status inferiors (the T-pronoun) is also used horizontally to address intimates, and vice versa.

Historically, a continuing change in pronominal usage can be seen from the Middle Ages onward in Europe. Medieval usage was based entirely on considerations of status. Between equals, pronominal usage was always reciprocal, with the mutual V-pronoun exchanged between members of the upper classes, and the mutual T-pronoun between members of the lower. Between classes, V was used upwards and T downwards.

Considerations of solidarity entered later, and at first were confined only to conversations between social equals. For a number of centuries, one said T to those with whom one was equal and solidary, and V to those with whom one was equal but not solidary – continuing at the same time the universal vertical usage of V to superiors and T to inferiors.

As long as solidarity was a relevant dimension only in horizontal relationships – between social equals – the system was in equilibrium. However, the solidarity and status dimensions are independent, and the equilibrium of the system was destroyed when the solidarity criterion began to be applied vertically as well as horizontally. It is evident that problems arise in cases where status relations in a dyad would dictate one form of address and solidarity relations another. In the nineteenth century the status criterion seemed to prevail in such conflicts, with intimates of higher status (e.g. parents, elder brothers) receiving the V-pronoun, and strangers of lower status (e.g. waiters) receiving the T-pronoun. This situation seems to have slowly reversed itself, with considerations of solidarity gaining the upper hand. In fact, Brown has noticed a tendency in European languages in recent times to avoid nonreciprocal usage of second person pronouns by using only the solidarity dimension as relevant to the choice of pronoun. Thus, in this evolving unidimensional system, there is an increasing tendency to address all intimates, regardless of status, with the T-pronoun, and all strangers with the V-pronoun.

It is the goal of the present study to investigate the semantics of social relations underlying the usage of the second person pronouns in Yiddish, as it was spoken in Eastern Europe before World War II. Several questions were held in mind.

1. Do we find, in all cases of the nonreciprocal pattern, that there is a pronoun of one type (the T-pronoun) which is directed both downward and to intimates, and that there is a pronoun of another type (the V-pronoun) which is directed both upward and to nonintimates?

2. Was pronominal usage in this traditional society of the late nineteenth and early twentieth centuries similar to that which Brown and Gilman outlined for earlier stages of Western European society?

3. What were the relative roles of ascribed and achieved criteria in the determination of social status, as reflected in pronominal usage? (Vertical usage of the V-pronoun should reveal dimensions of status. In addition, to the extent that ascribed status is dominant over achieved, dyadic situations of long-term, nonreciprocal patterns of address should not be uncommon.)

Yiddish has two second person pronouns – the singular *du* and the plural *ir*.[1]

---

1. Given the regional origins of our informants, it is not necessary to consider such variations as the use of a polite *Sie* in Western Yiddish, and the plural *er*, instead of *ir*, which was found in much of Poland, Bohemia, Moravia, and western Hungary. (I am grateful to Dr. Uriel Weinreich for pointing out these variant forms to me.)

As in earlier forms of German, *ir* (cf. *Ihr*) can be used as a singular pronoun of address when speaking to a single individual distant from the speaker on either the status or solidarity dimensions, in addition to the normal use of this pronoun in addressing two or more individuals, regardless of their social relationship to the speaker. The usage is thus, grammatically, analogous to the *tu* and *vous* of French, the *ty* and *vy* of Russian, etc. It is clear, then, that we will be concerned with the use of *du* and *ir* in *dyadic* situations, when the speaker faces a single individual and must decide which of the two pronouns is appropriate. It is the contention here that the linguistically obligatory decision forces the speaker to attend to those characteristics of the addressee which are relevant to placing him on the status and solidarity dimensions, as defined by the society. Since the nonlinguistic behavior involved in all dyadic confrontations is also based on such decisions, however, we cannot introduce language as the prime determinant of the choice made.

There were 22 informants in the study, all of whom were born, and spent their youth in the Eastern European Jewish community, and presently reside in southeastern Michigan. The writer interviewed 13 individuals (using both Yiddish and English in the interviews), and gave questionnaires to the others. The interview followed the lines of the questionnaire (see below). The informants had left Europe in three main migration periods: pre-World War I, post-World War I, and Post-World War II. The mean age of the informants was about 56. The range in age was 25–73, with all informants but one being older than 40. The informants were born in the Ukraine (Russia), Poland, Lithuania, and Latvia, with heaviest representation from the first-named area. Most of them came from families of merchants or small businessmen – predominant occupations in the community under study. (No major differences in pronominal usage on the basis of regional origin or occupation were revealed in this sample.) As was usual in those days, most informants were at least *bi*lingual, speaking the vernacular of the national state in which they resided in addition to Yiddish.

Since Yiddish is not, for the majority of the informants, their major language of communication in America today, an attempt was made to reinstate the set of speaking Yiddish in its native environment in the past. Because the average age of leaving Europe was 21 years, this meant, to a great extent, establishing the set of viewing social relations through the eyes of a young person from the perspective of middle or old age. In questions directed to the informant in the second person ('What would you say...') the interviewer attempted to determine the age of the speaker which was being used as point of reference for the answer. Many questions were phrased or re-phrased in the third person ('What would one say...') in an attempt to avoid this problem.

Dyadic situations were presented to the informants (see Table 1), and they were asked to indicate whether the appropriate pronouns would be *du* or *ir*, or

The Maydem Marionette Theater presents a parody on the Song
of Songs (shir hashirim): 'The Song of the Umbrella' (shir hashirem)
(circa 1936).

whether they were not sure. The situations and a tabulation of responses are presented below.[2]

An examination of the data reveals that we must refer to earlier stages of Western European history to find parallels for such pronominal usage. The society had certainly not reached the unidimensional solidarity semantic towards which present European usage seems to be moving. As we shall see, conflicts in the cases of addressing solidary superiors and nonsolidary inferiors seem to have been resolved both on the bases of status and solidarity, with ascribed status and the solidarity of family ties appearing to play the most important roles.

We may begin by examining a paradoxical case of nonreciprocal use of the two pronouns which, at first glance, seems to contradict Brown's 'linguistic universal' of the linkage of intimacy and condescension, on the one hand, versus distance and deference, on the other. Several informants made reference to the 'uneducated' lower classes, who said *du* to everyone, regardless of status or solidarity. Thus, for example, it was reported that a drayman might say *du* to a well-to-do burgher, while the latter, following the solidarity rule, would still say *ir* to this stranger. Thus we have a non-reciprocal situation in which the T-pronoun is given upward, and the V-pronoun downward. However, the contradiction is resolved if we consider the lower-class speaker to be using a different system of pronominal usage – namely, one in which the distinction between the T- and V-forms no longer exists, as is the case in English. If this is indeed the case, the fact that the drayman says *du*, rather than *ir*, does not affect our argument, there being but a single form in his speech.

All of the informants in this study had the pronominal distinction in their speech, and none were of the uneducated lower class. Thus our findings may not be applicable to the entire Yiddish community.

The speech of the well-to-do burgher in the example above gives us our first case of the resolution of a conflict presented by a system out of equilibrium, as described above. In such a system, the solidarity rule works vertically as well as horizontally, and the merchant faces the dilemma of addressing an inferior with whom he is not intimate. The decision is in the direction of solidarity over status.

A similar, though more complicated case is reflected in the responses to Situation 17, where the informants agreed without exception that they would say *ir* to a beggar. This issue also touches upon a central ethic of the community, discussed by many students of Eastern European Jewry (cf. Zborowski and Herzog 1952). Many informants explained that the poor have dignity; that they make it possible for the rich to perform the highly valued good deed of giving;

2. The writer wishes to thank Dr. Roger Brown for permission to adapt some items of his questionnaire for use in this study.

Table 1.

Dyadic situations	Pronouns (D = *du*, I = *ir*, ? = not certain)	Number of informants[3]
1. You to your mother and your mother to you.	D–D	21
	I–D	1
2. You to your father and your father to you.	D–D	20
	I–D	2
3. You to your grandmother and your grandmother to you.	D–D	15
	I–D	4
	I–I	1
4. You to your grandfather and your grandfather to you.	D–D	13
	I–D	6
	?–D	1
5. You to an older relative whom you are meeting for the first time, and such an unfamiliar older relative to you.	D–D	2
	I–D	14
	?–D	3
	I–I	2
6. You to an aunt who lives in the same town, and she to you.	D–D	12
	I–D	10
7. You to an uncle who lives in the same town, and he to you.	D–D	13
	I–D	9
8. You to your husband (or wife), and your husband (or wife) to you.	D–D	22
9. You to your father-in-law, and your father-in-law to you.	I–D	17
	I–I	1
10. You to your mother-in-law, and your mother-in-law to you.	I–D	18
11. You to a brother- or sister-in-law.	D	18
	I	0
	?	1
12. You to the spouse of a brother- or sister-in-law.	D	16
	I	1
	?	2
13. You to a Rabbi, and a Rabbi to you.	I–D	8
	I–I	9
	I–?	4
14. Suppose you are in a strange town, and you need to have your shoes repaired. You find a shoemaker who is older than you. What will you say to him?	D	0
	I	22
15. Suppose you find a shoemaker who is roughly your own age. What will you say to him?	D	0
	I	22
16. Suppose you find a shoemaker who is younger than you are, but is no longer a boy. What will you say to him?	D	2
	I	19
	?	1
17. What would you say to a beggar, and what would a beggar say to you?	I–D	1
	I–?	4
	I–I	16

3. Number of informants does not add to 22 for every situation, as some informants felt unable to respond to certain situations on the basis of their own personal experience, and were not willing to make general normative statements in such cases.

Table 1. (*cont.*)

Dyadic situations	Pronouns (D = *du*, I = *ir*, ? = not certain)	Number of informants[3]
18. Suppose that a boy has been introduced to a young lady his own age just a few minutes ago. However, after only a very short conversation, he feels for her a very great sympathy and attraction. What would he say to her?	D	2
	I	17
	?	1
19. Suppose a boy and a girl have known each other for some time, and like each other very much. But they are not engaged. What will they say to each other?	D	18
	I	2
	?	1
20. What would a boy say to his fiancée?	D	22
21. Suppose you were invited to the home of a Rabbi. There you are introduced to his son, a boy of about seven years old. What would you say to him?	D	21
	I	1
22. What would you say to first cousins of your own age with whom you grew up?	D	22
23. What would you say to first cousins of your own age whom you are meeting for the first time at a family celebration?	D	20
	I	1
	?	1
24. Suppose you have begun to work on a new job. What would you say to your coworkers who are of the same age as you and come from the same town?	D	4
	I	14
	?	3
25. What would you say to them if they came from a different town?	D	3
	I	16
	?	2
26. What would you say to them if they were older than you?	D	0
	I	21
	?	1
27. What would your older coworkers say to you, as a new worker?	D	8
	I	11
	?	3
28a. Suppose a new man comes to work on a job, and that he is younger than the boss. What will the boss say to him, and what will he say to the boss?	D–I	10
	?–I	3
	I–I	8
b. Will it be any different after five years?	Yes	3
	No	7
	Maybe	8
29a. Suppose a new man comes to work on a job, and that he is *older* than the boss. What will the boss say to him, and what will he say to the boss?	D–I	1
	?–I	1
	I–I	18
b. Will it be any different after five years?	Yes	3
	No	6
	Maybe	8
30. Suppose a childhood friend grows up to become your boss at the place where you work. What will you say to him, and what will he say to you?	D–D	14
	?–D	1
	I–?	1
	I–D	1
31. What would you say to a Yiddish-speaking *am* (wetnurse) or to a maid working in your house, and what would she say to you?	D–D	1
	?–D	1
	D–I	8
	I–D	1
	?–I	2
	I–I	7

Table 1. (*cont.*)

Dyadic situations	Pronouns (D = *du*, I = *ir*, ? = not certain)	Number of informants[3]
32. What would you say to a person of your same age and sex whom you speak to, but do not know well?	D	2
	I	20
33. Suppose you meet someone later in life whom you knew as a child. As children together you said *du* to one another. However, you never really liked this person, never felt sympathetic with him. You said *du* in the past because everyone did at that age. What would you say to him if you were to meet again today?	D	13
	I	5
	?	1

In conclusion the informants were asked the following questions:

1. Up to what age should an adult say *du* to a child? (Mean response = 18.3 years.)

2. How long (roughly) do you think one should know someone before starting to say *du*? (Range of responses: from one month to indefinite, or never switch to *du*.)

3. How do two people change from saying *ir* to saying *du* to each other? Do you know of any rules that were followed? Was there any ceremony ever involved in changing from *ir* to *du*? (Many informants pointed out that the individual of greater age or status must inititate the change, if there is to be one; but that such changes were rare. Few were able to report any ceremony involved in the switch.)

that it would be crude and insulting to address them with *du*. It would seem that by their social function of making alms-giving possible they paradoxically acquire an increased status in the community.

The sphere of employer–employee relations gives us a better opportunity to examine the relative roles of status and solidarity in a conflict situation. Here we can deal with three variables: relative status, relative age, and length of association between individuals. Of relevance here are Situations 28 and 29 in the list above.

Situation 28 deals with relations between a boss and a worker who is younger than he. This is another case of status inferiority plus non-solidarity. The youth and subordinate position of the new worker should predispose the employer to say *du* to him, while the fact that he is a stranger should put him in the *ir* category. Informants split almost 50–50 in this case, although all agreed, of course, that the young worker would say *ir* to his boss.

Entirely different, however, is the case of the relations between an employer and a new worker older than he. Here age sways the balance, and all informants but one agreed that the boss would say *ir* to the older man, regardless of his subordinate position as far as employment is concerned. Only a crude individual – a *grobian* – it was stated, would say *du* to an older man, even if he was an employee. In no case, however, would the employee say *du* to the boss.

In both cases – regardless of relative age – informants doubted that the situation would change after five years. Only three informants, in each case, stated that the mutual *du* could be introduced if employer and employee were to become close friends.

Brown and Ford, in analyzing address in American English, have suggested that 'it is to be expected in a society whose values are more strongly linked to achieved personal attributes than to ascribed attributes...that occupation would prevail over age in the determination of deference' (1961: 377). In the traditional Yiddish community, where values were at least as strongly linked to ascribed personal attributes (age, family history, inherited wealth, etc.) as achieved ones (learning, earned wealth, etc.), it is not surprising to find hints that age sometimes prevailed over occupation in the determination of deference.

The importance of ascribed personal attributes is also reflected in the difficulty of changing from the pronominal usage with which a dyad has begun. This applies not only to the work situation described above. All informants stressed the fact that many years of friendship could not easily move a relationship between two adults from mutual *ir*, or nonreciprocal *ir-du*, to mutual *du*; just as many years of estrangement, or a change in social position, could not change a mutual *du* relationship established in childhood (Situations 30 and 33). Few informants were able to remember a specific ceremony, such as the German *Bruderschafttrinken*, employed to mark a switch to the intimacy of mutual *du*. If ascribed characteristics are more important than achieved, it stands to reason that relationships will maintain for years the distinction reflected in their initial pronominal usage; the achieved characteristics of solidarity can rarely wash away the ascriptions of status. Only such dramatic events as living through a crisis together seem to have the force of breaking this rule.

The reader will, of course, realize another sort of exception. As Situations 18, 19, 20, and 8, reveal, living together through the crisis called 'falling in love' or 'getting married', is also sufficient to change a dyad from mutual *ir* to mutual *du*. All informants agreed that husbands and wives addressed each other with *du*, although some remembered remnants of the earlier custom of mutual *ir* between marriage partners.[4]

This brings us to the realm of family relations (Situations 1–12, 22, 23). In the core of the family, solidarity prevails over status. Almost all informants were on a mutual *du* basis with their parents, and with their grandparents if they lived in the same town and were in close daily contact. This matter of close daily contact seems to be almost as important as kinship in the determination of solidarity. Informants split on the use of *du* in addressing aunts and uncles living in the same town, and would almost never say *du* to an older relative met for the first time. Thus, as we move away from the interacting nuclear family and

---

4. For interesting reports of other forms of address used between marriage partners, see Liberman (1954) and Elzet (1955).

The Opera Division of the Jewish Musical Institute presents *Carmen*, by Georges Bizet, in four acts... with 3 choruses, a symphony orchestra, and a ballet.

its close extensions, status prevails over solidarity. By the time we reach in-laws, universal use of *ir* is agreed upon.

At least two aspects of solidarity, however, are important here – the ascribed ties of kinship and the 'achieved' ties of intimacy. They can be examined by holding status constant. Compare Situations 23 and 32. When dealing with individuals of the same age, most informants would say *du* to first cousins, even upon their first meeting, but would continue to say *ir* to slight acquaintances even after continued contact.

Thus it would seem that kinship takes precedence over familiarity in determining solidarity. Within the family, long-established intimacy takes precedence over the status of age in determining pronominal usage, but, in the absence of such intimacy, the status rule of age takes over.

We have yet to examine carefully the role of very high status. About one half of the informants reported that some Rabbis would say *du* to everyone, regardless of age or status (Situation 13). This is an example of the exceptional status of a speaker enabling him to ignore all characteristics of those whom he addresses, for his pronominal system is unidimensional.

In sum, then, it seems that ascribed status, and, if exceptional, achieved status prevail over solidarity in the semantics of pronouns of address in the Yiddish of our informants. The exception is the strong solidarity of kinship, which is also based on ascribed, rather than achieved values. (The central role of the family in Eastern European Jewish society has been frequently commented upon.) The general picture resembles that drawn by Brown and Gilman for nineteenth century Europe, retaining situations of nonreciprocal address. The 'linguistic universal' linking intimacy and condescension, distance and deference, was again found to hold true.

REFERENCES

Brown, R., Ford, Marguerite (1961), 'Address in American English', *J. Abnorm. Soc. Psychol.* 62: 375–385.

Brown, R., Gilman, A. (1960), 'The pronouns of power and solidarity', in *Style in Language*, ed. by T. Sebeok. New York, Wiley.

Elzet, Y. (1955), 'Vegn a bimkem farn vort "vayb" un dem vaybs nomen', *Yidishe shprakh* 15: 83–85.

Liberman, Kh. (1954), 'Fun vanen shtamt di vendung tsu der froy "tsi herstu"?', *Yidishe shprakh* 14: 24–29.

Zborowski, M. Herzog, Elizabeth (1952), *Life is with People: The Jewish Little Town of Eastern Europe*. New York, International Universities Press.

צו אלע עלטערן און דערציער!

בּאַלד צוויי יאָר עקזיסטירט אין ווילנע

אַ ספּעציעלע שול פֿאַר גייסטיק - אָפּגעשטאַנענע קינדער

דאָ לערנען זיך קינדער, וואָס קענען אין דער אַלגעמיינער שול קיין אָרט ניט געפֿינען, ווייל די אַרבעט דאָרט איז ניט צוגעפֿאַסט פֿאַר זייערע פֿעאיקייטן. ניט האַבנדיק קיין באַזונדערע שול פֿאַר זיך, זיינען זיי פֿאַרמשפּט צו בלייבן אָן עלעמענטאַרע בילדונג און דערציאונג און צו ווערן אויפן גאַנצן לעבן אַ לאַסט פֿאַר זייער משפּחה און פֿאַר דער געזעלשאַפֿט.

מיט גרויס ליבשאַפֿט און אויפמערקזאַמקייט ווערט יעדעס פֿון די קינדער באַהאַנדלט אין זייער אייגענער אַנשטאַלט. דאָ האָבן זיי אַ מעגלעכקייט זיך רואיק און בהדרגה צו אַנטוויקלען און אפֿשר אין עטלעכע יאָר אַרום זיך אויסצוגלייכן מיט זייערע גלייכלעכע חברים פֿון דער אַלגעמיינער שול.

דורך דעם ווילנער שטאָטלער פֿסיכאָלאָגישן קאַבינעט זיינען שוין דורכגעגאַנגען אַ פֿאָר הונדערט יידישע קינדער, וואָס געהערן צו דער ספּעציעלער שול. די שול, וואָס האָט זיך ערשט פֿאַר צוויי יאָרן געעפֿנט מיט 13 קינדער, פֿאַרמאָגט שוין היינט דריי קלאַסן, אין וועלכע עס קומען כּסדר צו קינדער פֿון די שולן פֿון אַלע ווילנער צענטראַלעס.

גרויס איז די נויט פֿון דער שול. די קהילה האָט איר עד-היום קיין שום סובסידיע ניט געגעבן. דאָס רוב קינדער געהערן צו די צומווייניקסטן באַמיטלטע שיכטן. די גאַנצע זאָרג פֿאַר דער שול ליגט אויף דער

געזעלשאַפֿט פֿאַר ספּעציעלער דערציאונג,

וואָס איז דאָ ניט לאַנג געוואָרן געגרינדעט.

די געזעלשאַפֿט שטעלט זיך בּרייטע אויפֿגאַבּן: זאָרגן פֿאַר גייסטיק-אָפּגעשטאַנענע קינדער, פֿאַר שווער-דערציעוודיקע, פֿאַר פֿאַרוואָרלאָזטע, - אויך פֿאַר קינדער מיט שפּראַך-פֿעלערן און פֿעלערן פֿון חושים. — זי פֿירט אויך אַן אויפֿקלערונגס-אַרבעט צווישן דער באַפֿעלקערונג, אָרדנט איין פֿאַרטראָגן און שמועסן וועגן די פּראָבּלעמען פֿון דער ספּעציעלער דערציאונג.

פֿאַר דער קורצער צייט פֿון איר עקזיסטענץ האָט די געזעלשאַפֿט באַוויזן אַרייצוציען אין איר אַרבעט מענטשן פֿון פֿאַרשיידענע ריכטונגען און אָנשי-אונגען, וועלכע זיינען פֿאַראייניקט דורך דער גרויסער אויפֿגאַבּע:

פֿסיכיש געזונט צו מאַכן דאָס יידישע קינד.

די געזעלשאַפֿט מוז פֿאַרברייטערן איר טעטיקייט. אָבּער דערצו זיינען ניטיק מענטשן און מיטלען. מיר ווענדן זיך צו דער יידישער ווילנע:

פֿאַרשרייבּט זיך פֿאַר מיטגל'ידער פֿון דער געזעלשאַפֿט פֿאַר ספּעציעלער דערציאונג!

העלפֿט דער געזעלשאַפֿט אויסצובּויען די ספּעציעלע שול!
העלפֿט דער געזעלשאַפֿט צו פֿירן איר וויכטיקע אַרבעט!

סעקרעטאַריאַט פֿון דער געזעלשאַפֿט:
קאַלעיאָווע 15. II. 3. טעל. 704. אָן זונטאָג און מיטוואָך פֿון 7-9 אז.
Odezwa T-wa Specjalnego Wychowania.   druk. d. krejnes, wilno

אויפרוף וועגן דער ספּעציעלער שול
Announcement about the school
for mentally retarded children
קול קורא בענין בית-הספר לילדים
נחשלים
Возвание о школе для умственно
отсталых детей

1930

The Society for Special Education treats each (retarded) pupil with love and care...providing an opportunity for quiet and gradual development and, perhaps ultimately, for catching up with...regular schools.

Bilingualism and Dialect Mixture Among Lubavitcher Hasidic Children

GEORGE JOCHNOWITZ

Hasidism (from Hebrew *ḥasid*, 'pious') is a pietist movement that spread through the Jewish communities of Eastern Europe during the eighteenth century. The Hasidim (adherents to Hasidism) are organized into tightly knit groups each centered on a highly respected rabbi, who is generally known by the name of the town in which he lives. There have been seven Lubavitcher rabbis since Hasidism appeared in Belorussia, although only four of them (the second through the fifth) resided and taught in Lubavitch, Belorussia. The name 'Lubavitcher', however, has been retroactively applied to the first rabbi, and has followed the sixth rabbi, Joseph Isaac Schneersohn, from Lubavitch through Leningrad, Riga, and Warsaw to Brooklyn. The current (and seventh) leader of the community, Rabbi Menachem Mendel Schneerson, son-in-law of his predecessor, is still known as the Lubavitcher Rabbi, and his followers are still the Lubavitcher Hasidim.

The informants interviewed for this study of Lubavitcher usage were all tenants vacationing during the summer of 1967 at a bungalow colony owned by my family. With one exception, all informants were Lubavitcher: A. B. is a Bobover Hasid, but his wife is of a Lubavitcher family, and their children go to Lubavitcher schools.

There follows a list of the informants who participated in the study. The initials used to identify them are not their own. The letters *gf, gm, fa, mo,* and *dau* stand for grandfather, grandmother, father, mother, and daughter, respectively. *Y, R, P, E, F, U, Geo,* and *G* stand for Yiddish, Russian, Polish, English, French, Ukrainian, Georgian, and German, respectively. It should be added that all the informants had studied Hebrew and that many, particularly the men and boys, could read and speak it quite well. Children below the age of six were not interviewed, nor were those (mostly teenagers) who spent the summer elsewhere.

The informants are divided into three groups: grandparents, parents, and children – there were no single or childless informants above the age of eighteen.

Informant	Family position	Year born	Birthplace	Spent childhood in	First language	Easiest	Other
A.A.	gf	1909	Petrikov, Belorussia	Same	Y	Y	R(E)
B.A.	gm (parents of B.B.)	?	?	?	Y	Y	RE
A.B.	fa	1915	Myślenice, Poland	Same	Y	Y	PRG (FE)
B.B.	mo	1931	Klimovič, Belorussia	Same and Uzbekistan	R	R	YFE
C.B.	son	1953	France	Cleveland and Brooklyn	Y	Y	E
D.B.	dau	1954	Cleveland	Brooklyn	Y	Y	E
E.B.	dau	1957	Brooklyn	Same	Y	E	
F.B.	dau	1960?	Brooklyn	Same	Y	Y	E
A.C.	fa	1915	Dołhinów, Poland (now Belorussia)	Vilna	Y	Y	PRE
B.C.	mo	1930	Kurzeniec, Poland (now Belorussia)	Same and Samarkand, Uzbekistan	R	R	YE
C.C.	dau	1955	Brooklyn	Same	Y	E	
A.D.	fa	1930	Nevel', Russian SFSR	Same	Y	Y	(E)
B.D.	mo	1932	Nevel'	Central Asia	R	R	YE
C.D.	dau	1954	Brooklyn	Same	Y	E	
D.D.	son	1955	Brooklyn	Same	Y	Y	E
E.D.	son	1957	Brooklyn	Same	Y	Y	E
F.D.	dau	1961	Brooklyn	Same	Y	Y	E
A.E.	gm (mother of B.F.)	?	Čirkas, Ukraine	Same	Y	Y	RU
A.F.	fa	1912	Klimovič	Same	Y	Y	(RE)
B.F.	mo	1923	Krimenčug, Ukraine	Crimea and Caucasus	R	R	YE
C.F.	son	1949	Paris	Philadelphia and Brooklyn	Y	E	
D.F.	son	1951	Paris	Philadelphia and Brooklyn	Y	E	
E.F.	son	1953	New York	Philadelphia and Brooklyn	Y	E	
F.F.	dau	1954	Philadelphia	Brooklyn	Y	E	
G.F.	dau	1956	Philadelphia	Brooklyn	Y	E	
A.G.	fa	?	Leningrad	Kazakhstan	Y	Y	RE
B.G.	mo	1935	Kaunas	?	Y	YR	FE
C.G.	son	1954	Paris	Brooklyn	Y	Y	E
D.G.	dau	1955	Paris	Brooklyn	Y	E	
E.G.	son	?	Brooklyn	Same	Y	Y	E
F.G.	dau	1961	Brooklyn	Same	Y	Y	E

Informant	Family position	Year born	Birthplace	Spent childhood in	First language	Easiest	Other
A. H.	gf	1916	Lagóisk, Belorussia	Belorussia	Y	Y	R
B.H.	gm (parents of B.I.)	1910	Głębkie, Poland (now Belorussia)	Belorussia	Y	Y	R(E)
A.I.	fa	?	?	?	Y	Y	?
B.I.	mo	1933	Kharkov	Samarkand	R	Y	F
C.I.	dau	1956	Canada	Brooklyn	Y	E	
D.I.	dau	1959	Brooklyn	Same	Y	Y	E
E.I.	son	1961	Brooklyn	Same	Y	Y	E
A.J.	fa	1913	Rokiškis Lithuania	Georgian SSR	Y	Y	(E)
B.J.	mo	1924	Nevel'	Same and Moscow	R	R	YE
C.J.	dau	1954	Brooklyn	Same	Y	E	
D.J.	dau	1955	Brooklyn	Same	E	E	Y
A.K.	fa	1923	Georgian SSR	Same	Y	Y	Geo R
B.K.	mo	1933	Montreal	Same	E	E	Y
C.K.	dau	1956	Brooklyn	Same	E	E	Y
D.K.	son	1957	Brooklyn	Same	E	E	Y
E.K.	dau	1960	Brooklyn	Same	E	E	(Y)

One set of grandparents (the A's) live in Albany, N.Y., and another (the H's) live in Montreal. The remaining informants all reside in the Crown Heights section of Brooklyn.

In Crown Heights, roughly half the inhabitants are black; the other half are Jewish. The Jews are often Orthodox, and most of these are Hasidic. Although the Lubavitchers are the largest single Hasidic denomination there, they are nevertheless only one of several. Most Lubavitchers here immigrated in the late 1940s and early 1950s. Almost all came from the Soviet Union. The language of the community is the northeastern (Lithuanian-Belorussian) dialect of Yiddish, hereafter NEY. The Lubavitchers are the only sizeable group in Crown Heights speaking this particular variant of Yiddish. Polish and Hungarian dialects of Yiddish prevail among the other Hasidim. The non-Hasidic Jews in the neighborhood are products of earlier waves of immigration and, generally, speak English rather than Yiddish. The Negroes, of course, speak English.

Among non-Hasidic Jews, Yiddish very commonly receded rapidly after the first generation in the United States. In addition, Jews from various parts of Eastern Europe mixed freely with each other, and dialectal peculiarities tended to be replaced by Standard Yiddish forms. The Lubavitchers, on the other hand, support an independent school system, and, since their school day is a long one, the children's opportunities for meeting non-Lubavitcher neighbors are reduced. They all worship at the Lubavitcher synagogue. The twenty-six children interviewed for this study all answered 'yes' when asked the question 'Are most of your friends Lubavitcher Hasidim?'

What is most striking is that education in secular colleges and universities is not encouraged. Boys, in particular, are discouraged from going to college. This situation is drastically different from the one that prevails among the non-Hasidic Jews in America. The Lubavitchers, of course, devote a great deal of energy to pursuing their religious training. The men in the community continue to study religious subjects in depth all their lives.

NEY was spoken in a large, relatively uniform dialect area that includes all of Belorussia, Latvia, Lithuania, and the northeastern corner of Poland. It is separated from other dialects of Yiddish by a bundle of grammatical, phonological, and lexical isoglosses (Weinreich 1965: 4–5). The vocalism of Standard Yiddish is closer to that of NEY than to that of any other Yiddish dialect, although the consonantism, vocabulary, gender system, and the life of NEY include many nonstandard features. Moreover, despite the relative uniformity of NEY, there are some internal divisions, which are discussed below.

The first part of this study deals with the following questions about the Yiddish of Lubavitcher children: (1) Do the children exhibit as much diversity as their parents when speaking Yiddish or is there a general American Lubavitcher Yiddish developing? (2) If such a dialect is indeed developing, do the other Yiddish dialects heard in Crown Heights influence it? (3) Is the Yiddish of American-born Lubavitcher children closer to Standard Yiddish than to that of their parents? And (4) What role does English play in the Yiddish of these children?

My second concern is with the English spoken by these children. As noted above, the Yiddish of previous waves of immigration has receded rapidly in the United States. Most second-generation American Jews of Yiddish-speaking backgrounds speak Yiddish with difficulty, if at all. The situation is quite different among the Lubavitchers, whose children speak Yiddish fluently and well. If this is the case, do they speak English as well as Yiddish? If they do not, what types of interference are found? Do the children speak English with a New York City accent? And finally, does English show signs of replacing Yiddish, if at a slower rate than in non-Hasidic Jewish communities, or will it be maintained indefinitely, as with Pennsylvania German in Lancaster County?

A century ago, Lubavitchers were by and large restricted to northern and eastern Belorussia. The Russian Revolution and the horrors of World War II, however, produced vast dislocations. Many informants who are now in the parents' generation spent their formative years in the Caucasus region or in Central Asia, particularly in the Uzbek S.S.R. Nevertheless, the Yiddish of the parents not only is NEY but often shows characteristics peculiar to northern or eastern Belorussia.[1]

Except for the problems involving sibilants and *r*s (see below), all the items the informants were asked about were suggested by Uriel Weinreich's article, already cited. Weinreich includes ten maps, which point out differences between Belorussian Yiddish and the rest of NEY, and discusses local variation within Belorussian Yiddish. I have chosen these items to show as many differences as possible between the dialects of the various adults and, thus, to determine how much dialect leveling has taken place among the children.

The area in northeastern Belorussia that was the original home of the Lubavitcher Hasidim was part of a much larger area where no distinction between hushing and hissing sibilants and affricates was made. This phenomenon, called *sábesdiker losn* in Yiddish, at one time covered most of the territory of NEY. It is

...the confusion of the hushing series of phonemes (*š, ž, č*) with the hissing phonemes (*s, z, c*), which are distinguished in all other dialects. The exact manner of rendition of the single set varies locally, but nowhere in this area is there an opposition of the two series in Yiddish. This dialect feature has come to be known as *sábesdiker losn* 'solemn speech' (literally 'Sabbath language'), a phrase which in general Yiddish is *šabesdiker lošn*, with two *š*'s and an *s* (Weinreich 1952: 362).

Sábesdiker losn, although once widespread, is rare in contemporary Yiddish. 'The derision with which this feature was regarded by other Yiddish speakers sent it reeling back under the impact of "general Yiddish" dialects from the south' (Weinreich 1952: 374). A few of the Lubavitcher informants would sporadically use a hissing instead of a hushing sibilant, or vice versa, on rare occasions. Only one informant, B.J., consistently lacked a distinction in one environment, albeit a very limited one: there was no /z ~ ž/ distinction before /i/. Thus *zilber* 'silver' is pronounced /žilber/, but /ž/ and /ž/ are distinguished before the other vowels, and the remaining sibilants are distinguished in all positions.

As might have been expected, there was no trace whatever of *sábesdiker losn* in the speech of the children. The disappearance of this stigmatized characteristic is analogous to the loss of /ʌy/ in items such as *bird* in the English of many New Yorkers (see Labov 1966).

An apical trill [r] or flap [r] is the common way of producing the phoneme /r/ in Belorussian Yiddish, although a velar fricative [ʎ], a uvular trill [ʀ], or a uvular fricative [ʁ] are widespread in Yiddish. Henceforth, all apical *r*s will be written [r], and all velar and uvular *r*s will be written [ʀ].

Of the five informants who were grandparents, two of them, A.E. and A.H., use [ʀ]. A.E. is not from Belorussia but from the Ukraine, where [ʀ] is more common. B.H., A.H.'s wife, uses [r], as does B.I., the daughter of the H's. A.E.'s daughter, B.F., also consistently uses [r]. I do not know what realization of /r/

1. Three informants, A.B., A.E., and B.K., do not speak NEY but Central (Polish) Yiddish, South-eastern (Ukrainian) Yiddish, and Standard Yiddish, respectively. The phonology of B.K.'s Yiddish shows traces of interference from English.

B.F.'s father used, but it seems irrelevant, since B.F. states that her first language was Russian and that she learned Yiddish from her husband, A.F., who uses [r]. B.I. too feels that Russian is the easiest language for her. The remaining grandparents, A.A. and B.A., use [r], as do their children.

Our sample of grandparents is too small to permit us to draw any definite conclusions, but the scanty evidence present points to the fact that within the Soviet Union, perhaps because of Russian influence, [r] was replacing [ʀ].

If this tendency existed in the Soviet Union, it certainly was not transplanted to the United States. Three of the sixteen parents have [ʀ], as compared with eight of the twenty-six children.

Parents A.J., A.B., and B.G. use [ʀ]. A.J.'s children, C.J. and D.J., use [r], as does their mother. B.G.'s husband, A.G., and their daughters, D.G. and F.G., use [r]. The G.'s sons agree with their mother and use [ʀ].

A.B. is the one informant who speaks Central (Polish) Yiddish rather than NEY. The B. children speak the NEY of their mother. Except for the eldest child, C.B., who agrees with his mother in using [r], the remaining B. children who were interviewed use [ʀ]. The B. children are like the D. children in this respect: the eldest D. child interviewed, C.D., uses [r]; her siblings, D.D., E.D., and F.D., who were interviewed, and their little brother, G.D., who was too young to be interviewed, consistently use [ʀ]. This is somewhat surprising since neither D. parent was ever heard to say [ʀ] – the elder D.s always use [r].

As for vowels, the oldest pronunciation of what Max and Uriel Weinreich denominate vowel 54[2] found in NEY is [u] in northern Belorussia. [uj], found in much of northern, eastern, and central Belorussia, is a later innovation, and [oj], which is also the Standard Yiddish realization of this vowel, is found in the southern and western parts of Belorussia and elsewhere in the NEY area.

Vowel 54 occurred in the following words on the questionnaire: *bojx* 'belly', *bloj* or *blojer* (the latter before a masculine noun) 'blue', *groj* or *grojer* 'gray', *gedojern* 'to last', *zojer* 'sour', and *mojl* 'mouth'. The following pronunciations were recorded for these words. (If an informant volunteered two pronunciations in response to a question, they are both counted. This explains the uneven totals obtained for the different words.)

'Belly':	*bojx*		*bujx*		*bux*		*boex*[3]	
	ad	ch	ad	ch	ad	ch	ad	ch[4]
	6	9	13	16	1	0	1	0

The *bux* and *boex* forms were produced by A.E. and A.B., respectively. Both of these informants speak a dialect of Yiddish other than NEY.

---

2. Max and Uriel Weinreich have used a system of numbered subscripts to identify vowels etymologically with their Proto-Yiddish equivalents. These subscripts are listed by Marvin I. Herzog (1965) on p. 161 and are explained in n. 1, p. 228.

3. Here and below in the transliteration of Yiddish forms the character *x* represents the voiceless velar fricative.

4. These abbreviations stand for *adults* and *children*.

'Blue':

bluver		*blo(er)*		*blow*		*bloj(er)*		*bluj(er)*		*blui(er)*	
ad	ch	ad	ch	ad	ch	ad	ch	ad	ch	ad	ch
1	0	9	0	1	0	12	23	0	1	1	1

A.E. and A.B. said *bluver* and *bluer*, respectively. One child, C.G., said *blu*.

'Gray':

ser		*gro(er)*		*groj(er)*		*grej(er)*		*gru(er)*	
ad	ch	ad	ch	ad	ch	ad	ch	ad	ch
1	1	3	0	11	10	1	12	1	1

As was the case for *blu(er)*, A.B. and C.G. produced *gru(er)*; *ser* is of Slavic etymology.

'To last':

gedowern		*gedoern*		*gedujern*		*gedojern*		*geduern*		*ø*	
ad	ch	ad	ch	ad	ch	ad	ch	ad	ch	ad	ch
1	0	2	0	6	4	8	14	3	0	0	8

A.B. produced *gedowern*, and eight children did not know the world at all.

'Sour':

zowe		*zujer*		*zojer*		*zuer*		*zuver*		*zover*	
ad	ch	ad	ch	ad	ch	ad	ch	ad	ch	ad	ch
1	0	8	18	7	7	5	0	1	0	1	0

A.B. produced *zowe* and A.G. *zover*.

'Mouth':

mowel		*mujl*		*mojl*		*mul*	
ad	ch	ad	ch	ad	ch	ad	ch
1	0	9	15	9	8	2	3

A.B. produced *mowel*.

The forms listed above indicate two clear tendencies. First, [u] and [o] as realizations of Proto-Yiddish Vowel 54 are relatively uncommon among adults and decidedly rare among children. The type [o] does not occur among the children at all. And second, particularly in the words for 'sour' and 'mouth', the children do not favor Standard Yiddish [oj] over [uj]. It is also interesting that eight children do not know the word *gedojern* and that twelve children but only one adult say *grej* for 'gray'. It is evident in these cases that English has a stronger effect on the Yiddish of Lubavitcher children than does Standard Yiddish.

The modern reflex of Proto-Yiddish Vowel 42 is normally /ej/ in NEY and /oj/ in Standard Yiddish. In the word *ojx* 'also', there seems to have been confusion with and contamination by Vowel 54 (Herzog 1965: 201). The pronunciations /oːx/ and /owex/ in Central Yiddish indicate the existence of two separate Proto-Yiddish forms: one with Vowel 42 and one with Vowel 54.[5]

5. I am indebted to Max Weinreich for this insight.

Perhaps this is the reason that *ojx* as well as *ejx* is heard among the Lubavitchers. The alternate forms *ojxet* and *ejxet* also exist.

'Also':	*ojx*		*ojxet*		*ejx*		*ejxet*	
	ad	*ch*	*ad*	*ch*	*ad*	*ch*	*ad*	*ch*
	6	1	0	3	13	7	1	15

Two facts are apparent from these data: the children differ from the adults in preferring the forms ending in -*et*, and the standard pronunciations with /oj/ are less common among the children than the adults.

In the word for 'public' the results are slightly different.

'Public':	*ojlom* or *ojlem*		*ejlom* or *ejlem*	
	ad	*ch*	*ad*	*ch*
	5	9	18	10

The reason for this difference becomes clear when we learn that six children (but no adults) were totally unfamiliar with this word as Yiddish, and knew it only as a Hebrew word meaning 'world'. NEY speakers traditionally say [ejlom] or [ejləm] even when speaking Hebrew, but the standard Ashkenazic Hebrew pronunciation seems to be gaining among the young.

In northern Belorussia, final unstressed vowels are reduced to /e/, which is realized as [ə].

'Public':	*ejlom* or *ojlom*		*ejlem* or *ojlem*	
	ad	*ch*	*ad*	*ch*
	18	12	5	7

'Sheet':	*lajlax*		*lajlex*	
	ad	*ch*	*ad*	*ch*
	3	8	16	17

In the case of 'public', there is no evidence to show the spread of standard /-om/ over /-em/. Standard *lajlax* is less uncommon among the children than among the adults, but the evidence is inconclusive.

The word *gix* 'rapid', probably in origin a hypercorrect form that spread from the Southwest, has replaced *gex* in much of Belorussia. Perhaps this should be considered a case of lexical rather than phonological variation.

'Rapid':	*gix*		*gex*	
	ad	*ch*	*ad*	*ch*
	13	12	10	15

The children show less preference than the adults for the prestige form *gix*.

One child, C.D., regularly uses [-un] rather than [-n] or [-ən] for her infinitive endings: thus [esun] rather than [esn] 'to eat'. Another child, E.I., said *nejvun* for 'pot cover', apparently from *an ejvn* 'an oven' (see below). No other informant ever produced final unstressed [-un], although Max Weinreich tells me that this form does exist in Belorussian Yiddish.

In summation so far, it may be said that in pronunciation, Lubavitcher children, by and large, show loyalty to the regional forms of northern Belorussia. The only exceptions to this pattern were the abandonment of /u/ or /o/ for Vowel 54, which were already rare among the adults, and the lack of *sábesdiker losn*, which was almost dead among the adults. The presence of speakers of other Yiddish dialects in Crown Heights (or even within their own group, e.g. A.B., A.E., and B.K.) and the influence of the Yiddish radio have had no effect upon the phonology of the children, unless the change [r] > [ʀ] is the result of dialect contact. The occurrence of /ej/ in the word for 'gray' is an indication of contamination from English.

In gender, NEY, unlike the other dialects of Yiddish, lacks the neuter category. Only A.B. and B.K., who are not NEY speakers, ever used the neuter article; none of the children was ever heard using it. Although the lack of the neuter is common to all NEY, in Belorussian Yiddish there are additional words with nonstandard genders, for example, *di teler* 'the plate', *di fencter*[6] 'the window', and *der mojl* 'the mouth'. In other dialects, *teler* is masculine, *fencter* is masculine or neuter, and *mojl* is feminine. Our informants use the following genders in these words.

'Plate':	masc.		fem.		neuter	
	ad	*ch*	*ad*	*ch*	*ad*	*ch*
	6	10	14	16	0	0

'Window':	masc.		fem.		neuter	
	ad	*ch*	*ad*	*ch*	*ad*	*ch*
	3	8	14	14	2	0

'Mouth':	masc.		fem.		neuter	
	ad	*ch*	*ad*	*ch*	*ad*	*ch*
	18	11	3	14	1	0

Thus, the majority of the adults use the Belorussian Yiddish genders. The children's results are not clear unless we consider the results obtained from the word *bord* 'beard'. This word is feminine everywhere in Yiddish except for the extreme northwestern corner of the NEY territory – an area that none of our informants comes from.

'Beard':	masc.		fem.		neuter	
	ad	*ch*	*ad*	*ch*	*ad*	*ch*
	0	11	20	15	0	0

6. Here and below in the transliteration of Yiddish forms, the character *c* represents the voiceless dental affricate.

Since *der bord* is nonstandard and uncommon in Yiddish and since no adult in the group says it, there is no reason for eleven children to use this form. There can be only one explanation. About two-fifths of the children seem to use the masculine, and three-fifths the feminine, no matter what the historical gender may be. Let us see how many informants use only the masculine, or only the feminine, for each of the four words in question.

All masculine		All feminine	
ad	*ch*	*ad*	*ch*
0	6	1	13

Since there are only four words involved, the fact that a given informant considers them all masculine or feminine is in itself of no importance. What is striking, however, is the discrepancy between the number of adults (1 out of 21) and of children (19 out of 47) who exhibit this pattern. It is probable that except for the words for male and female beings, where everyone seems to make a distinction, most of the nineteen children who used only one gender in these words do not distinguish gender in nouns at all. One child, G.F., says *di mojl*, *di teler*, *der fencter*, and *der bord*. Her parents, A.F. and B.F., say *der mojl*, *der teler*, *di fencter*, and *di bord*. It is likely that G.F. has little if any feeling for gender. If gender is indeed disappearing from the children's Yiddish, it is a remarkable finding, and one worthy of further investigation. Unfortunately, I did not anticipate this result and did not include enough items on the questionnaire to test it. I did not remark the consistent use of only one gender until I examined my notes when the summer was over and the informants had gone home.

The following are the data obtained from the items on the questionnaire concerning idiomatic and lexical variation.

'It hurts me':	*s'iz mir tut vej*		*s'tut mir vej*		*s'tut vej mir*	
	ad	*ch*	*ad*	*ch*	*ad*	*ch*
	7	12	12	12	1	1

The Standard Yiddish form is *s'tut mir vej*. If anything, it is more common in the adults' generation.

'Floor':	*padloge*		*brik*		*pol*		*dil*		*flor*		ø	
	ad	*ch*	*ad*	*ch*	*ad*	*ch*	*ad*	*ch*	*ad*	*ch*	*ad*	*ch*
	7	0	11	8	4	9	3	0	0	4	0	5

The fact that nine children simply said *flor* (obviously from English 'floor') or could not think of a Yiddish word probably indicates that some of the parents themselves use *flor* when not being questioned. At least four different words for 'floor' are current among the adults. This no doubt causes confusion or misunderstanding, and thus explains the decline of some of the Yiddish words. The words *dil* and *padloge* do not exist among the children at all.

'Ceiling'

lubis		dax		baltn		balkn		patalók		sufít		stol'e		stel'e		ruf		
ad	ch	ad	ch	ad	ch	ad	ch	ad	ch	ad	ch	ad	ch	ad	ch	ad	ch	ad
1	0	1	6	7	0	3	3	8	6	1	0	4	2	4	0	0	2	0

In this case, eight different words were produced by the adults. Four of these, *lubis, sufít, baltn,* and *stel'e,* seem to have vanished among the children. The word *dax* is Yiddish for 'roof', not 'ceiling'. One adult, as opposed to six children, gave this response. He immediately corrected himself and changed his answer to *stel'e.* If we add the *dax, ruf* (= 'roof') and zero columns, we find that a total of fifteen children did not think of a Yiddish word for 'ceiling'. William Labov tells me that words for 'ceiling', 'floor', 'porch', and other peripheral parts of a house are unstable in a great many other immigrant languages, and are replaced by the English terms.

'Pot cover': Only three responses other than *dekl* were made for this item. A child, E.I., said *nejvun* (see above), and two adults, A.A. and A.B., said *kriške* and *štercl,* respectively.

'Short': Everyone answered *kurc* except for A.B., who used Central Yiddish *korc,* and A.E., her granddaughter G.F., and another child, D.I., who said *kirc,* a form found in a narrow strip just south of the NEY area. The geographical distribution and history of this and other pronunciations of *kurc* are discussed in detail by Max Weinreich (Weinreich, ed. 1965: 73–86). D.I. immediately corrected herself to *kurc,* which she said she liked better. Since D.I.'s parents are both NEY speakers, *kirc* is an unlikely form for her.

'Hanukkah top':

	drejdl		*gor*	
	ad	ch	ad	ch
	15	23	6	1

Seven adults and twelve children who had answered *drejdl* responded affirmatively when asked if they recognized *gor* as a synonym. The word *gor* is a northern Belorussian form.

'Store':

	klejt		*krom*		*gevélb*		*gešéft*		*stor* or ∅	
	ad	ch	ad	ch	ad	ch	ad	ch	ad	ch
	6	2	14	15	2	0	3	1	0	12

The results here are analogous to those found for 'floor' and 'ceiling'. All the adults and most of the children are aware that *stor* is an English loan, but the feeling that Yiddish should be kept pure is apparently not very strong.

'Duck':

	entl		*kačke*		∅	
	ad	ch	ad	ch	ad	ch
	13	2	12	13	0	3

The word *entl* is an eastern Belorussian form. In this case, as was also true for 'Hanukkah top', the Standard Yiddish words are overwhelmingly favored by the children.

'Cows':	*behejmes*		*ki*		*fi*		*ø*	
	ad	ch	ad	ch	ad	ch	ad	ch
	19	20	5	4	1	0	1	1
'To love':	*lib hobn*		*holt hobn*		*libn*		*glajxn*	
	ad	ch	ad	ch	ad	ch	ad	ch
	17	16	5	3	3	2	2	7

In Belorussian Yiddish, the everyday word for 'cows' is *behejmes*, as opposed to general Yiddish *ki*. Although *holt hobn* is found in all the NEY area, it is not favored by our informants. A.H. said that *holt hobn* was for objects and *lib hobn* for things. A.C. said that as a child he used only *holt hobn*, but now uses *lib hobn* for people.

It appears, then, that lexical forms that are rare among the adults are even more uncommon among the children. Thus, items such as *dil* 'floor' were not found among the children; other lexical items such as *gor* 'Hanukkah top' and *entl* 'duck' are on their way out. As for gender, there can be no doubt that at least some of the children are unsure in their handling of many nouns. It would be most interesting to study this question in detail some years from now.

Summing up all my results, so far I would judge that Standard Yiddish has had no effect on the Yiddish of Lubavitcher children, although the elimination of rare lexical items necessarily favors standard forms. But interference from English is unmistakable.

The question, 'Which language is easiest for you?' elicited the following responses:

Grandfathers			*Grandmothers*			*Fathers*			*Mothers*			*Sons*			*Daughters*		
Y	R	E	Y	R	E	Y	R	E	Y	R	E	Y	R	E	Y	R	E
2	0	0	3	0	0	8	0	0	1	5	1	6	0	4	5	0	11

These data show a marked discrepancy between the answers of the male and female informants. The majority of the males find Yiddish easier; the females lean toward Russian and English, depending upon where they were born, although the three grandmothers find Yiddish easier. The religious education of the boys is much more extensive and profound than that of the girls. All the boys below roughly the age of thirteen attend a Lubavitcher primary school where the language of instruction is Yiddish and the curriculum wholly oriented toward the study of the Bible and the Talmud. Upon graduation, the boys enter the Lubavitcher High School, where Yiddish is the language of instruction during the morning when religious subjects are taught, and English, for the first time, is used in the afternoon for secular studies. The English-speaking teachers of the afternoon sessions are not necessarily members of the Lubavitcher community. The girls, on the other hand, attend Lubavitcher schools where religious education in Yiddish during the morning and secular classes in English after lunch is the pattern from the very beginning. Thus, the girls encounter English as a language of instruction some eight years before the boys do.

Except in the K. family, where B.K. is a native speaker of English, Yiddish is the first language the children learn. The boys often speak Yiddish to each other; but the girls definitely prefer English and invariably use it when speaking to each other. This is perhaps surprising, since they always use Yiddish when speaking to their parents, to preschool children, and occasionally to their brothers. It seems reasonable, however, to assume that the next generation of Lubavitcher children will learn English as their first language.

The fact that five mothers[7] but no fathers found Russian easier than Yiddish reflects an analogous pattern of education that must have existed in the preceding generation. Women occasionally use Russian when speaking to each other, but always address their husbands in Yiddish. (None of the informants, incidentally, can speak Belorussian.)

Solomon Poll found a similar situation among a group of Hasidim of Hungarian origin who live in the Williamsburg section of Brooklyn. 'Hungarian is used much more frequently among women than among men' (Poll 1965: 135). The group Poll studied differs from the Lubavitchers in some important ways. For example, he states that 'the Hasidim feel that the establishment of the State of Israel represents a great threat to their ultra-Orthodox beliefs' (Poll 1965: 137). This statement is totally untrue as far as the Lubavitchers are concerned. They are both emotionally and intellectually committed to a strongly pro-Israel policy. There is, in fact, a Lubavitcher settlement called Kfar Chabad in Israel.

The position of Yiddish is apparently stronger within the group that Poll studied than it is among the Lubavitchers. 'Presently only Yiddish is cultivated as the vernacular. It is used in almost every aspect of the lives of the ultrareligious Jews. Thus it is and will remain a tool of communication among the ultrareligious group in America for the foreseeable future' (Poll 1965: 152). Poll's conclusion probably is generally valid for the Lubavitchers too, but at least one segment of the Crown Heights community – girls between the ages of seven and twenty – prefer speaking English, and, as a consequence, in the next generation Yiddish may become the second rather than the first language.

William Labov's *The Social Stratification of English in New York City* supplied the English part of the questionnaire used in this study. The children and one adult (B.K., who was born in Montreal) read the word list, the list of minimal pairs, and 'When I was nine or ten,...' found in the appendix of Labov's work

7. B.B. is not counted among the mothers; she could not say whether Russian or Yiddish was easiest for her.

No accent		Possible accent		Little accent		Unmistakable accent	
C.C.	1955	C.D.	1954	C.B.*	1953	E.B.	1957
F.F.	1954	C.F.*	1949	D.B.	1954	F.B.	1960?
G.F.	1956	E.F.*	1953	D.F.*	1951	D.D.*	1955
C.K.	1956	D.G.	1955			E.D.*	1957
E.K.	1960	C.I.	1956			F.D.	1961
		D.I.	1959			C.G.*	1954
		C.J.	1954			E.G.*	1959?
		D.J.	1955			D.I.	1959
		D.K.*	1957			E.I.*	1961
Boys	*Girls*	*Boys*	*Girls*	*Boys*	*Girls*	*Boys*	*Girls*
0	5	3	6	2	1	5	4

(Labov 1966: 596–597). Two minimal pairs were altered for the present study – *tin* ~ *ten* and *pin* ~ *pen* were replaced by *ten* ~ *tan* and *pen* ~ pan, respectively. (Since the adults, except for B.K., are not native speakers of English and all have foreign accents to some degree, they were not given the English part of the questionnaire.) I have divided the children into four categories as follows: no foreign accent, possible accent, little accent, and unmistakable accent. I am not sure what criteria were involved in making these judgments, which were impressionistic and subjective. But my wife, who like myself is a native speaker of American English, fully agrees with these evaluations. In the above list, boys' names are followed by asterisks, and the year of birth is included.

Four or five of the nine children (E.G., who looks about eight or nine, did not know his age) in the *unmistakable accent* column were born in 1959 or after; only two of the seventeen children in the other three categories were born in or after 1959. Except for D.J. and the three K. children interviewed, Yiddish was the first language of the children. Their English improves as they grow older. Most of the informants, including E.B., were also tenants during the summer of 1966. At that time, E.B. consistently used a uvular [ʀ] in English. I was startled to hear her use nothing but an American *r* when I saw her again in July, 1967. Despite this radical improvement, E.B. remains on the *unmistakable accent* list.

Five of the younger children had difficulty with the questionnaire because they had not yet fully mastered the art of reading English. Of the remaining twenty-one, only one, D.D., did not pronounce normal American *r*'s in preconsonantal position. D.D., moreover, did not have [ʒ] in words such as *verse* or *hurt*, which he pronounced [vœs] and [hœt]. Prevocalic *r* is a source of greater difficulty. Five children consistently use [ʀ] and one [r] here. Three or four of the other children produce a normal [ʒ], even in casual conversation.

The omission of /r/ before consonants is best dealt with in terms of the five styles distinguished in Labov's study: *A*-casual speech; *B*-careful speech;

C-reading style: *D*-word lists; and *D'*-minimal pairs (Labov 1966: 90–98). The consonant, he found, is least likely to be dropped in style *D'* in New York City English (Labov 1966: 238). This observation also holds true among Lubavitcher children. Except for D.D., all the children distinguished between *dock* and *dark*, and between *cod* and *card*, by pronouncing [ɹ] in the second word of each pair. D.D. and three others, however, pronounced *sauce* and *source* as homonyms. In style *C* the results also remain consistently in agreement with Labov's findings. Eight children always pronounce *r* is this style, but twelve fluctuate between the presence and absence of this sound. D.D., of course, has no preconsonantal *r*.

I have no data on the remaining styles, but casual observation leads me to believe that *r*s are increasingly dropped as the style becomes increasingly informal. There seemed to be no child, however, who was totally *r*-less, even in the most casual speech. In fact, while the pattern of using more *r*s in formal speech agrees with Labov's findings, the Lubavitcher children use *r*s to a greater extent in all styles than do most young New Yorkers (Labov 1966: 342–345).

The vowel /eh/ in the noun *can* (e.g. a tin can) is phonetically realized as [ɪə], [ɛə], [æ ⊥ ə], etc. It is, in the speech of most New Yorkers, phonemically different from the /æ/ in the verb *can*. Since the /eh/ vowel is stigmatized, particularly when realized as a high vowel, it is rarer in more formal styles. Labov found low vowel realization of /eh/, or replacement of /eh/ by /æ/, to be particularly prevalent among Jews (Labov 1966: 295–301).

A failure to distinguish between /ɛ/ and /æ/ or /eh/ is classically typical of a Yiddish accent in English. Four children did not distinguish *ten* from *tan*, and two confused *pen* and *pan*. But the pair *said~ sad* caused no such difficulty.

As was the case with *r*, Lubavitcher children favor the more formal variants. Only four children distinguished between the stressed vowels in *I can* and *a tin can* when reading the list of minimal pairs. Six children never used /eh/ and thus showed no /æ~ eh/ distinction in styles *C*, *D*, or *D'*. Of the nineteen children who kept /æ/ separate from /eh/, fifteen of them produced a nonnative vowel, usually [ɛː], for /eh/. Seven of these fifteen did not always produce a normal [æ], the vowel tending to be too high. The six children (all girls) with no /æ~ eh/ distinction, however, all produced perfect [æ]'s.

There was no one who produced a good /eh/ who had trouble with /æ/. Yet Yiddish has neither sound. Lubavitcher children have adopted the /æ/ of General American speech, but young members of the Lubavitcher community have not learned the /eh/ of their neighbors.

The four children who have an /æ~ eh/ distinction and who nevertheless pronounce both sounds without foreign interference are four of the five F. children interviewed. The youngest child, G.F., on one occasion had slight difficulty with /eh/, but generally pronounces the vowel as well as her elder siblings. The F. family lived in Philadelphia for some years, where an /æ~ eh/ distinction also exists. Yet in other respects the F. children sound like New

Yorkers and not Philadelphians. They occasionally drop *r*s, and their /ow/ and /æw/ phonemes have none of the [əw] and [æɪw] quality of Philadelphia speech. Thus the F. children have lost their Philadelphia accents, but in moving to New York they have retained a distinction that most New Yorkers possess, although it is lacking in the Crown Heights Lubavitcher community.

In New York City speech, *bored* and *bawd* are very commonly both pronounced /bohd/. According to Labov, the /oh/ phoneme is realized as something between [ʊə] and [ɔə]. In the speech of young New Yorkers, he finds, the /oh/ and /uh/ phonemes are merging (Labov 1946: 359–364). Effects of the merger are noticeable among the Lubavitcher children. Nine children make a distinction between *sure* and *shore*; eight do not. Only three, however, distinguish between *poor* and *pour*.

The high /oh/ vowel common in New York City speech is somewhat stigmatized and is certainly as foreign to the phonemic system of Yiddish as /eh/ is. Yet fourteen of the children consistently used /oh/ wherever it might be expected. Three of the F. children departed from this pattern in the word *chocolate* in whose first syllable /a/ occurred. This no doubt reflects the Philadelphia pattern, where high /oh/ is common, but where /a/ is the stressed vowel in *chocolate*.

Three children occasionally use [ɐ] rather than [oə]. One of these is C.C., who favors prestige pronunciations; the other two were members of the K. family. A third K. child, D.K., had no /oh/ or /ɔ/ phoneme at all – *caught* and *cot* are both /kat/ in his speech. D.K. agrees with his mother B.K. in this respect. B.K. is from Montreal, where no /a~/ɔ distinction is made. Finally, four children produced a nonnative sounding [ɹo] instead of /oh/. This is a smaller number than had difficulty with /æ/ and /eh/.

To turn to another feature of pronunciation that is a mark of group affiliation in New York City, ten children always pronounced the *th* sounds as fricatives. Twelve children used fricatives most of the time, but sometimes used stops /t, d/ or affricates /tθ, dð/. One child, C.G., had a majority of stops and only produced fricatives when he was being especially careful. And one child, E.I., used only stops and had no /θ/ or /ð/ in his speech.

A few matters may be noted briefly: (1) In a process analogous to the merger of *poor* and *pour*, *beer* and *bear* are becoming homophonous in the speech of young New Yorkers. Only three children distinguished between these words. (2) The words *mirror* and *nearer* rhymed for nine children and did not for twelve. (3) *Voice* and *verse* were always distinguished. The stigmatized /ʌy/ is unknown among the Lubavitcher children. (4) The sequences /ay/ and /aw/ are realized as [ɑɪ] or [ɒɪ] and [æu], respectively. This is typical of the speech of many young New Yorkers. (5) *Finger* and *singer* rhymed in the speech of all the children. (6) *Which* and *witch*, and *do* and *dew*, were always homophonous.

To sum the whole matter up, Lubavitcher children are as fluent in English as they are in Yiddish. Their English pronunciation improves as they grow older, and girls above the age of eight speak English with little or no foreign accent. Boys, whose education is much more religiously oriented, have more trouble with English. The fact that girls prefer English and boys Yiddish is precisely analogous to the situation among the parents, where the women prefer Russian and the men Yiddish.

Despite the relative isolation of the Lubavitcher community and the fact that none of the parents was born in New York, Lubavitcher children speak English with a New York accent, with the reservation that prestige markers are more prevalent. Yet the F. children show traces of Philadelphia speech, and the K. children reflect the Montreal pronunciation of their mother. Children's pronunciation, after the earliest years, in general mirrors the speech of their peers, not that of their parents. Yet it is only natural that the K. children, whose mother is the single native speaker of English among the adults, should model their speech after their mother's. The speech of Lubavitcher children is probably particularly subject to non-New York influences because there is no native English-speaking adult population to provide a counterinfluence.

The teenage girls who will be the mothers of the next generation speak English very well. There is no doubt that in another generation the English of Lubavitcher children will be absolutely native. Religion, however, is the central fact in Lubavitcher life, and religious education and discussion is exclusively in Yiddish. It is therefore reasonable to conclude that the Lubavitcher community will remain bilingual indefinitely.

REFERENCES

Herzog, M. I. (1965), 'The Yiddish language in northern Poland: Its geography and history', *International Journal of American Linguistics* 31 (2): 161, 201, 228.

Labov, W. (1966), *The Social Stratification of English in New York City*, 90–98, 238, 295–301, 345, 359–364, 596–597. Washington, D.C.

Poll, S. (1965), 'The role of Yiddish in American ultra-Orthodox and Hassidic communities', *YIVO Annual of Jewish Social Studies* 13: 135, 137, 152.

Weinreich, U. (1952), '*Sábesdiker losn* in Yiddish: a problem of linguistic affinity', *Word* 8: 362, 374.

Weinreich, U., editor (1965), 'The dynamics of Yiddish dialect formation', in *The Field of Yiddish: Studies in Language, Folklore, and Literature*, second vol., 73–86. New York.

Invitation to a literary–musical soiree; program includes the presentation of a play by Sholem Aleykhem, piano, violin, dance, etc. (late 1930s).

Epilogue:
Contributions of the Sociology of Yiddish to the
General Sociology of Language

JOSHUA A. FISHMAN

THE MAX WEINREICH HERITAGE

Sociolinguistic research on Yiddish has already contributed significantly to the sociology of language in general. Indeed, much of it has followed Max Weinreich's vision that research on Yiddish that is of general theoretical interest is better research and, therefore, ultimately also more useful to the world of Yiddish per se. For over a third of a century Weinreich pointed to various topics of great general interest that could more conveniently or definitively be studied via Yiddish materials than via data drawn from other language communities (see e.g. Vaynraykh 1937, 1953, 1959, 1967, 1973), guaranteeing thereby that research on Yiddish would be of more than routine interest to the language sciences as a whole. Finally, Weinreich also focused the combined sophistication of the language sciences on the field of Yiddish per se and, particularly in his magnum opus *Di geshikhte fun der yidisher shprakh* (1973), provided an unsurpassable example of how the circle could be completed and renewed ad infinitum: the contributor (Yiddish) could benefit from contributions from the language sciences more generally, and, as a result, make even further noteworthy contributions. The present review is an attempt to expand upon the latter approach, but to do so particularly in connection with sociological-sociolinguistic theory, rather than in connection with the sociohistorical or the linguistic-sociolinguistic issues that interested Weinreich most. Thus, this paper seeks to answer the questions: 'where are we in connection with the sociology of Yiddish?' and 'where should we be heading?' in such a way as to be most responsive to Max Weinreich's views mentioned above.

PERSPECTIVE ON THE SOCIOLOGY OF YIDDISH

Most students come to the sociology of Yiddish with a far more restricted view of the 'uses and users' of the language than is warranted. Their intellectual, emotional, and usage interactions with Yiddish have been skewed, either by partisan bias (positive or negative) or by simple lack of opportunity to note or to study the true variety of uses and users that obtains. Stewart's (1968) ordered dimensions of language evaluations (standardization, autonomy, historicity, and vitality), when applied to Yiddish alone (rather than to a variety of languages, as one would normally do), enable the student to realize that what some consider to be a standard language, others take as a mere vernacular, dialect, creole, etc. However, not only can these evaluative dimensions be put to orientational use *vis-à-vis* the synchronic as well as the diachronic variability of Yiddish reality (standardization and autonomy being later stages of all sociolinguistic development than either the sense of vitality or historicity, in Yiddish as well as in other languages), but they also can themselves be used as guides to research. Which of these dimensions do different (Jewish and non-Jewish) samples attribute to Yiddish today? Do these dimensions reveal an orderly progression in children's sociocognitive development *vis-à-vis* Yiddish (e.g. among Hasidic or other ultra-Orthodox children today)? Can these dimensions be utilized (as is? with additions/deletions?) to differentiate the various ideological positions *vis-à-vis* Yiddish, e.g. those expressed at the 1908 Tshernovits Language Conference (Rothstein 1977)? Thus far Stewart's dimensions have been much cited but they have not been tested, refined, revised, or even much utilized via empirical research. The field of Yiddish could benefit from such research and would contribute to general sociolinguistic theory in so doing. Suffice it to say it is my impression that 'in the real world' Stewart's dimensions will arrange themselves in theoretically unexpected ways and that attitudinal reality is far more complex and inconsistent than theoretical parsimony, and, therefore, much more interesting and challenging.

YIDDISH IN SMALL-GROUP INTERACTION: UNITS AND PARAMETERS

The first 'technical problem' that students must face in connection with the sociology of Yiddish is that of the units and parameters (dimensions) in terms of which language use is to be analyzed. It has always been my preference to find such basic units at the small-group, face-to-face level and to build upon them for higher levels of analysis (community, region, nation) as well. The basic goal, at the outset, is to derive units and dimensions by means of which it can become clear that *the same interlocutors* do *not* speak (write) to each other *in the same way* on all occasions. Several systematic and parsimonious accounts of 'ways' and 'occasions' have been developed within the sociology of language (for four such, namely those of Labov, Erwin-Tripp, Grimshaw, and Fishman, see Fishman 1971) and the sociology of Yiddish could utilize and refine any one of them. Thus far only Herman (1968) has reported empirical work in this connection, indicating that Yiddish in Israel is utilized much more frequently in *private* than in *public* interactions and in *emotional* rather than in *task* oriented situations (English too has been shown to be subject to the same constraints in Israel, although to a lesser degree; see Rosenbaum, Nadel, Cooper, and Fishman, 1977). All in all, the sociology of Yiddish is still quite deficient with respect to empirical research on the basic notion of the sociolinguistic repertoire. This is highly regrettable, because it is in this area, rather than in connection with most of those that follow, that the foundations of the entire sociolinguistic enterprise are being and will be laid.

Weinreich's work itself is replete with linguistic *examples* of the sociolinguistic repertoire among users of Yiddish (usually, Yiddish-plus-other-languages), both in Eastern Europe and in the United States. However, examples and systematic empirical demonstrations are not one and the same, certainly not insofar as the theoretical refinement of units and parameters is concerned.

Whatever the basic model followed, the usual finding is that of variability in 'ways' across 'occasions', when interlocutors are kept constant (although their status-role relations with each other may nevertheless vary). However, even when 'occasions' are maximally dissimilar and when the 'ways' involve maximally dissimilar languages, the transition from one to the other is, nevertheless, usually less than complete. To some extent this may be a reflection of a pervasive familiarity that serves to narrow inter-occasional distance for interlocutors who speak/write Yiddish to each other at least on some occasions. To some extent, however, this may also reflect a basic tendency for varieties within a common repertoire to share (that is to minimize the number of separate) features, this being a reflection of a tendency within the language apparatus per se, which the pervasive familiarity syndrome within Ashkenaz (within all Jewry? within all self-perceived minorities?) merely intensifies. At any rate, and particularly if we are concerned with intra-Yiddish variation across a range of occasions from extremely informal to extremely formal, the result is a tension system between the need to mark varieties vividly so that they can be recognizably different for different occasions, and the tendency to keep the differences between them minimal, particularly in view of the pervasive familiarity which is so omnipresent at least between Yiddish users. The resulting tension is not unknown in other speech communities (see e.g. Ma and Herasimchuck 1971), but it is one that certainly could be clarified with wide-reaching implications indeed from within the field of Yiddish.

My own observations among 'educated' speakers of Yiddish whose intimacy-variety is broadly southern (Bessarabian, Podolian) is that transitions to increased formality are marked by proportionally more realizations of *a* for *o* (tate/tote, mame/mome, kalt/kolt), of *u* for *i* (puter/piter, muter/miter, shvues/shvies), of initial *h for* ♯ (halb/♯olb, hamer/♯amer/♯emer, heys/♯eys), and of *ay* for *a:* (zayn/za:n, mayn/ma:n, vayb/va:b). On the other hand, no such transitions seem to occur (or if they do, they occur at a far lower rate of

20־יאריקער יובל פֿון יידישן לערער־פֿאראיין אין ווילנע

1935 – 1915

Sz. BASTOMSKI, Wilno, Stefańska 24. (Poland) :אדרעס פֿון יובל־קאָמיטעט

צום יואיק לוסנרדעוקנ ונאראנ ווילנא

זייער חשובער פֿריינד!

יובל־קאָמיטעט

אין דעצעמבער 1935 ווערט 20 יאָר, זינט ס'איז געגרינדעט געוואָרן דער יידישער
לערער פֿאראיין אין ווילנע.

ש. באַסטאָמסקי

ס'איז ניט נאָר אַ יום־טוב פֿון דער ווילנער יידישער לערערשאַפֿט, נאָר גלייכצייטיק
אויך אַ וויכטיקע דאַטע אין דער יידישער פֿראָפֿעסיאָנעלער און קולטור־באַוועגונג בכלל.

י. גראָסמאַן

אין יאָר 1915, נאָכדעם ווי די צאַרישע מאַכט האָט פֿאַרלאָזן ווילנע, איז געגרינדעט
געוואָרן דער ווילנער יידישער לערער־פֿאראיין. דאָס איז געווען די צייט, ווען ס'איז
געלייגט געוואָרן דער גרונטשטיין פֿון די יידיש־וועלטלעכע שולן.

ל. סוהרבאַוויטש

מ. יאָפֿע

מ. לעווינסקי

דער ווילנער יידישער לערער־פֿאראיין איז געווען דער איניציאַטאָר און דער אַקטיוו־
סטער בויער פֿון אַ גאַנצער ריי שולן און אַנדערע קולטור־אַנשטאַלטן אין ווילנע און ווילנ(ער געגנט.

י. מהרשק

דער ווילנער יידישער פֿאראיין האָט מיטגעהאָלפֿן צו גרינדן די ערשטע אָרגאַניזציע
פֿון דער יידיש־וועלטלעכער שול אין ווילנע (צ. ב. ק.) און אויך מיטגעווירקט צו אָרגאַניזירן
די ערשטע קולטור באַראַטונגען אין וואַרשע (אין 1919), אַלס רעזולטאַט פֿון וועלכע ס'איז
געשאַפֿן געוואָרן די צענטראַלע יידישע שול־אָרגאַניזציע (צ.י.ש.א.).

י. סטויצקי

א. סליעפֿ

ג. פֿלודערמאַכער

ח. פֿיפֿקאָ

אָמע ראָזענטאַל

די פֿארוואַלטונג פֿון ווילנער יידישן לערער־פֿאראיין האָט באַשלאָסן צו באַצייכענען די
דאָזיקע וויכטיקע דאַטע דורך אַרויסגעבן אַ זאַמלבוך, געווידמעט דער געשיכטע און טעטיק־
פֿון פֿאראיין, שאַפֿן אַ הילפֿס־פֿאָנד ביים פֿאראיין און איינאָרדענען אַ פֿיערלעכע
יובל־אַקאַדעמיע.

ז. רייזען

מ. ראבֿיטאָוויטש

י. שער

מיר נעמען זיך דערמיט דעם כבוד אייך צו פֿאַרבעטן צו דער **יובל־פֿיערונג**, וואָס
וועט פֿאַרקומען שבת דעם 25־סטן יאַנואַר 1936 אין זאַל פֿון דער קאָנסערוואַטאָריע (קאַנסקע 1).

מיט פֿריינדלעכן גרוס
יובל – קאָמיטעט

פֿאַרבעטונג צו דער פֿייערונג לכבוד דעם 20־יאַריקן יובילייי פֿון יידישן לערער־פֿאראיין
Invitation to the celebration of the 20th anniversary of the Yiddish Teachers Association
הזמנה לחגיגת מלאת 20 שנה לאיגוד המורים האידיים
Приглашение на празднование двадцатилетнего юбилея Союза еврейских учителей

Twentieth anniversary of the Yiddish Teachers Association (Vilna), organized in 1915 when the Czarist
government withdrew, initiator of a long list of Yiddish schools and cultural institutions.

realization or at far later, i.e. more extreme, levels of formality stressing) either for *o/u* (zog/zug, foter/futer, montik/muntik) or for *e/ey* (lebm/leybm, teg/teyg, ze/zey). Regardless of the underlying explanatory approach to phenomena of this type, it would seem to be insufficient to posit that the first series consists of 'markers' (stereotypes) whereas the second merely consists of 'variables', precisely because the speakers in question (as well as their interlocutors) are often as aware of the latter as of the former even in any superficial discussion of the issue. Indeed, variation within the latter series is considered pejoratively (affectatious and unnatural) whereas variation within the former is obviously capable of positive interpretation (cultured, courteous, etc.).

Similar contributions remain to be made with respect to the repertoire of occasions, particularly since their ethnographic exploration (i.e. their explication as viewed from within) is still in its infancy in the general field and entirely absent in the Yiddish sociolinguistic enterprise. What kinds of occasions will bring about what kinds/degrees of transition in the two series suggested above? The answer to this question would be stimulating indeed.

YIDDISH USAGE ACROSS SOCIAL STRATA AND SECTORS

If the former topic usually pertains to the repertoire range as realized with the *same* interlocutors (normally with those with whom intimacy relations are most clearly recognized, i.e. within closed networks), then the present topic pertains to the repertoire range that is realized across the full gamut of *different* interlocutors with whom Yiddish is utilized (i.e. within open networks as well). As a result, this topic often involves greater attention to variation between Yiddish and other languages (rather than or in addition to the focus on intra-Yiddish variation emphasized above). Basically, however, the two topics are closely interconnected, with the range between intimacy occasions (nonstatus stressing, personal interactions, closed networks in home and neighborhood domains) and formality occasions (status stressing, transactional interactions, open networks in work and education domains) merely being more extended than before. Fortunately, there has been Yiddish related research in this latter connection, although not nearly as much as one would care to have.

Slobin (1963) demonstrated the formality–informality continuum via an analysis of the pronoun of address system (du/ir). His study would benefit from empirical replication in a variety of Yiddish using networks today, both where the coterritorial languages also make similar distinctions (e.g. Spanish, French) as well as where they do not (e.g. English, Hebrew). Indeed, given all of the work that has gone into Tu–Vu inquiries in the past fifteen years the studies conducted have seldom, if ever, been pursued in structurally contrastive bilingual settings particularly such in which one of these languages – in our case Yiddish – was weakening for certain speakers but not for others. In addition, such inquiries would be of interest if they also included native and non-native speaker status as part of their study design. A similarly fruitful line of research is that undertaken by Ronch (1969) who demonstrated that, among elderly Yiddish–English bilinguals in New York, Yiddish appears to be normatively more expected in family, friendship, and 'Jewish domains' and English in work, education, and government domains, even when their interlocutors on all occasions are Yiddish–English bilinguals (albeit largely different ones in each domain). Seemingly, if a semantic differential study were done in the context of Yiddish–English (or of Yiddish–*X*lish) connotative images, on the order of Fertig and Fishman's study of Spanish and English among Puerto Ricans in New York City (1969), Yiddish would probably score as softer and weaker. How it would score relative to the good–bad and active–passive dimensions is more doubtful, and, at any rate, what we need is evidence rather than speculation. The general point here is that both semantic differential scores *and* sociofunctional data have never been obtained on the languages of bilingual networks, and the field of Yiddish is one of the contexts in which this could be done.

LANGUAGE REFLECTIONS OF SOCIOCULTURAL PROCESSES

Weinreich himself was the master in this area (see particularly his presentation of Yiddish as a key to and as product of the way of the SHaS in his 1973 vol. 1). He fully anticipated Ferguson's diglossia notion by well over six years, not only in terms of *inveynikste tsveyshprakhikayt* concerns (1953; further developed in 1959, the same year in which Ferguson's more famous paper was published), but also in terms of the use of H as a stylistic variable within L itself, thus a continuum of Hness in L, rather than merely an H vs L dichotomy. However, this topic does not end here. Weinreich's attempts to clarify the historically changing normative views as to when Yiddish was more appropriate and when Loshn Koydish was more appropriate have been probabilistically elaborated (Fishman, 1977b) and applied to a consideration of systematic orthographic preferences (Fishman 1973), thus going beyond the lexical and morphosyntactic realm in which Weinreich found his data. Still lacking, however, is a full-blown review of Jewish ideological and social class factors in the evaluation of Yiddish, either in years long since gone by (e.g. late nineteenth and early twentieth centuries) or currently. Herman's demonstration (1972) that Yiddish is much more acceptable to Ashkenazi youngsters in Israel than to Sefardi ones, and to religious (*dati*) and traditional (*mesorati*) youngsters than to secular (*ḥolani*) ones, merits replication and re/dis-confirmation far and wide. Indeed, the whole topic of Yiddish '*awareness*' (that is: cognitions relative to Yiddish, or what is known, believed, suspected), and Yiddish *attitudes* (i.e. what is desired, felt, sought for, with respect to Yiddish), remains largely unexplored, whether among Yiddish speakers, those ignorant of Yiddish, or even non-Jews. Not so long ago Yiddish (even the very *name* 'Yiddish') seems to have been considered 'funny' in some Jewish circles. This itself is the reflection of sociocultural processes among its speakers, erstwhile speakers, and more distant acquaintances. The fact that such reactions are rarer today than they were, and may have been replaced by and large by far different ones, makes it all the more urgent that the former reactions (among whom? how explicated?) be documented and that the replacements be carefully monitored. Although the field of language attitude research is now quite fully developed (see, e.g. Cooper and Fishman 1977), it is still rare for investigators to stick with the same population over time and to try to account for attitudes and attitude changes empirically. Research on Yiddish could make a real contribution here (Macaulay 1975).

Although Dr. Kh. Spivak is upset that ignorant critics have claimed to note gaps in the Hebrew–Yiddish dictionary that he and Yehoyesh have just published, the poet Yehoyesh, speaking in verse, is unconcerned, (*Der groyser kundes*, June 23, 1911)

If I could pick the populations to monitor most closely (from the point of view of variance in connection with ongoing sociocultural processes), I would select the ultra-Orthodox in the United States and in Israel. The proportion of native born and entirely fluent (if not native) speakers of the coterritorial languages among them is now great enough for cognitive and functional questions (and, therefore, for rationales and answers) to arise that were not necessary before. The appearance of a non-Yiddish speaking Orthodoxy must have a very definite impact on the phenomenology of Yiddish among Yiddish speaking Orthodoxy, both in the United States and Israel, just as the appearance of Yiddish speaking nonbelievers had initially and continues to have to this very day (Poll 1965) on the latter. The major problem in studying Orthodox populations, however, is that they are resistant to study even at the participant observation/ethnographic level. Rich though this level is, it nevertheless benefits, as does all research at whatever level, from cross-methodological buttressing (see, e.g. Ma and Herasimchuck 1971; Hofman and Fisherman 1971; Rosenbaum, Nadel, Cooper, and Fishman 1977). The goal in this area remains that of finding a speech-network that can be studied *as a whole*, so that variations in language beliefs, language feelings, and language usage can be studied in relation to variations in role repertoire, both within and without the usage (speech and writing) network. In both countries ultra-Orthodoxy is beginning to accept and to enact national (citizenship) roles, to interact more with non-Orthodox Jews as well as with non-Jews, to be more exposed to standard Yiddish-in-print, to be more exposed to modern(ized) Hebrew for purposes of traditional Jewish scholarship and piety. All of these social processes, differentially enacted, may well have differential consequences *vis-à-vis* knowing, using, and liking Yiddish. Their synchronic and diachronic delineation for an intact speech network would represent quite an advance in the state of the sociolinguistic art today.

LANGUAGE CONSTRAINTS AND LANGUAGE CONTRIBUTIONS TO WORLD VIEW

Within the language sciences the Whorfian hypothesis has occupied an increasingly marginal position during the past two decades. Having contributed several times to the marginalization of this hypothesis (most recently Fishman and Spolsky 1977), I am aware, nevertheless, of the power that this position still commands among those who hold to it – both within academia and, particularly, without its walls. Within the Yiddishist fold there is not only an endless reservoir of anecdotal observation concerning the absolute untranslatability and irreplaceability of Yiddish, but even firmer conviction as to its significance for the Jewish personality, the authenticity and the very physical being of the speakers. These views need to be studied, both thematically and developmentally, i.e. they need to be studied as quasimystic experiences rather than for objective validity. One interesting population to study in this connection (perhaps even more interesting than the activists studied by Hesbacher and Fishman 1965) are Yiddish literati. The latter have both a vested interest in claiming the absolute uniqueness or coidentity of Yiddish and their own personal creativity/identity, on the one hand, and a self-serving conflicting interest in being translated into English, Hebrew, French, Spanish or other coterritorial and wider-communicational languages, on the other. The often unverbalized collision between these two positions would seem to be ripe for exploration and would represent a sociolinguistic contribution to dissonance theory as well.

MULTILINGUALISM

Almost every sociolinguistic consideration of Yiddish is bound to be in the context of multilingualism. Seemingly, this phenomenon has commonly obtained with respect to the social setting of Yiddish-using communities for well-nigh the entire millennium in which the language has existed. For our purposes, here, this poses the problem of whether a *separate* topic such as multilingualism might still be fruitful if all other topics indicated in this review are also to be retained. Although the decision in this connection is likely to be a somewhat arbitrary one, my preference is to retain this topic and to utilize it for a consideration of the sociological concomitants of the genesis, spread and functional specification of Jewish languages in general and of Yiddish in particular. The most relevant *general* literature is not only that which deals with the social foundations of pidginization–creolization (Grimshaw 1971; Mintz 1971) but that concerned with elitist (specialist) – mass differences in interaction with other speech/writing communities (e.g. Tanner 1967; Pool 1972) and with sociocultural and symbolic continuity and change more generally (Turner 1974). The sociological counter-part of linguogenesis leads us to the entire topic of differences between linguistically more homogeneous and linguistically less heterogeneous Yiddish using networks, on the one hand, as well as to the differences between more interacting and less interacting networks (*vis-à-vis* non-Jews and non-Yiddish using Jews), on the other hand. Obviously, although the two sets of factors *do* go hand in hand on many occasions, they do *not* do so constantly. This is an issue of general theoretical importance which researchers working with Yiddish networks might help clarify. The initial acquisition of some Germanic varieties by Jews had to imply interactions that had not previously existed. The internal 'Judaization' of these varieties had to result from the utilization for intragroup purposes of varieties that had previously served intergroup purposes alone. These 'Judaized' varieties then became available also to individuals (women, children and many men as well) who lacked inter-(ethnic) group contacts but for whom the acceptance of these varieties represented a (further) *multilingualization* of their repertoires, at least initially. Aspects of these processes are available for study

י. גערשטיינס כאָר

כ״ג דער זש.

„פּריז פֿון דער רעאַל־יזמאָעע"

באַגריסט די דעלעגאַטן און געסט פֿון דעם אַלוועלטלעכן צוזאַמענפֿאָר פֿון ייִדישן וויסנשאַפֿטלעכן אינסטיטוט אין ווילנע

אונדזער כאָר האָט זיך געגרינדעט אין פֿעברואַר 1932; ער איז
אַ געמישטער. די זינגער רעקרוטירן זיך פֿון אַרבעטער, אַנגעשטעלטע
און שטודירנדיקער יוגנט. ביי דער היינטיקן טאָג ציילט דער כאָר 68 מיט־
גלידער. אַחוץ אַ מאַן 5, זיינען דאָס אַלע געוועזענע שילער פֿון
ייִדיש־וועלטלעכע שולן. אונדזער כאָר פֿאַרמאָגט אַ רעפּערטואַר פֿון
צענדליקער לידער: פֿאָלקס־לידער און ווערק פֿון די קאָמפּאָזיטאָרן
אַנצעוו, ארכאַנגעלסקי, באָראָדין, גאָלדפֿאַדן, גלוק, געלבאַרט, גרע־
טשאַנינאָוו, דאַרגאָמיזשסקי, הירשין, וויינער, זילבערטס, טשייקאָווסקי,
ליאוו, מענדעלסאָן, סען־סאַנס, פֿאָזנער, פֿאַלאַנסקי, קאַנטסקי, רובין,
שומאַן און שקליאַר צו די טעקסטן—אָריגינעלע און איבערגעזעצטע—
פֿון מ. בראָדערזאָן, א. גאָלדפֿאַדן, מ. ל. האַלפּערן, ד. האָפֿשטיין,
ש. וואָלמאַן, ל. ניידוס, ב. סאַראַבסקי, י. ל. פּרץ, אי. פּעפֿער, ש. קאַ־
האַן, א. רייזען און ב. שאַפֿיר. דער כאָר האָט צוויי מאָל געזונגען
פֿאַרן מיקראָפֿאָן פֿון דעם ווילנער ראַדיאָ. דער היינטיקער איז דער
צעגטער עפֿנטלעכער אַרויסטריט פֿון כאָר.

דער צוזאַמענשטעל פֿון כאָר:

סאָפּראַנען: ס. אלבערטס, ח. אנדערוואָשצהסקי, מ. בערנשטיין, ס. גאָלדשמידס, מ. דאַרגאָ־
זשאַנסקי, כ. רושאַנסקי, ל. דושין, ב. הענדלער, ר. וויינשטיין, ס. זשורער, מ. סורעץ, ס. סורעץ,
י. סדיק, ח. סטשערנע, ד. ליפּאָהיקוויטש, פּ. מוסקאַ, ס. פֿאַיאַרער, ס. פֿריירנשטיין, ב. קאַריסקי,
אַ. רוויטנסטיין, מ. סוסטער, ג. סמוקלער, ב. ספּיסטאַלניק. אַלס: א. בצנדער, ג. בערנשטיין
ל. גאָרדאָן, ר. גרעגבדזער, ג. דעזיגעניטשעק, ג. סורעץ, מ. יאַקאָבסאָן, פּ. יאַקאָבסאָן, ס. יונגערמאַן,
ה. יצרוביכמאַהויסט, ס. מאַגילניק, מ. עפֿראָן, מ. פֿרוושאַן, נ. סוטערמאַן, ח. קאָהאָן, ב. קאַמעל, ב. ראָפֿפֿעס,
א. סוטאַשטעק, ב. סטילער, ס. סמעַרקאָוויטש, י. סעסקין. טענאָרן: י. אנגל, ד. גאָלאָמב, נ. גער־
שאַטער, ע. ליוגומסקי, ס. מאַטוז, סקיבין, מ. עלפֿערדאַהויסס, א. ראָדקין, מ. רוויגנסקי. באַסן: ב. באַסעל,
ח. בראַידע, ש. גרילאַן, ס. גורהויסס, ז. הערבלון, ה. זאָלשטאַנסקי, ז. זידער, מ. זידעל, ש. זשאַ־
ווזרסקי ד. יאַקאָבסאָן, י. מאַסלאָווסקי, ב. מיקטאָם, א. קאָצלבונג, ק. קאַפּאַנסקי, פּ. רוודין.

אַקאָמפּאַניאַטאָרין—רחל סיליון.

א קאָנצערט־פּראָגראַם פֿון גערשטיינס כאָר

Program of a concert by J. Gerstein's Choir

תוכנית קונצרט של מקהלת י. גרשטיין

Программа концерта хора Герштейна

today as Yiddish speaking Jews differentially adopt English and Hebrew, not only via interaction with 'outside' networks but also via interaction with each other, within their own networks. The adoption and adaptation of other vernaculars ('multilingualization') thus has varying rather than constant sociological concomitants, and it is this fact that requires patient illumination. Who adopts from the outside, who adopts from the inside, who adapts, how does adaptation facilitate more widespread adoption, what are the restraints upon adaptation – these are all good general issues to which the sociology of Yiddish could make major post-Weinreichian empirical contributions.

LANGUAGE MAINTENANCE AND LANGUAGE SHIFT

If various theoretical issues in multilingualism research are still largely unstudied in conjunction with the sociology of Yiddish, the topic of language maintenance and language shift is among the most studied of all. Indeed, if Yiddish has almost always functioned within a context of multilingualism it has, particularly in modern times, repeatedly lived in the shadow of displacement and replacement, and, even more, been presumed to live in such a shadow without hope of surviving 'a blink of history' by its very own users and champions (Howe 1976). The very process of intranetwork adoption of coterritorial internetwork languages, mentioned above as part of the story of linguogenesis, has, however, obviously also been part of the story of linguocide for Yiddish and remains so today, even though over four million Jews could justifiably claim Yiddish as their mother tongue.

So many studies of Yiddish language maintenance have been so consistently negative for so long a time that the differential character of language shift has been rather overlooked. As a result, the *relative* contributions of a variety of 'hard' demographic factors (e.g. heterogeneity of origin, age, educational-occupational status, and settlement concentration) to differential retention of Yiddish have yet to be studied *vis-à-vis* each other, much less relative to the contribution of 'softer' behavioral-ideological-attitudinal factors *vis-à-vis* language retention. An encompassing study of all of these factors in a few contrasted communities would have major value for the sociology of language maintenance and language shift more generally (Fishman 1965a, 1966, 1969, 1972b, 1977a), in addition to its importance for the sociology of Yiddish in particular.

Somewhat more differentiated data *have* been collected in conjunction with Israeli student *attitudes* toward Yiddish (Cooper and Fishman 1977), Israeli police attitudes toward Yiddish (Fisherman and Fishman 1975), and Israeli

◄ J. Gerstein's chorus (organized 1932) greets and presents a program in honor of the delegates and guests of the World Conference of the Yiddish Scientific Institute (Yivo), 1935.

קאָמוניסטישע פּאַרטיי פון ליטע. סעקציע פון קאָמינטערן.
פּראָלעטאַריער פון אַלע לענדער, פאַראייניקט זיך!

כאַוויירים אַרבעטער, פּויערים, קעמפּער, אַרבעטנדיקע אינטעליגענץ, אַלע אַרבעטנדיקע!

דעם 21 סן יולי קלייבט זיך צונויף דער סאָלקס־סיים. דאָס אַרבעטנדיקע פאָלק פון ליטע. וואָס האָט זיך באַפרייט פון דער פאַשיסטישער רעזשים, וויל זיך פולשטענדיק בא־פרייען פון קאַפּיטאַליסטישער קנעכטשאַפט. אין גאַנצן לאַנד קומען מער רייזיקע מיטינגען פון אַרבעטער, פּויערים און סאָלדאַטן, אויף וועלכע זיי פאָדערן אַיינצורן צו סאָוועטן־מאַכט, סטאַליניש קאָנסטיטוציע. און אַנשליסן ליטע צו די סאָוועטישע, סאָציאַליסטישע רעפּובליקן. אָן עמעסן ווויליזיין פון די אַרבעטנדיקע, איניפּבלי פון דער סאָלקס־קולטור, קען געבן נאָר אַ פרייע, סאָוועטישע ליטע, וואו ס׳וועט ניט זיין קיין עקספּלואַטאַציע פון מענטש דורך מענטש, קיין אַרבעטסלאָזיקייט. אונדזער פאָטערלאַנד וועט פולשטענדיק זיין זיכער, ווען זי וועט זיין פאַראייניקט צו דער גרויסער און פעסטער מישפּאָכע פון ראַטן־פאַרבאַנד. אויסקלייבנדיק די בעסטע פאַרשטייער אין סאָלקס־סיים. האָבן די אַרבעטנדיקע פראָלעגנשטעלם זייערע פאָדערונ־גען און זיי ווייזן, אַז די פאָרשטייער פון פאָלק וועלן זייערע פאָדערונגען באַפרידיקן.

כאַוויירים און כאַווערטעס!

דער ווילנער געביט־קאָמיטעט פון דער קאָמוניסטישע פּאַרטיי אין ליטע רופט אַלע אַרבעטער, פּויערים, קעמפּער, אַרבעטנדיקע אינטעליגענץ, אַלע אַרבעטנדיקע דעם 21 סן יולי אין צוזאַמענהאַנג מיט דער עפענונג פון פאָלקס־סיים 12 אַזייגער אויף לוקישקער פּלאַץ אויף אַ

מיטינג - דעמאָנסטראַציע,

קעדיי צו באַגריסן דעם פאָלקס - סיים און צו פאָדערן אַרויסזאָגן
די פאָדערונגען.

זאָל לעבן דער פאָלקס־סיים!

זאָל לעבן אַ ראַטן־ליטע!

זאָל לעבן די קאָמוניסטישע פּאַרטיי פון ליטע!

זאָל לעבן די רויטע־אַרמי אונדזער באַפרייערין!

זאָל לעבן דער ראַטנפאַרבאַנד!

זאָל לעבן דער פירער און לערער פון אַלע אַרבעטנדיקע דער
באַזער סטאַלין!

ווילנער קאָמיטעט
פון דער קאָמוניסטישער פּאַרטיי אין ליטע.

„Expresso" Spaustuvė Vilniuje

רוף צו דער דעמאָנסטראַציע אויף לוקישקער פּלאַץ

1940 20/VII   Call for the demonstration at Lukishki Square

קריאה להפגנה בכיכר לוקישקי

Призыв к демонстрации на Лукишской площади

radio listening preferences (Kaẓ 1972; Nadel and Fishman 1977). These have consistently pointed to the improvement of attitudes (but not usage) as higher educational levels are attained. For whatever reason, the attitudinal-affective 'end of Yiddish' seems further away than either many of its friends or most of its enemies have assumed.

Israel itself represents a rich mine for the sociological study of Yiddish-related attitudes, and one that must be fully exploited if only in order that the sociology of Yiddish not be reduced to the sociology of Yiddish in America. Interestingly enough, the dissolution of traditional Jewish diglossia (Fishman 1967, 1977b, 1979), on the one hand, and the influx of Hebrew and English language roles and influences, on the other hand (Cooper and Fishman 1977; Allony-Fainberg 1977; Nadel and Fishman 1977; Ronen et al. 1977), have led not only to the weakening of Yiddish use in Israel but also to a rekindling of nostalgia for it among those who once spoke or heard it. Although the slang of the younger generation apparently loses its Yiddishisms more rapidly than any other of its manifold non-Hebrew borrowings (Kornblueth and Aynor 1974), that of the older generation seems to be particularly retentive of Yiddishisms (Ben-Amoẓ and Ben-Yehuda 1972). By and large, the attitudinal response to Yiddish is nonideological; *vis-à-vis* Hebrew it reveals neither the pained and conflicted ambivalence of Byalik (Bileẓky 1970) nor the forebodings as to the future of Hebrew voiced by Kaẓenelson (1960). However, a haloization seems to be setting in *vis-à-vis* Yiddish in some Israeli youth circles, with increasingly favorable attitudes coexisting side-by-side with decreasing utilization of the language (Fishman 1974).

Because of this interesting discontinuity between attitude and use which Yiddish in Israel so strikingly reveals (even more so than in the United States, as well as more so than other Diaspora-derived Jewish languages in Israel), it would appear to be a very favorable setting for further language-attitude research. This discontinuity is an important topic for sociolinguistic (and for social science) research more generally and a real contribution could be made in this connection via the patient exploration of Yiddish attitude/use phenomena. The coavailability of several other Diaspora-derived Jewish vernaculars, on the one hand, as well as several non-Jewish vernaculars brought by Jews as mother tongues from the Diaspora, all of which are seemingly moving toward extinction as mother tongues among Jews in Israel, makes possible a number of intriguing contrasts not easily available elsewhere for the student of language attitude vs. language use differentials. Although Irish data (Committee 1975) implies that the gap between positive attitudes and negative usage can be maintained for

---

◄ The Communist Party of Lithuania, soon after the Soviet occupation, appeals to 'Comrade workers, peasants, fighters, working intellectuals, all workers "to attend a demonstration"' and concludes 'Long live Stalin, the leader and teacher of all workers.'

quite some time (indeed, over several generations), it would be highly desirable to find out what its upper limit might be. Can all vernaculars live on eternally at a purely affective level, as have classical Latin, Greek, and Hebrew, or only those with a certain ethnodynamic configuration? If, as I suspect, the latter is true, does Yiddish fit this configuration more today than it did in yesteryear (Segalman 1968)?

LANGUAGE POLICY AND LANGUAGE PLANNING

Little attention has been given to official recognition/de-recognition of Yiddish in the world. All such action (whether in Versailles treaty negotiations pertaining to Poland and the Baltic states, during the Menshevik or early Bolshevik regimes, or in conjunction with the expenditure of American bilingual education funds in Hasidic neighborhoods today) proceeds via political conflict, bargaining, negotiating, and compromise. The records of such processes relative to Yiddish are in a particularly unsystematized and unanalyzed state and deserve to be rescued from oblivion.

The situation with respect to corpus planning is, surprisingly, similarly primitive. Given all the concern evidenced by Yiddishist intellectuals during the past (three quarters of a) century for proper Yiddish orthography, for rejection of recent Germanisms, and for *ausbau* from German (wherever possible) more generally, for purification *vis-à-vis* Slavisms and Americanisms (and, in Latin America, *vis-à-vis* Spanishisms, but much more rarely in Israel *vis-à-vis* Ivritisms), there has been next to no sociological (and even very little linguistic-sociolinguistic) study of any of these phenomena. Other than Yudel Mark's somewhat loaded survey (Anon [Yudl Mark] 1959) of the reactions to 'Yivo spelling' on the part of 172 Yiddish writers, journalists, and teachers (the nature of his sample of respondents and the definition of the universe from which this sample was selected both being curiously ignored) and David Gold's informal study of the personal spelling habits of most Yivo-affiliated Yiddish specialists (1977), no studies come to mind of the interaction between differential knowledge, attitudes, and usage *vis-à-vis* the entire corpus planning enterprise in the modern Yiddish period (note, however, Shekhter 1969 and 1975 for fine examples of the prevalent mode of textual analyses in this connection). The intriguing questions in this respect are not so much the extent to which corpus planning has penetrated into widespread written/spoken usage (which by all general indications could be expected to be relatively negligible; see, e.g. Rubin et al. 1977), but the extent to which it is known, liked and, used in even the most specialized circles. Studies of lexical and orthographic planning in Israel (e.g. Hofman 1974a, 1974b; Alloni-Fainberg 1974; Rabin 1971; Seckbach 1974) have not only indicated how shallow much corpus planning 'success' may be when status planning sanctions are not authoritatively implemented, but have provided models for exploring such topics in the Yiddish field as well. However, the Yiddish case lends itself most particularly to the study of patterned evasion or rejection of corpus planning, i.e. of language activists and language elites who not only do not know, do not like and/or do not attempt to use the products of corpus planning, but whose rejection of these products is often consciously rationalized as being in *defense* of the language (and, therefore, reflective of their stewardship thereof) rather than as an abandonment of it. Such patterned evasion/rejection of language planning by its purported custodians has only been *fleetingly* mentioned elsewhere (see, e.g. Rabin 1971 re Hebrew; Geerts et al. 1976 re Dutch; Gunderson 1976 re Norwegian; Wexler 1974 re Ukrainian and White Russian; Rubin et al. 1977 re India and Indonesia; and O'Murchu 1976 re Irish) but has not heretofore received the focused attention that it deserves.

CONCLUSIONS

A rather substantial amount of sociological-sociolinguistic research has already been done with respect to Yiddish-using (speaking, writing, understanding or even merely mother-tongue claiming) populations. Indeed, that which *has* already been done is sufficient in quantity and in quality for the sociology of Yiddish to appear as a recognizable field of study, research and publication. However, as such, its greatest contribution and its soundest development would obtain if it could simultaneously advance our understanding of topics of general theoretical interest. The underlying purpose of this review has been to suggest a few of the many promising areas in which this can be done.

REFERENCES

Anon [Yudl Mark] (1959), 'Rezultatn fun an ankete vegn oysleyg', *Yidishe shprakh* 19: 83–96.

Alloni-Fainberg, Yafa (1974), 'Official Hebrew terms for parts of the car: A study of knowledge, usage and attitudes', *International Journal of the Sociology of Language* 1: 67–94. (Also in *Advances in Language Planning*, ed. by J. A. Fishman, 493–518. The Hague, Mouton.)

Allony-Fainberg, Yaffa (1977), 'The influence of English on formal terminology in Hebrew', in *The Spread of English: The International Sociology of English as an Additional Language*, ed. by Joshna A. Fishman, Robert L. Cooper and Andrew W. Conrad, 223–228. Rowley (Mass.), Newbury House

Ben-Amoz, Don and Ben-Yehuda, Netiva (1972), *Milon olami le-ivrit meduberit*. Jerusalem, Levin-Epstein.

Bileẓky, Y. H. (1970), *H. N. byalik ve-yidish*. Tel Aviv, Perets Farlag.

Committee on Irish Language Attitudes Research (1975), *Main Report*. Dublin, Government Stationer.

Cooper, Robert L., Fishman, Joshua A. (1977), 'A study of language attitudes', in *The Spread of English: The International Sociology of English as an Additional Language*, ed. by Joshua A. Fishman, Robert L. Cooper and Andrew W. Conrad, 239–276. Rowley (Mass.), Newbury House.

Fertig, Sheldon, Fishman, Joshua A. (1969), 'Some measures of the interaction between language, domain and semantic dimension in bilinguals', *Modern Language Journal* 52: 244–249.

Fisherman, Haya, Fishman, Joshua A. (1975), 'The "official languages" of Israel: Their status in law and police attitudes and knowledge concerning them', in *Multilingual Political Systems, Problems and Solutions*, ed. by Jean-Guy Savard and Richard Vigneault, 498–535. Quebec City, Laval University Press.

Fishman, Shikl (1965a), 'Language maintainance and language shift in certain urban immigrant environments: the case of Yiddish in the United States', *Europa Ethnica* 22: 146–158.

— (1966), *Language Loyalty in the United States*. The Hague, Mouton.

— (1966), 'Bilingualism with and without diglossia; diglossia with and without bilingualism', *Journal of Social Issues* 23 (2): 29–38.

— (1969), 'Language maintenance and language shift: Yiddish and other immigrant languages in the United States', *Yivo Annual of Jewish Social Science* 14: 12–26.

— (1971), *Advances in the Sociology of Language*, vol. 1. The Hague, Mouton.

— (1972b), 'Language maintainance and language shift as a field of inquiry: revisited', in his *Language and Sociocultural Change*, ed. by Anwar Dil, 76–133. Stanford, Stanford University Press.

— (1973), 'The phenomenological and linguistic pilgrimage of Yiddish' (some examples of functional and structural pidginization and de-pidginization), *Kansas Journal of Sociology* 9: 127–136. (Also in his *Advances in the Creation and Revision of Writing Systems*, 293–306. The Hague, Mouton, 1977.)

— (1974), 'Vos ken zayn di funktsye fun yidish in yisroel?' *Yidisher Kemfer* April: 40–46.

— (1979), 'The sociolinguistic "normalization" of the Jewish people', in *Archibald Hill Festschrift*, ed. by M. A. Jazayery, E. C. Polome and W. Winter, vol. 4, 223–231. The Hague, Mouton.

— (1977a), 'The spread of English as a new perspective for the study of language maintainance and language shift', in *The Spread of English: The International Sociology of English as an Additional Language*, ed. by J. A. Fishman, Robert L. Cooper and Andrew W. Conrad, 108–136. Rowley (Mass.), Newbury House.

— (1977b), 'Yiddish and Loshn Koydesh in traditional Ashkenaz: On the problem of societal allocation of macro-functions', in *Language in Sociology*, ed. by Albert Verdoodt and Rolf Kjolseth, 39–48. Louvain, Peeters.

Fishman, Joshua A., Spolsky, Bernard (1977), 'The Whorfian hypothesis in 1975: a socio-linguistic re-evaluation', in *Language and Logic in Personality and Society*, ed. by Harwood Fisher and Rogelio Diaz-Guerrero. New York, Academic Press.

Geerts, G., van der Broeck, J., Verdoodt, A. (1977), 'Successes and failures in Dutch spelling reform', in *Advances in the Creation and Revision of Writing Systems*, ed. by J. A. Fishman, 179–246. The Hague, Mouton.

Gundersen, Dag (1977), 'Successes and failures in the modernization of Norwegian spelling', in *Advances in the Creation and Revision of Writing Systems*, ed. by J. A. Fishman, 247–266. The Hague, Mouton.

Gold, David (1977), 'Successes and failures in the standardization and implementation of Yiddish spelling and Romanization', in *Advances in the Creation and Revision of Writing Systems*, 307–370. The Hague, Mouton.

Grimshaw, Allen D. (1971), 'Some social forces and some functions of pidgin and creole languages', in *Pidginization and Creolization of Languages*, ed. by Dell Hymes, 427–446. New York, Cambridge University Press.

Herman, Simon (1968), 'Explorations in the social psychology of language choice', in *Readings in the Sociology of Language*, ed. by J. A. Fishman, 492–511. The Hague, Mouton.

— (1972), *Israelis and Jews: A Study in the Continuity of an Identity*. New York, Random House.

Hesbacher, Peter, Fishman, Joshua A. (1965), 'Language loyalty: its functions and concomitants in two bilingual communities. *Lingua* 13: 145–165.

Hoffman, Gerard, Fishman, Joshua A. (1970), 'Life in the Neighborhood', *International Journal of Comparative Sociology* 12: 85–100.

Hofman, John E. (1974a), 'The prediction of success in language planning; the case of chemists in Israel', *International Journal of the Sociology of Language* 1: 39–66.

— (1974b), 'Predicting the use of Hebrew terms among Israeli psychologists', *International Journal of the Sociology of Language* 3: 53–66.

Hofman, John E., Fisherman, Haya (1971), 'Language shift and maintainance in Israel', *International Migration Review* 5: 204–226. (Also in *Advances in the Sociology of Language*, ed. by J. A. Fishman, vol. 2, 342–364. The Hague, Mouton, 1972.)

Howe, Irving (1976), *World of Our Fathers: The Journey of the East European Jews to America and the Life they Found and Made*. New York, Harcourt Brace Jovanovich.

Kaz, Elihu et al. (1972), *Tarbut yisrael 1970*, 2 vols. Jerusalem, Israel Institute of Applied Social Research and Communications Department, Hebrew University.

Kazenelson, K. (1960), *Mashber ha-ivrit ha-modernit*. Tel Aviv, Anach.

Kornblueth, Ilana, Aynor, Sarah (1974), 'A study of the longevity of Hebrew slang', *International Journal of the Sociology of Language* 1: 15–38.

Ma, Roxana, Herasimchuck, Eleanor (1971), 'The linguistic dimensions of a bilingual neighborhood', in *Bilingualism in the Barrio*, ed. by J. A. Fishman, R. L. Cooper and R. Ma, 347–464. Bloomington, Indiana University Language Sciences Monographs.

Macaulay, Ronald K. S. (1975), 'Negative prestige, linguistic insecurity and linguistic self-hatred', *Lingua* 36: 147–161.

Mintz, Sidney W. (1971), 'The socio-historical background to pidginization and creolization', in *Pidginization and Creolization of Languages*, ed. by Dell Hymes, 427–446. New York, Cambridge University Press.

Nadel, Elizabeth, Fishman, Joshua A. (1977), 'English in Israel: A sociolinguistic study', in *The Spread of English: The International Sociology of English as an Additional Language*, ed. by Joshua A. Fishman, Robert L. Cooper, and Andrew W. Conrad, 137–167. Rowley (Mass.), Newbury House.

O'Murchi, Mairtin (1977), 'Successes and failures in the modernization of Irish spelling', in *Advances in the Creation and Revision of Writing Systems*, ed. by J. A. Fishman, 267–289. The Hague, Mouton.

Poll, Simon (1965), 'The role of Yiddish in American ultra-orthodox and Hasidic communities', *Yivo Annual of Jewish Social Research* 13: 125–152.

Pool, Jonathan (1972), 'National development and language diversity', in *Advances in the Sociology of Language*, vol. 2, 213–230. The Hague, Mouton.

Rabin, Chaim (1971), 'Spelling reform – Israel 1968', in *Can Language be Planned?*, ed. by Joan Rubin and Bjorn H. Jernudd, 95–122. Honolulu, University Press of Hawaii.

Ronch, Judah et al. (1969), 'Word naming and usage for a sample of Yiddish–English bilinguals', *Modern Language Journal* 53: 232–235.

Ronen, Miriam, Seckbach, Fern, Cooper, Robert L., Fishman, Joshua A. (1977), 'Foreign loanwords in Hebrew newspapers', in *The Spread of English: The International Sociology of English as an Additional Language*, ed. by Joshua A. Fishman, Robert L. Cooper, and Andrew W. Conrad, 229–235. Rowley (Mass.), Newbury House.

Rosenbaum, Yehudit, Nadel, Elizabeth, Cooper, Robert L., Fishman, Joshua A. (1977), 'English on Keren Kayemet Street', in *The Spread of English: The International Sociology of English as an Additional Language*, ed. by Joshua A. Fishman, Robert L. Cooper, and Andrew W. Conrad, 179–194. Rowley (Mass.), Newbury House.

Rothstein, Jay (1977), 'Reactions of the American Yiddish press to the Tshernovits Language Conference of 1908 as a reflection of the American Jewish experience', *International Journal of the Sociology of Language* 13: 103–120.

Rubin, Joan, Jernudd, Bjorn, Das Gupta, Jyotirindra, Fishman, Joshua A., Ferguson, Charles A. (1977), *Language Planning Processes*. The Hague, Mouton.

Shekhter, Mordkhe (1969), 'The "hidden standard"; a study of competing influences in standardization', in *Field of Yiddish III*, ed. by M. Herzog et al., 284–304. The Hague, Mouton.

— (1975), 'Der yivo un yidish', *Yidishe shprakh* 34: 2–23.

Seckbach, Fern (1974), 'Attitudes and opinions of Israeli teachers and students about aspects of modern Hebrew', *International Journal of the Sociology of Language* 1: 105–124.

Segalman, Ralph (1968), 'Hansen's law revisited', *Dimensions* 2 (4): 28–31.

Slobin, Dan I. (1963), 'Some aspects of the use of pronouns of address in Yiddish', *Word* 19: 193–202.

Stewart, Wiliam A. (1968), 'A sociolinguistic typology for describing national multilingualism', in *Readings in the Sociology of Language*, ed. by J. A. Fishman, 531–545. The Hague, Mouton.

Tanner, Nancy (1967), 'Speech and society among the Indonesian elite: a case study of a multilingual community', *Anthropological Linguistics* 9 (3): 15–40.

Turner, Victor (1974), 'Metaphors of anti-structure in religious culture', in his *Dramas, Fields and Metaphors: Symbolic Action in Human Society*, 273–300. Ithaca, Cornell University Press.

Vaynraykh, Maks (1937), 'Le Yiddish comme objet de la linguistique générale', Communication au IVe Congrès International de Linguistes, à Copenhague, le 27 août 1936. Institut Scientifique Juif (Yivo), Wilno.

— (1953), 'Yidishkayt and Yiddish: on the impact of religion on language in Ashkenazic Jewry', in *Mordecai M. Kaplan Jubilee Volume*, 481–514. New York, Jewish Theological Seminary. (Also in *Readings in the Sociology of Language*, ed. by J. A. Fishman, 382–413. The Hague, Mouton, 1968.)

— (1959), 'Inveynikste tsveyshprakhikayt, in ashkenaz biz der haskole; faktn un bagrifn', *Goldene Keyt* 35: 3–11. (Translated into English (1972) in *Voices from the Yiddish*, ed. by Irving Howe and Eliezer Greenberg. Ann Arbor, University of Michigan Press.)

— (1967), 'The reality of Jewishness vs. the ghetto myth: The sociolinguistic roots of Yiddish', in *To Honor Roman Jakobson*, 211–221. The Hague, Mouton.

— (1973), *Geshikhte fun der yidisher shprakh*, 4 vols. New York, Yivo. (English translation of vols. 1 and 2 by Shlomo Noble and Joshua A. Fishman, University of Chicago Press, 1980).

Wexler, Paul (1974), *Purism and Language*. Bloomington (Indiana), Indiana University Language Sciences Monographs.

Original Sources*

PART I SOCIOHISTORICAL PERSPECTIVE

The Reality of Jewishness versus the Ghetto Myth: The Sociolinguistic Roots, MAKS VAYNRAYKH (MAX WEINREICH), reprinted from *To Honor Roman Jakobson*, The Hague, Mouton, 1967, 211–221.

The Yiddish Language: Its Cultural Impact, YUDL (YUDEL) MARK, reprinted from *American Jewish Historical Quarterly*, 1969, 59, 201–209.

Vegn der natsyonaler role fun yidish un der yidisher kultur [Concerning the Ethnonational Role of Yiddish and Yiddish Culture], SHMUEL NIGER, reprinted from *Yidish in undzer lebn* [Yiddish in Our Life]. New York, Workmen's Circle Educational Department, 1950, 5–14.

Ume veloshn: yidish folk, yidish loshn [People and Language: Jewish Nationality and Yiddish Language], AVROM GOLOMB, reprinted from *Yorbukh fun der nayer yidisher shul y. l. perets in meksike* [Yearbook of the New Jewish School in Mexico (named after) Y. L. Perets], 1962, 13.

PART II ORTHODOXY: THEN AND NOW

A Defense of Yiddish in Old Yiddish Literature, YISROEL TSINBERG (ISRAEL ZINBERG), reprinted from *Yivo Annual of Jewish Social Sciences*, 1946, 1, 283–293.

Yidishkeyt un yidish [Jewishness and Yiddish], SORE SHENIRER, reprinted from *Beys yankev*, 1931, 8, 71–72.

Di rekht fun 'loshn ashkenaz' bay dintoyres [The Rights of Yiddish in Suits in Rabbinic Courts], and Der vilner goen un yidish [The Sage of Vilna and Yiddish], YITSKHOK RIVKIND, reprinted from *Pinkes*, 1927, 1, 156–157.

Geule fun loshn [Redemption of Language], SHLOYME BIRNBOYM (SOLOMON BIRNBAUM), reprinted from *Beys yankev*, 1931.

The Role of Yiddish in American Ultra-Orthodox and Hassidic Communities, SOLOMON POLL, reprinted from *Yivo Annual of Jewish Social Sciences*, 1955, 13, 125–152.

Who Needs Yiddish?, SHIMON SUSHOLTZ, reprinted from *The Jewish Observer*, 1976, June, 18–20.

PART III MODERNIZATION MOVEMENTS
AND MODERN ATTITUDES

Di fir klasn [The Four Categories], Y. M. LIFSHITS, reprinted from *Kol mevaser*, 1863, 2, 323–328, 364–366, 345–380, 392–393 (including Yankev Shmuel Bik's letter to Tuvye Feder [1815] and the editor's [Aleksander Tsederboym's] comments).

* All articles which are not listed are being published for the first time in this volume.

Matesyohu mizes un di polemik vegn yidish [Matesyohu Mizes (Mattathias Mieses) and the Polemic about Yiddish], G. KRESL, reprinted from *Goldene keyt*, 1957, 28, 143–163.

Zhitlovsky and American Jewry, EMANUEL S. GOLDSMITH, reprinted from *Jewish Frontier*, 1975, November, 14–17.

Mir bashuldikn un monen akhrayes! [We Accuse and Demand Responsibility!], ZERUBOVL, reprinted from *Yidish in erets yisroel* [Journal of the League for the Rights of Yiddish in the Land of Israel], 1936, 7–18.

Der blik az yidish iz der tamtsis fun yidishkayt—di sakone fun der formule 'lingvistish-sekularistish' [The View that Yiddish is the Quintessence of Jewishness—The Danger of the Formulation 'Linguistic-Secularistic'], LEYBESH LERER (LEIBUSH LEHRER), reprinted from *Yidishkayt un andere problemen* [Jewishness and Other Problems]. New York, Farlag Matones, 1940, 68–94.

An ofener briv tsu undzer yidishistisher inteligents [An Open Letter to Our Yiddishist Intelligentsia], BEN-ADIR, Bucharest, Frayland Liga, 1947, reprinted from *Afn shvel*, 1942, 2, 13/14 (4/5), 3–5.

Who Needs Yiddish? A Study in Language and Ethics, JOSEPH C. LANDIS, reprinted from *Judaism*, 1964, 13, (4), 1–16.

PART IV HISTORIC MOMENTS

Attracting a Following to High-Culture Functions for a Language of Everyday Life: The Role of the Tshernovits Language Conference in the 'Rise of Yiddish', JOSHUA A. FISHMAN, reprinted from *Language Spread: Studies in Diffusion and Social Change*, edited by Robert L. Cooper, 1981, Arlington, Center for Applied Linguistics. Prepared originally for presentation at the Ford Foundation and Center for Applied Linguistics sponsored Conference on Language Spread, University of Aberystwith, Wales, September 12–14, 1978. (The revised article published in this volume was prepared with the assistance of the Memorial Foundation for Jewish Culture.)

Di yidishe shprakh af der tog-ordenung fun der sholem-konferents in pariz, 1919 [The Yiddish Language on the Agenda of the Peace Conference in Paris, 1919], YOYSEF TENENBOYM, reprinted from *Yivo-bleter*, 1957/58, 41, 217–229.

Tsu der efenung fun der yidish-katedre in yerushelayemer universitet [On the Inauguration of the Yiddish Chair at the University in Jerusalem], M. SHNEYERSON, M. SHVABE, B. DIANBURG, D. PINSKI, KH. GRINBERG, L. SIGL, D. SADAN, reprinted from *Goldene keyt*, 1951, 11, 187–202.

Address at the Dedication of the Leivick House in Israel, May 14, 1970, GOLDE MEYER (GOLDA MEIR), reprinted from *Yiddish*, 1973, 1(1), 4–5.

Deklaratsye fun der velt-konferents far yidish un yidisher kultur in yerushelayem...dem 23stn–26stn oygust 1976 [Declaration of the World Conference for Yiddish and Yiddish Culture in Jerusalem...August 23–26, 1976], reprinted from *Barikht fun der velt-konferents far yidish un yidisher kultur* [Minutes of the World Conference for Yiddish and Yiddish Culture]. Tel-Aviv, World Bureau for Yiddish and Yiddish Culture, 1977, 232–233.

PART V FORMAL INSTITUTIONS OF LANGUAGE: THE PRESS, LITERATURE, THEATER, SCHOOLS

Der 'bund' un der gedank vegn a yidish-veltlekher shul [The 'Bund' and the Idea of a Yiddish-Secular School], KH. SH. KAZHDAN, reprinted from *Fun kheyder un 'shkoles' biz tsisho* [From the kheyder (= Traditional Orthodox Elementary Schools) and 'shkoles' (= Russified Schools) to Tsisho (= Socialist-Nationalist Yiddish schools)]. Mexico City, Mendelson Fund, 1956, 268–288.

Tsvey shprakhn–eyn eyntsike literatur [Two Languages–One Literature], BAL-MAKHSHOVES, reprinted from *Geklibene verk* [Selected Works]. New York, Tsiko, 1953, 112–123.

Lererkursn far yidish in lodzher geto [Yiddish Courses for Teachers in the (Nazi) Ghetto of Lodz], Y. L. GERSHT, reprinted from *Yivo-bleter*, 1947, 40(2), 17–23.

The Night of the Murdered Poets, JUDAH L. GRAUBART, reprinted from *The Reconstructionist*, 1974, 40(2), 17–23.

The American Yiddish Press at Its Centennial, B. Z. GOLDBERG, reprinted from *Judaism*, 1970, 20 (2), 224–228.

Ida Kaminska and the Yiddish Theater, HAROLD CLURMAN, reprinted from *Midstream*, 1968, 14, 53–57.

Yiddish in the University, LEONARD PRAGER, reprinted from *The Jewish Quarterly*, 1974, 22(1–2) (79–80), 31–40.

PART VI MAINTENANCE AND SHIFT

Di yidishe shprakh in undzer privat-lebn [The Yiddish Language in Our Private Life], M. OLGIN, reprinted from *Fragn fun lebn*, 1911, 39–49.

The Struggle for Yiddish During World War I: The Attitude of German Jewry, ZOSA SZAJKOWSKI, reprinted from *Yearbook of the Leo Baeck Institute*, 1964, 131–158.

Di shprakhn bay yidn in umophengikn poyln [The Languages of Jews in Independent Poland], YANKEV LESHTSHINSKI, reprinted from *Yivo-bleter*, 1943, 22, 147–162.

Lebediker untergang [Lively Death] and A loshn af tomid, nisht af dervayl [A Language for Always, Not Just for a While], YANKEV GLATSHTEYN, reprinted from *In der velt mit yidish* [In the World with Yiddish]. New York, Congress for Jewish Culture, 1972, 429–432, 433–436.

Yiddish in Melbourne, F. MANFRED KLARBERG, reprinted from *Jewish Journal of Sociology*, 1970, 12 (1), 59–73.

PART VII SOCIOLINGUISTIC VARIATION AND PLANNING

Vegn zhargon oysleygn [About Spelling Zhargon (=Yiddish)], SHOLEM ALEYKHEM (ALEICHEM), reprinted from *Di yidishe folks-bibliotek*, 1888, 1, 474–476.

Undzer mame-loshn [Our Mother Tongue], G. ZELIKOVITSH, reprinted from *Literarishe briv* [Literary Letters]. New York, Hebrew Publishing Company, 1909, 45–46.

Vegn litvishn dialekt in kongres-poyln [Concerning the Litvak (=Northeastern) Dialect in Congress Poland], NOTE BERLINER, and Zeyer gerekht [Absolutely Right], B. (=SHLOYME BIRNBOYM), reprinted from *Beys-yankev*, 1938, 8, 71–72, 42–43.

The 'Hidden Standard': A Study of Competing Influences in Standardization, MORDKHE SHEKHTER (SCHAECHTER), reprinted from *The Field of Yiddish*, 1969, 3, 284–304.

Politics and Linguistics in the Standardization of Soviet Yiddish, RACHEL ERLICH, reprinted from *Soviet Jewish Affairs*, 1973, 3(1), 71–79.

Some Aspects of the Use of Pronouns of Address in Yiddish, DAN I. SLOBIN, *Word*, 1963, 19, 193–202.

Bilingualism and Dialect Mixture Among Lubavitcher Hasidic Children, GEORGE JOCHNOWITZ, reprinted from *American Speech*, 1968, 43, 182–200.

Epilogue: Contributions of the Sociology of Yiddish to the General Sociology of Language, JOSHUA A. FISHMAN, revised and expanded version of an article published in *The Field of Yiddish*, 1980, 4, 475–498.

Index*

Agnon, Sh"ay, 37
Aḥad Ha-'am, 19, 25n, 27
Ambivalence toward Yiddish, 1, 7–9, 13–16
Assimilation, 11n, 12n, 18n, 19–20, 23, 35, 51
Attitudes to Yiddish, 1–2, 4–5, 6–10, 12–24, 25, 39n, 58n, 740, 744–745, 749–752
Ausbau languages, 3n, 56, 57n, 752
Authenticity movements, Jewish, 4
Autonomists. *See* Cultural autonomy

Bal-makhshoves, 5n
ben Yehuda, Eliezer, 18n, 59
Berditshevski, Mikhe Yoysef, 37
Berliner, Note, 57n
Bilingualism. *See* Multilingualism/bilingualism
Birnbaum, Nathan. *See* Birnboym, Nosn
Birnboym, Nosn, 9n, 54
Birnbaum, S(olomon) A. *See* Birnboym, Shloyme
Birnboym, Shloyme, 25, 54
Bund(ism), 17, 25, 45
Byalik, Khayim Nakhmen, 37, 751

Committee for the Implementation of the Standardized Yiddish Orthography, 26
Componentiality, 1, 3
Congress for Jewish Culture, 26
Contrastivity, 1, 3–4
Cultural autonomy, 12, 16–19, 23, 45, 740

Dialects, 61–63
Diaspora, languages of. *See* Jewish languages
Dictionaries, 55, 56n, 62, 745
Diglossia, 6, 11n, 20n, 21n, 32n, 39n, 55, 744, 751
Dimensions of language use, 740–741, 744
Dubnov, Shimen, 16

Dubnow, Simeon. *See* Dubnov, Shimen

Educational role, 7, 13n, 16, 26, 28, 32n, 35, 40–48, 51, 53–55, 742

Fellman, Jack, 57n
Ferguson, Charles A., 744
Fertig, Sheldon, 744
Fishman, Joshua A., 744

German, link with, 11n, 13, 21n, 50, 56–58, 61, 752
Gerstein, J., 748
Gold, David, 752
Goldfadn, Avrom, 35, 39
Golomb, Avrom, 46n
Gordin, Y. L., 39
Graetz, Heinrich, 13
Grammar, 5n, 57n
Gutskov, K., 39

Hapgood, Hutchins, 38n
Hasidism, 7–9, 49
Haskole (Enlightenment), 12–13, 16, 35, 50, 57n
Hebraism, 19–20, 21n, 27, 35
Hebrew, 2, 6, 12n, 13, 20–1, 27, 32, 45, 46n, 53, 57–59, 61; modern Hebrew, 2, 4, 59, 746, 751. *See also* Ivrit; Literature
Hebrew Language Committee, 57n
Hebrew University, Jerusalem, 26–28
Herman, Simon, 740, 744
Hersch, L., 51
Hirshbeyn, Perets, 39
History of Yiddish language, 1–28
Howe, Irving, 18n

* Only 'The Sociology of Yiddish: A Foreword', pp. 1–97, and 'Epilogue: Contributions of the Sociology of Yiddish to the General Sociology of Language', pp. 739–756, are indexed. Names of authors whose Yiddish works are cited are transliterated in accordance with the Yiddish pronunciation of their names.

איך בין ניט קיין יידישיסט, וועלכער גלויבט, אז דאָס
שוין אליין שטעלט מיט זיך פאַר אַן אַבסאָלוטן ווערט.
בער אַ גמרא־ייד בין איך יאָ, און איך וויים, אז היילי־
ייט און אבסאָלוטקייט זיינען ניט אלעמאָל אידענטיש.
י הלכה האָט פאָרמולירט צוויי אידעען פון קדושה: 1)
רפי קדושה; 2) תשמישי קדושה. זי האָט אָפּגעפסקנט,
ז מען דאַרף ראַטעווען פֿון אַ שרפה שבת, ניט נאָר די
פר תורה נאָר אויך דאָס מענטעלע, אין וועלכן זי איז
יינגעוויקלט; ניט בלויז די תפילין, נאָר אויך דעם זעקל,
ין וועלכן זי ליגן. ממילא, יידיש ווי אַ שפראַך, ניט
וקנדיק וואָס זי איז ניט פאַררעכנט צווישן גופי קדושה,
עהערט זיכער צום קלאַס פון תשמישי־קדושה, וועלכע
ינען אויך היילי...

באַשיצן מיט אַלע
...חות. איז דען
ייליקסטע ספרי...
...ון זיינען נאָך אלץ
שפראַך האָט דער
...מ״א, דער מהרש...
שינער און אנד...
תורה געלערנט.
עזעריטישער מג...
עשה בראשית
אבן די יידישע
וריישאפט אויסג...
שיבות זייערע ש...
ער הייליק, כאָט...
אר אַן אָפּגעליט...
...ן תשמישי־קדושה.
ויפהאַלטן דעם זכות!